Where Psychologists Work

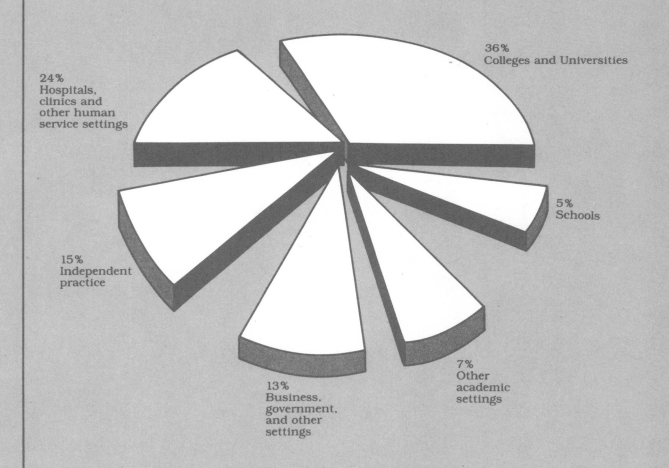

36%
Colleges and Universities

24%
Hospitals,
clinics and
other human
service settings

5%
Schools

15%
Independent
practice

7%
Other
academic
settings

13%
Business,
government,
and other
settings

Psychology

SECOND EDITION

Psychology

SECOND EDITION

Spencer A. Rathus

St. John's University
Jamaica, N.Y.

Holt, Rinehart and Winston
New York Chicago San Francisco Philadelphia
Montreal Toronto London Sydney
Tokyo Mexico City Rio de Janeiro Madrid

Publisher   John L. Michel
Senior Acquisitions Editor   Nedah Abbott
Assistant Editor   Alison Podel
Senior Project Manager   Arlene D. Katz
Production Manager   Pat Sarcuni
Art Director   Lou Scardino
Managing Editor   Edward Cone
Text Design   Caliber Design Planning, Inc.
Cover Design   Lou Scardino
Photo Research   Cheryl Mannes
Cover Art   Jack Tworkov, "RED & GREEN WITH YELLOW STRIPE" (1964)

Library of Congress Cataloging in Publication Data

Rathus, Spencer A.
    Psychology.

    Bibliography: p.
    Includes indexes.
        1. Psychology. I. Title. [DNLM: 1. Psychology.
BF 121 F235p]
    BF121.R34 1984   150   83-10647
    ISBN 0-03-063177-7

Copyright © 1984 by CBS College Publishing
Address correspondence to:
383 Madison Avenue
New York, N.Y. 10017
All rights reserved
Printed in the United States of America
Published simultaneously in Canada
4 5 6 7   039   9 8 7 6 5 4 3 2 1

CBS College Publishing
Holt, Rinehart and Winston
The Dryden Press
Saunders College Publishing

Copyright Acknowledgments

FIGURE 1.1 (p. 7 and end papers) Data from Strapp, J. and Fulcher, R. "The Employment of APA Members," AMERICAN PSYCHOLOGIST, 36, pp. 1263–1314. Copyright 1981 by American Psychological Association. Reprinted by permission of the publisher.
QUESTIONNAIRE (pp. 30–31) Reprinted from Crowne, D. P. and Marlow, D. JOURNAL OF CONSULTING PSYCHOLOGY, p. 351, Table 1. Copyright 1960 by American Psychological Association. Reprinted by permission of publisher and authors.
NEWS ITEM (p. 35) Copyright 1981 by The New York Times Company. Reprinted by Permission.

FIGURE 2.11 (p. 58) From INTRODUCTION TO PSYCHOLOGY, Sixth Edition, by Ernest R. Hilgard, Richard C. Atkinson, and Rita L. Atkinson © 1975 by Harcourt Brace Jovanovich, Inc. Reproduced by Permission of the publisher.
NEWS ITEM (p. 59) Copyright 1981 Time Inc. All rights reserved. Reprinted by permission from TIME.
NEWS ITEM (p. 66) Copyright 1981 by Newsweek, Inc. All Rights Reserved. Adaptation Reprinted by Permission.
NEWS ITEM (p. 68) Copyright 1979 by Newsweek, Inc. All Rights Reserved. Adaptation Reprinted by Permission.

(Copyright Acknowledgments continued on p. 624)

To Allyn
My New Daughter

Preface

Writing a textbook can engulf you. Family and friends have a way of asking that you play the basic role of citizen by attending dinner, going to an occasional film, taking a turn at mowing the lawn, and remembering to close the refrigerator door. Under normal circumstances, requests like these are perfectly reasonable. But composing a book like *Psychology* demands that you lock yourself into your study, spend evenings at the library, and develop a hearing deficit that permits you to ignore most household events except for an occasional emergency. In my case, it also requires bumping into walls and wearing a perpetual distracted look.

Composing the second edition of *Psychology*, like writing the first edition, was one of the most demanding yet rewarding challenges of my career as a psychologist. Frankly, when I had completed the first edition, I thought that the hard part was over. Revisions, I told myself, would come easy. Not so. Psychology is such a dynamic, evolving field that the second edition required as much work as the first. Keeping up with the literature is a full-time job, as any instructor of psychology will gladly testify. Only three years have elapsed since the writing of the first edition, but research and theory in many areas of psychology have advanced so rapidly that in the current edition it was necessary for me to integrate the findings of literally hundreds of studies carried out since 1980. In addition, I integrated the comments and suggestions of dozens of colleagues who used the first edition in the classroom and reviewed early drafts of the second.

Changes in psychology and suggestions from colleagues have led me to extensively rework many of the chapters in the second edition. For example, Chapter 2 (Biology and Behavior) contains additional material on the roles of hormones in athletic competition and in regulation of the menstrual cycle. Chapter 11 (Abnormal Behavior) now contains a critical comparison of the DSM-II and the DSM-III, and a discussion of the increasingly controversial insanity plea. A comprehensive section on sex roles and sex differences was added to Chapter 13 (Sexual Behavior). Similar examples can be found throughout the text.

As with the first edition, I also set myself the task of making clear the many meanings of psychology. Psychology continues to touch almost every aspect of our lives and I sought to emphasize this relevance. Yet psychology remains a science with strict rules and procedures for determining what is truth and what is fiction. Psychology even provides guidelines for deciding what we can use as evidence. Thus this book is also a recounting of the continuing human endeavor to replace superstition with science, and to place facts and logic before folklore and the emotional appeal.

Coverage

The second edition of *Psychology* still provides instructors with a comprehensive and balanced textbook that communicates in content and form the excitement, relevance, and true scientific nature of psychology. It provides students with a straightforward introduction to the basic research areas within psychology, such as physiological psychology, sensation and perception, learning and memory, cognitive processes, motivation and emotion, and personality and social psychology. With that knowledge as a base, the text also makes explicit for students many of psychology's evolving applications in the areas of human growth and development, states of consciousness, stress and adjustment, abnormal behavior and psychotherapy, and sexual behavior.

Because no introductory survey textbook can pursue every important area within the broad science of psychology in the depth these areas deserve, *Psychology* is succinct in presentation. A number of areas are combined to receive single chapter coverage: Sensation and Perception (Chapter 3); Learning and Memory (Chapter 5); Language, Thought, and Intelligence (Chapter 6); Motivation and Emotion (Chapter 7); and Personality Theory and Measurement (Chapter 9). Clear, concise, accurate coverage of these areas permits full chapter treatment of topics that immediately touch students' lives: States of Consciousness (Chapter 4), including sleep and dreams, drugs, meditation, biofeedback, and hypnosis; Stress and Adjustment (Chapter 10); and Sexual Behavior (Chapter 13), including the sexual revolution, sex roles and differences, varieties of sexual experience, and sexual problems or dysfunctions. The applied areas of psychology, as all areas, are treated with academic rigor. Great emphasis is placed on research methodology and up-to-date research findings.

The Writing Style

The second edition of *Psychology*, as the first, was deliberately written with the needs of the student in mind. But the second edition had the advantage of feedback from dozens of instructors and hundreds of students. I believe that their input has enabled me to retain the engaging and motivating qualities of the first edition, while avoiding frivolity and condescension. Colleagues and students have helped me in my continuing quest to craft the language and the vocabulary so that they are accessible to the student. It is my belief that even the most abstract concepts can be presented in energetic prose that is easy to retain when one writes and rewrites according to the suggestions of the readers.

Psychology was also explicitly written for the instructor—the instructor who wants to teach from a textbook that is:

easily understood
interest-arousing
clearly written
accurate and up-to-date
succinct in presentation
well-illustrated
comprehensive and balanced
applied as well as theoretical

Learning Aids

The central task of a textbook is to provide students with clear information in a format that promotes learning. *Psychology* contains six specific elements designed to meet this goal:

Chapter Outlines

Each chapter begins with an outline that helps organize the subject matter for the student. Care was taken to present the heads used in the chapter outline in a succinct and clear manner.

"Truth-or-Fiction?" Sections

"Truth-or-Fiction?" sections follow the chapter outline. These sections stimulate student interest by challenging "common knowledge" and folklore. Many students consider themselves "psychologists"; even by the age at which they first attend college they have already observed human behavior for many years. The "Truth-or-Fiction?" sections cause them to reflect upon the accuracy of their observations, and to reconsider whatever conclusions they may have drawn about "human nature."

Glossary Items Defined in the Margins

Technical terms are defined in the margins of the text, at the points where they occur in the text. Research shows that most students do not make use of a glossary that appears at the back of a book. Moreover, ready access to glossary items permits students to maintain concentration on the chapter—they need not flip back and forth between different sections of the book.

Technical terms are written phonetically to help students pronounce them properly. They will not have to "unlearn" embarrassing mispronunciations through verbal errors made in the classroom. The lucid marginal definitions for technical terms are repeated in two or more chapters, as needed. This repetition gives the instructor flexibility in the sequencing of reading assignments. All technical terms are boldfaced on the pages where they appear. They are also listed in the index, and pages on which they appear are boldfaced in the index, allowing students to readily locate their definitions.

Illustrations

A generous supply of photographs, figures, and drawings illustrates the themes and research findings presented in the text. Figure captions are extensive when needed to reinforce the explanatory function of illustrations and to permit rapid review of subject matter when students seek information by thumbing through the pages.

Chapter Summaries

Traditional end-of-chapter summaries review the material in a logical step-by-step manner. Care was taken to include as many of the boldfaced key terms in each chapter as possible.

"Truth-or-Fiction Revisited" Sections

"Truth-or-Fiction Revisited" sections complete each chapter. In this way, each chapter comes full circle, and provides a sense of psychological closure, by returning to the issues raised in the chapter-opening "Truth-or-Fiction?" sections. By now, the material has been discussed in the text and reviewed in the summary. "Truth-or-Fiction Revisited" sections provide students with immediate feedback as to whether erroneous views have been dispelled. They serve as a reminder that psychology is an empirical science.

Features

Even with the best of learning aids, an introductory text will succeed only if it also stimulates the interest of students and encourages them to read the text content. *Psychology* uses five features deliberately designed to motivate students and help them apply psychological principles to their own lives. These include:

Applications

While *Psychology* avoids deceivingly simple answer to complex human problems, it does offer numerous indications of how psychological principles and research have been applied in such areas as:

weight loss
methods of relaxation and
   meditation
decision making

cutting down and quitting
   smoking
day care
insomnia

test anxiety
rape prevention
suicide prevention

News Items

Most introductory psychology students are likely to "update" their psychological knowledge in future years from news reports. Relevant news articles from sources like *Time* magazine and the *New York Times* supply interesting highlights for the students and also provide the instructor an opportunity to show how psychological information is reported in such articles. In this way the student will become a more sophisticated and discriminating consumer of popularized media reports.

Questionnaires

"Know thyself," wrote the bard. *Psychology* contains a number of questionnaires that students can use under the guidance of their instructors to increase their self-knowledge. Questionnaires and checklists will help students explore what motivates them to drink alcohol, whether they have "Type A" personalities, whether they have an internal or external locus of control, whether they are sensation seekers, what sexual anxieties they have, and how self-assertive they are. They can discuss the implications of their findings with their instructors.

Topics of High Current Interest

Psychology pays special attention to topics of student relevance and interest, including love; adult development; death and dying; sex roles, sex differences, and sexism; drug abuse; obesity; behavior modification; stress and its management; meditation, biofeedback, and hypnosis; and the reciprocal impact we and the environment have on one another. But in each case the focus is on psychological theory and research findings so that "common sense"—which too often could be labeled common *non*sense—is replaced by solid scientific analysis.

Psychological Controversies

Although psychologists have gathered data which have reshaped our thinking about human behavior, many controversies remain. For example, *Can* human behavior be controlled by electrical stimulation of the brain? *Does* acupuncture provide relief from pain? *Can* people have freedom of choice, or is freedom only an illusion? *Do* apes really show facility with language? *Is* rape a victim-precipitated crime? Issues like these are discussed in a stimulating point-counterpoint fashion.

The Ancillaries

The needs of today's instructors and students demand a full and broad array of ancillary materials to make teaching and learning more effective. *Psychology* is accompanied by a complete, convenient, and carefully conceived package: an Instructor's Manual, a Student Study Guide, a Test Bank, a Computerized Test Bank Tape, and a Slide Set. To provide instructors with a coherent, unified, time-saving package, I participated in the writing and coordination of the ancillaries myself, rather than assign them to people less familiar with the text. They occupied my attention fully, as did the text. No mere afterthoughts, they were planned as helpful items right from the start of this project.

The Instructor's Manual

The organization of the *Instructor's Manual* parallels that of the text. Each chapter of the manual offers Teaching Objectives, a list of appropriate slides, Lecture Notes, Discussion Questions, and Commentary for the Materials for Student Distribution. There is a separate section of detailed information on test construction.

The Whole Psychology Catalogue   A unique section called *The Whole Psychology Catalogue* contains news items, questionnaires, demonstrations, and activities that can be easily reproduced by adopters of the text for classroom distribution and use.

The Study Guide

The *Study Guide*, like the Instructor's Manual, is organized into chapters that correspond to the text. Each chapter contains an Overview, Learning Objectives, list of Key Terms, Exercises, a programed Chapter Review, and three 20-item Multiple Choice Tests. The tests were carefully crafted to provide students with an accurate assessment of their achievement in psychology. The grades on these tests are highly valid predictors of actual course grades for students whose instructors take advantage of the comprehensive Test Bank.

Sections on Test Anxiety and Careers in Psychology The Study Guide also features two unique sections. The first, "Test Anxiety," is a detailed presentation that supplements the material on test anxiety presented in Chapter 10 of the text. The second, "Aiming Toward a Career in Psychology," complements the text's discussion of psychological specialties by explaining licensing requirements, APA accreditation, the process of gaining admission to graduate programs in psychology, and career opportunities at the associate's, bachelor's and master's levels, as well as at the doctoral level.

Test Bank

The *Test Bank*, written by Kenneth Heilman of the University of Wisconsin—Eau Claire and myself, contains nearly 3,000 multiple-choice test items. Each item is preceded by a block of codes which give the correct answer, text page reference and major subject area, and tell whether the item tests knowledge or application. A subject index is also provided at the beginning of the manual.

Computerized Test Bank

A Computerized Test Bank consisting of 8 floppy disks is also available. It includes approximately 3000 test items. These questions contained on the disks are similar to the questions which appear in the printed version of the Test Bank. With this system you will have the option of entering the program and adding or deleting questions at your discretion.

Slide Set

A slide set featuring 300 slides—double the number for the last edition, is free to schools adopting 100 or more copies. The slides, which are either full color, two-color, or black and white, consist of tables, graphs, line drawings, cartoons, photographs, demonstrations, and comparisons. Also included with the slide set is a descriptive resource guide.

But, however, lavishly produced, handsomely designed, and supportive of the teaching endeavor the ancillaries are for *Psychology*, it is the text that must first be judged of value as a teaching tool. I feel that the second edition of *Psychology* will continue to be perceived by users as capable of promoting a maximum of student understanding.

Acknowledgments

Many colleagues provided valuable suggestions and insights at various stages in the development of *Psychology* and its ancillaries. My sincere thanks to the following: Mark H. Ashcraft, Cleveland State University; Patricia Barker, Schenectady County Community College; Otto Berliner, SUNY—Alfred State College; Richard A. Block, Montana State University; C. Robert Borresen, Wichita State University; Theodore N. Bosack, Providence College; Carl L. Denit, Dutchess County College; Wendy L. Dunn, Coe College; John Foust, Parkland College; Marvin Goldstein, Rider College; Arthur Gutman, Florida Institute of Technology; George Herrick, SUNY—Alfred State College; Sidney Hochman, Nassau Community College; John H. Hummel, University of Houston; Sam L. Hutchinson, Radford University; Jarvel Jackson, McLennan Community College; Robert L. Johnson, Umpqua Community College; Eve Jones, Los Angeles City College; Mary-Louise Kean, University of California—Irvine; Richard Kellogg, SUNY—Alfred State College; Elaine LeVine, New Mexico State University; Charles Levinthal, Hofstra University; Robert MacAleese, Spring Hill College; Daniel Madsen, University of Minnesota—Duluth; Thomas Malloy, New Mexico State University; S. R. Mathews, Converse College; Richard McCarbery, Lorain College; Derrill McGuigan, Rider College; Leroy Metze, Western Kentucky University; Thomas Minor, SUNY at Stony Brook; Joel Morgovsky, Brookdale Community College; Walena C. Morse, West Chester State College; Jeffrey Nevid, St. Johns University; Joseph Palladino, Indiana State University—Evansville; John Pennachio, Adirondack Community College; Terry Pettijohn, Ohio State University—Marion; Gregory Pezzetti, Santa Ana College; Donis Price, Mesa Community College; Valda Robinson, Hillsborough Community College; Rene A. Ruiz, New Mexico State University; H. R. Schiffman, Rutgers University; Paul Wellman, Texas A&M; Richard Whinery, Ohio State University—Chillocothe; Robert Williams, William Jewel College; Keith A. Wollen, Washington State University.

I am grateful to John Michel, publisher, for his enthusiastic support of *Psychology*, and for the support he provided its author at many steps along the way. Dan Loch provided detailed and sound advice that aided me in integrating the suggestions of reviewers. Alison Podel, assistant editor, helped me with details too numerous to mention here. Suffice it to say that when I needed something, most of the time I dialed her number. My gratitude to Karen Thompson for marketing the second edition of this textbook, and to Nedah Abbott, Psychology Editor, for her words of encouragement. I owe a special debt to Arlene Katz, Senior Project Manager, who navigated the final manuscript through the sometimes choppy waters of production. Lou Scardino directed the art program for the book, and is to be credited for giving the text its visual impact. Pat Sarcuni ably managed the production of the book. A belated thank you to Marie Schappert for her expertise in marketing the first edition of *Psychology*. A debt of gratitude must be paid to Ray Ashton and Harry McQuillen, without whose faith and continued support this book would not exist in its present form.

The publishing professionals at Holt, Rinehart and Winston are a particularly able and inspiring group of individuals. It is a continuing privilege to work with them.

Contents

THREE

Sensation and Perception   79

SIX

Language, Thought, and Intelligence   213

SEVEN

Motivation and Emotion   255

EIGHT

Developmental Psychology   293

NINE

Personality: Theory and Measurement   341

TEN

Stress and Adjustment   387

ELEVEN

Abnormal Behavior   423

TWELVE

Psychotherapy   461

THIRTEEN

Sexual Behavior   499

FOURTEEN

Social Psychology   535

Psychology

SECOND EDITION

OUTLINE

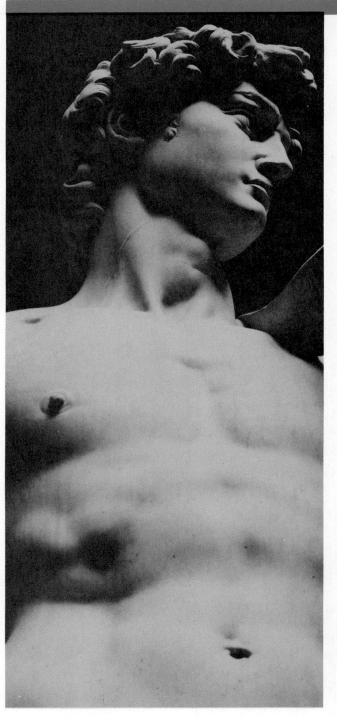

What Is Psychology?

- Psychology is the study of the mind.
- Psychologists attempt to control the behavior of other people.
- The single largest group of psychologists is employed by colleges and universities.
- Only people use tools.
- Alcohol causes aggression.
- You could survey twenty million Americans and still not predict accurately the outcome of a presidential election.
- So-called "talk-show therapy" is unethical.

What Is Psychology?

"What a piece of work is man!" wrote William Shakespeare. "How noble in reason! how infinite in faculty! in form, in moving, how express and admirable! in action how like an angel! in apprehension how like a god! the beauty of the world! the paragon of animals!"

You probably had no trouble recognizing yourself in Shakespeare's description—"noble in reason," "admirable," godlike in understanding, head and shoulders above all other animals. That's you to a "t," isn't it? But human behavior is greatly varied, and much of it is not so admirable. And a good deal of human behavior, even familiar behavior, is rather puzzling. Consider these examples:

Most adults on crowded city streets will not stop to help a person lying on the sidewalk, or to help a lost child. Why?

While most of us watch television, ride a bicycle, and jog or go for a swim, some people seek excitement by driving motorcycles at breakneck speed, climbing the outside of the World Trade Center, or skydiving. Why?

Most adults who smoke cigarettes or overeat know that they are probably jeopardizing their health. Yet they continue in their hazardous habits. Why?

Some children seem capable of learning more in school than others. Their teachers scan their records and find that more capable children usually have higher IQs—that is, higher scores on intelligence tests. But what is "intelligence"? Why do some people have, or seem to have, more of "it" than others?

A rapist or murderer claims to have committed his crime because another "personality" living in him took over, or because a dog prompted him with "mental messages." What is wrong with such people? What can be done about it?

"What a piece of work is man!" wrote William Shakespeare. Psychologists agree. Psychologists use the scientific method to study the observable behavior and mental processes of this most complex and subtle of animals. Michelangelo's *David*, pictured here, captures the awesome beauty and power of man.

Human behavior has always fascinated other human beings. Sometimes we are even "surprised at ourselves." Psychologists, like other people, are intrigued by the mysteries of behavior and make an effort to answer questions such as we have posed. But while most people try to satisfy their curiosity about behavior in their spare time, or through casual observations, psychologists make the study of behavior their lifework.

Psychology may be defined as a scientific approach to the study of behavior. As a science, it brings carefully controlled methods of observation, such as the survey and the experiment, to bear on its subject matter whenever possible. Most psychologists are interested primarily in human behavior, yet many of them focus much or all of their research on the behavior of animals ranging from rats and pigeons to flatworms and gorillas. Some psychologists believe that research findings about such animals can be **generalized** to humans. Others argue that people are so distinct from other animals that we can only learn about people by studying people. As with many such controversies, both views hold much truth. For instance, laboratory studies of the nerve cells of animals like the squid have given us much insight into the workings of the nerve cells of people (see Chapter 2). But only by studying people can we understand the purely human inventions of morality, values, and romantic love. Yet many psychologists study the behavior of lower animals simply because they enjoy doing so. They are under no obligation to justify their interests on the basis of generalizability to people.

Psychologists generally agree that psychology is the science of behavior, but they do not all agree on what behavior is. Some psychologists prefer to limit their definition to observable behavior—for example, to activities like pressing a lever, turning left or right, eating and mating, or even involuntary bodily functions like heart rate, dilation of the pupils of the eyes, blood pressure, or emission of a certain brain wave. All these behaviors can be measured by simple observation or by reliable laboratory instruments. Other psychologists prefer to extend the definition of behavior to include mental processes like images, concepts, thoughts, dreams, and emotions. The difficulty in studying mental processes is that they are private events that cannot be fully verified through use of laboratory instruments. They are usually assumed to be present on the basis of the **self-report** of the person experiencing them. However, psychologists have found that mental processes often can be at least partially verified by laboratory instruments. Dreams, for instance, are most likely to occur when certain brain waves are being emitted (see Chapter 4). Strong emotions are usually accompanied by increases in heart rate and rate of breathing, or respiration (see Chapter 7). In this way psychologists who study mental processes can often tie them to a number of observable behaviors. This allows them to verify self-reports with some confidence.

The Goals of Psychology

Psychology, like other sciences, seeks to explain, predict, and control the events it studies. Thus, psychology seeks to explain, predict, and control observable behavior and mental processes.

Psychologists attempt to explain or understand behavior in terms of psychological concepts like learning, motivation, emotion, intelligence, personality, and attitudes. When possible, concepts are interwoven into **theories.** Theories are sets of statements about events that involve assumptions about behavior, and derived explanations and predictions. Many psychological the-

Psychology The science that studies observable behavior and mental processes. (From the Greek *psyche*, meaning "soul" or "mind," and the Greek suffix *-logos*, meaning "word.")

Generalize To extend or spread.

Self-report (1) A subject's testimony about his or her own thoughts, feelings, or behaviors; (2) a method of investigation in which information is obtained through the report of the subject.

Theory A formulation of relationships underlying observed events. A theory involves assumptions and logically derived explanations and predictions. (From the Greek *theoria*, meaning "a looking at.")

Variable A condition that is measured or controlled in a scientific study. A variable can vary in a measurable manner.

Pure research Research conducted without concern for immediate applications. Also called *basic research*.

Applied research Research conducted in an effort to find solutions to particular problems.

ories also involve anatomical structures or biological processes. For instance, our responses to drugs like alcohol and marijuana reflect the biochemical actions of these drugs and our expectations or beliefs about the drugs, as we shall see in Chapter 4.

A satisfactory psychological theory must allow us to predict behavior. For instance, a satisfactory theory of hunger will allow us to predict when people will eat and not eat. A broadly satisfying, comprehensive theory should have a wide range of applicability. A broad theory of hunger might apply to human beings and lower animals, to normal weight and overweight people, and to people who have been deprived of food for differing lengths of time. If our observations cannot be adequately explained by or predicted from a given theory, we should consider revising or replacing that theory.

In psychology many theories have been found to be incapable of explaining or predicting new observations. As a result they have been revised extensively. For example, the theory that hunger results from stomach contractions may be partially correct for normal weight individuals, but it is inadequate as an explanation for feelings of hunger among the overweight. In Chapter 7 we shall see that stomach contractions are only one of many factors, or **variables,** involved in hunger. Contemporary theories also focus on biological variables, such as fat cells and brain structures, and psychological variables such as the presence of other people who are eating and the time of day.

The notion of controlling behavior is highly controversial. Some people erroneously think that psychologists seek ways to make people do their bidding—like puppets dangling on strings. This could not be farther from the truth. Psychologists are generally committed to belief in the dignity of human beings, and human dignity demands that people be free to make their own decisions and choose their own behavior. Psychologists are learning more all the time about the various influences on human behavior, but they apply this knowledge only upon request and in ways they believe will be helpful to an individual or an institution. Later in this chapter you will see that ethical standards prevent psychologists from using any method in research or practice that might harm or injure an individual. Psychologists also only engage in research with people who have consented to participate after receiving an explanation of the purposes and procedures of the study.

The remainder of this chapter provides an overview of psychology and psychologists. You will see that psychologists have diverse interests and fields of specialization. We discuss the major perspectives psychologists have used in attempting to explain behavior, and note the historical development of these perspectives. Then we explore methods psychologists use to test their theoretical assumptions and gather new information about behavior.

What Psychologists Do

Psychologists share a keen interest in behavior, but in other ways they may differ markedly. Some psychologists engage primarily in basic or **pure research.** Pure research has no immediate application to personal or social problems, and has thus been characterized as research for its own sake. Other psychologists engage in **applied research,** which is designed to find solutions to specific personal or social problems. Still other psychologists do not engage in research at all. They are concerned with applying psychological knowledge to help individuals change their behavior so that they can be more effective in meeting their goals. A number of psychologists are engaged primarily in teaching, disseminating psychological knowledge in classrooms, seminars, and workshops. Figure 1.1 shows that the single largest group of psychologists is employed by colleges and universities, but some of these psychologists counsel students rather than teach.

Many psychologists are involved in all the activities described above: research, **consultation,** and teaching. For example, professors of psychology usually conduct pure or applied research and consult with individuals or industrial clients as well as instruct in the classroom. Full-time researchers may be called upon to consult with industrial clients and to organize seminars or workshops in which they help others acquire some of their skills. Practitioners, like clinical and industrial psychologists, may also engage in research—which is usually applied—and teach in the classroom or workshop. Unfortunately for psychologists who teach, conduct research, and also carry on a practice, research into expanding the week to 250 hours does not look promising.

Let us now explore some of the specialties of psychologists. Although psychologists tend to wear more than one hat, let us suggest three broad areas of specialization: clinical services, research, and industry. Psychologists in all specialties are found on college and university faculties.

Psychologists in Clinical Services

Clinical Psychologists   Clinical psychologists specialize in helping people who are behaving abnormally adjust to the demands of life. Their clients' problems may range from severe anxiety or depression to sexual dysfunctions to loss of goals in life. Clinical psychologists are trained to evaluate problems through structured interviews and psychological tests. They help their clients

FIGURE 1.1   Specialties and Work Settings of Psychologists. A recent survey of members of the American Psychological Association (Stapp & Fulcher, 1981) showed that 45 percent identified themselves as clinical psychologists (see chart at left). The chart on the right shows that the single largest group of psychologists works in colleges and universities, while the next largest group works in hospitals, clinics, and other human service settings.

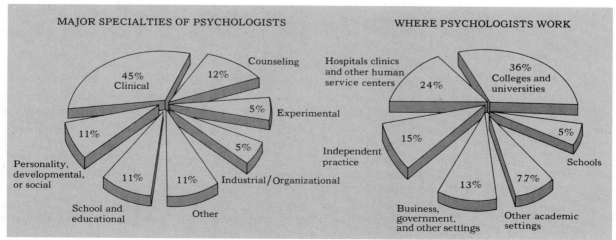

Psychotherapy The systematic application of psychological knowledge to the treatment of problem behavior. Psychotherapy frequently encourages clients to express feelings and develop insight into motives; see Chapter 12. (From the Greek *psyche,* meaning "soul" or "mind," and *therapeuein,* meaning "to treat.")

Behavior therapy Application of principles of learning (see Chapter 5) to the direct modification of problem behavior. In contrast to psychotherapy, behavior therapy may be conducted without the development of client self-insight; see Chapter 12.

Dyslexia (dis–LEGS–see–uh). Impaired reading ability. (From the Greek prefix *dys–,* meaning "bad," and *lexis,* meaning "speech.")

resolve their problems and change maladaptive behavior through the techniques of **psychotherapy** and **behavior therapy.** Clinical psychologists may work in institutions for the mentally ill or mentally retarded, in outpatient clinics, in college and university clinics, or they may establish private practices.

As you can see in Figure 1.1, clinical psychologists comprise the largest subgroup of psychologists. So it is not surprising that most lay people think of clinical psychologists when they hear the term psychologist. Many clinical psychologists divide their time between clinical practice, teaching, and research.

Counseling Psychologists   Counseling psychologists, like clinical psychologists, use interviews and tests to define their clients' problems. Clients of counseling psychologists typically have adjustment problems but do not behave in seriously abnormal ways. These problems may include difficulty making academic or vocational decisions, difficulty making friends in college, marital or family conflict, physical handicaps, or the adjustment problems of an offender who is returning to the community from prison. Counseling psychologists use various counseling methods to help clients clarify their goals and find ways of surmounting obstacles so that they can meet their goals. Counseling psychologists are often employed in college and university counseling and testing centers. They are also found in rehabilitation agencies.

School Psychologists   School psychologists are employed by school systems to help identify and assist students who encounter problems that interfere with learning. These problems range from social and family problems to emotional disturbance and learning disabilities like **dyslexia.** School psychologists define students' problems through interviews with teachers, parents, and students themselves, through psychological tests such as intelligence and achievement tests, and through direct observation of student behavior in the classroom. They consult with teachers, school officials, parents, and other professionals in an effort to help students overcome obstacles to learning. They help make decisions about placement of students in special education and remediation programs.

Educational Psychologists   Educational psychologists, like school psychologists, are concerned with optimizing classroom conditions to facilitate learning. But they usually focus on improvement of course planning and instruction methods for a school system rather than on the identification and assistance of children with learning problems.

Educational psychologists are often more concerned than school psychologists about theoretical issues relating to learning and child development. They are more likely to engage in pure and applied research and to hold faculty posts in colleges and universities. Some educational psychologists specialize in preparing standardized tests, such as the Scholastic Aptitude Tests.

Community Psychologists   Community psychologists are similar to clinical psychologists in their training and functions. However, they more often work in community agencies—such as community mental health centers—and they tend to focus on the prevention as well as the treatment of abnormal behavior. They consult with community organizations to develop ways of educating the public about personal and social problems like drug abuse and child abuse.

Psychologists in Research

Psychologists in all specialties may conduct pure or applied research. Still, there are a number of specialties in which psychologists are more likely to be engaged primarily in research and, quite often, in teaching.

Developmental Psychologists   Developmental psychologists study changes—physical, emotional, cognitive, and social—that occur in people throughout the life span. They attempt to sort out the relative influences of heredity and the environment on certain types of growth and to learn the causes of developmental abnormalities.

We find developmental psychologists conducting research on a wide variety of issues. These may include the effects of maternal use of aspirin or heroin on an unborn child, the value of breast-feeding as compared with bottle feeding, children's concepts of space and time, adolescent sexual behavior, and factors that may help the elderly adjust to forced retirement.

On Hurricanes, HIM-icanes, and Sex Roles

In May 1979 the World Meteorological Association decided at long last to give hurricanes men's as well as women's names. Since 1953 a number of "female" storms had done their damage. But beginning in 1979, storms named Frederick and David joined their "sisters" in devastating the islands of the Caribbean and the southern coastline of the United States.

The World Meteorological Association added men's names to this frightening roster in response to protests from women's groups. The women had been outraged by the exclusive use of women's names because of the implication that storminess and unpredictability were specifically female traits.

A sex role is a cluster of traits considered masculine or feminine in our culture. Personality and social psychologists are vitally concerned about sex roles. Later in this book you will see that they have found at least partial answers to a number of provocative questions:

- What traits have been considered masculine? What traits have been considered feminine?
- What traits do people attribute to the "healthy man" and to the "healthy woman"?
- Are women more emotional but less logical than men?
- Are women more talkative than men?
- Are men more aggressive than women?
- How do men and women compare in their verbal and math skills?
- Do women make natural mothers?

Sex roles have been changing in the United States. A number of men are becoming househusbands while their wives trek to the office each morning. For those who see men as aggressive, competi-

In recent years, men and women have felt more free to express traits considered part of the sex role of the opposite sex. In this scene from the film *Kramer vs. Kramer*, Dustin Hoffman learns that he can be warm and supportive of his son—that he can show traits that have been traditionally considered feminine—after his wife leaves them.

tive, and achievement-oriented, such a turnabout is puzzling. For those who believe the woman's place is in the home, it is almost blasphemous. Yet it would appear that an increasing number of people, men and women, are showing psychological androgyny. That is, they feel free to express traditionally masculine traits and traditionally feminine traits. They are self-assertive yet supportive, logical yet warm. Research seems to be suggesting that psychologically androgynous people may be better capable of adapting to a variety of life's challenges because of the wider range of traits they can bring to bear.

Personality Psychologists Personality psychologists attempt to determine influences on human thought processes, feelings, and behaviors and to explain both normal and abnormal behaviors. They are particularly concerned with human issues such as **anxiety,** aggression, **sex-typing,** and learning by observing others. Other topics of interest to personality psychologists include **repression** as a way in which we defend ourselves from feelings of anxiety and guilt, and the effects of TV violence.

Social Psychologists Social psychologists are primarily concerned with ways in which individuals and groups of people influence the behavior of other people. Whereas personality psychologists tend to look within the person for explanations of behavior, social psychologists tend to focus on social or external influences.

Social psychologists have historically focused on topics including attitude formation and attitude change, interpersonal attraction and liking, sex roles and **stereotypes,** obedience to authority, conformity to group norms, and group decision-making processes. Social psychologists, like personality psychologists, study the problem of human aggression.

Environmental Psychologists Environmental psychologists examine how behavior influences and is influenced by the social and physical environment. Like social psychologists, they are concerned with the effects of crowding on the behavior of city dwellers. Environmental psychologists study ways in which buildings and cities can be designed to better serve human needs. They also investigate the effects of **ambient** temperatures, noise, and air pollution on people and lower animals.

TABLE 1.1   Divisions of the American Psychological Association

General Psychology	Consumer Psychology
Teaching of Psychology	Theoretical and Philosophical Psychology
Experimental Psychology	Experimental Analysis of Behavior
Evaluation and Measurement	History of Psychology
Physiological and Comparative Psychology	Community Psychology
Developmental Psychology	Psychopharmacology
Personality and Social Psychology	Psychotherapy
The Society for the Psychological Study of Social Issues	Psychological Hypnosis
Psychology and the Arts	State Psychological Association Affairs
Clinical Psychology	Humanistic Psychology
Consulting Psychology	Mental Retardation
Industrial and Organizational Psychology	Population and Environmental Psychology
Educational Psychology	Psychology of Women
School Psychology	Psychologists Interested in Religious Issues
Counseling Psychology	Child and Youth Services
Psychologists in Public Service	Health Psychology
Military Psychology	Psychoanalysis
Adult Development and Aging	Clinical Neuropsychology
The Society of Engineering Psychologists	Psychology and the Law
Rehabilitation Psychology	Psychologists in Independent Practice

This constantly evolving list reflects the diversity of interests found among psychologists, as well as areas of social concern and individual specialties. Many psychologists are active in several divisions.

Environmental psychologists study relationships between behavior and the environment. They suggest that large cities may so overload us with stimulation that we might not notice this gentleman's leisurely stroll across New York's Fifth Avenue.

Experimental Psychologists   Psychologists in all specialties may conduct experimental research. However, those called experimental psychologists conduct research into fundamental processes relevant to all other specializations. These include the functions of the nervous system, sensation and perception, learning, and motivation, to name but a few. Experimental psychologists who focus on the biological foundations of behavior and seek to understand the relationships between biological changes and psychological events are called **physiological psychologists.**

   Experimental psychologists are more likely than other psychologists to engage in basic or pure research. Still, their findings are often applied by other specialists in psychological practice. Pure research in motivation, for example, has helped clinical and counseling psychologists devise strategies for helping people with weight problems. Pure research in learning has helped school and educational psychologists optimize learning conditions in the schools. In later chapters you will see that brain research has led to various attempts to control aggression in people and lower animals through techniques like electrical stimulation of certain parts of the brain (abbreviated ESB) and **psychosurgery.** Many aspects of this sort of research are in their infancy, and some work in this area has stimulated controversy. However, most of the controversy surrounds certain applications of research findings rather than the value of pure research itself.

Psychologists in Industry

Industrial Psychologists   Industrial psychologists are employed by business firms to apply psychological expertise to improve working conditions, enhance productivity, and counsel employees who encounter problems on the job. They help in innovation of concepts like **job sharing** and **flextime,** and evaluate the results. They assist in the processes of hiring and promotion. They may use psychological tests to help determine whether job applicants

Physiological psychologists (FIZZ–zee–oh–LODGE–uh–kull). Psychologists who study the relationships between biological processes, on the one hand, and observable behaviors and mental processes, on the other. (From the Greek *physis*, meaning "nature.")

Psychosurgery A controversial biological treatment of problem behavior in which specific areas or structures of the brain are destroyed. See Chapter 12.

Job sharing Dividing a full-time job into part-time work that is shared by two or more workers. Also called work sharing.

Flextime A flexible work schedule which attempts to meet worker as well as company needs.

One of the Major Participants in Experimental Psychology. To you this fellow may look like just another rat, but he and his fellow rodents have participated in countless thousands of experiments in physiological psychology, sensation and perception, learning and motivation. Although many consider learning to be rather simple and mechanical in the rat, some experiments suggest that rats can form cognitive maps of their world, as you will see in Chapter 5.

have abilities, interests, and traits that predict successful performance of certain job responsibilities.

Industrial psychology is currently a rapidly expanding specialization. Businesses have been learning that psychological expertise can help them increase productivity and worker involvement, while decreasing employee turnover and absenteeism.

Consumer Psychologists   Consumer psychologists study the behavior of consumers in an effort to predict and influence their behavior. Their functions include advising store managers how to lay out the aisles of a supermarket to increase impulse buying and how to arrange window displays to draw customers in. They also devise strategies for making newspaper ads and television commercials more effective. Interestingly, they have found that while some ads may catch the eye, like the photo of Brooke Shields on p. 13, you may remember the photo but forget the product when the ad is too sexy (LaChance and others, 1978; Schultz, 1978).

How Psychologists View Behavior

There's no place like home—for violence, that is. Consider the following statistics:

- Half of all American wives have been physically assaulted by their husbands at least once.
- In a given year, 16 of every 100 couples have conflicts that involve biting, kicking, punching, or worse.
- Each year more than a million American children are brought to the attention of authorities as victims of child abuse.

We know to avoid dark streets and alleyways and not to frequent unknown bars. We know that the world at large is a violent place, with open

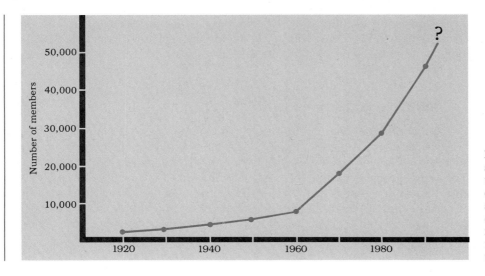

FIGURE 1.2 The profession of psychology has undergone a population explosion. The membership of the American Psychological Association has mushroomed from 228 in 1910 to well over 50,000 in the 1980s.

warfare and guerrilla conflict. But for many Americans, the most dangerous place is home. In *Behind Closed Doors: A Survey of Family Violence in America*, Murray Strauss and his colleagues (1979) report results of a survey of 2,143 people. They estimate that as many as eight million Americans are assaulted by family members each year.

Psychologists tend to view problems like human violence and aggression from a variety of perspectives, or broad psychological theories. When we are aware of the perspectives of psychologists, we have some insight into their basic assumptions about human nature. We can also, to some degree, predict the sort of research they prefer to conduct in their search for answers.

There are at least four major perspectives in contemporary psychology: the biological, the cognitive, the psychoanalytic, and the behavioral perspectives. Each of them has its own tradition and history. Let us have a look at each of them to see what they say about human nature. We shall also note what each perspective suggests about the origins and control of human aggression. While it is simplistic to make broad generalizations about these

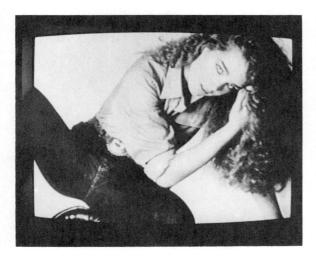

Consumer psychologists have found that if ads are too sexy, they may catch the eye but the reader may not be able to recall the name of the product. Does this photo of Brooke Shields in her Calvins help viewers recall the brand of jeans, or do they just remember Brooke Shields?

Determinants Factors that set limits.

Hormone A chemical substance that promotes development of bodily structures and regulates various bodily functions. (From the Greek *horman,* meaning "to stimulate" or "to excite.")

Genes The basic building blocks of heredity.

Morphine (MORE–feen). A narcotic derived from opium that produces feelings of well-being. (From *Morpheus,* the Greek god of dreams.)

perspectives, let us note that the first three—biological, cognitive, and psychoanalytic—tend to look within the person for explanations of behavior. The fourth—the behavioral perspective—tends to focus on the person's situation, or circumstances.

The Biological Perspective

Psychologists assume that every thought, fantasy, dream, and mental image is made possible by the nervous system, and especially by that central part of the nervous system we call the brain. Physiological psychologists seek links between measurable events in the brain—like the "firing" of brain cells—and mental processes. They have used techniques like electrical stimulation of certain sites in the brain to show that these areas are involved in a wide range of emotional and behavioral responses, like mating behavior and aggression.

Psychologists who focus on biological **determinants** of behavior also study the influence of hormones and genes. For instance, the **hormone** prolactin stimulates not only production of milk in rats but also maternal behavior. In lower animals, sex hormones not only cause development of the sexual organs, but also determine whether mating behavior will follow stereotypical male or female behavior patterns. **Genes** are the basic units of heredity. Psychologists are vitally interested in the extent of genetic influences on human traits and behaviors like intelligence, abnormal behaviors, criminal behaviors, and even the tendency to become addicted to drugs like alcohol and **morphine.** Recent studies (e.g., Buss & Plomin, 1975) have shown that identical twins (who share the same genetic endowment) are more likely than fraternal twins (who are no more closely related than other brothers and sisters) to share broad personality traits like sociability, emotionality, and level of activity. In Chapter 6 we shall see that the degree to which intelligence reflects heredity *("nature")* or environmental influences *("nurture")* is a hotly debated issue with political implications.

Physiological psychologists use ESB and other techniques to learn what parts of the brain are linked to such behaviors as mating and aggression. The monkey in this photo is exhibiting a rage response, not because the other monkey in the cage has provoked him, but because certain areas deep within his brain are receiving electrical stimulation.

The Biological Perspective and Aggression Electrical stimulation of the brain triggers aggressive behaviors and **rage responses** in a number of lower animals. Thus, some psychologists have suggested that human aggression may someday be controlled through ESB or other biological means of changing behavior. This concept conjures up the spectre of people being made into docile, compliant robots, then manipulated into doing the bidding of others. But this type of control actually may not be possible with people, since aggression seems less localized and mechanical in people than in lower animals. It is possible that certain areas in the brain may signal the sensation that the person is in a situation in which aggression is one of several possible responses. However, learning influences the probability that the person will actually respond aggressively.

Sociobiology **Sociobiology** is a recent offshoot of the biological perspective that became popular in the 1970s. Sociobiology views the gene as the "ultimate unit of life," or the "hereditary units . . . which either fail or prosper as a result of (natural) selection" (Leak & Christopher, 1982, pp. 313–314). Sociobiology argues that the underlying purpose of animal behavior is to contribute as many genes as possible to the next generation. That is, lower animals and—yes—people are motivated to have and raise as many offspring as possible. One of the conditions for raising offspring is establishing a **territory** which permits one to obtain food and attract a mate. More aggressive individuals are usually likely to be more successful at establishing such territories. Therefore, in such species, whatever genes are linked to aggressive behavior are more likely to be transmitted to the following generation. Human beings may be one such species, although our intelligence—our capacity to outwit other species—seems to be a more central factor in our survival.

Sociobiology has been severely attacked on various grounds. Many scientists argue that it is absurd to suggest that genes can harbor anything akin to an "intent" to be transmitted. Sociobiology also seems to suggest that aggressiveness is natural and desirable. Thus, efforts to control aggression can be seen as doomed to failure and even morally questionable, as interfering with the natural order of things.

The Cognitive Perspective

Psychologists with a **cognitive** perspective are interested in studying our mental processes. They investigate how we perceive and mentally represent the outside world, how we go about solving problems, how we dream and daydream. Cognitive psychologists attempt to study what we refer to as the **mind.**

Structuralism The beginning of psychology as a science is often set in the year 1879, when Wilhelm Wundt (1832–1920) established the first psychological laboratory in Leipzig, Germany. Wundt claimed that the mind was a natural event and could be studied scientifically, just as light, heat, and the flow of blood could also be studied scientifically. Wundt used the method of **introspection** to try to discover the basic elements of thought. When presented with various sights and sounds, he and his colleagues tried to look inward as objectively as possible to describe their sensations and feelings.

Wundt and his students—among them, Edward Bradford Titchener, who brought Wundt's methodology to Cornell University in the United States—

Rage response Stereotypical aggressive behavior that can be brought forth in lower animals by electrical stimulation of the brain.

Sociobiology A biological theory of social behavior which assumes that the primary purpose of behavior is to insure the transmission of an organism's genes from generation to generation.

Territory The particular area appropriated and defended by an animal, or pair of animals, for purposes of feeding and breeding.

Cognitive Having to do with mental processes. (From the Latin *cognitio*, meaning "knowledge.")

Mind That part of consciousness involved in perception and awareness. (From the Greek *menos*, meaning "spirit" or "force.")

Introspection A method of describing one's mental content as objectively as possible. (From the Latin *intro-*, meaning "inward," and *specere*, meaning "to look.")

Wilhelm Wundt.

William James.

founded the school of psychology known as **structuralism.** Structuralism attempted to define the makeup of conscious experience, breaking it down into sensations (like sight or taste), feelings, and images (like memories or dreams). The first school of psychology was cognitive in nature.

Functionalism   Toward the end of the nineteenth century, William James (1842–1910), a Harvard University physiologist and brother of the novelist Henry James, adopted a broader view of psychology that focused on the relationships between conscious experience and behavior. He described his views in the first psychology textbook, *The Principles of Psychology*, published in 1890 by the same publisher as the book you are now reading. Though it is almost 100 years old, some still consider James's book "the single greatest work in American psychology" (Adelson, 1982, p. 52). James argued that experience is fluid and continuous. It cannot be broken down into basic units as readily as the structuralists maintained.

James also noted how past experience teaches us to function more adaptively. Many of our functions, like lifting forks to our mouths and turning doorknobs, require our full attention at first. If you don't believe this, stand by with paper towels and watch a baby's first efforts at self-feeding. But with experience such activities can become **habitual,** or automatic through repetition. We can then carry them out without much attention at all, freeing ourselves to focus on other matters, such as our witty dinner conversation. James founded the school of **functionalism,** which addresses the ways in which experience permits us to function more effectively in our environment. Habitual responses are also part of the behavioral tradition, which we shall discuss soon. But because functionalism emphasizes personal experience, the functionalist school is considered to be within the cognitive tradition.

Gestalt Psychology   In the 1920s, another cognitive school was quite active in Germany: **Gestalt psychology.** In the 1930s, a group of noted Gestalt psychologists, among them Kurt Koffka, Wolfgang Köhler, and Max Wertheimer, left Europe to escape the Nazi threat. They carried on their work in the United States.

Gestalt psychologists argue that you cannot explain human perception in terms of basic units. They claim that we tend to perceive separate pieces of information as integrated wholes, or in terms of the contexts in which they occur. Note Figure 1.3. The dots in the centers of the configurations at the left are the same size, yet we may perceive them as being of different sizes because of the contexts in which they appear. The gray squares in the center figure are equally bright, but they may look different because of their different backgrounds. The second symbol in each line at the right is identical. But in the top row we may perceive it as a B, and in the bottom row as the number 13. The symbol has not changed, only the context in which it appears. In *The Prince and the Pauper*, Mark Twain dressed a peasant boy as a prince and the kingdom bowed to him. Do clothes sometimes make the man, or woman?

Gestalt psychologists were at one time involved in studying the role of **insight** in both human and animal problem solving. Their findings suggest that we often manipulate the mentally represented elements of problems until we group them in such a way that we believe that we shall be able to reach our goal. The manipulations may take quite some time in a sort of mental trial and error. But once the proper grouping has been found, we seem to perceive it all at once. The chimpanzee in Figure 1.4 is at first unsuccessful

Structuralism The school of psychology, founded by Wundt and his students, which argues that the mind consists of three basic elements—sensations, feelings, and images—which combine to form experience.

Habitual Having the nature of a habit, which is a response to a stimulus that becomes automatic with repetition.

Functionalism The school of psychology, founded by William James, that emphasizes the uses or functions of the mind rather than the elements of experience.

Gestalt psychology (gesh–TALT). The school of psychology that emphasizes the tendency to organize perceptions into wholes, to integrate separate stimuli into meaningful patterns. (*Gestalt* is a German word meaning "shape" or "form.")

Insight In Gestalt psychology, the sudden reorganization of perceptions, allowing the sudden solution of a problem.

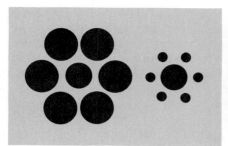

(A) Are the dots in the center of the configuration the same size? Why not take a ruler and measure their diameters.

(B) Which of the gray squares is brighter?

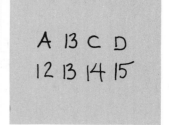

(C) Is the second symbol in each line the letter B or the number 13?

FIGURE 1.3. Gestalt psychologists have shown that our perceptions depend not only on our sensory impressions, but also on the context of our impressions. They argue that human perception cannot be explained in terms of basic units because we tend to interpret our perceptions of things as wholes, in terms of the contexts in which they occur. You will interpret a man's running in your direction very differently depending on whether you are on a deserted street at night or at a track in the morning.

in reaching for bananas hanging from the ceiling. Then it suddenly piles the boxes atop one another and climbs them to reach the banana. It seems that the chimp has experienced a sudden reorganization of the mental elements that represent the problem—that is, has had a "flash of insight." Have you ever sat pondering a problem for quite a while, and then suddenly the solution has appeared? Did it seem to "come out of nowhere"? In a flash? Was it difficult at that point to understand how it could have taken so long?

FIGURE 1.4 At first the chimpanzee cannot reach the bananas hanging from the ceiling. After some time has passed, it suddenly piles the boxes on top of one another to reach the fruit, behavior suggestive of a "flash of insight." Gestalt psychologists argue that behavior is often too complex to be explained in terms of learning mechanical responses to environmental stimulation.

When Gestalt psychologists undertook research into insight learning with chimpanzees, they assumed that the chimps had developed insight into problems when at first they floundered about and then, suddenly, they reached a goal in a burst of activity. But the chimps could not explain their problem-solving processes to us. As we shall see in Chapter 6, psychologists in recent years have taught chimps and gorillas to use many of the symbols of sign language. Within a few years, shall we learn more about the problem-solving processes of apes by communicating with them?

Cognitive Development Today the cognitive tradition in psychology has many different faces. For instance, Swiss psychologist Jean Piaget's (1896–1980) innovative study of the intellectual or cognitive development of children has inspired thousands of research projects by developmental and educational psychologists. The focus of this research is to learn how children and adults mentally represent and reason about the world.

As we shall see in Chapter 8, Piaget has shown us that the child's conception of the world seems to develop through various stages of sophistication. Although the role of experience is essential to children, their cognitive understanding also seems to develop according to something akin to an inner clock.

Humanistic Psychology **Humanistic psychology** is a recently developed school of psychology within the cognitive tradition. It stresses the importance of human consciousness, self-awareness, and the capacity to make choices. Consciousness is seen as the unifying force underlying our personalities. Humanists believe that to a large extent we "invent ourselves"—our ways of responding to the world—as we go through life.

The goals of humanistic psychology tend to be more applied than academic. Humanistic psychologists have been involved in devising ways to help people "get in touch" with their feelings and realize their potentials. Humanistic psychology reached the peak of its popularity in the 1970s with encounter groups, Gestalt therapy, meditation, and a number of other methods that have been referred to, collectively, as the Human Potential Movement. We shall discuss some of these techniques in Chapters 4 and 12.

The Cognitive Perspective and Aggression Cognitive psychologists assert that our behavior is influenced by our values, our perceptions of our situations, and by choice. People who believe that aggression is necessary and justified, as in wartime, are likely to act aggressively in that situation. People who believe that a particular war or act of aggression is unjust, or who oppose aggression under all circumstances, are less likely to behave aggressively. Piaget noted that the bases of our moral judgments change as we mature. For instance, five-year-old children might consider an act of aggression wrong simply because they have been told that aggression is bad. However, an eight-year-old child would also be likely to consider the motives of the aggressor. Acting in self-defense or to apprehend a criminal might be seen as right and just.

Cognitively-oriented psychotherapists note that we are more likely to respond aggressively to a provocation when our thoughts magnify the insult or otherwise stir feelings of anger. In Chapter 12 you will see how a number of explosive people gained control of aggressive impulses when they learned

Humanistic psychology The school of psychology that assumes the existence of the self and emphasizes the importance of consciousness and self-awareness.

to perceive a provocation as a problem demanding a solution rather than an insult demanding retaliation.

The Psychoanalytic Perspective

Each year, like clockwork, every television crime series has a show in which a *psycho* goes on a killing spree. At the show's conclusion a **psychiatrist** explains that the killer was "unconsciously" doing away with his own mother or father.

Perhaps a friend has tried to "interpret" a slip of the tongue you made, or asked you what you thought might be the symbolic "meaning" of a dream.

The notions that people are driven by deeply hidden impulses, and that verbal slips and dreams reflect unconscious wishes, are now themselves deeply imbedded in our culture. This is largely due to the influence of one man— Sigmund Freud (1856–1939). Freud, a Viennese physician who, like the Gestalt psychologists, fled to the United States in the 1930s to escape the Nazi tyranny, founded the school of psychology known as **psychoanalysis.** Although the psychoanalytic perspective is only one of many viewpoints in psychology, it has captured the imagination of the public. To many people, the psychoanalytic perspective is what psychology is all about. Yet it has been challenged repeatedly by experimental psychologists, and Freud's own followers have continually refined and modified psychoanalytic theory. In fact, if Freud were alive today, he might disown most of his followers, as he did members of his circle who made less radical changes during his lifetime.

In contrast with psychologists, who conducted research mainly in the laboratory, Freud, the physician, gained his understanding of human thoughts, emotions, and behavior through clinical interviews with his patients. He was astounded at how little insight his patients seemed to have into their motives. Some patients justified the most abominable behavior with absurd explanations. Others, by contrast, seized the opportunity to blame themselves for nearly every misfortune that had befallen the human species.

Freud came to believe that hidden impulses, especially primitive sexual and aggressive impulses, were more influential than conscious thought in determining human behavior. As you will see in later chapters, Freud thought that most of the mind was unconscious, consisting of a seething cauldron of conflicting impulses, urges, and wishes. People were motivated to gratify these impulses, but at the same time they sought to avoid condemnation by others and themselves. Thus, they would often delude themselves about their own motives.

Freud also devised a method of psychotherapy which is also called psychoanalysis. Psychoanalysis aims to help patients gain insight into many of their deep-seated conflicts and to find socially acceptable ways of expressing wishes and gratifying needs. Psychoanalytic therapy is a long-term process that can last several years.

The Psychoanalytic Perspective and Aggression   Freud believed that aggressive impulses were, in part, an inevitable result of the frustrations of daily life. Yet children, fearing their parents' disapproval and loss of love, would come to repress most aggressive wishes. But in his later years Freud became so despondent about the mass slaughter of World War I and other human tragedies that he **postulated** the existence of a death instinct, **thanatos.** Than-

Psychiatrist A physician who specializes in the application of medical treatments to abnormal behavior.

Psychoanalysis The school of psychology, founded by Sigmund Freud, that emphasizes the importance of unconscious motives and conflicts as determinants of human behavior. (Also the name of Freud's method of psychotherapy.)

Postulate To claim or assume. To take as self-evident.

Thanatos (THAN–uh–toes). In psychoanalytic theory, the death instinct. (A Greek word meaning "death.")

Sigmund Freud, at 29, and his Future Wife, Martha Bernays. Freud, a physician, gained his understanding of human behavior from clinical interviews with patients. He was astounded at how they deluded themselves about their true motives, and came to believe that the mind was mostly unconscious, a seething cauldron of conflicting impulses and wishes.

Behaviorism The school of psychology that defines psychology as the study of observable behavior only, and investigates relationships between stimuli and responses.

atos was the final expression of what Freud saw as the unconscious human wish to return to the stress-free days prior to birth. Not a very pretty picture of human nature.

Research has been somewhat hard on the psychoanalytic perspective. Still, psychoanalysts claim, with some justification, that their views have not been tested adequately in the laboratory. We shall expand our discussion and evaluation of psychoanalysis in later chapters.

The Behavioral Perspective

If you consistently reward a rat with food for turning right when it comes to a corner or choice-point in a maze, it will learn to turn right, at least when it has been deprived of food for a while. But what does the rat think or say to itself when it is learning to turn to the right? "Hmm, last time I was in this situation and turned to the right, I was given some food. Think I'll try that again"?

John B. Watson.

Does it seem somewhat ridiculous to try to place yourself in the "mind" of a rat? So it seemed to John Broadus Watson (1878–1958), the founder of American **behaviorism.** But he was asked to consider just such a question as one of the requirements for his doctoral degree, which he received from the University of Chicago in 1903. Watson bridled at the efforts of the structuralists and the functionalists to study "consciousness" during the early part of this century. He asserted that if psychology were to be a hard science, like physics or chemistry, it must study only observable, measurable behavior. It must not concern itself with mental events, or "elements of consciousness," that were accessible only to the organism experiencing them.

Watson argued that psychology should concern itself with measurable **responses** to environmental **stimuli.** He pointed to the laboratory experiments being carried out in Russia by Ivan Pavlov as a model. Pavlov had found that laboratory dogs would salivate when a bell was rung, if ringing the bell had been paired with feeding a number of times. Pavlov explained the salivation in terms of the laboratory conditions, or **conditioning,** that led to it—not in terms of the imagined mental processes of the dogs subjected to these conditions. Moreover, the response that Pavlov chose to study, salivation, was a public event that could be measured **reliably** by laboratory instruments. But it was absurd to try to determine what a dog, or a person, was thinking.

The behavioral perspective soon became firmly rooted in American psychology. Many psychologists condemned the cognitive and psychoanalytic perspectives for their efforts to portray processes that could not be seen, touched, or measured by any scientific instrument.

Harvard University psychologist B. F. Skinner introduced the concept of **reinforcement.** Organisms, he maintained, learned to behave in certain ways because they had been reinforced for doing so. Skinner demonstrated that laboratory animals would carry out all sorts of simple and complex behaviors because they had been reinforced for doing so. They will peck buttons (Figure 1.5) or turn in circles, then climb ladders and push toys across the floor (see Barnabus the rat in Chapter 5). Many psychologists adopted the view that one could fully explain—in principle—all human behavior as the complex summation of so many instances of learning through reinforcement. Nevertheless, as a practical matter, they recognized that trying to list even one person's complete history of reinforcement would be a hopeless task.

Response In behavioral theory, a movement or other observable reaction to a stimulus.

Stimuli (STIM–you–lie, or STIM–you–lee). Plural of *stimulus*. (1) A change in the environment that leads to a change in behavior (a response). (2) Any form of physical energy, like light or sound, that impinges on the sensory receptors of an organism. (A Latin word meaning "goad," "pang," "spur," or "incentive.")

Conditioning In behavioral theory, a simple form of learning in which responses become associated with stimuli. See Chapter 5.

Reliably Consistently.

Reinforcement In behavioral theory, a stimulus that follows a response and increases the frequency of the response. See Chapter 5.

FIGURE 1.5 A Couple of Examples of the Power of Reinforcement. In the photo on the left, we see how our feathered gift to city life has earned its keep in many behavioral experiments on the effects of reinforcement. Here the pigeon pecks the red button because pecking this button has been followed (reinforced) by the dropping of a food pellet into the cage. In the photo on the right, Magic Raccoon shoots a basket. Behaviorists teach animals complex behaviors, like shooting baskets, by first reinforcing approximations to the goal (or target behavior). As time progresses, closer approximations are demanded before reinforcement is given.

The Behavioral Perspective and Aggression   The behavioral perspective assumes that people acquire aggressive skills through reinforcement. People also display aggressive skills in response to social provocations, like insults, or in response to frustration when they have been reinforced for doing so in the past. People who are strong, well-coordinated, and—in our culture—male are more likely to have been reinforced for exhibiting aggressive responses.

Behaviorists would not speak of "believing in" aggressive behavior or of "choosing" to act aggressively. Beliefs and choices are private mental events and for behaviorists not appropriate for scientific discussion.

Behavior Therapy   Behaviorists suggest that aggressive behaviors can be modified by refusing to reinforce them. Nonreinforcement of learned responses is called **extinction.** ("Extinction" may sound rather final, but in Chapter 5 you will see that it may not be.) Aggressive people may also be taught alternate responses to aggression and then reinforced for displaying the nonaggressive responses. The concepts of extinction and of teaching alternate responses for problem behaviors has led to a revolution in the methods available to clinical, counseling, and school psychologists.

In behavior therapy, the focus is on directly instigating adaptive behavior rather than trying to uncover how maladaptive behaviors were acquired. It should be noted that some clients seen in therapy are vitally interested in gaining insight into the origins of their behavior. In such cases therapists may supplement their behavioral techniques with other methods, or refer their clients elsewhere. Still, behavior therapy is one of the most direct paths to modifying problem behavior.

Social Learning Theory   John B. Watson was a **radical behaviorist.** For him behaviorism was a philosophy of life as well as a broad guideline for psychological research. Not only did he despair of measuring mental processes in the laboratory, but he also denied their influence on behavior in his private conversations.

The behavioral perspective remains a dominant force in psychology, but few modern-day psychologists consider themselves radical behaviorists. Many contemporary adherents to the behavioral tradition, like Albert Bandura and Walter Mischel of Stanford University, are proponents of **social learning theory.** They believe that people's acquired skills and reinforcement histories play an important role in their future behavior. However, they argue that knowledge of people's values and expectations are also essential if we are to be able to explain and predict their behavior in a given situation. The concepts of "values" and "expectations" clearly have a cognitive flavor.

Cognitive Behavior Therapy   Many behaviorally-oriented clinical and counseling psychologists practice **cognitive behavior therapy.** In attempting to foster adaptive behavior patterns, they focus not only on teaching clients new observable or **overt** behavior, but also help clients overcome self-defeating thought patterns. For instance, it is usually self-defeating for a client to think "I'll never be able to handle this!" when faced with a new challenge. Such thoughts increase our level of anxiety and distract us from the task at hand. Cognitive behavior therapists help clients pinpoint such harmful thoughts and replace them with more rational and encouraging thoughts.

Some psychologists believe that the future of psychology will see the integration of the behavioral and cognitive perspectives. Behaviorism, they maintain, has served its historial purpose in highlighting the excesses of the cognitive approach. But it is inadequate to explain complex behavior in human beings—or even in laboratory rats.

How Psychologists Study Behavior

Do only people use tools? Does alcohol cause aggression? Does pornography lead to crimes of violence?

Many of us have expressed opinions on questions like these at one time or another. But psychology is a science. Within a science, assumptions about the behavior of cosmic rays, chemical compounds, cells, or people must be supported by evidence. Strong arguments, reference to authority figures, even tightly knit theories are not considered evidence in psychology. While psychology is a theoretical science, it is also an **empirical** science. Evidence must thus be based upon carefully controlled observations in the laboratory and elsewhere.

Psychologists gather evidence for their assumptions about behavior in a number of ways. In this section we examine the naturalistic observation method, the experimental method, the survey, the case study, and the correlational method.

The Naturalistic Observation Method

The next time you go to McDonald's or Burger King for lunch, have a look around. Pick out slender people and overweight people and observe whether they eat their burgers and fries differently. Do the overweight eat more rapidly? Chew less frequently? Leave less food on their plates? This is precisely the type of research psychologists have recently used to study the eating habits of normal- and over-weight people. In fact, if you notice some mysterious-looking people at McDonald's watching others over sunglasses and occasionally tapping the head of a partly concealed microphone, perhaps they are recording their observations of other people's eating habits—even as you watch.

This method of scientific investigation is called **naturalistic observation.** Psychologists and other scientists use it to observe behavior in the field, or "where it happens." They try to avoid interfering with the behaviors they are observing by using **unobtrusive** measures. As you see in Figure 1.6, Jane Goodall has observed the behavior of chimpanzees in their natural environment in order to learn about their social behavior, sexual behavior, use of tools, and other facts of chimp life. Her observations have shown us that (1) we were incorrect to think that only people use tools; and (2) kissing, as a greeting, is used by **primates** other than humans. But don't conclude that using tools or kissing are inborn or **instinctive** behaviors among primates. Chimps, like people, can learn from experience. It may be that they learned how to use tools and to kiss. The naturalistic observation method may tell us what is happening as we watch, but it is not the best method for determining the causes of behavior.

Other scientists have observed the Tasaday, a recently discovered primitive tribe in the Philippine Islands. Aggressive behavior is unknown among the Tasaday. It may be somewhat romantic to conclude that aggressive behavior results from civilization, especially since many other primitive tribes

Empirical Emphasizing or based on observation and experiment, in contrast to theory. (From the Greek *empeiria*, meaning "experience.")

Naturalistic observation A method of scientific investigation in which organisms are observed carefully in their natural environments.

Unobtrusive Avoiding interfering. (From the Latin *trudere*, meaning "to thrust.")

Primate (PRY–mate). A member of an order of mammals including people, apes, and monkeys.

Instinctive Inborn, natural, unlearned. (From the Latin *instinguere*, meaning "to impel" or "to instigate.")

FIGURE 1.6 Jane van Lawick Goodall has used the naturalistic observation method with chimpanzees, quietly observing them for many months in their natural environment. In using this method, scientists try to avoid interfering with the animals or people they observe, even though this sometimes means allowing an animal to be mistreated or to die from a curable illness. Goodall's observations have taught us that not only humans use kissing as a social greeting. In the photo at right, two chimps greet each other. Male chimps have been observed greeting females by kissing their hands. Very European? We also learn from Goodall that tools are used by primates other than human beings. The chimp in the photo to the left is using a stick to poke around in a termite hill and gather food.

have been known to be quite aggressive. Still, the findings on the Tasaday show that aggression is not universal among human beings. Thus, aggression may not be an unavoidable part of the human condition.

There are many problems with the naturalistic observation method. For instance, sometimes we see what we want to see. Kissing behavior among chimps seems to serve a social function similar to human kissing, but "kissing" by the kissing gourami, a tropical fish, seems to be a test of strength. We must be cautious in our interpretations.

We must also be certain that the animals or people we are observing represent the target **population,** such as citizens of the United States (rather than young business people in Southern California or white, middle-class Americans). Visitors from space who encountered only the Tasaday would gain an erroneous impression of the human potential for violence. Visitors who observed the Times Square area in New York might conclude that only men are sexually aroused by pornography, since very few women attend such films and are usually accompanied by men when they do. In Chapter 13 you will see that other types of observations lead to very different conclusions.

Finally, it is difficult to determine the causes of behavior through naturalistic observation. After visiting a few bars near the university where I teach, you might conclude that alcohol causes aggressive behavior as you duck to avoid the flying ashtrays and chairs. There is little doubt that aggression often accompanies drinking, but you will soon learn that alcohol may not cause aggression—at least among college males who are social drinkers.

Population A complete group of organisms or events.

The Experimental Method

Most psychologists would agree that the preferred method for answering research questions, such as whether alcohol causes aggression, is the experimental method. In an **experiment** a group of participants receives a **treatment,** such as a dosage of alcohol. The participants, or **subjects,** are then observed carefully to determine whether the treatment makes a difference in their behavior.

Experiments are used whenever possible in contemporary psychological research because they allow psychologists to directly control the experiences of animals and people in their effort to determine the results of a treatment. Experiments are usually undertaken to test a **hypothesis,** an assumption about behavior that is often derived from theory. For example, a psychologist assumes that alcohol leads to aggression by reducing fear of consequences or generally energizing the activity levels of drinkers. He or she then hypothesizes that the treatment of drinking alcohol will lead to measurable increases in aggression among provoked individuals.

Independent and Dependent Variables   In an experiment to determine whether alcohol causes aggression, experimental subjects would be given a quantity of alcohol and its effects would be measured. Alcohol would be considered an **independent variable,** a variable whose presence is manipulated by the experimenters so that its effects may be determined. The independent variable of alcohol may be administered at different levels, or doses, from none to a quantity sufficient to cause **intoxication.**

The measured results or outcomes in an experiment are called **dependent variables.** Their presence presumably depends on the independent variables. In an experiment to determine whether alcohol influences aggression, aggressive behavior would be a dependent variable. Other dependent variables of interest in an experiment on the effects of alcohol might include sexual arousal (see Chapter 4), visual-motor coordination, and performance on intellectual tasks such as defining words or numerical computations.

In an experiment on the relationships between temperature and aggression, temperature would be an independent variable and aggressive behavior would be a dependent variable. We might use various temperature settings, from below freezing to blistering hot, and study the effects of each. We might also use a second independent variable, such as provocation, and insult certain subjects but not others. Then we could also study the interaction between temperature and social provocation as they influence aggression.

Experiments can be quite complex, with several independent and dependent variables. Psychologists often use complex experimental designs and sophisticated statistical techniques to determine the effect of each independent variable, acting alone and in combination with others, on each dependent variable.

Experimental and Control Groups   Ideal experiments use experimental and control subjects, or experimental and control groups. **Experimental subjects** receive the treatment while **control subjects** do not. Every effort is made to ensure that all other conditions are held constant both for experimental and control subjects so that we can have confidence that the experimental outcomes reflect the treatments, and not chance factors or variation.

Experiment A method of scientific investigation that seeks to discover cause-and-effect relationships by introducing independent variables and observing their effects on dependent variables. (From a Latin word meaning "trial" or "test.")

Treatment In experiments, a condition received by participants so that its effects may be observed.

Subjects Participants in a scientific study. Many psychologists consider this term dehumanizing and no longer use it in reference to human participants.

Hypothesis (high–POTH–uh–sis). An assumption about behavior that is derived from theory and tested through research. (A Greek word meaning "groundwork" or "foundation.")

Independent variable A condition in a scientific study that is manipulated so that its effects may be observed.

Intoxication Drunkenness. (From the Latin *toxicare,* meaning "to smear with poison.")

Dependent variable A measure of an assumed effect of an independent variable.

Experimental subjects (1) Subjects receiving a treatment in an experiment. (2) More generally, participants in an experiment.

Control subjects Experimental participants who do not receive the experimental treatment, but for whom all other conditions are comparable to those of experimental subjects.

In an experiment concerning the effects of alcohol on aggression, experimental subjects would be given alcohol and control subjects would not. In a complex experiment different experimental groups might receive (1) different dosages of alcohol and (2) different types of provocations.

Blinds and Double Blinds One experiment on the effects of alcohol on aggression (Boyatzis, 1974) reported that men at parties where beer and liquor were served acted more aggressively than control subjects at parties where only soft drinks were served. But we must be cautious in interpreting these findings because the experimental subjects knew that they had drunk alcohol, and the control subjects knew that they had not. It is possible that increases in aggression that appeared to result from drinking may not have reflected the alcohol itself, but rather experimental subjects' expectations about the effects of alcohol. Other experiments show that people "act in stereotyped ways" when they think they have been drinking alcohol (Marlatt & Rohsenow, 1981). For instance, men will become less anxious in social situations, more aggressive, and more sexually aroused—even though they have drunk only a **placebo** like tonic water.

Well-designed experiments control for the possible effect of expectations about the treatment by creating conditions in which the experimental and control subjects are unaware of, or **blind** to, the treatment they have received. But researchers may also have expectations. They may, in effect, be "rooting for" a certain treatment. For instance, tobacco company executives may wish to show that cigarette smoking is harmless. For this reason it is useful if the people measuring the experimental outcomes are also unaware of who has received the treatment. Studies in which both subjects and experimenters are unaware of who has received the treatment are called **double-blind studies.**

In one well-designed study on the effects of alcohol, Alan Lang of the University of Wisconsin and his colleagues (1975) pretested a highball of vodka and tonic water to determine that it could not be discriminated by taste from tonic water alone. They recruited college men as subjects. Some subjects received vodka and tonic water while others received tonic water only. Of subjects who received vodka, half were misled into believing that they had

FIGURE 1.7

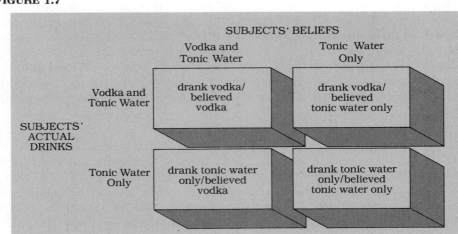

drunk tonic water only (Figure 1.7). Of subjects receiving tonic water only, half were misled into believing that their drink contained vodka. Thus half the subjects were blind to the treatment they received. Experimenters who measured aggressive responses were also blind as to which subjects had received vodka.

The research team found that men who believed that they had drunk vodka responded more aggressively to a provocation than men who believed that they had drunk tonic water only. The actual content of the drink was immaterial. That is, men who had actually drunk alcohol acted no more aggressively than men who had drunk tonic water only. The results of the Lang study differ dramatically from those reported by Boyatzis, perhaps because the Boyatzis study did not control for the effects of expectations or beliefs about alcohol.

Is it possible that alcohol does not cause aggression? That centuries of folklore have been in error? Quite possible. Other studies that control for the effects of expectations have shown that alcohol can even decrease aggressive behavior (Marlatt & Rohsenow, 1981). Actually, this finding should not be so surprising. We acknowledge that alcohol can lead to a stupor, even to passing out. Why should such a substance cause aggressive outbursts prior to its depressing effects on the nervous system? Psychology is an empirical science. Centuries of folklore may stimulate research into certain topics, but folklore is not acceptable evidence within science.

So what do we make of it? Why does belief that one has drunk alcohol increase aggression while alcohol itself may not? Perhaps alcohol gives one a certain social role to play in our culture—the role of the uninhibited social mover. Perhaps alcohol also provides an excuse for aggressive or other antisocial behavior. After all, the drinker can always claim, "It wasn't me, it was the alcohol." How do you think you will respond the next time someone says "It was the alcohol" to you?

Generalizing from Experimental Results Many factors must be considered in interpreting the results of experiments. In the Lang study the subjects represented a **sample** of male college students. The results may not extend to women. College men also tend to fall within a certain age range (about 18 to 22) and are more intelligent than the general population. We cannot be certain that the findings extend to older men of average intelligence, although it seems reasonable to **infer** that they do. Subjects in the Lang study reported themselves to be social drinkers. In Chapter 4 you will also see that some psychologists suggest that alcoholics differ genetically from people who can control their drinking. Whether or not this is so, we cannot be certain that college social drinkers represent people who do not drink at all or people who drink to excess.

There is a quip in psychology that experiments tend to be run with "rats, sophomores, and soldiers." Why? Because these subjects are readily available. Still, science is a conservative enterprise, and scientists are cautious about generalizing experimental results to populations other than those from which their samples were drawn.

Operational Definitions Our ability to generalize experimental results also relates to the operational definitions of the independent and dependent variables. The **operational definition** of a variable is limited to the methods used to create or measure that variable. For example, sexual arousal may be operationally defined as subjects' self-reports (based on introspection) that they

Sample Part of a population.

Infer (in–FUR). Draw a conclusion.

Operational definition. A definition of a variable in terms of the methods used to create or measure the variable. For example, an operational definition of intelligence is that which is measured by intelligence tests.

feel sexually aroused. This would also be considered a **subjective** definition of arousal since it depends on subjects' private feelings. Unfortunately, self-reports can fall prey to accidental or purposeful inaccuracies, as we shall see in the next section. Thus, psychologists prefer to use objective measures whenever possible. For this reason, many recent studies define sexual arousal in the male as size of erection and in the female as vaginal blood pressure. Both can be measured directly by objective laboratory instruments.

In the Lang study on alcohol and aggression, alcohol was operationally defined as a certain dose of vodka. Other types of drinks and other dosages of vodka might have had different effects. Aggression was operationally defined as selecting a certain amount of electric shock and administering it to another student participating in a psychological experiment. College men might behave differently when they drink in other situations, for example, when they are insulted by a supporter of an opposing football team or are threatened outside a bar. Still, some psychologists argue that subjects in a laboratory may

PorNO

Carrying placards with slogans like PorNO! groups such as Women Against Pornography have recently descended upon red-light districts in several cities to protest pornographic films and books that often portray women being raped, tortured, and killed.

As reported in *Time* magazine (August 27, 1979), 4,500 women marched through Minneapolis's red-light district behind the banner *Women Unite, Take Back the Night.* Later that fall, as reported in the *New York Times* (October 21, 1979), some 5,000 women marched through New York's garish Times Square area to protest the scores of adult bookstores and pornographic movie houses. One banner read *Stop Violence Against Women.* Outrage over pornography has united women of many political persuasions. As a Cleveland protester put it, "We all get raped and we all get beaten."

Pornography is a highly charged issue, but psychologists are committed to the objective study of all aspects of human behavior, including responses to pornography. Recent psychological experiments have addressed questions such as:

- Does pornography lead to crimes of violence?
- Does repeated exposure to pornography transform the average male into an insatiable Casanova?
- How do people who are repulsed by pornography differ from those who enjoy it or are indifferent to it?
- Is pornography for men only, or does it also sexually arouse women?

Some findings concerning the effects of pornography may surprise you, as you will see in Chapter 13. For instance, in experiments using vaginal blood pressure as the operational definition of sexual arousal, Julia Heiman (1975) found that pornography sexually aroused women as well as men. Howard and his colleagues (1973) used size of erection as their operational definition of sexual arousal and exposed college men to 15 daily 90-minute sessions of pornographic films. Continued exposure to pornography did not drive these men to sexual abandon. Rather, the average size of erection diminished as time went on. Pornography, like many other sources of stimulation, may lose some of its capacity to influence our behavior with the passage of time.

Psychologists, like other people, may harbor strong moral opinions on controversial issues such as pornography. But, as scientists, it is their responsibility to run their experiments without bias and to report the results objectively.

assign a meaning to the laboratory setting and their actions which makes them comparable to the real-life situation (e.g., Berkowitz & Donnerstein, 1982).

Does it sound as if we are speaking from both corners of our mouth? As if we're praising the Lang study, on the one hand, but telling you not to believe it, on the other? Not quite. The Lang study is worthy of praise for reasons discussed earlier. It has also been **replicated** to some degree with subjects other than college men and other dosages of alcohol. We can also say, with some justification, that only studies that control for the effects of expectations should receive our attention. Thus, the Lang study and studies showing similar results (see Chapter 4) are, in a sense, all we have on the behavioral effects of alcohol—despite centuries of folklore.

The Survey Method

In the good old days, when being "sound as a dollar" was a sign of good health, one had to wait until the wee hours of the morning to learn the results of local and national elections. Throughout the evening and early morning hours suspense would build as ballots from distant neighborhoods and states were tallied. Nowadays one barely becomes settled with an after-dinner cup of coffee on election night before the CBS News computer cheerfully announces (computers do not, of course, have emotions or make "cheerful" announcements, but they certainly seem rather smug at times) that it has examined the ballots of a "scientifically selected sample" and then predicts the next president of the United States. All this may occur with less than one percent of the vote tallied. Polls taken before elections also do their share of eroding wonderment and doubt—so much so that supporters of projected winners must sometimes be encouraged to actually vote on Election Day so that predictions will be borne out.

Just as computers and pollsters predict election results and report national opinion on the basis of scientifically selected samples, psychologists conduct **surveys** in order to learn about behavior that cannot be observed in the natural setting or studied experimentally. Surveys may employ interviews, questionnaires, and psychological tests. By distributing questionnaires and analyzing answers with a computer, psychologists can survey many thousands of people at a time.

In the late 1940s and early 1950s Alfred Kinsey of Indiana University and his colleagues published two surveys of sexual behavior, based on interviews, that shocked the nation: *Sexual Behavior in the Human Male* (1948) and *Sexual Behavior in the Human Female* (1953). Kinsey reported that masturbation was practically universal in his sample of men at a time when masturbation was still widely thought to impair physical or mental health. He also reported that about one woman in three still single at age 25 had engaged in premarital intercourse.

The survey was the appropriate method for attaining these data, since Kinsey wished to learn what was happening in the United States rather than study the causes of sexual behavior in depth. And if Kinsey had tried to use the naturalistic-observation method, he and his colleagues might have been tossed into jail as Peeping Toms.

Psychologists also commonly use surveys to learn about people's values (e.g., Yankelovich, 1981), whether married people are as happy as single people (e.g., Campbell, 1975; Schultz, 1980), whether attitudes toward having large families are changing, and so on. They may use psychological tests, like in-

Replicate Repeat or duplicate. In science, research must be reported in sufficient detail to permit other investigators to replicate it.

Survey A method of scientific investigation in which large samples of people are questioned.

telligence and aptitude tests, to learn how people who are successful in college differ from those who are not, or if men and women differ in verbal or math skills. Psychologists also use tests to learn how the personalities of people who show abnormal or criminal behavior differ from "normals."

Interviews, questionnaires, and psychological tests are not foolproof, of course. People may inaccurately recall their behavior or may purposefully misrepresent it. For instance, they may wish to ingratiate themselves with their interviewers by answering in what they perceive to be the socially desirable direction. Other people may wish to exaggerate their problems, possibly to draw attention to themselves or, so to speak, as a "cry for help." For these reasons some commonly used psychological tests have items built into them called **validity scales.** Validity scales are sensitive to misrepresentations and alert the psychologist when test results may be deceptive.

Because of such problems many psychologists prefer to observe behavior directly when possible. But it is not always possible—as in surveys of sexual behavior, or when samples of thousands of people are required.

QUESTIONNAIRE

The Social Desirability Scale

Do you say what you think, or do you tend to misrepresent your beliefs to earn the approval of others? Do you answer questions honestly, or do you say what you think other people want to hear?

Telling others what we think they want to hear is making the socially desirable response. Falling prey to social desirability may cause us to distort our beliefs and experiences in interviews or on psychological tests. You can complete the following test devised by Crowne and Marlowe (1960) to gain insight into whether you have a tendency to produce socially desirable responses. Read each item and decide whether it is true (T) or false (F) for you. Try to work rapidly and answer each question by writing a T or F in the blank space. Then turn to the scoring key in Appendix B to interpret your answers.

T   F

_____ 1. Before voting I thoroughly investigate the qualifications of all the candidates.

_____ 2. I never hesitate to go out of my way to help someone in trouble.

_____ 3. It is sometimes hard for me to go on with my work if I am not encouraged.

_____ 4. I have never intensely disliked anyone.

_____ 5. On occasions I have had doubts about my ability to succeed in life.

_____ 6. I sometimes feel resentful when I don't get my way.

_____ 7. I am always careful about my manner of dress.

_____ 8. My table manners at home are as good as when I eat out in a restaurant.

_____ 9. If I could get into a movie without paying and be sure I was not seen I would probably do it.

_____ 10. On a few occasions, I have given up something because I thought too little of my ability.

_____ 11. I like to gossip at times.

The *Literary Digest* Survey: A Case Study in the Importance of Random Sampling   You recall President Landon, don't you? Elected in 1936, he defeated the incumbent president, Franklin D. Roosevelt? If this sounds wrong, it may be because it is wrong. Roosevelt defeated Landon in a landslide of about 11 million votes. Still, the *Literary Digest*, a popular magazine of the day, had predicted a Landon victory.

The *Digest*, you see, had phoned the voters it surveyed. Today telephone sampling is a widely practiced and reasonably legitimate technique. But the *Digest* poll was taken during the Great Depression, when Americans who had telephones were decidedly higher in socioeconomic status than Americans without phones. Americans at higher income levels are also more likely to vote Republican, and Alf Landon was heading the Republican ticket. No surprise, then, that the people sampled said they would vote overwhelmingly for Landon.

Survey samples must accurately represent the population they are meant to reflect. One way to accomplish this is through a **random sample.** In a random sample, each member of a population has an equal chance of being

_____ 12. There have been times when I felt like rebelling against people in authority even though I knew they were right.

_____ 13. No matter who I'm talking to, I'm always a good listener.

_____ 14. I can remember "playing sick" to get out of something.

_____ 15. There have been occasions when I have taken advantage of someone.

_____ 16. I'm always willing to admit it when I make a mistake.

_____ 17. I always try to practice what I preach.

_____ 18. I don't find it particularly difficult to get along with loudmouthed, obnoxious people.

_____ 19. I sometimes try to get even rather than forgive and forget.

_____ 20. When I don't know something I don't mind at all admitting it.

_____ 21. I am always courteous, even to people who are disagreeable.

_____ 22. At times I have really insisted on having things my own way.

_____ 23. There have been occasions when I felt like smashing things.

_____ 24. I would never think of letting someone else be punished for my wrong-doings.

_____ 25. I never resent being asked to return a favor.

_____ 26. I have never been irked when people expressed ideas very different from my own.

_____ 27. I never make a long trip without checking the safety of my car.

_____ 28. There have been times when I was quite jealous of the good fortune of others.

_____ 29. I have almost never felt the urge to tell someone off.

_____ 30. I am sometimes irritated by people who ask favors of me.

_____ 31. I have never felt that I was punished without cause.

_____ 32. I sometimes think when people have a misfortune they only got what they deserved.

_____ 33. I have never deliberately said something that hurt someone's feelings.

Source: Crowne, D. P., and Marlowe, D. A new scale of social desirability independent of pathology, *Journal of Consulting Psychology*, 1960, 24, p. 351, Table 1. Copyright 1960 by the American Psychological Association. Reprinted by permission.

"Would you say Attila is doing an excellent job, a good job, a fair job, or a poor job?"

selected to participate. Researchers can also use a **stratified sample,** which is drawn so that known subgroups in the population are represented proportionately in the sample. For instance, 12 percent of the United States population is black. Thus, a racially stratified sample would be 12 percent black. As a practical matter, a large randomly selected sample will show reasonably accurate stratification. In any event an appropriately selected random sample of 1,500 Americans will represent the general United States population reasonably well. But a haphazardly drawn sample of 20 million may not.

The Kinsey studies on sexual behavior did not adequately represent blacks, poor Americans, the elderly, and other groups. Recent magazine surveys of sexual behavior run by *Redbook* (Tavris & Sadd, 1977) and *Cosmopolitan* (Wolfe, 1981) asked readers to fill out and return questionnaires. Although many thousands of readers responded, did they represent the general American population? Probably not. They may have represented only a subgroup of readers of these magazines who were willing to fill out candid questionnaires about their sexual behavior. Shere Hite (1976, 1981) distributed well over 100,000 questionnaires for each of her surveys of sexual behavior, but had returns of about 3,000 for the 1976 report, and about 7,000 for the 1981 report. Do the people who returned her questionnaires accurately represent those who received them? What do you think?

The Case Study Method

Sigmund Freud developed psychoanalytic theory largely on the basis of **case studies,** or carefully drawn biographies of the lives of individuals. In the

Stratified sample A sample drawn such that known subgroups within a population are represented in proportion to their numbers in the population.

Case study A carefully-drawn biography that may be obtained through interviews, questionnaires, and psychological tests.

historical case study the task is to reconstruct a person's past on the basis of memories, records, and, perhaps, interviews with people who have known the person. Of course there are bound to be gaps in memory, and people may distort their pasts because of social desirability or other factors. Interviewers may also be subtly biased and indirectly encourage **interviewees** to fill in gaps in ways that are consistent with their theoretical perspectives.

Jean Piaget used the case study method to study the cognitive development of children. He observed and played with them for thousands of hours, noting how they responded to objects and questions at various stages of development.

The case study is used in the clinic when a psychologist helps individuals, agencies, or business firms change their behavior so that they can more effectively meet the challenges in their lives. Clinical suggestions are based on laboratory research when possible, but clinical practice is also sometimes an art in which psychologist and client agree that a treatment has been helpful on the basis of the client's self-report.

The case study can be used quite scientifically in clinical practice if the psychologist repeatedly applies and removes a treatment, attempts to control for variables such as client expectations, or takes repeated measures through behavioral observations, psychological tests, or structured interviews (Hayes, 1981; Kazdin, 1981). If the treatment leads to consistent changes in the client, it may be concluded that these are not chance fluctuations in behavior. But this approach is unlikely to be used in clinical practice. Some "treatments," such as helping a client gain insight into the meaning of events that occurred prior to the age of five, cannot be repeatedly applied then removed. In other cases rather concrete treatments may be used to help clients quit smoking, lose weight, or resolve sexual problems. But it would be harmful to the client to reinstate these problems—even with the intention of resolving them a second time—to determine whether treatment has been effective. But psychologists encourage laboratory experiments in these problem areas so that they will know that their treatments are backed by research whenever possible.

The Correlational Method

Are people with higher intelligence more likely to do well in school? Are people with lighter eye color at greater risk for behaving abnormally?

Research has shown consistently that people who attain higher scores on intelligence tests tend, as a group, to obtain higher scholastic averages. In Chapter 6 you will see that there is a controversy over just what intelligence tests measure. Still, the scores obtained on them are related to overall academic achievement.

What of light eyes and the risk for abnormal behavior? Psychologist David Cohen (1978) of the University of Texas surveyed students from his classes over the years. He operationally defined "risk for" abnormal behavior as a student's report that the student, or a close relative, had been hospitalized for abnormal behavior. (Note that the use of the **criterion** of "a close relative" implies that abnormal behaviors can, to some degree, be inherited. We shall explore this notion in Chapter 11.) Cohen found that among college women—not men—a combination of dark hair, light eyes, and lefthandedness placed the student at greater risk. Dark-haired, light-eyed, lefthanded women readers should not be overly concerned since the number of women surveyed who fit this description was small—seven in fact. But there was a relationship

Interviewees Persons who are interviewed.

Criterion Standard, means for making a judgment.

Correlational research A method of scientific investigation that studies the relationships between variables. Correlational research can imply but cannot show cause and effect because no experimental treatment is introduced.

Informed consent The term used by psychologists to indicate that a person has agreed to participate in research after receiving information about the purposes of the study and the nature of the treatments.

Confidential Secret, not to be disclosed.

Ethics The system of morals of, in this case, the profession of psychology.

Remediation The process of helping people overcome deficiencies.

Lesion (LEE–shun). An injury that results in impaired behavior or loss of a function. (From the Latin *laedere*, meaning "to harm" or "to injure.")

between this combination of traits and "risk for" abnormal behavior, which, Cohen speculates, might have reflected some biological differences between these women and others.

Studies of the relationships between intelligence and achievement, or between eye color and abnormal behavior, are examples of **correlational research***. In correlational research, one or more variables are mathematically linked, or correlated, to one or more other variables.

Correlational research may suggest but does not show cause and effect. For instance, does higher intelligence cause greater academic achievement? Does greater achievement lead to higher intelligence test scores? It may seem obvious to you that higher intelligence leads to greater achievement, but research has shown that children placed in richly stimulating Head Start programs at an early age later obtain higher scores on intelligence tests! The relationship between intelligence and achievement may not be so simple as you might have thought. And Cohen does not suggest that light eye color causes abnormal behavior. Unknown biological factors may account for both, when they are found together along with several other variables.

Ethics in Psychological Research and Practice

Psychologists adhere to a number of ethical standards in research and practice. For instance, psychologists will not undertake research methods or treatments which they believe are harmful to subjects or clients (American Psychological Association, 1981). Human subjects must provide **informed consent** before they participate in research programs. Psychologists treat the records of research subjects and clients as **confidential.**

Ethics limit the types of research that psychologists may conduct. For example, how can we determine whether early separation from one's mother impairs social development? One research direction is to observe the development of children who have been separated from their mothers from an early age. But it is difficult to draw conclusions from such research because the same factors that led to the separation, such as family tragedy or irresponsible parents, rather than the separation itself, may have led to the observed outcomes.

Scientifically, it would be more sound to run experiments in which children are purposefully separated from their mothers at an early age and compared with children who are not. But psychologists would not seriously consider such research because of ethical standards.

Yet experiments on the effects of early separation from the mother have been carried out with monkeys and other animals. As you will see in later chapters, this research has shown that early separation may lead to the development of social deficits. But it has also suggested possible avenues of **remediation.**

Experiments with infant monkeys highlight some of the dilemmas faced by psychologists and other scientists when they contemplate research with people or animals that has or may have harmful effects. Psychologists and biologists who study the workings of the brain have destroyed sections of the brains of laboratory animals to learn how these areas of the brain influence behavior. For instance, as you will see in Chapter 7, a **lesion** in one part of a

---

* The mathematics of the *correlation coefficient* are discussed in Chapter 6 and in Appendix A.

brain structure will cause a rat to overeat. A lesion elsewhere will cause the rat to go on a crash diet. Psychologists generalize to people from experiments like these in the hope that we may find solutions to persistent human problems, such as obesity. But psychologists must still face the ethical dilemma of subjecting animals to harm. Generally speaking, psychologists do so only when they believe that the eventual benefits of their research to people justify the harm done to animals. Still, tradition and law suggest that "there is a limit to the amount of pain an animal should endure in the name of science" (Larson, 1982).

The Use of Deception A number of psychological experiments have required deception of human subjects. In the Lang (Lang and others, 1975) study on alcohol and aggression, the researchers had to (1) misinform half their subjects about the beverage they had drunk; and (2) mislead subjects to believe that they were giving other participants electric shock when they were actually only pressing switches on a dead control board. (Pressing these switches was the operational definition of aggression in the study.)

We saw that students in this study who believed they had drunk vodka were more aggressive than students who believed they had not. The actual content of the beverages was immaterial. But this study could not have been

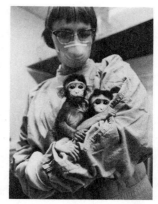

Now and then psychologists and other scientists must do animals some harm if they are to answer research questions that may yield important benefits for people. Justifying such harm is a major ethical dilemma.

On-Air Psychologists—Healers or Exploiters? On the Ethics of "Talk-Show Therapy"

Bob is in his 40s, and by most standards successful—a corporate executive who adores his children and the woman he has been married to for more than 20 years. But anguish creeps into his voice when he confides to a psychologist what he has taken great pains to hide from the world: that he gets a secret, scary pleasure from trying on his wife's lingerie. Bob is worried that his family will find out and terrified that he might be seriously disturbed. The therapist makes a gentle inquiry into his background, and finally pronounces his fetish harmless, "a little eccentric, but nothing more than that." Tell your wife, she urges soothingly. "It will take a tremendous burden off you—and it may lose its forbidden pleasure."

It is an intimate conversation between doctor and distressed—but this time, there is nothing private about it. The "patient" is on her office telephone. Clinical psychologist Toni Grant is in a sound studio at KABC radio in Los Angeles, listening

to him on headphones and murmuring her advice into a microphone .... And as they talk, 122,000 listeners in the Los Angeles area—at home washing dishes, typing in their offices, or driving on the freeways—are hanging on to every word ....

Each weekday afternoon from one to four, when "Dr. Toni"—as she is referred to by her listener/callers—officiates at her radio show, the switchboard is aglow with calls from the lonely and the lovelorn, the timid and the tempest-tossed seeking salve for their wounded psyches....

"Go get in touch with who you are," she coos to a distraught housewife whose husband of 17 years has just walked out the door. "Women like you don't want to be loved," she informs a 43-year-old woman with a history of abusive boyfriends....

Some professionals see the benefits of these kinds of call-in shows outweighing the potential harm—provided the shows are handled responsibly. Dr. Patricia Keith-Spiegel, professor of psychology at California State University–Northridge, and former chairperson of the American Psychological Association's ethics com-

mittee, believes they offer a tremendous potential for public education about emotional problems, and may help to "demystify the image of the therapist as a cold, objective bearded man with a foreign accent." Others point out that they provide an individual with a broader perspective on his or her personal problems by showing that those problems are shared by others....

Psychology talk shows, nonetheless, raise serious ethical questions for the profession and for the public. To score high in the ratings, the hosts are frequently pressed to take as many calls as possible and to issue quick, often speculative judgments....

Until recently, the APA's code of ethics forbade "psychological services for the purpose of diagnosis, treatment or personal advice" except "in the context of a professional relationship." But ... the APA has revised its guidelines. Diagnosis and therapy—except in the [psychologist's] office—are still prohibited, but personal advice may be given out in print or over the airwaves.

Debrief To receive information about a just-completed procedure.

Breathalyzer A device that measures the quantity of alcohol in the body by analyzing the breath.

run without deceiving the subjects. Foiling their expectations or beliefs was at the heart of the experiment.

Despite their use of deception, I believe the Lang study was ethical. Its potential benefits outweigh the possible harmful effects of the deceptions. I also find it preferable that subjects only thought they were shocking other people. After all, would we prefer them actually to deliver painful electric shock?

The code of ethics of the American Psychological Association requires that research participants who are deceived be **debriefed** afterward to help eliminate any harmful effects. After the study, Lang's subjects were informed of the deceptions and their purposes. Students who had actually drunk alcohol were given coffee and a **breathalyzer** test, so that the researchers could be sure that they were not leaving the laboratory in an intoxicated state.

Psychologists use deception in research only when the research could not be run without it. As with other ethical dilemmas, deception is used when the psychologist believes that its benefits will outweigh its potential harm.

Psychologists are human, of course, and capable of making errors. Occasionally human and animal research participants have been exposed to more harm than anticipated. But when psychologists make every effort to minimize possible harmful effects of research that they believe is important, they are acting ethically.

Summary

Psychology is a scientific approach to the study of behavior. Some psychologists limit their definition of behavior to observable behavior, while others include mental processes like images, concepts, thoughts, and dreams. Psychology seeks to explain, predict, and control behavior. But psychologists consider it unethical to control the behavior of other people. They do help clients modify their behavior for their own benefit.

Behavior is explained through psychological theories, which are sets of statements that involve assumptions about behavior. Explanations and predictions are derived from theories. Theories are revised, as needed, to accommodate new observations. If necessary, they are discarded. Some psychologists engage in basic or pure research, which has no immediate applications. Others engage in applied research, which seeks solutions to specific problems.

Psychologists are found in clinical services, in research, and in industry. Many wear several hats and teach as well. Psychologists in clinical services include clinical, counseling, school, educational, and community psychologists. Psychologists who primarily conduct research include developmental, personality, social, experimental, and physiological psychologists.

Psychologists in industry include industrial and consumer psychologists.

Psychologists tend to view behavior from various perspectives, or broad psychological approaches. There are four major approaches in contemporary psychology: biological, cognitive, psychoanalytic, and behavioral.

Biologically oriented psychologists search for relationships between behavior and biological processes, explaining behavior in terms of events in the brain and elsewhere.

Cognitively oriented psychologists are most concerned with mental processes—how we perceive and mentally represent the world. Scientific psychology's origins are usually traced to the year 1879, when Wilhelm Wundt established the first psychological laboratory to study the mind through introspection or looking inward. A number of movements may be considered cognitive: structuralism, functionalism, Gestalt psychology, humanistic psychology, and the developmental approach of Jean Piaget.

Sigmund Freud's psychoanalytic perspective is based on clinical interviews and stresses the importance of unconscious processes as determinants of human behavior. Freud taught that we are motivated to gratify basic impulses in a way that allows us to escape social disapproval or self-condemnation.

The behavioral perspective was originated by John B. Watson in response to what he considered the mentalistic excesses of the cognitive and psychoanalytic perspectives. Watson insisted that psychology focus on observable behavior only. He suggested focusing on the situational determinants of responses rather than mental processes since the latter are private subjective events. Contemporary social learning theorists appear to be attempting a reconciliation of the behavioral and cognitive perspectives, while so-called radical behaviorists prefer to avoid any discussion of cognition.

Theory may lead to predictions, or hypotheses, about behavior, but psychologists confirm or disconfirm hypotheses through empirical research. The naturalistic observation method studies behavior where it happens—in the "field." Experiments are used to seek cause and effect, or the effects of independent variables on dependent variables. These variables comprise operational definitions of the conceptual variables of the experimenters; for instance, in one study an ounce of vodka may be the operational definition of alcohol. Experimental subjects are given a treatment, while control subjects are not. Blinds and double blinds may be used to control for the effects of the expectations of the subjects and the researchers themselves. Results can be generalized only to populations that have been adequately represented in research samples.

Surveys may employ interviews, questionnaires, and psychological tests to learn about behavior that cannot be observed directly. It is important to use random or stratified samples to represent the population one is surveying. Case studies are carefully drawn biographies of the lives of individuals. Correlational research shows relationships between variables, but does not determine cause and effect.

Ethical standards of psychologists prevent mistreatment of human and animal subjects. Records of human behavior are kept confidential. Human subjects are required to give informed consent and are debriefed after studies in which deception was necessary. Limits are set on the discomfort that may be imposed on animals.

Truth or Fiction Revisited

- *Psychology is the study of the mind.* False. While psychology may be translated from its Greek roots as the study of the soul or mind, scientific psychology is defined as the study of behavior. Some psychologists restrict their definition of behavior to observable behavior, but others include mental processes like thoughts, images, and dreams.
- *Psychologists attempt to control the behavior of other people.* False. Psychologists attempt to explain and predict behavior, and to help people or groups marshal their own resources to meet the challenges in their own lives more effectively. Psychologists may also help clients clarify their goals, but they do not tell them what their goals ought to be.
- *The largest single group of psychologists is employed by colleges and universities.* True. The next largest group is employed in clinics, hospitals, or other human services settings.
- *Only people use tools.* False. Naturalistic observation methods have found that chimpanzees and other animals also use tools.
- *Alcohol causes aggression.* False. But people who drink may act aggressively because of their beliefs about the effects of alcohol.
- *You could survey 20 million Americans and still not predict accurately the outcome of a presidential election.* True. It is most important that a sample represent the population it is meant to represent. If the sample is not representative, sample size is immaterial.
- *So-called "talk-show therapy" is unethical.* Not necessarily—so long as it is used for giving responsible advice, and not for diagnosis or therapy.

OUTLINE

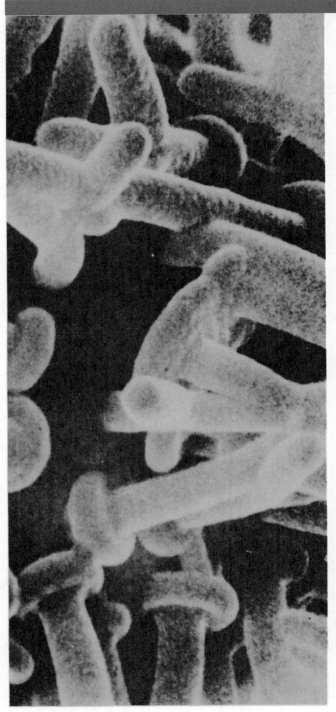

Biology and Behavior

TRUTH OR FICTION?

- Some cells in your body stretch all the way from your spinal cord to your big toe.
- In order to study nerve cells from the inside, scientists have created glass tubes so narrow that you could place 20,000 of them on the head of a pin.
- The human brain is larger than that of any other animal.
- Many men who are paralyzed below the waist can still achieve erection and ejaculate.
- Armed only with crossed fingers and a radio transmitter, a scientist stopped the raging charge of a two-ton bull.
- Fear can give you indigestion.
- If a surgeon were to stimulate a certain part of your brain electrically , you might swear in court that someone had stroked your leg.
- If a certain area in your brain were damaged, you would lose the ability to speak but could still understand written or spoken language.
- Some people are genetically identical.

Long ago and far away our universe began with a "big bang" that sent count-less atoms and other particles hurling at fantastic speeds into every corner of space. For fifteen to twenty billion years, galaxies and solar systems have been condensing from immense gas clouds, sparkling for some eons, then winking out. Human beings have only recently evolved on an unremarkable rock cir-cling an average star in a typical spiral-shaped galaxy.

Since the beginning of time, the universe has been in flux—changing. Change has brought life and death and countless challenges. Some creatures have adapted successfully to these challenges and continued to evolve. Others have not met the challenges and have become extinct, falling back into the distant mists of time. Some have left fossil records. Others have disappeared without a trace.

At first human survival on planet Earth required a greater struggle than it does today. We fought predators like the leopard. We foraged across parched lands for food. We may have warred with creatures very much like ourselves—creatures who failed to meet the challenges of life and whose bones are now being unearthed on digs in Africa. Yet we prevailed. The human species has survived and continues to pass on its unique characteristics from generation to generation through genetic material whose complex chemical codes are only now being cracked.

Yet what is passed on from generation to generation? The answer is: biological or **physiological** structures. There is no evidence that we can in-herit thoughts or ideas or images or plans. But we inherit physiological struc-tures that serve as the material base for our observable behaviors, our emo-tions, and our cognitions—our thoughts, images, and plans.

Just how our mental processes and observable behaviors are linked to physiological structures is the fascinating question being answered piece by piece by a group of psychologists called **physiological psychologists.** Through systematic probing of the brain and other structures, physiological psychol-ogists in recent years have seemed perpetually on the threshold of exciting discoveries. For instance, they are experimenting with "brain foods" that may enhance our abilities to learn and remember; with chemical substances pro-duced in our own brains that we may someday put to use to treat mental illness and needless pain (Miller, 1982); with controlling aggression and ov-ereating by stimulating certain parts of the brain with electric currents.

Such research has changed our very way of conceptualizing what it is to be human. It seems at once to hold the promise of great advances in human welfare and the threat of advanced methods of behavior control or brain con-trol. In this chapter we explore the work of physiological psychologists as they unlock the mysteries of:

1. *Neurons.* Neurons are the building blocks of the nervous system. There are billions of neurons in the body, all transmitting messages of one kind or another.
2. *The nervous system.* Neurons join to form a nervous system with subdivi-sions that are responsible for muscle movement, perception, automatic functions like heartbeat and breathing, and psychological phenomena like thoughts and feelings.
3. *The cerebral cortex.* The cerebral cortex is the large, wrinkled mass inside your head that you think of as your brain. Actually, it is only one part of the brain—the "human" part, perhaps.
4. *The endocrine system.* Through secretion of hormones, the endocrine sys-

Physiological Having to do with the biological functions and vital processes of living organisms.

Physiological psychologists Psychologists who study the relationships between biolog-ical processes, on the one hand, and observable behav-iors and mental processes, on the other.

tem controls functions ranging from growth in children to production of milk in nursing women.

5. *Heredity.* Within every cell of your body are hundreds of thousands of genes. These complex chemical substances determine just what type of creature you are, from the color of your hair to your body temperature and the fact that you have arms and legs rather than wings or fins.

Neurons

Let us begin our journey in a fabulous forest of nerve cells that can be visualized as having branches, trunks, and roots very much like trees. As in other "forests," many of these nerve cells ("trees") are next to one another. But unlike other forests, these "trees" also lie end to end; their "roots" are intertwined with the "branches" of many nerve cells, or other "trees" below. Messages can be transmitted from nerve cell to nerve cell, or "tree" to "tree." Nerve cells communicate through chemical substances, called **neurotransmitters,** that are transmitted from the "branches" of one to the "roots" of the next. Neurotransmitters may lead to chemical changes in the receiving nerve cell that cause the message to travel along its "trunk," be translated back into neurotransmitters in its "branches," and then travel through the small spaces between nerve cells to be received by the "roots" of yet other nerve cells.

Each "tree" in this forest is a nerve cell, or **neuron,** that transmits and coordinates messages in the form of nervous impulses. (See photographs of neurons in Color Plate 2.1.) The nervous system also contains billions of **glial cells.** Glial cells outnumber neurons. Their functions appear to include nourishment and direction of the pattern of growth of neurons, and the removal of waste products from the nervous system. But neurons occupy center stage in the nervous system. The messages transmitted by neurons somehow account for phenomena ranging from perception of an itch from a mosquito bite and the coordination of a skier's vision and muscles to the composition of a concerto and the solution of an algebraic equation.

The Makeup of Neurons

Neurons vary according to their functions and their location in the body. Some in the brain are only a fraction of an inch in length, while others in the legs are several feet long. But every neuron is a single nerve cell with a number of common features: a cell body, or **soma,** dendrites, and axon (Figure 2.1). The cell body contains the nucleus, which uses oxygen to create energy to carry out the work of the cell and performs maintenance chores. Anywhere from a few to several hundred short fibers, or **dendrites,** extend from the cell body to receive incoming messages from up to 1,000 adjoining neurons. In the analogy of the neuron to a tree, dendrites serve as the roots. An **axon** extends trunklike from the cell body. An axon may be quite short or extend several feet if it is carrying messages from the toes upward. Like tree trunks, axons too may branch and extend in different directions. Axons end in smaller branching structures that are aptly named **terminals.** At the tips of the axon terminals are swellings called **bulbs** (Figure 2.2). Neurons carry messages in one direction only, from the dendrites or cell body through the axon to the axon terminals. The messages are then transmitted from the terminal bulbs to other neurons, to muscles, or to glands.

Neurotransmitters Chemical substances involved in the transmission of neural impulses from one neuron to another.

Neuron (NEW–ron). A single nerve cell. (A Greek word meaning "nerve.")

Glial cells (GLEE–al). Cells that produce myelin and engage in housekeeping chores for neurons.

Soma A cell body. (A Greek word meaning "body.")

Dendrites Rootlike structures attached to the soma of a neuron. Dendrites receive impulses from other neurons. (From the Greek *dendron,* meaning "tree.")

Axon A long, thin part of a neuron that transmits impulses to other neurons from small branching structures called terminals.

Terminals Small, branching structures at the tips of axons.

Bulbs Swellings at the ends of terminals.

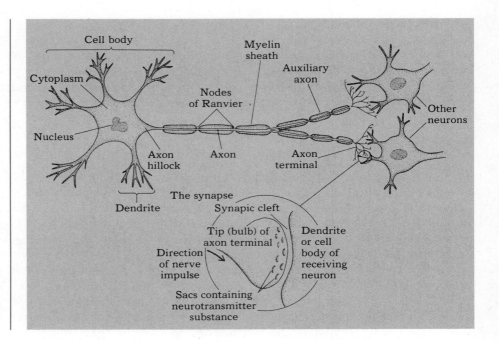

FIGURE 2.1 The Anatomy of a Neuron. "Messages" enter neurons through dendrites, are transmitted along the trunklike axon, and then are sent through axon terminals to muscles, glands, and other neurons.

Myelin Many neurons are wrapped tightly with white, fatty **myelin sheaths.** Myelin is produced by glial cells. Myelin sheaths insulate the axon from electrically charged atoms, or ions, found in the bodily fluids that encase the nervous system, and facilitate the transmission of messages. Myelin does not uniformly coat the surface of an axon. It is missing at points called **nodes of Ranvier,** where the axon is exposed. Neural messages, or impulses, seem to "jump" quite rapidly from node to node rather than travel more slowly through the length of the axon.

The process of myelinization is not complete at birth. The growth of myelin is part of the maturation process that leads to the abilities to crawl and walk during the first year of life. It may be that babies are not physiologically "ready" to engage in visual-motor coordination and other types of learning until the coating process has been completed. In the disease multiple sclerosis, myelin is replaced with a hard fibrous tissue that throws off the timing of nerve impulses and interferes with muscular control. If neurons that control breathing are afflicted, the person can die from suffocation.

Afferent and Efferent Neurons If someone steps on your big toe, the sensation is registered by receptors or sensory neurons near the surface of your skin. Then it is transmitted to the spinal cord and brain through **afferent neurons** that are perhaps two to three feet long. In the brain, subsequent messages may be buffeted about by associative neurons that are only a few thousandths of an inch long. You experience the pain through this process and perhaps entertain some rather nasty thoughts about the perpetrator who is now apologizing and begging for understanding. Long before you arrive at any logical conclusions, however, motor neurons, or **efferent neurons,** will have sent messages back to your toe and foot so that you have withdrawn them and begun an impressive hopping routine. Other efferent neurons may have stimulated glands, so that by now your heart is beating more rapidly, you are sweating, and the hairs on the backs of your arms may have even

Myelin sheath (MY–uh–lin). A fatty substance that encases and insulates axons, permitting more rapid transmission of neural impulses. (From the Greek *myelos,* meaning "marrow.")

Node of Ranvier A noninsulated segment of a generally myelinated axon.

Afferent neurons Neurons that transmit messages from sensory receptors to the spinal cord and brain. Also called sensory neurons. (From the Latin *afferre,* meaning "to carry.")

Efferent neurons Neurons that transmit messages from the brain or spinal cord to muscles and glands. Also called motor neurons. (From the Latin *efferre,* meaning "to carry outward.")

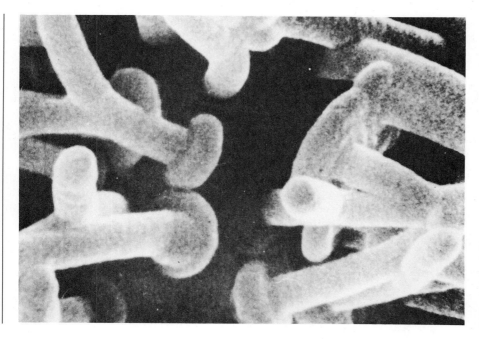

FIGURE 2.2 A much-enlarged photograph of axon terminals, showing the terminal bulbs or buttons. The bulbs are also referred to as synaptic knobs.

become erect! Being a sport, you may say, "Oh, it's nothing." But considering all the neurons involved, it was really quite a bit, wasn't it?

In case you think that afferent and efferent neurons will be hard to distinguish because they sound pretty much the SAME to you, simply remember that they are the "SAME." That is, Sensory = Afferent, and Motor = Efferent. But don't tell your professor I let you in on this **mnemonic** device.

A Psychological Controversy: Do We Lose Brain Cells as We Grow Older?

I've waited awhile, but now I'll come out with it. Although you have many billions of neurons, practically all of them were present at birth and they have probably been dying off at the rate of several thousand a day. Yes, the brain and other parts of the nervous system grew larger as you matured, but this has been largely due to the development of existing neurons (such as the growth of myelin sheaths), the thickening of dendrites and axon terminals, and the growth of glial cells.

No doubt about it, you're losing some cells. But don't despair: We probably have more cells than we need. And many brain functions seem to be duplicated in different groups of cells. And if you started with, say, 12 billion neurons in the brain and were losing 10,000 a day, or three million a year, it would take a while to make a dent. Yet Marian Diamond (1978) of the University of California maintains that we have no basis for affixing any number to the daily loss of brain cells. She claims that no reports of loss of brain cells have been supported by adequate research methodology. And she warns that one sinister effect of theorizing that we lose vast numbers of brain cells as we age is that it seems to justify the tossing of elderly workers onto the scrap heap of forced retirement.

Diamond and her colleagues decided that it was high time that a careful study on brain-cell counts was done. Rats journey through the life cycle more

Mnemonic (neh–MON–ick). Aiding memory, usually by linking chunks of new information to well-known schemes. See Chapter 5. (From the Greek *mnemon,* meaning "mindful.")

Neurons **43**

rapidly than we slowpoke humans, and so they compared the numbers of cells in the occipital lobes of rats' brains at the ages of 26 days (weaning), 41 days (onset of puberty), 108 days (young adulthood), and 650 days (old age).

The occipital lobes were cut into thin slices and stained so that neurons could be differentiated under the microscope from glial cells. The greatest decrease in neurons and glial cells occurred prior to 108 days, or young adulthood. Decreases at later ages were trivial by comparison. We must be cautious in generalizing from rats to people, but these findings suggest that intellectual deficits found in some elderly people may have little if anything to do with loss of brain cells.

Diamond also reports that rats raised in enriched environments—with ladders, mazes, tunnels, and many companions—developed thicker cerebral cortexes with larger numbers of glial cells than rats raised in plain cages with just a couple of companions. Not only does the brain shape our experience. Experience to some degree can also shape the brain.

The Neural Impulse

In the late 1700s, Italian physiologist Luigi Galvani engaged in a shocking experiment in a rainstorm. While his neighbors had the sense to remain indoors, Galvani and his wife were out on the porch connecting lightning rods to the heads of dissected frogs whose legs were connected by wire to a well of water. When lightning blazed above, the frogs' muscles contracted repeatedly and violently. This is not a recommended way to prepare frogs' legs— Galvani was demonstrating that **neural impulses** are electrical in nature.

Neural impulses travel somewhere between two (in nonmyelinated neurons) and 225 miles an hour (in myelinated neurons). This speed is not impressive when compared with that of an electric current, which travels at the speed of light—over 186,000 miles per second. But distances in the body are short, and a message will travel from a toe to the brain in perhaps one-fiftieth of a second.

Neural impulse The electrochemical discharge of a nerve cell, or neuron.

Polarize To ready a neuron for firing by creating an internal negative charge in relation to the body fluid outside the cell membrane.

Resting potential The electrical potential across the neural membrane when it is not responding to other neurons.

Permeability The degree to which a membrane allows a substance to pass through it.

Depolarize To reduce the resting potential of a cell membrane from about −70 millivolts toward zero.

Action potential The electrical impulse that provides the basis for the conduction of a neural impulse along an axon of a neuron.

An Electrochemical Process   The process by which neural impulses travel is electrochemical. In a resting state, there is a relatively greater number of positively charged sodium ions (Na+) in the body fluid outside the neuron than in the fluid within the neuron. Positively charged potassium (K+) ions and negatively charged chlorine (Cl−) ions are more plentiful inside. This difference in electrical charge **polarizes** the neuron with a negative **resting potential** of about −70 millivolts in relation to the body fluid outside the cell membrane.

When the neuron is stimulated by other neurons, the cell membrane changes its **permeability** to allow sodium ions to enter. Consequently the area of entry becomes positively charged or **depolarized** with respect to the outside (Figure 2.3). The inside of the cell at the disturbed area is said now to gain an **action potential,** or positive charge, of about +40 millivolts. This inner change causes the next section of the cell to become permeable to sodium ions; but sodium ions are pumped out of the area of the cell previously affected, which then returns to its resting potential. In this way the neural impulse is transmitted in steps along the axon. Because the impulse is created anew at each step, its strength does not change. As noted earlier, neural impulses are conducted more rapidly along myelinated axons because they jump from node to node.

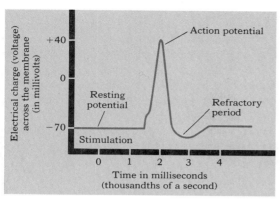

FIGURE 2.3 When a section of a neuron is stimulated by other neurons, the cell membrane becomes permeable to sodium ions so that an action potential of about +40 millivolts is induced. This action potential is transmitted along the axon. Eventually the neuron fires (or fails to fire) according to the all-or-none principle.

An impulse may be conducted along the length of a neuron in less than one thousandth of a second. Then it may "fire," or transmit the "message" to other neurons, muscles, or glands. A neuron may transmit several hundred such messages in a second. Yet, in accord with the **all-or-none principle,** each time a neuron fires it transmits an impulse of the same strength. Neurons fire more frequently when they have been stimulated by a number of other neurons, and frequency of firing seems related to the strength of the message being sent.

For a thousandth of a second or so after firing, a neuron enters a **refractory period** during which it is less responsive to stimulation from other neurons. The refractory period is apparently a time of recovery. When we realize that such periods of recovery may take place 1,000 times per second, it seems a rapid recovery indeed.

All-or-none principle The fact that a neuron fires an impulse of the same strength whenever its action potential has been triggered.

Refractory period A phase following firing during which a neuron's action potential cannot be triggered.

Fantastic Voyage: On Getting into Neurons (Literally)

In the film *Fantastic Voyage* Raquel Welch and her comrades are reduced to microscopic size and injected, along with a submarine, into the bloodstream of a sick man so that they can seek out the source of the disease and cure him. That, of course, is science fiction. You couldn't possibly get into the bloodstream, or into a much narrower neuron, to engage in scientific research, could you?

In the 1930s getting into a narrow human neuron was out of the question. But British scientist John Young found that the aquatic fellow responsible for that Italian dish *calimari*—that is, the squid—had some neurons a full millimeter in diameter. It was a relatively simple matter for Englishmen Alan Hodgkins and Andrew Huxley to construct microelectrodes that could be placed within squid neurons to observe their electrical activity.

But you can place 20,000 human neurons on the head of a pin! At the cell body, a human neuron is only about one-thousandth of an inch wide. Still,

scientists have recently constructed glass tubes, called micropipettes, that are so small that they can be inserted into human neurons (Chase, 1978). Filling these tubes with a fluid conductor permits direct observation of the electrical impulses that pass through. Through this technique, cats can move about freely while the electrical activity in a single neuron is being monitored.

Among the more fascinating findings with the micropipette is that the muscles of cats and people undergo a mysterious but adaptive paralysis during rapid-eye-movement (REM) sleep, the stage of sleep during which we do most of our dreaming. The interiors of the neurons that control the muscles become more negatively charged and therefore cannot discharge. And so our muscles tend to remain relaxed during REM sleep. Otherwise we might begin to act out the themes of our dreams and might awaken or even hurt ourselves.

The Synapse and Neurotransmitters

Synapse (SIN–apps). A space or junction between the terminal bulbs of an axon and the dendrites or soma of another neuron. (From the Greek *synapsis,* meaning "junction" or "connection.")

The "branches," or axon terminals, of one neuron do not actually touch the "roots," or dendrites, of another. There is a small space between neurons called the **synapse** or synaptic cleft (Figure 2.1). In the bulbs at the tips of the axon terminals are sacs or synaptic vesicles that contain neurotransmitters. When a neural impulse reaches the axon terminal, the neuron "fires" by releasing the neurotransmitters from these vesicles into the synaptic cleft. From there they influence the receiving neuron to become depolarized. If adequate quantities of neurotransmitters are released by the first and other cells, the receiving neuron will also fire.

Excitatory synapse A synapse into which neurotransmitters are released that influence receiving neurons in the direction of firing by increasing depolarization of their cell membranes.

Inhibitory synapse A synapse into which neurotransmitters are released that influence receiving neurons *not* to fire by encouraging changes in their membrane permeability in the direction of the resting potential.

Excitatory and Inhibitory Synapses There are excitatory and inhibitory synapses. **Excitatory synapses** influence receiving neurons in the direction of firing. **Inhibitory synapses** influence them in the direction of not firing. Neurons may be influenced by up to 1,000 other neurons, all of which pour forth neurotransmitters from their synaptic vesicles. The additive stimulation received from all these cells determines whether a particular neuron will also fire and "participate" in the transmission of the "message."

Acetylcholine (uh–see–till–CO–lean). A neurotransmitter that controls muscle contractions. Abbreviated *ACh.*

Effects of Certain Transmitters A number of neurotransmitters have been identified and shown to be involved in processes ranging from muscle contraction to emotions. Excesses or deficiencies of neurotransmitters have been linked to diseases and abnormal behavior.

Acetylcholine (ACh) controls muscle contractions, as is highlighted by the effects of curare. **Curare** is a poison that was extracted from plants by South American Indians and used in hunting. If an arrow tipped with curare pierced the skin and the poison entered the body, it would prevent ACh from lodging within receptor sites in neurons, resulting in paralysis. The victim would be prevented from contracting the muscles used in breathing and die from suffocation.

Curare (cue–RAH–ree). A substance extracted from South American plants that causes motor paralysis. In small doses, curare is a muscle relaxant. South American Indians dipped arrowheads in curare for use in hunting and warfare.

Deficiencies of **dopamine** are linked to Parkinson's disease, a disorder in which patients progressively lose control over their muscles. They come to show muscle tremors and jerky, uncoordinated movements. The drug L-Dopa, a substance that the brain converts to dopamine, helps slow the progress of Parkinson's disease. On the other hand, excesses of dopamine have been linked to schizophrenia. As you will see in Chapter 12, the drug chlorpromazine, which is used in treatment of schizophrenia, is thought to work by blocking the action of dopamine. Not surprisingly, chlorpromazine may have "Parkinsonian" side effects, which are usually then treated by additional drugs, adjustment of the dose of chlorpromazine, or switching to another drug.

Dopamine (DOPE–uh–mean). A neurotransmitter that is involved in Parkinson's disease and may play a role in schizophrenia. See Chapter 11.

Norepinephrine (nor–ep–pee–NEFF–rin). A neurotransmitter whose action is similar to that of the hormone *epinephrine,* and which may play a role in depression. See Chapter 11.

Norepinephrine is chemically similar to the hormone epinephrine, which we shall discuss later in the chapter. Norepinephrine, like epinephrine, also speeds up the heartbeat and other bodily processes. Deficiencies of epinephrine have been linked to depression (Ellison, 1977).

Serotonin A neurotransmitter, deficiencies of which have been linked to anxiety and insomnia.

Deficiencies of another neurotransmitter, **serotonin** have been linked to anxiety (Ellison, 1977) and insomnia (Carlson, 1981) in adults, and to aggressive behavior in children (Bland, 1982).

There you have it—a fabulous "forest" of neurons in which countless billions upon billions of vesicles are pouring neurotransmitters into synaptic clefts at any given time, when you are involved in strenuous activity, now as you are reading this page, even as you are passively watching television. This

Brain Food and the Junk–Food Syndrome

Come now! Is there really such a thing as brain food? Isn't all that stuff about fish, for instance, just folklore?

It may be that fish is not in the swim of things as a brain food, but other foods, like liver, eggs, and soybeans may very well be "brain foods"—foods that influence brain activity through enhancing the production of certain neurotransmitters (Wurtman, 1978).

Soybeans, for example, are rich in lecithin. Lecithin raises the blood level of choline, and this eventually raises the amount of acetylcholine (ACh) in the brain.

The neurotransmitter serotonin helps us moderate pain and get to sleep. Serotonin deficiencies have also been linked to childhood misconduct and poor academic performance (Bland, 1982). "Junk foods" like candy, ice cream, sugared cereal, soft drinks, and cookies are high in calories but low in nutrition—especially minerals and the vitamins and proteins that are needed to maintain an adequate level of serotonin. Foods high in protein contain the amino acid tryptophan, from which the body produces serotonin, and B vitamins are used in the conversion of tryptophan to serotonin.

Applications of these discoveries are coming slowly, but early research with oral choline has helped psychiatric patients cope with a movement disorder (called tardive dyskinesia) that seems linked to long-term use of drugs that are prescribed in treatment of psychotic behavior (see Chapter 12). Dietetic changes (replacing some "empty-calorie" junk foods with more nutritious fare) has led to improved school performance and lessened violence in a number of children (Bland, 1982).

It may be somewhat early to try to pick and choose foods that can guarantee that we shall become healthy, wealthy, and wise. On the other hand, it seems reasonable to ask ourselves whether we and our children are making some effort to limit junk foods and take in adequate amounts of proteins, vitamins, and minerals.

---

microscopic picture is repeated several hundred times every second. The combined activity of all these neurotransmitters determines which messages will be transmitted and which will not. Your experience of your perceptions, your thoughts, and your control over your body is very different from the electrochemical process we have described. Yet somehow these many electrochemical events become "translated" into your psychological sense of yourself and of the world.

The Nervous System

There was a time during my childhood when it seemed to me that it was not a very good thing to have a "nervous" system. For instance, if your system were not so nervous, you might be less likely to jump at strange noises.

At some point I learned that a nervous system was not a system that was nervous, but a system of nerves that were involved in thought processes, heart beat, visual-motor coordination, and so on. I also learned that the human nervous system was more complex than that of any other animal, and that our brains were larger than those of any other animal. Now this last piece of business is not exactly true. A human brain weighs about three pounds, but elephant and whale brains may be four times as heavy. Still, our brains comprise a greater part of our body weight than do those of elephants or whales. Our brains weigh about one-sixtieth of our body weight. Elephant brains weigh about one-thousandth of their total weight, and whale brains a paltry one-10,000th of their weight. So if we wish, we can still find figures which can make us proud.

The brain is but one part of the nervous system. A **nerve** is a bundle of axons that is capable of concentrated transmission of messages. The cell bod-

Nerve A bundle of axons from many neurons.

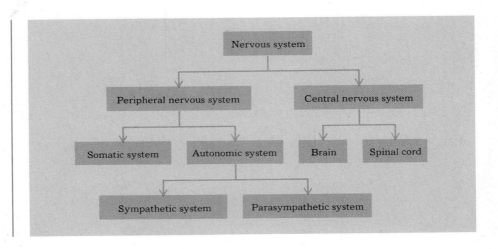

FIGURE 2.4 Divisions of the Nervous System.

Nuclei (NOO–klee–eye). Plural of *nucleus*. A group of neural cell bodies found in the brain or spinal cord.

Ganglia Plural of *ganglion*. A group of neural cell bodies found elsewhere in the body other than the brain or spinal cord.

Central nervous system The brain and spinal cord.

Peripheral nervous system (pair–IF–fur–al). The part of the nervous system consisting of the somatic nervous system and the autonomic nervous system.

Spinal cord A column of nerves within the spine that transmits messages from sensory receptors to the brain, and from the brain to muscles and glands throughout the body.

Spinal reflex A simple unlearned response to a stimulus that may involve as few as two neurons. (From the Latin *reflectere*, meaning "to bend back" or "to reflect.")

Interneuron A neuron that transmits a neural impulse from a sensory neuron to a motor neuron.

Gray matter In the spinal cord, the neurons and neural segments that are involved in spinal reflexes. They are gray in appearance.

White matter In the spinal cord, axon bundles that carry messages back and forth from and to the brain.

ies of these neurons are not considered part of the nerve. The cell bodies are gathered into clumps called **nuclei** in the brain and spinal cord, and **ganglia** elsewhere.

The nervous system consists of the brain, the spinal cord, and nerves linking them to receptors in the sensory organs and effectors in the muscles and glands. As shown in Figure 2.4, the brain and spinal cord compose what we refer to as the **central nervous system.** The sensory (afferent) neurons that receive and transmit messages to the brain and spinal cord, and the motor (efferent) neurons that transmit messages from the brain or spinal cord to the muscles and glands compose the **peripheral nervous system.** There is no deep, complex reason for labeling the two major divisions of the nervous system in this way. It is just geography. The peripheral nervous system extends more into the edges or periphery of the body.

Let us now examine the nature and functions of the central and peripheral nervous systems.

The Central Nervous System

The central nervous system consists of the spinal cord and the brain.

The Spinal Cord   The **spinal cord** is a column of nerves about as thick as a thumb. It transmits messages from receptors to the brain, and from the brain to muscles and glands throughout the body (Figure 2.5). The spinal cord is also capable of some "local government" of responses to external stimulation through **spinal reflexes.** A spinal reflex is an unlearned response to a stimulus that may involve only two neurons—a sensory (afferent) neuron and a motor (efferent) neuron. In some reflexes a third neuron, called an **interneuron,** transmits the neural impulse from the sensory neuron through the spine to the motor neuron (Figure 2.6).

The spinal cord includes both gray matter and white matter. The **gray matter** consists of small, unmyelinated neurons that are involved in spinal reflexes. The **white matter** is composed of bundles of longer, myelinated (and thus whitish) axons that carry messages back and forth to and from the brain. As you can see in Figure 2.6, a cross section of the spinal cord shows the gray matter, which includes cell bodies, to be distributed in something of a butterfly-shaped pattern. (In fact, if you turn to the inkblot shown on page 380,

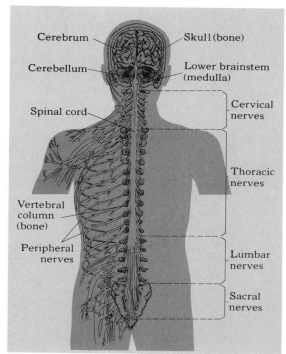

FIGURE 2.5 A View of the Nervous System from the Back. Note that the spinal cord is protected by a column of bones called vertebrae. The brain is protected by the skull.

you can see why physiologists, nurses, and physicians often say that this inkblot reminds them of the spinal cord or gray matter.)

We engage in many reflexes. We blink in response to a puff of air. We swallow when food accumulates in the mouth. A physician may tap the leg below the knee to see if we will show the knee-jerk reflex, a sign that the nervous system is operating adequately. Urinating and defecating are reflexes that occur in response to pressure in the bladder and the rectum. Parents typically spend a number of weeks or months in toilet training infants, or

FIGURE 2.6 A cross-section of the spinal cord, showing a sensory neuron, interneuron, and motor neuron—a combination involved in many spinal reflexes.

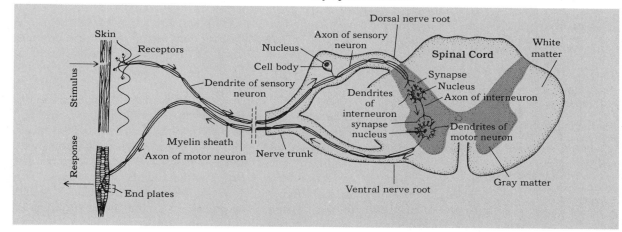

teaching them to involve their brains in the process of elimination. We could suggest that learning to inhibit these reflexes makes civilized conversation possible.

Sexual response also involves many reflexes. Adequate stimulation of the genital organs will lead to erection in the male, vaginal lubrication in the female (both are reflexes which make sexual intercourse possible), and orgasm (another reflex) in both sexes. These processes *can* be quite mechanical, not involving the brain at all, but most often they are not. Feelings of passion, memories of an enjoyable sexual encounter, and sexual fantasies usually contribute to sexual response by transmitting messages from the brain to the genitals through the spinal cord (Rathus, 1983). Awareness of pleasurable sexual sensations in the genitals also works to heighten sexual response, but is not biologically required. (In fact, some people can reach orgasm without touching the genitals—through fantasy alone—usually by imagining sexual stimulation of the genitals by an exciting sex partner.)

Although sexual response in humans is rarely fully mechanical, we can, as noted, respond purely on a reflexive level. Some men and women have spinal cord injuries that prevent genital sensations from reaching the brain. But genital stimulation in many instances can still lead to the reflexes of sexual arousal and orgasm (Money, 1960; Comarr, 1970). In experiments with dogs in which messages were prevented from reaching the brain by way of the spinal cord, the animals have achieved erection, shown pelvic thrusting, and ejaculated (Hart, 1967). After ejaculation, in fact, they were usually responsive to additional sexual stimulation *earlier* than dogs whose spinal columns were intact. It seems that the brain can inhibit sexual response as well as promote it. Many men paralyzed below the waist have similarly achieved erection and ejaculated in response to genital stimulation, although they have not experienced sexual sensations. In this way, even paralyzed people often have sexually active relationships and become parents. Do they "enjoy" their sexual activity? Why not? They achieve common sexual goals with their partners and observe the pleasure their partners experience.

The Brain   Every show has a star, and the brain is the undisputed star of the human nervous system. The size and shape of your brain are responsible for your large, delightfully rounded head. In all the animal kingdom, you (and about five billion other human beings) are unique because of the capacities for learning and thought made possible by the human brain. (See Color Plate 2.2 for a photograph of the human brain.)

Let us have a look at the brain, as shown in Figure 2.7. We shall begin with the back of the head, where the spinal cord rises to meet the brain, and work our way forward. The backmost part of the brain, or hindbrain, consists of three major structures: the medulla oblongata, the pons, and the cerebellum.

Many nerves that connect the spinal cord to higher levels of the brain pass through the **medulla oblongata.** The medulla oblongata is vital in the control of basic functions like heartbeat and respiration. The **pons** lies forward of the medulla. Like the medulla, it is involved in respiration. The pons, which means "bridge" in Latin, transmits information concerning bodily movement.

Behind the pons lies the **cerebellum,** which means "little brain" in Latin. The two hemispheres of the cerebellum are involved in maintaining balance and in controlling motor (muscle) behavior. Injury to the cerebellum may lead to lack of motor coordination, stumbling, and loss of muscle tone.

Medulla oblongata (meh–DULL–ah). An oblong-shaped area of the hindbrain involved in heartbeat and respiration.

Pons A structure of the hindbrain that is involved in respiration.

Cerebellum A part of the hindbrain involved in muscle coordination and balance.

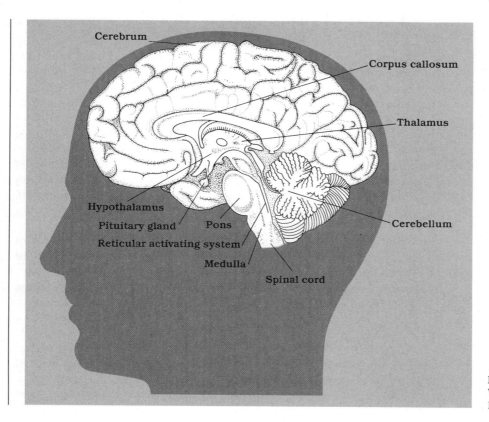

FIGURE 2.7 A Cutaway View of the Human Brain.

The **reticular activating system** (RAS) begins in the hindbrain and ascends through the region of the midbrain into the lower part of the forebrain. The RAS is vital in the functions of attention, sleep, and arousal. Injury to the RAS may leave an animal **comatose.** Electrical stimulation of the RAS wakens sleeping animals, and certain drugs called central nervous system depressants, like alcohol, are thought to work in part by lowering RAS activity.

Sudden loud noises will stimulate the RAS and awaken a sleeping animal or person. But the RAS may become selective, or acquire the capacity to play a filtering role through learning. It may allow some messages to filter through to higher brain levels and awareness, while screening out others. For example, the parent who has primary responsibility for child care may be awakened by the stirring sounds of an infant while louder sounds of traffic or street noise are filtered out. The other parent, by contrast, may usually sleep through even loud cries. But if the first parent must be away for several days, the second parent's RAS may quickly acquire sensitivity to noises produced by the child. This sensitivity may rapidly fade again when the first parent returns.

Also located in the midbrain are areas involved in vision and hearing. These include the area that controls eye reflexes such as dilation of the pupils and eye movements.

The five major areas of the frontmost part of the brain, or forebrain, are the thalamus, the hypothalamus, the basal ganglia, the limbic system, and the cerebrum.

The **thalamus** is located near the center of the brain. It consists of two joined lobes that have egg or football shapes. The thalamus serves as a relay station for incoming sensory stimulation—sights, sounds, touches, and the

Reticular activating system A part of the brain involved in attention, sleep, and arousal. (From the Latin *rete,* meaning "net.")

Comatose In a coma, a state resembling sleep from which it is difficult to be aroused.

Thalamus An area near the center of the brain that is involved in the relay of sensory information to the cortex, and in the functions of sleep and attention. (From the Greek *thalamos,* meaning "inner chamber.")

Hypothalamus A bundle of nuclei below the thalamus involved in body temperature, motivation, and emotion. See Chapter 7. (From the Greek *hypo-*, meaning "under," and *thalamos.)*

Basal ganglia Ganglia located between the thalamus and cerebrum that are involved in motor coordination.

Limbic system A group of structures that form a fringe along the inner end of the cerebrum. They are involved in memory and motivation. (From the Latin *limbus,* meaning "border" or "fringe.")

Epilepsy Temporary disturbances of brain functions that involve sudden neural discharges. (From the Greek *epilepsia,* meaning "seizure.")

Cerebrum The large mass of the forebrain, which consists of two hemispheres. (Latin word meaning "brain.")

position of the body—which it then transmits to an appropriate section of the cerebral cortex. For instance, the thalamus relays sensory input from the eyes to the visual areas of the cerebral cortex. The thalamus also seems involved in controlling sleep and attention, in coordination with other brain structures, including the RAS.

The **hypothalamus** is a tiny bundle of nuclei located beneath the thalamus and above the pituitary gland. The hypothalamus is about the size of a pea and weighs only four grams, yet it is vital in the control of body temperature, motivation, and emotion. Experimenters learn many of the functions of the hypothalamus by implanting electrodes in various parts of it and observing the behavioral effects when a current is switched on. In this way it has been found that the hypothalamus is involved in hunger, thirst, sex, and aggression. We shall learn more about the hypothalamus later in this chapter and in Chapter 7.

The **basal ganglia** are buried between the thalamus and the cerebrum and are involved in coordination of movement. Their deterioration has been linked to Parkinson's disease.

The **limbic system** is the name given a group of structures that lie along the inner edge of the cerebrum. The limbic system is found in mammals only. It is involved in memory (the storage of information), and in the drives of hunger, sex, and aggression. A part of the limbic system is sometimes removed in an effort to control **epilepsy,** or seizures that stem from sudden neural discharges. People who have had such operations can recall material learned prior to them, but cannot permanently store new information. Destruction of certain areas of the limbic system leads monkeys and other mammals to show docile behavior. Destruction of other areas will lead to a rage reaction at the slightest provocation.

The **cerebrum** is the crowning glory of the brain. Only in human beings does the cerebrum comprise such a large proportion of the brain (Figure 2.7).

FIGURE 2.8 The Corpus Callosum. This thick fiber bundle connects the two hemispheres of the brain. Surgeons may treat severe epilepsy by severing the corpus callosum.

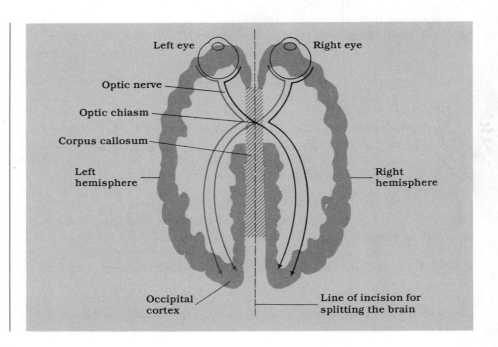

Left eye Right eye

Optic nerve

Optic chiasm

Corpus callosum

Left hemisphere

Right hemisphere

Occipital cortex

Line of incision for splitting the brain

The surface of the cerebrum is wrinkled, or convoluted, with ridges and valleys. This surface is the **cerebral cortex.** The convolutions allow a great deal of surface area to be packed into the brain. We shall explore the cerebral cortex in depth in a later section of this chapter.

Valleys in the cortex are called **fissures.** A most significant fissure practically divides the cerebrum in half (Figure 2.8). The hemispheres of the cerebral cortex are connected only by the **corpus callosum** (Latin for "thick body" or "hard body"), a thick fiber bundle. Later we shall see that severing the corpus callosum leads to some interesting behavior.

The Peripheral Nervous System

The peripheral nervous system consists of sensory and motor neurons that transmit messages to and from the central nervous system. The two main divisions of the peripheral nervous system are the somatic nervous system and the autonomic nervous system.

The Somatic Nervous System The **somatic nervous system** transmits messages about stimulation of the muscles, skin, and joints to the central nervous system. As a result, we can experience pressure, pain, and changes in temperature. Messages from the brain and spinal cord to the somatic nervous system control voluntary body movements, like raising a hand, winking, or running, and the minor involuntary muscle movements that maintain our posture or balance.

The Autonomic Nervous System *Autonomic* means "automatic." The **autonomic nervous system** (ANS) regulates the glands and **involuntary** activities like heartbeat, respiration, digestion, and dilation of the pupils of the eyes. While these activities will all occur on a purely autonomic basis, we can exert conscious control over respiration. In Chapter 4 we shall see that people have also learned to gain conscious control over other autonomic functions, such as heartbeat, through biofeedback training.

The ANS has two branches or divisions, the **sympathetic** and the **parasympathetic.** These branches have largely opposing effects but can also work together. Many organs and glands are stimulated by both branches of the ANS (Figure 2.9). In general, the sympathetic division is most active during processes that involve the spending of bodily energy from stored reserves, such as in a fight-or-flight response to a predator. The parasympathetic division is most active during processes that replenish reserves of energy, as during eating (Levitt, 1981). For instance, when we are afraid, the sympathetic division of the ANS accelerates the heart rate. But when we relax, it is the parasympathetic division that decelerates the heart rate. The parasympathetic division stimulates digestive processes, but the sympathetic branch inhibits digestive activity. Since the sympathetic division predominates when we feel fear or anxiety, fear or anxiety can lead to indigestion.

In sexual activity, a small amount of anxiety (characterized by sympathetic activity), as on a first date, can enhance sexual response by generally activating the body. However, the reflexes of erection and vaginal lubrication are largely under parasympathetic control. For that reason, too much anxiety (sympathetic activity) can inhibit erection or lubrication from occurring. Ejaculation, ironically, is largely under sympathetic control. Even though a great deal of anxiety can inhibit erection, it can produce early or premature eja-

Cerebral cortex The wrinkled surface area of the cerebrum, often called "gray matter" because of the appearance afforded by the many cell bodies. *(Cortex* is a Latin word meaning "bark.")

Fissures. Valleys.

Corpus callosum A thick bundle of fibers that connects the two hemispheres.

Somatic nervous system The divison of the peripheral nervous system that connects the central nervous system with sensory receptors, muscles, and the surface of the body.

Autonomic nervous system The division of the peripheral nervous system that regulates glands and involuntary activities like heartbeat, respiration, digestion, and dilation of the pupils. Abbreviated *ANS.* (From the Greek *autonomos,* meaning "independent.")

Involuntary Automatic, not consciously controlled.

Sympathetic The branch of the ANS that is most active during emotional responses that spend the body's reserves of energy, such as fear and anxiety. (From the Greek *syn-,* meaning "together," and *pathos,* meaning "feeling.")

Parasympathetic The branch of the ANS that is most active during processes that restore the body's reserves of energy, like digestion. Parasympathetic activities are frequently, but not always, antagonistic to sympathetic activities. (From the Greek *para-,* meaning "alongside," and *sympathetic.)*

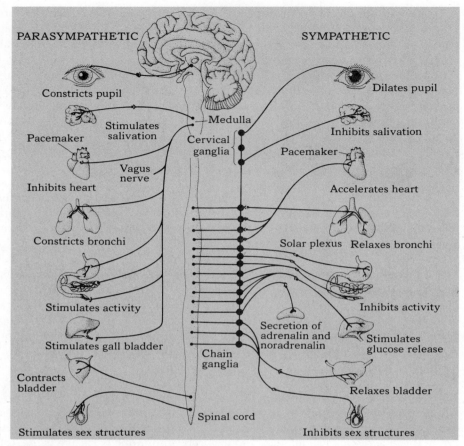

PARASYMPATHETIC   SYMPATHETIC

Constricts pupil — Dilates pupil

Stimulates salivation — Inhibits salivation

Pacemaker — Pacemaker

Medulla

Cervical ganglia

Vagus nerve

Inhibits heart — Accelerates heart

Constricts bronchi — Solar plexus   Relaxes bronchi

Stimulates activity — Inhibits activity

Stimulates gall bladder — Secretion of adrenalin and noradrenalin   Stimulates glucose release

Chain ganglia

Contracts bladder — Relaxes bladder

Spinal cord

Stimulates sex structures — Inhibits sex structures

FIGURE 2.9   Activities of the Two Branches of the Autonomic Nervous System (ANS). The parasympathetic branch of the ANS generally acts to replenish stores of energy in the body. It is connected to organs by nerves that originate near the top and bottom of the spinal cord. The sympathetic branch is most active during activities that expend energy. Its neurons collect in clusters or chains of ganglia along the central portion of the spinal cord. The two branches of the ANS frequently have antagonistic effects on the organs they service.

culation. In Chapter 13 we shall see that treatment of premature ejaculation and other problems that are linked to high levels of sympathetic activity involves lessening the person's level of anxiety.

In Chapter 7 we shall learn more about the role of the ANS in motivation and emotion. In Chapter 10 we shall see how prolonged overarousal of the ANS is stressful and can lead to various psychological and medical problems.

The Cerebral Cortex

Just where is that elusive piece of business you think of as your "mind"? Thousands of years ago it was not generally thought that the mind had a place to hang its hat within the body. It was common to assume that the body was inhabited by demons or souls that could not be explained in terms of substance at all. After all, if you look inside a human being, the biological structures you find do not look all that different in quality from those of many lower animals. So it seemed to make sense that those qualities which made us distinctly human—thinking, planning, talking, dreaming, composing—were unrelated to substances that you could see, feel, and actually weigh on a scale.

The ancient Egyptians attributed control of the human being to a little man, or **homunculus,** who dwelled within the skull and sort of pressed the buttons that regulated our behavior. The Greek philosopher Aristotle thought that the soul had set up living quarters in the heart. After all, serious injury to the heart could be said to cause the soul to take flight from the body.

Through a variety of accidents and research projects, we have come to recognize that "mind," or consciousness, dwells essentially within the brain. Within the brain, it is located largely in the cerebral cortex. Different sorts of bodily injuries have distinct effects. It became increasingly apparent that injuries to the head can lead to impairments of consciousness and awareness, such as loss of vision and hearing, general confusion, or loss of memory. Experiments in stimulating or destroying specific areas in animal brains and human brains (experiments are not intended to harm people, but local injuries are sometimes unavoidable in operations that are intended to save life or cure certain disorders) have also shown that certain areas of the brain are associated with specific types of sensations or activities.

From the perspective of physiological psychologists today, the mind is a manifestation of the brain. Without the brain, in other words, there is no mind. Within the brain lies the potential for self-awareness and purposeful activity. The brain somehow gives rise to the mind. Whether thought is then self-initiated, merely responsive to external stimulation, or reflects an ongoing interaction between people and the environment is a hotly debated issue in psychology. But it is generally agreed that for every **phenomenological** event, like a "thought" or a "feeling," there are accompanying, underlying neurological events.

When you realize that a neuron may fire 1,000 times a second, and that thoughts may involve the firing of millions or billions of neurons, you can understand that it will never become practical to try to explain a thought in terms of the firing of a particular combination of neurons. Yet while we shall never be able to outline precisely the substance of all the effects of the "mind," it is assumed that the mind is generally based on the substance of the brain. All this adds to the fascination of the work of physiological psychologists.

We have seen that sensation and muscle activity involve many parts of the nervous system. But the essential human activities of thought and language involve the hemispheres of the cerebrum.

The Geography of the Cerebral Cortex

Each of the two hemispheres of the cerebral cortex is divided into four parts or lobes, as shown in Figure 2.10. The **frontal lobe** lies in front of the central fissure, and the **parietal lobe** lies behind. The **temporal lobe** lies below the side, or lateral, fissure, across from the frontal and parietal lobes. The **occipital lobe** lies behind the temporal lobe and behind and below the parietal lobe.

When light strikes the retinas of the eyes, neurons in the occipital lobe fire and we "see." Direct artificial stimulation of the occipital lobe also produces visual sensations. You would "see" flashes of light if neurons in the occipital region of the cortex were stimulated with electricity, even if it were pitch black out or your eyes were covered. The hearing or auditory area of

Homunculus
(ho–MUN–cue–luss). Latin for "little man." A homunculus within the brain was once thought to govern human behavior.

Phenomenological
(fen–NOM–men–no–LODGE–ick–al). Having to do with subjective, conscious experience. (From the Greek *phänomenon,* meaning "appearance.")

Frontal lobe The lobe of the cerebral cortex that lies to the front of the central fissure.

Parietal lobe
(par–RYE–uh–tal). The lobe that lies just behind the central fissure. (From the Latin *paries,* meaning "wall.")

Temporal lobe The lobe that lies below the lateral fissure, near the temples of the head.

Occipital lobe
(ox–SIP–it–tal). The lobe that lies behind and below the parietal lobe, and behind the temporal lobe. (From the Latin *ob-,* meaning "in the way" or "against," and *caput,* meaning "head.")

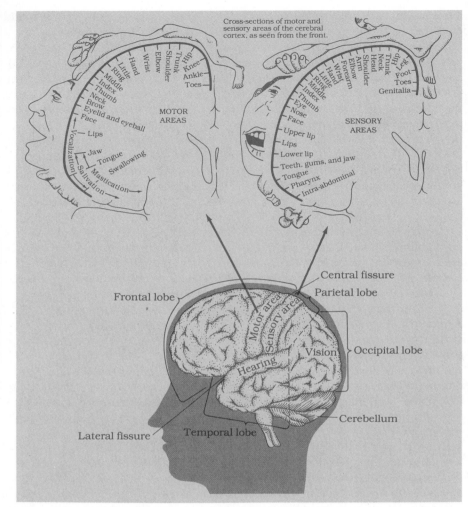

FIGURE 2.10   The Geography of the Cerebral Cortex. The cortex is divided into four lobes: frontal, parietal, temporal, and occipital. The visual area of the cortex is located in the occipital lobe. The hearing or auditory cortex lies in the temporal lobe. The sensory and motor areas face each other across the central fissure. What happens when surgeons stimulate areas of the sensory or motor cortex during operations?

Sensory cortex The section of cortex that lies just behind the central fissure in the parietal lobe. Sensory stimulation is projected in this section of cortex.

the cortex lies in the temporal lobe along the lateral fissure. As we shall see in Chapter 3, sounds cause structures in the ear to vibrate. Messages are relayed to the auditory area of the cortex, and when you hear a noise, neurons in this area are firing.

Just behind the central fissure in the parietal lobe lies an area of **sensory cortex** in which the messages received from skin senses all over the body are projected. These sensations include heat and cold, touch, pain, and movement. Neurons in different parts of this sensory cortex fire depending on whether you wiggle your finger or raise your leg. And if a brain surgeon were to stimulate the proper area of your sensory cortex with a small probe known as a "pencil electrode," you might testify in court that someone had touched your arm or leg. Figure 2.10 suggests how our faces and hands are sort of overrepresented on this cortex as compared with, say, our trunks and legs. For this reason, our faces and hands are relatively more sensitive to touch.

The **motor cortex** lies in the frontal lobe, just across the valley of the central fissure from the sensory cortex. Neurons in the motor cortex fire when we move certain parts of our body. If a surgeon were to stimulate a certain area with a pencil electrode, you would raise your leg. Raising the leg would be sensed in the sensory cortex, and you might have a devil of a time trying to figure out whether you had "intended" to raise that leg! How do you like this as an example of brain control?

Thought, Language, and the Cortex

Areas of the cerebral cortex that are not primarily involved in sensation or motor activity are called **association areas.** Their functions appear largely to involve learning, thought, memory, and language.

Association areas in the frontal lobes, for example, involve memory functions required for simple problem solving. Monkeys with **lesions** in these areas have difficulty remembering which of a pair of cups holds food when the cups have been screened off from them for a few seconds (Bauer & Fuster, 1976; French & Harlow, 1962). Stimulation of many association areas with pencil electrodes during surgery leads people to recall memories vividly, along with the emotions linked to them (Penfield, 1969). It is as if the person were being shown a film of the past inside the head.

Some association areas seem involved in integrating sensory information. Certain neurons in the visual area of the occipital lobe fire in response to visual presentation of vertical lines. Others fire in response to horizontal lines. Although single cells may respond only to part of the visual field, association areas "put it all together" so that you see a box, or an automobile, or a roadmap, and not a confusing array of verticals and horizontals.

The left and right hemispheres of the brain tend to duplicate each other's functions to some degree, but they are not entirely equal. For the nine of ten people who are right-handed, the left hemisphere contains language functions and dominates. For about half the people who are left-handed, the right hemisphere is dominant. The left hemisphere thus contains language functions for about 95 percent of us.

The language areas of the cortex are located near the intersections of the frontal, temporal, and parietal lobes. When one particular language area has been damaged, as can happen during a stroke, afflicted people may not be able to understand spoken or written language. Damage to another language area may make it difficult for people to express themselves through speech. **Aphasia** is the term given to such language problems.

Many years ago it was discovered that patients with injuries to one hemisphere of the brain would show sensory or motor deficits on the opposite side of the body. Experimentation since that time has made it clear that sensory and motor nerves crisscross in the brain. The left hemisphere controls functions on the right side of the body, and the right hemisphere controls functions on the left side of the body.

As you can see in Figure 2.11, recent research (e.g., Ornstein, 1977) suggests that the dominant (usually the left) hemisphere is somewhat more involved in intellectual undertakings that require logic and problem solving, or the comprehension and production of speech. The nondominant (usually

Motor cortex The section of cortex that lies in the frontal lobe, just across the central fissure from the sensory cortex. Neural impulses in the motor cortex are linked to muscular responses throughout the body.

Association areas Areas of the cortex involved in learning, thought, memory, and language.

Lesion An injury that results in impaired behavior or loss of a function.

Aphasia Impaired ability to comprehend or express oneself through speech. (From the Greek *a-*, meaning "not," and *phasis*, meaning "utterance.")

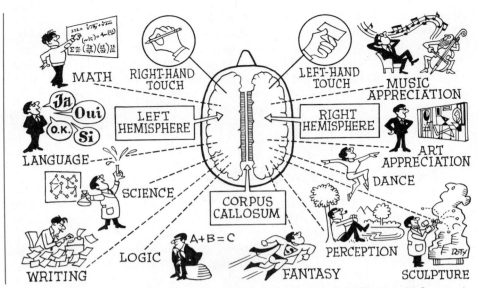

FIGURE 2.11 Some of the Specializations of the Left and Right Hemispheres of the Cerebral Cortex. It is well established that sensory and motor functions crisscross in the brain. The localization of logical vs. artistic functions is more speculative.

right) hemisphere is relatively more concerned with esthetic responses and imagination.

A number of studies suggest that the hemispheres of the brain may be more specialized in men than in women (Goleman, 1978). Observations of brain-injured adults suggest that men with damage to the dominant hemisphere are more likely to show verbal deficiencies than women with similar damage. Men with damage to the nondominant hemisphere are also more likely than similarly damaged women to show spatial relations deficits. If such biological differences in brain organization exist, they may help explain why many women outperform men in verbal skills that also involve some spatial organization, such as reading, spelling, and articulation of speech. But men might then excel at more specialized spatial tasks like imagining mathematical functions rotating in space or interpreting roadmaps. However, we should keep in mind that research in specialization of the hemispheres of the cortex is in its infancy. In Chapter 13 we shall see that cognitive differences between the sexes are quite small, and that differences within the sexes outweigh differences between the sexes.

Divided-Brain Experiments: When Two Hemispheres Stop Talking to One Another

A number of patients suffering from severe cases of epilepsy have undergone **split-brain operations** to try to confine the disorder to one hemisphere of the cerebral cortex, rather than allow one hemisphere to agitate the other through transmitting a "violent storm of neural impulses" (Carlson, 1981). The surgeon severs the corpus callosum, the thick band of nervous fibers that, in the main, connect the hemispheres. These operations do seem to help epi-

Split—brain operation An operation in which the corpus callosum is severed, usually in an effort to control epileptic seizures.

Three Pioneers of the Brain

The human brain is a whole universe, and of all the questions that it can conceive, none is more mysterious or intriguing than precisely how it works. For tracing some of the elusive answers through the intricate corridors of consciousness and perception, three scientists were awarded Nobel Prizes in 1981. For his pioneering research into the differing functions of the brain's two cerebral hemispheres, Roger Sperry of the California Institute of Technology, won half the prize. The other half was divided between David Hubel and Torsten Wiesel, professors of neurology, for discovering how images are transferred from the eye's retina to the brain.

Sperry's research, carried out over three decades, forms the theoretical basis for much of the modern research into how the brain processes information. Previously it was thought that one hemisphere of the brain was dominant, and the other was a minor one that lacked the capacity for higher mental functions. Working first with test animals, Sperry surgically severed the corpus callosum. He discovered that the animals could still perform learned tasks when stimulated solely in one hemi-

sphere, but that the other hemisphere could be taught to perform similar tasks, demonstrating that each hemisphere, independently, contained the ability to learn.

Sperry then studied epileptics who had undergone similar surgery to control seizures. Surprisingly, the patients had suffered no obvious changes in mental capacity. Sperry's test procedures proved that each cerebral hemisphere in such patients had its own separate world of consciousness, perceptual existence,

Roger Sperry.

emotions, thoughts, and memory. In subsequent research, the right hemisphere, far from being inferior to the left, as was once thought, proved clearly superior in some respects, including the capacity for intuitive thinking, interpreting auditory impressions, and comprehending spatial relationships. Said the Nobel Committee of Sperry's achievements: "He has provided us with an insight into the inner world of the brain which hitherto had been almost completely hidden from us."

Hubel and Wiesel have provided a road map of a small portion of that world. By measuring electrical impulses given off by the neurons of the visual cortex, the researchers discovered that the cells in the cortex are arranged in a regular pattern in columns organized into equally regular "hypercolumns." Each cell within each column, they discovered, has a specific responsibility to perceive and analyze incoming images according to contrast, linear patterns and movement on the retina. Within the columns, the analysis also occurs in a formal sequence. Eventually all this information is relayed to the higher centers in the brain where the "full picture," or visual impression, is assembled and a memory of it is stored.

lepsy patients. People who have undergone them wind up with two brains that function somewhat independently, yet under most circumstances their behavior remains perfectly normal. But some of the effects of two hemispheres that have stopped talking to one another can be rather intriguing.

Gazzaniga (1967, 1972) has shown that split-brain patients whose eyes are closed may be able to describe verbally an object like a key that is held in one hand, but cannot do so when the object is held in the other. As shown in Figure 2.12, if a split-brain patient handles a key with his left hand behind a screen, **tactile** impressions of the key are projected into the right hemisphere, which has little or no language ability. Thus he will not be able to describe the key. If it were held in his right hand, he would have no trouble describing it because sensory impressions would be projected into the left hemisphere of the cortex, which contains language functions. To further confound matters, if the word *ring* is projected into the dominant (left) hemisphere while the patient is asked what he is handling, he will say "ring," not "key."

Tactile Of the sense of touch. (From the Latin *tangere*, meaning "to touch.")

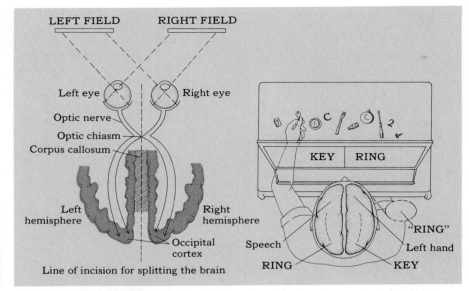

FIGURE 2.12 In the drawing on the left, we see that visual sensations in the left visual field are projected in the occipital cortex of the right hemisphere. Visual sensations from the right visual field are projected in the occipital cortex in the left hemisphere. In the split-brain experiment diagrammed on the right, a subject with a severed corpus callosum handles a key with his left hand and perceives the written word *key* with his left eye. The word "key" is projected in the right hemisphere. But speech is usually a function of the left (dominant) hemisphere. The written word "ring," perceived by the right eye, is projected in the left hemisphere. So, when asked what he is handling, the split-brain subject reports "ring," not "key."

A Psychological Controversy: Can Behavior Be Controlled by Electrical Stimulation of the Brain?

Some years ago, José Delgado astounded the world by stepping into a bullring armed only with a radio transmitter, a cape, and, perhaps, crossed fingers (Figure 2.13). As he describes his experiment in *Physical Control of the*

FIGURE 2.13 Brave bulls are dangerous animals which will attack an intruder in the arena. Even in full charge, however, a bull can be stopped abruptly by radio-triggered electrical stimulation of the brain. After several stimulations, there is a lasting inhibition of aggressive behavior.

Mind (1969), Dr. Delgado implanted a radio-controlled electrode in the limbic system of a "brave bull," a variety bred to respond with a raging charge when it sees any human being. But when Delgado pressed a button on a transmitter, sending a signal to a battery-powered receiver attached to the bull's horns, an electrical impulse went into the bull's brain and the animal would cease his charge. After several stimulations, the bull's naturally aggressive behavior disappeared.

Here seemed the dawn of a new age of brain control. An experiment with a monkey produced even more astonishing results. Electrical stimulation of one part of her brain (ESB) caused her to (1) stop whatever she was doing; (2) alter expression; (3) turn her head; (4) stand on two feet and circle; (5) climb up and down a pole; (6) growl; and then (7) attack another monkey (Delgado, 1969).

Since these early days, ESB has been used with people to address various problems. For instance, Robert Heath of Tulane University claims that ESB helped some severely disturbed schizophrenic patients (Valenstein, 1978). Cancer or trauma patients suffering from unrelenting pain are using ESB to block pain messages in the spinal cord before they reach the brain (Restak, 1975). It has even been suggested that electrodes be used to block criminal behavior. Electrodes implanted in habitual criminals would be monitored by a distant computer. When the computer interpreted data like muscle tension and heavy breathing to mean that a crime was being considered, it could use ESB to cause the criminals to forget what they were about to do!

But psychologist Elliot Valenstein (1978) is not quite so impressed with the potential of ESB. He notes, for example, that the bull in the Delgado demonstration did not really have its aggressive tendencies eliminated by ESB. Rather, the electrical impulses caused the bull to circle to the right. The bull might have been more confused than pacified.

Also, behavior resulting from ESB does not perfectly mimic natural behavior. ESB-provoked behavior is stereotyped and compulsive. For instance,

And Now . . . Brain Transplants?

In recent years we have grown accustomed to hearing about heart, kidney, and lung transplants, but what of brain transplants? According to Don Marshall Gash (1981) of the University of Rochester, we may be transfering human tissue to human brains within a decade or so to treat injuries to the brain and illnesses like Parkinson's disease.

Researchers have recently grafted neurons from fetal rats into the brains of injured or diseased rats. In one application, vasopressin neurons have been transplanted into rats that have defective vasopressin neurons. Vasopressin is the antidiuretic hormone (ADH) that causes the kidney to increase reabsorption of water. Without vasopressin, rats and people must almost continually drink and excrete water.

Dopamine neurons have also been transplanted with some success. In Parkinson's disease there is a gradual loss of dopamine neurons. When dopamine neurons from fetal rats were transplanted to brain sites in adults where loss of these neurons had occurred, they grew vigorously and to some degree reversed the loss of motor control.

Fetal rat neurons were used because adult neurons will not survive transplanting. But the brains of the recipient rats are unlikely to reject transplanted neurons, in contrast to the rejection problems encountered in heart and kidney transplants.

Problems remain, including a major ethical issue: Where would the donor neurons come from? Gash suggests one possible answer—brains may be tolerant enough not to reject implants from closely related animals. If this notion strikes you as bizarre, remember that we have already considered using the hearts and other organs of related species.

an animal whose "hunger" has been prodded by ESB may eat one kind of food only. And ESB in the same site may produce different behaviors at different times. A rat may eat when receiving ESB on one occasion, but drink on another. ESB may not be quite so predictable as had been thought.

The sites for producing pleasant or unpleasant sensations in people may vary from person to person and from day to day. According to Valenstein, "The impression that brain stimulation in humans can repeatedly evoke the same emotional state, the same memory, or the same behavior is simply a myth. The brain is not organized into neat compartments that correspond to the . . . labels we assign to behavior" (1978, p. 31).

Still, experimentation with ESB goes on. Many are more optimistic than Valenstein about its potential.

The Endocrine System

Here are some things you may have heard about hormones and behavior. Are they truth or fiction?

- Some obese people actually eat very little, and their excess weight is caused by "glands."
- A boy whose growth was "stunted" began to catch up with his agemates after receiving injections of "growth hormone."
- A woman who becomes anxious and depressed just before menstruating is suffering from "raging hormones."
- Some East German women athletes who earned gold medals in the 1976 Olympics were accused of using hormone injections against the rules.
- People who receive injections of adrenalin often report that they feel "as if" they are about to experience some emotion, but they're not sure which one.

Let us consider each of these items. The obese may often attribute their weight problems to glands, but most of the time they simply eat too much. Growth hormone, a secretion of the **pituitary gland,** can promote growth. Women may become somewhat more anxious or depressed at the time of menstruation, but the effects of hormones have been exaggerated. Later in this section we shall see that women's response to menstruation reflects their attitudes as well as biological changes. The women athletes were found to be using steroids; these hormones are produced by the **adrenal cortex,** and in greater quantity in men. They promote resistance to stress and muscle growth in both men and women. Finally, adrenalin, a hormone produced by the **adrenal medulla,** does generally arouse people and thereby heighten general emotional responsiveness. In Chapter 7 you will see that the specific emotion to which this arousal is attributed may depend on the person's situation.

Ductless Glands

The body contains two types of glands: glands with **ducts** and glands without ducts. A duct is a tube that carries substances to specific locations. Saliva, sweat, and tears (the name of a new singing group?) all reach their destinations by ducts. Psychologists are more likely to show interest in the substances secreted by ductless glands because of their behavioral effects (see the summary in Table 2.1). The ductless glands constitute the **endocrine**

Pituitary gland The body's "master gland," which secretes growth hormone, prolactin, antidiuretic hormone, and others.

Adrenal cortex One of the two adrenal glands located above the kidneys. The adrenal cortex produces steroids. (From the Latin *ad-*, meaning "at" or "near," and *renes*, meaning "kidneys.")

Adrenal medulla One of the adrenal glands. The adrenal medulla produces adrenalin.

Duct A tube or channel. (From the Latin *ducere*, meaning "to lead.")

Endocrine system Ductless glands that secrete hormones and release them directly into the bloodstream.

system of the body, and they secrete substances called **hormones** (from the Greek horman, meaning "to stimulate" or "to excite").

Let us now examine the functions of several glands of the endocrine system.

TABLE 2.1   An Overview of Some Major Glands of the Endocrine System

Gland	Hormone	Major Effects
Pituitary		
ANTERIOR LOBE	Growth hormone	Causes growth of muscles, bones, and glands
	Adrenocorticotrophic hormone (ACTH)	Regulates adrenal cortex
	Thyrotrophin	Causes thyroid gland to secrete thyroxin
	Follicle-stimulating hormone	Causes formation of sperm and egg cells
	Luteinizing hormone	Causes ovulation, maturation of sperm and egg cells
	Prolactin	Stimulates production of milk
POSTERIOR LOBE	Antidiuretic hormone (ADH)	Inhibits production of urine
	Oxytocin	Stimulates uterine contractions during delivery and release of milk during nursing
Pancreas	Insulin	Enables body to metabolize sugar, regulates storage of fats
	Glucagon	Increases levels of sugar and fats in blood
	Somatostatin	Regulates secretion of insulin and glucagon
Thyroid	Thyroxin	Increases metabolic rate
Parathyroid	Parathormone	Increases blood calcium level
Pineal	Melatonin	Regulates reproductive behavior and growth of secondary sex characteristics
Adrenal		
CORTEX	Steroids	Increases resistance to stress, regulates carbohydrate metabolism
MEDULLA	Adrenalin (Epinephrine)	Increases metabolic activity (heart and respiration rates, blood sugar level, etc.)
	Noradrenalin (Norepinephrine)	Raises blood pressure, acts as neurotransmitter
Testes	Testosterone	Promotes growth of male sex characteristics
Ovaries	Estrogen	Regulates menstrual cycle
	Progesterone	Promotes growth of female reproductive tissues, maintains pregnancy
Uterus	(Several)	Maintains pregnancy

Growth hormone A pituitary hormone that regulates growth.

Prolactin (pro–LACK–tin). A pituitary hormone that regulates production of milk and, in lower animals, maternal behavior.

Antidiuretic hormone (ant–eye–dye–you–RET–ick). A pituitary hormone that inhibits the production of urine. Abbreviated *ADH.*

Oxytocin (ox–see–TOE–sin). A pituitary hormone that stimulates labor. (From the Greek *oxys,* meaning "quick," and *tokos,* meaning "birth.")

Pancreas (PAN–kree–us). A gland behind the stomach whose secretions influence the level of sugar in the blood.

Insulin A pancreatic hormone that stimulates the metabolism of sugar.

Glucagon A pancreatic hormone that increases the levels of sugar and fat in the blood.

The Pituitary Gland

The pituitary gland is located just below the hypothalamus. It is so central to the body's functioning that it is referred to as the master gland. The anterior (front) and posterior (back) lobes of the pituitary gland produce or secrete many hormones, some of which are listed in Table 2.1.

Growth hormone regulates the growth of muscles, bones, and glands. An excess of growth hormone can lead to *giantism,* a condition in which people may grow two to three feet taller than they would normally. Children whose growth patterns seem abnormally slow often catch up to their agemates when growth hormone is administered by a physician. A recently discovered substance, growth hormone releasing factor (or GRF), is produced by the hypothalamus and thought to cause the pituitary to produce growth hormone (Slade & Biddle, 1982).

Prolactin largely regulates maternal behavior in lower mammals, such as rats, and stimulates production of milk in women. As you will see in Chapter 7, transfusion of blood from a new mother rat to another female rat will cause the recipient to display typical mothering behaviors.

When the fluid level of the body is low, the hypothalamus stimulates the pituitary gland to secrete **antidiuretic hormone,** which is abbreviated *ADH* and also referred to as *vasopressin.* ADH then inhibits production of urine in order to conserve fluid.

Oxytocin stimulates labor in pregnant women. Obstetricians may induce labor or increase the strength of uterine contractions during labor by injecting pregnant women with oxytocin.

FIGURE 2.14   Location of Major Glands of the Endocrine System.

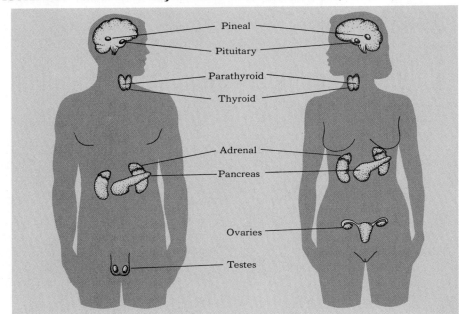

The Pancreas

The **pancreas** is influential in controlling the level of sugar in the blood and the urine through the hormones **insulin** and **glucagon.** One form of diabetes (diabetes mellitus) is characterized by excess sugar in the blood (**hyperglycemia**) and in the urine, a condition that can lead to coma and death. Diabetes stems from inadequate secretion or utilization of insulin. People who do not secrete enough insulin of their own may need to inject this hormone daily in order to control diabetes.

The condition **hypoglycemia** is characterized by too little sugar in the blood. Symptoms of hypoglycemia include shakiness, dizziness, and lack of energy, a **syndrome** that is easily confused with anxiety. Many people have sought help for anxiety and learned through a series of blood tests that they are actually suffering from hypoglycemia. This disorder is generally controlled through dietary restrictions.

The Thyroid Gland

Thyroxin is produced by the thyroid gland. Thyroxin affects the body's **metabolism,** or rate of using oxygen and producing energy. Some people who are overweight are suffering from a condition known as **hypothyroidism,** which results from abnormally low secretions of thyroxin. Deficiency of thyroxin can lead to **cretinism** in children, a disorder characterized by stunted growth and mental retardation. Adults who secrete too little thyroxin may feel tired and sluggish, and may put on weight. People who produce excesses of thyroxin may develop **hyperthyroidism,** a disorder characterized by excitability, insomnia, and weight loss.

The Adrenal Glands

The adrenal glands, located above the kidneys, have an outer layer, or cortex, and an inner core, or medulla. The adrenal cortex is regulated by the pituitary hormone ACTH. The cortex secretes as many as 20 different hormones known as **steroids.** As noted in the box "In Sports, 'Lions vs. Tigers,' " anabolic (artificial) steroids have been used to enhance athletic prowess.

Adrenalin, also known as epinephrine, is secreted by the adrenal medulla. It acts on the sympathetic branch of the ANS and on the RAS to arouse the body in preparation for threats and stress. As noted earlier and in Chapter 7, adrenalin is also implicated in general emotional arousal.

The Testes and the Ovaries

Did you know that if it were not for the secretion of the male sex hormone **testosterone** about 6 weeks after conception, we would all develop into females? Testosterone is produced by the testes and, a few weeks following fertilization of an ovum, it stimulates prenatal differentiation of male sexual organs. During puberty it promotes development of **secondary sexual characteristics** such as the beard and deep voice, the growth of muscle and bone, and the sperm-producing ability of the testes.

Testosterone levels vary slightly with stress, time of the day or month, and other factors, but are maintained at fairly even levels by the hypothalamus,

Hyperglycemia (high–purr–gly–SEEM–me–uh). A disorder caused by excess sugar in the blood. (From the Greek *hyper-*, meaning "above," and *glykys*, meaning "sweet.")

Hypoglycemia A disorder caused by too little sugar in the blood. (From the Greek *hypo-*, meaning "under.")

Syndrome (SIN–drome). A cluster of symptoms characteristic of a disorder.

Thyroxin (thigh–ROCKS–sin). The thyroid hormone which increases metabolic rate. (From the Latin *thyroides*, meaning "shield-shaped.")

Metabolism (met–TAB–bowl–ism). In organisms, a continuous process that converts food into energy. (From the Greek *metabole*, meaning "change.").

Hypothyroidism A condition caused by a deficiency of thyroxin and characterized by sluggish behavior and a low metabolic rate.

Cretinism A condition caused by thyroid deficiency in childhood and characterized by mental retardation and stunted growth.

Hyperthyroidism A condition caused by excess thyroxin and characterized by excitability, weight loss, and insomnia.

Steroids Hormones produced by the adrenal cortex that increase resistance to stress and regulate carbohydrate metabolism.

Adrenalin A hormone produced by the adrenal medulla that stimulates sympathetic ANS activity. Also called *epinephrine.*

Testosterone A male sex hormone produced by the testes that promotes growth of male sexual characteristics and sperm.

Secondary sexual characteristics Physical traits, other than the genitals, that differentiate the sexes.

In Sports, "Lions vs. Tigers"

When Don Schollander swam the 400–meter freestyle in 4 minutes, 12.2 seconds at the 1964 Olympics, he set a world record and took home a gold medal. Had he clocked the same time against the women racing at the 1980 Moscow Games, he would have come in fifth. In the pool and on the track, women have closed to within 10 percent or less of the best male times, [but] ... physiologists, coaches, and trainers generally agree that while women will continue to improve their performances, they will never fully overcome inherent differences in size and strength. In sports where power is a key ingredient of success, the best women will remain a stroke behind or a stride slower than the best man.

Muscle vs. Fat A man's biggest advantage is his muscle mass. Puberty stokes male bodies with the hormone testosterone, which adds bulk to muscles. A girl's puberty brings her an increase in fat. When growth ends, an average man is 40 percent muscle and 15 percent fat; a woman 23 percent muscle, 25 percent fat. Training reduces fat, but no amount of working out will give a woman the physique of a man. Male and female athletes sometimes try to build bigger muscles by use of anabolic steroids—artificial male hormones that stimulate muscle growth—even though they may be dangerous and all major sports have outlawed them.

Bulging muscles alone can't make a woman as strong as a man. Men have larger hearts and lungs and more hemoglobin in their blood, which enables them to pump oxygen to their muscles more efficiently than women can. A man's wider shoulders and longer arms also increase a man's leverage, and his longer legs move him farther with each step. Although highly conditioned women can achieve pound-for-pound parity with men in leg strength, their upper-body power is usually only one-half to two-thirds that of an equally well-conditioned male athlete.

A few sports make a virtue of anatomy for women. Extra body fat gives a woman English Channel swimmer better buoyancy and more insulation from the cold, and narrow shoulders reduce her resistance in the water. As a result, women have beaten the fastest male's round trip by a full three hours. In long-distance running contests, women may also be on an equal footing with men ... Under the body-draining demands of extended exertion, a woman's fat may provide her with deeper energy reserves ....

Tough Women athletes have dispelled the myths about their susceptibility to injury. The uterus and ovaries are surrounded by shock-absorbing fluids—far better protected than a man's exposed reproductive equipment. And the bouncing of the breasts doesn't make them more prone to cancer, or even to sagging. As for psychological toughness, Penn State sports psychologist Dorothy Harris says that "if you give a woman a shot at a $100,000 prize, you discover that she can be every bit as aggressive as a man."

Going one-on-one with a man is not the goal of most women in sports. "It's like pitting lions against tigers," declares Joan Ullyot. "Women's achievements should not be downgraded by comparing them to men's."

---

pituitary gland, and testes. Low blood levels of testosterone signal the hypothalamus to produce releasing hormones. Releasing hormones, in turn, signal the pituitary to secrete luteinizing hormone which then stimulates the testes to secrete testosterone. Conversely, high blood levels of testosterone signal the hypothalamus not to secrete releasing hormones, so that further testosterone is not produced.

Estrogen A generic term for several female sex hormones that promote growth of female sexual characteristics and regulate the menstrual cycle.

Progesterone (pro–JESS–ter–own). A female sex hormone that promotes growth of the sexual organs and helps maintain pregnancy.

Menstruation The monthly shedding of the lining of the uterus by women who are not pregnant. (From the Latin *menstruus*, meaning "monthly.")

The ovaries produce **estrogen** and **progesterone.** Estrogen is a generic name for several female sex hormones that lead to development of reproductive capacity and development of female secondary sexual characteristics at puberty. Progesterone also has multiple functions. It stimulates growth of the female reproductive organs and maintains pregnancy. As is the case with testosterone, estrogen and progesterone levels influence and are also influenced by hormones of the hypothalamus and pituitary gland.

Hormonal Regulation of the Menstrual Cycle While testosterone levels remain fairly stable, estrogen and progesterone levels vary markedly and regulate the menstrual cycle. Following **menstruation**—sloughing off of the inner lining of the uterus—estrogen levels increase, leading to the development of an ovum (egg cell) and growth of the inner lining of the uterus. The ovum is released by the ovary when estrogens reach peak blood levels. Then the inner lining of the uterus thickens in response to secretion of progesterone, gaining the capacity to support an embryo if fertilization should occur. If the ovum is not fertilized, estrogen and progesterone levels drop suddenly, triggering menstruation once more.

A Psychological Controversy: Does Premenstrual Syndrome Doom Women to Misery?

For several days prior to and during menstruation, many people have felt that "raging hormones" doom women to irritability and poor judgment—two facets of **premenstrual syndrome.** This view, as noted by Karen Paige (1973) has cost women many opportunities to assume responsible positions in society:

> Women, the old argument goes, are eternally subject to the whims and wherefores of their biological clocks. Their raging hormonal cycles make them emotionally unstable and intellectually unreliable. If women have second-class status, we are told, it is because they cannot control the implacable demands of that bouncing estrogen (p. 41).

Do women show behavioral and emotional deficits prior to and during menstruation? The evidence is mixed.

Bardwick (Bardwick, 1971; Ivey & Bardwick, 1968) found women's moods to be most positive halfway through their menstrual cycles (during release of an ovum). But women have been found to show greater anxiety, depression, and fatigue for several days before menstruating. Dalton (1972, 1980) reported that women are more likely to commit suicide or crimes, call in sick at work, and develop physical and emotional problems before or during menstruation.

Dalton (1968) also reported that the grades of English schoolgirls decline during the eight-day period prior to and including menstruation. However, investigators in the United States have found no decline in academic performance at this time (Bernstein, 1977; Rodin, 1976; Sommer, 1972, 1973).

There is evidence showing a link between hormone levels and mood in women. Paige (1971) studied women whose hormone levels were kept rather even by birth-control pills or whose hormone levels varied throughout the cycle. She found that women whose hormone levels fluctuated appeared to show somewhat greater anxiety and hostility prior to and during menstruation. However, they did not commit crimes or wind up on mental wards. Other studies suggest that even among women who report premenstrual syndrome, the symptoms are most often mild (Moos, 1968; Brooks and others, 1977). Moreover, environmental stressors, like exams, trigger greater variations in mood than do the phases of the menstrual cycle (Wilcoxon and others, 1976).

We must note also that women may be responding to negative cultural attitudes toward menstruation as well as to menstrual symptoms themselves. In some societies, menstruating women have been consigned to special living quarters because of expectations of foul temper (Paige, 1977). The historical view of menstruation as a time of pollution (Fisher, 1980; Paige, 1978) may make women highly sensitive to internal sensations at certain times of the month as well as concerned about discreet disposal of the menstrual flow. Other research (Paige, 1973) shows that women who do not share highly traditional cultural attitudes—including attitudes about the debilitating nature of menstruation—are less likely to show mood changes throughout the different phases of the menstrual cycle.

The Sexual Brain

At birth, they looked like girls, and they were raised as girls. The 18 children in the Dominican Republic did household chores, baby-sat and stayed close to their mothers, while their brothers planted crops, played in the river and cheered at cockfights. The children never doubted that they were girls. But their sexual identity was shattered at puberty. After a surge of male sex hormones, their voices deepened, their muscles developed and their genitals turned masculine. The "girls" became men.

These children were suffering from a rare genetic disease that leads to deficiency in male hormones during the prenatal period. Unfortunate natural "experiments" such as these and carefully designed laboratory experiments with lower animals show the impact of sex hormones on prenatal development and, at least in the case of lower animals, on social behavior and learning.

Man's close animal relatives respond to hormones in their social behavior. In a series of experiments, Robert Goy of the University of Wisconsin gave female rhesus monkeys male hormones before birth. They became male in appearance but with ovaries instead of testes. They played rough-and-tumble games (analogous to tomboy play) less frequently than males but more than normal females. They usually chose male playmates, as males do. When Goy exposed female monkeys to male hormones for shorter periods, they compromised: they didn't prefer male friends, but roughhoused as often as before. Goy concludes that hormones may determine different traits depending on when the fetus or infant monkey is exposed to them. "Each psychosexual characteristic may have an underlying neural system and develop at different times," he says.

Hormones may be subtle enough to hone even the fine points of behavior. Female mice who develop in the uterus between two males act more aggressively and stake out territory more often than sisters who develop away from males. They were probably influenced by the male hormones produced by their brothers.

"Critical Period" To influence behavior, hormones probably affect the brain during its "critical period." At this stage in development the brain is impressionable, and hormones cause permanent changes in it just as they permanently alter sex organs, says UCLA physiologist Roger Gorski. If male rats do not get male hormones early in life, for instance, they arch their backs like mating females and will not mount females even if they later receive hormones.

The greatest difference between male and female rat brains exists in the area that controls aspects of reproduction. Here, a group of cells called the sexually dimorphic nucleus is five to eight times larger in males. Castrated males, deprived of hormones, have smaller nuclei than normal males, and females given testosterone have larger nuclei than usual.

Thinking Ability The meaning of these differences in brain structure isn't yet clear. One hint, says Bruce McEwen of Rockefeller University, is that the cerebral cortex of rats can receive hormones during the critical period. This region controls thought, so the action of hormones might affect males' and females' thinking ability. Indeed, experiments suggest male and female rats do have different learning abilities. Males run mazes better than females, just as human males, as a group, seem slightly better at spatial tasks than females [see Chapter 13]. When female rats get male hormones during their critical period, though, they run the maze like males, reports William Beatty of North Dakota State University.

In an experiment on learning, Beatty taught his rats to run to the end of their box when a light went on. Otherwise, they got an electric shock. Females picked up the trick sooner than males. If they received male hormones during early development, however, their performance got worse. Similarly, males prevented from getting male sex hormones before birth and at puberty learned as rapidly as females. Such experiments promise to bring together physiology and psychology, providing insight into how hormones sculpt the brain and influence behavior.

Tomboy: Given male hormones, a female rhesus monkey roughhouses with a male.

However, some hormonal changes at time of menstruation can cause some very real and painful problems. For instance, **prostaglandins,** which cause uterine contractions, may in some women cause painful cramping. In such cases prostaglandin-inhibiting drugs, like Motrin and Indocin, are showing promise in helping women (Rathus, 1983). Unfortunately, the medical establishment has often treated women's menstrual complaints as **hysterical.** And so many women have not received what medical help is available (Toufexis, 1981).

In summary, (1) hormone levels seem to exert some influence over mood shifts in women, but most often these shifts are minor; (2) evidence that women show performance deficits prior to and during menstruation is unreliable; (3) traditional views of (perfectly harmless) menstrual flow as polluting may contribute to any problems women may encounter; but (4) some women experience very real menstrual discomfort, like menstrual cramping, and such problems need to be treated medically.

Heredity

Spend a moment or two reflecting on some facts of life:

- People cannot breathe underwater (without special equipment).
- People cannot fly (again, without some rather special equipment).
- Fish cannot learn to speak French or do an Irish jig even if you raise them in enriched environments and send them to finishing school (which is why we look for tunas that taste good, not for tunas with good taste).
- Chimpanzees and gorillas can learn to use sign language.

People cannot breathe underwater or fly (without oxygen tanks, airplanes, or other devices) because of the structures they have inherited. Fish are similarly limited by their **heredity** and cannot speak French or do a jig. Although the language ability of apes is a controversial topic (as we shall see in Chapter 6), some psychologists believe that chimpanzees and gorillas are capable of understanding and expressing some verbal concepts through American sign language (Bazar, 1980). But chimps and gorillas have shown no ability to speak, even though they can make sounds. They have probably failed to inherit humanlike speech areas of the cerebral cortex.

Genetics and Behavior Genetics

Heredity, or the biological transmission of traits from one generation to another, plays a significant role in the determination of traits we consider human, and inhuman. The structures we inherit at once make our behaviors possible and place limits on them. The field within the science of biology that studies heredity is called **genetics. Behavior genetics** is a specialty that bridges the sciences of psychology and biology. It is concerned with the transmission of structures and traits that give rise to behavior.

Nature and Nurture   Behavior geneticists are attempting to sort out the relative importance of **nature** (heredity) and **nurture** (environmental influences) in the development of various behavior patterns. Psychologists are especially interested in the roles of nature and nurture in intelligence (Plomin & DeFries,

Prostaglandins Hormones that cause uterine contractions, and hence cramping.

Hysterical Reflecting psychological "excitability" rather than biological problems. See Chapter 11.

Heredity The tranmission of characteristics from one generation to another through genes. (From the Latin *heres*, meaning "heir.")

Genetics The branch of biology that studies heredity. (From the Latin *genesis*, meaning "birth.")

Behavior genetics The study of the genetic transmission of structures and traits that give rise to behavior.

Nature In behavior genetics, heredity.

Nurture In behavior genetics, environmental influences on behavior, including factors like nutrition, culture, socioeconomic status, and learning.

Extraversion A trait in which a person directs his or her interest to persons and things outside the self. See Chapter 9.

Neuroticism A trait in which a person is given to anxiety, foreboding, and avoidance reactions. See Chapters 9 and 11.

Genes The basic building blocks of heredity, which consist of deoxyribonucleic acid.

Chromosomes Genetic structures consisting of genes which are found in the nuclei of the body's cells.

1980), abnormal behavior patterns like schizophrenia, and social problems like sociopathy and aggression. We shall be pursuing these particular themes throughout this book. Recent research has also suggested that heredity is a major factor in personality traits such as **extraversion** (Loehlin and others, 1982), **neuroticism** (Scarr and others, 1981), and shyness (Kagan, 1982; Plomin, 1982).

In a general sense it can be argued that all behavior reflects the influences of both nature and nurture. All organisms inherit a range of structures that set the stage for certain behaviors. Yet environmental influences such as nutrition and learning also figure in to whether genetically possible behaviors will be displayed. A potential Shakespeare who is raised in an impoverished neighborhood and never taught to read or write is unlikely to create a *Hamlet*. For this reason it may be most accurate to state that behavior represents an interaction between nature and nurture.

Let us now turn our attention to the building blocks of heredity: *genes* and *chromosomes*.

Genes and Chromosomes

The building blocks of heredity are called **genes.** Genes are composed of large, complex molecules of deoxyribonucleic acid, which has several chemical components. You can breathe a sigh of relief, for behavior geneticists refer to this acid simply as DNA. As you can see in Figure 2.15, DNA takes the form of a double spiral, or helix.

Twenty thousand or more genes constitute segments of rod-shaped **chromosomes**—genetic structures found in the nuclei of the body's cells. A normal human cell contains 46 chromosomes. A little math will show you that each cell then contains hundreds of thousands of genes.

FIGURE 2.15   The Double Helix of DNA.

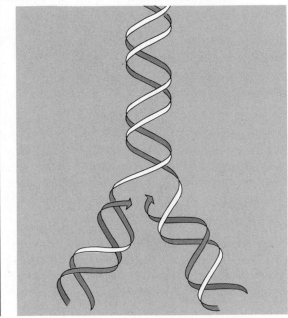

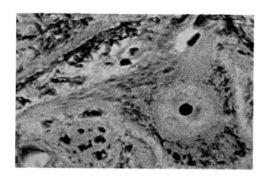
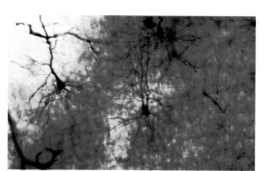

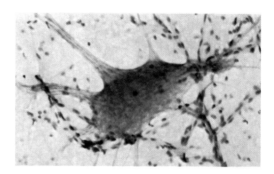

Color Plate 2.1 Neurons take many different forms in different portions of the nervous system. Above left: the large cell body is a motor neuron (multipolar) from the grey matter in the spinal cord. Above right: a pyramidal neuron in the cerebral cortex. Right: one large multipolar neuron from the myenteric (intestinal) plexus.

Color Plate 2.2 A photo of a human brain split from top to bottom.

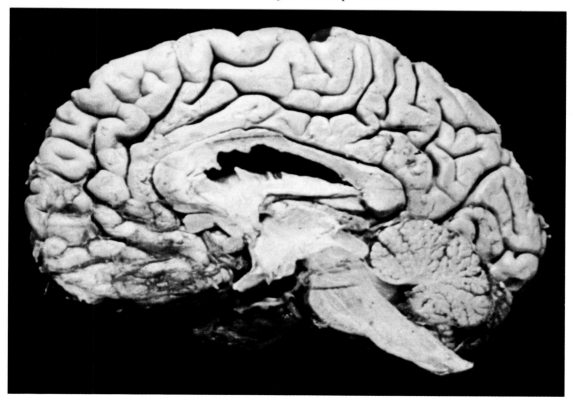

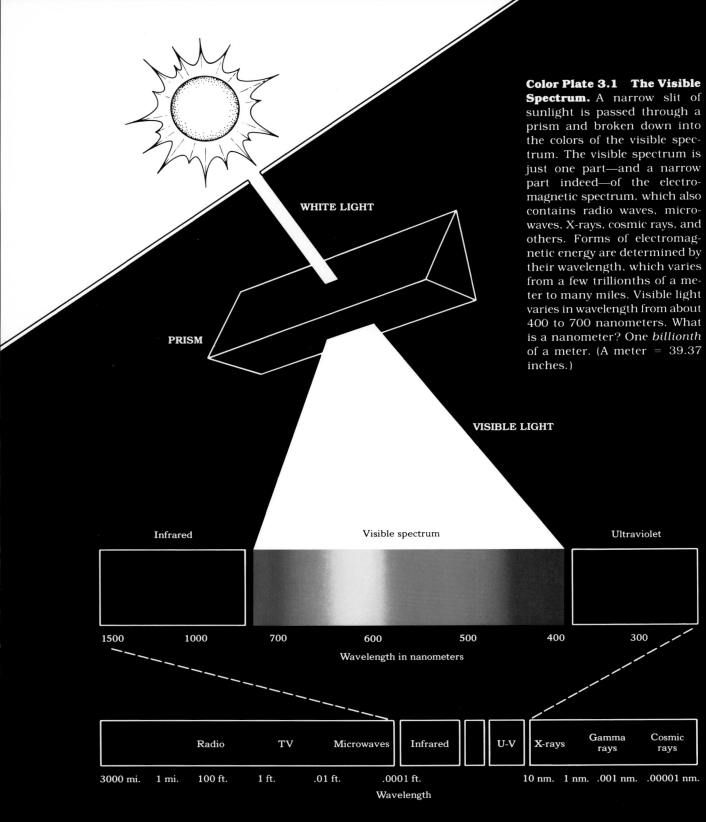

Color Plate 3.1   The Visible Spectrum. A narrow slit of sunlight is passed through a prism and broken down into the colors of the visible spectrum. The visible spectrum is just one part—and a narrow part indeed—of the electromagnetic spectrum, which also contains radio waves, microwaves, X-rays, cosmic rays, and others. Forms of electromagnetic energy are determined by their wavelength, which varies from a few trillionths of a meter to many miles. Visible light varies in wavelength from about 400 to 700 nanometers. What is a nanometer? One *billionth* of a meter. (A meter = 39.37 inches.)

WHITE LIGHT

PRISM

VISIBLE LIGHT

| Infrared | Visible spectrum | Ultraviolet |

1500   1000   700   600   500   400   300

Wavelength in nanometers

| Radio | TV | Microwaves | Infrared | | U-V | X-rays | Gamma rays | Cosmic rays |

3000 mi.   1 mi.   100 ft.   1 ft.   .01 ft.   .0001 ft.   10 nm.   1 nm.   .001 nm.   .00001 nm.

Wavelength

The electromagnetic spectrum

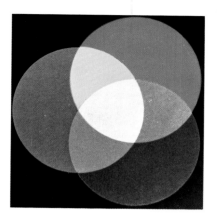

Color Plate 3.2 Additive Color Mixtures Produced by Lights of Three Colors: Red, Green, and Blue. In the early 1800s British scientist Thomas Young discovered that white light and all the colors of the spectrum could be produced by adding various combinations of three basic colors and varying their intensities.

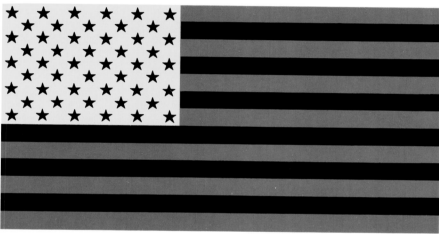

Color Plate 3.3 Three Cheers for the. . .Green, Black, and Yellow? Don't be concerned, we can quickly restore Old Glory to its familiar hues. Just stare at the center of this picture for 30 seconds. Then remove the book quickly and stare at a sheet of white paper and you will see a more familiar picture. This is an afterimage. You can blink a couple of times to maintain the afterimage for a longer period of time.

Afterimages like this led Ewald Hering to doubt the trichromatic theory of color vision and to suggest the opponent-process theory in its place. As the text points out, there is now evidence that leads us to believe that both theories have some validity.

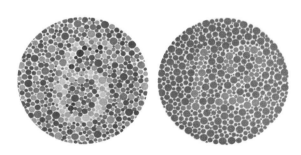

Color Plate 3.4 Two plates from a Test for Color Blindness. Can you see the numbers in these illustrations? A person with red-green color blindness would not be able to see the 6, and a person with blue-yellow color blindness would not be able to discriminate the 12.

Figure 1

Children's art provides insight into their cognitive development. In Figure 1, a three-year-old girl scribbles a person and a few flowers. The color dominates the form and is arbitrary, not realistic.

In Figure 2, drawn at the age of five, the size of the object seems to represent its perceived importance, not the actual size of the sensory image in relation to others. Visual motor coordination has improved, but color usage remains somewhat arbitrary.

Figure 2

Figure 3

At age nine, in Figure 3, the colors are muted and more representational. Intellect controls impulsivity. Visual motor coordination has improved further, and the relations among object in size and space are more realistic, suggesting increased knowledge of part-whole relationships. The nine-year-old also projects appropriate life and movement into the figures, suggesting accurate understanding of cause-effect relationships and of temporal sequences.

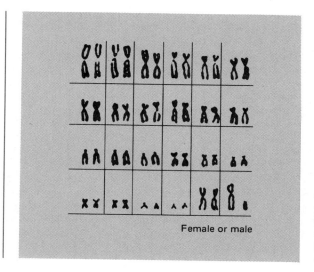

FIGURE 2.16 The 23 Pairs of Human Chromosomes. Sex is determined by the twenty-third pair of chromosomes. Females have two X sex chromosomes, while males have an X and a Y sex chromosome.

Female or male

We receive 23 chromosomes from our fathers and 23 chromosomes from our mothers. When a sperm cell fertilizes an ovum they join into 23 pairs of chromosomes (Figure 2.16). The composition of the twenty-third pair determines our sex. We all receive an X chromosome (so called because of the "X" shape) from our mothers. If we also receive an X chromosome from our fathers, we develop into females. If we receive a Y chromosome (named after the "Y" shape) from our fathers, we develop into males.

Traits are determined by pairs of genes. Sometimes a trait may result from an "averaging" of the genetic instructions. But many genes carry **dominant traits** or **recessive traits.** Brown hair, for instance, is dominant over blond hair. So if one parent carries genes for only brown hair, and the other for only blond hair, the children will invariably have brown hair. But brown-haired parents may also carry recessive genes for blond hair, as shown in Figure 2.17. If the recessive gene from one parent should combine with the recessive gene from the other, the recessive trait will be shown. In the example given in Figure 2.17, the child will have blond hair. Brown eyes are similarly dominant over blue eyes, and brown-eyed persons may carry recessive genes for blue eyes.

The fertilized ovum that carries genetic messages from both parents is called a **zygote.** Now and then a zygote divides into two and each grows into an individual with the same genetic makeup. These are known as identical or **monozygotic twins.** If the woman produces two ova in the same month, and they are fertilized, they develop into fraternal or **dizygotic twins.** Identical or monozygotic twins are important in the study of the relative influences of heredity and environment in areas of psychological interest like intelligence, schizophrenia, and sociopathy. Differences between monozygotic twins are the result of environmental influences (of nurture, not nature).

Genetic Abnormalities

Occasionally children do not have the normal complement of 46 chromosomes, and behavioral as well as physical abnormalities result.

In **Down's syndrome,** also called mongolism, the twenty-first pair of chromosomes has an extra, or third, chromosome. For that reason, this dis-

Dominant trait In genetics, a trait that is expressed.

Recessive trait In genetics, a trait that is not expressed when the gene or genes involved have been paired with dominant genes. But recessive traits are transmitted to future generations and expressed if paired with other recessive genes.

Zygote (ZY–goat). A fertilized egg cell. (From the Greek *zygon,* meaning "yoke"—two things harnessed together.)

Monozygotic twins Identical twins. Twins who develop from a single zygote, thus carrying the same genetic instructions. (From the Greek *monos,* meaning "single.")

Dizygotic twins Fraternal twins. Twins who develop from separate zygotes. (From the Greek *di-,* meaning "two.")

Down's syndrome A genetic abnormality characterized by slanted eyelids and mental retardation, and caused by an extra chromosome in the twenty-first pair. Also called *mongolism.*

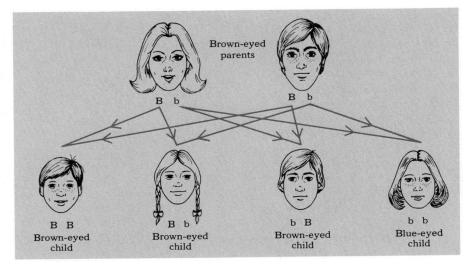

Brown-eyed parents

B b   B b

B B
Brown-eyed child

B b
Brown-eyed child

b B
Brown-eyed child

b b
Blue-eyed child

FIGURE 2.17 Two brown-eyed parents each carry a recessive gene for blue eyes. Their children have an equal opportunity of receiving genes for brown eyes and blue eyes. In such cases, 25 percent of the children show the recessive trait—blue eyes. The other 75 percent show the dominant trait, or brown eyes. But two of three who show brown eyes carry the recessive trait for transmittal to future generations. If a blue-eyed person has a child with someone who has brown eyes but carries a recessive gene for blue eyes, what is the probability that the child will have blue eyes?

order is also called *Trisomy 21*. Persons with Down's syndrome have eyes with an upward slant and thickened eyelids—hence the somewhat inaccurate descriptive term "mongolism." They are also mentally retarded.

An extra Y sex chromosome is associated with heightening of male secondary sexual characteristics in men labeled "supermales." XYY males are somewhat taller than average and develop heavier beards. At one point it was speculated that XYY syndrome was linked to aggressive criminal behavior. In Chapter 11 you will see that evidence for this assertion is sketchy at best.

Other disorders have been attributed to defective genes. One of them, **phenylketonuria** (PKU), is transmitted by a recessive gene. Therefore, if both parents are carriers, PKU will be transmitted to about one child in four (as in Figure 2.17). Children with PKU cannot metabolize *phenylpyruvic acid*, which builds up in their bodies and leads to mental retardation. We have no cure for PKU, but it can be detected in newborn children through blood or urine analysis. Children with PKU who are placed on diets low in phenylalanine, the substance that is converted into phenylpyruvic acid, right after birth show little or no mental deficiency.

Amniocentesis   Today pregnant women who have reason to suspect genetic abnormalities in their children are likely to have an **amniocentesis** about 15 weeks following conception (Figure 2.18). Fluid is withdrawn from the amniotic sac containing the fetus. Fetal cells that have sloughed off into the fluid are then examined microscopically for chromosomal abnormalities. Amniocentesis is commonly done with women who become pregnant past the age of 35 because the chances of Down's syndrome increase dramatically as women age.

Phenylketonuria
(fee–nill–key–tone–NEW–ree–uh). A genetic abnormality caused by phenylpyruvic acid and characterized by mental retardation.

Amniocentesis
(am–knee–oh–cent–TEE–sis). A method for determining the presence of genetic abnormalities in an unborn child by examining fluid drawn from the amniotic sac. (From the Greek *amnion*, meaning "lamb," and *kentesis*, meaning "tapping," as by a needle.)

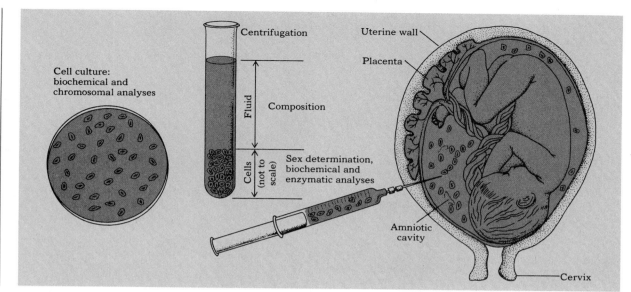

FIGURE 2.18 Amniocentesis. This modern method for examining the chromosomes sloughed off by a fetus into amniotic fluid permits the prenatal identification of certain hereditary diseases. Amniocentesis also allows parents to learn the sex of their unborn child. Would you want to know?

Amniocentesis also permits parents to learn the sex of their unborn child through examination of the twenty-third pair of chromosomes. However, amniocentesis carries some risks, and it would be unwise to have the procedure done solely for this purpose. If you were having an amniocentesis, would you want to know the sex of your unborn child, or would you prefer to wait?

Experiments in Selective Breeding

You need not be a psychologist to know that animals can be selectively bred to enhance desired traits over the generations. Simply compare wild African dogs with varieties as diverse as the Great Dane, the tiny, nervous Chihuahua, and the pug-nosed, white-trimmed Boston terrier. We breed our cattle and chickens bigger and fatter, so that they provide the most food calories for the minimum amount of feed. It also seems that we can selectively breed animals to enhance the presence of traits that are of more interest to psychologists, such as intelligence (although "intelligence" in lower animals does not correspond directly to human intelligence), aggressiveness, and even preference for alcohol over water (Eriksson, 1972).

Rats, for example, have been bred selectively for maze-learning ability (Rosenzweig, 1969; Tryon, 1940). Though limited in scope, maze-learning ability involves some capacity to profit from experience to meet the requirements of one's situation.

In such studies, an initial group of rats is tested for maze-learning ability by measuring the number of mistakes they make in repeated trials as they learn to find a food goal. Rats making the fewest mistakes are labeled B_1,

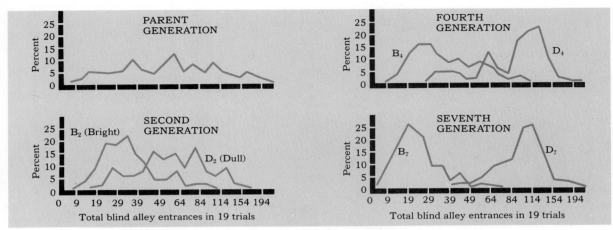

FIGURE 2.19   Selective Breeding for Maze-Learning Ability in Rats. In the Tryon study, the offspring of maze-bright rats were inbred for six generations. So were the offspring of maze-dull rats. As the generations became further removed, there was progressively less overlap in the maze-learning ability of the offspring of the two groups, even though environmental influences were held as constant as possible for all offspring. Is maze-learning ability in rats similar to intelligence in human beings?

signifying the first generation of "maze-bright" rats. "Maze-dull" rats are labeled D_1. The total distribution of errors, or blind-alley entrances, made by the first (parent) generation is shown in Figure 2.19. These errors were made over a series of 19 runs in the Tryon study.

Maze-bright rats from the first generation were then bred with other maze-bright rats, while maze-dull rats were similarly interbred. The second graph in Figure 2.19 shows how the offspring (B_2) of the maze-bright parents compared with the offspring (D_2) of the maze-dull parents in numbers of errors (blind-alley entrances). The offspring of the maze-bright rats, as a group, clearly made fewer errors than the offspring of the maze-dull, although there was considerable overlap between groups. The brightest offspring of the maze-bright were then interbred as were the dullest of the maze-dull for six consecutive generations. Fortunately for experimental psychologists, rat generations are measured in months, not decades. Throughout these generations, the environments of the rats were kept as constant as possible. Dull rats were often raised by bright mothers, and vice versa, so that a critic could not argue that the maze-learning ability of bright offspring could be attributed to an enriched environment provided by a bright mother.

After six generations there was little overlap in maze-learning performance between maze-bright and maze-dull rats. The (spatial relations) superiority of the maze-bright rats did not generalize to all types of learning tasks. We also cannot emphasize too strongly that maze-learning ability in rats is not comparable to the complex groupings of behavior that define human intelligence. Still, experiments such as these suggest that it would be foolhardy to completely overlook possible genetic influences on human intelligence.

Some breeds of dogs, like Doberman pinschers and German shepherds, have been bred to be more aggressive than other varieties. Within breeds, however, dogs have been selectively bred to show high or low activity levels.

Chickens have also been selectively bred for aggressiveness (consider the "sport" of cockfighting) and for level of sexual activity (McClearn & DeFries, 1973; Scott & Fuller, 1965).

Genetic counseling Advice or counseling concerning the probability that a couple's offspring will have genetic abnormalities.

Genetics and the Future

The future of selective breeding and other methods for modifying living organisms seems at once promising and frightening. On the positive side, selective breeding practices have given birth (literally) to superchickens, superwheat, and super fir trees. These are oversized organisms that mature early, reproduce early, and are more disease resistant than their ancestors. There may be yet more promise in genetic engineering, in which the genetic structures of organisms are changed by direct manipulation of their reproductive cells. Even as you are reading this page, biologists and corporations are rushing to the patent office with new life forms—mostly microscopic—that they hope will be marketable in some fashion or another.

On another level, **genetic counseling** has become more common. In this procedure, information about a couple's genetic backgrounds is compiled to determine the possibility that their union may result in genetically defective children. Some couples whose natural children would be at high risk for genetic diseases elect to adopt.

Some fear that increasing control of genetics will make possible future scenarios like that portrayed by Aldous Huxley in his still powerful 1932 novel *Brave New World.* Through a fictitious method called "Bokanovsky's Process," egg cells from parents who are identically suited for certain types of labor are made to "bud." From these buds up to 96 people with identical genetic make-ups can be developed—filling whatever labor niches are required by society.

In the novel the director of a "hatchery" is leading a group of students on a tour. One student is foolish enough to question the advantage of Bokanovsky's Process:

"My good boy!" The Director wheeled sharply round on him. "Can't you see? Can't you see?" He raised a hand; his expression was solemn. "Bokanovsky's Process is one of the major instruments of social stability!"

Major instruments of social stability (wrote the student).

Standard men and women; in uniform batches. The whole of a small factory staffed with the products of a single bokanovskied egg.

"Ninety-six identical twins working 96 identical machines!" The voice was almost tremulous with enthusiasm. "You really know where you are. For the first time in history." He quoted the planetary motto. "Community, Identity, Stability." Grand words. "If we could bokanovskify indefinitely the whole problem would be solved."

Through Bokanovsky's Process we might be able to eliminate certain genetic disorders. We might even be able to lower the incidence of crime, aggression, and abnormal behaviors. But I ask those of you who think that all this might be a good idea to consider that from none of these "bokanovskified" eggs would there emerge a Shakespeare, a Beethoven, or an Einstein. Perhaps we would avoid tyrants, but we would also be bereft of geniuses and individuals who might shape the world in ways we cannot foresee.

And those of you who think that genetic research ought to be stopped should consider that there is no such thing as bad knowledge—only bad use of knowledge.

Summary

The nervous system consists of neurons, which transmit information through neural impulses, and glial cells, which serve support functions. Neurons have a cell body (soma), dendrites, which receive transmissions, and axons. From axon terminals neurotransmitters travel across synapses to other neurons. Many neurons have fatty myelin sheaths, which are missing at the nodes of Ranvier. Neural impulses can jump from node to node. Afferent neurons transmit sensory messages to the central nervous system, and efferent neurons conduct messages from the central nervous system that stimulate glands or cause muscles to contract. Although it has been estimated that we lose several thousand neurons daily through the aging process, there is little evidence for this view.

Neural transmission is electrochemical. An electric charge is conducted along an axon through a process that allows sodium ions into the cell and then pumps them out. The neuron has a resting potential of -70 millivolts, and an action potential of $+30$ to $+40$ millivolts. Excitatory synapses stimulate neurons to fire; inhibitory neurons influence them not to. Neurons fire on an all-or-none principle. Neurons may fire up to 1,000 times per second, and a refractory (insensitive) period follows each firing. Important neurotransmitters include acetylcholine, dopamine, and noradrenalin (or norepinephrine).

The brain and spinal cord compose the central nervous system. Reflexes involve the spinal cord, but not the brain. The somatic and autonomic systems compose the peripheral nervous system. The hindbrain includes the medulla, pons, and cerebellum. The reticular activating system begins in the hindbrain and continues into the forebrain. Important structures of the forebrain include the thalamus, hypothalamus, limbic system, and cerebrum. The hypothalamus is involved in controlling body temperature and regulating motivation and emotion.

The somatic nervous system transmits sensory information about muscles, skin, and joints to the central nervous system; it also controls muscular activity from the central nervous system. The autonomic nervous system (ANS) regulates the glands and involuntary activities like heartbeat, digestion, and dilation of the pupils. The sympathetic division of the ANS dominates in activities that expend the body's resources, such as fleeing from a predator, and the parasympathetic division dominates during processes that build the body's reserves, like eating.

The cerebral cortex is divided into the frontal, parietal, temporal, and occipital lobes. The visual cortex is in the occipital lobe, and the auditory cortex is in the temporal lobe. The sensory cortex lies behind the central fissure in the parietal lobe, and the motor cortex lies in the frontal lobe, across the central fissure from the sensory cortex. Association areas of the cortex are involved in thought and language. The language areas of the cortex lie near the intersection of the frontal, temporal, and parietal lobes in the dominant hemisphere. For right-handed people the left hemisphere of the cortex is dominant; for half the left-handed people the right hemisphere is dominant. Split-brain patients may be able to describe a screened-off object like a pencil that is held in the hand connected to the dominant hemisphere, but cannot do so when the object is held in the other hand.

The endocrine system consists of ductless glands that secrete hormones. The pituitary gland secretes growth hormone, prolactin, ADH, and oxytocin. The pancreas secretes insulin, which enables the body to metabolize sugar. The adrenal medulla secretes adrenalin (epinephrine), which increases metabolic rate. Sex hormones secreted by the testes and ovaries are responsible for prenatal sexual differentiation, and female sex hormones regulate the menstrual cycle.

Genetics is concerned with transmission of traits from generation to generation. Genes are the basic building blocks of heredity and consist of DNA. Twenty thousand or more genes make up each chromosome. People have 46 chromosomes. They receive 23 from the father and 23 from the mother. Dominant traits are expressed, while recessive traits may not be. A fertilized egg cell is a zygote. Identical twins are monozygotic, while fraternal twins are dizygotic.

Down's syndrome is caused by an extra chromosome on the twenty-first pair. "Supermales" have XYY sex chromosomal structure. Phenylketonuria is transmitted by a recessive gene and controlled by diet.

Experiments show that rats can be selectively bred for maze-learning ability, but we cannot assume that maze-learning ability in rats corresponds directly to human intelligence.

Truth or Fiction Revisited

- *Some cells in your body stretch all the way from your spinal cord to your big toe.* True. Some neurons do, while other neurons are only a few thousandths of an inch long.
- *In order to study nerve cells from the inside, scientists have created glass tubes so narrow that you could place 20,000 of them on the head of a pin.* True. These tubes are called micropipettes.
- *The human brain is larger than that of any other animal.* False. Elephant and whale brains are larger, but our brains have a higher brain-to-body-weight ratio.
- *Many men who are paralyzed below the waist can still achieve erection and ejaculate.* True. These sexual responses are reflexes that do not require input from the brain. It is only necessary that the appropriate section of the spine be intact.
- *Armed only with crossed fingers and a radio transmitter, a scientist stopped the raging charge of a two-ton bull.* True. Electrical stimulation of the bull's limbic system stopped the charge.
- *Fear can give you indigestion.* True. Fear stimulates (and is stimulated by) the sympathetic branch of the ANS, but digestion involves parasympathetic activity. These two branches of the ANS service many of the same organs and have largely opposing effects.
- *If a surgeon were to electrically stimulate a certain part of your brain, you might swear in court that someone had stroked your leg.* True. Stimulation of areas of the sensory cortex leads to the perception of sensation in corresponding parts of the body.
- *If a certain area in your brain were damaged, you would lose the ability to speak but could still understand the written or spoken language.* True. This is one form of aphasia.
- *Some people are genetically identical.* True. They are identical or monozygotic twins. Monozygotic twins are important in studies of the relative influence of nature and nurture on certain behavior patterns.

OUTLINE

Sensation and Perception

- White sunlight is actually composed of all the colors of the rainbow.
- On a clear, dark night you could probably see the light from a single candle burning 30 miles away.
- We all have blind spots in our eyes.
- We need two eyes in order to perceive depth.
- "Motion pictures" do not move at all.
- The advertising slogan for the film *Alien* was accurate: "In space, no one can hear you scream."
- Onions and apples have the same taste.
- An American columnist underwent a painless appendix operation in China while he was fully awake. His only anesthetic was twirling needles.

Five thousand years ago in China, give or take a day or two, an arrow was shot into the air. Where did it land? Ancient records tell us precisely where: in the hand of a fierce warrior and master of the martial arts.

As the story was told to me, the warrior had grown so fierce because of a chronic toothache. The persistent pain had simply ruined his disposition.

On one fateful day our hero watched as invading hordes assembled on surrounding hills. His troops were trembling, and he raised his arms in wild gestures in an effort to boost their morale in the face of the invaders' superior numbers. A slender wooden shaft lifted into the air from a nearby rise, arced, and then descended—right into the warrior's palm. His troops cringed and muttered among themselves, but our hero said nothing. Although he saw the arrow through his palm, he did not scream. He did not run. He did not even complain.

He was astounded. His toothache had vanished. His entire jaw was numb.

Meanwhile the invaders looked on—horrified. They, too, muttered among themselves. What sort of warrior could look upon an arrow through his hand with such indifference? Even with a growing smile? If this was the caliber of warrior in this village, they'd be better off traveling west and looking for a brawl in ancient Sumer, or in Egypt. They sounded the retreat and withdrew.

Our warrior received a hero's welcome back in town. A physician offered to remove the arrow without a fee—a tribute to bravery. But our warrior would have none of it. The arrow had done wonders for his toothache and he would permit no meddling. He had discovered already that if the pain threatened to return, he need only twirl the arrow and it would recede once more.

But things were not so rosy on the home front. His wife was thrilled to find him jovial once more, but the arrow put a crimp into romance. When he put his arm around her, she was in dire danger of being stabbed to death. Finally she gave him an ultimatum: It was she or the arrow.

Placed in deep conflict, our warrior consulted a psychologist who then huddled with the physician and the village elders. After much todo, they asked the warrior to participate in an experiment. They would remove the arrow and replace it with a pin that the warrior could twirl as needed. If the pin didn't do the trick, they could always fall back on the arrow, so to speak.

To his wife's relief, the pin worked. And here, in ancient China, lay the origins of the art of **acupuncture**—the use of needles to relieve pain and treat a variety of ills ranging from **hypertension** to some forms of blindness.

I confess that this tale is not entirely accurate. To my knowledge, there were no psychologists in ancient China. (Their loss.) Moreover, the part about the warrior's wife is fictitious. But it is claimed that acupuncture, as a means for dealing with pain, originated in ancient China when a soldier was, in fact, wounded in a hand by an arrow and discovered that a chronic toothache had disappeared. The Chinese, historians claim, then set out to "map" the body by sticking pins here and there to learn how they influenced the perception of pain.

Control of pain is just one of the many issues that interest psychologists who study the closely related concepts of sensation and perception. **Sensation** is the stimulation of sensory receptors and the transmission of sensory information to the central nervous system (the spinal cord or brain). Sensory receptors are located in sensory organs like the eyes and ears, and, as we shall see, in the skin and elsewhere in the body. Their stimulation is mechanical, resulting from the presence of light, sound, touch, and so on.

Acupuncture
(ACK–you–PUNK–tyour). The ancient Chinese practice of piercing parts of the body with needles in order to deaden pain and treat illness. (From the Latin *acus*, meaning "needle.")

Hypertension High blood pressure. See Chapter 10.

Sensation The stimulation of sensory receptors and the transmission of sensory information to the central nervous system. (From the Latin *sensus*, meaning "sense.")

Perception is not mechanical at all. Perception is the process by which sensations are organized into an inner representation of the world, providing you with your own internal picture or map of reality. Perception results from much more than sensation. It involves learning and expectations and ways in which we organize incoming information about the world. Perception is an active process through which we make sense of sensory stimulation. A human shape and a twelve-inch ruler may stimulate paths of equal length among the sensory receptors in our eyes. But whether we interpret the human shape to be a foot-long doll or a full-grown person 15 to 20 feet away is a matter of perception.

In this chapter we shall see that your personal map of reality—your ticket of admission to a world of changing sights, sounds, and other sources of sensory input—depends largely on the "five senses" of vision, hearing, smell, taste, and touch. There are also a number of other senses that alert you to your own body position without your having literally to watch every step you take. We shall explore the nature of each of these senses, and we shall find that highly similar sensations may lead to quite different perceptions in different people—or among the same people in different situations. For perception is an active process in which people interpret sensory input according to the situation and their own expectations.

Vision

Our eyes are said to be our "windows on the world." We consider information from vision more essential than that from hearing, smell, taste, and touch. Studies in **visual capture** have shown, for example, that when we perceive a square object through lenses that distort it into a rectangle, we report the object to be a rectangle even when we can feel it with our hands (Rock & Victor, 1964). Because vision is our dominant sense, we consider blindness our most debilitating sensory loss. An understanding of vision requires discussion of the nature of light and of the master of the sensory organs, the eye.

Light

The Bible tells us that in the beginning the **light** was set apart from the dark. The light was good and the potential for evil lay in darkness. In almost all cultures light is a symbol of goodness and knowledge. We describe capable people as being "bright" or "brilliant." If we are not being complimentary, we label them as "dull." People who aren't "in the know" are said to be "in the dark." Just what is this stuff called light?

Visible light is actually just one small part of a spectrum of electromagnetic energy (see Color Plate 3.1) that is described in terms of wavelengths. These wavelengths vary from those of cosmic rays, which are only a few trillionths of an inch long, to some radio waves that extend for many miles. Radar, microwaves, and X-rays are also forms of electromagnetic energy shown in Color Plate 3.1.

You have probably seen rainbows or seen light broken down into several colors as it filtered through your windows. Sir Isaac Newton, the British scientist, discovered that sunlight could be broken down into different colors by means of a triangular solid of glass called a **prism** (Color Plate 3.1). When I

Perception The process by which sensations are organized into an inner representation of the world—a psychological process through which we interpret sensory information. (From the Latin *percipere*, meaning "to take hold of," or "to comprehend.")

Visual capture The tendency of vision to dominate the other senses.

Light Electromagnetic energy of various wavelengths. The part of this spectrum of energy that stimulates the eye and produces visual sensations. (From the Latin *lux*, meaning "light.")

Visible light The band of electromagnetic energy that produces visual sensations. (Usually simply referred to as *light*.)

Prism A transparent triangular solid that breaks down visible light into the colors of the spectrum. (From the Greek *prisma*, meaning "something sawed," referring to the construction of a prism.)

Hue The color of light, as determined by its wavelength. (From the Old English *hiw,* meaning "appearance.")

Amplitude Height. The extreme range of a variable quantity.

Absolute threshold The minimal amount of energy that can produce a sensation.

Psychophysicist A person who studies the relationships between physical stimuli, like light or sound, and their perception.

took introductory psychology, I was taught that I could remember the colors of the spectrum, from longest to shortest wavelengths, by using the mnemonic device, *Mr. Roy G. Biv* (red, orange, yellow, green, blue, indigo, violet). I must have been a backward student because I found it easier to recall them in reverse order, using the meaningless acronym *vibgyor.*

The wavelength of visible light determines its color, or **hue.** The wavelength for red is longer than that for orange, and so on through the spectrum.

To gain a clearer idea of the meaning of waves of light, think for a moment of waves crashing down on a shore. The wavelength—or length or waves—corresponds to the frequency with which they hit the shore—or *how often* a new wave comes. But waves also have height, or **amplitude.** Light waves of greater "height" or amplitude are seen as brighter, or more intense.

Absolute and Difference Thresholds: Two Psychophysical Concepts

The weakest amount of light that a person can see is called the **absolute threshold** for light. It may also be defined as the amount of physical energy required to activate the visual sensory system. Beneath this threshold, detection of light is impossible (Haber & Hershenson, 1980).

Psychophysicists run experiments to determine the absolute threshold for vision by presenting visual stimuli of progressively greater intensity. They begin with an intensity of light that is not detectable, increase it step by step, and ask subjects to report "Yes, I see it" when they can detect a visual stim-

TABLE 3.1   Absolute Thresholds and Other Characteristics of Our Sensory Systems

Sense	Stimulus	Receptors	Threshold
Vision	Electromagnetic energy	Rods and cones in the retina	A candle flame viewed from a distance of about 30 miles (48 km) on a clear, dark night
Hearing	Sound pressure waves	Hair cells on the basilar membrane of the inner ear	The ticking of a watch from about 20 feet (6 m) away in a quiet room
Taste	Chemical substances dissolved in saliva	Taste buds on the tongue in the mouth	About one teaspoon of sugar dissolved in 2 gallons of water
Smell	Chemical substances in the air	Receptor cells in the upper nasal cavity (the nose)	About one drop of perfume diffused throughout a small house (1 part in 500 million)
Touch	Mechanical displacement or pressure on the skin	Nerve endings located in the skin	The wing of a fly falling on a cheek from a distance of about 0.4 inch (1 cm)

Source: Adapted from Galanter (1962).

TABLE 3.2 Weber's Constant for Various Sensory Discriminations

Sense	Type of Discrimination	Weber's Constant
Vision	Brightness of a light	1/60
Hearing	Pitch (frequency) of a tone	1/333
	Loudness of a tone	1/10
Taste	Difference in saltiness	1/5
Smell	Amount of rubber smell	1/10
Touch	Pressure on the skin surface	1/7
	Deep pressure	1/77
	Difference in lifted weights	1/53

ulus. The relationship between the intensity of the light (a physical stimulus) and its perception (a psychological event) is considered *psychophysical*—it bridges psychological and physical events.

As you can see in Table 3.1, absolute thresholds have been determined for the sense of vision, hearing, taste, smell, and touch.

How much of a difference in intensity between two lights is required before you will perceive one as brighter than the other? The minimum required difference in intensity is defined as the **difference threshold** for light. Psychophysicist Ernst Weber discovered through laboratory research that the difference threshold for perceiving differences in the intensity of light is about two percent (actually closer to one-sixtieth) of their intensity. This fraction, one-sixtieth, is known as **Weber's constant** for light. It has also been called the **just noticeable difference,** or *jnd*, for light, indicating that people can perceive a difference in intensity when the brightness of a light is increased or decreased by one-sixtieth. Remarkably, Weber's constant (1/60) for light holds whether we are comparing two quite bright or rather dull lights. However, it becomes inaccurate when we compare extremely bright or extremely dull lights.

As you can see in Table 3.2, Weber's research in psychophysics touched on many senses. He derived difference thresholds for different types of sensory stimulation.

The Eye: Our Living Camera

Would it be possible to see without eyes? What if the visual area of a person's occipital lobe were in working order but the eyes were not functional? Brain-surgery patients report "seeing" flashes when their visual cortex is stimulated by a pencil electrode. Could direct stimulation of the visual cortex compensate for loss of eyesight?

An Experiment in Artificial Vision In a recent experiment in artificial vision (Dobelle and others, 1976), a strip of Teflon with 64 electrodes was attached from the outside to the visual cortex of blind people (Figure 3.1). When electricity passed through an electrode, a portion of the cortex was stimulated, and the subject drew a corresponding dot on a piece of paper. However, there was no one-to-one correspondence between points on the visual cortex and the image projected on the computer screen. The visual cortex must first be "mapped" through computer-aided trial-and-error stimulation before any image can be projected onto the cortex in a meaningful array of points.

Difference threshold The minimal difference in intensity that is required between two sources of energy so that they will be perceived as different.

Weber's constant The fraction of the intensity by which a source of physical energy must be increased or decreased so that a difference in intensity will be perceived.

Just noticeable difference The minimal amount by which a source of energy must be increased or decreased so that a difference in intensity will be perceived.

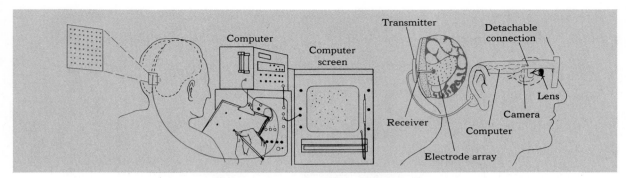

FIGURE 3.1 An Experiment with Artificial Vision. In the near future, will we be able to provide people with artificial vision so long as the visual cortex in their occipital lobes is intact? In the experiment shown in this figure, the visual cortex of the blind person to the left is being "mapped" with the aid of a computer, so that a visual image shown on the screen can be directly projected onto his visual cortex. In the drawing to the right, a futuristic artificial vision system is shown in which a miniature television camera is implanted in a blind person's eye cavity. A computer in the glasses codes camera impressions in accordance with the person's visual-cortex map. The coded impression is then projected onto his visual cortex. Thus the blind person "sees."

In this experiment, after the computer had been programed to project accurately a point from the television screen onto the visual cortex through firing the appropriate electrode, simultaneous firing of the proper electrodes enabled the subject to "see" a simple line drawing. Figure 3.1 suggests that in the future blind people may be capable of "seeing" at least outlines of images through the simultaneous firing of thousands of electrodes in the visual cortex. This would require more detailed strips of Teflon or another material, and extensive computer mapping of an individual's visual cortex.

Those of us who are fortunate enough to possess those magnificent optical instruments called eyes need not be directly concerned about artificial vision. The projection of images using our natural visual systems involves millions of points. And most "mapping" of the cortex—or the capacity to relate images to objects—seems to be largely complete by birth, or shortly afterward. (Note the box, "How Well Do Newborn Babies See?")

FIGURE 3.2 The Human Eye, a Camera, and a Projected Image. In both the eye and a camera, light enters through a narrow opening and is projected onto a sensitive surface.

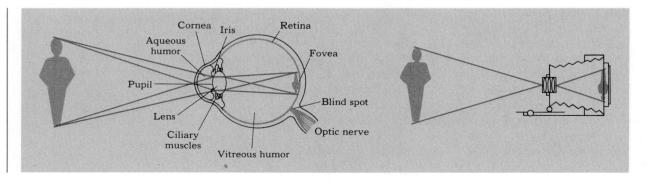

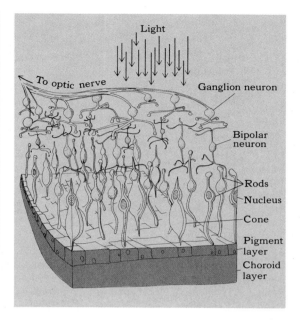

FIGURE 3.3 The Retina of the Human Eye. After light travels through the vitreous humor of the eye, it finds its way through ganglion neurons and bipolar neurons to the photosensitive rods and cones. These photoreceptors then transmit sensory input back through the bipolar neurons to the ganglion neurons. The axons of the ganglion neurons form the optic nerve, which transmits sensory stimulation through the brain to the visual cortex of the occipital lobe.

The Structure of the Eye Consider the major parts of the eye that are shown in Figure 3.2. As with a film or television camera, light enters through a narrow opening and is projected onto a sensitive surface. Light first passes through the transparent **cornea.** The amount of light that passes is determined by the size of the opening of the muscle called the **iris.** The opening in the iris is called the **pupil.** Pupil size adjusts automatically to the amount of light. The more intense the light, the smaller the opening. We must also adjust the amount of light allowed into a camera according to its brightness.

Once light passes through the iris, it encounters the **lens.** The lens adjusts or accommodates to the image by changing its thickness. Changes in thickness permit projection of a clear image of the object onto the retina. (Camera lenses do not automatically adjust to the image. We must manually adjust the position of the lens until the image is clear.) If you hold a finger at arm's length, then slowly bring it toward your nose, you will feel tension in the eye as the thickness of the lens accommodates to keep the retinal image in focus (Haber & Hershenson, 1980). When people "squint" to bring an object into focus, they are adjusting the thickness of the lens.

The **retina** is like the film or image surface of the camera. But rather than being composed of film that is sensitive to light (photosensitive), the retina consists of photosensitive cells, or **photoreceptors,** called *rods* and *cones.* The retina (Figure 3.3) contains several layers of cells: the rods and cones, **bipolar cells,** and **ganglion cells.** Light travels past the ganglion cells and bipolar cells and stimulates the rods and cones. The rods and cones then send neural messages through the bipolar cells to the ganglion cells. The axons of the ganglion cells constitute the **optic nerve.** The optic nerve conducts the sensory input to the brain and, eventually, the visual area of the occipital lobe.

The **fovea** is the most sensitive area of the retina (see Figure 3.2). The **blind spot,** by contrast, is insensitive to visual stimulation. The blind spot is the part of the retina where the axons of the ganglion cells congregate to form the optic nerve (Figure 3.4).

Cornea (CORE–knee–uh). Transparent tissue forming the outer surface of the eyeball. (From the Latin *cornu,* meaning "horn" and referring to the appearance of the cornea.)

Iris A muscular membrane whose dilation regulates the amount of light that enters the eye.

Pupil The apparently black opening in the center of the iris, through which light enters the eye. (From the Latin *pupilla,* meaning one's figure as reflected in the eye of another.)

Lens A transparent body between the iris and *vitreous humor* that focuses an image on the retina. (From the Latin *lentil,* referring to the shape of a lens.)

Retina The area of the inner surface of the eye that contains rods and cones. (Probably from the Latin *rete,* meaning "net.")

Photoreceptors Cells that respond to light.

Bipolar cells Neurons that conduct neural impulses from rods and cones to ganglion cells.

Ganglion cells Neurons whose axons form the optic nerve.

Optic nerve The nerve that transmits sensory information from the eye to the brain. (From the Greek *optikos,* meaning "seeing.")

Fovea (FOE–vee–uh). A rodless area near the center of the retina where vision is most acute. (A Latin word meaning "pit.")

Blind spot The area of the retina where axons from ganglion cells meet to form the optic nerve. It is insensitive to light.

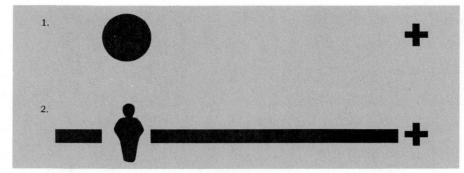

FIGURE 3.4   A Disappearing Act—Locating the Blind Spot. Look at Drawing 1. Close your right eye. Then move the book back and forth about one foot from your left eye while you stare at the plus sign. You will notice the circle disappear. When the circle disappears it is being projected onto the blind spot of your retina, the point at which the axons of ganglion neurons collect to form the optic nerve. Then close your left eye. Stare at the circle with your right eye, and move the book back and forth. When the plus sign disappears, it is being projected onto the blind spot of your right eye. Now look at Drawing 2. You can make this figure disappear and "see" the black line continue through the spot where it was by closing your right eye and staring at the plus sign with your left. When this figure is projected onto your blind spot, your brain "fills in" the line, which is one reason that we're not usually aware that we have blind spots.

Rods and Cones   **Rods** and **cones** are the photoreceptors in the retina (Figure 3.5). Over 100 million rods and six million cones are distributed across the retina. The fovea contains cones only. Cones then become more sparsely distributed as you work forward from the fovea toward the lens. Rods, by contrast, are absent at the fovea but distributed more densely as you approach the lens.

Rods are sensitive to the intensity of light only. They allow us to see in "black and white." Cones provide color vision. If you are a camera buff, you know that black-and-white films are generally "faster," or more responsive to light, than color film. In the same way, rods are more sensitive than cones to light. Therefore, under dim illumination, as during nighttime, objects appear to lose their color.

Dark Adaptation   Have you ever entered a movie theater on a bright afternoon and had to feel your way to a seat by holding onto the backs of the chairs near the aisle? You may have thought at first that the theater was too dark. But after several minutes you were able to see other people clearly, even in the darkest recesses of the theater. Adjusting to lower lighting is called **dark adaptation.**

Figure 3.6 shows the amount of light that is needed for detection as a function of the amount of time spent in the dark. The cones and rods adapt at different rates. The cones, which permit perception of color, reach their maximum adaptation to darkness in about 10 minutes. The rods, which allow perception of light and dark only, are more sensitive and continue to adapt to darkness for up to about 45 minutes.

Visual Acuity   You may recall from geometry that an acute angle is a sharp angle. Your **visual acuity** is the sharpness of your vision—your ability to discriminate visual details.

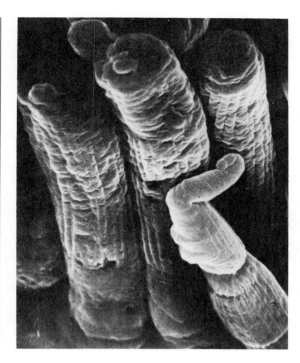

FIGURE 3.5 A Much (Much!) Enlarged Photograph of Several Rods and a Cone. Cones are usually upright fellows. However, the cone at the bottom right of this photo has been bent by the photographic process. You have more than 100 million rods and six million cones distributed across the retina of each eye. Only cones provide sensations of color. The fovea of the eye is populated by cones only, which are then distributed more sparsely as you work forward toward the lens. Rods, by contrast, are absent at the fovea and become more densely packed as you work forward.

In basketball, the "Big E" may be Elvin Hayes, but in the field of visual acuity, the big E is the first letter on the Snellen Chart (Figure 3.7), which you may have seen on numerous eye examinations. If you were to stand 20 feet from the Snellen Chart and could only discriminate the E, we would say that your vision is "20/200." This would mean that you can see from a distance of

FIGURE 3.6 This illustration shows the amount of light necessary for detection as a function of the amount of time spent in the dark. Cones and rods adapt at different rates. Cones, which permit perception of color, reach maximum dark adaptation in about 10 minutes. Rods, which permit perception of dark and light only, are more sensitive than cones. Rods continue to adapt for up to about 45 minutes.

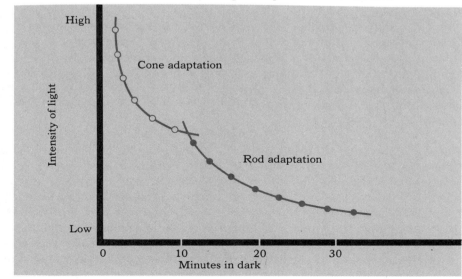

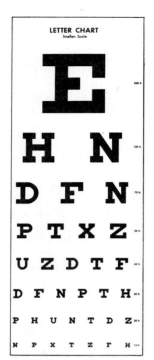

LETTER CHART
Snellen Scale

FIGURE 3.7 The Snellen Chart.

20 feet what a person with normal vision can discriminate from a distance of 200 feet. In such a case you would be quite **nearsighted.** You would have to be unusually close to an object to discriminate its details. A person who could read the smallest line on the chart from 20 feet would have 20/15 vision and be somewhat **farsighted.** It is not unusual for eyes to differ somewhat in their visual acuity, although people tend to be generally nearsighted or farsighted when their vision is not normal.

You may have noticed that elderly people often hold newspapers or books at a distance. As you grow older, the lenses of the eyes become relatively brittle, making it more difficult to accommodate to, or focus on, objects. This condition is called **presbyopia,** from the Greek for "old man." The lens structure of elderly people with presbyopia differs from that of farsighted young people. Still, the effect of presbyopia in the elderly is to make it difficult to perceive nearby visual stimuli.

If you are nearsighted in youth, you may welcome presbyopia, since your vision will tend to normalize. But people who had normal visual acuity in their youth typically find that they must use corrective lenses to read. And people who were initially farsighted often suffer from headaches linked to eyestrain during the later years.

Color Vision

For most of us the world is a place of brilliant colors. Adults with normal color vision can discriminate up to 150 color differences across the visible spectrum (Bornstein & Marks, 1982). How do we do it? As noted earlier, different colors have different wavelengths. Although we can vary the physical wavelengths of light in a continuous manner, from shorter to longer, changes in color seem to be discontinuous. But why is it that our perception of a color may shift suddenly from blue to green, even though the change in wavelength is smaller than that between two blues? Why is it that even though people from different cultures may classify colors in ways that seem strange to us (the primitive Hanunoo speak of "dark," "light," "dry," and "wet" colors), people from all cultural backgrounds divide the regions of the visible spectrum into similar groupings that correspond to the reds, yellows, greens, and blues shown in Color Plate 3.1?

Our ability to perceive color depends on the eye's transmission of different messages to the brain when lights of different wavelengths stimulate the cones in the retina. In this section we explore and evaluate two theories of how lights of different wavelengths are perceived as being of different colors: *trichromatic theory* and *opponent-process theory.* Then we discuss the problems of some individuals who are blind to some or all the colors of the visible spectrum.

Trichromatic Theory   *Tri* is a word root meaning "three" (a tricycle has three wheels), and *chromatic* derives from the Greek *chroma,* meaning "color." **Trichromatic theory** is based on an experiment that was run by British scientist Thomas Young in the early 1800s. As you can see in Color Plate 3.2, Young projected three lights of different colors onto a screen so that they partly overlapped. He found that he could create any color from the visible spectrum by simply varying the intensities of the lights. When all three lights fell on the same spot, they created white light, or the appearance of no color at all. The three lights manipulated by Young were red, green, and blue–violet.

Nearsighted Capable of seeing nearby objects with greater acuity than distant objects.

Farsighted Capable of seeing distant objects with greater acuity than nearby objects.

Presbyopia Brittleness of the lens, a condition which permits greater visual acuity with distant objects.

Trichromatic theory (try–chrome–MAT–tick). The theory that color vision is made possible by three types of cones, some of which respond to red light, some to green, and some to blue.

Just How Well Do Newborn Babies See?

Newborn babies don't seem to see much. They can look rather glassy-eyed. One eye may even be looking off to the side while the other appears to be staring vacantly ahead. Yet, according to psychologist Daphne Maurer of McMaster University and her husband Charles (1976), newborn babies see quite a bit better than you might think.

Naturally, you can't ask a newborn baby to report how well it sees, but you can train filtered lights and a movie camera on the baby's eye. Reflections from objects in the environment are recorded on film and show what the baby was looking at.

The Maurers found that newborn babies will stare at almost any object presented for minutes—golf balls, wheels, checkerboards, bull's-eyes, circles, triangles, even lines. Moving objects seem to be most captivating, as measured by the amount of time spent looking at them.

Babies have their preferences. They'll watch black and white stripes when given the chance rather than, say, gray blobs. This finding allowed the Maurers to measure visual acuity in the newborn. As black and white stripes become narrower, they eventually take on the appearance of that dull gray blob. As they are progressively narrowed, we can assume that babies can still discriminate them when they are preferred to an actual blob.

Various studies using such methods suggest that newborn infants are nearsighted, with their visual acuity somewhat poorer than 20/100. But the Maurers remind us that newborn infants, unlike adults or older children, are not motivated to "perform." If they were, they might show greater acuity.

Newborn infants also see best through the centers of their eyes. They do not have the peripheral vision of adults. Nor do they focus normally (that is, show adequate accommodation of the lenses) until

they are four months old. For this reason they see most clearly objects placed no more than about a foot away. Nor do newborns have the muscular control to aim both eyes at an object. One eye may be staring off to the side while the other fixates on an object straight ahead.

Other recent studies have found that infants may see most if not all the colors of the visible spectrum by two to three months of age. At the age of four months, infants prefer the colors blue and red as measured by amount of time spent looking at them—just as college students do (Bornstein & Marks, 1982).

Every year some 50,000 children are found to have strabismus. In this condition the eye muscles do not work together. The child seems to be looking at an object with one eye only. Unfortunately, note the Maurers, many strabismus operations are not performed until a child is two or three years old, at which point perfect correction may no longer be possible. They recommend that children be brought to a specialist if their eyes are not converging properly on an object by the age of six months.

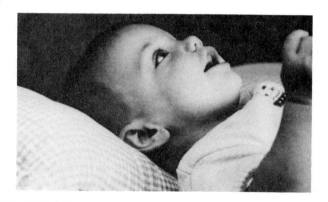

German physiologist Hermann von Helmholtz saw in Young's discovery an explanation of color vision. Von Helmholtz suggested that the eye must have three different types of photoreceptors or cones. Some must be sensitive to red light, some to green, and some to blue. We see other colors when two different types of color receptors are stimulated. The perception of yellow, for example, would result from the simultaneous stimulation of receptors for red and green. Trichromatic theory is also known as the Young-Helmholtz theory, after Thomas Young and Hermann von Helmholtz.

Opponent-Process Theory   In 1870, Ewald Hering proposed the **opponent-process theory** of color vision. Opponent-process theory also holds that there are three types of color receptors, but they are not theorized to be red, green, and blue. Before reading on, why don't you try a brief experiment? Look at

Opponent-process theory
The theory that color vision is made possible by three types of cones, some of which respond to red or green light, some to blue or yellow, and some to the intensity of light only. Red-green cones would not be able to transmit sensations of red and green at the same time.

the strangely colored American flag in Color Plate 3.3 for at least half a minute. Then look at a sheet of white or gray paper. What has happened to the flag? If your color vision is working properly, and if you looked at the miscolored flag long enough, you should see a flag composed of the familiar red, white, and blue. The flag you perceive on the white sheet of paper is an **afterimage** of the first. (If you didn't look at the green, black, and yellow flag long enough the first time, you may wish to try it again. It will work any number of times.)

Hering suggested that afterimages are made possible by three types of color-receptors: red-green, blue-yellow, and a type that perceives differences in brightness from light to dark. A red-green cone could not transmit messages for red and green at the same time. Hering would perhaps have said that when you were staring at the green, black, and yellow flag for 30 seconds, you were disturbing the balance of neural activity. The afterimage of red, white, and blue would then have represented the eye's attempt to reestablish a balance.

Evaluation Recent evidence suggests that both theories of color vision may be partially correct (Hurvich & Jameson, 1974; Hurvich, 1978). Research with **microspectrophotometry** supports trichromatic theory. Microspectrophotometry is a modern method for analyzing the sensitivity of single cones to light of different wavelengths. This research shows that some cones are sensitive to blue, some to green, and some to yellow-red parts of the spectrum—consistent with trichromatic theory.

But studies of the bipolar and ganglion neurons suggest that messages from the cones are transmitted to the brain in an opponent-process fashion. Some neurons that transmit messages to the visual centers in the brain, for example, are excited or "turned on" by green light but inhibited or "turned off" by red light. Others can be excited by red light but are inhibited by green light. It may be that there is then a "neural rebound effect" that would help explain afterimages. With such an effect, a green-sensitive ganglion that had been excited by green light for half a minute or so might switch briefly to inhibitory activity when the light is shut off. The effect would be to perceive red, even though no red light were being shone (Haber & Hershenson, 1980).

These theoretical updates allow for the afterimage effects with the green, black, and yellow flag, and are also consistent with Young's experiments in mixing lights of different colors.

Color Blindness If you can discriminate the colors of the visible spectrum, you have normal color vision and are labeled a **trichromat.** This means that you are sensitive to red-green, blue-yellow, and light-dark. People who are totally color-blind are called **monochromats** and are sensitive to light-dark only. Total color-blindness is quite rare. The fully color-blind see the world as trichromats would on a black-and-white television set or in a black-and-white movie.

Partial color blindness is more common than total color blindness. Partial color blindness is a sex-linked trait that strikes mostly males. The partially color-blind are called **dichromats.** Dichromats can discriminate only two colors, red and green, or blue and yellow, and the colors that are derived from mixing these colors. Color Plate 3.4 shows the types of tests that are used to diagnose color blindness.

A dichromat might put on one red sock and one green sock, but would not mix red and blue socks. Monochromats might put on socks of any color.

They would not notice a difference so long as the socks did not differ in intensity, or brightness.

When we selectively breed cats and dogs, we are interested in producing coats of certain colors. But if cats and dogs bred human beings, they would not be concerned about our color, because cats and dogs are monochromats.

Depth Perception

Think of the problems you might have if you could not judge depth or distance. You might bump into other people, thinking them farther away than they are. An outfielder might not be able to judge whether to run toward the infield or the fence to catch a fly ball. You might give your front bumper a workout in stop-and-go traffic. Fortunately, both *monocular and binocular cues* help us perceive the depth of objects. Let us examine a number of them.

Monocular Cues   Now that you have considered how difficult it would be to navigate through life without depth perception, ponder the problems of the artist who attempts to portray three-dimensional objects on a two-dimensional canvas. Artists use **monocular cues,** or cues that can be perceived by one eye, to create an illusion of depth. These cues—including perspective, clearness, interposition, shadows, texture gradient, and motion parallax—cause certain objects to appear more distant from the viewer than others.

Because of **perspective,** or the tendency to perceive parallel lines as converging as they recede, objects that are farther away look smaller. The distances between far-off objects also appear smaller than equivalent distances between nearby objects. However, as we shall see when we discuss *size constancy*, we learn that distant objects that appear small will actually be larger when they are close by. In this way, their relative size also becomes a cue as to their distance from us.

The two engravings in Figure 3.8 represent impossible scenes in which the artists use principles of perspective to fool the viewer. In the engraving to the left, *Waterfall*, note that the water appears to be flowing away from the

Monocular cues Stimuli suggestive of depth that can be perceived with one eye only. (From the Greek *monos*, meaning "single," and the Latin *oculus*, meaning "eye.")

Perspective A monocular cue for depth based on the convergence (coming together) of receding parallel lines.

"Excuse me for shouting—I thought you were further away."

"I'll explain it to you, Stevie. It's called perspective."

FIGURE 3.8   Two Impossible Engravings. In *Waterfall*, to the left, how does Dutch artist M. C. Escher suggest that fallen water flows back upward, only to fall again? In *False Perspective*, to the right, how did English artist William Hogarth use monocular cues for depth perception to deceive the viewer?

Chezt-Yord (1970) by Victor Vasarley. How does the artist use monocular cues for depth perception to lend this picture a three-dimensional quality?

fall in a zigzag to the upper right and left because the stream becomes gradually narrower and the stone sides of the aqueduct appear to be stepping down. However, given that it arrives at the top of the fall, it must actually somehow be flowing upward. The spot from which it falls is no farther from the viewer than is the collection point from which it appears to (but does not) begin its flow backward. In the engraving at the right, *False Perspective*, not all things become smaller as they recede into the distance. Thus, what at first seems to be background suddenly becomes foreground, and vice versa.

The clearness of an object also suggests its distance from us. We learn that we can perceive more details of nearby objects. Artists may then depict objects they wish the viewer to perceive as nearby more clearly. Note that the "distant" hill in the Hogarth engraving (Figure 3.8) is given less detail than are the nearby plants at the bottom of the picture. Note, too, how Vasarley uses clearness (crispness of line) to help provide a three-dimensional effect in Chezt-Yord (above).

We learn that nearby objects can block our views of more distant objects. **Interposition,** or the apparent placing of one object in front of another, thus makes objects appear closer (Figure 3.9). In the Hogarth engraving (Figure 3.8), which looks closer: the trees in the background (background?) or the moon sign hanging from the building (or is it buildings?) to the right? How does the artist use interposition to fool the viewer?

Interposition A monocular cue for depth based on the fact that a nearby object obscures vision of a more distant object behind it.

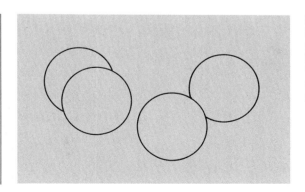

FIGURE 3.9 The Effects of Interposition. The four circles are all the same size. Which circles appear closer? The complete circles or the circles with chunks bitten out of them?

Shadows or highlights also add to the illusion of depth as shown in the tektite photograph (Figure 3.10). Another monocular cue is **texture gradient.** A gradient is a progressive change, and closer objects are perceived as having progressively rougher textures. In the Hogarth engraving (Figure 3.8), the building just behind the large fisherman's head has a rougher texture and thus seems closer than the building with the window from which the woman is leaning. Our surprise is thus heightened when the moon sign is shown as hanging from both buildings.

If you have ever driven in the country, you have probably noticed that distant objects, like mountains and stars, appear to move along with you. Objects at an intermediate distance seem stationary. But nearby objects, like roadside markers, rocks and trees, seem to go by quite rapidly. The tendency of objects to seem to move backward or forward as a function of their distance is known as **motion parallax.** We learn to perceive objects that appear to move with us as being at greater distances.

Earlier we noted that nearby objects cause the lens to accommodate or bend more to bring them into focus. The sensations of tension in the eye muscles also provide a monocular cue to depth, especially when we are within about four feet of the objects.

Binocular Cues **Binocular cues,** or cues that involve both eyes, also help us perceive depth. Two binocular cues are *retinal disparity* and *convergence*.

Try a brief experiment. Hold your index finger at arm's length. Now gradually bring it closer, until it almost touches your nose. If you keep your eyes relaxed as you do so, you will see two fingers. An image of the finger will be projected onto the retina of each eye, and each image will be slightly different since the finger will be seen at different angles. The difference between the projected images is referred to as **retinal disparity,** and serves as a binocular cue for depth perception (see Figure 3.11). Note that the closer your finger comes, the farther apart the "two fingers" appear. Closer objects have greater retinal disparity.

If we try to maintain a single image of the approaching finger, our eyes must turn inward, or converge on it, giving us a "cross-eyed" look. **Convergence** is associated with feelings of tension in the eye muscles and provides another binocular cue for depth. The binocular cues of retinal disparity and convergence are strongest at near distances.

FIGURE 3.10 The role of shading in the perception of depth. The surfaces of pieces of natural glass called Tektite appear to be pock-marked by small craters. But if the photo is turned upside down, the craters become bumps or mounds.

Texture gradient A monocular cue for depth based on the perception that closer objects appear to have rougher (more detailed) surfaces.

Motion parallax A monocular cue for depth based on the perception that nearby objects appear to move more rapidly in relation to our own motion. (From the Greek *para-*, meaning "alongside," and *allassein*, meaning "to change.")

Binocular cues Stimuli suggestive of depth that involve simultaneous perception by both eyes.

Retinal disparity A binocular cue for depth based on the difference of the image cast by an object on the retinas of the eyes as the object moves closer or farther away.

Convergence A binocular cue for depth based on the inward movement of the eyes as they attempt to focus on an object that is drawing nearer.

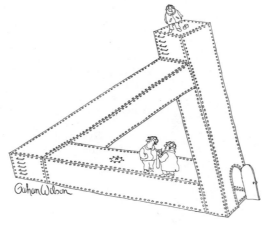

"Let's have another look at the blueprint."

FIGURE 3.11   Retinal Disparity and Convergence as Depth Cues. As an object or your finger nears your eyes, you begin to see two images of it due to retinal disparity. If you maintain perception of a single image, your eyes must converge on the object.

Perceptual Constancy

The image of a dog or cat seen from 20 feet might occupy the same amount of space on your retina as an inch-long insect crawling in the palm of your hand. Yet you would not perceive the dog or cat to be as small as the insect. Through your experiences you have acquired **size constancy,** or the tendency to see the same object as being the same size even though the size of its image on the retina varies as a function of its distance. You know that an object seen at a great distance will appear much larger when it is nearby, yet still be the same size. We may joke that people or cars look like ants from airplanes, but we know that they remain people and cars.

A case study highlights evidence that size constancy is learned. Turnbull (1961) found that an African pygmy, Kenge, thought that buffalo perceived

Size constancy The tendency to perceive an object as being the same size even as the size of its retinal image changes according to its distance.

To Perceive the Impossible Drawing

What's wrong with each of these drawings? Each has firm lines. Each has interesting shapes. In fact, if you look at just one corner of any of the drawings, it makes perfect sense. But take a critical view of the endless staircase. What would happen if you were ever to start walking up this staircase? Would you ever reach the top? Or what would happen if a ball rolled down these stairs and managed to turn all the corners? Would it ever reach bottom?

In each case the artist, working in two dimensions, has used perceptual cues carefully to encourage us to perceive a three-dimensional figure. Note that any one segment of these drawings makes perfect sense. It's just when you put it all together that you realize that . . . well, you can't put it all together, can you? That would be impossible.

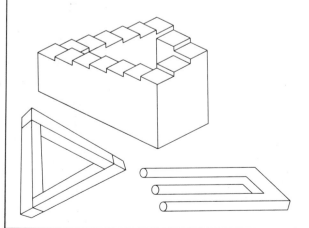

across an open field were some form of insect. Kenge normally did not view large animals from great distances because he lived in a thick forest. For this reason he had not developed size constancy.

We also have **color constancy,** or the tendency to think of an object as retaining its color even though lighting conditions may alter its appearance. Your bright orange car may edge toward yellow-gray as the hours wend their way through twilight to nighttime. But when you finally locate it in the parking lot you will still think of it as orange. You expect an orange car and still judge it "more orange" than the (faded) blue and green cars to either side. However, it would be fiercely difficult to find it in a parking lot filled with yellow and red cars similar in size and shape.

We also perceive objects as maintaining their shapes, even if we perceive them from different angles so that the shape of the retinal image changes dramatically. This tendency is called **shape constancy.** You perceive the top of a coffee cup or a glass to be a circle, even though it is a circle when seen from above only. When seen from an angle, it is an ellipse. When seen on edge, the retinal image of the cup or glass is the same as that of a straight line. So why would you still describe the rim of the cup or glass as a circle? Because you have labeled it circular or round and know that it will look circular when seen from above. Such labels and expectations make the world a stable place. Can you imagine the chaos that would prevail if we described objects as they stimulated our sensory organs with each changing moment, rather than according to stable conditions?

In another example, a door is a rectangle only when viewed straight on (Figure 3.12). When we move to the side or open it, the left or right edge comes closer and appears larger, changing the retinal image to a trapezoid. Yet we continue to think or doors as being rectangles.

Perceptual Organization

Just what do you see in Figure 3.13? Random splotches of ink or a rider on horseback? If you perceive a horse and rider, it is not because of the precision of the drawing. Rather it is because of the principle of **closure,** or the tendency to perceive a complete or whole figure, even when there are gaps in the sensory input.

FIGURE 3.12 Shape Constancy. When closed, this door is a rectangle. When open, the retinal image is trapezoidal. But due to shape constancy, we still perceive the door as rectangular.

FIGURE 3.13 Meaningless splotches of ink or a horse and rider? This figure illustrates the Gestalt principle of closure.

FIGURE 3.14 How many animals and demons can you find in this Escher print? Do we have white figures on a black background, or black figures on a white background? Figure-ground perception is the tendency to perceive geometric forms against a background.

Earlier in the century Gestalt psychologists, discussed in Chapter 1, noted that we tend to integrate bits and pieces of sensory stimulation into meaningful wholes. They attempted to formulate rules that governed this integrative process. Max Wertheimer, in particular, discovered many such rules. As a group, these rules are referred to as the laws of **perceptual organization.** Let us examine a number of these rules, beginning with those concerning figure-ground perception.

Figure-Ground Perception Take a look at Figure 3.14—a nice leisurely look. How many people, objects, and animals can you find in this Escher print? If your eye is drawn back and forth so that sometimes you are perceiving white figures on a dark background, and then dark figures on a white background, you are experiencing figure-ground reversals. That is, a shift is occurring in your perception of what is figure and what is ground, or backdrop. Escher was able to have some fun with us because of our tendency to try to isolate geometric patterns or figures from a background. However, in this case the "background" is as meaningful and detailed as the·"figure." Therefore, our perceptions shift back and forth.

The Rubin Vase In Figure 3.15 we see a Rubin vase, one of psychologists' favorite illustrations of figure-ground relationships. Note that the figure-ground relationship in part A of the figure is unclear, or ambiguous. There are no cues that suggest that the white or the black area must be the figure. For this

Perceptual organization
The tendency to integrate perceptual elements into meaningful patterns.

FIGURE 3.15   The Rubin Vase. A favorite drawing used by psychologists to demonstrate figure-ground perception. Part *A* is ambiguous, with neither white nor black clearly figure or ground. In *B* and *C* the white areas are clearly the figures.

Proximity Nearness. The perceptual tendency to group together objects that are near one another. (From the Latin *proximus*, meaning "nearest.")

Similarity The perceptual tendency to group together objects that are similar in appearance.

reason, our perception may shift from seeing the vase as the figure and then seeing two profiles as the figure.

There is no such problem in part B. Since it seems that a white vase has been brought forward against a black ground, we are more likely to perceive the vase than the profiles. In part C we are more likely to perceive the profiles than the vase because the figure of the vase is broken into patches of black and white. The profiles have greater potency in part C, yet we can still perceive the vase if we wish, despite the breakdown into black and white sections, because prior stimulation has led us to search it out. Why not have fun with some friends by covering parts B and C and asking them what they see? (They'll catch on to you quickly if they can see all three drawings at once.)

The Necker Cube   Perceptual shifts could occur with the Rubin vase because the figure and ground relationship was ambiguous. The Necker cube (Figure 3.16) provides another example of how an ambiguous drawing can lead to perceptual shifts.

Hold this page at arm's length and stare at the center of the figure for 30 seconds or so. Try to allow your eye muscles to relax. (The feeling is of your eyes "glazing over.") After a while you will notice a dramatic shift in your perception of these "stacked boxes" so that what was once a front edge is now a back edge, and vice versa. This dramatic perceptual shift is made possible by the fact that the outline of the drawing permits two interpretations.

FIGURE 3.16   A Stack of Necker Cubes.

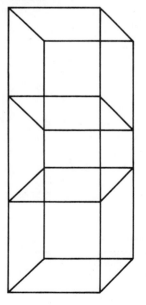

Some Other Gestalt Rules for Organization   Gestalt psychologists have also noted that our perceptions are guided by rules or laws of *proximity, similarity, continuity,* and *common fate.*

Verbally describe part A of Figure 3.17 without reading further. Did you say that part A consisted of six lines or of three groups of two (parallel) lines? If you said three sets of lines, you were influenced by the **proximity,** or nearness, of some of the lines. There is no other reason for perceiving them in pairs or subgroups: all lines are parallel and of equal length.

Now describe part B of the figure. Did you perceive the figure as a six by six grid, or as three columns of x's and three columns of o's? According to the law of **similarity,** we perceive similar objects as belonging together. For

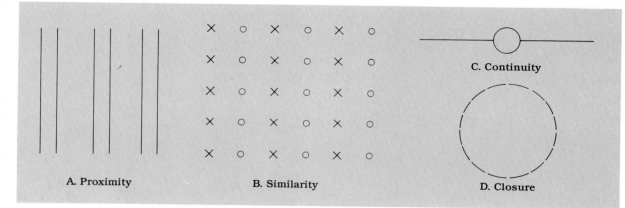

FIGURE 3.17   Some Gestalt Laws of Perceptual Organization.

this reason, you may have been more likely to describe part B in terms of columns than rows or a grid.

What about part C? Is it a circle with two lines stemming from it, or is it a (broken) line that goes through a circle? If you saw it as a single (broken) line, you were probably organizing your perceptions according to the rule of **continuity.** That is, we perceive a series of points or a broken line as having unity.

According to the law of **common fate,** elements seen moving together are perceived as belonging together. A group of people running in the same direction appear unified in purpose. Birds flying together seem to be of a feather. (Did I get that right?)

Part D of Figure 3.17 provides another example of the law of closure. The arcs tend to be perceived as a circle, or circle with gaps, rather than as just a series of arcs.

Visual Illusions

Psychologists, like magicians, enjoy pulling a rabbit out of the hat now and then. There are a number of visual **illusions,** or deceptive pictures, that psychologists enjoy showing students to demonstrate how the rules of visual perception can deceive us.

On p. 100 is an *op art* picture by Bridget Riley. When you fixate your gaze on any point in the picture, the surrounding areas seem to be in motion. *Current*, like many other op artworks, uses a moiré pattern. In such a design two almost identical patterns—in this case, wavy lines—are placed next to each other.

The Hering-Helmholtz and Müller-Lyer illusions (Figure 3.18) are named after the people who originated them. In the Hering-Helmholtz illusion, the horizontal lines are straight and parallel. However, the radiating lines cause them to appear bent outward near the center. The two lines in the Müller-Lyer illusion are the same length, but the line on the left, with its reversed arrow heads, looks longer.

The Hering-Helmholtz and Müller-Lyer illusions can probably be explained by the rule of size constancy. Because of experience and lifelong use of perceptual cues, we tend to perceive the Hering-Helmholtz drawing as

Continuity The tendency to perceive a series of points or lines as having unity.

Common fate The tendency to perceive elements that move together as belonging together (birds that flock together are assumed to be of a feather).

Illusions Sensations that give rise to misperceptions. (From the Latin *illudere*, meaning "to mock" or "to play with.")

Current, an op art picture by Bridget Riley, 1974. Synthetic polymer on composition board.

three-dimensional. We perceive the two parallel lines as curving across the apparently receding cone formed by the radiating lines.

To follow the explanation for the Müller-Lyer illusion, imagine the lines as the corners of a room as seen from inside a house (at left) and outside a house (at right). In this example, the reverse arrowheads to the left are lines where the walls meet the ceiling and floor. We perceive the lines as extending

FIGURE 3.18 The Hering-Helmholtz and Müller-Lyer Illusions.

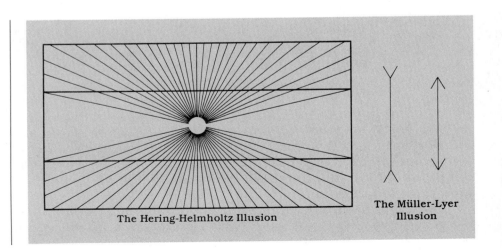

The Hering-Helmholtz Illusion

The Müller-Lyer Illusion

toward us; they push the corner away from us. The arrowheads to the right are lines where exterior walls meet the roof and foundation. We perceive them as receding from us; they push the corner toward us. The vertical line to the left is thus perceived as farther away. Since the lines are equal in length, the principle of size constancy encourages us to perceive the line to the left as longer.

Figure 3.19 is known as the Ponzo illusion. In this illusion, the two horizontal lines are the same length. But do you perceive the top line as being longer? The rule of size constancy may also afford insight into this illusion. Perhaps the converging lines strike us as parallel lines receding into the distance, like the train tracks in the cartoon on p. 92. If so, we assume from experience that the horizontal line at the top is farther "down" the "track." Again, the rule of size constancy tells us that if two objects appear to be the same size, and one is farther away, the farther object must be larger. So we perceive the top line as larger.

Now that you are an expert at explaining these visual illusions, have a look at Figure 3.20. First take some bets as to whether all three cylinders are equal in height and width. Then get a ruler. Once you have made some money, however, try to explain why the cylinders to the right look progressively larger.

Perception of Movement

Have you ever been on a train that began to pull out of the station while the train on the adjacent track remained stationary? If your own train did not lurch as it accelerated, you might have thought at first that the other train was moving. Or you might not have been certain whether your train was moving forward or the other train was moving backward.

The visual perception of movement is based on change of position relative to other objects. To early scientists, whose only instrument for visual observation was the naked eye, it seemed logical that the sun circled the earth. You have to be able to imagine the movement of the earth around the sun as seen from a theoretical point in outer space—you cannot observe it directly.

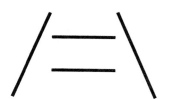

FIGURE 3.19   The Ponzo Illusion. The two horizontal lines in this drawing are equal in length, but the top line is perceived as longer. Can you use the principle of size constancy to explain why?

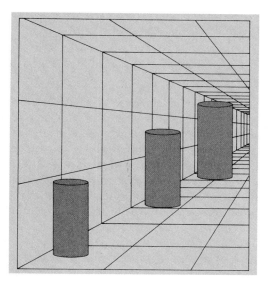

FIGURE 3.20.   In this drawing, the three cylinders are the same size, yet they appear to grow larger toward the top of the picture. Can you use the principle of size constancy to explain why?

On Subliminal Perception: Hidden Persuaders Strike Again

When atomic scientist J. Robert Oppenheimer addressed the American Psychological Association in 1955, he expressed the belief that the physicist's ability to control nuclear power was "trivial" in comparison to the psychologist's ability to control human behavior (Adams, 1982).

Soon afterward, New Jersey market researcher James Vicary made headlines when he claimed that he had used "subliminal perception" to cause people to buy popcorn and Coca-Cola *without knowing that their behavior had been influenced.* Vicary had repeatedly flashed the words POPCORN and DRINK COCA-COLA across the screen too rapidly for the Fort Lee audience to perceive on a conscious level. Yet they must have perceived the message on a level below that of conscious awareness, or subliminally, because they bought 58 percent more popcorn and 18 percent more Coke after these messages were displayed.

Since the mid-1950s, subliminal perception has had a spotty record of use. Soon after his initial experiment, the word BLOOD and pictures of a skull were used subliminally to increase audience arousal at a horror movie. The practice fell from favor when exposed by Vance Packard in his alarming bestseller, *The Hidden Persuaders.*

In recent years, a death mask was flashed on the screen to heighten audience response to *The Exorcist,* an indiscretion for which Warner Brothers was sued in the 1970s by a teenager who fainted during the film and broke his jawbone and several teeth in the process. In the 1970s, the subliminal message GET IT was also used in a television toy commercial until the Federal Communications Commission got wind of this abuse and threatened harsh action. Several stores have even tried mixing subliminal messages ("I am honest," "I will not steal") in with the background music by means of a sound mixer in order to cut down on shoplifting (*Time* magazine, 1979).

Research psychologist Lloyd Silverman of the Veterans Administration Regional Office in New York City has run numerous experiments in which depressed and schizophrenic patients show some improvement after being flashed brief subliminal messages (Silverman and others, 1982). Several studies with more than 200 subjects, for example, have shown that male schizophrenic patients show more socially appropriate behavior and perform more normally on Rorschach tests (see Chapter 9) after being repeatedly shown the subliminal message MOMMY AND I ARE ONE. Schizophrenics, according to psychoanalytic theory, harbor unconscious fantasies of undoing their early separation from their mothers, so this message is reassuring.

In an experiment carried out in Israel, tenth-grade students presented with the subliminal message *MOMMY AND I ARE ONE* showed significantly higher scores on subsequent achievement tests than control subjects (Ariam & Siller, 1982). The investigators argue that subliminal message enhances adaptation among normal persons as well as psychiatric populations.

The psychological community has not accepted this research uncritically. Rutgers University psychiatrist Donald Spence doubts that people can even perceive such a subliminal message: "It is asking a great deal of the human organism to expect subjects not only to take in a five-word sentence but to interpret it in a very particular way." Many studies (e.g., Haspel & Harris, 1982), in fact, have failed to replicate Silverman's findings.

Apparently many psychologists still consider the evidence for the hidden persuaders to be far from persuasive.

So, how do you determine which train is moving when your train is pulling out of the station (or that other train is pulling in!)? One way is to look for objects you know are stable, like station platform columns, houses, signs, or trees. If you are stationary in relation to them, your train is not moving. But observing people walking on the station platform may not provide the answer, since they are also changing their position relative to stationary objects. As suggested earlier, you might try to sense the motion of the train in your body. You would know from experience how to do these things quite well, although it might be more difficult to phrase explanations for them.

We have been considering the perception of real movement. Psychologists have also studied several types of apparent movement, or illusions of movement. These include the *autokinetic effect* and *stroboscopic motion.*

The Autokinetic Effect   If you were to sit quietly in a dark room and stare at a point of light projected onto the far wall, after a while it might appear that the light had begun to move, even if it remained quite still. The tendency to perceive a stationary point of light as moving in a dark room is called the **autokinetic effect.**

In one interesting experiment on the autokinetic effect (Block & Block, 1951), subjects were asked to judge how far the point of light moved. They provided estimates over a series of trials. The light, of course, did not move at all. Prejudiced subjects arrived at their final judgments more rapidly than nonprejudiced subjects. They were quicker to jump to their conclusion, given the same (erroneous) evidence.

Stroboscopic Motion   In **stroboscopic motion,** the illusion of movement is provided by the presentation of a rapid progression of images of stationary objects (Beck and others, 1977). In a sense, a motion picture does not move at all. Motion pictures do not consist of images that move. Rather, the audience is shown 16 to 22 pictures or frames per second, like those in Figure 3.21. Each frame differs slightly from that preceding it. Showing them in rapid succession then provides the illusion of movement.

At the rate of at least 16 frames per second, the "motion" in a film seems smooth and natural. With fewer than 16 or so frames per second, the movement looks choppy and unnatural. That is why slow motion is achieved through filming perhaps 100 or more frames per second. When they are played back at about 22 frames per second, movement seems slowed down yet smooth and natural.

Hearing

Consider the advertising slogan for the recent science fiction movie *Alien: "IN SPACE, NO ONE CAN HEAR YOU SCREAM."* It's true. For space is an almost perfect vacuum, and hearing requires a medium through which sound can travel, like air or water.

Sound, or **auditory** stimulation, travels through the air like waves. Sound is caused by changes in air pressure that result from vibrations. These vibrations, in turn, can be created by a tuning fork, your vocal cords, guitar strings, or the clap of a book thrown down on a desk.

Figure 3.23 suggests the way in which a tuning fork creates sound waves. During a vibration back and forth, the right prong of the tuning fork moves to the right. In so doing, it pushes together, or compresses, the molecules of air immediately to the right. Then the prong moves back to the left, and the air

Autokinetic effect The tendency to perceive a stationary point of light in a dark room as moving. (From the Greek *autos*, meaning "self," and *kinein*, meaning "to move.")

Stroboscopic motion A visual illusion in which the perception of motion is generated by a series of stationary images that are presented in rapid succession. (From the Greek *strobos*, meaning "twisted around," and *skopein*, meaning "to see.")

Auditory Having to do with hearing. (From the Latin *audire*, meaning "to hear." What is meant by "auditing" a course?)

Figure 3.22   Briefly define each of the words in this list. Then turn to Figure 3.24 on p. 105.

fox   _____

wolf   _____

puma   _____

deer   _____

bear   _____

beaver   _____

FIGURE 3.21   Frames from a Motion Picture. In a motion picture, viewing a series of stationary images at the rate of about 16 to 22 per second provides the illusion of movement. This form of apparent movement is termed stroboscopic motion.

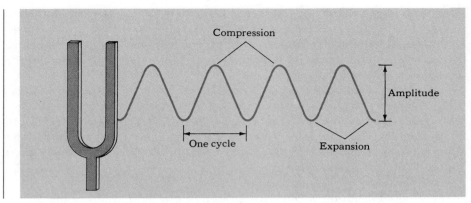

FIGURE 3.23 The vibration of the prongs of a tuning fork alternately compress and expand air molecules, sending forth waves of sound.

On Aroused Pupils and Dirty Words

Psychologists have run some classic experiments that show that our sensory organs respond to our emotions and interests as well as to sensory input. For example, our pupils tend to open, or dilate, when we are actively interested or pleasantly aroused. So what turns you on is readily apparent to someone who is tracking the dilation of your pupils.

Response to Nudes, Landscapes, and Infants
Eckhard Hess (1965, 1975) measured pupil dilation in college men and women in response to photographs. College men's pupils dilated most widely when they looked at photos of nude women. But the men were rather unresponsive to nude men, landscapes, and infants. College women's pupils showed some dilation when they viewed nude men, but showed more dilation in response to photos of infants, suggesting greater interest in the latter.

Perceptual Defense or Lack of Certainty?
Elliott McGinnies (1949) found that most of us can read common words like *table* or *chair* aloud after an exposure of only one-tenth of a second. But most people required about two-tenths of a second before they could read "dirty" words like *whore* aloud. Moreover, subjects showed more anxiety, as measured by sweat in the palm of the hands, when

words like *whore* were shown. McGinnies and other psychologists concluded that people could not consciously perceive the objectionable words because of a perceptual defense process that narrows attention when we are threatened by disturbing stimulation. Yet the presence of sweat showed that perception had occurred on an unconscious level, and suggested that perceptual defense served to protect us from the anxiety that might attend conscious recognition.

But many psychologists challenge the explanation of perceptual defense if not McGinnies's research results. Some have pointed out that people may require more time to respond to *whore* than *chair* simply because they are more used to seeing the latter in print. Others point out that it is less socially acceptable to say *whore* aloud than *chair*. For this reason, many subjects might have needed more time to be certain they would be saying aloud the word that was shown, and not a misinterpretation. Simple fear of saying the "dirty" words aloud could also have caused the sweat in the palms.

Still other critics have noted that some people perceive dirty words more readily than *table* or *chair*. Sweat in the palms, for them, may simply signal surprise at finding these words in a psychological experiment.

molecules to the right expand. By vibrating back and forth, the tuning fork actually sends air waves in many directions. A cycle of compression and expansion is considered one wave of sound. Sound waves can occur many times in one second. The human ear is sensitive to sound waves that vary from frequencies of 20 to 20,000 cycles per second.

Pitch and Loudness

Frequency   The frequency of a sound, or the number of cycles per second, is expressed in the unit **Hertz,** abbreviated *Hz*. One cycle per second is one Hz. The greater the number of cycles per second (Hz), the higher the **pitch** of the sound. The pitch of women's voices is usually higher than those of men because women's vocal cords are usually shorter than those of men and consequently vibrate at a greater frequency. The strings of a violin are shorter than those of a viola or bass viol. They vibrate at greater frequencies and we perceive them as higher in pitch.

Amplitude   The loudness of a sound is determined by the height, or amplitude, of sound waves. The higher the amplitude of the wave, the greater the loudness. Figure 3.25 shows records of sound waves that vary in frequency and amplitude. Frequency and amplitude are independent dimensions. Sounds both high and low in pitch can be either high or low in loudness.

The loudness of a sound is usually expressed in the unit **decibel,** abbreviated *dB*, which is named after the inventor of the telephone, Alexander Graham Bell. Zero dB is equivalent to the threshold of hearing. How loud is that? About as loud as the ticking of a watch 20 feet away in a very quiet room (see Table 3.1).

The decibel equivalents of many familiar sounds are shown in Figure 3.26. Twenty dB is equivalent in loudness to a whisper at five feet. Thirty dB is roughly the limit of loudness at which your librarian would like to keep your college library. You may suffer hearing damage if exposed protractedly

Hertz (hurts). A unit expressing the frequency of sound waves, named after the German physicist Heinrich Hertz. One Hertz, or *1 Hz*, equals one cycle per second.

Pitch The highness or lowness of a sound, as determined by the frequency of the sound waves. (The voice of a soprano is higher in pitch, but not necessarily in loudness, than that of a bass singer.)

Decibel A unit expressing the loudness of a sound. (From the Latin *deci-*, meaning "tenth," and *bel*, named for Alexander Graham Bell.) Abbreviated *dB*.

Figure 3.24

Use each of the words in the following list in a brief sentence:

endure	_____
cope	_____
carry	_____
lift	_____
bear	_____
manage	_____

How did you use the word "bear"? Would you have used it in the same way if the list had been the one shown in Figure 3.22?

If you defined "bear" as an animal in Figure 3.22 (p. 103), you may have been influenced by the context of the word. After all, the words above and below in Figure 3.22 were names of animals. But in the present list, the word "bear" was among several verbs suggestive of carrying burdens. So it would not be surprising if your short sentence involved "bearing a burden" of some kind or other.

Our perception of sensory stimulation is influenced by the context of the stimulation as well as the stimulation itself. The word "bear" is rough and wooly only in the forest. The context of a stimulus creates an expectation about the meaning of the stimulus. Gestalt psychologists refer to such expectations as *sets*.

Would you like another example? Read the following words aloud rapidly: MacArthur, Macduff, Macbeth, Macintosh, Macpherson, Machine. (Now rewrite the words and try it on a friend.)

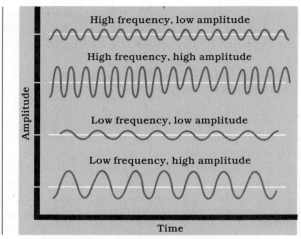

FIGURE 3.25 Sound Waves of Different Frequencies and Amplitudes. Which sounds have the highest pitch? Which are loudest?

FIGURE 3.26 Decibel Ratings of Some Familiar Sounds.

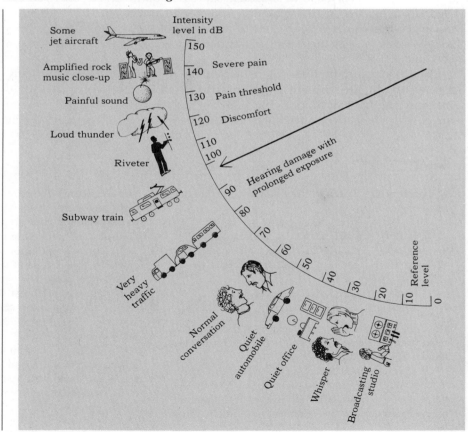

to sounds of 85–90 dB. In Chapter 14, we shall learn more about the effects of noise, and about "noise pollution."

When musical sounds (also called tones) of different frequency are played together, we also perceive a third tone that results from the difference in their frequencies. If the combination of tones is pleasant, we say that they are in harmony, or **consonant** (from Latin roots meaning "together" and "sound"). Unpleasant combinations of tones are labeled **dissonant** ("the opposite of" and "sound"). The expression that something "strikes a dissonant chord" means that we find it disagreeable.

Overtones and Timbre   In addition to producing the specified musical note, instruments like the violin also produce a number of tones that are greater in frequency. These more highly pitched sounds are called **overtones.** Overtones result from vibrations elsewhere in the instrument and contribute to the quality or richness—the **timbre**—of a sound. A $200 machine-made violin will produce the same musical notes as a $100,000 Stradivarius. But professional musicians require more expensive instruments because of the richness of their overtones—their timbre.

Noise   **Noise** is a combination of dissonant sounds. When you place a spiral shell to your ear, you do not hear the roar of the ocean. Rather, you hear the reflected noise in your vicinity. **White noise** consists of many different frequencies of sound. Yet white noise, this mixture, can lull us to sleep if the loudness is not too great.

Now let us turn our attention to the marvelous instrument that senses all these different "vibes": the human ear.

The Ear

The human ear is good for lots of things—catching dust, combing your hair around, hanging jewelry from, and nibbling. It is also admirably suited for sensing auditory stimulation, or hearing. It is shaped and structured to capture sound waves, to vibrate in sympathy with them, and to transmit all this business to centers in the brain. In this way you can not only hear something, you can also figure out what it is.

You have an outer ear, a middle ear, and an inner ear. The outer ear is shaped to funnel, or channel, sound waves to the **eardrum** (see Figure 3.27), a thin membrane that vibrates in response to sound waves and thereby transmits them to the middle and inner ears. The middle ear contains three small bones, the "hammer," the "anvil," and the "stirrup," which also transmit sound by vibrating. These bones were given their names (actually the Latin *malleus*, *incus*, and *stapes*, which translate as hammer, anvil, and stirrup) because of their shapes.

The stirrup is attached to another membrane, the **oval window,** which transmits vibrations into the bony tube within the inner ear called the **cochlea** (from the Greek for "snail"). The cochlea, which has the shape of a snail shell, contains fluids that vibrate against the **basilar membrane** that lies coiled within the spiral of the cochlea. The **organ of Corti,** sometimes referred to as the command post of hearing, is attached to the basilar membrane. Thousands of receptor cells project like hair from the organ of Corti and bend in

Consonant In harmony. (From the Latin *con-*, meaning "with," and *sonus*, meaning "sound.")

Dissonant Incompatible, discordant. Not in harmony. (From the Latin *dis-*, meaning "the opposite of.")

Overtones Tones of a higher frequency than those played. Overtones result from vibrations throughout a musical instrument.

Timbre (TIM–ber). The quality or richness of a sound. The quality that distinguishes the sounds of one musical instrument from those of another. (From the Greek *tympanon*, meaning "drum.")

Noise A combination of dissonant sounds. (From the same Greek word from which "nausea" is derived: *nausia*, meaning "seasickness.")

White noise Discordant sounds of many frequencies, often producing a lulling effect. When you put your ear to a shell you hear white noise, not the sound of the sea.

Eardrum A thin membrane that vibrates in response to sound waves, transmitting them to the middle and inner ears.

Oval window A membrane that transmits vibrations from the stirrup of the middle ear to the cochlea within the inner ear.

Cochlea (COCK–lee–uh). The bony tube within the inner ear that contains the basilar membrane and the organ of Corti.

Basilar membrane A membrane that lies coiled within the cochlea.

Organ of Corti The receptor for hearing which lies on the basilar membrane in the cochlea. It contains the receptor cells that transmit auditory information to the auditory nerve.

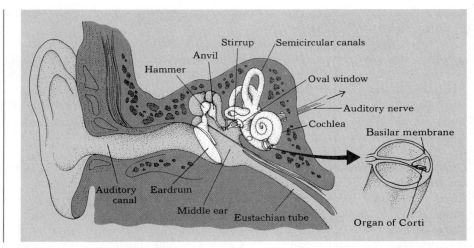

FIGURE 3.27 The Human Ear. The outer ear funnels sound to the eardrum. Inside the eardrum, vibrations of the "hammer, anvil, and stirrup" transmit it to the inner ear. In the inner ear, vibrations in the cochlea transmit the sound to the auditory nerve by way of the basilar membrane and the organ of Corti.

response to the vibrations of the basilar membrane. The bending of these receptor cells generates a neural impulse that is transmitted by the **auditory nerve** to the brain. Finally, within the brain this auditory input is projected onto the hearing areas of the temporal lobes of the cerebral cortex.

Locating Sounds

How do you balance the loudness of a stereo set? You sit between the speakers and adjust the volume until the sound seems equally loud in each ear. If the sound to the right is louder, the musical instruments will be perceived as being toward the right, rather than straight ahead.

There is a resemblance between balancing a stereo set and locating sounds. A sound that is louder in the right ear is perceived as coming from the right. A sound from the right side also reaches the right ear first. Loudness and sequence of stimulating the ears both provide directional cues.

But it may not be easy to locate a sound that is directly in front, in back, or overhead. Such sounds are equally loud in and distant from each ear. So what do we do? Simple—usually we turn our heads slightly to determine in which ear the sound increases. If you turn your head a few degrees to the right and the loudness increases in your left ear, the sound must be in front of you. Of course we also use vision and general knowledge in locating the source of sounds. If you hear the roar of jet engines, most of the time you will make money by betting that the airplane is overhead.

Theories of Hearing

We know that sounds are heard because they cause vibration in parts of the ear and information about these vibrations is transmitted to the brain. But what determines the loudness and pitch of our perceptions of these sounds?

Auditory nerve The axon bundle that transmits neural impulses from the organ of Corti to the brain.

The loudness and pitch of sounds appear related to the number of receptor neurons on the organ of Corti that fire, and how often they fire. Psychologists are generally agreed that sounds are perceived as louder when more of these sensory neurons fire, but they are not so certain about the perception of pitch. Two theories have been advanced to explain pitch discrimination: *place theory* and *frequency theory*.

Place Theory   According to **place theory,** the pitch of a sound is determined by the place along the basilar membrane that vibrates in response to it. Different spots along the membrane would then be sensitive to tones of differing frequencies. There is one exception: The entire membrane appears responsive to tones that are low in frequency (Von Békésy, 1957).

Frequency Theory   According to **frequency theory,** the frequency with which receptor neurons fire corresponds to the frequency of the sound. Individual neurons would not be capable of firing rapidly enough to transmit information about sounds of higher frequencies, however. It has been suggested that this limitation can be overcome through a **volley principle.** According to the volley principle, groups of neurons may take turns firing at high frequencies in order to transmit information about sounds of high frequency.

Place theory and frequency theory both seem to have something to offer. Future theories of pitch discrimination may incorporate elements from each.

Smell

You could say that people are sort of underprivileged when it comes to the sense of smell. Dogs, for instance, devote about seven times as much area of the cerebral cortex to the sense of smell. Male dogs sniff to determine where the territories of other dogs leave off and to determine whether female dogs are sexually receptive. Dogs can even make a living sniffing out marijuana in closed packages and suitcases.

Still, smell has an important role in human behavior. If you did not have a sense of smell, an onion and an apple would taste the same to you! As lacking as our senses of smell may be when we compare them to those of the dog, we can detect the odor of 1/1,000,000th of a milligram of vanilla in a liter of air (Levitt, 1981).

Odors are detected by sites on receptor neurons in the **olfactory** membrane high in each nostril. An odor is a sample of the actual substance being sensed. When a number of molecules of that substance, perhaps as few as 100 or so, come into contact with the olfactory membrane, the substance is smelled. According to various theories, there are between four and seven basic odors. These include flowery, minty, **musky, camphoraceous, ethereal, pungent,** and **putrid.**

The sense of smell tends to adapt rather rapidly to odors, even **noxious** odors. This may be fortunate if you are using a locker room or an outhouse. But it may not be so fortunate if you are being exposed to fumes from paints or other chemicals, since you may lose awareness of them even though they remain harmful.

Place theory The theory that the pitch of a sound is determined by the section of the basilar membrane that vibrates in response to it.

Frequency theory The theory that the pitch of a sound is determined by the frequency with which receptor cells fire in response to the sound.

Volley principle A modification of frequency theory: The hypothesis that groups of neurons may be able to achieve the effect of firing at very high frequencies by "taking turns" firing—that is, by firing in volleys. Receptor cells would not otherwise be able to fire with adequate frequency to create the perception of very high pitches.

Odor The characteristic of a substance that makes it perceptible to the sense of smell. (A Latin word meaning "smell.")

Olfactory Having to do with the sense of smell. The olfactory membrane located high in each nostril is the receptor for smell. (From *odor* and the Latin *facere*, meaning "to make.")

Musky Having the strong, penetrating odor of musk, which is secreted by many animals.

Camphoraceous (kam–for–RAY–shuss). Having the odor of camphor, a substance that protects fabrics from moths.

Ethereal Having the odor of chemical compounds called ethers.

Pungent Having a sharp, piercing odor.

Putrid Having a rotten, foul-smelling odor.

Noxious (NOCK–shuss). Harmful, injurious. (From the Latin *noxa*, meaning "injury.")

Some Recent Studies in Olfaction: "The Nose Knows"

Let us now turn our attention to some recent research concerning the sense of smell. We shall have a brief look at *menstrual synchrony* and olfactory messengers otherwise known as *pheromones*.

Menstrual Synchrony   In Chapter 2 we saw that the menstrual cycle is regulated by hormones. In 1971, psychologist Martha McClintock reported on the phenomenon of **menstrual synchrony.** She monitored the menstrual cycles of 135 women and found that the cycles of friends and roommates converged from an average of 8.5 days apart to within five days during one school year. McClintock also found that the cycles of women who spent more time with men were shorter.

To demonstrate that menstrual synchrony is caused by odor, San Francisco State University psychologist Michael Russell and his colleagues (1977) recruited a colleague, Genevieve, with a regular 28-day cycle, who did not shave her underarms or use deodorants. The researchers then dabbed "essence of Genevieve" on the lips of five women subjects three times weekly over a period of four months. During this brief period the women's cycles converged from an average of 9.3 days apart to 3.4 days. Four of the women's cycles synchronized within one day of Genevieve's. A control group of six women dabbed with alcohol showed no synchronization.

In a more recent study with laboratory rats, McClintock (1979) caused the reproductive cycles of female rats to converge by circulating air between their cages. The sense of smell was the only source of "contact" between the animals.

Pheromones: Has Science Found a Magic Potion?   For centuries people have searched for a magic potion—some formula that could cause others to fall in love with you, or at least be wildly attracted to you. Some scientists suggest that these potions may exist. They are **pheromones.**

Many organisms, from insects through mammals, are sexually aroused by these chemical secretions. They are produced by other members of the species and are detected through the sense of smell. Animals use pheromones to gather food, mark territories, sound alarms, maintain pecking orders, and send out sexual cues. Pheromones induce mating behavior mechanically in insects (Robinson & Robinson, 1979), but—perhaps to the chagrin of romantics—their sexual role becomes less vital as we rise through the ranks of the animal kingdom.

Mammals secrete pheromones in the vagina. Male mice attempt to mate with other males when urine from the female, containing pheromones, is smeared on their backs (Connor, 1972). Male mice (Cooper, 1978) and male guinea pigs (Beauchamp, 1981) show less sexual arousal when their sense of smell is blocked. Vaginal secretions also arouse male monkeys (Michael and others, 1971), but monkeys seek sexual activity even when nose drops have blocked their sense of smell (Goldfoot and others, 1978). Cognitive functioning is more complex among monkeys than mice. Monkeys are more responsive than mice to the sight of another monkey, past experience with another monkey, and observation of other monkeys involved in sexual activity.

Some people also apparently respond to pheromones, but, like monkeys, we do not need them. We can respond sexually to a glimpse of a loved one,

Menstrual synchrony The convergence of the menstrual cycles of women who spend time in close quarters. (From the Latin *syn-*, meaning "together" and *chronos*, meaning "time.")

Pheromones (FAIR–oh–moans). Chemical secretions detected by the sense of smell that stimulate stereotypical behaviors in other members of the same species.

an erotic photo, a whiff of perfume or cologne that stirs a memory, or a lover's voice (Rathus, 1983). But still consider the case of **exaltolide,** a musky substance that is highly concentrated in the urine of adult men. Its odor is more detectable by and appealing to adult women than to children or men (Hassett, 1978). Moreover, women are most sensitive to exaltolide when they are ovulating (thus capable of conceiving).

Morris and Udry (1978) ran an experiment with married couples in which women smeared various perfumes on their breasts at bedtime. One perfume contained suspected pheromones. The couples tracked their sexual activity. One couple in five showed significantly more frequent sexual activity when they used the pheromone-laced perfume, although they did not know when the substance was being used. Pheromone-sensitive couples also engaged in sexual relations more frequently at the time of ovulation.

In other studies (Durden-Smith, 1980), photos of men and women have been rated more attractive when a suspected pheromone was in the air. People have dallied longer in pheromone-sprayed telephone booths. Although a suspected male pheromone could not be perceived consciously, women were more likely to sit on a waiting room chair that had been sprayed. Most of the sprayed seats in a theater were also occupied by women. Thus, pheromones may play some role in the sex lives of people who are sensitive to them, even if they are unnecessary.

Perfume manufacturers are betting that pheromones can play a significant role. The substance used in the studies reported by Durden-Smith, **alpha androstenol,** is extracted from human sweat. You can find it in British sex shops where a small bottle sells for $24, or in the United States, where Jovan is marketing a new cologne, Andron, which contains a synthetic version of this suspected pheromone.

Taste

Your cocker spaniel may jump at the chance to finish off your ice cream cones, but your Siamese cat may turn up her nose at this golden opportunity. Why? Dogs can perceive the taste quality of sweetness, as can pigs, but cats cannot (Dethier, 1978).

There are four primary taste qualities: sweet, sour, salty, and bitter. The "flavor" of a food involves its taste, but is more complex. As noted earlier, apples and onions have the same taste—or the same mix of taste qualities— but their flavor is vastly different. After all, you wouldn't chomp into a nice cold onion on a warm day, would you? The flavor of a food depends on its odor, texture, and temperature, as well as its taste. If it were not for odor, heated tenderized shoe leather might just pass for your favorite steak dish.

Taste is sensed through **taste cells,** or receptor neurons that are located on **taste buds.** You have about 10,000 taste buds, most of which are located near the edges and back of your tongue. As noted in Figure 3.28, taste buds tend to specialize a bit. Some, for example, are more responsive to sweetness, while others react to several tastes. Receptors for sweetness lie at the tip of the tongue and receptors for bitterness lie toward the back of the tongue. Sourness is sensed along the sides of the tongue, and saltiness overlaps the areas sensitive to sweetness and sourness (Figure 3.28). This is why people perceive a sour dish to "get them" at the sides of the tongue.

Exaltolide
(eggs–SALT–oh–lied). A musky substance that is suspected to be a sexual pheromone.

Alpha androstenol
(an–DROSS–ten–all). A sexual pheromone extracted from sweat.

Taste cells Receptor cells that are sensitive to taste.

Taste buds The sensory organs for taste. They contain taste cells and are located on the tongue.

A New Whodunit: The Case of the Smelly T-Shirts

Now, who would pay you $10 to wear a T-shirt for 48 hours, extracting a promise that you would jog around or do pushups for at least an hour during this period? Psychologists, of course, trying to learn how sensitive we are to one form of air pollution—body odor. Body odor, as your TV set will gladly inform you through a thousand commercials, is one of America's mortal sins, although many foreign cultures do not find such odors to be offensive. (Which is one reason these cultures are foreign to us?)

Following these two-day exercises, subjects peeled the shirts off and returned them to the experimenters (McBurney and others, 1977) in tightly sealed plastic bags. In a procedure that demonstrates unparalleled commitment to the advancement of psychology, students then smelled the shirts and rated them for relative offensiveness.

There was general agreement as to which shirts smelled worse. Anonymous owners of the most putrid were rated as dirtier, less intelligent, less healthy, fatter, and less appealing to the opposite sex. Yet they were also rated stronger, more industrious, and more athletic. Apparently they were seen as tough and hard-working, but mindless and dirty drones.

Subjects also rated their own shirts as least offensive. When you live with yourself for a long time, it seems you become more tolerant—or less likely to make a stink.

Schleidt and Hold (1981) found that married couples in West Germany, Italy, and Japan could identify T-shirts worn to bed for a week by their mates—even when blindfolded. Apparently the nose knows its mate. In these studies both men and women generally considered male odors more noxious than female odors, although they also generally rated their mates' odor as less offensive than their own.

There was one exception. The Japanese women considered their husbands' body odors more noxious than their own. Why? The researchers speculate that the reason is linked to the fact that in Japan marriages are still frequently arranged by families. That is, the Japanese don't always get to sniff out a mate for themselves.

By eating hot foods and scraping your tongue, you regularly kill off many taste cells. But you need not be alarmed at this unintentional display of oral aggression. Taste cells are the rabbits of the sense receptors, reproducing at the rate of complete renewal every week or so.

FIGURE 3.28 Taste buds on different areas of the tongue are sensitive to different primary taste qualities.

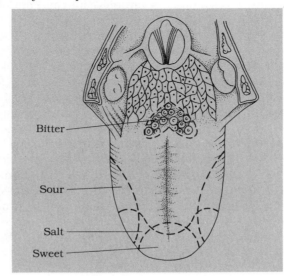

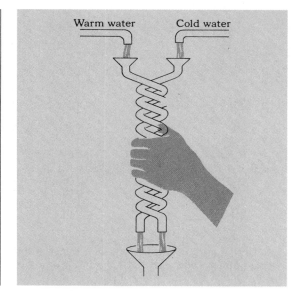

FIGURE 3.29 People perceive hotness when receptors for warmth and coldness are stimulated simultaneously. Would you be able to hold on to the coils if you perceived intense heat, even if you knew that one coil was filled with warm water and the other with cold water?

The number of taste cells declines with age. The elderly may spice their food more heavily than the young because their sense of taste has grown less sensitive. Since food is less savory, the elderly may also eat less and become malnourished.

Touch

You may think of yourself as having *a* sense of touch, but your skin actually discriminates among four kinds of skin sensations: pressure, warmth, coldness, and pain. How it does so is not perfectly clear. It has been generally believed that there are four kinds of sensory receptors in the skin, one for each type of sensation. But recent research suggests that some nerve endings may receive more than one type of sensory input.

Although we have receptors that are sensitive to warmth and to coldness, we have none that are sensitive to hotness. A classic experiment in sensation and perception showed that simultaneous stimulation of receptors for warmth and coldness led to perception of hotness. As shown in Figure 3.29, two coils were intertwined. Warm water was run through one of them, and cold water through the other. Yet people who grasped the coils simultaneously, as shown in the figure, felt heat so intense that they had to let go at once. Knowing that the heat was phony made no difference. The perception of burning heat was quite convincing. I'll bet my cash that you would let go of the coils on each trial, too.

Now let us turn our attention to the consideration of an important psychological issue concerning perception of pain: Does acupuncture provide relief from pain?

"Feel-O-Vision": A New Type of Skin Flick?

In the near future some blind people may be reading, and engaging in other "visual" tasks, with their backs. It might only be necessary that readily portable versions of equipment being studied by Paul Bach-y-Rita (1972) be developed.

Bach-y-Rita used a grid of 400 tiny vibrators (20 by 20) that stimulated the backs of blind people. They were sensed through nerve endings sensitive to pressure. A "picture" with only 400 points does not allow very fine discrimination (or much "fine tuning," if your prefer). Still, it's more than enough to allow people to read the letters of the alphabet, be aware of large nearby objects like cars and people, and, possibly, big cracks in the pavement.

If this sounds unworkable to you, ask a friend to spell out some words on your back with his or her fingers. No, I have no suggestions for what the words might be.

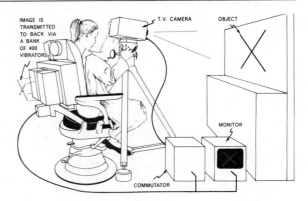

"Feel-o-vision." This blind person is "reading," thanks to a grid of 400 vibrators that transmit the visual pattern shown on the TV monitor onto her back.

A Psychological Controversy: Does Acupuncture Provide Relief from Pain?

Thousands of years ago the Chinese began mapping the body to learn where pins might be placed to deaden pain elsewhere. Much of the Chinese practice of acupuncture was unknown in the West, even though Western powers occupied much of China during the 1800s. But early in the 1970s, *New York Times* columnist James Reston underwent an appendectomy in China, with acupuncture the only anesthetic. He reported no discomfort. In 1972 the National Institutes of Health (NIH) undertook research to determine whether acupuncture was effective in the control of pain. And in 1975 the NIH reported that acupuncture was no more effective than hypnosis or sugar pills—that is, **placebos.**

Yet hypnosis, as you will see in Chapter 4, and sugar pills may be quite effective in controlling pain. Despite the NIH conclusion, there have been numerous clinical reports that acupuncture is effective with people (Pool, 1973), and there is experimental evidence that it reduces perception of pain in cats and mice (Levitt, 1981). Neurosurgeon J. Lawrence Pool (1973) reports that just placing needles in certain bodily locations sometimes removes pain. At other times the needles are twirled about 120 times a minute.

Pool also notes that "a modern treatment is not to move the needle or needles but to run through them a small direct electric current" (1973, p. 161). Levitt (1981) points out that such "stimulation-produced **analgesia**" (SPA) has been used successfully with many pain patients suffering from cancer or nerve or brain damage. Activating an implanted electrode (which is an electrified "needle") for 15 to 30 minutes can provide hours of relief from pain.

All of this is very nice, but we still need to know *how* acupuncture (or SPA) works—when and if it does. As Levitt points out, "One obstacle to the general acceptance of acupuncture has been the lack . . . of an explanation for the means by which needles inserted at one site could engender analgesia at

Placebos Bogus treatments that control for the effect of expectations. See Chapter 1.

Analgesia (an–al–GEE–zee–uh). A state of not feeling pain, though fully conscious. (From the Latin *an-*, meaning "without," and *algos*, meaning "pain.")

a distant location" (1981, p. 165). Let us discuss two explanations of the possible analgesic effects of acupuncture: *gate theory* and *endorphins*.

Gate Theory   According to the "gate theory" of pain, originated by Melzack (1973), twirling needles may activate nerves that prevent other nerves from transmitting pain messages to the brain. The mechanism is analogous to shutting down a "gate" in the spinal cord. It is something like too many calls flooding a switchboard at once. The flood prevents any calls from getting through.

Endorphins   **Endorphins** (short for endogenous morphine) are substances produced by the nervous system that are similar in chemical composition and effect to the narcotic pain-killer morphine. Acupuncture and SPA may serve as analgesics by causing endorphins to be released (Levitt, 1981).

There is supportive evidence. The drug *naloxone* is known to block the pain-killing effects of morphine. The analgesic effects of SPA (Akil and others, 1976) and acupuncture are also blocked by naloxone. Therefore, it may well be that the analgesic effects of SPA and acupuncture can be linked to the morphinelike endorphins.

Interestingly, the so-called placebo effect—that is, the way in which expectation of relief sometimes leads to relief from pain and other problems—has also occasionally been attributed to release of endorphins. In future years we may well find ways of controlling pain without drugs, acupuncture, or other external means. We may learn how to control release of our bodies' own pain-killing systems more or less directly.

Kinesthesis and the Vestibular Sense

Try a brief experiment. Close your eyes. Then touch your nose with your index finger. If you weren't right on target, I'm sure you came close. But how? You didn't see your hand moving, and you (probably) didn't hear your arm swishing through the air.

You were able to bring your finger to your nose through your kinesthetic sense, called **kinesthesis,** after the Greek words for "motion" *(kinesis)* and "perception" *(aisthesis)*. Kinesthesis is the sense that informs you about the position and motion of parts of the body. Sensory information is fed back to the brain from sensory organs in the joints, tendons, and muscles.

Imagine going for a walk without kinesthesis. You would have to watch the forward motion of each leg to be certain you had raised it high enough to clear the curb. And if you had tried our brief experiment without the kinesthetic sense, you would have had no sensory feedback until you felt the pressure of your finger against your nose (or cheek, or eye, or forehead), and you probably would have missed dozens of times.

Before we leave kinesthesis, let's try another brief experiment. Close your eyes. Then "make a muscle" in your right arm. Could you sense the muscle without looking at it or feeling it with your left hand? Of course you could. It is also kinesthesis that senses muscle contractions.

Your **vestibular sense** informs you whether you are upright (physically, not morally). Sensory organs located in the **semicircular canals** (Figure 3.27) and elsewhere in the ears monitor your body's motion and position in rela-

Endorphins Substances produced by the nervous system that have an analgesic effect.

Kinesthesis (kin–ness–THEE–sis). The sense that informs about the position and motion of parts of the body.

Vestibular sense (vest–TIB–you–lar). The sense that informs about body position relative to gravity. Also called the sense of equilibrium. (From the Latin *vestibulum,* meaning "entrance hall," reflecting the location of the vestibular sensory organs in the "entranceway" of the ear.)

Semicircular canals Structures of the inner ear that monitor bodily movement and position.

tionship to gravity. They tell you whether you are falling and provide cues as to whether your body is changing speeds, as in an accelerating airplane or automobile.

Extrasensory Perception

Imagine how rich you could grow if you had **precognition,** that is, if you were able to perceive future events. Perhaps you would check next month's stock market reports and know in advance what stocks to buy or sell. Or you could make Superbowl or World Series bets with perfect safety.

Or think of the power you would have if you were capable of **psychokinesis,** that is, of manipulating or moving objects from a distance. You may have gotten a glimpse of the types of things that could happen with psychokinesis from films like *The Power, Carrie,* and *The Fury.*

Precognition and psychokinesis are two concepts associated with **extrasensory perception** (ESP)—the perception of objects or events through means other than sensory organs. Two other concepts are **telepathy,** or the direct transmission of thoughts or ideas from person to person, and **clairvoyance,** or the perception of objects that do not stimulate the sensory organs. An example of clairvoyance is "knowing" what card is to be dealt next, although it is still in the deck and unknown to the dealer.

ESP is extremely controversial, and most psychologists do not believe that it is an appropriate area for scientific inquiry. Scientists study natural events and ESP smacks of the supernatural, perhaps of the occult. ESP also has sensationalistic aspects, as in films like *Carrie.* ESP for many also has the flavor of a nightclub act in which a blindfolded "clairvoyant" on stage calls out the contents of an audience member's pocketbook.

Other psychologists believe that our minds should remain open about ESP, as suggested in the quote from *Hamlet:* "There are more things in heaven and earth, Horatio,/ Than are dreamt of in your philosophy." They might argue that we do not know how gravity works, yet some force holds us to planet Earth. At one time those who claimed that the Earth circles the sun were considered heretics. Now this astronomical fact is known to every schoolchild. The issue for these scientists is not whether ESP has a sensationalistic flavor, or is believed in by "weirdos" and "quacks." The issue is whether ESP can be demonstrated in the scientist's laboratory.

Perhaps the best known of the respected ESP researchers was the late Joseph Banks Rhine, of Duke University (1971), who studied ESP for several decades, beginning in the late 1920s. In a typical experiment in clairvoyance, Rhine would use a pack of 25 so-called Zener cards, which contained five sets of the five distinct cards shown in Figure 3.30. A subject guessing which of the five patterns was about to be turned up would be correct 20 percent of the time (one time in five) by chance alone. Rhine found that there were many subjects whose percentage of guesses was consistently significantly greater than the 20 percent chance rate. He concluded that some individuals apparently possessed some degree of ESP.

More recent studies have been done in clairvoyance with automated equipment, like random number generators. Other studies have been done in psychokinesis. As of today, there are many studies that claim that individuals have performed tasks requiring ESP at above-chance levels of success. How-

Precognition Ability to foresee the future. (From the Latin *prae-,* meaning "before," and *cognitio,* meaning "knowledge.")

Psychokinesis Ability to manipulate objects or events by thought processes.

Extrasensory perception Perception of objects and events without sensation; abbreviated *ESP.* A controversial area of investigation. (From the Latin *extra-,* meaning "outside.")

Telepathy Direct transference of thought from one person to another.

Clairvoyance Ability to perceive things in the absence of sensory stimulation. (A French word meaning "clearsightedness.")

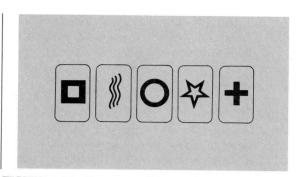

FIGURE 3.30 Zener Cards. Zener cards have been used in research on clairvoyance to determine whether some people can guess which card is about to be turned up at above-chance levels.

ever, these studies have not been accepted by an appreciable segment of the scientific community.

There are many reasons for this skepticism, as noted by Hansel (1979), and they go beyond simply feeling that ESP is not an appropriate area of inquiry. For one, negative results are rarely reported by ESP researchers. Therefore, we would expect *some* low-frequency findings (like an individual with a high success rate at ESP tasks for a period of several days) to surface in the literature. In other words, if you flip a coin indefinitely, eventually you will flip 10 heads in a row. The odds against this are overwhelming, but if you report your "success," and do not report the weeks of failure, you give the impression that you have unique coin-flipping ability.

Second, it has not been easy to replicate ESP experiments. Subjects who have "shown" ESP with one researcher have failed to do so with another, or have refused to participate in a study with another. Third, some researchers, including a colleague of Rhine, have been found tampering with data or equipment. (Rhine himself was never accused of fraud.)

For these and other reasons, as noted, ESP research has not received much credibility. To be fair, science has shown, again and again, that "There are more things in heaven and earth" than there were once thought to be. But science has not yet found that ESP is one of those things. For the time being, the great majority of psychologists prefer to study perception that involves sensation. What is life without some sensation?

Summary

Sensation is the stimulation of sensory receptors (neurons) and the transmission of sensory information to the central nervous system. Perception reflects learning and expectations; it is the active organization of sensations into a representation of the world.

Vision is our dominant sense. Visible light is one part of a spectrum of electromagnetic energy. The absolute threshold for a stimulus, like light, is the lowest intensity at which it can be detected. The minimum difference in intensity that can be discriminated is the difference threshold. Difference thresholds are expressed in Weber's constants.

The eye senses and transmits visual stimulation to the occipital lobe of the cerebral cortex. After passing through the cornea, pupil size determines the amount of light that can pass through the lens. The lens focuses light as it projects onto the retina, which is composed of photoreceptors called rods and cones. The fovea is the most sensitive part of the eye. The fovea is populated by cones only, which permit perception of color. Rods are spaced most densely near the lens and transmit sensations of light and dark only. Rods are more sensitive than cones to lowered lighting, and continue to adapt to darkness once cones have reached peak adaptation.

Visual acuity is sharpness of vision. As people age, the lens becomes brittle, resulting in presbyopia, a condition similar to farsightedness.

There are two theories of color vision. According to trichromatic theory, there are three types of cones, some sensitive to red, others to blue or green light. Opponent-process theory proposes three types of color receptors: red-green, blue-yellow, and light-dark. Opponent-process theory better accounts for afterimages, but both theories seem to have some validity. Color-blind people who can see light and dark only are called monochromats. Dichromats, who can discriminate only two colors (red and green, or blue and yellow), are more common.

Depth perception involves monocular and binocular cues. Monocular cues include perspective, clearness, interposition, texture gradient, motion parallax, and accommodation. Binocular cues include retinal disparity and convergence.

We develop size, color, and shape constancy through experience. That is, we assume that objects retain their size, shape, and color despite their distance, position, or lighting conditions.

Gestalt rules of perceptual organization influence our grouping of bits of sensory stimulation. These rules concern figure-ground relationships, proximity, similarity, continuity, common fate, and closure. Visual illusions use perceptual cues as well as twists on rules for organization to deceive the eye.

We perceive real movement by sensing movement across the retina and movement of objects in relation to one another. Distant objects appear to move more slowly than nearby objects, whereas middle-ground objects may give the illusion of moving backward. The autokinetic effect is the tendency to perceive a point of light in a darkened room as moving. Stroboscopic motion, used in films, is the perception of a series of still pictures as moving.

Auditory stimulation, or sound waves, require a medium. Sound waves alternately compress and expand molecules of the medium—creating vibrations. The human ear can hear sounds varying in frequency from 20 to 20,000 cycles per second. The greater the frequency, the higher the pitch of a sound. The loudness of a sound is measured in decibels (dB). Noise is a combination of dissonant sounds.

The eardrum vibrates in sympathy to sound, and transmits auditory stimulation through the bones of the middle ear to the cochlea of the inner ear. The basilar membrane of the cochlea transmits stimulation to the organ of Corti, and from there sound travels to the brain by the auditory nerve. Sounds seem louder when more neurons of the organ of Corti fire. But two theories are competing to account for the perception of pitch: place theory and volley theory.

Odors are detected by the olfactory membrane in each nostril. An odor is a sample of the substance being smelled. The sense of smell adapts rapidly to odors, even unpleasant ones. Menstrual synchrony depends on the sense of smell. Pheromones, detected by the sense of smell, help control sexual behavior in lower animals, but are unnecessary with people.

There are four primary taste qualities: sweet, sour, salty, and bitter. Flavor involves the odor, texture, and temperature of food, as well as its taste. Taste is sensed through taste cells, which are located in taste buds on the tongue.

Touch involves four skin sensations: pressure, warmth, coldness, and pain. Perception of hotness is caused by simultaneous stimulation of warmth and coldness receptors. If acupuncture is effective in relieving pain, it may work by way of gate theory or by releasing endorphins.

Kinesthesis is the sensing of bodily position and movement, and relies on sensory organs in the joints, tendons, and muscles. The vestibular sense is housed primarily in the semicircular canals of the ears and informs us whether we are in an upright position.

There has been speculation as to whether extrasensory perception (perception without sensation) is possible. Evidence in this area has fallen into disrepute because of underreporting of experimental failures, failure to replicate research with positive results, and cases of fraud.

Truth or Fiction Revisited

- *White sunlight is actually composed of all the colors of the rainbow.* True. White light can be broken down into its components—the visible spectrum—by a prism.
- *On a clear, dark night you could probably see the light from a single candle burning 30 miles away.* True. This degree of brightness approximates the absolute threshold for light.
- *We all have blind spots in our eyes.* True. It is at the spot where axons of ganglion cells gather to form the optic nerve.
- *We need two eyes in order to perceive depth.* False. There are several monocular (one-eyed) cues for depth perception.
- *"Motion pictures" do not move at all.* True. Stroboscopic motion—presentation of a series of still pictures—creates the illusion of movement.
- *The advertising slogan for the film* Alien *was accurate: "In space, no one can hear you scream."* True. Sound waves require a medium like air or water, and space is an almost perfect vacuum.
- *Onions and apples have the same taste.* True. But their flavor, which includes their odor and other cues, is vastly different.
- *An American columnist underwent a painless operation in China while he was fully awake. His only anesthetic was twirling needles.* True, according to James Reston's self-report. The technique used is called acupuncture.

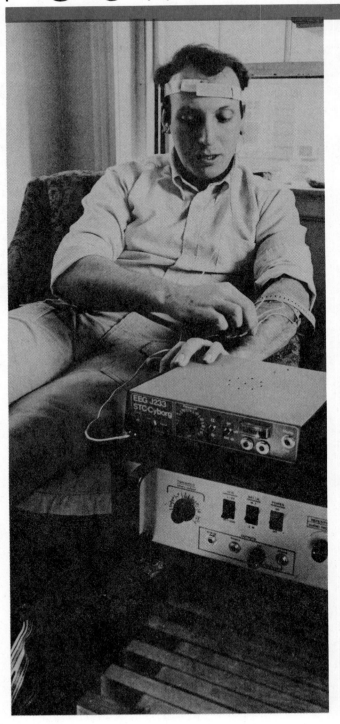

OUTLINE

States of Consciousness

TRUTH OR FICTION?

- There is no such thing as consciousness.
- Most people have about five dreams during an eight-hour period of sleep.
- Coca-Cola once "added life" through a powerful but now illegal stimulant.
- Heroin was once used as a cure for addiction to morphine.
- People have managed to bring high blood pressure under control through meditation.
- You can learn to increase or decrease your heart rate consciously.
- A hypnotized man experienced no pain when his arm was amputated.

It is a well-known fact of life that the few individuals who have gained insight into the mysteries of the universe wear flowing robes, have long beards streaked with white, and set up shop on some distant mountaintop. A sag in their shoulder telegraphs their weariness with knowledge and the burdens of the world.

These sages are hard to meet. You've got to wait for the end of the monsoon season, or for a thaw, to make the journey. Then you must enlist one of the last guides who recalls the route. Such guides would typically prefer to watch their donkeys graze in the backyard than make any darn fool trip. But they can be persuaded. (If they couldn't, I'd have to find another tale.)

So it is not surprising that psychologist Robert Ornstein's (1972) recounting of the experiences of a group of American travelers who were seeking just such a wise old man describes them as scrambling and stumbling through the Himalayan mountains. As you would expect, the trip was long and arduous. Many would have turned back. But these hardy travelers were searching for the scoop on heightened consciousness, for the key to inner peace and harmony.

Finally, the travelers found themselves at the feet of the venerable **guru.** They told him of the perils and pitfalls of their journey, of the singular importance they attached to this audience. They implored the guru to share his wisdom, to help them open their inner pathways.

The guru said, "Sit, facing the wall, and count your breaths."

This was it? The secret that had been preserved through the centuries? The wisdom of several lifetimes? The prize for which our seekers had risked life and limb and bank account?

Yes, in a sense this was. Counting your breaths is one method of **meditation**—one way of narrowing your *consciousness* so that the stresses of the outside world can fade away.

In this chapter we shall explore meditation and other states of consciousness. Some of them, like sleep, are quite familiar to you. Others, like meditation, biofeedback, and hypnosis may seem more exotic. It is also in this chapter that we deal "consciousness-altering" drugs. But first we shall tackle the $64,000 question: What *is* consciousness? This is a dangerous undertaking for at least two reasons. First, some psychologists believe that the science of psychology should not deal with the question of consciousness at all. Second, the meanings of the word are quite varied.

The $64,000 Question: What *Is* Consciousness?

In 1904, William James wrote an intriguing article entitled, "Does Consciousness Exist?" Think about that. *Does consciousness exist?* Do you feel that *you* have consciousness? That you are conscious or aware of yourself? Of the world around you? Would you bear witness to being conscious of, or experiencing, thoughts and feelings? I would bet that you would. And so, to be sure, would William James. But James did not think that consciousness was a proper area of study for psychologists. It smacked of religion and philosophy, not of science. Consciousness was not a *thing* to James. Rather, it was "a mere echo, the faint rumor left behind by the disappearing (concept of the) 'soul' " (James, 1904, p. 477).

As noted in Chapter 1, John Watson, the "father of modern behaviorism," insisted that only observable, measurable behavior was the proper province

Guru (GOO–roo). A spiritual adviser or teacher. (A Sanskrit word meaning "venerable.")

Meditation As a method for coping with stress, a systematic narrowing of attention that slows the metabolism and helps produce feelings of relaxation. (From the Latin *meditare.)*

of psychology. In "Psychology as the Behaviorist Views It," published in 1913, Watson declared, "The time seems to have come when psychology must discard all references to consciousness" (p. 163). The following year Watson was elected president of the American Psychological Association, which further cemented these ideas in the minds of many psychologists.

Despite such objections, and despite the problems involved in defining (much less measuring) consciousness, we shall attempt to explore the meanings and varieties of this most intriguing concept. Many psychologists, especially cognitive psychologists, believe that we cannot meaningfully discuss human behavior without referring to the concept of consciousness.

The Meanings of Consciousness

The word *consciousness* has several meanings. Let's have a look at a few of them.

Consciousness as Sensory Awareness   One meaning of consciousness is **sensory awareness** of the environment. The sense of vision permits us to be "conscious" of, or to see, the sun gleaming in the snow on the rooftops. The sense of hearing allows us to be conscious of, or to hear, a concert.

We are more conscious of, or have greater awareness of, those things to which we pay attention. Many things are going on nearby and in the world at large, yet you are conscious of, or focusing on, the words on this page (perhaps).

Subliminal stimuli, discussed in the last chapter, are not perceived "consciously" in that we are not aware of them. However, they stimulate our sensory receptors and may be capable of influencing our behavior.

Sensory awareness Knowledge of the environment through perception of sensory stimulation—one definition of consciousness.

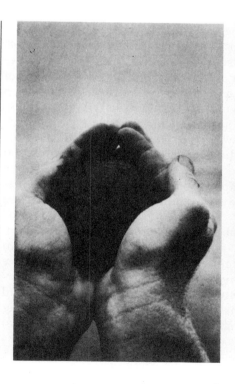

One of the definitions of consciousness is sensory awareness. These people are enhancing their "consciousness" of the environment through sensory awareness exercises.

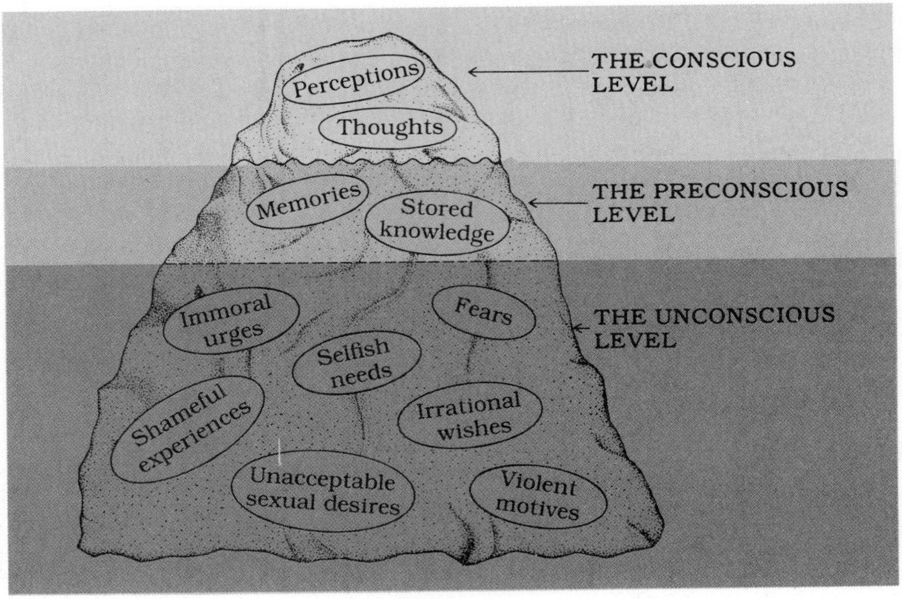

FIGURE 4.1 According to Sigmund Freud, many memories, impulses, and feelings exist below the level of conscious awareness. We could note that any film that draws an audience seems to derive its plot from items that populate the unconscious.

Consciousness as Direct Inner Awareness   Close your eyes. Imagine spilling a can of bright red paint across a black tabletop. Watch it spread across the black, shiny surface, then spill onto the floor. Although this image may be vivid, you did not "see" it literally. Your eyes and no other sensory organs were involved. You were conscious of the image through **direct inner awareness.**

We are conscious of, or have direct inner awareness of, thoughts, images, emotions, and memories. We are conscious of, or know of, the presence of all these cognitive processes without using our senses.

Sigmund Freud, the founder of psychoanalysis, differentiated thoughts and feelings of which we are conscious, or aware, from those which are preconscious and unconscious (see Figure 4.1). **Preconscious** material is not currently in awareness, but is readily available. As you answer the following questions, you will summon up "preconscious" information: What did you eat for dinner yesterday? About what time did you wake up this morning? What's happening outside the window or down the hall right now? What's your phone number? We can make these preconscious bits of information conscious simply by directing our inner awareness, or attention, to them. We had not been aware of them because our attention had been focused elsewhere—presumably on matters that were more important, or at least more timely.

According to Freud, still other mental events are **unconscious,** or unavailable to awareness under most circumstances. Freud believed that certain memories were painful and certain impulses (primarily sexual and aggressive impulses) were unacceptable. Therefore, we would place them out of awareness, or **repress** them, to escape feelings of anxiety, guilt, and shame. Freud theorized the very process of repression to be unconscious, or automatic. After all, you can't choose to stop thinking about an unacceptable impulse and, at the same time, be unaware that it ever existed.

Direct inner awareness Knowledge of one's own thoughts, feelings, and memories, without use of sensory organs—another definition of consciousness.

Preconscious In psychoanalytic theory, descriptive of material that is not in awareness but can be brought into awareness by focusing one's attention. (The Latin root *prae-* means "before.")

Unconscious In psychoanalytic theory, descriptive of ideas and feelings that are not available to awareness.

Repress In psychoanalytic theory, to eject anxiety-provoking ideas, impulses, or images from awareness, without awareness that one is doing so.

Still, people do sometimes choose to stop thinking about distracting or unacceptable ideas. This conscious method of putting unwanted mental events out of awareness is termed **suppression.** We may suppress thoughts of a date when we need to study for a test. (We may also try to suppress thoughts of an unpleasant test when we are on a date so that the evening will not be ruined.)

Some bodily processes are **nonconscious**—incapable of being experienced either through sensory awareness or direct inner awareness. The growing of hair and the carrying of oxygen in the blood are nonconscious. We can see that our hair has grown, but have no sense receptors that provide sensations related to the process. We can feel the need to breathe but we cannot directly experience the exchange of carbon dioxide and oxygen.

Consciousness as Personal Unity: The Sense of Self   To the newborn, this world must seem a confusing disarray of sensory inputs. But gradually we begin to sort things out and better organize our perceptions. We also learn to differentiate us from that which is not us. We develop a sense of being persons, individuals. There is a totality to our impressions, thoughts, and feelings that comprises our conscious existence—our continuing sense of **self** in a changing world.

In this usage of the word, consciousness *is* self. Cognitive psychologists view a person's consciousness as an important determinant of the person's behavior. Humanistic psychologists (see Chapters 1 and 9) view consciousness—self-awareness and the sense of being a person—as the essence of what it means to be human. Traditional psychoanalysts tend to stress the relative importance of *un*conscious processes in determining human behavior (see Chapter 9). Behaviorists (see Chapter 1) have stressed the importance of environmental or situational determinants of behavior. But social learning theorists, who place themselves largely within the behavioral tradition, have argued that the prediction of behavior requires knowledge of elements of a person's experience, like values and expectations, that have the flavor of a continuing conscious sense of self. These matters will be discussed further in Chapters 9 and 10.

Consciousness as the Waking State   The least controversial meaning of the word *consciousness* describes the normal waking state, as opposed, for example, to sleep. From this perspective, sleep, meditation, the hypnotic "trance," and the disordered perceptions that can accompany use of consciousness-altering drugs are considered **altered states of consciousness.**

For the remainder of this chapter we shall explore various states of consciousness and the agents that bring them about. These states and agents include sleep and dreams, a number of drugs, meditation, biofeedback, and hypnosis.

Sleep and Dreams

Sleep has always been a fascinating topic. After all, we spend about one-third of our adult lives sleeping. Most of us complain when we do not sleep at least six hours or so, but some people sleep for an hour or less a day and lead otherwise healthy and normal lives.

Suppression The deliberate, or conscious, placing of certain ideas, impulses, or images out of awareness.

Nonconscious Descriptive of bodily processes, such as the growing of hair, of which we cannot become conscious. We may "recognize" that our hair is growing but cannot directly experience the biological process.

Self The totality of impressions, thoughts, and feelings. The sense of self is another definition of consciousness. See Chapter 9.

Altered states of consciousness States other than the normal waking state, including sleep, meditation, the hypnotic "trance," and the distorted perceptions produced by use of some drugs.

Why do we sleep? Why do we dream? Why do some of us have trouble getting to sleep, and what can we do about it? We don't have all the answers to these questions, but we have learned a great deal in the past couple of decades. In this section we explore the stages and functions of sleep, dreams, and sleep disorders, including insomnia and night terrors.

The Stages of Sleep

When I was an undergraduate psychology student, I first heard that psychologists studied sleep by "connecting" people to the **electroencephalograph** (EEG), a device that measures the electrical activity of the brain. I had a gruesome image of people somehow being "plugged in" to the EEG. Not so. Electrodes are simply attached to the scalp or other areas with tape or paste. Later, once the brain activity under study has been duly recorded, they are simply removed. A bit of soap and water and you're as good as new.

The EEG provides psychologists with some interesting scrawls that show the frequency and strength of the electric currents of the brain (see Figures 4.2 and 4.4). A trip from a high point to a low point, and back, is called a cycle. During the deepest stage of sleep—or stage 4 sleep—only about one to three of these cycles occur each second. So the printouts in Figure 4.2 show what happens over a period of 15 seconds or so. During stage 4 sleep, the brain emits slow but strong **delta waves.** Delta waves reach relatively great height or amplitude, when compared with other brain waves. Their amplitude reflects their strength. The strength or energy of brain waves is expressed in the electric unit **volts.**

Figure 4.2 shows five stages of sleep: four stages of **non-rapid-eye-movement** (NREM) sleep, and one stage of **rapid-eye-movement** (REM) sleep. When we close our eyes and begin to relax before going to sleep, our brains emit many **alpha waves.** Alpha waves are low-amplitude brain waves of about

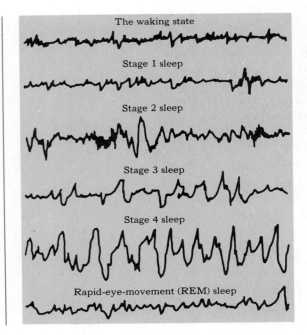

The waking state

Stage 1 sleep

Stage 2 sleep

Stage 3 sleep

Stage 4 sleep

Rapid-eye-movement (REM) sleep

FIGURE 4.2 The Stages of Sleep. This figure illustrates typical EEG patterns for the stages of sleep. During REM sleep, EEG patterns resemble those of the lightest stage of sleep, stage 1 sleep. For this reason, REM sleep is often termed *paradoxical sleep.* As sleep progresses from stage 1 to stage 4, brain waves become slower and their amplitude increases. Dreams are most vivid during REM sleep. Night terrors tend to occur during stage 4 sleep.

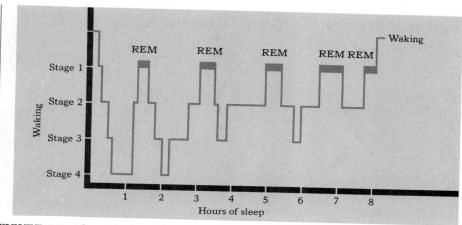

FIGURE 4.3 Sleep Cycles. This figure illustrates the alternation of REM and non-REM sleep for the typical sleeper. There are about five periods of REM sleep during an eight-hour night. Sleep is deeper earlier in the night, and REM sleep tends to become prolonged toward morning.

eight–twelve cycles per second. (Through biofeedback training, discussed later in the chapter, people have been taught to relax by purposefully emitting alpha waves.)

As we enter stage 1 sleep, our brain waves slow down from the alpha rhythm and enter a pattern of **theta waves.** Theta waves have a frequency of four–six cycles per second, and are accompanied by slow, rolling eye movements. The transition from alpha waves to theta waves may be accompanied by a **hypnagogic state,** during which we may experience brief hallucinatory, dreamlike images that resemble vivid photographs. These images may be somehow linked to creativity. Stage 1 sleep is the lightest stage of sleep. If we are awakened from stage 1 sleep, we may feel that we have not slept at all.

After 30 to 40 minutes of stage 1 sleep, we undergo a rather steep descent into sleep stages 2, 3, and 4 (see Figure 4.3). Stage 4 is the deepest stage of sleep, from which it is most difficult to be awakened. During stage 2, **sleep spindles** appear. These are rather short bursts of rapid brain waves of a frequency of 13–16 cycles per second. During stages 3 and 4, we produce the slower delta waves.

After perhaps half an hour of deep stage 4 sleep, we begin a relatively rapid journey back upward through the stages until we enter REM sleep (Figure 4.3). REM sleep derives its name from the *rapid eye movements,* observable beneath our closed lids, that characterize this stage. During REM sleep we produce relatively rapid, low-amplitude brain waves that resemble those of light stage 1 sleep. REM sleep is also called paradoxical sleep. This is because the EEG patterns observed during REM sleep suggest a level of arousal similar to that of the waking state (Figure 4.2). However, we are difficult to awaken during REM sleep. If we are awakened during REM sleep, we report that we have been dreaming 80 percent of the time. (We also dream during NREM sleep, but less frequently. We report dreaming only about 20 percent of the time when awakened during NREM sleep.)

As you can see from Figure 4.3, we tend to undergo five trips through the different stages of sleep each night. These trips include about five periods of REM sleep. Our first journey through stage 4 sleep is usually longest. Sleep tends to become lighter as the night wears on. Our periods of REM sleep tend

Theta waves Slow brain waves produced during the hypnagogic state.

Hypnagogic state (hip–nuh–GAHDGE–jick). The drowsy interval between waking and sleeping, characterized by brief, hallucinatory, dreamlike experiences.

Sleep spindles Short bursts of rapid brain waves that occur during stage 2 sleep.

Sleep and Dreams **127**

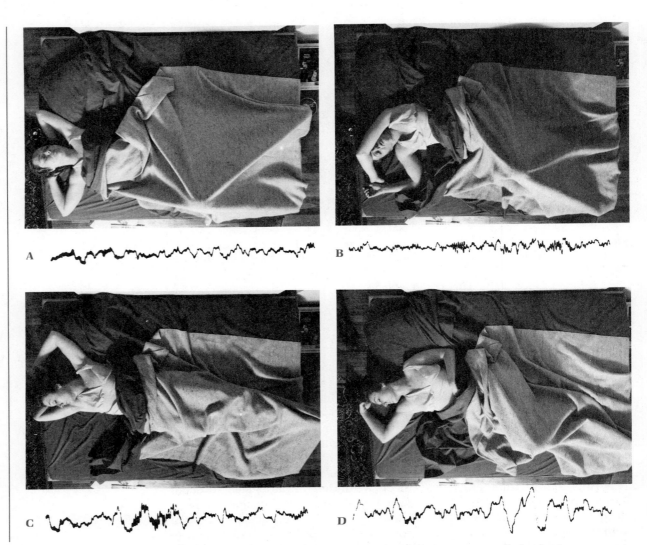

FIGURE 4.4 A. In the first of normal sleep's four stages, small, fast brain waves appear on the EEG record. B. In the second stage, the brain shows short bursts of activity as light sleep begins to deepen. C. In the third stage, larger, slower brain waves appear as the half-hour descent to deep sleep continues. D. The fourth stage, with large delta waves, is followed by ascent to lighter sleep, then to dreaming (REM sleep).

to become longer, and, toward morning, our last period of REM sleep may last upwards of half an hour.

Now that we have some idea of what sleep is like, let us examine the issue of *why* we sleep.

Functions of Sleep

One outdated theory of the reasons for sleep suggested that sleep allowed the brain to rest and recuperate from the stresses of working all day. But the EEG has shown that the brain is active all night long. Moreover, at least during REM sleep, the brain waves are quite similar to those of light sleep and the waking state. So the power isn't switched off at night.

But what of sleep and the rest of the body? Most researchers would not contest the view that sleep helps rejuvenate a tired body (Levitt, 1981). Most of us have had the experience of going without sleep for a night and feeling "wrecked" the following day. Perhaps the following evening we went to bed early to "get our sleep back." Research also suggests that increased physical exertion leads to a greater proportion of time spent in NREM sleep (Walker and others, 1978). Hartmann (1973) suggests that many proteins are synthesized during NREM sleep, and that these proteins may be linked to the restorative effects of sleep. However, no one has yet discovered a relationship between sleep and the restoration of specific chemical substances.

Let us continue our study of the functions of sleep by turning to research concerning long versus short sleepers and the effects of sleep deprivation.

Long vs. Short Sleepers

Ernest Hartmann (1973) of Tufts University compared people who slept nine hours or more a night ("long sleepers") with people who slept six hours or less ("short sleepers"). He found that short sleepers tended to be more happy-go-lucky. They spent less time ruminating and were energetic, active, and relatively self-satisfied. The long sleepers were more concerned about personal achievement and social causes. They tended to be more creative and thoughtful, but were also more anxious and depressed. Hartmann also found that in general we tend to need more sleep during periods of change and stress, such as a change of jobs, an increase in work load, or an episode of depression. So it may be that sleep helps us recover from the stresses of life.

Hartmann also found that long sleepers spend proportionately more time in REM sleep than do short sleepers. Subtracting the amount of REM sleep experienced by both types of sleepers dramatically closed the gap between them. Perhaps REM sleep is at least partially responsible for the restorative function. Since much REM sleep is spent in dreaming, it has been speculated that dreams may somehow promote recovery.

Sleep Deprivation

What will happen to you if you miss sleep for one night? For several nights? If you cut down from, say, your normal seven to ten hours to just five and one half? Anecdotal and research evidence offers some suggestions.

In 1959 disc jockey Peter Tripp remained awake for eight days. Toward the end of this episode, he became so paranoid that he could not be given psychological tests (Dement, 1972). However, 17-year-old Randy Gardner remained awake for 264 consecutive hours (11 days), and did not show serious psychological disturbance (Levitt, 1981).

In another anecdote, 10 of 11 military cadets who were ordered to engage in strenuous activity for 100 hours developed visual hallucinations, and most developed problems in balance and movement (Opstad and others, 1978). But, as noted by Levitt (1981), these cadets were also deprived of rest and food, not just sleep. According to sleep researcher Wilse Webb, carefully-controlled experiments with people who remain sleepless for several consecutive days result in few serious disturbances. Most often, participants show temporary problems in attention, confusion, or misperception (Goleman, 1982). These cognitive lapses may reflect brief episodes of borderline sleep. Participants may also show fine hand tremors, droopy eyelids, problems in focusing the eyes, and heightened sensitivity to pain. But there are few, if any, horror stories.

What if we were to decide that we wanted to spend a bit more of our lives in the waking state—to work, to study, to play, perchance to daydream? Would any ill effects attend curtailing our sleep to, say, five and one half hours a night? Webb followed 15 college men who restricted their sleep to five and one half hours for 60 days. For the first few weeks, they showed an increase in deep sleep but a decrease in REM sleep. But by the end of the first 30 days, they returned to the original level of deep sleep, but REM sleep remained at a below-normal level.

Over the 60 days the men showed little dropoff in ability to remember or to compute numbers. They did show less vigilance on one psychological test, as measured in terms of numbers of responses. But Webb suggests that this deficit may have reflected decreased motivation to perform well, rather than a falling off of perceptual sharpness. It is particularly interesting that the men reported falling asleep in class or feeling drowsy during the first week only. After that they reported *less* drowsiness than prior to the study. Did the study encourage them to permanently change their life styles? No. Despite the lack of ill effects of restricting sleep, all participants returned to their normal seven or eight hours when the study was complete.

Deprivation of REM Sleep   In some studies, animals or people have been deprived of REM sleep. With people, REM-sleep deprivation is accomplished by monitoring EEG records and eye movements and waking subjects during REM sleep.

Animals deprived of REM sleep learn more slowly and forget what they have learned more rapidly (Hartmann & Stern, 1972; Pearlman & Greenberg, 1973). There is too much individual variation to conclude that people deprived of REM sleep learn more poorly than they would otherwise (McGrath & Cohen, 1978). But it does seem that such deprivation interferes with human memory— that is, the retrieval of information that has been learned earlier (Cipolli & Salzarulo, 1978; Bloch and others, 1979).

There is some recent research concerning possible links between REM sleep and various forms of abnormal behavior such as hallucinations and depression (see Levitt, 1981, p. 270). But this research is in its early stages, and it would be premature to draw any conclusions.

In any event, people deprived of REM sleep tend to show *REM-rebound.* That is, they tend to spend more time in REM sleep during subsequent sleep periods. They catch up.

As noted earlier, it is during REM sleep that we tend to dream. Let us now turn our attention to dreams, a mystery about which people have theorized for centuries.

Dreams

Just what is the stuff of dreams? **Dreams** are a form of cognitive activity that occur during sleep. Like vivid memories and daytime fantasies, dreams involve visual images in the absence of external visual stimulation. Some dreams are so realistic and well organized that we feel that they must be real—that we simply cannot be dreaming this time. You may have had such a dream on the night before a test. The dream would have been that you had taken the

Dreams A sequence of images or thoughts that occur during sleep. Dreams may be vague and loosely plotted, or vivid and intricate.

test and now it is all over. (Ah, what disappointment then prevailed when you woke up to realize that such was not the case!) Other dreams are disorganized and unformed.

Dreams are most vivid during REM sleep. Then they are most likely to have clear imagery and coherent plots, even if some of the content is fantastic. Plots are vaguer and images more fleeting during NREM sleep. You may well have a dream every time you are in REM sleep. Therefore, if you sleep for eight hours and undergo five sleep cycles, you may have five dreams. Upon waking, you may feel that time seemed to expand or contract during your dreams, so that during ten or 15 minutes your dream content ranged over days or weeks. But dreams tend to take place in "real time": 15 minutes of events fills about 15 minutes of dreaming. Your dream theater is quite flexible: you can dream in black and white and in full color.

Theories of the Content of Dreams   You may recall dreams involving fantastic adventures, but according to Calvin Hall (1966), who has interviewed hundreds of dreamers and recorded the content of thousands of dreams, most dreams are simple extensions of the activities and problems of the day. Hall links dreams to life stresses. If we are preoccupied with illness or death, sexual or aggressive urges, or moral dilemmas, we are likely to dream about them. The characters in our dreams are more likely to be friends and neighbors than spies, monsters, and princes.

Sigmund Freud theorized that dreams reflected unconscious wishes and urges. He argued that through dreams we could express impulses that we would censor during the day. Moreover, the content of dreams was symbolic of unconscious fantasized objects, such as genital organs (see Table 4.1). In

TABLE 4.1   Dream Symbols in Psychoanalytic Theory

Symbols for the Male Genital Organs

airplanes	fish	neckties	tools	weapons
bullets	hands	poles	trains	
feet	hose	snakes	trees	
fire	knives	sticks	umbrellas	

Symbols for the Female Genital Organs

bottles	caves	doors	ovens	ships
boxes	chests	hats	pockets	tunnels
cases	closets	jars	pots	

Symbols for Sexual Intercourse

climbing a ladder	entering a room
climbing a staircase	flying in an airplane
crossing a bridge	riding a horse
driving an automobile	riding a roller coaster
riding an elevator	walking into a tunnel or down a hall

Symbols for the Female's Breasts

apples	peaches

Freud theorized that the content of dreams symbolized urges, wishes, and objects of fantasy that we would censor in the waking state.

Incubus (INK–cue–bus). (1) A spirit or demon thought in medieval times to lie on sleeping people, especially on women for sexual purposes. (2) A nightmare.

Succubus (SUCK–cue–bus). A female demon thought in medieval times to have sexual intercourse with sleeping men.

Chapter 12 we shall see that a major part of Freud's method of psychoanalysis involved interpretation of the dreams of his clients. Freud also believed that dreams "protected sleep" by providing imagery that would help keep disturbing, repressed thoughts out of awareness.

The view that dreams "protect sleep" has been challenged by the observation that disturbing events of the day tend to be followed by related disturbing dreams—not protective imagery (Foulkes, 1971). Our behavior in dreams is also generally consistent with our waking behavior (Carrington, 1972; Cohen, 1973). Most dreams, then, are unlikely candidates for the expression (even disguised) of repressed urges. The moralistic liver tends to be the moralistic dreamer.

Hobson and McCarley (1977) suggest that dreams reflect activation of the pons and automatic integration of this activity by the cerebral cortex. The dream's content reflects the neural activity of parts of the cortex involved in vision, hearing, and memory. From this perspective, dreams reflect biological rather than psychological activity. Even so, there might still be a greater than chance tendency to dream about events of the day, since these events would have been represented more recently in the cortex.

Nightmares Have you ever dreamt that something heavy was on your chest and watching as you breathed? Or that you were trying to run from a terrible threat but couldn't gain your footing or coordinate your leg muscles?

In the Middle Ages such nightmares were thought to be the work of demons called incubi and succubi (singular: **incubus** and **succubus**). By and

In the Middle Ages nightmares were thought to be the work of demons who were sent to pay sleepers for their sins. In this picture, "Nightmare," by Fuseli, a demon sits upon a woman who is dreaming a nightmare, and threatens to suffocate her.

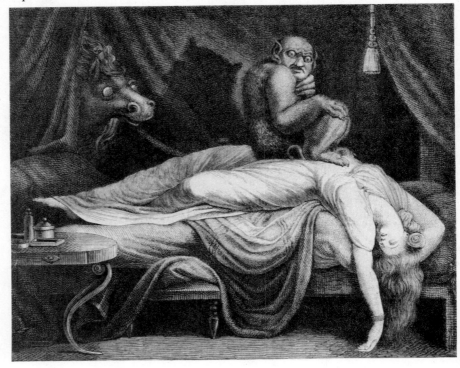

large, they were seen as a form of retribution. That is, they were sent to pay you for your sins. They might sit on your chest and observe you fiendishly (how else would a fiend observe, if not "fiendishly"?), as suggested in Fuseli's "Nightmare," or they might try to suffocate you. If you were given to sexual fantasies or behavior, they might have sexual intercourse with you.

Nightmares, as most pleasant dreams, are generally products of REM sleep. We shall discuss the more disturbing "night terrors" under the section on sleep disorders.

The Dreamer's Paralysis Why don't we engage in muscular activity and thrash about when we dream? Of course, it is fortunate that we don't. If we did, we might wake up frequently, and we could also hurt ourselves.

But still, our brains are active when we dream, and the content of many dreams involves strenuous activity. Does some biological or psychological process prevent our muscles from acting in accord with our dreams? According to UCLA researcher Michael Chase (1981), the answer is yes. During REM sleep, which is when we do most of our dreaming, motor neurons are barraged by a chemical that inhibits them from responding to excitatory messages. It may be that abnormal functioning of this chemical is involved in various sleep disorders, ranging from sleepwalking to narcolepsy (paralytic attacks during the waking state).

In any event, the normal functioning of this chemical saves our bed partners, and ourselves, a good deal of wear and tear.

Sleep Disorders

There are a number of sleep disorders. Some, like insomnia, are all too familiar. Others, like narcolepsy, seem somewhat exotic. In this section we shall discuss insomnia, narcolepsy, apnea, sudden infant death syndrome, and the deep-sleep disorders—night terrors, bedwetting, and sleepwalking.

Insomnia **Insomnia** refers to three types of sleeping problems: difficulty falling asleep (sleep-onset insomnia), difficulty remaining asleep through the night, and awakening prematurely in the morning. Perhaps 30 million Americans suffer from insomnia (Clark and others, 1981), with women complaining of the disorder more frequently than men. Millions of sleeping pills are downed each evening.

As a group, people who suffer from insomnia show higher levels of autonomic activity as they try to get to sleep and as they sleep (Haynes and others, 1981; Johns and others, 1971; Monroe, 1967). Persons with sleep-onset insomnia obtain higher anxiety scores on questionnaires and show more muscle tension in the forehead than nonsufferers (Haynes and others, 1974). Personality tests also find poor sleepers to be more depressed and **ruminative** than good sleepers, more concerned about physical complaints, and more shy and retiring (Freedman & Sattler, 1982; Marks & Monroe, 1976; Monroe & Marks, 1977). Insomnia comes and goes with many people, increasing during periods of anxiety and tension.

Insomniacs (that's a word that will keep you awake) tend to compound their sleep problems through their efforts to somehow force themselves to get to sleep (Kamens, 1980; Youkilis & Bootzin, 1981). Their concern heightens autonomic activity and muscle tension. You cannot force or will yourself to get to sleep. You can only set the stage for it by lying down and relaxing when

Insomnia A term for three types of sleeping problems: (1) difficulty falling asleep, (2) difficulty remaining asleep, and (3) waking early. (From the Latin *in–*, meaning "not," and *somnus*, meaning "sleep.")

Ruminative Given to prolonged turning over of thoughts. (From the Latin *ruminare*, meaning "to chew [the cud]" as a cow does.)

Tolerance Habituation to a drug, with the result that increasingly higher doses of the drug are needed to achieve similar effects.

Autogenic training A method for reducing tension involving repeated suggestions that the limbs are becoming warmer and heavier and that one's breathing is becoming more regular.

you are tired. If you focus on sleep too closely, it will elude you. Yet millions go to bed each night dreading the possibility of sleep-onset insomnia.

How (and How Not) to Get to Sleep at Night *Sleeping pills.* No question about it: The most common method for fighting insomnia in the United States is popping pills. Sleeping pills may be effective—for a while. They generally work through reducing arousal. At first lowered arousal may be effective in itself. Focusing on changes in arousal may also distract you from your efforts to somehow *get* to sleep. Expectation of success may also help.

But there are problems with sleeping pills. First, you attribute your success to the pill and not yourself, creating dependency on the pill rather than self-reliance. Second, you develop **tolerance** for sleeping pills. With continued usage you must progressively increase the dose to achieve the same effects. Third, high doses of these chemicals can be dangerous, especially if mixed with an alcoholic beverage or two. Sleeping pills and alcohol both depress the activity of the central nervous system, and their effects are additive.

Relaxation. Recently, psychological methods for coping with insomnia have been developed. These methods reduce tension directly, as with muscle relaxation exercises. They also involve cognitive elements which distract us from striving to get to sleep.

Focusing on releasing muscle tension has been shown to reduce the amount of time needed to fall asleep and the incidence of waking during the night. It increases the number of hours slept and leaves us feeling more rested in the morning (Lick & Heffler, 1977; Weil & Gottfried, 1973). A common method for easing muscle tension is progressive relaxation, which we shall discuss in Chapter 10. Biofeedback training (Haynes and others, 1977) and **autogenic training** (Nicassio & Bootzin, 1974) have also been used successfully. Biofeedback is discussed later in this chapter. In autogenic training, one reduces muscle tension by focusing on suggestions that the limbs are growing warm and heavy and that the breathing is becoming regular. These methods also provide one with something on which to focus other than trying to fall asleep.

Coping with exaggerated fears. You need not be a sleep expert to realize that convincing yourself that the day will be ruined unless you get to sleep *right now* will increase, rather than decrease, bedtime tensions. As noted earlier, sleep does seem to restore us, especially after physical exertion. But we often exaggerate the problems that will befall us if we do not sleep. Here are some beliefs that increase bedtime tension, and some alternatives that you can think if they apply to you:

Exaggerated Belief	**Alternative Belief**
If I don't get to sleep, I'll feel wrecked tomorrow.	Not necessarily. If I'm tired, I can go to bed early tomorrow night.
It's unhealthy for me not to get more sleep.	Not necessarily. Some people do very well on only a few hours of sleep.
I'll wreck my sleeping schedule for the whole week if I don't get to sleep very soon.	Not at all. If I'm tired, I'll just go to bed a bit earlier. I'll get up about the same time with no problem.
If I don't get to sleep, I won't be able to concentrate on that big test tomorrow.	Possibly, but my fears may be exaggerated. I may just as well relax or get up and do something enjoyable for a while

Avoiding ruminating in bed. Don't plan or worry about tomorrow in bed. When you lie down for sleep, you may organize thoughts for the day for a few minutes, but then allow yourself to relax or engage in fantasy. If an important idea comes to you, jot it down on a handy pad so that you won't lose it. But if thoughts persist, get up and follow them elsewhere. Let your bed be a place for relaxation and sleep—not your study. Even a waterbed is not a think tank.

Establishing a regular routine. Sleeping late can encourage sleep-onset insomnia. Set your alarm for the same time each morning and get up, regardless of how many hours you have slept. By sticking to a regular time for rising, you'll be indirectly encouraging yourself to get to sleep at a regular time as well.

Using fantasy. Psychologist Jerome Singer (1975) notes that fantasies or "daydreams" are almost universal and may occur naturally as we fall asleep. You can allow yourself to "go with" fantasies that occur at bedtime, or purposefully use fantasies to get to sleep. You may be able to ease yourself to sleep by focusing on a sun-drenched beach, with waves lapping on the shore, or on a walk through a mountain meadow on a summer day. You can construct your own "mind trips" and paint their details finely. With mind trips you conserve fuel and avoid lines at airports.

Narcolepsy   In **narcolepsy,** which is in a sense the mirror image of insomnia, the person falls suddenly, irresistibly asleep. Narcolepsy afflicts as many as 100,000 people in the United States and seems to run in families. The "sleep attack" lasts about 15 minutes, after which the person awakens, feeling refreshed. Despite being refreshing, these sleep episodes are dangerous and

Narcolepsy A sleep disorder characterized by uncontrollable seizures of sleep during the waking state. (From the Greek *narke,* meaning "sleep," and *lepsia,* meaning "an attack.")

How Do You Beat Insomnia? Simple—Just Stay Awake as Long as You Can

What if you had tried everything to get to sleep?—counting sheep, drinking warm milk, even relaxation training at the Temple University Behavior Therapy Unit, and nothing helped? How would you react if your therapist then suggested that you had been going about it backwards—that you should be trying to stay awake as long as you could?

These are the instructions L. Michael Ascher (Ascher & Efran, 1978) gave five insomniacs at the university clinic when all else—including relaxation training—had failed. The five were given rationales for staying awake that sounded logical. Some were told that it would allow them to learn more about their bedtime thoughts. Others were simply told to extend their relaxation exercises into the wee hours.

Guess what: All five clients "failed" at their new assignments. They fell asleep too quickly to accomplish these goals. During a two-week assessment period, their sleep-onset time fell to an average of six to 15 minutes from a pretreatment average of 29 to 90 minutes. In a follow-up experiment (Turner & Ascher, 1979), it was found that instructions to re-

main awake were as effective as more established methods of relaxation training, establishing a regular routine, and avoiding naps.

Why were instructions to remain awake effective? Do we chalk it up to the general perversity of human nature? Not at all. Insomniacs tend to become trapped in a vicious cycle in which anxiety over not sleeping increases bodily tensions. These tensions then confirm the appropriateness of their anxiety and their expectations of failure. Instructions to remain awake remove clients "from this system"—from the vicious cycle of focusing on falling asleep and thereby heightening tension (Ascher & Efran, 1978).

This form of therapy is not unique to insomnia. Psychiatrist Viktor Frankl (1975) long used this method with many anxiety-related problems. It is called *paradoxical intention.* Sometimes we are more effective at achieving our ends when we try not to achieve them. But don't carry this beyond its limits—after all, you're not likely to do well in a course by cutting all classes and never cracking the textbook.

frightening. They can occur while a person is driving or engaged in work with sharp tools. They may also be accompanied by sudden collapse of muscle groups or the entire body (see Figure 4.5); sleep paralysis, in which the person cannot move during the transition from the waking state to sleep; and hallucinations as of a person or object sitting on the chest.

The causes of narcolepsy are unknown, but it is thought to be a disorder of REM-sleep functioning. Stimulants and antidepressant drugs have helped many narcolepsy sufferers.

Apnea   **Apnea** is a potentially dangerous sleep disorder that afflicts as many as one million men, primarily the overweight. In apnea, sleepers stop breathing periodically through the night, as many as 500 times! At such times they may suddenly sit up, gasp to begin breathing again, then fall back asleep. Such sleepers are stimulated nearly but not quite to waking by the buildup of carbon dioxide.

Causes of apnea may include anatomical deformities that clog the air passageways, like a thick palate, or a defect in the breathing centers of the brain. Apnea can be treated by use of **tranquilizers** and, sometimes, surgery.

Sudden Infant Death Syndrome (SIDS)   **SIDS,** or crib death, kills 6,000 to 7,000 children during the first year of life in the United States each year. The child goes to sleep, apparently in perfect health, and is found dead in the morning. New parents often live in dread of SIDS, checking their infants regularly through the night to see that they are breathing. If they stop breathing, but are stimulated, they usually begin breathing again. Parents of children who die from SIDS also typically experience strong guilt that they failed to monitor or catch their children in time. Cribs and monitors are available that will sound an alarm if the infant stops breathing.

SIDS is all the more frightening because its causes, like those of sleep apnea, are unknown. But it may reflect the infant's immature nervous system or defects in the respiratory centers of the brain. The risk also seems greatest when the infant has a cold.

Deep-Sleep Disorders: Night Terrors, Bed-Wetting, and Sleepwalking
Night terrors, bed-wetting, and sleepwalking all occur during deep (stage 3 or 4) sleep, are more common among children, and may reflect immaturity of the nervous system.

Night terrors are similar to but more severe than nightmares. Night terrors usually occur during deep sleep while nightmares take place during REM sleep. Night terrors occur early during the night while nightmares are usually events of the morning hours (Hartmann, 1981). The dreamer may suddenly sit up with a surge in the heart and respiration rates, talk incoherently, and move about wildly. The dreamer is never fully awake, returns to sleep, and may recall a brief image, as of someone pressing on the chest. But, in contrast to the nightmare, memories of the episode are not vivid. Night terrors are often decreased by a minor tranquilizer at bedtime, which reduces the amount of time spent in stage 4 sleep.

Bed-wetting is often seen as a stigma that reflects parental harshness, or the child's attempt to punish the parents, but this disorder, too, may stem from immaturity of the nervous system. In most cases, bed-wetting resolves itself before adolescence, often by age eight. Behavior therapy methods that condition children to awaken when about to urinate have been helpful. The

FIGURE 4.5 In a narcolepsy experiment at Stanford, this poodle barks, nods, then falls suddenly asleep. The causes of narcolepsy are unknown, but it is thought to be a disorder of REM sleep functioning.

antidepressant drug *imipramine* often helps by increasing bladder capacity. But often all that is needed is reassurance that no one need be "to blame" for bed-wetting and that most children "outgrow" the disorder.

As many as 15 percent of children sleepwalk at least once. Sleepwalkers may roam about almost nightly, while their parents fret about the accidents that could befall them. Sleepwalkers typically do not remember their excursions, but may respond to questions while they are up and about. Mild tranquilizers and maturity typically put an end to sleepwalking.

We have noted that drugs often play a role in the treatment of sleep disorders. But drugs are used "recreationally" or to "expand consciousness" as well as to treat problems. Let us now turn our attention to a number of such drugs.

Drugs

The world is a supermarket of consciousness-altering chemical substances, or drugs. America is flooded with hundreds of drugs that distort perceptions and change mood—drugs that take you up, let you down, and move you across town. Some people use drugs because their friends do, or because their parents tell them not to. Some are seeking pleasure. Others, like our Himalayan travelers, are seeking inner truth. We go off on our internal trips, and many times drugs provide both the vehicle and the fuel.

Following a dropoff in popularity during the 1960s, alcohol has reasserted its dominance among drugs used on college campuses. The majority of college students have tried marijuana, and perhaps one in five smokes it regularly. Many Americans take **depressants** to get to sleep at night and **stimulants** to get going in the morning. Valium, a minor tranquilizer used to relieve anxiety and tension, is the most widely prescribed drug in the world. Heroin may literally be the opium of the lower classes, while cocaine is the toy of the well-to-do. Despite laws, moral pronouncements, medical warnings, and an occasional exaggerated horror story, drugs are very much with us.

We shall deal with some general issues in drug use and abuse, and then turn our attention to specific drugs.

Depressant A drug that lowers the rate of activity of the nervous system. (From the Latin *de–*, meaning "down," and *premere*, meaning "to press.")

Stimulant A drug that increases activity of the nervous system.

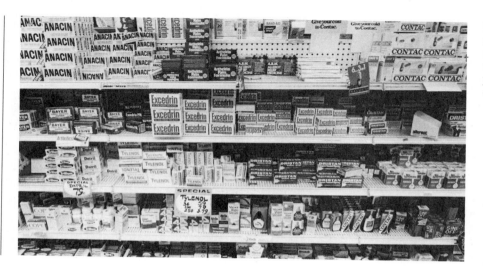

We are a drug-oriented society. This is just a sampling of the vast array of drugs available without prescription at the local drugstore.

Drugs   **137**

Alcoholism Drinking that persistently impairs personal, social, or physical well-being.

Dependence Habitual use of a drug. Dependence may be physiological or psychological.

Addiction Physiological dependence on a drug. Addiction reflects bodily changes that stem from prolonged use of certain drugs.

Abstinence syndrome A characteristic cluster of symptoms that results from sudden decrease in the level of usage of an addictive drug. (From the Latin *abstinere,* meaning "to hold back.")

Psychoactive Giving rise to psychological effects.

Delirium tremens A condition characterized by sweating, restlessness, disorientation, and hallucinations. The "D.T.s" occur in some chronic alcohol users when there is a sudden decrease in usage. (From the Latin *de–,* meaning "from," and *lira,* meaning "line" or "furrow"—suggesting that one's behavior is away from the beaten track or norm.)

Disorientation Gross confusion. Loss of sense of time, place, and the identity of people.

Hallucinations (hal–loose–sin–NAY–shuns). Perceptions in the absence of sensation. (From the Latin *hallucinari,* meaning "to wander mentally.")

Use and Abuse Where does drug *use* end and *abuse* begin? If we use the legal status of a drug as our criterion, the use of prohibited substances like heroin, LSD, and marijuana constitutes abuse. But if we focus on whether one's use of the drug interferes with ability to meet the demands of daily life, abuse is not so easy to define. For example, the American Psychiatric Association (1980) defines alcohol abuse, or **alcoholism,** as drinking that repeatedly interferes with physical, personal, or social well-being. If you are missing work because you are drunk, or "sleeping it off," your behavior fits the definition. From this perspective, the amount of the drug being used is not the central factor. It is whether the person's pattern of use interferes with other areas of life.

Dependence, Addiction, and the Abstinence Syndrome Drug **dependence** is generally defined as habitual use of a drug. Dependence has been confused with **addiction,** but addiction has a more specific meaning. Addiction is *physiological* dependence on a drug. Addiction implies that protracted use of the drug leads to bodily changes with certain biological and psychological effects. The central effect is the occurrence of withdrawal symptoms, or an **abstinence syndrome,** when the level of usage is suddenly decreased. Addictive drugs have characteristic abstinence syndromes. The abstinence syndrome for alcohol includes anxiety, tremors, restlessness, weakness, rapid pulse, and high blood pressure. A frequent effect of addiction is tolerance. When the body becomes habituated to a drug, higher doses may be required to achieve similar effects.

People may become *psychologically* dependent on a drug even if it is nonaddictive. Psychological dependence is defined as repeated use of the substance as a way of dealing with stress. One may become psychologically dependent on a drug without increasing tolerance. Many regular marijuana users show a *reverse* tolerance for the marijuana "high." With regular usage, they require relatively *less* marijuana to achieve this high.

Physiological Effects and Expectations Our response to a substance reflects (a) the physiological effects of that substance, and (b) our *expectations* about its effects. Consider the case of reverse tolerance for the marijuana high. It may be that some of the **psychoactive** substances in marijuana smoke take a long time to be metabolized by the body. The effects of new doses would then be added to those of the substances remaining in the body. But regular users also *expect* certain effects. These expectations may interact with even mild bodily cues present in slight intoxication, producing effects previously attained only through higher doses.

Once people have become psychologically dependent on a substance, they also show concern or anxiety over going without it. Many signs of anxiety—shakiness, rapid pulse, sweating, and so on—overlap with abstinence syndromes that result from addiction. Thus people may believe that they are addicted to a substance when they are only psychologically dependent. Still, there are some aspects of abstinence for certain drugs that are unmistakably physiological. One example is **delirium tremens** ("the D.T.s"), which are experienced by some chronic alcoholics when they suddenly decrease or suspend usage. D.T.s are characterized by heavy sweating, restlessness, **disorientation,** and terrifying **hallucinations**—often of creepy, crawling animals.

Causal Factors in Drug Dependence

Cummings provides a striking example of how dependent people can become on a substance—in this case, water. A group of hospitalized alcoholics "moved their cots into the bathroom while the staff looked on, baffled. After several days it was found that these alcoholics had substituted water for alcohol. If one drinks eight gallons or more of water per day, the **pH** level of the blood is altered and one becomes **intoxicated.** The consequence of this was that the patients had to move their cots to the bathroom to be near the spout and the toilet, because eight gallons of water per day results in constant drinking and urinating" (1979, p. 1121). Numerous psychological and physiological causes for dependence on certain substances have been advanced.

Psychoanalytic Views   Psychoanalytic explanations of substance abuse propose that drugs help people control or express unconscious needs and impulses. Alcoholism, for example, may reflect the need to remain dependent on an overprotective mother, or the effort to reduce emotional conflicts, or to cope with unconscious homosexual impulses.

Behavioral/Social Learning Views   Learning theorists suggest that first usage of tranquilizing agents like Valium and alcohol usually results from observing others or receiving a recommendation. But subsequent usage is reinforced by the drugs' positive effects on the mood and their reduction of unpleasant sensations like anxiety, fear, and tension. Avoidance of withdrawal symptoms for addicted people is also reinforcing. Carrying the substance around is reinforcing because one can then avoid worrying about having to go without it. Some people will simply not leave the house without taking Valium along. After all, *something* upsetting could occur *sometime* during the day.

Genetic Predispositions   There is growing evidence that people can have a genetic predisposition toward addiction to certain substances (Vaillant, 1982). For example, rats have been selectively bred to show preference for alcohol over other beverages (Sigovia-Riquelma and others, 1971). Moreover, the biological children of alcoholics who are raised by adoptive parents are more likely to develop alcohol-related problems than are the natural children of the adoptive parents (Goodwin and others, 1973; Goodwin, 1979). Cummings (1979) argues that not everyone can become addicted to heroin. Of newborn children of addicted mothers, about 92 percent show an abstinence syndrome, but the other eight percent do not. Cummings states that this difference cannot be attributed to the quantity of heroin used by the mother.

Prenatal Factors   The prenatal environment may also play a role. Julien (1978) reports that small amounts of alcohol drunk by mothers during certain stages of pregnancy can predispose the child to alcohol-related problems.

Let us now consider the effects of some specific substances, beginning with alcohol.

Alcohol

No drug has meant so much to so many as alcohol. It's our dinnertime relaxant, our bedtime **sedative,** our cocktail party social facilitator. We celebrate holy days, applaud our accomplishments, and express joyous wishes

pH A chemical symbol expressing the acidity of a solution. Abbreviation for "hydrogen power."

Intoxicated Drunk.

Sedative A drug that soothes or quiets restlessness or agitation. (From the Latin *sedare,* meaning "to settle.")

Two facets of alcohol. No drug has meant so much to so many as alcohol. Yet for many, alcohol is a central problem of life.

with alcohol. The young assert their maturity with alcohol. The elderly use it to stimulate circulation in peripheral areas of the body. Alcohol kills germs on surface wounds. Some pediatricians even swab the painful gums of teething babies with alcohol.

Alcohol is the tranquilizer you can buy without prescription. It is the relief from anxiety you can swallow in public without criticism or stigmatization. A man who pops a Valium tablet may look weak. A man who chugalugs a bottle of beer may be perceived as "macho."

No drug has been so abused as alcohol. Perhaps 10 million Americans are alcoholics. Compare this figure to the 200,000 who use heroin regularly, or the 300,000 to 500,000 who abuse sedatives. The greatest number of problem drinkers is found among men aged 30–34 and 45–49, and among women aged 21–24 and 45–49 (Cahalan, 1970). Excessive drinking has been linked to loss of employment and downward movement in social status (Vaillant & Milofsky, 1982). Yet half of all Americans use alcohol, and despite widespread marijuana use, it is the drug of choice among adolescents.

Effects of Alcohol Adolescent and adult samples expect that alcohol will have a number of effects, including reducing tension, diverting one from worrying, enhancing pleasure, increasing social ability, and transforming experiences for the better (Brown and others, 1980; Christiansen and others, 1982). What *does* alcohol do?

Chemically, alcohol is a depressant. It slows the activity of the central nervous system. It relaxes and deadens minor aches and pains. It may release people from normal inhibitions by reducing fear of consequences and by providing an excuse for unacceptable behavior. ("It wasn't me, it was the alcohol.") We shall pursue this important issue below. Alcohol also induces feelings of elation and **euphoria** that may help wash away self-doubts and self-criticism.

Alcohol also intoxicates. Increased quantities impair cognitive functioning, jumble the speech, and reduce motor coordination. Many people compensate for the effects of alcohol on cognitive tasks by focusing on them more carefully, especially if they are not highly intoxicated (Williams and others, 1981). Despite our efforts to compensate for deterioration in motor coordination, alcohol is clearly implicated in perhaps half of our automobile accidents.

Euphoria (you–FOR–ree–uh). Feelings of well-being, elation. (From the Greek *euphoros*, meaning "healthy.")

As a food, alcohol is fattening. Yet chronic drinkers may be malnourished. Though high in calories, alcohol does not contain nutrients like vitamins and proteins. A diet low in protein can lead to **cirrhosis of the liver,** which afflicts many alcoholics. In this disease, connective fibers replace active liver cells, impeding circulation of the blood. Drinking can also rupture small blood vessels, especially in the nose, leading to swelling and redness. Chronic drinking has been linked to heart disease, high blood pressure, and brain damage. Even moderate drinking by a pregnant woman can harm the fetus.

Drinking as a Strategy   We tend to think of excessive drinkers, or people who act antisocially when they drink, as "victims" of alcohol. Yet recent theory and evidence suggests that many so-called victims may purposefully use drinking as an excuse for failure and antisocial behavior.

In one experiment, volunteers were given the chance to drink alcohol (supposedly in a taste test) after having to write an essay that ran counter to their actual attitudes (Steele and others, 1981). Subjects who drank more heavily were likely to maintain their pre-experimental attitudes. Subjects who drank less showed more attitudinal change after writing the essays. The researchers theorize that some of us may drink as a way of allowing us to live with actions that run counter to our attitudes. In Chapter 1 we already saw how people tend to attribute socially unacceptable aggressive behavior to alcohol.

In another experiment (Tucker and others, 1981), volunteers were given cognitive tasks. Some had access to study materials and, consequently, had a high expectation of success. Others did not have study materials available. Subjects who could use study aids drank less than subjects who could not. The researchers suggest that subjects who were more likely to fail used alcohol as a *self-handicapping strategy.* That is, if they did fail, they could attribute their failure to the alcohol.

Hull (1981) notes that alcohol also lowers self-awareness. When we drink, we become less sensitive to personal and social standards and expectations, and less aware of our deviation from them. Thus we are less likely to experience self-criticism, feelings of guilt, and shame for behavior we would not accept when sober. It is a short step to adopting drinking as a way of life when we seek excuses for doing things that would otherwise be unacceptable.

It should be noted that regardless of how or why one starts drinking, regular drinking can lead to physiological dependence. Once one has become addicted to alcohol, one will be motivated to drink in order to avoid withdrawal symptoms. Still, even when alcoholics have been "dried out"—withdrawn from alcohol—many return to drinking. Perhaps they are still seeking to use alcohol as an excuse for failing to live up to their expectations.

Let us now examine some experiments that suggest how we use drinking as a strategy in the area of sexual behavior.

Alcohol and Sex   Note this exchange between Macduff and a porter, two characters in Shakespeare's *Macbeth*:

> *Porter:* Drink, sir, is a great provoker of three things.
> *Macduff:* What three things does drink especially provoke?
> *Porter:* **Marry,** sir, **nose-painting,** sleep, and urine. **Lechery,** sir, it provokes and unprovokes; it provokes the desire, but takes away the performance.

Does alcohol stir the sexual appetite? *Does* it inhibit sexual response ("take away the performance")? In a study of 20,000 readers of *Psychology Today,*

Cirrhosis of the liver (sir–ROW–sis). A disease caused by protein deficiency in which connective fibers replace active liver cells, impeding circulation of the blood. Alcohol does not contain protein; therefore, persons who drink excessively may be prone to this disease. (From the Greek *kirrhos,* meaning "tawny," referring to the yellow-orange color of the diseased liver.)

Marry In this quote, an alternate spelling for the name Mary—used to avoid disrespect to the Virgin Mary. In Shakespearean times, *Marry* was the equivalent of *My goodness.*

Nose–painting Redness of the nose caused by rupture of small blood vessels.

Lechery Unrestrained indulgence of sexual desires. (May derive from the Greek *leichein,* meaning "to lick.")

Drugs   **141**

three of five respondents wrote that alcohol increased their sexual pleasure. Women reported these enhancing effects more often than men (Athanasiou and others, 1970). Many people believe that alcohol either increases or does not affect their sexual response, as did a group of male alcoholics studied by Wilson and his colleagues (1978).

Recent studies of response to sexually explicit films suggest that men who *believe* they have drunk alcohol (when they have not) show increases in sexual arousal, as measured by size of erection and subjective feelings of arousal. But men who have *actually* drunk alcohol, without knowing it, show decreased sexual response (Briddell & Wilson, 1976). As noted in Chapter 1, such studies are made possible by inability to taste vodka when mixed with tonic water. In this way, subjects can be led to believe they have drunk alcohol when they have not, and vice versa. Similar research shows that alcohol also decreases women's response to sexually explicit films (Wilson & Lawson, 1978). Thus our beliefs about the effects of alcohol may diverge markedly from its actual effects. The "sexy" feeling we may experience after a few drinks may stem from sensations we expect rather than arousal that is stimulated by alcohol.

Many of us may drink, or encourage dates to drink, to lower inhibitions. However, there is no evidence that alcohol directly reduces feelings of guilt. In experiments similar to those described above, men who *believed* they had drunk alcohol, when they had not, spent significantly more time looking at sexually explicit pictures than men who *believed* they had not drunk alcohol. Researchers conclude that drinking may have served as an excuse for prolonged looking at these pictures (Lang and others, 1980; Lansky & Wilson, 1981). Alcohol may provide us with an excuse for an assortment of behaviors we consider deviant.

Dim lights, candles, soft music, a little wine work wonders—sometimes. Why may wine stoke the fires of love? Is it because alcohol stimulates sexual arousal, or because a person who accepts an invitation for a drink may see himself or herself as participating in a seduction?

Treatment of Alcoholism Treatment of alcoholism has been a frustrating endeavor. *Detoxification*, or helping an addicted alcoholic safely through the abstinence syndrome, is a generally straightforward medical procedure, requiring about one week (Rada & Kellner, 1979). But assisting the alcoholic to then learn to cope with life's stresses through measures other than drinking is the heart of the problem. Several treatments have been tried, most with little documented success.

Medication. The drug *disulfuram* (brand name Antabuse) has been used most widely with alcoholics. Mixing Antabuse with alcohol can cause feelings of illness. However, current maintenance doses of Antabuse are usually too low to have this result, and there is little convincing evidence of the drug's effectiveness (Miller & Hester, 1980).

Alcoholics Anonymous. Many people consider Alcoholics Anonymous (AA), a nonprofessional organization, to be most effective with alcoholics. At AA, alcoholics undergo a conversion in identity to that of a "recovered alcoholic." This conversion requires confession of one's drinking sins to a group of alcoholics, and the making of a public commitment not to touch another drop. The new identity becomes confirmed with the passing of each sober day, and recovered alcoholics often help other alcoholics undergo a similar conversion.

While AA commonly cites a success rate of 75 percent, this figure includes only persons who remain in treatment. As many as 90 percent of those who attend AA meetings drop out after a handful of meetings (Miller, 1982).

Behavior Therapy. Behavior therapy is proving to be helpful to many alcoholics. A variety of methods which will be explained in depth in Chapter 12 show promising success rates. These include aversion therapy, relaxation training, covert sensitization, instruction in social skills, and self-monitoring (Elkins, 1980; Miller & Mastria, 1977; Olson and others, 1981).

A number of behavior therapists recommend a treatment strategy referred to as *controlled social drinking* instead of total abstinence (Miller & Muñoz, 1983). Critics argue that if an alcoholic, or a recovered alcoholic, has just one drink, he or she will go on an uncontrolled drinking binge. Yet research undertaken in the early 1970s by Mark and Linda Sobell suggested that controlled social drinking was a feasible goal for many alcoholics (Sobell & Sobell, 1973; Sobell and others, 1972). Eighty-five percent of the Sobell's subjects were engaging in successful controlled social drinking at a two-year follow-up.

But now, more than a decade afterward, a follow-up of the Sobells' 20 subjects reported in the July 9, 1982 issue of *Science* found that most subjects had returned to uncontrolled drinking on several occasions, and that only *one* had successfully continued to moderate his drinking. Four of the original 20 had died from alcohol-related causes (Pendery, Maltzman, & West, 1982). According to psychologist Alan Marlatt (in Fisher, 1982), there were shortcomings in both the studies run by the Sobells and by the Pendery group. In each case, for example, the follow-ups may have been biased because they were conducted by investigators who had an interest in showing a particular outcome. The next chapter in this debate remains to be written.

Marijuana

The *Cannabis sativa* plant grows wild in many parts of the world. This would arouse little interest but for the fact that **marijuana** is produced from it. Marijuana stirs interest because it helps some people relax and can elevate

Marijuana The dried vegetable matter of the *Cannabis sativa* plant. (A Mexican–Spanish word.)

Why Do You Drink?

Do you drink? If so, why? To enhance your pleasure? To cope with your problems? To help you in your social encounters? Half of all Americans use alcohol for a variety of reasons. Perhaps as many as one user in 10 is an alcoholic.

To gain insight into your reasons for using alcohol, respond to the following items writing T in the blank space if an item is true or mostly true for you, or an *F* if an item is false or mostly false for you. Then turn to the answer key in Appendix B.

T   F

_____ 1 I find it very unpleasant to do without alcohol for some time.

_____ 2 Alcohol makes it easier for me to talk to other people.

_____ 3 I drink to appear more grown up and more sophisticated.

_____ 4 When I drink, the future looks brighter to me.

_____ 5 I like the taste of what I drink.

_____ 6 If I go without a drink for some time, I am not bothered or uncomfortable.

_____ 7 I feel more relaxed and less tense about things when I drink.

_____ 8 I drink so that I will fit in better with the crowd.

_____ 9 I worry less about things when I drink.

_____ 10 I have a drink when I get together with the family.

_____ 11 I have a drink as part of my religious ceremonies.

_____ 12 I have a drink when a toothache or some other pain is disturbing me.

_____ 13 I feel much more powerful when I have a drink.

_____ 14 You really can't blame me for the things I do when I have been drinking.

_____ 15 I have a drink before a big test, date, or interview when I'm afraid of how well I'll do.

_____ 16 I find I have a drink for the taste alone.

_____ 17 I've found a drink in my hand when I can't remember putting it there.

_____ 18 I'll have a drink when I feel "blue" or want to take my mind off my cares and worries.

Psychedelic
(sigh–kuh–DELL–lick). Causing hallucinations, delusions, or heightening perceptions.

Hallucinogenic Giving rise to hallucinations.

Delta–9–tetrahydrocannabinol
(tet–truh–hide–row–can–NAB–in–all). The major active ingredient in marijuana. Abbreviated *THC*. Its name describes its chemical composition.

Resin (RAH–zin). The saplike substance of plants.

Hashish (hah–SHEESH). A drug derived from the resin of Cannabis sativa. Often called "hash."

Glaucoma An eye disease characterized by increased fluid pressure within the eye. A cause of blindness. (From the Greek *glaukos,* meaning "gleaming"—referring to the appearance of the diseased eye.)

---

the mood. It also sometimes produces mild hallucinations, which is why marijuana is classified as a **psychedelic** or **hallucinogenic** drug.

The major psychedelic substance in marijuana is **delta-9-tetrahydrocannabinol** which, perhaps to save energy, is usually referred to as THC. Other substances with possible psychedelic effects that are found in marijuana include *cannabichromene* and *cannabidol*. THC is found in the branches and leaves of male and female plants, but is concentrated highly in the **resin** of the female plant. **Hashish,** or "hash," is derived from this sticky resin. It is more potent than marijuana, although the effects are similar.

In the last century, marijuana was used almost as aspirin is used today for headaches and minor aches and pains. It could be bought without prescription in any drugstore. Today marijuana use and possession are illegal in most states, but medical applications are being explored. Marijuana is known to decrease nausea and vomiting among cancer patients receiving chemotherapy. It appears to help **glaucoma** sufferers by reducing fluid pressure in

_____ 19 I can do better socially and sexually after having a drink or two.
_____ 20 Drinking makes me do stupid things.
_____ 21 Sometimes when I have a few drinks, I can't get to work.
_____ 22 I feel more caring and giving after having a drink or two.
_____ 23 I drink because I like the look of a drinker.
_____ 24 I like to drink more on festive occasions.
_____ 25 When a friend or I have done something well, we're likely to have a drink or two.
_____ 26 I have a drink when some problem is nagging away at me.
_____ 27 I find drinking pleasurable.
_____ 28 I like the "high" of drinking.
_____ 29 Sometimes I pour a drink without realizing I still have one that is unfinished.
_____ 30 I feel I can better get others to do what I want when I've had a drink or two.
_____ 31 Having a drink keeps my mind off my problems at home, at school, or at work.
_____ 32 I get a real gnawing hunger for a drink when I haven't had one for a while.
_____ 33 A drink or two relaxes me.
_____ 34 Things look better when I've had a drink or two.
_____ 35 My mood is much better after I've been drinking.
_____ 36 I see things more clearly when I've been drinking.
_____ 37 A drink or two enhances the pleasure of sex and food.
_____ 38 When I'm out of alcohol, I immediately buy more.
_____ 39 I would have done much better on some things if it weren't for alcohol.
_____ 40 When I have run out of alcohol, I find it almost unbearable until I can get some more.

Sources: Items adapted from (1) general discussion of expectancies about alcohol in Christiansen and others (1982) and (2) smokers' self-testing items analyzed by Leventhal and Avis (1976).

the eye. It may offer some relief from **asthma.** But there are side effects, as noted in the "Marijuana Update."

Effects of Marijuana   A survey of 150 marijuana smokers found reports of different sensations at differing levels of intoxication (Tart, 1971). The early stages of intoxication are frequently characterized by restlessness, which gives way to calmness later on. Fair to strong intoxication is linked to reports of heightened perceptions, and increases in self-insight, creative thinking, and **empathy** for the feelings of others. Strong intoxication was linked to perceiving time as passing more slowly, and increased awareness of bodily sensations, such as heart beat. Smokers also reported that strong intoxication heightened sexual sensations and that a song might seem to last an hour rather than a few minutes. Visual hallucinations were not uncommon. Strong intoxication may cause smokers to experience disorientation. If the mood is euphoric, loss of identity may be interpreted as harmony with the universe.

Asthma (AS–muh). A condition marked by recurrent attacks of labored breathing accompanied by wheezing. (A Greek word meaning "panting.")

Empathy Ability to understand and share another person's feelings. (From the Greek _en–,_ meaning "in," and _pathos,_ meaning "feeling.")

Marijuana Update: The National Academy of Sciences Report

In 1980 nearly 25 million Americans spent $24 billion to smoke marijuana regularly. Another 25 million have tried the drug. One reason that marijuana is the most widely used illegal substance in the U.S. is the tenacious belief that occasional joints do little, if any, harm. In February 1982 the Institute of Medicine of the National Academy of Sciences, chaired by Arnold Relman, editor of the prestigious *New England Journal of Medicine*, issued a long-awaited 188-page report on marijuana's effects. Based on an analysis of 1,000 research studies, the Institute concluded that widespread use of the drug "justifies serious national concern." But after its 15-month study, the academy had to admit that as yet there is insufficient research to conclude that marijuana causes irreversible long-term damage to mental functioning and physical health.

Some excerpts from the committee report:

Effects on the Nervous System and on Behavior [Marijuana's] most clearly established acute effects are on mental functions and behavior. With a severity directly related to dose, marijuana impairs motor coordination and affects tracking ability and perceptual functions important for safe driving and the operation of other machines; it also impairs short-term memory and slows learning. Other acute effects include euphoria and other mood changes, but there are also disturbing mental phenomena, such as brief periods of anxiety, confusion, or psychosis.

. . . [The] long-term effects of marijuana on the human brain and on human behavior remain to be defined.

Effects on the Cardiovascular and Respiratory Systems There is . . . no evidence to indicate that a permanently [harmful] effect on the normal cardiovascular system occurs. There is good evidence to show that marijuana increases the work of the heart, usually by raising heart rate and, in some persons, by raising blood pressure. This rise in workload poses a threat to patients with hypertension, cerebrovascular disease, and coronary atherosclerosis.

Marijuana smoke . . . has many chemical components (including carbon monoxide and "tar") and biological effects similar to tobacco smoke, but also some unique ingredients. This suggests the strong possibility that prolonged heavy smoking of marijuana, like tobacco, will lead to cancer of the respiratory tract and to serious impairment of lung function.

Effects on the Reproductive System [THC] appears to have a modest reversible suppressive effect on sperm production in men, but there is no proof that it [impairs] male fertility . . . . There is convincing evidence that marijuana interferes with ovulation in female monkeys. [But] no satisfactory studies of the relation between use of marijuana and female fertility and child bearing have been carried out. Although [THC] is known to cross the placenta readily and to cause birth defects when administered in large doses to experimental animals, no adequate clinical studies have been carried out to determine if marijuana use can harm the human fetus.

Conclusions Our major conclusion is that what little we know for certain about the effects of marijuana on human health—and all that we have reason to suspect—justifies serious national concern . . . . Our major recommendation is that there be a greatly intensified and more comprehensive program of research into the effects of marijuana on the health of the American people.

As noted in *Time* magazine, on March 8, 1982: "Medical science's uncertainty about the serious risks of marijuana has apparently been noted by at least one segment of the population. Also released in 1982 was a University of Michigan study that revealed regular marijuana use among 17,000 high school seniors across the country has dropped from a high of 11 percent in 1978 to seven percent in 1981. The most frequently cited reason: the teenagers' concern about possible adverse effects of marijuana smoking on physical and psychological health."

But some smokers encounter negative experiences with strong intoxication. Marijuana increases the heart rate. This increase combined with heightened awareness of bodily sensations leads some smokers to fear that their hearts will "run away" with them. Some smokers find disorientation threatening, and fear failure to regain their identities. High levels of intoxication occasionally induce nausea and vomiting. Needless to say, smokers with such experiences smoke infrequently, or just once.

Some people report that marijuana helps them socialize at parties. But the friendliness characteristic of early stages of intoxication may give way to self-absorption and social withdrawal as the smoker becomes higher (Mendelson and others, 1974).

The Langley Porter Study In a recent study at the Langley Porter Psychiatric Institute in San Francisco, Reese Jones and his colleagues (1976) measured

Marijuana, a mild psychedelic, can relax one, provide feelings of euphoria, and enhance sensory pleasure. Perhaps one in five college students smokes marijuana regularly.

the effects of controlled marijuana administration to 53 experienced male volunteers over an 11- to 13-day period. Three groups of subjective effects were identified, as noted in Table 4.2.

Sedative effects were most noticeable during the first few days of smoking. They decreased rapidly throughout the remainder of the study, suggesting

TABLE 4.2 Subjective Effects of Marijuana Use

Group I: Sedative Effects (Most prominent during first few days)

Thinking seemed fuzzier	Arms or legs felt weaker
Thoughts moved slower	Stomach felt heavier
Harder to concentrate	Mouth and throat felt drier
Felt it was harder to talk	Lips felt numb
Movements seemed slower	Eyesight worse than usual
Body felt more unsteady	Eyelids felt as if they were closing

Group II: Good Feelings (Increased regularly during study)

Felt more at peace	Felt it was easier to talk
Had greater love for others	Liked to talk more
Liked having people around more	Noticed things more
Felt more relaxed	Saw comical side of things more
Felt extreme well-being	Felt happier and sillier
Thinking seemed clearer	Liked answering these questions

Group III: Tension and Anxiety (Greatest at beginning and after discontinuation of marijuana at end of study)

Body felt worse than usual	Perspired more
Felt more tense than usual	Stomach felt more jittery
Noticed bodily feelings more than usual	Was less hungry than usual
	Had more on mind than usual
Body felt more energetic	Noticed feelings more than usual
Body felt hotter	Felt more irritable than usual

Source: Jones and others (1976).

that regular smokers come to tolerate marijuana's sedative effects. "Good feelings" increased slightly but regularly throughout the study, suggesting a reverse tolerance for these effects (which may reflect buildup of substance-related chemicals in the body). "Tension-anxiety" sensations were greatest during the early days of the study and for several days after marijuana was discontinued. The authors suggest that the last group of sensations may constitute an abstinence syndrome for heavy smokers who suddenly decrease usage. This interpretation implies that marijuana can be addictive, and is controversial. Most other researchers believe that marijuana is not addictive, although, of course, people may become psychologically dependent on the substance. Furthermore, in a recent Jamaican study, people who had smoked marijuana heavily reportedly showed no withdrawal symptoms when they abstained for six days (Rubin & Comitas, 1975).

Marijuana and Amotivational Syndrome   Some have feared that marijuana can lead to **amotivational syndrome**—that is, destroy achievement motivation and melt away ambition. These fears have been fueled by correlational evidence that heavy smokers in the college ranks do not strive to succeed as strenuously as do nonsmoking or infrequently smoking classmates. But we cannot confuse correlation with cause and effect. Other studies suggest that people who choose to smoke heavily already differ from those who do not. For instance, heavy smokers may be more concerned with emotional experience and fantasy than intellectual performance and self-control. Their approach to life could underlie both relative lack of ambition and regular use of marijuana.

Large-scale Latin American studies also find no causal relationship between marijuana use and amotivational syndrome. Heavy smokers in Jamaica (Rubin & Comitas, 1975) and Costa Rica (Coggins, 1976) had no difficulty finding or holding jobs. But these studies have been criticized because almost all subjects held routine, undemanding jobs. Neither smokers nor nonsmokers showed ambition to climb the educational or occupational ladder. Also, Latin American smokers do not typically inhale marijuana smoke as deeply, or hold it in their lungs as long, as do U.S. smokers (Davison & Neale, 1982). Such studies will have to be replicated with a wide spectrum of smokers and nonsmokers in the United States before we can place much stock in them.

Cigarettes

All cigarette packs sold in the United States carry this message: "Warning: The Surgeon General Has Determined That Cigarette Smoking Is Dangerous to Your Health." Cigarette advertising has been banned on the radio and television. In 1982, Surgeon General C. Everett Koop declared that "Cigarette smoking is clearly identified as the chief preventable cause of death in our society and the most important public health issue of our time."

In that year, 430,000 people would die from cancer, and the Surgeon General's report argued that 30 percent of these deaths were attributable to smoking (Toufexis, 1982). Cigarette smoking can cause cancer of the lungs, larynx, oral cavity, and esophagus, and may contribute to cancer of the bladder, pancreas, and kidneys. Cigarette smoking is also linked to death from heart disease, chronic lung and respiratory diseases, and other illnesses. Pregnant women who smoke risk miscarriage, premature birth, and birth defects. Once it was thought that smokers' ills tended to focus on men, but today women smokers have a 30 percent greater risk of dying from cancer than do women nonsmokers.

Second-hand smoke is also a problem. People trapped in close quarters with smokers show increased levels of carbon monoxide in the blood. These quantities are sufficient to trigger asthma attacks and to distress people suffering from heart disease (Doyle, 1974). Because of the effect on nearby nonsmokers, smoking has been banished from many public places, like elevators. Many restaurants now reserve sections for nonsmokers.

So it's no secret that cigarette smoking is dangerous. Although the percentage of Americans who smoke has fallen off in recent years, many millions still smoke. And according to a University of Michigan study, 20 percent of high school seniors smoked regularly in 1981. *Why?* Are smokers unaware of the risks they take? How do we explain this all-too-frequently fatal attraction to cigarettes? First let us examine the components of tobacco smoke. Then we shall consider why people smoke and how they may be able to cut down or quit their habits.

Components of Tobacco Smoke: Where There's Smoke, There's Chemicals Tobacco smoke contains *carbon monoxide*, *hydrocarbons* (or *"tars"*), and *nicotine.*

Oxygen is carried throughout the body by a substance in the blood called **hemoglobin.** But when carbon monoxide combines with hemoglobin, it impairs the blood's ability to supply the body with oxygen. One result: shortness of breath. Some **hydrocarbons** have been shown to cause cancer in laboratory animals.

Nicotine is a stimulant that can cause cold, clammy skin, faintness and dizziness, nausea and vomiting, and diarrhea—all of which account for the occasional discomforts of the novice smoker. But nicotine also stimulates discharge of the hormone **epinephrine.** Epinephrine (also called adrenalin) creates a burst of autonomic activity, including rapid heart rate and release of sugar into the blood. It also provides a sort of mental "kick." Nicotine is responsible for the stimulating properties of cigarette smoke, but its effects are short-lived. In the long run it can contribute to fatigue.

Why People Smoke If smoking is so dangerous, why do people smoke? Are smokers singularly unaware of smoking's perils? Let us examine a number of reasons for smoking:

1. *Rationalization.* It has been known for many years by smokers and nonsmokers alike that there are links between smoking and cancer. But, as found by Pervin and Yatko (1965), smokers tend to **rationalize** their smoking. They are more likely than nonsmokers to report that a cure for cancer will be found in the near future. They may feel that their own level of smoking is within a safe range.
2. *Rites of passage.* For the young, smoking may still be seen, in some groups, as a way of asserting maturity and independence. In one classic study (Weir, 1967), male college students perceived men shown smoking in photos as rugged, daring, and adventurous. They were more likely to perceive nonsmokers as timid, shy, and awkward. In another report from the 1960s, Mausner (1966) found that many young women smokers were reluctant to quit, in part, because smoking fit the self-image of the bright, sophisticated, career-oriented woman. However, in the 1980s, peer pressure seems to be

Hemoglobin The substance in the blood that carries oxygen.

Hydrocarbons Chemical compounds consisting of hydrogen and carbon.

Nicotine A stimulant found in tobacco smoke. (From the French name for the tobacco plant, *nicotiane.*)

Epinephrine (epp–pin–NEFF–rin). Another name for adrenalin, the hormone secreted by the adrenal medulla. (From the Greek *epi–*, meaning "on," and *nephros*, meaning "kidney." What are the roots of the word *adrenalin?*)

Rationalize To find excuses for unacceptable behavior. See Chapters 9 and 10.

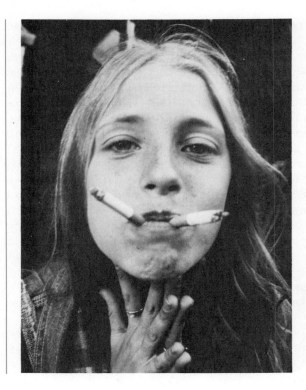

For some adolescents, smoking has been a symbol of having come of age, of being daring, rugged, and adventurous. Yet according to one recent survey, it may be that most high school students today disapprove of smoking cigarettes.

favoring *not* smoking. According to one 1980 survey, 74 percent of high school seniors thought their peers would disapprove of their smoking (*ADAMHA News*, February 9, 1981).

3. *Observational learning and conformity.* We tend to be influenced by the behavior of others. In an American Cancer Society survey (Lieberman Research, 1967), 19 percent of nonsmokers reported that their friends smoked. But 56 percent of the friends of smokers smoked also. Successful quitters are less likely to be married to smokers (Schwartz & Dubitsky, 1968).

4. *Addiction.* There is considerable controversy as to whether regular smokers simply develop strong psychological dependence on cigarettes, or become addicted to them. The withdrawal symptoms from smoking cigarettes (nervousness, drowsiness, anxiety, energy loss, headaches, fatigue, irregular bowels, lightheadedness, insomnia, dizziness, cramps, palpitations, tremors, and sweating) do mimic an anxiety state. However, Stanley Schachter (1977) has shown that regular smokers adjust their smoking in order to maintain fairly even levels of nicotine in their bloodstream. Thus we know that smokers will avoid drops in nicotine levels. Changes in nicotine level are short-term affairs. Still, they constitute a real and measurable bodily change that results from use of cigarettes, and people who are unwilling to experience the results of this dropoff could be considered addicted.

It has also been found that nicotine is excreted more rapidly when the urine is highly acid. Stress increases the amount of acid in the urine. For this reason, smokers may need to smoke more when under stress to maintain the same blood nicotine level. They may *believe* that smoking is helping them cope with stress. However, recent research (Silverstein, 1982) suggests strongly that the "calming effect" attributed to cigarette smoking may amount to nothing more than suspension of the withdrawal symptoms of addicted smokers. The only source of stress with which smokers may be "coping" is the stress of withdrawal.

5. *Pleasure.* Some people find pleasure in the handling of cigarettes, their taste, or in the surge of stimulation provided by nicotine. Regardless of why you or your classmates smoke, there are a number of ways of cutting down and quitting.

Quitting Smoking When it comes to stopping smoking, common sense is also good psychology. A University of Missouri study found that people who successfully cut down smoking by at least 50 percent were more highly motivated and committed to cutting down than were would-be reducers (Perri and others, 1977). David Premack (1970) believes that humiliation is a prime motivator for those who succeed. At some point we become humiliated by our inability to quit. Perhaps we torch a hole into a favorite piece of clothing or see our children fiddling with cigarettes. We then resolve to be reborn or purified as nonsmokers (Sarbin & Nucci, 1973). Our belief that we can cut down or quit is also important (Blittner and others, 1978).

Given the determination to quit, you or your friends may find it helpful to try some of the following suggestions:

- Tell your family and friends that you're quitting—make a public commitment.
- Think of specific things to tell yourself when you feel the urge to smoke: how you'll be stronger, free of fear of cancer, ready for the marathon, etc., etc.
- Tell yourself that the first few days are the hardest—after that, withdrawal symptoms weaken dramatically.
- Remind yourself that you're "superior" to nonquitters.
- Start when you wake up, at which time you've already gone eight hours without nicotine.
- Go on a smoke-ending vacation to get away from places and situations in which you're used to smoking.
- Throw out ashtrays and don't allow smokers to visit you at home for a while.
- Don't carry matches or light other people's cigarettes.
- Sit in nonsmokers' sections of restaurants and trains.

A Magic Cure for Smoking?

What if there were a magic cure for smoking? A cure that was guaranteed to help you through the abstinence syndrome . . . with just one hitch?

The hitch? Some side effects. For two to three days after taking the cure, some people complain of nervousness and drowsiness, some of headaches, insomnia, or constipation. But these side effects are usually gone within a week. Considering the alternatives—fear of cancer and heart disease, the cost of cigarettes, the humiliation of not being able to quit—wouldn't "the cure" be worth it?

The "magic" cure exists and is readily available. It's called stopping smoking. I've simply described some common withdrawal symptoms. Sarbin and Nucci (1973) point out that we need not look upon these symptoms as awful. They are, after all, signs that the body is recovering from the effects of smoking.

Our interpretation of bodily sensations is central in coping with abstinence from any drug. It is also central in curbing overeating. We can interpret temporary, unpleasant sensations as signs that we are *winning*—not as disasters that must be avoided at all costs. After all, we wouldn't be experiencing them if we had not marshalled our will power to take action that we felt was good for us.

- Fill your days with novel activities—things that won't remind you of smoking.
- Use sugar-free mints or gum as substitutes for cigarettes (don't light them up).
- Buy yourself presents with all that cash you're socking away.

It's true that there is a high relapse rate for quitters. Be on guard: We are most likely to relapse—that is, return to smoking—when we feel highly anxious, angry, or depressed (Shiffman, 1982). But when you are tempted, you can decrease the chances of relapsing by using almost any strategy (Shiffman, 1982), like reminding yourself of reasons for quitting, having a mint, or going for a walk. And also keep in mind a note of encouragement from Stanley Schachter (1982): Despite high relapse "rates," millions of Americans have quit and been able to stay away from cigarettes permanently.

Amphetamines

Amphetamines are a group of stimulants that were first used by soldiers during World War II to help them remain alert through the night. Truck drivers have used them to drive through the night. But amphetamines have become more widely known through students who have used them for all-night cram-sessions, and through dieters. One of their effects is reduction of hunger.

Amphetamines and a related stimulant, Ritalin, have been found effective in calming **hyperactive** children and increasing their attention span. A combination of stimulants and behavior therapy may be most effective with them (Gittelman-Klein, 1976). This paradoxical effect of stimulants may be explained by assuming that children may behave hyperactively because of immaturity of the cerebral cortex. The amphetamines then stimulate the cortex to exercise control over more primitive centers in the lower brain.

Called speed, uppers, bennies (for Benzedrine), and dexies (for Dexedrine), these drugs are often used for the euphoric "rush" they can produce, especially in high doses. (The so-called antidepressant drugs, which we shall discuss in Chapter 12, do not produce any euphoric rush.) Some people swallow amphetamines in pill form or inject liquid Methedrine, the strongest form, into their veins. They may stay awake and "high" for days on end. Such highs must come to an end. People who have been on prolonged highs sometimes "crash," or fall into a deep sleep or depression. Some people commit suicide when crashing.

People can become psychologically dependent on amphetamines, especially when they are using them to cope with depression. Tolerance develops rapidly, but opinion is mixed as to whether they are addictive. High doses may cause restlessness, hallucinations, paranoid delusions (see Chapter 11), insomnia, loss of appetite, and irritability.

Opiates and Opioids

Opiates are a group of **narcotics** derived from the opium poppy. The ancient Sumerians gave this poppy its name: It means "plant of joy." The opiates include morphine, heroin, codeine, demerol, and similar drugs whose major medical application is **analgesia.** In this section we discuss morphine, heroin, and the **opioid** methadone. Opioids are similar to opiates in chemical structure and effect, but are artificial (synthesized in the laboratory).

Amphetamines (am–FET–uh–means). Stimulants derived from *al-pha–methyl–beta–phenyl–ethyl–amine,* a colorless liquid consisting of carbon, hydrogen, and nitrogen.

Hyperactive More active than normal.

Opiates (OH–pee–ates). A group of addictive drugs derived from the opium poppy that provide a euphoric "rush" and depress the nervous system.

Narcotics Drugs used to relieve pain and induce sleep. The term is usually reserved for opiates. (From the Greek *narke,* meaning "numbness" or "stupor.")

Analgesia A state of not feeling pain, although fully conscious.

Opioid (OH–pee–oid). A synthetic (artificial) drug similar in chemical composition to opiates.

Morphine **Morphine** was introduced at about the time of the Civil War in the United States and the Franco-Prussian War in Europe. It was used to deaden pain from wounds, and used quite liberally. Addiction to morphine became known as the "soldier's disease." There was little stigma attached to this disease until morphine became a restricted substance.

Morphine and heroin can have distressing abstinence syndromes, beginning with flu-like symptoms and progressing through tremors, cramps, chills alternating with sweating, rapid pulse, high blood pressure, insomnia, vomiting, and diarrhea. However, the syndrome can be quite variable from person to person. Many American soldiers who used heroin in Vietnam are reported to have stopped with little trouble when they returned home.

Heroin **Heroin** was given its name because when it was derived it was hailed as "the hero" that would cure addiction to morphine. But heroin, like the other opiates, is a powerful depressant that can provide a euphoric rush and is highly addictive. Users of heroin find it so pleasurable that they claim it eradicates any thought of food or sex. Heroin was soon used to treat so many "problems" that it became known as G.O.M. ("God's own medicine").

Heroin is illegal. Because the penalties for possession or sale are high, it is also very expensive. For this reason many addicts support their "habits" through dealing (selling heroin), prostitution, or selling stolen goods. But heroin does not directly stimulate criminal or aggressive behavior. On the other hand, people who use heroin regularly may be more likely than nonusers to engage in *other* criminal behavior as well. Considering the legal penalties for heroin use, most users are willing to take high risks.

Although regular users develop tolerance for heroin, high doses can cause drowsiness, stupor, altered time perception, and impaired judgment. A number of addicts die from so-called overdoses, but as Davison and Neale (1982) point out, "overdose victims" often show no evidence of having taken more than the usual dose (about 10 milligrams). Coroners often list the cause of death as heroin overdose if the victim is known to be a user and death by natural causes, suicide, or violence has been ruled out.

Davison and Neale suggest that alcohol or **quinine** may contribute to these deaths. As noted earlier, alcohol and heroin are both depressants, and they have additive effects. Since 1939, when many New York City addicts contracted malaria from an epidemic of contaminated needles, heroin has been "cut" (diluted) with quinine, a medicine used to treat malaria. But quinine can kill by flooding the lungs with fluid, a finding disclosed by autopsies of some "overdose victims."

Methadone **Methadone** has been used to treat heroin addiction in the same way heroin was used to treat morphine addiction. This synthetic narcotic is slower acting than heroin and does not provide the thrilling rush. Most addicts so treated simply swap addictions. Because they are unwilling to undergo withdrawal symptoms, or to contemplate a life style devoid of drugs, they must be maintained indefinitely on methadone.

If methadone is injected, rather than taken orally, it can provide many addicts with sensations similar to those of heroin. Another drug, *naloxone*, prevents users from becoming high if they later take heroin. Some addicts are placed on naloxone after being withdrawn from heroin. However, former addicts can choose not to take naloxone, and, again, drugs like naloxone do not provide former addicts with the desire to undertake a heroin-free life style.

Morphine An opiate introduced at about the time of the U.S. Civil War.

Heroin An opiate. Heroin, ironically, was used as a "cure" for morphine addiction when first introduced.

Quinine (KWY–nine). A medicine used to treat malaria.

Heroin is a highly addictive derivative of opium that provides a euphoric "rush." This young male is injecting heroin into a vein.

Cocaine

No doubt you've seen commercials claiming that Coke adds life. Given its caffeine and sugar content, "Coke"—Coca-Cola, that is—should provide quite a lift. But Coca-Cola hasn't been "the real thing" since 1906. At that time the manufacturers discontinued use of the coca leaves from which the soft drink derived its name. Coca leaves contain **cocaine,** a stimulant that produces a state of euphoria, or high, reduces hunger, deadens pain, and bolsters self-confidence.

Cocaine is brewed from coca leaves as a "tea," breathed in ("snorted") in powder form, and injected ("shot up") in liquid form.

"Song of Praise" As reported in *Time* magazine:

> A cocaine high is an intensely vivid, sensation-enhancing experience—though there is no evidence, as is often claimed, that it is aphrodisiacal .... Says a Manhattan ballerina, "It makes you shiver in tune with the raw, volcanic energy of New York. It bleeds your sense till you see the city as an epileptic rainbow, trembling at the speed of light." Test programs at UCLA have shown that lab monkeys will forgo both food and sex in favor of an injection of a cocaine solution (July 6, 1981, p. 59).

Users of cocaine are often devoted and well-to-do: Its price per ounce is about 70 times that of the finest beluga caviar and five times that of gold. Despite the expense, perhaps 20–30 percent of young adults have tried cocaine at least once (Kelly, 1980).

Cocaine—also called *snow* and *coke*, like the slang term for the soft drink—has been used as a local anesthetic since the early 1800s. It came to the attention of one Viennese neurologist in 1884, a young chap named Sigmund Freud, who used it to fight depression and published an early supportive article, "Song of Praise."

Dependence Cocaine is not addictive, but users can become highly psychologically dependent. Overdoses can lead to restlessness and insomnia, tremors, severe headaches, nausea, convulsions, psychotic reactions (hallucinations and delusions), and—though rarely—respiratory and cardiovascular collapse. Repeated "snorting" constricts blood vessels in the nose, drying the skin, and, at times, exposing cartilege and perforating the nasal septum. These problems require cosmetic surgery.

Having noted these potential problems, it must be admitted that moderate cocaine use has not been shown to be of major medical concern. Although cocaine has been unavailable to the general public since the Harrison Narcotic Act of 1914, it is still commonly the anesthetic of choice for surgery on the nose and throat. Cocaine, by the way, is a stimulant, *not* a narcotic. Its classification as a narcotic was only a legality—bringing the drug under the prohibitions of the narcotics act.

Barbiturates and Methaqualone

If its name ends in *-tal*, it may well be a **barbiturate,** like amobarbital, phenobarbital, pentobarbital, and secobarbital. Barbiturates are depressants with a number of medical uses, including relief of anxiety and tension, deadening of pain, and treatment of epilepsy, high blood pressure, and insomnia.

Barbiturates are highly addictive, and lead rapidly to psychological dependence.

Methaqualone, sold under the brand names Quaalude and Sopor, is a depressant similar in effect to barbiturates. Methaqualone is also addictive and quite dangerous.

Psychologists are generally opposed to using barbiturates and methalqualone for anxiety, tension, and insomnia. They lead rapidly to dependence and do nothing to teach the individual how to alter disturbing patterns of behavior. Many physicians, too, have become concerned by barbiturates. They now prefer to prescribe minor tranquilizers like Valium and Librium for anxiety and tension, and yet other drugs for insomnia. However, as you will see in Chapter 12, it is now thought that minor tranquilizers may also be addictive. Their prescription still does nothing to help the person change sources of stress in his or her life.

Barbiturates and methaqualone are popular as street drugs because they relax the muscles and produce a mild euphoric state. High doses of barbiturates result in drowsiness, motor impairment, slurred speech, irritability, and poor judgment. An addicted person who is withdrawn abruptly may experience severe convulsions and die. High doses of methaqualone may cause internal bleeding, coma, and death. Because of additive effects, it is dangerous to mix alcohol and other depressants at bedtime, or at any time.

LSD

LSD is the **acronym** for lysergic diethylamide acid, a synthetic hallucinogenic drug. Users sometimes just call it "acid." Supporters claim that LSD "expands consciousness" and opens new worlds. Sometimes people believe they achieved great insights while using LSD, but when it wears off they often cannot apply or recall these discoveries exactly.

As a powerful hallucinogenic, LSD produces vivid and colorful hallucinations. LSD "trips" can be somewhat unpredictable. Some regular users have only "good trips." Others have one bad trip and swear off. Regular users who have had no bad trips argue that people with bad trips were psychologically unstable prior to using LSD. In fairness, Barber's review of the literature (1970) suggests that rare psychotic symptoms are usually limited to people with a history of psychological problems.

Flashbacks Some LSD users have **flashbacks**—distorted perceptions or hallucinations that occur days, weeks, or longer after usage but mimic the LSD "trip." It has been speculated that flashbacks stem from chemical changes in the brain produced by LSD, but Heaton and Victor (1976) and Matefy (1980) offer a psychological explanation for flashbacks.

Heaton and Victor (1976) found that users who have flashbacks are more oriented toward fantasy and allowing their thoughts to wander. They are also more likely to focus on internal sensations. If they should experience sensations similar to a past trip, they may readily label them flashbacks and allow themselves to focus on them indefinitely, causing an entire replay of the experience to unfold.

Matefy (1980) found that users who have flashbacks show greater capacity to become fully engrossed in role-playing, and hypothesized that flashbacks may be nothing more than enacting the role of being on a trip. This does not necessarily mean that people who claim to have flashbacks are lying.

Methaqualone An addictive depressant. Often called "ludes."

LSD Lysergic acid diethylamide. A hallucinogenic drug.

Acronym A word formed from the first letters of other words. *Amphetamine* is an acronym. See Chapter 5 for a discussion of acronyms as aids to memory. (From the Greek *akros*, meaning "at the end," and *onyma*, meaning "name.")

Flashbacks Distorted perceptions or hallucinations that occur days or weeks after LSD usage but mimic the LSD experience.

They may be more willing to surrender personal control in response to internal sensations for the sake of altering their consciousness and having peak experiences. Users who do not have flashbacks prefer to be more in charge of their thought processes and have greater concern for meeting the demands of daily life.

Other Hallucinogenics   Other hallucinogenic drugs include **mescaline** (derived from the peyote cactus) and **phencyclidine** (PCP). Regular use of hallucinogenics may lead to tolerance and psychological dependence. But hallucinogenics are not known to be addictive. High doses may induce frightening hallucinations, impaired coordination, poor judgment, mood changes, and paranoid delusions.

Let us now consider a number of ways of altering consciousness that do not rely on drugs.

Meditation: When Eastern Gods Meet Western Technology

So, back to our mountaintop and our venerable guru. Counting your breaths is one form of concentrative meditation. Let us begin our discussion of meditation by defining two broad types of meditation: concentrative and mindful.

Meditation: Concentrative and Mindful

In **concentrative meditation,** people attempt to alter their state of consciousness by detaching themselves from the external environment and the intrusive flow of thought. They do so by restricting their attention to a single or repetitive image, sound, movement, or thought.

In **mindful meditation,** as practiced in certain zen traditions, the person purposefully focuses on all "distractions"—random thoughts and images, odors, the play of light, bodily sensations, and so on. These images are perceived "passively," supposedly without response. (But recall from Chapter 3 that perception itself is an active process, influenced by expectations.) Through total passive absorption with the present, one is believed to transcend the present and achieve *nirvana*—a oneness with the universe that requires complete negation of self-awareness.

Let us return to concentrative meditation. Counting breaths is one way of practicing this form of meditation. The yogis stare intently at a pattern on a vase or mandala (note an example of a mandala on p. 354 in Chapter 9). The ancient Egyptians stared at an oil-burning lamp—the origin of the fable of Aladdin's magic lamp. Islamic mystics of Turkey, referred to as "whirling dervishes," may concentrate on their body movements or the rhythm of their breathing.

A Cognitive View of Meditation

While these concentrative and "mindful" methods vary, they seem to have a common cognitive thread: Through passive observation, the normal relationship between the person and the environment is altered. Problem-

People use many forms of meditation to try to expand inner awareness and experience inner harmony. The effects of meditation, like the effects of drugs, reflect the bodily changes induced by meditation *and* the meditator's expectations.

solving, planning, worry, awareness of the events of the day are suspended. In this way consciousness—that is, the normal focuses of attention—is altered and a state of relaxation is often induced. Meditators may report that they have "merged" with the object of meditation (the vase or a repeated phrase, for example) and then transcended it, leading to "oneness with the universe," rapture, or some great insight. Psychology has no way of measuring "oneness with the universe," but psychologists can measure bodily changes, as we shall see. It is reasonable to believe that the effects of meditation, like the effects of drugs, reflect whatever bodily changes are induced by meditation *and* one's expectations about meditation.

Let us now turn our attention to some recent research on **Transcendental Meditation** (TM), a simplified form of concentrative meditation brought to the United States by the Maharishi Mahesh Yogi in 1959. Hundreds of thousands of Americans practice TM by repeating **mantras,** words or sounds that are thought to have the capacity to help one achieve an altered state of consciousness.

TM and Dr. Benson

All this meditating business had been going on for centuries. But why, Herbert Benson of Harvard Medical School wanted to know, should a serious scientist waste his time on such far-out stuff? There had been fantastic claims for TM—from the expanding of inner awareness to the "liberating of inner energy" and the lowering of high blood pressure. TM had all the trappings of

Transcendental Meditation
The simplified form of meditation brought to the U.S. by the Maharishi Mahesh Yogi. Abbreviated *TM.*

Mantra (MON–truh). A word or sound that is repeated in TM. (A Sanskrit word that has the same origin as the word *mind.)*

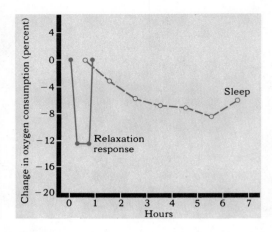

FIGURE 4.6 Comparison of the Change in Oxygen Consumption Which Occurs during the "Relaxation Response" with That Which Occurs during Sleep. The decreased metabolism of the relaxation response endures while the response is being elicited.

a wacky new religion. So Benson (1975) was skeptical when the Maharishi's disciples showed up at his lab and asked that he scientifically verify their ability to lower their blood pressure.

Though skeptical, Benson was also curious, and he did look into TM. With a vengeance. He studied practitioners ranging in age from 17 to 41. Business people, students, artists. People who had practiced TM for nine years, novices who had practiced a few weeks.

Benson's findings made him do an about-face. While TM yielded no scientific evidence of expanding consciousness, it did produce what Benson labeled a **relaxation response.** During TM the body's metabolic rate dramatically decreased. This lowered rate of oxygen consumption—or **hypometabolism**—differed from that in sleep. The drop-off in metabolism was steeper during TM (see Figure 4.6), taking minutes rather than hours to reach the lowest point. Further, oxygen consumption decreased by 10 to 20 percent during TM, as compared with the typical eight percent for sleep. The blood pressure of people with hypertension decreased (Benson and others, 1973). In fact, people who meditated twice daily tended to show normalized blood pressure through the entire day. Meditators produced more frequent alpha waves—brain waves associated with feelings of relaxation, but infrequent during sleep. Benson's subjects also showed lower heart and respiration rates and a decrease in blood lactate—a substance whose presence has been linked to anxiety (Pitts & McClure, 1967).

Relaxation response Benson's term for a group of responses which can be brought about by meditation. They involve lowered activity of the sympathetic branch of the autonomic nervous system.

Hypometabolism A condition characterized by a dramatically lowered rate of metabolism that can be induced by meditation.

A Cautionary Note We find no major fault with Benson's research. TM does appear helpful for people with hypertension and as a general relaxing agent. But keep in mind that we have no scientific evidence that TM or other forms of meditation produce a special state of consciousness. Moreover, formerly anxious and tense individuals who practice TM have also *chosen* to alter their stress-producing life styles by taking time out for themselves once or twice a day. Just taking this time out may be quite helpful. A number of studies have also suggested that other forms of relaxing, including just *sitting quietly*, may achieve most of the measurable effects of meditation.

Still, if you wish to try meditating, the following instructions for simple concentrative meditation may be of help.

Trying Concentrative Meditation

In concentrative meditation, what you *don't* do is more important than what you do. Limit your awareness to a repeated or constant stimulus that holds some attraction for you. It may be a phrase, your breathing, a pleasant sight or odor, a mantra. Adopt a passive "what happens, happens" attitude. (Don't try to force it.) Make your environment quiet and predictable. Assume a comfortable sitting position or lie back with your head raised on a pillow. Try meditating once or twice a day for 10 to 20 minutes.

For a concentrative device, Benson suggests "perceiving" the word *one* on every outbreath. This means "thinking" the word, but less actively than usual (good luck). Carrington suggests thinking or perceiving the word *in* while you are inhaling, and *out* or *ah–h–h* while exhaling.

If you are using a mantra, you can prepare for meditation and say the mantra aloud several times. Enjoy it. Then say it softer and softer. Close your eyes and think only the mantra. Allow the thinking to become "passive" so that you only "perceive" the mantra. Again, adopt a passive "what happens, happens" attitude. Continue to perceive the mantra. It may grow louder or softer, disappear for a while and then return. Allow yourself to drift. What happens, happens.

Some additional suggestions (from Carrington, 1977): Don't eat for an hour before meditating. Avoid drinks with caffeine for at least two. Seat yourself before a pleasant object, like a green plant or burning incense. Avoid facing direct light. Change your position as necessary. It's kosher to scratch or yawn. Play for time if you're interrupted: yawn, stretch, move slowly. You can check your watch through half-closed eyes.

Above all, "take what you get." You can't force relaxation. You can only set the stage for it and allow it to happen. If disruptive thoughts come in while

Are Mantras Magic Words or Just Nice Sounds?

Om, shalom, holy, easy, calm, relax, one—people use many words when they are meditating. Some are everyday words. Others are more exotic. Some people have wondered if special words, or mantras, have magical qualities for inducing a meditative state.

In Transcendental Meditation there are 16 mantras, including *ieng* and *om*. TM instructors assign novices their own mantra, supposedly on the basis of individual traits and needs. But initiating interviews are brief, and the insight of TM instructors is variable. Still, many initiates believe in the specialness of their own mantra and adhere to a pledge of secrecy about it. Of course, sincere belief that your mantra is special may be all that is needed for you to act, think, and feel as if it were. This is the so-called placebo effect. As noted in Chapter 3, a sugar pill is also a placebo, and sometimes the placebo, because of our expectations, earns effects that can't be differentiated from "the real thing."

TM mantras are soothing in sound. They have open vowels and soft consonants like *r*'s, *m*'s, and *ng*'s. They sound foreign and mysterious. Any mantra, TM or not, can help you focus your awareness and minimize distractions from intruding thoughts. Benson (1975) suggests the word *one*. He notes that it is soft, easy to think, effective, and meaningless. Carrington (1977) counters that *one* is very meaningful, suggesting one God, the unity of life, or personal unity. It is also reminiscent of the Sanskrit *om*, which has religious meanings for some people. Still, if it works for you, it works.

Choice of a mantra is a personal matter. If you are trying meditation, there is no reason not to use one mantra for a while and then switch if it doesn't do the job for you. But consistent use of a mantra can give it more potency as a cue to induce feelings of relaxation. Carrington (1977) suggests mantras like *ah-nam, shi-rim,* or *ra-mah*. Or try *one* or *om*. Don't use words like *klutz* or *rats*.

you are meditating, you can try to allow them to "pass through." Don't get wrapped up in trying to squelch them. (Note also alternate methods of relaxation discussed in Chapter 10.)

Biofeedback: Getting in Touch with the Untouchable

There is little we can take for granted in life. But two decades ago psychologists were rather secure in their distinction between *voluntary* and *involuntary* functions. Voluntary functions, like lifting an arm or leg, were conscious. They could be directly willed. But other functions, like heart rate and blood pressure, were involuntary or autonomic. Thus they were beyond conscious control. We could no more consciously control blood pressure than, say, purposefully emit alpha waves.

Once in a while, to be sure, we heard tales of strange "Yoga" experts or other exotics who could make their hair stand literally on end or "will" their cheeks to stop bleeding after a nail had been put through. But such episodes were viewed as horror stories or stage tricks. Serious scientists went back to serious research.

Headline: *Lab Rats "Expand Consciousness" at Rockefeller University?*

"Serious scientists" went back to "serious research" except for a handful of pioneering psychologists like Neal E. Miller of Rockefeller University. In the late 1960s, Miller trained laboratory *rats* to voluntarily increase or decrease their heart rates (Miller, 1969). His procedure was simple. There is a "pleasure center" in the hypothalamus of the rat. When a small burst of electricity stimulates this center it must be quite reinforcing: rats will do whatever they can to reap this bit of shock, like learning to press a lever.

Miller implanted electrodes in the rats' pleasure centers. Some rats were then given electric shock whenever their heart rates happened to increase. Other rats received shock when their heart rates were momentarily lower. One group of rats was consistently "rewarded" (that is, shocked) when their heart rates showed an increase. The other group was consistently rewarded for a decrease. After a single 90-minute training session, rats altered their heart rates by as much as 20 percent in the direction for which they had been "rewarded."

Biofeedback Training (BFT): A Definition

Miller's research was an early example of **biofeedback training** (BFT). Biofeedback is simply a system that provides, or "feeds back," information about a bodily function to an organism. Miller used electrical stimulation of the brain to feed back information to rats when they had engaged in a targeted bodily response (that is, raised or lowered their heart rates). Somehow the rats then used this information to raise or lower their heart rates voluntarily.

Similarly, people have learned to voluntarily change various bodily functions that were once considered beyond their control. But electrodes are not implanted in people's brains. Rather, people hear a "blip" or observe some other signal that informs them when the targeted response is being displayed.

Biofeedback training The systematic feeding back to an organism of information about a bodily function so that the organism can gain control of that function. Abbreviated *BFT*.

Some Human Applications   People, for instance, can learn to emit alpha waves (and feel somewhat more relaxed) through feedback from an EEG. A "blip" may increase in frequency whenever alpha waves are being emitted, and the person is asked by the psychologist simply to "make the blip go faster." An **electromyograph** (EMG), which monitors muscle tension, is commonly used to help people become more aware of muscle tension in the forehead and elsewhere, and learn to lower this tension. Through other instruments people have learned to lower their heart rates, their blood pressure, and the amount of sweat in the palm of the hand. All of these changes are relaxing.

People have also learned to elevate the *temperature* of a finger. Why bother, you ask? Limbs become subjectively warmer when more blood flows into them. Increasing the temperature of a finger—that is, altering patterns of blood flow in the body—helps some people control headaches which stem from too great a flow of blood into the head.

BFT "Strategies"   *How* do rats increase their heart rate? *What* do people do when a therapist asks them somehow to make a "blip" go faster in order to emit more alpha waves?

In keeping with scientists' preferences for discussing publicly observable behavior, rather than private events, we shall make no effort to delve into the consciousness of rats. Human self-reports must be treated cautiously, too, since they are often unreliable. But it seems that people use various cognitive strategies to change those BFT signals (Qualls & Sheehan, 1981). Many of these strategies involve fantasy, or imagery. For instance, to lower the heart rate one person may imagine looking at a grey screen while another imagines lying on a beach.

> **Electromyograph** An instrument that measures muscle tension. Abbreviated *EMG*. (From the Greek *mys*, meaning "mouse" and "muscle"—reflecting similarity between the movement of a mouse and the contraction of a muscle.)

Biofeedback is a system that provides, or "feeds back," information about a bodily function to an organism. Through biofeedback training, people have learned to gain voluntary control over normally involuntary functions.

Wait! you say? Who needs BFT? Just ask people to picture a grey screen or lying on a beach if you want them to relax? Good point. Many psychologists do precisely that, often with good results. However, BFT has helped many people become more aware of a number of functions in a quite efficient manner. That is, if people are not aware of muscle tension, biofeedback signals of some sort will rapidly increase awareness.

In any event, BFT is in its infancy both in the laboratory and in psychological treatment. There is little doubt that we shall hear of many exciting applications in the next few years.

Hypnosis

Perhaps you have seen films in which Dracula hypnotized victims into a stupor. Then he could get on with a bite in the neck with no further nonsense. Perhaps a fellow student labored to place a friend in a "trance" after reading a book on hypnosis. Or perhaps you have seen an audience member hypnotized in a nightclub act. If so, chances are this person acted as if he or she had returned to childhood, imagined that a snake was about to have a nip, or lay rigid between two chairs for a while.

A Brief History

Hypnosis, derived from the Greek word for sleep, has only recently become a respectable subject for psychological inquiry. It seems to have begun in its modern forms with Franz Mesmer in the eighteenth century. Mesmer asserted that the universe was connected by forms of magnetism—which may not be far from the mark. But he claimed that people, too, could be drawn to one another by "animal magnetism." (No bullseye here.) Mesmer used bizarre props to bring people under his "spell." He did manage a respectable cure rate for minor ailments. But we skeptics are more likely to attribute his successes to the placebo effect than to animal magnetism.

During the second half of the last century, hypnosis contributed to the formation of psychoanalytic theory. Jean Martin Charcot, a French physician, had believed that **hysterical disorders,** such as hysterical blindness and paralysis, were caused by physical problems. But when students were able to stimulate a normal woman to display hysterical symptoms through hypnosis, Charcot began to pursue psychological causes for hysterical behavior. One of his students, Pierre Janet, suggested that hysterical symptoms represented subconscious thoughts breaking through a "weakness" in the nervous system.

The notion of subconscious roots for hysterical disorders was developed in Vienna, Austria. The physician Josef Breuer discovered that a female patient felt better about personal problems when he encouraged her to talk and express her feelings freely while hypnotized. Sigmund Freud later suggested that hypnosis was one avenue to the unconscious. (Dreams were another.) Freud used Breuer's talk method, **catharsis,** to help patients relive troubling experiences and release the tension that had been produced by them. But, after a while, Freud switched from hypnosis to free association to promote self-insight and catharsis, for reasons discussed in Chapter 12.

Hypnotism Today   Today hypnotism retains its popularity in nightclubs, but is also used as an anesthetic in dentistry, childbirth, even surgery. (See the

Hypnosis (hip–NO–sis). A condition in which people appear highly suggestible and behave as though they are in a trance. (From the Greek *hypnos*, meaning "sleep.")

Hysterical disorders Disorders in which a bodily function is lost because of psychological rather than biological reasons. See Chapter 11.

Catharsis (kuh–THAR–sis). Free expression of feelings. (A Greek word meaning "purification"—suggesting that such expression of feelings is psychologically healthful.)

box "On Hypnosis and Pain.") Psychologists may use hypnosis to help teach clients how to relax or help them imagine vivid imagery in techniques like systematic desensitization, which we shall discuss at length in Chapter 12. Police use hypnosis to prompt the memories of witnesses. But courtroom testimony by hypnotized people has been challenged because witnesses may pick up on suggestions accidentally or purposefully communicated by the hypnotist (Press and others, 1981).

The Process of Hypnosis

The state of consciousness called the "hypnotic trance" is usually induced by asking subjects to narrow attention to a small light, a spot on the wall, an object held by the hypnotist, or just the hypnotist's voice. There are verbal suggestions that the limbs are becoming warm, heavy, and relaxed. (Suggestions of warmth and heaviness can induce blood flow into the limbs and help calm activity of the sympathetic division of the autonomic nervous system. It has been shown that *expecting* certain bodily changes—like changes in heart rate and skin temperature—can produce changes in that direction [Pennebaker & Skelton, 1981].) Subjects are also told that they are becoming sleepy or falling asleep.

Hypnosis is *not* sleep, as shown by differences in EEG recordings for the hypnotic trance and the stages of sleep. But the word *sleep* is understood by subjects to suggest a hypnotic trance, and has a track record of success.

Hypnotic Suggestibility   Hypnosis is most successful with people who understand what is expected of them during the "trance state." People who are readily hypnotized are said to have hypnotic suggestibility. Generally speaking, they have positive attitudes and expectations about hypnosis, and are highly motivated to become hypnotized (Barber and others, 1974). Like LSD users who claim to experience flashbacks, people with high hypnotic suggestibility enjoy daydreaming, and have highly vivid and absorbing imagination styles (Crawford, 1982).

Changes in Consciousness Brought about by Hypnosis

Hypnotists and hypnotized subjects report that hypnosis can bring about some or all of the following changes in consciousness. As you read them, keep in mind that all changes in "consciousness" are inferred from changes in observable behavior and subject self-report. This caution has implications for certain theories of hypnosis that we shall discuss in the following section.

Subjects Become Passive   When being hypnotized, or in a trance, subjects await instructions and appear to suspend planning.

Attention Becomes Narrowed   Subjects may focus on the hypnotist's voice or a spot of light and avoid attending to background noise or intruding thoughts. It is claimed that subjects may not hear a loud noise behind the head if directed not to. (However, objective measures of hearing *do* suggest that subjects do not show any reduction in auditory sensitivity; rather they *report* greater deafness [Spanos and others, 1982].) Subjects may be instructed to show heightened memory, or **hypermnesia,** by focusing on selected details and then reconstructing an entire memory. This is the method used in police

Hypermnesia
(high–purr–KNEE–she–uh).
Greatly enhanced memory.

investigations. (Such a method prompts recall, we may note, even when people are *not* in a "trance.")

Subjects Become Suggestible   Subjects may respond to suggestions that an arm is becoming lighter and will rise, or that the eyelids are becoming heavier and must close. They may act as though they cannot unlock hands clasped by the hypnotist, or bend an arm "made rigid" by the hypnotist.

Subjects Assume Unusual Roles   Most subjects expect to play sleepy, relaxed roles, but they may also be able to play roles calling for increased strength or alertness, such as riding a bicycle with less fatigue than usual (Banyai & Hilgard, 1976). In **age regression** subjects may play themselves as infants or children. Research shows that many supposed childhood memories and characteristics are played inaccurately. Nonetheless, some subjects show excellent recall of details like hair style or speech pattern. A subject may speak a language forgotten since childhood.

Subjects Suspend Reality Testing   Hypnotized subjects may act as though hypnotically induced hallucinations and delusions are real. In the "thirst hallucination," for example, subjects act as if parched even if they have just had a drink.

Subjects Show Posthypnotic Amnesia   Subjects act as though they cannot recall events that took place under hypnosis, or that they were hypnotized, if so directed. The hypnotist may later direct subjects to recall these experiences.

Subjects Follow Posthypnotic Suggestions   Subjects may follow instructions according to prearranged cues of which they are supposedly unaware. For instance, a subject may be directed to fall again into a deep trance upon the single command, "Sleep!"

Theories of Hypnosis

Psychoanalytic Theory   According to Sigmund Freud's psychoanalytic theory, the hypnotic trance represents **regression.** Hypnotized adults suspend "ego functioning," or conscious control of their behavior. They permit themselves to return to childish modes of responding that emphasize fantasy and impulse, rather than fact and logic.

Role Theory   Theodore Sarbin (1972) offers a **role theory** view of hypnosis (Sarbin & Coe, 1972). He points out that the changes in behavior that are attributed to the hypnotic trance can be successfully imitated when subjects are instructed to behave *as though* they were hypnotized. We cannot be hypnotized unless we are quite familiar with the hypnotic "role"—the set of behaviors that supposedly constitute the trance. Sarbin is not suggesting that hypnotic subjects *fake* the hypnotic role, but rather that they allow themselves to enact this role under the hypnotist's directions.

Research findings that "suggestible" hypnotic subjects are motivated to enact the hypnotic role (Barber and others, 1974), are good role players, and have vivid and absorbing imagination styles (Crawford, 1982) would all seem supportive of role theory. The fact that the behaviors shown by "hypnotized"

On Hypnosis and Pain

In 1842 London physician W. S. Ward amputated a man's leg after using a rather strange anesthetic: hypnosis. According to reports, the patient experienced no discomfort. Several years later operations were being performed routinely under hypnosis at the infirmary in London. Today hypnosis is commonly used as an anesthetic in dentistry, childbirth, even some forms of surgery.

However, recent research (Barber and others, 1974) suggests that hypnosis may not be the perfect anesthetic after all. Many patients who have been hypnotized report some pain. Others are administered analgesic (pain-relieving) drugs along with hyp-notic suggestions. It also turns out that many internal organs are not particularly sensitive to pain (some register no pain at all). In such cases only a local anesthetic is required to deaden the pain of skin incisions. It is not surprising that hypnosis and a local anesthetic are a potent combination.

We must also keep in mind that anxiety and the expectation of severe pain can compound any painful experience. Witness the muscle tension and anxiety of many dental patients just sitting in the waiting room! Any procedure that dramatically changes our expectations can also reduce pain.

---

subjects can be mimicked by role players means that we need not resort to the concept of the "hypnotic trance"—an unusual and mystifying altered state of awareness—to explain hypnotic events.

Neodissociation Theory   Ernest Hilgard (1977) explains hypnotic phenomena through **neodissociation theory.** This is the view that we can selectively focus our attention on one thing (like hypnotic suggestions) and still perceive other things "subconsciously." In a sense, we do this all the time. We are not fully conscious, or aware, of everything going on about us. Rather, at any moment we selectively focus on events, like tests, dates, or television shows, that seem important or relevant. But while taking a test we are peripherally aware of the color of the wall or the sound of rain.

When people are hypnotized, they selectively attend to the hypnotist, yet they perceive other events "subconsciously" or peripherally. When told to forget they were hypnotized, they focus on other matters. But the experience of hypnosis can be focused on afterward. Let us assume a person in a "trance" is given the posthypnotic suggestion to fall into a trance again upon hearing "Sleep," but not to recall the fact that he or she was given this command. Upon "waking" the person does not focus on the posthypnotic suggestion. But hearing the command "Sleep!" leads to rapid refocusing of attention and return to the "trance." These thoughts are all, in a sense, separated or dissociated from each other. Yet the person's attention can focus rapidly on one, then another.

Police hypnotists ask witnesses to focus on the events of a crime that they may have perceived "subconsciously" at the time. They focus carefully and can, perhaps, better recall some details.

According to Hilgard, this subconscious level of perception functions as though we had "hidden observers" in us. Hilgard has run experiments in which hypnotized subjects immersed their left hands into buckets of ice water and verbally reported no sensation. But through **automatic writing** with the right hand, these subjects recorded painful coldness. Similarly, subjects have not responded to sudden loud noises when hypnotized, but their "hidden observers" have recorded them through automatic writing.

Note that role theory and neodissociation theory are not suggesting that the sometimes remarkable phenomena of hypnosis do not occur. Rather they

Neodissociation theory A theory that explains hypnotic events in terms of subconscious perception of events. People can focus selectively on hypnotic suggestions, but still perceive outside sources of stimulation.

Automatic writing Writing about perceived stimulation while the major portion of a person's attention is focused elsewhere.

suggest that we do not need to explain these events through an altered state of awareness called a trance. Hypnosis may not be special at all. Rather it is *we* who are special—through our great imaginations, our role-playing ability, and our capacity to divide our consciousness—concentrating now on one event we deem important, concentrating later on another.

Summary

Consciousness has several meanings, including (1) sensory awareness; (2) direct inner awareness of cognitive processes; (3) personal unity or the sense of self; and (4) the waking state. Freud differentiated among ideas that are conscious, preconscious (available to awareness by focusing on them), and unconscious (unavailable to awareness under ordinary circumstances).

Electroencephalograph (EEG) records show different stages of sleep characterized by different brain waves. We have four stages of non-rapid-eye-movement (NREM) sleep and one of REM sleep. Stage 1 sleep is lightest, and stage 4 is deepest. Most dreams occur during REM sleep. Most dreams are extensions of the events of the day.

Sleep apparently serves a restorative function, although we do not know quite how, or how much sleep we need. Anxious and tense people are more likely to suffer from insomnia. Psychological methods for dealing with insomnia include relaxation and distraction from the "task" of falling asleep. Other sleep disorders include narcolepsy, apnea, sudden infant death syndrome (SIDS), and the deep-sleep disorders of night terrors, bedwetting, and sleepwalking.

Various drugs alter consciousness. Physiological dependence, or addiction, is known by presence of an abstinence syndrome upon withdrawal. Psychological dependence is resorting to a drug under stress. Some people may have genetic predispositions to become addicted to certain drugs.

Alcohol is an addictive, intoxicating depressant. Alcohol provides people with an excuse for failure or antisocial behavior, but does not directly induce antisocial behavior. Marijuana is a hallucinogenic. The active ingredients, including THC, often produce heightened and distorted perceptions, relaxation, feelings of empathy, and reports of new insights. Hallucinations are possible. Long-term effects of marijuana are unknown.

Cigarette smoke contains carbon monoxide, hydrocarbons, and the stimulant nicotine. Regular smokers adjust their smoking to maintain a consistent blood level of nicotine, suggestive of addiction. Amphetamines are stimulants that produce feelings of euphoria when taken in high doses. But high doses may also cause restlessness, insomnia, psychotic symptoms, and a "crash" upon withdrawal. Opiates like heroin are depressants that reduce pain, but they are also bought on the street because of the euphoric rush they provide. They are highly addictive. The stimulant cocaine was used in Coca-Cola prior to 1906. Now it is an expensive, illegal drug. Barbiturates are highly addictive depressants used to treat epilepsy, high blood pressure, anxiety, and insomnia. LSD is a hallucinogenic drug that produces vivid hallucinations. So-called LSD flashbacks may reflect psychological factors, like interest in attending to internal sensations and fantasy.

In meditation, one focuses on an object or objects in order to merge with and then transcend them, thereby expanding consciousness. We cannot measure "transcendental" effects, but Transcendental Meditation lowers high blood pressure and induces hypometabolism.

Biofeedback informs an organism when a targeted biological response is occurring, such as lowered heart rate or emission of alpha waves. Through biofeedback training, people and lower animals have learned to control a number of autonomic functions.

Hypnosis in its modern form was originated by Mesmer, who explained the trance through "animal magnetism." Hypnotized people typically become passive, narrow attention, become suggestible, assume unusual roles, suspend reality testing, show posthypnotic amnesia, and follow posthypnotic suggestions. Current theories of hypnosis deny the existence of a special trance state. Rather, they focus on our abilities to enact roles with which we are familiar, and to divide our awareness, so that now we focus on one event, and now another—as our attention is redirected by the hypnotist.

Truth or Fiction Revisited

- *There is no such thing as consciousness.* No simple true or false answer is possible. Many people would argue that consciousness exists because of their personal experience of being conscious. However, consciousness cannot be observed or measured directly. Therefore many psychologists prefer not to study it, and some would argue that since we cannot demonstrate that consciousness exists through scientific means, we ought not to discuss it. But many other psychologists, primarily cognitive psychologists, believe that human consciousness must be studied if we are to learn about human nature.

- *Most people have about five dreams during an eight-hour period of sleep.* True. People have most dreams during REM sleep and we undergo about five periods of REM sleep during eight hours of sleep.

- *Coca-Cola once "added life" through a powerful but now illegal stimulant.* True. Prior to 1906, Coca-Cola used the stimulant cocaine. However, to the credit of the Coca-Cola company, cocaine was discontinued as soon as questions were raised about it—long before it became illegal.

- *Heroin was once used as a cure for addiction to morphine.* True. At the time it was not recognized that heroin was also highly addictive.

- *People have managed to bring high blood pressure under control through meditation.* True. Meditation can lower blood pressure in hypertensive people.

- *You can learn to increase or decrease your heart rate consciously.* True. People have learned to control many autonomic functions through biofeedback.

- *A hypnotized man experienced no pain when his arm was amputated.* True, according to reports of observers. However, we cannot directly observe another person's private experiences—such as that of pain. We can only say that many hypnotized people act *as though* they are not having pain under surgery.

FIVE

OUTLINE

Learning and Memory

- Dogs can be trained to salivate when a bell is rung.
- During World War II a Harvard psychologist proposed that we train pigeons to guide missiles to their targets.
- People actually *learn* to feed hard-earned cash into slot machines, even when there has been no payoff for hours.
- Rats can be trained to climb a ramp, cross a bridge, climb a ladder, pedal a toy car, and do several other tasks—all in proper sequence.
- All of our experiences are perfectly and permanently imprinted on the brain so that proper stimulation can cause us to remember them exactly.
- There is no such thing as a photographic memory.
- There is no limit to the amount of information you can store in your long-term memory.
- The poison strychnine, in small doses, helps laboratory rats remember newly learned maze routes.

In Aldous Huxley's futuristic novel, *Brave New World*, the Director of the Central London Hatchery and Conditioning Center is leading a group of visitors on a tour. The year is 632 A.F. (that is, after Ford, or 632 years after the birth of Henry Ford, the originator of many techniques of mass production in the Twentieth Century).

Five classes of people populate the London of the future—Alphas, Betas, Gammas, Deltas, and Epsilons. The Alphas are the brightest. Administrators are drawn from their rank. Epsilons are least intelligent and supply menial laborers. But Epsilons are happy. Selective breeding, oxygen deprivation prior to birth, and early learning or **conditioning** combine to lead them to want only what the central planners of the brave new world decree that they should have, and not to want what it is decreed they should not have. That, notes the Director, "is the secret of happiness and virtue—liking what you've got to do. All conditioning aims at that: making people like their unescapable social destiny."

The tour arrives at the Neo-Pavlovian Conditioning Rooms, where the visitors witness a demonstration of one step in the conditioning of Delta children. Deltas belong to the **caste** just above Epsilons, and also primarily supply laborers. The social destiny of Deltas requires them to be able to focus exclusively on their assigned physical labor and not on higher forms of human activity such as reading or even the appreciation of beauty or nature.

"Set out the books," commands the Director.

In silence the nurses obeyed his command. Between the rose bowls the books were duly set out—a row of nursery quartos opened invitingly each at some gaily colored image of beast or fish or bird.

"Now bring in the children."

They hurried out of the room and returned in a minute or two, each pushing a kind of tall dumbwaiter laden, on all its four wire-netted shelves, with eight-month-old babies, all exactly alike (a Bokanovsky Group, it was evident) and all (since their caste was Delta) dressed in khaki.

"Put them down on the floor."

The infants were unloaded.

"Now turn them so that they can see the flowers and books."

Turned, the babies at once fell silent, then [crawled] toward those clusters of sleek colors, those shapes so gay and brilliant on the white pages. . . . Small hands reached out uncertainly, touched, grasped, unpetaling the . . . roses, crumpling the . . . pages of the books. The Director waited until all were happily busy. Then, "Watch carefully," he said. And, lifting his hand, he gave the signal.

The Head Nurse, who was standing by a switchboard at the other end of the room, pressed down a little lever.

There was a violent explosion. Shriller and ever shriller, a siren shrieked. Alarm bells maddeningly sounded.

The children started, screamed; their faces were distorted with terror.

"And now," the Director shouted (for the noise was deafening), "now we proceed to rub in the lesson with a mild electric shock."

He waved his hand again, and the Head Nurse pressed a second lever. The screaming of the babies suddenly changed its tone. There was something desperate, almost insane, about the sharp spasmodic yelps to which they now gave utterance. Their little bodies twitched and stiffened; their limbs moved jerkily as if to the tug of unseen wires.

"We can electrify that whole strip of floor," bawled the Director in explanation. "But that's enough," he signalled to the nurse.

Conditioning A simple form of learning in which associations are learned between stimuli and responses. See classical and operant conditioning.

Caste A rigid class distinction based on birth rather than achievement. (From the Latin *castus*, meaning "pure.")

The explosions ceased, the bells stopped ringing, the shriek of the siren died down from tone to tone into silence. The stiffly twitching bodies relaxed, and what had become the sob and yelp of infant maniacs broadened out once more into a normal howl of ordinary terror.

"Offer them the flowers and the books again."

The nurses obeyed, but at the image of the roses, at the mere sight of those gaily colored images of pussy and cock-a-doodle-doo and baa-baa black sheep, the infants shrank away in horror; the volume of their howling suddenly increased.

"Observe," said the Director triumphantly, "observe."

Books and loud noises, flowers and electric shocks—already in the infant mind these couples were compromisingly linked; and after 200 repetitions of the same or a similar lesson would be wedded indissolubly. What man has joined, nature is powerless to put asunder.

"They'll grow up with what psychologists used to call an 'instinctive' hatred of books and flowers. Reflexes unalterably conditioned. They'll be safe from books and botany all their lives." The Director turned to his nurses. "Take them away again."

Still yelling, the khaki babies were loaded on to their dumbwaiters and wheeled out, leaving behind them the smell of sour milk and a most welcome silence.

Brave New World, fortunately, is a work of fiction, not of fact. But the Director's program for teaching Delta infants to cringe at the sight of books and flowers has a realistic ring. It is clearly consistent with what we know of **classical conditioning,** a simple form of learning in which an originally neutral stimulus comes to bring forth, or **elicit,** the response usually brought forth by another stimulus by being paired repeatedly with that other stimulus. In *Brave New World*, the Director repeatedly paired books and flowers with stimuli that elicited fear (loud noises and electric shocks). The result was that the children learned to respond to the books and flowers as if they were loud noises and electric shocks.

This type of classical conditioning described so vividly in *Brave New World* is more specifically termed **aversive conditioning.** In aversive conditioning a neutral stimulus is paired repeatedly with an aversive stimulus. Eventually, the previously neutral stimulus acquires aversive properties itself. *Brave New World* is a work of fiction and shows how the learning discoveries of psychologists may be perverted. But many psychologists today use aversive conditioning to help clients gain control over "bad habits," as we shall see in Chapter 12. For example, clients who want to stop smoking cigarettes may use the technique of **rapid smoking,** or inhaling every six seconds, so that (previously desired) cigarette smoke takes on an aversive quality. Electric shock and nausea-producing drugs have also been used to help people gain control over problem drinking.

In this chapter we discuss learning and memory. We may as well admit at the outset that the very definition of **learning** stirs controversy in psychology. The concept may be defined in different ways. From a cognitive perspective, learning is *the process by which* experience leads to a relatively permanent change in behavior. Learning is *made evident* by behavioral change, but is defined as an internal, and not directly observable, process. From a behaviorist perspective, learning *is* the change in behavior that stems from experience. The behaviorist definition is **operational.** Learning is defined in terms of the measurable events or changes in behavior by which it is known.

Classical conditioning A simple form of learning in which one stimulus comes to bring forth the response usually brought forth by a second stimulus, by being paired repeatedly with the second stimulus.

Elicit To bring forth, evoke. (From the Latin *e-*, meaning "out," and *lacere*, meaning "to entice.")

Aversive conditioning An instance of classical conditioning in which a previously desirable or neutral stimulus acquires aversive (repugnant) properties by being paired repeatedly with an aversive stimulus.

Rapid smoking An example of aversive conditioning designed to reduce the appeal of cigarettes. Cigarettes are inhaled rapidly, making the smoke aversive.

Learning (1) The process by which experience leads to a relatively permanent change in behavior. (2) The behaviorist definition: a relatively permanent change in behavior that results from experience.

Operational Defined in terms of the operations required to measure a concept.

Some behaviorists prefer to use the term "acquisition of responses" rather than learning because learning can have a cognitive meaning. Let us be aware that there is a controversy about how to define learning. However, this controversy should not affect your study of the three major forms of learning that are discussed in the chapter: *classical conditioning*, *operant conditioning*, and *cognitive learning*.

Learning would do us little good if we could not remember what we had learned. For this reason, this chapter also discusses memory. We may define **memory** as the processes by which learning is maintained over the passage of time. Memory is actually a complex group of processes that do not all seem to operate according to the same set of rules. (When you have completed the chapter, you may think that we should speak of memo*ries*, not simply of *a* memory.) We shall attempt to sort out truth from fiction, myth from reality in our study of memory. We shall see that we can use many strategies to improve memory, and that memory, like other cognitive processes, involves biological changes. In our exploration of this strange biology, we shall observe life in a goldfish bowl. We shall also learn, at long last, what makes the worm turn—or, more precisely, what made a number of worms turn in the laboratories of certain psychologists.

Classical Conditioning

We have a distinct preference for having teachers grade our papers with A's rather than F's. We are also (usually) more likely to stop our cars for red than green traffic lights. Why? We are not born with instinctive attitudes toward the letters A and F. Nor are we born knowing that red means stop and green means go. We learn the meanings of these symbols through association. We come to understand their intended meanings through words that explain them.

Studies at the Soviet Military Medicine Academy: Pavlov's Research Goes to the Dogs

Learning through association can also occur automatically, as Russian scientist Ivan Pavlov (1849–1936) discovered in research with laboratory dogs. A physiologist, Pavlov was attempting to identify neural receptors in the mouth that triggered a response from the salivary glands. But his research efforts were hampered by the fact that the dogs often salivated at undesired times, as when a laboratory assistant inadvertently clinked a food tray.

Because of its biological makeup, a dog will salivate if meat is placed on its tongue. Salivation in response to meat is unlearned, a **reflex**. Reflexes are elicited by a certain range of stimuli. A **stimulus** may be defined as a change in the environment, like dropping meat on the tongue or a traffic light's changing from green to red. Reflexes are simple, unlearned responses to stimuli. Pavlov discovered that reflexes can also be learned, or conditioned, through association. His dogs began salivating in response to clinking food trays because this noise, in the past, had been paired repeatedly with the arrival of food. The dogs would also salivate when an assistant entered the laboratory. Why? In the past the assistant had brought food.

When we are faced with novel events, we sometimes have no immediate way of knowing whether or not they are important. When we are striving for

Memory Processes by which learning is maintained over time.

Reflex A simple unlearned response to a stimulus.

Stimulus (1) A change in the environment that leads to a change in behavior. (2) Any form of physical energy, such as light or sound, that impinges on the sensory receptors of an organism.

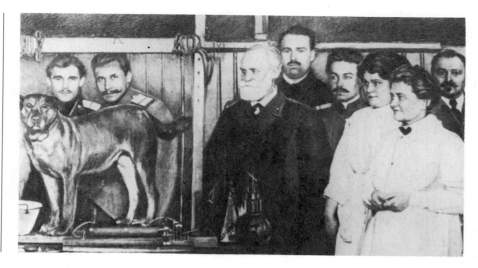

Ivan Pavlov, his assistants, and a furry expert salivator at the Soviet Military Medicine Academy early in the century.

concrete goals, we often ignore the unexpected, even when the unexpected is just as important, or more important, than the goal. So it was that Pavlov at first looked upon this uncalled-for canine salivation as an annoyance, an impediment to his research. But in 1901 he decided that his "problem" was worth looking into. Then he set about to show that he could train, or condition, his dogs to salivate when he wished and in response to any stimulus he chose.

Pavlov termed these trained salivary responses "conditional reflexes." They were *conditional* upon the repeated pairing of a previously neutral stimulus (like the clinking of a food tray) and a stimulus (in this case, food) that predictably evoked the target response (in this case, salivation). Today conditional reflexes are more generally referred to as **conditioned responses** (CRs). They are responses to previously neutral stimuli that are learned, or conditioned.

Pavlov demonstrated conditioned reflexes by strapping a dog into a harness like the one in Figure 5.1. When meat was placed on the dog's tongue, it salivated. He repeated the process several times with one difference. He preceded the meat by half a second or so with the ringing of a bell on each occasion. After several pairings of meat and bell, Pavlov rang the bell but did *not* follow the bell with the powder. Still the dog salivated. It had learned to salivate in response to the bell.

Conditioned response In classical conditioning, a learned response to a previously neutral stimulus. A response to a conditioned stimulus. Abbreviated *CR*.

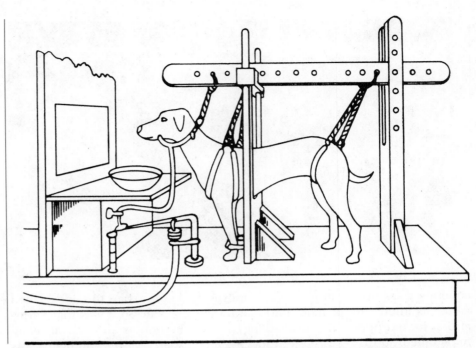

FIGURE 5.1 Pavlov's Demonstration of Conditioned Reflexes in Laboratory Dogs. From behind the two-way mirror at the left, a laboratory assistant rings a bell and then places meat on the dog's tongue. After several pairings, the dog salivates in response to the bell alone. A tube collects saliva and passes it to a vial. The quantity of saliva is taken as a measure of the strength of the animal's response.

Why? Explanations for the learning of conditioned responses are made in terms of describing the conditions of learning: The dog learned to salivate in response to the bell *because* the ringing of the bell had been paired with meat. Psychologists do *not* say that the dog "knew" that food was on the way. We cannot speak meaningfully about what a dog "knows." We can only outline the conditions under which targeted behaviors will reliably occur.

Stimuli and Responses in Classical Conditioning: US, CS, UR, and CR

Unconditioned stimulus A stimulus that elicits a response from an organism without learning. Abbreviated *US*.

Unconditioned response An unlearned response. A response to an unconditioned stimulus. Abbreviated *UR*.

Orienting reflex An unlearned response in which an organism attends to a stimulus.

Conditioned stimulus A previously neutral stimulus that elicits a conditioned response because it has been paired repeatedly with a stimulus that already elicited that response. Abbreviated *CS*.

In the demonstration described above, the meat is an unlearned or **unconditioned stimulus** (US). Salivation in response to the meat is an unlearned or **unconditioned response** (UR). The bell was at first a meaningless or neutral stimulus. It might have produced an **orienting reflex** in the dog because of its distinctness. But it was not yet associated with food. Then, through repeated association with the meat, the bell became a learned or **conditioned stimulus** (CS) for the salivation response. But salivation in response to the *bell (or CS)* is a learned or conditioned response (CR). A CR is a response similar to a UR, but the response elicited by the CS is by definition a CR, not a UR.

Types of Classical Conditioning   Most types of classical conditioning occur most efficiently when the conditioned stimulus (CS) is presented about 0.5 seconds before the unconditioned stimulus (US). But conditioning can also take place if the CS and US are presented at the same time, or if the CS is

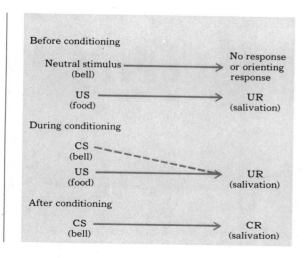

FIGURE 5.2 **A Schematic Drawing of Classical Conditioning.** Before conditioning food elicits salivation. The bell, a neutral stimulus, elicits no response or an orienting response. During conditioning, the bell is rung just before meat is placed on the dog's tongue. After several repetitions, the bell, now a CS, elicits salivation, the CR.

presented a few seconds before the US. Learning is less efficient, and sometimes does not take place, when the US is presented prior to the CS. Presenting the US prior to the CS is referred to as **backward conditioning.**

Extinction and Spontaneous Recovery

By "updating" expectations, classical conditioning helps oganisms adapt to a changing environment. A dog may learn to associate a new scent (CS) with the appearance of a dangerous animal. It can then take evasive action when it perceives the scent. A child may learn to associate hearing a car pull into the driveway (CS) with the arrival of its parents (US). Thus the child may come to squeal with delight (CR) when it hears the car.

Extinction   But times can change. The once dangerous animal may no longer be a threat. (What a puppy perceives as a threat may lose its power to menace once the dog matures.) After moving to a new house the child's parents may commute by public transportation. The sounds of a car in a nearby driveway may signal a neighbor's, not a parent's, homecoming. When conditioned stimuli (like the scent or the sound of a car) are no longer followed by unconditioned stimuli (a dangerous animal, a parent's homecoming), they lose their ability to elicit conditioned responses. In this way, the organism adapts to a changing environment. The process by which CSs lose the ability to elicit CRs because the CSs are no longer associated with USs is termed **extinction.**

In experiments in the extinction of CRs, Pavlov found that repeated presentations of the CS (or bell), without the US (meat), would lead to extinction of the CR (salivation in response to the bell). *Why?* It is tempting to say that the animal learns that hearing the bell no longer *means* that meat is on the way. But we cannot know what bells or other stimuli "mean" to animals. We can only make note of the observable behavior they display when presented with a stimulus. For this reason, the scientific explanation of Pavlov's experiment must be along these lines: The dog no longer salivates because the bell (CS) was presented repeatedly in the absence of the meat (US). Therefore, the salivation response to the bell (CR) was extinguished. When we say that a response has been extinguished, rather than that a stimulus has "lost its meaning," we are referring to observable events.

Backward conditioning A conditioning procedure in which the unconditioned stimulus is presented prior to the conditioned stimulus.

Extinction (eggs–STINK–shun). In classical conditioning, repeated presentation of the conditioned stimulus without the unconditioned stimulus, leading to suspension of the conditioned response.

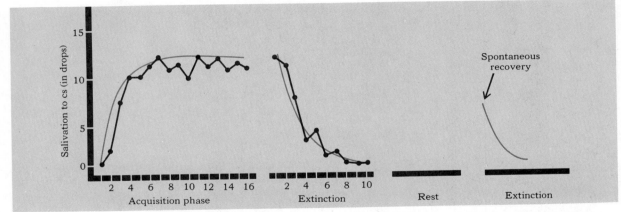

FIGURE 5.3 Learning and Extinction Curves. Actual data from Pavlov (1927) are presented in black, and idealized curves are presented in brown. In the acquisition phase, a dog salivates (shows a CR) in response to a bell (CS) after only a few trials in which the bell is paired with meat (the US). Afterward, the CR is extinguished in about 10 trials in which the CS is not followed by the US. After a rest period, the CR recovers spontaneously. A second series of extinction trials then leads to more rapid extinction of the CR.

Figure 5.3 shows that a dog conditioned by Pavlov began to salivate (show a CR) in response to a bell (CS) after only a couple of pairings of the bell with meat (the US). Continued pairings of the stimuli, or **trials,** led to increased salivation, measured in number of drops of saliva. After seven or eight trials, salivation leveled off at 11 to 12 drops. Then salivation to the bell (CR) was extinguished through several trials in which the CS (bell) was presented without the meat (US). After about 10 extinction trials, the CR (salivation in response to the bell) was no longer shown.

Spontaneous Recovery What would happen if we were to allow a day or two to pass after we had extinguished the CR (salivation response to a bell) in a laboratory dog, and then we again presented the CS (bell)? Where would you place your money? Would the dog salivate or not?

If you bet that the dog would again show the CR (salivate in response to the bell), you were correct. Organisms tend to show **spontaneous recovery** of extinguished CRs merely as a function of the passage of time. For this reason, the term *extinction* may be a bit misleading. When a species of animals becomes extinct, all members of that species capable of reproducing have died. The species vanishes permanently. But the experimental extinction of CRs does not lead to the permanent eradication of CRs. Rather, it seems that they inhibit that response. The response does remain available for future performance.

Consider Figure 5.3 again. When spontaneous recovery of the CR does occur, the strength of the response (in this case, the number of drops of saliva) is not as great as it was at the end of the series of acquisiton trials. A second set of extinction trials will also extinguish the CR more rapidly than did the first series of extinction trials. Although the CR is at first weaker the second time around, pairing the CS with the US once more will build response strength rapidly.

Spontaneous recovery, like extinction, is adaptive. What would happen if the child heard no car in the driveway for several months? It could be that

Trial In classical conditioning, a presentation of the stimuli. In conditioning trials, both the conditioned stimulus and the unconditioned stimulus are presented. In extinction trials, the conditioned stimulus is presented alone.

Spontaneous recovery In classical conditioning, the eliciting of a conditioned response by a conditioned stimulus after some time has elapsed following the extinction of the conditioned response.

the next time a car entered the driveway the child would associate the sounds with a parent's homecoming (rather than the arrival of a neighbor). This expectation could be appropriate. After all, *something* had systematically changed in the neighborhood when no car had entered the nearby driveway for so long. In the wilds a waterhole may contain water for only a couple of months during the year. But it is useful for animals to associate the waterhole with the thirst drive from time to time so that they will return to it and learn when.

As time passes and the seasons change, things sometimes follow circular paths and arrive at where they were before. Spontaneous recovery seems to provide a mechanism whereby organisms are capable of rapidly adapting to intermittently recurring situations.

Generalization and Discrimination

No two things are exactly alike. Traffic lights are hung at slightly different heights, and shades of red and green differ slightly. The barking of two dogs differs, and the sound of the same animal differs slightly from bark to bark. Adaptation requires that we respond similarly to stimuli that are equivalent in function, and that we respond differently to stimuli that are not.

Generalization   Pavlov noted that responding to different stimuli as though they are functionally equivalent is adaptive for animals. Rustling sounds in the undergrowth differ, but rabbits and deer do well to flee when they perceive any of many varieties of rustling. Sirens differ but people do well to become vigilant, or to pull their cars to the side of the road, when any siren is heard.

In a demonstration of **stimulus generalization,** Pavlov first conditioned a dog to salivate when a circle was presented. During each acquisition trial, the dog was shown a circle (CS), then given meat (US). After several trials the dog exhibited the CR of salivating when presented with the circle alone. Pavlov demonstrated that the dog also exhibited the CR (salivation) in response to closed geometric figures like ellipses, pentagons, and even squares. The more closely the figure resembled a circle, the greater the strength of the response (the more drops of saliva that flowed).

Discrimination   Organisms must also learn (1) that many stimuli that are perceived as similar are functionally different; and (2) to respond adaptively to each. During the first couple of months of life babies can discriminate the voices of their mothers from those of others, and will often stop crying when they hear Mother, but not when they hear a stranger's voice.

Pavlov showed that a dog conditioned to salivate in response to circles could be trained *not* to salivate in response to ellipses. The type of conditioning that trains an organism to show a CR in response to a narrow range of stimuli (in this case, circular rather than elliptical geometric figures) is termed **discrimination training.** Pavlov trained the dog by presenting it with circles and ellipses, but associating the meat (US) with circles only. After a while, the dog no longer showed the CR (salivation) in response to the ellipse. Instead the animal showed **stimulus discrimination**. It showed the CR in response to circles only.

Pavlov then discovered that he could make the dog behave as though it were quite anxious by increasing the difficulty of the discrimination task. After the dog showed stimulus discrimination, Pavlov showed the animal increasingly rounder ellipses. Eventually the dog could no longer discriminate them

Stimulus generalization
The eliciting of a conditioned response by stimuli that are similar to the conditioned stimulus.

Discrimination training
Teaching an organism to show a conditioned response only to one of a series of similar stimuli, accomplished by pairing that stimulus with the unconditioned stimulus and presenting similar stimuli in the absence of the unconditioned stimulus.

Stimulus discrimination
The eliciting of a conditioned response by only one of a series of similar stimuli.

from circles. Then the animal put on an infantile show. It urinated, defecated, barked profusely, and snapped at laboratory personnel.

Perhaps we would also turn nasty if we could no longer make the discriminations necessary for survival. Consider how you might behave if you could barely discriminate between a greenish-red and a reddish-green traffic light, but a person dressed in unmistakable blue was ready to hand you a traffic ticket every time you made an error.

Daily living requires appropriate generalization and discrimination. No two hotels are alike, but when traveling from one city to another it is adaptive to expect to stay in some hotel. It is encouraging that green lights in Washington have the same meaning as green lights in Honolulu. But returning home in the evening requires the ability to discriminate our homes or apartments from those of others. If we could not readily discriminate our mates from those of others, we might rapidly land in divorce court.

Higher-Order Conditioning   In **higher-order conditioning,** a previously neutral stimulus comes to serve as a CS after being paired repeatedly with a stimulus that has already become a CS. Pavlov demonstrated higher-order conditioning first by conditioning a dog to salivate (show a CR) in response to a bell (a CS). He then paired the shining of a light repeatedly with the bell. After several pairings, shining the light (the higher-order CS) came to elicit the response (salivation) that had been elicited by the bell (the first-order CS).

Consider children who learn that their parents are about to arrive when they hear a car in the driveway. It might be the case that a certain cartoon show comes on television a few minutes before the car enters the driveway. The television show can come to elicit the expectations that their parents are coming by being paired repeatedly with the car's entering the driveway. In another example, a boy may burn himself touching a hot stove. After this experience, the sight of the stove may serve as a CS for eliciting a fear response. But hearing the word "stove" may elicit a cognitive image of the stove, and so hearing the word alone may evoke a fear response.

Through classical conditioning we learn to associate stimuli so that a simple, usually passive response made to one is then made in response to the other. Let us now turn our attention to operant conditioning, in which organisms learn to engage in certain behaviors because of their effects. The sight of a hypodermic syringe may elicit a fear response because a person had a painful injection. This is an example of classical conditioning. But subsequent avoidance of injections is operant behavior. The person avoids injections because this behavior has the effect of reducing fear.

Operant Conditioning

Higher-order conditioning A form of classical conditioning in which a previously neutral stimulus comes to elicit the response brought forth by a *conditioned* stimulus by being paired repeatedly with that conditioned stimulus.

Operant conditioning A simple form of learning in which an organism learns to engage in behavior because it is reinforced.

Instrumental conditioning Another term for operant conditioning, reflecting the fact that in operant conditioning behavior is *instrumental* in achieving certain effects.

In **operant conditioning,** an organism learns to operate on the environment, or to engage in certain behavior, because of the *effects* of that behavior. Operant conditioning is also known as **instrumental conditioning,** or instrumental learning, because the learned behavior is *instrumental* in achieving certain effects.

We begin this section with the historic work of Columbia University psychologist Edward L. Thorndike. Then we examine the more recent work of Harvard University psychologist B. F. Skinner.

Edward L. Thorndike and the Law of Effect

During the 1890s there was something of a mystery in the neighborhood of Columbia University in New York City. Stray cats were disappearing from the streets and alleyways. It turned out that many of them were brought to the quarters of a doctoral student, Edward Thorndike, as subjects for experiments in learning by trial and error.

Thorndike placed the cats in so-called "puzzle boxes." If the animals managed to pull a string in the cage a latch would open, allowing the cat to escape from the box and reach a bowl of food that had been placed outside.

When first placed in a puzzle box, the cat would try to squeeze through any opening and claw and bite at the confining bars and wire. It would claw at any feature it could reach inside or outside the box. The cat would seem to pay little or no attention to the food outside.

Through this **random trial-and-error** behavior it might take three to four minutes before the cat would first chance upon the response of pulling the string. But pulling the string would have the immediate effect of opening the cage and allowing the cat to reach the food. When later replaced in the cage, the cat would again take nearly three to four minutes to happen upon pulling the string, a response that would again release the animal. But as the trials proceeded, the cat would take less and less time to pull the string. After seven or eight trials, it would pull the string within a few seconds after being placed in the box.

Edward L. Thorndike.

"Stamping In" and "Stamping Out" Responses   Thorndike explained the cat's learning to pull the string in terms of his **law of effect.** According to this law, in a certain situation (like being placed in the puzzle box), a particular response (like pulling the string) would be "stamped in," or strengthened, by a reward (escaping the box and eating). Briefly, rewards would stamp in S–R (stimulus–response) connections. Punishments, by contrast, would "stamp out" connections between stimuli and responses. Organisms would learn *not* to engage in responses that had been punished. Later we shall see that the effects of punishment on learning are less certain.

B. F. Skinner and associates at the Harvard University laboratory.

B. F. Skinner and Reinforcement

"What did you do in the war, Daddy?" used to be a familiar question to many who served during America's conflicts. Some stories involve heroism, others involve the unusual. B. F. Skinner's story, as related in his autobiography *The Shaping of a Behaviorist*, is among the unusual.

Project Pigeon   During World War II Skinner proposed "Project Pigeon," the systematic training of pigeons to guide missiles to their targets. In their training, the pigeons would be **reinforced** for pecking at targets projected onto a screen (see Figure 5.4). Then they would be placed in missiles. Pecking at similar targets displayed on a screen would correct the flight path of the missile, resulting in a "hit" and a sacrificed pigeon. But plans for building the necessary missile—for some reason called the *Pelican* and not the *Pigeon*—were scrapped. The pigeon equipment was too bulky, and, as Skinner lamented, his suggestion was not taken seriously. Apparently the Defense Department concluded that Project Pigeon was for the birds.

Random trial-and-error
Referring to the behavior that occurs prior to learning what behavior is rewarded or reinforced. The implication is that in a novel situation the organism happens upon the first "correct" (reinforced) response by chance.

Law of effect Thorndike's principle that responses are "stamped in" or "stamped out" because of their effects.

Reinforce To follow a behavior with a stimulus that increases the frequency of that behavior.

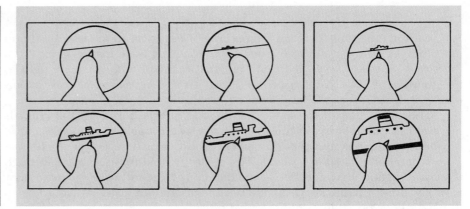

FIGURE 5.4. During World War II, B. F. Skinner suggested training pigeons to guide missiles to their targets. In an operant conditioning procedure, the pigeons would be reinforced for pecking targets projected on a screen. Afterward, in combat, pecking at the on-screen target would keep the missile on course.

Operant Behavior   Project Pigeon may have been scrapped, but the principles of learning Skinner applied to the project have found wide application in operant conditioning. In classical conditioning, an organism learns to associate stimuli. One previously neutral stimulus (the CS) comes to elicit the response brought forth by another stimulus (the US) because they are paired repeatedly. But in operant conditioning an organism learns to *do* something, because of its effects or consequences.

This is **operant behavior,** behavior that manipulates the environment. In classical conditioning, involuntary responses like salivation or eyeblinks are often conditioned. In operant conditioning, *voluntary* responses like pecking at a target, pressing a lever, or many of the athletic skills required in playing tennis are usually acquired, or conditioned.

In operant conditioning, organisms engage in operant behaviors, also known simply as **operants,** that result in presumably desirable consequences such as food, a hug, an A on a test, attention, or social approval. Some children learn to conform their behavior to social codes and rules to earn the attention and approval of their parents and teachers. Other children, ironically, may learn to "misbehave" since misbehavior also results in attention from other people. Children may especially learn to be "bad" when their "good" behavior is routinely ignored.

Skinner Boxes and Cumulative Recorders   In order to study operant behavior efficiently, Skinner devised an animal cage termed the Skinner box (see Figure 5.5). Unlike Thorndike's puzzle box, a "correct" response does not result in the animal's escaping, having to be hunted down, and replaced in the box. The animal remains in the box, but the response desired by the trainer, like pressing a lever, results in a food pellet's being dropped into the cage.

Skinner further mechanized Thorndike's method for studying behavior by making use of a **cumulative recorder,** as shown in Figure 5.6. Not only is the trainer freed from chasing the subject after each correct response, but the trainer need not even be present when correct responses are made. In the examples used, the lever in the Skinner box is connected to the recorder so that the recording pen moves upward with each correct response. The paper

Operant behavior Voluntary responses that are reinforced.

Operant An "operant" is the same as an operant behavior.

Cumulative recorder An instrument that records the frequency of an organism's operants (or "correct" responses) as a function of the passage of time.

FIGURE 5.5. One of the stars of modern psychology, an albino rat, earns its keep in a Skinner box. The animal presses a lever because of reinforcement—in the form of food pellets—that is delivered through the spout of the feeder. The habit strength of this operant can be measured as the frequency of lever pressing.

moves continuously to the left at a slow but regular pace. In the sample record shown in Figure 5.6, lever pressings (which record correct responses) were at first few and far between. But after several reinforced responses, lever pressing came fast and furious. When the rat is no longer hungry, the lever pressing will drop off and then stop.

The First "Correct" Response　In operant conditioning, it matters little how the first response that is reinforced comes to be made. The organism can happen upon it by chance, as in random trial-and-error learning. The organism can also be physically guided into the response. You may command your dog to "Sit!" then press its backside down until it is in a sitting position. Finally you reinforce sitting with food or a pat on the head and a kind word.

FIGURE 5.6　A Cumulative Recorder. Paper moves continuously to the left while a pen automatically records each targeted response by moving upward. When the pen reaches the top of the paper, it is automatically reset to the bottom.

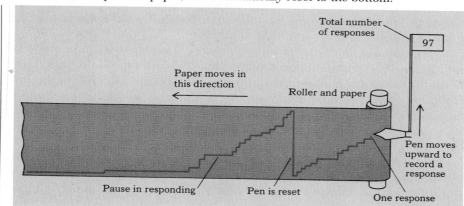

Animal trainers use physical guiding or coaxing to bring about the first "correct" response. Can you imagine how long it would take to train your dog if you waited for it to sit or roll over and then seized the opportunity to command it to sit or roll over? You would both age significantly in the process.

People, of course, can be verbally guided into desired responses when they are learning tasks like running a machine, spelling, or adding numbers. But they then need to be informed when they have made the correct response. Knowledge of results is often all the reinforcement that motivated people need to learn new skills.

Reinforcers   Reinforcers increase the probability that an operant will be repeated. How do we know whether a stimulus is a reinforcer? Any stimulus that increases the probability that responses preceding it will be repeated serves as a reinforcer. Reinforcers include food pellets when an organism has been deprived of food, water when it has been deprived of liquid, the opportunity to mate, and the sound of a bell that has been previously associated with eating. (Yes, a CS can serve as a reinforcer.)

Skinner distinguished between positive and negative reinforcers. **Positive reinforcers** increase the probability that an operant will occur when they are applied. Food and approval usually serve as positive reinforcers. **Negative reinforcers** increase the probability that an operant will occur when they are *removed*. People often learn to plan ahead so that they need not fear that things will go wrong. Fear acts as a negative reinforcer because *removal* of fear increases the probability that the behaviors preceding it (such as planning ahead or fleeing a predator) will be repeated.

Greater reinforcers prompt more rapid learning than do lesser reinforcers. You will probably work much harder for $1,000 than for $10. (If not, get in touch with me—I have some chores that need to be taken care of.) With sufficient reinforcement, operants become a **habit.** They show a high probability of recurrence in a certain situation.

We can also distinguish between primary and secondary or conditioned reinforcers. **Primary reinforcers** are effective because of the biological makeup of the organism. Food, water, adequate warmth (positive reinforcers), and pain (a negative reinforcer) all serve as primary reinforcers. **Secondary reinforcers** acquire their value through being associated with established reinforcers. For this reason they are also termed **conditioned reinforcers.** We may seek money because we have learned that it may be exchanged for primary reinforcers. Money, attention, social approval, all are conditioned reinforcers in our culture. We may be suspicious of, or not "understand," people who are not interested in money or the approval of others. Part of "understanding" others lies in being able to predict what they will find reinforcing.

Positive reinforcer A reinforcer that, when *presented*, increases the frequency of an operant. Food and approval are usually positive reinforcers.

Negative reinforcer A reinforcer that, when *removed*, increases the frequency of an operant. Pain, anxiety, and disapproval are usually negative reinforcers—that is, organisms will learn to engage in responses that permit them to *avoid* these reinforcers.

Habit A learned response that shows a high frequency of recurrence under certain conditions.

Primary reinforcer An unlearned reinforcer, such as food, water, warmth, or pain.

Secondary reinforcer A stimulus that gains reinforcement value through association with other, established reinforcers. Money and approval are secondary reinforcers.

Conditioned reinforcer Another term for a secondary reinforcer.

FIGURE 5.7 Understanding other people includes being able to predict what they will find reinforcing. In this Dagwood cartoon, Dagwood apparently finds money more reinforcing than the praise of his boss, Mr. Dithers.

Extinction and Spontaneous Recovery in Operant Conditioning Extinction in classical conditioning results from repeated presentation of the CS without the US, so that the CR becomes inhibited. In operant conditioning, extinction results from repeated performance of operant behavior without reinforcement. After a number of trials, the operant behavior also becomes inhibited (is no longer shown).

After some time has passed, however, an organism will usually again perform the operant when placed in a situation in which the operant had been previously reinforced. Spontaneous recovery of learned responses occurs in operant as well as classical conditioning. If the operant is reinforced at this time, it quickly regains its former strength.

Baseball Magic? Superstitious Behavior in People and Birds

Have you ever watched the typical baseball pitcher closely? He usually does a good deal of fidgeting before releasing the ball. If you analyze the "fidgeting" carefully, you often find that he engages in a complex ritual before letting the ball go. Some pitchers touch their caps, tug their ear lobes, cross themselves, bow their heads, or undergo a whole series of similar behaviors. This series of acts may have been performed so many times that it is now habitual, that is, it occurs without thinking. But if someone were to prevent the pitcher from engaging in these behaviors, he might protest that he simply couldn't pitch without them.

Similarly, golfer Gary Player always wears black. Race car driver Mario Andretti never signs autographs with a green pen. Hockey player Bobby Orr touched every teammate on the shoulder before a game.

In an article "Baseball Magic" we are told that former Brooklyn Dodger pitcher Alan Foster once forgot his shoes on a road trip and used his roommate's (Gmelch, 1971). He pitched a no-hitter, and he and the shoes became inseparable. Rube Waddell, a member of the old Philadelphia Athletics, had to carry a hairpin when he pitched. If he won he kept the hairpin. If he lost he searched the streets until he found another.

Why do athletes and other people develop superstitious behavior? According to B. F. Skinner, it may be because the honored object or magical act (like wearing the borrowed shoes) was once accidentally associated with desired consequences (like pitching a no-hitter). In this way the superstitious response is reinforced.

In an experiment on creating "superstitious" behavior, Morse and Skinner (1957) intermittently dropped food pellets into the cages of food-deprived pigeons regardless of the birds' behavior. It seems that most pigeons were reinforced by the pellets for whatever they were doing at the time. A bird who had been circling circled more frequently. Another, who had been pecking, jerked its head repeatedly.

All this, of course, is limited to pigeons and a few athletes. You're too intelligent to have any superstitions, aren't you?

"THIS IS A STICKUP!"

"THIS IS A STICKUP!"

"THIS IS A STICKUP!"

Reinforcers versus Rewards and Punishments **Rewards,** like reinforcers, are stimuli that increase the frequency of behavior. But rewards are also considered pleasant events. Skinner preferred the concept of reinforcement to that of reward, because reinforcement does not suggest trying to "get inside the head" of an organism (person or lower animal) to guess what it would find pleasant or unpleasant. A list of reinforcers is arrived at **empirically,** by observing what sorts of stimuli will increase the frequency of the behavior of organisms.

Punishments are aversive events that suppress or decrease the frequency of the behavior with which they are associated. (Recall that *negative reinforcers* are defined in terms of *increasing* the frequency of behavior, although the increase occurs when the negative reinforcer is *removed.* A punishment *decreases* the frequency of a behavior when it is *applied.*) Punishment, like rewards, can influence the probability that behavior will be shown. But many learning theorists agree that punishment is usually undesirable, especially in raising children:

1. *Punishment does not suggest an alternate, acceptable form of behavior.*
2. *Punishment tends to suppress undesirable behavior only under circumstances in which its delivery is guaranteed.* It does not take children long to learn that they can "get away with murder" with one parent, or one teacher, but not with another.
3. *Punishment can create anger and hostility.* Adequate punishment will almost always suppress unwanted behavior—but at what cost? A child may express accumulated feelings of hostility against other children.

Reward A pleasant stimulus that increases the frequency of the behavior it follows. (Why did Skinner prefer to use the term "reinforcement"?)

Empirically By trial or experiment, rather than by logical deduction.

Punishment An unpleasant stimulus that suppresses the behavior it follows. (What is the difference between a negative reinforcer and a punishment?)

4. *Punishment may generalize too far.* For example, the child who is punished severely for bad table manners may stop eating altogether. Overgeneralization is more likely to occur when the child does not know exactly why he or she is being punished, and when the child has not been shown alternate, acceptable behaviors.

5. *Punishment may be modeled as a way of solving problems or coping with stress.* Later in this chapter, and in Chapter 9, we shall see that one way in which children learn is by observing others. Even though children may not immediately perform the behavior they observe, they may perform it later on, even much later on as adults, when their circumstances are similar to those of the **model.**

It is preferable to focus on rewarding children for desirable behavior than to punish them for unwanted behavior. By ignoring their misbehavior, or by using **time out** from positive reinforcement, we can consistently avoid reinforcing children for misbehavior.

To reward or positively reinforce children for desired behavior takes time and care. Simply never using punishment is not enough. First, we must pay attention to them when they are behaving well. If we take their desirable

Model An organism that engages in a response that is imitated by another organism.

Time out In operant conditioning, a method for decreasing the frequency of undesired behaviors: an organism is removed from a situation in which reinforcement is available when unwanted behavior is shown.

Self-Stimulation? Shocking!

What if the most intense form of positive reinforcement, the greatest imaginable pleasure, were to be found deep within your own brain? What would it be like if you could locate this source of pleasure and "switch it on" at will?

This may sound like the stuff of science fiction, but more than 20 years ago experiments by James Olds and Peter Milner (Olds, 1969; Olds & Milner, 1954) suggested that such areas do exist within the brains of people and other mammals. With a bit of trial and error, they can be located and switched on rather easily.

Olds and Milner discovered accidentally (how many important discoveries are made by accident!) that mild electrical stimulation of an area of the hypothalamus of the rat would reinforce whatever the rat was doing at the time. For this reason, they labeled this area the "pleasure center" of the rat.

Olds and Milner found that a rat that could stimulate its own pleasure center, as by pressing a lever in a Skinner box, would learn to do so rapidly. It would then stimulate itself repeatedly, up to 100 times a minute and over 1,900 times an hour.

Rats will perform complex behaviors to receive such stimulation. They will learn mazes with very few errors. If you deprive them of food for 24 hours, they will still choose brain stimulation over food. Now, that's reinforcement.

As noted in Chapter 2, a number of brain surgery patients have reported intense pleasure when certain areas of the brain were stimulated with pen-

cil electrodes. Findings like these have led to a few cases in which severely disturbed psychiatric patients have been able to use electrical self-stimulation of the brain to improve their moods.

But as also noted in Chapter 2, the responsiveness of specific areas of the brain to stimulation is not as predictable in people as in lower animals. In people, the physical effects of brain stimulation also interact with expectations and learning. It is unlikely that it will ever be as easy to "switch on" people as it is to switch on rats.

A rat with an electrode implanted in its "pleasure center" presses a lever to stimulate itself. In public, yet!

behavior for granted, and act as if we are aware of them only when they misbehave, we may be encouraging misbehavior. Second, we must carefully physically or verbally guide them into making the desired responses. We cannot teach children table manners by waiting for them to exhibit proper responses by random trial-and-error and then reinforcing them. If we waited by holding a half gallon of ice cream behind our backs as a reward, we would have wet dining room floors long before we had children with table manners.

Discriminative Stimuli   B. F. Skinner might not have been able to get his pigeons into the drivers' seats of missiles during the war, but he had no problem training them to respond to traffic lights. Try the following experiment for yourself.

Find a pigeon. Or sit on a park bench, close your eyes, and one will find you. Place it in a Skinner box with a button on the wall. Drop a food pellet into the cage whenever it pecks the button. (Soon it will learn to peck the button whenever it has not eaten for a while.) Now place a small green light in the cage. Turn it on and off intermittently throughout the day. Reinforce button-pecking with food whenever the green light is on, but not when the light is off. It will not take long for this clever city pigeon to learn that it will gain as much by grooming itself or squawking and flapping around as it will by pecking the button when the light is off.

The green light will have become a **discriminative stimulus.** Discriminative stimuli act as cues. They provide information as to when an operant (in this case, pecking a button) will be reinforced (in this case, by a food pellet being dropped into the cage).

As noted above, operants that are not reinforced tend to become extinguished. For the pigeon in our experiment, pecking the button *when the light is off* becomes extinguished.

A moment's reflection will suggest many ways in which discriminative stimuli influence our behavior. Would you rather ask your boss for a raise when she is smiling or when she is frowning? Wouldn't you rather answer the telephone when it is ringing? Do you think it wise to try to get smoochy when your date is blowing smoke in your face or chugalugging a bottle of antacid tablets? One of the factors involved in gaining social skills is learning to interpret social discriminative stimuli (smiles, tones of voice, body language) accurately.

Schedules of Reinforcement   Some responses are maintained by **continuous reinforcement.** You probably become warmer every time you put on heavy clothing. You probably become less thirsty every time you drink water. But if you have ever watched people throwing money down the maws of slot machines, or "one-armed bandits," you know that behavior can also be maintained by **partial reinforcement.**

There is some folklore about gambling that is based on solid learning theory. You can get a person "hooked" on gambling by fixing the game to allow heavy winnings at first. Then you gradually space out the gambling behaviors that are reinforced until the gambling is maintained by very infrequent winning—or even no winning at all.

New operants or behaviors are acquired most rapidly through continuous reinforcement, or, in some cases, through "one-trial learning" that met with great reinforcement. So-called **pathological gamblers** often experienced a "big win" at the racetrack or casino or in the lottery in their late teens or

Discriminative stimulus In operant conditioning, a stimulus that indicates when an operant will be reinforced.

Continuous reinforcement A schedule of reinforcement in which every correct response is reinforced.

Partial reinforcement One of several reinforcement schedules in which not every correct response is reinforced.

Pathological gambler A person who gambles habitually, despite consistent losses. A compulsive gambler.

early twenties (Greene, 1982). But once the operant has been acquired, it can be maintained by tapering off to a schedule of partial reinforcement.

There are four basic schedules of reinforcement. They are determined by changing either the *interval* of time that must elapse between correct responses before reinforcement is made available, or the *ratio* of correct responses to reinforcements. If the interval that must elapse between correct responses, before reinforcement becomes available, is zero seconds, the reinforcement schedule is continuous. A larger interval of time, such as one or 30 seconds, is a partial reinforcement schedule. A one-to-one (1:1) ratio of correct responses to reinforcements is a continuous reinforcement schedule. A higher ratio, such as a 2:1 or 5:1 ratio, would be a partial reinforcement schedule.

The four basic types of schedules of reinforcement are *fixed interval*, *variable interval*, *fixed ratio*, and *variable ratio* schedules.

In a **fixed interval schedule,** a fixed amount of time, say one minute, must elapse between the previous and subsequent times that reinforcement is made available for correct responses.

In a **variable interval schedule,** varying amounts of time are allowed to elapse between making reinforcement available. In a three-minute variable interval schedule, the mean amount of time that would elapse between reinforcement opportunities would be three minutes, but each interval might vary from, say, one to five minutes or from two to four minutes.

With a fixed interval schedule, an organism's response rate falls off after each reinforcement, as if it has learned that it must wait a while before reinforcement will be made available. But the response rate remains rapid on the more unpredictable variable interval schedule.

In a **fixed ratio schedule,** reinforcement is provided after a fixed number of correct responses have been made.

In a **variable ratio schedule,** reinforcement is provided after a variable number of correct responses has been made. In a 10:1 variable ratio schedule, the mean number of correct responses that would have to be made before a subsequent correct response would be reinforced is 10, but the ratio of correct responses to reinforcements might be allowed to vary from, say, 1:1 to 20:1 on a random basis.

Fixed ratio and variable ratio schedules maintain a high response rate. With a fixed ratio schedule, it is as if the organism learns that it must make several responses before being reinforced. It then "gets them out of the way" as rapidly as possible. With a variable ratio schedule, reinforcement can come at any time. This unpredictability also maintains a high response rate.

Shaping

If you are teaching disco-type maneuvers to people who have never danced, do not wait until they have performed a perfect Latin hustle before telling them they're on the right track. The fox-trot will be back in style before they have learned a thing.

We can teach complex behaviors by **shaping,** or at first reinforcing small steps toward the behavioral goals. At first it may be wise to smile and say "Good" when a reluctant newcomer gathers the courage to get out on the dance floor, even if your feet get flattened by his initial clumsiness. If you are teaching someone to drive a car with a standard shift, at first generously reinforce the learner simply for shifting without stalling.

But as training proceeds, we come to expect more before dispensing reinforcement. We reinforce **successive approximations** to the goal. If you

Fixed interval schedule A schedule in which a fixed amount of time must elapse between the previous and subsequent times that reinforcement is available.

Variable interval schedule A schedule in which a variable amount of time must elapse between the previous and subsequent times that reinforcement is available.

Fixed ratio schedule A schedule in which reinforcement is provided after a fixed number of correct responses.

Variable ratio schedule A schedule in which reinforcement is provided after a variable number of correct responses.

Shaping In operant conditioning, a procedure for teaching complex behaviors that at first reinforces approximations to the target behavior.

Successive approximations In operant conditioning, behaviors that are progressively closer to a target behavior.

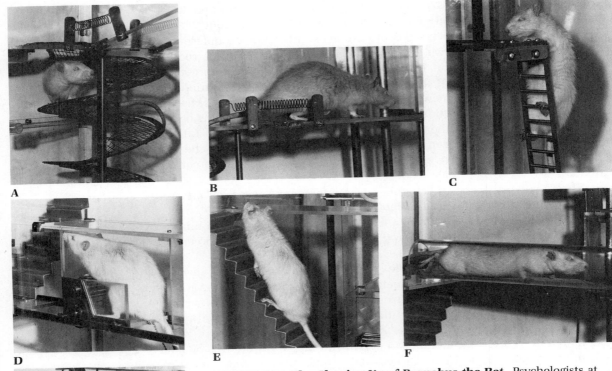

FIGURE 5.8   The Shaping Up of Barnabus the Rat. Psychologists at Columbia University (Pierrel & Sherman, 1963) shaped Barnabus to perform a complex behavioral chain by reinforcing each behavior in sequence. The sequence proceeded from last to first so that each reward would trigger the next behavior in the chain. In these photos you see Barnabus (a) climb a spiral ramp, (b) cross a bridge, (c) climb a ladder, (d) pedal a toy car, (e) climb steps, (f) crawl through a tube, and (g) ride an elevator to return to the starting platform. Finally, Barnabus presses a lever to attain a food pellet (not shown). Complex behavior for a rat?

want to train a rat to climb a ladder, first reinforce it (with a food pellet) when it turns toward the ladder. Then wait until it approaches the ladder before using reinforcement. Then do not drop a food pellet into the cage until the rat touches the ladder. In this way the rat will reach the top of the ladder more quickly than if you had waited until the target behavior had first occurred by random trial and error. This method of shaping was used to train one rat, Barnabus, to engage in the complex behavioral sequence shown in Figure 5.8.

Learning to drive a new standard-shift automobile to a new job also involves a complex sequence of operant behaviors. At first we actively seek out all the discriminative stimuli or landmarks that cue us when to turn—signs, buildings, hills, and valleys. We also focus on shifting to a lower gear as we slow down so that the car won't stall. But after many repetitions these responses, these chains of behavior, become "habitual" and we need pay very little attention to them.

Have you ever driven home from school or work and been suddenly unsettled as you got out of your car that you couldn't recall exactly how you had returned home? Your entire trip may seem "lost." Were you in great danger? How could you allow such a thing to happen. Actually, it may be that your responses to the demands of the route and to driving your car had become so habitual that you did not have to focus much awareness on them. You were able to think about dinner, a problem at work, or the weekend as you drove. But if something unusual, like hesitation in your engine or a severe rainstorm, had occurred on the way home, you would have deployed as much attention as was needed to arrive home. Your trip was probably quite safe, after all.

Applications of Operant Conditioning   People have efficiently trained animals and influenced each other's behavior since the dawn of history. *Brave New World* showed us how a fictional world abused principles of operant conditioning. But in the real world these principles have led to a number of recent beneficial applications.

Principles of operant conditioning are used in biofeedback training, which was discussed in Chapter 4. Through biofeedback training, people and lower animals have learned to control autonomic responses to attain reinforcement. The rats in Neal Miller's laboratory, for example, were reinforced by mild shock in the pleasure centers of their brains when they accelerated or decelerated their heart rates. As part of a program of therapy to enhance their well-being, people have learned to manipulate their heart rates, blood pressure, galvanic skin response, even the emission of certain brain waves.

When people receive biofeedback training, the reinforcement is *information*, not electric current in the brain. Perhaps a "bleep" sound changes in pitch or frequency of occurrence to signal that they have modified the autonomic function in the target direction. Biofeedback has also been used with

Can Masochism Be Explained through Principles of Learning?

Why is it that some people are *masochistic*, that they seem to derive pleasure from stimulation that most of us would consider painful? In the case of sexual masochism, it may be that guilt encourages the individual to seek punishment for sexual acts so that they can be enjoyed. Receiving punishment constitutes "making amends," so that now—with the price paid—it is "all right" to experience pleasure.

But Pavlov ran a series of experiments that suggests that some cases of masochism may reflect conditioning. He trained dogs to seek shocks that were strong enough to make rigid the muscles of untrained animals.

Pavlov began by associating feeding with a weak electric shock in the leg. The process was repeated daily so that the shock came to serve as the CS for the US of food. After repeated pairings, the shock alone elicited salivation (the CR). In addition, Pavlov also increased the shock gradually on a daily basis. The dogs eventually tolerated and even sought out high levels of shock, whether or not they were hungry.

This experiment has been replicated many times, in the United States as well as Russia. Once they have undergone such training, many animals will learn to perform operants that result in high levels of electric shock. The shock becomes a secondary or conditioned reinforcer, even at high levels.

Why do trained animals seek electric shock? Pavlov theorized that the "neural connection" between the shock and salivation had grown so strong that there was no longer a neural path between the stimulus of the shock and a pain response. There is little physiological evidence to support the neural-connection hypothesis. Nor can we know whether the trained animals did or did not encounter pain. We can only observe how they behaved. The animals' behavior suggests that high levels of shock had, in fact, become conditioned positive reinforcers.

accident patients who have lost neuromuscular control of various parts of the body. A "bleep" informs them when they have contracted a muscle group or sent an impulse down a neural pathway. By learning to change the bleeps, they also gradually regain voluntary control over the damaged function.

Behavior therapists also apply operant conditioning to foster desired responses, such as social skills, and to extinguish unwanted behaviors, such as social withdrawal in a mental hospital. Several techniques are discussed in Chapter 12. Here let us briefly note that therapists may show clients how to refuse unreasonable requests through modeling the response and through verbal instruction (coaching). They reinforce client self-assertiveness by offering approval and informing them of the appropriateness of their behavior. In **token economies,** when institutionalized mental patients engage in appropriate social behaviors, they are reinforced by receiving tokens, such as poker chips. These tokens are conditioned reinforcers and may be exchanged by the patient for snacks and privileges.

B. F. Skinner has been instrumental in developing an educational practice called **programed learning.** Programed learning is based on the assumption that any complex task, involving conceptual learning as well as motor skills, can be broken down into a number of small steps. These steps can be shaped individually and combined in sequence to form the correct behavioral chain. Programed learning does not punish errors. Instead, correct responses are reinforced. Everyone earns "100," but at his or her own pace. Programed learning also assumes that it is the task of the teacher (or program) to structure the learning experience so that errors will not be made.

Operant Conditioning and Human Behavior   In a political essay written in 1822, British philosopher Jeremy Bentham wrote that "Nature has placed mankind under the governance of two sovereign masters, pain and pleasure" (p. 33). He added that the effectiveness of pain and pleasure in influencing behavior would depend on their (1) intensity; (2) duration; (3) certainty; and (4) immediacy (p. 64). Intense, enduring, certain, and immediate reinforcers do shape behavior more effectively than do weak, brief, uncertain, and delayed reinforcers, especially during the early stages of learning.

But are we "under the governance" of punishments and rewards? Is all human behavior controlled by reinforcement? This is a complex and troubling question. It is true that human behavior *can* be acquired through reinforcement. In one study, for example, college students were reinforced by another person's agreement whenever they expressed an opinion (Verplanck, 1955). Without being aware of the experimental procedure, the students significantly increased their frequency of stating opinions. In other "experiments," professors have been reinforced for behaviors like telling jokes by student attention or smiles. The frequency of the targeted behaviors has increased dramatically, again without awareness of the conditioning process.

But some psychologists believe that principles of conditioning explain *all* human behavior. They assert that our behavior is the inevitable outcome of our biological potentials and our **reinforcement histories.** This behaviorist view regards conditioning as the basic unit of all human learning. Human learning is seen as wholly mechanical and determined by reinforcement.

Opposing psychologists will usually agree that conditioning procedures can be used to shape *some* human behavior. Parents and teachers can use conditioning to toilet train children or help them associate written letters with spoken sounds. But these psychologists argue that with people reinforcers do

Token economy The awarding of fixed numbers of tokens for specified desirable behaviors in an institutional setting. The tokens may be exchanged for privileges.

Programed learning A method of learning based on operant conditioning principles, in which complex tasks are broken down into simple steps. The proper performance of each step is reinforced. Incorrect responses are not punished, but go unreinforced.

Reinforcement history The summation of one's reinforced learning experiences, which, in operant conditioning, is assumed to account for current behaviors.

not work for mechanical reasons. Adults may work for money and social approval, but this does not mean that money and social approval mechanically shape their behavior. Rather, these reinforcers, and others, provide a person with information as to whether a desired response has been made. The person then has the choice of whether or not to display that response. Some people also choose to engage in nonreinforced behavior because of their own moral values. For instance, people may donate money anonymously to charity.

Behaviorists counter that in such instances self-approval is a conditioned reinforcer that was acquired according to principles of learning, and that controls behavior as fully as food pellets controlled Barnabus the Rat. You may think of yourself as making conscious choices and having freedom. But behaviorists argue that your choices, and even your thoughts (which some would describe as **covert** verbal behaviors), are fully determined by your reinforcement history.

What do you think? Is human behavior controlled by reinforcement, or is there such a thing as personal freedom? We shall deal with this issue again when we discuss human personality in Chapter 9.

Let us now turn our attention to the field of **cognitive learning.** Cognitive research suggests that much learning, by humans and lower animals, is not so mechanical after all.

Covert Hidden or concealed.
Cognitive learning Learning that involves mental representation of the world. Examples of cognitive learning include problem solving by insight, the formation of cognitive maps, latent learning, and observational learning.

Cognitive Learning

About 60 years ago German Gestalt psychologist Wolfgang Köhler became convinced that not all forms of learning could be explained by mechanical conditioning when one of his chimpanzees, Sultan, went bananas. Sultan had learned to use a stick to rake in bananas placed outside his cage. But now Herr Köhler (pronounced *hair curler*) placed the banana beyond the reach of the stick. He gave Sultan two bamboo poles that could be fitted together to make a single pole long enough to retrieve the delectable reward. The set-up was similar to that shown in Figure 5.9.

FIGURE 5.9 Gestalt psychologist Wolfgang Köhler ran experiments with chimpanzees that suggest that not all learning is mechanical. This chimp must retrieve a stick outside the cage and attach it to a stick he already has before he can retrieve the distant circular object. While fiddling with two such sticks, Sultan, another chimp, seemed to suddenly recognize that the sticks could be attached. This was an example of learning by insight.

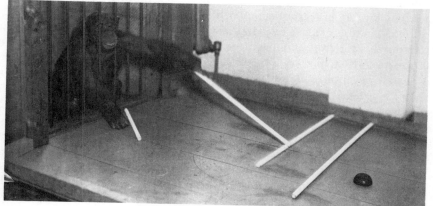

As if to make this historic occasion more dramatic, Sultan at first tried to reach the banana with one pole. When he could not do so, he returned to fiddling with the sticks. Köhler left the laboratory after an hour or so of frustration (his own as well as Sultan's). An assistant was assigned the thankless task of observing Sultan. But soon afterward Sultan happened to align the two sticks as he fiddled. Then, in what seemed a flash of inspiration, Sultan fitted them together and pulled in the elusive banana.

Köhler was summoned to the laboratory. When he arrived the sticks fell apart, as if on cue. But Sultan regathered them, fit them firmly together, and actually tested the strength of the fit before retrieving another banana.

Learning by Insight

Köhler was impressed by Sultan's rapid "perception of relationships" and used the term **insight** to describe it. He noted that such insights were not learned gradually through reinforced trials. Rather they seemed to occur "in a flash" when the elements of a problem had been arranged appropriately. Sultan also proved himself immediately capable of stringing several sticks together to retrieve various objects, not just bananas. This seemed no mechanical generalization. It appeared that Sultan understood the principle of the relationship between joining sticks and reaching distant objects.

Psychologists in the United States soon demonstrated that not even the behavior of rats was as mechanical as most behaviorists suggested. E. C. Tolman (1948), a University of California behaviorist, showed that rats behaved as if they acquired **cognitive maps** of mazes. While they would learn many paths to a food goal, they would typically choose the shortest. But if the shortest path was blocked, they would quickly switch to another. The behavior of the rats suggested that they learned *places in which reinforcement was available*, not a series of mechanical motor responses.

Bismarck, one of University of Michigan psychologist N. R. F. Maier's laboratory rats, provided further evidence for learning by insight (Maier & Schneirla, 1935). Bismarck had been trained to climb a ladder to a tabletop where food was placed. On one occasion Maier used a mesh barrier to prevent Bismarck from reaching his goal. But as shown in Figure 5.10, a second ladder to the table was provided. The second ladder was in clear view of the animal. At first Bismarck sniffed and scratched and made every effort to find a path through the mesh barrier. Then Bismarck spent some time washing his face, an activity that apparently signals frustration in rats. Suddenly Bismarck jumped into the air, turned, ran down the familiar ladder, around to the new ladder, up the new ladder, and then claimed his just desserts.

It is difficult to explain Bismarck's behavior through conditioning. It seems that Bismarck suddenly perceived the relationships between the elements of his problem so that the solution occurred by insight. He seems to have had what Gestalt psychologists have termed "an Aha!-experience."

Latent Learning

Many behaviorists argue that organisms acquire only those responses, or operants, for which they are reinforced. However, E. C. Tolman showed that rats learn about their environments in the absence of reinforcement.

Tolman trained some rats to run through mazes for standard food goals, while other rats were permitted to explore the same mazes for several days

Insight In Gestalt psychology, a sudden perception of relationships among elements of the "perceptual field," permitting the sudden solution of a problem.

Cognitive map A mental representation or "picture" of the elements in a learning situation, such as a maze.

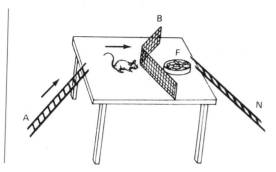

FIGURE 5.10 Bismarck has learned to reach dinner by climbing ladder *A*. But now the food goal *F* is blocked by wire mesh barrier *B*. Bismarck washes his face for a while, but then, in an apparent flash of insight, runs back down ladder *A* and up new ladder *N* to claim his just desserts.

without food goals or other rewards. The rewarded rats could be said to have found their ways through the mazes with fewer errors (fewer "wrong turns") on each trial run. But, in a sense, the unrewarded rats had no correct or incorrect turns to make, since no response led to a reward.

After the unrewarded rats had been allowed to explore the mazes for 10 days, food rewards were placed in a box at the far end of the maze. The previously unrewarded explorers reached the food box as quickly as the rewarded rats after only one or two reinforced trials (Tolman & Honzik, 1950).

Tolman concluded that rats learned about mazes in which they roamed even when they were unrewarded for doing so. He distinguished between learning and performance. Rats would acquire a cognitive map of a maze and, even though they would not be motivated to follow an efficient route to the far end, they would learn rapid routes from end to end, just by roaming about within the maze. But this learning might be hidden, or **latent,** until they were motivated to follow the rapid routes for food goals.

Observational Learning

How many things have you learned from watching other people in real life, in films, and on television? From films and television we may have gathered vague ideas about how to sky dive, ride surfboards, climb the outside of the World Trade Center, run a pattern to catch a touchdown pass in the Superbowl, and dust for fingerprints, even if we have never tried these activities.

Social learning theorist Albert Bandura has run numerous experiments (e.g., Bandura and others, 1963) that show that we acquire operants through observing the behavior of others. We may need some practice to refine these skills, but we acquire the basic "know-how" through observation. We may also choose to allow these skills to lie latent. For example, we may not imitate aggressive behavior unless we are provoked and believe that we are more likely to be rewarded than punished for aggressive behavior.

Observational learning may account for most human learning. It occurs when we as children observe parents cook, clean, or repair a broken appliance. Observational learning takes place when we watch teachers solve problems on the blackboard or hear them speak in a foreign language. Observational learning does not appear to be mechanically acquired through reinforcement. We can learn in this way without engaging in overt responses at all. It appears sufficient to pay attention to the behavior of others.

As noted at the beginning of the chapter, it would be of little use to discuss how we learn if we were not capable of remembering what we learn

Latent Hidden or concealed. In latent learning, learning is not exhibited at the time of learning. But it is demonstrated when adequate reinforcement is introduced. (From the Latin *latere,* meaning "to lie hidden.")

Observational learning Acquiring operants, which may or may not be performed, through observing others engaged in them. Observational learning occurs without emission and reinforcement of a response.

from second to second, from day to day, or, in many cases, for a lifetime. Let us now turn our attention to the subject of memory. How do we remember things? How much can we remember? How can we improve our ability to remember?

Memory

Are you in a betting mood? I bet that I can show you how to memorize the lines and shapes that correspond to the numbers 1–9 in Figure 5.11—practically instantaneously. Check them out for a minute to see if you think you can do it. Then turn to Figure 5.12.

Memory is a most important area of investigation in psychology. Without memory, or the abilities to store and retrieve information, learning would profit us little. There would be no point to reading this book, or any other, if you could not remember it. How could you play Space Invaders if you forgot how to use the "joystick" after every shot? What would life be like if you could not remember your name, your address, your family, friends, and plans?

The Structure of Memory

Before the turn of the century, William James was intrigued by the fact that some memories were unreliable, "going in one ear and out the other," while others could be recalled for a lifetime:

> The stream of thought flows on, but most of its elements fall into the bottomless pit of oblivion. Of some, no element survives the instant of their passage. Of others, it is confined to a few moments, hours, or days. Others, again, leave vestiges which are indestructible, and by means of which they may be recalled as long as life endures (1890).

James observed correctly that there were different types or structures of memory. Each holds impressions or "elements of thought" for different lengths of time. Modern psychologists classify memory according to three such structures: *sensory memory*, *short-term memory (STM)*, and *long-term memory (LTM)*.

Sensory Memory

The world is a constant display of sights and sounds and other sources of sensory stimulation, but only some of these are remembered. Memory first requires that you pay attention to a stimulus or image, whether a new name,

FIGURE 5.11 How quickly can you memorize the shapes that correspond to each number, 1 to 9? After you have pondered this question for a while, turn to Figure 5.12.

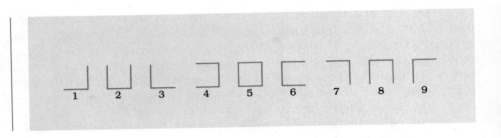

Memory:
The Unreliable Witness

Psychologist Jean Piaget vividly remembered an attempt to kidnap him from his baby carriage along the Champs Elysées. He recalled the gathered crowd, the scratches on the face of the heroic nurse who saved him, the policeman's white baton, the assailant running away. However vivid, Piaget's recollections were false. Years later the nurse confessed that she had made up the entire story.

A Creative Blend of Fiction and Fact Many social scientists believe that most early childhood memories are dreamlike reconstructions of stories told by parents and friends. Now [psychologist] Elizabeth Loftus . . . has a sobering message for grownups. Their memories are almost as unreliable as children's. They are so encrusted with experiences, desires and suggestions that they often resemble fiction as much as fact. In *Eyewitness Testimony* (1980), Loftus made a strong case against the reliability of remembrances of court witnesses. In her latest work, *Memory* (1981) she indicts human recollections in general.

One problem with memory is that people do not observe well in the first place. Surprisingly often, people fail a simple test: picking out the exact copy of a real penny in a group of 15 possible designs. More important, people forget some facts and "refabricate" the gaps between the ones they do not remember accurately. They tend to adjust memory to suit their picture of the world. One example: in tests involving observations of a black man with a hat and a white man carrying a razor, people often recall the razor being in the black's hands. . . .

Hypnosis and Truth Serums Hypnosis and "truth serums" can also produce as much fiction as fact. "Far from dredging up reality," writes Loftus, "hypnosis encourages a person to relax, to cooperate, and to concentrate." Suggestibility is so heightened that people may remember events that never occurred. Studies show that after taking truth drugs, people can lie competently, garble facts and invent stories to please their questioners. Other Loftus arguments:

- Hearing memory is apparently stronger in humans than touch, sight or smell memory. Patients who have been under total anesthesia can sometimes recall words spoken during an operation.

- Most people can not easily remember more than six or seven items in a series—a fact that bodes ill for the postal service's plan to replace five-digit zip codes with nine-digit ones. A Loftus tip: Mental shopping lists should be set up with the important purchases at the beginning or the end. As memory dims, the items in the middle tend to fade first.

- Slight stress improves memory. Heavy stress erodes it. People who are about to subject themselves to danger—mountain climbing, parachute jumping, etc.—perform poorly at mental tasks.

- Alcohol and marijuana seem to affect information storage more than retrieval. That is, memory may work well at the time, but some things that occur while a person is under the influence may not be recalled. Senility works in a similar way, eroding ability to store new information.

- Any severe shock can produce memory loss. Rats forget tricks when given electric jolts. Amnesia, which can be the result of physical or emotional shock, is often selective. One woman, a professor of English, forgot the events and dates of her own life, but remembered those of English literature well enough to teach.

- For a few people, sexual intercourse brings sudden loss of memory lasting several hours. Dr. Richard Mayeux, of New York's Neurological Institute, has reported treating two cases of one-time memory loss and confusion after sex. Mayeux believes that this phenomenon may be related to hypertension, but is not particularly worrisome.

The Permanence of Long-Term Memories One of the questions in memory research is whether long-term memories are held permanently in the brain. Freud thought so. He believed that these memories lie deep in the unconscious, undisturbed by surface mental distortions. The late neurosurgeon Wilder Penfield agreed. His famous discovery, found accidentally while examining an epileptic woman, showed that electrical stimulation of the brain could trigger a re-experience of past events. Penfield took this as an indication of a "permanent imprint" of experience on the brain.

Loftus argues otherwise, finding that electrical stimulation of the brain produces the same mix of fiction and fact found in most unassisted attempts at recollection. Her conclusion: There is no evidence that "true" memories exist, like Platonic essences, beneath confused and adapted ones. "Unfortunately," she writes, "we are simply not designed that way." All memories, even those dredged up by psychoanalysis or hypnosis, are apt to be skewed. Or, as Santayana might have put it, those who remember the past are condemned to revise it.

Sensory memory The structure of memory first encountered by incoming information, in which sensory input, such as a visual stimulus, is maintained for only a fraction of a second.

Sensory register Another term for *sensory memory*.

Encode To transform sensory input into a form which is more readily processed by memory.

FIGURE 5.12 The nine shapes in Figure 5.11 form this familiar tic-tac-toe grid when the numbers are placed inside them and they are arranged in numerical order, three shapes to a line. This method for recalling the shapes collapses nine chunks of information into one meaningful chunk. You encode them by thinking of the tic-tac-toe grid; then simply "read" the grid, shape by shape, numbering each one as you do so.

1	2	3
4	5	6
7	8	9

a vocabulary word, or an idea. Paying attention somehow separates it from all the stimuli you find irrelevant, and are less likely to retain. So if you are reading this section while you are watching *General Hospital*, you may recall more about the trials and tribulations of Luke and Laura than about the structure of memory.

Note what happens when you perceive a visual stimulus, such as this list of 10 letters:

THUNSTOFAM

The visual impression lasts for only a fraction of a second in what is called **sensory memory,** or the **sensory register.** If the letters had been flashed on a screen for, say, one-tenth of a second, your ability to list them on the basis of sensory memory would be rather meagre. The trace of their image would already have vanished, and you would probably recall only three or four of them.

Recollection of all 10 letters would depend on whether you had successfully transformed or **encoded** the list of letters into a form in which it could be processed further by memory. Below we shall see that one way of enhancing recall would be to read (or "mentally say") the list of letters as a word. Chances of recollection would have been further enhanced by repeating the "word" to yourself, or rehearsing it.

George Sperling (1960) demonstrated the existence of sensory memory in a series of important experiments run about 25 years ago. In a typical procedure, three rows of numbers and letters like those below were flashed on a screen for about one-tenth of a second:

6	G	R	2
V	L	7	4
9	K	5	T

Viewers were asked what they had seen. On the average they remembered about three and one-half numbers and letters. After that, presumably, the sensory image faded or decayed and no more numbers were remembered.

FIGURE 5.13 The Structure of Memory. Sensory information impacts upon the sensory memory. If we attend to it, it is transferred to short-term memory (STM). Otherwise, the trace may decay. Once in STM, rehearsal stores the memory in long-term memory (LTM), unless it is first displaced by other chunks of information. Once in LTM, memories may be retrieved through appropriate search strategies. But if the memory is organized poorly, or misfiled, it may be lost.

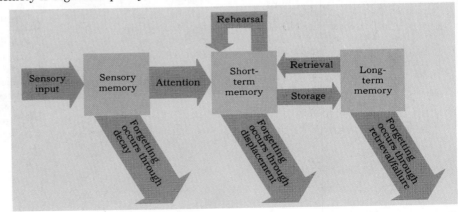

But if Sperling pointed an arrow before, during, or after presentation at the row he wanted viewers to report, they were usually successful. Arrows pointed prior to the display led to best recall. Perhaps they guided the subjects to focus their attention on the "relevant" material.

Sperling found that if he delayed pointing the arrow for a few fractions of a second after the display, subjects were much less successful in reporting the target row. If he allowed a quarter of a second to elapse, the arrow did not aid recall at all. Apparently stimuli decay in the sensory register within that amount of time.

Short-Term Memory

If you focus attention on a stimulus in the sensory register, you will tend to retain it in **short-term memory** for up to 30 seconds or so after the trace of the stimulus decays. In short-term memory the image tends to fade significantly after 10 to 12 seconds if it is not repeated or rehearsed (Keele, 1973). It is possible to focus on maintaining a visual image in the short-term memory (Fisher & Karsh, 1971), but it is more common to encode visual stimuli as sounds, or auditory stimulation. Then the sounds can be rehearsed.

Encoding   Let us now return to the task of remembering the list of 10 letters shown at the beginning of this section. If you had coded them as the three-syllable word THUN-STO-FAM, you would probably have recalled them by mentally rehearsing (saying to yourself) the three-syllable "word" and then spelling it from the sounds. Transforming a visual stimulus into sounds in order to remember it is known as using an **acoustic code**.

A few minutes later, if someone asked whether the letters had been upper case (THUNSTOFAM) or lower case (thunstofam), you might have recalled them in either case. You had used an acoustic code to help recall the list and upper and lower case letters sound alike. When asked to list the letters, you might have said "s-t-o-w" rather than "s-t-o" since "stow" is an actual word that sounds like "sto."

A more elaborate way of coding the letters could have involved recognizing that they serve as an **acronym** for the familiar phrase, "THe UNited STates OF AMerica." In order to recall the 10 letters, you would then have had to "picture" the phrase and "read aloud" the first two letters of each word in the phrase. Since this phrase code is more complex than simply seeing the list as a single word, it might have taken you longer to recall (actually, to reconstruct) the list of 10 letters. But by using the phrase you would probably remember the list of letters longer. The phrase is meaningful, and thus more likely to be recalled than the meaningless "word" THUNSTOFAM.

THUNSTOFAM is not too difficult to remember. But what if the visual stimulus had been TBXLFNTSDK? This list of letters cannot be pronounced as they are. You would have had to have found a complex acronym in order to code these letters, and within a fraction of a second. Most likely an impossible task. To aid recall you would probably have chosen to try to repeat or rehearse the letters rapidly, to read each one as many times as possible before the stimulus trace faded. You would have visualized each letter as you said it, and tried to return to it before it decayed.

Auditory stimuli can be maintained longer in short-term memory than can visual stimuli (Keele, 1973). So you would probably try to use an acoustic code to remember the letters TBXLFNTSDK, rehearsing sounds. But in an effort

Short-term memory The structure of memory that can hold a sensory stimulus for up to thirty seconds after the trace decays. About seven chunks of information may be maintained at once in short-term memory.

Acoustic code A code in which visual or other stimuli are transformed into sounds that may be rehearsed. (From the Greek *akoustikos*, meaning "hearing.")

Acronym A name composed of the initial letters of that which it represents.

to recall these letters, you might mistakenly report them as "TVXLFNTSTK." This would be an understandable error since the incorrect *V* and *T* sound, respectively, like the correct *B* and *D*.

The Serial Position Effect Note that you would also be likely to recall the first and last letters in the series, *T* and *K*, more accurately than the others. Why? The tendency to recall more accurately the first and last items in a series than the intervening items is known as the **serial position effect.** This effect may occur because we pay more attention to the first and last stimuli in a series. They serve as the visual or auditory boundaries for the other stimuli. It may also be that the first item is likely to be rehearsed more frequently (repeated more times) than any other item. The last item is likely to have been rehearsed most recently, and so least likely to have faded through decay.

Chunks of Information: Is 7 a Magic Number or Did the Phone Company Get Lucky? Rapidly rehearsing 10 meaningless letters is not an easy task. With TBXLFNTSDK there are 10 **chunks** of information that must be maintained simultaneously in short-term memory. With THUNSTOFAM there are only three chunks to digest at once—much easier on the digestion.

Psychologist George Miller noted that the average person was comfortable in digesting about seven integers at a time, the number of integers in a telephone number. (The three-digit area code prefix is usually recalled as a separate chunk of information.) "My problem is that I have been persecuted by an integer," Miller (1956) wrote. "For seven years [the number seven] has followed me around, has intruded in my most private data, and has assaulted me from the pages of our most public journals." Most people have little trouble recalling five chunks of information, as in a post office zip code. Some can remember nine which is, for all but a few, an upper limit. So seven chunks, plus or minus one or two, is for Miller the "magic" number.

How, then, do children learn the alphabet, which is 26 chunks of information? How do they learn to associate letters of the alphabet with spoken sounds? The 26 letters of the alphabet cannot be spoken like a word or phrase. There is nothing about the shape of an *A* to indicate its sound. Nor does the visual stimulus *B* sound like a *B*. Children learning the alphabet and learning to associate letters (visual stimuli) with sounds do so by **rote.** It is mechanical associative learning that requires time and repetition. If you think that learning the alphabet by rote is a simple child's task, now that it is behind you, try learning the Russian or Hebrew alphabet.

If you had recognized THUNSTOFAM as an acronym for the first two letters of each word in the phrase "THe UNited STates OF AMerica," you would have reduced the number of chunks of information that have to be recalled. We could consider the phrase a single chunk of information, and the rule that we must use the first two letters of each word of the phrase as another chunk.

Reconsider Figures 5.11 and 5.12. In Figure 5.11 you were asked to learn nine chunks of visual information. Perhaps you could have used the acoustic codes "L" and "Square" for chunks three and five, but no obvious codes are available for the other seven chunks. But once you looked at Figure 5.12, you realized that you need only recall perhaps two chunks of information. One is the familiar tic-tac-toe grid. The other is the rule that each shape is the shape of a section of the grid, if read like words on a page (from upper left to lower right). The number sequence 1–9 presents no problem since you learned this series by rote many years ago, and have rehearsed it in countless calculations since.

Interference in Short-Term Memory   Every time I have looked up a phone number and am trying to dial, rehearsing the number repeatedly, it is guaranteed that someone will ask me the time of day. Unless I say "Just a minute!" and jot down the number on my cuff before I answer, it's back to the phonebook again. Attending to new numbers, even briefly, impairs my ability to keep the phone number in short-term memory.

In an experiment with college students, Lloyd and Margaret Peterson (1959) showed how such interference can play havoc with short-term memory. They asked students to remember three-letter combinations, like HGB, an easy three chunks of information. Then they asked students to count backward from a number like 181 by 3's (that is, 181, 178, 175, 172, and so on). The students were told to stop counting and to report the letter sequence after various brief intervals of time had passed, as shown in Figure 5.14. The percentage of combinations recalled accurately fell dramatically within just a few seconds. After 18 seconds of interference, the letter sequences had been **displaced** by counting in almost all of these bright young students.

Eidetic Imagery   Some people have short-term memories that are capable of storing many more than seven or nine chunks of information. Only about 5 percent of children tested are capable of what has been called photographic memory, or **eidetic imagery** (Haber, 1980). Even then this ability declines with age. These children can view a complex picture for 20–30 seconds, have the picture removed as they continue to observe a gray (neutral) background, and then respond accurately to questions about details of the picture for many minutes (Haber, 1969). The accuracy of their responses suggests that they are still "seeing" the picture.

Figure 5.15 provides an example of a test of eidetic imagery. Children are asked to look at the top drawing in the series for 20–30 seconds, after which it is removed. The children then continue to observe a neutral background. Several minutes later they are shown the middle drawing. When asked what they see, many report "a face." A face would be seen only if the children

Displace In memory theory, to cause chunks of information to be lost from short-term memory by the adding of too many new items.

Eidetic imagery (eye–DET–tick). The capacity to remember visual sensory input, such as pictures, with exceptional clarity and detail. Also called "photographic memory." (From the Greek *eidos*, meaning "shape" or "that which is seen.")

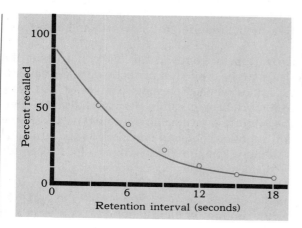

FIGURE 5.14   Decrease in ability to recall three-letter combinations while counting backward for 18 seconds. Subjects in this experiment were bright college students.

FIGURE 5.15   A Test of Eidetic Imagery. Children look at the left drawing for 20–30 seconds, after which it is removed. Now the children look at a neutral background for several minutes. Then they are shown the middle drawing. When asked what they see, children with the capacity for eidetic imagery report "a face." The face is seen only by children who retain the first image and fuse it with the image in the center, thus perceiving the image on the right.

fuse the retained first-seen top image with the later-seen middle image, yielding the bottom image (Haber, 1980).

Eidetic imagery appears remarkably clear and detailed. It appears to be essentially a perceptual phenomenon in which acoustic coding is not involved.

Long-Term Memory

Think of your **long-term memory** as a vast storehouse of information containing names, dates, places, what Johnny did to you in second grade, what Susan said about you when you were 12. Psychologists are not certain how much of what you experience and think about becomes stored in long-term memory.

How Much of What We Experience or Think Is Stored in Long-Term Memory?   Some psychologists argue that every perception and idea is stored permanently. The only question is whether we shall receive appropriate stimulation to help us retrieve this information. These psychologists often point to the work of neurosurgeon Wilder Penfield (1969). By electrically stimulating parts of the brain, many of his patients reported rather vivid remembrance of things past.

Other psychologists like Elizabeth Loftus (1980, 1981) note that the memories "released" by Penfield's probes were not perfectly detailed. Patients also seemed to recall more specifics when the events were ones that were important to them. We may be more likely to store permanently those perceptions and thoughts that are important or meaningful to us. We recall material better when we pay more attention to it, and encode it in a meaningful, rehearsable form. In the box "Memory: The Unreliable Witness" (p. 195), Loftus also argues that memories are distorted by our biases and needs.

How Much Information *Can* Be Stored in Long-Term Memory?   There is no evidence for any limit to the amount of information that can be stored

Long-term memory The memory structure capable of relatively permanent storage. Losses in long-term memory are thought to reflect failures at retrieval rather than decay or displacement.

in long-term memory. New information may replace older information in the short-term memory, but there is no evidence that memories in long-term memory are lost by displacement. Long-term memories may last days, years, or, for all practical purposes, a lifetime. From time to time it may seem that we have forgotten, or "lost," a memory in long-term memory, such as the names of elementary or high-school classmates. But it is more likely that we simply cannot find the proper cues to help us retrieve the information. (See the box, "Whatever Happened to the Class of 1965?") If it is lost, it usually becomes lost only in the same way as when we misplace an object but know that it is still somewhere in the house or apartment. It is "lost" but not eradicated or destroyed.

Elaborative rehearsal A method for increasing the probability of recalling new information by relating it to already well-known material.

Transferring Information from Short-Term to Long-Term Memory   How is information transferred from short-term to long-term memory? By and large, the more often chunks of information are rehearsed, the more likely they are to be transferred to long-term memory (Rundus, 1971). But pure rehearsal, with no attempt to make information meaningful by linking it to past learning, is no guarantee of permanent storage (Craig & Watkins, 1973).

A more effective method is purposefully to relate new material to information that has already been solidly acquired. (Recall that the nine chunks of information in Figure 5.11 were made easier to reconstruct once they were associated with the familiar tic-tac-toe grid in Figure 5.12.) Relating new material to well-known material is known as **elaborative rehearsal** (Postman, 1975). For example, have you seen this word before?

FUNTHOSTAM

Whatever Happened to the Class of 1965?

What's the name of your first-grade teacher? Of the first boy or girl you ever kissed? Of that hunk or fox that sat next to you in ninth-grade math? Chances are that with a bit of concentration you can recall quite a bit more than you might think.

In an article called "Those Unforgettable High-School Days," Harry Bahrick and his colleagues (1975) found that recent graduates could recall an average of 47 names of schoolmates. People who had been out of school for at least 40 years could recall the names of an average of 19 schoolmates. The size of the school was unrelated to the number of names recalled.

On a recognition test, former students were shown photos of schoolmates interspersed with four times as many photos of strangers. Recent graduates correctly identified former schoolmates 90 percent of the time, while subjects out of school for at least 40 years correctly identified former schoolmates 75 percent of the time. But a chance level of recognition would have been only 20 percent, showing rather solid long-term memory for the older subjects.

Psychologists have also found that being in the proper context dramatically increases recall (Estes, 1972; Tulving, 1974; Watkins and others, 1976). Have you ever walked the halls of an old school and been assaulted by memories of faces and names that you thought were gone forever? Have you ever walked through your old neighborhood and recalled the faces of people, or aromas of cooking that were so real that you could salivate?

Because we tend better to remember information in the context in which it was learned, it is probably better to take tests in the same room, and at the same desk, in which the subject-matter was taught. But if you can only do a long-division problem in your classroom and nowhere else, the chances are that you haven't done a good job of learning the principles involved. Textbooks ask you to solve numbers of problems with variations in details just so that you will not be "stuck" in the context of a particular problem. Varying the context and details of the problem prevents you from solving it mechanically and forces you to show that you can apply the principles and rules involved.

Say it aloud. Do you know it? If you had used an acoustic code alone to "memorize" THUNSTOFAM, the meaningless word you first saw on page 196, it might not have been easy to recognize FUNTHOSTAM as an incorrect spelling. But let us assume you had used a code that involved the "meaning" of THUNSTOFAM, a **semantic code.** Then you would have associated it with the phrase "The United States of America," and would have scanned the spelling of the words in the phrase to determine the correctness of FUNTHOSTAM. Of course, you would have found it incorrect.

You may recall that English teachers encouraged you to use new vocabulary words in sentences to help you remember them. Each new usage is an instance of elaborative rehearsal. You are building extended semantic codes that will help you retrieve their meanings in the future. Foreign-language teachers may suggest that learning classical languages "exercises the mind" so that we shall understand English better. Not exactly. The mind is not analogous to a muscle that responds to exercise. But the meanings of many English words are based on foreign tongues. A person who recognizes that *retrieve* stems from roots meaning "again" *(re-)* and "find" (*trouver* in French) is less likely to forget that *retrieval* means "finding again" or "bringing back."

Before proceeding to the next section, let me ask you to cover the above part of this page. Now, which of the following words is correctly spelled: *retrieval* or *retreival?* The spellings sound alike, so an acoustic code for reconstructing the correct spelling would fail. But a semantic code, such as the spelling rule "*I* before *e* except after *c*," would allow you to reconstruct the correct spelling: retr*ie*val.

Organization in Long-Term Memory The storehouse of long-term memory is usually well-organized. Items are not just piled on the floor or thrown into closets. We tend to gather information about rats and cats into a certain section of the warehouse, perhaps the animal or mammal section. We gather oaks, maples, and eucalyptus into the tree section.

Information tends to be organized according to a *hierarchical structure*, as shown in Figure 5.16. A **hierarchy** is an arrangement of items (or chunks

FIGURE 5.16 The Hierarchical Structure of Long-Term Memory. Where are whales filed in the cabinets of your memory? Your classification of whales may influence your answers to these questions: Do whales breathe underwater? Are they warm-blooded? Do they nurse their young?

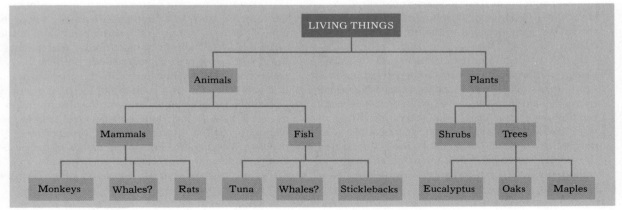

A mother whale and her young calf. Are whales classified as mammals or as fish in the structure of your memory?

of information) into groups or classes according to common or distinct features. As we work our way up the hierarchy shown in Figure 5.16, we find more-encompassing or **superordinate** classes to which the items below belong. For example, all mammals are animals, but there are many types of animals other than mammals.*

When items are correctly organized in long-term memory, you are more likely to recall accurate information about them. For instance, do you remember whether whales breathe underwater? If you did not know that whales are mammals (or, in Figure 5.16. **subordinate** to mammals), or knew nothing about mammals, a correct answer might depend on some remote instance of rote learning. You might recall some details from a documentary on whales, for example. But if you *did* know that whales are mammals, you would be able to "remember" that whales do not breathe underwater by reconstructing information you know about mammals, the group to which whales are subordinate. Similarly, you might "remember" that whales, because they are mammals, are warm-blooded, nurse their young, and are a good deal more intelligent than, say, tunas and sticklebacks, which are fish.

Had you incorrectly classified whales as fish, you might have searched your memory and constructed the incorrect answer that they do breathe underwater.

Forgetting

What do DAR, RIK, BOF, and ZEX have in common? They are all **nonsense syllables.** Nonsense syllables are meaningless syllables three letters in length. Their usage was originated by German psychologist Hermann Ebbinghaus (1850-1909), and they have been used by many psychologists to study memory and forgetting.

* A note to biological purists: Figure 5.16 is not intended to accurately reflect phyla, classes, orders, and so on. Rather it shows how an individual's classification scheme might be organized.

Superordinate Descriptive of a higher (including) class or category in a hierarchy.

Subordinate Descriptive of a lower (included) class or category in a hierarchy.

Nonsense syllables Meaningless syllables, three letters in length, used by psychologists to study memory.

Oh Gee, It's on the Tip of My Tongue . . .

Have you ever been so close to recalling something that you felt it was "on the tip of your tongue"? But you still could not quite put your finger on it? This is a frustrating experience, like reeling in a fish but having it drop off the line just before it breaks the surface of the water. Psychologists term this experience the *tip-of-the-tongue phenomenon,* or *TOT.*

In a TOT experiment, Brown and McNeill (1966) defined some rather unusual words for students, like *sampan,* which is a small riverboat used in China and Japan. Students were then asked to recall the words they had learned. Students often had the right word "on the tips of their tongues," but many reported words similar in meaning, like *junk, barge,* or *houseboat.* Other students reported words that sound similar, like *Saipan, Siam, sarong,* and *sanching. Sanching,* by the way, is not an actual word.

Brown and McNeill concluded that our storage systems are indexed according to both the sounds and the meanings of words, according to both acoustic and semantic codes. By scanning words that are similar in sound and meaning to the word that is on the tip of the tongue, we often eventually retrieve the word for which we are searching.

Recognition In memory theory, the easiest memory task, identifying objects or events as having been encountered before.

Paired associates Nonsense syllables presented in pairs in experiments that measure recall. After viewing pairs, subjects are shown one member of each pair and asked to recall the other.

Recall Retrieval or reconstruction of learned material.

Since they are intended to be meaningless, remembering nonsense syllables should depend on simple acoustic coding and rehearsal, rather than on elaborative rehearsal, semantic coding, or other ways of making learning meaningful. Nonsense syllables provide a means of measuring simple memorization ability in studies of the three basic memory tasks of *recognition, recall,* and *relearning.* Studying these memory tasks has led to several conclusions about the nature of forgetting.

Recognition   To measure **recognition,** one type of memory task, psychologists may ask subjects to read a list of nonsense syllables. Then the subjects read a second list of nonsense syllables and indicate whether they recognize any of the syllables as having appeared on the first list. Forgetting is defined as failure to recognize a nonsense syllable that has been read before.

Recognition is the easiest type of memory task. This is why multiple-choice tests are easier than fill-in-the-blank or essay tests. We can recognize or identify photos of former classmates more easily than we can recall their names (Tulving, 1974).

Recall   Psychologists often use lists of pairs of nonsense syllables, called **paired associates,** to measure **recall,** a second memory task. A list of paired associates is shown in Figure 5.17. Subjects read through the lists, pair by pair. Later they are shown the first member of each pair and asked to recall the second. Recall is more difficult than recognition. In a recognition task, one simply indicates whether an item has been seen before, or which of a number of items is paired with a stimulus (as in a multiple-choice test). But in a recall task, the person must retrieve a syllable, with another syllable serving as a cue.

Retrieval is made easier if the two syllables can be meaningfully linked, even if the "meaning" is stretched a bit. Consider the first pair of nonsense syllables in Figure 5.17. The image of a WOMan smoking a CEG-arette may make CEG easier to retrieve when the person is presented with the cue, WOM.

It is easier to recall vocabulary words from foreign languages if you can construct a meaningful link between the foreign and English words (Atkinson, 1975). The *peso,* pronounced *pay-so,* is a unit of Mexican money. A link can be formed by finding a part of the foreign word, like the *pe* (pronounced *pay)* in *peso,* and construct a phrase like "You pay with money." When you read

FIGURE 5.17 Psychologists often use paired associates, like those below, to measure recall. Retrieving CEG in response to the cue WOM is made easier by an image of a WOMan smoking a "CEG-arette."

WOM	CEG
GOR	NIF
XAR	MUP
JEK	BAC
HOK	MIB

or hear the word *peso* in the future, you recognize the *pe-* and retrieve the link or phrase. From the phrase, you then reconstruct the translation, "a unit of money."

A similar method for prompting recall involves use of acronyms. As noted in our discussion of "Thunstofam," acronyms are words that are constructed from the first letter or letters of the chunks of material to be retrieved. In Chapter 2 we saw that the acronym SAME can help us recall that *s*ensory neurons are also called *a*fferent neurons, and *m*otor neurons are also termed *e*fferent. In Chapter 3 we saw that the acronym ROY G. BIV can help us recall the colors of the visible spectrum. One of my favorite acronyms remains CREEP. This was the abbreviation the press ascribed to the Committee to *REE*lect the *P*resident during Richard Nixon's reelection campaign in 1972.

In Chapter 4 we noted that some people who are hypnotized show **posthypnotic amnesia.** They are unable, for example, to recall previously learned word lists (Kihlstrom, 1980). Spanos and his colleagues (1980, 1982) hypothesize that posthypnotic amnesia occurs when hypnotized subjects interpret the suggestion not to recall information as an "invitation" to keep their attention *away from* retrieval cues. A hypnotized person might be told that he or she would not be able to recall the colors of the spectrum upon "awakening." This suggestion might be interpreted as an invitation *not* to focus on the acronym Roy G. Biv.

Relearning: Is Learning Easier the Second Time Around? **Relearning** is a third method of measuring retention. Do you remember having to learn all the state capitals in grade school? What were the capitals of Wyoming and Delaware? Even when we cannot recall or recognize material that had once been learned, we can relearn it more rapidly the second time, like Cheyenne for Wyoming and Dover for Delaware. Similarly, as we go through our thirties and forties we may forget a good deal of our high school French or geometry. But we could learn what took months or years much more rapidly the second time around.

Since time is saved when we relearn things we had once known, this method of measuring retention is also known as measuring **savings.** Quickly, now. What are the capitals of Wyoming and Delaware?

Why People Forget

When we do not attend to, encode, and rehearse sensory input, we may forget it through decay of the trace of the image. Material in short-term memory can be lost through displacement, as may happen when we try to remember several new names at a party.

According to **interference theory,** we also forget material in short-term and long-term memory because newly learned material interferes with it. The two basic types of interference are *retroactive interference* (also called *retroactive inhibition)* and *proactive interference* (or *proactive inhibition.)*

Retroactive Interference In **retroactive interference** new learning interferes with the retrieval of old learning. A medical student may memorize the bones in the leg through rote repetition. Later he or she may find that learning the names of the bones in the arm makes it more difficult to retrieve the names of the leg bones, especially if the names are similar in sound or in relative location on each limb.

Posthypnotic amnesia (am–KNEE–she–uh). Inability to recall material presented while hypnotized, according to a suggestion of the hypnotist.

Relearning Another measure of retention. Material is usually relearned more quickly than it is learned initially.

Savings Another term for relearning—referring to the fact that one usually "saves" time the second time material is learned.

Interference theory The view that we may forget material placed in memory because other learning interferes with its retrieval.

Retroactive interference The interference by new learning in ability to retrieve material learned previously. (From the Latin *retro-*, meaning "backward.")

Proactive Interference   In **proactive interference** older learning interferes with the capacity to retrieve more recently learned material. High school Spanish may "pop in" when you are trying to retrieve college French or Italian words. All three are Romance languages, with similar roots and spellings. Old German vocabulary words would probably not interfere with your ability to retrieve more recently learned French or Italian because many German roots and sounds differ markedly from those of the Romance languages.

In terms of motor skills, you may learn how to drive a standard shift on a car with three forward speeds and a clutch that must be let up slowly after shifting. Later you learn to drive a car with five forward speeds and a clutch that must be released rapidly. For a while you make a number of errors on the five-speed car because of proactive interference. (Old learning interferes with new learning.) If you return to the three-speed car after driving the five-speed car has become "natural," you may stall it a few times. This is because of retroactive interference (new learning interfering with the old).

Repression   According to Sigmund Freud, we are motivated to forget painful memories and unacceptable ideas because they produce anxiety, guilt, and shame. (In terms of operant conditioning, anxiety, guilt, and shame serve as negative reinforcers. We learn to do that which is followed by their removal—in this case, not to think about certain events and ideas.) In Chapter 11 we shall see that psychoanalysts believe that repression is at the heart of disorders like **psychogenic amnesia.**

Retrograde Amnesia   In retrograde amnesia, a source of trauma, like a head injury or an electric shock, prevents recent perceptions or ideas from being remembered. In this case it seems that the shock interferes with all the processes of memory. Paying attention, encoding, and rehearsal are all prevented.

It may also be that some perceptions and ideas must be allowed to rest undisturbed for a while if they are to be remembered (Gold & King, 1974). A football player who is knocked unconscious, or a victim of an auto accident, may be unable to recall events for several minutes prior to the trauma. The football player may not recall taking to the field. The accident victim may not recall entering the car.

Now that we have looked at how and why we forget, let us consider ways of improving our ability to remember.

Some Methods for Improving Memory

Who among us has not wished for a better memory from time to time? If we could remember more, we might earn higher grades, charm people with our stock of jokes, or even pay our bills on time. Psychologists once believed that one's memory was fixed, that one had a good or poor memory and was stuck with it (Singular, 1982). But today psychologists have found that there are a number of ways in which we can all improve our memories, such as the following.

The Method of Loci   You might be better able to remember your shopping list if you imagine meat loaf in your navel, or a strip of bacon draped over your nose. This is a meaty example of the **method of loci.** With this method you select a series of related images, like the parts of your body or the furniture in your home. Then you imagine an item from your shopping list, or another list you want to remember, attached to each image.

By placing meat loaf or a favorite complete dinner in your navel, rather than a single item like chopped beef, you can combine several items into one chunk of information. At the supermarket you recall the (familiar) ingredients for meat loaf, and simply recognize whether or not you need each one.

Mediation   In the method of **mediation,** you link two items with a third that ties them together. What if you are having difficulty remembering that John's wife's name is Tillie? Laird Cermak (1978) suggests that you can mediate between John and Tillie as follows. Reflect that the *john* is a slang term for bathroom. Bathrooms often have ceramic *tiles*. *Tiles*, of course, sounds like *Tillie*. So it goes: John-bathroom-tiles-Tillie.

Mnemonics   In a third method of improving memory, **mnemonics,** chunks of information are combined into a format, such as an acronym, jingle, or phrase. Recalling the phrase "Every Good Boy Does Fine" has helped many people remember the musical keys E, G, B, D, F.

How can you remember how to spell *mnemonics?* Simple—just be willing to grant "aMNesty" to those who cannot.

The Biology of Memory

The Search for the Engram   Early in this century most psychologists believed that **engrams** were responsible for memory. Engrams were hypothesized electrical circuits in the brain that corresponded to the memory trace—a neurological process that was somehow thought to parallel a perceptual experience. But physiological psychologists like Karl Lashley spent many fruitless years searching for these circuits or the parts of the brain in which they might be housed (Lashley, 1950).

Current research into the biology of memory has been focusing on the possible roles of so-called **memory molecules.** Let us examine a few experiments that are suggestive of the importance of memory molecules.

The Worm Turns, *or*, How Some Worms Got Fed Up (Literally) with Learning   A flatworm has an unusual sex life. It has both male and female sex organs. When the pickings in the outside world don't look very promising, it may just mate with itself and produce more flatworms—which are no less strange-looking.

The flatworm can also *regenerate.* If you cut it in half, the head part will grow a new tail, and, more remarkably, the tail part will grow a new head, complete with a new brain.

In their efforts to locate memory functions in the flatworm, James McConnell and his colleagues (1959) devised a research program based on its ability to regenerate. Where would you think a flatworm's memory is located? Heads or tails?

To find out, the McConnell group conditioned some worms to scrunch up when a light was shone. Flatworms normally save "scrunching" for the stimulus of electric shock, but the researchers paired the light with shock.

Mediation A method of improving memory by linking two items with a third that ties them together.

Mnemonics (neh–MON–nicks). A method of improving memory in which chunks of information are combined into a format like an acronym, jingle, or phrase.

Engram (1) An assumed electrical circuit in the brain that corresponds to a memory trace. (2) An assumed chemical change in the brain that accompanies learning. (From the Greek *en-*, meaning "in," and *gramma*, meaning "something that is written or recorded.")

Memory molecule Molecules whose chemical compositions are thought to change with experience, forming a chemical basis for memory.

The flatworm can mate with itself, regenerate lost parts, and, possibly, learn "roadmaps" by eating worms that have already found the way.

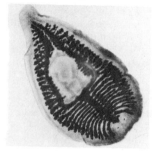

After repeated pairings, the light became a CS that elicited the response usually evoked by the shock (US).

After the classical conditioning, the worms were cut in half and given time to regenerate. As expected, the head part that grew a new tail scrunched up when a light was shone. But so did the tail part after a new head was regenerated! Memory of the light-shock association was not stored in the head alone.

In follow-up studies, the McConnell group fed chopped-up flatworms who had learned the light-shock association to other flatworms. The cannibal worms apparently got "fed up" with learning. They often scrunched up when the light was shone, even though they had not been conditioned to do so. In other experiments, flatworms were trained, by operant conditioning, to turn to the right or left at choice points in mazes. Then they were chopped up and fed to untrained worms. The untrained worms then learned to turn right or left (assuming that they were expected to turn in the same direction as their dinner) more rapidly than did untrained worms who had not been given this "brain food."

Where were memories stored in the worms that regenerated new heads? *What* did the cannibal worms eat that helped them learn mazes more rapidly than their fellows did? Additional studies by McConnell and his colleagues (1970) suggest that memories might have been stored and transmitted in molecules of **ribonucleic acid** (RNA). RNA is a protein, or **amino acid,** that is similar in structure to DNA. DNA, as noted in Chapter 2, is involved in the transmission of the genetic code from one generation of animals to another. The body's DNA is basically fixed, so that we don't suddenly become different people, but RNA is changeable.

The McConnell group transferred molecules of RNA from flatworms who had learned the light-shock association to untrained worms. The untrained worms then learned the light-shock association in fewer pairings than did worms who did not receive RNA.

Before you conclude that the best way to earn an A is to grind up your professor for dinner, we must note that McConnell's studies have not always been successfully replicated. For one thing, flatworms are not easy to condition. Similar experiments in transferring "memory molecules" between the brains of higher animals, like mice and rats, have also not consistently led to the predicted results.

But other research on the possible role of proteins in learning and memory, in which scientists have experimentally manipulated protein formation, is also suggestive of the role of memory molecules.

Life in a Goldfish Bowl: The Consolidation of Learning University of Michigan biochemist Bernard Agranoff taught goldfish that sometimes it is better to be left in the dark (Pines, 1975). He flashed a light and then the fish were given electric shock. The shock was turned off when the fish swam to the other side of the tank. After several trials the fish learned to swim to the other side of the tank whenever the light was flashed. This is an example of **avoidance learning:** by swimming across the tank the fish avoided the shock. (To be technical, the CS of light came to elicit the fear response elicited by the US of shock. Fear then acted as a negative reinforcer. The fish swam across the tank when they saw the light because they could avoid the shock in this way.)

Ribonucleic acid (rye–bow–NEW–klee–ick). A substance that is involved in transmitting genetic information, and possibly in memory formation. Abbreviated *RNA.*

Amino acid (uh–ME–no). Protein involved in metabolism.

Avoidance learning An operant conditioning procedure in which an organism learns to exhibit an operant that permits it to avoid an aversive stimulus.

Agranoff found that he could interfere with the fishes' learning by injecting **puromycin**—a chemical that impairs protein formation in the brain—after the fish were taught to associate light and electric shock. They subsequently made no effort to swim across the tank when the light was shone.

Agranoff reasoned that the puromycin prevented **consolidation** of the fishes' learning. It had prevented the memory of the association from becoming fixed in long-term memory. If, on the other hand, Agranoff waited for an hour before injecting puromycin, the learning was apparently consolidated. The fish would swim to safety as soon as the light was shone.

At the University of California at Irvine, James McGaugh's research seems to serve as the mirror image of Agranoff's. McGaugh (McGaugh and others, 1980) injected **strychnine** into laboratory rats following conditioning. In large doses, strychnine is poisonous. In the smaller doses used by McGaugh, strychnine apparently promoted protein formation and helped the rats consolidate their learning of mazes. Here, too, the injection had to be given within an hour, while the new memories were apparently still being consolidated.

Current research into the chemistry of memory also involves antidiuretic hormone, which is secreted by the pituitary gland and involved in the thirst drive (see Chapters 2 and 7). Volunteers have received a synthetic form of antidiuretic hormone, or **vasopressin,** through nasal sprays and have shown significant improvement in recall. Excess vasopressin, unfortunately, can have serious side effects, such as constriction of the blood vessels. But research into the effects of similar chemicals, which may have fewer side effects, is underway.

The Future of Learning and Memory   Research into the biology of memory is in its infancy, but what an exciting area of research it is. What would it mean to you if you could read for a half hour to an hour, pop a pill, and cause your new learnings to become consolidated in long-term memory? You would never have to reread the material; it would be at your fingertips for a lifetime. It would save a bit of study time, would it not?

The search for memory molecules, like so many other psychological endeavors, remains in its infancy.

Puromycin A chemical substance that inhibits protein formation in the brain, and is thought to inhibit consolidation of learning.

Consolidation In memory theory, the fixing of information in long-term memory.

Strychnine (STRICK–nine). A poison that, in small doses, aids the consolidation of learning.

Vasopressin Another term for *antidiuretic hormone.*

Summary

Learning may be defined as the process by which experience leads to relatively permanent changes in behavior. In classical conditioning, a previously neutral stimulus (the conditioned stimulus, or CS) comes to elicit the response evoked by a second stimulus (the unconditioned stimulus, or US) by being paired repeatedly with the second stimulus. A response to a US is called an unconditioned response (UR), and a response to a CS is termed a conditioned response (CR).

Classical conditioning occurs efficiently when the CS is presented about 0.5 seconds before the US. In backward conditioning, the US is presented first. After a US-CS association has been learned, repeated presentation of the CS (for example, a bell) without the US (meat powder) will extinguish the CR (salivation). But extinguished responses may show spontaneous recovery as a function of time that has elapsed since the end of the extinction process. In stimulus generalization, organisms show a CR in response to a range of stimuli similar to the CS. In stimulus discrimination, organisms learn to show a CR in response to a more limited range of stimuli by pairing only the limited stimulus with the US.

In operant conditioning, an organism learns

to emit an operant that is reinforced. Initial "correct" responses may be performed by random trial and error, physical or verbal guiding. Reinforced responses occur more frequently. In shaping, successive approximations to the target response are reinforced. Positive reinforcers increase the probability that operants will occur when they are applied. Negative reinforcers increase the probability that operants will occur when they are removed. Primary reinforcers have their value because of the biological makeup of the organism. Secondary reinforcers, like money and approval, acquire their value through association with established reinforcers.

Rewards are pleasant stimuli that increase the frequency of behavior. Punishments are aversive stimuli that suppress the frequency of behavior. Many learning theorists prefer treating children's misbehavior by ignoring it or using time out from positive reinforcement rather than by using punishment. Punishment fails to teach desirable responses, creates hostility, can lead to overgeneralization, and serves as a model for aggression.

A discriminative stimulus indicates when an operant will be reinforced. In operant conditioning, operants are extinguished when they are shown repeatedly without reinforcement. Continuous reinforcement leads to most rapid acquisition of new responses, but operants are maintained most economically through partial reinforcement. There are four basic schedules of reinforcement. In a fixed interval schedule, a specific amount of time must elapse since a previous correct response before reinforcement again becomes available. In a variable interval schedule, the amount of time is allowed to vary. In a fixed ratio schedule, a fixed number of correct responses must be performed before one is reinforced. In a variable ratio schedule, this number is allowed to vary.

Research in cognitive learning suggests that not all behavior can be explained through conditioning. Köhler showed that apes can learn through sudden reorganization of perceptual relationships, or insight. Tolman's work with rats suggests that they develop cognitive maps of the environment and that operant conditioning teaches places where reinforcement is available, rather than mechanically increasing the frequency of oper-

ants. Tolman's latent learning studies suggest that organisms learn in the absence of reinforcement. Bandura and others have shown that people learn by observing others, without emitting reinforced responses of their own.

Memory may be divided into sensory, short-term, and long-term memory. A stimulus is maintained in sensory memory only for a fraction of a second. It then decays unless it is attended to and encoded. In short-term memory a perception or image may be maintained by auditory rehearsal of the encoded version. About seven (plus or minus two) chunks of information may be maintained in short-term memory at once. New chunks of information may displace older chunks that have not been transferred to long-term memory. Long-term memories are organized in a hierarchical structure. Accurate organization aids the retrieval process, and the reconstruction of information that is not simply acquired by rote learning. Appropriate cues must be used if information is to be retrieved.

Retention is tested through three types of memory tasks which, in order of ascending difficulty, are recognition, recall, and relearning (savings). Recall is often measured through use of paired associates of nonsense syllables. According to interference theory, people forget because learning can interfere with retrieval of other learnings. In retroactive interference, new learning interferes with old learning. In proactive interference, old learning interferes with new learning. Freud suggested that we also forget threatening or unacceptable material through repression, or motivated forgetting. In retrograde amnesia, shock or other trauma prevents recently learned material from being recalled, probably by interfering with consolidation.

Memory may be improved by the method of loci, through mediation, or through mnemonics. In each method incoming information is associated with already-known material or a format constructed for the occasion. "Every Good Boy Does Fine" is a mnemonic device for memorizing the musical keys, E, G, B, D, F.

Early in the century it was thought that engrams—electrical circuits in the brain corresponding to memory traces—made memory possible. Present research into the biology of memory focuses on the roles of neurotransmitters and RNA.

Truth or Fiction Revisited

- *Dogs can be trained to salivate when a bell is rung.* True. Pavlov accomplished this by repeatedly pairing a bell with the presentation of meat to laboratory dogs.

- *During World War II a Harvard psychologist proposed that we train pigeons to guide missiles to their targets.* True. B. F. Skinner proposed to accomplish this through operant conditioning. But the Defense Department apparently thought that the project was for the birds. It never got off the ground.

- *People actually* learn *to feed hard-earned cash into slot machines, even when there has been no payoff for hours.* True. Persistent, nonreinforced behavior may be maintained by unpredictable partial reinforcement schedules.

- *Rats can be trained to climb a ramp, cross a bridge, climb a ladder, pedal a toy car, and do several other tasks—all in proper sequence.* True. In chaining, each individual response is shaped. The animal is then reinforced for performing them in sequence. The final response in the sequence is usually shaped first, and the remaining tasks are then shaped in backward order.

- *All of our experiences are perfectly and permanently imprinted on the brain so that proper stimulation can cause us to remember them exactly.* False. It seems that what we remember is a blend of truth and fiction, skewed by our biases and needs.

- *There is no such thing as a photographic memory.* False. This phenomenon is called eidetic imagery, and is found in about five percent of children. The capacity is lost by adulthood.

- *There is no limit to the amount of information you can store in your long-term memory.* True, so far as we know. Long-term memories tend to be lost through poor organization or lack of adequate retrieval cues, but apparently not through decay or displacement.

- *The poison strychnine, in small doses, helps laboratory rats remember newly learned maze routes.* True. Strychnine helps them consolidate their learning.

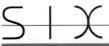

SIX

OUTLINE

Language, Thought, and Intelligence

- Psychologists have been able to teach chimpanzees and gorillas how to use sign language.
- Deaf children do not babble.
- Thought is not possible without language.
- Dogs can learn the concepts of roundness and squareness.
- The only way to solve a problem is to keep plugging away at it.
- A person's "IQ" is the same thing as his or her intelligence.
- There is no such thing as an unbiased intelligence test.
- High intelligence runs in families.

When I was in high school, I remember being taught that human beings differed from other creatures that walked, swam, or flew over the earth because we were the only ones to use language and tools. Then I found out that lower animals used tools too. Otters use rocks to open clam shells. Chimpanzees throw rocks as weapons and have been filmed, in the wild, using sticks to dig out grubs for food.

In recent years, our exclusive claim to the use of language has also been challenged. Advanced primates like chimps and gorillas have been taught abstract **symbols** (as in Figure 6.1), and have used these symbols to communicate by making signs with their hands or pressing keys on an electric typewriter.

Language makes possible the efficient communication of large amounts of complex knowledge from one person to another, and from one generation to another. According to psychologist Roger Brown, "The important thing about language is that it makes life experiences cumulative; across generations and within one generation, among individuals. Everyone can know much more than he (or she) could possibly learn by direct experience" (1970, p. 212). Or, as one of my college English professors could not resist saying about the novels we read, we receive **vicarious** experience.

Language provides many of the basic units of thought, and thought is central to intelligent behavior. Chimps and gorillas may have acquired the ability to communicate a few symbols. Even so, the extraordinarily larger human capacities to acquire, manipulate, use, and create language clearly separate us from lower animals more so than any other factors. Other animals may be stronger, run faster, smell more keenly, even live longer, but only we

FIGURE 6.1 Operant conditioning was used to teach a chimp named Sarah (left) to communicate through plastic symbols. Psychologists reinforced Sarah for selecting the proper symbols, or for following instructions made with symbols. Here Sarah will follow directions to place the apple in the pail and the banana in the dish. Lana (right) was taught to express simple ideas by pressing keys on a computer-controlled keyboard.

have produced literature, music, mathematics, and science. Only we have begun to explore the reaches of space that surround the tiny rock called Earth. Our ability to manipulate the symbols of language has made this exploration possible.

In this chapter we shall first survey efforts to teach language to apes since these attempts afford insight into our own use of language. Next we shall discuss the building blocks and structure of language. We shall explore theories of language acquisition in an effort to learn why people can use language but tuna fish and turtles cannot. This will prepare us for a discussion of how language and thought are intertwined in the formation of concepts and in problem solving. Finally, we shall examine the meanings of intelligence and see how intelligence is measured. As you might be aware from the continuing publicity over "IQ tests," the definition and measurement of intelligence have become controversial issues.

On Language and Apes: Going Ape over Language?

Some of us may know people who insist that their dogs understand every word they say. But when we look closely we find what the animals respond to is their human owner's excitement and a few words or commands—like "Sit," "Lunchtime," or "Out"—that have been paired repeatedly with certain acts or events. Even when dogs respond to the command "Speak," they do so with a doglike howl, bark, yap, or whine. They do not speak at all. Nor has anyone ever had a talking pet cat, horse, or elephant. So it was guaranteed that the weight of evidence of human history would make us skeptical of the first startling reports that chimpanzees had been taught to communicate by abstract symbols.

Washoe   However, close observation showed that Washoe, a female chimp raised by Beatrice and Allen Gardner (1972), had learned a good deal of **Ameslan,** the language of the deaf. The Gardners and their assistants raised Washoe from the time she was a year of age. Instead of speaking to her, they used signs. Washoe learned signs for actions, like *come, gimme,* and *tickle;* signs for things, like *apples, flowers,* and *toothbrush;* and other signs, like *more.* By the age of five, Washoe could use more than 160 signs. She could combine them to form simple sentences, although her word order was somewhat haphazard.

Many of Washoe's sentences were **duos,** simple two-word sentences. Her duos were largely **telegraphic,** like those of young children. Note these examples: *More tickle, More banana,* and *More milk.* As time passed Washoe showed some ability to sign longer sentences, like *Come gimme drink* and *Gimme toothbrush hurry.*

Sarah   Ann and David Premack (1975) taught another female chimp, Sarah, to communicate by arranging symbols on a magnet board (see Figure 6.1). Eventually Sarah learned simple telegraphic sentences like *Place orange dish.* The Premacks consider their work with Sarah a demonstration of the role of **operant conditioning** in the learning of language. Sarah was **reinforced** for selecting the proper symbols to make a request and for following instructions that were communicated by symbols.

Ameslan Acronym for *American Sign Language.*

Duo (DO–oh). A simple two-word sentence.

Telegraphic Referring to speech in which only the essential words are used, as in a telegram.

Operant conditioning A simple form of learning in which an organism learns to engage in behavior that is reinforced. See Chapter 5.

Reinforce In operant conditioning, to follow a behavior with a stimulus that increases the frequency of that behavior.

Lana   Another chimp, Lana, was trained to communicate by means of a keyboard controlled by a computer (Rumbaugh and others, 1973; Rumbaugh, 1977; Rumbaugh and Savage-Rumbaugh, 1978). Lana learn to manipulate about 100 keys, each of which showed a different symbol. She would press various combinations of keys to communicate simple ideas (Figure 6.1).

Koko   Perhaps the most impressive claims for teaching language to an ape come from Francine Patterson, who taught several hundred signs to a gorilla named Koko. Patterson (1978) claims that Koko has earned scores on intelligence tests just below those of children of comparable ages, at around ages five, six, and seven. She also asserts that Koko's use of language is almost human. Koko insults, lies, and, at times, does the exact opposite of what she is told to do.

A Psychological Controversy: Can Apes Really Understand Language?

Many apes have learned to manipulate their hands into Ameslan signs or to press a certain key to obtain a reward. But do these behaviors suggest an *understanding* of language? People understand that symbols (like words) stand for objects and ideas. Two-year-old children string signs (words) together in original combinations that show an understanding of rules of grammar. Many psychologists question whether apes show as much understanding of language as even young children.

Nim, the subject of Herbert Terrace's research, signs with his teacher *me* (photo upper left), *hug*, upper right, and *cat* (lower left). Notice that while Nim is signing *me* the teacher is signing *you*. While Nim is signing *hug*, the teacher is signing *Nim*. And while Nim is signing *cat*, the teacher is signing *who?*

Adventures with Koko

What is the worst insult you can think of? How about "You dirty toilet devil" or "Rotten stink"?

These are just samples of the insults reportedly used by Koko, in reference to her trainer and companion, Francine Patterson (1978). At the time Koko was a seven-year-old female gorilla. Gorillas, of course, are incapable of speech, but Koko is reported to have made these insults in Ameslan, the sign language used by some 200,000 deaf Americans. Koko learned to use some 375 signs regularly, including signs for *friend, airplane, lollipop, belly button,* even *stethoscope.*

The first meeting between Patterson and Koko was not promising. The 20-pound Koko, barely a year old, bit Patterson on the leg. Koko will grow to 250 pounds and be extremely strong, but gorillas are not the wild, aggressive animals portrayed by old Hollywood films. Instead they are usually calm and quite shy.

Since their first meeting, Patterson was friend, trainer, and mother to Koko in her mobile home on the Stanford University campus. She taught Koko sign language through the "molding technique." She would physically guide Koko's hand into the correct sign for an object while the object was present.

IQ Tests   Patterson carefully tracked Koko's performance on intelligence tests constructed for people. Koko's IQ scores have ranged between 84 and 95, just below those of average children. Patterson suggests, however, that a "cultural bias" may be built into these tests. One question asked where one could run to find shelter from rain, to a spoon, hat, house, or tree. Koko answered tree and the correct answer, of course, is house. We might be tempted to side with Koko, since gorillas in the wild are more likely to encounter trees than houses. But keep in mind that Koko lived in a (mobile) house, not a tree. So I

would consider tree a wrong answer for Koko—even at the risk of being called an "ape-ist." Still Koko's reported IQ scores seem surprisingly high for a nonhuman.

Although Koko cannot speak, she learned to understand speech as well as Ameslan. It became necessary for people to spell out words like *c-a-n-d-y* that they did not wish Koko to understand.

Patterson often took Koko and a young male gorilla, Mike, on short auto trips for novel stimulation. Now and then Koko signed *Go there* to avoid returning home, or *Hurry go drink* when they passed a vending machine.

Signing between Apes   Koko and Mike lived at opposite ends of the mobile home. On one occasion Koko could see that Mike was trying to find the proper signs to be let in to play with her. After a while Koko signed *Mike think hurry*. When Mike finally succeeded, Koko signed *Good know Mike*.

Koko may have empathized with the plights of others. When she saw a horse with a bit in the mouth, she signed *Horse sad*. Asked why, she signed *Teeth*. When shown a photograph of another gorilla struggling to avoid a bath, Koko, who also dislikes baths, signed *Me cry there*. When Patterson asked Koko if she was an animal or a person, Koko signed without hesitation *Fine animal gorilla*.

Understanding of Language or an Elaborate Trick?   Patterson's conclusions about Koko's language ability have not escaped criticism. Many researchers argue that Koko, like other apes who have been taught "language," shows no understanding of grammar and may simply be an excellent imitator of her teacher. Many psychologists believe that the ape's use of language is akin to an elaborate trick to gain a reward.

Herbert Terrace of Columbia University, who sought to show that apes can conquer **syntax** and string words together into original sentences, has concluded that apes cannot master even the basics of grammar. Nor do apes show spontaneous conversation as human children do. They use language in response to their teachers only. After reviewing videotapes and reports of others who taught language to apes, he wrote, "The closer I looked, the more I regarded the many reported instances of language as elaborate tricks for obtaining rewards" (Terrace, 1980). Chimpanzees do not show as much comprehension of the importance of word order as human children do (e.g., Fodor and others, 1974), suggesting that these apes do not share the **intuitive** human grasp of grammar.

Syntax The rules in a language for placing words in proper order to form meaningful sentences. (From the Latin *syntaxis*, meaning "joining together.")

Intuitive That which is known without conscious use of reasoning. (From the Latin *in*–, meaning "in," and *tueri*, meaning "to look at" or "to watch." The word "tuition" also derives from *tueri*.)

In *Speaking of Apes*, the husband-and-wife team of **linguist** Thomas Sebeok and **anthropologist** Donna Jean Umiker-Sebeok (1980) suggests that much of the language usage of these apes may be an example of the "Clever Hans Effect." Clever Hans was the name given a German circus horse at the turn of the century. Hans could tap out, with his hoofs, the answers to problems posed by his trainer. A German psychologist finally recognized that Hans was not actually solving problems. Instead, he was responding to a host of unintended stimuli emitted by his trainer—including patterns of breathing, the size of his pupils, and changes in facial expression. Apes, who are more intelligent than horses, ought also to be able to use cues emitted by their trainers to arrive at a "correct" response.

Ulric Niesser (1982) concludes that "language is uniquely our own.... There have been several concerted attempts to bestow sign language upon apes ... and they have essentially failed.... The published reports of these studies present no convincing demonstration of anything beyond what other animals can be trained to do: make isolated responses to isolated stimuli, or produce repetitive behavior in the hope of a food reward" (p. 45).

Having noted appropriate skepticism, let us end this section on a positive note. Psychologist Stanley Milgram (1982) considers teaching sign language to apes a major accomplishment of psychology. "Psychologists," he writes, "have learned to do something that has eluded human beings since prehistory—namely, communicate better with animals. By teaching primates elements of sign language, thus bypassing their inadequate vocal apparatus, we've ... gained new insight into animal cognition" (p. 50).

Now that we have more reason to appreciate the singularly human capacity to grasp the rules of grammar, let us turn our attention to the basics of language to see how language works.

The Basics of Language

Psychologists who study the ways in which we perceive and acquire language are called **psycholinguists.** One of the functions of psycholinguists is to analyze the basic components of language.

Ameslan is a language without sound since it is intended for use by deaf people. But the components of other languages do include sound: *phonology* (sounds), *morphology* (units of meaning), *syntax* (word order), and *semantics* (the meanings of words and groups of words).

Phonology

Phonology is the study of the basic sounds in a language. There are 26 letters in the English alphabet, but more than 40 basic sounds or **phonemes.** These include the *t* and *p* in *tip*, which a psycholinguist may designate with the /t/ and /p/ phonemes. The *o* in *go* and the *o* in *gone* are different phonemes—that is, they sound different—although they are spelled with the same letter. English speakers who learn French may be confused because the *o* phoneme, as in the word *go*, has various spellings in French, including *o, au, eau,* even *eaux.*

At one time or another, you may have heard someone trying to be humorous or witty by speaking English with a mock German or Japanese accent. Why can these two languages be mocked so readily in English? One answer is that different languages may use different phonemes. English speakers learning French, Spanish, or German must practice different-sounding "rolling *r*'s." German has two throaty phonemes, both spelled *ch*, which are not found in English, French, and Spanish. French and German have no *th* phonemes. So French and German speakers often compensate by pronouncing the word *the* with a sort of *zh* sound. Japanese has no *r* phoneme. For this reason, many Japanese pronounce the English words *right* and *wrong* as *light* and *long*.

Morpheme The smallest unit of meaning in a language.

Morphology

Morphemes are the smallest units of meaning in a language. A morpheme consists of one or more phonemes pronounced in a certain order. The words *dog* and *cat* are morphemes, but not all morphemes are words. The words *dogs* and *cats* each consist of two morphemes. Adding a *z* phoneme to *dog* makes the word plural. Adding an *s* sound to *cat* serves the same function.

An *ed* morpheme at the end of a verb places it in the past tense, as with *add* and *added*, and with *subtract* and *subtracted*. A *ly* morpheme at the end of an adjective often makes the word an adverb, as with *strong* and *strongly* and *weak* and *weakly*. Now, if you remember that adjectives modify things and adverbs modify actions, you are talking about syntax.

Syntax

since feeling is first
who pays any attention
to the syntax of things
will never wholly kiss you ...
                    —e.e. cummings

These four lines from an e.e. cummings poem are confusing because the *syntax* permits at least two interpretations. How would the meaning be changed if we were to place a question mark at the end of the third line and remove the fourth? What would happen to the meaning if we placed *he* or *she* before the word *who?* Cummings delighted in phrasing poetry to allow various interpretations. He toyed with the syntax of English. Syntax concerns the customary arrangement of words in phrases and sentences in a language. Syntax deals with the ways words are to be strung together, or ordered, into phrases and sentences. The precise rules for word order are the *grammar* of a language.

In English, statements usually follow the pattern subject, verb, and object of the verb. Note this example:

The young boy (subject) → has brought (verb) → the book (object).

The sentence would be confusing if it were written "The young boy *has* the book *brought*." But this is how the sentence would be written in German. German syntax differs from that of English. In German, a past participle ("brought") is placed at the end of the sentence, while the helping verb ("has") follows the subject. German vocabulary also has a way of producing long, polysyllabic words for which English would use several separate words.

Mark Twain, the American humorist, wrote an essay "The Awful German Language" to describe the horrors of trying to learn German syntax, or word order. Twain presents the following quote from a German newspaper to make

Although English and German have common origins, the syntax and many other features of the languages are quite different. After several months of struggling with German syntax and trying to memorize the gender of German nouns, American humorist Mark Twain wrote, "The inventor of the language seems to have taken pleasure in complicating it every way he could think of."

All German nouns have gender or sex—male, female, or neuter (none). In English, only nouns that are actually male (like *man* or *boy* or *ram*) would be referred to by pronouns like *he* or *him*. But, as Mark Twain noted in *A Tramp Abroad* (1880), the sex of German nouns is not always assigned so logically:

"A tree is male, its buds are female, its leaves are neuter; horses are sexless, dogs are males, cats are females,—Tom-cats included, of course; a person's mouth, neck, bosom, elbows, fingers, nails, feet, and body are of the male sex, and his head is male or neuter according to the word selected to signify it, and *not* according to the sex of the individual who wears it,—for in Germany all the women wear either male heads or sexless ones; a person's nose, lips, shoulders, breast, hands, and toes are of the female sex; and his hair, eyes, chin, legs, knees, heart, and conscience haven't any sex at all. The inventor of the language probably got what he knew about a conscience from hearsay."

Of course, the rules of German gender seem natural to a native-born German, even if they seem arbitrary to us. In French all things are either male or female, including rocks and avocados.

his point. The faint-of-heart may wish to skip to the next section. For the stouthearted, here is a literal, word-by-word translation:

In the daybeforeyesterdayshortly after eleveno'clock Night, the inthistownstandingtavern called "The Wagoner" was downburnt. When the fire to the onthedownburninghouseresting Stork's Nest reached, flew the parent storks away. But when the bytheraging, firesurrounded Nest itself caught Fire, straightway plunged the quickreturning Mother-stork into the flames and died, her wings over her young ones outspread.

Semantics

Semantics concerns the meanings of a language. It is the study of the relationship between language and the objects or events language depicts. Words that sound and are spelled alike can have different meanings, depending on their usage. Compare these sentences:

A rock sank the boat.
Don't rock the boat.

In the first sentence, *rock* is a noun and the subject of the verb *sank*. The sentence probably means that the hull of a boat was ripped open by an underwater rock, causing the boat to sink. (It could also be that someone hurled a rock at the boat, but the rock would have to be rather large, and the hurler rather burly.) In the second sentence, *rock* is a verb. The sentence probably means that someone needs to be warned not to stand in a small boat or move about in it too rapidly. The second sentence could also be a figure of speech in which a person is being warned not to change things— not to "make waves" or "upset the apple cart."

Or compare these sentences:

The chicken is ready for dinner.
The lion is ready for dinner.
The shark is ready for dinner.

Semantics The study of the relationships between language and objects or events. The study of the meaning of language. (From the Greek *sema*, meaning "sign" or "symbol.")

The first sentence probably means that a chicken has been cooked and is ready to be eaten. The second sentence probably means that a lion is hungry, or about to devour its prey. Our interpretation of the phrase "is ready for dinner" reflects our expectations concerning chickens and lions. Whether or not we expect a shark to be eaten or to do some eating would reflect on our seafood preferences or on how recently we had seen the movie *Jaws*.

Now that we have looked at the structure of language, we can better appreciate the "child's task" of acquiring language. In the following section, we trace language development from birth.

Outcry over "Wuf Tickets": Black English vs. Standard Usage in the Courtroom

Many of the black kids at Ann Arbor's Green Road Housing Project in Michigan do not talk much like their well-to-do white classmates at the neighborhood King elementary school. Some of it is simple pronunciation: "We do maf work" for "We do mathematics work." Some of the differences lie in odd verb tenses: "She-ah hit us" for "She will hit us." More often the difference involves the verb "to be." Green Roaders say, "He be gone" when they mean, "He is gone a good deal of the time"; "He been gone" when they mean, "He's been gone a long while"; and "He gone" when they mean, "He is gone right now." Some is pure idiom. "To sell wolf tickets" (pronounced wuf tickets) means to challenge somebody to a fight.

Such speech, widely known as Black English, is customarily pounced upon by teachers trying to teach standard English usage. Though that would seem a normal part of pedagogy, a small group of Green Road parents felt that teachers were expressing their disapproval of Black English too harshly, causing student embarrassment and hurting the children's chances to learn. The parents filed a federal suit in Michigan's Eastern District Court, demanding that school authorities "recognize" Black English as a formal dialect with historic roots and grammatical rules of its own.

A Bridge to Standard English Like most Green Road parents, the plaintiffs want their children to use standard English, but they insisted that the school respond more sympathetically to the dialect in teaching. "Language is like clothing," said University of Michigan professor Daniel Fader, testifying on behalf of the children. "When you take it away from the child, you leave him naked." As attorney Gabe Kaimowitz insisted, "We're looking for use of Black English as a bridge to get kids to use standard English."

The suit divided Detroit's black community. "A mountain out of a molehill," said Detroit N.A.A.C.P. President Larry Washington. "The dominant language of this country is English," added Washington. "If our children are to increase their chances, that's what they have to be taught." School officials decided that the suit was unnecessary and cited as evidence an existing volunteer training course in the techniques of teaching standard English to Black English speakers.

Sensitivity Courses After three weeks of argument, U.S. District Judge Charles W. Joiner concluded that the school had not been as sympathetic as it should have been. In a 43-page opinion that is expected to serve as a precedent for other legal challenges, Joiner provided the first judicial opinion that Black English is a distinct dialect, not just slovenly talk, and ordered the Ann Arbor school district to prepare a plan for teaching Black English speakers. All teachers at the King school will now be required to take "sensitivity courses" in how to steer small pupils tactfully away from "wuf tickets" and into the verb "to be."

Cooing Unlearned verbalizations that are thought to express pleasure in newborn infants.

Babbling The child's first vocalizations that have the sound of speech.

Language Development

I have been told by a friend who has three young children that the most fascinating thing he experienced with each of them was how they learned to talk. As he put it, "One day, nothing; the next, they seemed to be talking in complete sentences." Although a child's use of language does seem at times to develop by leaps and bounds, we can point to a number of markers such as the following.

Crying and Cooing

Newborn children, as parents are well aware, have one highly effective form of verbal expression: crying and more crying. But by a couple of months of age, children also begin **cooing.** Cooing, like crying, is unlearned. Cooing appears associated with feelings of pleasure or positive excitement.

Parents soon learn that different cries and coos have different meanings and indicate different things: hunger, gas, or pleasure at being held or rocked. Crying and cooing are not true language. In true language, sounds (or signs, in the case of Ameslan) are symbols. Cries and coos do not represent objects or events. By about eight months of age, cooing decreases markedly. By about the sixth month, children have already begun to *babble*.

Babbling

Babbling is the first vocalizing that sounds like human speech. Babbling children utter phonemes found in several languages, including the throaty German *ch*, the clicks of certain African tribes, and rolling *r*'s (Atkinson and others, 1970; McNeill, 1970). Babbling appears to be inborn. Deaf children babble even though they cannot hear the speech of others. Reinforcements for babbling like adult smiling or pats on the stomach can increase its frequency (e.g., Rheingold and others, 1959).

TABLE 6.1 Some Milestones in Language Development

Approximate Age	Language Performance
Birth	Cries
12 weeks	Coos, gurgles
16 weeks	Differentiates sounds and responds to human sounds
20 weeks	Makes vowel and consonant sounds
6 months	Babbles single syllable (ma, mu, da, di)
8 months	Reduplicates babbles (mama, didi), intonates
12 months	Understands some words as symbols
18 months	Still babbles, utters 2–50 words, not many joined
24 months	Shows vocabulary of 50+ words (especially nouns), uses two-word phrases
30 months	Shows fastest vocabulary increase—daily additions
36 months	Shows 1,000-word vocabulary, 80% of which is intelligible to strangers

The ages in this table are approximations. Parents need not assume that their children will have language problems if they are somewhat behind. Source: Adapted from Lenneberg (1967).

From these beginnings, children seem to single out the types of phonemes used consistently in the home within a few months. By the age of nine or 10 months these phonemes are repeated regularly. "Foreign" phonemes begin to drop out.

The Holophrase

By about 18 months of age, children usually produce dozens of words, like *no*, *cookie*, *mama*, *hi*, and *eat*. Others, like *allgone* and *bye-bye*, may not be found in the dictionary, but function as words.

Single words are called **holophrases** when they are used to express complex meanings. For example, *mama* may be used by the child to signify, "Come here, mama," and *eat* may be used to signify "I want to eat."

"He has some teeth, but his words haven't come in yet."

The Duo

Toward the end of the second year, children begin to speak in simple two-word sentences called duos. Many duos consist of an *open class word* and a *pivot word*.

Open class words usually express concrete concepts that can be described in a single word (Dale, 1976). *Mommy*, *Daddy*, *car*, and *milk* are open class words. **Pivot words** tend to be small, like *go*, and are attached to the (usually larger) open class words. "Mommy go," "Daddy go," and "Car go" are duos with the pivot word in the second position. In "More milk" the pivot word is in the first position. Pivot words usually stand for phrases. In the duo "Car go," *go* stands for "is going." In the duo "More milk," *more* stands for "I want more."

Duos are examples of telegraphic speech, in which only essential words are used. In the duo "That ball" (Table 6.2), the words *is* and *a* are implied. Duos appear at about the same time in the development of languages other than English (Slobin, 1973). The limited importance of environmental influences supports the view that the human tendency to develop language according to universal processes is **innate.**

Holophrase A single word used to express complex meanings. (From the Greek *holos*, meaning "whole," and *phrazein*, meaning "to speak.")

Open class words Words that usually express concepts that can be described in a single word.

Pivot words Small words that usually stand for phrases and modify open class words.

Innate Existing at birth. Unlearned, natural. (From the Latin *in–*, meaning "in," and *nasci*, meaning "to be born.")

Yum-Yum, Da-Da, Wa-Wa, and Poo-Poo

If you are around infants, you are likely to hear baby talk like *yum-yum*, *da-da*, *wa-wa*, and *poo-poo*. If the babies do not babble these sounds, their parents probably will.

Landreth (1967) notes that when parents speak to children in baby talk, they usually simplify their speech and use sound duplicates like *yum-yum*, *bye-bye*, *mama*, *dada*. Parents also use diminutive forms of words, by adding *ee* phonemes. *Dog* becomes *doggie* and *horse* becomes *horsey*. Parents may also use dramatic exaggerations, brief sentences, concrete nouns, and talk to themselves out loud—as in, "Now, what does Mommy have for Baby?" (Shenker, 1971).

Now and then we hear that parents should not overdo baby talk with infants. The rationale is that children learn language by imitating parents, and that baby talk does not serve as the best of models.

There is no evidence that baby talk is damaging. Learning by imitation is only a partial explanation of language acquisition in children. In any event, most adults follow rules of grammar when they talk to their children, even if that talk is baby talk (Newport, 1976; Snow, 1972). Parental talking also stimulates greater production of infant sounds (Blank, 1974).

The message seems clear enough. Baby talk is just fine for parents and for babies. If you want to use baby talk with your children, go ahead and enjoy it.

TABLE 6.2   Some Uses of Children's Two-Word Sentences (Duos)

Type of Sentence	Example	Understanding Suggested by Sentence
Naming and locating	That ball. There car.	Objects exist that have names.
Negating	Milk allgone. No eat.	Objects may become used up or leave; people may *not* do things.
Demanding and wishing	Want Mommy. More milk.	Objects can be brought back or quantities increased.
Describing events	Mommy go. Daddy sit. Doggie bark.	People and animals and objects engage in actions.
Describing objects	Pretty Mommy. Big glass.	People and objects have traits or qualities.
Indicating possession	Mommy cup. My shoe	People possess objects.
Questioning	Where Mommy? Where milk?	People can provide information if stimulated to do so.

Duos, while brief and telegraphic, still show an early understanding of syntax. The child will say "Sit chair" to tell a parent to sit in a chair, not "Chair sit." (Apes do not reliably make this distinction.) The child will say "My shoe," not "Shoe my," to show possession. "Mommy go" means Mommy is leaving, while "Go Mommy" expresses the wish for Mommy to go away. For this reason, "Go Mommy" is not heard frequently.

Toward More Complex Language

Between the ages of two and three, children's vocabularies leap impressively from about 250 to 1,000 words. Sentence structure expands to include several words. Children show understanding of the rules of grammar. This understanding enables them to form the plurals of words they hear for the first time by adding *s* or *z* phonemes. They also form the past tense of words they hear for the first by adding *d* or *ed*.

Children's lack of knowledge of irregular words (words that do not conform to the usual grammatical rules) can produce some charming "errors." A child of two and a half may report that he or she has just seen some *gooses* or *sheeps* at the farm. The child may add that his or her arm *hurted* because he or she was *hitted* by Johnny.

In an experiment designed to show that preschool children are not just clever mimics but have actually grasped rules of grammar, Berko (1958) showed children pictures of nonexistent animals, as in Figure 6.2. She first showed them a single animal and said, "This is a wug." Then she showed them a picture of two animals and said, "Now there are two of them." Then she said, "There are two _____," asking the children to finish the sentence. Ninety-one percent of the children said "wugs," correctly pluralizing the bogus word. This percentage was approximated in similar language tasks.

As language develops beyond the third year, children begin to use pronouns like *it* and *she* accurately. They gain facility with prepositions like *in*, *before* or *on*, which represent physical or temporal relationships among ob-

This is a wug   Now there are two of them.   There are two _____.

FIGURE 6.2 Many bright, sophisticated college students are unfamiliar with "wugs." Here are several wugs—actually, make-believe animals used in a study to learn whether preschool children can form the plurals of unfamiliar nouns.

jects and events. During the early school years children come to understand words that describe relationships between people, like *uncle* or *aunt*. Aunt Elizabeth is no longer simply the person designated repeatedly as Aunt Elizabeth. She is now understood to be Aunt Elizabeth *because* she is Mother's sister. Another sister of Mother's could now be expected to be labeled an aunt.

Theories of Language Development

Countless billions of children have learned the languages spoken by their parents. They have continued to pass these languages down, with minor changes, from generation to generation. We know of some of the biological structures involved in using language, like the speech centers in the brain and the vocal cords. Our understanding of the psychological processes involved in language development, however, remains largely speculative. Theories of language development may be divided broadly into learning theories and psycholinguistic theory.

Learning Theories

Classical Conditioning **Classical conditioning** may be involved in children's learning that words are signs for objects and activities. The word *cereal*, for example, may become the conditioned stimulus (CS) for cereal (the unconditioned stimulus, or US), if the word is paired repeatedly with perception of the cereal. After conditioning has occurred, the word *cereal* (the CS) may elicit an image of cereal (a conditioned response, or CR). According to learning theorist O. Hobart Mowrer (1960), many mental images are conditioned responses that are elicited by conditioned stimuli, in this case, words.

There is no doubt that children can learn words for objects by pairing perception of the object with a name. Yet children as well as adults also learn words for abstract qualities (like "goodness"), complex events, and thought processes. We cannot simply point to truth, goodness, Western civilization, the creation of the universe, or memory, and name these things. For this reason, classical conditioning is at best a partial explanation for language acquisition.

Operant Conditioning When children begin to speak, parents frequently become excited and hug and kiss them. They shower them with reinforcing attention (Brown & Hanlon, 1970). Reinforcement tends to increase the frequency of behavior, including language-related behavior. Some psychologists (e.g., B. F. Skinner, 1957) have argued that language development can be largely explained by operant conditioning.

Classical conditioning A simple form of learning in which one stimulus comes to elicit the response usually brought forth by a second stimulus by being paired repeatedly with the second stimulus. See Chapter 5.

Model As a verb, to engage in a behavior that is imitated by another.

Observational learning A form of cognitive learning in which responses are acquired by observing others engage in them. It is not necessary that the learner emit the response, or that it be reinforced. See Chapter 5.

Psycholinguistic theory The view that language learning involves an interaction between environmental influences and an inborn tendency to acquire language. The emphasis is on the innate tendency.

Language Acquisition Device In psycholinguistic theory, neural "prewiring" that is presumed to facilitate the child's learning of grammar. Abbreviated *LAD*.

We do observe parents shaping their children's verbal behavior. They **model** certain sounds or words clearly, like *Mama* or *Dada*, and encourage children to repeat them. At first they reinforce children simply for approximating the sounds. Later on they may require that the children utter the sound clearly, while pointing to the right person, before reinforcement is given. Some theorists suggest that our biological makeup is such that sound production is "self-reinforcing" in children. They suggest that children enjoy babbling and other sounds for their own sake, even when nobody else is present or rewards them.

Critics argue that operant conditioning, like classical conditioning, can only partially explain language development. Children do not appear to learn rules of grammar by trial-and-error behavior and reinforcement. Instead, they appear to show insight into language structure. This insight allows them to produce sentences spontaneously. According to principles of operant conditioning, children might be limited to utterances for which they have been previously reinforced.

Observational Learning One of my friends has an eight-year-old nephew whose speech is sprinkled with double negatives (as in "Yes, we don't have no bananas") and frequent "Way to go!" exclamations—just as his father's speech is. Children can learn by observing their parents and other people. **Observational learning** may help explain why, during the first year, children begin to emphasize repetition of phonemes used by their parents, and why the accents, vocabularies, and grammatical peculiarities of some children tend to be similar to those of their parents. We also observe parents encouraging children to observe and imitate their verbal behavior by repeating words and sentences.

Observational learning can also provide only a partial explanation for language acquisition. Observational learning does not explain why children babble sounds they have not heard, or why they make certain overgeneralizations in their speech. When a child says "Mommy goed away" rather than "Mommy went away," or "I dood it" rather than "I did it," it is not because parents were observed or heard to make these errors. It is because the child is applying grammatical rules, as they are understood, in his or her own speech (Ervin-Tripp, 1964).

Psycholinguistic Theory

According to **psycholinguistic theory,** language acquisition involves an interaction between environmental influences, like parental speech and reinforcement, and an inborn tendency to acquire language (Chomsky, 1968, 1980; Rosenthal, 1980). Noam Chomsky labels this inborn tendency the **Language Acquisition Device,** or *LAD*. He believes that the LAD is a "prewiring" of the nervous system that makes it well suited to learn basic rules of grammar.

Parents naturally influence children to learn their particular language. Parents may naturally use reinforcement and other principles of learning theory. Yet children's ability to grasp the syntax of a language basically reflects their neural prewiring, or LAD.

Critics of Chomsky argue that he may overestimate children's intuitive grasp of grammar (Premack & Premack, 1972). Also, no one has yet shown how the hypothetical LAD is wired, or prewired.

On a broad level, it makes perfect sense that language development involves learning through experience and *some* kind of neural prewiring. Goldfish, flatworms, and rats, despite the best of environments, do not learn language. It seems foolish to think that we simply have not yet found an efficient way to teach them English or French. It is safe to assume that they lack the "prewiring." Apes, on the other hand, may be partially prewired to use language. Partial prewiring could explain why they gain some facility with Ameslan, even though their syntax remains unreliable. And, of course, they are not prewired to develop speech.

Language and Thought

Now all these theories may be of little moment to a 20-month-old who has just polished off her plate of chocolate chip cookies and exclaims "Allgone!" What does her use of "Allgone" suggest about her thought processes? Would she have known that there were no cookies left if she did not have a word to express this idea? Do you think in words? Can you think *without* using language? Would you be able to solve problems without using words or sentences?

According to Jean Piaget (1976), whose theory of cognitive development will be discussed in Chapter 8, language is merely a reflection of a person's knowledge of the world. Language is not necessary for the acquisition of much of this knowledge. It is possible to have the concepts of roundness or redness even when we do not know or use the words *round* or *red*.

The Linguistic Relativity Hypothesis

Language may not be fully necessary for thought, but some psychologists suggest that language structures the way we perceive the world (Whorf, 1956; Sapir, 1921). This view is termed the **linguistic relativity hypothesis.** We may have some concept of snow even if we have no words for snow. If our language, like the language of Eskimos, had many words for snow, depending on whether the snow was hard-packed, falling, melting, etc., our ability to think about snow might be enhanced. Garo, a Burmese language, uses several words for rice, depending on whether the rice is husked or unhusked, and on how it is prepared. In English we have hundreds of words to describe different colors, but those who speak Shona use only three words for colors. People who speak Bassa use only two words for colors (Gleason, 1961), corresponding to light and dark, or white and black. The Hopi Indians have two words for flying objects, one for birds and an all-inclusive word for anything else that may be found traveling through the air.

Does this mean that the Hopi are limited in their ability to think about bumblebees and airplanes that fly overhead? Are English speakers limited in their ability to think about skiing conditions? Are those who speak Shona and Bassa "color-blind" for all practical purposes?

Probably not. People who use only a few words to distinguish colors seem to perceive color variations in the same way as people with dozens of words (Rosch, 1974; Bornstein & Marks, 1982). For example, the Dani of New Guinea, like the Bassa, use only their words for dark and light in labeling colors. Still, they have no difficulty in distinguishing the many colors of the

Linguistic relativity hypothesis The view that language structures the way in which one perceives the world. As a consequence, one's thoughts would be limited by the concepts available in his or her language.

Concept A symbol that stands for groups of objects, events, or ideas with common properties. (From the Latin *conceptus*, meaning "conceived.")

spectrum in matching and memory tasks. English-speaking skiers, who are concerned about different skiing conditions, have developed a comprehensive special vocabulary, including *powder* and *corn snow*.

Critics of the linguistic relativity hypothesis argue that vocabulary suggests the range of concepts that the speakers of the language have deemed important. But this does not mean people cannot make distinctions for which there are no words. Hopi Indians flying from New York to San Francisco nowadays would not think that they are flying inside a bird or a bumblebee, even if they have no word for airplane.

Concepts and Concept Formation

What's black and white and read all over? This riddle was used quite often when I was younger. Since the riddle was spoken, you would probably assume that "read" meant "red" when you heard it. And so, in seeking an answer, you would scan your memory for an object that was red even though it was black and white. The answer to the riddle, "newspaper," would meet with a good groan.

The word *newspaper* is a **concept.** Concepts are symbols. They stand for groups of objects, events, or ideas that have common properties. Newspapers are indeed black and white, most of the time. They are usually read, although they can also be used for sopping up spills, paper-training your dog, and kindling and fanning fires. Material, color, shape, and purpose—these are some of the types of properties that most newspapers share. If a newspaper had full-color photos (as some do), or was made of glossy paper (as newsletters of some professional organizations are), we might think of it as an unusual newspaper.

Riddles often reveal and rely upon concept confusion with words. What is the relationship between concepts and words?

Concepts and Words

Words are concepts, but not all concepts are words. For instance, a dog can respond to the concept of *roundness* even though it cannot understand that the word "round" symbolizes the concept. This can be demonstrated through operant conditioning, as in the following example. Allow a dog to choose one of three pathways, one with a circle above it, and the other two with a square and a triangle. Alternate the size and position of these geometric figures, but reinforce the dog with food for taking the pathway marked by the circle. The round circle will become a discriminative stimulus, and the dog will reliably take the pathway marked by the circle—at least when it has been deprived of food for a while.

FIGURE 6.3 Where does figure *A* belong? With *B* or with *C?* Most adults prefer to classify objects according to form rather than color concepts, and would thus choose *C.* Why not try this on a few adults and find out for yourself?

Concepts and Classes

Some concepts, like *animal*, *activity*, and *event*, are quite general. They refer to large groups or classes of objects or events that have only a few properties in common. Flatworms, birds, and chimps all fit into the animal category, for example. Other concepts, like *Boston terrier*, *microcomputer*, and *chocolate seven-layer cake*, are more specific. There are fewer instances of the concept *Boston terrier* than there are of *animal*, but Boston terriers share more properties with one another than do animals in general.

Hierarchies of Concepts   Everyone who takes a job in modern corporate America joins a **hierarchy.** You report to or are *subordinate* to your boss. If you yourself are a boss, you will have subordinates or people who report to you. Concepts also follow a hierarchy. Some concepts are **subordinate** to, or contained by, others. The concepts *dog* and *bird* are said to be subordinate to, or contained by, the concept *animal*. Other concepts are **superordinate** to, or contain, others. The concept *animal* is superordinate to the concepts *dog*, *bird*, *chimp*, and *flatworm*.

Subordinate concepts possess all the properties ascribed to superordinate concepts. Dogs, birds, chimps, and flatworms each possess all the properties that pertain to animals, even if they differ markedly from one another in many obvious ways. Superordinate concepts do not have all the properties possessed by each subordinate concept. Birds, for instance, have all the properties of animals in general, but also have feathers and fly. Dogs, chimps, and flatworms do not have feathers or fly, but they are still animals.

Consider people for a moment. The concept *teacher* is subordinate to the concept *person*. Those things that are true of persons, like bleeding when scratched, making errors, and having emotions, are also true of teachers. But as you can see in Figure 6.4, it may be that some students place teachers in a special category. Sadly, none of my students ever seem surprised when I make errors in the classroom.

Concepts permit us to make generalizations about the world around us without having directly to experience every object or event. If you have learned that Boston terriers are affectionate and somewhat "nervous," you will expect to find these properties in a new Boston terrier.

Knowledge of groups or classes allows us to make certain decisions efficiently. You may decide to buy a dog rather than a cat, or an Irish setter rather than a Doberman pinscher, because you know something about those classes of animals.

Assimilation and Accommodation   According to Jean Piaget, our conceptual development involves the processes of **assimilation** and **accommoda-**

FIGURE 6.4   You may classify teachers as people, and therefore assume that what is true of people will also hold for teachers. But children have to learn to classify concepts according to "adult" schemata.

Concept and Concept Formation   **229**

tion. Assimilation is the inclusion of a new object or event into an existing concept, or, in Piaget's terminology, into an existing **schema.** Parents usually let children know they are trying to include too many four-legged animals into the "doggy" schema when they refer to horses as "big doggies." The creation of a new schema, like "horseys," is an example of accommodating to new events, or changing one's way of grouping information.

Concept Formation

Simple Concepts   Many simple concepts, like *dog* and *red,* may be taught by association. Many lower animals learn to respond to such concepts. The animals are reinforced for engaging in target behaviors in the presence of simple concepts used as discriminative stimuli. With children, words can be used as discriminative stimuli. For instance, "flash cards" with pictures on them of different types of dogs, or **positive instances** of the concept, "dog," are shown to a child as one says the word "dog" or the sentence, "This is a dog." **Negative instances,** that is, things which are *not* dogs, are then shown to the child while one says, "This is *not* a dog." Of course, things that are *negative instances* of one concept may be *positive instances* of another. So in teaching a child, one may be more likely to say, "This is *not* a dog, it's a *cat,*" rather than simply, "This is not a dog."

Complex Concepts   More abstract concepts, like *uncle* or *square root,* may have to be learned through verbal explanations that involve more basic concepts. If one points to *uncles* (positive instances) and *not uncles* (negative instances) repeatedly, a child may eventually learn that uncles are males, or even that they are males who are not their own fathers. However, it is doubtful that this show-and-tell method would ever teach them that uncles are brothers of a parent. The concept *uncle* is best taught by explanation after a child understands the concepts *parent* (or at least *Mommy* and *Daddy)* and *brother.*

Concepts that are still more abstract, like *justice, goodness,* and *beauty,* may require complex verbal explanation and the presentation of many positive and negative instances. These concepts are so abstract and instances of them are so varied that no two people may agree on their definition. Of, if their definitions coincide, they may argue over positive versus negative instances. An action that seems just to you may seem unjust to me. What seems a beautiful work of art to me may impress you as meaningless masses of colors. Thus, the phrase "Beauty is in the eye of the beholder."

Schema (SKI–muh). According to Piaget, a hypothetical mental structure that permits the classification and organization of new information. (Both a Greek and Latin word meaning "plan" or "form.")

Positive instances Examples of a concept.

Negative instances Events that are *not* examples of a concept. Concept formation is aided by presentation of both positive and negative instances of the concept.

Concept Formation and Hypothesis Testing   Experiments in concept formation suggest that people often acquire concepts through the active process of *hypothesis testing* (Bourne and others, 1971; Bruner and others, 1956; Horton & Turnage, 1976). Let us try a brief experiment to see how you might acquire the concept *zed*—or learn what "zeds" are so that you can describe them.

Let us imagine that we sit across a table from one another with a box of plastic shapes between us, like those in Figure 6.5. These are the rules: I ask you to pick out a piece, and each time you do so, I tell you whether or not it is a zed. When you can single out all the pieces that are zeds without making errors, I'll know that you have learned what zeds are.

You select *A1,* the small colored triangle, and I say, "No, that's not a zed." Then you pick out *B2,* and I say, "Yes, that's a zed." Do you pick out the third piece at random or on the basis of some hypotheses about what zeds might

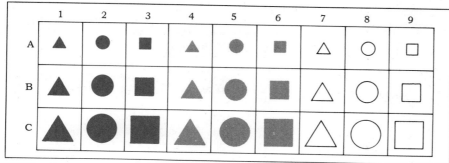

FIGURE 6.5 Geometric Forms of the Type Used by Psychologists in Experiments on Concept Formation. Let's imagine we are seeing how long it takes you to learn what *daks* are. You select pieces B1 and B4 and find that these are both daks. What hypotheses do you now consider about the definition of a dak? Then you select C4 and learn that this is not a dak. Does this finding affect your hypotheses? What piece would you select next to gain further information? Why? (What hypothesis are you seeking to confirm?)

be? Have you already eliminated several hypotheses about zeds? For instance, you know already that the following hypotheses are false: All zeds are gray, all zeds are white, all zeds are square. Can you eliminate any other hypotheses at this point?

Next you pick out *B5*, and I say yes. What's your hypothesis? Do you next pick out *B8*? If you do, I say no. How do you react? You continue to select pieces. *C5* is no. *B4* is yes. *B3* is yes. *B7* is no. Would you now be able to identify those pieces that are *zed* or *not zed* without making further errors? You would if your current hypothesis is that zeds are medium-sized and brown or gray.

Studies like these suggest that even young children may use hypothesis testing to speed learning of concepts like shapes and colors. When you show a child a square and say "Square," the child may try to understand what accounts for the squareness of the figure. Is it the figure's boxiness, its size, its color, or what? After being shown several figures that are square, and several figures that are not, the child appears to develop a concept of squareness that involves other concepts like *boxy* and *sides as long as one another*. It may be many years before the child's definition involves sophisticated concepts like *closed geometric figure, four sides equal in length*, and *right angles*.

Problem Solving

One of the pleasures I derived from taking my own introductory psychology course lay in showing friends the textbook and getting them involved in the problems in the section on problem solving. First, of course, I struggled with the problems myself. It's that time, now. And it's your turn. Get some scrap paper, take a breath, and have a go at the following problems. The answers will be discussed in the following pages, but don't peek. *Try* the problems first.

1. Provide the next two letters in the series for each of the following:
   a. ABABABAB??
   b. ABDEBCEF??
   c. OTTFFSSE??

TABLE 6.3   Water Jar Problems

Problem Number	Three Jars Are Present with the Listed Capacity (in Ounces)			Obtain This Amount of Water
	Jar A	Jar B	Jar C	
1	21	127	3	100
2	14	163	25	99
3	18	43	10	5
4	9	42	6	21
5	20	59	4	31
6	23	49	3	20
7	10	36	7	3

For each problem, how can you use some combination of the three jars given, and a tap, to obtain precisely the amount of water shown? Adapted from Abraham S. Luchins and Edith H. Luchins, *Rigidity of Behavior* (Eugene: University of Oregon Press, 1959), p. 109.

2. Draw straight lines through all the points in Figure A below, using only *four* lines. Do not lift your pencil from the paper or retrace your steps. (Answer shown on page 235.)
3. Move three matches in figure B below to make four squares of the same size. You must use *all* the matches. (Answer shown on page 235.)
4. You have three jars, A, B, and C, which hold the amounts of water, in ounces, shown in Table 6.3. For each of the seven problems in Table 6.3, use the jars in any way you wish to arrive at the indicated amount of water. Fill or empty any jar as often as you wish. How do you obtain the desired amount of water in each problem? (The solutions are discussed on p. 234.)

If you are like most other problem solvers, you used three steps to solve parts *a* and *b* of Problem 1. First, you sought to uncover the structure of the various elements, or *cycles*, in each series. Series *1a* has repeated cycles of two letters: *AB, AB*, and so on. Series *1b* may be seen as having four cycles of two consecutive letters: *AB, DE, BC*, and so on.

Second, you searched for *rules* that governed the advance of each series. In series *1a*, the rule is simply to repeat the cycle. Series *1b* is more complicated, and different sets of rules can be used to describe it. One correct set of rules is that odd-numbered cycles (*1 and 3*, or *AB* and *BC*) simply repeat the last letter of the previous cycle (in this case *B*) and then advance by one letter according to the alphabet. The same rule applies to even-numbered cycles (*2 and 4*, or *DE* and *EF*).

Third, you used the rules uncovered to *generate* the next letters in the series: *AB* in series *1a*, and *CD* in series *1b*.

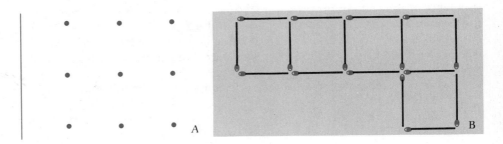

Question: What alternate sets of rules could you have found to describe these two series? Would you have generated the same answers from these rules?

Now, how about part *c* of Problem 1? Were you seeking a pattern of letters that involved cycles and the alphabet? If so, it may be because parts *a* and *b* were solved by this approach.

Mental Sets

The tendency to respond to a new problem with the same approach that helped solve earlier, similar-looking problems is termed a **mental set.** Mental sets usually make our work easier, but they can mislead us when the similarity between problems is illusory, as in part *c* of Problem 1. But here is a clue: Part *c* is no alphabet series. Each of the letters in the series *stands* for something. If you can discover what they stand for (that is, discover the rule), you will be able to generate the ninth and tenth letters. (The answer is in Figure 6.7 on page 235.)

Stages in Problem Solving

You're starved but you're on a diet. You've already eaten your allotted number of calories for the day. What do you do?

For millions of people, this problem is all too familiar. According to psychologist Donald M. Johnson (1944), people tend to use three stages in solving problems, whether the problem concerns dieting, selecting a house, or moving matchsticks about to create a design. These stages include (1) preparation; (2) production; and (3) evaluation.

We prepare ourselves to solve a problem by familiarizing ourselves with its elements and clearly defining our goals. In the dieting problem, we know that we can reduce feelings of hunger by eating. Unfortunately, we shall also gain weight by eating. We then try to produce a number of alternate solutions in which we can reduce hunger without gaining weight. No, finding a magician is not the solution. Eating low-calorie preplanned snacks when we feel hungry could be a solution. An alternative is to interpret feelings of hunger as signs that we are winning the battle of the bulge! After all, we are not likely to encounter feelings of hunger when we consistently overeat. When we believe that our solutions meet our goals, we evaluate our solutions as correct.

In parts *a* and *b* of Problem 1, the search for cycles and for the rules governing the cycles served as preparation for producing possible solutions.

Incubation How did you do with problems 2 and 3? If you produced solutions that did not meet the goals, you may have become frustrated and thought, "The heck with it! I'll come back to it later." This attitude suggests a fourth stage of problem solving: **incubation.** An incubator warms chicken eggs for a while so that they will hatch. Incubation in problem solving refers to standing back from the problem for a while as some mysterious process in us seems to continue to work on it. Later, the answer may occur to us as "in a flash."

There are fascinating tales of scientists, artists, and philosophers who came away muttering from seemingly impossible problems. Later, they seemed to receive a flash of inspiration in strange settings, perhaps while walking through the woods, or while soaking in the tub. After many frustrating at-

Mental set (1) Readiness to respond to a situation in a set manner. (2) In problem solving, a tendency to respond to a new problem with an approach that was successful with problems that are similar in appearance.

Incubation In problem solving, a hypothesized process that sometimes occurs when one stands back from a frustrating problem for a while. Sometimes the solution "suddenly" is realized when the problem has been allowed "to incubate."

tempts at trying to construct a method for measuring precisely the volume of an odd-shaped object, like a crown, Archimedes, the Greek philosopher, was struck by the solution while lingering in his tub. Suddenly he realized that one could mark the line of the water in a tub, and then submerge the object, with all its nooks and crannies and points and dents. The volume of the water that rose above the line (which was displaced) would equal precisely the volume of the odd-shaped object beneath the surface.

Some psychologists suggest that the incubation effect occurs because we have been working on the elements of the problem unconsciously. Such an answer, unfortunately, is no answer. If we cannot observe the rules by which "unconscious" problem solving occurs, they remain outside the realm of scientific discussion. One possible solution to the incubation problem is that standing back from the problem provides us with some distance from unprofitable but persistent mental sets.

Consider Problem 7 about the water jar. What if we had tried all sorts of solutions involving the three water jars, and none worked? What if we were then to stand back from this water jar problem for a day or two? Is it not possible that with a little distance we might suddenly recall a 10, a 7, and a 3—three elements of the problem—and realize that we can arrive at the correct answer by using only two water jars? Our solution might seem too easy, and we might check Table 6.3 cautiously, to make certain that the numbers are there, as remembered. Perhaps our incubation period would have done nothing more than unbind us from the mental set that the case 7 *ought* to be solved by the formula $B - A - 2C$.

While we are discussing mental sets and the water jar problems, have another look at water jar case number 6. The formula $B - A - 2C$ will solve this problem. Is that how you solved it? But note also that the problem could have been solved more efficiently by using the formula $A - C$. If the second formula did not occur to you, it is probably because of the mental set you acquired from solving the first five problems.

Functional Fixedness

What is a pair of pliers? A tool for grasping, a paperweight, or a weapon? A pair of pliers could function as any of these, but your tendency to think of them as a grasping tool is fostered by your experience with them. You have probably used a pair of pliers only for grasping things. The tendency to think of an object in terms of its name or one narrow type of usage is termed **functional fixedness.** Functional fixedness can be similar to a mental set in that it can make it difficult for us to use familiar objects to solve problems in novel ways.

In a classic experiment in functional fixedness, Birch and Rabinowitz (1951) placed subjects in a room with electrical equipment, a switch and a relay, and asked them to solve the Maier two-string problem. In this problem, a person is asked to tie together two dangling strings. But, as shown in Figure 6.6, they cannot be reached simultaneously.

In the experiment, either the switch or the relay can be used as a weight for one of the strings. If the weighted string is sent swinging, the subject can grasp the unweighted string and then wait for the weighted string to come his or her way. Subjects given prior experience with the switch as an electrical device were significantly more likely to use the relay as the weight. Subjects given prior experience with the intended function of the relay were signifi-

Functional fixedness The tendency to view an object in terms of its name or familiar usage. Creative problem solving often requires conceiving novel functions for familiar objects.

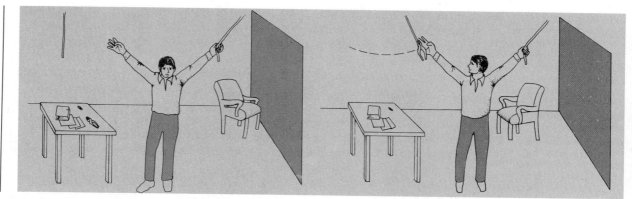

FIGURE 6.6   The Maier Two-String Problem. A person is asked to tie two dangling strings together, but he cannot reach them both at once. He is allowed to use any object in the room to help him—paper clips, tissue paper, a pair of pliers, a chair, tape. He can solve the problem by taping the pliers to one string and sending it swinging back and forth. Then he grabs the stationary string and catches the moving string when it swings his way. After removing the pliers the strings are tied together. Functional fixedness could impede solution of the problem by causing the person to view the pliers as a grasping tool only, and not as a weight.

cantly more likely to use the switch as a weight. Subjects given no prior experience with either device showed no preferences for using one or the other as the weight.

You may know that soldiers in survival training in the desert are taught to view insects and snakes as sources of food rather than as pests or threats. But it would be understandable if you chose to show civilian functional fixedness for as long as possible if you were stuck in the desert.

Creativity in Problem Solving

A creative person may be more capable of solving problems to which there are no preexisting solutions, no tried and tested formulas. When I was an undergraduate, a favorite professor remarked that there is nothing new

FIGURE 6.7   Answers to Problems on Pages 231-232. For problem 1C, note that each of the letters is the first letter of the numbers one through eight. Therefore, the two missing letters are *NT*, for *n*ine and *t*en. The solutions to problems 2 and 3 are shown in this illustration.

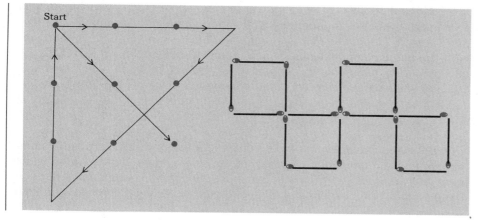

under the sun, only novel combinations of old elements. The core of **creativity** was the ability to generate many novel combinations of existing elements.

My professor's view of creativity was similar to that held by many psychologists. Mednick (1962), for example, argues that creativity is the ability to make unusual and sometimes remote associations to the elements of a problem, so that new combinations that meet the goals may be generated.

In the two-string problem, the ability to associate a switch or a relay with the quality of weight rather than their intended electronic functions requires some creativity. Tying the switch or relay to the end of the string is a new combination of the familiar elements in the problem, one that meets the requirements of the situation.

Convergent Thinking and Divergent Thinking   According to Guilford (1959; Guilford & Hoepfner, 1971), creativity demands divergent thinking rather than convergent thinking. In **convergent thinking,** thought is limited to present facts as the problem solver tries to narrow thinking to find the best solution. In **divergent thinking,** the problem solver associates more fluently and freely to the various elements of the problem. The problem solver allows "leads" to run a nearly limitless course to determine whether they will eventually combine as needed. "Brainstorming" is a popular term for divergent thinking when carried out by a group.

Successful problem solving may require both divergent and convergent thinking. At first divergent thinking generates many possible solutions. Convergent thinking is then used to select the most probable solutions and to reject the others.

Factors in Creativity   What factors contribute to creativity? Guilford (1959) has noted that creative people show flexibility, fluency (in generating words and ideas), and originality. Getzels and Jackson (1962) found that creative schoolchildren tend to express rather than inhibit their feelings, and to be playful and independent. Conger (1977) concurs that creative people tend to be independent and nonconformist. But independence and nonconformity do not necessarily make a person creative.

Nevertheless, creative children are often at odds with their teachers because of their independence. Faced with the chore of managing upwards of 30 pupils, teachers too often label quiet and submissive children as "good" children. These studies of creativity may also explain in part why there have been many more male than female artists throughout history, even though Maccoby and Jacklin (1974) found no sex differences in creativity. As Conger has noted, traits like independence and nonconformity are more likely to be discouraged in females than in males, because such traits are inconsistent with the passive and compliant social roles traditionally ascribed to females. Because of the women's movement, the numbers of women in the creative arts and sciences are growing rapidly today.

Intelligence and Creativity

Intelligence and creativity sometimes, but not always, go hand in hand. Persons low in intelligence are often also low in creativity, but high intelligence is no guarantee of creativity (Crockenburg, 1972). But it sometimes happens that people of only moderate intelligence excel in creativity, especially in fields like art and music.

Tests that measure intelligence are not useful in measuring creativity. As you will see on the following pages, intelligence test questions usually require convergent thinking to focus in on the answer. On an intelligence test, an ingenious answer that differs from the designated answer is wrong. Tests of creativity are oriented toward determining how flexible and fluent thinking can be. Here, for example, is an item from a test used by Getzels and Jackson (1962) to measure associative ability, a factor in creativity: "Write as many meanings as you can for each of the following words: (a) duck; (b) sack; (c) pitch; (d) fair." Those who write several meanings for each word, rather than only one, are rated as more potentially creative.

Intelligence

What form of life is so adaptive that it can survive in desert temperatures of 120° F, or Arctic climes of −40° F? What form of life can run, walk, climb, swim, live underwater for months on end, and fly to the moon and back? I won't keep you in suspense any longer. Human beings are that form of life. But our naked bodies do not allow us to be comfortable in these temperature extremes. It is not brute strength that allows us to live underwater or travel to the moon. We attribute our success in adapting to these different conditions, and in challenging our physical limitations, to our **intelligence.**

You have heard about intelligence since you were a young child. At an early age we gain impressions of how intelligent we are as compared to other family members and schoolmates. Expressions like "That's a smart thing to do" and "What an idiot!" are heard each day. We think of some people as "having more" intelligence than others. We associate intelligence with academic success, advancement on the job, and appropriate social behavior. Psychologists and others use intelligence as a **trait** or characteristic in an effort to explain why people do (or fail to do) things that are adaptive and inventive.

Despite our sense of familiarity with the concept of intelligence, intelligence cannot be seen, touched, or measured physically. For this reason, intelligence is subject to various definitions, and ideas and theories about intelligence are some of the most controversial issues found in psychology today.

In this section we discuss various definitions of intelligence. We see how intelligence is measured and examine the determinants of intelligence—heredity and environment.

Defining Intelligence

Psychologists generally distinguish between **achievement** and intelligence. Achievement is what a person has learned, the knowledge and skills that have been gained by experience. Achievement involves specific content areas like English, history, and math. Psychologists use achievement tests to measure what students have learned in academic areas. We would not be surprised to find that a student who has taken Spanish, but not French, would score better on a Spanish than a French achievement test. The strong relationship between achievement and experience seems obvious.

Intelligence is not so easy to define (Green, 1981). Most psychologists would agree that intelligence in some way allows people to achieve in academia. Intelligence, then, has something to do with *learning ability*. But psychologists disagree about what learning ability is and how people acquire it.

Intelligence A complex and controversial concept. (1) Defined by David Wechsler as the "capacity . . . to understand the world . . . and . . . resourcefulness to cope with its challenges." (2) Defined operationally as the trait or traits required to perform well on an intelligence test. (From the Latin *inter,* meaning "among," and *legere,* meaning "to choose." Intelligence implies the capacity to make adaptive choices.)

Trait A distinguishing quality or characteristic of personality that is presumed to account for consistency in behavior. (From the Latin *trahere,* meaning "to draw a line.) See Chapter 9.

Achievement That which is attained by one's efforts and presumed to be made possible by one's abilities. (From the Middle French *achever,* meaning "to finish.")

Historical Views of Intelligence   In 1904 British psychologist Charles Spearman suggested that the various behaviors we consider intelligent have a common, underlying factor. He labeled this factor **g,** for "general intelligence." He supported this view by noting that people who excel in one area generally show the capacity to excel in others. He noted, however, that even the most capable people seemed more capable in some areas—perhaps music or business or poetry—than in others. For this reason, he also suggested that **s,** or specific factors, accounted for individual abilities.

American psychologist Louis Thurstone (1938) analyzed data from various tests of individual abilities and concluded that Spearman had oversimplified the concept of intelligence. Thurstone's data suggested the presence of seven basic or **primary mental abilities,** instead of a single underlying trait (see Table 6.4). Thurstone suggested that a person might have high word fluency and be able to think rapidly of words that rhyme, yet not be efficient at solving mathematical problems (Thurstone & Thurstone, 1963).

This view may strike a sympathetic chord in you. Most of us know people who are "good at" math but "poor in" English, and vice versa. Nonetheless, there does seem to be some underlying link between various mental abilities. The data still show that the person with excellent reasoning ability is likely to have a larger-than-average vocabulary and better-than-average numerical ability. There are few, if any, people who excel 99 percent of the population in one mental ability, yet are excelled by 80 or 90 percent of the population in others.

David Wechsler, the developer of widely used intelligence tests for adults and children defined intelligence as a general or "global capacity" (1939, p. 3). Later he described intelligence as the "capacity of an individual to understand the world around him and his resourcefulness to cope with its challenges" (1975, p. 139). Intelligence, to Wechsler, involved both a cognitive representation of the world and effective behavior.

Behavioral Views   Many behaviorally-oriented psychologists prefer not to make assumptions about unobservable mental processes and mental abilities. They may prefer to speak about intelligence in terms of verbal skills or the number and quality of responses that are available to an individual in various situations.

An Operational Definition   Edwin Boring, an historian of psychology, once made the offhand remark that intelligence is "the capacity to do well in an intelligence test" (Rice, 1979). This wry definition is quite enough for those who try to avoid some of the controversies about intelligence altogether. They define intelligence *operationally*, in terms of the operations used to measure it. Intelligence, from this perspective, is defined as what is measured in intelligence tests.

Contemporary Conceptions of Intelligence: Laypersons and Experts   Yale University psychologist Robert J. Sternberg and his colleagues (Sternberg and others, 1981; Sternberg, 1982) asked people at a supermarket, waiting for trains, and studying in a college library to list behaviors characteristic of intelligence. The conceptions of the laypersons were then compared to those of "experts," psychologists with doctoral degrees who were engaged in research in intelligence.

TABLE 6.4   Louis Thurstone's Primary Mental Abilities

Ability	Brief Description
Spatial ability	Visualizing forms and spatial relationships
Perceptual speed	Grasping perceptual details rapidly, perceiving similarities and differences between perceived stimuli
Numerical ability	Computing numbers
Verbal meaning	Knowing the meanings of words
Memory	Recalling information (words, sentences, etc.)
Word fluency	Thinking of words quickly (rhyming, doing crossword puzzles, etc.)
Reasoning	Deriving rules from examples (as in problems *1a* to *1c* on page 231), or providing examples of rules and principles

Perhaps the major finding was that laypersons and experts share very similar conceptions of intelligent behavior. Mathematical analysis showed that three major factors underlay each group's conception of intelligence. Each group agreed that verbal ability and problem-solving ability were crucial to the definition of intelligence. Laypersons also included a factor that the researchers label social competence, however, while experts included a broader category of practical intelligence (see Table 6.5). All in all, the two groups structured their conception of intelligence in highly similar ways. Although experts may be at odds in their efforts to define intelligence, laypersons apparently understand quite well what the experts are talking about.

TABLE 6.5   Basic Factors Involved in Laypersons and Experts' Conceptions of Intelligence

Laypersons	Experts
1. Practical Problem-Solving Ability 　Reasons logically and well 　Identifies connections among ideas 　Sees all aspects of a problem 　Keeps an open mind	1. Verbal Intelligence 　Displays a good vocabulary 　Reads with high comprehension 　Displays curiosity 　Is intellectually curious
2. Verbal Ability 　Speaks clearly and articulately 　Is verbally fluent 　Converses well 　Is knowledgeable about a particular field of knowledge	2. Problem-Solving Ability 　Able to apply knowledge to problems at hand 　Makes good decisions 　Poses problems in an optimal way 　Displays common sense
3. Social Competence 　Accepts others for what they are 　Admits mistakes 　Displays interest in the world at large 　Is on time for appointments	3. Practical Intelligence 　Sizes up situations well 　Determines how to achieve goals 　Displays awareness to world around him or her 　Displays interest in the world at large

Data adapted from Sternberg and others, 1981, pp. 45–46.

Measuring Intelligence

There may be theoretical disagreements about the nature of intelligence, but thousands of intelligence tests are administered by psychologists and educators every day. The results of these tests are often used to make vital decisions about academic careers. First we discuss the *reliability* and *validity* of intelligence tests, and then we discuss a number of individual and group intelligence tests.

Reliability and Validity Intelligence is thought to be a relatively stable trait. It does not change much from day to day or week to week. A test that measures intelligence should yield consistent or stable results. The consistency of a means of measurement is known as its **reliability.** Psychologists use statistical techniques, especially the *correlation coefficient*, to study the reliability of tests.

Correlation coefficients and other statistics are explored in Appendix A. Here let us note that a **correlation coefficient** is a number that indicates how strongly two or more things, like height and weight, or taxes and government spending, are related. Correlation coefficients vary from -1.00 (a perfect negative correlation) to $+1.00$ (a perfect positive correlation). In order for an intelligence test to be considered reliable, correlations between a group's test results on two separate occasions should be positive and high (about $+.90$).

There are different ways of showing a test's reliability. **Test-retest reliability** is shown by comparing scores of tests taken on different occasions. The measurement of test-retest reliability may be confused by the fact that people often improve their scores from one occasion to the next because of increasing familiarity with the testing procedure and the test items. In **split-half reliability,** results on half the items on a test may be correlated with scores from the other half. In **alternate-form reliability,** scores on one form of a test are correlated with scores on another form of the test. Of course, it must be shown that the forms of the test are indeed comparable.

The **validity** of a test is the degree to which it measures what it is supposed to measure. A valid intelligence test should measure intelligence, not

TABLE 6.6 Interpretations of Some Correlation Coefficients

Correlation Coefficient	Interpretation
$+1.00$	A perfect positive correlation, as between temperature on the Fahrenheit scale and temperature on the centigrade scale
$+0.90$	High positive correlation, adequate for test reliability
$+0.60$ to 0.70	Moderate positive correlation, usually adequate for test validity
$+0.30$	Weak positive correlation, unacceptable for adequate test reliability or validity
$+0.00$	No correlation between variables (no association indicated)
-0.30	Weak negative correlation
-0.60 to -0.70	Moderate negative correlation
-0.90	High negative correlation
-1.00	A perfect negative correlation

height, musical ability, or interests. We determine whether an intelligence test is valid by correlating the intelligence test scores with an external measure or **criterion** of intelligence. First, we ask what more intelligent people can do that less intelligent people cannot do, and we then find out whether the intelligence test actually predicts that type of behavior, or criterion.

For example, psychologists generally assume that intelligence is one of the factors responsible for academic success. As a result, intelligence test scores have been correlated with school grades, which serve as the external measure of intelligence, or criterion, to see if the scores are valid. Intelligence tests correlate from about +0.60 to +0.70 with school grades (Lavin, 1965; McCall, 1975). This correlation does not approach a perfect positive relationship. This suggests that factors in addition to performance on intelligence tests contribute to academic success. Motivation and adjustment are two of them (Scarr, 1981). Yet most psychologists consider a correlation coefficient of +0.60 to be a reasonably adequate suggestion of validity.

By these standards, many individual and group intelligence tests have adequate reliability and validity. The Stanford-Binet Intelligence Scale (SBIS) and the Wechsler scales for adults and children are the most widely used and well-respected individual intelligence tests. The SBIS and Wechsler scales yield scores called **intelligence quotients, or IQs.** Each of them has been carefully developed and revised over the years. Each has been used by thousands of educators to help make decisions about tracking and guiding children. Each has been accused of discriminating against racial minorities like Hispanic and black children, against the foreign-born, and against socially or economically deprived children. We shall examine these and other tests and the controversy surrounding them.

Alfred Binet.

Criterion Standard. Means of making a judgment.

Intelligence quotient (1) Originally, a ratio obtained by dividing a child's score (or "mental age") on an intelligence test by his or her chronological age. (2) Generally, a score on an intelligence test.

IQ Abbreviation for *intelligence quotient.* A score on a test—*not* a trait.

Mental age The accumulated months of credit that a test-taker earns on the Stanford Binet Intelligence Scale.

The Stanford-Binet Intelligence Scale The SBIS originated through the work of Frenchmen Alfred Binet and Theodore Simon early in this century. The French public school system sought an instrument that could identify children who were unlikely to profit from the regular classroom setting so that they could receive special attention. The Binet-Simon scale came into use in 1905. Since that time, it has undergone great revision and refinement.

The Binet-Simon scale was meant for use with children and yielded a score called a **mental age,** or MA. The ability to solve intellectual problems increases with age, at least through childhood. The MA shows the intellectual level at which a child is functioning. A child with an MA of six is functioning, intellectually, like the average child aged six.

TABLE 6.7   Some Items from the First Binet-Simon Scale

Naming objects pointed to in pictures
Repeating series of numbers (digits)
Comparing the heaviness of different weights, placing a series of weights
  in order from lightest to heaviest
Repeating sentences
Explaining how objects, like a fly and butterfly, differ from each other
Drawing designs from memory
Completing sentences with words left out
Constructing sentences including three words given by the examiner
Defining abstract words (concepts)

Source: Adapted from Willerman (1977).

Binet also recognized that the best way to learn how the typical child of a certain age functioned intellectually was to administer his test to thousands of children of different ages. This method of determining standards for performance is termed the **standardization** of a test. Binet determined **empirically** how many items would be answered correctly by children of different age groups. In taking the test, children earned "months" of credit for each correct answer. Their MA was determined by adding the years and months of credit they attained.

Louis M. Terman of Stanford University adapted the Binet-Simon scale for use with American children. The first version of the *Stanford* Binet Intelligence Scale (SBIS) was published in 1916. The SBIS yielded an intelligence quotient rather than simply an MA, and American educators developed interest in learning the IQs of their pupils.

The IQ reflects the relationship between a child's mental age and actual or **chronological age,** or CA. The IQ is computed by the formula IQ = (Mental Age/Chronological Age) × 100, or

$$IQ = \frac{MA}{CA} \times 100$$

Using this formula, you can readily see that a child with an MA of 6 and a CA of 6 would have an IQ of 100. Children who can handle intellectual problems as well as older children will earn IQs above 100. For instance, an eight-year-old who does as well on the SBIS as the average 10-year-old will attain an IQ of 125. Children who do not answer as many items correctly as other children of their age will attain MAs that are lower than their CAs. Consequently, their IQ scores will be below 100.

Since adults do not make gains in problem-solving ability from year to year in the same dramatic way children do, the above formula is not used in arriving at their IQ scores. For adults, IQ scores are derived from comparing their performances with those of other adults.

TABLE 6.8   Subtests from the Wechsler Adult Intelligence Scale

Verbal Subtests	Performance Subtests
1. *Information:* "What is the capital of the United States?" "Who was Shakespeare?"	7. *Digit symbol:* Learning and drawing meaningless figures associated with numbers.
2. *Comprehension:* "Why do we have zip codes?" "What does 'A stitch in time saves nine' mean?"	8. *Picture completion:* Pointing to the missing part of a picture.
3. *Arithmetic:* "If 3 candy bars cost 25¢, how much will 18 candy bars cost?"	9. *Block design:* Copying pictures of geometric designs using multicolored blocks.
4. *Similarities:* "How are good and bad alike?"	10. *Picture arrangement:* Arranging cartoon pictures so that they tell a meaningful story.
5. *Digit span:* Repeating series of numbers forwards and backwards.	11. *Object assembly:* Putting pieces of a puzzle together so that they form a meaningful object.
6. *Vocabulary:* "What does canal mean?"	

Items for subtests 1, 2, 3, 4, and 6 are similar to test items on the Wechsler Adult Intelligence Scale.

The Wechsler Scales   David Wechsler has developed a series of scales for use with adults (Wechsler Adult Intelligence Scale), school-age children (Wechsler Intelligence Scale for Children), and younger children (Wechsler Preschool and Primary Scale of Intelligence). The Wechsler scales group test questions into a number of separate subtests (such as those shown in Table 6.8). Each subtest measures a different type of intellectual task, so that it can be readily determined how well a person does on one type of task (such as defining words) as compared with another (such as using blocks to construct geometric designs). In this way the Wechsler scales help the psychologist study a person's relative strengths and weaknesses, as well as providing a measure of overall intellectual functioning.

As you can see in Table 6.8, Wechsler described some of his scales as measuring essentially *verbal* tasks, and others as assessing *performance* tasks. In general, verbal subtests require knowledge of verbal concepts, while performance subtests require familiarity with spatial relations concepts. But the two groupings are not necessarily so easily distinguished. For example, the ability to name the object being pieced together in subtest 11, a sign of word fluency and general knowledge as well as of spatial relations ability, helps the person construct it rapidly. In any event, Wechsler's scales permit the com-

FIGURE 6.8   Items resembling those in the performance subtests of the Wechsler Adult Intelligence Scale.

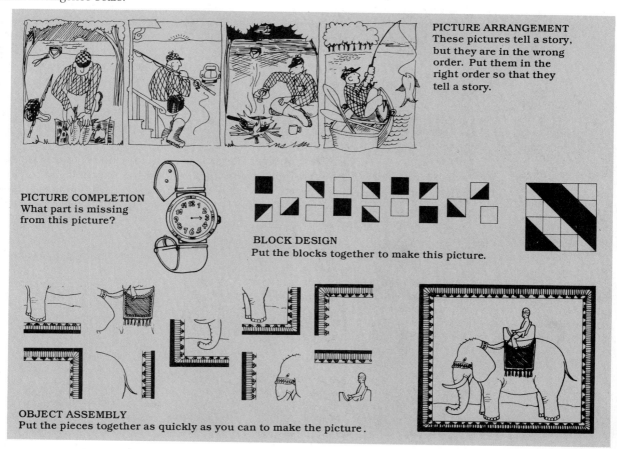

PICTURE ARRANGEMENT
These pictures tell a story, but they are in the wrong order. Put them in the right order so that they tell a story.

PICTURE COMPLETION
What part is missing from this picture?

BLOCK DESIGN
Put the blocks together to make this picture.

OBJECT ASSEMBLY
Put the pieces together as quickly as you can to make the picture.

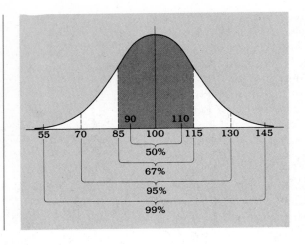

FIGURE 6.9 Approximate Distribution of IQ Scores. Wechsler defined the deviation IQ so that 50 percent of scores would fall within the broad average range of 90–110. This bell-shaped curve is referred to as a *normal curve* by psychologists. It describes the distribution of many traits, including height.

Deviation IQ A score on an intelligence test that is derived by determining how far an individual's score deviates from the norm. On the Wechsler scales, the mean IQ score is defined as 100, and approximately two of three scores fall between 85 and 115.

putation of verbal and performance IQs. It is not unusual for nontechnically-oriented college students to attain higher verbal than performance IQs.

Wechsler also introduced the concept of the **deviation IQ.** Instead of using mental and chronological ages to compute an IQ, Wechsler examined the distribution of the number of correct answers attained by subjects of different ages. He assigned IQ scores on the basis of how much a person's number of correct answers deviated from the average number of correct answers attained by people of the same age. The average test result at any age level is defined as an IQ score of 100. Wechsler then distributed IQ scores so that the middle 50 percent of them would fall within the broad average range from 90 to 110.

As you can see in Figure 6.9, most people's IQ scores cluster around the average. Only five percent of the population have IQ scores of above 130 or below 70. Table 6.9 indicates the labels that Wechsler assigned to various IQ scores, and the approximate percentages of the population who attain IQ scores at those levels.

Group Tests   The SBIS and Wechsler scales are administered to one person at a time. This one-to-one ratio is optimal. It allows the psychologist to facilitate performance (within the limits of the standardized directions) and to observe the test taker closely. In such a setup, psychologists do more than mechanically score answers and compute IQs. They can be alert to factors

TABLE 6.9   Variations in IQ Scores

Range of Scores	Percent of Population	Brief Description
130 and above	2	Very superior
120–129	7	Superior
110–119	16	Bright normal
100–109	25	High average
90–99	25	Low average
80–89	16	Dull normal
70–79	7	Borderline
Below 70	2	Intellectually deficient

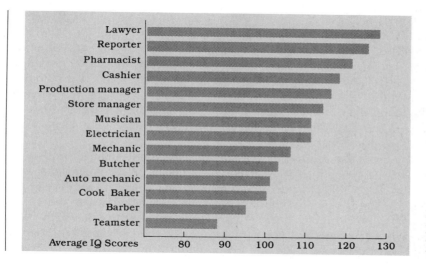

FIGURE 6.10 Average IQ scores for people in various occupations, according to the Army Alpha group intelligence test.

that impair performance, such as language difficulties, illness, or a noisy or poorly lit room. But large institutions with few psychologists, like the armed forces and the public schools, have also wished to estimate the intellectual functioning of their charges. They have asked psychologists to provide tests that can be administered to large groups of inductees and schoolchildren.

Two such tests were rapidly developed for use with the armed forces: the *Army Alpha*, for people who can read, and the *Army Beta*, for people who cannot read or have problems with English. (See Figure 6.10 for the average IQ scores of people in various occupations, according to the Army Alpha Test.)

Group tests for schoolchildren, first developed during World War I, were administered to four million children by 1921, a couple of years after the war had ended (Cronbach, 1975). At first these tests were heralded as remarkable instruments because of their easing of the huge responsibilities of school administrators. But as the years passed they came under increasing attack because many administrators relied on them completely to track children. They did not seek other sources of information about the children's abilities and achievements (Reschly, 1981).

Such use and misuse of intelligence tests has led psychologists like Leon Kamin to complain, "Since its introduction to America the intelligence test has been used more or less consciously as an instrument of oppression against the underprivileged—the poor, the foreign born, and racial minorities" (in Crawford, 1979, p. 664). Despite such criticisms, group tests are administered to as many as 10 million children a year in the United States, although some states, like California, and some cities have outlawed them (Bersoff, 1981). Let us explore further some of the controversy concerning the use of both individual and group intelligence tests.

The Testing Controversy

I was almost one of the testing casualties. At 15 I earned an IQ test score of 82, three points above the track of the special education class. Based on this score, my counselor suggested that I take up bricklaying because I was "good with my hands." My low IQ, however, did not allow me to see that as desirable.

This brief testimony, offered by black psychologist Robert L. Williams (1974, p. 32), echoes the sentiments of many psychologists. They feel that intelligence tests have been used to discriminate against blacks and others—or at least that the results of intelligence tests are given too much weight in educational decision making. It has been charged that some psychologists who freely admit that intelligence cannot be sensed or measured directly forget this admission as soon as they begin to compare test scores. At such times they make decisions as though an IQ were a person's intelligence instead of a score on a test.

Intelligence tests, critics point out, all measure performances, skills, and achievements. The vocabulary and arithmetic subtests on the Wechsler scales, for example, clearly reflect achievement in language skills and computational ability. It is generally assumed that the broad types of achievement measured by these tests reflect intelligence. Yet we cannot rule out the possibility that they also strongly reflect cultural familiarity with the concepts required to respond correctly to test questions. In particular, the tests seem to reflect middle-class white culture in the United States (Garcia, 1981).

If scoring well on intelligence tests requires a certain type of cultural experience, the tests are said to have a **cultural bias.** Children raised to speak Black English in black neighborhoods could be at a disadvantage, not because of differences in intelligence, but because of cultural differences. For this reason, psychologists like Raymond B. Cattell (1949) have tried to construct **culture-fair** intelligence tests. Some culture-fair tests do not rely on language at

It's a *BITCH*—The Black Intelligence Test of Cultural Homogeneity, That Is

Many have complained that commonly used intelligence tests are culturally biased in favor of middle-class white children. They contain concepts that are more familiar to whites than blacks. What would happen if an intelligence test were culturally biased in favor of black children? Would whites still outperform blacks?

Vocabulary is the single best predictor of overall intelligence test scores. Black psychologist Robert L. Williams (1974) developed an "intelligence test" consisting of 100 words likely to be more familiar to blacks than to whites. Why not try a few items to see how "intelligent" you are?

Instructions: Circle the letter that indicates the correct meaning of the word or phrase.

1. *the bump*
   a. a condition caused by a forceful blow
   b. a suit
   c. a car
   d. a dance
2. *running a game*
   a. writing a bad check
   b. looking at something
   c. directing a contest
   d. getting what one wants from another person or thing
3. *to get down*
   a. to dominate
   b. to travel
   c. to lower a position
   d. to have sexual intercourse
4. *cop an attitude*
   a. leave
   b. become angry
   c. sit down
   d. protect a neighborhood
5. *leg*
   a. a sexual meaning
   b. a lower limb
   c. a white
   d. food

The "correct" answers are: 1–d, 2–d, 3–d, 4–b, 5–a. How did you do? Williams gave the BITCH to 100 white and 100 black adolescents, and the blacks outperformed the whites.

Certainly the BITCH is not a valid intelligence test. It does not predict academic success. But it dramatically highlights the importance of trying to choose test items with which all test takers have had an opportunity to become familiar.

all. Instead, they evaluate reasoning ability through geometric designs, as shown in Figure 6.11.

Culture-fair tests have not lived up to their promise. First, middle-class white children still outperform blacks on them. Second, they do not appear as valid as other intelligence tests. They do not predict academic success as accurately, and academic success remains the central concern of educators.

There may really be no such thing as a culture-fair or culture-free intelligence test. Motivation to do well, for example, could be considered a cultural factor. Because of socioeconomic differences, black children in America often do not have the same motivation as whites to do well on tests. Highly motivated children attain higher scores on intelligence tests than do less well-motivated children (Zigler & Butterfield, 1968). Even basic familiarity with pencils and paper is a cultural factor. Again, white children in the United States are more likely to be familiar with these materials than are blacks.

Some of the controversy over using intelligence tests in the public schools might be diffused if they were viewed as broad achievement tests—which, of course, they are—rather than direct measures of intelligence. It would be clearly understood that they measure a child's performance in certain areas on a given day. The focus might be on using follow-up techniques, perhaps more extensive individual testing or interviews, to more fully outline a child's academic strengths and weaknesses, including factors like motivation and adjustment, and to determine the best strategies to help enhance the child's

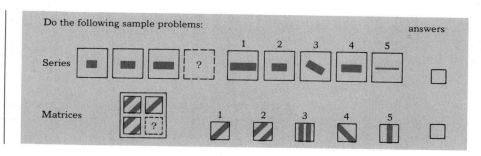

FIGURE 6.11 Sample Items from Raymond Cattell's Culture-Fair Intelligence Test.

Determinant A factor that defines or sets limits.

Zygote A fertilized egg cell. See Chapters 2 and 8.

academic performance. Then testing would promote equal opportunity instead of excluding some children from privileges (Gordon & Terrell, 1981). It is irresponsible to make major decisions about children's lives on the basis of an isolated test score attained in an impersonal group-testing situation.

The Determinants of Intelligence

In 1969 Arthur Jensen, an educational psychologist at the University of California, published an article called "How Much Can We Boost IQ and Scholastic Achievement?" in the *Harvard Educational Review*. Filled with statistics, jargon, and 123 pages long, the article gained national visibility because of Jensen's assertion that 80 percent of the variability in IQ scores is inherited. This may seem like nothing to get excited about, yet Jensen became the focus of campus demonstrations and was sometimes booed loudly in class. *Why?*

As a group, blacks score about 15 points below whites on intelligence tests, and Jensen had asserted that this difference was largely genetically determined. If so, the difference could never be decreased.

Protests from the black community were echoed by many whites, including many prominent psychologists and other scientists. "Jensen-*ism*" became equated with racism and fascism. Jensen's article suggested that there would be a permanent underprivileged class of blacks. Consider this emotional condemnation from behavior geneticist Jerry Hirsch: "It perhaps is impossible to exaggerate the importance of the Jensen disgrace.... It has permeated both science and the universities and hoodwinked large segments of government and society" (1975, p. 3).

Crawford (1979) suggested that Jensen's views met with virulent opposition from scientists and laypersons because they are incompatible with a basic American belief. American children are supposed to be able to grow up to be whatever they want to be, even President. Crawford cited a statement of this faith which he attributed to Abraham Lincoln: "If my father's son can become President, so can your father's son." (If Lincoln had made this remark today, surely he would have added "or daughter.")

What do psychologists know about the **determinants** of intelligence? What are the roles of heredity and environment?

Intelligence and Heredity In Chapter 2 we saw that rats have been bred selectively for maze-learning ability. "Maze-bright" parent rats tend to have maze-bright litters, and "maze-dull" parents tend to have maze-dull litters. But, as noted in that chapter, we must be cautious about generalizing such

findings to people. Maze-learning ability in rats is not directly comparable to human intelligence.

Psychologists generally prefer to rely on studies comparing the links between intelligence (as measured by IQ scores) and heredity in humans. It would, of course, be unethical and impractical to run experiments in which we selectively breed people on the basis of IQ scores or other factors. Still, we can examine the IQ scores of closely and distantly related people who have been raised together or apart. If heredity is involved in human intelligence, closely related people ought to have more similar IQs than distantly related or unrelated people, even when they are raised separately.

Figure 6.12 shows the results of 52 studies of IQ and heredity in human beings, as summarized by the journal *Science*. The outside lines show the range of correlations of IQ scores for pairs of people, and the center line shows the average correlation for the pairs.

Identical twins develop from one **zygote,** and their heredity is identical. Figure 6.12 shows that the IQ scores of identical twins are more alike than the scores for any other pairs, even when the twins have been reared apart. The average correlation is about +.90. Correlations between the IQ scores of

FIGURE 6.12 Summary of findings of 52 studies concerning the relationship between IQ scores and heredity. Outside lines show the range of correlations for pairs of individuals in each group, and the center line shows the average correlation within the group. A question mark follows the data concerning "identical twins reared apart" because it was recently revealed that British psychologist Cyril Burt, whose research contributed to these figures, had falsified much of his data. Generally speaking, however, more recent research remains consistent with this summary.

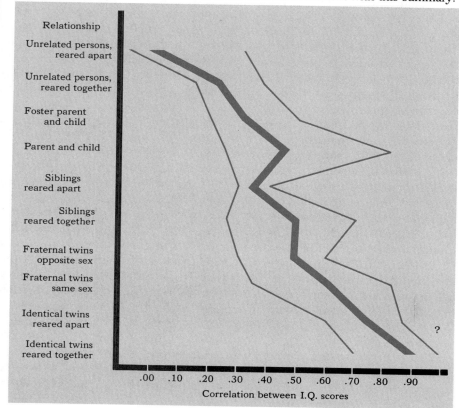

fraternal twins (twins that develop from separate zygotes), siblings, and parents and children are generally comparable, as is their degree of genetic relationship. The correlations tend to vary from the upper +.40s to the upper +.50s. Correlations between the IQ scores of children and their biological parents are higher than those between children and foster parents.

Note that there is no relationship between the IQ scores of unrelated people who are raised separately. This is as it should be since such pairs share neither heredity nor environment. But there is an average correlation in the +.30s for siblings separated at an early age and reared apart. And there is an average correlation in the +.70s for identical twins who were separated at an early age and raised apart.

These studies provide strong evidence for the role of heredity in IQ scores. Note, however, that genetic pairs (like identical twins) reared together show higher correlations between IQ scores than similar genetic pairs (like other identical twins) who were reared apart. This finding holds for identical twins, siblings, and unrelated people. *For this reason, the same group of studies strongly suggests that the environment also plays an important role in the attaining of IQ scores.*

Intelligence and the Environment   Social behavior and intellectual functioning are both adversely influenced by early deprivation. Undernourished South African children have scored some 20 IQ points lower than children with adequate diets (Stock & Smythe, 1963). Children moved from impersonal orphanages to settings where they received individual attention showed average increases in IQ scores of 28 to 29 points (Skeels, 1966).

Even studies with rats selectively bred for maze-brightness and maze-dullness have provided evidence for the importance of experience to learning ability. Cooper and Zubek (1958) provided young rats descended from maze-bright and maze-dull parents with different early environments. Some rats from each group were raised in a dull, featureless environment. Others were reared in rat amusement parks with ramps, ladders, wheels, and toys. Rats raised in the impoverished environment did poorly on maze learning tasks in adulthood, regardless of their parentage. But rats raised in the "amusement park" later learned mazes relatively rapidly. An enriched early environment caused the performances of rats with maze-dull parents to move closer to those of rats with maze-bright parents.

Studies of Head Start programs, which offer children from impoverished backgrounds educational experiences to help prepare them for entering elementary school, suggest that environmental enrichment can enhance learning ability in people. In a New York City study, adolescent boys who had participated in Head Start attained average SBIS scores of 99. Boys similar in background, but who did not have preschooling, earned an average SBIS score of 93 (Palmer, 1976). In another study, 20 black children were provided with enriched day care from the age of six weeks (Heber and others, 1972). By the age of five, their IQ scores averaged about 125, as compared with an average of 95 for children from similar backgrounds who did not receive day care.

Studies by Scarr and Weinberg (1976, 1977) also suggest the importance of environmental influences on IQ scores, even though they do not rule out a role for heredity. Black children who were adopted before the age of one by white parents who were above average in income and education showed IQ scores some 15 to 25 points higher than those attained by black children raised by their natural parents (Scarr & Weinberg, 1976). Still, the adoptees' average IQ scores, about 109, remained somewhat below those of their adoptive parents' natural children, which were about 115 (Scarr & Weinberg, 1977). Even so, the presumably enriched early environment appeared to close much of the gap between the scores of blacks and whites.

Race and Intelligence: A Concluding Note   It is challenging and somewhat dangerous to try to draw conclusions about the relationship between race and intelligence. As Charles Crawford noted, "The conflict over the issue of heredity, environment, and intelligence has become irrational and . . . the source of this irrationality is . . . the possibility of a conflict between basic American values and scientific findings" (1979, p. 664). The American values in question concern equal opportunity. As Herrnstein (1971) pointed out, differences in the heredity of intelligence could make equal opportunity an empty promise for those people who do not have the intellectual means to take advantage of it.

There seems to be ample evidence that *both* heredity and environment influence intelligence (Plomin & DeFries, 1980). Heredity provides the physiological potential for intelligent behavior. An impoverished environment may prevent some from living up to their potential, but an enriched environment encourages others to wring every last drop from their potential, minimizing any differences in heredity.

Studies in race and IQ appear to suggest, at least as the matter stands today, that we cannot ignore the possibility that some of the differences in IQ scores between the races may be related to heredity. Still, the studies of Head Start programs and adoptees strongly suggest that an enriched early environment can close the gap between any racial differences in IQ.

Perhaps we need not be concerned with "how much" of a person's IQ is due to heredity and how much is due to environment. Psychology has traditionally supported the dignity of the individual. Therefore, it might be more appropriate for us to try to identify children *of all races* whose environments seem to place them at high risk for failure to develop their potential, and then do what we can to enrich these environments.

Summary

Apes have recently been taught to use symbols to communicate, but it seems that only people have an intuitive grasp of grammar and use language spontaneously. Psycholinguists study the ways in which we perceive and acquire language.

There are several basic components of language: phonology, morphology, syntax, and semantics. Phonology is the study of the basic sounds of a language. English has more than 40 basic sounds, or phonemes. Morphemes are the smallest units of meaning in a language. They consist of one or more phonemes pronounced in a particular order. Syntax is the system of rules that determines how words are strung together into sentences. Semantics concerns the meanings of a language; it is the study of the relationship between language and objects or events.

Newborn children cry and begin to coo by about two months. Babbling, the first vocalizations that have the sound of speech, appears at about six months and contains phonemes found in many languages. At about 18 months children produce holophrases—single words that express complex meanings. Duos follow toward the end of the second year. Duos usually consist of a pivot word (like *go)* and an open class word (like

Mommy). Pivot words generally stand for phrases while open class words describe concepts that are normally expressed in a single word. Between two and three, children's vocabulary leaps from about 250 to 1,000 words. Children of two and a half may overgeneralize in their formation of plurals and the past tense by adding *s* and *ed* to irregular words. Still, preschool children show remarkable understanding of grammatical rules.

Many theories, including learning theory and psycholinguistic theory, attempt to account for language development. Classical conditioning may be involved in children's learning to associate words with objects, events, and situations. A word may be a CS for an object (US). Reinforcement increases the frequency of language-related behaviors and shows children when they have made desired verbal responses. Children also imitate the speech they observe parents and others using. But learning theory cannot account for the child's apparent intuitive grasp of syntax and grammar. Psycholinguistic theory asserts that some sort of neural prewiring (a "Language Acquisition Device") underlies these human abilities.

Thought is possible without language, but language facilitates thought. According to the linguistic relativity hypothesis, language structures (and limits) the way in which we perceive the world. Critics argue that a vocabulary may suggest the concepts deemed important by the users of a language, but do not prevent users from making distinctions for which there are no words.

Concepts are symbols that stand for groups of objects, events, or ideas that have common properties. Words are concepts, but not all concepts correspond to words. Concepts permit us to generalize without experiencing each instance of the concept. Some concepts contain, or are superordinate to, others. According to Piaget, concept development involves assimilation (inclusion of new events into existing concepts) and accommodation (changing one's way of conceptualizing events).

Concepts may be formed through presentation of positive and negative instances, or through explanation using other concepts. We may actively seek to acquire new concepts through hypothesis testing.

Problem solving involves stages of preparation, production, and evaluation. First we familiarize ourselves with the elements of the problem. Then we try to produce alternate solutions. Finally, we evaluate whether a solution has met our goals. When we cannot find a solution, distancing ourselves from the problem sometimes allows the solution to "incubate." Incubation may permit the breaking down of misleading mental sets. A mental set is the tendency to solve a new problem in ways in which similar problems were solved in the past. Functional fixedness is the tendency to perceive an object in terms of its intended function or name, and can prevent novel use of familiar objects.

Achievement is what a person has learned. Intelligence is presumed to underlie achievement, and has been defined by Wechsler as "capacity . . . to understand the world . . . and . . . resourcefulness to cope with its challenges." Spearman believed that a common factor, *g*, underlay all intelligent behavior, but that people also have specific abilities, or *s* factors. Thurstone suggested that there are seven primary mental abilities, including word fluency and numerical ability. Laypersons see intelligence as involving problem-solving ability, verbal ability, and socially appropriate behavior.

Intelligence tests must be reliable and valid, features that are expressed in terms of correlation coefficients. Reliability is the consistency of a test. Validity is the degree to which a test measures an external criterion—that which it is supposed to measure. Validity studies typically correlate intelligence with academic success. Intelligence tests yield scores called intelligence quotients, or *IQs.*

The Stanford-Binet Intelligence Scale, originated by Alfred Binet, derives IQ scores by dividing children's mental age scores by their chronological ages, then multiplying by 100. The Wechsler scales use deviation IQs, which are derived by comparing a person's performance to that of agemates. Wechsler scales contain verbal and performance subtests. Some psychologists argue that intelligence tests are culturally biased in favor of middle-class white children, and efforts have been made to develop culture-fair or culture-free tests. However, culture-fair tests are weaker predictors of academic success.

Evidence suggests that both heredity and environment are determinants of intelligence. Enrichment of the child's early environment appears to markedly close the IQ gap between children of lower socioeconomic status and middle-class children.

Truth or Fiction Revisited

- *Psychologists have been able to teach chimpanzees and gorillas how to use sign language.* This is partially true. These apes have been taught to produce signs for objects, but do not show a grasp of grammar or use language spontaneously.
- *Deaf children do not babble.* False, they do. Babbling appears to be innate.
- *Thought is not possible without language.* False. But language permits more efficient thinking. It enables us to manipulate words that stand for concepts.
- *Dogs can learn the concepts of roundness and squareness.* True. Through operant conditioning, dogs will learn to respond to round or square shapes as discriminative stimuli. However, they show no evidence of understanding that words stand for concepts.
- *The only way to solve a problem is to keep plugging away at it.* False. When a persistent but unprofitable mental set impedes our problem-solving ability, it may be helpful to stand back from the problem for a while and allow the elements of the problem to "incubate." In this way the solution sometimes comes to us "in a flash."
- *A person's "IQ" is the same thing as his or her intelligence.* False. An IQ is an intelligence quotient, that is, a score on an intelligence test. A person's intelligence is assumed to be a trait of that person.
- *There is no such thing as an unbiased intelligence test.* This is most likely true. Adequate performance reflects motivation, adjustment, and basic familiarity with objects like pencils and paper, as well as intelligence. The first three factors are more likely to be found among the culture of middle-class children than among that of children from lower socioeconomic status.
- *High intelligence runs in families.* Not necessarily—it is accurate to say that high *IQs* run in families, but IQs are scores on intelligence tests, not intelligence per se. Families share heredity but are also generally reared in similar environments. The simple finding that high (or low) IQ scores run in families does little to sort out the relative influences of heredity and environment.

OUTLINE

Motivation and Emotion

- Of 2,000 Americans polled in a recent survey, more than half were overweight.
- Overweight people are more sensitive to stomach pangs than are normal-weight people.
- Eating salty pretzels can make you thirsty.
- Stimulating male rats in a certain part of the brain causes them to engage in sexual foreplay.
- Women make natural mothers.
- You can fool a lie detector by squiggling your toes.
- Romantic love is found in every culture in the world.
- Taking a date to a horror film or for a roller coaster ride may stimulate feelings of passion.

"Some say the world will end in fire," wrote the poet Robert Frost. "Some say in ice." For many years we have been unnerved by movies that have had the world ending in fire, ice, and everything in between. *The Poseidon Adventure, Earthquake, The Towering Inferno, When Worlds Collide, The War of the Worlds, The Beast from 20,000 Fathoms, The Omen, Black Sunday.* In such films and novels we've been plagued by bees, giant ants, spiders, grasshoppers, green slime, comets, floods, hurricanes, blizzards, shipwrecks, monsters, terrorists, cosmic disasters, international disasters, occult disasters—disasters of every flavor and every size, of every conceivable and some not-so-conceivable misfortune that could befall the human species.

Most of us would rather avoid such fates, so how do we account for their huge success on the silver screen? What motivates us to flock to the audience of every film from *Jaws* to *Juggernaut?*

We do not have the final answer to this question. But here are some speculations that have been advanced by psychologists, religious leaders, politicians, film critics, and your friendly neighborhood bartender:

> Life is filled with vague anxiety and persistent pressures. Disaster films provide us with a temporary focus for our fears, anxieties, and frustrations.
>
> Audiences can purge their aggressive impulses by enjoying disasters that are happening to others.
>
> We are seeking coping strategies. We learn how to deal with our own problems by observing the heroes and the heroines.
>
> Disaster films make our own problems seem trivial.
>
> Disaster films heighten awareness of the fragility of life, rendering our own existences more precious.
>
> Most of us lead sedentary lives with uncomfortably low levels of arousal. Disaster films raise our arousal to more optimum levels so that we feel full of vim and vigor.
>
> Afterward, our dates may interpret their high levels of arousal from the movie as attraction to us.
>
> We have an instinctive drive to throw away money.
>
> We're grateful it's not happening to us.
>
> Charlton Heston is cute.
>
> They're fun.

In this chapter we shall explore the closely related issues of motivation and emotion. We begin with a few basic definitions. Then we discuss Maslow's concept of a human hierarchy of motivating needs. We explore physiological drives, stimulus motives, and social motives. Finally, we explore various theories of emotion and examine a number of emotions, including that most idealized human emotion—love.

Motives, Needs, Incentives, and Drives

The psychology of motivation is concerned with the *whys* of behavior. Why do we eat, drink, make love? Why do we strive to get ahead, to earn the approval of others? Why do we try new things? **Motivation** is a hypothesized state within an organism that propels the organism toward a goal. We can be motivated by *needs* and by *incentives*.

Needs are states of physical deprivation. For instance, when we have not eaten or drunk for a while, we tend to develop needs for food and water. We speak of the body as having needs for oxygen, fluids, calories, vitamins, minerals, and so on.

Motivation A state within an organism that propels the organism toward a goal. (From the Latin *movere*, meaning "to move.")

Need A state of deprivation.

Needs give rise to **drives,** such as the drives of hunger and thirst. Drives are the psychological **correlates** of needs. We *experience* drives of hunger and thirst when we have gone without food and water. Drives arouse us to action. Drive level usually increases with the length of time we have been deprived. We are usually more highly aroused by the hunger drive when we have not eaten for several hours than when we have not eaten for, say, one hour.

An **incentive** is an object, person, or situation perceived as capable of satisfying a need. Money, food, a sexually attractive person, social approval, and attention all can act as incentives that motivate behavior. A rat with an equal need will run down a maze more rapidly when it whiffs Limburger cheese than when it has learned to expect Purina Rat Chow. A dog will eat steak more rapidly than it will eat Purina Dog Chow. I'll show that I have nothing against the Purina folks by adding that you are probably more motivated to buy Purina Dog Chow when it is on a limited-time-only, half-price sale. That is, you may respond to the financial *incentive.*

Let us now turn our attention to psychologist Abraham Maslow's (1963) scheme for organizing and understanding human motives.

Abraham Maslow and the Hierarchy of Needs

Abraham Maslow (1908–1970) was fond of asking graduate students, "How many of you expect to achieve greatness in your careers?" He would prod them to extend themselves because he believed that people are capable of doing more than responding to physical needs and seeking belongingness and social approval. As a humanistic psychologist, Maslow believed that we were separated from lower animals by our capacity for **self-actualization,** or self-initiated striving to become whatever we believe we are capable of being. In fact, he saw self-actualization to be as essential a human need as hunger.

Maslow organized human needs into a **hierarchy** from physiological needs, like hunger and thirst, through self-actualization (see Figure 7.1). He believed that our lives would naturally travel up through this hierarchy so long as we did not encounter insurmountable social or environmental hurdles. Maslow was optimistic about human nature. He believed that people behaved antisocially only when their needs were frustrated, particularly their needs for love and acceptance.

Maslow's needs hierarchy includes:

1. *Physiological needs:* hunger, thirst, elimination, warmth, fatigue, pain avoidance, sexual release.
2. *Safety needs:* protection from the environment through housing and clothing, security from crime and financial hardship.
3. *Love and belongingness needs:* love and acceptance through intimate relationships, social groups, and friends. Maslow believed that in a generally well-fed society, like ours, much frustration stemmed from failure to meet needs at this level.
4. *Esteem needs:* achievement, competence, approval, recognition, prestige, status.
5. *Cognitive understanding:* novelty, understanding, exploration, knowledge.
6. *Aesthetic needs:* music, art, poetry, beauty, order.
7. *Self-actualization:* fulfillment of our unique potentials.

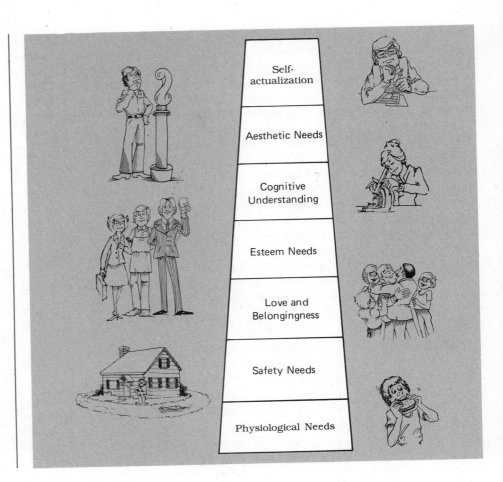

FIGURE 7.1 Maslow's Hierarchy of Needs. Maslow believed that we progress to higher psychological needs, such as understanding, aesthetics, and self-actualization, once basic survival needs are met. Where do you fit in this picture?

Maslow predicted that if we were to experience two incompatible needs, we would first direct our behavior to meet the lower need. We are less concerned about social recognition or completing a novel when we are starving or have been waiting in line for half an hour to use the bathroom. Other psychologists, like Carl Rogers, have noted that people may seek high-level fulfillment even when lower needs have not been met. Some artists and writers devote themselves fully to their art, even at the price of a struggle with poverty.

Physiological Drives

Certain bodily needs must be met if we are to survive. We need oxygen, food, drink, proper temperatures, to eliminate waste products, and so on. Such physiological needs give rise to **physiological drives**—aroused conditions within the organism that motivate behavior directed toward attaining goals that will reduce these needs. Because physiological drives are unlearned, they are also referred to as **primary drives.** Although sexual behavior leads to survival of the species rather than survival of the individual, sex is also a primary drive.

The *behavior* that people use to satisfy many of the drives is strongly influenced by learning. Eating meat or fish, drinking coffee or tea, kissing lips or rubbing noses are all learned preferences.

Physiological drives Unlearned drives with a biological basis, such as hunger, thirst, and avoidance of pain.

Primary drives Another term for *physiological drives.*

Are You a Self-Actualizer?

Where do you stand in your journey up through Maslow's hierarchy of needs? Are you still literally hungry? Are you seeking security? Are you searching for acceptance, competence, and prestige? Or are you knocking on the door of self-actualization?

Maslow (1971) identified eight characteristics of self-actualizing people. How many of them describe you?

- Experiencing life in the present, the here and now. Neither focusing excessively on past pleasures nor wishing days away while rushing toward future goals.
- Making growth choices rather than fear choices. Taking reasonable risks to develop your unique potential.
- Getting to know yourself. Looking inward, searching for your talents and values.
- Striving toward honesty in interpersonal relationships. Stripping away the game playing and social facades that block the development of intimacy.
- Becoming self-assertive, self-expressive. Maslow writes that the self-actualizer "dares to listen to himself . . . at each moment in life, and to calmly say, 'No, I don't like such and such' " (1971, p. 47).
- Striving toward new goals. Becoming the best you can be.
- Involving yourself in meaningful, rewarding activities. By doing so we may have "peak experiences"—brief moments of joy and fulfillment.
- Being open to new experiences. Being willing to change opinions or to try new paths.

Homeostasis   Certain mechanisms in the body are triggered when we are in a state of deprivation. These mechanisms then motivate us, through sensations like hunger, thirst, and cold, to act to restore the prior balance. The bodily tendency to maintain a steady state is called **homeostasis.**

Homeostasis works much like a domestic thermostat. When the room temperature drops below the set point, the heating system is triggered. The heat stays on until the set point is restored. Psychologists in this century have learned that the homeostatic systems of the body involve fascinating interactions between physiological and psychological processes.

In this section we explore the drives of hunger, thirst, sex, and pain. Then we address a controversial issue: whether there is a primary maternal drive in humans.

Hunger

Some of us may bounce up and down in weight because of cycles of overeating and dieting, but for most of us body weight remains remarkably constant over the years (Keesey, 1980). What are the body mechanisms that regulate the hunger drive? What psychological processes are at work? Why do many of us continue to eat when we have already supplied our bodies with the needed nutrients?

The Mouth   Let us begin with the mouth—an appropriate choice since we are discussing eating. The acts of chewing and swallowing provide some sensations of **satiety.** If they did not, we might eat for a long time after we had taken in enough food because it takes the digestive tract time to metabolize food and provide signals to the brain by way of the bloodstream.

In classic **sham** feeding experiments with dogs, a tube was implanted in the animals' throats so that any food swallowed fell out of the body. Even though no food arrived at the stomach, the animals stopped feeding after a brief period (Janowitz & Grossman, 1949). However, they resumed feeding sooner than animals whose food did reach the stomach. Let us proceed to the stomach, too, to search for further regulatory factors in hunger.

Homeostasis (home–me–oh–STAY–sis). The tendency of the body to maintain a steady state, such as body temperature or level of sugar in the blood. (From the Greek *homos*, meaning "same," and *stasis*, meaning "standing.")

Satiety (SAY–she–uh–tea). The state of being satisfied. Fullness.

Sham False, pretended. (A variation of the word "shame.")

Hypothalamus A bundle of nuclei beneath the thalamus in the brain that are involved in regulation of body temperature and a number of drives, including thirst, hunger, and sex. See Chapter 2.

Lesion An injury that results in impaired behavior or loss of a function.

Ventromedial nucleus A central area on the underside of the hypothalamus that appears to function as a stop-eating center. (From the Latin *venter*, meaning "belly," and *medius*, meaning "middle.")

Hyperphagic (high–purr–FAY–jick). Characterized by excessive eating. (From the Greek *hyper-*, meaning "over," and *phagein*, meaning "to eat.")

Stomach Contractions An empty stomach will lead to stomach contractions that we call hunger pangs, but these pangs are not as influential as had once been thought. People and animals whose stomachs have been removed will still regulate food intake to maintain a normal weight level.

This finding led to the discovery of many other regulatory mechanisms, including blood sugar level, the hypothalamus, even receptors in the liver.

Blood Sugar Level When we are deprived of food, the level of sugar in the blood drops. The deficit is communicated to the **hypothalamus,** a small bundle of nuclei near the middle of the brain (see Chapter 2) that are involved in regulating hunger, the sex drive, body temperature, and other functions. The drop in blood sugar apparently indicates that we have been burning energy and need to replenish it by eating.

Let us examine evidence that suggests that the brain may have centers that signal us when to start and stop eating.

Experiments with the Hypothalamus: The Search for "Start Eating" and "Stop Eating" Centers in the Brain If you were just reviving from a surgical operation, fighting your way through the fog of the anesthesia, food would probably be the last thing on your mind. But when you operate on rats and make a **lesion** in the **ventromedial nucleus** (VMN) of the hypothalamus, they will grope toward their food supplies as soon as their eyes open. Then they eat vast quantities of Purina Rat Chow or whatever else they can find.

It may be that the VMN functions like a stop-eating center in the rat's brain (Novin and others, 1976). If you electrically stimulate the VMN—or "switch it on"—a rat will stop eating until the current is turned off. When the VMN is lesioned, the rat becomes **hyperphagic.** It will continue to eat until it has mushroomed to about five times its normal weight (see Figure 7.2). Then it will level off its eating and maintain the higher weight. It is as if the set point of the stop-eating center were raised to be triggered at a much higher level (Keesey & Powley, 1975; Powley, 1977).

FIGURE 7.2 A Hyperphagic Rat. This rodent winner of the basketball look-alike contest went on a binge after it received a lesion in the ventromedial hypothalamus. Its body weight is about five times normal. But now it is eating only enough to maintain its pleasantly plump stature, so you need not be concerned that it will eventually burst. If the lesion had been made in the lateral hypothalamus, the animal might have become the "Twiggy" of the rat world.

VMN-lesioned rats are also more sensitive than normal rats to the taste of food. They will eat even greater amounts of food if sugar or fat is added, but will eat less if the food is stale or bitter (Levitt, 1981).

It may be that the **lateral hypothalamus** is a start-eating center in the rat brain. If you electrically stimulate the lateral hypothalamus, the rat will start to eat. If you make a lesion in the lateral hypothalamus, the rat may stop eating altogether—that is, become **aphagic.** But if you force-feed an aphagic rat for a while, it will begin to eat on its own, but then level off at a lower body weight. It is like turning the thermostat down from, say, 70° F to 40° F.

Receptors in the Liver Other research suggests that receptors in the liver are also important in regulating hunger (Friedman & Stricker, 1976; Schwartz, 1978). These receptors appear sensitive to the blood sugar level. In a state of food deprivation, blood sugar is low, and these receptors send rapid messages to the brain. After a meal the blood sugar level rises, and their rate of firing decreases.

While many areas of the body work in concert to regulate the hunger drive, this is only part of the story. In human beings the hunger drive is more complex. Psychological as well as physiological factors play an important role, as we shall see in our discussion of the problem of obesity.

Obesity

We need food to survive, but food means more than survival for many of us. Food is a symbol of family togetherness and caring. We associate food with the nurturance of the parent-child relationship, with visits home at Thanksgiving. Friends and relatives offer food when we enter their homes. Saying no may be interpreted as a personal rejection. Bacon and eggs, coffee with cream and sugar, meat and mashed potatoes, seem part of what it is to be American, part of sharing American values and agricultural abundance.

But an enormous number of us are paying the price of abundance: obesity. Some findings of a 1981 Lou Harris poll:

- Of 2,000 people surveyed, 36 percent admitted to being overweight.
- When they reported their heights and weights, another 22 percent exceeded recommended weights for their age group. *A total of 58 percent were overweight.*
- Of those who admitted to being overweight, 39 percent were currently dieting. Another 42 percent had dieted in the past but given it up. Only 19 percent had never tried to lose weight by dieting.
- For the admittedly overweight, "sweets" were hardest to resist. Seventy-six percent reported problems resisting candy, ice cream, cake, and cookies. Only 26 percent had trouble controlling intake of starches like bread and potatoes. Seventeen percent were tempted by soft drinks, and 11 percent said that beer and liquor contributed to weight problems.

With few exceptions, America idealizes slender heroes and heroines. For the many Americans who measure more-than-up to television and film idols, food may have replaced sex as the central source of guilt. We feel guilt when we binge, then repent and resolve to diet. Perhaps we stick to starvation diets for a while and drop a few pounds. Then we too often return to our fattening ways and are struck by guilt again.

Lateral hypothalamus An area at the side of the hypothalamus that appears to function as a start-eating center. (From the Latin *lateris*, meaning "side.")

Aphagic (uh–FAY–jick). Characterized by undereating.

Arteriosclerosis (are–TEAR–ce–oh–scler–ROW–sis). A disease characterized by thickening and hardening of the arteries.

Gout A disease characterized by swelling and severe pain, particularly in the big toe.

Fat cells Cells that store fats.

Adipose tissue Containing animal fat. (From the Latin *adipis,* meaning "fat.")

Internal eaters People who eat predominantly in response to internal stimuli, like hunger pangs.

External eaters People who eat predominantly in response to external stimuli, like the sight or smell of food or the time of day.

The obese are motivated to lose weight for more than social reasons. They encounter more than their fair share of illnesses, including heart disease; **arteriosclerosis,** diabetes, and **gout.**

Why do so many of us overeat? Is obesity a physiological problem, a psychological problem, or both? Research suggests that there are psychological features to the problem of obesity, in addition to any physiological factors.

On Fat Cells and Obese People   Obese people may be sabotaged by microscopic units of life within their bodies in their efforts to maintain a slender profile: **fat cells.** No, fat cells are not overweight cells. They are cells that store fat, otherwise called **adipose tissue..** Hunger may be related to the amount of fat stored in these cells. As time passes after a meal, the blood sugar level drops. Fat is then drawn from these cells to provide further nourishment. At some point, the hypothalamus is signaled of the fat deficiency in these cells, triggering the hunger drive.

People with more adipose tissue than other people will feel food-deprived earlier, even though they may be of equal weight. This is presumably because more signals are being sent to the brain. Obese people, and *formerly* obese people, generally have more adipose tissue than people of normal weight. It may be for this reason that many people who have dieted successfully complain that they are hungry constantly as they try to maintain normal weight levels.

Why do some of us have more fat cells than others? We inherit different numbers of fat cells, so there may be some truth to the notion that some people are born with a greater disposition toward gaining weight than others. But the number of fat cells may also be influenced by childhood and adult dietary habits (Brownell, 1982; Sjøstrøm, 1980). Obese children develop more adipose tissue. And so childhood obesity may cause the adult dieter to feel persistent hunger, even after leveling off at a new desired weight.

But while fat cells may play a role in triggering internal sensations of hunger, they cannot compel us to eat. As we shall see in the following section, obese people seem to be *less* sensitive than normal-weight people to internal sensations of hunger.

Internal and External Eaters: Out of Sight, Out of Mouth?   During the late evening news, just as I'm settling in for sleep, a Burger King "Aren't You *Hungry?*" or frozen pizza ad assaults me from the television set. Juicy meat, gooey cheese, and drippy sauce do me in. My stomach growlings are all the evidence I need that the hunger drive can be triggered by external stimuli, such as the sight of food, as well as by chemical imbalances and signals within the body.

While such commercials may stir most of our appetites, overweight people seem to be more responsive than normal-weight people to external stimulation. People who respond predominantly to their own internal stimuli are referred to as **internal eaters.** Those who must be tied to the bedpost when they see a food commercial or catch a whiff of kitchen aromas are **external eaters.** Any of us may occasionally respond to an especially appealing incentive, like a slice of chocolate cream cheese pie (sorry, you externals). But external eaters are decidedly more swayed by external stimulation, as many experiments have shown. We shall describe just a couple of classic studies.

Balloons may not sound like your favorite breakfast treat. Still, Stunkard (1959) managed to recruit obese and normal-weight subjects for a study in which they swallowed stomach balloons after an all-night fast. Such balloons, filled slightly with water, will signal stomach contractions to a monitor. Subjects reported whether they were hungry every 15 minutes. Normal-weight subjects were more likely than the obese to report hunger when their stomachs contracted. They were significantly more likely to respond to internal stimulation.

In another study, Schachter and Gross (1968) involved students in paper-and-pencil tasks in the late afternoon, when they were likely to be anticipating dinner. After 50 minutes, each student was left a box of Wheat Thins and given additional tasks. The students did not know that the researchers' only interest was the number of Wheat Thins they would eat during a second time period. The researchers had left a doctored clock with students during the 50-minute period. As a consequence, some students believed only 25 minutes had passed, while others believed that an hour and 40 minutes had gone by, which meant that dinnertime was very near. Obese students were slaves to the clock. Those who believed it was dinnertime ate twice as many Wheat Thins during the second time period as those who believed it was earlier in the afternoon. The belief manipulation had no such effect on normal-weight students. Hunger in the overweight was triggered by the mere expectation of food. Other studies have found that the overweight are also more responsive to the sight and smell of food and to the presence of other people who are eating.

Why are obese people more responsive than the normal-weight to external stimulation? Psychologist Stanley Schachter (1971) observed similarities between the eating behavior of hyperphagic rats and obese people that led him to wonder whether many of the obese are troubled by faulty neural regulation of hunger because of problems in the hypothalamus.

Faulty hypothalamus or simple overeating? Whatever the triggers of their overeating, these minibikers weigh in at 700 pounds each.

Heavy people, like hyperphagic rats, are more sensitive than the normal-weight to the taste of food (Schachter, 1971; Schachter & Rodin, 1974). They eat relatively larger quantities of sweet foods, like vanilla milkshakes, but lower quantities of bitter foods. Obese people also take larger mouthfuls, chew less, and finish their meals more rapidly than normal-weight people (LeBow and others, 1977; Marston and others, 1977).

But the faulty neural mechanism theory has not yet been directly supported as a factor in obesity in human beings. For the moment we can note only that the eating behavior of obese people resembles that of hyperphagic rats. It is also possible that early dietary habits promote the greater sensitivity to external cues found among the obese (Rodin & Slochower, 1976).

Many other factors, such as emotional states, may also play a role in obesity. For example, dieting efforts may be impeded by negative emotional states like depression (Baucom & Aiken, 1981).

But now, some good news for people who would like to lose a few pounds. Psychological research has led to a number of helpful suggestions for people who would like to lose some weight and keep it off. Following a self-help manual can be successful (Wing and others, 1982).

How To Lose Weight: An Abbreviated Manual   There is no mystery about it. Losing weight means burning more calories than you consume. You can accomplish that by eating less, exchanging some high-calorie foods (like ice cream and butter) for low-calorie foods (like vegetables and diet margarine), and by exercising more. Here are a number of suggestions:

- *Establish calorie-intake goals and heighten awareness of whether you are meeting them.* Acquire a book that shows how many calories are found in foods and keep a diary of your calorie intake.
- *Use low-calorie substitutes for high-calorie foods.* Fill your stomach with

Some external sources of stimulation that may motivate eating.

celery rather than cheese cake and burritos. Eat preplanned low-calorie snacks rather than binge on a jar of peanuts or a container of ice cream.

- *Establish eating patterns similar to those of internal eaters.* Take small bites. Chew thoroughly. Take a five-minute break between helpings. Ask yourself if you're still hungry. If not, stop eating. Don't be afraid to leave your meal unfinished—children are no longer starving in China.

- *Avoid sources of external stimulation (temptations) to which you have succumbed in the past.* Shop at the mall with the Alfalfa Sprout, not the Gushy Gloppe Shoppe. Plan your meal before entering a restaurant and avoid ogling that tempting full-color menu. Attend to your own plate, not the sumptuous dish at the next table. (Your salad probably looks greener to them, anyhow.) Shop from a list. Walk briskly through the supermarket, preferably after dinner when you're no longer hungry. Don't be sidetracked by pretty packages (fattening things may come in them). Keep out of the kitchen. Study, watch TV, write letters elsewhere. Keep fattening foods out of the house. Prepare only enough food to remain within your calorie-intake goals.

- *Exercise to burn more calories.* Reach for your mate, not your plate (to coin a phrase). Jog rather than eat an unplanned snack. Build exercise routines by a few minutes each week.

- *Reward yourself when you've met a weekly calorie-intake goal—but not with food.* Imagine how great you'll look in that new swimsuit next summer.

- *Mentally rehearse solutions to problem situations.* Consider how you will politely refuse when cake is handed out at the office party. Rehearse your next visit to parents or other relatives—the ones who tell you how painfully thin you look and who try to stuff you like a pig. Imagine how you'll politely refuse seconds, and thirds, despite all their protestations.

- *Above all, if you slip from your plan for a day, do not catastrophize.* Do not tell yourself you're a failure and then go on a binge. Consider the *weekly* trend, not just a day, and resume your strategies the following day.

You may find other useful suggestions in the section on self-control techniques in Chapter 12.

Diet Pills: Too Much of a Miracle?

Forget aspirin, penicillin, or tranquilizers. The true wonder drug, in the eyes of all too many people, is the one that promotes weight loss. For a while amphetamines seemed to provide that miracle, until doctors began warning of their severe side effects, which include increased blood pressure and heart rate, a dependency on the drugs, and bouts of depression when the pills are withdrawn. Now magical diet potions are being promoted and . . . can be had for the asking at almost any drug counter.

These . . . products contain two familiar ingredients, benzocaine and phenylpropanolamine (PPA). Benzocaine is a local anesthetic that has long been used to soothe skin irritations and itching. Added to special chewing gums or candy, it presumably dulls the taste buds and discourages eating. PPA, a drug related to the amphetamines, has enjoyed a long history as a nasal decongestant in cold remedies. In such popular diet pills as Dexatrim, Prolamine, Spantrol, and Appedrine (which also contain caffeine), manufacturers say that it depresses the brain's "appetite center" in the hypothalamus.

But do the drugs really work? Yes, say the pharmaceutical houses. . . . Yet many doctors are unconvinced. The *Medical Letter*, a highly regarded bulletin for physicians, notes that in one published study of 66 obese patients, the greatest weight loss was achieved not by anyone on PPA but by someone who had been given a placebo. Says *Letter* Consulting Editor Dr. Martin Rizack: "If someone really wants to lose weight, you can give them almost anything and probably get an effect. . . ."

Most specialists still feel that the real answer to shedding pounds is changing lifestyles. Says Cleveland Dr. Victor Vertes: "These drugs are not going to burn calories. You've got to curb your calorie intake. And for long-term weight control, they're completely useless. You can't take them for the rest of your life."

Thirst

Our bodies need fluids as well as food in order to survive. We may survive without food for several weeks, but will only last for a few days without water. It has been speculated that thirst is a stronger drive than hunger because animals who have been deprived of food and water will typically drink before eating, when given the opportunity to do both. Critics of this view note that hungry animals must take in fluids to produce saliva and other digestive fluids before eating.

Physiological mechanisms maintain a proper fluid level in the body. When there is excess fluid, we are not likely to feel thirsty and our bodies form urine. When there is a fluid deficiency, we are likely to experience a thirst drive and our bodies are less likely to form urine.

Since we may experience thirst as dryness in the mouth and throat, it was once thought that receptors in the mouth and throat played a major role in determining thirst or satiety. But it seems that receptors in the kidney and hypothalamus play more central roles in regulating the thirst drive.

Regulation of Thirst in the Kidneys When the body is depleted of fluids, the flow of blood through the kidneys drops off. In response to this decreased flow of blood, the kidneys secrete the hormone **angiotensin.** Angiotensin, in turn, signals the hypothalamus of fluid depletion.

The Role of the Hypothalamus: On Shrivelled Cells and Salty Pretzels Osmoreceptors in the hypothalamus can also detect fluid depletion from changes that occur within the brain. The brain, like the rest of the body, becomes fluid-depleted. Fluid depletion causes the osmoreceptor cells to shrivel, which in and of itself may trigger thirst.

Another osmoreceptor signal involves the concentration of chemicals in bodily fluids. As the volume of water in the body decreases, the concentration of chemicals in the water, such as sodium (which combines with chlorine to make salt) increases. (Think of a pool of salt water evaporating in the sun. The salt does *not* evaporate, only the water, and the remaining water becomes increasingly salty. If all the water evaporated, there would be nothing left but a crust of salt.) An increasing concentration of salt can also signal the osmoreceptors that the body's water supply is falling.

In a classic experiment, an injection of a salt solution into a goat's hypothalamus triggered heavy intake of fluids, even though the goat had just drunk its fill (Andersson, 1971). (Injection of salt-free water caused the animal *not* to drink, apparently by "fooling" the osmoreceptors into behaving as though there were a higher level of fluids throughout the body.) Did you ever wonder why bartenders are usually happy to provide customers with "free" salty peanuts and salty pretzels? As the salt is dissolved into bodily fluids, the customer becomes thirsty again, even though he or she may also be making frequent trips to the bathroom in order to urinate.

The hypothalamus responds to signs of dehydration transmitted by osmoreceptors in at least two ways: (1) It signals the pituitary gland to secrete **antidiuretic hormone (ADH).** ADH causes the kidneys to slow urine formation—a water-conservation measure. (2) The hypothalamus signals the cerebral cortex. As a result, we experience the thirst drive.

Our responses to thirst are varied and largely learned. Some of us go to the tap for water. Others brew coffee or tea. Still others prefer juice or a soft

Angiotensin (an–gee–oh–TEN–sin). A hormone that signals the hypothalamus of bodily depletion of fluids. This hormone is secreted by the kidneys in response to decreased flow of blood.

Osmoreceptors Receptors in the hypothalamus that are sensitive to depletion of fluids. (From the Greek *othein*, meaning "to push"—referring to the pressure exerted by fluids.)

Antidiuretic hormone A pituitary hormone that inhibits production of urine. Abbreviated *ADH.*

drink. The time of day, social custom, and individual preferences all play a role in deciding which fluids will be drunk.

External cues may also stimulate us to drink, as they can stimulate us to eat—even in the absence of internal cues for thirst. Watching someone squeeze an orange or hearing a cork pop can make us desire orange juice or champagne. We may also drink alcohol to earn the approval of drinking buddies or for whatever incentives the sensations of intoxication may provide.

Receptors in the Mouth and Throat   Receptors in the mouth and throat do play some role in thirst, after all. Once we have begun drinking, they monitor the amount of fluid we have taken in. At some point they signal the hypothalamus, "Stop, enough." But if we have not reversed the internal processes that signal dehydration, we shall soon feel thirsty again (Adolph, 1941).

Drinking, like eating, has complex origins. It can be motivated by a combination of internal and external cues.

Sexual Motivation

We may describe people as "hungering" or "thirsting" for sex, but the sex drive differs from hunger and thirst in that sex may be necessary for the survival of the species, but not for the survival of the individual (despite occasional claims to the effect, "I'll simply *die* unless you . . .").

But there are also important similarities between the hunger, thirst, and sex drives. All three can be triggered by external cues as well as internal processes. The sex drive, for example, can be triggered by the sight (or memory) of a loved one, a whiff of perfume, attractive strangers, provocative photographs or films, or a wink.

In Chapter 3 we noted that chemicals detected through the sense of smell—pheromones—play a major role in sexual behavior among lower animals, and appear to play a motivational role in the sexual behavior of some human beings. In the following section, we focus on the organizing and activating influences of sex hormones.

Sex Hormones: Organizing and Activating Influences   In Chapter 2 we saw that sex hormones promote sexual differentiation and regulate the menstrual cycle. They also have **organizing effects** and **activating effects** on sexual behavior. They may predispose people and lower animals toward masculine or feminine mating patterns (an organizing effect). And they influence the sex drive and facilitate sexual response (activating effects).

Male rats who have been castrated at birth—and thus deprived of testosterone—make no effort to mate as adults. But when they receive *female* sex hormones in adulthood, they become receptive to the sexual advances of other *males* and assume typical female mating stances (Harris & Levine, 1965). Male rats who are castrated in adulthood also show no sexual behavior. But if they receive injections of testosterone, they resume **stereotypical** male sexual behaviors.

Female mice, rats, cats, and dogs are receptive to males only during **estrus,** when female sex hormones are plentiful. The sexual organs of female rodents exposed to large doses of testosterone **in utero** (because they share the uterus with many brothers, or because of injections) become somewhat masculinized in appearance, and these females are predisposed toward masculine mating behaviors. If they are given testosterone as adults, they attempt

Organizing effects The possible *directional* effects (that is, heterosexual or homosexual) of sex hormones.

Activating effects The arousal-producing effects of sex hormones.

Stereotypical Fixed, conventional.

Estrus The periodic sexual excitement of many female mammals, during which they are receptive to sexual advances by males. (From the Greek *oistros,* meaning "frenzy.")

In utero (YOU–terr–oh). Latin phrase meaning "in the uterus."

Mount To assume a stereotypical mating stance (applies to male members of many species).

Antiandrogen Acting in opposition to male sex hormones (androgens).

Menopause The end of menstruation. (From the Greek *men*, meaning "month," and *pauein*, meaning "to cause to stop"—referring to the end of monthly discharges from the uterus.)

Instinctive Inborn. Responding to a situation in an unlearned, stereotypical manner.

Negative reinforcer A reinforcer that increases the freqency of a behavior when *removed*. An aversive stimulus, like pain or fear. See Chapter 5.

to **mount** other females about as often as males do (Goy & Goldfoot, 1975). The earlier doses of testosterone may have permanently organized the brain in the masculine direction, predisposing them toward masculine sexual behaviors in adulthood, when "activated" by additional testosterone.

Testosterone is also important in the behavior of human males. Men who are castrated or given **antiandrogen** drugs usually show gradual loss of sexual desire and of the capacities for erection and orgasm. Still, many castrated men remain sexually active for years, suggesting that for many people fantasies, memories, and other cognitive stimuli are as important as hormones in sexual motivation. Beyond minimal levels, there is no clear link between testosterone level and sexual arousal. For example, sleeping men are *not* more likely to have erections during surges in the testosterone level (Schiavi and others, 1977).

Unlike females of most other species, women are sexually responsive during all phases of the menstrual cycle, even during menstruation itself, when hormone levels are low, and even after **menopause.** But androgens may influence female as well as male sexual response. Women whose adrenal glands and ovaries have been removed (so that they no longer produce androgens) may gradually lose sexual interest and the capacity for sexual response. But an active and enjoyable sexual history seems to ward off this outcome, suggestive of the importance of cognitive and experiential factors in human sexual motivation.

Pain

Pain is a signal that something is wrong. It motivates escape or avoidance behavior—any activity, **instinctive** or learned, that will lead to reduction of the pain. Such activities may include rubbing a stubbed toe, removing a splinter, fighting back, or taking two aspirin tablets. Pain can act as a **negative reinforcer** (see Chapter 5). That is, removal of pain reinforces the behavior that preceded it.

There is evidence that experience and attitudes influence perception of pain. Melzack and Scott (1957) reared puppies in isolation from other dogs and most sources of sensory stimulation. A control group was exposed to the scrapes, nips, and barks that puppies encounter from others of their kind. After several months, the control animals showed normal howls and withdrawal in response to painful stimulation. But the puppies raised in isolation responded less strongly to pain and were less likely to withdraw from it.

Among people, attitudes that pain is unbearable make unavoidable pain, such as that from a toothache or broken bone, more difficult to cope with. In Chapter 10 we shall note recently devised psychological methods for coping with the catastrophizing thoughts, muscle tension, and feelings of helplessness that often attend painful experiences.

The "Maternal Drive"—Do Women Make Natural Mothers?

We often hear that men are naturally clumsy at child-rearing tasks like making faces, saying "Goo," feeding infants, and changing diapers. Women, however, supposedly make "natural" mothers. Consider the expression "A mother *knows.*" Somehow a mother *knows* how to raise children properly. *Do* mothers "know"? If so, *how* do they know? Does maternal behavior reflect a primary drive in human beings, or is it learned?

The Maternal Drive in Lower Animals   In many lower animals, parental behavior is **innate** and governed by hormones. For example, the *male* members of some species of fish will guard their young in their mouths at time of danger when they are influenced by certain hormones. But when the levels of these hormones drop off, their own young will become just another meal if they have not yet swum off on their own.

Maternal behavior in rats also appears largely under the control of hormones: estrogen, progesterone, and **prolactin.** Hormones are carried in the bloodstream. When the blood from a new mother rat is transfused into another female rat, the second female will also show maternal behaviors (Terkel & Rosenblatt, 1972). But at least one situational factor also triggers mechanical maternal behaviors in rats. Female rats will show maternal behaviors in response to being presented a litter of rat pups. *And so will males.* Male rats presented with a litter will maintain a nest and hover above the pups in a typical nursing stance.

Maternal Behavior among Primates   With monkeys, learning plays a more prominent role. At the University of Wisconsin Primate Center, Harry F. Harlow and his colleagues (Harlow & Harlow, 1966; Ruppenthal and others, 1976) reared female monkeys in isolation. At maturity they did not show normal sexual or social interests or behaviors. If they bore children, they frequently showed lack of interest and impatience. This pattern of neglect and abuse was termed the "motherless-mother syndrome." This syndrome suggests that mothering is learned among primates, and that important related learnings occur at early ages.

Gorillas are yet more advanced primates. Female gorillas raised in captivity often do not have the opportunity to observe adult gorillas functioning in natural social groups. They must often learn how to raise offspring by observing human models going through the motions if they are to be successful mothers.

Maternal Behavior among Humans   Human beings are also primates, the most advanced primates. (We write the textbooks.) With people, as other primates, sexual and mothering behaviors must also be learned.

If maternal behaviors are learned, why does parenthood often seem to come naturally to women but not to men? Others direct our growth in particular directions by providing early socialization messages and experiences. Girls are usually given dolls and guided into play that prepares them for the caretaking roles their parents expect them to assume in adulthood. Given this background, it is not surprising that so many women seem to take "naturally" to motherhood. (Even so, of the at least one million cases of child abuse reported to authorities in the United States each year, a sizeable number of them reflect maternal abuse rather than paternal abuse.) If the Pittsburgh Steelers had all been urged to change **siblings'** diapers and baby sit during adolescence, they, too, might fit the mothering role "naturally."

Stimulus Motives

Physical needs give rise to the drives of hunger and thirst. In these cases, and in the case of pain, we are motivated to *reduce* stimulation that impinges upon us. The sex drive is a bit different. We are usually motivated temporarily

Innate Inborn.

Prolactin A hormone involved in the secretion of milk in mammals, and, among lower mammals, in the regulation of maternal behavior.

Siblings Brothers and sisters.

Stimulus motives Motives to increase the stimulation impinging on an organism.

Sensory deprivation (1) In general, insufficient sensory stimulation. (2) A research method for systematically decreasing the stimuli that impinge upon sensory receptors.

to increase the amount of sexual tension we experience (for instance, by prolonged fantasies or by making love). By so doing, sexual release through orgasm is frequently more pleasurable. Then, after orgasm, sexual tension is reduced.

In the so-called **stimulus motives,** our goals are to *increase* the amount of stimulation impinging upon us. These motives include sensory stimulation, activity, exploration, and manipulation of the environment.

Stimulus motives are also generally considered innate. We shall see that people may be motivated to seek the level of stimulation that produces an *optimal level of arousal*—that is, a general level of activity or motivation at which we feel our best and behave most effectively.

Some stimulus motives provide a clear evolutionary advantage. People and lower animals who are motivated to learn about and manipulate the environment are more likely to survive until sexual maturity. They are more likely to pass on whatever genetic codes may underlie these motives to subsequent generations.

Sensory Stimulation and Activity

During the 1950s some lucky students at McGill University were paid $20 a day (which, with inflation, would be nearly $100 today) for doing absolutely nothing. How would you like such "work"? Don't answer too quickly. According to the results of such experiments in **sensory deprivation,** which were run by Bexton, Heron, and Scott (1954), you might not like it much at all. In fact, you might find it intolerable.

FIGURE 7.3   A Participant in a Sensory Deprivation Experiment. He sees, hears, and touches "no evil"—or anything else, for that matter. Experimental conditions like these do not produce a restful vacation. Volunteers quickly become bored and irritable, and many quit after only a few hours despite financial incentives to continue. Apparently we have strong motives for sensory stimulation.

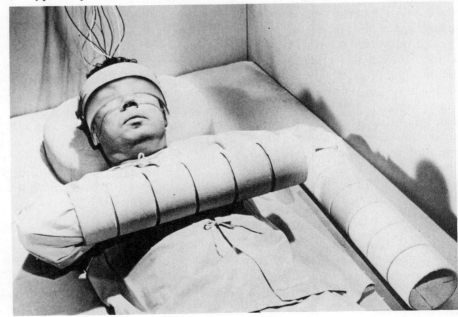

Student volunteers were placed in isolation booths. In these quiet cubicles, they were blindfolded, their arms were bandaged, and they could hear nothing but the dull continuous hum of the air conditioning (Figure 7.3). With nothing to do, many students fell asleep for a while. After a few hours of sensory-deprived wakefulness, most students felt bored and irritable. As time went on, they became increasingly uncomfortable. A number of them reported visual hallucinations which were usually restricted to simple images of dots and geometric shapes (Zubek, 1973).

Many subjects quit during the first day despite the financial incentive and the desire to contribute to scientific knowledge. Those who remained found it temporarily difficult to concentrate on even the simplest problems after several days of sensory deprivation. All in all, the experimental conditions did not provide a relaxing vacation. Instead, they proved to be a nightmare of boredom and disorientation.

Some people seek higher levels of stimulation and activity than others. John may be content to sit by the TV set all evening, while Marsha doesn't feel right unless she's out on the tennis court or jogging. Cliff isn't content unless he has ridden his motorcycle over back trails at breakneck speeds, and Janet feels exuberance in the chest when she's catching the big wave or diving freefall from an airplane. One's preference for tennis, motorcycling, or skydiving will reflect one's geographical location, social class, and learning experiences. But it may just be that the levels of arousal at which we are comfortable would be too high or low for other people. It may also be that these levels are determined to some degree by innate factors.

Exploration and Manipulation

Have you ever brought a dog or cat into a new home? At first they may show general excitement. New kittens are even known to hide under a couch or bed for a few hours. But then they will begin to explore every corner of the new environment. When placed in novel environments, many animals appear to possess an innate motive to engage in exploratory behavior.

Once familiar with the environment, lower animals and people appear motivated to seek **novel stimulation.** For example, when they have not been deprived of food for a great deal of time, rats will often explore unfamiliar arms of mazes rather than head straight for the section of the maze in which they have learned to expect food. Animals who have just **copulated** and thereby reduced their sex drives will often show renewed interest in sexual behavior when presented with a novel sex partner. And monkeys will learn how to manipulate gadgets for the incentive of being able to observe novel stimulation through a window (see Figure 7.4).

The question has arisen as to whether people and animals seek to explore and manipulate the environment *because* these activities may help them reduce primary drives, like hunger and thirst, or whether they will engage in these activities for their own sake. Many psychologists do believe that such stimulating activities are reinforcing in and of themselves. Monkeys do seem to get a kick from "monkeying around" with gadgets (see Figure 7.5). They will learn how to manipulate hooks and eyes and other mechanical devices without any external incentives whatsoever (Harlow and others, 1950). Children will engage in prolonged play with "busy boxes"—boxes filled with objects that honk, squeak, rattle, and buzz—even though manipulation does not result in food, ice cream, or even hugs from parents.

Novel stimulation (1) New or different stimulation. (2) A hypothesized primary drive to experience new or different stimulation.

Copulate (COP–you–late). To have sexual intercourse. (From the Latin root for "couple.")

FIGURE 7.4 People and lower animals are motivated to explore the environment and seek novel stimulation. This monkey has learned to unlock a door for the privilege of viewing a model train.

FIGURE 7.5 These young rhesus monkeys appear to monkey around with gadgets just for the pleasure of monkeying around. No external incentives or reinforcers are needed. Human children similarly enjoy manipulating gadgets that honk, squeak, rattle, and buzz.

QUESTIONNAIRE

Are You a Sensation Seeker?

Are you content reading or watching TV all day, or must you catch the big wave or bounce the bike across the dunes of the Mohave Desert? For a number of years, University of Delaware psychologist Marvin Zuckerman (1980) has been working with sensation-seeking scales that measure the level of stimulation or arousal a person will seek, and predict how well the person will fare in sensory-deprivation studies.

Zuckerman and his colleagues (1978) find four factors involved in sensation seeking: (1) seeking of thrill and adventure; (2) disinhibition (that is, the tendency to act out on impulses); (3) seeking of experience; and (4) susceptibility to boredom. Other studies show that high sensation seekers are less tolerant of sensory deprivation. They are also more likely to become involved in drugs and sexual experiences, to show public drunkenness, and to volunteer for high-risk activities and unusual experiments (Kohn and others, 1979; Malatesta and others, 1981; Zuckerman, 1974).

To gain insight into your own sensation-seeking tendencies, try this shortened version of one of Marvin Zuckerman's sensation-seeking scales. For each of the 13 items, circle the choice, A or B, that best describes your behavior, tastes, or ideas. Then compare your responses to those in the answer key in Appendix B.

1. A. I would like a job that requires a lot of traveling.
   B. I would prefer a job in one location.
2. A. I am invigorated by a brisk, cold day.
   B. I can't wait to get indoors on a cold day.

The Search for Optimal Arousal

Some drives, like hunger and thirst, are associated with higher levels of **arousal** within an organism. When we eat or drink to reduce these drives, we are also lowering the associated level of arousal. At other times we act to increase our levels of arousal, as in going to a horror film, engaging in athletic activity, or seeking a new sex partner.

How can we explain the apparently contradictory observations that people and lower animals sometimes act to reduce arousal and at other times act to increase arousal? Some psychologists attempt to reconcile these differences by suggesting that we seek levels of arousal that are optimal for us at certain times of the day.

Our levels of arousal can vary from quite low (see Figure 7.6), as in when we are sleeping, to quite high, as when we are frightened or intensely angered. Psychologists also hypothesize that we each have optimal levels of arousal at which we are likely to feel best and function most effectively in various situations. People whose optimal levels of arousal are relatively low may prefer sedentary lives. People whose optimal levels of arousal are high may seek activities like skydiving and motorcycling, intense problem solving (as of a difficult crossword puzzle), or vivid daydreaming. Psychologists Donald Fiske and Salvatore Maddi argue that people behave in ways that increase the impact of stimulation upon them when their levels of arousal are too low, and act to decrease the impact of stimulation when their levels are too high (Maddi, 1980). The types of activity they will engage in also depend on factors like needs for meaningfulness and for variety.

Arousal (1) A general level of activity or preparedness for activity in an organism. (2) A general level of motivation in an organism. (From the Middle English *rousen*, meaning "to cause to rise"—referring to the causing of game to rise from cover during a hunt.)

---

3. A. I get bored seeing the same old faces.
   B. I like the comfortable familiarity of everyday friends.
4. A. I would prefer living in an ideal society in which everyone is safe, secure, and happy.
   B. I would have preferred living in the unsettled days of our history.
5. A. I sometimes like to do things that are a little frightening.
   B. A sensible person avoids activities that are dangerous.
6. A. I would not like to be hypnotized.
   B. I would like to have the experience of being hypnotized.
7. A. The most important goal in life is to live it to the fullest and experience as much as possible.
   B. The most important goal in life is to find peace and happiness.
8. A. I would like to try parachute-jumping.
   B. I would never want to try jumping out of a plane, with or without a parachute.
9. A. I enter cold water gradually, giving myself time to get used to it.
   B. I like to dive or jump right into the ocean or a cold pool.
10. A. When I go on a vacation, I prefer the comfort of a good room and bed.
    B. When I go on a vacation, I prefer the change of camping out.
11. A. I prefer people who are emotionally expressive even if they are a bit unstable.
    B. I prefer people who are calm and even-tempered.
12. A. A good painting should shock or jolt the senses.
    B. A good painting should give one a feeling of peace and security.
13. A. People who ride motorcycles must have some kind of unconscious need to hurt themselves.
    B. I would like to drive or ride a motorcycle.

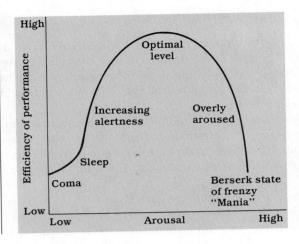

FIGURE 7.6 Our optimal levels of arousal lie somewhere in between sleep and a state of panic. People whose optimal levels of arousal are high will seek more stimulation than people whose optimal levels are low.

The Yerkes-Dodson Law A former National Football League linebacker was reported to work himself into such a frenzy before a game that other players gave him a wide berth in the locker room. Linebacking is a relatively simple football job, requiring brute strength and something called "desire" more so than does, say, quarterbacking. This particular linebacker was no stronger than many others, but his level of motivation—or desire—helped his team reach the Superbowl on many occasions.

According to the Yerkes-Dodson law (see Figure 7.7), a high level of motivation increases performance on a relatively simple task, whether the task is linebacking or solving a series of simple math problems. A high level of motivation may help explain how 118-lbs Martha Weiss lifted the front end of a 4,500-lbs Cadillac to rescue a trapped eight-year-old, according to a December 6, 1979 Associated Press story.

When a task is complex it seems helpful to keep one's level of motivation at lower levels. True, there are some complexities to the linebacker's job. Through experience, the linebacker must acquire the capacity to predict or "read" the play. But the quarterback's job is more complicated. He must call the plays, sometimes change them at the line of scrimmage because of an unexpected defensive realignment, and "keep a cool head" as his receivers

FIGURE 7.7 The Yerkes-Dodson Law. An easy or simple task may be facilitated by a high level of arousal or motivation. A highly aroused 118-pound woman lifted the front end of a 4,500-pound Cadillac to rescue a child. But a complex task, like quarterbacking a football team or attempting to solve a math problem, requires attending to many variables at once. For this reason, a complex task is usually carried out more efficiently at a lower level of arousal.

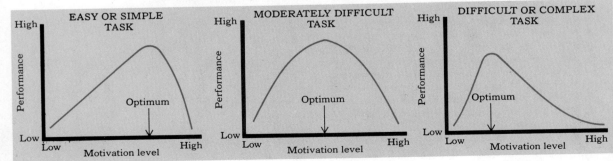

try to break into the open and defenders try to break through the offensive line and tackle him.

"Cool" linebackers and "hotheaded" quarterbacks don't do well in the professional ranks. Instead, linebackers must "psych themselves up" and quarterbacks must "maintain their cool." Some linebackers convince themselves that the opposing team represents evil in the universe, while some quarterbacks approach their job with computer-like level-headedness.

Social Motives

Social motives Learned or acquired motives.

The dollar may no longer be as strong an incentive as it used to be for America's young adults. In a recent survey of 23,000 *Psychology Today* readers, money and job security were rated less important than "intangibles" in career decisions (Renwick & Lawler, 1978). Opportunities to do things that make workers feel good about themselves, to accomplish something, to learn, to develop skills and abilities—all were rated more important than money.

Money, job security, and achievement provide **social motives**. These are secondary, rather than primary, motives—motives that are acquired through social learning. Like physiological drives and stimulus motives, social motives prompt goal-directed behavior. Psychologist Henry Murray (1938) constructed a list of 20 human motives that consist largely of social motives (see Table 7.1). We are each moved by a number of social motives, although the priorities we give these motives will vary, as will the goals we seek to satisfy the motives.

TABLE 7.1   List of Motives Compiled by Henry Murray

Motive	Definition
Abasement:	To surrender. To comply and accept punishment. To apologize, confess, atone. Self-depreciation. Masochism.
Achievement:	To overcome obstacles, to exercise power, to strive to do something difficult as well and as quickly as possible.
Affiliation:	To form friendships and associations. To greet, join, and live with others. To co-operate and converse sociably with others. To love. To join groups.
Aggression:	To assault or injure another. To murder. To belittle, harm, blame, accuse or maliciously ridicule a person. To punish severely. Sadism.
Autonomy:	To resist influence or coercion. To defy an authority or seek freedom in a new place. To strive for independence.
Avoidance:	To avoid blame, ostracism or punishment by inhibiting asocial or unconventional impulses. To be well-behaved and obey the law.
Counteraction:	Proudly to refuse admission of defeat by restriving and retaliating. To select the hardest tasks. To defend one's honour in action.
Defendance:	To defend oneself against blame or belittlement. To justify one's actions. To offer extenuations, explanations and excuses. To resist 'probing.'
Deference:	To admire and willingly follow a superior allied Other. To co-operate with a leader. To serve gladly.
Dominance:	To influence or control others. To persuade, prohibit, dictate. To lead and direct. To restrain. To organize the behavior of a group.
Exhibition:	To attract attention to one's person. To excite, amuse, stir, shock, thrill others. Self-dramatization.
Harmavoidance:	To avoid pain, physical injury, illness, and death. To escape from a dangerous situation. To take precautionary measures.
Infavoidance:	To avoid failure, shame, humiliation, ridicule. To refrain from attempting to do something that is beyond one's powers. To conceal a disfigurement.
Nurturance:	To nourish, aid or protect a helpless other. To express sympathy. To 'mother' a child.
Order:	To arrange, organize, put away objects. To be tidy and clean. To be scrupulously precise.
Play:	To relax, amuse oneself, seek diversion and entertainment. To 'have fun,' to play games. To laugh, joke and be merry. To avoid serious tension.
Rejection:	To snub, ignore or exclude another. To remain aloof and indifferent. To be discriminating.
Sentience:	To seek and enjoy sensuous impressions.
Sex:	To form and further an erotic relationship. To have sexual intercourse.
Succorance:	To seek aid, protection or sympathy. To cry for help. To plead for mercy. To adhere to an affectionate nurturant parent. To be dependent.
Understanding:	To analyse experience, to abstract, to discriminate among concepts, to define relations, to synthesize ideas.

FIGURE 7.8 Tapping Fantasies in Personality Research. This is one card of the Thematic Apperception Test which is commonly used to assess the need for achievement. What is happening in this picture? What is the person thinking and feeling? What is going to happen? Your answers to these questions reflect your own needs as well as the content of the card.

The Need for Achievement

We all know people who strive constantly to get ahead, to "make it," to earn vast sums of money, to invent, to accomplish the impossible. These people have a high need for achievement, abbreviated **n ach.**

TAT Assessment of *N Ach* Psychologist David McClelland (1958) discovered that we can assess *n ach* through people's fantasies as well as their activities. One method involves use of the **Thematic Apperception Test** (TAT), originated by Henry Murray. The TAT contains cards with pictures and drawings that are subject to various interpretations. Subjects are shown one or more TAT cards and asked to construct stories about the pictured theme, what led up to it, what the characters are thinking and feeling, and what is likely to happen.

One TAT card shows a boy with a violin (see Figure 7.8). He may be staring into space, or his eyes may be almost closed. Consider two stories that could be told about this card:

Story 1: "He's upset that he's got to practice because his instructor is coming by and he hasn't yet learned his lesson for the week. But he'd rather be out playing with the other kids, and he'll probably sneak out to do just that."

Story 2: "He's thinking, 'Someday I'll be the world's greatest violinist. I'll be playing at Lincoln Center and the crowd'll be cheering.' He practices several hours every day."

You need not be a psychologist to see that the second story suggests more achievement motivation in the storyteller than does the first.

N ach The need for achievement. The need to master, to accomplish difficult things.

Thematic Apperception Test A test devised by Henry Murray to measure needs through fantasy production. Abbreviated *TAT.* See Chapter 9.

The Slump of the Secure Player

A team of psychologists has mustered statistical evidence to show that long-term contracts take some hustle out of professional baseball players.

Multiyear contracts became commonplace in 1977, two years after a federal arbitration panel ruled that players were no longer bound indefinitely to the teams that originally signed them, a decision that made it advantageous for owners to tie up their stars. Richard O'Brien and other psychologists at Hofstra University studied how the ruling affected players' performance. The researchers examined the records of 38 pitchers during the three years before and after they signed contracts for three

or more years, comparing their play with that of 38 randomly chosen pitchers who signed only single-season contracts for the same period.

As long as they had to get their contracts renewed each year, the players who eventually won long-term berths improved steadily, from an average of 3.66 earned runs scored against them per game in 1974 to 2.91 in 1976. After signing their long-term agreements, however, their earned run averages (ERAs) climbed to an average of 4.04 three years later. The pitchers with one-year contracts showed no consistent pattern during the six years.

The researchers recommend that owners combine a base salary with incentive payments for achieving

goals such as a specified ERA or batting average. Negotiated performance targets, they say, "would allow equitable rewards for productive seasons for all players."

Just before the findings were published, the Baltimore Orioles' ace pitcher, Jim Palmer, provided independent support for that consclusion in a *New York Times* interview. Having a long-term contract himself, Palmer noted that "up until 1975, my next year's salary always depended on every pitch I threw. I never relaxed. I never took anything for granted. It would seem to be hard for some players to have that kind of intensity after signing a multiyear contract. Some players are making a lot more money than they should."

Behavior of Individuals with High *N Ach* Classic studies find that people with high *n ach* earn higher grades than people of comparable learning ability but low *n ach*. They are more likely to earn high salaries and be promoted than are low-n-ach people with similar opportunities. They perform better at math problems and unscrambling anagrams (such as decoding RSTA into STAR or RATS*). Mothers with high *n ach* tend to encourage their children to think and act independently, while low-n-ach mothers tend to be more protective and restrictive. High n-ach-parents encourage their children to develop high *n ach* and are more likely to applaud their children's accomplishments (McClelland and others, 1953).

McClelland (1965) found that 83 percent of high-n-ach college graduates took positions characterized by risk, decision making, and the chance for great success, such as business management, sales, or businesses of their own making. High-n-ach individuals seem to prefer challenges and are willing to take moderate risks to achieve their goals. They see their fate as in their own hands.

A strong need for achievement can have a negative side. For instance, one study at a midwestern community college found that students with high *n ach* were more likely than their low-n-ach classmates to cheat to earn high grades (Johnson, 1981).

Getting Ahead at AT&T A recent report by industrial psychologist Douglas Bray (1982) finds that factors similar to *n ach*—including need for advancement and great investment in one's work—are of moderate importance in predicting advancement through the managerial ranks at American Telephone and Telegraph. However, two other factors are more important: administrative skills (consisting of organizational ability, decision making, and creativity) and interpersonal skills (leadership, communication ability, and adaptability). *N ach* is an important element in success, but not the only factor.

---

*You can always count on a psychologist not to miss an opportunity to throw a few rats into his book.

The Need for Affiliation

Affiliation Association or connection with a group. (From the Latin *filius*, meaning "son.")

N aff The need for affiliation.

Theory of social comparison The view that people look to others for cues as to appropriate behavior when they are in confusing situations.

Leadership motive syndrome A cluster of needs including strong needs for power and self-control and a low need for affiliation.

The need for **affiliation,** abbreviated **n aff,** prompts us to make friends, join groups, and to prefer to do things with others rather than go it alone.

N aff contributes to the social glue that creates families and civilizations. In this sense, it is certainly a healthy trait. Yet it seems that our *n aff* is often increased by anxiety, as when people "huddle together "in fear of some outside force.

The Schachter Studies on Anxiety and *N Aff* In a classic experiment on the effects of anxiety on *n aff,* Stanley Schachter (1959) manipulated subjects' anxiety by leading them to believe that they would receive either painful electric shocks (the high anxiety condition) or mild electric shocks (the low anxiety condition). Subjects were then asked to wait while the shock apparatus was supposedly being set up. Subjects could choose to wait alone or in a room with others. The majority (63 percent) of subjects who expected a painful shock chose to wait in a room with other people. Only one-third (33 percent) of the subjects who expected a mild shock chose to wait with others.

In a related experiment, Schachter found that "misery may love company," but company of a special sort. Highly anxious subjects were placed in two social conditions. In the first, they could choose either to wait alone or with other subjects who would also receive painful shocks. Sixty percent of these subjects chose to affiliate, that is, to wait with others. In the second condition, highly anxious subjects could choose to wait alone or with people they believed were not involved with the study. In this second condition, no one chose to affiliate. Schachter concluded that misery loves company so long as the company is just as miserable.

Social Comparison Theory Why did Schachter's subjects wish to affiliate only with people who shared their misery? Schachter explained their choice through the **theory of social comparison.** This theory holds that in an ambiguous situation—that is, a situation in which we are not certain as to what we should do or how we should feel—we will affiliate with people with whom we can compare feelings and behaviors. Schachter's anxious recruits could compare their reactions with those of other "victims," but not with people who had no reason to feel anxious. His highly anxious subjects may also have resented uninvolved people for "getting away free."

The Need for Power

Another social motive is the need for power—to control other organizations and other people. The need for power has both its positive and negative features since power can be used either for good or bad purposes. In one recent study it was found that group leaders with a high need for power may impede group decision making by failing to promote full discussion of all the facts concerning a business situation and by not encouraging full consideration of members' proposals (Fodor & Smith, 1982).

For a number of years, Harvard psychologist David McClelland and his colleagues have studied a "motivational profile" referred to as the **leadership motive syndrome.** People with this profile show a cluster of needs that includes high needs for power and self-control, and low *n aff.* People high in the leadership motive syndrome often rise quickly through the military or corporate ranks, assuming that they also have managerial skills. But they also often pay a price.

Leadership Motive Syndrome and Illness People with this motivational profile are also at high risk for developing illness, especially when they are under the stress of having their need for power inhibited or frustrated (McClelland & Jemmott, 1980). On a physiological level, the need for power is often linked to prolonged activity of the sympathetic branch of the autonomic nervous system (McClelland and others, 1980). Prolonged sympathetic activation can lead to high blood pressure (McClelland, 1979) and the breaking down of the body's immune systems (McClelland and others, 1982).

We shall learn more about behavior patterns that lead to stress and illness in Chapter 10. At this point let us note that David McClelland (1982) suggests that one of the major achievements of contemporary psychology has been the development of strategies for coping with this type of behavior. We shall also describe these strategies in some detail in Chapter 10.

Emotion

Emotions color our lives. We are green with envy, red with anger, blue with sorrow. The poets paint a thoughtful mood as a brown study. Positive emotions like love and desire can fill our days with pleasure, but negative emotions like fear, depression, and anger can fill us with dread and make each day an intolerable chore.

Emotions as Responses, Motives, and Goals An emotion can at once be a response to a situation (in the way that fear is a response to a threat) and have motivating properties (in the way that anger can motivate us to act aggressively). An emotion can also be a goal in and of itself. We may behave in ways that will lead us to experience joy or feelings of love.

Definition of Emotion We define an **emotion** as an aroused state that has physiological, situational, and cognitive components. While no two people experience emotions in exactly the same way, it is possible to make some generalizations. Fear, for example, frequently involves **sympathetic** arousal (rapid heartbeat and breathing, sweating, muscle tension), the perception of a threat, and beliefs to the effect that one is in danger (see Table 7.2). Anger may involve both sympathetic and **parasympathetic** arousal (Funkenstein, 1955), a frustrating or provocative situation (like an insult), and belief that the provocateur ought to be paid back. Depression often involves predominantly parasympathetic arousal, a situational component of loss, failure, or inactivity, and cognitions of helplessness and worthlessness. Joy, grief, jealousy, disgust, embarrassment, liking—all have physiological, situational, and cognitive components.

The box on the use of devices that can distinguish between truth and lies—at least according to their manufacturers—highlights the link between autonomic arousal and emotion.

The Range of Emotional and Behavioral Responsiveness People who might label themselves as experiencing similar emotions do not necessarily feel or act in the same ways. Fearful people do not all show the same degree

Emotion An aroused state that has physiological, situational, and cognitive components.

Sympathetic Of the sympathetic division of the autonomic nervous system. See Chapter 2.

Parasympathetic Of the parasympathetic division of the autonomic nervous system. See Chapter 2.

TABLE 7.2   Components of Three Common Emotions

Emotion	Components		
	Physiological	**Situational**	**Cognitive**
Fear	Sympathetic arousal	Environmental threat	Belief in danger, desire to avoid
Anger	Sympathetic and parasympathetic arousal	Frustration or provocation	Desire to hurt provocateur
Depression	Parasympathetic arousal	Loss, failure, or inactivity	Thoughts of helplessness, worthlessness

Emotions have physiological, situational, and cognitive components.

of arousal or run away. Angry people do not all become flushed or act aggressively.

Why do people who supposedly "have" the same emotion feel and act differently. These differences may at least in part reflect the uniqueness of the cognitive components of our feeling states (Sommers, 1981). In Chapters 10 and 12 we shall see that many psychologists help clients relieve distressing emotions by showing them how to alter their cognitions.

Classification of Emotions

How many emotions are there? What are they? These questions have prompted many speculations and observations. One investigator surveyed Roget's thesaurus and found more than 400 English words that named emotions (Davitz, 1969). But these were not all distinct emotions since there were many instances of overlap.

From a study of infants, Bridges (1932) suggested that at first people show only one basic emotion: a **diffuse** excitement. During the first few months of life, this excitement differentiates into 11 emotions. Another investigator argued that there are eight basic emotions (Plutchik, 1962). Others, including behaviorist John B. Watson, endorse three basic human emotions: joy or happiness, anger, and fear. These emotions prompt distinct behavioral tendencies: joy motivates approach, anger motivates fighting, and fear prompts fleeing.

Yet another classification approach involves the search for factors that allow us to group emotions meaningfully. Russell and Mehrabian (1977) suggest that focus on three factors permits such grouping: the intensity of the emotion (degree of arousal), the presence of positive or negative feelings, and the tendency to express dominance or submission. From this perspective, anger is intense, negative, and gives rise to the tendency to dominate. Fear is also intense and negative, but prompts submissive behavior. But as yet, the number of "basic" human emotions remains in dispute (Izard, 1978).

Expression of Emotions

A number of emotions are "basic" in the sense that they are found in different cultures, but their expression can vary from culture to culture. The expression of emotions may be influenced by learning as well as innate factors (Averill, 1978).

Diffuse Spread out.

Just What Do Lie Detectors Detect?—Lies or Arousal?

The use of devices to sort out truth from lies has a lengthy, if not laudable, history. As told by Burke Smith (1967, p. 25):

> The Bedouins of Arabia once required conflicting witnesses to lick a hot iron; the one whose tongue was burned was considered to be lying. The ancient Chinese, it is said, made someone who was being questioned chew rice powder and spit it out; if the powder was dry, the suspect was guilty. In ancient Britain a suspect who could not swallow a "trial slice" of bread and cheese was also found to be guilty.

These methods may sound primitive, even bizarre, but they are consistent with modern knowledge. Anxiety concerning being caught in a lie is linked to sympathetic arousal, and one sign of sympathetic arousal is dryness in the mouth, or lack of saliva. The emotions of fear and guilt are also linked to sympathetic arousal and, hence, dryness in the mouth.

The Polygraph   Modern-day lie detectors, or *polygraphs* (see Figure 7.9), monitor four indicators of sympathetic arousal while a witness or suspect is being examined: heart rate, blood pressure, respiration rate, and galvanic skin response (GSR). But many questions have been raised about use of the polygraph, especially since it is frequently used in the hiring process in industry and in helping to establish guilt or innocence in the courtroom.

Supporters of the polygraph claim that they are accurate in more than 90 percent of cases (Podlesny & Raskin, 1977), but conflicting research suggests that polygraphs do not approach this high accuracy rate (Lykken, 1981), and that they are sensitive to more than lies. In one experiment, subjects were able to reduce the accuracy rate to 25 percent by thinking about exciting or disturbing events during

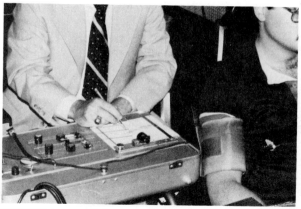

FIGURE 7.9   A "Lie Detector." The polygraph monitors heart rate, blood pressure, respiration rate, and GSR (sweat in the palms of the hands). Is the polygraph sensitive to lying only? Is it foolproof? Because of the controversy surrounding these issues, polygraph evidence is no longer admitted in many courtrooms.

the interview (Smith, 1971). Other subjects were yet more successful at poking holes in the accuracy rate. They dropped it to 10 percent by tensing and relaxing their toes while being interviewed.

There are other problems. One is the great variability in the reliability of the human judges of polygraph responses (Szucko & Kleinmuntz, 1981). Another is the possibility that sociopaths (discussed in Chapter 11), who show little anxiety or guilt, may escape detection because their lying is usually accompanied by low levels of arousal. Because of problems such as these, polygraph evidence is no longer admitted as evidence in many courtrooms. Polygraph interviews are still often conducted in criminal investigations and in job interviews. But these practices are being questioned as well.

Smiling appears to be a universal sign of friendliness and approval (Ekman & Oster, 1979). Baring the teeth may be a universal sign of anger (Darwin, 1872). But other gestures and facial expressions can have decidedly different meanings from culture to culture. A lowered brow is a sign of social dominance in Western society (Keating and others, 1981). And in Greece, an elderly woman's spitting on a child is an expression of admiration of the child's beauty (Triandis, 1976)!

In an often-cited study, Klineberg (1938) reported that Chinese authors had their characters display emotions through some surprising gestures and expressions. A man showed anxiety or disappointment (not approval) by clapping his hands. A woman showed anger (not surprise) when her eyes grew round and open. A man showed happiness (not puzzlement) by scratching his ears and cheeks. Other characters showed surprise (not disdain) by sticking out their tongues.

The Facial Feedback Hypothesis We recognize that emotional states are *reflected* by facial expressions, but the **facial feedback hypothesis** argues that the causal relationship between emotions and facial expressions can work in the opposite direction. Inducing experimental subjects to smile, for example, leads them to report more positive feelings (Kleinke & Walton, 1982), and to rate cartoons as more humorous (Laird, 1974). When subjects are induced to frown, they rate cartoons as being more aggressive (Laird, 1974). When subjects pose expressions of pain, they also rate electric shocks as more painful (Colby and others, 1977; Lanzetta and others, 1976). As Charles Darwin noted more than 100 years ago, "The free expression by outward signs of an emotion intensifies it. On the other hand, the repression, as far as possible, of all outward signs softens our emotions" (Darwin, 1872, p. 22).

What is the link between facial feedback and emotion? It seems that posing intense facial expressions, as those signifying fear, leads to increased activity of the autonomic nervous system (Zuckerman and others, 1981). Our perception of heightened activity of the autonomic nervous system then leads to self-report of heightened emotional activity. Additional research also suggests that perception of the facial *movement* involved in showing emotions may lead us to conclude that our emotional responsiveness has increased (McCaul and others, 1982).

You may have heard the British expression "to keep a stiff upper lip" as a way of handling stress. It may well be that a "stiff" lip will lower the experience of emotion so long as the lip is relaxed rather than quivering with fear or tension. But when a lip is stiffened through strong muscle tension, facial feedback could heighten autonomic activity and the perception of emotional response. In the following section we shall see that the facial feedback hypothesis is related to the James-Lange theory of emotion.

Theories of Emotion

How is it that we come to feel emotions like joy or anger, love or fear? Several theories have attempted to explain emotional responses.

The James-Lange Theory Just before the turn of the century, William James of Harvard University suggested that our emotions follow, rather than cause, our overt behavioral responses to events. This view was also proposed by a contemporary of James, the Danish physiologist Karl G. Lange. For this reason, it is referred to as the James-Lange theory of emotion.

According to James and Lange, we become angry *because* we act aggressively. We become afraid *because* we run away. They hypothesized that the makeup of the body is such that certain external stimuli will trigger specific patterns of arousal and activity, like fighting or fleeing. Emotions are simply the cognitive representations (or by-products) of automatic physiological and behavioral responses.

Walter Cannon (1927) criticized the James-Lange theory on several grounds. The most telling criticism is directed toward the assertion that each emotion has distinct physiological correlates. Cannon noted, correctly, that the physiological arousal that accompanies Emotion A is not as distinct from the arousal that accompanies Emotion B as the theory asserts.

FIGURE 7.10 The James-Lange Theory of Emotion. According to the James-Lange theory, events trigger specific arousal patterns and actions. Emotions result from appraisal of our actions.

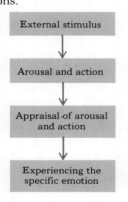

External stimulus

↓

Arousal and action

↓

Appraisal of arousal and action

↓

Experiencing the specific emotion

Today the James-Lange theory is considered to be of mainly historical interest. Still, it is of some value. It suggests that by acting in a certain way we can induce desired emotional responses. Perhaps we can overcome the emotion of fear by somehow approaching, rather than running from, dreaded objects or situations. Perhaps we can overcome the emotion of depression by engaging in, rather than withdrawing from, activities that we normally enjoy, such as bicycling or attending concerts. (This is noted in the box on using

Must You Remain Loyal to Depression, or Can You Use Pleasant Events To Lift Yourself Out of the Dumps?

Some people act as though they want to remain faithful to the emotion of depression. Becky's romance had recently disintegrated, and after some weeks had passed, friends became concerned that she remained weepy and withdrawn. Finally, despite her protests, they talked her into going with them to a rock concert by that new group The Naked and the Dead.

It took some time for Becky to focus on the music and the excitement of the crowd, but after a while she began clapping and shouting with her friends. Afterwards, feelings of depression returned, but they were not so intense. Becky pushed herself to get out and do things. She eventually dated others and dwelled less on the past.

Becky's friends had encouraged Becky to "get out and do things" because, like many people, they shared an assumption (consistent with the James-Lange theory) that by acting in a certain way we may come to experience the emotions usually linked with that activity. According to University of Oregon psychologist Peter Lewinsohn, one way to fight depression is to engage in pleasant events that are incompatible with depression. A number of researchers have shown that there is a significant correlation between mood and the number and type of pleasant activities with which we become involved (e.g., Lewinsohn & Graf, 1973; Lewinsohn & Libet, 1972; Rehm, 1978).

Here is a partial list of activities found by Lewinsohn and Graf to be linked with positive emotions:

Laughing
Being relaxed
Thinking about something good in the future
Thinking about people I like
Breathing clean air
Seeing beautiful scenery
Sitting in the sun
Having spare time
Listening to music
Seeing good things happen to my family or friends
Watching wild animals
Being with happy people
Being with friends
Having a frank and open conversation
Being with someone I love
Having a lively talk
Doing a project in my own way
Reading stories, novels, poems, or plays
Having peace and quiet
Wearing clean clothes
Smiling at people
Kissing
Watching people
Having sexual relations
Petting, necking
Complimenting or praising someone
Meeting someone new
Seeing old friends
Expressing my love to someone
Having coffee, tea, a soft drink with friends
Planning or organizing something
Planning trips or vacations
Learning to do something new

Would these activities work for you? First consider that there is a wide variety of preferences, and so we may profit from constructing our own lists. Also, experiments in using pleasant activities to lift one's mood have shown mixed results. For instance, Reich and Zautra (1981) found that engaging in pleasant activities increases feelings of well-being, but tends to relieve distress only for people under considerable stress. Biglan and Craker (1982) found that engaging in pleasant events increased the activity level of four depressed women, but did not improve self-reports of mood. So there are no guarantees.

Emotions are complex, involving physiological, situational, and cognitive factors. Still, if you have been down in the dumps for a while and can't think of a good reason to stay there, it may help you to engage in some activities that seem incompatible with depression. Like chicken soup, it can't hurt. Try it—you may like it.

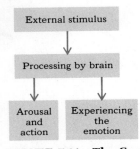

FIGURE 7.11 The Cannon-Bard Theory of Emotion. According to the Cannon-Bard theory, events are processed by the brain. The emotion, arousal, and action are then triggered simultaneously.

pleasant events to counter feelings of depression.) Sound farfetched? These assumptions underlie many effective behavior therapy practices that are currently used in clinics across the world. There is a kernel of truth in many outdated theories.

The Cannon-Bard Theory Walter Cannon was not content merely to critique the James-Lange theory. He (Cannon, 1927) and Philip Bard (1934) suggested that an event would trigger bodily responses (arousal and action) and the experience of an emotion simultaneously. As shown in Figure 7.11, when an event is perceived (processed by the brain), the brain stimulates autonomic and muscular activity (arousal and action) *and* cognitive activity (experiencing of the emotion). According to the Cannon-Bard theory, emotions *accompany* bodily responses. Emotions are not produced *by* bodily changes, as in the James-Lange theory.

The central criticism of the Cannon-Bard theory focuses on whether (1) bodily responses (arousal and action) and (2) emotions are actually stimulated simultaneously. For example, pain or the perception of danger may trigger arousal before we begin to experience distress or fear. Also, many of us have had the experience of having a "narrow escape," and then becoming aroused and shaky afterwards, when we have finally had time to consider the damage that might have occurred.

What is needed is a theory that allows for an ongoing interaction of external events, physiological changes (such as autonomic arousal and muscular activity), and cognitive activities. We need not be overly concerned with which must come first—the chicken, the egg, or the egg salad.

The Schachter-Singer Theory According to Stanley Schachter (1971), emotions have generally similar patterns of bodily arousal. They vary along a weak-strong dimension that is determined largely by the level of arousal. The label we *attribute* to an emotion depends upon our cognitive appraisal of our situation. This appraisal is based on many factors, including our perception of external events and the ways in which other people seem to be responding to those events (see Figure 7.12). Given the presence of other people, we engage in *social comparison* (see page 278) to arrive at an appropriate response.

In a classic experiment, Schachter and Jerome Singer (1962) showed that arousal can be labeled quite differently, depending on a person's situation. The investigators told subjects that their purpose was to study the effects of a vitamin on vision. Half the subjects received an injection of adrenalin, a hormone that increases autonomic arousal (see Chapter 2). A control group received an injection of an inactive **saline** solution. Subjects given adrenalin then received one of three "cognitive manipulations," as shown in Table 7.3.

Saline Containing salt. (From the Latin *sal,* meaning "salt.")

Table 7.3 Injected Substances and Cognitive Manipulations in the Schachter-Singer Study

Group	Substance	Cognitive Manipulation
1	Adrenalin	No information given about effects
2	Adrenalin	Misinformation given: itching, numbness, etc.
3	Adrenalin	Accurate information: physiological arousal
4	Saline solution	None

Source: Schachter & Singer, 1962.

Group 1 was told nothing about possible emotional effects of the "vitamin." Group 2 was deliberately misinformed; group members were led to expect itching, numbness, or other irrelevant symptoms. Group 3 was informed accurately about the increased arousal they would experience.

After receiving injections and cognitive manipulations, subjects were asked to wait, in pairs, while the experimental apparatus was being set up. Subjects did not know that the person with whom they were waiting was a confederate of the experimenter. The purpose of the confederate was to model a response that the subject would believe resulted from the injection.

Some subjects waited with a confederate who acted in a happy-go-lucky manner. He flew paper airplanes about the room and tossed paper balls into a wastebasket. Other subjects waited with a confederate who acted angrily, complaining about the experiment, tearing up a questionnaire, and departing the waiting room in a huff. As the confederates worked for their Oscars, real subjects were observed through a one-way mirror.

Subjects in Groups 1 and 2 were likely to imitate the behavior of the confederate. Those exposed to the **euphoric** confederate acted jovial and content. Those exposed to the angry confederate imitated that person's complaining, aggressive ways. But Groups 3 and 4 were less influenced by the behavior of the confederate.

Schachter and Singer concluded that Groups 1 and 2 were in an ambiguous situation. They experienced arousal from the adrenalin injection but had no basis for attributing it to any event or emotion. Social comparison with the confederate led them to attribute their arousal either to happiness or anger, whichever was displayed by the confederate. Group 3 expected arousal from the injection with no particular emotional consequences. They did not imitate the confederate's display of happiness or anger because they were not in an ambiguous situation. Group 4 experienced no physiological arousal for which they needed an attribution, except, perhaps, for some induced by observing the confederate. Group 4 subjects also failed to imitate the confederate.

Now happiness and anger are quite different emotions. Happiness is a positive emotion and anger, for most of us, is a negative emotion. Yet Schachter and Singer suggest that any physiological differences between these two emotions are so slight that a different cognitive appraisal of a situation can lead one person to label arousal as happiness and another person to label arousal as anger. This view could not be farther removed from the James-Lange theory, which holds that each emotion has specific and readily recognized bodily sensations. The truth may lie somewhere in between.

In science it must be possible to attain identical or similar results when experiments are replicated. The Schachter and Singer study has been replicated with *different* results. For instance, in studies by Rogers and Deckner (1975) and Maslach (1978), subjects were less likely to imitate the behavior of the confederate, and more likely to apply negative emotional labels to their arousal, even when exposed to a euphoric confederate. Perhaps there is something negative about the ambiguity of having an "emotion" without an explanation for it.

Evaluation   What do we make of all this? As noted at the outset of the section on emotion, emotions do seem to be influenced by physiological, situational, and cognitive factors. The patterns of arousal that lead us to believe we are experiencing certain emotions may be more specific than suggested by Schachter and Singer, but less specific than suggested by James and Lange. Our situa-

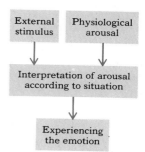

FIGURE 7.12   The Schachter-Singer Theory of Emotion. According to the Schachter-Singer theory, events and arousal are appraised by the person. The emotional response stems from the person's appraisal.

Euphoric Characterized by feelings of well-being, elation.

Love A strong, pleasant emotion that has many meanings. Note the "types" of love presented in this section.

Romantic love An intense, positive emotion that involves arousal, a cultural setting that idealizes love, the actual or fantasized presence of an attractive person, and belief that one is "in love."

tions, and our appraisals of our situations, are also influential, and when our situations are ambiguous, we are at least somewhat more likely to interpret them by social comparison.

There is no reason to insist that any particular component of emotional response—physiological, situational, or cognitive—is more crucial than others in determining emotional response. What is crucial is that people gather information from all three sources in determining appropriate behavior and arriving at emotional labels. The fact that none of the theories we have discussed applies to *all* people in *all* situations is comforting. Our emotions are not quite so easily manipulated as theorists have suggested.

Now let us turn our attention to an enigmatic and always fascinating human emotion—love.

Love

What makes the world go round? **Love,** of course. Love is one of the most deeply stirring emotions, the ideal for which we will make great sacrifice, the emotion that launched a thousand ships in the Greek epic *The Iliad.*

For thousands of years, poets have sought to capture love in words. A seventeenth century poet wrote that his love was like "a red, red rose." In Sinclair Lewis's novel *Elmer Gantry*, love is "the morning and the evening star." Love is beautiful and elusive. It shines brilliantly and heavenly. Passionate or **romantic love** can also be earthy and sexy, involving a solid dose of sexual desire. Love is often seen as self-sacrificing. According to Steck and colleagues (1982), college undergraduates see the desire to help or care for the loved one as more central to the concept of love than is concern for how the loved one can meet one's own needs.

Despite the importance of love in our lives, researchers have not paid much attention to the concept until recent years. Anthropologists had noted that romantic love is not found in all cultures, and that many foreigners have wondered how Westerners can develop such passionate and exclusive feelings

Love is one of the most deeply stirring emotions. Romantic love appears to exist only in cultures that idealize the concept.

for another person. Let's look at how the concept of romantic love evolved in our Western culture.

The Greek Heritage of Four Types of Love   The concept of love can be traced back at least to the classical Greeks, who had four concepts related to the modern meaning of love: *storge, agape, philia,* and *eros.* **Storge** is translated as attachment and affection, the emotion that binds parents and children. **Agape** is similar to generosity and charity. It implies the wish to share one's bounty, and is epitomized by anonymous donations to charity. **Philia** is close in meaning to friendship. It is based on liking and respect and involves the desire to do and share things with another person.

   Eros is closest in meaning to passionate or romantic love. Sigmund Freud used the concept of *eros* to describe a basic life instinct, which he thought motivated most human behavior (see Chapter 9). Freud believed, literally, that *eros* "makes the world go round." Our own concept of romantic love does not imply any basic life instinct. Still, romantic love can be an important determinant of behavior—in societies that believe in the concept.

Romantic Love in Contemporary Western Culture: A Role-Playing Approach   In order to experience romantic love, in contrast to attachment or sexual arousal, one must be exposed to a culture that idealizes the concept. In Western culture, romantic love blossoms with the fairy tales of Sleeping Beauty, Cinderella, Snow White, and all their princes charming. It matures with romantic novels, television tales and films, and the personal tales of friends and relatives about dates and romances (Udry, 1971).

Storge (STORE–gay). Feelings of attachment and affection.

Agape (AH–gah–pay). Feelings of generosity, charity.

Philia (FEEL–ee–uh). Feelings of friendship.

Eros The Greek concept of love closest in meaning to romantic love, emphasizing sexual desire.

Consider an analogy: In Chapter 4 we noted that there is probably no such thing as a hypnotic "trance." Rather, one must understand what is expected of a person in a "trance" in order to play the role of a hypnotized person. In the same way, romantic love may not reflect any natural inner state. A person must have experience with a culture that idealizes the concept of love in order to successfully play the role of a person who is "in love." This does not mean that we are being "phony" when we enact the role of someone in love. It simply means that we require a clear concept of a certain pattern of behavior before we can enact it.

Unlike the Greeks, we use the label "love" to describe everything from affection to sexual intercourse ("making love") because "love" is a more socially acceptable word for polite conversation. During adolescence, lust is often labeled love. We use the label "love" to describe lust because sexual desire in the absence of a committed relationship is often viewed as primitive.

We retain much of a double standard toward sexual behavior. Women often justify sexual experiences as involving someone they love. Men usually need not justify sexual desires, and so need not attribute passion to love.

Defining Romantic Love   Definitions of romantic love vary. Psychoanalysts generally speak in global concepts, such as Erich Fromm's "craving for complete fusion . . . with one other person. (Love) is by its very nature exclusive" (1956, p. 44). Erik Erikson also sees love as the merging of two identities. To Erikson, mature love is possible only after one has established **ego identity** (see Chapters 8 and 9).

Others have avoided unmeasurable concepts like the merging or fusing of identities, and define romantic love in terms of the behavior of lovers. Rubin (1970) observed that lovers express the desire to be together, claim to feel lost when apart, have romantic interest in the loved one only (exclusivity), are preoccupied with the loved one, and do what they can to help the loved one. Romantic lovers are also sexually aroused by one another and **idealize** one another (Driscoll and others, 1972). They magnify each other's positive features and overlook their flaws.

Social psychologists Ellen Berscheid and Elaine Walster (Berscheid & Walster, 1978; Walster & Walster, 1978) define love in terms of physiological response and cognitive appraisal of that response. Love, to them, involves intense arousal and some reason to label that arousal love.

Let us define romantic love in terms of physiological, situational, and cognitive components. Romantic love is an intense, positive emotion that involves (1) arousal; (2) a cultural setting that idealizes love; (3) the actual or fantasized presence of a person considered attractive; and (4) the *belief* that one is "in love."

On Love and Arousal: If My Heart Is Pounding, It Must Mean I Love You
The Roman poet Ovid suggested that young men (his interests were admittedly sexist) might open their ladies' hearts by taking them to the gory gladiator contests. The women could attribute the pounding of their hearts and the butterflies in their stomachs to the nearness of their dates, and conclude that they were inspired by them. Research does suggest that strong arousal in the presence of a reasonably attractive person may lead us to believe that we are experiencing desire (Istvan & Griffitt, 1978). But if the person is decidedly *un*attractive, we may attribute our arousal to revulsion or disgust (White and others, 1981).

Are You in Love?
The Love Scale

The following love scale was developed at Northeastern University in Boston. To compare your own score (or scores, if you have been busy) with those of Northeastern University students, simply think of your dating partner or partners and fill out the scale with each of them in mind. Then compare your scores to those in Appendix B.

The Love Scale

Directions: Circle the number that best shows how true or false the items are for you according to this code:

7 = definitely true	4 = not sure,	3 = somewhat false
6 = rather true	or equally true and false	2 = rather false
5 = somewhat true		1 = definitely false

1. I look forward to being with _____ a great deal.
   definitely false 1 2 3 4 5 6 7 definitely true
2. I find _____ to be sexually exciting.
   definitely false 1 2 3 4 5 6 7 definitely true
3. _____ has fewer faults than most people.
   definitely false 1 2 3 4 5 6 7 definitely true
4. I would do anything I could for _____.
   definitely false 1 2 3 4 5 6 7 definitely true
5. _____ is very attractive to me.
   definitely false 1 2 3 4 5 6 7 definitely true
6. I like to share my feelings with _____.
   definitely false 1 2 3 4 5 6 7 definitely true
7. Doing things is more fun when _____ and I do them together.
   definitely false 1 2 3 4 5 6 7 definitely true
8. I like to have _____ all to myself.
   definitely false 1 2 3 4 5 6 7 definitely true
9. I would feel horrible if anything bad happened to _____.
   definitely false 1 2 3 4 5 6 7 definitely true
10. I think about _____ very often.
    definitely false 1 2 3 4 5 6 7 definitely true
11. It is very important that _____ cares for me.
    definitely false 1 2 3 4 5 6 7 definitely true
12. I am most content when I am with _____.
    definitely false 1 2 3 4 5 6 7 definitely true
13. It is difficult for me to stay away from _____ for very long.
    definitely false 1 2 3 4 5 6 7 definitely true.
14. I care about _____ a great deal.
    definitely false 1 2 3 4 5 6 7 definitely true.

Total Score for Love Scale: _____

Despite the saying, love does not seem to be "blind"—just a bit near-sighted. Let us consider a couple of experiments on arousal and feelings of passion. In one study, male college students rated the attractiveness of *Playboy* nudes (Valins, 1966). Each rater was wired so that he could monitor his own heartbeat (he believed) through a microphone and earphone set. Heart sounds accelerated in frequency when certain slides were being shown. In general, subjects rated models as more attractive when the heartbeats were more rapid.

There was one catch. Valins had doctored the feedback arrangement so that raters were *not* listening to their own heartbeat. Instead, they were hearing heart beats that were accelerated or slowed down for randomly selected models. The men may have attributed what they believed to be their own hearts racing to the slide being shown. As a consequence, perhaps they believed that this woman *must* be particularly appealing to them.

Rapid heartbeat, of course, does not only signify passion. It is also one sign of fear. Can university students confuse feelings of fear with sexual attraction? Impossible, you say? Quite possible, according to a Canadian study with male subjects (Dutton & Aron, 1974).

This study got a rise out of subjects—a rise of 230 feet, to be precise. Some subjects were interviewed by a woman on a spindly bridge that swayed high above the rocky canyon of the Capilano River in Vancouver. In this unlikely setting they answered questions and wrote stories in response to TAT pictures. The men also received the phone number of the interviewer in case they wished to learn more about the study. Other subjects were interviewed by the same woman on a lower and apparently safer bridge. Subjects who had gotten high—230 feet high, that is—wrote TAT-based stories that contained more sexual content, and phoned their interviewer more frequently afterward.

Wait, you say. The sexual content of the stories and the phone calls might have reflected only the height of the bridge and had nothing to do with the presence of the woman interviewer? The investigators anticipated this objection, so they arranged for another group of male subjects to be interviewed on the two bridges by men. Subjects interviewed by men wrote stories devoid of sexual content and made few calls afterward, regardless of the bridge on which they had been interviewed. And so the presence of the woman was required. Dutton and Aron reasoned that the male subjects interviewed by men could not attribute their arousal, which apparently stemmed from the height of the spindly bridge, to sexual desire. But men interviewed by a woman could attribute their physiological responses to her presence. In this way, feelings of fear somehow took on the meaning of passion.

Many sources of arousal may lead us to respond more positively to members of the opposite sex. A horror movie or a roller coaster ride may just stimulate your date's passion. It is also possible that there is, after all, a love potion. It's called adrenalin.

Summary

A motive is a state within an organism that leads to goal-directed behavior. A need is a state of deprivation. Maslow hypothesized that people have a hierarchy of needs, including an innate need for self-actualization. His hierarchy includes physiological, safety, love and belongingness, and esteem needs, and needs for cognitive understanding, aesthetics, and self-actualization.

Physiological or primary drives are unlearned and generally function according to a homeostatic principle—the body's tendency to maintain a steady state. Hunger is regulated by several internal mechanisms, including stomach contractions, blood sugar level, receptors in the mouth and liver, and by the hypothalamus. The ventromedial hypothalamus functions as a stop-eating center. Lesions in this area lead to hyperphagia in rats; the rats grow to several times their normal body weight, but eventually level off. The lateral hypothalamus has a start-eating center.

Obese people, like hyperphagic rats, are more responsive than normal-weight people to external cues.

Thirst is regulated by level of blood flow and the concentration of chemicals, like sodium, in the blood. Dehydration leads the kidneys to produce the hormone angiotensin, which signals the hypothalamus. Osmoreceptors in the hypothalamus detect lowered local flow of blood, which stems from dehydration or increased concentration of sodium. The hypothalamus then stimulates the pituitary to secrete antidiuretic hormone, which slows urine formation, and also signals the cortex, which prompts the thirst drive.

In lower animals the sex drive is largely controlled by sex hormones, and females are sexually receptive only when in estrus. Cognitive factors are relatively more influential among higher animals, and sex hormones are not required—above a certain minimum standing level—for people to become sexually aroused.

The hormone prolactin plays a major role in inducing instinctive mothering behavior in lower animals like rats. Among primates, maternal behavior is learned.

Stimulus motives are also innate. Sensory deprivation studies show that lack of stimulation is aversive. People and many lower animals have needs for stimulation and activity, for exploration and manipulation. There is evidence that we seek personal optimal levels of arousal, at which we feel best and function most efficiently. According to the Yerkes-Dodson law, high levels of motivation facilitate performance of simple tasks, but impede performance of complex tasks.

Social motives are secondary or learned. They include needs for achievement (n ach), affiliation, and power. People with a high n ach accomplish more than people of comparable ability with lower n ach.

An emotion is an aroused state with physiological, situational, and cognitive components. Emotions motivate behavior and also serve as goals. The expression of some emotions, like smiling, seems universal and is probably innate. Other emotions, like surprise, find different expression in different cultures. Facial expressions can heighten emotional response, perhaps through autonomic and muscular feedback. Lie detectors are sensitive to arousal, not just lies, and therefore somewhat unreliable.

According to James-Lange theory, emotions are specific reactions to characteristic events. Cannon-Bard theory proposes that processing of events by the brain gives rise both to the emotion and bodily responses. According to Schachter and Singer, emotions reflect physiological arousal and situational factors that prompt cognitive appraisal and labeling. As an emotion, romantic love involves arousal, actual or fantasized presence of an attractive person, a cultural setting that idealizes love, and belief that one is in love.

Truth or Fiction Revisited

- *Of 2,000 Americans polled in a recent survey, more than half were overweight.* True. Fifty-eight percent were.
- *Overweight people are more sensitive to stomach pangs than are normal-weight people.* False. Normal-weight people are more sensitive to internal cues for hunger.
- *Eating salty pretzels can make you thirsty.* True. Increased concentrations of salt cause the hypothalamus to trigger the thirst drive.
- *Stimulating male rats in a certain part of the brain causes them to engage in sexual foreplay.* True. Sexual behavior patterns seem largely instinctive among lower animals.
- *Women make natural mothers.* False. They must learn maternal behavior.
- *You can fool a lie detector by squiggling your toes.* True. According to one study, toe-squiggling will fool the polygraph method most of the time.
- *Romantic love is found in every culture in the world.* False. It is found only in cultures that idealize the concept.
- *Taking a date to a horror film or for a roller coaster ride may stimulate feelings of passion.* True. The heightened autonomic arousal could be attributed to your charming presence.

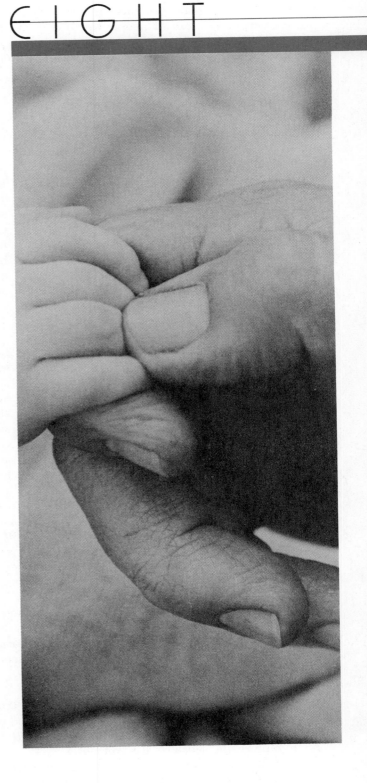

EIGHT

OUTLINE

Theories of Development

Prenatal Development
The First Trimester
The Second Trimester
The Third Trimester

Infancy and Childhood
Reflexes
Perceptual Development
Attachment
The Effects of Social Deprivation
Identification and Sex Typing

Cognitive Development
Jean Piaget
Piaget's Stages of Cognitive Development
Kohlberg's Levels and Stages of Moral
Development

Adolescence
Changes in the Male
Changes in the Female
Adolescent Behavior and Conflicts

Adult Development
Young Adulthood
Middle Adulthood
Late Adulthood

Summary

Truth or Fiction Revisited

Developmental Psychology

- You can determine the sex of your child.
- A newly fertilized egg cell wanders around the womb with no visible means of support.
- Newborn infants prefer human faces to other forms of visual stimulation.
- Children placed in day-care facilities grow less attached to their mothers.
- A four-year-old child may believe that the sky is blue because someone has painted it.
- Adolescents are biologically capable of reproduction when they first ejaculate or have their first menstrual period.
- Sexual morality is the central concern of the identity crisis of adolescence.
- Forced retirement may be a death sentence.

On a summerlike day in October, Elaine and her husband Dennis rush out to their jobs as usual. While Elaine, a buyer for a New York department store, is arranging for dresses from the Chicago manufacturer to arrive in time for the spring line, a very different drama is unfolding in her body. Hormones are causing a follicle (egg container) in one of her **ovaries** to rupture and release an ovum. For a day or so following **ovulation,** Elaine will be capable of becoming pregnant. When it is released, the ovum will begin a slow journey down a four-inch-long **fallopian tube** to the **uterus.** It is within this tube that one of Dennis's sperm cells will unite with it.

Like many other couples, Elaine and Dennis made love the previous night. But unlike most other couples, their timing and methodology were quite purposeful. Elaine's **gynecologist** had been tracking the consistency of her **vaginal mucus** with a **viscometer,** an instrument in his office. The viscometer had predicted that her mucus would be thinnest at about midnight. When the mucus is thinnest, sperm cells with Y sex **chromosomes** are likely to arrive in the fallopian tubes before sperm with X sex chromosomes do. If a sperm with a Y sex chromosome unites with an ovum, all of which contain X sex chromosomes, the woman will conceive a boy. In the past, two of Dennis's sperm, each containing an X sex chromosome, had resulted in Elaine's conceiving daughters.

When Elaine and Dennis made love, he ejaculated hundreds of millions of sperm, with about equal numbers of Y and X sex chromosomes. By the time of conception only a few thousand had survived the journey to the fallopian tubes. Of these, eight of ten carried Y sex chromosomes. Several bombarded the ovum, attempting to penetrate. Only one succeeded. The fertilized ovum, or **zygote,** is $1/175$th of an inch long—a tiny stage for the drama yet to unfold.

The genetic material from Dennis's sperm cell combines with that in Elaine's egg cell. Later Dennis and Elaine will be pleased to learn that the sperm carried a Y sex chromosome, after all. Other genetic instructions determine that the being conceived this morning will grow arms rather than wings, a mouth rather than gills, and hair rather than scales. From the moment of conception, your stamp as an individual distinct from all others—with the possible exception of an identical twin—has been assured: whether you will have yellow or black hair, someday grow bald or develop a widow's peak, or have a straight or curved nose. We do not know exactly how much influence genetic instructions have on traits like timidity, social shyness, and intelligence. Still, the effects of heredity are felt to some degree here as well (e.g., Kagan, 1982; Plomin & DeFries, 1980; Scarr and others, 1981).

Developmental psychologists would be pleased to study the behavior of Dennis and Elaine's new son from the moment of conception through his lifetime. There are a number of reasons for this. One approach to the explanation of adult behavior lies in the discovery of early influences and developmental sequences. One answer to the question of *why* we behave in certain ways lies in outlining the development of behavior patterns over the years.

There is continuing interest in sorting out what human behavior is the result of nature (heredity) and of nurture (environmental influences). What effects do genetics, early interactions with parents and **siblings,** and experiences in the school and the community have on traits like aggressiveness and intelligence? Clearly, the effects of nature and nurture interact in our development. Heredity matters little if one starves to death while an infant, and a rich environment cannot turn a rhesus monkey into a Shakespeare.

Ovaries Female reproductive organs located in the abdomen that produce female reproductive cells, or *ova.* (*Ovum* is a Latin word meaning "egg.")

Ovulation The releasing of an ovum (female reproductive cell) from an ovary.

Fallopian tube A tube that conducts ova from an ovary to the uterus.

Uterus The hollow organ within females in which the unborn child develops. (A Latin word.)

Gynecologist (guy–nah–KOLL–oh–jist). A physician who specializes in women's health problems. (From the Greek *gyne,* meaning "woman.")

Vaginal mucus Secretions that moisten and protect membranes within the female organ of sexual intercourse.

Viscometer An instrument that measures the viscosity (stickiness) of vaginal mucus.

Chromosomes Genetic structures composed of genes that are found within the nuclei of cells. People typically have 23 pairs of chromosomes. See Chapter 2.

Zygote A fertilized ovum.

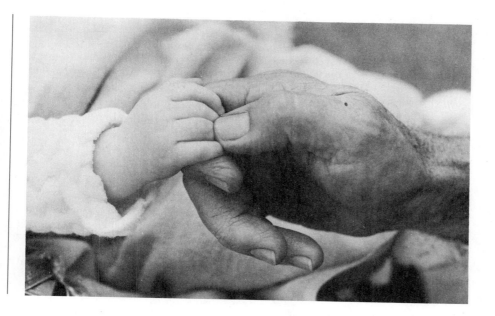

Developmental psychologists also seek insight into the causes of developmental abnormalities. This avenue of research can yield answers to pressing questions of health and psychological well-being. For instance, should pregnant women avoid smoking cigarettes and drinking alcohol? Is it safe for the **fetus** if pregnant women use aspirin for a headache, or **tetracycline** to ward off a bacterial invasion? What are the effects of social deprivation at an early age? Need we be concerned about placing our children in day-care centers while we work? What conflicts and disillusionments can we expect as we journey through the decades of the 30s, 40s, and 50s? What are the effects of forced retirement on the elderly? The information acquired by developmental psychologists can help us make decisions about how we raise our children and lead our own lives.

Of course, there is another very good reason for studying human development. Thousands of psychologists enjoy it.

Theories of Development

On a descriptive level, psychologists observe and record the growth and development of children and adults as faithfully as possible. But psychologists also try to explain and predict growth and development through developmental theories. For example, psychoanalytic theory views growth and development in terms of **psychosexual development** (see Table 8.1). According to psychoanalytic theory, each **stage** of development—oral, anal, and so on—is ushered in by biological changes. Each stage is characterized by particular behaviors and holds a distinct potential for the development of various traits and conflicts.

Table 8.1 shows three stage theories of development: Freud's stages of psychosexual development, Erik Erikson's stages of psychosocial development, and Jean Piaget's stages of intellectual development. The theories of Freud and Erikson primarily address the development of personality traits

Siblings Brothers and sisters.

Fetus The unborn child from the third month following conception through childbirth. (A Latin word meaning "bringing forth.")

Tetracycline An antibiotic drug.

Psychosexual development Sigmund Freud's characterization of development, in which the sexual implications of maturing biological structures are emphasized. See Chapter 9.

Stage A distinct period of life that is qualitatively different from other stages. Stages follow one another in an orderly sequence.

TABLE 8.1   An Outline of Three Major Stage Theories of Development

Approximate Age	Sigmund Freud: Psychosexual Development	Erik Erikson: Pyschosocial Development	Jean Piaget: Intellectual Development
Birth–1 year	Oral	Trust vs. mistrust	Sensorimotor
1–2 years	Anal	Autonomy vs. doubt	
2–3 years	Phallic	Initiative vs. guilt	Preoperational
3–4 years			
4–5 years			
5–6 years			
6–7 years	Latency	Industry vs. inferiority	Concrete operational
7–12 years			
Adolescence	Genital	Ego identity vs. role diffusion	Formal operational
Early adulthood		Intimacy vs. isolation	
Middle adulthood		Generativity vs. stagnation	
Later adulthood		Ego integrity vs. despair	

It should be noted that these stages are not totally age-bound; different people may enter different stages at somewhat different ages, and it is possible that many individuals will not reach the formal operational stage of intellectual development. Entering a new stage also does not mean that all characteristics of the earlier stage have been left behind; a person may cope with issues involving trust or mistrust of others for many years. Jean Piaget's stages of intellectual development are described in detail later in this chapter, while Freud and Erikson are discussed in greater depth in Chapter 9.

and interpersonal relationships. Piaget's theory addresses the ways in which we come to develop a cognitive representation of the world.

Each stage within a stage theory is a relatively **discrete** period of life that differs, in quality, from other periods. Stages follow one another in a certain sequence.

Not all developmental theories are stage theories. Social learning theorists view human development as a continuous process in which the effects of learning mount gradually, with no major sudden qualitative changes. In general, stage theorists tend to place more emphasis on nature and **maturation.** They point out that the environment, even when enriched, profits us little until we are mature enough, or **ready,** to develop in a certain direction. Social learning theorists place more emphasis on the role of the environment, or nurture.

Prenatal Development

The Chinese are nine months older than we are when they are the same age. Why? The Chinese date a person's age from the assumed time of conception rather than birth. The first nine months are eventful, indeed.

Discrete Separate and distinct.

Maturation Changes that result from heredity and minimal nutrition but do not appear to require learning or exercise. A gradual, orderly unfolding or developing of new structures or behaviors as a result of heredity. (From the Latin *maturatio,* meaning "ripening.")

Ready In developmental psychology, referring to a stage in the maturation of an organism when it becomes capable of engaging in a certain response.

For the nine months following conception, the single cell formed by the union of sperm and egg will multiply—becoming two, then four, then eight, and so on, forming tissues and organs and structures that gradually take the unmistakable shape of a human being. The nine months of **prenatal** development are divided into three **trimesters** of three months each.

The First Trimester

After fertilization the zygote divides repeatedly, even while it is undergoing the journey to the uterus with no source of outside nourishment. Three to four days are required to reach the uterus. Then this mass of dividing cells wanders about the uterus for another three to four days before beginning to become implanted in the uterine wall. Implantation requires another week or so. The period from conception to implantation is the **period of the ovum.**

Prenatal Prior to birth. (From the Latin *nasci*, meaning "to be born.")

Trimester A group of three months.

Period of the ovum Up to the first two weeks of life, before the developing "ovum" (now fertilized) has become securely implanted in the uterine wall.

FIGURE 8.1   Human Embryos and Fetuses Shown at about One-Third Smaller Than Their Actual Sizes. Prenatal development is cephalocaudal; that is, the head develops first and the rest of the body follows. Eyes and ears can be seen by the beginning of the fourth week. A "tail" disappears by the eighth week.

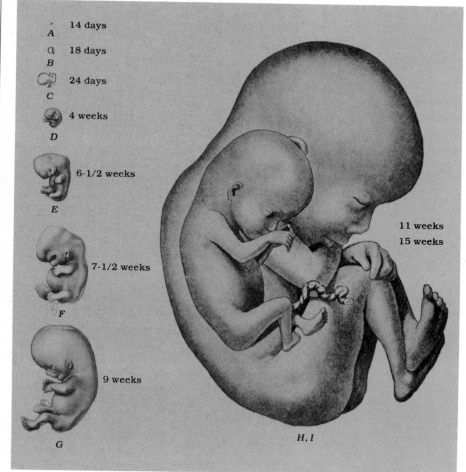

A   14 days
B   18 days
C   24 days
D   4 weeks
E   6-1/2 weeks
F   7-1/2 weeks
G   9 weeks

11 weeks
15 weeks

H, I

Embryonic period Approximately the third through the eighth weeks following conception. (From the Greek *embryon,* meaning "thing newly born.")

Androgens Male sex hormones. See Chapters 2 and 7.

Amniotic sac (am–knee–AH–tick). A sac within the uterus that contains the embryo or fetus.

Amniotic fluid Fluid within the amniotic sac that protects the embryo or fetus from being jarred or injured. Amniotic fluid is formed largely from the unborn child's urine.

The **embryonic period** lasts from implantation until about the eighth week of development. At about three weeks a primitive heart begins to beat and pump blood. It will continue to beat without rest every minute of every day for perhaps 80 or 90 years. "Arm buds" and "leg buds" begin to appear toward the end of the first month. By the end of the second month the limbs are elongating and facial features are forming—in an embryo about one inch long. During the second month the nervous system begins to transmit messages, and the kidneys begin to filter acid from the blood.

The fetus begins to turn and respond to external stimulation at about the ninth or tenth week. By the end of the third month fingers and toes appear fully formed. The eyes can be clearly distinguished, and the sex of the fetus can be determined visually.

Hormones and Prenatal Sexual Differentiation   At about five to six weeks, primitive sexual organs that cannot be distinguished have been formed. By about the seventh week, the genetic code (XY or XX) begins to assert itself, leading to changes in the internal and external sexual organs. If a Y chromosome is present, testes will form and begin to produce male sex hormones. These **androgens** lead to further development of internal and external male sexual organs.

In the absence of male sex hormones, the internal and external sexual organs will become female. Female sex hormones are not needed to induce these changes. If an embryo with an XY chromosomal structure were prevented from producing androgens, it would develop as a female—despite the genetic code.

The Amniotic Sac   The unborn child—embryo and fetus—develops within an **amniotic sac,** a protective environment in the mother's uterus. The sac is surrounded by a clear membrane and contains **amniotic fluid,** which sus-

A remarkable photograph of a living fetus within the mother's uterus.

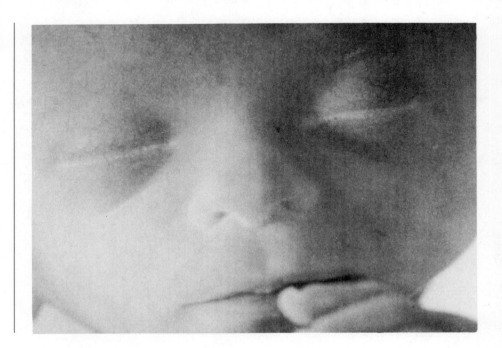

pends the developing child. Amniotic fluid serves as a "shock absorber," preventing the child from being damaged by the mother's movements.

The Placenta   The **placenta** is a mass of tissue that permits the fetus to exchange nutrients and wastes with the mother. The fetus is connected to the placenta by the **umbilical cord.** The mother is connected to the placenta by the system of blood vessels in the uterine wall.

The circulatory systems of mother and fetus do not mix. A membrane in the placenta permits only certain substances to pass through, such as oxygen and nutrients (from the mother), carbon dioxide (from the fetus), some microscopic disease organisms—including those that cause **syphilis** and **German measles**—and some drugs, including aspirin, narcotics, alcohol, and tranquilizers. (See Table 8.2).

Ultimately the placenta passes from the mother's body after delivery. For this reason it is also called the "afterbirth."

The Second Trimester

The second trimester is characterized by further maturation of fetal organ systems and dramatic gains in size. Between the ends of the first and second trimesters, the fetus advances from one *ounce* to two *pounds* in weight and grows three or four times in length, from about four to 14 inches.

During the second trimester, soft, downy hair grows above the eyes and on the scalp. The skin turns ruddy because of blood vessels that show through the surface. (During the third trimester, fatty layers will give the red a pinkish hue.)

Placenta (pluh–CENT–uh). A membrane that permits the exchange of nutrients and waste products between the mother and her developing child, but does not allow the maternal and fetal bloodstreams to mix. (From the Greek *plakous*, meaning "flat object.")

Umbilical cord A tube between the mother and her developing child through which nutrients and waste products are conducted. (From the Latin *umbilicalis*, meaning "situated at the navel.")

Syphilis A sexually transmitted disease.

German measles A disease that can cause nerve damage in unborn children.

TABLE 8.2   Possible Effects on the Fetus of Certain Agents during Pregnancy

Agent	Possible Effect
Heavy sedation during labor	Brain damage, asphyxiation
Alcohol	Mental retardation, addiction, undersize
Heroin	Addiction, undersize
Aspirin (large doses)	Respiratory problems, bleeding
Tetracycline	Yellow teeth, deformed bones
Streptomycin	Deafness
Rubella (German measles)	Mental retardation, nerve damage impairing vision and hearing
Paint fumes (substantial exposure)	Mental retardation
Vitamin A (large doses)	Cleft palate, eye damage
Vitamin D (large doses)	Mental retardation
Cigarettes	Undersize, premature delivery, fetal death
X rays	Malformation of organs
Thalidomide	Deformed or absent limbs
Diethylstilbestrol (DES) —a form of estrogen formerly used to help maintain pregnancy.	Cervical cancer

A variety of chemical and other agents have been found harmful to the fetus, or are strongly implicated in fetal damage. Pregnant women should consult their physicians about their diets, vitamin supplements, and use of any drugs—including drugs available without a prescription.

Fetal Movement In the middle of the fourth month, the mother usually detects the first fetal movements. She suddenly feels that the baby is "alive," although, of course, it has been alive since conception. By the end of the second trimester, the fetus moves its limbs so vigorously that the mother may complain of being kicked. It opens and shuts its eyes, sucks its thumb, alternates between periods of wakefulness and sleep, and perceives lights and sounds. It also hiccoughs and turns somersaults, all of which are clearly perceived by the mother—often at four A.M.

Amniocentesis As noted in Chapter 2, it is at about the fifteenth week of pregnancy that many women who are concerned that their fetuses may be harboring genetic abnormalities undergo **amniocentesis.** Fetal cells sloughed off into the amniotic fluid are removed by a syringe, and their chromosomal makeup is examined. The presence of Down's syndrome, Tay-Sachs disease, cystic fibrosis, and other disorders—plus the sex of the fetus—may be detected.

The Third Trimester

During the last three months the organ systems of the fetus continue to mature. The fetus gains nearly six pounds and grows in length by 50 percent. Newborn boys average about seven and one half pounds and newborn girls about seven pounds.

During the seventh month, the fetus normally turns upside down in the uterus so that delivery will be head-first. As the fetus grows it becomes somewhat cramped in the uterus, and movement is somewhat constricted. Many women become concerned that their fetuses are markedly less active during the ninth month than previously, but most of the time this change is not linked to any problems.

In recent years, awareness of the risks to the fetus posed by maternal use of pain-reducing medications during labor and delivery has increased. Since such drugs can depress the nervous system activity of the fetus, and the breathing of the newborn, women today tend to use them sparingly. However, so-called **regional anesthetics,** such as the **epidural**—in contrast to **general anesthetics**—have less of an effect on the child.

Infancy and Childhood

From the dark and private prenatal world, **neonates** are thrust into a room filled with light, noise, incomprehensible movements, and cold. Mucus and blood that may clog the respiratory tract are wiped away when the newborn's head appears. A suction device is usually applied to the nose and mouth to aid breathing. When the baby is completely out of the mother's body, the suctioning is usually repeated and the umbilical cord is clamped and cut. The stump of the cord will dry up and usually drop off the baby within several days. (Whether the baby winds up with an "inny" or an "outy" has nothing to do with the preferences or expertise of the physician.)

The baby is given silver nitrate or antibiotic eyedrops to prevent eye infections that could stem from passage through the vagina. The baby also receives a vitamin K injection since newborns do not manufacture this vitamin. Vitamin K helps prevent bleeding.

In response to complaints that hospitals are cold, impersonal places to have babies, some babies today are delivered in dimly lit hospital rooms that resemble bedrooms. Some even have bedroom furniture. Rather than whisking the baby away to a nursery after the umbilical cord is cut, the neonate is often placed on the mother's abdomen for a while and, in some instances, allowed to remain in the mother's room until discharge from the hospital. Some researchers argue that this early closeness promotes bonding, or **attachment,** between mother and child (e.g., Kennell and others, 1974; Ringler and others, 1975). They report that mothers who spent more time with their newborn infants showed greater attachment (spending more time with their infants, and kissing, soothing, and talking to them more frequently) at follow-ups of one month, one and two years. Critics note that adoptive parents and fathers also develop strong attachments to children, and that there may be no particular **critical period** for mother-infant bonding (Rutter, 1979).

Early closeness is often desired by the mother, and there are no reasons, other than hospital procedures, why mothers should not be allowed to spend as much time with their **infants** as they wish. Rather than being left to pace in the waiting room, fathers are now often present at the delivery and may help their wives through the process by guiding them in breathing and relaxation exercises.

Reflexes

If soon after your birth you had been held gently, face down in comfortably warm water, you would not have drowned. Instead of breathing in, you would have exhaled slowly through the mouth and engaged in swimming motions. This response is inborn, or innate, and just one of many **reflexes** with which children are born. Reflexes are stereotypical responses that are elicited by certain types of stimuli without involving higher brain functions.

Several months later, this swimming reflex, like many other reflexes, will have ceased to exist. But even at six to 12 months of age, children can learn readily how to swim. The transition from reflexive swimming to learned swimming is reasonably smooth.

A number of other reflexes are shown in Table 8.3. Such reflexes have survival value. Since newborn children do not "know" that it is necessary to eat in order to live or to reduce feelings of hunger, it is fortunate that they have **rooting** and sucking reflexes. Aside from those listed in the table, children have sneezing, coughing, yawning, blinking, and many other reflexes. (It is guaranteed that you will learn about the **sphincter** reflex if you dress in expensive new clothes and hold an undiapered neonate on your lap for a while.) Pediatricians largely learn about the adequacy of the newborn child's neural functioning by testing its reflexes.

As children develop, their muscles and neural functions mature, and they learn to coordinate sensory and motor activity. Many reflexes tend to drop out of their storehouse of responses, and other processes, like the elimination of wastes, come under voluntary control.

Perceptual Development

Newborn children spend up to 18 to 20 hours a day sleeping and do not have much opportunity to learn about the world. Still, they seem capable of perceiving the world reasonably well soon after birth (Haber & Hershenson, 1980).

Attachment (1) The tendency of infants or young organisms to remain close to other organisms, especially when fear-inducing stimuli are introduced. (2) A general description of the closeness of many parent-child relationships, involving sharing of strong, positive emotions.

Critical period A period in an organism's development when it is capable of certain types of learning.

Infant A very young organism, a baby. (From Latin roots meaning "not yet speaking.")

Reflex A simple unlearned response to a stimulus.

Rooting The turning of an infant's head toward a touch, as by the mother's nipple.

Sphincter A ringlike muscle that circles a bodily opening, such as the anus. An infant will exhibit the sphincter reflex (have a bowel movement) in response to intestinal pressure. (A Greek word meaning "the act of closing.")

TABLE 8.3   Some Major Reflexes Present at Birth

Reflex	Stimulus	Response	Meaning	Comments
Moro or Startle	Any loud noise, bumping crib, sudden loss of support, jerking blanket	Legs draw up, back arches, arms brought forward in hugging or embracing motion, symmetrical movements	Absence indicates immaturity, or edema of brain or brain damage. Presence indicates awareness of equilibrium.	Basic reflex lost 3–6 months after birth, can appear in modified form even in adult
Grasp or Palmar; Plantar	Any object placed on palms or soles	Hands grasp object with firm grip, then let go, toes curl downward	Absence indicates neural depression	No thumb involved, reflex lost by 12 months; infant can sustain own weight when lifted
Sucking (accompanies swallow reflex)	Touch lips	Sucking movements	Absence indicates immaturity, narcosis, brain injury, or retardation	Lost if not stimulated, generalized at first but becomes more efficient as times goes by
Rooting	Touch cheek	Head turns toward touch	Prepares infant for sucking	Inexperienced mothers will touch cheek to push it toward nipple, infants will root (i.e., turn the other way)
Withdrawal	Heat (bottle), pinprick (diaper)	Recoil from pain and cry	Absence indicates neural immaturity or damage	Serves as a protective device against harmful stimuli
Babinski	Any foot (sole) stimulation	Fanning (spreading) of toes	Persistence indicates lack of myelination or other malfunction	Leaves at 4–6 months; convenient for noting cerebration progress

Source: Turner and Helms (1983).

Visual Development   Neonates are able to discriminate between light and dark and to respond to color (Bornstein and others, 1976). Newborns can fixate on a light and within days can follow, or track, a moving light with their eyes (McGurk and others, 1977). After four months or so infants appear to focus as efficiently as adults do (Salapatek, 1975).

Response to Complex Visual Stimulation and the Human Face   Newborn children appear more intrigued by complex rather than by simple visual stim-

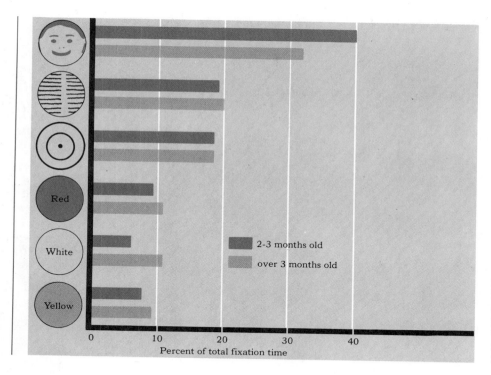

FIGURE 8.2 Infant Preferences for Visual Stimuli. Infants appear to prefer complex to simple visual stimuli, especially figures similar to the human face.

Legend in figure: 2-3 months old / over 3 months old

X-axis: Percent of total fixation time (0, 10, 20, 30, 40)

uli, as measured by **fixation time,** or the amount of time spent gazing at an object. However, fixation time decreases when stimuli become overly complex (Greenberg & Blue, 1977). In classical studies run by Fantz (1961), infants fixated longer on visual stimuli that resembled the human face, as compared to nonhuman but equally complex configurations, including "scrambled" facial features. It may be that even the perceptual system of the infant encourages social behavior.

Fear of Strangers   Although children seem intrigued by novel faces during the first few months of life, many children show fear of strangers at about six or eight months of age. Perhaps by this age they begin to realize that other people may not be so predictable as their parents.

Depth Perception   Infants also show depth perception by the time they are able to crawl about, as well as the good sense to avoid crawling off ledges and tabletops into open space. Note the setup (Figure 8.3) in the classic "visual cliff" experiment run by Walk and Gibson (1961). An infant crawls about freely above the portion of the glass with a checkerboard pattern immediately beneath, but hesitates to crawl out over the portion of the glass beneath which the checkerboard has been dropped by about four feet. Since the glass alone would support the infant, this is a "visual" rather than an actual cliff.

Eighty-one percent of the infants studied by Walk and Gibson refused to venture onto the visually unsupported glass surface, even when their mothers beckoned from the other side. Infants also seem distressed when placed on the visually unsupported surface at the age of 55 days (several months before they can crawl), as measured by increases in heart rate (Campos and others, 1970).

Fixation time The amount of time spent looking at a visual stimulus. A measure of interest in infants.

FIGURE 8.3   The Classic Visual Cliff Experiments. This young explorer has the good sense not to crawl out onto an apparently unsupported surface, even when Mother beckons from the other side. Rats, pups, kittens, and chicks also will not try to walk across to the other side. (So don't bother asking why the chicken crossed the visual cliff.)

Hearing   When children are born, hearing may be impaired by amniotic fluid and mucus in the ears. But hearing typically improves dramatically within a few hours or days. Newborn infants will turn their heads toward unusual sounds and suspend other activities. An old-fashioned way of testing hearing in the newborn is to see if they are startled by loud noises, or if loud noises produce increases in heart rate.

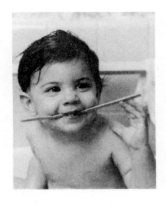

Smell   Neonates can discriminate distinct odors, such as those of onions and licorice. Infants breathe more rapidly and are more active when presented with powerful odors, and they will turn away from unpleasant odors as early as from 16 hours to five days of age (Rieser and others, 1976).

Taste   Shortly after birth infants show the ability to discriminate taste. They will suck liquid solutions of sugar and milk but grimace and refuse to suck salty or bitter solutions. Infants can clearly discriminate sweetness on the day following birth. The tongue pressure of one-day-old infants sucking on a nipple correlates with the amount of sugar in their liquid diet.

Sensitivity to Pain   Newborn infants appear rather insensitive to pain, which may reflect an adaptive response to the birth process. However, their sensitivity increases dramatically within a few days.

FIGURE 8.4 **The Development of Locomotion in Infants.** At birth, infants appear to be bundles of aimless "nervous energy." They have reflexive responses, but also engage in random muscular movements. Random movement is replaced by purposeful activity as they mature. Infants develop locomotion, or movement from place to place, in an orderly sequence of steps. Practice helps infants learn to coordinate muscles, but maturation is essential. During the first six months, cells in the motor and sensorimotor areas of the brain mature to allow activities like crawling and, later, walking. The times in the figure are approximate: An infant who is a bit behind may develop with no problems at all, and a slightly precocious infant will not necessarily become another Albert Einstein (or Rudolph Nureyev).

Attachment

When your newborn infant smiles at you, it may be for reasons other than your charm. Infants at this age smile reflexively when their cheeks are stroked, or in response to internal stimulation. But within a couple of months children show social smiling. They gratify their parents—especially their mothers—by appearing to be happy that they are there. Smiling at Mother, clinging to her, crying when she leaves—these and other behaviors are interpreted as signs of attachment.

Mother-infant attachment appears to thrive when the mother shows affection toward the child and is responsive to its needs and signals. Infants also seem to influence the process of attachment, however. Almost any infant activity that earns a response from an adult—like smiling, crying, moving, sneezing, and even soiling the diapers—may promote attachment (Bowlby, 1958).

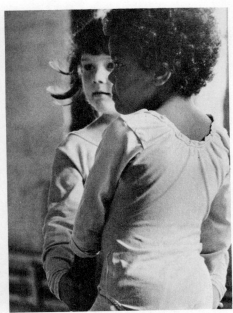

Conditioned reinforcer A stimulus that acquires reinforcement value through being paired with a reinforcer. See Chapter 5.

But *why* do children become attached to their parents, especially their mothers? Is attachment learned? Is it instinctive? Let us examine three views of attachment, and then examine the influences on attachment of day care and group child-rearing (as found in the *kibbutz).*

A Behavioral View of Attachment: Mothers as Reinforcers Early in this century, behaviorists argued that attachment behaviors were learned through laws of conditioning. It was usually Mother who fed the infant and tended to other primary needs. So it was understandable that the infant would learn to approach its mother to meet its needs. Presence of the mother led the infant to have good feelings, since Mother would reduce the baby's primary drives.

From this perspective, a child's mother becomes a **conditioned reinforcer.** Because of repeated association with primary reinforcers, the mother herself acquires reinforcing properties. The mother's attention and approval—even her presence—can come to shape the child's future behavior.

Some Notes on the Art of Being a Crybaby

Parents may be convinced that a major reason for infant crying is to let parents know they are around and in top voice—especially at about 3:00 A.M. Infants actually cry for a variety of reasons ranging from hunger to indigestion and fatigue. Careful attention to the type of cry and to the behavior associated with it may allow parents to learn to determine why their child is crying that way (Turner & Helms, 1979).

Here are some samples of infant crying:

• A loud, insistent cry associated with flexing and kicking the legs may indicate colicky pain (due to gas or other sources of distress in the digestive tract).

• A fretful cry associated with passing of air and green stool may indicate indigestion.

• A fretful cry associating with putting the fingers in the mouth and flexing and tensing the legs may signal hunger.

• A whining cry associated with listlessness and little movement may suggest illness and weakness.

• A shrill, sharp cry associated with a great deal of movement, or hardly any movement, may indicate injury.

The Harlows' View of Attachment: Mother as a Source of Contact Comfort Research begun by University of Wisconsin psychologist Harry F. Harlow in the 1950s threw doubt on the behaviorist view that attachment was learned and mechanical. Harlow had noted that infant rhesus monkeys raised without mothers or companions appeared to become attached to pieces of cloth in their cages. They clung to them as though they were security blankets. Could it be, Harlow wondered, that monkeys cling **instinctively** to soft and cuddly things? He conducted an ingenious series of experiments to investigate this question (Harlow, 1959).

In one study, Harlow placed rhesus monkey infants in cages with two substitute, or **surrogate,** mothers, as shown in Figure 8.5. One mother was made from wire mesh from which extended a baby bottle that fed the infant. The other surrogate mother may not look much more maternal to you, but "she" was made of soft, cuddly terry cloth. Infant monkeys, as you can see from the graph in Figure 8.5, spent most of their time clinging to the cloth mother. Very disloyal, you may think, since the wire mother "fed" them. From studies like these, Harlow concluded that monkeys—and perhaps humans— have a physiological need for **contact comfort.** It may be that the way to a monkey's heart is through its skin, not its stomach.

Instinctively Without learning; naturally.

Surrogate Substitute. (From the Latin *surrogare,* meaning "to elect in place of another.")

Contact comfort (1) The pleasure attained from physical contact with another. (2) A hypothesized primary drive to seek physical comfort from contact with another.

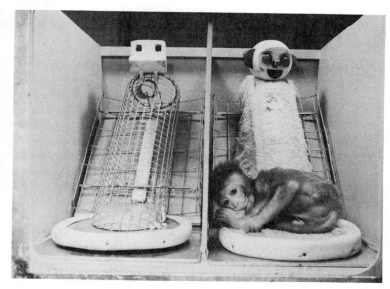

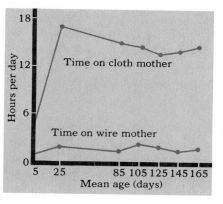

FIGURE 8.5 Attachment in Infant Monkeys. Although this rhesus monkey infant is fed by the "wire mother," it spends most of its time clinging to the soft, cuddly, "terrycloth mother." It knows where to get a meal, but contact comfort is apparently a more central determinant of attachment in infant monkeys (and infant humans?) than is the feeding process.

FIGURE 8.6 Security. With its terrycloth surrogate mother nearby, this infant rhesus monkey will apparently feel secure enough to explore the "bear monster" placed in its cage. But infants with only wire surrogate mothers, or with no mothers, remain cowering in a corner when the bear or other "monsters" are introduced.

Harlow and Zimmerman (1959) found that a surrogate mother made of terry cloth could also serve as a comforting base from which a rhesus infant could explore the environment. Toys like oversized wooden insects and stuffed bears were placed in cages with infants and their surrogate mothers (see Figure 8.6). When the monkeys were alone or had only wire surrogate mothers as companions, they cowered in fear so long as the "insect monster" or "bear monster" was present. But when the terry-cloth mothers were present, the infants clung to them for a while and then explored the intruding "monster." It may be that among humans, too, strong bonds of mother-infant attachment provide a secure base from which infants feel encouraged to express their curiosity motives.

The attachment of infant monkeys for their mothers does not seem to diminish if they are rejected. Harlow and Harlow (1966) exposed infant monkeys to different forms of "rejection" from their surrogate mothers, including being blown off by streams of compressed air and being catapulted across the cage by a spring. The infants waited until these dangers had apparently subsided and then returned to their mothers, clinging as tightly as before. It may also be that abusive human mothers will not alienate the affections of their infants.

One surrogate mother did discourage her infant from clinging—by being "coldhearted." Ice water was pumped through her, destroying the comfort of contact.

Imprinting: An Ethological View of Attachment   **Ethologists** have argued that for many animals attachment occurs during a critical period of life. In this period, young animals form an instinctive attachment to the first moving object they encounter. The unwritten rule seems to be, "If it moves, it must be mother." It is as if the image of the moving object becomes "imprinted"

Ethologist A scientist who studies behavior patterns of various species. (From the Greek *ethos*, meaning "character" or "disposition.")

FIGURE 8.7 Imprinting. Quite a following? Konrad Lorenz may not look like Mommy to you, but these goslings became attached to him because he was the first moving object they perceived and followed. This type of attachment process is referred to as imprinting.

upon the young animal. In fact, the process of forming an attachment in this manner is called **imprinting.**

Ethologist Konrad Lorenz (1952) became well known when pictures of a "family" of young geese following him were made public (see Figure 8.7). How did Lorenz acquire his "following"? He was present when the goslings underwent their critical period shortly after hatching, and he allowed them to follow him. The critical period for geese and many other animals seems bounded at one end by the age at which they first engage in locomotion and, at the other end, by the age at which they develop fear of strangers. The extent of the goslings' attachment was shown in various ways. They followed "Mommy" persistently, ran to Lorenz when frightened, honked with distress at his departure, and tried to overcome barriers placed between them and Lorenz (Sluckin, 1970). If you substitute crying for honking, it all sounds rather human.

If imprinting occurs with human children, it cannot follow the same mechanics that apply, say, to geese and ducks. Only 25 to 50 percent of children develop fear of strangers. When they do, it occurs at about six to eight months of age, *prior to* independent locomotion, or crawling, which usually occurs a month or two later.

But it is unlikely that children undergo imprinting. People have few, if any, instincts. In general, the higher the species, the greater the proportion of behavior that reflects learning rather than heredity. Human attachments can also develop prior to and long after the middle of the first year of life.

Imprinting A process occurring during a critical period in the development of an organism, in which that organism responds to a stimulus in a manner that will afterwards be difficult to modify.

Infancy and Childhood **309**

A Psychological Issue: Does Day Care Interfere with Mother-Child Bonds of Attachment?   Between seven and eight million American preschool children are now placed in supervised group settings known as day care. About half of today's American mothers spend the day on the job, and the ideals of the women's movement and increased financial pressure are likely to swell this number. So it is not surprising that we have become vitally concerned about the effects of day care on children—especially when many people fear that reducing the amount of time parents and children spend together may loosen the bonds of attachment.

Kagan and his colleagues (1976, 1980) compared the social, cognitive, and language development of children placed in day care with that of children who remained at home. The children were followed from the ages of three and one half months to 29 months.

Although day-care children were separated from their mothers for several hours each workday, the researchers found no measurable differences in mother-child bonds of attachment. They concluded that the quality of the mother-child relationship was more important than the quantity—that is, the number of hours spent together.

Two points are significant in this study. First, the children all came from intact homes, so it cannot be assumed that children whose parents are separated or widowed will do equally well in day care. Second, the day-care caretakers were all rated highly competent by the researchers. Parents considering day care should not hesitate to examine the credentials of those to whom they intend to entrust their children.

Growing Up in the Kibbutz: What Are the Effects of Raising Children in Groups on Parent-Child Attachment?   About three percent of the Israeli population live in collective farm settlements known as **kibbutzim.** In the kibbutz, children are raised in group settings from shortly after birth through adolescence (Bronfenbrenner, 1973). Children spend their first year in a nursery, then advance to a toddler's house. The same group of children remains together from infancy, and their bonds of attachment grow very strong.

Parents visit and play with their children frequently, but their primary care is entrusted to a child-rearing specialist, or **metapelet.** Because parents are not involved in training chores, this arrangement reduces early parent-child conflict. Despite the reduced parent-child contact, kibbutz life does not seem to impair parent-child bonds of attachment (Maccoby & Feldman, 1972). In fact, parent-child relations seem more cordial in the kibbutz. As noted by Rabkin and Rabkin (1974), group life also "shields the child from overprotective or domineering parents who might block his efforts to become independent." It may also be that the kibbutz experience encourages children to be more generous and cooperative (Shapira & Madsen, 1974).

The Effects of Social Deprivation

According to psychoanalyst Erik Erikson, a child's relationships during the first year of life are crucial. They determine whether the child will develop trust in people and the world, and come to perceive them as basically "good" and willing to meet his or her needs. The alternative is a basic sense of mistrust which may permanently hamper future relationships. Even when children's material needs are met, the development of social skills may be impaired if they do not receive adequate social stimulation. Children raised in institutions

Kibbutz (key–BOOTS). An Israeli collective farm. Plural: *kibbutzim,* pronounced key-boots-SEEM. (A Hebrew word.)

Metapelet (meh–TAP–eh–let). An Israeli child-rearing specialist. (A Hebrew word.)

(like orphanages) where they have not suffered in a material sense, but have received little social stimulation, show retarded social and intellectual development (Spitz & Wolff, 1946; Provence & Lipton, 1962).

Studies of children in orphanages are limited in that they are correlational. The factors that led to their placement in the institution, such as family disruption, may also have led to—or added to—their developmental problems. Ethical considerations prevent us from conducting experiments in which we randomly assign human infants to home life or institutions. However, experiments of this kind with rhesus monkeys show results that are consistent with those of the correlational studies with people.

Experiments with Infant Monkeys   As noted earlier, terry-cloth surrogate mothers provide infant monkeys with contact comfort and encourage them to explore the environment. But they do not promote normal social behavior. Harlow (1965) found that rhesus infants raised with terry-cloth mothers later avoided contact with other monkeys. They cowered and refused to respond to them. As adults, socially deprived rhesus males showed little interest in approaching sexually receptive females. Socially deprived rhesus females seemed equally unimpressed with any show of attention by adult males, even when they were in **estrus.** As noted in Chapter 7, if "motherless mothers" later had children of their own, they tended to ignore or abuse them (Ruppenthal and others, 1976).

There seems to be a link between the amount of time an infant rhesus monkey has been deprived and its capacity to recover from social deprivation. Monkeys raised without social stimulation for the first three months of life tend to adjust rapidly when placed in a community cage. But if they have been isolated for six months or more, they tend to sit clutching themselves and rocking back and forth in corners.

Overcoming Social Deprivation   Numerous efforts have been made to learn whether the damage social deprivation does to human and monkey infants can be overcome. When monkeys deprived for six months or more are placed with older monkeys, they tend to remain socially withdrawn and apathetic (Erwin and others, 1974). But Suomi and Harlow (1972) found that deprived monkeys placed with younger, three-to-four-month-old females for a couple of hours a day show greater likelihood of recovery. They may ignore the younger monkeys at first, even abuse them. But when the younger monkeys persist in their efforts to initiate social interaction with their deprived elders, many of the deprived monkeys begin to play with the youngsters within a few weeks. Many of them eventually expand their social contacts to rhesus monkeys of various ages and both sexes.

In an article in the *American Journal of Psychiatry*, Suomi, Harlow, and McKinney wrote of the young female monkeys who had eventually coaxed many deprived elders out of their asocial ways: "We are all aware of the existence of some therapists who seem inhuman. We find it refreshing to report the discovery of nonhumans who can be therapists" (Suomi and others, 1972, p. 932).

Six months of social deprivation seriously impairs the social development of rhesus monkeys, unless drastic "curative" measures are taken—such as using monkey therapists. And the success of this treatment is far from guaranteed. But Kagan and Klein (1973) report that human infants may be able to recover fully from 13 or 14 months of deprivation. The natives in an

Estrus The period during which many female mammals are capable of conceiving and are receptive to sexual advances by males.

FIGURE 8.8 "**Monkey Therapists.**" In the left photo, a three- to four-month-old rhesus monkey "therapist" tries to comfort a monkey who was raised in social isolation. The deprived monkey remains withdrawn. She clutches herself in a ball and rocks back and forth. The right photo was taken several weeks afterward and shows that deprived monkeys given young "therapists" can learn to play and adjust to community life. Is it possible that socially deprived people would profit from younger, rather than older, therapists?

isolated Guatemalan village believe that fresh air and sunshine will make children ill. Children are thus kept in windowless huts until they can walk, and are played with infrequently. The children behave apathetically during their isolation and are physically and socially retarded when they do start to walk. However, by the age of three they act as well coordinated as other children. By the age of 10 they show no social or intellectual deficits when compared with American children of the same age (Kagan, 1972).

The Skeels and Dye Study   A classic experiment with retarded children in an orphanage provided dramatic evidence of the ability of children to recover from deprivation (Skeels & Dye, 1939). A group of retarded 19-month-old children considered unlikely candidates for adoption was placed in the care of mildly retarded, institutionalized older girls. The girls spent a great deal of time playing with, talking to, and generally mothering them. When the children were able to walk they were given stimulating toys and an enriched nursery school experience. Children who remained in the orphanage continued to receive relatively little social stimulation.

Four years after being placed with the surrogate mothers, the "retarded" children showed an average gain of 32 IQ points on standardized intelligence tests. Children remaining in the orphanage showed an average *decrease* of 21 points. Later Skeels (1966) reported that most children placed with surrogate mothers had been graduated from high school and about one-third had attended college. These children were generally well-adjusted. Most had married and were raising children who showed no intellectual or social deficits. But most children left in the orphanage had not advanced beyond grammar school, and many had remained in some type of institutional setting.

Identification and Sex Typing

Like mother like daughter, like father like son—at least often, if not always. Why is it that little boys (often) grow up to behave according to the cultural stereotypes of what it means to be male? That little girls (often) grow up to behave like female stereotypes? Let us examine various views of **identification** and **sex typing**.

Biological Views   As noted in Chapters 2 and 7, sex hormones appear to some degree to masculinize or feminize the brain as well as to exert organizing and activating effects on sexual behavior. Hormonal influences at certain critical periods—particularly during prenatal development—may create predispositions toward developing a number of the **stereotypical** masculine or feminine traits discussed in Chapter 13. However, there are no reliable correlations between such traits and levels of sex hormones among adults.

Psychoanalytic Views   According to Sigmund Freud, sex typing is just one aspect of identification. That is, children become like their same-sex parents and other important adults by internalizing, or bringing inward, what they perceive as their personality traits and behavior patterns. Part of this process is continuous. Children gradually learn about and internalize the values and morals of their parents and others. But to Freud, sex typing was largely influenced by sexual feelings, especially during the phallic stage, as we shall see in Chapter 9.

Freud wrote that both boys and girls identified with their mothers during the first year of life because mothers usually held primary responsibility for gratifying infants' needs. But during the phallic stage, at about age five or six, sex typing (or, to Freud, sexual identification) was prompted by a combination of love for the parent of the same sex and fear of consequences of *not* becom-

Identification (1) In psychoanalytic theory, the unconscious assumption of the behavior and values of another person. (2) In social learning theory, broad imitation of another person's behavior.

Sex-typing The process by which children acquire the behavior patterns stereotypical of people of their sex.

Stereotypical Conventional, fixed, traditional.

Social learning theorists argue that sex typing involves processes of identification and socialization. Most children strive to broadly imitate the behavior of the same-sex parent. Parents and other adults provide children with messages about the types of activities that are appropriate for them, and reinforce them for engaging in them. Boys are usually socialized into aggressive, competitive roles, while girls are typically socialized into dependent, caretaking roles.

ing like the same-sex parent. However, it seems that sex typing occurs earlier than Freud believed. Boys and girls show a firm sense of being male or female by about 18 to 36 months of age (Money & Ehrhardt, 1972; Money, 1977).

Social Learning Views   Social learning theorists tend to view identification as a broad, continuous learning process in which children are influenced by rewards and punishments to imitate their parents, particularly the parent of the same sex (Bronfenbrenner, 1960; Kagan, 1958). In identification one not only imitates a certain behavior pattern, but also tries to become broadly like the model.

Whom are children likely to imitate? Probably the people who seem to be competent and exercise efficient control of resources (like food, pets, and toys) that are of value to them (Bandura and others, 1963). In this way children may identify with both parents up to a point. But children are also likely to learn that they will be more effective at imitating the behavior of people who are similar to them. A little boy, for instance, may come to feel that he would have difficulty giving birth to babies before he fully understands the mechanics of the problem. A girl will learn at an early age that only women can carry and bear children.

Children are also influenced by **socialization.** Others provide messages about how we are expected to behave. They reward us for behavior they consider appropriate, and punish (or fail to reinforce) us for behavior they consider inappropriate. Girls are given dolls while they still sleep in cribs. They are encouraged to rehearse care-taking behaviors as preparation for tra-

---

Noneducational Television Can Be Educational, Indeed, *or*, "I'm Popeye, the Sailor Woman"?

What do Popeye, the Pink Panther, and Bugs Bunny have in common—aside from fat bank accounts? They're all *male*. In a study of children's TV shows, Sternglanz and Serbin (1974) found that several shows have all-male casts and that among shows with "coed" heroes, males outnumber females two to one.

Children who watch TV are learning more than how to rescue Olive Oyls and trap roadrunners. Female TV characters are portrayed as less active than males and more likely to follow directions of others (especially males). Females' activities have less impact than those of males. Male characters are more likely to conceive and carry out plans, be aggressive, and just have fun.

Commercials also support sex-role stereotypes. In their study of 199 TV commercials, McArthur and Resko (1975) found that 70 percent of the male characters were portrayed as authorities on their products, as compared with 14 percent of females. Male figures were significantly more likely to back claims with scientific and other arguments. Men were more often shown as capable problem-solvers, while women more frequently acted ignorant, passive, and flustered. The woman's place was still in the home—

only 13 percent of male product users were shown using home products, as compared to one-third of the females.

Walstedt, Geis, and Brown (1980) provided disconcerting experimental evidence that TV portrayals of sex-role stereotypes affect viewers. They showed one group of women four commercials in which women were portrayed as unconfident and dependent. In one example an actress was flustered when she learned that her husband preferred a product other than the one she used, and she promised to act according to his preferences in the future. Another group of women were shown commercials identical in content and dialogue, but women acted in the dominant, authoritative roles. After being shown these commercials, both groups of women were rated for self-confidence and independence while delivering an impromptu speech and rating cartoons. Women shown commercials in which actresses played stereotypical feminine roles showed significantly less self-confidence and independence.

Television apparently educates children in ways we may not have expected. It seems to endorse and perpetuate sex-role stereotypes.

ditional feminine adult roles. Boys are given athletic equipment, cars, and guns, and encouraged to compete aggressively. Boys are handled more frequently than girls, while girls are spoken to more often.

Schools also spur the socialization process. Even in a nursery school which proclaimed a commitment to breaking down traditional **sex-role** stereotypes, girls were still complimented on their clothing more frequently than boys were, particularly when they wore dresses (Joffee, 1971). In high school, girls are more likely to be assigned courses in homemaking, secretarial work, and dancing. Boys are more frequently guided into shop courses and pre-professional studies (Naffziger & Naffziger, 1974).

Cognitive Views   From a cognitive perspective, identification and sex typing stem in some degree from the child's sense of **gender identity,** or the acquired self-concept of being male or being female. The child is usually motivated to live up to sex-role stereotypes and imitate the behavior of adult role models of the same gender. Children consider themselves masculine or feminine according to how well their perceptions of their own personality traits fit the masculine and feminine stereotypes (Kagan, 1964).

Children apparently learn which behaviors are considered masculine and feminine by observing the relative frequencies with which adult men and women perform them. In one experiment, eight- and nine-year-old boys and girls observed adult males express random preferences for certain members of 16 pairs of items, such as for a banana over an apple, or a toy cow over a toy horse (Perry & Bussey, 1979). Then the children showed "their own" preferences. Boys selected an average of 14 of the 16 items chosen by adult males, while girls chose only three of 16 of these items. The children were apparently motivated to make choices that they thought were appropriate for their genders. A second experiment by Perry and Bussey (1979) suggests that children imitate same-sex adults only when they believe that the adult is behaving appropriately for his or her gender.

Cognitive Development

Did you know that if you remove a teddy bear from the sight of a three-month-old child it no longer exists? (As far as the infant is concerned: "Out of sight, out of existence.") Did you know that if you ask a four-year-old child, "Why is the sky blue?" he or she may answer, "Because Mommy painted it," or "Because blue's my favorite color."

If these ways of looking at the world do not impress you as logical, your impression is quite correct. Cognitive changes that occur during adolescence make it difficult for us to remember our thought processes during childhood. Cognitive functioning develops over a number of years, and children have many charming but illogical ideas about the world. Swiss psychologist Jean Piaget (1896-1980) has contributed significantly to our understanding of children's cognitive development.

Jean Piaget

During his early 20s, Jean Piaget obtained a job at the Binet Institute in Paris. His initial task was to develop a standardized version of the Binet intelligence test in French. In so doing, he questioned many children with po-

TABLE 8.4   Piaget's Stages of Cognitive Development

Stage	Approximate Age	Description
Sensorimotor	Birth to 2 years	Behavior suggests child lacks language and does not use symbols, or mental representations of objects in environment. Simple responding to the environment (reflexes) ends, and intentional behavior—such as making interesting sights last—begins. Child learns to seek hidden object (object permanence) and begins to acquire basics of language.
Preoperational	2 to 7 years	Child begins to represent world mentally, but thought is egocentric. Child does not focus on two aspects of situation at once (lack of conservation). Child shows animism, artificialism, immanent justice.
Concrete operational	7 to 12 years	Child shows conservation concepts, can adopt viewpoint of others, can classify objects in series (for example, from shortest to longest), and shows comprehension of basic relational concepts (such as one object being larger or heavier than another).
Formal operational	12 years and above	Mature, adult thought emerges. Thinking seems characterized by deductive logic, consideration of various possibilities before attempting to solve a problem (mental trial and error), abstract thought (for instance, philosophical consideration of moral principles), and forming and testing of hypotheses.

tential items and became intrigued by their *incorrect* answers. Another investigator might have shrugged them off and forgotten them. Young Piaget realized that there were methods to his children's madness. The wrong answers seemed to reflect consistent, if illogical, cognitive processes.

Piaget hypothesized that children's cognitive processes develop in an orderly sequence (1963). While some children may be more advanced than others at particular ages, the developmental sequence does not vary. Piaget identified four major stages of cognitive development (see Table 8.4): *sensorimotor, preoperational, concrete operational,* and *formal operational.* We shall return to these stages in detail in the following pages.

Piaget's View of Human Nature   Piaget regarded maturing children as budding scientists who actively intend to learn about and take intellectual charge of their worlds. In the Piagetian view, children who squish their food and laugh enthusiastically are often acting as miniature physicists. In addition to enjoying earning a response from parents, they are studying the texture and consistency of their food. (Parents, of course, often prefer that their children would practice these experiments in the laboratory, not the dining room.)

Piaget's view of human nature differs markedly from formal psychoanalytic thought, which views children and adults as largely irrational and at the mercy of instinctive impulses. It also varies markedly from the early behaviorist view that people react to environmental stimuli rather than intend to interpret the world. Piaget saw people are actors, not reactors—as purposefully forming cognitive representations of and seeking to manipulate the world.

Piaget's View of Intelligence: Assimilation and Accommodation   Piaget described human thought or intelligence in terms of *assimilation* and *accom-*

Jean Piaget (1896–1980).

modation. **Assimilation** is responding to a new stimulus through a reflex or old habit. Infants, for example, usually try to place new objects in their mouths to suck, feel, or explore them. Piaget would say that the child is assimilating a new toy to the sucking **schema.** A schema is a way of looking at, or mentally representing, the world.

Accommodation is the creation of new ways of looking at the world. Children (and adults) accommodate to objects and situations that cannot be integrated into existing schemata. The ability to accommodate to novel stimulation advances as a result of both maturation and learning, or experience.

Newborn children merely assimilate environmental stimulation according to reflexive schemata. Reflexive behavior, to Piaget, is not characteristic of intelligence. True intelligence involves dealing with the world through a smooth, fluid balancing of the processes of assimilation and accommodation. As the child matures and gains experience, assimilation takes on the character of play. Accommodation becomes more sophisticated in that the child comes to imitate the ways in which other people cope with novel events (Cowan, 1978). Let us now return to the stages of cognitive development.

Piaget's Stages of Cognitive Development

As we explore many of the milestones of cognitive development, we shall integrate them with the four stages of development hypothesized by Jean Piaget. Remember that statements about cognitive development are always *inferred* from children's observable behavior. In this sense, cognitive development remains theoretical. But the concept does provide us with a meaningful way of interpreting and predicting the behaviors of children which appear to reflect intellectual processes.

The Sensorimotor Stage The newborn infant is capable only of assimilating novel stimulation to existing reflexes, such as the rooting and sucking reflexes. But by the time an infant has reached the age of one month, it will already show purposeful behavior by repeating behavior patterns that are pleasurable, such as sucking its hand. Within the first few months the infant begins to coordinate vision with grasping, so that it simultaneously looks at what it is holding or touching.

A three- or four-month-old infant may become fascinated by its own hands and legs. It may become absorbed in watching itself open and close its fists. The infant becomes increasingly interested in acting upon the environment to make interesting results (such as the sound of a rattle) last. Behavior becomes increasingly intentional, purposeful. Between four and eight months of age the infant explores cause-and-effect relationships, such as the thump that can be made by tossing an object, or the way kicking can cause a hanging toy to bounce.

Prior to eight months or so, out of sight is literally out of mind. Objects are not yet mentally represented. For this reason a child will make no effort to search for an object that has been removed or placed behind a screen. But after nine months or so, as you can see in Figure 8.9, infants realize that objects removed from sight still exist and attempt to find them. In this way they show what is known as **object permanency.**

During the second year of life, children begin to show interest in how things are constructed. It may be for this reason that they persistently touch and finger their parents' and their own faces. Toward the end of the second

Assimilation According to Piaget, the inclusion of a new event into an existing schema.

Schema According to Piaget, a hypothetical mental structure that permits the classification and organization of new information. New information may be "integrated" into existing *schemata* (the plural of *schema.*)

Accommodation According to Piaget, the modification of schemata so that information that is inconsistent with existing schemata can be integrated or understood.

Object permanency Recognition that objects removed from sight still exist, as demonstrated in young children by continued pursuit.

FIGURE 8.9 Object Permanency. To the infant at top, who is in the early part of the sensorimotor stage, out of sight is truly out of mind. Once a sheet of paper is placed between the infant and the toy elephant, the infant loses all interest in it. From evidence of this sort, Piaget concluded that the toy is not mentally represented. The bottom series of photos shows a child in a later part of the sensorimotor stage. This child does mentally represent objects, and pushes through a towel to reach an object that has been screened from sight.

Sensorimotor stage The first of Piaget's stages of cognitive development, characterized by coordination of sensory information and motor activity, early exploration of the environment, and lack of language.

Preoperational stage The second of Piaget's stages, characterized by illogical usage of words and symbols, spotty logic, and egocentrism.

year, children begin to engage in mental trial and error before they try out overt behavior. For instance, when they look for an object you have removed, they will no longer begin their search in the last place it was seen. Rather, they may follow you, assuming that you are carrying the object even though it is not visible. It is as though they are anticipating failure in searching for the object in the place where it was most recently seen.

Since the first stage of development is dominated by learning to coordinate perception of the self and of the environment with motor (muscular) activity, Piaget termed it the **sensorimotor stage.** The sensorimotor stage comes to a close at about the age of two, with the acquisition of the basics of language.

The Preoperational Stage The **preoperational stage** is characterized by children's early usage of words and symbols to represent objects and the relationships among them. But be warned—any resemblance between the logic of children between the ages of two to seven and your own very often appears purely coincidental. Children may use the same words as adults do, but this does not mean that their views of the world are similar to adults' (Piaget, 1971).

For one thing, preoperational children are decidedly **egocentric.** They cannot understand that other people do not see things as they do. They often perceive the world as a stage that has been erected to meet their own needs or for their own amusement. For instance, when asked "Why does the sun shine?" they may respond, "To keep me warm." Preoperational children also show **animism.** That is, they tend to attribute life and intentions to inanimate objects, such as the sun and the moon. They also show **artificialism,** the belief that environmental features like rain and thunder were designed and constructed by people. Examples of egocentrism, animism, and artificialism are shown in Table 8.5.

To gain further insight into preoperational thinking, first consider these two problems: Imagine that you pour water from a low wide glass into a tall, thin glass. Now, does the tall, thin glass contain more than, less than, or the same amount of water as was in the low, wide glass? I won't keep you in suspense. If you said the same (with possible minor exceptions for spilling a drop and evaporation), you were correct. Now that you're rolling, here is the other problem. If you flatten a ball of clay into a pancake, do you wind up with more, less, or the same amount of clay? If you said the same, you are correct once more. To arrive at the correct answers to these questions, you must understand the law of **conservation.** This law holds that properties of substances like their weight and mass remain the same—that is, weight and mass are *conserved*—even if you change their shape or arrangement.

Conservation requires the ability to think about, or **center** on, two aspects of a situation at once, such as height and width. Conserving the weight or mass of a substance requires recognition that a change in one dimension

Egocentric According to Piaget, assuming that others view the world as does oneself.

Animism The belief that inanimate objects move because of will or spirit. (From the Latin *animas*, meaning "breath" or "soul.")

Artificialism The belief that natural objects have been created by human beings.

Conservation According to Piaget, recognition that certain properties of substances remain constant even though their appearance may change. For example, the weight and mass of a clay ball are "conserved" even if it is flattened into a pancake.

Center According to Piaget, to focus one's attention.

TABLE 8.5   Examples of Preoperational Thought

Sample Questions	Typical Answers
Egocentrism	
Why does the sun shine?	To keep me warm.
Why is there snow?	For me to play in.
Why is grass green?	Because that's my favorite color.
What are TV sets for?	To watch my favorite shows and cartoons.
Animism	
Why do trees have leaves?	To keep them warm.
Why do stars twinkle?	Because they're happy and cheerful.
Why does the sun move in the sky?	To follow children and hear what they say.
Where do boats go at night?	They sleep like we do.
Artificialism	
What causes rain?	Someone emptying a watering can.
What is the sky blue?	It has been painted.
What is the wind?	A man blowing.
What causes thunder?	A man grumbling.

Source: Turner and Helms (1983).

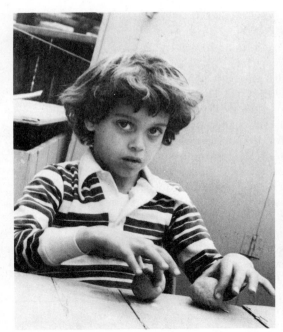

FIGURE 8.10 Conservation of Mass. This young lady has rolled two clay balls. In the photo at the left, she agrees that both have the same amount (or mass) of clay. In the photo at the right, she (gleefully) flattens one clay ball. Now, when asked which piece has more clay, she says that the flattened one does. Why? She is looking down on the clay and centering on the greater width of the flattened piece. Since she is in the preoperational stage, she does not recognize that, despite the change in shape, the mass of the clay has been conserved. Does she think that any clay was taken away from the "smaller" piece, or that any was added to the "larger" piece? No—ask her. Does this make any difference. Not to a preoperational child. She sees no inconsistency at all.

can compensate for a change in another. But the girl in Figure 8.10, who is in the preoperational stage, focuses only on *one dimension at a time.* When she is first presented with the two balls of clay, shown at the left, she agrees that they have the same amount of clay. Then she flattens one ball into a pancake, as shown at the right. Asked which piece now has more clay, she points to the pancake. Why? When she looks down on both pieces of clay, the pancake is wider. The preoperational child focuses on the most apparent dimension of the situation only—in this case, the greater width of the flattened piece of clay. She does not recognize that the decrease in height compensates for the gain in width. By the way, if you ask her whether any clay has been added or taken away in the flattening process, she will readily reply no. But if you then repeat the question as to which piece has *more* clay, she will again point to the pancake.

If all this sounds rather illogical, that is because it is illogical—or, to be precise, preoperational. But if you have any doubts concerning its accuracy, borrow a brilliant four- or five-year-old and try the clay experiment for yourself.

After you have tried the experiment with the clay, try the following. Make two rows with five pennies each. In the first row, place the pennies about half an inch apart. In the second row, place the pennies two to three inches apart. Ask a four- to five-year-old child which row has more pennies. What do you predict the child will answer? Why?

Piaget (1962) found that the moral judgment of preoperational children is usually **objective.** In judging how guilty people are for their misdeeds, preoperational children center on the amount of damage done. Older children and adults, by contrast, usually focus on the intentions or motives of the wrongdoer.

To demonstrate objective moral judgements, Piaget would tell children stories about people and ask them which character was naughtier, and why. Barry, for instance, is helping his mother set the table when he accidentally bangs the dining room door into a tray and breaks nine cups and six plates. Harmon breaks three cups as he sneaks into a kitchen cabinet to find forbidden cookies. Who is naughtier, Barry or Harmon? The typical four-year-old will say that Barry is naughtier. Why? He broke more china.

The Stage of Concrete Operations   By about the age of seven, the typical child is entering the stage of **concrete operations.** In this stage, which lasts until about the age of 12, children show the beginnings of the capacity for adult logic. However, their logical thought, or operations, generally involve tangible objects rather than abstract ideas. Concrete operational children can center simultaneously on two dimensions or aspects of a problem. This attainment has implications for moral judgments, conservation, and other intellectual undertakings.

Children now become **subjective** in their moral judgments. They center on the motives of wrongdoers as well as the amount of damage done when assigning guilt. Concrete operational children judge Harmon more harshly than Barry, since Barry was trying to help his mother when he broke the plates and cups.

Concrete operational children show understanding of the laws of conservation. The girl in Figure 8.10, now a few years older, would say that the flattened ball still has the same amount of clay. If asked why, she might reply, "Because you can roll it up again like the other one." An answer to this effect also suggests awareness of the concept of **reversibility**—recognition that many processes can be reversed or undone, so that things can be restored to their previous condition. Centering simultaneously on the height and the width of the clay, she recognizes that the loss in height compensates for the gain in width.

Concrete operational children can conserve *number* as well as weight and mass. They recognize that there is the same number of pennies in each of the rows described earlier, even though one row may be spread out to look longer than the other.

Children in this stage are less egocentric. They acquire the abilities to take on the roles of others and view the world, and themselves, from other peoples' perspectives. They recognize that people see things in different ways because of different situations and different sets of values.

During the concrete operational stage, children's own sets of values begin to emerge and acquire stability. Children come to understand that feelings of love between them and their parents can endure even when someone feels angry or disappointed at the moment.

The Stage of Formal Operations   The stage of **formal operations** is the final stage in Piaget's scheme. It begins at about the time of **puberty,** and is the stage of cognitive maturity. Not all children enter this stage at about the time of puberty, and some people never reach it.

Objective According to Piaget, objective moral judgments focus, or center, on the amount of damage done rather than on the motives of the actor.

Concrete operations Piaget's third stage, characterized by logical thought concerning tangible objects, conservation, and subjective morality.

Subjective According to Piaget, subjective moral judgments center on the motives of the perpetrator.

Reversibility According to Piaget, recognition that processes can be undone, that things can be made as they were.

Formal operations Piaget's fourth stage, characterized by abstract logical thought—deduction from principles.

Puberty The period of physical development during which changes occur that lead to reproductive capacity.

Syllogism (SILL–oh–jism). A form of reasoning in which a conclusion is drawn from two statements or premises. (From the Greek *syn-*, meaning "together," and *logizes-thai*, meaning "to reason.")

Formal operational children (and adults) think abstractly. They become capable of solving geometric problems about circles and squares without reference to what the circles and squares may represent in the real world. Children derive rules for behavior from general principles and can focus, or center, on many aspects of a situation at once in arriving at judgments and solving problems.

In a sense, it is during the stage of formal operations that people tend to emerge as theoretical scientists—even though they may see themselves as having little or no interest in science. As Cowan notes, it is in this stage that children "discover the world of the hypothetical" (1978, p. 249). They become aware that situations can have many different outcomes, and they can think ahead, systematically "trying out" different possibilities. Children—adolescents by now—also conduct "experiments" to determine whether their hypotheses are correct. These experiments are not carried out in the laboratory. Rather, adolescents may experiment with different tones of voice, ways of carrying themselves, and ways of treating others to see which sorts of behavior are most effective for them.

Children in this stage can reason deductively, or draw conclusions about specific objects or people once they have been classified accurately. Consider this **syllogism:** "All men are mortal. Socrates is a man. Therefore Socrates is mortal." Formal operational children can follow this logic in which a statement is made about a class or group of objects ("All *men* are mortal"). Then a particular object or event (in this case, Socrates) is assigned to that class—that is, *"Socrates* is a man." Finally, it is concluded, or deduced, that what is true for the class (men) is also true for the particular object or event (Socrates)—that is, "Socrates is mortal."

Adolescents can be somewhat proud of their new logical abilities. A new sort of egocentrism can develop in which adolescents emotionally press for acceptance of their logic without recognition of the exceptions, or practical problems, that are often considered by adults. Consider this example. "It is wrong to hurt people. Industry A occasionally hurts people (perhaps through pollution or economic pressures). Therefore, Industry A must be severely punished or dismantled." This thinking is not illogical. However, by impatiently pressing for immediate major changes or severe penalties, it may not fully consider various practical problems, such as thousands of resultant layoffs.

College students are sometimes insulted by what may seem an implication that they reached their intellectual height by the age of 12 or so. But this is a misreading of Piaget's intentions. Piaget meant that we have by and large developed the basic intellectual tools to deal with life's problems and enhance our lives by about this age. Knowledge will still be acquired, experience will still build upon experience, and our emotional responses will still undergo changes. What was very pressing at age 12 or 15 may seem less so later on—and what was unimportant then may gain value in our eyes.

Evaluation of Piaget's Views on Cognitive Development Piaget is widely applauded at the descriptive level. Few psychologists disagree, for example, with Piaget's observations concerning the development of concepts like object permanency and conservation. But some psychologists argue that Piaget placed too much emphasis on the role of maturation in the development of these concepts. They suggest that attainment of these concepts can be accelerated through training (e.g., Siegler & Liebert, 1972; Miller and others, 1975).

Other psychologists take issue with the view that people actively strive to make sense of the environment. They argue that Piaget's descriptions of behavior do not show "how much" of a child's behavior is reactive to the environment and how much acts upon the environment. Behaviorists, as noted earlier, tend to see behavior as more reactive.

Still other psychologists argue that we cannot observe or directly measure a schema, or a mental event of any sort. They believe it unscientific to use concepts that cannot be directly tied to observable behavior. However, Piaget's supporters point out that schemata like object permanency are always defined in terms of what children say and do (such as seeking and finding a hidden object), and that theories may be allowed to use some concepts which are presumed to underlie observable behavior.

It is clear that Piaget's insights into children's behavior have profoundly influenced developmental psychology. The sheer number of experiments that have been undertaken to *disprove* certain of his views serves as testimony to this fact.

Kohlberg's Levels and Stages of Moral Development

Lawrence Kohlberg of Harvard University has contributed to our understanding of moral development among children and adults—one aspect of cognitive development. Before we formally discuss Kohlberg's views, read the following tale used by Kohlberg (1969) in much of his research, and answer the questions below.

> In Europe a woman was near death from a special kind of cancer. There was one drug that the doctors thought might save her. It was a form of radium that a druggist in the same town had recently discovered. The drug was expensive to make, but the druggist was charging 10 times what the drug cost him to make. He paid $200 for the radium and charged $2,000 for a small dose of the drug. The sick woman's husband, Heinz, went to everyone he knew to borrow the money, but he could only get together about $1,000 which was half of what it cost. He told the druggist that his wife was dying and asked him to sell it cheaper or let him pay later. But the druggist said: "No, I discovered the drug and I'm going to make money from it." So Heinz got desperate and broke into the man's store to steal the drug for his wife.

What do you think? Should Heinz have tried to steal the drug? Was he right or wrong? As you can see from Table 8.6, the issue is more complicated than a simple yes or no. Respondents offer many reasons for saying yes or no, and Kohlberg believes that these responses can be classified according to the level and stage of moral development they suggest.

According to Kohlberg, there are three levels of moral development and two stages within each level.

The Preconventional Level In the **preconventional level,** which applies to most children through about the age of nine, children base their moral judgments on the consequences of their behavior. For instance, stage 1 is oriented toward obedience and punishment. Good behavior is seen as that which involves obedience and allows one to avoid punishment.

In stage 2, good behavior is that which will allow people to satisfy their own needs and, sometimes, the needs of others. (Heinz's wife needs the drug; therefore, stealing the drug—the only way of attaining it—is not wrong.)

Preconventional level According to Kohlberg, a period during which moral judgments are based largely on expectation of rewards or punishments.

TABLE 8.6   Kohlberg's Levels and Stages of Moral Development

Levels	Stages	Illustrative Responses to Story of Heinz Stealing the Drug
Level I: Preconventional level	*Stage 1:* Obedience and punishment orientation.	It isn't really bad to take it—he did ask to pay for it first. He wouldn't do any other damage or take anything else, and the drug he'd take is only worth $200; he's not really taking a $2,000 drug.
	Stage 2: Naively egoistic orientation.	Heinz isn't really doing any harm to the druggist, and he can always pay him back. If he doesn't want to lose his wife, he should take the drug because it's the only thing that will work.
Level II: Conventional level	*Stage 3:* "Good-boy orientation."	Stealing is bad, but this is a bad situation. Heinz isn't doing wrong in trying to save his wife, he has no choice but to take the drug. He is only doing something that is natural for a good husband to do. You can't blame him for doing something out of love for his wife. You'd blame him if he didn't love his wife enough to save her.
	Stage 4: Respect for authority and social order. Orientation to "doing duty" and to showing respect for authority.	The druggist is leading a wrong kind of life if he just lets somebody die like that, so it's Heinz's duty to save her. But Heinz can't just go around breaking laws and let it go at that—he must pay the druggist back and he must take his punishment for stealing.
Level III: Postconventional level	*Stage 5:* Contractual legalistic orientation.	Before you say stealing is wrong, you've got to really think about this whole situation. Of course, the laws are quite clear about breaking into a store. And, even worse, Heinz would know there were no legal grounds for his actions. Yet, I can see why it would be reasonable for anybody in this situation to steal the drug.
	Stage 6: Conscience or principled orientation.	Where the choice must be made between disobeying a law and saving a human life, the higher principle of preserving life makes it morally right—not just understandable—to steal the drug.

Source: J. R. Rest. The Hierarchical Nature of Moral Judgment: The Study of Patterns of Comprehension and Preference with Moral Stages, *Journal of Personality* 41, no. 1 (1974), pp. 92–93. Copyright © 1974, by Duke University Press.

The Conventional Level   The **conventional level** of moral reasoning spans the ages of about nine through 15. At this level right and wrong are judged by conformity to conventional (family, church, societal) standards of right and wrong. According to the stage 3 "good-boy orientation," it is good to meet the needs and expectations of others. During this stage moral behavior is seen as what is "normal"—that is, what the majority does. (Heinz should steal the drug because that is what a "good husband" would do. It is "natural" or "normal" to try to help one's wife. *Or*, Heinz should *not* steal the drug because "good people do not steal.")

In stage 4 moral judgments are based on rules that maintain the social order. Showing respect for authority and doing one's duty are valued highly. (Heinz must steal the drug; it would be his responsibility if he let her die. He would pay the druggist when he could.) Many people do not mature beyond the conventional level.

Conventional level According to Kohlberg, a period during which moral judgments largely reflect social conventions. A "law and order" approach to morality.

The Postconventional Level In the **postconventional level,** moral reasoning is based on the person's own moral standards. In each instance, moral judgments are derived from personal values, not from conventional standards or authority figures. In stage 5's contractual, legalistic orientation, it is recognized that laws stem from agreed-upon procedures and that many rights have great value and should not be violated. But it is also recognized that there are circumstances in which existing laws cannot bind the individual's behavior. (Although it is illegal for Heinz to steal the drug, in this case it is the right thing to do.)

In stage 6's principled orientation, people choose their own ethical principles—such as justice, **reciprocity,** and respect for individuality. Behavior that is consistent with these principles is considered right. If a law is seen as unjust, or as contradicting the rights of the individual, it is wrong to obey it.

Postconventional people look to themselves as the highest moral authority. This point has created confusion, because to some it suggests that it is right for people to break the law or ignore social conventions whenever it is convenient. But this interpretation is inaccurate. Kohlberg means that postconventional people are obligated to do what they believe is right, even if it counters social rules or laws—even if it demands great personal sacrifice.

Not all people reach the postconventional level of moral reasoning. Those who are capable of postconventional moral judgments do not necessarily exercise this ability in all situations.

Adolescence

G. Stanley Hall, first president of the American Psychological Association, described **adolescence** as a time of *Sturm und Drang*—storm and pressure. He attributed the conflicts and distress of adolescence to biological changes. However, anthropologists like Ruth Benedict (1934) and Margaret Mead (1935) have found cross-cultural evidence that the problems of adolescence reflect cultural influences and expectations rather than hormonal changes or physical growth patterns.

Adolescence is bounded by the advent of puberty on the lower end. Puberty begins with the appearance of **secondary sexual characteristics,** such as the growth of bodily hair, deepening of the voice in males, and rounding of the breasts and hips in females. Puberty ends when the long bones make no further gains in length so that full height is attained. But adolescence ends with psychosocial markers, such as assumption of adult responsibilities. Adolescence is a psychological concept with biological correlates, but puberty is a biological concept.

Changes in the Male

At puberty, pituitary hormones stimulate the testes to increase output of testosterone. Testosterone causes the penis and testes to grow, and pubic hair appears. Typical ages are included in the discussion of the following marker events, but there is much individual variation—which most often is no cause for concern.

Underarm hair appears at about age 15. A beard does not develop for another two or three years. At 14 or 15 the voice deepens because of the growth of the "voice box," or **larynx.** By age 13 or 14 erections become frequent

Postconventional level According to Kohlberg, a period during which moral judgments are derived from moral principles and people look to themselves to set moral standards.

Reciprocity Mutual action. Treating others as one is treated.

Adolescence The stage bounded by the advent of puberty and the capacity to take on adult responsibilities. Puberty is a biological concept while adolescence is a psychobiological concept. (From the Latin *adolescere,* meaning "to increase to" or "to come to maturity.")

Secondary sexual characteristics Physical traits, other than the genitals, that differentiate the sexes.

Larynx (LAR–inks). The structure in the throat that contains the vocal cords.

Epiphyseal closure
(ep–pea–FEES–ee–al). The turning to bone of cartilage that at first separates the long end (epiphysis) of a bone from the main part.

and boys may ejaculate. Ejaculatory ability usually precedes the presence of mature sperm by at least a year, so that ejaculation is not evidence of reproductive capacity. Typically, girls also menstruate before they can reproduce.

Boys and girls undergo general growth spurts during puberty. Girls usually shoot up before boys, but individuals differ and some boys spurt earlier than some girls. The muscle mass increases in weight, and there are gains in shoulder width and chest circumference. At 20 or 21 men stop growing taller because testosterone also causes **epiphyseal closure,** preventing the long bones from making further gains in length.

Changes in the Female

In the female, pituitary secretions cause the ovaries to begin to secrete estrogen. Estrogen stimulates growth of breast tissue as early as ages eight or nine. Estrogen promotes growth of fatty and supportive tissue in the hips and buttocks and widens the pelvis, causing the hips to become rounded.

Small amounts of androgens produced by the female's adrenal glands (see Chapter 2), along with estrogen, stimulate growth of pubic and underarm hair. Excessive androgen production can darken or increase the quantity of facial hair. Estrogen and androgen work together to stimulate the growth of the female sexual organs.

As noted in Chapter 2, estrogen production becomes cyclical in puberty and regulates the menstrual cycle. First menstruation, or **menarche,** tends to occur between ages 11 and 14. But girls cannot become pregnant until ovulation first occurs, about two years later.

Estrogen typically brakes the female growth spurt some years earlier than testosterone brakes that of the male. Girls deficient in estrogen during their late teens may grow quite tall, but most tall girls reach their heights because of normal genetically determined variations.

Adolescent Behavior and Conflicts

In our society adolescents are "neither fish nor foul," as the saying goes—neither children nor adults. Although adolescents may be old enough to reproduce, and as large as their parents, they are often treated quite differently. They may not be eligible for driver's licenses until they are 16 or 17, and cannot attend R-rated films unless accompanied by an adult. They are prevented from working long hours. They are required to remain in school usually through age 16. They may not marry until they reach the "age of consent."

The message is clear. Adolescents are seen as an emotional, impulsive lot. They must be restricted for their own good.

According to Roger Gould's (1975) research with 524 men and women of various age groups, a major concern of 16- to 18-year-olds is parental domination and yearning for independence. Given the restrictions placed on adolescents, their yearning for independence, and a sex drive heightened by high levels of sex hormones, it is not surprising that many adolescents report frequent conflict with their families (see Table 8.7).

Ego Identity vs. Role Diffusion   According to psychoanalyst Erik Erikson, the major challenge of adolescence is the creation of an adult identity. This is accomplished primarily through choosing and developing a commitment to an occupation or a role in life.

TABLE 8.7 Issues Reported by Adolescents as Leading to Family Conflict Very Often during High School

Issues	Percent Reporting		
	General Frequency	Males	Females
1. Going around with certain boys or girls	15.3	11.9	20.5
2. Boy-girl relations in general	8.2	3.4	15.4
3. Getting to use the car	13.3	16.9	7.7
4. Time spent watching TV	10.2	10.2	10.3
5. Eating dinner with the family	19.4	20.3	17.9
6. Being home enough	15.3	10.2	20.5
7. Responsibility at home	11.2	11.9	10.3
8. Money	7.4	3.4	13.5
9. Understanding each other	11.6	10.3	13.5
10. Disobedience	7.1	3.4	12.8
11. Quarreling and fighting	10.2	6.8	15.4
12. Ridicule of ideas	5.4	1.7	11.4
13. Arguing	15.8	12.1	21.6
14. Attitudes toward parents	7.1	3.4	12.8
15. Favoritism	5.3	0.0	13.5
16. Rivalry between siblings	7.4	5.3	10.8
17. Schoolwork	7.4	5.3	10.8
18. Neglecting work	7.4	3.5	13.5
19. Religious or philosophical ideas	6.3	1.7	10.8
20. Church attendance	15.6	11.9	18.9

Source: *American Journal of Orthopsychiatry*, 40, no. 4 (1970), p. 661.

Erikson (1963) theorizes that adolescents experience a life crisis of *ego identity versus role diffusion.* If this crisis is resolved properly, adolescents develop a firm sense of who they are and what they stand for. This sense of **ego identity** can carry them through difficult times and color their achievements with meaning. If they do not resolve this life crisis properly, they may experience **role diffusion.** They then spread themselves thin, running down one blind alley after another, and placing themselves at the mercy of leaders who promise to give them the sense of identity they cannot mold for themselves.

One aspect of attaining ego identity is learning "how to connect the roles and skills cultivated earlier with the occupational prototypes of the day" (Erikson, 1963, p. 261)—that is, with jobs. But ego identity goes beyond occupational choice. It extends to sexual, political, and religious beliefs and commitments.

Waterman and Nevid (1977) found that the majority of first- and second-year State University of New York at Albany students surveyed were either in serious conflict about, or had not begun to consider seriously, occupational choices. The percentage of students who experience conflict, or an **identity crisis,** about occupational choice increases from the fall to the spring semester of the first year (Waterman & Waterman, 1971). Many of these students emerge from their identity crises to show commitment to career roles at some point during the college years (Waterman and others, 1974). Commitments made during college seem more stable than commitments made during high school. Many adolescents turn their attention to identity crises in the areas of religion and politics only after they have defined their occupational roles. Bread on the table seems to be the primary concern.

Menarche (men–NARK–key). The beginning of menstruation. (From the Greek *men,* meaning "month," and *arche,* meaning "beginning.")

Ego identity According to Erikson, a sense of who one is and what one stands for.

Role diffusion According to Erikson, the probable outcome if ego identity is not established during adolescence; characterized by confusion, insecurity, and susceptibility to the suggestions of others.

Identity crisis According to Erikson, a period of inner conflict during which one examines one's values and makes decisions about life roles.

Sexual Morality and Personal Identity on Campus

What are your views on premarital sex? Have you arrived at a clear set of personal beliefs that guide your sexual behavior?

For many college students sexual decision making—not occupational choice—occupies center stage in the evolution of ego identity. Occupational decisions can be postponed, at least for a while, but many college students face sexual decision making every week, or every weekend.

Caroline Waterman and Jeffrey Nevid (1977) surveyed 70 male and 70 female first- and second-year students at State University of New York at Albany. They sought to learn whether the students had developed a stable set of beliefs about premarital sex. They also wanted to determine whether these beliefs had grown out of a serious examination of the alternatives—or, as Erik Erikson labeled it, from an *identity crisis.*

Crisis or commitment in occupational choice, and in religious and political views were also investigated. For each of these areas—occupation, religion, politics, and sexual morality—student beliefs were assigned to one of four identity statuses based on Erikson's concepts:

According to Erikson, the fundamental challenge of adolescence is the creation of one's adult identity.

Identity Achievement Resolution of an identity crisis through development of a stable set of beliefs or a course of action.

Foreclosure Adoption of a set of beliefs without undergoing an identity crisis—for instance, accepting parental or peer values without personal examination or questioning.

Moratorium Serious examination of alternative values and possibilities while in the throes of a personal identity crisis.

Identity Diffusion Lack of stable beliefs or commitment, and absence of a search to develop a set of beliefs.

Waterman and Nevid found that sexual decision making was extremely important to first- and second-year students. The lowest incidence of identity diffusion involved sexual morality, while the highest involved political beliefs.

There were interesting sex differences in identity status in the area of sexual morality. Most men (64 percent) were foreclosers. Women, by contrast, were evenly split between identity achievers (39 percent) and foreclosers (39 percent). The majority of men expressed the belief that there is nothing wrong with premarital sex, but most of them had *never seriously examined* their beliefs about sexual morality. They had simply adopted the sexual double standard that is generally permissive toward male sexuality but restrictive of women.

Most women also endorsed premarital sex, but they were more likely than men to approve of premarital sex only within the bounds of affectionate relationships. In arriving at their beliefs, the women more frequently underwent an identity crisis in which they had rejected less permissive parental values.

Although most men and women shared the same beliefs, they had arrived at them by vastly different routes. The issue, in short, was less stressful for the men.

Adult Development

Human development continues through the years of adulthood, with people showing changing concerns and involvements. Many theorists, like Erik Erikson and Daniel Levinson, believe that these concerns are patterned such that we can speak of stages of adult development. Psychologists have different schemes for dividing the adult years, but we may be able to use three broad categories without causing too much conflict: young adulthood, middle adulthood, and late adulthood.

Young Adulthood

Roger Gould's (1975) sample reported the 20s to be fueled with ambition. In her book *Passages*, Gail Sheehy (1976) labeled the 20s the **Trying Twenties**—a period during which people strive to advance themselves in the career world.

Establishing Pathways in Life Sheehy interviewed 115 people drawn largely from the middle and upper classes, including many managers, executives, and other professionals. The young adults in her sample were concerned about establishing their pathways in life, finding their places in the world. They were generally responsible for their own support, made their own choices, and were largely free from parental influences.

Sheehy noted that during the 20s we often feel "buoyed by powerful illusions and belief in the power of the will (so that) we commonly insist . . . that what we have chosen to do is the one true course in life" (1976, p. 33). This "one true course" usually turns out to have many swerves and bends. As we develop, what seemed important one year can lose some of its allure in the next. That which we hardly noted can gain prominence. We can also be influenced in unpredictable ways by chance encounters with people who gain sudden influence in our lives (Bandura, 1982).

Intimacy vs. Isolation According to Erikson (1963), a central task of young adulthood is the establishment of intimate relationships. Young adults who have evolved a firm sense of identity during adolescence are now ready to fuse their identities with those of other people through relationships like marriage and the construction of abiding friendships.

Erikson warns that we may not be capable of committing ourselves to others until we have established our own life roles. This may be one reason that teenage marriages suffer a much higher divorce rate than those formed in adulthood. People who do not reach out to develop intimate relationships may risk retreating into isolation and loneliness.

The Challenge of the Thirties Gould (1975) noted that the ages of 29 to 34 were commonly characterized by self-questioning: "Where is my life going?" "Why am I doing this?" Sheehy (1976) labeled the 30s the **Catch Thirties**— the first period of major reassessment in life. During the 30s we often find

Trying Twenties Sheehy's term for the third decade of life, when people are frequently occupied with advancement in the career world.

Catch Thirties Sheehy's term for the fourth decade of life, when many people undergo major reassessments of their accomplishments and goals.

TABLE 8.8   **Some Developmental Tasks of Young Adulthood**

Choosing and courting a mate	Learning how to manage a home
Learning to live harmoniously with a marriage partner	Establishing a career or seeking an advanced degree
Starting a family and taking on the role of parent	Assuming some civic responsibility
Meeting the needs of one's children	Making friends and belonging to a social group

Young adulthood spans some 20 years, from about age 20 to age 40, and according to developmental psychologist Robert J. Havighurst (1972) of the University of Chicago, it involves a number of developmental tasks that most people must meet if they are to adjust well.

According to Erikson, establishing intimate relationships is a central task of young adulthood. People who do not reach out to others risk retreating into isolation.

that the life styles we adopted during the 20s do not fit as comfortably as we had anticipated.

One response to the disillusionments of the 30s, according to Sheehy, "is the tearing up of the life we have spent most of our 20s putting together. It may mean striking out on a secondary road toward a new vision or converting a dream of 'running for president' into a more realistic goal. The single person feels a push to find a partner. The woman who was previously content at home with children chafes to venture into the world. The childless couple reconsiders children (see the box, "At Long Last Motherhood"). And almost everybody who is married . . . feels a discontent" (1976, p. 34).

Many people make major life changes in their 30s, 40s, and even later in life (Sheehy, 1981). Making successful life changes requires risk-taking, but risk-taking in itself is no guarantee of success. Successful life-changers also show foresight, the ability to summon up both stereotypically masculine (like ambition) and feminine (like tenderness) traits, and strong belief in their purpose.

According to Daniel Levinson and his colleagues (1978), the second half of the 30s is characterized by settling down. Sheehy similarly found that young adults who had successfully ridden out the storm of reassessments of the Catch Thirties began the process of "rooting" at this time. They felt a need to plant roots, to make a financial and emotional investment in their homes. Their concerns became more focused on promotion or tenure, career advancement, and long-term mortgages.

How Did I Get to Be . . . Thirty-Five?

Realizing that you're no longer as young as you used to be isn't easy. In *Passages* Gail Sheehy writes that women enter midlife about five years earlier than men do, at 35 rather than 40. Entering midlife triggers a sense of urgency, of a "last chance" to do certain things.

But what is so special about the age of 35? As Sheehy notes:

- Thirty-five is the average age at which women send the youngest child off to school.
- Thirty-five is the beginning of the so-called "age of infidelity."
- Thirty-five is the average age at which married women reenter the work force.
- Thirty-four is the average age at which divorced women remarry.
- Thirty-five is the age at which wives most frequently run away.
- Thirty-five brings nearer the end of the childbearing years.

At Long Last Motherhood

Like many women of her generation, Anne Fowler went through her 20s believing it was more blessed to live than to conceive. A dedicated, and upwardly mobile, teacher at Granada High School in Livermore, California, she always wanted a family. But she could never figure out how to have babies without hurting her career. Last year, at the age of 31, she stopped trying. Giving up the race for promotions—at least temporarily—Fowler and her husband decided to have their first child. "My mother told me that if people thought everything through, nobody would *ever* have children," she laughs ...

They have traveled and worked late and dressed to succeed, and now they are seeking "something more." Increasingly, women over 30 are becoming mothers for the first time.... "There is a profound baby hunger around these days among women who have put off having children," says psychiatrist Donald A. Bloch....

More than 3.6 million babies were born in the United States in 1980. For the most part this baby boomlet reflects the fact that, with the post–World War II baby-boom generation reaching adulthood, there are simply more potential mothers than ever before. In the last seven years the number of women of childbearing age has swelled by 6.7 million to 51.9 million. And though the overall U.S. birthrate has not risen, the rate among women in their early 30s *has* grown. What's more, the number of first births among women of that age has jumped by 37 percent in recent years. The trend is sharpest among urban professional women....

What made so many women postpone having children until now was a complex of social and economic factors. The feminist movement illuminated alternate paths women could take besides marriage and motherhood, and better methods of birth control provided the freedom of choice to pursue them. Changing sexual mores also played a part, while inflation and recession made it difficult for couples to feel secure enough financially to start a family. Women put off pregnancy while they advanced in their careers, saved for a house, [or] earned a doctorate....

Back to the Family Throughout it all, however, counterpressures were pushing women toward motherhood. Medical breakthroughs like amniocentesis may have made later pregnancies safer and less stressful. But there was still no way of getting around the ultimate deadline of menopause. "These women don't suddenly discover God, motherhood, and apple pie," says sociologist Norma Wikler, coauthor of a study of older mothers called *Up Against the Clock.* "They have deferred and deferred and now see that deadline approaching." Other experts see traces of renewed traditionalism at work, along with peer pressure and a bit of back-to-the-family faddishness. "I think it's sort of a contagion that's going on," says New York psychologist Iris Fodor. "My patients see their friends having babies and they want their own."

Middle Adulthood

There is some point between the ages of 35 and 45 when most of us realize that life may be more than halfway over. There may be more to look back upon than forward to. We'll never be president or chairperson of the board. We'll never play shortstop for the Dodgers or dance in the New York City Ballet.

The Midlife Crisis The middle-level, middle-aged businessperson looking ahead to another 10 to 20 years of grinding out accounts in a Wall Street cubbyhole may encounter a severe midlife depression. The housewife with two teenagers, an empty house from eight to three, and a fortieth birthday on the way may feel that she is coming apart at the seams. Both are experiencing a **midlife crisis,** a feeling of entrapment and loss of purpose that afflicts many middle-aged people. It propels some into extramarital affairs just so they can feel that they remain physically attractive.

The early 40s mark a turning point for men. Men in their 30s still consider themselves part of the Pepsi Generation, older brothers to youths in their 20s. At about 40 some marker event—physical illness, a change on the job, the obituary of a contemporary—leads men to recognize that they are a full generation older than 20-year-olds (Levinson and others, 1978). They mourn their own youth and begin to adjust to the specter of old age and the finality of death.

Midlife crisis A crisis experienced by many people near age 40 when they realize that life may be halfway over. They may feel trapped in meaningless life roles.

The Dream Levinson's term for the overriding drive of youth to become someone important, to leave one's mark on history.

Generativity vs. Stagnation   Erikson (1963) labels the life crisis of the middle years as that of generativity versus stagnation. If we come through this crisis positively, we may maintain or enhance our creativity, newly embrace family values, and pursue the Eriksonian ideal of helping to shape the new generation enthusiastically. This shaping may involve our own children, but it may extend to working to make the world a better place. For those who weather this crisis, experience may combine with strength to heighten productivity.

The Dream: Inspiration or Tyrant?   Until midlife the men studied by Levinson and his colleagues (1978) were largely under the influence of **the Dream**—the overriding drive of youth to become, to be the great novelist or scientist, to leave one's mark on history. At midlife men must come to terms with the discrepancy between their actual achievements and the Dream.

The Dream, you see, may tell the author that the merely memorable novel is inadequate—it must be a masterpiece. The Dream may lead all of us, not just men, to belittle our accomplishments. Middle-aged people who free themselves from the tyranny of the Dream find it more possible to enjoy the passing pleasures of the day.

The Empty Nest Syndrome   You may think that parents would give a sigh of relief when the last child goes off to college, gets married, or moves into an apartment. After all, now there is time to devote to themselves. But parents, particularly mothers who have allowed themselves to become too wrapped up in their children's lives, often feel that there is not much to live for when their children leave home (Bart, 1970).

"Now, see here, Harley. I was forty once, and I never went through any mid-life crisis!"

According to Harbeson:

Too many married women arrive at middle age without having looked and planned far enough ahead, and experience difficulties in making the transition from motherhood to socially useful occupations.... [There] are an appalling number of unhappy over-40 women [who] could be helped if they could find a sufficient purpose for their lives. These women are simply at a loss to know what to do with themselves when they reach the point where their children are no longer dependent on them. Usually, they are the ones who have been the most devoted mothers.... Too often their only relief is in some form of occasional social diversion which provides them an escape (1971, p. 139).

Such women are said to be suffering from the **empty nest syndrome.**

According to Sheehy (1976), mothers of grown children usually expect that the appropriate path for filling their lives with new meaning lies in the cultivation of interests that had been allowed to lie dormant when their families came along. Slightly more than half the American women whose children have left the nest are now in the work force. Some have returned to college.

A study of life satisfaction among Americans was optimistic. Men and women with children over 17 reported more general life satisfaction and more positive feelings than parents of younger children (Campbell, 1975). They were also much more satisfied than people who had never married.

Late Adulthood

Most people say that as you get old you have to give up things. I think you get old because you give up things.
—Senator Theodore Francis Green, age 87, *Washington Post*, June 28, 1954

The idea that society can provide only a limited number of jobs, and that the elderly are the logical ones to be left out, is no longer tenable. There are unlimited goods and services needed and desired in American society. Among the greatest resources that could be channeled toward these ends are the experience, skill and devotion of America's elderly millions.
—Mae Rudolph, *Family Health*, March 1970

How old would you be if you didn't know how old you was?
—Satchel Paige, ageless Baseball pitcher

The true test of maturity is not how old a person is but how he reacts to awakening in the midtown area in his shorts.
—Woody Allen, *Without Feathers*

Late adulthood begins at the age of 65. One very obvious reason that developmental psychologists have become concerned with the later years is the so-called "demographic imperative" (Neugarten, 1982). More of us are swelling the ranks of the elderly in our nation's population all the time, significantly changing age distribution. Improved health care and knowledge about the importance of diet and exercise appear to have combined so effectively that more Americans than ever before are aged 65 or above.

At the time of the first census, conducted in 1790, half of all Americans were age 16 or younger. In 1970 the median age was under 28, but it is likely to be 35 by year 2000 and nearly 40 by 2030. At that time more than 50 million of an American population of some 300 million (one person in six) will be 65 or above. Today only about one person in 10 is aged 65 or above.

Empty nest syndrome A sense of depression and loss of purpose experienced by some parents when the youngest child leaves home.

Late adulthood The last stage of life, beginning at age 65.

Another reason for increased interest in the later years is the recognition that, in a sense, *all* development involves aging. Developmental psychologist Bernice Neugarten (1982) suggests that development and aging are similar, perhaps synonymous, terms.

A third reason for studying the later years is to learn what we can to optimize them and promote the health and psychological well-being of the elderly. Psychologists have found that the later years can be more than the stage for preparing to die.

Some Changes That Occur during Late Adulthood A number of changes occur during the later years which lead to many problems for the elderly. Changes in calcium metabolism lead to increased brittleness in the bones and increased risk of breaks from falls and other accidents. The skin becomes less elastic, subject to wrinkles and folds.

The senses become less acute. Not only do the elderly see and hear less acutely, they may also use more spice to flavor their food. The elderly require more time—known as **reaction time**—to respond to stimuli. It takes elderly drivers longer to respond to traffic lights, other vehicles, and changing road conditions.

The elderly also show some decline in general intellectual ability as measured by scores on standardized intelligence tests. This drop-off is most noticeable on timed items, such as those found on several of the "perform-ance" scales of the Wechsler Adult Intelligence Scale (see Chapter 6). Loss of sensory acuity and loss of motivation to do well may contribute to lower scores. For instance, nursing home residents who are rewarded for remem-bering recent events show improved scores on standard cognitive memory tests (Langer and others, 1979; Wolinsky, 1982). In some cases, apparently "irreversible cognitive changes" may reflect psychological disorders like depression (Albert, 1981). Such changes are not primarily cognitive; nor are they irreversible. If the depression is treated properly intellectual perform-ances may also improve.

However, the elderly often combine years of experience with high levels of motivation on the job. In these cases forced retirement can be an arbitrary and painful remedy for no sin other than turning 65 or 70. (See the box "It Takes a Long Time to Become Young".) According to Kimmel:

> Up to the age of 65 there is little decline in learning or memory ability; factors of motivation, interest, and lack of recent educational experience are probably more important in learning complex knowledge than age per se. Learning may just take a bit longer for the elderly and occur more at the individual's own speed instead of at an external and fast pace (1974, p. 381).

Despite the changes that occur with aging, one survey of persons aged 70–79 found that 75 percent were generally satisfied with their lives (Neugar-ten, 1971). A more recent study of persons who had been retired for from 18 to 120 months found that 75 percent rated retirement as mostly good (Hen-drick and others, 1982). Over 90 percent were generally satisfied with life and more than 75 percent reported their health to be good or excellent.

Theories of Aging Although it may be hard to believe that it will happen to us, to date everyone who has walked the Earth has aged—which is not necessarily a bad fate, considering the alternative. Why do we age? Various factors, some of which are theoretical, apparently contribute to aging.

Reaction time The amount of time required to respond to a stimulus.

It Takes a Long Time To Become Young

Is youth purely a matter of chronological age, or does attitude have something to do with it? In *It Takes a Long Time to Become Young*, film director and writer Garson Kanin (1978) argues that too many people are tossed arbitrarily into the human wastebasket by forced retirement policies when they turn 65 or 70.

Kanin cites data from the U.S. Bureau of Labor Statistics showing that the mean life span of forced retirees is only 30 to 40 months. One of three marriages breaks up after a forced retirement, and the suicide rate among forced retirees is 12 times greater than the norm for others in this age group.

Kanin argues that personal choice or demonstrated inability to perform are the only legitimate reasons for retirement—at 82 or 42. The older worker's experience often compensates for lowered stamina.

Kanin tells the story of a Connecticut town that lost its electrical power. After several days of fruitless poking around, the retired engineer who installed the system was consulted. He surveyed the situation, tapped his mallet once, and there was light. He sent the town a bill for $1,000.02—$.02 for tapping and $1,000 for knowing where to tap. Wisdom does not come cheap.

The opportunity to engage in meaningful work is a major objective of the senior rights movement and groups like the Gray Panthers.

Heredity plays a role. **Longevity** runs in families. People whose parents and grandparents lived into their 80s and 90s have a greater chance of reaching these years themselves.

Environmental factors affect aging. For instance, it seems that people who exercise regularly tend to live somewhat longer. Disease, stress, obesity, and cigarette smoking are among the factors that can contribute to an early death. According to Yale University psychologist Judith Rodin, elderly people also show better health and psychological well-being when they can exert control over their own lives (Rodin & Langer, 1977; Wolinsky, 1982). Unfortunately, their decline in health and finances results in some of the elderly being placed in nursing homes and surrendering their independence. But even in the nursing home, they fare better when they are kept well-informed and allowed to make decisions on matters that affect them.

There are a number of biological theories of aging. The **cellular aging theory** suggests that the DNA within cells, which carries the genetic code of

Longevity A long span of life.

Cellular aging theory The view that aging occurs because bodily cells lose the capacity to reproduce and maintain themselves.

FIGURE 8.11   Phases of Retirement. Many of us look forward to retirement, but retirement is not always smooth or straightforward. Early enjoyment frequently gives way to disenchantment as expectations are not met. We may then change our expectations and make adjustments (reorient ourselves), and enter a more stable period. Retirement can terminate through new work, illness, or death.

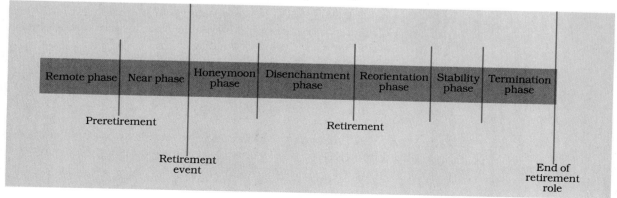

the individual (see Chapter 2), suffers damage from external factors (like ultraviolet light) and random internal changes. As the person ages, the ability to repair DNA decreases. Eventually damages and other changes accumulate to the point where affected cells can no longer reproduce or serve their bodily functions. Another view is that waste products within cells eventually accumulate so that many cells are poisoned and no longer capable of functioning. These views are somewhat speculative at this time.

Living Arrangements of the Elderly Since persons in late adulthood tend to spend 80 to 90 percent of their time at home (Hansen, 1975), their living arrangements are extremely important. About 25 percent of the elderly live in rural areas, 33 percent in inner cities, and 40 percent in older lower-middle-class neighborhoods within cities (Hendrick & Hendrick, 1977). The majority own their own homes. Mobile homes and senior citizen hotels are becoming more popular. Only about five percent live in nursing homes and institutions. Retirement communities, which began in Florida, have sprung up in most Sunbelt states. The elderly feel that these communities offer protection from street crime and other city problems (Leslie & Leslie, 1977). Although moving requires many adjustments, the relocating of retirees does not appear particularly stressful when adequate plans have been made and the retirees are financially secure (Hendrick and others, 1982).

On Death and Dying Death is the last great taboo. Psychiatrist Elisabeth Kübler-Ross comments on our denial of death in her book *On Death and Dying:*

> We use euphemisms, we make the dead look as if they were asleep, we ship the children off to protect them from the anxiety and turmoil around the house if the [person] is fortunate enough to die at home, [and] we don't allow children to visit their dying parents in the hospitals (1969, p. 8).

From her work with terminally ill patients, Kübler-Ross found some common responses to news of impending death. She identified five stages of dying through which many patients pass: *denial, anger, bargaining, depression,* and *final acceptance.* Elderly people who suspect that death is approaching may undergo similar experiences.

In the denial stage people feel, "It can't be me. The diagnosis must be wrong." Denial usually gives way to anger and resentment toward the young and healthy and, sometimes, toward the medical establishment—"It's unfair. Why me?" Then people may try to bargain with God to postpone death, promising, for example, to do good deeds if they are given another six months, another year. With depression come feelings of hopelessness and loss—grief at the specter of leaving loved ones and life itself. Ultimately an inner peace may come, a quiet acceptance of the inevitable. This "peace" does not resemble happiness; it is nearly devoid of feeling.

The final hours pose a towering challenge. Kübler-Ross argues that this challenge could be better met if death and dying were dealt with as facts of life rather than denied—if the dying were helped to die in dignity in their homes rather than in an anonymous hospital.

Lying Down to Pleasant Dreams . . . The American poet William Cullen Bryant lived from 1794 to 1878, yet never in adulthood could he recapture the majesty of his poem "Thanatopsis," composed at age 18.

"Thanatopsis" could be said to express Erik Erikson's goal of **ego integrity** (as opposed to despair) during the later years. Ego integrity derives from wisdom, from the acceptance of one's own life span as occurring at a certain point in human history and having limits. We spend most of our lives accumulating relationships and things; Erikson argues that adjustment to the later years requires the wisdom to let go.

Erikson was optimistic about people. He believed that it is possible to maintain a basic sense of trust through life, that we can live in such a way that when our time comes to "join the innumerable caravan"—the countless billions who have died before us—we can depart life with dignity and integrity. We can accept the full circle of our own brief life cycle in the history of humankind.

Live, the poet writes, so that

> ...when thy summons comes to join
> The innumerable caravan that moves
> To the pale realms of shade, where each shall take
> His chamber in the silent halls of death,
> Thou go not, like the quarry-slave at night,
> Scourged to his dungeon, but, sustained and soothed
> By an unfaltering trust, approach thy grave
> Like one who wraps the drapery of his couch
> About him, and lies down to pleasant dreams.

Bryant, of course, wrote "Thanatopsis" at 18, not 85. At that advanced age his feelings, his pen, might have differed. But literature and poetry, unlike science, need not reflect reality. They can serve to inspire and warm us.

Ego integrity A firm sense of identity, characterized by the wisdom to accept the fact that life is limited and the ability to let go.

Summary

Human growth and development begin when a sperm cell carrying an X (female) or Y (male) sex chromosome combines with an ovum to become a fertilized ovum, or zygote. For up to two weeks the zygote divides as it travels through the fallopian tube and then within the uterus. Then it becomes implanted in the uterine wall and gains mass as it continues to divide and differentiate. It is connected to the mother by the umbilical cord. Nutrients and oxygen travel to the fetus from the mother via a permeable membrane called the placenta, and wastes are removed from the baby's bloodstream via the placenta. Various substances can pass through the placenta, so mothers should take drugs and other substances with caution.

Development within the uterus and after birth reflects nature (heredity) and nurture (environmental influences). Certain learnings are possible only when the person has become ready through maturation.

Infants are born with certain reflexes—stereotyped responses elicited by certain stimuli without involving higher brain functions. Reflexes like rooting and sucking promote survival and cease when the infant has learned survival behaviors. Newborn children spend most of the day sleeping. They can see better than is usually presumed and show greater interest in complex visual stimuli—especially human faces—than in simple stimuli. They are capable of depth perception by the time they can crawl. Infants can hear at birth, unless hearing is impeded by fluid in the ears. They can discriminate between different tastes shortly after birth and prefer sweet tastes, as measured by force of, and amount of time spent in, sucking.

Early in the century behaviorists argued that children become attached to their mothers through conditioning—because their mothers fed them and attended to their other needs. Harlow's studies with rhesus monkeys suggest that an innate motive called contact comfort may be more important. Rhesus infants become more attached to terry-cloth mothers than to wire mothers that feed them, as measured by time spent clinging to the "mothers."

Animals like geese and ducks show a critical period during which they will become attached to a moving object that they follow. This process is called imprinting. There is little evidence that human children have critical periods for forming bonds of attachment.

Day care has not been shown to alter mother-child bonds of attachment or a child's cognitive functioning. Children raised in groups in the kibbutz also become attached to their parents.

Social deprivation in rhesus monkeys leads to disturbances in social and sexual behavior. Exposure to young, persistent female companions has been shown to help deprived monkeys overcome social deficits. Social deprivation also impairs social and intellectual functioning in humans. Deprived children placed with surrogate mothers have shown an ability to make significant gains in intellectual and social functioning.

Children become like their parents and acquire stereotypical sex-role behaviors through various processes. It may be that (prenatal) hormonal influences play a role in sex typing. Children also identify with parents—internalizing their behavioral tendencies. It may be that at first they identify with the mother and later (usually) identify with the parent of the same sex. Socialization—the messages and experiences provided children by their elders—also encourages acquisition of stereotypical sex-roles. Children appear to acquire a gender identity at an early age. Once this identity is established, it appears that they imitate behaviors that they believe are appropriate for persons of their gender.

Piaget saw children as scientists trying to make sense of the perceptual world. He defined intelligence as involving the processes of assimilation (interpreting events according to existing cognitive structures or schemata) and accommodation (modifying existing schemata to permit understanding of new events, concepts, and relationships). Piaget's scheme for understanding cognitive development includes four stages: sensorimotor (prior to use of language and symbols); preoperational (characterized by egocentric thought, animism, artificialism, and inability to center on more than one aspect of a situation); concrete operational (characterized by conservation, less egocentrism, reversibility, and subjective moral judgments); and formal operational (characterized by capacity for abstract logic.)

Kohlberg hypothesizes three levels (preconventional, conventional, and postconventional) of moral judgment and two stages within each of these. In the preconventional level, judgments are made on the basis of the consequences of behavior. In the conventional level, judgments reflect the perceived need to maintain the social order. In the postconventional level, judgments are derived from personal ethical principles and the self is seen as the highest moral authority.

Adolescence, which begins with puberty and ends with the assumption of adult responsibilities, is often stressful in our society. The changes that lead to the capacity to reproduce and secondary sexual characteristics are stimulated by testosterone in the male and by estrogen and androgens in the female. According to Erikson, ego identity—or the defining of a life role—is the major challenge of adolescence.

The chapter divides adulthood into three categories: young adulthood, middle adulthood, and late adulthood. Young adults in their 20s strive to establish pathways in the business world and to develop intimate relationships. The 30s is a time of reassessment for many young adults, and at about age 35 or so, many young adults plant roots. Middle adulthood is a time of crisis and reassessment for many, involving recognition that life may be more than halfway over. Many middle-aged men must face up to the fact that they will never achieve the Dream—the overriding drive of youth to become, to leave one's mark on history. Many people encounter the empty nest syndrome when the youngest child leaves home.

The elderly show less sensory acuity and their reaction time increases. Apparent decreases in general cognitive functioning and memory may, in part, reflect lack of motivation or psychological problems, like depression. We do not know why people age. Heredity and environmental factors (like stress and smoking) play a role, and it is possible that DNA breakdowns within cells gradually accumulate such that cells can no longer repair themselves or reproduce. Maintaining responsibility may delay aging. In most job situations experience can compensate for loss of quickness and stamina. Forced retirement is linked to higher mortality and divorce rates. Kübler-Ross identifies five stages of dying among terminally ill patients: denial, anger, bargaining, depression, and final acceptance.

Truth or Fiction Revisited

- *You can determine the sex of your child.* Not with certainty. However, new methods that involve tracking the viscosity of the vaginal mucus provide greater-than-chance probabilities that parents can determine whether they will have a girl or boy.

- *A newly fertilized egg cell wanders around the womb with no visible means of support.* True. This so-called period of the ovum ends with implantation of the zygote in the uterine wall.

- *Newborn infants prefer human faces to other forms of visual stimulation.* True. They fixate longer on human faces than on other forms or patterns.

- *Children placed in day-care facilities grow less attached to their mothers.* False. It seems that the quality of the mother-child relationship, rather than the amount of time spent together, determines the strength of the bonds of attachment.

- *A four-year-old child may believe that the sky is blue because someone has painted it.* True. Piaget terms this sort of preoperational thinking "artificialism."

- *Adolescents are biologically capable of reproduction when they first ejaculate or have their first menstrual period.* False. Mature sperm and ova are not necessarily present in early ejaculations or menstrual flows.

- *Sexual morality is the central concern of the identity crisis of adolescence.* False. Occupational choice seems to be a more central concern.

- *Forced retirement may be a death sentence.* True. The mortality rate is higher among forced retirees than among other members of the same age groups.

OUTLINE

Personality: Theory and Measurement

- Some psychologists claim that the human mind is like a vast submerged iceberg, only the tip of which rises above the surface into awareness.
- Women who compete with men in the business world are suffering from penis envy.
- Some psychoanalysts feel that you have inherited mysterious memories that date back to ancient times.
- Obese people are jolly.
- We may believe that we have freedom of choice, but behaviorists argue that our preferences and choices are actually forced upon us by the environment.
- A psychologist could write a believable personality report about you without interviewing you, testing you, or, in fact, having any idea who you are.
- Psychologists can always determine whether a person has told the truth on a personality test.

Personality and Personality Theories

There is an ancient Islamic tale about several blind men who encounter an elephant for the first time. Each touches a different part of the elephant, but each is stubborn and claims that he alone has grasped the true nature of the beast. One grabbed our gray friend by the legs and then described the elephant as firm, strong, and upright, like a pillar. To this the blind man who had touched the ear of the elephant objected. From his perspective, the animal was broad and rough, like a rug. The third man had become familiar with the animal's trunk. He was astounded at the gross inaccuracy of the others. Clearly the elephant was long and narrow, he declared, like a hollow pipe.

Each of this trio had come to know the elephant from a different perspective. Each was blind to the beliefs of his fellows, and to the real nature of the elephant—not only because of his physical limitations, but also because his initial encounter had led him to think of the elephant in a certain way.

So it is that different ways of encountering human beings have led psychologists to view people from different perspectives. Various theories of human **personality** have been advanced. Because personality is not something that can be touched directly, theories of personality may differ as widely as the blind men's concepts of the elephant.

Personality psychologist Walter Mischel (1981) notes that people do not even agree on what the word *personality* means. Some equate personality with liveliness, as in, "She's got a lot of personality." Others characterize a person's personality as consisting of the most striking or dominant traits, as in a "shy personality," or a "happy-go-lucky personality."

But Mischel notes that a "common theme" runs through most personality definitions that are spawned by psychologists: "The distinctive patterns of behavior, including thoughts and emotions, that characterize each individual's adaptation to the situations of his or her life" (1981, p. 2). Personality deals with the ways in which people differ. Personality theories may include discussion of internal variables like thoughts and emotions, as well as observable behavior.

Personality theories seek to explain how people develop distinctive patterns of behavior, and to predict how people with certain patterns will respond to the demands of life. In this chapter we shall explore four major approaches to the study of personality: psychoanalytic theory, trait theory, social learning theory, and self theory. All attempt to explain behavior, but they differ vastly in their willingness to swim beneath the surface of observable behavior in their efforts to do so. Then we shall explore psychological methods of measuring personality.

Personality The distinct patterns of behaviors, including thoughts and feelings, that characterize a person's adaptation to life. (From the Latin *persona*, meaning "actor's face mask.")

Psychoanalytic theory Sigmund Freud's perspective, which emphasizes the importance of unconscious motives and conflicts as determinants of behavior.

Psychoanalytic Theory

What if we had four, not three, men who were not blind, but who held different theories of the elephant's personality?

The person with the **psychoanalytic theory** might walk around the elephant a few times, scratching his beard. "What we have here," he would say finally, "is the mere surface of the elephant, although I grant you it is a rather large surface. But you cannot hope to understand our mammoth friend by studying those floppy ears or that threatening trunk." The elephant snorts.

"The essential elements of personality dwell deep within that gray head, beneath that flab." The elephant taps the ground.

"You see, there are forces at work deep inside the elephant. They are so deep that the beast is not aware of them. Yet they determine his behavior. To understand this elephant, we shall have to find a couch, a very large couch . . ."—the elephant glares impatiently—"have him lie down on it, and start him talking. It may take years, but this is one way for us to learn about forces that reside deep within his unconscious mind."

"My what?" asks the elephant.

"Your unconscious mind."

"But I'm not aware of any unconscious mind," protests the elephant.

"Aha!" exclaims the psychoanalyst. "I rest my case."

Psychodynamic Descriptive of Freud's view that various forces move through the personality and determine behavior.

Sigmund Freud

He was born with a shock of dark hair—in Jewish tradition, the sign of a prophet. In 1856, in a Czechoslovakian village, an old woman told his mother that she had given birth to a great man. The child was raised with great expectations. In manhood, Freud himself would be cynical about this notion. Old women, after all, would earn greater favors through good tidings than through forecasts of doom. But, in a sense, the prophecy about Freud may have been realized. Few have shaped our thinking about human nature as deeply as the bearded, compassionate psychoanalyst from Vienna.

Freud's view of personality is **psychodynamic.** He taught that personality is characterized by a dynamic struggle. Basic drives such as hunger, sex, and aggression come into conflict with social pressures to behave according to laws, rules, and moral codes. The laws and social rules become internalized. We make them parts of ourselves. After doing so, the dynamic struggle becomes a clashing of opposing *inner* forces. The major struggles lie *within*. At any given moment our observable behaviors, as well as our thoughts and emotions, represent the outcome of these inner clashes.

Sigmund Freud taught that human personality is characterized by a dynamic struggle as basic physiological drives come into conflict with laws and social codes.

The Geography of the Mind: Warming Up to the Human Iceberg

Freud was trained as a physician. Early in his practice, he was astounded to learn that some people apparently experienced loss of feeling in a hand or paralysis of the legs without any medical disorder being present. These strange symptoms often disappeared once patients had recalled and discussed distressful events and feelings of guilt or anxiety that seemed to be associated with the symptoms. For a long time these events and feelings were hidden beneath the surface of awareness. Even so, they had the capacity to profoundly influence the behavior of patients.

Conscious, Preconscious, and Unconscious From this sort of clinical evidence, Freud concluded that the human mind was like an iceberg. Only the tip of an iceberg rises above the surface of the water, while the great mass of it darkens the deep. Freud came to believe that people, similarly, were only aware of a small number of the ideas and the impulses that dwelled within their minds. Even though our perceptions of our own experiences may seem full and rich, Freud argued that the greater mass of the mind, our deepest images, thoughts, fears, and urges, remained beneath the surface of conscious awareness, where little light illuminated them. He labeled the region that poked through into the light of awareness the **conscious** part of the mind. He called the regions that lay below the surface the preconscious and the unconscious.

The **preconscious** mind contains elements of experience that are presently out of awareness, but can be made conscious simply by focusing on them. The **unconscious** mind is shrouded in mystery. It contains biological instincts and urges that we only partially perceive as hunger, thirst, sexuality, and aggression. Some unconscious urges cannot be experienced consciously because mental images and words could not portray them in all their color and fury. Other unconscious urges, which are largely sexual and aggressive in nature, may be kept below the surface by *repression*.

Repression has been called motivated forgetting. It is the ejecting of unacceptable ideas from awareness. Repression protects us from recognizing impulses we would consider inappropriate in light of our moral values. Repression occurs automatically; the process itself takes place without awareness. So, you ask, how do we know when we have repressed something? We

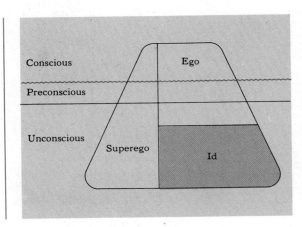

FIGURE 9.1 The Human Iceberg. According to psychoanalytic theory, only the tip of human personality rises above the surface of the mind into conscious awareness. Material in the preconscious can become conscious if we direct our attention to it, but unconscious material tends to remain shrouded in mystery.

do not know. By definition we cannot know. After all, if we knew that we were repressing the momentary angry impulse to destroy a loved one, we wouldn't be protecting ourselves very well from awareness of the impulse.

The unconscious is the largest part of the mind. It is here that the dynamic struggle between biological drives and social rules is fiercest. As drives seek expression, and internalized values exert counterpressures, the resultant conflict can give rise to various psychological disorders and behavioral outbursts (see the box on "The Catharsis Controversy"). Since we cannot view the unconscious mind directly, Freud developed a method of mental detective

The Catharsis Controversy

Think of a person as a steam engine, and of aggressive impulses as steam. What will happen if there is a persistent buildup of steam (aggressive impulses), but there is no safety valve? Eventually there may be an uncontrollable outburst of aggression.

The steam-engine analogy is often used to communicate some of Sigmund Freud's concepts about unconscious human impulses and the hazards of denying them expression. Freud believed that it was inevitable that aggressive impulses would accumulate as we experienced the frustrations of daily life. These frustrations might stem from fighting our ways through crowds on the way to work, from petty conflicts in the office, from being ignored by an attractive person of the opposite sex.

Given the model of the steam engine, it is easy to understand why Freud also believed that one way to avert a serious aggressive outburst would be to en-

courage "aggression" on a smaller scale—as the saying goes, to help a person to "let off excess steam." Freud encouraged patients in psychoanalysis to express their frustrations and anger verbally rather than through physical aggression. Other theorists have suggested that "letting off steam" can take many forms, including watching contact sports, engaging in athletic activity of one's own, aggressive fantasies, sarcasm, and wit (showing "oral aggression" or "a biting tongue").

This is the catharsis hypothesis, the notion that an outlet for hostile impulses will avert large-scale outbursts. What does psychological research show about the effectiveness of "letting off steam" as a way of averting greater aggression later on?

In typical experiments, subjects are provoked through insults by confederates of the experimenter. Then they are given the opportunity to retaliate through administering an electric shock to their provocateurs. Of course, the "shock machine" they are using does nothing more than record the intensity of the shock they selected and its duration—that is, the objective measures of aggression.

In some studies of this kind, subjects who believe they have delivered shocks (behaved aggressively) to people who insulted them have shown reportedly pleasant reductions in arousal, and have been less likely to engage in aggression when given a subsequent opportunity to act aggressively (Doob & Wood, 1972; Hokanson & Burgess, 1962; Hokanson and others, 1963; Konečni, 1975). But other studies (e.g., by Geen and others, 1975) have found that aggressive behavior can lead to increased, rather than decreased, aggression later on.

Aggression does not mechanically lead to pleasant reductions of arousal or to reduction of the likelihood of future violence. People, it seems, must believe that their aggression is justified under the circumstances. If they do not, they may feel guilty, leading to an increase in emotional arousal (Geen and others, 1975). This increased arousal then spurs additional violence.

Freud viewed people as analogous to steam engines: Aggressive impulses would naturally build as a result of day-to-day frustrations. People who did not "let off steam" by verbally expressing hostile feelings or finding other acceptable outlets might be subject to aggressive outbursts. These people have been prompted to express hostile impulses by pounding pillows. Does such a "cathartic" experience decrease the probability of interpersonal aggression afterwards?

work called **psychoanalysis.** In psychoanalysis people are prompted to talk about anything that "pops" into their minds while they are comfortable and relaxed. People may gain **self-insight** by pursuing some of the thoughts that pop into awareness. But they may also be motivated to avoid discussing threatening subjects. The force of repression that has made unacceptable thoughts and feelings unconscious also prompts **resistance,** the desire to avoid thinking about or discussing them. Repression and resistance may make psychoanalysis a tedious process that lasts for years, or decades. Yet Freud used this painstaking method with many clients to arrive at his conclusions about the geography of the mind.

The Structure of Personality

When is a structure not a structure? When it is a mental or **psychic structure.** Sigmund Freud labeled the clashing forces of personality psychic structures. They could not be seen or measured directly, but their presence was suggested by observable behavior, expressed thoughts and emotions. Freud hypothesized the existence of three psychic structures: the *id, ego,* and *superego.*

Freud suggested that each of us is influenced by an id that demands instant gratification without regard for moral scruples and the needs of others. Robert Louis Stevenson had a dream in which a similar idea was expressed, and he developed it into the novel *Dr. Jekyll and Mr. Hyde.* In one film version of the tale, Dr. Jekyll, shown at right, is a loving, considerate person—suggestive of ego functioning. The monstrous Mr. Hyde, shown at left, is suggestive of the id. Stevenson's wife was horrified by the concept and destroyed an early version of the manuscript. But Stevenson was so enthralled by the idea that he rewrote the book.

The Id The **id** is the psychic structure present at birth. It represents physiological drives and is fully unconscious. Freud described the id as "a chaos, a cauldron of seething excitations" (1964, p. 73). The conscious mind might find it inconsistent to love and hate the same person at the same time, but Freud believed that conflicting emotions could dwell side by side in the id. In the id we could experience hatred for our mothers for failing to immediately gratify all of our needs, even at the same time we loved them.

The id follows what Freud termed the **pleasure principle.** It demands instant gratification of instincts without consideration of law, social custom, or the needs of others. If Freud had lived to watch the television show *Sesame Street*, he might have thought that the Cookie Monster represented the id quite well.

The Ego The **ego** begins to develop during the first year of life, largely because not all of a child's demands for gratification can be met immediately. The ego "stands for reason and good sense" (Freud, 1964, p. 76), for rational ways of coping with frustration. It curbs the appetites of the id and makes plans that are in keeping with social convention so that a person can find gratification yet avoid the disapproval of others. The id lets you know that you are starving. The ego creates the idea of walking to the refrigerator, heating up some blueberry cheese tacos, and pouring a glass of milk.

The ego is guided by the **reality principle.** It takes into account what is practical and possible, as well as what is urged. Within Freudian theory, it is the ego that provides the conscious sense of self.

Although most of the ego is conscious, some of its business is carried out unconsciously. For instance, the ego also acts as a watchdog or censor that screens the impulses of the id. When the ego senses that socially unacceptable impulses—impulses which we would rather not admit to having—are rising into awareness, it may use psychological defenses to prevent them from surfacing. Repression is one such psychological defense, or **defense mechanism.** Other defense mechanisms will be explored in Chapter 10. Freud suspected that persistent feelings of nervousness and nameless anxieties could represent unconscious, repressed feelings of hostility toward loved ones.

The Superego The **superego** develops throughout middle childhood, usually incorporating the moral standards and values of parents and significant members of the community through **identification.**

The superego functions according to the **moral principle.** The superego can hold forth shining examples of ideal behavior or of an ideal self. But the superego also acts like the conscience or "voice within"—like an internal moral guardian. Throughout life the superego monitors the intentions of the ego and hands out judgments of right and wrong. It floods the ego with feelings of guilt and shame when the verdict is in the negative.

The ego hasn't an easy time of it. It stands between id and superego, braving the arrows of each. It strives to satisfy the demands of the id and the moral sense of the superego. The id may urge, "You are sexually aroused!" But the superego may warn, "You're not married." The poor ego is caught in the middle.

From the Freudian perspective, a healthy personality has found ways to gratify most of the id's demands without seriously offending the superego. Most of the remaining demands of the id are contained or repressed. If the ego is not a good problem solver, or if the superego is overly strict, the ego

Id The psychic structure, present at birth, that represents physiological drives and is fully unconscious. (A Latin word meaning "it.")

Pleasure principle The governing principle of the id—the seeking of immediate gratification of instinctive needs.

Ego (EE–go). The second psychic structure to develop, characterized by self-awareness, planning, and the delay of gratification. (A Latin word meaning "I.")

Reality principle Consideration of what is practical and possible in gratifying needs—characteristic of the ego.

Defense mechanism In psychoanalytic theory, an unconscious function of the ego that protects it from anxiety-evoking material by preventing accurate recognition of this material.

Superego The third psychic structure, which functions as a moral guardian and sets forth high standards for behavior.

Identification In psychoanalytic theory, the unconscious assumption of the behavior of another person, usually the parent of the same sex.

Moral principle The governing principle of the superego, which sets moral standards and enforces adherence to them.

Intrapsychic Referring to the psychodynamic movement of psychic energy among the mental structures hypothesized by Freud.

Eros In psychoanalytic theory, the basic instinct to preserve and perpetuate life.

Libido (lib–BEE–doe). (1) In psychoanalytic theory, the energy of Eros; the sexual instinct. (2) Generally, sexual interest or drive.

Erogenous zone An area of the body that is sensitive to sexual sensations.

Psychosexual development In psychoanalytic theory, the process by which libidinal energy is expressed through different erogenous zones during different stages of development.

Oral stage The first stage of psychosexual development, during which gratification is hypothesized to be attained primarily through oral activities, like sucking and biting.

Weaning Accustoming the child to surrender sucking the mother's breast or a baby bottle. (From the Old English *wenian*, meaning "to accustom.")

will be in some hot water. Trying to negotiate an end to conflict is never easy. When the conflict is *within* a person, or **intrapsychic,** it can be especially difficult.

Psychosexual Development

Freud, himself a physician, stirred controversy within the medical establishment of his day by arguing that sexual impulses, and their gratification, were central factors in the development of personality—even among children. Freud did not believe that children desired sexual intercourse. But he did insist that their most basic ways of relating to the world, such as suckling their mothers' breasts and moving their bowels, involved intense sexual feelings.

Freud believed that one of the major instincts of the id was **Eros,** the instinct to preserve and perpetuate life. Eros contained a certain amount of energy, which Freud labeled **libido.** This energy was psychological in nature and involved sexual impulses, so Freud considered it *psychosexual*. This libidinal or psychosexual energy would be expressed through sexual feelings in different parts of the body, or **erogenous zones,** as the child developed. Freud saw human development as a process of **psychosexual development.** He hypothesized five stages of psychosexual development: oral, anal, phallic, latency, and genital.

The Oral Stage   During the first year of life, a child experiences much of its world through the mouth. If it fits, into the mouth it goes. This is the **oral stage** of psychosexual development. Freud argued that oral activities like sucking and biting bring the child sexual gratification as well as nourishment.

Freud believed that children would encounter conflicts during each stage of psychosexual development. During the oral stage conflict would center around the nature and extent of oral gratification. Early **weaning** could lead

Freud, himself a physician, stirred controversy within the medical establishment of his day by portraying children as having sexual feelings and curiosities.

to frustration. Excessive gratification, on the other hand, could lead an infant to expect it would automatically be handed everything in life. Inadequate or excessive gratification in any stage could lead to **fixation** in that stage, and the development of traits characteristic of that stage. Oral traits include dependency, gullibility, and optimism or pessimism.

Freud theorized that adults with an **oral fixation** could experience exaggerated desires for "oral activities" like smoking, overeating, alcohol abuse, and nail biting. Like the infant whose very survival depends on the mercy of an adult, adults with oral fixations may be disposed toward clinging, dependent interpersonal relationships.

Note that according to psychoanalytic theory our traits and "fixations" have little to do with conscious choice or self-concept. Rather, we are portrayed as being largely at the mercy of events that occurred long before we could weigh alternatives and make decisions about how we would behave. Freud's own "oral fixation," cigar smoking, may have contributed to the cancer of the mouth and jaw that killed him in 1939. His illness lingered for many years during which time he underwent several operations. Freud seemed to fare better during brief periods when he managed not to smoke. But he would not permanently forgo this source of "oral gratification."

The Anal Stage During the **anal stage,** sexual gratification is attained through contraction and relaxation of the **sphincter** muscles that control elimination of waste products. The process of elimination, which was controlled reflexively during most of the first year of life, comes under voluntary muscular control, even if such control at first is not reliable. The anal stage is said to begin in the second year of life.

In Freud's view, the events of the anal stage may confuse children about the meaning of their waste products. Children may be given the idea that their waste products are valuable because their parents make an event of placing them on the potty and encouraging them to "be good" and "do it" (that is, produce wastes). But children also receive the message that their wastes are dirty. Parents may show disgust when cleaning up after the child who is less than successful at learning sphincter control.

According to Freud, it is during the anal stage that children learn to delay the gratification of eliminating whenever they feel the urge. The general issue of self-control may become a source of conflict between parent and child. **Anal fixations** may stem from this conflict and lead to two sets of anal traits. So-called **anal retentive** traits involve excessive use of self-control. They include perfectionism, a strong need for order, and exaggerated neatness and cleanliness. **Anal-expulsive** traits, on the other hand, "let it all hang out." They include carelessness, messiness, even **sadism.**

In the film and television series *The Odd Couple*, Oscar Madison and Felix Ungar share an apartment after their wives have thrown them out. Oscar is messy. He drops everything everywhere, like a truck of junk on a bumpy road. Felix is excessively neat, the type who will follow a smoker around the room with an ashtray.

According to psychoanalytic theory, both Felix and Oscar are fixated in the anal stage of psychosexual development. Their behavior patterns reflect the opposing ways in which they have learned to adjust to a strict toilet-training process.

Felix became very well housebroken. His personality type is anal-retentive. He has a place for everything and everything is in its place. Neatness and

Fixation In psychoanalytic theory, arrested development. Attachment to objects of a certain stage when one's development should have advanced so that one is attached to objects of a more advanced stage.

Oral fixation Attachment to objects and behaviors characteristic of the oral stage.

Anal stage The second stage of psychosexual development, when gratification is attained through anal activities, like eliminating wastes.

Sphincter A ringlike muscle that circles and controls the contraction of a bodily opening.

Anal fixation Attachment to objects and behaviors characteristic of the anal stage.

Anal retentive Descriptive of behaviors and traits that have to do with "holding in," or with the expression of self-control. A Freudian personality type.

Anal expulsive Descriptive of behaviors and traits that have to do with unregulated self-expression, such as messiness. A Freudian personality type.

Sadism Attaining gratification from inflicting pain on or humiliating others. (After the French Marquis de Sade.)

Phallic stage The third stage of psychosexual development, characterized by a shift of libido to the phallic region. (From the Greek *phallos*, meaning "image of the penis.")

Clitoris (KLIT–or–riss). An external female sexual organ which is highly sensitive to sexual stimulation. (From the Greek *kleitoris*, meaning "hill.")

Oedipus complex (ED–uh–puss). A conflict of the phallic stage in which the boy wishes to possess his mother sexually and perceives his father as a rival in love.

Electra complex A conflict of the phallic stage in which the girl longs for her father and resents her mother.

Displaced Transferred. See the defense mechanism of displacement in Chapter 10.

Latency stage The fourth stage of psychosexual development, characterized by repression of sexual impulses.

Genital stage The mature stage of psychosexual development, characterized by preferred expression of libido through intercourse with an adult of the opposite sex.

Incest taboo The cultural prohibition against marrying or having sexual relations with a close blood relative. (From the Latin *in–*, meaning "not," and *castus*, meaning "chaste.")

spelling both count. But Oscar rebelled. His slovenliness probably symbolizes his resentment at being forced to use the potty when it was still difficult for him to exercise self-control. His personality is anal-expulsive. He is unkempt, disorganized, and careless.

The Phallic Stage   Children are said to enter the **phallic stage** during the third year of life. During this stage the major erogenous zone is the phallic region (the **clitoris** in girls). Parent-child conflict is likely to develop over masturbation, which parents may treat with punishment and threats. During the phallic stage children may develop strong sexual attachments to the parent of the opposite sex and begin to view the same-sex parent as a rival for the other parent's affections. Boys may want to marry Mommy, and girls may want to marry Daddy.

Feelings of lust and jealousy are difficult for little children to handle. Home life would be tense indeed. So these feelings remain largely unconscious, although their influence is felt through fantasies about marriage and through vague hostilities toward the same-sex parent. Freud labeled this conflict in boys the **Oedipus complex,** after the legendary Greek king who unwittingly killed his father and married his mother. Similar feelings in girls give rise to the **Electra complex.** According to Greek legend, Electra was the daughter of the king Agamemnon. She longed for him after his death and sought revenge against his slayers—her mother and her mother's lover.

The Oedipus and Electra complexes become resolved by about the ages five or six. Children then repress their hostilities toward and identify with the parent of the same sex. Identification leads to playing the social and sexual roles of the same-sex parent, and internalizing that parent's values. Sexual feelings toward the opposite-sex parent are repressed for a number of years. When they emerge during adolscence, they are **displaced** onto socially appropriate members of the opposite sex.

The Latency Stage   By the age of five or six, Freud believed that children would have been in conflict with their parents over sexual feelings for several years. The pressures of the Oedipus and Electra complexes would motivate them to repress all sexual urges. In so doing they would enter the **latency stage,** a period of life during which sexual feelings would remain unconscious. They would use this period to focus on schoolwork and to consolidate earlier learning, most notably, of appropriate sex-role behaviors. Also, during the latency stage it is not uncommon for children to prefer playmates of their own sex.

The Genital Stage   Freud wrote that we enter the final stage of psychosexual development, or **genital stage,** at puberty. Adolescent males again experience sexual urges toward their mothers, and adolescent females toward their fathers. But the **incest taboo** provides ample motivation for keeping these impulses repressed and displacing them onto other adults or adolescents of the opposite sex. But boys might still seek girls "just like the girl that married dear old Dad." Girls might still be attracted to men who resemble their fathers.

People in the genital stage prefer, by definition, to find sexual gratification through intercourse with a member of the opposite sex. Sigmund Freud was an Orthodox Jew who believed that the primary purpose of human sexuality was to follow the Biblical command to "be fruitful and multiply." The thrust of Eros was aimed at the perpetuation of the human species. So it is not surprising that this most traditional psychological thinker would assume that proper adult sexuality meant sexual intercourse—preferably within a lasting union that would provide for the care and well-being of children. In Freud's view, oral or anal stimulation, masturbation, and homosexual activity would all represent **pregenital** fixations and immature forms of sexual conduct. They would not be in keeping with the life instinct Eros.

Pregenital Characteristic of stages less mature than the genital stage.

Cognitive vs. Psychoanalytic Views of Religious Conversion: Do We Suddenly See the Light, or Do We Strive to Keep a Lid on the Id?

Each year thousands of parents in the United States are shocked to learn that their children have become Hare Krishnas or "Moonies," or joined some other religious cult or sect. They cannot understand why their children have foresaken not only their early religious learnings, but also their families. Now and then we hear of parents who have their children kidnapped and "deprogrammed" in an effort to have them return to the family and fold.

Why is it that people undergo the dramatic experience of religious conversion? Cognitive and psychoanalytic perspectives offer quite different explanations. From the cognitive view, religious conversion represents a conscious effort to put an end to uncertainty about the nature of man and the universe. The type of person who is ripe for conversion would probably show great concern with basic religious and political questions during adolescence. From a psychoanalytic perspective, religious conversion represents a defense against an upsurge of unconscious Oedipal hatred toward the father (Freud, 1927/1964). By converting to a new religion, a person is submitting to a powerful father figure (God), and keeping the lid on impulses from the id. The psychoanalytic view suggests that converts would encounter more traumatic events during childhood and adolescence, giving rise to feelings of hostility which would then be controlled through conversion.

In a study of the cognitive and psychoanalytic views of religious conversion, psychologist Chana Ullman (1982) interviewed 40 religious converts and 30 nonconverts. Ullman expected that converts would show less tolerance of uncertainty and greater concern about basic religious issues than would nonconverts—thus supporting the cognitive view. But she found that converts and nonconverts could not be distinguished on these variables.

Instead, in keeping with the psychoanalytic view, Ullman found that 77 percent of the religious converts, as compared with 23 percent of the nonconverts, reported problematic relationships with their fathers, including a frequent incidence of father absence. Note these excerpts from interviews with converts: "My relationship with (my father) was to keep from antagonizing him or causing any trouble," and "He did not understand anything you did, you could do nothing right . . . and I started hating him" (Ullman, 1982, p. 192). Converts were also more likely than nonconverts to report specific traumatic events during childhood and adolescent stress.

In additional findings, 80 percent of the converts reported emotional turmoil just before converting (such as "I thought I was going crazy" or "I had suicidal thoughts"). The same percentage reported that their conversion provided relief from anxiety, anger, or depression.

Ullman concludes that her study highlights the roles of stress and anxiety in precipitating religious conversion. Although her study cannot reveal what may have been occurring with her subjects on an unconscious level, it does seem to provide strong evidence that childhood trauma and a rejecting or absent father figure also contribute to the likelihood of conversion. As Ullman writes, "In many religious conversion cases, the experience may be seen as an attempt to gain the approval, protection, or guidance of an authority figure, as suggested by the original psychoanalytic hypothesis" (1982, pp. 191–192).

Why do people undergo religious conversions? Are they searching for answers to cognitive uncertainty, or are they attempting to maintain control over unconscious impulses?

Karen Horney.

A Psychological Controversy: Do Women Who Compete with Men Suffer from Penis Envy?

Psychoanalytic theory in many ways has been a liberating force, allowing people to admit the importance of sexuality in their lives. But it has also been claimed that Freud's views are repressive of women. The **penis-envy** hypothesis has stigmatized women who compete with men in the business world as failing to have resolved the Electra complex.

Freud believed that little girls envy boys their penises. The root of this envy supposedly lay in the "fact" that the clitoris is not so sensitive to sexual stimulation as the penis. So when little girls masturbated, they would inevitably be disappointed. They would envy the sexual superiority of their brothers and male playmates. They would resent their mothers for bringing them into the world so "ill-equipped," as Freud (1964) wrote in *New Introductory Lectures on Psychoanalysis*, and develop the wish to marry their fathers as a substitute for not having penises of their own.

Through a series of developmental transformations, the wish to marry the father would evolve into the desire to marry another man and bear children. A baby, especially a male child, would symbolize something growing from the genital region and bring some psychological satisfaction. Freud declared that the ideally adjusted woman would accept her husband's authority, symbolizing surrender of the wish to have a penis of her own.

Freud warned that retaining the wish to have a penis would lead to maladjustment. Persistent jealousy would cause women to develop masculine traits. They might even become competitive and self-assertive, or at worst, homosexual.

These assumptions have been attacked strongly by women and by modern-day psychoanalysts. Karen Horney (1967), a **neo-Freudian,** contended that little girls do not feel inferior to little boys, and that the penis-envy hypothesis was not supported by the evidence of actual observations of children. Horney wrote that Freud's view reflected a Western cultural prejudice that women are inferior to men—and not sound psychological theory.

There is also no evidence for the assertion that the clitoris is less sensitive than the penis. The clitoris is similar in embryonic origin and function to the sexually sensitive tip of the penis (Rathus, 1983). The incidence of masturbation among women may not be so high as the incidence for men (Hunt, 1974), but this difference is more likely to reflect childhood training than biological differences between the sexes.

Psychologist Phyllis Chesler (1972) argues that there has been a historic prejudice against self-assertive, competent women, one shared by mental-health professionals. Many people, as we shall see in Chapter 13, want women to remain passive and submissive, emotional, and dependent on men. In Freud's day these prejudices were more extreme. Psychoanalytic theory, in its original form, reflected the belief that motherhood and family life were the only proper avenues of fulfillment for women.

Penis envy In psychoanalytic theory, jealousy of the male sexual organ attributed to girls in the phallic stage.

Neo-Freudian A person who views behavior largely from the psychoanalytic perspective, but who generally attributes more behavior to conscious motives and reasoned decision-making.

Evaluation of Freud's Psychoanalytic Theory

Freud's psychoanalytic theory has had tremendous appeal and has been a major contribution to twentieth century thought. It is the richest of personality theories, explaining many varieties of human behavior and traits. But despite its richness, Freud's work has been criticized on many grounds.

Psychic determinism The view that behavior is not arbitrary, but is determined by the outcome of the clashing of psychic forces.

Some followers of Freud, like Erik Erikson, have argued that Freud placed too much emphasis on human sexuality and neglected the relative importance of social relationships. Others, like Alfred Adler and Erich Fromm, argued that Freud placed too much emphasis on unconscious motives. Adler and Fromm assert that people consciously seek self-enhancement and intellectual pleasures, rather than simply attempting to gratify the dark demands of the id.

A number of critics note that "psychic structures" like the id, ego, and superego have no substance. They are little more than useful fictions, poetic ways to express inner conflict. It is debatable whether Freud ever attributed substance to the psychic structures. He, too, may have seen them more as poetic fictions than as "things." If so, his critics have the right to use other descriptive terms and write better "poems."

Nor have the stages of psychosexual development escaped criticism. People may begin to masturbate as early as the first year of life, rather than in the "phallic stage." As parents can testify from observing their children play "doctor," the latency stage is not so sexually "latent" as Freud believed. Much of Freud's thinking concerning the Oedipus and Electra complexes remains simple speculation. His views of female sexuality and sex-role behavior reflect the ignorance and prejudice of his times.

Once we have catalogued our criticisms of Freud's views, what of merit is left? A number of important things. In his doctrine of **psychic determinism** Freud pointed out that behavior is determined and not arbitrary. He pointed out that childhood experiences can have far-reaching effects on adult personality. He noted that people have defensive ways of looking at the world. Our cognitive processes can be distorted by our efforts to defend ourselves against anxiety and guilt. If these ideas no longer impress us as unique or innovative, it is largely because of the powerful influence of Sigmund Freud.

We're Number One! On Basking in Reflected Glory

Every fall football mania sweeps college campuses like the brisk September air. From the ivy halls of Yale and Harvard to the Big Ten stadiums of Michigan and Ohio, "fans of championship teams gloat over their team's accomplishments and proclaim their affiliation with buttons on their clothes, bumper stickers on their cars, and banners on their public buildings. Despite the fact that they have never caught a ball or thrown a block . . . fans . . . claim for themselves part of their team's glory; . . . the shout is always 'We're number one,' never, 'They're number one!' " (Cialdini and others, 1976).

Why is it *"we're,"* not *"they're,"* number one? Is it an expression of loyalty to the home team? Or do fans "bask in the reflected glory" of winners, but dissociate themselves from losers?

In one study, psychologists on several prominent football campuses observed student behavior on the Mondays after football games (Cialdini and others, 1976). On Mondays following victories, significantly higher percentages of students wore clothing with school insignias or mascots as compared to the Mondays following defeats. But this could just have meant that students liked their schools better after victories.

To find out whether students were more likely to identify with their schools after victories, investigators asked students to describe the outcome of the game. When their team won, students were likely to write *"We* won." But when the home team lost, students more frequently referred to the team as "They," not "We." That is, *"We* won" but *"They* lost."

According to the personality concept of identification, we attempt to identify or associate ourselves with people who are powerful, successful, and admired, but to dissociate ourselves from losers. When we identify with winners, their success becomes *our* success, providing a boost to our self-esteem. As children we tend to identify with our parents, because they seem capable of manipulating the environment enough to yield rewards we ourselves have difficulty attaining. Identifying with a loser only boosts the agony of defeat.

Analytical psychology
Jung's psychoanalytic theory, which emphasizes the collective unconscious and archetypes.

Collective unconscious
Jung's hypothesized store of vague racial memories.

Archetypes
(ARE–keh–types). Basic, primitive images or concepts hypothesized by Jung to reside in the collective unconscious. (From the Greek *archein,* meaning "to begin," and *typos,* meaning "figure" or "model.")

Mythical Descriptive of traditional, fictitious stories often intended to explain natural phenomena or human origins. (From the Greek *mythos,* meaning "legend.")

Other Psychoanalytic Theories

A number of personality theorists are intellectual descendents of Sigmund Freud. Their theories, like Freud's, include roles for unconscious motivation, for motivational conflict, and for defensive responses to anxiety-evoking ideas and urges that involve repression and cognitive distortion of reality (Wachtel, 1982). In other respects, they differ markedly. We discuss the psychodynamic views of Carl Jung, Alfred Adler, and Erik Erikson.

Carl Jung and Analytical Psychology

Carl Jung (1875–1961) was a Swiss psychiatrist who once had been a favorite of Freud's and a member of his inner circle. But he fell into disfavor with Freud when he developed his own psychoanalytic theory which he termed **analytical psychology.** Jung, like Freud, was intrigued by unconscious processes. He believed that we not only have a *personal* unconscious, which contains repressed memories and impulses, but also an inherited **collective unconscious,** which contains primitive images, or **archetypes,** reflections of the exciting history of our species.

Archetypes   Archetypes include vague mysterious **mythical** images. Examples of archetypes are the All-Powerful God, the young hero, the fertile and nurturing mother, the wise old man, the hostile brother, even fairy godmothers, wicked witches, and themes of rebirth or resurrection. Archetypes themselves remain unconscious, but Jung declared that they influence our thoughts and emotions and render us responsive to cultural themes in stories and films. Archetypes are somewhat accessible through the interpretation of dreams.

Jung believed that within each of us reside shadowy parts of the personality which may unfold gradually as we mature. He believed that we all

Carl Gustav Jung.

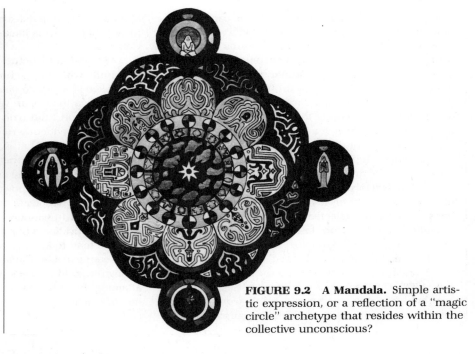

FIGURE 9.2   A Mandala. Simple artistic expression, or a reflection of a "magic circle" archetype that resides within the collective unconscious?

have an **animus,** a masculine, aggressively competitive aspect to our personalities, and an **anima,** which is feminine, soft, supportive, and passive. Cultural influences make it likely that men will express the animus more so than women will, and women the anima. But we are all seen as richly multifaceted.

The Self Jung downplayed the importance of the sexual instinct. He saw it as but one of several important instincts. Despite all of his interest in the collective unconscious, Jung also granted more importance to conscious motives than Freud did. Jung believed that one of the archetypes is a **self,** a conscious, unifying force of personality that gives conscious direction and purpose to human behavior. According to Jung, heredity dictates that the self will persistently strive to achieve a wholeness or fullness. This striving takes many forms. Some people become intrigued by mystical patterns like the magic-circle archetype, or **mandala.** Others seek to express this unity through religious experience, or through inner voyages fueled by drugs or meditation.

Jung believed that an understanding of human behavior must incorporate the facts of self-awareness and self-direction as well as the impulses of the id and the mechanisms of defense. But the same Jung who insisted that importance must be attached to fully conscious functions went even further than Freud in constructing an involved, poetic inner life. Many of Jung's ideas cannot be verified through scientific study. They remain at the level of theoretical, even spiritual, speculation.

Alfred Adler

Alfred Adler and Individual Psychology

Alfred Adler (1870–1937), another follower of Freud, also believed that Freud had placed too much emphasis on sexual impulses. Adler believed that people are basically motivated by an **inferiority complex.** In some people feelings of inferiority may be based on physical problems and the need to compensate for them. But Adler believed that all of us harbor some feelings of inferiority, and that these feelings give rise to a **drive for superiority.** For instance, the English poet Lord Byron, with a crippled leg, became a champion swimmer. Beethoven's encroaching deafness may have spurred him on to greater musical accomplishments.

Adler, like Jung, believed that self-awareness plays a major role in the formation of personality. Adler spoke of a **creative self,** a self-aware aspect of personality that strives to overcome obstacles and develop the individual's potential. Because this potential is uniquely individual, Adler's views have been termed **individual psychology.**

Erik Erikson and Psychosocial Development

Erik Erikson, as Jung and Adler before him, believed that Freud had placed undue emphasis on sexual instincts. Erikson taught that social relationships are more crucial determinants of personality. Erikson, for example, found the general climate of the mother-infant relationship more important than the details of the feeding process or sexual feelings that might be stirred by the mother's nearness.

Psychosocial Development For this reason, Erikson proposes stages of psycho*social* rather than psycho*sexual* development. Rather than labeling a stage after an erogenous zone, Erikson labeled stages after the traits that might be

Animus (AN–uh–mus). Jung's term for a masculine archetype of the collective unconscious. (A Latin word meaning "soul" or "disposition.")

Anima (AN–uh–muh). Jung's feminine archetype.

Self In analytical psychology, a conscious, unifying force to personality that provides people with direction and purpose.

Mandala (MON–duh–luh *or* man–DOLL–uh). In the Hindu and Buddhist traditions, a circular design symbolizing the wholeness or unity of life. (A Sanskrit word meaning "circle.")

Inferiority complex Feelings of inferiority hypothesized by Adler to serve as a central motivating force.

Drive for superiority Adler's term for the desire to compensate for feelings of inferiority.

Creative self According to Adler, the self-aware aspect of personality that strives to achieve its full potential.

Individual psychology Adler's psychoanalytic theory, which emphasizes feelings of inferiority and the creative self.

TABLE 9.1   Erik Erikson's Stages of Psychosocial Development

Time Period	Life Crisis	The Task
Infancy	Trust vs. mistrust	Coming to trust the mother and the environment, to associate surroundings with feelings of inner goodness
Early childhood	Autonomy vs. shame and doubt	Developing the wish to make choices and the self-control to exercise choice
Preschool years	Initiative vs. guilt	Adding planning and "attacking" to choice; being active
Grammar-school years	Industry vs. inferiority	Mastering fundamentals of technology, skills, productivity
Adolescence	Ego identity vs. role diffusion	Connecting skills and social roles to career objectives
Young adulthood	Intimacy vs. isolation	Committing the self to another; experiencing sexual love
Middle adulthood	Generativity vs. stagnation	Guiding and encouraging the younger generation; being creative
Late adulthood	Ego integrity vs. despair	Accepting the time and place of one's own life cycle; exhibiting wisdom and dignity

Source: Erikson (1963), pp. 247-269.

Erik Erikson.

developed during that stage (Table 9.1). The first stage of **psychosocial development** is the stage of trust versus mistrust because of the two possible major outcomes: (1) A warm, loving relationship with the mother (and **significant others**) during infancy may lead to a sense of basic trust in people and the world. (2) A cold, nongratifying relationship may lead to a pervasive sense of mistrust. Erikson extended Freud's five developmental stages to eight to include the changing concerns of various stages of adulthood (discussed in Chapter 8).

Erikson was as traditional as Freud in his beliefs about proper sexual behavior. For Erikson, as for Freud, sexual intimacy should take place within a heterosexual union that provides for the well-being of the next generation.

Trait Theory

Once the psychoanalytically oriented student of personality finishes his description of the elephant, the second personality student walks around the elephant deliberately to study the low-hung belly and the thick legs.

"No," he says to the psychoanalyst. "You're digging too deep. Everything we need to know about our elephant is right here, right here in this massive belly. Our fat friend"—the elephant snorts—"is basically relaxed and jolly. He simply loves to eat—"

"Deep," interrupts the psychoanalyst. *"Deep."*

"—he loves to eat and he gets along with everybody. He's not athletic or courageous, he's not scholarly or artistic. We know all this from these rolls of flab. He loves everyone."

"You, I don't like at all," notes the elephant.

Psychosocial development Erikson's theory of personality and development, which emphasizes social relationships and eight stages of growth.

Significant others Persons who have a major impact on one's development, including parents, peers, and lovers.

Traits from Allport to Cattell

If asked to describe yourself you would probably mention one or more of your **traits.** Traits are personality elements that are inferred from behavior and account for behavioral consistency. Freud linked certain traits to his stages of psychosexual development. We use traits to describe others. If you describe a friend as "shy," it may be because you observed some social anxiety or withdrawal in early meetings. In personality trait theory, traits are assumed to endure, to underlie and account for behavior in various situations. Similarly, you would probably predict consistent social anxiety and withdrawal for your "shy" friend and might be surprised if he or she acted assertively.

Gordon Allport   According to psychologist Gordon Allport (1937, 1961), traits were rooted in the nervous system of the person. Allport considered them "neuropsychic" structures. They steered or guided people to behave consistently in various situations. For example, the trait of sociability may steer a person to invite friends along when going out, to share confidences when writing letters, and to make others feel welcome and comfortable at family gatherings. A person who lacks the trait of sociability would be disposed to behave very differently in these situations.

Allport labeled traits according to the roles they play in directing behavior. In rare cases a trait may be so outstanding and pervasive that it seems to steer practically all aspects of a person's behavior. Such a powerful trait is a **cardinal trait.** Allport (1937) offered the following adjectives as examples of cardinal traits from historic and literary figures: *Christ-like,* **Machiavellian, Napoleonic,** and **Sadistic.**

Central traits define the outstanding characteristics of the person. They are the sort that might be mentioned in a letter of recommendation, such as "well-groomed," "honest," and "hard-working." **Secondary traits** are less influential and less noticeable. Rather than generally guiding the behavior of the individual, they appear to occur in a small range of situations and to govern a limited number of responses. Our total pattern of traits is termed our **personality structure.**

More than 40 years ago Allport and Odbert (1936) catalogued some 18,000 human traits from a search through word lists of the sort found in dictionaries. Some were physical traits, like short, white, and brunette. Others were behavioral traits, like shy and emotional. Still others were moral traits, like honest. This exhaustive list has served as the basis for personality research by many other psychologists.

Raymond Cattell   Psychologists like Raymond Cattell (1965) have used statistical techniques to reduce this universe of innumerable traits to smaller lists that show commonality in meaning. Cattell also distinguished between surface traits and source traits. **Surface traits** describe characteristic ways of behaving like cleanliness, stubbornness, thrift, and orderliness. We may observe that these traits tend to form meaningful patterns that are suggestive of underlying traits. (Cleanliness, stubbornness, and so on were all referred to as *anal retentive* traits by Freud.)

Cattell refined the Allport catalogue by removing unusual terms and grouping the remaining traits into 16 central **source traits**—the underlying traits from which surface traits are derived. Cattell argued that psychological measurement of a person's source traits would enable us to predict his or her

Trait An aspect of personality that is inferred from behavior and assumed to give rise to behavioral consistency.

Cardinal trait Allport's term for pervasive traits that guide practically all of a person's behavior.

Machiavellian Characterized by craftiness and deceitfulness in the attainment of one's goals. (After Italian statesman Niccolo Machiavelli.)

Napoleonic Governed by the needs for power and aggression.

Sadistic Attaining gratification by inflicting pain on others.

Central traits Outstanding, noticeable (but not necessarily all-pervasive) characteristics of a person.

Secondary traits Traits that appear in a limited number of situations and govern a limited number of responses.

Personality structure One's total pattern of traits.

Surface traits Cattell's term for characteristic, observable ways of behaving.

Source traits Cattell's term for underlying traits from which surface traits are derived.

Beachhead in the Pacific: Erik Erikson's Search for Self-Identity

For the United States, World War II in the Pacific meant island hopping and a bloody miniature war on each island. Ever nearing the Japanese home islands, American marines landed on hostile sands, drew enemy fire, gained difficult beachheads, and gradually cleared the islands of the enemy. During this war, as during other wars, some chose to make their contribution through the medical corps, to follow the battles and try to minimize the human wreckage, rather than add to it themselves.

One young medical corpsman, strongly opposed to the bloodshed, was stuck one night on such a beachhead. Soldiers around him struggled through the night to prevent them all from being swept back into the ocean as enemy fire raged. Shells burst into light, illuminating the corpses and the embattled alike. The air around them was punctured by the crack of enemy bullets whistling by before whacking into sand—or flesh—with dead thuds. Promised air and naval support failed to arrive. Soldiers cursed their commanders, the navy, the island, the human species. Resentments combined with fear, and the medical corpsman's level of arousal grew such that his perceptions and memories became clouded and unreal.

Later he recalled that he had been required to unload ammunition rather than tend to the sick and wounded. He recalled a superior officer screaming profanities. His last memory of that night was of someone handing him an automatic rifle.

When he awoke in the field hospital the next day, he was plagued by jumpiness, anxiety, and vicious headaches. No physical ailments could be found, but his condition worsened. Finally he was sent stateside and referred for treatment to the Mount Zion Veterans' Rehabilitation Clinic in San Francisco, where he was treated by a psychoanalyst named Erik H. Erikson.

Erik Erikson and Self-Identity Erikson worked with this and many other soldiers suffering from what came to be known as *battlefield neurosis*. They had all recently returned from the battlefields of the Pacific theater. They experienced intense anger and anxiety, especially when startled or awakened from recurrent battlefield nightmares.

Erikson (1963) gradually learned our medical corpsman's history. Parental violence and his mother's drinking had wracked his childhood. During one drunken rage she had threatened him with a gun. He took it from her and threw it out the window. He left home that day and vowed never to drink, curse, or carry a gun. He confirmed his own sense of identity by rejecting these aspects of his mother's behavior. Nonviolence, sobriety, self-control, clean speech—all became central aspects of the corpsman's *self-identity*, his sense of who and what he was as an individual.

That tragic night in the Pacific his nerves had been strung taut. He had been confronted with the cursing of a respected officer. A rifle had been thrust

Marines landing on a Pacific island during World War II, (above) from the film *The Sands of Iwo Jima.*

Introversion A source trait characterized by intense imagination and the tendency to inhibit impulses.

Extraversion A source trait characterized by tendencies to be socially outgoing and to express feelings and impulses freely.

Neuroticism Eysenck's term for emotional instability. (This definition is not fully consistent with the meanings of the terms *neurotic* and *neurosis,* as discussed in Chapter 11.)

behavior in various situations. Cattell believed that the major work of a personality theorist lay in helping refine the list of source traits.

Others Many personality theorists have worked to uncover and define central or source traits. For instance, Edwards (1954) isolated 15 source traits and Gough (1954) identified 10. British psychologist Hans J. Eysenck (Eysenck & Rachman, 1965) has focused much of his research on the relationships between two source traits: **introversion-extraversion** and stability-instability, otherwise called **neuroticism.** These source traits or personality dimensions, and a number of surface traits that reflect different combinations of these source traits, are shown in Figure 9.3.

into his hands. He had spun out of control and his self-identity as a good and honorable person had been shaken.

His battlefield neurosis had little to do with fear or cowardice. Erikson sensed that many such soldiers had engaged in behavior incompatible with their self-identities. They had lost touch with who and what they were. Successful adjustment to stress requires maintaining a stable sense of self. When self-identity is threatened by disease, tragedy, or awareness that our behavior is incompatible with our self-definition, we may encounter anxiety, panic, and feelings of alienation. We feel cut adrift from life's purposes and meaning.

The Personal Background of a Psychoanalyst

Erikson's interpretation of the corpsman's problems reflected his own identity problems as a child in Europe, as related in his autobiography (Erikson, 1975). His natural father had deserted his mother just before his birth. Young Erikson was raised by his mother and his stepfather, Theodor Homburger, a

American folk hero John Wayne and other soldiers attempt to establish a beachhead.

physician. But his mother and stepfather did not want young Erikson to feel different, so they did not tell him about his natural father for many years.

Though his mother and stepfather were Jewish, Erikson's blond hair and blue eyes resembled those of his natural father, a Dane. In his stepfather's synagogue he was considered a Gentile. To his classmates he was a Jew. He felt different from other children and alienated from his family. He fantasized that he was the offspring of special parents who had abandoned him. "Who am I?" was a question that permeated his early quest for identity.

As he grew and developed, Erikson faced another identity issue: "What am I to do in life?" His stepfather encouraged him to follow in his footsteps and pursue medicine. But Erikson sought his own path. As a youth he studied art and traveled through Europe, leading the bohemian life of an artist. It was a period of serious questioning and soul-searching—a personal drama that Erikson would later label an *identity crisis.*

The turmoil of his personal search for identity oriented Erikson toward his life's work: psychotherapy. He left his wanderings and plunged into psychoanalytic training under the tutelage of Sigmund Freud's daughter, Anna Freud.

Out of the chaos of his own identity problems Erikson had forged a personally meaningful life pattern. To Erikson, the creation of a personality was not merely the inevitable outcome of the interplay of environmental forces and intrapsychic conflict. He had fashioned his own personality through a series of conscious and purposeful acts. Or so it seemed to him. Sigmund Freud might have argued that even these conclusions were inevitable given the twists and turns his life had taken.

Can we to some degree fashion our personalities, or are they the inevitable outcomes of the forces acting upon us from early childhood? What do you think?

Evaluation of Trait Theory

Trait theory continues to generate useful psychological research, but may be criticized on several grounds. Trait theory is more descriptive than explanatory. It focuses on describing existing traits rather than tracing their origins or investigating how they may be modified. The "explanations" provided by trait theory have been criticized as **circular explanations.** If we say that John failed to ask Marsha on a date *because* of shyness, we have contributed little to our understanding of the causes of John's behavior.

Allport argued that traits were *neuropsychic structures,* somehow embedded in the person's nervous system. Critics have argued that Allport

Circular explanation An explanation that merely restates its own concepts instead of offering additional information.

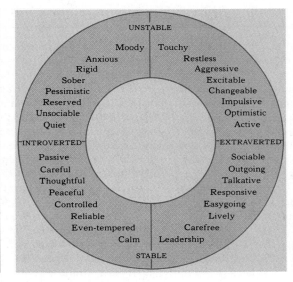

FIGURE 9.3 **Eysenck's Personality Dimensions.** Various personality traits fall within the two major dimensions of personality suggested by Hans Eysenck.

The diagram shows a circle divided by two axes. The vertical axis runs from UNSTABLE (top) to STABLE (bottom), and the horizontal axis runs from INTROVERTED (left) to EXTRAVERTED (right).

Upper-left quadrant (Unstable/Introverted): Moody, Anxious, Rigid, Sober, Pessimistic, Reserved, Unsociable, Quiet

Upper-right quadrant (Unstable/Extraverted): Touchy, Restless, Aggressive, Excitable, Changeable, Impulsive, Optimistic, Active

Lower-left quadrant (Stable/Introverted): Passive, Careful, Thoughtful, Peaceful, Controlled, Reliable, Even-tempered, Calm

Lower-right quadrant (Stable/Extraverted): Sociable, Outgoing, Talkative, Responsive, Easygoing, Lively, Carefree, Leadership

Private self-consciousness The tendency to take critical note of one's own behavior, even when unobserved by others.

Type In personality theory, a personality pattern in which a number of traits cluster together in a meaningful way.

Humor In this usage, a bodily fluid. (A Latin word meaning moisture.)

failed to specify where and how these traits were embedded. In this sense, traits have no more substance than do Freud's psychic structures. Still, a number of psychologists argue that diverse traits like social shyness, aggressiveness, and neuroticism vary from person to person in ways that suggest that inborn factors play an important role (see Chapters 2 and 8).

A basic assumption of trait theory is that human behavior tends to be largely consistent from one situation to another. But research suggests that behavior varies more from situation to situation—at least for some people—than trait theory would allow (Bem & Allen, 1974; Mischel, 1977, 1981). People who are high in **private self-consciousness**—who carefully monitor their own behavior, even when others are not observing them—also try to show consistent behavior from situation to situation (Fenigstein and others, 1975; Scheier and others, 1978; Underwood & Moore, 1981). But other people show greater variability in behavior.

Types from Hippocrates to Sheldon and Eysenck

Are obese people jolly? Are athletic people assertive and outgoing? Are slender, bespectacled people scholarly and socially withdrawn? The "fat, jolly type," the "athletic type" and the "cerebral type" are some of the personality stereotypes prevalent in our culture. Some people assume that people with a certain appearance or body build also have certain attitudes and act in a certain way.

Types are clusters of traits. Type theorists assume that traits cluster together so that we can speak of people as belonging to one personality type or another. The notion that people fall into types is not new. Hippocrates, the physician of the Golden Age of Greece, suggested that there were four types of people (see Table 9.2). Each type was determined by the individual's dominant bodily fluid or **humor.**

Psychologists no longer make use of Hippocrates' types. Hippocrates' notion that types are determined by bodily "humors" is a naive view of human biology and psychology. But the names of Hippocrates' types have remained in use as descriptive terms. Even today we find people described as "melancholy" or "sanguine" in literature and common usage.

Can we make inferences about people's personalities from their physiques? Some people harbor stereotypes of the "athletic type," the "cerebral type," and so on.

TABLE 9.2   The Typology of Hippocrates (circa 400 B.C.)

Type	Dominant Fluid	Base Temperament
Choleric	Yellow bile	Restless, irritable, hot-blooded
Melancholic	Black bile	Depressed, sad
Sanguine	Blood	Cheerful, optimistic
Phlegmatic	Phlegm	Calm, inactive

Hippocrates, the physician of the Golden Age of Greece, suggested that there were four basic types of people. Each type was determined by the person's dominant humor, or bodily fluid.

Constitutional Theory   More recently, American physician William Sheldon (1942) theorized that there are three basic personality types. Each type is linked to a certain physique or constitution, as noted in Figure 9.4. For this reason, types are referred to as **somatotypes.**

In Sheldon's **constitutional theory** an obese person is **endomorphic.** Sheldon predicted that endomorphs would be found to be pleasure-loving, relaxed, and sociable. Sheldon also asserted that there were **mesomorphic** and **ectomorphic** types, roughly equivalent to "athletic" and "intellectual" types. Mesomorphs would be outgoing, domineering, and assertive. Ectomorphs would be contemplative, intense, and inhibited.

Sheldon did not claim that people perfectly fit into one personality type. Rather, their physiques (and personalities) might contain elements from two or more types, as represented on a scale of one through seven for each type. A pure mesomorph, for example, would be rated 1–7–1, while the average person would be rated 4–4–4. Sheldon did claim that behavior could be predicted once a person had been classified according to how much he or she had been influenced by each type of physique.

Eysenck's Personality Types   Carl Jung was first to distinguish between introverts and extraverts. Hans Eysenck (1960) added the dimension of neuroticism to introversion-extraversion and has described a number of personality types according to where they are "situated" along these dimensions (refer to Figure 9.3). For instance, an anxious type would be high both in introversion and neuroticism; that is, preoccupied with his or her own thoughts and emotionally unstable. Where would you place athletes and artists in terms of the dimensions of introversion-extraversion and neuroticism?

Somatotypes Sheldon's term for personality types hypothesized to be consistent with stereotypical physiques.

Constitutional theory Sheldon's view that one's physique is a determinant of one's personality structure.

Endomorphic (END–doe–mor–fik). According to constitutional theory, an obese and sociable somatotype. (From the Greek *endon,* meaning "within," and *morphe,* meaning "form.")

Mesomorphic (MEZZ–oh–mor–fik). A muscular, athletic, and courageous somatotype. (From the Greek *mesos,* meaning "middle.")

Ectomorphic (ECK–toe–mor–fik). A slender, tall, and cerebral somatotype. (From the Greek *ektos,* meaning "outside.")

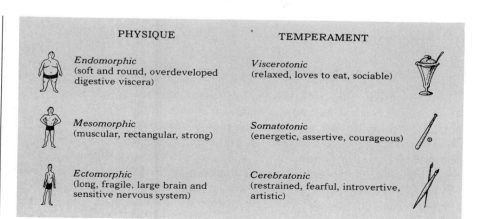

PHYSIQUE

Endomorphic (soft and round, overdeveloped digestive viscera)

Mesomorphic (muscular, rectangular, strong)

Ectomorphic (long, fragile, large brain and sensitive nervous system)

TEMPERAMENT

Viscerotonic (relaxed, loves to eat, sociable)

Somatotonic (energetic, assertive, courageous)

Cerebratonic (restrained, fearful, introvertive, artistic)

FIGURE 9.4   Sheldon's Constitutional Theory. Sheldon believed that our temperaments are determined largely by our physiques. Are obese people jolly?

On Cockpits and Cocktails: A Comparison of Pilots, Artists, and Writers

What *don't* airline pilots, creative artists, and writers have in common? According to Raymond Cattell's Sixteen Personality Factors Scale, which measures the source traits he isolated, pilots are more stable, conscientious, tough-minded, practical, controlled, and relaxed than the other two groups (see Figure 9.5). But artists and writers are more intelligent, sensitive, and imaginative. You might prefer to have artists at a cocktail party, but pilots—at least those in the group tested by Cattell—seem to have the stable and controlled personality profile you would prefer to have in charge in the cockpit.

A major criticism of the trait approach is that behavior varies more widely from situation to situation than traits (examples of "personal variables") would allow. By contrast, the social learning approach to personality theory has focused on situational variables. But current social learning theorists believe that behavior is determined by an interaction between personal and situational variables.

FIGURE 9.5 Three Personality Profiles According to Cattell's 16 Personality Factors.
How do the traits of pilots, artists, and writers compare? Where would you place yourself along these 16 personality dimensions?

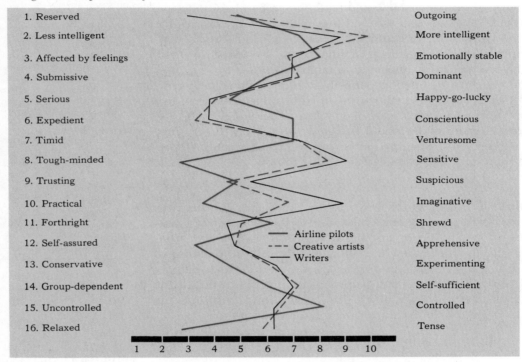

Evaluation of Type Theory

Type theory, like trait theory, underestimates the importance of situational influences in determining behavior. It also underestimates the importance of individual differences among people assigned to a given type. Sheldon's typology has received some support through research. But Mischel (1981) points out that the people rating subjects' physiques in these studies, or reporting on the temperaments of acquaintances, may have had **experimenter bias.** They may have been aware of cultural stereotypes concerning physique and personality and may have distorted their ratings or information to fit the stereotypes.

Experimenter bias A distortion of findings that stems from experimenter expectations.

Social Learning Theory

The psychoanalyst chides the trait theorist: "Wonderful, you've described this elephant as rotund, plump, obese, but how, my friend, did he become so huge? What motivated him to gorge himself so?" The elephant casts a pointed glance. "Little ghosts, perhaps? Vague cosmic forces? It is clear to anyone who cares to reflect that our fat friend is fixated in the oral stage."

"A *biting* insight," comments the trait theorist.

"The *what* stage?" asks the elephant.

"The oral stage," repeats the psychoanalyst. "Under stress he is obviously under the control of oral impulses from the id."

"Id, shmid!" barks the social learning theorist. "What's all this stuff about psychic structures?" He addresses the trait theorist: "And what's this garbage about a personality *structure?* You can't observe or measure psychic structures or personality structures. You pretend to be scientific, but you're both engaged in witch hunts for imaginary structures inside an imaginary mind.

"If you want to be scientific, pull out the camera and the tape measure. Let's agree to stick to what we can all see, hear, and feel—the elephant's eating behaviors and the details of the situations in which he stuffs his nose."

"I'm not sure I see the improvement," says the elephant.

"Rather than trying blindly to dig down deep within the elephant, let's pay some attention to the circumstances under which he eats."

The Behaviorist Challenge

At Johns Hopkins University in 1924, psychologist John B. Watson announced the battle cry of the **radical behaviorist** movement: "Give me a dozen healthy infants, well-formed, and my own specified world to bring them up in and I'll guarantee to take any one at random and train him to become any type of specialist I might suggest—doctor, lawyer, merchant-chief and, yes, even beggar-man and thief, regardless of his talents, penchants, tendencies, abilities, vocations, and the race of his ancestors" (p. 82).

So it was that Watson sounded the behaviorist argument that situational variables, or environmental influences—not internal, personal variables—are the significant shapers of human preferences and behaviors. Watson argued that unseen, undetectable mental structures must be rejected in favor of that which can be seen and measured.

Modern-day social learning theorists like Walter Mischel (1981) and Julian Rotter (1972) agree that discussions of human nature should be tied to observable experiences and behaviors when possible. However, they assert that personal variables must also be considered if human behavior is to be adequately explained and predicted.

In this section we first focus on the determinants of behavior according to social learning theory. Then we discuss two human issues from the social learning perspective: the nature of freedom and the learning and performance of aggressive responses.

Personal and Situational Variables

Rather than focusing on mental structures and traits, social learning theorists focus on human behavior. The performance of behavior is assumed to depend on personal and situational variables (see Figure 9.6). **Personal**

Radical behaviorist A person who does not believe in "mind" or other mentalistic concepts.

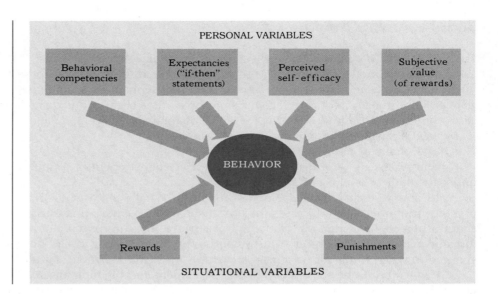

FIGURE 9.6 Social Learning Theory. According to social learning theory, personal and situational variables interact to determine behavior.

variables include *behavioral competencies, expectancies, perceived self-efficacy*, and *the subjective value of rewards*. **Situational variables** include rewards and punishments.

Behavioral Competencies **Behavioral competencies** are skills. They include academic skills like reading and writing, athletic skills like swimming and tossing a football properly, social skills like knowing how to ask someone out on a date, job skills, and many others. Behavioral competencies tend to be acquired through operant conditioning and observational learning (discussed in Chapter 5). In the case of operant conditioning, we learn to engage in certain responses (operants) in certain situations because they have been reinforced. In the case of observational learning, which is a more sophisticated and efficient form of learning, we learn to engage in responses that we observe other people perform. We are more likely to imitate these responses if they are reinforced in the people we observe.

Primary and conditioned reinforcers (see Chapter 5) can lead to the acquisition of skills. Primary reinforcers include food, liquid, a comfortable temperature, and removal of pain. Conditioned reinforcers gain their reinforcement value through association with established reinforcers. Conditioned reinforcers can become generalized when they are paired with several primary reinforcers. Then they are referred to as **conditioned generalized reinforcers.** Conditioned generalized reinforcers like money, attention and social approval can exert powerful influences on behavior. Mischel (1981) notes that many people seem to learn to seek money for its own sake. They work to pile up "paper profits" even though they never trade them in for primary reinforcers.

Radical behaviorists equated learning with behavior, but social learning theorists usually distinguish between the learning and performance of skills. We may acquire a skill (learn how to do something) just by observing another person. We may then choose not to perform this response until we believe that we will be reinforced for it. We are more likely to engage in aggressive behavior, for example, when we believe that it is appropriate or will be socially

Personal variables In social learning theory, determinants of behavior that are within the person.

Situational variables In social learning theory, determinants of behavior that are outside the person.

Behavioral competencies Skills.

Conditioned generalized reinforcers Stimuli that (1) have acquired reinforcement value through pairing with established reinforcers; and (2) reinforce a wide variety of behaviors. Examples include money and social approval.

tolerated. This is one reason that girls, for whom aggressive behavior is almost always deemed inappropriate, are less likely than boys to respond aggressively to a provocation.

Expectancies **Expectancies,** or "if-then" statements, are personal predictions about the outcome (or reinforcement contingencies) of engaging in a response. Expectancies are related to past experience in similar situations. Some expectancies may be acquired mechanically through principles of classical conditioning. Assume that we encountered pain by falling off a bicycle or pleasure from eating a piece of cake. Now we have the opportunity to ride a bicycle or eat another piece of cake. The associated pain or pleasure is perceived as an image, such as a mental picture of scraping your hands and knees or of the deep chocolate flavor of the cake. The nature of the image (negative or positive) influences us either not to repeat (not to ride a bicycle recklessly) or to repeat (eat another piece of cake) the response.

A more active cognitive process, problem solving, may also be brought to bear in arriving at expectancies. In problem solving we relate a current situation to past similar situations. We engage in cognitive "trial and error," predicting the outcomes of various responses. When we have had experience with several related situations or problems, and have used many types of responses, we are more likely to arrive at accurate expectancies.

Perceived Self-Efficacy According to social learning theorist Albert Bandura, the probability that we shall begin or persist in operant behavior is also related to our **perceived self-efficacy,** or the degree to which we believe that our efforts will bring about a positive outcome. As noted by Bandura and his colleagues Linda Reese and Nancy Adams:

> In their daily lives people must make decisions about whether to attempt risky courses of action or how long to continue, in the face of difficulties, those they have undertaken. Social learning theory posits that ... people tend to avoid situations they believe exceed their coping capabilities, but they undertake and perform assuredly activities they judge themselves capable of managing. ...
>
> Self-judged efficacy also determines how much of an effort people will make and how long they will keep at a task despite obstacles or adverse experiences. ... Those who have a strong sense of efficacy exert greater effort to master the challenges ... (1982, p. 5).

In Chapter 10 we shall review research that suggests that people can be helped to improve their performances by increasing their perceived self-efficacy. Believing in oneself may not be the whole story, but self-belief *in combination with* adequate skills seem to make for strong efforts.

Subjective Value of Rewards The subjective value of a reward tends to depend on past experience with it or similar rewards. Because of experience, our feelings about the reward may be positive or negative. If you became nauseated the last time you drank a glass of iced tea, its subjective value as an incentive may diminish, even on a hot day.

Subjective value will also depend on social motives. A person with a high need for achievement *(n ach)* will work harder for an A in a course than will a person with a low *n ach*—assuming that the low-n-ach individual has not been promised a new car as a reward for an A. Ten dollars may also have greater subjective value as a reward to a poor person than to a rich person.

Expectancies Personal predictions about the outcomes of potential behaviors. "If-then" statements.

Perceived self-efficacy (EFF–fee–kah–see). A person's belief that he or she can achieve his or her goals through his or her own efforts. (From the Latin *efficere,* meaning "to bring to pass.")

A Psychological Controversy: Is Our Behavior an Expression of Free, Conscious Choice, or Is Choice Only an Illusion?

The radical behaviorist outlooks of John B. Watson and B. F. Skinner largely discard the notions of free will, choice, and self-direction. From their perspective, even our telling ourselves that we have free will is determined by the environment as surely as is our becoming startled at a sudden noise.

Let us define freedom as the right to do what you *want* to do. Most of us tend to assume that our wants somehow originate within us. But Skinner suggests that environmental influences, such as parental approval and social custom, shape us into *wanting* to do certain things and *not wanting* to do others.

In his novel *Walden Two* Skinner (1948) describes a utopian society in which people are happy and content because they are allowed to do whatever they please. However, they have been trained or conditioned from early childhood to engage in prosocial behavior and to possess prosocial attitudes. For this reason they *want* to behave in a decent, kind, and unselfish way. But they look upon themselves as being free.

Skinner elaborated his beliefs about people and society in *Beyond Freedom and Dignity* (1972). According to Skinner, adaptation to the environment requires acceptance of behavior patterns that ensure survival. If the group is to survive, it must construct rules and laws that will aid the cause of social harmony. Other people are then systematically rewarded for following these rules and laws and punished for disobeying them. Nobody is really free, although we may think of ourselves as having come freely together to establish the rules and then as choosing to follow them.

Some object to radical behaviorist notions because they degrade the importance of human consciousness and choice. Others argue that people are not so blindly ruled by pleasure and pain. People have rebelled against

Do radical behaviorists see people as similar to R2D2 and C3PO from the *Star Wars* film series? Charming and entertaining, but rather mechanical when all is said and done?

With violent films so common, it may be more difficult to explain why most people who watch them remain nonviolent than it is to explain why a minority imitate the aggressive behavior they observe.

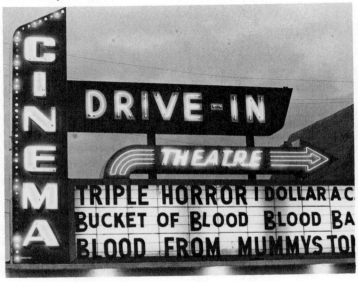

the so-called necessity of survival by choosing pain and hardship over pleasure, or death over life. For instance, in Dickens' novel *A Tale of Two Cities*, the hero sacrifices his life to save that of another man.

The radical behaviorist defense might be that the apparently individual choice of pain or death is forced upon the altruist just as inevitably as conformity to social custom is forced upon others. The altruist was also shaped by external influences. Those influences simply differed from those that affect most of us.

It may not be possible to resolve this issue logically. How can we know the difference between freedom and the illusion of freedom? How do we differentiate between a "real want" and a "perceived want"?

In any event, many social learning theorists reject the radical behaviorist ideas of Watson and Skinner. They see people as influencing the environment, just as the environment influences them. They view behavior as stemming from an ongoing interaction between personal and situational variables. **Interactionism** focuses on the ways that variables influence one another. From an interactionist perspective, we need not be concerned about whether the environment first shapes us or we first shape the environment. We need not worry about which came first—the chicken or the egg. It is enough to note that chickens and eggs develop from each other and are essential to each other's existence.

Copycats, Models, TV, and Rewards: Social Learning Perspectives on Aggression

Can we be expected to act in a civilized manner when we are exposed to a persistent bombardment of violence in TV shows and films? In Florida, in 1977, a teenaged boy killed an elderly woman. The defense claimed that he was not guilty by reason of insanity. Why? He had become "addicted" to TV violence and could no longer differentiate between fantasy and reality. (He was found guilty.)

In 1974 a nine-year-old California girl was raped with a bottle by four other girls who admitted they had been given the idea by the TV movie *Born Innocent*. The victim's family sued the network and the local station that had screened the film. The courts, however, chose not to award damages. Such a precedent might interfere with the right to free expression as guaranteed by the First Amendment to the Constitution.

It cannot be argued that TV violence directly caused these crimes. After all, with a few unfortunate exceptions, the millions who watch television do *not* imitate antisocial behavior. But it does seem that aggressive behavior in humans is largely learned. Social learning theory explains the acquisition of aggressive responses through operant conditioning and observational learning.

Operant Conditioning of Aggressive Responses A number of learning theorists (Dollard and others, 1939) once believed that frustration mechanically aroused an aggression drive, and that aggressive behavior was rewarding because it reduced that drive. Today it is generally believed that frustration is discomforting because it is usually linked to highly elevated arousal and disconcerting thoughts. Thus we are motivated to engage in behavior that reduces overarousal and to thoughts that we have surmounted obstacles to goals. Sometimes these goals may be reached through aggressive responses.

Model In social learning theory, an organism that exhibits behaviors that others will imitate, or acquire, through observational learning.

But a wide range of behavioral options is available, including socially appropriate self-expression.

Aggressive behavior may be reinforced in some people, especially the strong and well-coordinated, because it may remove sources of frustration or external threats and earn the respect of peers. Social provocations can also lead to unpleasant increases in tension and arousal. There is some evidence that aggression can lead to pleasant declines in blood pressure (Kahn, 1966), one measure of arousal, when we believe that aggression is justified (Geen and others, 1975).

But do children happen upon *initial* aggressive responses by trial and error, as rats learn to press a lever for food in a cage? Research suggests that observational learning is a more common way of acquiring aggressive responses.

Observational Learning of Aggressive Responses   Children learn not only from the effects of their own behavior, but also from observing the behavior of their parents and other adults (Bandura, 1973). In fact, children are more likely to imitate what their parents do than to heed what they say. If adults say they disapprove of aggression, but smash furniture or slap each other when frustrated, children are likely to develop the notion that this is the way to handle frustration.

Children will also imitate the aggressive behavior they see on television, whether the aggressive **models** are cartoons or real people (Bandura and

Children will imitate the behavior of adult models in certain situations, as shown in these pictures from a classic study by Bandura and his colleagues (1963). In the top row, an adult model strikes a clown doll. The next two rows show a boy and a girl imitating the aggressive behavior.

others, 1963). The probability of aggression increases when the models are similar to the observers, and when the models are rewarded for acting aggressively.

There are various explanations for the influence of television:

1. *Television violence increases the level of arousal of viewers.* We are more likely to engage in many forms of behavior, including aggressive behavior, when we have high levels of arousal. Osborn and Endsley (1971) used **galvanic skin response** (GSR) as their measure of arousal and found that violent shows led to significantly higher levels of arousal among four- and five-year-olds than did nonviolent shows.

2. *Television violence may serve as a catalyst for aggression.* Mass media analysts (e.g., Felsenthal, 1976) suggest that television violence may act as a **catalyst** with some viewers. It may **disinhibit** the expression of aggressive impulses that would otherwise have been controlled. In related experiments, subjects who observe a confederate of the experimenter shock another confederate then deliver more shock to the second group of confederates themselves (Doob & Wood, 1972).

3. *Television violence teaches viewers aggressive skills.* Many police officers report that criminals frequently admit to imitating methods of operation observed on television (Mankiewicz & Swerdlow, 1977).

4. *Television violence may desensitize viewers to violence.* Media violence apparently has the effect of decreasing viewers' emotional response to subsequent violence (Geen, 1981; Thomas and others, 1977). Boys who watch television many hours a day show less emotional response to violent boxing films, as measured by GSR, than do boys who watch television less frequently (Cline and others, 1973). The researchers in this study did not control the number of hours the boys watched television. It may be that boys who chose to watch less frequently were also more responsive to portrayals of violence than were chronic viewers. Still, American children have the opportunity to watch hundreds or thousands of violent assaults on television each year. It may be that they learn to perceive violence as humdrum or commonplace. If so, their own attitudes toward violence could become less condemnatory, and they might place less value on restraining their own aggressive urges.

While most psychologists agree that television violence contributes to aggression (NIMH, 1982; Parke and others, 1977), some psychologists believe that this conclusion is premature. They argue that most evidence is correlational, not experimental (e.g., Kaplan & Singer, 1976), and that the incidence of violent crime in the United States cannot be linked conclusively to the introduction of television (Hennigan and others, 1982).

Other psychologists note that there is a circular relationship between viewing media violence and aggressive behavior (Eron, 1982; Fenigstein, 1979). Television violence, they assert, contributes to aggressive behavior, and aggressive children are also more likely to watch more violent television. Eron found that aggressive children are less popular than nonaggressive children. He theorizes that aggressive children watch more television because their peer relationships are less fulfilling and because the high incidence of television violence tends to confirm their own aggressiveness (1982, p. 210).

It may be that television violence is one factor among many that contribute to aggressive behavior. Eron (1982) argues that parental rejection and the use of physical punishment by parents also contribute to aggression in

Galvanic skin response A sign of sympathetic arousal detected by sweat present in the palm of the hand. The more sweat in the palm, the greater the amount of electricity that is conducted across the palm. Abbreviated *GSR*. (After Italian physicist Luigi Galvani.)

Catalyst (CAT–uh–list). An agent that hastens or facilitates a reaction. (From the Greek *kata*, meaning "down," and *lyein*, meaning "to loosen.")

Disinhibit In social learning theory, to cause the occurrence of a usually inhibited behavior (generally as a consequence of observing a model engage in that behavior).

youngsters. It may be that harsh experiences in the home further confirm the viewer's notion that the world is filled with violence, and encourage further reliance on the television for companionship.

Evaluation of Social Learning Theory

Critics of social learning theory allow that it has given rise to precise statements about many situation-response relationships. They contend, however, that social learning theory has failed to derive satisfying statements about the development of traits and to account for self-awareness. It may also be that social learning theory—like its intellectual forebear, radical behaviorism— has not always paid sufficient attention to genetic differences among people. It appears naive to deny the role of heredity in the performance of, say, intelligent behavior, or in the development of abnormal behavior. These issues are expanded in Chapters 6 and 11.

But social learning theorists may be beginning to repair these theoretical flaws. Mischel (1981) stresses that today's social learning theorists view people as active, not merely as mechanical reactors to environmental pressures (as Watson saw them). Cognitive functioning has become an appropriate area of study for many contemporary social learning theorists (Wilson, 1982). In the area of abnormal behavior, social learning theorists Gerald Davison and John Neale (1982) may speak for many of their fellows when they suggest that inherited or physiological factors often interact with situational stress to give rise to abnormal behavior.

Social learning theory has also contributed to the formation of many strategies for helping people change maladaptive behavior. These strategies are collectively termed behavior therapy, and you will learn more about them in Chapters 10 and 12.

Self Theory

"Gentlemen, gentlemen," the self theorist reproves. "There may be some truth in what each of you has to say, but our elephant friend doesn't feel that you've gotten to the core of his being. None of you has asked *him* about his impressions of himself. He must feel quite left out."

"Like a specimen under a microscope," says the elephant.

"Creative," comments the trait theorist.

"Penetrating," remarks the psychoanalyst.

"A predictable response," sighs the social learning theorist.

The self theorist continues. "The elephant's behavior may be influenced by unconscious dynamic forces within him. He does appear to possess traits. And his reinforcement history may explain some of his peanut- and popcorn-inhaling behaviors. There are also environmental influences: He lies in the shade and wades in the pool when it's hot. Perhaps he had to learn that within our culture it is expected that elephants will fear mice—" The elephant trumpets and rears on his back legs.

"All these things are true, but they are not the *essence* of the elephant," summarizes the self theorist. "They are not his *self.*"

"*His* self?" mocks the trait theorist. "A rather poor grammarian."

"Don't blame him," says the social learning theorist. "It's our educational system these days."

"It may reflect some deep-seated conflict," notes the psychoanalyst. *"His* is possessive. *Him* ends in *m,* the first letter in *mother."*

The self theorist is undaunted. "Gentlemen," he proceeds, "I am convinced that self-awareness is the guiding principle in the elephant's personality. I don't buy that his sense of self is but the tip of his personality, floating above the deep reaches of the unconscious," he remarks to the psychoanalyst. "Note that I did not say that he was self*ish,"* he says to the trait theorist. "Nor do I believe that his freedom of choice is only an illusion," he says to the social learning theorist. "His sense of self is inborn. It will urge him to develop his unique potential."

"Fellows," the trait theorist addresses the psychoanalyst and social learning theorist, "I'm thirsty. Let's get something to wet our whistles."

"Just the stimulus I needed," agrees the social learning theorist.

"A little oral gratification never hurt," nods the psychoanalyst.

Moments later the elephant and self theorist are quite alone. "Your ideas sound good to me," consoles the elephant.

Carl R. Rogers.

Carl Rogers and the Concept of the Self

"My experience in therapy and in groups makes it impossible for me to deny the reality and significance of human choice. To me it is not an illusion that man is to some degree the architect of himself," wrote self theorist Carl Rogers (1974, p. 119). According to a survey of clinical and counseling psychologists (Smith, 1982), Rogers is the single most influential psychotherapist of recent years.

"I" and "We" and "Me" and "Us": Some Notes on a Minor Failure to Communicate

What would you do if you wanted to express the idea that you had a stomach cramp, but each time you complained the doctor examined every member of your family? Or imagine the plight of a gentleman who has been driven wild with desire but cannot express his feelings accurately. Every time he professes his love for his girl friend, she becomes indignant. She protests that she is simply not interested in group sex.

In her novel *Anthem,* Ayn Rand (1946) described a man with a similar problem. He had difficulty making himself understood to other people—and to himself.

In the futuristic society of Rand's novel, the rulers wish to encourage unselfish, group-oriented behavior. They have stricken the words *I* and *Me* from the language. Equality 7–2521, the hero of the story, can refer to himself only as "We" or "Us." But collectivism, Rand's term for any system of government that places the group above the individual, does not control Equality 7–2521 fully. Why not? As Equality puts it, "We were born with a curse."

Anthem tells of Equality's increasing friction with society and his eventual break from the group. But not until the climax of the novel, when Equality stumbles across "ancient" writings in a prehistoric house, does he find the concepts to talk and think precisely about his center of awareness, his self. *I.*

What is Equality's "curse"? Ayn Rand suggests that something inborn in Equality, something inborn in each of us, strives to develop and be expressed. This something ultimately defines us as individuals, or as selves. Ayn Rand was not a psychologist, but her assumptions about human nature resemble those of humanistic psychologists like Carl Rogers and Abraham Maslow.

Humanistic psychologists theorize that the self is the basic feature of personality. The self is an inborn, fluid way of organizing perceptions and experiencing the world. The self is influenced by experience. Its growth can be stunted when conditions are antagonistic to its development. But humanistic psychology begins with the assumption of the self. The self is because it is. The limits of the self separate that which is psychologically you from that which is not.

Humanistic Emphasizing the importance of self-awareness and the freedom to make choices.

Gestalt In this usage, a quality of wholeness. See Chapter 1 for a discussion of Gestalt psychology.

Values A person's sense of what is important or desirable. (From the Latin *valere*, meaning "to be strong.")

Innate Inborn, natural, unlearned.

Self-actualization In humanistic theory, the innate tendency to strive to realize one's potential. Self-initiated striving to become all one is capable of being.

The view that people tend to shape themselves through freedom of choice and action is considered **humanistic.** Self theory is basically humanistic, but psychologists from other schools may also show a humanistic bent. Erik Erikson's view that we strive consciously to cope with identity crises and to invent ourselves is also humanistic. Many social learning theorists who stress the importance of personal cognitive variables as determinants of behavior see themselves as humanistic.

Rogers defines the self as an "organized, consistent, conceptual **gestalt** composed of perceptions of the characteristics of the 'I' or 'me' and the perceptions of the relationships of the 'I' or 'me' to others and to various aspects of life, together with the values attached to these perceptions" (1959, p. 200). Your self is your center of experience. It is your ongoing sense of who and what you are, your sense of how and why you react to the environment, and how you choose to act upon the environment. Your choices are made on the basis of your **values,** and your values are also parts of your self.

To Rogers the sense of self is inborn or **innate.** The self provides the experience of being human in the world. It is the guiding principle behind personality structure and behavior.

Self-Actualization

Humanistic personality theorists like Carl Rogers and Abraham Maslow believe that organisms are genetically programed to grow, unfold, and become themselves. This central tendency, termed **self-actualization,** is a characteristic of life itself.

It could be said that self-actualization functions as a cardinal trait. It is the steering principle that underlies behavior. Self-actualization renders behavior organized, meaningful, and whole.

A trip to the West Coast once provided Rogers a poetic natural image for the self-actualizing tendency. He became caught up in the drama of life's capacity to develop, to grow, to strive toward distant goals and keep itself on course despite the harshest of environments:

According to humanistic psychologists like Carl Rogers, we each view the world and ourselves from a unique frame of reference. What is important to one person may have little value to another.

During a vacation weekend some months ago I was standing on a headland overlooking one of the rugged coves which dot the coastline of northern California. Several large rock outcroppings were at the mouth of the cove, and these received the full force of the great Pacific combers which, beating upon them, broke into mountains of spray before surging into the cliff-lined shore. As I watched the waves breaking over these large rocks in the distance, I noticed with surprise what appeared to be a tiny palm tree on the rocks, no more than two or three feet high, taking the pounding of the breakers. Through my binoculars I saw that these were some type of seaweed, with a slender "trunk" topped off with a head of leaves. As one examined a specimen in the interval between the waves it seemed clear that this fragile, erect, top-heavy plant would be utterly crushed and broken by the next breaker. When the wave crunched down upon it, the trunk bent almost flat, the leaves were whipped into a straight line by the torrent of water, yet the moment the wave had passed, here was the plant again, erect, tough, resilient. It seemed incredible that it was able to take this incessant pounding hour after hour, day after night, week after week, perhaps, for all I know, year after year, and all the time nourishing itself, extending its domain, reproducing itself; in short, maintaining and enhancing itself in this process which, in our shorthand, we call growth. Here in this palmlike seaweed was the tenacity of life, the forward thrust of life, the ability to push into an incredibly hostile environment and not only hold its own, but to adapt, develop, become itself (Rogers, 1963, pp. 1–2).

The Self-Concept and Frames of Reference

Our self-concepts are our impressions of ourselves and our evaluation of our adequacy. It may help to think of us as rating ourselves along various scales or dimensions, like good–bad, intelligent–unintelligent, strong–weak, and tall–short.

Rogers states that we all have unique ways of looking at ourselves and the world, or unique **frames of reference.** It may be that we each use a different set of dimensions in defining ourselves, and that we judge ourselves according to different sets of values. To one person achievement–failure may be the most important dimension. To another person the most important dimension may be decency–indecency. A third person may not even think in terms of decency.

Self-Esteem and Positive Regard

Rogers assumes that we all develop a need for self-regard or **self-esteem** as we grow and become aware of ourselves. Self-esteem tends first to reflect the esteem others hold for us. We are likely to seek the love and approval of parents and other important people in our lives.

Parents are likely to help their children develop self-esteem when they show them **unconditional positive regard,** when they accept them as people of intrinsic merit regardless of their behavior of the moment. But when parents show **conditional positive regard** for their children, accepting them only when they behave in a desired manner, children may learn to disown the thoughts, feelings, and behaviors that parents have rejected. Conditional positive regard may lead children to develop **conditions of worth**—that is, to think that they are worthwhile only if they behave in certain ways.

Since each of us is thought to have a unique potential, children who develop conditions of worth must become disappointed in themselves to some

Frame of reference One's unique patterning of perceptions and attitudes, according to which one evaluates events.

Self-esteem One's evaluation and valuing of oneself.

Unconditional positive regard A persistent expression of esteem for the value of a person, but not necessarily an unqualified acceptance of all of the person's behaviors.

Conditional positive regard Judgment of another person's value on the basis of the acceptability of that person's behaviors.

Conditions of worth Standards by which the value of a person is judged.

Congruence According to Rogers, a fit between one's self-concept and one's behaviors, thoughts, and feelings. (From the Latin *congruens*, meaning "coming together.")

Self-ideal A mental image of what we believe we ought to be.

Discrepancy Lack of agreement, inconsistency.

degree. We cannot fully live up to the wishes of others and remain true to ourselves. This does not mean that the expression of the self inevitably leads to conflict. Rogers was optimistic about human nature. He believed that we hurt others or act in antisocial ways only when we are frustrated in our efforts to develop our potentials. But when parents and others are loving and tolerant of our differentness, we, too, shall be loving—even if some of our preferences, abilities, and values differ from those of our parents.

But children in some families learn that it is bad to have ideas of their own, especially about sexual, political, or religious matters. When they perceive their parents' disapproval, they may come to see themselves as rebels and label their feelings as selfish, wrong, or evil. If they wish to retain a consistent self-concept, and self-esteem, they may have to deny many of their genuine feelings, or disown parts of themselves. In this way the self-concept becomes distorted. According to Rogers, anxiety often stems from partial perception of feelings and ideas that are inconsistent with the distorted self-concept. Since anxiety is unpleasant, we may deny that these feelings and ideas exist.

Psychological Congruence and the Self-Ideal

When we accept our feelings as our own, we experience psychological integrity or wholeness. There is a "fit" between our self-concepts and our behavior, thoughts, and emotions, which Rogers calls **congruence.**

According to Rogers, the path to self-actualization requires getting in touch with our genuine feelings, accepting them as ours, and acting upon them. This is the goal of Rogers's method of psychotherapy, client-centered therapy, which we shall discuss in Chapter 12. Here suffice it to say that client-centered therapists provide an atmosphere in which clients can cope with the anxiety that may attend focusing on disowned parts of the self.

Rogers also believes that we have mental images of what we are capable of becoming, or **self-ideals.** We are motivated to reduce the **discrepancy** between our self-concepts and our self-ideals. But as we undertake the process of actualizing ourselves, our self-ideals may gradually grow more complex. Our goals may become higher or change in quality. The self-ideal is something

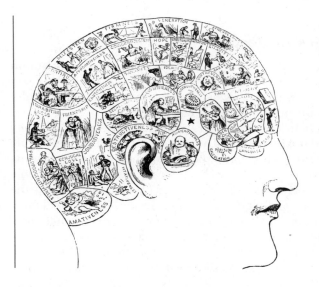

FIGURE 9.7   A Phrenologist's Map of the "Mental Functions."

like a carrot dangling from a stick strapped to a burro's head. The burro strives to reach the carrot, as though it were a step or two away, without recognizing that its own progress also causes the carrot to advance. Rogers believes that the process of striving to meet meaningful goals, the good struggle, is what yields human happiness.

Maslow notes that as we actualize ourselves we may now and then encounter **peak experiences.** Peak experiences are brief moments of rapture that seem to tell us that what we are doing is right for us, that we are on the proper path. The artist may encounter such rapture upon completing a sketch that captures his or her visual experience. The machinist may find it in visualizing a more efficient way to complete an assembly-line task. We may encounter peak experiences at the birth of our children, or when our research yields major findings. We are all unique. What provides you with a peak experience may be meaningless to a friend or co-worker.

Evaluation of Self Theory

Perhaps the most telling criticism of self theory is that the central concept of self-actualization cannot be proved or disproved. Like an id, or a trait, a self-actualizing force cannot be observed or measured directly. It must be inferred from its supposed effects.

Self-actualization, like trait theory, yields circular explanations for behavior. When we observe someone apparently engaged in positive striving, we gain little insight by attributing this striving to self-actualization. We have done nothing to explain the origins of the actualizing tendency. And when we observe someone who is not engaged in growth-oriented striving, it seems **gratuitous** to "explain" this outcome by suggesting that the self-actualizing tendency has been blocked or frustrated. It may simply be that self-actualization is an acquired need rather than an innate need, and that it is found in some, but not all, of us.

Self theory, like social learning theory, has little to say about the development of traits and personality types. Self theory assumes that we are unique, but does not predict the traits, abilities, and interests we shall develop.

Measurement of Personality

Measures of personality are used to make important decisions, such as whether a person is suited for a certain type of work, for a particular class in school, or for a drug to reduce agitation. As part of their admissions process, graduate schools will often ask professors to rate prospective students on scales that assess traits like intelligence, emotional stability, and cooperativeness. Students may take tests of **aptitudes** and interests to gather insight into whether they are suited for certain occupations. It is assumed that students who share the aptitudes and interests of people who are well-adjusted in certain positions are likely to be well-adjusted themselves in those positions.

If you had wanted to learn about your personality early in the last century, an "expert" might have measured the bumps on your head with a **caliper.** This method, termed **phrenology,** was based on the erroneous belief that traits, abilities, and mental functions dwelled in specific places in the head, and could be measured from the outside. Figure 9.7 shows a "map" of these functions, as used by many phrenologists.

Peak experience In humanistic theory, a brief moment of rapture that stems from the realization that one is on the path to self-actualization.

Gratuitous (grat–TOO–it–tuss). Without cause or justification.

Aptitude A natural ability or talent. (From the Latin *apere*, meaning "to grasp" or "to reach.")

Caliper An instrument consisting of a pair of curved movable legs that is used for measuring the diameter or thickness of something.

Phrenology The analysis of personality by measurement of the shapes and protuberances of the skull. (From the Greek *phrenos*, meaning "brain.")

Behavior rating scale A systematic means for recording the frequency with which target behaviors occur.

Reliability Consistency. See Chapter 6 for a discussion of several types of reliability in testing.

Validity The degree to which a test measures or predicts what it is supposed to measure or predict, as determined by correlating a test score with an external criterion.

Criterion Standard, basis for making a judgment.

Objective tests Tests whose items must be answered in a specified, limited manner. Tests whose items have concrete answers that are labeled correct.

Standardized Given to a large number of respondents so that data concerning the usual responses can be accumulated and analyzed.

Forced-choice format A method of presenting test questions that requires a respondent to select one of a number of possible answers.

Today's personality measures are more scientific, if not more interesting. They involve using a sample of behavior, usually in the form of the self-report, to predict future behavior. Some measures are **behavior rating scales** that assess overt behavior in settings like the classroom or mental hospital. With behavior rating scales, trained observers usually check off each occurrence of a specific behavior within a certain time frame, say, a 15-minute period. More frequently used objective and projective tests will be discussed in this section.

Reliability and Validity

Since important decisions are made on the basis of personality measures, they must be *reliable* and *valid*. The **reliability** of a measure is its consistency. A measure of height would not be reliable if a person appeared taller or shorter every time a measurement was taken. A reliable personality measure, like a good tape measure, must yield similar results on different testing occasions. In general, a longer test is more reliable than a shorter test. A 100-word spelling test is likely to be more reliable than a 10-word spelling test.

The **validity** of a test is the degree to which it measures what it is supposed to measure. In order to determine whether a test is valid, we see whether it actually predicts an outside standard or **criterion.** Tests of musical aptitude, for example, should predict whether a person can learn to play a musical instrument. Written tests that measure anxiety should predict whether a person shows symptoms of anxiety like rapid heartbeat, sweat in the palms of the hands, shakiness, and so on.

Objective Tests

Objective tests present respondents with a **standardized** group of test items in the form of questionnaires. Respondents are limited to a specific range of answers. One test may request that respondents indicate whether items are true or false for them. Another may ask respondents to select the preferred activity from groups of three.

Some tests have a **forced-choice format** in which respondents are asked to indicate which of two statements is more true of them, or which of several activities they prefer. They are not given the option of answering "none of the above." Forced-choice formats are frequently used in interest inventories that help predict whether one would be well-adjusted in a certain occupation. The following item is similar to those found in interest inventories:

I would rather
  a. be a forest ranger
  b. work in a busy office
  c. play a muscial instrument

A forced-choice format is also used in the Edwards Personal Preference Schedule, which measures the relative strength of social motives (like achievement, nurturance, and others discussed in Chapter 7), by pitting them against one another consecutively in groups of two.

The Minnesota Multiphasic Personality Inventory (MMPI) The MMPI contains 566 items presented in a true-false format. The MMPI is widely used by clinical and counseling psychologists to help diagnose abnormal behavior problems of the sort that will be discussed in Chapter 11. Accurate measurement of the client's problems should lead to appropriate treatment.

The MMPI has been given to thousands of individuals over the last few decades. This wide usage has permitted psychologists to compare the test records of clients with those of people who are known to have had certain problems. A similar test record is suggestive of the presence of similar problems. Psychologists may also send completed tests to computer scoring services that compare the test record to thousands of records in the computer's memory. Figure 9.8 shows a computer test report based on the MMPI of a 27-year-old barber who consulted a psychologist because of depression and difficulty making decisions. Computer test reports also usually contain a "warning" to the effect that they are not intended to be a substitute for the clinician's personal judgment.

The MMPI is usually scored for the four **validity scales** and ten **clinical scales** described in Table 9.3. The validity scales indicate whether there is reason to believe that the test results represent the client's thoughts, emotions, and behaviors. The validity scales in Table 9.3 assess different **response sets,** or biases in answering the questions. People with high "L" scores, for example, may be attempting to present themselves as excessively moral and well-behaved. People with high "F" scores may be attempting to present themselves as bizarre, or answering haphazardly. In one study, F-scale scores were positively correlated with conceptual confusion, hostility, presence of **hallucinations** and other unusual thought patterns as measured on a behavior rating scale (Smith & Graham, 1981). Many personality measures have some kind of validity scales. The clinical scales of the MMPI assess the problems shown in

Validity scales Groups of test items that indicate whether a person's responses accurately reflect that individual's traits.

Clinical scales Groups of test items that measure the presence of various abnormal behavior patterns.

Response set A tendency to answer test items according to a bias—for instance, to make oneself seem perfect or bizarre.

Hallucinations Perceptions in the absence of sensory stimulation. See Chapter 11.

TABLE 9.3   MMPI Validity and Clinical Scales Commonly Reported

Scale	Abbreviation	Definition
Validity Scales		
Question	?	Corresponds to number of items left unanswered
Lie	L	Lies or is highly conventional
Frequency	F	Exaggerates complaints, answers haphazardly
Correction	K	Denies problems
Clinical Scales		
Hypochondriasis	Hs	Expresses bodily concerns and complaints
Depression	D	Is depressed, pessimistic, guilty
Hysteria	Hy	Reacts to stress with physical symptoms; lacks insight
Psychopathic Deviate	Pd	Is immoral, in conflict with law, involved in stormy relationships
Masculinity/Femininity	Mf	Has interests characteristic of stereotypical sex roles
Paranoia	Pa	Is suspicious, resentful
Psychasthenia	Pt	Is anxious, worried, high-strung
Schizophrenia	Sc	Is confused, disorganized, disoriented
Hypomania	Ma	Is energetic, active, easily bored, restless
Social Introversion	Si	Is introverted, timid, shy, lacking self-confidence

Roche MMPI Computerized Interpretation Service

The response of this patient to the test indicates that he understood the items and that he correctly followed the instructions. However, it appears that he is somewhat self-critical. He may be somewhat more likely than the average person to admit to symptoms and psychological problems even when they are minimal. This suggests that he may be willing to accept professional assistance.

This patient shows a personality pattern which occurs frequently among persons who seek psychiatric treatment. Feelings of inadequacy, sexual conflict and rigidity are accompanied by a loss of efficiency, initiative, and self-confidence. Insomnia is likely to occur along with chronic anxiety, fatigue, and tension. He may have suicidal thoughts. Patients with this pattern are likely to be diagnosed as depressives or anxiety reactions. The basic characteristics are resistant to change and will tend to remain stable with time. Among medical patients with this pattern, a large number are seriously depressed, and others show some depression, along with fatigue and exhaustion. There are few spontaneous recoveries, although the intensity of the symptoms may be cyclic.

There are unusual qualities in this patient's thinking which may represent an original or eccentric orientation or perhaps some schizoid tendencies. Further information is required to make this determination.

He is concerned, to an unusual degree, with bodily functions and health. He may overreact to illness, and complain unreasonably about relatively minor ailments. Medical patients with this characteristic tend to be frustrating to their physicians because they complain of pains and disorders that are vague, difficult to identify, and may have no organic basis. Although some of these patients have a genuine physical illness, there is a strong psychological component, and they tend to be egocentric, demanding, and pessimistic.

He appears to be an idealistic, inner-directed person who may be seen as quite socially perceptive and sensitive to interpersonal interactions. His interest patterns are quite different from those of the average male. In a person with a broad educational and cultural background this is to be expected and may reflect such characteristics as self-awareness, concern with social issues, and an ability to communicate ideas clearly and effectively. In some men, however, the same interest pattern may reflect rejection of masculinity accompanied by a relatively passive, effeminate, noncompetitive personality.

FIGURE 9.8 An MMPI Report Written By a Computer. Computer interpretation of test results allows clinicians to use their time more efficiently. Computer reports usually include a statement suggesting that they are not intended as a substitute for the clinicians's own judgment.

Table 9.3, as well as stereotypical masculine or feminine interests and introversion.

MMPI scales were constructed empirically, on the basis of actual clinical data, rather than on the basis of psychological theory. A test-item bank of several hundred items was derived from questions often asked in clinical interviews. Here are some of the items that were used:

My father was a good man . . . . T F
I am very seldom troubled by headaches . . . . T F
My hands and feet are usually warm enough . . . . T F
I have never done anything dangerous for the thrill of it . . . . T F
I work under a great deal of tension . . . . T F

Schizophrenic
(skit–so–FRAIN–nick). Characteristic of a major thought disorder. See Chapter 11 for a full discussion.

The items were administered to clients and psychiatric patients with known clinical symptoms, like depression or **schizophrenic** symptoms. Items that successfully set apart people with these problems were included on scales

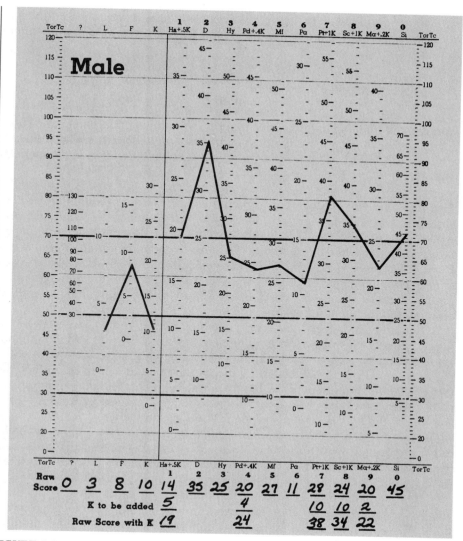

	TorTc	?	L	F	K	1 Hs+.5K	2 D	3 Hy	4 Pd+.4K	5 Mf	6 Pa	7 Pt+1K	8 Sc+1K	9 Ma+.2K	0 Si	TorTc
Raw Score		0	3	8	10	14	35	25	20	27	11	28	24	20	45	
K to be added						5			4			10	10	2		
Raw Score with K						19			24			38	34	22		

FIGURE 9.9   An MMPI Personality Profile. This profile was attained by the depressed barber. On this form, scores at the standard level of 50 are average for males, and scores above the standard score of 70 are considered abnormally high. The "raw score" is the number of items answered in a certain direction on a given MMPI scale. K is the correction scale. A certain percentage of the K-scale score is added onto several clinical scales to correct for denial of problems.

with appropriate names. The barber whose test record was scored and interpreted by computer (Figures 9.8, 9.9) scored abnormally high on the F, Hs, D, Pt, Sc, and Si scales. The computer's memory was scanned and it was reported that people who score in such a pattern tend to show the behaviors indicated in Figure 9.8.

The California Psychological Inventory   Another Personality Inventory, the California Psychological Inventory (CPI), is widely used in research and clinical practice to assess 18 dimensions of normal behavior, such as achievement, dominance, flexibility, self-acceptance, and self-control.

Interest Inventories The Strong-Campbell Interest Inventory and the Kuder Preference Record are two of the tests widely used to predict adjustment in various occupations.

Projective Tests

You may have heard that there is a personality test that asks people what a drawing or inkblot looks like, and that they commonly answer "A bat." There are a number of such tests, the best known of which is the Rorschach inkblot test, named after its originator, Swiss psychiatrist Hermann Rorschach (1884–1922).

The Rorschach Inkblot Test The Rorschach test is a **projective test.** In projective techniques there are no clear, specified answers. People are presented with **ambiguous** stimuli, like inkblots or vague drawings, and may be asked to report what these stimuli look like to them, or to tell stories about them. Since there is no concrete proper response, it is assumed that people *project* their own personalities into their responses. The meanings they attribute to these stimuli are assumed to reflect their personalities as well as the drawings or blots themselves.

Actually the facts of the matter are slightly different. There may be no single "correct" response to the Rorschach inkblot shown in Figure 9.10, but some responses would clearly not be in keeping with the features of the blot. Figure 9.10 could be a bat or a flying insect, the pointed face of an animal, the face of a jack-o'-lantern or many other things. But responses like "an ice cream cone," "diseased lungs" or "a metal leaf in flames" are not suggested by the features of the blot and may suggest personality problems.

The idea that ambiguous stimuli might be used to mirror the personality did not originate with Rorschach. In the early 1500s, Renaissance artist and inventor Leonardo da Vinci suggested that people showed individual differences in personality in their interpretations of cloud formations.

The Rorschach (1921) inkblot test contains 10 cards. Five are in black and white and shades of gray. Five use a variety of colors. Subjects are given the cards, one by one, and asked what they look like, or what they could be.

FIGURE 9.10 A Rorschach Inkblot. What does this look like? What could it be?

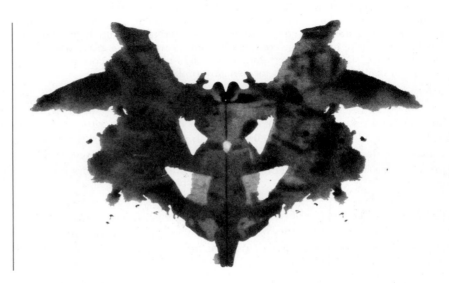

TABLE 9.4 Meanings Commonly Attributed to Certain Types of Content in Rorschach Responses According to Psychoanalytic Theory

Content	Interpretation
Animals	Immaturity, poor human relationships; high percentage of animal responses is normal for children
Anatomy	Concern about bodily problems, hostility
Plants	Femininity, nurturance (sexism, anyone?)
Blood	Aggression, hostility
Clouds	Intense anxiety, usually free-floating
Sex (e.g., penis, vagina)	Emotional disturbance; however, common among normal college students and other sophisticated individuals
Human (people)	Interest in other people

They can give no, one, or several responses to each card. They can hold the card upside down or sideways.

Responses are scored according to the *location, determinants, content,* and *form level.* The location is the section of the blot chosen—the whole card, or a major or minor detail. Determinants include features of the blot like shading, texture, or color that influence the response. The content is the *what* of the response, for instance a bat, a jack-o'-lantern, or a human torso. (Table 9.4 indicates the meanings attributed to certain types of content, according to many psychoanalytically oriented testers.) Form level indicates whether the response is consistent with the shape of the blot and the complexity of the response. A response that reflects the shape of the blot is a sign of adequate **reality testing.** A response that richly integrates several features of the blot is a sign of high intellectual functioning. The Rorschach is thought to provide insight into a person's intelligence, interests, cultural background, degree of introversion or extraversion, level of anxiety, reality testing, and a host of other variables.

The Thematic Apperception Test (TAT)   The TAT was developed in the 1930s by psychologist Henry Murray at Harvard University. It consists of drawings, like that shown in Figure 9.11, that are open to a variety of interpretations. Subjects are given the cards one at a time and asked to make up stories about them.

As noted in Chapter 7, Henry Murray has been a major contributor to the study of social motives. The TAT has been widely used in research in social motives as well as in clinical practice. In an experiment described in Chapter 7, need for achievement was assessed from subjects' responses to a card of a boy and a violin. The notion is that we are likely to some degree to be preoccupied with our needs, and that our needs will be projected into our responses to ambiguous situations. The TAT is also widely used to assess attitudes toward other people, especially parents, lovers, and spouses.

A Psychological Controversy: Can You Write a Personality Report That Applies to Everyone?

Take this brief personality test. Indicate whether each item is mostly true or false for you. Then read the report below to learn everything you always wanted to know about your personality but were too intelligent to ask.

Reality testing The capacity to perceive one's environment and oneself according to accurate sensory impressions.

FIGURE. 9.11 A Thematic Apperception Test Card. What is happening in this picture? What are the people thinking and feeling? How will it turn out?

1. I can't unclasp my hands.. T F
2. I often mistake my hands for food .... T F
3. I never liked room temperature .... T F
4. My throat is closer than it seems .... T F
5. Likes and dislikes are among my favorites .... T F
6. I've lost all sensation in my throat .... T F
7. I try to swallow at least three times a day............................. T F
8. My squirrels don't know where I am tonight .... T F
9. Walls impede my progress.. T F
10. My toes are numbered.. T F
11. My beaver won't go near the water .... T F

Total number of items marked true (T): _____

If your total number of items marked true was between zero and 11, the following personality report applies to you:

> The personality test you have taken has been found to predict inner potential for change.... In the past it has been shown that people with similar personality scores ... have a strong capacity for change.... You have a great deal of unused potential you have not yet turned to your advantage....
>
> The test also suggests that you display ability for personal integration and many latent strengths, as well as the ability to maintain a balance between your inner impulses and the demands of outer reality. Therefore, your personality is such that you have a strong potential for improvement (Halperin & Snyder, 1979, pp. 142–143).

That's you all right, isn't it? I shouldn't be surprised if you thought it sounded familiar. Psychologists Keith Halperin and C. R. Snyder (1979) administered a phony 50-item personality questionnaire to women in an introductory psychology course at the University of Kansas. The items weren't as silly as the 11 you answered, which were thrown together by Daniel Wegner (1979) and some friends during their graduate-school days. Still, the test was meaningless. Then the students rated the same personality report, which included the paragraphs cited above, for accuracy. The average rating was "quite accurate"!

Halperin and Snyder then administered a therapy program to women who had received the phony report and to women who had not. Believe it or not, women who had received the report, which underscored their capacity for change, showed greater improvement from the treatment than women who had not. When you believe you have the capacity to improve your lot, you are probably more likely to succeed.

The tendency to believe a generalized (but phony) personality report has been labeled the **Barnum effect.** It is probably the Barnum effect that makes fortune-tellers a living. Some psychologists argue that people who would credit such reports are simply gullible. But Layne (1979) counters that these reports are actually quite accurate, even if they do apply to many people. Reports like this may increase the recipient's perceived self-efficacy, and encourage people to harness their potential.

Circus magnate P. T. Barnum once declared, "There's a sucker born every minute." But in the case of the Barnum effect, it may simply be that most of us share the ability to make major improvements in our lives.

Evaluation of Measures of Personality

It seems clear that personality measures can provide useful information to help people make decisions about themselves and others. But in general, psychological tests should not be the sole criteria for making important decisions.

For example, single scales of the MMPI are reasonably accurate measures of the presence of a trait, like depression. But one could not justifiedly hospitalize a person for fear of suicide solely on the basis of a high D-scale score on the MMPI. Similarly, combinations of high MMPI scale scores seem to reflect certain clinical pictures in some populations, but not in others. A typical study found that a combination of high scores on the D, Pt, and Sc scales was likely to suggest severe disturbance in college males, but not college females (Kelley & King, 1979). The MMPI is also troubled by the fact that abnormal validity scale scores do *not* invalidate the test when respondents are highly disturbed.

The Rorschach inkblot test, for all its artistic appeal, has had major difficulties with validation. Some clinics no longer allow its use, and some doctoral programs in clinical psychology no longer require students to learn how to use it. The TAT has been consistently shown to be a useful research tool, but its clinical validity has also met with criticism.

Barnum effect The tendency to believe that a generalized personality report or prediction about oneself is accurate. (After circus magnate P. T. Barnum.)

Psychological tests should not be used as the sole means for making important decisions. But tests that are carefully chosen and interpreted may provide useful information for supplementing other sources of information.

Summary

Personality can be defined as "the distinctive patterns of behavior, including thoughts and emotions, that characterize each individual's adaptation to the situations of his or her life." The four major current personality theories include psychoanalytic, trait, social learning, and self theory.

Psychoanalytic theory, originated by Sigmund Freud, assumes that we are driven largely by unconscious motives and intrapsychic conflict. The unconscious id is the psychic structure present at birth. The id represents psychological drives and operates according to the pleasure principle, seeking instant gratification. The ego is the sense of self or "I." The ego develops through experience and operates according to the reality principle. It takes into account what is practical and possible in gratifying the impulses of the id. The superego is the moral sense, a partly conscious psychic structure that develops largely through identification with others. Defense mechanisms protect the ego from anxiety by repressing unacceptable ideas or distorting reality.

People undergo psychosexual development as psychosexual energy, or libido, is transferred from one erogenous zone to another during childhood. There are five stages of development: oral, anal, phallic, latency, and genital. Fixation in the oral stage may lead to oral traits like dependency and gullibility. Anal fixation may result in cleanliness–messiness, or perfectionism–carelessness. Children eventually identify with the same-sex parent through resolution of the Oedipus and Electra complexes of the phallic stage.

Carl Jung's analytical psychology features a collective unconscious and a number of archetypes. Alfred Adler's individual psychology features the inferiority complex and the compensating drive for superiority. Erik Erikson's psychosocial development highlights the importance of early social relationships rather than the gratification of childhood sexual impulses.

Trait theory adopts a descriptive approach to personality. Traits are assumed to underlie behavior and to account for behavioral consistency. Gordon Allport saw traits as neuropsychic structures. Cardinal traits dominate the personality. Raymond Cattell distinguished between surface traits (characteristic ways of behaving that seem linked in an orderly manner) and source traits (underlying traits from which surface traits are derived). Cattell constructed a test that measures 16 source traits.

Types are clusters of traits. William Sheldon hypothesized three basic human physiques, each of which was linked to certain traits: endomorphic (round and jolly), mesomorphic (muscular and athletic), and ectomorphic (lean, fragile, and scholarly).

Social learning theorists evolved within the behavioral tradition and place more emphasis on situational determinants of behavior. John Watson, the father of modern behaviorism, rejected notions of mind and personality altogether. Modern social learning theorists consider behavior to reflect personal variables, like behavioral competencies (skills), expectancies, perceived self-efficacy, and the subjective value of rewards, and situational variables, like rewards and punishments.

Humanistic self theory begins with the assumption of the existence of the self. The self is an organized and consistent way in which a person perceives his or her "I" to relate to others and the world. The self is innate and will attempt to become actualized (develop its unique potential) when the person receives unconditional positive regard. Conditions of worth lead to a distorted self-concept, disowning parts of the self, and, often, anxiety.

In personality measurement, psychologists take a sample of behavior to predict future behavior. A good test is reliable (yielding consistent results) and valid (it predicts a criterion—that which it is supposed to measure).

In objective tests, people respond to a standardized set of test items in specific, limited ways (as in multiple-choice tests or true–false tests). The MMPI is an objective personality test that uses a true–false format to assess abnormal behavior. It contains validity scales as well as clinical scales and has been validated empirically.

Projective tests present ambiguous stimuli and permit the subject a broad range of response. The foremost projective technique is the Rorschach inkblot test, although the TAT is widely used in research and clinical practice.

Truth or Fiction Revisited

- *Some psychologists claim that the human mind is like a vast submerged iceberg, only the tip of which rises above the surface into awareness.* True. Followers of Sigmund Freud's psychoanalytic theory believe that most of the mind is unconscious.

- *Women who compete with men in the business world are suffering from penis envy.* False. This view of Freud's has been severely criticized by many other psychologists, including contemporary followers of Freud, as reflective of ignorance and prejudice.

- *Some psychoanalysts feel that you have inherited mysterious memories that date back to ancient times.* True. Carl Jung and his followers believe that there is a collective unconscious that contains racial memories.

- *Obese people are jolly.* Not necessarily. This stereotype is consistent with Sheldon's constitutional theory, but people's personalities cannot be readily typed according to physique.

- *We may believe that we have freedom of choice, but behaviorists argue that our preferences and choices are actually forced upon us by the environment.* True. Contemporary social learning theorists, however, suggest that behavior reflects personal variables as well as environmental variables, and that freedom of choice is more than an illusion.

- *A psychologist could write a believable personality report about you without interviewing you, testing you, or, in fact, having any idea who you are.* Possibly. Research into the so-called Barnum effect suggests that the majority of people will agree with broadly stated personality descriptions of themselves.

- *Psychologists can always determine whether a person has told the truth on a personality test.* False. However, some tests, like the MMPI, have built-in validity scales that frequently suggest when test-takers have not answered test items accurately.

OUTLINE

Stress and Adjustment

- Too much of a good thing can make you ill.
- Our emotional problems stem almost completely from external pressures that we have little or no ability to change or control.
- Some people are dedicated to the creation of their own stress.
- It is possible for people to be literally scared to death.
- Some people drink alcohol purposefully to handicap themselves in their ability to cope with conflict or failure.
- When you are about to undergo a serious operation, learning the grisly details of the surgery and the expected course of recuperation may make the experience less stressful.
- If you tell people just to allow their muscles to relax, many will have no idea what to do.
- People who make decisions on the basis of inspiration and gut-level feelings wind up with fewer regrets than people who methodically add up all the pluses and minuses.

Stress

Yes, too much of a good thing *can* make you ill. You may think that marrying Mr. or Ms. Right, finding a prestigious job, moving to a new home, quitting smoking, and winning the lottery—all in the same year—would propel you into a state of bliss. It's possible. But these events could also lead to headaches, high blood pressure, or asthma. As pleasant as they may be, they all involve significant life changes. And according to Thomas Holmes and Richard Rahe (1967) of the University of Washington, life changes cause **stress.**

Stress is a concept borrowed from physics. In physics stress is defined as a pressure or force exerted on a body. The crushing of tons of rock against the earth, the smashing of one car into another, the stretching of a rubber band—all are types of physical stress. Psychological forces, or stresses, also "press," "push," or "pull." We may feel "crushed" by the "weight" of a major decision. We may feel "smashed," or as though we are "stretched" to the point of "snapping."

In psychology, then, stress is the demand made on an organism to adapt, to cope, to **adjust.** Some stress is necessary to keep us alert and occupied. Sensory deprivation experiments show that the absence of stimulation is unpleasant—so much so that we may invent our own by hallucinating. Each of us functions best at moderate levels of stress that some call a "healthy tension." But stress that is too intense or too prolonged can overtax our adjustive capacity and lead to physical or psychological harm.

In this chapter we explore many sources of stress: life changes, pain and discomfort, anxiety, frustration, conflict, and Type A behavior. We shall see that stress can lead to physiological problems which Hans Selye calls "diseases of adaptation." We discuss defensive methods of coping with stress that reduce the immediate impact of **stressors** but do not confront their origins. Finally, we discuss more active coping methods that modify or eliminate stressful circumstances, or fundamentally change self-defeating ways of responding to stress.

Stress and Life Changes: "Going through Changes"

It is the "last" straw that will break the camel's back. Similarly, stresses in the form of life changes can pile atop each other until we can finally no longer cope. Although there are individual differences in coping ability, Holmes and Rahe (1967) were able to find some **normative data** concerning the number of life changes that will tax many of us to the limit.

Holmes and Rahe gave marriage an arbitrary weight of 50 **life-change units** and asked people from all walks of life to assign units to other life changes, using marriage as a baseline. Most events shown in Table 10.1 were rated less stressful than marriage, but a few were considered more stressful. These include death of a spouse (100 units) and divorce (73 units). Positive events, for example, outstanding personal achievement and a vacation, also made the list.

The Holmes and Rahe list has not gone unchallenged. For instance, positive events may be less disturbing then negative events, even when the number of life-change units assigned to them is rather high (Lefcourt and others, 1981). Also, many of the changes listed by Holmes and Rahe actually

---

Stress The demand made on an organism to adjust. (From the Latin *strictus,* meaning "bound tight.")

Adjust To respond to stress. To behave in ways that meet the demands of the environment. (From the Latin *ad-,* meaning "toward," and *just,* meaning "right.")

Stressor An event or stimulus that acts as a source of stress.

Normative data Information concerning the behavior of a population.

Life-change units Numbers assigned by raters to various life changes that reflect the amount of stress caused by each.

TABLE 10.1   Scale of Life-Change Units

Life Event	Life-change units		
Death of one's spouse	100	Change in responsibilities at work	29
Divorce	73	Son or daughter leaving home	29
Marital separation	65	Trouble with in-laws	29
Jail term	63	Outstanding personal achievement	28
Death of a close family member	63	Wife beginning or stopping work	26
Personal injury or illness	53	Beginning or ending school	26
Marriage	50	Change in living conditions	25
Being fired at work	47	Revision of personal habits	24
Marital reconciliation	45	Trouble with one's boss	23
Retirement	45	Change in work hours or conditions	20
Change in the health of a family member	44	Change in residence	20
Pregnancy	40	Change in schools	20
Sex difficulties	39	Change in recreation	29
Gain of a new family member	39	Change in church activities	19
Business readjustment	39	Change in social activities	18
Change in one's financial state	38	Mortgage or loan of less than $10,000	17
Death of a close friend	37	Change in sleeping habits	16
Change to a different line of work	36	Change in number of family get-togethers	15
Change in number of arguments with one's spouse	35	Change in eating habits	15
Mortgage over $10,000	31	Vacation	13
Foreclosure of a mortgage or loan	30	Christmas	12
		Minor violations of the law	11

How many life-changes units did you "earn" during the past year? Holmes and Rahe linked one's number of life-change units to risk for medical problems. Source: Holmes and Rahe (1967).

involve clusters of changes. For instance, "gain of new family member" is not a single event. Having children is often linked to problems in calming them when they cry, frequent minor illnesses, lack of sleep, added financial burdens, lack of personal freedom, and many other demands (Weinberg & Richardson, 1981). The degree of stress linked to an event will also reflect the meaning the event has for the individual. Pregnancy, for example, can be a positive or negative life change, depending on whether one wants to have a child.

Still, Holmes and Rahe found that people who "earned" 300 or more life-change units according to their scale within a year were at greater risk for illness. Eight of 10 developed medical problems, as compared with only one of three people whose life-change units totals for the year were below 150. Other researchers have found that life changes are linked to relapses among persons who show major psychological disorders, such as **schizophrenia** (Rabkin, 1980).

While the links between life changes and illness may seem quite convincing, it is correlational rather than experimental (Monroe, 1982). The data show that a high total of life-change units is related to medical and psychological disorders. It may seem logical that these changes caused the disorders, but the life changes were not manipulated experimentally and rival explanations of the data are also possible. For instance, it might just be that people who are predisposed toward medical or psychological problems lead lives that involve greater degrees of change. Still, life changes do require adjustments.

Schizophrenia A major psychological disorder in which thought processes are impaired and emotions are not appropriate to the situation. See Chapter 11.

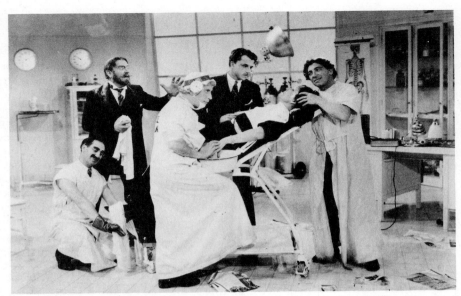

An outing to the dentist's office is usually more stressful than suggested in this scene from the Marx Brothers film, *A Day at the Races*. Pain and discomfort tax our ability to adjust. Psychologists suggest that we can minimize our discomfort by controlling catastrophizing thoughts and spacing painful tasks or chores as best we can.

Pain and Discomfort

Pain and discomfort impair performance and coping ability. Athletes report that pain interferes with their ability to run, swim, and so forth, even when the source of the pain does not directly weaken them.

In an experiment on the effects of pain on performance, psychiatrist Curt Richter (1957) first recorded the amount of time rats could swim to stay afloat in a tub of water. In water at room temperature, most rats could keep their noses above the surface for about 80 hours. But when Richter blew **noxious** streams of air into their faces, or kept the water uncomfortably hot or cold, the rats could remain afloat for only 20 to 40 hours. When the rats were **traumatized** by having their whiskers noisily chopped off while inside a black bag before being placed in the water, some managed to remain afloat for only a few minutes. Yet the clipping itself had not physically weakened them. Rats that were allowed several minutes to recover from the clipping before being launched swam for the usual 80 hours. Later we shall see that psychologists recommend that we space aggravating tasks or chores so that discomfort does not build to the point where it compounds stress and impairs our performance.

In Chapter 14 we shall see that people who experience discomfort from heat, crowding, and pollution often show more antisocial behavior. The discomforts of city life can also lead us to be less concerned with the plights of others, even of children.

Anxiety

"Up-tight," "shook up," "jumpy," "on edge," "butterflies in the stomach"—these are just some of the colorful expressions used to describe the unpleasant sensations we associate with **anxiety.** Anxiety may be thought of

Noxious Harmful, injurious.

Traumatize In psychology, to injure or wound psychologically.

Anxiety (1) A negative emotion characterized by persistent fear and dread. (2) A general emotional response to stress.

as a general emotional response to stress, but anxiety is also a source of stress. As other emotions (see Chapter 7), anxiety can have situational, physiological, and cognitive components. Anxiety is also a source of motivation that, as other sources of motivation, leads to goal-directed behavior. In the case of anxiety, the goal is usually to reduce or eliminate the anxiety (Spielberger, 1966, 1972).

Trait vs. State Anxiety Anxiety is sometimes thought of as a trait or personality variable. People who show **trait anxiety** may experience persistent feelings of dread and foreboding—cognitions that something terrible is about to happen. They are chronically worried and concerned. They experience rapid heart beat and respiration rate, muscle tension, and so forth, even when they perceive no environmental threat. Certainly when things are going well they are likely to be less anxious than when things are going poorly, but they show some anxiety even under the best of circumstances. I recall one friend saying about another, "Gail is the type of person who, if she were given a million dollars, would say, 'Good grief, how am I going to spend all that?' "

Sigmund Freud suggested that persistent anxiety of this sort was a form of **neurotic anxiety.** Neurotic anxiety represented the vague sensing of the danger that unacceptable, unconscious impulses might break loose into awareness. For example, resolution of the Oedipus complex requires that men **repress** sexual impulses toward their mothers and hostile impulses toward their fathers. Perception of Oedipal wishes would cause guilt because of the incest taboo and recognition of the wish to hurt a loved one—one's father.

Freud wrote that neurotic anxiety could become generalized, or **free-floating.** We might be anxious all, or almost all, of the time as we tried to keep a lid on our boiling impulses. What we observe, of course, in the case of free-floating anxiety is frequent or persistent anxiety. It has not been shown that such anxiety reflects efforts to repress unacceptable wishes. It could also reflect failure to pinpoint all the environmental and self-imposed stressors acting on one, or even be due to a highly active autonomic nervous system (see Chapter 2).

State anxiety, by contrast, refers to a temporary condition of arousal that is clearly triggered by a specific situation (Shedletsky & Endler, 1974). We might experience state anxiety on the eve of a final exam, before a big date, on a job interview, or while waiting in the dentist's office. Different people experience state anxiety in somewhat different situations (Mellstrom and others, 1976). The presence of state anxiety depends on our unique learning histories and what a situation—such as learning to use a microcomputer—means to us, as well as whether the situation produces physical pain or discomfort. In the following section we focus more on the cognitive components of anxiety and other negative emotions, and see how they can compound the stress we experience.

Irrational Beliefs and Self-Imposed Stress "There is nothing either good or bad, but thinking makes it so." In writing these lines, Shakespeare did not mean that injuries and misfortunes do not discomfort us. He did mean that our cognitive responses to unfortunate circumstances can heighten our discomfort.

New York psychologist Albert Ellis (Ellis & Harper, 1975; Ellis, 1977) shared Shakespeare's view. He noted that our beliefs about events, as well as the events themselves, fashion our reaction to them, creating anxiety, depression, and other stressful emotions.

Trait anxiety Anxiety as a personality variable, or persistent trait.

Neurotic anxiety In psychoanalytic theory, feelings of anxiety that stem from unconscious concern that unacceptable ideas or impulses may break loose into awareness or be expressed in behavior.

Repress To eject from consciousness.

Free-floating Chronic, persistent. Not tied to particular events.

State anxiety A temporary condition of anxiety that may be attributed to a situation.

Catastrophize
(kuh–TASS–tro–fize). To exaggerate or magnify the noxious properties of events such that adjustment efforts may be hampered. To "blow out of proportion." (From the Greek *kata*-, meaning "down," and *strephein,* meaning "to turn.")

A person might be fired from a job and be miserable about it. It would be natural to assume that losing the job had caused the misery. But Ellis points out that beliefs, even if they are rapidly fleeting, actually account for much of the misery. Let us examine the situation according to Ellis's A-B-C approach: Losing the job is an *Activating event*. The eventual outcome, or *Consequence*, is misery. But between the activating event and the consequences lies a set of *Beliefs*, such as the following: "What an important job this was," "Losing this job means I'm worthless," "My family will starve." The process works this way:

Activating events $\longrightarrow$ Beliefs $\longrightarrow$ Consequences

These beliefs tend to **catastrophize** the extent of the loss and contribute to anxiety. Extensive focusing on them, or ruminating, may also distract the person from planning what to do next.

Ellis examined his early experiences as a clinical psychologist and concluded the following: (1) People in our culture are likely to harbor several of the irrational Beliefs listed below; and (2) these Beliefs are responsible for a good deal of self-imposed stress in the forms of anxiety, depression, and impaired interpersonal relationships. How many of these irrational Beliefs do you harbor? Are you willing to challenge them?

Irrational Belief 1. You must have sincere love and approval almost all the time from the people you find significant.

Irrational Belief 2. You must prove yourself thoroughly competent, adequate, and achieving. Or you must at least have real competence or talent at something important.

Irrational Belief 3. Things must go the way you would like them to go, because you need what you want. Life proves awful, terrible, and horrible when you do not get what you prefer.

Irrational Belief 4. Others must treat everyone in a fair and just manner. When people act unfairly or unethically they are rotten. They deserve damnation and severe punishment and the universe must see to it that they get this kind of retribution.

Irrational Belief 5. When dangers or fearsome things exist in your world, you must continually preoccupy yourself with and be upset about them.

Irrational Belief 6. People and things should turn out better than they do. It is awful and horrible if you do not immediately find solutions to life's hassles.

Irrational Belief 7. Your emotional misery comes almost completely from external pressures that you have little or no ability to change or control. Unless these pressures change, you cannot help making yourself feel anxious, depressed, self-downing, or hostile.

Irrational Belief 8. It is easier to avoid facing life's difficulties and responsibilities than to undertake more rewarding forms of self-discipline. You need immediate comfort and cannot go through present pain to achieve future gain.

Irrational Belief 9. Your past life influenced you immensely and remains all-important. If something once strongly affected you, it has to keep determining your feelings and behavior today. (Yet, many psychologists today have come to believe that many early traumatic experiences can be "outgrown.")

Irrational Belief 10. You can achieve happiness by inertia and inaction, or by passively and uncommittedly "enjoying yourself."

One study found that the irrational belief that one must be loved by, and earn the approval of, practically everyone was endorsed by 65 percent of anxious subjects, as compared with only two percent of nonanxious subjects (Newmark and others, 1973). Another found that college men who believe that it is awful to be turned down for a date show more social anxiety than men who are less likely to catastrophize rejection (Gormally and others, 1981).

People whose marriages are distressed are also more likely than people with functional marriages to harbor a number of irrational beliefs (Eidelson & Epstein, 1982). They are more likely to believe that any disagreement is destructive, that their partners should be able to read their minds (and know what they want), that their partners cannot change, that they must be perfect sexual partners, and that men and women differ dramatically in personality and needs. It is rational, and adjustive to a marriage, for partners to recognize that no two people can agree all the time, to express their wishes rather than depend on "mind-reading," to believe that we all can change (although change may come slowly), to tolerate intermittent sexual frustrations and blunders, and to treat each other as equals.

Let us return to Ellis's basic irrational beliefs. Ellis recognizes that it is understandable that we would like to have the approval of others, but it is irrational to believe that we cannot survive without it. It would be nice to be competent in everything we undertake, but it's not absolutely necessary—unless we convince ourselves that it is. There is a kernel of truth to most of these irrational beliefs, but many people create or compound their own stress by exaggerating their importance or necessity.

Childhood experiences may explain the origins of irrational beliefs, but it is our own irrational beliefs that cause us misery *now. Here. Today.* If we wish to change the way we feel about our lives and ourselves, we must find rational alternatives for our irrational beliefs. We shall suggest a number of helpful strategies for doing so as the chapter progresses.

Frustration

You may wish to play the line for the varsity football team but weigh only 120 lbs. or are a woman. You may have been denied a job or educational opportunity because of your ethnic background. Now and then the urge to gratify an impulse or two may be frustrated by your moral code.

We all encounter **frustration,** the thwarting of a motive to attain a goal (see Figure 10.1). And frustration is another source of stress. Many sources of frustration are obvious. Adolescents are used to being too young to wear makeup, drive, go out, spend money, drink, or work. Age is the barrier that requires them to delay gratification. No wonder G. Stanley Hall characterized adolescence as a period of storm and stress.

We may also be frustrated if our goals are set too high, or if our self-demands are irrational. As Albert Ellis noted, if we try to earn other people's approval at all costs, or insist on performing perfectly in all of our undertakings, we are doomed to failure, frustration, and misery. We may condemn ourselves if we must displease a friend or parent when we express our own ideas. We may judge ourselves harshly if we only show gradual improvement in a difficult academic subject, rather than earn consistent A's.

Frustration (1) The thwarting of a motive. (2) The emotion produced by the thwarting of a motive.

FIGURE 10.1 A Model for Frustration. A person *(P)* has a motive *(M)* to reach a goal *(G)*, but is frustrated by a barrier *(B).*

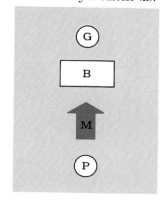

Most college students will have little difficulty understanding the frustration these students are encountering in their long registration lines. Frustration results from thwarting a motive to reach a goal. In this case student motives to eat lunch and get out and enjoy the sun are being blocked by the need to keep their place in line if they wish to get into preferred courses.

Tolerance for frustration Ability to delay gratification, to maintain self-control when a motive is thwarted.

Conflict A condition characterized by opposing motives, in which gratification of one motive prevents gratification of the other. (From the Latin *com-*, meaning "together," and *fligere*, meaning "to strike.")

FIGURE 10.2   An Approach–Approach Conflict.

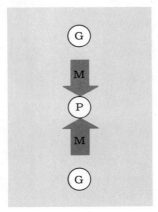

Anxiety and fear may also serve as barriers that prevent us from acting effectively to meet our goals. A high-school senior who wishes to attend an out-of-state college may be frustrated by fear of leaving home. A young adult may be frustrated from asking an attractive person out on a date by fear of rejection (a common fear, as we shall see in Chapter 14). A woman may be frustrated in her desire to move up the corporate ladder by fear that co-workers, friends, and family may view her assertiveness as compromising her femininity. In Chapter 13 we shall see that such concerns have led many women to fear the prospect of success.

Getting ahead is often a gradual process that demands that we must be able to live with some frustration and delay gratification. Yet our **tolerance for frustration** may fluctuate. Stress heaped upon stress can lower our tolerance, just as Richter's rats, stressed from their close shaves, sank quickly to the bottom of the tub. We may laugh off a flat tire on a good day. But if it is raining, or if we have just waited for an hour in a gas line, the flat may seem like the last straw. People who have encountered frustration but learned that it is possible to surmount barriers or find substitute goals are more tolerant of frustration than those who have never experienced it, or those who have experienced excesses of frustration.

Conflict

Have you ever felt "damned if you did and damned if you didn't"? Regretted that you couldn't do two things, or be in two places, at the same time? Wanted to go to a film but had to study for a test? This is **conflict**—being torn in two or more directions by opposing motives. Conflict is frustrating and stressful. Conflict may also be looked at as a type of frustration in which the barrier to achieving a goal is an opposing impulse or motive. Let us consider four types of conflict.

Approach-Approach Conflict An **approach-approach conflict** (Figure 10.2) is the least stressful form of conflict. Here each of two goals is positive and within reach. You may not be able to decide between pizza or tacos, Tom or Dick, or a trip to Nassau or Hawaii. In such cases you may **vacillate** for a while before making a decision.

When you have made your choice, there may be some regrets, especially if that choice falls short of expectations. You may be nauseated by the pizza. Tom may grind his teeth. It may rain in Nassau. Still, once a choice is made you are likely to become more active or work harder as you are nearing your goal. If it is satisfying, you are not likely to be too regretful about the road not taken (see the Robert Frost poem on p. 396).

Avoidance-Avoidance Conflict An **avoidance-avoidance conflict** (Figure 10.3) is more stressful. You may be fearful of visiting the dentist, but also fear that your teeth will decay if you do not. You may not want to contribute to the Association for the Advancement of Lost Causes, but fear that your friends will consider you cheap or uncommitted if you do not. Each goal is negative in an avoidance-avoidance conflict.

When an avoidance-avoidance conflict is highly stressful, and no resolution is in sight, some people withdraw from the conflict by focusing their attention on other matters or by suspending behavior altogether. In *How To Save Your Own Life*, novelist Erica Jong (1977) portrays a woman in such a conflict who does not wish to remain in a barren marriage but is reluctant to end it because she fears having to swim alone in the social world once more. The persistent stress becomes so depressing that she cannot get out of bed in the morning to begin the day. Only at that low ebb does she resolve to get divorced.

Approach-Avoidance Conflict One goal can produce both approach and avoidance motives, as in the **approach-avoidance conflict** (Figure 10.4). People and things have their pluses and minuses, their good points and their bad points. Cream cheese pie may be delicious, but oh, the calories! Why are so many attractive goals immoral, illegal, or fattening? The unconscious conflicts theorized by Freud have approach and avoidance motives. For example, boys are theorized to wish to possess their mothers sexually, but the wish is frustrated by fear of retaliation by their fathers.

Approach-avoidance conflicts may also lead to vacillation. And we tend to exaggerate the positive features of distant goals that seem repulsive when they are nearby. Many couples repeatedly break up, then reunite. When they are apart—feeling lonely and sexually frustrated—they recall each other fondly and swear that they would make it work "this time" if they got together again. Perhaps they cannot even recall their sources of discontent. But after they again spend time together, they may find themselves facing the same old aggravations. "How could I have ever believed this _____ (you fill it in) would change," they may each think. "This time we're going to *stay* apart."

Double Approach-Avoidance Conflict The most complex form of conflict is the **double approach-avoidance conflict** (Figure 10.5), in which each of two or more goals has its positive and negative aspects. Should you study on the eve of an exam or go to a film? "Studying's a drag, but I won't have to worry about flunking. I'd love to see the movie, but I'd just be worrying about how I'll do tomorrow." Should you take a job or advanced training when you

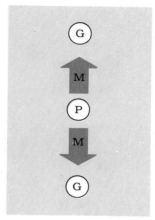

FIGURE 10.3 An Avoidance–Avoidance Conflict.

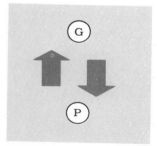

FIGURE 10.4 An Approach–Avoidance Conflict.

Approach-approach conflict Conflict involving two positive but mutually exclusive goals.

Vacillate (VASS–sill–late). To move back and forth. (From the Latin *vacillare*, meaning "to sway to and fro.")

Avoidance-avoidance conflict Conflict involving two negative goals, with avoidance of one requiring approach of the other.

Approach-avoidance conflict Conflict involving a goal with positive and negative features.

Double approach-avoidance conflict Conflict involving two goals, each of which has positive and negative aspects.

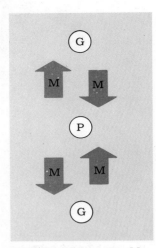

FIGURE 10.5 A Double Approach–Avoidance Conflict.

complete your college program? If you opt for the job cash will soon be jingling in your pockets, but later you might wonder if you reached your potential. By furthering your education you may have to delay the independence and gratification that are afforded by earning a living, but you may find a more fulfilling position later on.

All forms of conflict entail motives that aim in opposite directions. When one motive is much stronger than the other—as when you feel "starved" and are only slightly concerned about your weight—it will probably not be too stressful to act in accord with the powerful motive and, in this case, eat. But when each conflicting motive is powerful you may encounter high levels of stress and confusion about the proper course of action. At such times you are faced with the need to make a decision. But making decisions can also be stressful, especially when there is no clear correct choice. But later in the chapter we shall present some methods for decision making that psychologists have found can afford some help.

Type A Behavior

In *Type A Behavior and Your Heart*, cardiologists Meyer Friedman and Ray H. Rosenman (1974) proposed that millions of us behave as though we were dedicated to the continuous creation of our own stress. As a result of research into the origins of heart disease, Friedman and Rosenman identified the so-called **Type A behavior** pattern. They suggest that Type A behavior is a stronger predictor of heart disease than smoking, lack of exercise, poor diet, or obesity.

Type A people are highly driven, competitive, and impatient (Matthews and others, 1982). They feel rushed and under pressure. They order their lives as though one eye were glued firmly to the clock. They are not only prompt, but frequently early for appointments (Strahan, 1981). They eat, walk, and talk rapidly, and experience great irritation when they are stuck in a line. They are merciless in their self-criticism when they fail at a task (Brunson & Matthews, 1981). Type A people find it difficult just to go out on the tennis court and bat the ball back and forth. They watch their form, perfect their strokes, and demand regular self-improvement. All in all, Albert Ellis's second irrational

Type A behavior Stress-producing behavior, characterized by perfectionism and a sense of time urgency.

The Road Not Taken

Poet Robert Frost often used nature as a way of describing feelings and conflicts that occur within people. In "The Road Not Taken," he recalls a decision he once made in order to resolve an approach-approach conflict. With gentle self-mockery he explains how he rationalized his choice:

Two roads diverged in a yellow wood,
And sorry I could not travel both
And be one traveler, long I stood
And looked down one as far as I could
To where it bent in the undergrowth;

Then took the other, as just as fair,
And having perhaps the better claim,

Because it was grassy and wanted wear;
Though as for that the passing there
Had worn them really about the same,

And both that morning equally lay
In leaves no step had trodden black.
Oh, I kept the first for another day!
Yet knowing how way leads on to way,
I doubted if I should ever come back.

I shall be telling this with a sigh
Somewhere ages and ages hence:
Two roads diverged in a wood, and I—
I took the one less traveled by,
And that has made all the difference.

belief—that you must be perfectly competent and achieving in everything you undertake—seems to be the motto of Type A people.

When you designate some people as Type A, you are practically obligated to designate others as Type B. Friedman and Rosenman are no slackers. They define Type B's as people who relax more readily than Type A's. Type B's are less ambitious and impatient. They pace themselves rather than hurry and scurry. They focus more on the quality of life. Type A's perceive time as passing more rapidly than do Type B's, and they work more quickly (Yarnold & Grimm, 1982). Type A's earn higher grades and more money than Type B's of equal intelligence (Glass, 1977), but Type B's smoke less, have lower **serum choles-terol** levels and fewer heart attacks (Friedman & Rosenman, 1974).

While the evidence seems clear that Type A people are at greater risk for a number of physical ailments than are Type B's, it must be pointed out that the evidence—as that which links life changes to medical and psychological disorders—is correlational, not experimental. For both practical and ethical reasons, no researcher has randomly assigned a group of subjects to Type A behavior patterns and measured the results. People who were already Type A were compared with people who were already Type B. It may seem unlikely, but we cannot rule out the possibility that predisposition toward certain medical problems also somehow promotes Type A behavior. It may also be that personality factors, such as values, beliefs, and attitudes, lead both to Type A behavior and physical ailments. The Type A behavior pattern in itself may not be the culprit. Later we shall see that methods for coping with Type A behavior address these attitudes as well as Type A behavior.

Physiological Response to Stress

How is it that too much of a good thing, or that anxiety, frustration, or conflict can make you ill? Why do Type A people run a greater risk of heart attacks than Type B's? We do not yet have all the answers, but those we have suggest that the body, under stress, is very much like a clock with an alarm system that does not shut off until its energy is dangerously depleted.

General Adaptation Syndrome

Hans Selye (1976) noted that the body's response to different stressors shows some similarities, whether the stressor is a bacterial invasion, a perceived danger, a major life change, an inner conflict, or a wound. He labeled this response the **general adaptation syndrome** (GAS). The GAS consists of three stages: an alarm reaction, a resistance stage, and an exhaustion stage.

The **alarm reaction** is triggered by the impact of a stressor. It mobilizes or arouses the body in preparation for defense. Cannon (1929) had earlier termed this alarm system the **fight-or-flight reaction.** It is characterized by activity of the sympathetic branch of the autonomic nervous system, as described in Chapter 2 (also see Table 10.2). It provides more energy for muscular activity, which can be used to fight or flee from a source of danger, and decreases the body's vulnerability to wounds. The fight-or-flight reaction is inherited from a long-ago time when many stressors were life-threatening. It was triggered by a predator at the edge of a thicket, by a sudden rustling in the undergrowth. Once the threat is removed, the body returns to a lower state of arousal.

Serum cholesterol (co–LESS–ter–all). A fatty substance (cholesterol) in the blood (serum) which has been linked to heart disease.

General adaptation syndrome Selye's term for a hypothesized three-stage response to stress. Abbreviated *GAS.*

Alarm reaction The first stage of the GAS, which is "triggered" by the impact of a stressor and characterized by sympathetic activity.

Fight-or-flight reaction Cannon's term for a hypothesized innate adaptive response to the perception of danger.

Are You Type A or Type B?

Are you Type A or Type B? Type A's are ambitious, hard driving, and chronically discontent with their current achievements. Type B's, by contrast, are more relaxed, more involved with the quality of life, and—according to cardiologists Meyer Friedman and Ray Rosenman—less prone to heart attacks.

The following checklist was developed from descriptions of Type A people by Friedman and Rosenman (1974) and by Matthews and her colleagues (1982). It will help give you insight into whether you are closer in your behavior patterns to the Type A or the Type B individual. Simply place a checkmark under the Yes if the behavior pattern is typical of you, and under the No if it is not. Try to work rapidly and leave no item blank. Then turn to the scoring key in Appendix B.

DO YOU: | | YES | NO

1. Strongly accent key words in your everyday speech? _____ _____
2. Eat and walk quickly? _____ _____
3. Believe that children should be taught to be competitive? _____ _____
4. Feel restless when watching a slow worker? _____ _____
5. Hurry other people to get on with what they're trying to say? _____ _____
6. Find it highly aggravating to be stuck in traffic or waiting for a seat at a restaurant? _____ _____
7. Continue to think about your own problems and business even when listening to someone else? _____ _____

Our ancestors lived in situations in which the alarm reaction would not be activated for long. They fought or ran quickly or, to put it bluntly, they died. Sensitive alarm reactions contributed to survival. Our ancestors did not spend years in the academic grind or carry 30-year mortgages. Contemporary pressures may activate our alarm systems for hours, days, or months at a time, so that highly sensitive systems may now be a handicap.

If the alarm reaction mobilizes the body and the stressor is not removed, we enter the adaptation or **resistance stage** of the GAS. The level of arousal is not as high as in the alarm reaction, but it is still greater than normal. In this stage the body attempts to restore lost energy and repair whatever damage has been done.

If the stressor is still not adequately dealt with, we may enter the final or **exhaustion stage** of the GAS. Our capacity for resisting stress varies, but

Resistance stage The second stage of the GAS, characterized by prolonged sympathetic activity in an effort to restore lost energy and repair damage. Also called the *adaptation stage.*

Exhaustion stage The third stage of the GAS, characterized by weakened resistance and possible deterioration.

TABLE 10.2 Components of the Alarm Reaction

Respiration rate increases	Digestion slows
Heart rate increases	Sugar is released from the liver
Blood pressure increases	
Muscles tense	Adrenalin is secreted
Blood shifts away from the skin	Blood coagulability increases

The alarm reaction is triggered by various types of stressors. It is essentially defined by activity of the sympathetic branch of the autonomic nervous system, and prepares the body to fight or flee from a source of danger.

8. Try to eat and shave, or drive and jot down notes at the same time?
9. Catch up on your work on vacations?
10. Bring conversations around to topics of concern to you?
11. Feel guilty when you spend time just relaxing?
12. Find that you're so wrapped up in your work that you no longer notice office decorations or the scenery when you commute?
13. Find yourself concerned with getting more *things* rather than developing your creativity and social concerns?
14. Try to schedule more and more activities into less time?
15. Always appear for appointments on time?
16. Clench or pound your fists, or use other gestures, to emphasize your views?
17. Credit your accomplishments to your ability to work rapidly?
18. Feel that things must be done *now* and quickly?
19. Constantly try to find more efficient ways to get things done?
20. Insist on winning at games rather than just having fun?
21. Interrupt others often?
22. Feel irritated when others are late?
23. Leave the table immediately after eating?
24. Feel rushed?
25. Feel dissatisfied with your current level of performance?

all of us, as even the strongest of Richter's rats, eventually become exhausted when stress persists indefinitely. Continued stress at this time may lead to deterioration, to what Selye terms "diseases of adaptation"—from allergies and hives to ulcers and heart disease—and ultimately to death.

Voodoo Death: A Case Study in Exhaustion?   Some years ago Walter Cannon (1957) became fascinated by voodoo "magic." He pored over records of apparently healthy Caribbean islanders who had died within hours or days of being told that voodoo curses had been placed on them. Cannon did not believe that they had been killed by the curses themselves. Rather, he suggested that these deaths might be attributed to prolonged overarousal of the fight-or-flight mechanism—that is, to overarousal of the sympathetic branch of the autonomic nervous system.

Some recipients of the curses might also have suffered from underlying heart or circulatory problems. In these cases the "curse" may have precipitated an attack. Others might simply have become overexhausted as they resisted the stressful belief that they were doomed. Perhaps these people had been scared to death—quite literally.

A Pain in the Neck: A Note on Headaches   At least 47 percent of the American population suffer from regular or occasional headaches (Schwab and others, 1974). Most headaches result from muscle tension (Brown, 1977). We are likely to contract muscles in the shoulders, neck, forehead, and scalp during the first two stages of the GAS. Persistent stress can lead to persistent muscle tension and persistent muscle-tension headaches.

Most other headaches, including the severe **migraine headache,** stem from changes in the blood supply to the head. These changes may be induced by barometric pressure, pollen, specific drugs, the chemical monosodium glutamate (MSG) which is often used to enhance the flavor of food, especially in Oriental restaurants, and the **tyramine** found in red wines. Tyramine is used by physicians to treat *low* blood pressure, and it can create pounding headaches, from elevated blood pressure, in normal persons.

Regardless of the original source of the headache, we can unwittingly propel ourselves into a vicious cycle: Headache pain is a stressor that can lead us to increase, rather than relax, muscle tension in the neck and shoulders. In this way we may compound headache pain. Muscle relaxation exercises that we shall discuss later in the chapter often relieve headache pain. Biofeedback training which alters the flow of blood to the head has been used effectively to treat migraine headache (Blanchard and others, 1980, 1982). People who are sensitive to MSG or tyramine can ask that MSG be left out of their Oriental dishes and can switch to a white wine.

Some Effects of Chronic Stress: When Psychological Factors Affect One's Physical Condition

Chronic stress can lead to a number of **psychosomatic** or **psychophysiological** problems in addition to headaches. Herbert Benson (1975) has shown that chronic stress can lead to high blood pressure, or **hypertension.** Hypertension, in turn, can lead to disorders like **arteriosclerosis,** strokes, and kidney malfunctions. Selye (1976) theorizes that chronic stress may play a role in inflammatory diseases, like arthritis; premenstrual distress; digestive diseases, like colitis; and even metabolic diseases like diabetes and **hypoglycemia.**

Why, under stress, do some of us develop **ulcers,** others develop hypertension, and still others suffer no bodily problems? It may be that there is an interaction between stress and predisposing biological and psychological differences between individuals (Davison & Neale, 1982).

Ulcers may afflict one person in 10 and cause as many as 10,000 deaths each year in the United States (Weiss, 1975). People who develop ulcers under stress often have higher **pepsinogen** levels than those who do not (Weiner and others, 1957), and heredity may contribute to pepsinogen level (Mirsky, 1958). Research with laboratory rats suggests that intense approach-avoidance conflict may also contribute to ulcers (Sawrey and others, 1956; Sawrey & Weisz, 1956).

Hypertension may afflict 10 to 30 percent of Americans (Seer, 1979). Blood pressure appears to be higher among blacks than whites, and also higher among both blacks and whites who tend to hold in, rather than express, feelings of anger (Harburg and others, 1973). However, Shapiro and Goldstein (1982) argue that the evidence that links hypertension to any particular personality pattern is not convincing.

Some 37 percent of **asthma** cases are linked predominantly to psychological factors, but 86 percent of asthma patients studied also show a history of respiratory infection (Rees, 1964). Such evidence again suggests an interaction between the psychological and the physiological.

Migraine headache A severe headache, usually occurring on just one side of the head, that stems from increased blood supply to the head and is often accompanied by nausea and impaired vision. (From the Greek *hemi-*, meaning "half," and *kranion,* meaning "skull.")

Tyramine (TIE–rah–mean). A crystalline chemical found in a number of foods that is used in the medical treatment of *low* blood pressure. Thus it can cause hyptertension in normal people.

Psychosomatic Having to do with physical illnesses that have psychological origins or are intensified by stress.

Psychophysiological Psychosomatic.

Hypertension High blood pressure.

Arteriosclerosis Hardening and thickening of the arteries leading from the heart.

Hypoglycemia A metabolic disorder characterized by a low level of sugar in the blood. See Chapter 2.

Ulcer An open sore, as in the lining of the stomach. (From the Greek *helkos,* meaning "wound.")

Pepsinogen A substance that helps the body digest proteins.

Asthma Recurrent attacks of difficult breathing and wheezing.

Coping with Stress

Many techniques for coping with stress are essentially defensive. They reduce the immediate impact of the stressor, but at some personal or social cost. This cost includes socially inappropriate behavior (as in alcoholism, aggression, or regression), avoidance of problems (as in withdrawal), or self-deception (as in use of **defense mechanisms** like rationalization or denial). **Defensive coping** grants us time to marshall our resources, but it does not deal with the source of stress or improve the effectiveness of our response to stress. In the long run, defensive methods can be harmful if we do not use the chance they provide to find more active ways of coping.

Direct or **active coping** begins with accepting responsibility for our own behavior, including our thoughts and our emotional responses. It includes manipulating the environment to change or eliminate sources of stress. When we cannot change the environment, it involves directly modifying cognitive and physiological responses so that the impact of stressors is reduced.

Let us explore a number of defensive and active methods for coping with stress.

Defensive Coping

In this section we discuss various methods of defensive coping. These include the use of alcohol and other drugs, aggression, withdrawal, fantasy, and the defense mechanisms of regression, denial, repression, rationalization, reaction formation, projection, intellectualization, displacement, and sublimation. Freud labeled the latter group of defensive measures "mechanisms" in keeping with the trend in his day to think of human functions in machinelike terms. He also believed that defense mechanisms operated unconsciously to protect the ego from the anxiety that might stem from recognition of unacceptable ideas and impulses. (Today many psychologists who have been influenced by computer science discuss human cognitive functioning in terms of "information processing.") But Freud's "mechanisms" may also be viewed as habitual (and not necessarily unconscious) ways of responding to stress that are reinforced by their reduction of discomfort, anxiety, or frustration.

Defense mechanisms are used by normal and abnormal people alike. They become problems when they are the only means used to cope with stress.

Alcohol and Other Drugs

Alcohol and a number of other drugs, including tranquilizers, act as central nervous system depressants that can directly blunt feelings of tension, anxiety, and frustration. Recent studies noted in Chapter 4 also suggest various cognitive effects of alcohol that help people cope with stress. Some behavioral scientists (e.g., Hull, 1981; Steele and others, 1981) argue that these cognitive effects allow people to decrease the negative feelings that stem from recognizing that their behavior has been inconsistent with their values or attitudes.

As noted in Chapters 1 and 4, people also often blame alcohol for inappropriate aggressive or sexual behavior. Tucker and his colleagues (1981) found that subjects used alcohol consumption as a "self-handicapping strategy." Subjects involved in a difficult experimental task drank more when they were denied access to materials that could have aided them in the task. It may well be that they drank in order to provide themselves with an external excuse for failure: "It wasn't me—it was the alcohol." An external excuse for failure may also have allowed them to maintain their self-esteem.

Consistent use of alcohol to cope with stress constitutes psychological dependence on alcohol. People may become dependent on many drugs in order to blunt awareness of stress or distort perception of what has become—for them—an unpleasant reality. Unfortunately, many drugs have negative effects, as noted in Chapter 4. Also, the drugs do nothing to help people find direct, active ways of dealing with sources of stress.

Aggression

Violence is often used to cope with threats and, sometimes, as a response to frustration. In warfare and in self-defense, aggressive behavior is usually positively valued. But most violence in our society is frowned upon, and its benefits are usually short-lived. Attacking a police officer who is writing you a traffic ticket will not earn a judge's understanding approval. Aggressive behavior, except for rare instances, heightens rather than reduces interpersonal conflict by creating motives for retaliation.

Withdrawal

When you are intensely frightened, or feel helpless, or believe that any decision would be futile, you may feel pressed to withdraw from the situation. Withdrawal can be emotional, as in showing loss of interest, or physical, as in moving or changing one's life style.

During the 1960s and early 1970s many thousands of college students dropped out because middle-class standards and values had lost their mean-

During the 1960s an epidemic of "existential neurosis" swept the college campuses. Many students experienced a crisis in their values and lost their sense of direction.

ing in the face of the Vietnam conflict and social unrest. Hirsch and Keniston (1970) unearthed a common factor among 31 academically successful dropouts from Yale University: loss of respect for their fathers. A conflict of values between the acquisition of material goods and the wishes to right injustice and explore the meaning of life had apparently led to their withdrawal. Money, the club, climbing the corporate ladder had become meaningless to them.

Withdrawal and Existential Neurosis   The crisis in values encountered by the Yale dropouts led to what Salvatore Maddi (1967) termed an **existential neurosis.** This neurosis is characterized by confusion, uncertainty, anxiety, depression, and the feeling that life has become meaningless and empty.

Many other students also encountered a crisis in values during this period of social upheaval. Some expressed their distaste for the middle-class job and traditional family structure by joining communes or moving to neighborhoods like the Haight-Ashbury district in San Francisco. They took up farming and poured their energies into arts and crafts. Some took to Eastern-style religious movements. Still others joined the drug subculture.

Temporary withdrawal can be healthy and productive, giving us the opportunity to find more effective means of coping. But prolonged withdrawal may also exclude us from arenas of life in which we could eventually find meaningful rewards.

Fantasy

Fantasy is not for children only. Have you ever daydreamed about the future, testing career and marital choices through cognitive trial and error? Fantasy serves many functions and is useful so long as it does not become an indefinitely prolonged substitute for effective action.

Defensive Coping or Strategy for Success? How Psychologists Have Learned To Use Fantasy To Cope with Pain and Discomfort   Some torturers of the Spanish Inquisition complained that their victims seemed indifferent to pain (Bernheim, 1964). They stretched the rack tighter or struck again with the tongue of the lash, but their prisoners only muttered unclear words beneath their breaths. What were they? Magic charms?

Probably not. They were probably prayers or phrases from poems that the sufferers found could be repeated and visualized to distract them from their pain. Many of us may also repeat comforting words or focus on the face of a loved one or pleasant past experiences when we are under stress. They distract us from our ordeals. Psychologists have found that we can also distract ourselves from pain by focusing on environmental details, like counting ceiling tiles or hairs on a finger, or describing the clothing of passers-by (Kanfer & Goldfoot, 1966; McCaul & Haugtvedt, 1982).

We may also suffer less from an unavoidable painful episode if we can integrate our discomfort into a narrative fantasy (Beers & Karoly, 1979; Knox, 1972). What? You fell from your bike and gashed your leg, and now you're waiting to be sewed up in an emergency room? What a bore. Didn't your gash really stem from an Alpine ski chase in which you soared above crevices and swerved past trees with enemy agents hot in pursuit? Can't you picture darting past this rock, that tree, flying across that gully while the ice air lashes your face? Too bad other patients have so little appreciation of your experience.

Existential neurosis (eggs–sis–TEN–shull). Maddi's term for feelings of anxiety and depression that are hypothesized to reflect loss of purpose.

Stress can sometimes lead us to regress, or adopt behavior characteristic of younger people or children. Under severe stress, this woman is crawling up into a ball, putting her hand to her mouth, and clutching a stuffed animal.

Defense Mechanisms

Regression   You may have been trying to explain a fine point in physics to your roommate for an hour. Then your roommate, who had "yessed" you all during the explanation, asks a question that shows that nothing you said was understood. You slam your book on the desk, shout "Jerk!" and stamp out of the room.

If you are six years old, this behavior is normal. For a college student, it is **regression**—returning to an earlier way of behaving under stress. You may know people who quit smoking or biting their nails but have returned to these habits before a big exam or after a fight with a date. These, too, are examples of regression. A psychoanalyst might consider them regression to the oral stage.

Regression Return, under stress, to a form of behavior characteristic of an earlier stage of development. A defense mechanism. (From the Latin *re-*, meaning "back," and *gradi*, meaning "to go." What are the roots of the word *progress?*)

Denial A defense mechanism in which threatening events are misperceived to be harmless.

Denial   Many people simply deny sources of danger. Many smokers refuse to believe that they risk cancer. A person may vaguely perceive that the company is going downhill, but maintain a complacent attitude until the layoff notice arrives. Hackett and Cassem (1970) found that many cardiac patients respond with an "It can't happen to me" attitude when the patient in the next bed dies. Kübler-Ross (1969) found that many terminally ill patients greet news of impending death with **denial.**

Denial reduces the immediate impact of stressors, but denies us the chance to take effective action to ward off real threats.

Repression Repression is the thrusting out of awareness of unacceptable ideas or urges that are often sexual or aggressive. Repression occurs unconsciously; we are not aware of when we are repressing unacceptable ideas. Freud theorized that repression is a normal aspect of personality development, which permits us to place certain conflicts behind us and move ahead. But repressing the fact that an important paper is due in two weeks is not adjustive.

Repression must be contrasted with **suppression**—the conscious decision not to focus on a distressing topic. French existentialist Albert Camus was obsessed with the idea that life is ultimately hopeless because of the inevitability of death. Characters in his novels could not experience happiness because of this obsession. A critic of Camus's psychology noted that while all of us will die, most of us suppress this eventuality so that we may enjoy the pleasures of everyday life.

Rationalization The smoker justifies his or her habit by saying, "I just can't quit." The prostitute says, "Why condemn me? I'd be out of business if wives were doing their job." These are **rationalizations**—ways of explaining unacceptable behavior that exonerate us from blame and guilt. We may also rationalize to cut our losses: "So the date didn't work out—we were too different to develop a relationship anyhow."

Rationalizations sometimes contain a kernel of truth. There may be a thin line between rationalization and rational thinking. After all, if the couple had been more compatible, perhaps the date would have worked out better.

But rationalization may also be used to justify criminal behavior. Maital (1982) found that people who cheat on their income tax returns often rationalize that government programs cost more than they're worth or that they pay more than their fair share of taxes. And muggers have been known to blame their victims: "Don't look at me. He was dumb for walking down that street alone with all that cash."

Reaction Formation Have you ever thought that someone who was sickeningly sweet and overpolite might be sitting on a hotbed of hostility? Has anyone denied feelings so strongly that you suspected they were actually present? Perhaps so. Freud theorized that another avenue for dealing with unacceptable impulses is **reaction formation**—taking an exaggerated position that opposes our true feelings.

Some people who go on crusades against pornography may be struggling to contain sexual impulses of their own. They may believe that their concerns are logical, but we may wonder why they become so aroused when others, who share their rational concerns, do not find it necessary to wholly dedicate themselves to the destruction of erotic materials.

Projection A motion picture projector thrusts an image onto a screen. A person from a society without projectors might think that the image had originated in the screen.

Freud suggested that we sometimes deal with our own unacceptable impulses through **projection**—attributing them to other people, and disowning them as parts of ourselves. An angry person may perceive the world as a hostile place. A sexually frustrated person who believes that sex is evil may interpret the innocent gestures of others as sexual advances.

Suppression The conscious placing of stressful or threatening events or ideas out of awareness. *Not* a defense mechanism.

Rationalization A defense mechanism in which an individual engages in self-deception, finding justifications for unacceptable ideas, impulses, or behaviors.

Reaction formation A defense mechanism in which unacceptable ideas and impulses are kept unconscious through the exaggerated expression of opposing ideas and impulses.

Projection A defense mechanism in which unacceptable ideas and impulses are cast out, or attributed, to others. (From the Latin *pro-*, meaning "forward," and *jacere*, meaning "to throw." What is the origin of the word *jet?*)

Intellectualization A defense mechanism in which threatening events are viewed with emotional detachment.

Displacement A defense mechanism in which ideas or impulses are tranferred from a threatening or unsuitable object to an acceptable object. (What is the role of displacement in the resolutions of the Oedipus and Electra complexes, discussed in Chapter 9?)

Sublimation A defense mechanism in which primitive impulses—usually sexual and aggressive—are channeled into positive, constructive activities.

Prosocial Characterized by concern for others.

Neo-Freudians Theorists in the psychoanalytic tradition who usually place less emphasis than Freud did on (1) the importance of sexual impulses, and (2) unconscious determinants of behavior. See Chapter 9.

Ego analysts A term descriptive of many Neo-Freudians, suggesting they attribute more importance to (conscious) ego functioning than Freud did.

Intellectualization Physicians who become emotionally involved with patients may not be able to undertake painful diagnostic and surgical procedures to save their lives. Instead, they try to distance themselves from their patients' immediate discomfort so that they can apply their knowledge and skills without excessive arousal. Similarly, psychologists who become as upset as a client over a family dispute would not be effective at suggesting coping behavior. **Intellectualization** is cognitive focusing on stress that permits emotional detachment.

While intellectualization permits us to solve problems rationally, excessive intellectualization may prevent us from experiencing life fully. Constant intellectualizers may impress us as cold, distant, or machinelike.

Displacement Freud considered **displacement** an essential aspect of developing mature sexual relationships. He argued that we develop lasting attachments to adults of the opposite sex by transferring, or displacing, onto them emotions first experienced toward our own parents. Displacement is adjustive because it permits us to substitute attainable goals for unattainable goals.

Aggressive impulses may be displaced onto targets less threatening than the person who provoked us. There is the old tale about the man who was scolded by his boss and took it out on his wife. She then scolded the child who, in turn, kicked the dog. The dog chased the cat, the cat chased the mouse, and so on. Some microscopic form of life may still be bearing the brunt of the boss's wrath.

Sublimation Why do we build cities, sculpt statues, write poems and novels? Are our motives noble, or do they have a darker basis?

Freud suggested that these creative acts represented **sublimation**—the channeling of socially unacceptable impulses into socially productive behavior. Sublimation permits one to escape self-criticism from recognition of, or acting out on, primitive impulses. An artist, for example, may gratify sexual impulses by working with nude models while also earning a high income and critical acclaim.

This dim view of human creativity has sparked much criticism. As noted in Chapter 9, many psychologists argue that noble behavior can reflect fully conscious, **prosocial** wishes. Even contemporary followers of Freud, known as **neo-Freudians** or **ego analysts,** believe that motives can stem from the (conscious) ego as well as from the (unconscious) id.

Active Coping

Fate, chance, luck, destiny—how many of us allow ourselves to be blown about by the wind, to endure conflict and frustration, to experience ceaseless anxiety, or engage in Type A behavior on the "fast track" to success and heart disease? How many of us, in the words of Henry David Thoreau, lead "lives of quiet desperation"?

In Shakespeare's *Julius Caesar*, Cassius and Brutus listen as crowds honor Caesar as a god. But they know Caesar is only made of flesh and blood. Cassius, in fact, had once saved Caesar from drowning. So whose fault was it that Caesar now stood upon the "narrow world" like a colossal statue while others seemed petty and fretted about beneath his legs. Cassius says to Brutus:

Men at some time are masters of their fates:
The fault, dear Brutus, is not in our stars,
But in ourselves, that we are underlings.

Similarly, if we are unhappy with our lots in life—if we are assaulted by stress heaped upon stress—it is up to us to do something about it. Rather than show socially inappropriate behavior, like aggression or regression— rather than withdraw from the social arena or use self-deception, we must bear the responsibility of coping actively if we wish to be the masters of our fates.

Perceived Self-Efficacy and Locus of Control: Taking Responsibility for Your Own Behavior

Self-Efficacy Psychologist Albert Bandura (1982) argues that our **perceived self-efficacy**—that is, our perceptions of our capacities to bring about change— influence our behavior, our thought patterns, even our emotional arousal.

In studies in which the level of perceived self-efficacy is manipulated but ability remains comparable, people in whom high levels of perceived self-efficacy have been induced complete experimental tasks more successfully and show lower emotional arousal in the process. People with higher levels of perceived self-efficacy are less likely to relapse when they have quit smoking or lost weight (Condiotte & Lichtenstein, 1981; Marlatt & Gordon, 1980), are more effective in athletic competition (Weinberg and others, 1980), and are more likely to seriously consider nontraditional and challenging career options (Betz & Hackett, 1981).

When intelligence and aptitudes are held constant, it appears that people with higher perceived self-efficacy regulate problem-solving behavior more effectively and bounce back more readily from failure. In these ways it seems that life's challenges may be less stressful for them.

The relationship between perceived self-efficacy and performance also appears to be a two-way street. While high perceived self-efficacy contributes to successful performances, Feltz (1982) found that improved performance (in women who were back-diving) also contributed to perceptions of self-efficacy.

Locus of Control Julian Rotter (1966) defines a concept closely related to that of self-efficacy: **locus of control.** People who believe that they can exert a significant influence over whether or not they will attain reinforcements are said to show "internal control." That is, they perceive the area, or locus, of control to be within themselves. People who see control outside their own hands are said to show "external control."

It is easy to attribute success to internal factors. If you carry the ball 70 yards for a touchdown, it is your clear thinking and catlike agility that does the deed. If you fumble the ball, it's someone else's fault or plain bad luck. Most of us tend to credit ourselves for our successes and blame others for our shortcomings (Fitch, 1970; Lau & Russell, 1980). There are exceptions: People prone to depression are likely to blame themselves to excess for failures and shortcomings (see Chapter 11).

Persons who show internal control, or "internals," are more effective at meeting new challenges (Rotter, 1975). "Internals" who quit smoking show lower relapse rates than "externals." Internals show less disturbance than externals when faced with unavoidable stresses such as spinal cord injury

Perceived self-efficacy In social learning theory, the degree to which an individual believes that he or she can influence the environment, or change the self, so that he or she can achieve his or her goals.

Locus of control The place (locus) to which an individual attributes control over the receiving of reinforcers— either inside or outside the self.

Locus of Control Scale

Do you believe that you are in charge of your own life? That you can exert an influence on other people and the environment to reach your goals? Or do you believe that your fate is in the "stars"? That you are ruled by luck, chance, and other people?

People who believe that they are in control of their lives are said to have an internal locus of control, or to be "internals." People who view their fates as being out of their hands are said to be "externals." Are you more of an "internal" or more of an "external"? To learn more about your perception of your locus of control, respond to the following questionnaire developed by Nowicki and Strickland (1973). These are the directions used by the authors of the questionnaire:

> We are trying to find out what men and women think about certain things. We want you to answer the following questions the way you feel. There are no right or wrong answers. Don't take too much time answering any one question, but do try to answer them all.
>
> One of your concerns during the test may be, "What should I do if I can answer both yes and no to a question?" It's not unusual for that to happen. If it does, think about whether your answer is just a little more one way or the other. For example, if you'd assign a weighting of 51 percent to "yes" and assign 49 percent to "no," mark the answer "yes." Try to pick one or the other response for all questions and not leave any blank.

Mark your responses to the questions by placing a check under the Yes/No columns. When you are finished, turn to Appendix B to score your test.

	YES	NO
1. Do you believe that most problems will solve themselves if you just don't fool with them?	___	___
2. Do you believe that you can stop yourself from catching a cold?	___	___
3. Are some people just born lucky?	___	___
4. Most of the time do you feel that getting good grades meant a great deal to you?	___	___
5. Are you often blamed for things that just aren't your fault?	___	___
6. Do you believe that if somebody studies hard enough he or she can pass any subject?	___	___
7. Do you feel that most of the time it doesn't pay to try hard because things never turn out right anyway?	___	___
8. Do you feel that if things start out well in the morning it's going to be a good day no matter what you do?	___	___
9. Do you feel that most of the time parents listen to what their children have to say?	___	___
10. Do you believe that wishing can make good things happen?	___	___
11. When you get punished does it usually seem it's for no good reason at all?	___	___
12. Most of the time do you find it hard to change a friend's opinion?	___	___
13. Do you think that cheering more than luck helps a team to win?	___	___
14. Did you feel that it was nearly impossible to change your parents' minds about anything?	___	___

15. Do you believe that parents should allow children to make most of their own decisions? _____ _____
16. Do you feel that when you do something wrong there's very little you can do to make it right? _____ _____
17. Do you believe that most people are just born good at sports? _____ _____
18. Are most of the other people your age stronger than you are? _____ _____
19. Do you feel that one of the best ways to handle most problems is just not to think about them? _____ _____
20. Do you feel that you have a lot of choice in deciding who your friends are? _____ _____
21. If you find a four-leaf clover, do you believe that it might bring you good luck? _____ _____
22. Did you often feel that whether or not you did your homework had much to do with what kinds of grades you got? _____ _____
23. Do you feel that when a person your age is angry with you, there's little you can do to stop him or her? _____ _____
24. Have you ever had a good-luck charm? _____ _____
25. Do you believe that whether or not people like you depends on how you act? _____ _____
26. Did your parents usually help you if you asked them to? _____ _____
27. Have you felt that when people were angry with you it was usually for no reason at all? _____ _____
28. Most of the time, do you feel that you can change what might happen tomorrow by what you did today? _____ _____
29. Do you believe that when bad things are going to happen they are just going to happen no matter what you try to do to stop them? _____ _____
30. Do you think that people can get their own way if they just keep trying? _____ _____
31. Most of the time do you find it useless to try to get your own way at home? _____ _____
32. Do you feel that when good things happen they happen because of hard work? _____ _____
33. Do you feel that when somebody your age wants to be your enemy there's little you can do to change matters? _____ _____
34. Do you feel that it's easy to get friends to do what you want them to do? _____ _____
35. Do you usually feel that you have little to say about what you get to eat at home? _____ _____
36. Do you feel that when someone doesn't like you there's little you can do about it? _____ _____
37. Did you usually feel that it was almost useless to try in school because most other children were just plain smarter than you were? _____ _____
38. Are you the kind of person who believes that planning ahead makes things turn out better? _____ _____
39. Most of the time, do you feel that you have little to say about what your family decides to do? _____ _____
40. Do you think it's better to be smart than to be lucky? _____ _____

(Shadish and others, 1981) or surgical operations (Shipley and others, 1978; Staub and others, 1971). Internals are more likely than externals to seek out information even about painful events, like operations. Experiments with laboratory rats suggest that knowing that a painful event is imminent results in less stress (as measured by less development of ulcers), perhaps because awareness permits the rats to brace themselves more effectively (Weiss, 1972).

Negative events, even from high school days, have more of a lingering effect on "external" than "internal" university students (Lefcourt and others, 1981). Lefcourt and his colleagues (1981) suggest that internal locus of control can help moderate the impact of negative events. In the following sections we examine several ways of moderating the impact of stressors, including controlling catastrophizing thoughts and lowering exhausting levels of bodily arousal.

Controlling Irrational and Catastrophizing Thoughts

Have you had any of these experiences?

1. You have difficulty with the first item on a test and become absolutely convinced that you will flunk.
2. You want to express your genuine feelings but think that you might make another person angry or upset.
3. You haven't been able to get to sleep for 15 minutes and assume that you will lie awake the whole night and feel "wrecked" in the morning.
4. You're not sure what decision to make, so you try to put your conflicts out of your mind by going out, playing cards, or watching TV.
5. You decide not to play tennis or go jogging because your form isn't perfect and you're in less than perfect condition.

This football player is catastrophizing his mistake on the last play. He is telling himself that he probably lost the game for his team and that the fans hate him. It would be more adjustive for him to tell himself that there is still time to win, that his teammates share the responsibility for the game outcome, and that fans have cheered him more frequently than they have booed him.

If you have had these or similar experiences, it may be because you harbor a number of the irrational beliefs isolated by Albert Ellis (see pages 392–393). These beliefs may make you overly concerned about the approval of others (experience 2, above) or perfectionistic (experience 5). They may lead you to think that you can best relieve yourself of certain dilemmas by pretending that they do not exist (experience 4), or that a minor setback will invariably lead to greater problems (experiences 1 and 3).

How, then, do we change irrational or catastrophizing thoughts? The answer is theoretically simple: We change these thoughts by changing them. However, it may take some work, and before we can change them we must often first become more aware of them.

Cognitive psychologist Donald Meichenbaum (1976) suggests a three-step procedure for controlling the irrational and catastrophizing thoughts that often accompany feelings of pain, anxiety, frustration, conflict, or tension:

1. Develop awareness of these thoughts through careful self-examination. Study the examples at the beginning of this section or in Table 10.3 to see if these experiences and thought patterns characterize you. (Also read Ellis's irrational beliefs carefully on pages 392–393 and ask yourself whether any of them tend to govern your behavior.) When you encounter anxiety or frustration, pay careful attention to your thoughts. Are they helping to point toward a solution, or are they compounding your problems?
2. Prepare thoughts that are **incompatible** with the irrational and catastrophizing thoughts, and practice saying them firmly to yourself. (If nobody is nearby, why not say them firmly aloud?)
3. Reward yourself with a mental pat on the back for effective changes in beliefs and thought patterns.

TABLE 10.3   Controlling Irrational, Catastrophizing Beliefs and Thoughts

Irrational, Catastrophizing Thoughts	Incompatible (Coping) Thoughts
"Oh my God, I'm going to lose all control!"	"This is painful and upsetting, but I don't have to go to pieces."
"This will never end."	"This will come to an end, even if it's hard to see right now."
"It'll be awful if Mom gives me that look."	"It's more pleasant when Mom's happy with me, but I can live with it if she isn't."
"How can I get out there? I'll look like a fool."	"So you're not perfect; it doesn't mean you'll look stupid. And if someone thinks you look stupid, you can live with that too. Just stop worrying and have some fun."
"My heart's going to leap out of my chest! How much can I stand?"	"Easy—hearts don't leap out of chests. Stop and think! Distract yourself. Breathe slowly, in and out."
"What can I do? There's nothing I can do!"	"Easy—stop and think. Just because you can't think of a solution right now doesn't mean there's nothing you can do. Take it a minute at a time. Breathe easy."

Do irrational beliefs and catastrophizing thoughts compound the stress you experience? Cognitive psychologists suggest that we can cope with stress by becoming aware of self-defeating beliefs and thoughts and replacing them with rational, calming beliefs and thoughts.

Rational restructuring The logical rethinking of threatening or anxiety-evoking events, so that coping strategies may be used instead of avoidance attempts or simple "floundering about.")

Coping with Test Anxiety by Controlling Irrational and Catastrophizing Thoughts   Have you or your friends experienced any of these thoughts while taking tests? "I just know I'm going to flunk." "I don't know what's wrong with me—I just can't take tests." "I know everything, but when I get in there my mind just goes blank." "The way I do on standardized tests, I'll just never get into graduate school."

Some students may use complaints of test anxiety as an excuse for performing poorly (Smith and others, 1982), but for many others, test anxiety is a frustrating handicap. Especially when we study diligently, test anxiety seems particularly cruel.

Yet we are not born with test anxiety. Test anxiety appears to reflect a combination of high bodily arousal and negative thoughts, including critical self-evaluations. People with high test anxiety show high levels of autonomic arousal during tests (Doerr & Hokanson, 1965) and are likely to report bodily sensations like dryness in the mouth and rapid heart rate (Galassi and others, 1981). On a cognitive level, they have more negative thoughts and are more self-critical than people with low or moderate test anxiety, even when they are performing just as well (Holroyd and others, 1978; Meichenbaum & Butler, 1980). Moreover, they allow their self-criticisms, and negative thoughts of the sort shown in Table 10.4, to *distract* them from working effectively on their tests (Arkin and others, 1982; Bandura, 1977; Sarason, 1978).

Marvin Goldfried and his colleagues (1978) have successfully treated test anxiety through **rational restructuring,** which is similar to the Meichenbaum technique discussed in the previous section. In rational restructuring, students first pinpoint self-defeating thoughts by imagining that they are taking tests and searching for the mental villains. Then they construct rational al-

TABLE 10.4   Percent of Positive and Negative Thoughts for Low and High Test Anxiety Groups of University Students

Thought	Low Test Anxiety Percent	High Test Anxiety Percent
POSITIVE THOUGHTS:		
Will do all right on test	71	43
Mind is clear, can concentrate	49	26
Feel in control of my reactions	46	23
NEGATIVE THOUGHTS:		
Wish I could get out or test was over	46	65
Test is hard	45	64
Not enough time to finish	23	49
Work I put into studying won't be shown by my grade	16	44
Stuck on a question and it's making it difficult to answer others	13	34
Mind is blank or can't think straight	11	31
Going to do poorly on test	11	28
Think how awful it will be if I fail or do poorly	11	45

High test-anxious students report fewer positive thoughts and more negative thoughts while taking tests. Moreover, their negative thoughts are linked to bodily sensations like dryness in the mouth and rapid heart rate. Source of data: Galassi, Frierson, and Sharer, 1981, pp. 56, 58.

TABLE 10.5 Self-Defeating Thoughts and Rational Alternatives for Decreasing Test Anxiety and Improving Grades

Self-defeating Thought	Rational Alternative
"I'm running out of time!"	"Time is passing, but just take it item by item. Getting bent out of shape won't help."
'This is impossible! Are all the items going to be this difficult?"	"Just take it item by item. Each item is different. Don't assume the worst."
"Everybody's smarter than I am!"	"Probably not, but maybe they're not handicapping themselves by catastrophizing and distracting themselves. Just do the best you can and then relax."
"I just can't do well on tests."	"That's true only if you believe it's true. Back to the items, one by one."
"If I flunk, everything is ruined!"	"You won't make yourself happy by failing, but it won't be the end of the world either. Just take it item by item and do the best you can."

Cognitive psychologists suggest that we cope with test anxiety by substituting rational alternatives for self-defeating thoughts.

ternatives for each of them (see Table 10.5). They practice the rational alternatives and mentally pat themselves on the back for improved performance.

Other research (Wilson & Linville, 1982) suggests that the academic performance of first-year college students improves when they are informed that grade point averages tend to increase as students reach their upperclass years. Perhaps they then attribute academic difficulties to adjusting to college life rather than personal inadequacy, and this "restructuring" of their performance permits them to be less self-critical.

Lowering Arousal

One reason that a squash does not become as aroused as a person when it is assaulted is that it does not catastrophize. Another reason is that it does not have an autonomic nervous system. Thus it has no alarm reaction.

Once you are aware that a stressor is acting upon you, and have developed a plan to cope with it, it is no longer helpful to have blood pounding so fiercely through your arteries. Psychologists and other scientists have developed many methods for teaching people to lower excessive bodily arousal. They include meditation and biofeedback (both discussed in Chapter 4), progressive relaxation and diaphragmatic breathing.

Meditation appears to facilitate adjustment to stress without decreasing awareness. In this way it does not reduce perception of potential threats. In one experiment, Orne-Johnson (1973) exposed meditators and nonmeditators to unpredictable loud noises. Meditators stopped showing a stress reaction—as measured by sweat in the palms of their hands (galvanic skin response, or GSR)—earlier than nonmeditators. In another experiment, Goleman and Schwartz (1976) used heart rate and GSR to measure stress reactions to a film that explicitly portrayed accidents and death. Meditators showed a greater alarm reaction than nonmeditators when the contents of the film were announced, but recovered normal levels of arousal more rapidly during the showings. Meditators in this study thus showed greater alertness to potential threat—a factor that could allow them to develop a plan for dealing with a stressor more rapidly—but also more ability to control arousal.

In one experiment with biofeedback, Sirota and his colleagues (1976) trained 20 women aged 21 to 27 to slow their heart rates voluntarily. Afterwards, the women reported a painful electric shock to be less stressful. In another biofeedback experiment, Gatchel and Proctor (1976) showed that college students who learned to slow their heart rates reduced their speech anxiety.

Meditation seems to focus on the cognitive components of a stress reaction, while biofeedback can be directed at various functions, such as heart rate and muscle tension. Progressive relaxation focuses on muscle tension, although the instructions to slow down breathing and develop mental imagery—for instance, feelings of heaviness in the limbs—promote other responses that are incompatible with an alarm reaction. Diaphragmatic breathing focuses on respiration rate. Yet all methods achieve somewhat similar effects: a combination of lowered arousal and cognitions of self-efficacy and internal locus of control.

Progressive Relaxation Edmund Jacobson (1938) of the University of Chicago noted that people tense their muscles when they are under stress, but are often unaware of it. He reasoned that if they could learn to relax these tensions they could lower the stress they experienced. But when he asked clients to focus on relaxing muscles, they often had no idea what to do.

Jacobson developed the method of **progressive relaxation** to teach people how to relax these tensions. In this method, people purposefully tense a muscle group before relaxing it. This sequence allows them to (1) develop awareness of their muscle tensions; and (2) differentiate between feelings of tension and relaxation. The method is "progressive" because people progress from one muscle group to another. Since its beginnings in the 1930s, progressive relaxation has undergone development by several behavior therapists, among them Joseph Wolpe of the Eastern Pennsylvania Psychiatric Institute (Wolpe & Lazarus, 1966).

Progressive relaxation decreases the sympathetic arousal of the alarm reaction (Paul, 1966b). It has been found useful with "diseases of adaptation" ranging from muscle-tension headaches (Tasto & Hinkle, 1973) to hypertension (Taylor and others, 1977). You can experience muscle relaxation in the arms by doing the following:

Settle down in a reclining chair, dim the lights, and loosen any tight clothing. Then use these directions to relax your arms. You can tape them or have a friend read them to you. For instructions concerning relaxation of your entire body, consult a behavior therapist or other helping professional who knows the techniques of progressive relaxation.

Settle back as comfortably as you can. Let yourself relax to the best of your ability.... Now, as you relax like that, clench your right fist, just clench your fist tighter and tighter, and study the tension as you do so. Keep it clenched and feel the tension in your right fist, hand, forearm ... and now relax. Let the fingers of your right hand become loose, and observe the contrast in your feelings.... Now, let yourself go and try to become more relaxed all over.... Once more, clench your right fist really tight ... hold it, and notice the tension again.... Now let go, relax; your fingers straighten out, and you notice the difference once more.... Now repeat that with your left fist. Clench your left fist while the rest of your body relaxes; clench that fist tighter and feel the tension ... and now relax. Again enjoy the contrast.... Repeat that once more, clench the left fist, tight and tense.... Now do the opposite of tension—relax and feel the difference. Continue relaxing like that for a while.... Clench both fists tighter and together, both fists tense, forearms tense, study the sensations ... and relax; straighten out your fingers and feel that relaxation. Continue relaxing your hands and forearms more and more.... Now bend your elbows and tense your biceps, tense them harder and study the tension feelings ... all right, straighten out your arms, let them relax and feel that difference again. Let the relaxation develop.... Once more, tense your biceps; hold the tension and observe it carefully.... Straighten the arms and relax; relax to the best of your ability.... Each time, pay close attention to your feelings when you tense up and when you relax. Now straighten your arms, straighten them so that you feel most tension in the triceps muscles along the back of your arms; stretch your arms and feel that tension.... And now relax. Get your arms back into a comfortable position. Let the relaxation proceed on its own. The arms should feel comfortably heavy as you allow them to relax.... Straighten the arms once more so that you feel the tension in the triceps muscles; straighten them. Feel that tension ... and relax. Now let's concentrate on pure relaxation in the arms without any tension. Get your arms comfortable and let them relax further and further. Continue relaxing your arms even further. Even when your arms seem fully relaxed, try to go that extra bit further; try to achieve deeper and deeper levels of relaxation (Wolpe & Lazarus, 1966, p. 177).

Diaphragmatic Breathing   Diaphragmatic breathing lowers arousal by slowing down breathing and, perhaps, by stimulating parasympathetic arousal (Harvey, 1978). As noted in Chapter 2, parasympathetic arousal to some degree counteracts sympathetic arousal, and may lead to feelings of relaxation.

Lie down on the back. Place your hands lightly on your stomach so that you feel it rise each time you inhale, and fall with every outbreath. To make breathing more regular, breathe through the nose only and take the same amount of time to inhale and exhale. You can also breathe diaphragmatically in a chair. Keep one hand on your chest at first to see that it remains still, and the other on your stomach to see that it rises and falls as you breathe in and out.

When you are tense, anxious, or in pain, diaphragmatic breathing may also help distract you. It gives you something to do with your hands, and you can use mental arithmetic ("one thousand one, one thousand two," etc.) to help monitor your breathing.

Changing the Pace of Your Daily Life

Stop driving yourself—get out and walk. Too often we jump out of bed to an abrasive alarm, hop into a shower, fight commuter crowds, and arrive at class or work with no time to spare. Then we first become involved in our hectic "day." Let us examine a number of methods for changing the pace of our daily lives. Some can help us with the Type A attitudes and behaviors discussed on pages 396-397. Others can help us recognize and cope with accumulating life changes.

Confronting the Value System That Supports Type A Behavior   The first step in coping with Type A behavior is confronting the value system that

"Choking," Athletes' Bugaboo, Is Tackled in New Way

Early in the 1976 football season, Penn State was facing its second loss in three games. With a fourth down on the Iowa 37-yard line and 50 seconds to play, coach Joe Paterno looked to his bench for a kicker. The choice was between two untested players, Matt Bahr, a sophomore, and Herb Menhardt, a freshman.

With 75,000 fans at Beaver Stadium watching anxiously, Paterno chose the 18-year-old Menhardt, who hooked the 54-yard kick wide to the left, leaving Iowa with a seven-six victory.

After that, Bahr got the starting job, which eventually landed him with the Pittsburgh Steelers. Menhardt went back to the bench, unable to cope with the first major failure of his life.

"I had to live with that kick for three years," said Menhardt, who quit football and did not return to the team until 1979. "Matt won the starting job and I had to accept being a failure. I had nightmares about it and all my so-called friends mocked me. I decided to give up on football. I knew I could kick, but I had to live with that one kick."

In a November 1979 game, Menhardt . . . was called on to make a last-second 54-yard field goal in a game at North Carolina State. He made it and Penn State won, nine–six.

That kick gave Menhardt the confidence he needed, and he went on to become one of the nation's leading kickers. In 1979 he finished with 14 field goals in 20 attempts, and 28 of 28 extra points. In 1980 he hit 15 of 21 field goals and converted all 28 extra-point attempts, placing him sixth nationally among kickers.

Devised by Psychology Students

What made the difference in Menhardt's career? It was a program developed by two Penn State graduate students to help athletes and scholars overcome "choking"—failure in pressure situations—on exams and to improve performance.

Menhardt worked in the summer of 1979 with Charles Stebbins and Kevin Hickey, doctoral students in psychology, and learned to relax and handle pressure. It was a practical approach: He . . . imagined succeeding in tense situations. He learned to approach difficult situations with a positive attitude, by telling himself, "I can do this."

"Everything just fell into place," he recalled. "The program took the burden and pressure of last-second field goals off my mind. It was like a placebo. It put you in the exact state you want to be in. Kicking is 60 percent mental, and now I have that part pretty well licked."

Last summer, after a refresher course, Stebbins said that Menhardt would be comfortable with 60-yard field goals under pressure.

Stebbins's program helps students to direct body activity properly. "This program goes far beyond mental training," said Menhardt, who plans to pursue a degree in sports psychology. "It concentrates on increasing peripheral vision, balance functions, response time, and other performance-related skills."

The technique involves a series of exercises in which the subject learns to relax the body's major muscle groups. It also includes deep breathing and repeating the word "relax."

The "stress principles and the ability to relax" then are applied to different situations—athletically, academically, and socially—to build confidence and internal discipline.

Stebbins assesses each player's problems and attempts to help him overcome his difficulty by simulating the problem situation.

Several professional sports teams have expressed interest in the program. A few pro football teams, a racing-car driver, and a few golfers are looking into using the techniques. The Olympic teams of three nations, including the United States, have also queried Stebbins, as have some musicians, singers, and dancers. Corporations in international management and accounting firms, including several on the Fortune 500 list, have asked about the program.

---

supports it. Do you place too much value on competing rather than cooperating? Do you spend all your time achieving, never appreciating? Must you always "do your best"—at play as well as at work? Or can you be more selective about your efforts?

It may be useful for Type A people to challenge the irrational idea that something awful will happen if they are less than perfect at all their undertakings. Suinn (1976) suggests relaxing for several minutes once or twice a day, using environmental engineering, and slowing down.

Using Environmental Engineering   You can change your personal environment to lower stress by adopting some of the following measures:

- Set your alarm clock lower or buy an alarm clock that makes a pleasant sound.

The Type A business executive is probably sending his blood pressure through the roof, but the Type B executive is capable of focusing on the quality of life and allowing himself to relax.

- Get up earlier to sit and relax, watch the morning news with a cup of tea, or meditate. This may mean going to bed earlier.
- Leave home earlier and take a more scenic route to work or school. Avoid rush-hour jams, if possible.
- Don't car-pool with last-minute rushers. Drive with a group that leaves earlier or use public transportation.
- Have a snack or relax at school or work before the "day" begins.
- Don't do two things at once. Avoid scheduling too many classes or appointments back to back.
- Use breaks to read, exercise, or meditate. Limit intake of stimulants like caffeine.
- Space chores. Why have the car and typewriter repaired, work, shop, and drive a friend to the airport all in one day?
- If rushed, allow unessential work to go to the next day.
- Set aside some time for yourself: for music, a hot bath, exercise, meditation, progressive relaxation. If your life will not permit this, get a new life.

Slowing Down

- Move about slowly when you awake. Stretch.
- Drive more slowly. This saves energy, lives, and traffic citations. It's also less stressful than racing the clock.
- Don't wolf lunch. Get out, make it an occasion.
- Don't tumble words out. Speak more slowly. Interrupt less frequently.

Recognizing and Controlling Hidden Life-Change Units Become aware of the hidden life-change units in your life. Variety is the spice of life, but too much spice sours the stomach.

Do not quit smoking and diet at the same time. A dramatic increase in income does not require that you immediately take on a new mortgage and move into a better neighborhood. If you suffer a tragic personal loss, it may be foolhardy to think that moving to a new job in a new city will promote adjustment.

Keeping a log of daily activities can help you track the hidden changes in your life. After a week or so, reflect. How many activities, people, and places differ from those of a few months ago? Are there major daily changes in sleeping, eating, or exercise routines? Are you a weekend runner or tennis player who tries to compensate for five sedentary weekdays by pushing your body through two days of strenuous weekend effort? Weekend athletes encounter major changes in recreational habits twice a week up to 52 times a year. How about your social life? Forcing yourself out of bed at 6:30 A.M. each weekday morning and staying up until 3:00 A.M. on weekends may give you chronic jet lag.

Making Decisions

When we are frustrated or in conflict, we must make decisions. We must understand the barriers that block our goals to determine whether we can overcome them and, if not, whether to search for potentially satisfying substitutes. When we are in conflict, we must carefully weigh the pluses and minuses of each possible course of action and then make a choice.

If we don't make choices, we sit on the fencepost. A personal experiment will convince you that sitting indefinitely on the fencepost causes a certain part of the anatomy to hurt. When we avoid making decisions we cannot resolve our conflicts, and conflict is painful.

Making decisions involves choosing among various goals or courses of action to reach goals. If decisions are to work out, we need to be able to predict the relative values of our goals, our ability to surmount the obstacles in our paths, and the costs of surmounting them. Janis and Mann (1977) suggest that a balance sheet can help us make more accurate predictions.

Using the Balance Sheet Experiments with the **balance sheet** show that it has helped high-school students choose a college and adults decide whether to go on diets and attend exercise classes (Janis & Wheeler, 1978). Balance sheet users show fewer regrets about "the road not taken" and are more likely to stick to their decisions. The balance sheet also increases the probability that people will respond to conflict with appropriate alertness—which Janis and Wheeler term **vigilance**—rather than deny conflict or become overly aroused.

Balance sheets help us list the pluses and minuses of any course of action. To use the balance sheet, jot down the following information for each choice (see Table 10.6): (1) projected **tangible** gains and losses for oneself; (2) projected tangible gains and losses for others; (3) projected self-approval or self-disapproval; and (4) projected approval or disapproval of others.

Meg was a 34-year-old woman whose husband beat her. She had married Bob at 27, and for two years life had run smoothly. But she had been bruised

Balance sheet An outline of positive and negative expectations concerning a course of action. An aid to effective decision making.

Vigilance Watchfulness. (From the Latin *vigil*, meaning "awake.")

Tangible Capable of being touched or felt. (From the Latin *tangere*, meaning "to touch.")

and battered, fearful of her life, for the past five. She sought psychotherapy to cope with Bob, her fears, her resentments, and her disappointments. The therapist asked if Bob would come for treatment too, but Bob refused. Finally, unable to stop Bob from abusing her, Meg considered divorce. But divorce was also an ugly prospect and she vacillated.

Table 10.6 shows the balance sheet, as filled out by Meg, for the alternative of divorce.

Meg's balance sheet supplied Meg and her therapist with a clear agenda of concerns to work out. It also showed that Meg's anticipations were incomplete. Would she really have no positive thoughts about herself if she divorced Bob? Would no one other than her mother applaud the decision? (And did she have an irrational need to avoid the disapproval of others?) Meg's list of negative anticipations pointed to the need to develop financial independence by acquiring job skills. Her fears about undertaking a new social life also seemed overblown. Yes, making new acquaintances might not be easy, but it was not impossible. It was, in fact, up to Meg. And what of Meg's feelings about herself? Wouldn't she be pleased that she had done what she thought was necessary, even if divorce also entailed problems?

Meg concluded that many of her negative anticipations were exaggerated. Many fears could be collapsed into an umbrella fear of change. Fear of change had also led her to underestimate her need for self-respect. Meg did divorce Bob, and at first she was depressed, lonely, and fearful. But after a

TABLE 10.6 Meg's Balance Sheet for the Alternative of Divorcing Bob

	Positive Anticipations	Negative Anticipations
Tangible gains and losses for me	1. Elimination of fear of being beaten or killed	1. Loneliness 2. Fear of starting a new social life 3. Fear of not having children owing to age 4. Financial struggle 5. Fear of personal emotional instability
Tangible gains and losses for others	1. Mother will be relieved	1. Bob might harm himself or others (he has threatened suicide if I leave)
Self-approval or self-disapproval		1. I might consider myself a failure because I could not help Bob or save our marriage
Social approval or social disapproval		1. Some people will complain marriage is sacred and blame me for "quitting" 2. Some men may consider me "that kind of woman"— an easy mark

When making a decision, weighing up the pluses and minuses for the various alternatives can lead to more productive choices and fewer regrets. Meg's balance sheet for the alternative of divorcing an abusive husband showed her psychologist that her list of positive anticipations was incomplete.

year she was working and dating regularly. She was not blissful, but had regained a sense of forward motion, took pride in being independent, and no longer dwelled in fear. It is fortunate that this story has a relatively happy ending. Otherwise, we would have had to look for another.

Are you now putting off making any decisions in your own life? Could using the balance sheet be of any help?

Summary

Stress is the demand made on an organism to adjust. Sources of stress include life changes, pain and discomfort, anxiety, irrational beliefs, frustration, conflict, and Type A behavior.

Positive as well as negative life changes require adjustment. People who earn more than 300 "life-change units" within a year, according to the Holmes and Rahe scale, are at high risk for medical or psychological disorders. Pain and discomfort impair our ability to perform, especially when severe demands shortly follow a traumatic experience. Psychologists have found that we can use fantasy to distract ourselves from pain and discomfort.

Trait anxiety is a personality variable, while state anxiety is situational. Freud hypothezised that neurotic anxiety (a form of trait anxiety) reflects difficulty in repressing unacceptable urges. Irrational beliefs can lead us to have unattainable interpersonal and personal goals—such as pleasing others or performing perfectly all the time. Frustration results from having unattainable goals or from barriers to reaching our goals. Conflict results from opposing motives. We often vacillate when we are in conflict. Approach-approach conflicts are least stressful. Double approach-avoidance conflicts are most complex.

Type A behavior is characterized by a sense of time urgency and high competitiveness. Type A people are at greater risk for heart attacks than are Type B's, who focus more on the quality of life. However, evidence is correlational, not experimental.

Under stress, Selye suggests we experience the general adaptation syndrome which consists of three stages: alarm, resistance, and exhaustion. Alarm and resistance involve overarousal of the sympathetic branch of the autonomic nervous system. Exhaustion involves parasympathetic dominance. Prolonged overarousal can lead to death or to psychophysiological disorders, including ulcers, asthma, and hypertension.

Defensive coping methods decrease the immediate impact of a stressor, but at some personal or social cost, such as socially inappropriate behavior, withdrawal, or self-deception. Defensive methods include use of alcohol and other drugs, aggression, withdrawal, fantasy, and several defense mechanisms. Defense mechanisms protect us from anxiety by helping keep unacceptable impulses out of awareness.

Direct or active coping methods manipulate the environment to remove sources of stress, or involve changing our cognitive or physiological responses to unavoidable stress. They avoid self-deception. The first step is accepting responsibility for one's responses to stress. People who perceive themselves capable of coping (as having self-efficacy or an internal locus of control) are less disturbed by stress and more effective in performance.

Major active coping methods include controlling irrational beliefs and catastrophizing thoughts, and lowering arousal. We can control self-defeating thoughts by becoming aware of them, constructing incompatible, rational alternatives, practicing the alternatives, and patting ourselves on the back for doing so. This cognitive method is also of use with test anxiety. Methods for lowering arousal include meditation, biofeedback, progressive relaxation, and diaphragmatic breathing.

We can cope with Type A behavior first by challenging Type A attitudes, then doing some environmental engineering and slowing down. Making decisions is often the way out of conflict. We can use the balance sheet more completely to list and weigh the pluses and minuses for the alternatives available to us.

Truth or Fiction Revisited

- *Too much of a good thing can make you ill.* True. The accumulation of a great number of life changes within a short period of time is highly stressful and increases the risk of medical or psychological disorders—even when many of the changes are positive.

- *Our emotional problems stem almost completely from external pressures that we have little or no ability to change or control.* False. This is one of the irrational beliefs identified by Ellis. It discourages us from trying to take charge of our lives.

- *Some people are dedicated to the creation of their own stress.* True. Type A people are characterized by a sense of time urgency and high competitiveness.

- *It is possible for people to be literally scared to death.* True. Cannon writes that victims of "voodoo" actually fell prey to prolonged overarousal of their autonomic nervous systems—a reaction triggered by fear.

- *Some people drink alcohol purposefully to handicap themselves in their ability to cope with conflict or failure.* True. It appears that then they can blame the alcohol rather than themselves for their shortcomings.

- *When you are about to undergo a serious operation, learning the grisly details of the surgery and the expected course of recuperation may make the experience less stressful.* True. Knowing the details apparently permits us to brace ourselves more effectively for the inevitable.

- *If you tell people just to allow their muscles to relax, many will have no idea what to do.* True. This is why Jacobson invented progressive relaxation, a technique that clearly teaches people the difference between muscle tension and relaxation.

- *People who make decisions on the basis of inspiration and gut-level feelings wind up with fewer regrets than people who methodically add up all the pluses and minuses.* False. People who use the balance sheet to weigh the pluses and the minuses have fewer regrets and are more likely to stick to their decisions.

ELEVEN

OUTLINE

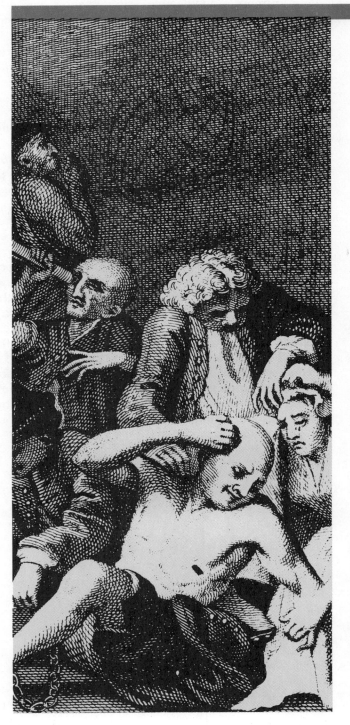

Abnormal Behavior

- A man shot the president of the United States in front of millions of television witnesses, yet was found not guilty by a court of law.
- Cavemen treated abnormal behavior by letting the sun shine in—or letting the evil spirits out. Therapy involved making a hole in the head.
- In the Middle Ages innocent people were drowned to prove that they were not possessed by the Devil.
- Mental disorders stem from physiological problems, such as chemical imbalances or metabolic disturbances.
- Depressed rats drive their neighbors to drink.
- In some mental disorders, people may see or hear things that are not actually there.
- Supermales can leap tall buildings at a single bound.
- Many Americans have changed their sex through surgery and hormone treatments.
- Strip-teasers are exhibitionists.
- Suicide is a sign of insanity.

The Ohio State campus lived in terror throughout the long fall session of a recent year. Four college women were abducted, forced to cash checks or obtain money with their instant-cash cards, then driven to unpopulated areas and raped. As told in *Time* magazine, a mysterious phone call led to the arrest of a 23-year-old drifter, William Milligan, who had been dismissed from the navy (Oct. 23, 1978, p. 102).

William was not the boy next door.

Several psychologists and psychiatrists who interviewed William concluded that 10 personalities resided within him, eight male and two female. His personality had been "fractured" by an abusive childhood. The personalities showed distinct facial expressions, vocal patterns, and memories. They even performed differently on personality and intelligence tests.

Arthur, the most rational personality, spoke with a British accent. Danny and Christopher were normal, quiet adolescents. Christene was a three-year-old girl. It was Tommy, a 16-year-old, who had enlisted in the navy. Allen was 18 and smoked. Adelena, a 19-year-old **lesbian** personality, had committed the rapes. Who had made the mysterious phone call? Probably David, aged nine, an anxious child personality.

The defense claimed that William was suffering from **multiple personality.** Several distinct personalities dwelled within him. Some were aware of the others; some believed that they were the sole occupants. Billy, the core personality, had learned to sleep as a child to avoid the abuse of his father. A psychiatrist asserted that Billy had also been asleep, in a "psychological coma," during the abductions. Therefore Billy should be found innocent by reason of **insanity.**

On December 4, 1978 Billy was found not guilty. But he did not walk away from the trial. He was given an indefinite term in an institution for the mentally ill. In 1982, John Hinckley was also found not guilty of the assassination attempt on President Reagan by reason of insanity. Expert witnesses testified that he was suffering from **schizophrenia.**

Multiple personality and schizophrenia are two types of abnormal behavior. In this chapter we first define abnormal behavior. Then we examine various explanations for, or "models" of, abnormal behavior. In our discussion of the demonological model, we shall see that if William Milligan or John Hinckley had lived in Salem, Massachusetts in 1692, just 200 years after Columbus had set foot in the New World, they might well have been hanged or burned as witches. At that time most people assumed that abnormal behavior was caused by possession by the Devil. Nineteen people lost their lives that year in that colonial town for allegedly practicing the arts of Satan.

Then we shall explore some issues involved in classifying abnormal behaviors. Finally, we discuss various patterns of abnormal behavior, including *anxiety disorders, dissociative disorders, somatoform disorders, affective disorders, schizophrenic disorders, personality disorders, psychosexual disorders,* and *suicide.*

Defining Abnormal Behavior

What is meant by abnormal behavior? Just being different is not sufficient cause to label a person abnormal. There is only one president of the United States at a given time, yet that person is not considered abnormal (usually).

Lesbian Female homosexual. (After the Greek island *Lesbos,* where homosexuality among women was idealized.)

Multiple personality A dissociative disorder in which a person appears to have two or more distinct personalities. The personalities may alternate in controlling the person. See *dissociative disorders* in this chapter.

Insanity A legal term descriptive of a person judged to be incapable of recognizing right from wrong or of conforming his or her behavior to the law. (From the Latin *in-,* meaning "not," and *sanus,* meaning "healthy.")

Schizophrenia (skits–oh–FREE–knee–uh). A psychotic disorder characterized by loss of control of thought processes and inappropriate emotional responses. See *schizophrenic and schizophreniform disorders* in this chapter.

The Insanity Plea: A Defense That Is on Trial

"Insanity" is a legal, not a psychological, term. People may be found insane, and thus not responsible for criminal behavior, if at the time of the offense they lacked the capacity to distinguish right from wrong, or they could not prevent themselves from engaging in the criminal acts.

You can readily see that this definition can lead to a hornet's nest of trouble. We cannot *know* whether other people understand right from wrong at any given moment or can control their behavior. We can only observe what they do (and listen to what they say) and draw our own conclusions. Judges and juries are not psychologists and psychiatrists. In the typical insanity defense, defense attorneys employ experts as witnesses, mental-health professionals who, on the basis of interviews or previous acquaintance with the client, usually testify that the accused was insane at the time of the act. The prosecution presents conflicting testimony from other expert witnesses to the effect that the accused was sane at the time of the crime.

Would-be presidential assassin John Hinckley (left) is just one of the many who have evaded criminal responsibility through the insanity plea. The defense claimed that Hinckley was living in a fantasy world that involved actress Jodie Foster (right), who played a young prostitute in the film *Taxi Driver*.

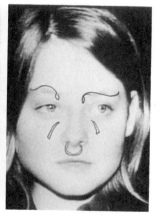

This type of back-and-forth "expert" testimony characterized the John Hinckley trial in 1982. Hinckley tried to assassinate President Ronald Reagan, claiming that he wished to impress movie actress Jodie Foster. The defense claimed that Hinckley was suffering from schizophrenia at the time and was therefore insane. He was portrayed as a "mental cripple" living in a "fantasy world." Influenced by the movie *Taxi Driver*, he had even sought young prostitutes on the streets of New York who seemed in need of help. (Jodie Foster had played a street prostitute in *Taxi Driver*, and she was "saved" by the movie's schizophrenic "hero.")

The prosecution then brought forth witnesses who testified that Hinckley was sane. Because well-trained professionals often have conflicting views about peoples' "mental states," which are private events, the public seems to be becoming somewhat skeptical of the insanity plea. Even some jury members who participated in the Hinckley decision were appalled that he had to be found not guilty. They argued that this was a case in which the presumption of innocence truly backfired; they would have had to prove "beyond a shadow of a doubt" that Hinckley was *sane* at the time of the crime in order to convict him—an impossible task.

Criminals who are found not guilty by reason of insanity are also often committed to mental institutions, rather than given concrete prison terms. They are theoretically eligible for release when they are no longer behaving abnormally. Thus the public fears that "sick" people will be walking the streets if they show no symptoms for a while, and that many criminals will fake a claim to insanity in hopes of earlier release from an institution.

Perhaps one way out of this morass, which would partly satisfy an aroused public, would be to institute a verdict of guilty *but* insane. This verdict would allow disturbed criminals to receive treatment that may in some instances prove helpful. But they would retain responsibility for their criminal acts and not be released from an institution simply because a judge now ruled them sane.

Only one person holds the record for running or swimming the fastest mile. That person is different from you and me but is not abnormal.

In order for someone's behavior to be labeled abnormal, someone else must be *disturbed* by it (Ullmann & Krasner, 1975)—whether that someone is the person showing the behavior, a family member, a police officer, or a psychologist. If nobody is disturbed by the behavior, nobody will bother to label

Paranoid Characterized by oversuspiciousness and delusions of grandeur or persecution. See *paranoia* and *delusions* in this chapter.

Hallucination A sensory experience in the absence of sensory stimulation. Confusion of imagined objects and events with reality.

Ideas of persecution Erroneous beliefs that one is being victimized or persecuted. See *delusion* in this chapter.

it abnormal. Behavior that meets one or more of the following criteria is likely to become labeled abnormal:

1. *Infrequent behavior.* Although rarity or statistical deviance is not sufficient for behavior to be labeled abnormal, it helps. Highly anxious or depressed people are not likely to be considered abnormal in a society in which nearly everyone is anxious or depressed.

2. *Socially unacceptable behavior.* Each society has standards or norms for acceptable behavior in a given context. In our society, walking naked is normal in a locker room, but abnormal on a crowded boulevard. Similarly, what is abnormal for one generation can be normal for another. Smoking marijuana and cohabiting without marriage were almost unheard of in the early 1960s, but scarcely raise an eyebrow today.

   What is normal in one society may be abnormal in another. Citizens of our society who assume that strangers will be hostile and try to take advantage may be considered overly suspicious, even **paranoid.** But among the Mundugumor, a cannibalistic tribe studied by the late anthropologist Margaret Mead (1935), perpetual suspicion was justified. Strangers, even male members of the same household, *were* hostile.

3. *Faulty perception or interpretation of reality.* I've heard it said that it's all right to say that you talk to God through prayer, but if you say that God talks back, you may be committed to a mental institution. Our society considers it normal to be inspired by religious beliefs, but abnormal to believe that God is speaking to you. "Hearing voices" and "seeing things" are considered **hallucinations.** Similarly, **ideas of persecution,** such as believing that the mafia or the CIA or the communists are "out to get you"—all are considered abnormal. (Unless they are out to get you, of course.)

"Is this a dagger which I see before me?" asks Macbeth in the Shakespearean play of that name. Macbeth—here played by Orson Welles—suffers from guilt following the murder of King Duncan. He wonders if he actually sees or is hallucinating the murder weapon, a dagger. Faulty perceptions suggest abnormal behavior.

Most of us may use defense mechanisms now and then to reduce the immediate impact of a stressor. But serious, persistent self-deception—as in remaining fully unmoved, through denial, at news of a relative's death—could be considered faulty perception and abnormal.

4. *Personal distress.* Anxiety, depression, exaggerated fears and other psychological states cause personal distress and can be considered abnormal. But anxiety and depression may also be appropriate responses to one's situation, for instance, a real threat or a loss. In such cases they are not abnormal unless they persevere indefinitely, long after the source of distress has been removed, or most people would have adjusted.

5. *Self-defeating behavior.* Behavior that leads to misery rather than happiness and fulfillment may be considered abnormal. From this perspective, chronic drinking that interferes with work and family life, and cigarette smoking that impairs health, may be labeled abnormal.

6. *Dangerous behavior.* Behavior that is dangerous to the self or others is considered abnormal. People who threaten or attempt suicide may be considered abnormal, as may people who threaten or attack others.

A Psychological Controversy: Is Homosexuality Abnormal?

Sometimes it is not clear whether or not a certain behavior pattern is normal. Politics then often enter the picture and professional groups may "flip-flop" on their judgments. One such group is the American Psychiatric Association, whose *Diagnostic and Statistical Manual of the Mental Disorders (DSM)*, is one widely used listing of abnormal behaviors. And one such flip-flop recently occurred in the case of **homosexuality,** or preference for sex partners of one's own sex.

From a statistical perspective, homosexuality is clearly abnormal. As you will see in Chapter 13, perhaps only two percent of the male population and one percent of the female population is exclusively homosexual (Hunt, 1974). Application of other standards is not so clear. Homosexuality was listed as abnormal (a "mental disorder") in the 1968 edition of the DSM, the DSM-II. In 1973 the members of the American Psychiatric Association voted that homosexuality was no longer a mental illness. Responding to requests from the homosexual community and others, it was decided that there was no evidence for homosexuality to be considered dangerous. If homosexuality were socially unacceptable, this could hardly be considered the fault of the homosexual. If homosexuality were self-defeating, it was only because of societal prejudice. This vote was probably an excellent choice. It eliminated one source of degradation for homosexuals and is consistent with evidence that homosexuals, as a group, are as well-adjusted as other segments of society (see Rathus [1983] for a review of the literature).

But the association entered a new "mental disorder" in the 1980 edition of the DSM, the DSM-III: **ego-dystonic homosexuality.** Homosexuality is "ego-dystonic" when it is inconsistent with the homosexual's self-concept. Then it is likely to cause personal distress. The new **diagnosis** legitimizes treatment by mental-health professionals of homosexuals who are in conflict about their sexual orientations. But it is ironic that most homosexuals would probably not be concerned about their sexual orientations if homosexuality were socially acceptable. (Note that there is no category called "ego-dystonic *heterosexuality*," which would apply to people who are discontent with their heterosexual orientation.)

Homosexuality Preference for sex partners of, and romantic relationships with, members of one's own sex. (From the Greek *homos,* meaning "same"—*not* the Latin *homo,* meaning "man.")

Ego-dystonic homosexuality Homosexuality that is inconsistent with one's self-concept. Homosexuality that causes personal distress. (From the Greek *dys-,* meaning "bad" or "ill," and *tonos,* meaning "tone" in the sense of the prevailing style.)

Diagnosis A decision or opinion concerning the nature of a diseased condition. (From the Greek *dia-,* meaning "between," and *gignoskein,* meaning "to know.")

Capricious
(cap–PREE–shuss). Given to abrupt changes, whimsical. (From the Latin *caput*, meaning "head," and the Italian *riccio*, meaning "hedgehog.")

There is also evidence that most members of the American Psychiatric Association still regard homosexuality as a mental disorder, despite the 1973 vote. Sixty-nine percent of the first 2,500 association members responding to a 1978 survey by the journal *Medical Aspects of Human Sexuality* said that homosexuality was an abnormal way of gratifying sexual needs. Sixty percent thought homosexuals less capable than heterosexuals of mature, loving relationships. Seventy percent asserted that homosexuals' problems are more likely to stem from inner conflict than societal prejudice.

Having struggled to define abnormal behaviors, let us discuss various views of their origins and treatment.

Normal vs. Abnormal: Historical and Contemporary Views

There are a number of historical and contemporary views or models of abnormal behavior. They include demonology and the medical, social learning, and sociocultural models. The organic and psychoanalytic models are offshoots of the medical model.

Demonology

Anyone who has read Homer's *Iliad* or *Odyssey* knows that the ancient Greek gods were a **capricious** lot. They drew humans into their own conflicts, often inspiring them to war to kill off the pets of rival gods. On the positive side, they could inspire poetry and art. The gods were also credited with creating human temperament, and punishing humans by causing confusion and madness.

Hippocrates, the Greek physician of the Golden Age of art and literature (fourth century B.C.), made the radical suggestion that abnormal behavior was not the work of the gods at all. Rather, it was caused by an abnormality of the

---

A Hole in the Head: Energy-Efficient Air Conditioning?

Archaeologists make a living digging into human history—literally. Among their findings—a number of human skeletons dating back to the Stone Age with egg-sized holes in the skull.

No, this was no primitive effort at air conditioning. Some of our ancestors apparently developed the notion that abnormal behavior represented invasion by evil spirits. They used the brutal method of breaking a pathway through the skull—called *trephining*—to let those irascible spirits out. Examination of these skeletons shows that some people survived trephining.

Was the practice successful? Well, most of the time it terminated the disturbing behavior. And the "patient." We also suspect that the threat of trephining persuaded many people to do their best to conform to the norms of their tribe or group.

Trephining. Our ancestors may have "air-conditioned" skulls in an effort to deal with abnormal behavior. The threat of trephining could certainly encourage conformity.

brain. This notion that bodily processes could affect thoughts, feelings, and behaviors was to lie dormant for about 2,000 years.

The Middle Ages   During the Middle Ages in Europe, and during the early days of American civilization along the rocky coast of Massachusetts, it was generally believed that abnormal behavior was a sign of **possession** by agents or spirits of the Devil. Possession could stem from **retribution,** signifying that God was punishing you for sins by having the Devil possess your soul. Wild agitation and confusion were attributed to retribution. Possession was also believed to result from deals with the Devil in which people traded their souls for earthly power or wealth. Such traders were called witches. Witches were held responsible for unfortunate events ranging from a neighbor's infertility to a poor crop.

In either case you were in for trouble. An **exorcist,** whose function was to persuade these spirits to find better pickings elsewhere, might pray at your side and wave a cross at you. If the spirits didn't call it quits, you might be beaten or flogged. If your behavior was still unseemly, there were other remedies, like the rack, which have powerful influences on behavior.

In 1484 Pope Innocent VIII ordered that witches be put to death. At least 200,000 accused witches were killed over the next two centuries. Europe was no place to practice strange ways. The goings-on at Salem were trivial by comparison.

There were ingenious "diagnostic" tests for ferreting out instances of possession. One involved dunking the suspect under water. Failure to drown was interpreted as support by the Devil—in other words, possession. Then you were in real trouble.

The Medical Model

Johann Weyer, a German physician, stood alone in the sixteenth century against the doctrine of possession. He argued that abnormal behavior stemmed from disorders of the body or the mind. This was the essence of the **medical model**—the view that abnormal behavior reflects an underlying illness. The organic model and the psychoanalytic model may be considered offshoots of the medical model.

Medical Model: Organic Version   In 1883 Emil Kraepelin published a textbook of psychiatry in which he developed the medical model further. Kraepelin argued that there were various forms of abnormal behavior, which, within the medical model, are commonly referred to as mental illnesses. (See Table 11.1 for a list of many of the commonly used terms concerning abnormal behavior that reflect the widespread influence of the medical model.) Each mental illness had specific origins, which he assumed were physiological. The

Possession According to superstitious belief, a psychological state induced by demons or the Devil in which a person exhibits abnormal behavior.

Retribution Deserved punishment for evildoing. (From the Latin *re-*, meaning "back," and *tribuere*, meaning "to pay." What is "tribute"?)

Exorcist (EGGS–or–sist). A person who drives away evil spirits through means like ritual prayers and beatings. (From the Greek *ex-*, meaning "out," and *horkizein*, meaning "to make one swear.")

Medical model The view that abnormal behavior is symptomatic of mental illness.

TABLE 11.1   **Some Commonly Used Terms Concerning Abnormal Behavior That Are Derived from the Medical Model**

Mental Illness	Diagnosis	Treatment
Mental Health	Mental Patient	Therapy
Symptoms	Mental Hospital	Cure
Syndrome	Prognosis	Relapse

Organic model The view that abnormal behavior is caused by biochemical or physiological abnormalities.

Syndrome A cluster or group of symptoms suggestive of a particular disorder. (From the Greek *syn-*, meaning "with," and *dramein*, meaning "to run.")

Neurotic Descriptive of disorders characterized chiefly by anxiety that is theorized to stem from unconscious conflict. A term whose usage is *not* recommended in the DSM–III.

Psychosis (sigh–CO–sis). A major disorder in which a person lacks insight and has difficulty meeting the demands of daily life and maintaining contact with reality.

assumption that biochemical or physiological problems underlie mental illness is the heart of the **organic model.**

Kraepelin argued that each mental illness, just like each physical illness, was typified by its own cluster of symptoms, or **syndrome.** Each mental illness had a specific outcome, or course, and would presumably respond to a characteristic form of treatment, or therapy.

Contemporary adherents to the organic model point out that certain mental disorders run in families, and are therefore transmitted from generation to generation by way of DNA (see Chapter 2). They also note that neurotransmitters and other chemical substances produce behavioral effects similar to those found in disorders like schizophrenia, as we shall see later in the chapter. Therefore, these disorders may reflect abnormally high or low levels of such substances.

According to the organic model, treatment requires medical expertise and involves controlling or curing the assumed underlying organic problem. The biological therapies discussed in Chapter 12 are largely based on the organic model.

Medical Model: Psychoanalytic Version   Sigmund Freud's psychoanalytic model argues that abnormal behavior, or mental illness, is symptomatic of underlying psychological problems. Consistent with psychoanalytic theory, these problems are viewed as largely unconscious conflicts that have childhood origins. The abnormal behavior (or "symptoms") often reflect difficulty in repressing primitive sexual and aggressive impulses.

Within Freudian theory, **neurotic** behavior and the experiencing of anxiety stem from the leakage of primitive impulses. Anxiety represents the impulse itself and fear of what might happen if the impulse were acted upon. In the case of **psychosis,** impulses are assumed to have broken through; behavior falls largely under the control of the id, rather than the ego or superego.

According to psychoanalytic theory, treatment (other than a sort of "band-aid" therapy) requires resolving the unconscious conflicts that are presumed to underlie the abnormal behavior. As you will see in Chapter 12, this can be a protracted process.

The medical model is a major advance over demonology. It led to the view that mentally ill people should be treated by qualified professionals rather than be punished. Compassion replaced hatred, fear, and persecution.

There are some problems with the medical model. For instance, the model suggests that the mentally ill, like the physically ill, may not be responsible for their own behavior. In the past, this view often led to hospitalization and suspension of responsibility (as in work and maintenance of a family life) among the mentally ill. This removal from the real world frequently decreased, rather than returned, ability to meet the demands of everyday life. But today even most adherents to the medical model encourage patients to remain in the community and maintain as much responsibility as they can.

The Social Learning Model

From a social learning point of view, abnormal behavior is not symptomatic of anything. Rather, it *is* the problem. Social learning theorists argue that abnormal behavior is acquired in the same way normal behaviors are acquired—through conditioning and observational learning. Why, then, do some people show abnormal behavior? Because their learning or reinforce-ment histories differ from those of most of us.

Acquiring Abnormal Behavior Patterns   A person who lacks social skills may never have had the chance to observe them. Or it may be that a minority subculture reinforced behaviors that are not approved by the majority. Pun-ishment for early exploratory behavior, or childhood sexual activity, may lead to anxiety concerning independence or sexuality in adulthood. Inconsistent discipline (random reinforcement of desirable behavior and unreliable pun-ishment for misbehavior) may lead to antisocial behavior. Children whose parents ignore or abuse them may come to pay more attention to their fan-tasies than the outer world, leading to schizophrenic withdrawal and inability to tell reality from fantasy.

Treatment   Since social learning theorists do not believe that abnormal be-havior reflects physiological or unconscious problems, they feel generally free to change or modify it directly. In Chapter 12 we shall see that they prefer *behavior therapy* to biological therapy or psychotherapy.

The Sociocultural Model

According to British psychiatrist R. D. Laing's **sociocultural model,** ab-normal behavior is a form of adjustment to an unjust society. Poverty, dis-crimination, and other social ills cause abnormal behavior. The schizophrenic flight into fantasy is a heroic act of defiance, not a sign of illness.

Sociocultural theorists argue that the "cure" to mental illness lies in changing society, not the person. They support their contention by pointing to evidence that mental illness is most common among the underprivileged.

Sociocultural model The view that society causes ab-normal behavior by subject-ing the individual to social pressures. Abnormal behav-ior is seen as a strategy for self-survival in a corrupting society.

Psych Ward: USSR

Let there be no doubt that Soviet authorities have turned our most humane branch of medicine into an instrument for achieving the main aim of their inter-nal policy—the suppression of dissent. . . . I appeal to you not for a moment to forget. . . .

—Your colleague, psychiatrist A. Koryagin

The above is an excerpt from a letter recently smug-gled out of Soviet labor camp 37 and addressed to psychiatrists in the West. As noted in *Newsweek* (Jan-uary 11, 1982), it is just one of a series of cries from Soviet dissidents who are trying, in vain, to have the Soviet Union alter its policy of using psychiatry as a political weapon. In June 1981, Anatoly Koryagin was sentenced to 12 years at hard labor for publicizing the internment of Soviet dissidents in mental hospi-tals.

A former Red Army Major General Pyotr Grigo-renko had been packed off to psych wards twice. He was stripped of Soviet citizenship in 1978 and found political asylum in the United States. Once in the US he underwent a series of psychological tests by Har-vard and Columbia psychiatrists to clear his name and expose this Soviet method of dealing with dissen-sion. The diagnosis: fully competent, if somewhat unbending.

The American psychiatrist who led the evalua-tion team sent a report on Grigorenko to their Soviet counterparts. The response? The Americans had made a "misdiagnosis" because of unfamiliarity with social norms in the Soviet Union.

In "The Myth of Mental Illness," psychiatrist Thomas Szasz (1960, 1974) claims that the label of *sick* has often been abused. We tend to label people "sick" when we do not understand, or when we dis-approve of, their behavior. According to Szasz, the sickness label is degrading; it denies victims basic competency. Rather than a diagnosis, the label "sick" becomes an insult and provides us with an excuse for throwing certain people away.

Consequence An outcome or result.

Antecedent (an–tea–SEED–dent). A happening or thing that occurs prior to another.

Eclectic Selecting from various systems or theories. (From the Greek *ek-*, meaning "out," and *legein*, meaning "to choose.")

Bipolar disorder A disorder in which the mood alternates between two extreme poles (elation and depression). Also referred to as *manic-depression*. See *affective disorders* in this chapter.

Dissociative neurosis A former term for *dissociative disorders*, emphasizing the theoretical role of unconscious conflict.

But we must note that low socioeconomic status is often a **consequence** rather than an **antecedent** of abnormal behavior.

Many psychologists look to more than one model to explain and treat abnormal behavior. They are considered **eclectic.** For example, many social learning theorists and behavior therapists believe that *some*, if not all, abnormal behavior patterns may reflect biochemical factors or an interplay of biochemistry and learning. These theorists are open to combining behavior therapy with, say, chemotherapy to treat schizophrenia and **bipolar disorder.** Similarly, a psychoanalyst may believe that a schizophrenic's disorganization represents control of the personality by the id rather than the ego and argue that only long-term psychoanalytic therapy can help the ego achieve permanent supremacy. But the psychoanalyst may be willing to use chemotherapy to calm agitation on a short-term basis.

We shall have more to say about the roles of these various models in explaining abnormal behaviors later on. But first let us explore some issues in classifying abnormal behaviors.

Classifying Abnormal Behavior

Toss some people, chimpanzees, seaweed, a few fish, and sponges into a room—preferably a well-ventilated room. Stir slightly. What do you have? It depends on how you classify this conglomeration.

Classify them as plants versus animals and you lump the people, chimps, fish, and, yes, sponges together. Classify them as stuff that carries on its business on dry land rather than underwater, and we throw in our lots with only the chimps. How about those that swim and those that don't? Then the chimps, the fish, and some of us are lumped together.

DSM-II vs. DSM-III: Categories in Flux

The way we classify things reflects the variables that we consider important. A common classification scheme is found in the DSM. The medical model (both organic and psychoanalytic versions) was considered quite important to the authors of earlier versions of the DSM. Consequently, the DSM-II (1968) contained several *neurotic* disorders (as shown in the left-hand column of Table 11.2).

"Neurosis": A Medical-Model View "Neurosis" translates literally as "a condition of the nerves"—suggesting an organic basis to this group of disorders. But no consistent organic basis has been found to underlie this group of problems. From a psychoanalytic perspective, the neuroses were *theorized* to stem from "neurotic conflict." But the neurotic conflict, which involved unconscious fear that primitive impulses might break loose, was a causal speculation, and not directly observable. The neuroses were simply lumped together and doubtful medical-model assumptions were used to label them, rather than observable common features.

Sleepwalking: A "Neurosis" or Simply a Problem That Is Usually First Evident in Childhood? Consider the case of sleepwalking (a problem discussed in Chapter 4). In the DSM-II, sleepwalking was classified as a **dissociative neurosis** because of the Freudian assumption that different aspects

TABLE 11.2   Old and Updated Labels for Some Classes of Abnormal Behaviors

DSM-II (1968)	DSM-III (1980)
Phobic neurosis	Phobic disorder
Anxiety neurosis	Generalized anxiety disorder
Obsessive-compulsive neurosis	Obsessive-compulsive disorder
Hysterical neurosis, dissociative type	Dissociative disorder
Hysterical neurosis, conversion type	Conversion disorder
Hypochondriacal neurosis	Hypochondriasis
Depressive neurosis	Dysthymic disorder

The DSM-III de-emphasizes the concept of neurosis. The DSM-III makes a greater effort to tie diagnostic categories to observable behavior.

of consciousness had become split apart, or *dissociated*, from one another, allowing unconscious impulses to be expressed while the person was asleep. However, since there is little measurable evidence for the Freudian view, sleep-walking has been "moved over" to a more descriptive, less theoretical, category in the DSM-III: disorders that begin in childhood.

According to psychoanalytic theory, the form a neurosis takes reflects a person's style of using defense mechanisms to adjust to the underlying conflict. Some neurotic people might show chronic anxiety *(anxiety neurosis)*. Some might show depression *(depressive neurosis)*. Still others might show dissociative neuroses, as in the cases of sleepwalking or multiple personality, the disorder attributed to William Milligan.

The DSM-III Emphasis on Observable Behavior   The DSM-III (1980) de-emphasizes the neuroses. Some are eliminated altogether, and alternate names for others are recommended, as shown, in part, in Table 11.2. For instance, dissociative and conversion disorders are no longer lumped together with anxiety disorders. Why not? Because their chief symptoms have little to do with anxiety. *For the authors of the DSM-III, it was more important that the list of disorders be based on observable behavior, than that it be consistent with the medical model.*

In any event, the DSM-III has not only changed some labels and moved some disorders around. It has also modified descriptions of diagnostic categories, tying them more clearly to observable behavior. The DSM-III specifies more precisely when a certain diagnosis should be made.

A DSM-III Advantage: Increased Diagnostic Reliability   We have a right to ask whether this fiddling with labels and disorders has had any measurable payoff. It could be argued that partial rooting out of medical-model influence is not an adequate justification. After all, changing names and descriptions creates adjustment problems for people who had become familiar with the older ways (DSM-III, pp. 9–10).

We can provide a partial answer to this question by referring to the *reliability* of diagnoses. A diagnosis is *reliable* if it will be made consistently in a given case. One study of the reliability of diagnoses made on the basis of an earlier version of the DSM was disappointing (Beck and others, 1962). The percentage of agreement between a pair of psychiatrists, for example, was 53 percent for the diagnosis of schizophrenia, and ranged from 38 to 63 percent for various **affective disorders.** The DSM-III has clarified diagnostic features for schizophrenia, and made major changes in the area of the affective disorders. One result: a pilot study of the reliability of diagnoses made on the basis of the DSM-III found an agreement rate of 81 percent for schizophrenic disorders and 83 percent for affective disorders (Spitzer and others, 1979).

Why, might we ask, don't we have a reliability rate of 100 percent? After all, important treatment decisions are made on the basis of diagnosis. There are at least three sources of error in diagnosis. Just one of these is imperfection in the diagnostic system. Second, we must deal with inconsistency in the presentation of problems by people who show or describe the disorders. Finally, the professionals who do the diagnosing differ in their training, ability, and outlooks. Keep in mind that there is also a good deal of diagnostic disagreement concerning physical disorders. For instance, we often seek "second opinions" when we are considering surgery or other major medical involvement.

In any event, the DSM-III seems to offer some improvements over earlier versions. But do not interpret this as a blanket endorsement of the DSM-III. In many ways it may still rely too strongly on the medical model. See Davison and Neale (1982) or Mehr (1983) for a fuller discussion.

Psychosis   The DSM-III uses the broad label *psychosis* to describe disorders in which **reality testing** is grossly impaired (p. 367). The DSM-II definition of psychosis focused on the frequent inability of psychotic people to meet the demands of everyday life. Psychotic people are now and then hospitalized for their own protection, and, sometimes, for the protection of society. But most

psychotic individuals are no threat to society, even when their disorders seem bizarre and frightening.

Organic psychoses. Some psychoses are known to have organic origins, while others are not. So-called **organic psychoses** can be linked firmly to physical abnormalities such as infections (like **encephalitis** or **meningitis),** trauma (like concussions), nutritional deficiencies (like **Korsakoff's syndrome),** intoxication (from drugs, metals like lead, etc.), and many others. In each case the psychological symptoms stem from known physical problems.

Functional psychoses. In the so-called **functional psychoses,** like schizophrenia and severe affective disorders, impaired reality testing cannot be linked to specific physical problems. We shall see, however, that research is uncovering possible links between functional psychoses and biochemical abnormalities.

So let us maintain some skepticism about the adequacy of categorizing schemes. In any event, the remainder of the chapter discusses many of the abnormal behaviors found in the DSM.

Anxiety Disorders

Anxiety disorders are characterized by nervousness, fears, feelings of dread and foreboding, and signs of sympathetic overarousal that include rapid heartbeat, muscle tension, and shakiness. We shall discuss three major anxiety disorders: phobic, generalized anxiety, and obsessive-compulsive disorders.

Phobic Disorder (Phobic Neurosis)

Phobic disorders, or *phobias*, are excessive, irrational fears of objects, situations, or activities. Some people have phobias for elevators and will not enter them. Yes, the cable *could* break. The ventilation *could* fail. One *could* be stuck in midair waiting for repairs. But these problems are infrequent, and it would be foolhardy to walk 40 flights of stairs twice daily to avoid them. Similarly, some people with phobias for needles will not receive injections, even when they are the recommended treatment for serious illness. Injections can be painful, but most people with phobias for needles would gladly suffer a pinch that would cause still greater pain if it would help them fight illness.

TABLE 11.3   **Some Exotic Species from the Museum of Phobias**

Name of Phobia	Definition
Ailurophobia	Fear of cats
Arachibutyrophobia	Fear of peanut butter sticking to the roof of your mouth
Belonophobia	Fear of pins and needles
Ergasiophobia	Fear of writing
Erythrophobia	Fear of blushing
Gephydrophobia	Fear of crossing bridges
Ophidiophobia	Fear of snakes
Pnigophobia	Fear of choking
Siderodromophobia	Fear of railways
Taphophobia	Fear of being buried alive
Triskedekaphobia	Fear of the number 13
Pantaphobia	Fear of—you guessed it—everything

Organic psychoses Psychotic disorders that are known to stem from biochemical or physiological abnormalities.

Encephalitis Inflammation of the brain.

Meningitis Inflammation of membranes (meninges) that envelop the brain and spinal cord.

Korsakoff's syndrome An alcohol-related disorder that is thought to reflect nutritional deficiency and is characterized by loss of memory (amnesia).

Functional psychoses Psychotic disorders that are hypothesized to stem from psychological conflict.

Phobic disorder (FOE–bick). Excessive, irrational fear. Fear that is out of proportion to the actual danger. Also called *phobia*. (From the Greek *phobos*, meaning "fear.")

Hans and Horses and Albert and Rats

Do you want to talk about conflict? Do you want to talk about drama? Do you want to talk about raw, unnerving fear? Well, my friends, forget about Frankenstein's monster. Forget about King Kong. Forget about income taxes and things that go bump in the night. For there in the heart of turn-of-the-century Vienna, that flourishing European capital of music and the arts, horses were biting people in the streets. Or so was convinced one petrified five-year-old boy by the name of Hans.

The Story of Little Hans   In 1908 a distraught physician wrote Sigmund Freud for advice. His son, Hans, would not leave the house for fear of horses, especially horses with blinders and black muzzles. So began a psychoanalysis by mail that would form the basis of the Freudian theory of phobias. Freud (1909) hypothesized that irrational fears symbolized unconscious conflicts.

From the age of three, Hans had shown increasing interest in his penis and other people's genitals. Caught touching himself, his mother had once warned that she would have a doctor cut it off if he did not stop. Later, perhaps for reassurance, he asked his parents if they had "weewee makers," to which they answered yes.

Hans enjoyed coming into bed with his parents, especially cuddling his mother, even though his father protested that this could be harmful. When he eventually learned that girls' weewee makers were not like his, Hans became quite distressed. When his father left for work in the morning, Hans developed fear that he would not return. At about this time he also developed his fear of horses.

A Psychoanalytic View of Phobias   From these and other glimpses of the boy's history, Freud concluded that the horse symbolized Hans's father, as we shall see. But first follow some complex reasoning:

Hans had presumably concluded that females did not have weewee makers because they had been castrated, just as Hans's mother had threatened him. Hans loved his mother and wished to spend as much time as he could with her. Perhaps he entertained some childish sexual fantasies about her. He sensed a rivalry with his father for his mother's love and became hostile toward him. This hostility was *projected* onto the father; Hans then experienced fear that he (Hans) might be harmed *by* his father. Why? As retaliation for Hans's wish to possess his mother. The fear that Hans encountered when his father left for work unconsciously reflected the possibility that Hans's *own* hostility might consume his father or drive him away.

In short, Hans was going through the Oedipus complex (see Chapter 9). Freud believed that all boys underwent this complex; they all wished to possess their mothers and destroy their rivals—namely, their fathers.

Conscious awareness of this conflict would have been too threatening for little Hans. He could not bear to think that his father might castrate him. But he could *displace* this fear onto an animal that had a large penis, as did his father, and whose blinders and black muzzle symbolized his father's spectacles and moustache. Hans could transform his castration anxiety into a phobia that horses would bite him. Horses, you see, do not castrate, they bite.

The Story of Little Albert   Some 12 years later, in the United States, John B. Watson was setting forth a learning theory explanation of phobias. His demonstration was a mini-experiment with an unlucky lad by the name of Little Albert. Albert was a phlegmatic fellow at the age of 11 months, not given to ready displays of emotion. But he did enjoy playing with a laboratory rat. Such are the toys to be found in psychologists' laboratories.

A Behavioral View of Phobias   Watson and his future wife, Rosalie Rayner (Watson & Rayner, 1920), set out to show that fears are acquired mechanically, by association. Using a method that some psycholo-

---

Agoraphobia
(AG–or–uh–FOE–bee–uh).
Fear of open, crowded places. (From the Greek *agora*, meaning "marketplace" or "place of assembly.")

Phobias may seriously interfere with one's life. A person may know that a phobia is irrational, yet still experience it. Although it could be argued that phobias involve faulty perception of the feared object, phobic people are not considered psychotic. The person's "irrationality" is usually limited to the phobic object.

Phobias are not uncommon in children and adults, and **agoraphobia** is the most common of them (Mahoney, 1980). Agoraphobia is a fear of open, busy places (like marketplaces). Agoraphobia can severely impair adjustment

gists have criticized as unethical, Watson startled Little Albert by clanging steel bars behind his head when the infant played with the rat. After seven pairings, Albert showed fear of the rat, even though clanging was suspended. Albert's fear also spread, or generalized, to objects similar in appearance to the rat, like a rabbit and his mother's coat's fur collar.

Somewhere there may be a gentleman in his 60s who cringes when he sees furry puppies, or furry muffs protecting the hands of girls in winter, and, of course, whenever rats are discussed on television.

Big Albert's fear of rats may never have extinguished. Extinction would require perceiving rats without painful consequences. But fear might have prevented Albert from facing rats. (Phobic people typically avoid the objects of their fears.) And avoidance behavior would have been reinforced by fear reduction.

Social Learning and Phobias   Social learning theorists suggest that phobias may also be acquired through modeling, or observational learning. If parents squirm, grimace, shudder, and squeal at mice, dogs, blood, or dirt on the kitchen floor, young observers may acquire the tendency to do likewise when they face these objects.

In an experiment on observational learning of fear, Bandura and Rosenthal (1969) hooked up a confederate to a frightening display of electrical equipment. As real subjects looked on, a buzzer was sounded. The confederate's arm shot up from the arm of the chair, as if in response to shock. The confederate also yowled and grimaced. But all this was an Academy Award performance, because no shock had been given. Still, after watching a number of repetitions, the observers began to show a high level of arousal in response to the buzzer, as assessed by physiological measures, even though they were never in any danger of being shocked.

Cognitive Factors   If such fears are acquired at a young age, we may later interpret our phobias as parts of our personalities. We may think that they were "always" there and always will be. We label ourselves as "people who fear (you fill it in)" and live up to the labels.

Psychologists Donald Meichenbaum (1977) and Michael Mahoney (1971) point out that phobic persons say frightening things to themselves when faced with the dreaded objects or situations: "I know I'll just drop dead!" "Oh my God, it's going to be awful!" "I've *got* to get out of here!" These thoughts are quite aversive and contribute to avoidance behavior.

Evaluation   What can we make of these views? Behaviorists Joseph Wolpe and Stanley Rachman (1960) accept Hans's father's behavioral descriptions, but challenge Freud's psychoanalytic *interpretation* of them. They find Freud's evidence for linking these events to an Oedipus complex flimsy and circumstantial. For instance, there is no evidence that Hans ever wished to possess his mother sexually. Hans never *expressed* any feelings of fear of, or hatred toward, his father. Nor was it unusual for light-colored horses to have black muzzles; thus there was no evidence that this feature of the animal tied it symbolically to the father.

Watson's experiment with Little Albert has also been challenged. For instance, half of the persons who are phobic cannot recall upsetting experiences in the situations that they find frightening (Keuthen, 1980). Also, some efforts to replicate Watson's experiment with Little Albert have failed (English, 1929). In science, experiments must be capable of being replicated if we are to accept their findings. Even if we did accept Watson's findings, they would not show that *all* phobias are acquired by association.

Evidence that fears can be acquired through observation and maintained through self-defeating expectations seems more firmly grounded. For example, Albert Bandura and his colleagues (Bandura, 1981; Bandura and others, 1982) have shown that the belief that we shall not be able to handle a potentially painful event arouses fear. When we believe that we shall not be able to cope with a threat, we tend to become preoccupied with it and magnify the potential danger. On the other hand, belief that we can cope with or control threatening events lessens our fear of them (Miller, 1980).

---

since some sufferers refuse to venture from their homes. Just a partial list of fairly familiar phobias includes **claustrophobia** (fear of tight places), **acrophobia** (fear of heights), fear of mice, snakes, and other creepy-crawlies, stage fright, and speech anxiety. Table 11.3 lists some phobias that may be less familiar. You could ask your professor whether memorizing them will earn you an A for achievement in this chapter—unless you have *erythrophobia*. (Out of consideration for students with *triskedekaphobia*, only 12 phobias are listed.)

Claustrophobia
(claws–tro–FOE–bee–uh). Fear of tight, small places. (From the Latin *claustrum*, meaning "box.")

Acrophobia
(ack–row–FOE–bee–uh). Fear of high places. (From the Greek *akros*, meaning "top.")

Generalized Anxiety Disorder (Anxiety Neurosis)

The central feature of **generalized anxiety disorder** is persistent anxiety of at least one month's duration. The anxiety cannot be attributed to a phobic object, situation, or activity. Rather, it seems free-floating. Symptoms may include motor tension (shakiness, inability to relax, furrowed brow, fidgeting, etc.), autonomic overarousal (sweating, dry mouth, racing heart, light-headedness, frequent urinating, diarrhea, etc.), feelings of dread and foreboding, and excessive vigilance, as shown by distractibility, insomnia, and irritability.

Theories of Generalized Anxiety   Psychoanalytic theory explains generalized anxiety as persistent difficulty in maintaining repression of primitive impulses. Social learning theorists suggest that generalized anxiety is often nothing more than fear that has been associated with situations so broad that they are not readily identified—for instance, social relationships or personal achievement. As noted in Chapter 10, social learning and cognitive theorists argue that generalized anxiety, like phobias, can be maintained by thoughts that one is in a terrible situation and helpless to change it.

There is some evidence that there may be a partial organic basis for persistent anxiety. Identical twins are significantly more likely than fraternal twins to share the diagnosis of anxiety disorder (Slater & Shields, 1969). We should note, however, that identical twins in the above study were reared together, and that parents often treat identical twins similarly (Nichols, 1978). But Scarr and her colleagues (1981) gave a battery of tests to adolescents and their parents in biologically related and adoptive families and found that **neuroticism** scores of parents and natural children correlated more highly than those of parents and adoptees.

Obsessive-Compulsive Disorder (Obsessive-Compulsive Neurosis)

An **obsession** is a recurring thought or image that seems irrational and beyond control. Obsessions are so strong and frequent that they interfere with daily life. They may include doubts as to whether one has locked the doors and shut the windows; impulses, such as the wish to strangle one's spouse; and images, such as one mother's recurrent fantasy that her children had been run over by traffic on the way home from school. In other cases, a 16-year-old boy found "numbers in my head" whenever he was about to study or take a test. A housewife became obsessed with the notion that she had soiled her hands with Sani-Flush and that it was spreading to everything she touched.

A **compulsion** is a seemingly irresistible urge to engage in an act, often repeatedly, such as lengthy, elaborate washing after using the bathroom. The impulse is frequent and forceful, interfering with daily life. Some men, called *exhibitionists*, report experiencing the compulsion to expose their genitals to women strangers. The woman who felt contaminated by Sani-Flush engaged in elaborate hand-washing rituals. She spent three to four hours daily at the sink and complained, "My hands look like lobster claws."

Psychoanalysts and social learning theorists broadly agree that compulsive behavior reduces anxiety. But psychoanalysts view obsessions as the leakage of unconscious impulses, and compulsions as acts that allow people to keep such impulses partly repressed. Social learning theorists focus on how obsessions and compulsions themselves may allow the person to avoid a feared or unwanted event. Social learning theorists also suggest that some obsessions or compulsions may be repeated because they have been reinforced.

Dissociative Disorders (Hysterical Neuroses, Dissociative Type)

The DSM-III lists three major dissociative disorders: *psychogenic amnesia, psychogenic fugue,* and *multiple personality.* In each case there is a sudden, temporary change in consciousness or self-identity.

Psychogenic Amnesia

In **psychogenic amnesia,** important personal information cannot be recalled. The memory problem cannot be attributed to organic problems such as a blow to the head or alcoholic intoxication. Thus it is *psycho*genic. The person may not be able to recall events for a number of hours after a stressful incident, as during warfare or in the case of the uninjured survivor of an accident. In generalized amnesia, people forget their entire lives. Amnesia may last for hours or years. Termination of amnesia is also sudden.

Bower (1981) wrote that Sirhan Sirhan, the assassin of Robert Kennedy, was amnesiac for his crime and could only reconstruct the events of the fateful day during hypnosis. As noted many times in this book, we cannot enter the mind of another person, and must therefore evaluate their claims—like Sirhan's claim of amnesia—on the basis of other evidence, such as behavioral observations and records of past behavior. People may claim amnesia for crimes in the hope that they will be treated as ill or insane, rather than as criminal. **Forensic psychologist** Arthur Centor (1982) argues that in 11 years of practice he has not seen *one* confirmed case of psychogenic amnesia. Claims of multiple personality are similarly suspect.

Claiming to have a disease in order to escape responsibility is known as **malingering.** Current research methods cannot guarantee that we can distinguish malingerers from people who have dissociative disorders.

Psychogenic Fugue

In **psychogenic fugue,** the person shows loss of memory for the past, travels suddenly from his or her home or place of work, and assumes a new identity. Either the person does not think about the past, or reports a past filled with bogus memories that are not recognized as false.

Multiple Personality

Multiple personality is the name given that most fascinating disorder, described in the case of William Milligan. Several "personalities," each with distinct traits and memories, "occupy" the same person, with or without awareness of the others. In the celebrated case that became the subject of the

Psychogenic amnesia A dissociative disorder marked by loss of memory of self-identity. Skills and general knowledge are usually retained.

Forensic psychologist A psychologist who assists, or testifies in, the courts. (From the Latin *forensis,* meaning "public.")

Malingering Pretending to be ill in order to escape duty or work. (From a French word meaning "sickly.")

Psychogenic fugue (fyoog). A dissociative disorder in which one experiences amnesia, then flees to a new location and establishes a new life style. (From the Latin *fugere,* meaning "to flee.")

Multiple Personality. In the film *The Three Faces of Eve*, Joanne Woodward played three personalities in the same woman: the shy, inhibited Eve White (above, left); the flirtatious and promiscuous Eve Black (above, right); and a third personality ("Jane") who was healthy enough to accept her sexual and aggressive impulses and still maintain her sense of identity.

film *The Three Faces of Eve* (see photos on this page), a timid housewife named Eve White harbored two other personalities: Eve Black, a sexually aggressive, antisocial personality, and Jane, an emerging personality who was able to accept the existence of her primitive impulses, yet show socially appropriate behavior. Finally, the three faces merged into one: Jane. Ironically, Jane (Chris Sizemore, in real life) reportedly split into 22 personalities later on. Chris Sizemore now tours college campuses, discussing her past. Another publicized case is that of Sybil, a woman with 16 personalities, played by Sally Field in a recent film.

Theories of the Dissociative Disorders

Psychoanalytic Theory According to psychoanalytic theory, dissociative disorders involve massive use of repression (see Chapter 10) to prevent recognition of unacceptable impulses. In psychogenic amnesia and fugue, the person forgets a profoundly disturbing event or impulse. In multiple personality, people express unacceptable impulses through alternate personalities.

Social Learning Theory Social learning theorists generally regard dissociative disorders as conditions in which people learn *not to think* about disturbing acts or impulses in order to avoid feelings of guilt and shame. Technically speaking, *not thinking about these matters* is negatively reinforced by *removal* of aversive stimuli—guilt and shame.

Cognitive Theory From a cognitive perspective, the dissociative disorders may be explained in terms of where one focuses attention at a given time. Consider dissociative disorders from the perspectives of the role-playing and neodissociative theories of hypnosis, discussed in Chapter 4. Perhaps all of us are capable of acting "as if" something had not happened, or "as if" we were someone else. Perhaps all of us are capable of dividing our awareness so that we become unaware, at least temporarily, of events that we usually focus more attention on. As suggested in Chapter 4, perhaps the marvel is *not* that attention can be divided, but that human consciousness normally integrates experience into a meaningful whole.

Somatoform Disorders

In **somatoform disorders,** people show or complain of physical problems, like paralysis, pain, or the persistent belief that they have a serious disease, yet no evidence of a physical abnormality can be found. In this section we shall discuss two somatoform disorders: *conversion disorder*, and *hypochondriasis*.

Conversion Disorder (Hysterical Neurosis, Conversion Type)

If you lost the ability to see at night, or if your legs became paralyzed, you would show understandable concern. **Conversion disorders** like night blindness are major losses of, or changes in, physical functioning. But some victims show indifference to them, a remarkable feature referred to as **la belle indifférence.** Conversion disorders "convert" a source of stress into a physical problem. They are rare and of short duration, but their existence led the young Sigmund Freud to believe that subconscious processes were at work in people, as discussed in Chapters 4 and 9.

During World War II a number of bomber pilots developed night blindness. They could not carry out their nighttime missions, although no damage to the optic nerves was found. In rare cases, women with large families have been reported to become paralyzed in the legs with no medical findings.

Somatoform disorders (so–MAT–toe–form). Disorders in which people complain of physical (somatic) problems, although no physical abnormality can be found.

Conversion disorders Disorders in which anxiety or unconscious conflicts are "converted" into physical symptoms which often have the effect of helping the person cope with anxiety or conflict.

La belle indifférence (lah bell an–DEEF–fay–ronce). A French term descriptive of the lack of concern sometimes shown by people with conversion disorders.

What, Me Hysterical? A Bit of Ancient (and All-too-Contemporary) Sexism

Conversion disorders were previously called *hysterical* conversion reactions. "Hysterical" or highly emotional, irrational people were thought likely to develop physical complaints as a result of stress. In an example of ancient sexism, such problems were apparently believed to be the exclusive province of women.

The Ancient Belief in the Wandering Uterus

Hysterical, you see, derives from the Greek word *hystera*, meaning "uterus" or "womb." The ancient Greeks viewed irritability and tension as female traits because some women encountered difficulties prior to and during menstruation (see Chapter 2). They attributed these problems to a wandering uterus! As the uterus roamed the body, they argued, it would cause pain and sensations in odd places. Men would never complain of such nonsense.

Of course, the Greeks had not met male pilots suffering from conversion blindness during World War II.

And Today . . . Unfortunately, many women today still find that legitimate physical complaints just prior to and during menstruation are treated as "hysterical" by a predominantly male medical establishment (see Rathus, 1983). We now know that hormonal changes that occur at various stages of a woman's menstrual cycle can cause many painful problems, and that these problems can often be alleviated if they receive proper treatment.

The DSM-III warns that even when the professional thinks that a complaint reflects a conversion disorder or hypochondriasis, every effort should be made to rule out a physical problem. A middle-aged woman with a "lump in the throat" was sent for psychological treatment because her physician thought the problem was "hysterical." The psychologist arranged for additional medical workup and a tumor was discovered. Physical complaints are not to be taken lightly.

Hypochondriasis
(high–poe–con–DRY–uh–sis).
Persistent belief that one has
a medical disorder despite
lack of medical findings.
(From a Greek word mean-
ing "the soft areas of the
body below the breast-
bone"—where anxious peo-
ple often feel a sense of
"heaviness.")

Dysthymic disorder
(dis–THIGH–mick). Feelings
of depression that persist for
at least two years. Also referred to as *depressive neurosis*.

Conversion disorders, like dissociative disorders, seem to serve a purpose. Their "blindness" may have afforded wartime pilots temporary relief
from stressful missions, or allowed them to avoid the guilt of bombing civilian
populations. The paralysis of a woman who prematurely commits herself to
a large family and a life at home may prevent her from engaging in house-
work—or in sexual intercourse—and becoming pregnant again. She "accom-
plishes" certain ends without having to admit to them or make decisions.

Hypochondriasis (Hypochondriacal Neurosis)

Persons with **hypochondriasis,** believe that they are suffering from one
or a host of serious diseases, although no medical evidence can be found.
Sufferers often become preoccupied with minor physical sensations, and
maintain an unrealistic belief that something is wrong despite medical reassurance. "Hypochondriacs" may go from doctor to doctor, seeking the one
who will find the causes of the sensations. The persistent fear may impair
work or home life.

Focusing on physical sensations and possible problems may serve the
function of taking the person's mind off other life problems. However, every
effort should be made to uncover real medical problems. Now and then a
supposed hypochondriac dies from something all too real.

Affective Disorders

The affective disorders are characterized by disturbance in expressed emotions. The disturbance generally involves depression or elation. We shall discuss three affective disorders: *dysthymic disorder*, *major depression*, and *bipolar disorder*.

Dysthymic Disorder (Depressive Neurosis)

Depression is the "common cold" of psychological problems, according
to Seligman (1973)—the most common psychological problem we face. Depressed people may feel sad, blue, or "down in the dumps." They may complain of lack of energy, loss of self-esteem, difficulty concentrating, loss of
interest in other people and usually enjoyable activities, pessimism, crying,
and thoughts of suicide.

Depression is a normal reaction to a loss or to exposure to unpleasant
events. One study found five major factors linked to feelings of depression:
marital discord, physical discomfort, incompetence, failure at work, and pressure at work (Lewinsohn & Amenson, 1978). UCLA psychologists Constance
Hammen and Arlene Mayol (1982) found that we are most likely to be depressed by events that are undesirable, and for which we feel responsible. In
addition to the factors found by Lewinsohn and Amenson, these include academic problems and dropping out of school; financial problems; unwanted
pregnancy; social problems, arguments, and fights; and conflict with the law.

But many people recover from losses less readily than the rest of us.
Other people seem to feel sad, helpless, guilty, and ashamed for little reason.
The DSM-III diagnoses depression as **dysthymic disorder** when it persists
for two years, even if intermittently relieved by normal moods, and when it is

not so severe that the person cannot meet most of the demands of daily life. We shall explore why depression may linger in some, when the rest of us seem to "snap back" from adversity, in the section on theories of depression.

Major Depressive Episode

To a large extent, the difference between dysthymic disorder and **major depression** is a matter of degree. In addition to the types of symptoms that define dysthymic disorder, people with major depression may show poor appetite and significant weight loss, agitation or severe **psychomotor retardation,** complaints of just "not caring" about anything anymore, and recurrent thoughts of death or suicide attempts.

Persons with major depression may also show impaired reality testing, or psychotic symptoms. These include delusions of unworthiness, guilt for imagined great wrongdoings, even ideas that one is rotting away from disease. There may also be hallucinations, as of the Devil administering just punishment or of strange sensations in the body.

Theories of Depression

Psychoanalytic Views Psychoanalysts suggest various explanations for depression. In one, depressed people are overly concerned about hurting others' feelings or losing their approval. They hold in rather than express feelings of anger. This anger-turned-inward is experienced as misery and self-hatred.

Social Learning Views Social learning theorists note similarities in behavior between people who are depressed and laboratory animals who are not reinforced for instrumental behavior. Inactivity and loss of interest result in each. Lewinsohn (1975) theorizes that depressed people often lack social and other skills that might lead to rewards. Some depressed people do have the social skills of nondepressed people, but they do not reinforce (credit) themselves as much as nondepressed people do for showing these skills (Gotlib, 1982).

Depression and Learned Helplessness Research stimulated by psychologist Martin Seligman and his colleagues has explored the links between depression and **learned helplessness.** In an early study, Seligman (1975) taught dogs that they were helpless to escape an electric shock by preventing them from leaving a cage in which they were shocked repeatedly. Later a barrier to a safe compartment was removed, allowing the animals a way out. But then when they were shocked again, the dogs made no effort to escape to safety. Apparently they had learned that they were helpless.

It can also be noted that the dogs were, in a sense, reinforced for doing nothing in this experiment. That is, the shock *eventually* stopped when the dogs were showing helpless behavior—inactivity and withdrawal. Thus they would have become likely to repeat their "successful behavior"—that is, doing nothing—in a similar situation. This helpless behavior resembles that of depressed people.

Further research suggests that the ways in which people interpret their shortcomings and failures can contribute to feelings of helplessness and, consequently, depression. From this perspective, cognitive factors play a central role in depression.

Depression and Attributional Style: Cognitive Factors   Depressed people tend to maintain low moods by attributing their failures and shortcomings to factors that they are helpless to change. Seligman and his colleagues note that when things go wrong, we may think of the causes of failure as *internal* or *external*, *stable* or *unstable*, *global* or *specific*.

Let us explain these various attributional styles through the example of having a date that does not work out. An internal attribution involves self-blame, as in "I really loused it up," whereas an external attribution places the blame elsewhere (as in "Some couples just don't take to each other," or, "She was the wrong sign for me"). Depressed people are more likely to attribute blame to internal causes—that is, to themselves—even when they are not to blame (Rizley, 1978).

A stable attribution ("It's my personality") suggests a problem that cannot be changed, while an unstable attribution ("It was the head cold") suggests a temporary condition. A global attribution of failure ("I have no idea what to do when I'm with people") suggests that the problem is quite large. A specific attribution ("I have problems making small talk at the very outset of a relationship") chops the problem down to a manageable size. A number of researchers (e.g., Miller and others, 1982; Peterson and others, 1981; Raps and others, 1982; Seligman and others, 1979) have found that many depressed people are more likely to attribute the causes of their failures to internal,

---

Headline: "Rats Take Dive!" Some Notes on Fight-Fixing at UCLA

They didn't sell popcorn. They didn't sell beer. But on the floor of the straw-covered arena, UCLA psychologist Gaylord Ellison's (1977) rats held wrestling match after match to determine who would be the champion—Numero Uno. For this is the way rats determine the pecking order of the colony. The winners earn the privileges of eating and choosing mates first.

One after another, rats in Ellison's experimental colonies paired off. First they would "stand and box." Then they would wrestle until one rat had been pinned to the ground. All this is normal rat behavior.

But this time Ellison was quite certain as to who the winners and losers would be. He had fixed the fights.

How? Ellison had injected some of the rats with a substance that depleted the norepinephrine (a neurotransmitter discussed in Chapter 2) available to their brains. The results? The "fixed" rats lost every match. They also showed behavior characteristic of depressed people. They appeared apathetic and withdrawn. They lay around listlessly in their burrows. Their appetites decreased and they lost weight.

Somehow the "depressed" rats were also socially disruptive. In one of Ellison's colonies, rats were given free access to water or alcohol solutions. Rats with lowered norepinephrine levels drank more water than alcohol. However, their colony-mates drank three times the amount of alcohol drunk by rats who did not have to live with norepinephrine-depleted rats. Does living with someone who is depressed eventually drive us to drink?

Stand and box   Top dog

---

stable, and global factors. These people not only exaggerate the amount of blame that should be attributed to them; they also view their problems as all but impossible to change. Is it any wonder that they are more likely than nondepressed people to feel helpless?

Organic Factors   Researchers are also searching for organic factors in depression. Seligman (1975), for example, found that dogs who had learned helplessness showed a decrease in the amount of norepinephrine (a neurotransmitter discussed in Chapter 2) available to the brain. Ellison (1977) found that rats with lowered levels of norepinephrine show behavior similar to that of depressed people (see box "Rats Take Dive!"). Helplessness and inactivity may therefore somehow lower norepinephrine levels. Once lowered, unfortunately, it could also be the case that norepinephrine deficiency tends to perpetuate inactivity.

As will be noted in Chapter 12, people whose depression has psychotic proportions often respond to antidepressant drugs. One effect of these drugs is the raising of norepinephrine levels, providing further evidence suggestive of a role for norepinephrine in depression. The relationships between depression and organic factors are complex and under intense study.

Bipolar Disorder (Manic-Depression)

In bipolar disorder, formerly known as manic-depression, there are mood swings from elation to depression. These cycles seem unrelated to external events. In the elated, or **manicky** phase, people may show excessive excitement or silliness, carrying jokes too far. They may show poor judgment, sometimes destroying property, and may be argumentative (Depue and others, 1981). Roommates may avoid them, finding them abrasive. Manicky people may speak rapidly and disclose unrealistically grand, delusional schemes. They may jump from topic to topic, showing **rapid flight of ideas.** They may show extreme generosity by making unusually large contributions to charity or giving away a car. They may not be able to sleep restfully or sit still.

Depression is the other side of the coin. Bipolar depressed patients often sleep more than usual and are lethargic. People showing major depression are more likely to show insomnia and agitation (Davison & Neale, 1982). They show social withdrawal and irritability. Some attempt suicide "on the way down," reporting that they fear again experiencing the full depths of depression.

Many researchers believe that bipolar disorder has an organic basis. It is more common among identical than fraternal twins and may well reflect excesses of norepinephrine. In Chapter 12 it will also be noted that the metal lithium helps flatten out manic-depressive cycles for many sufferers, apparently by lowering levels of norepinephrine.

Schizophrenic and Schizophreniform Disorders

Joyce was 19. Her boyfriend brought her into the emergency room because she had slit her wrists. When she was interviewed, her attention wandered. She seemed distracted by things in the air, or something she might be hearing. It was as if she had an invisible earphone.

She explained that she had cut her wrists because the "hellsmen" had told her to. Then she seemed frightened. Later she said that the hellsmen had

Manicky Elated, showing excessive excitement. (From the Greek *mania*, meaning "raging madness.")

Rapid flight of ideas Rapid speech and topic changes, characteristic of manicky behavior.

Autism Self-absorption. Absorption in daydreaming and fantasy. (From the Greek *autos*, meaning "self.")

Schizophreniform disorders (skits–oh–FRAY–knee–form). Disorders that resemble (have the *form* of) schizophrenic disorders, but whose symptoms are of relatively brief duration.

Brief reactive psychosis A psychotic episode less than two weeks in duration that follows a known stressful event.

Prognosis A prediction of the probable course of a disorder. (From the Greek *pro-*, meaning "forward," and *gignoskein*, meaning "to know.")

Delusions of grandeur (GRAND–your). Erroneous beliefs that one is a "grand" person, like Jesus or like a secret agent on a special mission.

warned her not to reveal their existence. She had been afraid that they would punish her for talking about them.

Her boyfriend told the psychiatrist that Joyce had been living with him for about a year. At first they had been together in a small apartment in town. But Joyce did not want to be near other people and had convinced him to rent a bungalow in the country. There she would make fantastic drawings of goblins and monsters during the days. Now and then she would become agitated and act as if invisible things were giving her instructions.

"I'm bad," Joyce would mutter, "I'm bad." She would begin to jumble her words. Ron, the boyfriend, would then try to convince her to go to the hospital, but she would refuse. Then the wrist-cutting would begin. Ron thought he had made the cottage safe by removing knives and blades. But Joyce would always find something.

Then Joyce would be brought to the hospital, have stitches put in, be kept under observation and medicated. She would explain that she cut herself because the hellsmen had told her she was bad and must die. After a few days she would deny hearing the hellsmen and insist on leaving the hospital.

Ron would take her home. The pattern continued.

When the admitting psychiatrist examined Joyce's wrists and heard that she believed she had been following the orders of "hellsmen," he began to suspect that she was suffering from a schizophrenic disorder. Schizophrenic behavior is characterized by disturbances in (1) thought; (2) perception and attention; (3) motor activity; (4) mood; and by (5) withdrawal and **autism.**

Schizophrenic vs. Schizophreniform Disorders

The DSM-III differentiates between schizophrenic and **schizophreniform disorders**—that is, disorders that resemble schizophrenic disorders but are assumed to be different because of duration. Schizophrenic disorders must have a duration of at least six months, and the person is likely to undergo a chronic course of deterioration. Schizophreniform disorders have a briefer duration (two weeks to six months), and the person is more likely to return to normal levels of functioning. A third diagnosis of **brief reactive psychosis** is used when the person has shown the disorder for less than two weeks, and the disorder follows a known stressful event.

In general, the more rapid the onset of the disorder, the more bizarre the behavior of the individual and the better the predicted outcome, or **prognosis.** The reasoning is that if the onset has been abrupt, especially in response to a stressor that can be identified, the disorder is less likely to reflect an unrelenting inner *process* of deterioration. Many researchers believe that biological processes are involved in schizophrenic disorders, but perhaps not in schizophreniform disorders and brief reactive psychoses. Researchers have found that people who show higher levels of stressful life events prior to the onset of the disorder (whose disorders are thus more likely to be *reactive)* do show a better prognosis (e.g., Harder and others, 1981).

Symptoms of Schizophrenic Disorders

Schizophrenic disorders are known primarily by disturbances in thought, which are largely inferred from verbal behavior. Schizophrenic persons may show illogical and incoherent thought processes, and they usually do not have insight that their thoughts and behavior are abnormal. They may have **delusions of grandeur,** persecution, or reference. With delusions of grandeur, the person may believe he is Jesus or a person on a special mission, or may have grand, illogical plans for saving the world. Persons with delusions of persecution may believe that they are being sought by the Mafia, CIA, FBI, or some other group or agency. A woman with delusions of reference expressed the belief that national news broadcasts contained coded information about her. A man with such delusions complained that neighbors had "bugged" his walls with "radios."

The perceptions of schizophrenics often include hallucinations—imagery in the absence of external stimulation that the schizophrenic cannot distinguish from reality. Joyce believed she heard "hellsmen." Others may see colors or even obscene words spelled out in midair. Auditory hallucinations are most common.

Motor activity may become wild and excited or slow to a **stupor.** There may be strange gestures and peculiar facial expressions. There may be *grooming*—as in repeatedly touching the hair or face or adjusting the clothing (Fairbanks and others, 1982). Emotional response may be **flat** or blunted, or inappropriate—as in giggling at bad news. Schizophrenics tend to withdraw from social contacts and become wrapped up in their own thoughts and fantasies.

Subtypes of Schizophrenia

The DSM-III lists three major types of schizophrenia: *disorganized* (called "hebephrenic" schizophrenia in the DSM-II); *catatonic*; and *paranoid*. The DSM-II category, *simple schizophrenia*, is now diagnosed as **schizotypal personality disorder** because of the absence of bizarre psychotic behaviors. Still persons with schizotypal personality disorders may show some "oddities" of thought, perception, and behavior, such as excessive fantasy and suspiciousness, feelings of being unreal, or odd usage of words (DSM-III, p. 312).

Disorganized Type **Disorganized schizophrenics** tend to have disorganized delusions and vivid, abundant hallucinations that are often sexual or religious. A 23-year-old female disorganized schizophrenic remarked "I see 'pennis.'" She pointed vaguely into the air before her. Asked to spell *pennis*, she replied irritatedly: "P–e–n–i–s." Apparently her social background was so inhibited that she had never heard the word for the male sexual organ spoken aloud; and so she mispronounced it. Extreme social impairment is common among disorganized schizophrenics. They also often show silliness and giddiness of mood, giggling and speaking nonsensically. They may neglect their appearance and hygiene, and lose control of their bladder and their bowels.

Catatonic Type **Catatonic schizophrenics** show striking impairment in motor activity. It is characterized by slowing of activity into a stupor that may change suddenly into an agitated phase. Catatonic individuals may hold unusual, even difficult postures for hours, even as their limbs grow swollen or stiff. A striking symptom is **waxy flexibility,** in which they maintain positions into which they have been manipulated by others. Immobile catatonic individuals usually will not respond to the speech of others. But after an episode of immobility they usually report that they heard what others were saying at the time.

Paranoid Type **Paranoid schizophrenics** are characterized by the content of their delusions. They usually show delusions of grandeur and persecution,

Stupor A condition in which the senses and thought are dulled. (From the Latin *stupidus*, meaning "stunned" or "amazed.")

Flat Monotonous, dull.

Schizotypal personality disorder (skit–so–TYPE–al). A disorder characterized by oddities of thought and behavior, but not involving bizarre psychotic symptoms. Formerly called *simple schizophrenia.*

Disorganized schizophrenics Schizophrenics who show disorganized delusions and vivid hallucinations. Formerly called *hebephrenic schizophrenics.*

Catatonic schizophrenics Schizophrenics who show striking impairment in motor activity. (From the Greek *kata*-, meaning "downward," and *tonos*, meaning "tension"—suggesting loss of muscle activity.)

Waxy flexibility A symptom of catatonic schizophrenia in which persons maintain postures into which they are placed.

Paranoid schizophrenia A type of schizophrenia characterized primarily by delusions—commonly of persecution—and by vivid hallucinations.

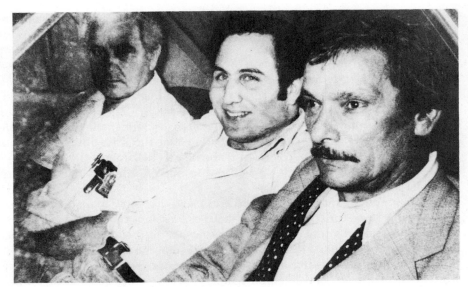

David Berkowitz, the "Son of Sam" Killer, smiles benignly upon his arrest in 1977. Does his response to arrest seem appropriate? Because of his inappropriate emotional responses and his claim that a dog had urged him to commit his crimes, many mental-health professionals considered him schizophrenic.

but may also show delusions of jealousy, in which they believe that a spouse or lover has been unfaithful. They may show agitation, confusion, and fear, and experience vivid hallucinations that are consistent with their delusions. The paranoid schizophrenic often constructs a complex or systematized delusion involving themes of wrongdoing or persecution.

A rarely used, related diagnostic category is **paranoia.** People may receive this diagnosis if they show a permanent, "unshakable" delusional system but do not show the confused, jumbled thinking or hallucinations suggestive of schizophrenia. Daily functioning in paranoia and in some cases of paranoid schizophrenia may be minimally impaired, or not impaired at all, so long as the person does not act on the basis of his or her delusions.

Possible Causes of Schizophrenia

Psychologists have investigated various factors that may contribute to schizophrenic disorders. In this section we consider socioeconomic, psychoanalytic, social learning, genetic, and biochemical possibilities.

Socioeconomic Status   Schizophrenia is most common among lower socioeconomic groups that inhabit the inner cities (e.g., Hollingshead & Redlich, 1958). Sociocultural theorist R. D. Laing argues that poverty and social injustice cause schizophrenia. According to him, schizophrenia "is a special sort of strategy that a person invents in order to live in an unlivable situation" (1964, p. 186).

Critics argue that Laing's view confuses correlation with cause and effect. It may be that the causal relationship between schizophrenia and social status, if any, works in the opposite direction. Schizophrenia may lead to lowered social status. There is considerable evidence that schizophrenics tend to drift downward in socioeconomic standing (Turner & Wagonfield, 1967).

Paranoia A major but rare disorder in which a person shows a persistent delusional system, but not the confusion of the schizophrenic.

Psychoanalytic Theory Psychoanalytic theorists view schizophrenia as the overwhelming of the ego by impulses of the id. The impulses are typically hostile or sexual. They threaten the ego and lead to intense intrapsychic conflict. Under this threat the person regresses to an early phase of the oral stage, **primary narcissism,** a state of self-absorption in which the infant has not yet learned that it and the world are separate and distinct. Fantasies become confused with reality, giving birth to hallucinations and delusions. Primitive impulses may carry more weight than social norms.

Critics point out that schizophrenic behavior is not that similar to infantile behavior. Moreover, psychoanalysts have not predicted accurately what sorts of early experiences will later cause schizophrenic disorders.

Social Learning Theory Social learning theorists explain schizophrenia through conditioning and observational learning. People show schizophrenic behavior when it is more likely than normal behavior to be reinforced. This may occur when the person is raised in a socially nonrewarding or punitive situation; inner fantasies then become more reinforcing than social realities.

In the hospital, patients may learn what is "expected" of them by observing other patients. Hospital staff may reinforce schizophrenic behavior by paying more attention to patients who behave bizarrely. This view is consistent with folklore that the child who disrupts the class earns more attention from the teacher than does the quiet, cooperative child.

Critics note that many of us grow up in socially punitive settings, but seem to show immunity to having socially appropriate responses extinguished. And some acquire schizophrenic behavior patterns without having had the opportunity to observe other schizophrenics.

Genetic Factors There is a decided tendency for schizophrenic disorders to run in families. Children of schizophrenic parents are at greater than normal risks for showing certain behaviors at early ages. In a research program referred to as the *New York Project*, for example, it has been found that these children show more difficulty in social relationships, more emotional instability, and less academic motivation than control children between the ages of 12 and 17 (Watt and others, 1982).

Persons with schizophrenic disorders constitute about one percent of the population, but children with two schizophrenic parents have about a 35 percent chance of becoming schizophrenic (Rosenthal, 1970). Most studies show that the identical twins of schizophrenics also show a high probability of being diagnosed as schizophrenic. A pair of individuals who receive the same diagnosis are called **concordant.** In various studies, the concordance rate for the diagnoses of the identical twins of schizophrenics has been found as high as 75 (Kallmann, 1946) to 86 percent (Essen-Möller, 1941). The concordance rate for fraternal twins, whose genetic endowments are not identical, has dropped off dramatically, but is still at above-chance levels.

It has been pointed out quite properly that the above studies have not controlled for environmental influences. Children raised in the same family have similar environments. Parents (and outsiders) often expect (and encourage) identical behavior from identical twins. To overcome this objection, studies have been done to determine whether the natural or adoptive parents of adopted children have a greater influence on the likelihood of their being judged schizophrenic (e.g., Heston, 1966; Wender and others, 1974). In such studies, the biological parent typically places the child at greater risk than

Primary narcissism (NAR–sis–izm). In psychoanalytic theory, the type of autism thought to describe the newborn child who has not yet learned that he or she and the world are separate and distinct. (From the mythical Greek figure *Narkissos,* who fell in love with his own reflected image.)

Concordant In agreement. (From the Latin *com*-, meaning "together," and *cor,* meaning "heart.")

Dopamine A neurotransmitter that seems implicated in the origins of schizophrenia. See Chapter 2. (Acronym for *dihydroxyphenylamine.*)

Amphetamines Stimulants whose overusage can lead to symptoms that mimic schizophrenia. See Chapter 4.

does the adoptive parent—even though the child has not been raised by the biological parent.

While evidence for a genetic role in schizophrenia seems strong, heredity cannot be the sole factor. If it were, there would be a 100 percent concordance rate for schizophrenia between pairs of identical twins. Genetics may establish a predisposition toward schizophrenia that at least sometimes must interact with other factors if the individual is to show a schizophrenic disorder. Perhaps heredity creates a predisposition for biochemical factors such as those discussed in the following section.

Biochemical Factors   Over the years numerous substances have been thought to play a role in schizophrenic disorders. Current theory and research focuses on the neurotransmitter **dopamine.**

The excess-dopamine theory of schizophrenia evolved from observation of the effects of **amphetamines**, a group of stimulants discussed in Chapter 4. Researchers are confident that amphetamines act by increasing the quantity of dopamine in the brain (see Chapter 2 for a fuller discussion of neurotransmitters). High doses of amphetamines lead to behavior that mimics paranoid

On Being Sane in Insane Places

What's one way to guarantee admission to a mental ward? Just show up at a hospital claiming to hear the words *empty, hollow,* and *thud.* Psychologist David Rosenhan (1973) of Stanford University coached volunteers—psychologists, physicians, a painter, and a housewife—to show up at different institutions with the single symptom. They claimed no other problems—just hearing *empty, hollow,* and *thud.*

Although the single symptom of hallucinations was not enough, according to the edition of the DSM (II) in use at the time, to make the diagnosis of schizophrenia, all but one of the phony patients was admitted with a diagnosis of schizophrenia. The other was admitted as showing a bipolar disorder. An early finding of the Rosenhan study was that many clinicians are quick to "jump at" a diagnosis on the basis of a prominent "symptom."

Following admission, the phony patients no longer claimed to hear voices and behaved normally in every way. But because they made no serious effort to gain discharge, they remained hospitalized for an average stay of 19 days. You can interpret this average stay as administrative and staff sloppiness, caution and concern for patients with possible serious problems, or a combination of both.

During their stays, no psychiatrists or other staff members became suspicious of the phony patients. But other *patients* had noticed that they were taking notes and later reported wondering if some of them were journalists or professors "checking up on the hospital."

Upon discharge the diagnosis was schizophre-

nia—"in remission" (that is, no longer showing symptoms). Even though the phony patients were totally symptom-free, the diagnosis of schizophrenia, once made, stuck like glue. Once people are admitted to the mental-health system and become "patients" and receive diagnostic labels, it may be that there is a tendency to treat the label and not the person. (How do *you* treat people once you label them "impossible," "not for me," or "one of *them?*")

Rosenhan's volunteers were not mistreated on their wards, but other patients were, sometimes for minor things like initiating verbal interaction. Even so, their movements, liberty, and privacy were restricted (one of the reasons that Thomas Szasz finds the concept of "mental illness" degrading). They might be observed while bathing or using the toilet. Staff avoided eye contact with them, apparently not allowing themselves to get "too close," and shepherded them mechanically from place to place and activity to activity.

Studies such as this find that some people can be warehoused rather than treated once admitted to a mental institution. Staff can also be quite insensitive to individual patient needs. Abuses like these—even when staff are well-intentioned—may now and then make the hospital experience more harmful than helpful. To correct such abuses, recent lawsuits have guaranteed that patients have a right to treatment. The community mental health movement has also made every effort to maintain patients in their homes, whenever possible, cutting the rolls of mental hospitals in half in recent years (Jones, 1975).

schizophrenia in normal people (Snyder and others, 1974). They also exacerbate the symptoms of schizophrenics (Angrist and others, 1974).

An additional, but also indirect, source of evidence for the excess-dopamine theory lies in the commonly held view that the **phenothiazines,** a class of drugs that are effective in many cases of schizophrenic and schizophreniform disorders, act by blocking the action of dopamine (Randrup & Munkvard, 1972). If lowering the quantity of dopamine in the brain reduces schizophrenic symptoms, it may be that these symptoms result from excess dopamine.

Future research may suggest that schizophrenia has multiple causes. Genetic biochemical factors may set the stage for some borderline individuals to display schizophrenic symptoms in response to impoverished environments or severe stressors. Other people may be so severely handicapped by biochemical factors that they will develop schizophrenic disorders under the most positive conditions.

Personality Disorders

Personality disorders, like personality traits, are enduring patterns of behavior. Personality disorders, however, are inflexible and maladaptive. They impair personal or social functioning, and are a source of distress to the individual or to others.

There are a number of personality disorders. We shall focus on the **antisocial personality,** but let us briefly note some other types that are similar to paranoia and schizophrenic disorders, but do not involve such gross impairment in reality testing. The *paranoid personality* is characterized by pervasive mistrust and suspicion. The *schizoid personality* is characterized by inability to form social relationships and absence of warm, tender feelings for others. Hallucinations and delusions are absent (as they also are in the schizotypal personality disorder, discussed earlier).

The Antisocial Personality

Persons with antisocial personalities are frequently referred to as **sociopaths** or **psychopaths.** Sociopathy is a fascinating social problem. The sociopath persistently violates the rights of others, shows indifference to commitments, and encounters conflict with the law. Cleckley (1964) notes that sociopaths often show a superficial charm and are at least average in intelligence. Perhaps their most striking feature, given their antisocial behavior, is their lack of guilt and low level of anxiety. Sociopaths seem largely undeterred

Phenothiazine (fee–no–THIGH–uh–zeen). A family of drugs that are effective in treatment of many cases of schizophrenia.

Personality disorders Enduring patterns of maladaptive behavior that are a source of distress to the individual or others.

Antisocial personality The diagnosis given a person who is in frequent conflict with society yet is undeterred by punishment and experiences little or no guilt and anxiety.

Sociopath A term for a person who shows an antisocial personality disorder.

Psychopath Another term for a person who shows an antisocial personality disorder.

TABLE 11.4   **Characteristics of the Antisocial Personality**

Persistent violation of the rights of others	History of delinquency
Irresponsibility as parents	History of running away
Lack of formation of enduring relationships or loyalty to another person	Persistent lying
	Sexual promiscuity
Failure to maintain good job performance over the years	Substance abuse
	Impulsivity
Failure to develop or adhere to a life plan	Inability to tolerate boredom
History of truancy	Onset of traits before age 15

Source: DSM-III (1980)

by punishment. Though they are likely to have earned disapproval, and often physical punishment, from others from childhood, they continue in impulsive, irresponsible styles of life.

A nineteenth-century mental-health worker described sociopaths as "morally insane." He realized that sociopaths suffered from no impairment in reality testing, but they seemed indifferent to the misery they inflicted.

Possible Causes of Sociopathy   Various factors appear to contribute to sociopathy, including a sociopathic father, lack of love and parental rejection during childhood, and inconsistent discipline.

Sociopathy tends to run in families. Early research in family influences, however, did not control for the possibility that the contributing factor was the family environment, and not genetics. Recent studies with adopted children found higher incidences of sociopathy among the biological rather than the adoptive relatives of sociopaths (Cadoret, 1978; Crowe, 1974; Hutchings & Mednick, 1974; Schulsinger, 1972).

Some researchers have suggested that one genetic factor in sociopathy was an extra Y sex chromosome. So-called **supermales,** with an XYY chromosomal structure, were thought to have a predisposition toward aggressiveness and crime. Supermales as a group are somewhat taller and more heavily bearded than XY males, but only about 1.5 percent of male delinquents and criminals tested show the XYY structure (Rosenthal, 1970). Moreover, there is no evidence that most supermales engage in crime or violence.

A more promising avenue of research, with genetic implications, suggests that sociopaths are unlikely to show anxiety or be deterred by punishment because they have lower-than-normal levels of arousal (Lykken, 1957, 1982). In typical experiments on this question, sociopaths of equal intelligence do not learn as rapidly as other subjects to avoid an impending electric shock. Once the levels of arousal of the sociopaths are increased by injections of adrenalin, they do engage in avoidance learning as rapidly as others (Schachter & Latané, 1964; Chesno & Kilmann, 1975). These findings tie in with the observation that many sociopaths are "thrill seekers"—taking high risks, racing motorcycles, fighting, and so on—who have no tolerance for boredom. It may be that dangerous, reckless activity raises their levels of arousal to more optimal and comfortable levels.

A genetically transmitted lower-than-normal level of arousal would not guarantee that a person would become sociopathic. It may also be necessary that a person be raised under conditions that do not foster development of the identity of a person who abides by the law and social norms. Punishment for deviation from the norm would then be unlikely to induce feelings of guilt and shame. The individual might be "undeterred" by punishment.

Before ending this section, we must note one further finding with sociopaths. The one form of punishment that does seem effective with many is loss of money (Schmauk, 1970). Do we need any further evidence that sociopaths are not out of touch with reality?

Supermale A male with XYY chromosomal structure.

Gender identity disorders Disorders in which a person's anatomic sex is inconsistent with his or her sense of being male or female.

Psychosexual Disorders

The DSM-III lists four classes of psychosexual disorders: *gender identity disorders, paraphilias, psychosexual dysfunctions,* and "others," which includes ego-dystonic homosexuality. In **gender identity disorders,** one feels uncomfortable with his or her anatomic sex. In the **paraphilias,** people show sexual arousal in response to unusual or bizarre objects or situations. We shall discuss sexual adjustment problems, or dysfunctions, in Chapter 13. We explored some issues concerning ego-dystonic homosexuality earlier. Here we shall focus on the gender identity disorder of *transsexualism* and on a number of paraphilias.

Transsexualism

About 30 years ago headlines were made when an ex-GI, now known as Christine Jorgensen, had a "sex-change operation" in Denmark. Since that time some 2,500 American transsexuals, including tennis player Dr. Renée Richards, have undergone sex-reassignment surgery. Sex-reassignment surgery is cosmetic. It cannot actually change one's gender by implanting reproductive organs of the opposite sex, but it can create the appearance of the external genitals of the opposite sex—more successfully with male-to-female than female-to-male transsexuals. After these operations, transsexuals can engage in sexual activity and reach orgasm, but they cannot have children.

Transsexualism is the persistent feeling that one is of the wrong sex. Transsexuals wish to be rid of their own genitals and live as members of the opposite sex. They do not see themselves as homosexuals, even though they are sexually attracted to members of their own anatomic sex. This is because they view nature's assignment as a mistake; they see themselves as "trapped" inside a body of the wrong sex.

Paraphilias (par–uh–FEEL–ee–uhs). Disorders in which people show sexual arousal in response to unusual or bizarre objects or situations. (From the Greek *para-,* meaning "alongside," and *philos,* meaning "loving.")

Transsexualism A gender identity disorder in which a person feels trapped in the body of the wrong sex. (The Latin prefix *trans-* means "across.")

Transsexualism. Physician Richard Raskin underwent sex reassignment surgery and became Renée Richards. A minor sensation was created when Renée competed as a woman on the women's tennis circuit. But Renée's game was less than spectacular, and she gradually faded from public notice.

The causes of transsexualism are unclear, but there are broad psychological and organic views. It may be that some transsexuals are raised by disappointed parents as children of the opposite sex. But it is also possible that some transsexuals have been influenced by prenatal hormonal imbalances. It may be that the human brain can be "masculinized" or "feminized" by sex hormones at certain stages of development in the womb, and that some fetuses are exposed to hormonal "imbalances" produced by themselves or their mothers at critical periods. (See Chapters 2 and 13 for further discussion of sex hormones.)

A recent study of 42 postoperative male-to-female transsexuals found that all but one would repeat the surgery, and the great majority found sexual activity more pleasurable as a "woman" (Bentler, 1976). Most female-to-male transsexuals rate their adjustment as positive, and are solid workers and tax payers (Person & Ovesey, 1974; Randall, 1969). Despite difficulties in surgically constructing structures that serve as external male sexual organs, a recently studied group of 22 postoperative female-to-male transsexuals were generally satisfied with their new bodies (Fleming and others, 1982).

Paraphilias: Variations in Choice of Sexual Object and Activity

The paraphilias we shall discuss include *fetishism*, *transvestism*, *zoophilia*, *pedophilia*, *exhibitionism*, *voyeurism*, *sexual masochism*, and *sexual sadism*.

Fetishism **Fetishism** is sexual response to a bodily part, like feet, or an inanimate object, such as an article of clothing. Sexual gratification is often achieved through masturbating in the presence of the object. Fetishes for undergarments and for objects made of leather, rubber, or silk are not uncommon.

Transvestism **Transvestism** is recurrent, persistent dressing in clothing usually worn by the opposite sex in order to achieve sexual excitement. Transvestism may range from wearing a single female undergarment in private to sporting full dress at a transvestite club. Most transvestites are heterosexual and married, but they seek additional sexual gratification through dressing as women.

Zoophilia **Zoophilia,** or *bestiality*, is sexual contact with animals as a preferred or exclusive means of achieving sexual arousal. Thus, a child or adolescent who shows some sexual response to an episode of rough-and-tumble play with the family pet is rarely showing zoophilia.

Pedophilia **Pedophilia** is actual or fantasized sexual activity with children as a preferred means of becoming sexually aroused. Most episodes are not coerced and involve exhibitionism or fondling rather than sexual intercourse.

Exhibitionism **Exhibitionism** is the repetitive act of exposing one's genitals to a stranger in order to surprise or shock, rather than sexually arouse, the victim. The exhibitionist is usually not interested in actual sexual contact with the victim. He may masturbate while fantasizing about or actually exposing himself.

Fetishism A variation of choice in sexual object in which a bodily part (like a foot) or an inanimate object (like an undergarment) elicits sexual arousal and is preferred to a person. (From the Portuguese *feitico*, meaning "a charm" as used in witchcraft.)

Transvestism Recurrent, persistent dressing in clothing worn by the opposite sex for purposes of sexual excitement. (From the Latin *trans-*, meaning "across," and *vestis*, meaning "garment.")

Zoophilia (zoe–oh–FEEL–ee–uh). Sexual contact with animals as a preferred source of sexual excitement. Also called *bestiality*.

Pedophilia (pea–doe–FEEL–ee–uh). Sexual contact with children as the preferred source of sexual excitement. (From the Greek *pais*, meaning "child," *philia*, meaning "loving.")

Exhibitionism The compulsion to expose one's genitals in public. (From the Latin *ex-*, meaning "out of," and *habere*, meaning "to hold.")

Professional strip-teasers and scantily-clad swimmers do not fit the definition of exhibitionist. Both groups may seek to sexually arouse, but usually not to shock, observers. The major motive of the strip-teaser may also be simply to earn a living.

Voyeurism   **Voyeurism** is repetitive watching of unsuspecting strangers while they are undressing or engaging in sexual activity as the preferred or exclusive means of achieving sexual arousal. We may enjoy observing spouses undress, or even the nudity in an R-rated film, without being diagnosed as voyeurs. In voyeurism, the "victim" does not know that he or she is being watched, and the voyeur prefers looking to doing.

Sexual Masochism   **Masochism** is named after the Austrian storyteller Leopold von Sacher-Masoch, who portrayed sexual satisfaction as deriving from pain or humiliation. The sexual masochist must receive pain or humiliation in order to achieve sexual gratification. It has been suggested that many masochists experience guilt about sex, but can enjoy sex so long as they see themselves as being appropriately punished for it.

Sexual Sadism   **Sadism** is named after the infamous Marquis de Sade, a Frenchman who wrote stories about the pleasures of achieving sexual gratification by inflicting pain or humiliation on others. In sadism, the person may not be able to become sexually excited unless he inflicts pain on his partner.

Psychological Explanations of the Paraphilias   According to psychoanalytic theory, paraphilias are defenses against anxiety. The exhibitionist, for example, has unconscious castration anxiety. His victim's shock at his exposure reassures him that he does, after all, have a penis. Fetishism, pedophilia, and so on protect him from fear of failure in adult heterosexual relationships.

Rathus (1983) offers a modified social learning view of fetishism and other paraphilias. First, a fantasized or actual event—like being sexually excited when discovered by a woman while urinating behind a bush—gives the person the idea that an unusual object or situation is sexually arousing. Second, the object is used in actuality or fantasy to heighten sexual arousal. Third, recognition of the "deviance" of the fantasy or act may cause feelings of anxiety or guilt. These feelings, if not extreme, may further increase emotional arousal in response to the object or activity. Heightened emotional response may then be *attributed* to the deviant object or activity. Fourth, orgasm reinforces the preceding behaviors and fantasies involving the object or activity. Fifth, in cases where a person is anxious about adult heterosexual relationships, the deviant object or activity may become the major or sole sexual outlet.

Suicide

Note a number of facts about suicide:

- Suicide is more common among college students than among nonstudents. About 10,000 college students attempt suicide each year.
- Suicide is the second leading cause of death among college students.
- Nearly 200,000 people attempt suicide each year in the United States. About one in 10 succeeds.

Voyeurism Attainment of sexual gratification through observing others undress or engage in sexual activity. (From the French *voir*, meaning "to see.")

Masochism Attainment of sexual gratification through receiving pain or humiliation.

Sadism Attainment of sexual gratification through inflicting pain or humiliation on sex partners.

- Three times as many women as men attempt suicide, but three times as many men succeed.
- Men prefer to use guns or hang themselves, but women prefer to use sleeping pills.
- Young blacks and native Americans are more than twice as likely as whites to commit suicide.
- Suicide is especially common among physicians, lawyers, and psychologists, although it is found among all occupational groups and at all age levels.
- No other cause of death leaves such feelings of guilt, distress, and puzzlement in friends and relatives.

Possible Causes of Suicide

Why do people take their own lives? An estimated 80 to 94 percent of suicides are linked to depression (Barraclough and others, 1969; Robins and others, 1959; Leonard, 1977; Schotte & Clum, 1982). Although most people who attempt suicide show hopelessness and despair, they do not appear out of touch with reality (Leonard, 1974).

Strongly suicidal women report finding life more dull, empty, and boring than do less or nonsuicidal women. They feel more anxious, angry, guilt-ridden, helpless, and inadequate than other women (Neuringer, 1982). In a Boston University study, college women who had attempted suicide were more likely than their peers to implicate their parents as a source of anger or conflict that led to the attempt (Cantor, 1976). They were also less likely to feel able to ask parents or others for help when they felt desperate or under great stress.

Suicide attempts are more frequent following a number of stressful life events, especially "exit events" (Slater & Depue, 1981). Exit events involve loss of social support—as in death, divorce, separation, a family member's leaving home, or the loss of an unrelated but significant person. People who consider suicide following stressful experiences have also been found less capable of solving problems than are those who do not consider suicide (Schotte & Clum, 1982). That is, they are less likely to think of more productive ways to cope with stress.

Some suicides are quite logical (Shneidman & Farberow, 1970), as in the case of a terminally ill patient in unrelenting pain, whose spouse has died and who feels like a burden to the family. Suicide may be ceremonial, as in the case of Japanese Samurai warriors who chose suicide over dishonor. A few suicides stem from thought disorders, as in paranoid schizophrenia or a "bad trip" induced by drugs. Joyce, discussed earlier, believed that "hellsmen" had ordered her to kill herself.

Myths about Suicide

Some believe that people who threaten suicide are only seeking attention. The serious just "do it." Actually 70 to 80 percent of suicides gave warnings within three months prior to the act (Stengel, 1964; Leonard, 1977). Forty percent of attempters had visited a mental-health worker the previous week (Yessler and others, 1961).

Some believe that those who fail at suicide attempts are only seeking attention. But 75 percent of successful suicides had made prior attempts (Cohen and others, 1966). Contrary to myth, discussion of suicide with a depressed person does not prompt suicide. In fact, extracting a promise that the person will not commit suicide before calling or visiting a mental-health worker seems to have prevented some cases of suicide.

Some believe that only insane people (meaning people who are out of touch with reality, or psychotics) would take their own lives. However, only a minority of suicides have thought disorders or psychotic affective disorders. Finally, most people with suicidal thoughts, contrary to myth, will *not* act on them. Suicidal thoughts at a time of great stress are not uncommon.

Preventing Suicide

If someone tells you he or she is considering suicide, you may feel frightened and flustered, or that an enormous burden has been placed on you. In such cases, your objective should be to encourage the person to consult a professional mental health worker, or to consult a worker yourself as soon as possible. But if the person refuses to talk to anyone else and you feel that you can't break free for a consultation, there are a number of things you can do:

- Draw the person out. Perhaps ask, "Why do you feel that way?" This gives you time to assess the danger and think.
- Be empathetic. Show that you understand how upset the person is. Do *not* say, "Don't be silly."
- Suggest that measures other than suicide might be found to solve the problem, even if they are not evident at the time.
- Ask how the person intends to commit suicide. People with concrete plans and the weapon are at greater risk. Ask if you might hold on to the weapon for a while. Sometimes the person says yes.
- Suggest that the person go *with you* to obtain professional help *now*. The emergency room of a general hospital, the campus counseling center or infirmary, the campus or local police will do. Some campuses have "hot lines" you can call. Some cities have suicide prevention centers with hot lines that people can use anonymously.
- Extract a promise that the person will not commit suicide before seeing you again. Arrange a concrete time and place to meet. Get professional help as soon as you are apart.
- Do *not* tell people threatening suicide that they're silly or crazy. Do *not* insist on contact with specific people, like parents or a spouse. Conflict with these people may have led to the suicidal thinking.

A Suicide-Prevention "Hot Line." At suicide prevention centers across the country, trained staff man hot lines around the clock. If someone you know threatens suicide, consult a professional as soon as possible.

In Chapter 12 we shall see how psychologists and other professionals help people who are showing various forms of abnormal behavior.

Summary

The term *abnormal* may be applied to behavior that is unusual or infrequent, socially unacceptable, involving faulty perception of reality, dangerous, self-defeating, or personally distressing. There are several models for explaining abnormal behavior: demonology (the most prevalent model throughout history), the medical model (organic and psychoanalytic subtypes), the social learning model, and the sociocultural model. Adherents to the medical model see abnormal behavior as symptomatic of underlying organic or psychoanalytic disorders. Social learning theorists see abnormal behaviors as acquired through principles of learning, but suggest that persons with abnormal behavior have unusual learning histories. Some psychologists are eclectic; they use more than one model to explain or treat abnormal behaviors.

A major system for classifying abnormal behavior is the DSM of the American Psychiatric Association. The DSM-III (1980) focuses more on observable behaviors than did the DSM-II (1968). The DSM-III de-emphasizes the concept of neurosis (presumed to stem from unconscious conflict), reorganizes and modifies categories, and relies relatively less heavily on the medical model than did the DSM-II. Homosexuality is no longer listed as a mental disorder.

Anxiety disorders are characterized by motor tension, feelings of dread, and high autonomic activity. They include irrational fears, or phobias; generalized (free-floating) anxiety; and obsessive–compulsive disorders, in which people are troubled by intrusive thoughts or impulses to repeat some activity.

The dissociative disorders include psychogenic amnesia (motivated forgetting), psychogenic fugue (forgetting plus fleeing and adopting a new identity), and multiple personality, in which a person behaves as if distinct personalities occupied the body. Somatoform disorders include conversion disorder and hypochondria. In a conversion disorder, there is loss of a bodily function with no organic basis. Hypochondriacs show consistent concern that they are suffering from illnesses, although there are no medical findings.

Affective disorders include dysthymic disorder, major depression, and bipolar disorder. In dysthymic disorder the person shows depressive behaviors for at least two years. Major depression may reach psychotic proportions, with grossly impaired reality testing. In bipolar disorder there are mood swings from elation to depression and back. Recent research emphasizes the possible roles of learned helplessness, attributional styles, and norepinephrine deficiency in depression. Bipolar disorder is thought to have a hereditary basis.

Schizophrenic disorders are characterized by disturbances in thought, perception, motor activity, mood, and by withdrawal and autism. Persons with rapid onset of schizophrenic symptoms are diagnosed as showing schizophreniform disorders or brief reactive psychoses. Their symptoms are usually more bizarre and they have better prognoses. There are three major types of schizophrenia: disorganized (formerly, hebephrenic); catatonic; and paranoid. A catatonic disorder is characterized by impaired motor activity, and paranoid schizophrenia is characterized by paranoid delusions. Recent research suggests that schizophrenia may have a hereditary basis, and much research is focusing on the excess-dopamine theory.

Sociopaths persistently violate the rights of others with little or no guilt or shame. Sociopaths may have lower-than-normal levels of arousal, which would help explain why they are undeterred by (most forms of) punishment and are often thrill-seekers.

Psychosexual disorders include gender identity disorders (as transsexualism), paraphilias, psychosexual dysfunctions, and ego-dystonic homosexuality. Transsexuals feel trapped in the body of the wrong sex and seek sex-reassignment surgery. In the paraphilias, people are sexually aroused by unusual or bizarre objects or situations.

Suicide is most often linked to feelings of depression and hopelessness. People who threaten suicide may well carry it out. Suicide prevention requires empathy, patience, and encouragement that solutions may be found to life's problems, and—most important—professional consultation as soon as possible.

Truth or Fiction Revisited

- *A man shot the president of the United States in front of millions of television witnesses, yet was found not guilty by a court of law.* True. John Hinckley was found not guilty of the attempted assassination of President Ronald Reagan by reason of insanity.

- *Cavemen treated abnormal behavior by letting the sun shine in—or letting the evil spirits out. Therapy involved making a hole in the head.* Anthropological evidence strongly suggests that this is the case. The practice is called trephining, and it was an early expression of the demonological model of abnormal behavior.

- *In the Middle Ages innocent people were drowned to prove that they were not possessed by the Devil.* True. It was believed that the Devil or his agents, within people they "possessed," would not take kindly to drowning and would keep the person afloat.

- *Mental disorders stem from physiological problems, such as chemical imbalances or metabolic disturbances.* Some do, like the organic psychoses. Schizophrenic and affective disorders may also have at least partial organic bases, but many others, like paraphilias, are not thought to.

- *Depressed rats drive their neighbors to drink.* It appears so. But it would be more accurate to say that the colony-mates of norepinephrine-depleted rats, whose *behavior* resembled that of depressed humans, increased their alcohol intake.

- *In some mental disorders, people may see or hear things that are not actually there.* True. These people are having hallucinations.

- *Supermales can leap tall buildings in a single bound.* False. So-called "supermales" have XYY sex chromosomal structure. They may be somewhat taller and more heavily bearded than the average male, but show little resemblance to the cartoon character, Superman.

- *Many Americans have changed their sex through surgery and hormone treatments.* Not exactly. About 2,500 transsexuals have undergone sex-reassignment surgery which provides the *appearance* of the external genitals of the opposite sex.

- *Strip-teasers are exhibitionists.* False. Exhibitionists attempt to surprise and shock their victims. Strip-teasers attempt to earn a living by sexually arousing their audiences.

- *Suicide is a sign of insanity.* False, the great majority of suicides may be depressed, but they are not out of touch with reality.

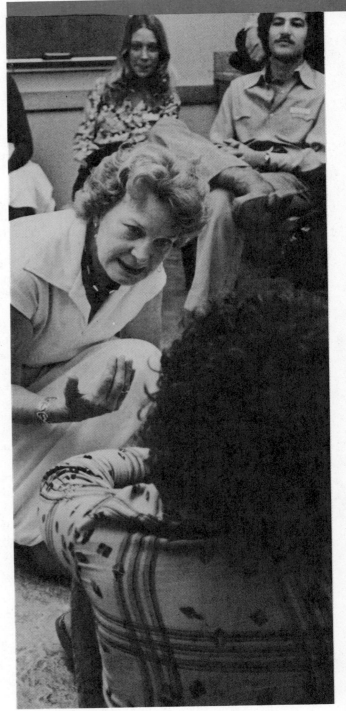

TWELVE

OUTLINE

Historical Overview
Asylums
Mental Hospitals
The Community Mental-Health Movement
The Helping Professionals
Insight-Oriented Therapies
Psychoanalysis
Client-Centered Therapy
Transactional Analysis
Gestalt Therapy
Cognitive Therapy
Behavior Therapy: Adjustment Is What You Do
Systematic Desensitization
Aversive Conditioning
Operant Conditioning
Assertiveness Training
Self-Control Techniques
Evaluation of Behavior Therapy
Group Therapy
Encounter Groups
Family Therapy
Evaluation of Group Therapy
Biological Therapies
Chemotherapy
Electroconvulsive Therapy
Psychosurgery
Summary
Truth or Fiction Revisited

Psychotherapy

- People in Merry Old England used to visit the local insane asylum for a fun night out on the town.
- The terms "psychotherapy" and "psychoanalysis" are interchangeable.
- You may be able to gain control over bad habits merely by keeping careful track of where and when you engage in them.
- Lying around in your reclining chair and fantasizing can be an effective way of confronting your fears.
- Smoking cigarettes can be an effective treatment for helping people to . . . stop smoking cigarettes.
- Staff members in a mental hospital induced reluctant patients to eat by ignoring them.
- Low fees are the most important factor to college students selecting a psychologist.
- The originator of a surgical technique intended to reduce violence learned that it was not always successful—when one of his patients shot him.

Brad is having an uplifting experience—literally. Six people who minutes ago were perfect strangers have cradled him in their arms and raised him into midair. His eyes are closed. Gently they rock him back and forth and carry him about the room.

Brad is no paralyzed hospital patient. He has just joined an encounter group. He hopes to be able to learn to relate to other people as individuals, not as passing blurs on the street or as patrons asking him to cash payroll checks at the bank where he works as a teller. The group leader had directed that Brad be carried about in order to help him break down his defensive barriers and establish trust in others.

Brad had responded to a somewhat flamboyant ad in the therapy section of the classifieds in New York's *Village Voice:*

> Come to life! Stop being a gray automaton in a mechanized society! Encounter yourself and others. New group forming. First meeting free. Call 212–555–0599. Qualified therapist.

Like many who seek personal help, Brad had little idea how to go about it. His group experience may or may not work out. For one thing, he has no idea about the qualifications of the group leader and did not know to ask. If he had answered other ads in the *Voice*, including some placed by highly qualified therapists, his treatment might have looked quite different. Brad could have been:

Lying on a couch talking about anything that pops into his head and exploring the hidden meanings of a recurrent dream.

Sitting face to face with a gentle, accepting therapist who places the major burden for what happens during therapy directly on Brad's shoulders.

Listening to a frank, straightforward therapist insist that his problems stem from self-defeating attitudes and beliefs, such as an overriding need to be liked and approved of at almost all costs.

Role-playing initiating a social relationship, including smiling at a new acquaintance, making small talk, and looking the person squarely in the eye.

The form of treatment, or psychotherapy, practiced by a psychologist or another helping professional is related to that practitioner's theory of person-

Members of encounter groups may undergo directed experiences designed to help them break down defensive barriers and develop trust in others.

ality or model of abnormal behavior. It is not (or ought not be) a matter of chance. In this chapter we explore the history of treatment of abnormal behavior. Then we describe and evaluate several of the major current psychological treatment approaches, including *psychoanalysis, client-centered therapy, cognitive therapy, behavior therapy,* and *group therapy.* These are all forms of **psychotherapy,** which is a systematic interaction between a therapist and a client that brings psychological principles to bear on influencing the client's thoughts, feelings, or behavior in order to help that client overcome abnormal behavior or adjust to problems in living.

Quite a mouthful? True. But note the essentials:

1. Psychotherapy is a *systematic interaction.* The therapist's theoretical viewpoint and the client's problems determine how the therapist and client will relate to each other.
2. Psychotherapy brings *psychological principles* to bear on the client's problems. Psychotherapy is based on principles concerning human motivation and emotion, learning, and personality. It is not based on, say, religious or biological principles, although there is no reason why psychotherapy cannot be compatible with both.
3. Psychotherapy influences *thoughts, feelings,* or *behavior.* Psychotherapy may be aimed at any or all of these aspects of human psychology.
4. Psychotherapy helps the client *overcome abnormal behavior* or *adjust* to problems in living. Psychotherapy is concerned with people who have been diagnosed as, say, anxious or depressed, but it is also used with people who seek help in adjusting to problems such as social shyness, loss of a spouse, or confusion about the direction of one's career. Let us note also that some individuals use psychotherapy, especially insight-oriented therapies, not because there is a problem, but to learn more about the self and achieve personal growth.

After exploring various psychotherapies, we shall turn our attention to the *biological therapies* that are used with some of the more severe forms of abnormal behavior, such as schizophrenic disorders and major depression. These include drug therapy *(chemotherapy), electroconvulsive shock therapy,* and *psychosurgery.*

Historical Overview

Ancient and medieval "treatments" of abnormal behavior often reflected the demonological model. They involved cruel practices like **trephining, exorcism,** or death by hanging or burning. Some people who could not meet the demands of everyday life were thrown into prisons. Others begged in city streets, stole crops and food animals from farms, or entered marginal societal niches occupied by prostitutes and petty thieves. A few might find their ways to monasteries or other retreats that offered a kind word and some support. Generally speaking, they died young.

Asylums

Asylums, which often had their origins in monasteries, were the first institutions meant primarily for the mentally ill. Their functions were human warehousing, not treatment. Asylums mushroomed in population until the

Psychotherapy A systematic interaction between a therapist and a client that brings psychological principles to bear on influencing the client's thoughts, feelings, or behavior in order to help that client overcome abnormal behavior or adjust to problems in living.

Trephining (treh–FINE–ing). Removal of a circular piece of the skull to let evil spirits out. A superstitious, prehistoric practice. (From *trepan,* a type of surgical saw.)

Exorcism The driving out of evil spirits by prayer and other means. See Chapter 11.

Asylum (uh–SIGH–lum). (1) An institution for the care of the mentally ill. (2) A safe place, or refuge. (From the Greek *a-,* meaning "without," and *sylon,* meaning "right of seizure." What does *political asylum* mean?)

Saturday Night at Bedlam

More than nine thousand people, without care or protection . . . "bound with galling chains, bowed beneath fetters and heavy iron balls attached to drag chains, lacerated with ropes, scourged with rods and terrified beneath storms of execration and cruel blows; now subject to jibes and scorn and torturing tricks; now abandoned to the most outrageous violations."

A medieval dungeon in the damp caverns beneath a turreted castle? No. These were the conditions found in many asylums in mid-nineteenth-century America as reported to Congress by New England schoolteacher Dorothea Dix.

And things were worse, much worse, at a London asylum by the name of St. Mary's of Bethlehem, which opened its gates to the unwary in 1547. Here the unfortunate were chained, whipped, and allowed to lie indefinitely in their waste products. Here the word *bedlam*, a bastardization of Bethlehem, had its origin. And there the ladies and gents of the British

St. Mary's of Bethlehem.

upper class might wend their way on a hazy afternoon or dull evening, taking in the sights.

The admission for stopping in to gander at the more violently disturbed? One penny.

daily stresses created by noise, overcrowding, and unsanitary conditions undoubtedly heightened the problems they were meant to ameliorate. Inmates were frequently chained and beaten. Some were chained for four decades.

Humanitarian reform movements began in the eighteenth century. In Paris, Philippe Pinel unchained the patients at the asylum known as La Bicêtre. The populace was amazed that most patients, rather than running amok, profited from kindness and greater freedom. Many were later able to function in society again. Reform movements were later led by the Quaker William Tuke in England, and by Dorothea Dix in America.

Mental Hospitals

Mental Hospitals gradually replaced asylums in the United States. By a typical year in the middle 1950s, over a million people resided, at least briefly, at state, county, Veterans Administration, or private facilities. Treatment, not warehousing, is the function of the mental hospital. Still, because of high patient populations and understaffing, many patients have received little attention. Even today, with somewhat improved conditions, it is not unusual for one psychiatrist to be responsible for the welfare of several hundred patients on a weekend.

The Community Mental-Health Movement

Since the 1960s, efforts have been made to maintain as many mental patients as possible in the community. The Community Mental-Health Centers Act of 1963 provided funds for creating hundreds of community mental-health centers, in which patients would be charged according to their ability to pay, in order to accomplish this goal. These centers attempt to maintain new patients as outpatients, to serve patients from mental hospitals who have

The unchaining of the patients at La Bicêtre—a landmark of the humanitarian reform movement.

been released to the community, and to provide other services as listed in Table 12.1. By the mid-1970s the number of patients living in mental hospitals had been cut nearly in half.

But is it all Valium and roses in the community? Critics note that many mental patients who had lived in hospitals for decades were discharged to "home" communities that seemed foreign and frightening. Some of them try to return to the protected world of the hospital and become trapped in a "revolving door" between the hospital and the community (Kohen & Paul, 1976).

The outlook for maintaining new patients in the community, rather than hospitalizing them, looks brighter. In a review of ten experiments in which seriously disturbed patients were randomly assigned either to hospitalization or some form of outpatient care, Kiesler (1982) did not find one case in which the outcomes of hospitalization were superior. The outpatient alternative was usually superior in terms of the patient's maintaining independent living arrangements, staying in school, and finding employment.

The Helping Professionals

Throughout history people in many roles have helped others to adjust, including priests and ministers, grandparents, witch doctors, palm readers, and wise men (and women). Today qualified professionals in these roles include psychologists, psychiatrists, and social workers, among others.

TABLE 12.1   Functions of the Community Mental-Health Center

Outpatient treatment
Short-term hospitalization
Partial hospitalization (e.g., patient sleeps in the hospital and works outside during the day)
Crisis intervention
Community consultation and education about abnormal behavior

The Community Mental-Health Centers Act provided funds for community agencies that attempt to intervene in mental-health problems as early as possible and maintain mental patients in the community.

Unfortunately, most states allow almost anyone to use the label *therapist*. This label indicates nothing about one's education and experience. People seeking effective therapy should never be shy about asking psychologists and others about their education and supervised experience. Here are some of the people who are genuinely qualified to help:

Psychologists   Psychologists have at least a master's degree and in many states must have a doctoral degree (Ph.D, Ed.D., Psy.D.) in order to use the label *psychologist*. The state will typically weigh the adequacy of the individual's education and supervised experience in psychology before granting a license to practice psychology. Psychologists use interviews, behavioral observations, and psychological tests to diagnose abnormal behavior problems, and psychotherapy to treat them. Most psychologists have been trained extensively in research methods. They are more likely than other helping professionals to be critically acquainted with psychological theory.

Psychiatrists   A psychiatrist is a licensed physician. Psychiatrists earn medical degrees and then undertake a psychiatric residency during which time they learn to apply medical skills, such as prescribing drugs, to treat abnormal behavior. Psychiatrists, like psychologists, may practice psychotherapy. Most psychiatrists rely on interviews for diagnostic purposes, but may refer patients to psychologists for psychological testing.

A view of Freud's consulting room at Berggasse 19 in Vienna. Freud would sit in the chair by the head of the couch while a client free associated. The cardinal rule of free association is that no thought is to be censored, no matter how trivial or personal.

Psychiatric Social Workers   Psychiatric social workers have an M.S.W. (Master of Social Work) degree and supervised experience in helping people adjust. Many offer psychotherapy, but social workers do not use psychological tests or prescribe medical treatments. Many specialize in marital or family problems.

Psychoanalysts   Once only physicians were admitted to psychoanalytic training, but today many psychologists and social workers also practice the form of therapy originated by Sigmund Freud. The practice of psychoanalytic therapy requires years of training beyond the doctoral level and completion of one's own psychoanalysis.

Insight-Oriented Therapies

Many forms of psychotherapy are based on the assumption that abnormal behavior can be remedied if people gain **insight** into their problems. Insight involves knowledge of the experiences that led to conflicts, problems like anxiety and depression, and maladaptive behavior. Insight also involves efforts to identify and *label* feelings and conflicts that lie beneath the level of conscious awareness. The assumption is that accurate self-knowledge is required if self-defeating behavior patterns are to be changed effectively.

Insight-oriented forms of psychotherapy that we shall examine include psychoanalysis, client-centered therapy, transactional analysis, gestalt therapy, and cognitive therapy.

Psychoanalysis: Where Id Was, There Shall Ego Be

You lie down on a couch in a slightly darkened room. Your **analyst** sits just behind you while you talk about anything that pops into your mind—no matter how trivial, no matter how personal. In order to avoid interfering with your self-exploration, your analyst may say little or nothing for session after session. But that is all right. After all, there are months of **psychoanalysis** ahead, perhaps years....

Psychoanalysis has three meanings. It is Freud's (1) theory of personality; (2) his method for investigating people's inner dynamics; and (3) his form of treatment or psychotherapy.

The Goals of Psychoanalysis   Psychoanalysis attempts to provide insight into many of the unconscious conflicts presumed to lie at the roots of a person's problems. It seeks to allow the client to express emotions and impulses that are theorized to have been dammed up by the forces of repression.

Freud was fond of saying, "Where id was, there shall ego be." In part he meant that psychoanalysis could shed some light on the inner workings of the client. But Freud did not believe we should become conscious of all primitive impulses and conflicts. Rather he sought to replace impulsive and defensive behavior with coping behavior. Impulses reflected urges of the id. Defensive behavior, such as timidly avoiding confrontations, represented the ego's compromising efforts to protect the client from these impulses and the possibility of retaliation. Coping behavior would allow the client to express at least part of these impulses in socially acceptable ways and achieve greater gratification.

Insight In psychotherapy, knowledge of one's underlying motives or impulses.

Analyst A person who practices psychoanalysis, Freud's method of psychotherapy. Short for *psychoanalyst.*

Psychoanalysis (1) Freud's method of psychotherapy. (2) The name of Freud's theory of personality. (3) Freud's method of conducting clinical research.

Abreaction In psychoanalysis, expression of previously repressed feelings and impulses to allow the psychic energy associated with them to spill forth. (The Latin prefix *ab-* means "away" or "from.")

Catharsis (kuh–THAR–sis). Another term for *abreaction*. See the discussion of catharsis as a means for averting violence in Chapter 9.

Free association In psychoanalysis, the uncensored uttering of all thoughts that come to mind.

Compulsion to utter The urge to express ideas and impulses—in psychoanalytic theory, a reflection of the seeking of expression by impulses within the id.

Resistance The tendency to block the free expression of impulses and primitive ideas—a reflection of the defense mechanism of repression.

Interpretation An explanation of a client's utterance according to psychoanalytic theory.

Wish fulfillment A primitive method used by the id to attempt to gratify basic instincts.

In this way a man with a phobia for knives might come to see that he had been repressing the urge to harm someone who had taken advantage of him. He might also find ways to confront his antagonist verbally. A woman with a conversion disorder—conversion paralysis of the legs—could see that her disability allowed her to avoid an unwanted pregnancy without feeling guilty. Perhaps she would also taste her resentment at being pressed into a stereotypical feminine sex role and decide to expand her options.

Freud also believed that psychoanalysis should permit the client to spill forth the psychic energy theorized to have been repressed by conflicts and guilt. He called this spilling forth **abreaction,** or **catharsis**. Abreaction would provide feelings of relief.

Free Association   Early in his development as a therapist, Freud found that his clients appeared to be able to focus on repressed conflicts and talk about them under hypnosis. Hypnosis seemed an efficient way of breaking through to topics of which clients were unaware in the normal waking state. (See Chapter 4 for a critical discussion of hypnosis.) But he found that many clients would deny the accuracy of this material once they were brought out of the "trance." Other clients found these revelations premature and painful. Freud then turned to **free association** as a more gradual method of breaking through the walls of defense that he believed had prevented the ego from gaining insight into unconscious processes.

In free association, the client is made comfortable, typically by lying on a couch, and asked to talk about any topic that comes to mind. No thought is to be censored—that is the cardinal rule. While psychoanalysts ask their clients to wander "freely" from topic to topic, they do not believe that the process *within* the client is fully free. Repressed impulses are continually seeking release. On a verbal level, they lead to a **compulsion to utter.** A client may begin free association by talking about various meaningless topics, but eventually the compulsion to utter will bring important repressed material to the surface.

But the ego maintains the tendency to repress unacceptable impulses and threatening conflicts. Clients will show **resistance** to recalling and talking about many frightening, threatening, or degrading ideas. Clients may claim "My mind is blank" when they are about to encounter such a thought. They may accuse the analyst of being too demanding or inconsiderate. They may "forget" their appointment when it seems that threatening material may be uncovered during that session.

During an analysis, the therapist observes this dynamic struggle between the compulsion to utter and resistance. Through discreet remarks, the analyst subtly tips the balance in favor of uttering. A gradual process of self-discovery and self-insight ensues. Now and then the analyst offers an **interpretation** of an utterance, showing how it suggests resistance, or, perhaps, the symbolic revelation of deep-seated feelings or conflicts.

Dream Analysis   Freud considered dreams the "royal road to the unconscious." As noted in Chapter 4, the psychoanalytic theory of dreams holds that they are determined by unconscious processes as well as the remnants or "residues" of the day. Unconscious impulses tend to be expressed in dreams as a form of **wish fulfillment.**

But unacceptable impulses, usually sexual or aggressive, are likely to be displaced onto objects and situations that reflect the era and culture of the

client. These objects then become **symbols** of the unconscious wishes. For instance, dream objects that are long and narrow may be **phallic symbols,** but whether the symbol takes the form of a spear, rifle, "stick shift," or spacecraft partially reflects one's cultural background.

In psychoanalytic theory, the perceived content of the dream is called its shown, or **manifest content.** The presumed hidden or symbolic content of the dream is referred to as its **latent content.** A man may dream that he is flying. Flying is the manifest content of the dream. Psychoanalysts usually interpret flying as symbolic of erection, so sexual potency might be involved in the latent content of such a dream. A list of psychoanalytic dream symbols is found in Table 4.1 (p. 131).

Freud often asked clients to jot down their dreams upon waking so that they could be interpreted during the psychoanalytic session.

Transference   Freud found that his clients responded not only to his appearance and behavior, but also according to what his appearance and behavior meant to them. A young woman might see Freud as a father figure and displace, or transfer, her feelings toward her own father onto Freud. Another woman might view him as a lover and, perhaps, act seductively. Men also showed this uncalled-for generalization of feelings, or **transference.** A man might also view Freud as a father figure, or, perhaps, a competitor. Freud discovered that he could also transfer feelings onto his clients—perhaps viewing a woman as a sex object or a young man as a rebellious son. He called this placing of clients into stereotypical roles in his own life **countertransference.**

Transference and countertransference lead to uncalled-for expectations of new people in our lives and may foster maladaptive behavior. We may expect our spouses to act like our opposite-sex parents and expect too much (or too little) from them. Or we may accuse them unjustly of harboring wishes and secrets we attributed to our parents. We may not give new friends or lovers a chance when we have been mistreated by someone from the past who played a similar role in our lives or our fantasies.

In any event, psychoanalysts are trained to be **opaque** concerning their own behavior and feelings so that they will not encourage client transference or express their own feelings of countertransference. Then, when the client acts accusingly, seductively, or otherwise inappropriately toward the analyst, the analyst can plead not guilty of encouraging the client's behavior and suggest that it reflects historical events and fantasies. In this way, transference behavior becomes grist for the therapeutic mill.

Symbol A sign that stands for, or represents, something else.

Phallic symbol A sign that represents the penis.

Manifest content In the psychoanalytic theory of dreams, the reported content of dreams.

Latent content In the psychoanalytic theory of dreams, the symbolized or underlying content of dreams.

Transference In psychoanalysis, the generalization to the analyst of feelings toward a person in the client's life.

Countertransference In psychoanalysis, the generalization to the client of feelings toward a person in the analyst's life.

Opaque (oh–PAKE). Literally, not permitting the passage of light; thus, in psychoanalysis, the hiding of feelings by the analyst. (From the Latin *opacus,* meaning "shaded.")

Insight-Oriented Therapies   **469**

Analysis of client transference is an important element of therapy. It provides client insight and encourages more adaptive social behavior. But it may take months or years for transference to develop fully and be resolved, which is one reason that psychoanalysis can be such a lengthy process.

Evaluation of Psychoanalysis   Psychoanalysis is difficult to evaluate for various reasons. As noted in Chapter 1, psychologists prefer experimental evidence whenever possible. But a sound experiment could require random assignment of people seeking therapy to psychoanalysis and a number of other therapies for comparison. A client might also have to remain in each form of therapy for years in order to attain a "true" psychoanalysis. People often seek psychoanalysis per se rather than psychotherapy in general. It would not be ethical, or even practical, to assign them randomly to assorted treatments or a no-treatment control group.

Self-insight and not behavioral change is the primary goal of psychoanalysis. Since each person's "self" insights must be unique, it could be impossible to measure objectively *how much* insight has been gained, and *whether* it is accurate.

Psychoanalysts therefore claim, with some justification, that clinical judgment must be the basis for evaluating the effectiveness of analysis. In any event, we·can note that there seems to be some consensus that psychoanalysis is most effective with well-educated, highly verbal and motivated clients. Psychoanalysis does not appear successful with psychotic disorders (Luborsky & Spence, 1971).

Note also the psychoanalytic focus on encouraging appropriate expression of repressed sexual and aggressive impulses. Some social thinkers have suggested that Freud's form of therapy may have been appropriate for repressed Victorians living in turn-of-the-century Vienna, but not for today's liberated, freely expressive Westerners. This is an interesting thought. Psychoanalysts could counter, of course, that many people remain repressed and conflicted, and that those who seem fully liberated may be "trying too hard" to deny unconscious conflicts and could also profit from analysis.

During the 1940s and 1950s, psychotherapy was almost synonymous with psychoanalysis. Few other approaches to psychotherapy had any impact (Garfield, 1981, 1982). But today, according to a recent survey of clinical and counseling psychologists, only about fourteen percent of psychotherapists report that they have a psychoanalytic orientation (Smith, 1982, p. 804). Sigmund Freud, once the model for almost all therapists, is currently rated only third in influence, following Carl Rogers and Albert Ellis, whom we discuss in the following pages (Smith, 1982, p. 807). The largest group of psychotherapists (41 percent) consider themselves eclectic (Smith, 1982, p. 804).

Client-Centered Therapy: Removing Roadblocks to Self-Actualization

Client-centered therapy
Carl Rogers's method of psychotherapy, which emphasizes the creation of a warm, therapeutic atmosphere that frees clients to engage in self-exploration and self-expression.

Client-centered therapy was originated by Carl Rogers (1951), who was rated as the most influential psychotherapist in a recent survey of 800 clinical and counseling psychologists (Smith, 1982). Rogers writes that abnormal behavior stems largely from roadblocks placed in the path of our own self-actualization. Because others show us selective approval when we are young, we learn to disown the disapproved parts of ourselves. We don masks and facades to earn social approval. We may learn to be seen but not heard—not even heard, or examined fully, by ourselves. As a result we may experience stress and discomfort and the feeling that we—or the world—are not real.

Client-centered therapy may provide insight into parts of us that we have disowned, allowing us to feel whole once more. Rogers stresses the importance of creating a warm, therapeutic atmosphere that encourages client self-exploration and self-expression. Therapist acceptance of the client is thought to lead to client self-acceptance and heightened self-esteem. Self-acceptance then frees the client to make choices and decisions that foster development of his or her unique potential.

Client-centered therapy is nondirective. The client takes the lead, listing and exploring problems. The therapist reflects or paraphrases important feelings and ideas of the client, helping the client get in touch with feelings and follow the strongest leads in the quest for self-insight. The effective client-centered therapist also shows *unconditional positive regard, empathetic understanding, genuineness,* and *congruence.*

The therapist shows **unconditional positive regard** for clients. They are respected as important human beings with unique values and goals, and provided with a sense of security that encourages them to follow their own feelings. Client-centered therapists believe strongly that people are basically *prosocial.* If people follow their own feelings, rather than act defensively, they should not be abusive or antisocial.

Empathetic understanding is shown by accurate reflection of the client's experiences and feelings. Therapists must view the world through their clients' eyes, or **frames of reference,** by setting aside their own values and listening carefully.

Genuineness is the therapist's honesty in relationships with clients. In contrast to the opaque psychoanalyst, client-centered therapists are supposed to be open about their feelings. It would be harmful to clients if their therapists could not truly accept and like them, even though their values may differ from those of the therapists. Client-centered therapists must be able to tolerate differentness because they believe that every client is different in important ways.

Successful client-centered therapists also show **congruence,** or a fit between their feelings and behavior. They serve as models of integrity to their clients.

Evaluation of Client-Centered Therapy

There is some difficulty in evaluating client-centered therapy because the goals of therapy—heightened self-esteem, self-acceptance, and self-actualization—pose measurement problems. The measurement of therapist traits, like empathetic understanding and genuineness, also poses research problems (Parloff and others, 1978). But if we rely on client self-report, there is some evidence that this form of therapy may foster self-esteem (Rogers & Dymond, 1954) and teach clients to relate to others more openly (Walker and others, 1960).

Like psychoanalysis, client-centered therapy seems most effective with well-educated, highly motivated and verbal people (Abramowitz and others, 1974; Wexler & Butler, 1976). There is no evidence of effectiveness with psychotic disorders. It has also not been shown consistently that positive therapy outcomes can be attributed to therapist traits like empathetic understanding and genuineness (Parloff and others, 1978). Despite the influence of Carl Rogers, only about nine percent of psychotherapists place themselves within the client-centered tradition (Smith, 1982, p. 804).

Unconditional positive regard Acceptance of the value of another person, although not necessarily acceptance of all of that person's behaviors.

Empathetic understanding Ability to perceive a client's feelings from the client's frame of reference. A quality of the good client-centered therapist.

Frame of reference One's unique patterning of perceptions and attitudes, according to which one evaluates events.

Genuineness Recognition and open expression of the therapist's own feelings. A quality of the good client-centered therapist.

Congruence A fit between one's self-concept and behaviors, thoughts, and emotions.

Transactional analysis A form of psychotherapy that deals with how people interact, and how their interactions reinforce attitudes, expectations, and "life positions." Abbreviated *TA*.

Inferiority complex Feelings of inferiority hypothesized by Alfred Adler to serve as a central motivating force. See Chapter 9.

"Parent" In TA, a moralistic "ego state."

"Child" In TA, an irresponsible, emotional "ego state."

"Adult" In TA, a rational, adaptive "ego state."

Transaction In TA, an exchange between two people.

Complementary In TA, descriptive of a transaction in which the ego states of two people interact harmoniously.

Transactional analysis (TA) is a popular form of therapy rooted in the psychoanalytic and humanistic traditions. According to Thomas Harris, author of *I'm OK—You're OK,* (1967) many of us suffer from the sort of **inferiority complex** that had been suggested by psychoanalyst Alfred Adler. Though adults, we may continue to see ourselves as dependent children. We may think other people are OK, but not see ourselves as OK. *I'm not OK—You're OK* is one of four basic "life positions," or ways of perceiving relationships with others.

A major goal of TA is to help people adopt the life position *I'm OK—You're OK,* in which they accept others and themselves. Unfortunately, people tend to adopt "games," or styles of relating to others that are designed to confirm one of the unhealthy life positions: I'm OK—You're not OK, I'm not OK—You're OK, or I'm not OK—You're not OK.

Psychiatrist Eric Berne, the originator of TA and author of *Games People Play* (1976), described our personalities as containing three "ego states": **Parent, Child,** and **Adult.** The "parent" is a moralistic ego state. The "child" is an irresponsible and emotional ego state. The "adult" is a rational ego state. (These are three hypothesized *ego states*, or ways of coping—They do not correspond to the concepts of id, ego, and superego.)

People tend to relate to each other as parents, children, or adults. A social exchange between two people is called a **transaction.** A transaction is said to fit, or be **complementary,** when a social exchange follows the same lines. In one type of complementary transaction, people relate as adults. But a transaction can also be complementary, even if upsetting, when two people relate as parent and child (Parent: "You shouldn't have done that"; Child: "I'm sorry, I promise it won't happen again"). Communication breaks down when the social exchange between the parties does not follow complementary lines (as in Figure 12.1). Note these examples:

> NATALIE (adult to adult): Did you have a good time tonight?
> HAL (child to parent): Why do you wanna know?

Or:

> BILL (adult to adult): Nan, did you see the checkbook?
> NAN (parent to child): A place for everything and everything in its place!

TA is often carried out with couples who complain of communication problems. It encourages people to relate to each other as adults.

TA also attempts to put an end to game playing. The most commonly played marital game is "If It Weren't for You" (Berne, 1976). People who play this game marry domineering mates who prevent them from going into things they would not have the courage to do anyhow, such as taking a more challenging job or moving to a new city. By playing "If It Weren't for You," they can blame their mates for their shortcomings and excuse their own timidity.

Evaluation of Transactional Analysis   There is little experimental evidence that TA is an effective form of psychotherapy. Yet it has a number of adherents in the helping professions, and many who have undergone TA claim that it has enhanced their relationships. Other professionals and some former clients express the view that TA is worthless or harmful. We shall have to await the results of carefully controlled research before we can pass judgment.

FIGURE 12.1   A Crossed Transaction. Natalie asks Hal, "Did you have a good time, tonight?" Hal replies, "Why do you wanna know?" Communication is thus broken off.

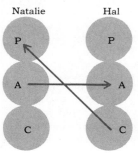

Games People Play

In *Games People Play* (1976), Eric Berne casts a cynical eye on some of the ways we interact with one another. He asserts that we play various "games" with other people that may provide us with excuses for failure or antisocial behavior, or that maneuver others into positions that "prove" that they're no good.

For instance, some clients play a sort of psychoanalytic game called "Archaeology." Archaeologists dig in the ruins of ancient civilizations. In this game, people dig into the ruins of their pasts to unearth the one crucial event that they assert will explain why they are having problems today. Why? Archaeology permits them to avoid getting on with the business of living and coping in the here and now.

In certain therapy groups, Berne noted, some clients take advantage of the Freudian view that no thought is to be censored by playing the game of "Self-Expression." In this group game, a client uses vulgar language and paints lurid images while other clients in the group also assume "liberated" roles and applaud his or her "honesty." One may ask, of course, why a "liberated" person would be trying so hard to be vulgar.

Some other games people play:

- "Look How Hard I've Tried"
- "I'm Only Trying to Help You"
- "Why Does This Always Happen to Me?"
- "Now I've Got You, You Son of a Bitch"
- "See What You Made Me Do"
- "You Got Me into This"
- "Kick Me"

Gestalt Therapy: Getting It Together

Like psychoanalysis and client-centered therapy, **gestalt therapy,** originated by Fritz Perls (1893–1970), aims to provide insight into how conflicting parts of the personality create distress. But unlike psychoanalysis, gestalt therapy focuses on "the here and now." Clients undergo exercises intended to make them more aware of current feelings and behavior, rather than explore the past. Unlike client-centered therapy, gestalt therapy is highly directive. The therapist leads the client through planned experiences.

One gestalt technique that increases awareness of internal conflict is the **dialogue.** Clients undertake verbal confrontations between opposing wishes and ideas. An example of these clashing personality elements is "top dog" and "underdog." One's top dog may conservatively suggest, "Don't take chances. Stick with what you have or you may lose it all." Your frustrated underdog may rise up and assert, "You never try anything. How will you ever get out of this rut if you don't take on new challenges?" Heightened awareness of the elements of conflict may clear the path toward resolution, perhaps through compromise.

Body language also provides insight into conflicting feelings. Clients may be instructed to attend to responses like furrows in the eyebrow and facial tension when they express ideas that they think they support wholeheartedly. In this way they often find that their body language suggests the presence of impulses that they have been denying.

In order to increase clients' understanding of opposing points of view, and to broaden their perspective, therapists may encourage them to argue ideas that are directly opposed to their own expressed ideas. They may also role play (act out) the behavior of important people in their lives to get more in touch with their points of view.

On Being a Wheel with Uncle Fritz   While many psychoanalysts may view dreams as the "royal road to the unconscious," Perls saw the stuff of dreams as disowned parts of the personality. He would often ask clients to role play the elements in their dreams to get in touch with these isolated parts. In

Fritz Perls.

Gestalt therapy Fritz Perls's form of psychotherapy, which attempts to integrate conflicting parts of the personality through directive methods designed to help the person perceive his or her whole self.

Dialogue A gestalt therapy technique in which clients verbalize confrontations between conflicting parts of their personality.

Gestalt Therapy Verbatim, Perls —known to clients and friends alike as Fritz— describes a session in which a client "Jim" is reporting a dream:

> JIM: I just have the typical recurring dream which I think a lot of people might have if they have a background problem, and it isn't of anything I think I can act out. It's the distant wheel—I'm not sure what type it is—it's coming toward me and ever-increasing in size. And then finally, it's just above me and it's no height that I can determine, it's so high. And that's—
> FRITZ: If you were this wheel, . . . what would you do with Jim?
> JIM: I am just about to roll over Jim. (1971, p. 127)

Perls encourages Jim to undertake a dialogue with the wheel. Jim comes to see that the wheel represents fears about taking decisive action. Through this insight the "wheel" becomes more manageable in size, and Jim is able to use some of the "energy" that he might otherwise have spent in worrying to begin to take charge of his life.

Evaluation of Gestalt Therapy   Gestalt therapy, like TA, has many adherents and clients who testify that it has helped them gain self-insight and engage in more productive behavior. But in some ways it seems more a philosophy of life than a form of therapy. It seems more a belief in the importance of what is here and being experienced, as opposed to reflection on the past and future. It emphasizes personal awareness and freedom. Perls expressed this philosophy in words that became a popular wall poster in the 1960s:

> I do my thing and you do your thing. I am not in this world to live up to your expectations. And you are not in this world to live up to mine. You are you and I am I. And if by chance we find each other, it's beautiful. If not, then not.

These words have a certain allure. In fact, they seem to fit the American ideal of "rugged individualism." Yet, they suggest that we needn't be concerned with working to improve interpersonal relationships, or with being sensitive to the needs of others. Some critics characterize this sort of thinking as now being out of date—a symptom or symbol of the "selfishness" of the "Me Decade" of the 1970s (Yankelovich, 1981).

As with TA, there is little experimental evidence supporting the effectiveness of gestalt therapy. Its appeal lies at least in part in its philosophy.

Cognitive Therapy

Cognitive therapy is the newest form of therapy presented in this book. Its name will be considered controversial by some. Its inclusion as an insight-oriented therapy may be considered controversial by others.

Cognitive therapy A form of therapy that focuses on how clients' cognitions (expectations, attitudes, beliefs, etc.) lead to distress and may be modified to relieve distress and promote adaptive behavior.

Controversy 1: What Do We Call "Cognitive Therapy"?   As noted in Chapter 1, many current theorists consider cognitive therapy to be a collection of techniques that belong within the province of behavior therapy. This group may prefer the name "cognitive *behavior* therapy" or argue that the name *behavior therapy* is sufficient. However, it seems that there is a difference in focus between many cognitive therapists and behavior therapists. To behavior therapists, the purpose of dealing with client cognitions is to change *overt* behavior. A cognitive therapist will agree that mental or cognitive change leads to overt behavioral change, but may assert that the cognitive change itself is the central and most important goal of therapy.

Another labeling problem exists in that some of the cognitive therapies, like **rational-emotive therapy** (see Chapter 10), already have names of their own. Adherents to rational-emotive therapy may, with justice, disapprove of being considered "one form of cognitive therapy."

Controversy 2: Is Cognitive Therapy an Insight-Oriented Therapy?
Another controversy is cognitive therapy's inclusion as an insight-oriented therapy. But cognitive therapists increase client awareness of the attitudes, attributions, and automatic types of thinking that tend to create and compound problems, as noted in the many examples in Chapters 10 and 11. In this way, insight into *current cognitions* is a primary goal of cognitive therapy. *Changing* these cognitions to reduce negative feelings like anxiety and depression, to provide more accurate perceptions of the environment, and to orient the client toward solving problems is a second goal.

Cognitive Therapy Methods   Having made my apologies, let us have a look at some cognitive therapy methods. These include cognitive restructuring and methods of enhancing coping skills. The founder of rational-emotive therapy, Albert Ellis—rated as the second most influential psychotherapist in the Smith (1982) survey—can be said to engage in cognitive restructuring when he shows clients how irrational beliefs (see Chapter 10) create anxiety, depression, and feelings of helplessness. Psychiatrist Aaron Beck (1976), who uses the term cognitive therapy, also focuses on clients' cognitive distortions, showing them, for example, how minimizing accomplishments and assuming the worst will heighten feelings of depression.

In Chapter 10 we also noted how becoming aware of and changing catastrophizing thoughts help provide us with coping ability under stress. (Consider the example of coping with test anxiety on pp. 412-413.) In the discussion of depression in Chapter 11, it was noted that internal, stable, and global attributions of failure lead to depression and feelings of helplessness. Cognitive therapists alert clients to all these cognitive distortions as a prelude to effective behavioral change.

Let us describe an experiment in the use of cognitive therapy in the control of anger and aggressive behavior in order to clarify some of these procedures.

Cognitive Therapy in the Control of Anger   Close your eyes. Imagine that you are pushing a cart down an aisle in a supermarket. Someone pushes into you, so hard that it seems purposeful, and then says, "What the hell's the matter with you? Why don't you watch where you're going!"

What would you think? Would you think, "This so and so can't treat me this way! People can't be allowed to act like that!" If so you would have made the cognitive "errors" of taking this person's rudeness personally and expecting others to live up to your own standards. Your attitudes might prompt you to violence, to behavior you might regret afterward.

Many cognitive therapists use a method called *running a movie* to get in touch with irrational beliefs and other cognitive errors that intensify negative feelings and prompt maladaptive behavior. In "running a movie" about the supermarket incident, a client would relive this upsetting experience in the imagination to search out fleeting thoughts that might otherwise barely be noticed.

Rational-emotive therapy Albert Ellis's form of cognitive psychotherapy, which focuses on how irrational expectations create anxiety and disappointment, and encourages clients to challenge and correct these expectations.

Novaco (1974) showed how cognitive restructuring and relaxation training helped 34 men and women deal with the supermarket-type of provocation more effectively. The participants typically exploded when they were frustrated. They picked fights in public places, destroyed valuable possessions, and assaulted marital partners.

Novaco's strategy included three phases: education, planning, and application training. In phase 1, participants were shown how anger is intensified by the irrational beliefs that mistakes should not be tolerated, that one must expect flawless behavior from others, and that an insult is a threat to one's own self-esteem. In phase 2, they were taught relaxation and deep breathing coping skills (as in Chapter 10, pages 413-415). They also learned rational alternatives for their irrational beliefs. In phase 3, participants imagined frustrating situations and practiced using rational beliefs and relaxation to arrive at adaptive, nonviolent responses. Treatment that involved both learning rational beliefs and relaxation training was more effective in lowering anger arousal and in promoting adaptive behavior outside the laboratory than either rational restructuring or relaxation alone.

Novaco's participants reported that the most effective aspect of treatment was cognitive restructuring of insults and other provocations. They came to see provocations as problems demanding a solution, rather than as threats requiring an immediate violent response.

Evaluation of Cognitive Therapy As noted in Chapters 10 and 11, there is an increasing body of evidence that cognitive factors play an important role in adjustment problems. They are particularly pertinent to feelings of anxiety and depression that are learned or acquired through experience. This is abundantly clear in phobias, where the client believes that a particular object or situation is awful and must be avoided, and in depressive reactions that are linked to internal, stable, and global attributions of failure. Cognitive approaches have already yielded many positive results with such adjustment problems.

We are still left with the question of whether we should differentiate between cognitive therapy and behavior therapy. The Novaco study of "cognitive therapy" also used muscle relaxation training, usually considered a behavior therapy technique. In another typical study—this one published in the journal *Behavior Therapy* (Jannoun and others, 1982)—it could be said that three of four components in the treatment of anxiety were essentially cognitive: self-monitoring to increase awareness of conditions under which anxiety occurs; reading instruction booklets about anxiety; and cognitive control of self-defeating thoughts. As in the Novaco study, the other treatment component was relaxation training. In the next section we discuss behavior therapy techniques, and you can consider for yourself whether a number of them have a strong cognitive flavor.

Behavior Therapy: Adjustment Is What You Do

Behavior therapy Systematic application of the principles of learning to the direct
modification of a client's
problem behaviors.

Behavior therapy—also called *behavior modification*—is the systematic application of principles of learning in order to promote desired behavioral changes. As suggested in the section on cognitive therapy, behavior therapists have increasingly come to incorporate cognitive processes in their theoretical outlook and cognitive procedures in their methodology (Wilson, 1982). For example, techniques like *systematic desensitization, covert sensitization, covert reinforcement,* and some others ask clients to engage in visual imagery or fantasy. However, behavior therapists insist that therapeutic outcome must be assessed in terms of observable, measurable behavior.

Behavior therapists rely heavily on principles of classical and operant conditioning and observational learning (described in Chapter 5). They help clients discontinue self-defeating behavior patterns, such as phobic avoidance of harmless stimuli, overeating, and smoking. They also help clients acquire adaptive behavior patterns, such as the social skills required to initiate relationships and to say no to insistent salespeople.

Behavior therapists may help clients gain "insight," but such insight usually involves increasing client awareness of the circumstances in which maladaptive behavior occurs, in contrast to the psychoanalytic search for its historic origins. Behavior therapists may be warm, supportive psychotherapists, but they do not, in contrast to client-centered therapists, argue that the warm therapeutic atmosphere is essential for positive changes to occur. Therapeutic change is seen to issue from the extinction or punishment of unwanted behavior, and the shaping and reinforcement of desired behavior.

About 17 percent of the clinical and counseling psychologists surveyed by Smith (1982) labeled themselves behavioral or cognitive-behavioral in orientation—the largest group of therapists who identified with a specific orientation. Behavior therapists Joseph Wolpe and Arnold Lazarus were ranked fourth and fifth among the 10 most influential psychotherapists (Smith, 1982, p. 807).

Let us look at a number of behavior therapy techniques.

Systematic Desensitization

Adam has a phobia for receiving injections. His behavior therapist treats him as he reclines in a comfortable padded chair. In a state of deep muscular relaxation, Adam observes slides projected onto a screen. A slide of a nurse holding a needle has just been shown three times, 30 seconds at a time. Each time Adam has shown no anxiety. So now a slightly more discomforting slide is shown: the nurse aiming the needle toward someone's bared arm. After fifteen seconds our armchair adventurer notices twinges of discomfort and raises a finger as a signal (speaking might disturb his relaxation). The projector operator shuts off the disturbing slide, and Adam spends two minutes imagining his "safe scene"—lying on a beach beneath the tropical sun. Then the slide is shown again. This time Adam views it for 30 seconds before feeling any anxiety.

Adam is undergoing **systematic desensitization,** a method for reducing phobic responses originated by psychiatrist Joseph Wolpe (1958, 1973). Wolpe assumed that maladaptive anxiety responses, like other behaviors, are learned or conditioned. He reasoned that they can be unlearned by **counterconditioning,** or by extinction (see Chapter 5). In counterconditioning, a response that is incompatible with anxiety is made to appear under conditions that usually elicit anxiety. Muscle relaxation is incompatible with anxiety. For this reason Adam's therapist is teaching Adam to experience relaxation in the presence of (usually) anxiety-evoking slides of needles.

Systematic desensitization is a gradual process. Clients learn to handle increasingly disturbing stimuli as anxiety to each one is counterconditioned. About 10 to 20 stimuli are arranged in a sequence or **hierarchy** according to

Systematic desensitization Wolpe's method for reducing fears by associating images of fear-evoking stimuli with deep muscle relaxation.

Counterconditioning The repeated pairing of a stimulus that elicits a certain response (such as fear) with a stimulus that elicits an antagonistic response (such as relaxation instructions) such that the first stimulus loses the capacity to elicit the problematic (fear) response.

Hierarchy An arrangement according to rank or class structure. In this case, stimuli are arranged according to the amount of fear they evoke.

Clients undergoing systematic desensitization. They engage in deep muscle relaxation while the therapist presents a graded series of fear-evoking stimuli.

their capacity to elicit anxiety. In imagination or by being shown photos the client travels gradually up through this hierarchy, approaching the **target** behavior. In Adam's case the target behavior was the ability to receive an injection without undue anxiety.

Psychological Controversies over Systematic Desensitization Psychoanalysts have argued that phobias are symptoms of unconscious conflicts, and that systematic desensitization of a "symptom" may only lead to the appearance of another symptom—that is, to **symptom substitution.** To behavior therapists, maladaptive behavior *is* the problem, not just a symptom of the problem. Evidence does suggest that systematic desensitization is effective in the great majority of treated cases (Paul, 1969a, Marks, 1982). To date, symptom substitution has not been shown to be a problem.

Other findings are of interest. One study found that a carefully ordered fear hierarchy was not needed in order to reduce phobic responses (Krapfl, 1967). Clients may not like it, but desensitization may work when the most fearful stimulus is presented first, or when items are presented in a randomly scrambled order. It may simply be that systematic desensitization works because clients *confront*, rather than avoid, fear-evoking stimuli. Counterconditioning may be icing on the theoretical cake.

It has been suggested that systematic desensitization may work because it provides clients with a chance to cognitively restructure the phobic object or situation—or, less technically, to change their minds about it (Kazdin & Wilcoxin, 1976). But some studies (e.g., Biran & Wilson, 1982) find that behavioral confrontation of the fear-evoking situations—in this study, of heights, elevators, or darkness—was more effective than cognitive restructuring.

Participant Modeling A behavioral alternative to systematic desensitization is **participant modeling,** which relies on observational learning. In this method, clients observe and then imitate people who do approach and cope with the objects or situations they fear. Bandura and his colleagues (1969) found that

Target Goal.

Symptom substitution The exchange of one symptom for another. The term refers to the psychoanalytic belief that a phobia is a symptom of an underlying disorder, and that removal of the phobia through behavioral techniques may lead to emergence of another symptom of the disorder.

Participant modeling A behavior therapy technique in which a client observes and imitates a person who approaches and copes with feared objects or situations.

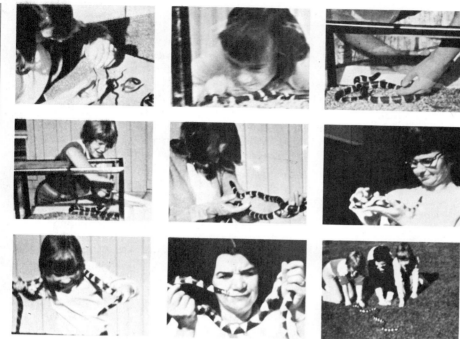

FIGURE 12.2 Participant Modeling. Participant modeling is a behavior therapy technique based on principles of observational learning. In these photos, people with an aversion for snakes observe and then imitate people who are unafraid. Parents often try to convince young children that something tastes good by eating it in front of them and saying "Mmm!"

participant modeling worked as well as systematic desensitization, and more rapidly, for a number of people who were afraid of snakes (see Figure 12.2).

In any event, systematic desensitization is a largely "painless" way to confront fears. And when given careful instructions, people seem capable of using it fully on their own—no therapist needed (Rosen and others, 1976).

Aversive Conditioning

You may have read the futuristic Anthony Burgess novel or seen the filmed version of *A Clockwork Orange.* The young antisocial "hero" of the tale, Alex, finds violence and rape to be superb pastimes. When he is caught, he is given the chance to undergo an experimental reconditioning program rather than serve a prison term. In this program, he watches films of violence and rape while he is throwing up as a result of being given an **emetic** drug. After his release, he feels ill whenever he considers violence. Unfortunately, Beethoven's music, which he had enjoyed, accompanies the films and feelings of nausea. Alex acquires an aversion for Beethoven as well.

In this novel, Alex undergoes a program of **aversive conditioning**—also called *aversion therapy*—which is available and used quite frequently today, although not in prisons. It is one of the more controversial procedures in behavior therapy. In aversive conditioning, painful or aversive stimuli are paired with self-defeating impulses—such as desire for a cigarette or to engage in antisocial behavior—in order to make the goal less appealing. In a typical procedure designed to help people control alcohol intake, tastes of different

Emetic Causing vomiting. (From the Greek *emein,* meaning "to vomit.")

Aversive conditioning A behavior therapy technique in which undesired responses are inhibited by pairing repugnant or offensive stimuli with them.

Whatever Happened to Little Albert, Anyhow?

Afraid of heights? Perhaps you should try munching away on your favorite treat while you climb the stairs.

John Watson and Rosalie Rayner (1920) taught Little Albert to fear a rat by clanging steel bars behind his head while he played with the animal. Sad to say, for Little Albert, they never taught him to unlearn his fear.

But University of California Professors Harold Jones and Mary Cover Jones (Jones, 1924; Jones & Jones, 1928) reasoned that if fears could be *conditioned* by painful experiences, they could be *counterconditioned* by pleasant experiences.

Two-year-old Peter feared rabbits intensely. The Joneses arranged for Peter to "confront" his fear—that is, be close to a rabbit—while engaging in some of his favorite activities, like munching merrily away on candy and cookies. They didn't just plop the rabbit in his lap. Had they done so, the cookies left on the plate, and those already eaten, might have decorated the walls. At first they merely placed the rabbit in the far corner of the room while Peter munched and crunched. Peter, to be sure, cast a wary eye, but the lad continued to eat.

Gradually the animal was brought closer. Eventually, Peter could eat treats and touch the rabbit at the same time. The Joneses theorized that the pleasure of eating was incompatible with fear and thus counterconditioned the fear.

No, I don't know how much weight and how many cavities Peter acquired while overcoming his fear of rabbits. But perhaps I should mention that most psychologists would *not* recommend going through life with a chocolate chip cookie in the mouth just in case we should happen across some upsetting stimulus.

Taste aversion The finding of the taste of a food to be repugnant.

alcoholic beverages are paired with nausea and vomiting. Tasting alcohol can also be paired with electric shock (Wilson and others, 1975), but there is evidence that we more readily develop a **taste aversion** from feeling ill than by being shocked (Cannon & Baker, 1981).

Aversive conditioning has been used with some success in treating problems as divergent as paraphilias (see Rathus, 1983), smoking cigarettes (see box on "Hot Smoke and Cold Turkey"), and retarded children's self-injurious behavior. It may seem paradoxical to use punishing aversive stimulation to stop children from hurting themselves, but people sometimes hurt themselves because of payoffs like sympathy and attention from others. If self-injury leads to more pain than anticipated, and no sympathy, it will probably be discontinued.

Hot Smoke and Cold Turkey

How do you use a hair dryer to quit smoking? Simple: Hook up the hose to a chamber with several lit cigarettes, and blow their smoke into the quitter's face. It works more effectively if the would-be quitter is smoking at the time, taking a puff every six seconds, to be precise.

But, you object, this procedure isn't pleasant at all. Quite right! It is *aversive conditioning*. Overexposure makes once-desirable cigarette smoke aversive. The quitter becomes motivated to avoid, rather than seek, cigarettes, and stops smoking on a target date. Many reports have shown a quit rate of 60 percent or higher at a six-month follow-up of former smokers (Lichtenstein and others, 1973; Schmahl and others, 1972; Delahunt & Curran, 1976; Sachs and others, 1979).

Rapid smoking, or inhaling every six seconds, remains the most widely researched aversion method for treating cigarette smoking (Lichtenstein, 1982). Rapid smoking has become popular because it is as effective as other methods and the apparatus is readily available—the quitter's own cigarettes. But rapid smoking raises the heartbeat and blood pressure, and decreases the blood's capacity to carry oxygen. True—these changes occur with normal smoking as well, but rapid smoking also produces heart abnormalities, as shown by the electrocardiogram, and intense discomfort (Lichtenstein & Glasgow, 1977). Rapid smoking should not take place without the informed consent of the smoker, medical approval, and a reasonable time limit.

In *A Clockwork Orange*, Alex's conditioned aversion to violence eventually "wore off." It is likely that the conditioning effects of aversive therapy do fade with the passage of time. After all, alcoholics cannot be made to feel nauseated every time they catch a whiff of alcoholic beverages in future months and years. But in many cases people seem to learn to avoid rather than seek out the problem objects or situations. It may also be that aversive conditioning provides the highly motivated people who undergo it with confirmation that *now* is the time for them to stop their self-defeating behavior.

Operant Conditioning

We usually prefer to relate to people who smile at rather than ignore us, and to take courses in which we do well rather than fail. We tend to repeat behavior that is reinforced. Behavior that is not reinforced tends to become extinguished. Behavior therapists have applied these principles of operant conditioning with psychotic patients as well as clients with milder problems.

The staff at one mental hospital were at a loss as to how to encourage withdrawn schizophrenic patients to eat regularly. Ayllon and Haughton (1962) observed that the staff were exacerbating the problem by coaxing patients into the dining room, even feeding them. The patients were apparently reinforced for uncooperativeness by increased staff attention. Some rules were changed. Patients who did not arrive at the dining hall within 30 minutes after serving were locked out. Staff could not interact with patients at mealtime. With uncooperative behavior no longer reinforced, patients quickly changed their eating habits. Patients were then required to pay one penny to enter the dining hall. Pennies were earned by interacting with other patients and showing other socially appropriate behaviors. These target behaviors also increased in frequency.

Many psychiatric wards and hospitals now use **token economies** in which tokens, like poker chips, must be used by patients to purchase television-watching time, extra visits to the canteen, or private rooms. The tokens are reinforcements for productive activities like making beds, brushing teeth, and socializing. While token economies have not eliminated all symptoms of schizophrenic disorders, they have encouraged many patients to become more active and cooperative.

We can often use the operant conditioning method of **successive approximations** in building good habits. Let us use a (not uncommon!) example: You wish to study three hours an evening, but can only maintain concentration for half an hour. Rather than attempting to increase study time all at once, you could do so gradually, say by five minutes an evening. After every hour or so of studying you could reinforce yourself with five minutes of people watching in a busy section of the library.

Assertiveness Training

Are you a person who can't say no? Do people walk all over you? Brush off those footprints and get some **assertiveness training!**

Assertive behavior may be contrasted with both *nonassertive* (submissive) behavior and *aggressive* behavior. Assertive people express their genuine feelings, stick up for their legitimate rights, and refuse unreasonable requests. But they do not insult, threaten, or belittle. Assertive people also do not shy away from meeting and constructing relationships with new people, and they express positive feelings such as liking and love.

Token economy A controlled environment in which people are reinforced for desired behaviors with tokens (like poker chips) that may be exchanged for privileges.

Successive approximations In operant conditioning, a series of behaviors that gradually become more similar to a target behavior.

Assertiveness training A collection of behavior therapy techniques that teach clients to express feelings, seek fair treatment, and improve social skills.

Assertiveness training aims to decrease social anxiety and enhance social skills by having clients refine appropriate social behavior in the therapeutic setting.

Self-monitoring Keeping a record of one's own behavior to identify problems and record successes.

Model To engage in behaviors that are imitated by others.

Feedback In assertiveness training, information as to the effectiveness of a response.

Behavior rehearsal Practice.

Broken record technique The unvarying repetition of a brief statement of one's position on an issue (usually a refusal) each time a request or argument is made.

Fogging A method of showing empathy while refusing a request: paraphrasing of the rationale for the request followed by refusal.

Assertiveness training aims to decrease social anxiety and enhance social skills through techniques like *self-monitoring*, *modeling*, and *behavior rehearsal*. In **self-monitoring**, the client keeps a record of upsetting social encounters in order to pinpoint instances of social avoidance, clumsiness, and feelings of frustration. The therapist may demonstrate or **model** more effective social behavior, then encourage the client to rehearse or practice this behavior while the therapist provides **feedback.** The therapist attends to the client's posture, facial expressions, and tone of voice as well as to the content of what the client is saying.

The therapist may also point out that various irrational beliefs may impede progress. If clients believe that it is awful to earn the disapproval of others, or to fumble at the first few attempts at behavioral change, they are likely to increase rather than decrease social anxieties. They need to learn to reward themselves for gradual gains rather than condemn themselves for imperfection.

Assertiveness training can be highly effective in groups. Group members can role play important people in the lives of other members, like potential dates, spouses, or parents. The trainee then engages in **behavior rehearsal** with the role player.

Two methods often taught clients who have difficulty refusing requests are the **broken record technique** and **fogging.** With the broken record technique, you express your position in a brief statement and repeat the statement, without variation, each time the request is made. If someone is trying to sell you insurance and refuses to accept a simple statement of noninterest, you may repeat "All my insurance needs are taken care of" each time a new request or comment is made. The salesperson will soon surrender. In fogging you "cloud" or soften the fact that you are saying no by first paraphrasing the other person's request to show understanding. If your spouse asks you to a film but you have more work to do first, you can fog by saying: "I know it's been a long week, and that you're dying to get out. I am, too. But I've got to get this done by the morning. Why don't we see it Monday night?"

"Well, I'm sorry if my remarks hurt your feelings, but I think it's a little unfair of you to blame me. I said those things on the advice of a highly qualified therapist."

What's wrong with this cartoon? It's true, of course, that psychotherapists of many persuasions encourage clients to express their genuine feelings. However, "qualified" psychotherapists also encourage clients to take responsibility for their own behavior—not to attribute their misdeeds to the suggestions of others.

Self-Control Techniques

Does it sometimes seem that mysterious forces are at work? Forces that delight in wreaking havoc with your New Year's resolutions and other efforts to take charge of bad habits? Just when you go on a diet, that juicy Big Mac stares at you from the TV set. Just when you resolve to balance your budget, that sweater goes on sale. Behavior therapists have developed a number of self-control techniques to help people cope with such temptations.

Functional Analysis of Behavior   Behavior therapists first engage in a **functional analysis** of the problem behavior to determine the stimuli that seem to trigger it and the reinforcers that seem to maintain it. In a functional analysis, you jot down each instance of the behavior in a diary. You note the time of day, location, your activity (including your thoughts and feelings), and reactions (yours and others').

Functional analysis serves a number of purposes. It makes you more aware of the environmental context of your behavior, can increase your mo-

Functional analysis A systematic study of behavior in which one identifies the stimuli that trigger it and the reinforcers that maintain it.

The Assertiveness Schedule

How assertive are you? Do you stick up for your rights, or do you allow others to walk all over you? Do you say what you feel, or what you think other people want you to say? Do you start up relationships with attractive people, or do you shy away from them?

     To find out just how assertive you are, take this self-report test of assertive behavior. Then turn to Appendix B to calculate your score and compare your assertiveness to that of a sample of 1,400 students drawn from 35 college campuses across the United States.

The Assertiveness Schedule

Directions: Indicate how well each item describes you by using this code:

3 very much like me	−1 slightly unlike me
2 rather like me	−2 rather unlike me
1 slightly like me	−3 very much unlike me

_____ 1. Most people seem to be more aggressive and assertive than I am.*

_____ 2. I have hesitated to make or accept dates because of "shyness."*

_____ 3. When the food served at a restaurant is not done to my satisfaction, I complain about it to the waiter or waitress.

_____ 4. I am careful to avoid hurting other people's feelings, even when I feel that I have been injured.*

_____ 5. If a salesman has gone to considerable trouble to show me merchandise that is not quite suitable, I have a difficult time saying "No."*

_____ 6. When I am asked to do something, I insist upon knowing why.

_____ 7. There are times when I look for a good, vigorous argument.

_____ 8. I strive to get ahead as well as most people in my position.

_____ 9. To be honest, people often take advantage of me.*

_____ 10. I enjoy starting conversations with new acquaintances and strangers.

_____ 11. I often don't know what to say to attractive persons of the opposite sex.*

tivation to change it, and can lead to significant behavioral change. In studies with highly motivated people, functional analysis alone has been found to increase the amount of time spent studying (Johnson & White, 1971) or talking in a therapy group (Komaki & Dore-Boyce, 1978), and to decrease the number of cigarettes smoked (Lipinski and others, 1975).

     Brian used functional analysis to learn about his nail biting. Table 12.2 shows a few items from his notebook. He discovered that boredom and humdrum activities seemed to serve as triggers for nail biting. He began to watch out for feelings of boredom as signals of times to practice self-control. He also planned to make some changes in his life so that he would feel bored less often.

     There are a number of self-control strategies aimed at (1) the stimuli that trigger behavior; (2) the behaviors themselves; and (3) reinforcers.

Strategies Aimed at Stimuli That Trigger Behavior

Restriction of the stimulus field. Gradually exclude the problem behavior from more environments. For example, for a while first do not smoke while

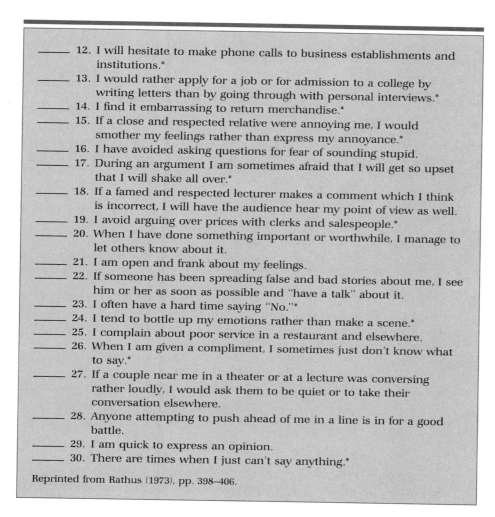

———— 12. I will hesitate to make phone calls to business establishments and institutions.*

———— 13. I would rather apply for a job or for admission to a college by writing letters than by going through with personal interviews.*

———— 14. I find it embarrassing to return merchandise.*

———— 15. If a close and respected relative were annoying me, I would smother my feelings rather than express my annoyance.*

———— 16. I have avoided asking questions for fear of sounding stupid.

———— 17. During an argument I am sometimes afraid that I will get so upset that I will shake all over.*

———— 18. If a famed and respected lecturer makes a comment which I think is incorrect, I will have the audience hear my point of view as well.

———— 19. I avoid arguing over prices with clerks and salespeople.*

———— 20. When I have done something important or worthwhile, I manage to let others know about it.

———— 21. I am open and frank about my feelings.

———— 22. If someone has been spreading false and bad stories about me, I see him or her as soon as possible and "have a talk" about it.

———— 23. I often have a hard time saying "No."*

———— 24. I tend to bottle up my emotions rather than make a scene.*

———— 25. I complain about poor service in a restaurant and elsewhere.

———— 26. When I am given a compliment, I sometimes just don't know what to say.*

———— 27. If a couple near me in a theater or at a lecture was conversing rather loudly, I would ask them to be quiet or to take their conversation elsewhere.

———— 28. Anyone attempting to push ahead of me in a line is in for a good battle.

———— 29. I am quick to express an opinion.

———— 30. There are times when I just can't say anything.*

Reprinted from Rathus (1973), pp. 398–406.

driving, then extend not smoking to the office. Or practice the habit only outside the environment in which it normally occurs (see box "Yoo Hoo, Ms. Nolan, Where Are You?").

Table 12.2 Excerpts from Brian's Diary of Nail Biting for April 14

Incident	Time	Location	Activity (Thoughts, Feelings)	Reactions
1	7:45 AM	Freeway	Driving to work, bored, not thinking	Finger bleeds, pain
2	10:30 AM	Office	Writing report	Self-disgust
3	2:25 PM	Conference	Listening to dull financial report	Embarrassment
4	6:40 PM	Living room	Watching evening news	Self-disgust

A functional analysis of problem behavior, like nail biting, increases awareness of the environmental context in which it occurs, spurs motivation to change, and, in highly motivated people, may lead to significant behavioral change.

Yoo Hoo, Ms. Nolan, Where Are You?

Youngsters may sneak a cigarette behind the garage or in the cellar, but this seems unlikely behavior for the sophisticated spouse of a psychologist. Or does it?

The wife of Ohio State University psychologist J. Dennis Nolan (1968) had tried quitting smoking several times, to no avail. Finally, the Nolans tried the strategy of *restriction of the stimulus field*. They limited Ms. Nolan's smoking to one place—a "smoking chair." The rules were simple: Ms. Nolan could smoke as often as she wished, but only in that chair. Also, smoking was the only activity permitted in the chair. The chair was placed in a remote corner of the basement so that Ms. Nolan would not be able to watch T.V. or converse while smoking.

In this way, smoking became dissociated from its usual triggers—eating, watching television, and so on. Ms. Nolan also became acutely aware of every moment of her smoking and had the opportunity to reflect on all the reasons for quitting. Her daily smoking dropped to seven cigarettes from a pretreatment mean of 24. After some weeks Ms. Nolan felt so humiliated by her treks to the basement and her inability to quit that she just stopped altogether.

But do not think that only damp basements work these wonders. University of Minnesota psychologist Alan Roberts (1969) used his bathroom to tackle his 23-year-old pack-a-day habit. Within several weeks, his smoking decreased by 75 percent. Then he developed a cold and quit altogether.

Avoidance of powerful stimuli that trigger habits. Avoid obvious sources of temptation. People who go window-shopping often wind up buying more than windows. If eating at The Pizza Glutton tempts you to forget your diet, eat at home or at The Celery Stalk instead.

Stimulus control. Place yourself in an environment in which desirable behavior is likely to occur. Maybe it's difficult to lift your mood directly at times, but you can place yourself in the audience of that uplifting concert or film. It may be difficult to force yourself to study, but how about rewarding yourself for spending time in the library?

Strategies Aimed at Behavior

Response prevention. Make unwanted behavior difficult or impossible. Impulse buying is curbed when you shred your credit cards, leave your checkbook home, and carry only a couple of dollars. You can't reach for the strawberry cream cheese pie in your refrigerator if you have left it at the supermarket (that is, have not bought it).

Competing responses. Engage in behaviors that are incompatible with the bad habits. It is difficult to drink a glass of water and a fattening milkshake simultaneously. Grasping something firmly is a useful competing response for nail biting or scratching.

Chain breaking. Interfere with unwanted habitual behavior by complicating the process of engaging in it. Break the chain of reaching for a readily available cigarette and placing it in your mouth by wrapping the pack in aluminum foil and placing it on the top shelf in the closet. Rewrap the pack after taking one. Put your cigarette in the ashtray between puffs, or put your fork down between mouthfuls of dessert. Ask yourself if you really want more.

Successive approximations. Gradually approach targets through a series of relatively painless steps. Increase studying by only five minutes a day. Decrease smoking by pausing for a minute when the cigarette is smoked halfway, or by putting it out a minute before you would wind up eating the filter. Decrease your daily intake of food by 50 to 100 calories every couple of days, or else cut out one type of fattening food every few days.

Strategies Aimed at Reinforcements

Reinforcement of desired behavior. Why give yourself something for nothing? Make pleasant activities, like going to films, walking on the beach, or reading a new novel contingent upon meeting reasonable, daily behavioral goals. Put one dollar away toward that camera or vacation trip each day you remain within your calorie limit.

Response cost. Heighten awareness of the long-term reasons for dieting or cutting down smoking by punishing yourself for not meeting a daily goal or for practicing a bad habit. Make out a check to your most hated cause and mail it at once if you bite your nails or inhale that cheesecake.

"Grandma's method." Remember Grandma's method for inducing children to eat their vegetables? Simple: No veggies, no dessert. In this method, desired behaviors, like studying and toothbrushing, can be increased by insisting that they be done before you carry out a favored or frequently occurring activity. For example, don't watch television unless you have studied first. Don't leave the apartment until you've brushed your teeth.

Covert sensitization. Create imaginary horror stories about problem behavior. Psychologists have successfully reduced overeating and smoking by having clients imagine that they become acutely nauseated at the thought of fattening foods, or that a cigarette is made from vomit. Some horror stories are not so "imaginary." Deliberately focusing on heart strain and diseased lungs every time you overeat or smoke, rather than ignoring these long-term consequences, may also promote self-control.

Covert reinforcement. Create rewarding imagery for desired behavior. When you have achieved a behavioral goal, fantasize about how wonderful you are. Imagine friends and family patting you on the back. Fantasize about the *Playboy* or *Playgirl* centerfold for a minute.

Response Cost. The thought of sending hard-earned cash to hated causes is enough to encourage many of us to practice self-control.

MOST HATED CAUSE!

Evaluation of Behavior Therapy

Behavior therapy has provided a number of strategies for treating anxiety, mild depression, social-skills deficits, and problems in self-control. They have proved effective for most clients in terms of quantifiable behavioral change. Behavior therapy has also been effective in helping manage institutionalized populations, including schizophrenics and the mentally retarded.

However, there is little evidence that behavior therapy alone is effective in treating the thought disorders involved in severe psychotic disturbance. There is also some question about why behavior therapy works. Is it because clients replace self-defeating habits with adaptive habits, or because they cognitively restructure disturbing stimuli and relationships? No broad, simple answer to this question is possible.

Still, behavior therapists can claim that experimental evidence supports the effectiveness of many of their treatment strategies. Behavior therapists have also been innovative with a number of problems—such as phobias and patient–management problems—for which there had not previously been effective treatments.

Group Therapy

When a psychotherapist has several clients with similar problems—whether stress management, adjustment to divorce, lack of social skills, or anxiety—it often makes sense to treat clients in groups of six to 12 rather than conduct individual therapy. The methods and characteristics of the group will reflect the needs of the members and the theoretical orientation of the leader. Clients may interpret each others' dreams in a psychoanalytic group. They may provide an accepting atmosphere for self-exploration in a client-centered group. Clients in a TA group may comment on the games played by others. Behavior therapy groups may undergo joint desensitization to anxiety-evoking stimuli or model and rehearse social skills.

There are several advantages to group therapy: (1) It is more economical, allowing several clients to be seen at once. (2) There is a greater fund of information and experience from which clients may draw. (3) Appropriate behavior receives the emotional support of several group members rather than just the therapist. (4) Group members who show improvement provide hope for others. (5) Group members can rehearse social skills in relating to one another in a relatively nonthreatening atmosphere. Still, many clients prefer individual therapy because they do not wish to disclose their problems to a group, are inhibited about relating to others, or desire individual attention. It is the responsibility of the therapist to explain that group disclosures must be kept confidential, to establish a supportive atmosphere, and to see that group members receive the attention they need.

As noted, many forms of therapy can be conducted individually or in groups. Encounter groups and family therapy can be conducted in group-format only:

Encounter Groups

Encounter groups are not appropriate for treating serious psychological problems. Rather, they are intended to promote personal growth through heightening awareness of one's own needs and feelings and those of others.

Encounter group A type of group that aims to foster self-awareness by focusing on how group members relate to each other in a setting that encourages open expression of feelings.

Many groups use touching exercises to help members grow comfortable with one another. This encourages them to be open about feelings and to try out new, adaptive behavior patterns.

This goal is sought through intense confrontations, or encounters, between strangers. Like ships in the night, group members come together out from the darkness, touch one another briefly, then sink back into the shadows of one another's lives. But something is thought to be gained from the contact.

Encounter groups stress interactions between group members in the here and now. Discussion of the past may be outlawed. Interpretation is out. Expression of general feelings toward others is encouraged. When group members think that a person's social mask is phony, they may descend en masse to rip it off.

Professionals recognize that encounter groups can be damaging when they urge overly rapid disclosure of intimate matters, or when several members attack one member in unison. Responsible leaders do not tolerate these abuses and try to keep groups moving in growth-enhancing directions.

Family Therapy

In **family therapy,** one or more families constitute the group. Family therapy may be undertaken from various theoretical viewpoints. One common viewpoint is the "systems approach," for which much credit can be given to family therapist Virginia Satir (1967). In Satir's method, the family system of interaction is analyzed (not in the psychoanalytic sense of the word) and modified.

It is often found that family members with low self-esteem cannot tolerate different attitudes and behaviors from other family members. Faulty family communications also create problems. It is also not uncommon for the family to present an "identified patient"—that is, the family member who has *the* problem and is *causing* all the trouble. However, family therapists usually

Family therapy A form of therapy in which the family unit is treated as the client.

"It's no use, Marvin. We tried tenderness and we tried Valium and you're still impossible."

assume that the identified patient is a scapegoat for other problems within and among family members. It is sort of a myth: Change the bad apple (identified patient) and the barrel (the family) will be functional once more.

The family therapist—who is often a specialist in this field—attempts to teach the family to communicate more effectively, and to encourage growth and the eventual **autonomy** of each family member. In doing so, the family therapist will also show the family how the identified patient has been used as a focus for the problems of other members of the group.

There are many other types of groups: marathon groups, sensitivity training, and psychodrama, to name just a few. Space limitations prevent us from examining each of them.

Evaluation of Group Therapy

An evaluation of group therapy must consider the intentions and goals of the various group formats. Generally speaking, it is easiest to demonstrate the effectiveness of behavior therapy groups because of the emphasis on mea-

Autonomy Self-direction.

"Relieving Hang-Ups Is My Game," *or* Psst, How About Some Therapy—Cheap?

What do you do when you feel the need for help? Do you ask friends for the name of a reliable helping professional, let your fingers do the walking through the yellow pages, or leaf through the classified ads of your newspaper?

In recent years psychologists and other helping professionals have begun to advertise their wares in news ads. But so have an assortment of "therapists," and helpers who run the gamut from respected professionals to massage experts, "sex surrogates," even "energy artists" who promise to do wonders with your "aura."

To what kind of ad would you respond if you were in the market for therapy? Psychologist Patricia Keith-Spiegel of California State University at Northridge showed mock news ads to hundreds of students to assess their selling power (Schaar, 1978). Some of them featured cutesy teasers like "My name is Lane, anxiety and depression relief is my game," or "Relieving personal hang-ups is my business." But students found these ads "too clever" to be effective. Money-back guarantees were also useless. Students understood that ethical psychotherapists cannot guarantee results, so this claim destroyed the ad's credibility.

Students responded favorably to ads suggesting that the psychotherapist was highly available, competent, and affordable—but not cheap. Cheap fees didn't draw the crowds, just as customers in a supermarket often prefer to pay a little more for a trusted brand name.

Because of the movement toward advertising, the American Psychological Association has drawn ethical guidelines. Psychologists may not:

- Mislead by presenting selected, favorable information
- Use endorsements by former clients
- Exaggerate the probability of a successful outcome
- Promise unique special abilities
- Use an emotional appeal

What if these standards were universal, so that ball players and actors could not endorse products on television commercials? Advertisers might actually have to focus on presenting useful information.

---

surable outcomes. Group desensitization, for example, works about as well as individual desensitization. A study of encounter groups suggests that they may hurt as many people as they help (Lieberman and others, 1973).

Generally speaking, people who desire a group experience should make certain that the leader is a qualified member of a helping profession, and that their personal goals are consistent with group goals and methods.

Biological Therapies

In the 1950s Fats Domino popularized the song "My Blue Heaven." Fats was singing about the sky and happiness. But today "blue heavens" is the street name for the 10 milligram dose of the most widely used prescription drug in the world: Valium. Family doctors commonly prescribe the **minor tranquilizer** Valium because the manufacturer once claimed that people could not become addicted to Valium nor readily kill themselves with Valium overdoses. Both of these assumptions now appear incorrect. Some people who have been using high doses of Valium are reported to go into convulsions when use is suspended. And now and then someone dies from mixing Valium with alcohol, or someone shows unusual sensitivity to the drug. But Valium, which comes in two milligram (white), five milligram (yellow), and 10 milligram (blue) tablets, remains prescribed more frequently than the most common antibiotics.

Minor tranquilizer A drug that relieves feelings of anxiety and tension.

Chemotherapy
(key–mow–THER–uh–pee).
The use of drugs to treat disordered behavior.

Major tranquilizer A drug
that decreases severe anxiety
or agitation in psychotic patients or in violent individuals.

Psychiatrists and other physicians prescribe Valium and many other drugs as chemical therapy, or **chemotherapy,** for various forms of abnormal behavior. In this section we discuss chemotherapy, *electroconvulsive therapy,* and *psychosurgery,* three biological or medical approaches to treating abnormal behavior.

Chemotherapy

If you visit a mental hospital, you will notice that many patients stroll up to the nurses' stations several times a day, toss pills from small paper cups into their mouths, and swallow them with water. Some patients have been taking the same pills for nearly twenty years. Some patients take pills to cope with feelings of anxiety, some to lift themselves from fearsome depressions, some to reduce violent agitation. Occasionally patients take pills because they, and perhaps the hospital staff, are afraid to learn what would happen if they stopped taking them.

In this section we discuss minor tranquilizers, major tranquilizers, antidepressants, and lithium.

Minor Tranquilizers   Valium is but one of many (many) minor tranquilizers. Others are listed in Table 12.3. These drugs are usually prescribed for outpatients who complain of anxiety or tension, although many people also use them as sleeping pills. They are theorized to influence the brain to lower sympathetic activity, thereby reducing the heart rate, respiration rate, and feelings of nervousness and tension.

Unfortunately, with regular usage people come to tolerate small dosages of these drugs very quickly. Dosages must be increased in order for the drug to remain effective. It is not unusual for the patient to become embroiled in a tug-of-war with the prescribing physician, if the physician becomes concerned about the dose the patient is using. In a typical confrontation, the physician wants the patient to cut down for his or her own benefit. The patient resents the physician for getting him or her "involved" with the drug and then playing the moralist.

Major Tranquilizers   Patients with schizophrenic and schizophreniform disorders are likely to be treated with **major tranquilizers**. Many of these drugs, including Thorazine, Mellaril, and Stelazine, belong to the chemical

---

TABLE 12.3   **Some Commonly Prescribed Psychiatric Drugs**

Minor Tranquilizers	Valium	Atarax
	Librium	Serax
	Miltown	Equanil
Major Tranquilizers	Thorazine	Mellaril
	Haldol	Stelazine
	Navane	Taractan
Antidepressants	Tofranil	Elavil
	Sinequan	Nardil
	Parnate	

class of **phenothiazines,** and are thought to act by blocking the action of dopamine in the brain. Research along these lines tends to support the excess-dopamine theory of schizophrenia, as noted in Chapter 11.

In most cases, these so-called antipsychotic drugs reduce agitation, delusions, and hallucinations (May, 1975; Watson and others, 1978). Major tranquilizers account in large part for the lessened need for various forms of restraint and supervision (padded cells, straitjackets, hospitalization, and so on) used with schizophrenic patients. More than any other single form of treatment, major tranquilizers have allowed hundreds of thousands of patients to lead largely normal lives in the community, holding jobs and maintaining family lives.

Unfortunately, in many cases the blocking of dopamine action leads to symptoms like those of Parkinson's disease, including tremors and muscular rigidity, as described in Chapter 2 (Calne, 1977; Levitt, 1981). These "side effects" can usually be controlled by drugs that are used for Parkinsonism. However, in a minority of patients long-term use of phenothiazines leads to motor problems that are not so readily controlled (Jus and others, 1976.)

Antidepressants **Antidepressant** drugs are often given patients with major depression. They are believed to work by increasing the amount of norepinephrine available in the brain, as noted in Chapter 11. Severely depressed people often have insomnia, and it is not unusual for antidepressant drugs, which have a strong **sedative** effect, to be given at bedtime.

Typically, antidepressant drugs like Tofranil and Elavil must "build up" to a therapeutic level, which may take 10 days to three weeks. For this reason, some patients are hospitalized during this period to prevent suicidal behavior. Overdoses of antidepressant drugs can be lethal. It can be a risky business to prescribe these drugs for depressed people who remain outpatients.

Lithium You could say that the ancient Greeks and Romans first used the metal lithium as a psychoactive drug. They would prescribe mineral water for patients with bipolar affective disorder. Although they had no inkling as to why this treatment was sometimes effective, it may have been because it contains lithium. A salt of the metal lithium, in tablet form, flattens out cycles of manicky behavior and depression for most persons with this disorder, apparently by moderating the level of norepinephrine available to the brain.

Since lithium is **toxic,** the dose must be carefully monitored through repeated analysis of blood samples during early phases of therapy. It may be necessary for persons with bipolar disorder to use lithium indefinitely, just as a medical patient with diabetes must continue use of insulin to control the illness.

Evaluation of Chemotherapy There is little question that major tranquilizers, antidepressants, and lithium have been found effective in helping patients with severe psychiatric disturbances. Problems in using these drugs are often related to their dosage and side effects.

Minor tranquilizers are frequently abused by overuse. Many people request them to dull the arousal that stems from anxiety-producing life styles or interpersonal problems. Rather than make the often painful decisions required to confront their problems and change their lives, they find it easier to pop a pill. At least for a while. Then they get involved in the vicious cycle

Phenothiazines A family of drugs that act as major tranquilizers and are effective in treating many cases of schizophrenic and schizophreniform disorders.

Antidepressant Acting to relieve depression.

Sedative A drug that relieves nervousness or agitation.

Toxic Poisonous.

of having to increase the dosage and cope with the worry of how dependent they have become on the drug. Many family physicians, and a few psychiatrists, find it easier to prescribe minor tranquilizers than to help patients examine their lives and modify anxiety-evoking conditions. The fact that many clients want pills, not conversation, does not ease the physician's lot.

Electroconvulsive Therapy

Electroconvulsive therapy (ECT) was introduced by Italian psychiatrist Ugo Cerletti in 1939 for use with psychiatric patients. Cerletti had noted that some slaughterhouses used electric shock to render animals unconscious. The shocks also produced convulsions, and, as other European researchers of the period, Cerletti erroneously believed that convulsions were incompatible with schizophrenia and other major disorders.

Electroconvulsive Therapy (ECT). In ECT electrodes are placed on each side of the patient's head and a current is passed between them. Sufficient voltage induces a seizure. ECT is used mostly in cases of major depression where antidepressant drugs fail. ECT is quite controversial: Many find it barbaric and nobody knows why it works.

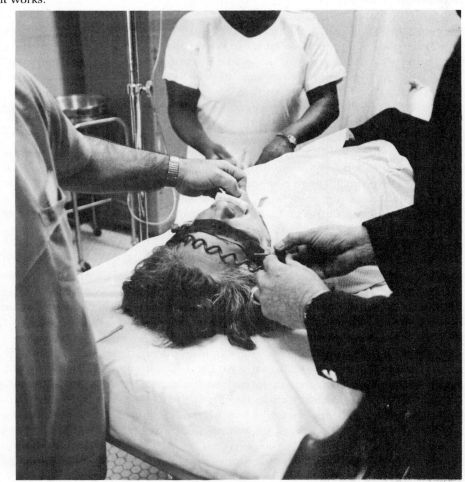

After the advent of major tranquilizers, use of ECT was generally limited to treatment of people with major depression. The discovery of antidepressant medications limited use of ECT even further—to patients who do not respond to these drugs.

ECT patients typically receive one treatment three times a week for several weeks. A current of 70 to 130 volts is passed through the head for 0.1 to 0.5 seconds (Kolb, 1977). ECT induces unconsciousness, and so patients would not recall the shock. Still, patients are usually put to sleep with a sedative prior to treatment. In the past, ECT patients had flailed about wildly during the convulsions, sometimes breaking bones. Today they are given muscle-relaxing drugs and convulsions are barely perceptible to onlookers. ECT is not given to patients with high blood pressure or heart ailments.

ECT is controversial for many reasons. First, ECT seems barbaric to many professionals. The thought of passing electric shock through the head and producing convulsions (even if they are suppressed by drugs) is distressing. Second are the side effects. ECT disrupts recall of recent memory, even though much memory can be regained as time passes after treatment (Cronholm & Ottosson, 1961; Squire and others, 1975). ECT may also reduce the drives of hunger and thirst (Prewett and others, 1978). Third, nobody knows *why* ECT works (Fink and others, 1974). For reasons like these, ECT was outlawed in Berkeley, California by voter referendum in 1982. It was the first time that a specific treatment found its way to the ballot box. Still, some helping professionals maintain that ECT is the treatment of choice when antidepressant drugs fail. Whether other localities follow the Berkeley example remains to be seen.

Psychosurgery

Psychosurgery is more controversial than ECT. It is a method for treating violently agitated people that could be said to have developed with the cavemen who practiced trephining. The contemporary technique called the prefrontal **lobotomy** involves severing the nerve pathways that link the prefrontal lobes of the brain to the thalamus. It was pioneered by the Portuguese neurologist Antonio Egas Moniz and was brought to the United States in the 1930s. This operation was performed on more than 1,000 mental patients by 1950.

Although prefrontal lobotomy often reduces violence and agitation, it is not universally successful. One of Dr. Moniz's failures shot him. This operation also has a host of side effects, including hyperactivity and distractibility, impaired learning ability, overeating, apathy and withdrawal, epileptic-type seizures, reduced creativity, and, now and then, death. Because of these side effects and the advent of major tranquilizers, psychosurgery has been largely discontinued.

In sum, biological forms of therapy, particularly chemotherapy, seem desirable for some major psychiatric disturbances that do not respond to psychotherapy, or to psychotherapy alone. But common sense as well as research evidence suggests that psychotherapy is preferable with problems like anxiety, mild depression, and interpersonal conflict. No chemical can show a client how to cope adequately with an interpersonal problem. It can only dull the pain of failure and put off the day when the client must eventually make decisions.

Psychosurgery Surgery that is intended to promote psychological changes or to relieve disordered behavior.

Lobotomy (lo–BOT–to–me). The severing or destruction of a lobe of the brain. A form of psychosurgery.

Summary

The history of treatment of abnormal behavior varies from ancient trephining and the exorcism of the Middle Ages to asylums and prisons, mental hospitals, and the contemporary community mental-health movement. Although many long-term patients encounter severe adjustment problems when they return from hospitals to the community, there is little evidence that hospitalization at the outset is superior to outpatient treatment.

Psychotherapy is the systematic use of psychological principles to help clients overcome abnormal behavior or adjust to problems in living. Many forms of psychotherapy, including psychoanalysis, client-centered therapy, transactional analysis and gestalt therapy are designed to foster self-insight. We have discussed cognitive therapy as an insight-oriented therapy because of the common view that cognitive change is the central feature of client gains. Behavior therapy helps clients substitute productive behavior for maladaptive behavior with or without benefit of self-insight.

Psychoanalysts attempt to shed light on unconscious conflicts that are presumed to lie at the roots of clients' problems, and to substitute coping behavior for impulsive behavior and avoidance of life's challenges. The major method is free association, in which clients utter what comes to mind without censorship. Psychoanalysis also focuses on the hidden meanings of dreams and the transference relationship between analyst and client.

Client-centered therapy is a nondirective method that provides clients with a warm, accepting atmosphere that enables them to explore and overcome roadblocks to self-actualization. Transactional analysis focuses on people's life positions (such as "I'm OK—You're not OK"), and how people play games to confirm unhealthy life positions. Gestalt therapy provides directed exercises that are designed to help clients integrate disowned parts of the personality. In the gestalt technique of dialogue, people undertake a verbal confrontation between conflicting parts of the personality.

Cognitive therapy focuses on how our attitudes, beliefs, and automatic cognitive responses to stress can heighten emotional distress and lead to maladaptive behavior. Cognitive therapy methods focus on increasing client awareness of cognitive distortions, and fostering cognitive restructuring and coping skills. Some include cognitive therapy as one feature of behavior therapy with the argument that *adaptive behavioral change* is the goal of cognitive therapy. Others assert that the cognitive change is most important.

The behavior therapist focuses on changing observable behavior rather than thoughts or feelings. Several behavior therapy techniques were discussed. These include systematic desensitization and modeling for reducing fears. In aversive conditioning undesired responses are decreased in frequency through punishment. Through operant conditioning methods, desired responses are reinforced and undesired responses are extinguished. In assertiveness training clients learn to express themselves and seek their legitimate rights. Clients are taught self-control methods for manipulating the antecedents and consequences of their behavior, and the behavior itself, to increase the frequency of desired responses and decrease the frequency of undesired responses.

Group therapy can be more economical than individual therapy. It permits the therapist to help several clients at once, and clients have each other's knowledge and emotional support as resources. There are many different kinds of groups. Encounter groups seek to promote personal growth through intense confrontations that deal with relating to other group members in the here and now. Family therapy usually uses a systems approach to boost family members' coping skills and self-esteem, and to promote the growth of each member.

Biological therapies have a distinct place in the treatment of abnormal behavior. Major tranquilizers have permitted thousands of schizophrenics to lead productive lives in the community. Antidepressants have relieved many instances of major depression, and lithium helps flatten out the cycles of bipolar affective disorder. Unfortunately, minor tranquilizers, used for anxiety and tension, are frequently abused. Electroconvulsive therapy is a controversial treatment that is still used in many cases to treat major depression when antidepressant drugs fail. Psychosurgery was once used to treat violently agitated patients, but its side effects and the advent of chemotherapy have made psychosurgery a very rare procedure today.

Truth or Fiction Revisited

- *People in Merry Old England used to visit the local insane asylum for a fun night out on the town.* True. People with severe disturbances were often chained and mistreated, and the public was frequently much amused.

- *The terms "psychotherapy" and "psychoanalysis" are interchangeable.* False. Psychoanalysis is just one type of psychotherapy, the type originated by Sigmund Freud.

- *You may be able to gain control over bad habits merely by keeping careful track of where and when you engage in them.* True. Self-monitoring of behavior has been shown to help highly motivated people increase the frequency of desired behaviors and decrease the frequency of unwanted behaviors.

- *Lying around in your reclining chair and fantasizing can be an effective way of confronting your fears.* True. In the behavior therapy technique of systematic desensitization, a client gradually travels up a hierarchy of fear-evoking stimuli while remaining as relaxed as possible.

- *Smoking cigarettes can be an effective treatment for helping people to ... stop smoking cigarettes.* True. The specific technique is rapid smoking, in which the person puffs every six seconds. It is effective in about 60 percent of cases.

- *Staff members in a mental hospital induced reluctant patients to eat by ignoring them.* True. They used operant conditioning to extinguish uncooperative patient behavior.

- *Low fees are the most important factor to college students selecting a psychologist.* False. Students prefer therapists who advertise high availability, show signs of competence, and request affordable but not cheap fees.

- *The originator of a surgical technique intended to reduce violence learned that it was not always successful—when one of his patients shot him.* True. Antonio Moniz, the originator of the prefrontal lobotomy, was shot by a former patient.

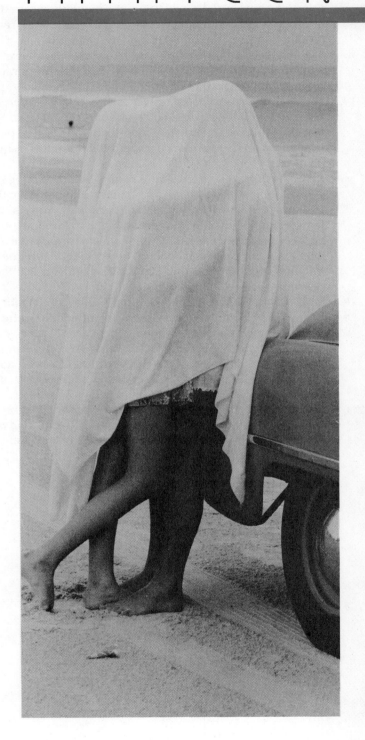

OUTLINE

Sexual Behavior

- Excessive masturbation can lead to mental illness.
- Most Americans learn about the birds and the bees through school sex education programs.
- Most women have entertained fantasies about imaginary lovers while engaging in sexual relations with their husbands.
- Men behave more aggressively than women do.
- Men have greater math and spatial relations abilities than women do.
- Sex offenders have histories of repeated exposure to pornography.
- Homosexuals suffer from hormonal imbalances.
- Sexual dysfunctions are rather rare occurrences.

Orgasm The height or climax of sexual excitement, involving involuntary muscle contractions, release of sexual tension, and, usually, intense subjective feelings of pleasure.

Coitus (CO–eet–tuss). Sexual intercourse.

Masturbation Self-stimulation of the sexual organs. (From the Latin *manus,* meaning "hand," and *stuprum,* meaning "defilement"—which offers insight into the history of attitudes toward masturbation.)

Procreation The production of offspring.

A Tale of Two Cultures

Offshore from the misty coasts of Ireland lies the small island of Inis Beag. From the air it is a green jewel, fertile and inviting. At ground level, things are not quite so warm.

The residents of Inis Beag do not believe that women experience **orgasm.** The woman who chances to find pleasure in sex is considered deviant (Messenger, 1971). Premarital sex is all but unknown. Women engage in **coitus** in order to conceive children and to appease their husbands' animal cravings. But they need not worry about being called on for frequent performances since the men of Inis Beag believe, erroneously, that sex saps their strength. Sex on Inis Beag is carried out in the dark—literally as well as figuratively— with the nightclothes on. The man lies on top in the so-called missionary position. In accord with local concepts of masculinity, he ejaculates as rapidly as he can. Then he rolls over and falls asleep. Once more the couple have done their duty.

If Inis Beag does not sound like your cup of tea, you may find the atmosphere of Mangaia more congenial. Mangaia is a Polynesian pearl of an island, lifting languidly from the blue waters of the Pacific. It is on the other side of the world from Inis Beag—figuratively as well as literally.

From an early age Mangaian children are encouraged to get in touch with their sexuality by stimulating their own genitals, or **masturbation** (Marshall, 1971). Mangaian adolescents are expected to engage in coitus. They may be found on secluded beaches or beneath the listing fronds of palms, diligently practicing techniques learned from village elders. When are Mangaian children old enough? When they are old enough.

Mangaian women are expected to climax, or reach orgasm, several times before their partners do. Young men want their partners to reach orgasm and compete to see who is more effective at bringing young women to multiple orgasms.

The residents of Inis Beag and Mangaia have similar anatomic features, but vastly different attitudes toward sex. Their attitudes influence both their sexual behavior and the pleasure they find—or do not find—in sex. Like eating, sexual activity is a natural function. Yet no other natural function has found such varied expression. No other natural function has been influenced so strongly by religious and moral beliefs, by cultural tradition, folklore, and superstition.

Throughout much of Western history sexual behavior has been viewed as indecent or sinful. The Judeo-Christian tradition has advanced the idea that **procreation** is the proper function of sex. Many people feel guilty about sexual activity, and many find no pleasure in sex. Others, who view themselves as the children of the "sexual revolution," may worry whether they have grown free enough in their sexual activity.

In this chapter we first explore American sexual behavior within and outside the institution of marriage. We examine sex roles, sex differences, and sexism. We discuss the controversial issues of pornography, homosexuality and rape, and attempt to sort out realities from myths. Finally, we explore patterns of sexual response and problems in sexual response that are labeled sexual dysfunctions. We shall see that while some sexual dysfunctions have physical origins, more often irrational beliefs and expectations create anxieties that interfere with natural sexual response. For this reason, sex therapists often focus more on clients' attitudes than on their sexual behavior.

American Sexual Behavior in Perspective: A Tale of Two Generations

In the late 1940s and 1950s the publication of a pair of scientific surveys of American sexual behavior shocked the nation. The "Kinsey reports" (Kinsey and others, 1948, 1953), which described the sexual behavior of 5,300 men and 5,940 women, contained no foul language or suggestive imagery. Yet they created such a stir that a congressional committee charged that they undermined the moral fiber of the country (Gebhard, 1976). We as a nation had not yet learned to discuss sex openly.

More recent sex surveys (e.g., Hite, 1976, 1981; Hunt, 1974; Tavris & Sadd, 1977; Wolfe, 1981) have elicited little public concern. Comparisons of sexual behavior of the 1940s and today must rely on the Kinsey reports and these recent surveys, yet they all have their shortcomings (Rathus, 1983). Kinsey's sample underrepresented blacks, the elderly, the poorly educated, southerners, and westerners. Kinsey's subjects were all interviewed by men, which may have had an inhibitory effect on women respondents. Morton Hunt's (1974) sample of 982 men and 1,044 women was drawn from phone listings in representative communities. But only about 20 percent of those contacted agreed to participate. Hunt's sample is thus likely to be a particularly open and frank group of volunteers. The high numbers of respondents to surveys run by magazines—such as the 100,000 people who responded to the *Redbook* survey (Tavris & Sadd, 1977) and the 120,000 who responded to the *Cosmopolitan* survey—actually comprise a low percentage of readers. Again, they are likely to be groups of open and frank volunteers.

Despite their limitations, these surveys and others provide some insight into the sexual practices of the American population. Let us have a look at American attitudes toward, and practice of, masturbation, petting, premarital coitus, and marital and extramarital sex over the past two generations.

Masturbation

> In solitude he pollutes himself, and with his own hand blights all his prospects for both this world and the next. Even after being solemnly warned, he will often continue this worse than beastly practice, deliberately forfeiting his right to health and happiness for a moment's mad sensuality.
>
> —J.W. Kellogg, M.D., *Plain Facts for Old and Young* (1882)

This portrayal of the masturbator by one of the fathers of American breakfast cereals was typical for its day. Epilepsy, cancer, heart attacks, insanity, sterility, itching, even warts—despite the lack of a shred of evidence, all were considered the lot of the masturbator. Kellogg, by the way, warned that certain foods, especially alcohol and coffee, might excite the sex organs. He recommended "unstimulating" grains instead. In case the issue comes up at a cocktail party, you are now an expert on the origins of corn flakes.

Such misinformation is not restricted to olden days. Recent samples of college students (Abramson & Mosher, 1975) thought that masturbation could be harmful. Each of 312 men interviewed by Masters and Johnson (1966) believed that "excessive" masturbation could lead to a mental disorder. Ironically, none believed that his own level of masturbation exceeded the danger point.

Inside Woody Allen

Despite widespread though groundless fears, most people have masturbated. Men report greater **incidence** of masturbation than women. Kinsey and his colleagues (1948, 1953) and Hunt (1974) found that nearly all adult males and about two-thirds of adult women surveyed had masturbated. Cotton's (1975) survey of college students found that 89 percent of males and 61 percent of females were masturbating. Another student sample (Miller & Lief, 1976) reported a **cumulative incidence** of 97 percent for males and 78 percent for females. Religious devoutness seems to inhibit masturbation. Still, Hunt found that even among regular churchgoers 92 percent of the men and 51 percent of the women have masturbated.

Incidence of masturbation has increased among the married. Forty percent of the married men and 33 percent of the married women interviewed by Kinsey and his colleagues reported masturbating. But in the 1970s Hunt found that 72 percent of his young husbands and 68 percent of his young wives masturbated. Married people masturbate when their spouses are absent or unavailable, or when they desire a change of pace.

Men and women report using fantasies such as those listed in Table 13.1 to increase sexual arousal when they masturbate. The great majority fantasize, and most often about coitus with a loved person. Fantasies seldom involve violence or homosexuality.

Misinformation about masturbation persists, but Americans today are less likely to consider masturbation wrong. Among Hunt's 18- to 24-year-olds, only 14 to 15 percent agreed that masturbation was wrong. However, nearly one in three of respondents aged 55 and above agreed that it was wrong.

Incidence The extent to which an event occurs. The number of people who have engaged in an event.

Cumulative incidence The occurrence of an event or act by a given time or age (such as the percentage of people who engage in premarital coitus by age 30).

TABLE 13.1   **Masturbation Fantasies Reported in the Hunt Study**

Fantasy	Incidence of Fantasy (Percents)	
	Men	Women
Having intercourse with a loved person	75	80
Having intercourse with strangers	47	21
Having intercourse with more than one person of the opposite sex at the same time........................	33	18
Doing sexual things you would never do in reality	19	28
Being forced to have sex.................................	10	19
Forcing someone to have sex............................	13	3
Having sex with someone of the same sex...............	7	11

Source of data: Hunt (1974), pp. 91–93.

These older subjects were in their 20s during Kinsey's surveys. Perhaps most Americans would now agree with Woody Allen's observation: He could not knock masturbation, since it meant having sex with someone he loved.

Contemporary scholars of sexual behavior agree that masturbation is neither physically nor mentally harmful. But people who believe that masturbation is harmful, wrong, or sinful may experience anxiety if they masturbate or consider masturbation.

Petting

Petting is touch or massage of another person's breasts or genitals. Some people include **fellatio** and **cunnilingus** as forms of petting, while others consider them separately. Petting can be used to provide pleasure or reach orgasm. When used to heighten sexual arousal as a prelude to coitus, petting is called **foreplay.**

Surveys suggest that many adolescents and young adults use petting as a halfway measure between sexual abstinence and coitus. It allows people to express affection and experience sexual excitement while avoiding pregnancy and maintaining virginity.

Kinsey found petting nearly universal among male adolescents. For college men who delayed marrying, petting became a major sexual outlet for many years. Petting was also common among females, especially those who delayed marriage. Ninety-four percent of women who remained single at age 20 had petted (Kinsey and others, 1953).

Hunt (1974) found petting nearly universal among adolescents in the 1970s. But Hunt's subjects began petting at younger ages than Kinsey's. They were less likely than Kinsey's subjects to use petting as a prolonged adjustment to the single life, since premarital coitus has become more common.

Both Kinsey and Hunt found that women who petted to orgasm prior to marriage were more likely to reach orgasm during the first year of marital coitus. Perhaps women who petted acquired sexual skills earlier. But it is also likely that women who petted prior to marriage were more open to their sexuality.

Petting Sexual interaction that does not include coitus.

Fellatio (fell–LAY–she–oh). Oral stimulation of the male genitals. (From the Latin *fellare*, meaning "to suck.")

Cunnilingus (cun–knee–LING–us). Oral stimulation of the female genitals. (From the Latin *cunnus*, meaning the female genitals, and *lingere*, meaning "to lick.")

Foreplay Sexual contact used to heighten sexual arousal in preparation for coitus.

TABLE 13.2 How Boys and Girls Learn the Facts of Life

	Percentages Reporting Source	
Main Source of Sexual Information	**Males**	**Females**
Friends	59	46
Reading	20	22
Mother	3	16
Father	6	1
School program	3	5
Adults outside the home	6	4
Brothers, sisters	4	6
Other sources, or No answer	7	7

How did you learn about the birds and the bees? Most of the people interviewed by Hunt in the 1970s learned about sex from friends and from reading. Parents and school programs apparently imparted relatively little information. Is it any surprise that sexual misinformation is widespread? Source of data: Hunt (1974), p. 122.

TABLE 13.3   Incidence of Premarital Intercourse among Different Age Groups (Percents)

	Age Group				
	18-24	**25-34**	**35-44**	**45-54**	**55 and over**
Men	95	92	86	89	84
Women	81	65	41	36	31

Source: Hunt (1974), p. 150.

Premarital Intercourse

The incidence of premarital coitus in Kinsey's day clearly reflected the sexual double standard that sexual activity is more acceptable for men than women. By age 20, 77 percent of the single men in Kinsey's sample, but only 20 percent of the single women, had engaged in premarital intercourse. By age 25, 83 percent of the single men and 33 percent of single women had done so.

Table 13.3 shows that the incidence of premarital intercourse seems to have exploded for young singles interviewed by Hunt, especially women. A survey of *Psychology Today* readers (Athanasiou and others, 1970) found that 79 percent of the male and 76 percent of the female respondents had engaged in premarital coitus. The *Redbook* survey (Tavris & Sadd, 1977) reported that 91 percent of single women aged 25 had engaged in premarital intercourse. Readers of these magazines may be somewhat better educated and more liberal than the general public. Still, it seems that the gap in sexual experience between unmarried men and women has been closing.

TABLE 13.4   Percentage of Men and Women Who View Premarital Intercourse as Acceptable

ACCEPTABLE BEHAVIOR	University of North Carolina Sample (1972)		Hunt Sample (1974)		Northeastern University Sample (1980)	
	Men	Women	Men	Women	Men	Women
FOR MALES						
Coitus when in love	92	92	82	68	92	97
Coitus with strong affection	87	75	75	55	89	82
Coitus without strong affection	55	32	60	37	49	24
FOR FEMALES						
Coitus when in love	100	100	77	61	92	91
Coitus with strong affection	89	72	66	41	92	91
Coitus without strong affection	62	26	44	20	32	24
Number of cases	107	68	982	1044	192	170

Sources: Bauman & Wilson (1976), Hunt (1974), Rathus (1980).

But it would be wrong to assume that Americans in large numbers have been climbing aboard the bandwagon of recreational sex. Fifty-four percent of the women in the Hunt study who had engaged in premarital coitus did so with one partner only—typically the man they wished to marry. So did 48 percent of a sample of 532 12- to 17-year-olds who visited a **contraceptive** clinic which Reichelt (1979) studied.

A sex-with-affection standard appears prevalent today, as noted in Table 13.4. Petting and premarital coitus are rated more acceptable for couples who are in love. In 1967, 85 percent of parents of college students in a CBS poll believed that all premarital coitus was morally wrong. But 63 percent of such parents in a recent poll (Yankelovich, 1981) agreed with the statement, "If two people love each other, there's nothing morally wrong with having sexual relations."

Hunt reports that most people who abstain from premarital coitus do so for moral or religious reasons. Other reasons mentioned include fear of being caught, of pregnancy, or of disease.

Marital Sex

Since Kinsey's day the marital bed has become a stage with more varied parts for the players. Kinsey's samples generally restricted coitus to the man-on-top, or missionary, position. Only one-third of the sample had also used the female-superior (woman-on-top) position, but this percentage doubled with the Hunt study. Today the rear (vaginal) entry, side-by-side, and sitting positions have become spices commonly included in the sexual diet.

Kinsey found that many husbands at lower educational levels engaged in a kiss or two and only brief bodily contact with their wives before coitus. Oral breast stimulation was often seen as "for babies, not for men." Oral-genital

Contraceptive Descriptive of a device that prevents pregnancy. (From the Latin *contra*, meaning "against," and *concipere*, meaning "to take in.")

There Is Nothing I Would Not Do, etc. is the title of a book by CBS newsperson Charles Osgood (1981). *P.O.S.S.L.Q.?* That's the title the US Census Bureau gives people who live together without benefit of marriage—Person of Opposite Sex Sharing Living Quarters.

There has been a profound increase in the numbers of (deep breath) P.O.S.S.L.Q.'s, or cohabitors, in recent years (Macklin, 1978; Glick & Spanier, 1980). In 1970, 523,000 couples lived together, but in 1978 more than twice this number—1,137,000—shared a residence. Children were present in 24 percent of these households.

Cohabiting vs. Married Couples How do cohabiting couples differ from the married? The difference in education between cohabiting and married women is surprising. Only 29 percent of married women continued their education past high school, but 53 percent of never-married cohabiting women had attended college (Glick & Spanier, 1980). Forty-six percent of cohabiting men as compared to 41 percent of married men had continued their education past high school.

Never-married cohabitors differ markedly from the married in employment status. Cohabiting men up through the age of 54 are less likely than married men in the same age group to be working. To some degree, especially among younger men, this difference reflects a greater tendency for cohabiting men to seek advanced education. But for many cohabiting men, a nontraditional approach to life style appears to encompass attitudes toward work as well as marriage.

For women the pattern is reversed. Cohabiting women are more likely than their married peers to work. For the woman, perhaps, the nontraditional behaviors of cohabiting and pursuing a career cluster together.

Cohabitation on Campus During the early 1960s a Columbia University student was found to be cohabiting with her boyfriend. She received such adverse publicity that she was forced to withdraw from school. But by the 1970s cohabitation became commonplace. Many factors contributed to this change, such as availability of birth control, decreased emphasis on maintaining virginity, relaxed college housing regulations, and the perception—correct or incorrect—that "everyone's doing it."

Perhaps one-fifth to one-third are. Macklin (1972) found that 25 percent of California State University at Northridge students, 36 percent at the University of Texas, 20 percent at the City University of New York (largely a commuter campus), 33 percent at Penn State, 23 percent at Arizona State, and 31 percent at Cornell had cohabited. Bower and Christopherson (1977) found that 25 percent of a sample of students from 14 state universities had cohabited.

Despite their "liberated" life style, cohabiting students seem traditional in many ways. They generally come from stable homes (Macklin, 1972). Their grades equal those of noncohabiting students. They are not more likely to use drugs. Ninety-six percent plan to marry someday, although probably at later ages than noncohabiting students (Bower & Christopherson, 1977). But they do not necessarily plan to marry their P.O.S.S.L.Q.'s.

Most cohabiting students thought their parents would disapprove of their life styles, but only seven percent of the students surveyed by Macklin thought cohabitation was morally wrong. Half the students who did not cohabit did not offer moralistic reasons. Rather, they had not found the right person, or their boyfriends or girlfriends lived too far away to make cohabitation feasible.

Ninety-six percent of Macklin's cohabiting students found their relationship sexually satisfying, and 90 percent considered their life style pleasurable and successful. But cohabitation is not a bed of roses. Most of Macklin's subjects tried to conceal cohabitation from their parents. Fifty-seven percent were jealous of their partners. Sixty-two percent felt "overinvolved" and isolated; 49 percent felt trapped at times. Sixty-two percent had feared pregnancy. Seventy-one percent had encountered conflicting desires concerning frequency of sexual activity, and 62 percent of the women had occasional difficulty reaching orgasm. This problem list seems as though it could have been compiled by young marrieds, although married couples are not likely to fear that their parents will discover that they are living together. Still, married couples may feel they must convince their parents that they can handle both college and marriage—and that they selected the right mate.

contact was viewed as unhealthy and repulsive. Yet Kinsey's college-educated husbands more often indulged in lengthy foreplay. They also more often recognized the importance of orgasm to women, and the link between foreplay and orgasm.

Hunt found that college-educated couples are still more likely to use oral sex than couples with high-school educations. But oral sex has become so popular among young couples that 90 percent of Hunt's couples under age 25 had used both fellatio and cunnilingus.

In the past it was often assumed that the "virile" man ejaculated quickly during intercourse. Most of the men in Kinsey's (1948) sample reached orgasm within two minutes after beginning coitus, many within 10 to 20 seconds. But women usually take longer to reach orgasm. This message may have been successfully communicated in more recent years, because Hunt's sample reported an average duration of coitus of about 10 minutes. Younger couples engaged in coitus for even longer periods.

Both Kinsey and Hunt found that coital frequency diminished with age, but Hunt's modern couples reported more frequent coitus at nearly all age levels. Hunt's 18- to 24-year-olds reported engaging in intercourse 3.25 times per week. This figure tapered off gradually to once weekly for couples aged 45 and above.

It is common for men and women to heighten their sexual excitement during marital intercourse with sexual fantasy. Some worry that they are being disloyal, but there is no evidence that these fantasies lead to unfaithfulness or loss of interest in one's mate. Sixty-five percent of a sample of married women from an affluent New York suburb reported using sexual fantasies during coitus (Hariton & Singer, 1974). The most common fantasy, reported by 56 percent, was of "an imaginary romantic lover." Other common fantasies included reliving another sexual experience (52%), doing something "forbidden" (50%), being overpowered (49%), making love in another setting (47%), and group sex (47%).

Hunt also found a link between perceived closeness of the marital relationship and the pleasure received from sexual relations. Marital coitus does not take place in an emotional vacuum—the closer the relationship, the more enjoyable the sex. Sexual pleasure may contribute to feelings of closeness, just as closeness may render sex more enjoyable.

Extramarital Sex

The sexual revolution has not liberated attitudes toward **extramarital sex.** The great majority of Americans still disapprove of it. Eighty to 98 percent of Hunt's subjects and 85 percent of respondents in a recent survey of *Ladies' Home Journal* readers (Schultz, 1980) believe that extramarital sex is wrong.

In both the Kinsey and the Hunt studies, the incidence of extramarital sex was about 50 percent for men and 20 percent for women aged 25 and above. About 20 percent of the *Ladies' Home Journal* readers (Schultz, 1980) also had affairs. The relatively liberal respondents to the *Redbook* survey (Tavris & Sadd, 1977) reported a 29 percent incidence of affairs. The *Redbook* survey found a significant link between work status and affairs. Twenty-four percent of all housewives in their late 30s, as compared with 53 percent of working women in the same age group, had had affairs. Traditionalists might seize upon this statistic as another reason that wives should stay at home. But working men are also likely to be more prone to affairs than "househusbands." Would men accept such a finding as a reason for them to remain in the home?

Little is known about the numbers of partners with whom married men have affairs. But the Kinsey, Hunt, and *Redbook* surveys all found that 40 to

Extramarital sex Sex involving a married person and someone other than his or her spouse.

Comarital sex Swinging among married couples.

50 percent of the women who had affairs did so with one partner only. About eight in 10 limited their activity to a handful (five or fewer) partners.

In "swinging," or **comarital sex,** husband and wife participate jointly in extramarital encounters with another couple or at swinging parties. Despite its capacity to make headlines, swinging seems rare. Only about two percent of Hunt's couples had "swung," and many of these only once. Four percent of the *Redbook* wives had tried it (Tavris & Sadd, 1977). But just two percent of a midwestern sample of 579 married adults from various income levels had (Spanier & Cole, 1975). One study (Gilmartin, 1975) found swingers to be relatively affluent and motivated by sexual novelty. Another study (Bartell, 1970) found that many swingers preserved marital stability by prohibiting emotional involvement with swinging partners.

Interestingly, Hunt found that people who had affairs usually found sex with their mates more pleasurable than sex with their lovers. Marital partners may lose a bit of novelty over the years, but they are more likely than strangers to know of their mates' sexual needs. Anxiety also inhibits human sexual response. Anxiety often attends illicit relationships and may interfere with the sexual fulfillment that married persons seek through them. In any event, the majority of Americans still report not having extramarital affairs.

TABLE 13.5   Stereotypical Sex-Role Traits

Instrumentality Cluster (Masculine Pole Perceived as More Desirable)

Feminine	Masculine
Nonaggressive	Aggressive
Dependent	Independent
Emotional	Not emotional
Submissive	Dominant
Dislikes math and science	Likes math and science
Noncompetitive	Competitive
Home-oriented	Worldly
Sneaky	Direct
Feelings easily hurt	Feelings not easily hurt
Has difficulty making decisions	Makes decisions easily
Not self-confident	Self-confident
Unable to separate feelings from ideas	Easily able to separate feelings from ideas

Warmth-Expressiveness Cluster (Feminine Pole Perceived as More Desirable)

Feminine	Masculine
Doesn't use harsh language	Uses harsh language
Talkative	Not talkative
Tactful	Blunt
Gentle	Rough
Empathetic	Not empathetic
Vain	Not vain
Neat	Sloppy
Strong need for security	Little need for security
Enjoys art and literature	Doesn't enjoy art and literature
Easily expresses tender feelings	Doesn't easily express tender feelings

Based on responses from 74 college men and 80 college women. Adapted from Broverman, I.K., and others. Sex-role sterotypes: A current appraisal. *Journal of Social Issues, Vol. 28(2),* 63.

Sex Roles and Sex Differences

"Why Can't a Woman Be More Like a Man?" You may recall this song title from the musical *My Fair Lady*. In the song, Henry Higgins laments that women are emotional and fickle while men are logical and dependable. The emotional woman is a **stereotype**—a fixed conventional idea about a group. The logical man is also a stereotype.

In this section we first explore stereotypes and sex roles of men and women in our culture. Then we discuss the ugly side of sex-role stereotyping—sexism. Finally, we examine evidence concerning actual cognitive and personality sex differences.

Sex Roles and Stereotypes

Cultural stereotypes of men and women encompass more traits than emotionality and logic. They involve clusters of stereotypes that we call **sex roles**—complex groups or clusters of ways in which men and women are expected to behave. Laypeople tend to see the traditional feminine stereotype as soft and fragile, coy, supportive, and "ladylike." The typical masculine stereotype is perceived as tough, protective, gentlemanly, heading the house, and providing for the family (Myers & Gonda, 1982).

In one study of the cultural conception of masculine and feminine sex roles, Inge Broverman and her colleagues (1972) had undergraduate psychology students list traits and behaviors that they thought differentiated men from women. A list of 122 traits, each of which was mentioned at least twice, was generated. Each trait was made into a bipolar scale, such as:

Not at all aggressive . . . . . . Very aggressive

Another group of students indicated which pole of the scale was more descriptive of the "average" man or woman. Only traits which achieved a 75 percent agreement rate were retained. Many of the 41 traits that met this standard are shown in Table 13.5.

Further analysis broke the list down into two broad factors. One centered around competency in the realm of objects, including the business world (which we label "instrumentality"). The second involved emotional warmth and expression of feelings (the Brovermans' "warmth-expressiveness cluster"). Other samples then rated the items as more desirable for men or women (Broverman and others, 1972; Elman and others, 1970). In general, masculine traits in the instrumentality cluster were rated as more desirable for men, while feminine traits in this cluster were rated as more desirable for women. The people in this study felt it was desirable for women to be less rational than men, less aggressive, less competitive, and less dominant, but more emotional and dependent. The ideal woman was also seen as neater, gentler, more empathetic, and more emotionally expressive than a man.

Sexism

Sexism is the prejudgment that a person, because of gender, will possess negative traits. These traits may prevent adequate performance in certain types of jobs or social situations. Until recently, sexism excluded women from many occupations, with medicine and law being the most visible examples.

Stereotype A fixed, conventional belief about a group.

Sex roles Complex groups or clusters of ways in which men and women are expected to behave in given social settings.

Sexism The prejudgment that a person, on the basis of his or her sex, will possess negative traits or perform inadequately. A form of prejudice.

Sexism may lead us to interpret the same behavior in different ways when shown by women or by men. We may see the male as "self-assertive," but the female as "pushy." We may view him as "flexible," but her as "fickle" and "indecisive." He may be "rational," when she is "cold." He is "tough" when necessary, but she is "bitchy." When the businesswoman dons stereotypical masculine behaviors, the sexist reacts negatively by branding her abnormal or unhealthy.

Sexism can also make it difficult for men to show stereotypical feminine behaviors. A "sensitive" woman is simply sensitive, but a sensitive man may be seen as a "sissy." A woman may seem "polite," when a man showing the same behavior is labeled "passive" or "weak." Only recently have men begun to gain footholds in occupational domains restricted largely to women in this century, such as nursing, secretarial work, and teaching elementary school.

The women's movement has pressed for social and legal demands for equal treatment for women, and for the right of women to select social and occupational roles according to their talents and interests, rather than their sex. But no movement has yet sprung up to declare war on the stereotypes that restrict men.

Let us examine some studies of the power of sexism.

Women in the Professional Ranks? Oops, There Goes the Neighborhood! Once women have gained footholds in traditional male preserves like medicine and engineering, do sexists say, "I guess I was wrong about women's abilities, after all"? Not according to a study at the University of Tulsa (Touhey,

Women and the Executive Suite

The day when women will routinely run big companies is still a long way off. But propelled by affirmative-action laws, the feminist movement and the rising consciousness of corporations themselves, women executives have come a long way in the last decade. Women now occupy one-fourth of the managerial and administrative positions in private industry. The number of women who are corporate officers of the 1,300 largest US companies—judged too tiny to count 10 years ago—stood at 477 in 1981, and the number of women directors of those companies now exceeds 300. And women are likely to move even more rapidly into the towers of corporate America in the future. Twenty-six percent of all today's Master-of-Business-Administration hopefuls are female—compared with 3.5 per cent in 1971—and the proportion is sometimes higher at the most prestigious schools....

Women joining the ranks today get a fairer deal, but many of the old barriers remain. "Men will accept women in certain staff jobs, where their talent and dedication can help," says consultant Betty Lehan. "[But] let the women try to invade the male turf and whap-o, the curtain comes down...."

Threat Experts trace some male hostility to the fact that certain men feel threatened when they have to work with women. Radcliffe president Matina S. Horner, who once reported that many women feared success, now theorizes that men resent situations where they have to cooperate with women. In a study of 150 pairs of undergraduates, Horner found women performed at peak efficiency when working on word games with male partners. But the men usually displayed "a sense of psychological impotence" or "assertive authoritarianism." The Center for Research on Women at Wellesley College found that such sexism may have a "tip-

ping" point, increasing as the number of women executives grows.... "As the proportion of women increases, their presence is more likely to be seen as a true threat," says co-author Carol Weiss.

Women managers, especially young ones, often find themselves unequipped for corporate combat—and a few feel psychologically trapped. "In the textbooks, you get the picture that a successful manager should be aggressive, decisive, independent, and creative," says Clare Wherley (of) Western Electric.... "But culturally, the successful *woman* is not supposed to be that way...."

Perhaps the worst pressure to which women executives are subjected is the double standard that requires them to perform flawlessly without complaint—and in fact, in many cases, to outperform males in comparable jobs to stay even. And those who do succeed can be subject to the intimation that they used their sexuality to get ahead.

1974). The Touhey study suggests, rather, that sexists downgrade the value of the profession, as if the profession must be lowering its standards when women are admitted. College students downgraded the prestige of architecture, college teaching, medicine, and science when they received exaggerated reports that these professions were being flooded by women. Medicine's prestige dropped most precipitously. Women students shared men's sexist expectations; they also downgraded these fields.

The Inferiority of the Talented Woman: The Bem Study   Psychologists Sandra and Daryl Bem (1973) had college students rate the quality of professional articles in several fields. When the same article was attributed to a woman, it received lower ratings than when it was attributed to a man. Women raters were as guilty as men at assuming male superiority. This rating pattern was maintained with works of art as well as essays.

There was one exception. When told a work by a woman artist had won a contest, women raters judged it more favorably than when it was attributed to a man. Why? The Bems suggest that we are trained to be suspicious of the woman aspirant in a man's milieu. But when a woman does outdistance her male competitors, other women stand ready to rise and applaud her. Perhaps they think she must be something special to compete with men.

Sad to say, she probably must be. Being just as good as a man may not yet be good enough for a woman.

Women in increasing numbers are pursuing careers that have been traditionally labeled masculine.

Sex-Role Stereotypes and Judgments of Mental Health   The above studies were carried out with college students. Would we expect knowledgeable mental-health professionals like psychologists, psychiatrists, and social workers to show fewer stereotypical attitudes? In the mid 1980s, with the increased attention sexism has received, they might. But a little more than 10 years ago, it seemed that one answer to the question "Why Can't a Woman Be More Like a Man?" was that she might be labeled mentally unhealthy.

The Brovermans and their colleagues (Broverman and others, 1970) gave mental-health workers a list of bipolar traits similar to those in Table 13.5 and asked them to identify the pole that typified the "healthy adult woman" and the "healthy adult man." The healthy woman was described as submissive, dependent, vain, emotional, and disinterested in math and science. But the healthy man was described as competitive, independent, firm, objective, decisive, and skilled in the worlds of business and science. It does not require lengthy consideration to conclude that the healthy man has a more positive stereotype than the healthy woman. Women professionals were as guilty of stereotyping as their male counterparts.

Other mental-health workers were simply asked to describe the "healthy adult person," sex unspecified. They chose adjectives typifying the healthy man, not the healthy woman. In other words, a soft, feminine female may be seen as a healthy woman, but not as an adult. However, as noted earlier, it may be that mental-health workers in the mid 1980s have become more aware of past stereotypical expectations.

Women and Fear of Success   Still, given the stereotype of the "healthy" woman that has prevailed in our culture, we can understand that a number of women have feared that forging ahead in the business world might compromise their femininity—at least in the eyes of others. In one type of study, Matina Horner (1972) provided college students with brief glimpses into the

Fear of success In psychological research, fear that achievement in a given area will be inconsistent with one's sex role, thereby compromising one's "femininity" or "masculinity."

lives of others, and asked them to write brief stories about the characters—how they felt, how others would react, and what their futures would hold. Note the following examples:

> *Capsule 1.* After first-term finals, Tom finds himself at the top of his medical school class.
> *Capsule 2.* Ron is with his girlfriend, Betty, when they find out he has been admitted to graduate school.

Then she repeated the procedure with the following "minor" changes:

> *Modified Capsule 1.* After first-term finals, Ann finds herself at the top of her medical school class.
> *Modified Capsule 2.* Betty is with her boyfriend, Ron, when they find out she has been admitted to graduate school.

In response to modified capsule 1, most women wrote stories suggesting that Ann would encounter social problems, or that she had come by her grades illegitimately. Ann might lose friends, remain single, become more and more socially isolated. Her grades might have reflected computer error, or the generosity of a powerful male benefactor who was her lover. But Tom's success was typically attributed to intelligence and hard work. Tom would find happiness, social acceptance, and wealth.

Horner concluded that women storytellers were projecting their own **fear of success** into their tales. Our culture tends to see high achievement and femininity as incompatible. The achieving woman might fear she will "lose" her femininity. Teachers and parents reward girls for good grades, but also often expect them to find husbands or to plan "feminine" careers at the proper age. They may fear that a serious career would disrupt family life or a husband's career. If Ron is admitted to graduate school, most storytellers assume that Betty will follow him and, perhaps, work to help put him through. If Betty is admitted to graduate school, many storytellers write that she may have to choose between Ron and the academic opportunity.

Some studies (e.g., Mednick & Puryear, 1976) report that recent samples of college women seem to show less fear of success than their counterparts of the 1960s. On the other hand, a recent survey of 23,000 relatively liberal *Psychology Today* readers (Renwick & Lawler, 1978) found that the husband's career almost always comes first when both spouses work.

Let us note also that at least one recent report (Janda and others, 1978) found that men tend to show similar fear of success about entering professions like nursing. Perhaps they fear that such work would compromise their "masculinity." Both sexes have been painfully restricted by cultural stereotypes.

Toward Psychological Androgyny

We usually think of masculinity and femininity as opposite poles of one continuum (Storms, 1979). The more masculine a person is, the less feminine he or she must be, and vice versa. This is why women who compete with men in the business world are not only seen as more masculine than other women, but also as less feminine.

But in recent years many psychologists have argued that masculinity and femininity comprise independent personality dimensions. A person who shows stereotypical masculine "instrumentality" traits can also show stereotypical feminine "warmth-expressiveness" traits (see Table 13.5). Such people show **psychological androgyny**.

Recent research suggests that people who are psychologically androgynous are well-adjusted because they can summon a wider range of traits to meet the demands of various situations. Such studies have shown that psychologically androgynous people of both sexes show "masculine" independence under group pressures to conform and "feminine" **nurturance** in interactions with a kitten or a baby (Bem, 1975; Bem, Martyna, & Watson, 1976). They feel more comfortable performing a wider range of activities, including (the "masculine") nailing of boards and (the "feminine") winding of yarn (Bem & Lenney, 1976; Helmreich and others, 1979). They are more accepting of nontraditional occupational roles (Motowidlo, 1982). They show greater maturity in moral judgments, greater self-esteem (Flaherty & Dusek, 1980; Spence and others, 1975), and greater ability to bounce back from failure experiences (Baucom & Danker-Brown, 1979). Psychologically androgynous women rate stressful life events as less undesirable than do feminine women (Shaw, 1982).

Sandra Bem (1974) has found that about 50 percent of her samples of college students have adhered to their own sex-role stereotypes on her test for measuring psychological androgyny. About 15 percent have been cross-typed (described by traits stereotypical of the opposite sex), and 35 percent have been androgynous. The incidence of psychological androgyny is probably higher among college students than among the general population. Yet many young people seem to be challenging stereotypical sex roles and deciding that they are free both to show instrumentality and to express feelings.

In this section we have explored cultural stereotypes and sexism. Let us now turn our attention to research concerning actual sex differences in cognitive functioning and personality.

Sex Differences: Vive La Différence or Vive La Similarité?

Differences in Cognitive Functioning   It was once believed that men were more intelligent than women because of their greater knowledge of world affairs and skill in science and industry. We now recognize that greater male knowledge and skill reflected the systematic exclusion of women from world affairs, science, and industry. Two generations of experience with assessment of intelligence have dispelled myths about overall differences in cognitive functioning between the sexes. Still, in their review of cognitive and personality differences between the sexes, Maccoby and Jacklin (1974) found persistent suggestions that women are somewhat superior to men in verbal ability. But men appeared somewhat superior in math and visual-spatial abilities (Table 13.6).

Three factors should caution us not to attach too much importance to these cognitive gender differences. First, they are small (Hyde, 1981). Second, they represent group differences, and variation in these skills is larger within, than between, the sexes. Despite group differences, millions of men excel the "average" woman in writing and spelling skills, and millions of women outdistance the "average" man in mathematics and spatial relations. Third, the small differences that appear to exist may reflect cultural expectations and environmental influences, not innate potential (Tobias, 1982). Women receiving even brief training in various visual-spatial skills, such as rotating geometric figures, show no performance deficit in these skills when compared to men (Stericker & LeVesconte, 1982). So-called ability tests actually measure

Psychological androgyny
Possessing personality traits attributed to both men and women. Possession of "instrumental" and "expressive" traits. (From the Greek *andros*, meaning "man," and *gyne*, meaning "woman.")

Nurturance
(NUR–chew–rants). The quality of promoting the development or upbringing of. (From the Latin *nutrire*, meaning "to nourish.")

TABLE 13.6 Vive la Différence? Just How Different Are the Two Sexes?

Differences Borne Out by Some Research Studies	Differences about Which There Is Greater Doubt	Assumed Differences Which Research Has Shown to Be False
Males tend to be more aggressive than females	Females are more timid and anxious than males?	Females are more sociable than males.
Females have greater verbal ability than males.	Males are more active than females?	Females are more suggestible than males.
Males have greater visual-spatial ability than females.	Males are more competitive than females?	Males have higher self-esteem than females.
Males have greater ability in math than females.	Males are more dominant than females?	Females lack achievement motivation.
		Males are more logical than females.

It has been commonly assumed that there are great differences between men and women, and that these differences reflect heredity or the natural order of things. Yet psychological research has shown the supposed differences to be much smaller than had been assumed. And those differences that remain, such as greater math ability in males and greater verbal ability in females, may reflect cultural expectations and not heredity.

Source: Based on data from Maccoby & Jacklin (1974).

achievement at a certain point in time. Neither men nor women should feel limited by cultural stereotypes or large-scale studies of comparisons of cognitive skills.

Differences in Personality In almost all cultures, with a couple of fascinating exceptions (Ford & Beach, 1951; Mead, 1935), it is the men who march off to war and who battle for glory and shaving-cream-commercial contracts in the arenas. In psychological studies, boys and men consistently behave more aggressively than girls and women.

But there are a couple of exceptions in experiments in which the measure of aggression was willingness to deliver electric shock. In the first experiment (Taylor & Epstein, 1967), in which men and women shocked each other when they failed to respond quickly to a stimulus, women generally chose lower levels of shock than men. However, when men violated **sex norms** of treating women favorably (by setting high levels of shock for women), women retaliated by setting shock levels as high as the men's. In the second experiment (Richardson and others, 1979), women's level of retaliation was influenced by the presence or absence of others. When women were observed by a person who remained silent, they set relatively low shock levels. However, when they were alone or in the presence of another woman who encouraged them, they set higher levels of shock as time went on. Thus it appears that women's relatively lower level of aggressiveness, when provoked, at least in part reflects cultural expectations and fear of social disapproval.

Despite the stereotype of women as gossips and "chatterboxes," research in communication styles suggests that men in many situations spend more time talking than women do. Men are also more likely to introduce new topics and to interrupt others (Deaux, 1976; Kramer, 1974). Yet women do seem more willing to reveal their feelings and personal experiences (Cozby, 1973). Women are less likely than men to curse—with the exception of women who are

Sex norms Social rules or conventions that govern the ways in which males and females interact.

bucking sex-role stereotypes. As noted in Table 13.5, use of harsh language is considered a masculine trait.

Women appear to require less **personal space** than men do. They tend to stand and sit closer to one another than men do, as noted in naturalistic observation studies of window shoppers and visitors to art exhibits (Bell and others, 1978), and in experiments (Sussman & Rosenfeld, 1982). Women also prefer to have friends sit next to them, while men prefer friends to sit across from them (Sommer, 1969; Fisher & Byrne, 1975). Social psychologists suggest that differences in seating preferences and personal space requirements reflect greater male competitiveness. Men, that is, perceive close encounters as confrontations in which they face potential adversaries. Thus, they need to keep an eye on them from a safe distance. Pieces of evidence provide some confirmation of this view. Anxious people (Karabenick & Meisels, 1972) and violent people (Kinzel, 1970) appear to seek more personal space than do the nonanxious and nonviolent. Personal space requirements also decrease when we grow more attracted to and trusting of members of the opposite sex (Allgeier & Byrne, 1973; Byrne and others, 1970; Edwards, 1972).

In a statistical analysis of 46 studies on **gender** and conformity, Cooper (1979) concluded that women do tend to conform to group pressures more so than males do. Conformity among women appears linked to acceptance of the stereotypical feminine role. Bem (1975) found that psychologically androgynous women are less likely to conform than are women who score as highly "feminine" on her sex-role inventory.

Clearly, there are important anatomical differences between the sexes. However, in many cases it seems that differences in personality and cognitive functioning are small, if they exist at all. The French have a saying, "Vive la différence." For those who have felt restricted by their sex roles, perhaps we can now exclaim, "Vive la similarité."

Varieties of Sexual Experience

We all possess a similar sexual biological makeup, and most readers will have been exposed to reasonably similar cultural beliefs and expectations about sex. Still, our sexual preferences may vary significantly, and sex can be used in the expression of anger and violence as well as in the expression of love. In this section we explore three varieties of sexual experience that are also major social issues: pornography, homosexuality, and rape.

Pornography

Since the late 1960s, when the Supreme Court ruled that prohibiting **explicit** sexual materials violated freedom of expression, **pornography** has been a boom industry in the US. Sections of major American cities—like Times Square in New York and the "Combat Zone" in Boston—garishly display their sex films and other wares. In just a few years we have developed "porno classics" like *Deep Throat* and *The Devil in Miss Jones*. Marilyn Chambers, the willowy star of the porno film *Behind the Green Door*, was fired as "the Ivory Soap girl" for appearing in the movie. Ivory Soap wished to retain its image as 99 and 44/100ths percent pure.

Some people complain that the availability of **erotica** has led to a breakdown in moral standards. Women's groups have argued that pornography

Personal space A psychological boundary that surrounds a person and permits that person to maintain a protective distance from others.

Gender One's classification according to sex.

Explicit (eggs–PLISS–sit). Clearly shown. Leaving nothing implied.

Pornography (pour–NOG–graph–fee). Explicit, uncensored portrayals of sexual activity that are intended to excite the observer sexually. (From the Greek *porne*, meaning "prostitute," and *graphein*, meaning "to write.")

Erotica Sexual material that stimulates a sexual response.

inspires crimes of violence against women. In this section we review research bearing on two important questions concerning pornography: What are the effects of pornography? Does pornography inspire antisocial behavior?

What Are the Effects of Pornography? In the 1960s, congress created a presidential Commission on Obscenity and Pornography to review research on pornography and conduct its own studies. The Commission concluded that married couples exposed to pornography reported feeling sexually aroused, but were not motivated to try observed sexual activities that were "deviant" for them (Abelson and others, 1970). More recent studies with participants ranging from middle-aged couples to college students have attained similar results (Brown and others, 1976; Fisher & Byrne, 1978; Hatfield and others, 1978; Heiby & Becker, 1980; Herrell, 1975; Mann and others, 1973; Schmidt & Sigüsch, 1970; Schmidt and others, 1973; Schmidt, 1975). Observers were sexually aroused and may have been motivated to masturbate or engage in sexual activity with their usual sex partners. But they did not lose self-control or become notably distressed or disturbed.

But these were generally "one-shot" experiments. What of people who have prolonged exposure to pornography? Howard and his colleagues (1973) exposed male college students to pornography for 90 minutes a day over a 15-day period. Personality variables as measured by psychological tests showed no change at the end of the study. Sexual arousal was measured by self-report and a **penile strain gauge,** which measures size of erection. Sexual arousal according to both measures was highest at the outset of the study. Then it waned gradually. Toward the end of the study many men reported increasing boredom and stated they would not have completed the study except for the financial incentive ($100) or their commitment to the research. Too much pornography did not drive these observers to abandon. Rather, it became a crashing bore.

It is folklore that men are most sexually responsive to explicit, "hard-core" sexual materials and fantasies. Women, however, are considered more romantic, and thus more likely to be sexually aroused by affectionate, "soft-core" themes. But in an often-cited study, psychologist Julia Heiman (1975) found that hard-core erotica is not for men only. She played audiotapes with romantic or sexually explicit content while college students' responses were measured by the penile strain gauge and the **vaginal photoplethysmograph.** She found that explicit sex, with or without romantic trappings, was sexually arousing to both women and men. But don't conclude that romance is an old-fashioned waste of time. Both college men and women report a greater liking of stories that combine sex with romance (Schmidt and others, 1973). Physical arousal alone does not mean that your date will say yes. Without romance, your dates are likely to disappear before sexual arousal becomes an issue.

Does Pornography Inspire Antisocial Behavior? The president's Commission surveyed over 3,000 mental-health professionals, including psychologists and psychiatrists. Eighty percent of them reported never seeing a case in which pornography seemed to be a causal factor in antisocial behavior. Only seven percent felt they had definitely encountered such a case. Only 12 percent thought that "obscene" books played a causal role in juvenile delinquency.

How do we summarize these results? By noting that the overwhelming majority of mental-health workers found little connection between pornog-

Penile strain gauge An instrument that measures the size of erection.

Vaginal photoplethysmograph (FOE–toe–pleth–THIZZ–mow–graph). An instrument that measures sexual arousal in women as a function of reflected light in the vaginal wall. The amount of light is related to blood pressure. (From the Greek *phos*, meaning "light," *plethyein*, meaning "to increase," and *graphein*, meaning "to write.")

Some glimpses of erotica in San Francisco.

raphy and antisocial behavior? Or by arguing that a significant minority had seen such cases? The data can be used to support either conclusion. But the data are also subject to all of the errors in self-report discussed in Chapter 1.

In a Danish study, Kutchinsky (1973, 1976) found a steady, substantial drop-off in the incidence of sexual offenses including exhibitionism, voyeurism, and pedophilia after restrictions against pornography were lifted in 1967. (There was no change in the incidence of rape, but Kutchinsky claims that rape had been rare in Denmark in any case.) Unfortunately, the Danish "experiment" was uncontrolled. It may be that the same factors that led to lifting of restrictions against pornography also contributed to the drop-off in sexual offenses. One factor could have been a liberalized attitude toward sexuality. Potential offenders might have found ready access to alternate sexual outlets.

Surveys of convicted sex offenders in the US (e.g., Goldstein, 1973; Goldstein and others, 1971) have found offenders to report *less* exposure to pornography than reference groups of nonoffenders. Rapists and pedophiles reported little or no discussion of sex at home during childhood. An implication is that repression of sexuality at early ages can trigger antisocial behavior later on. But we must interpret this data with caution also. It involved self-reports of convicted offenders rather than direct observations of behavior. Convicted offenders could believe that they would gain favorable treatment from authorities by appearing as "normal" as possible. They would also recognize that exposure to pornography is not considered normal in our culture. Thus, they might be motivated to underreport such exposure.

These research studies have all had major shortcomings. Still, none of them supports the view that pornography *does* lead to antisocial behavior. However, a couple of recent well-controlled experiments with aggressive-erotic films give us reason for concern, even though normal men and women are usually more sexually aroused by films that portray affectionate coitus than by films showing sex with aggression (Malamuth, 1981).

In one study (Donnerstein, 1980), 120 college men were either provoked or treated neutrally by a male or female confederate of the experimenter. Subjects were then shown neutral, erotic, or aggressive-erotic films. In the latter film, a man forced himself into a woman's home and raped her. Subjects were then given the opportunity to aggress against the male or female confederate of the experimenter through a fake electric shock apparatus. The measure of aggression was the intensity of the shock chosen. As expected, provoked subjects selected higher shock levels. But even nonprovoked men shown aggressive-erotic films showed greater aggression toward women confederates. And provoked men who were shown aggressive-erotic films chose the highest shock levels against women.

A second study (Malamuth and others, 1980) found that college men and women usually reported greater sexual response to a story about mutually-desired sex than to a story about rape. But in variations of the study, Malamuth and his colleagues portrayed the rape victim as experiencing an involuntary orgasm, with or without pain. The addition of the involuntary orgasm raised student self-reports of sexual arousal to levels that equalled the response to mutually-desired sex. Women subjects were most responsive when the woman in the story did not have pain, but men were most aroused when she did. The researchers speculate that the woman's orgasm legitimized the violence. Thus, the sexual responsiveness of the observers was **disinhibited.** The story may have reinforced the cultural myth that some women need to be dominated and will be "turned on" by an overpowering man. Exposure to aggressive-erotic films may increase violence, even among normal college men.

However, even these well-controlled experiments have some limitations. For example, they both involved selection of a (phony) electric shock in a laboratory. Neither measured violence against women outside the lab. Still, if legislation were to be considered to answer the legitimate concerns of women who argue against the availability of aggressive-erotic materials, it might be that the Swedish approach of outlawing portrayals of *violence* rather than of sexual behavior could be considered. There remains no evidence that pornography without violence stimulates antisocial behavior.

On *Playboy* Centerfolds and Academic Averages

Who displays his *Playboy* centerfold on the wall? Who leaves it in the magazine or at the newsstand? Psychologists Richard Miller and Gary Carson (1975) peeked into the dorm rooms of 169 male campus residents at Utah's Weber State College to determine whether *Playboy*-type photos adorned the walls.

Dean's list men, it turned out, were less likely to pin them up. Students with high grade-point averages decorated their walls less frequently than students with a C average or below. Varsity team members were more likely to "decorate" their walls than were the less athletically inclined.

Does *Playboy* "art" distract college men from the academic life? Or do the more intellectually oriented have less interest in these photos? There is no evidence that more academically oriented people have less interest in sex. We would bet that the A student is simply more likely to undrape his fantasies in his mind than on his walls.

Homosexuality

Definition and Incidence of Homosexuality   **Homosexuality,** or a homosexual *orientation*, is defined as sexual preference for members of one's own sex. Sexual activity with members of one's own sex may reflect limited sexual opportunities rather than homosexuality. For instance, adolescent boys may masturbate one another while fantasizing about girls, and men in prisons may similarly turn to each other as sexual outlets.

Kinsey estimated that as many as 37 percent of the men and 13 percent of the women in his sample had had at least one homosexual encounter, while only about four percent of his male and one to three percent of his female subjects had a homosexual orientation. About two percent of the men and one percent of the women in the Hunt study had a homosexual orientation.

Homophobia   Although the American Psychiatric Association no longer regards homosexuality as a mental disorder (see Chapter 11), studies found that most Americans as recently as during the 1970s still regarded homosexuals as "sick" (Steffensmeier & Steffensmeier, 1974), "sinful" (Pattison, 1974), and "dangerous" (Morin & Garfinkle, 1978).

Some people show an extreme intolerance and fear of homosexuals that has been labeled **homophobia.** Homophobia has been linked to traditional family ideology, including belief in male dominance and the need for women to sacrifice for their husbands and children (Krulewitz & Nash, 1980). Perhaps highly traditional people would have the "most to lose" if stereotypical sexual patterns were suddenly distorted. Some men may hate homosexuals because they are attempting to bolster their own hypermasculine images (Mosher & O'Grady, 1979). Perception of homosexuality might lead them to fear "it" could happen to them.

Homosexuality Preference for sexual activity and the forming of romantic relationships with members of one's own sex. (From the Greek *homos*, meaning "same.")

Homophobia Strong negative feelings toward homosexuals.

In recent years, homosexuals (and their families) have become more open about expressing their sexual orientations and demanding equal rights.

Stereotypes of the Homosexual   Most people assume that a person's sexual orientation, **heterosexual** or homosexual, is part of his or her sex role (Storms, 1980). That is, a "masculine" man would have a sexual preference for women, and a "feminine" woman would prefer men. Homosexuals would thus be expected to have undergone role reversals, so that a **gay male** would show stereotypical feminine traits and a **lesbian** would be masculine. This presumed link has led to the cultural stereotypes of the swishy, effeminate gay male and the butch lesbian. Certainly there are a number of homosexuals who adhere to these stereotypes—just as heterosexuals largely adhere to their own stereotypes. But the majority of homosexuals do not.

It is often assumed that within each homosexual couple, one partner assumes an aggressive, masculine pattern of sexual behavior, and the other a passive, feminine pattern. But most homosexuals assert that they do not conform either to traditional masculine or feminine roles in their social or sexual interactions.

Adjustment of Homosexuals   Despite the slings and arrows of an often outraged society, it seems that homosexuals are about as well-adjusted as heterosexuals. Saghir and Robins (1973) could not distinguish gay males from heterosexuals in terms of anxiety, depression, and psychosomatic complaints like headaches and ulcers. Adelman (1977) found that professionally employed lesbians were somewhat more socially isolated than professional heterosexual women, but could not otherwise be differentiated. Other studies find more anxiety, tension, and depression among heterosexual women than among lesbians (Reiss and others, 1974; Siegelman, 1972, 1979; Wilson & Greene, 1971). Siegelman (1979) concludes that the similarities between lesbians and heterosexual women outweigh the differences, but lesbians are more self-accepting and goal-directed. Lesbians may achieve greater self-worth and a stronger self-identity through their work. Married women who work often see their jobs as secondary to their husbands'.

Bell and Weinberg (1978) found that the adjustment of San Francisco homosexuals was linked to their life styles. Homosexual "close couples" who lived as though married appeared at least as well-adjusted as married people. Homosexuals who led other life styles showed various levels of adjustment. Older homosexuals who lived by themselves and had few if any sexual contacts were poorly adjusted (as are many heterosexuals who lead a similar life style).

Causes of Homosexuality   The origins of homosexuality are complex and controversial. It was once thought that homosexuality might be genetically transmitted. Kallmann (1952) found a 100 percent **concordance** rate for homosexuality among the **probands** of 40 identical twins. However, more recent studies (e.g., Parker, 1964; Zuger, 1976; McConaghy & Blaszczynski, 1980) have failed to replicate Kallmann's findings.

Sex hormones are known to influence the mating behavior of lower animals (see Chapters 2 and 7). It was thought that gay males might be deficient in testosterone while lesbians might have lower-than-normal levels of estrogen and higher-than-normal levels of androgens in their bloodstreams. However, recent studies have shown no reliable differences in current hormone levels between heterosexuals and homosexuals (Meyer-Bahlburg, 1977, 1979). However, prenatal sex hormones can "masculinize" or "feminize" the brain. In people it is possible that prenatal hormonal influences create a basic predisposition toward heterosexuality or homosexuality (Money, 1977). Social learning experiences would then help determine whether this disposition is expressed in behavior or in fantasy.

Psychoanalytic theory (Bieber and others, 1962; Bieber, 1976) suggests that homosexuals resolve the Oedipus and Electra complexes, which were discussed in Chapter 9, differently from the heterosexual majority. In men this faulty resolution stems from a "classic pattern" of a close-binding mother and a detached-hostile father. But we should note that many gay males have had excellent relationships with both parents and that the childhoods of many heterosexuals have fit the "classic pattern."

Social learning theory suggests that pleasurable early sexual interactions with people of our own sex may induce a homosexual orientation. However, many gay males and lesbians felt their preferences before they had had any overt sexual contacts (Bell and others, 1981). And many others had numerous homosexual experiences in childhood, but never doubted their heterosexual orientations.

The causes of human homosexuality are indeed mysterious—as mysterious as the causes of human heterosexuality.

Forcible Rape

Forcible rape is the seeking of sexual gratification against the will of one's sex partner. There were more than 75,000 reported cases of rape in 1980. Since it has been estimated that only one rape in five is reported, it may be that 350,000 to 400,000 rapes take place in the United States each year.

If we add to these figures instances in which women are subjected to forced kissing and petting, the numbers grow even more alarming. For example, nearly 70 percent of 282 women in one college sample had been assaulted (usually by dates and friends) at some time since entering college (Kanin & Parcell, 1977).

In most off-campus sexual assaults, rapists and their victims are usually between 15 and 25 and from the lower socioeconomic classes. Most rapes occur indoors, and about 85 percent of these take place in the victim's home (Hursch, 1977). At least one-third of rapists and victims were at least casually acquainted. About 50 percent of rapists have previous arrests, and many have long records of violence as juvenile offenders (Amir, 1971).

A Psychological Controversy: Is Rape A Victim-Precipitated Crime? Who is responsible for rape? The victim or her assailant?

This question may sound absurd, but there is a long history of blaming women for the troubles that befall them. As noted by Brownmiller (1975), laws have generally been framed for the convenience of men. Rape has been viewed as a crime against *a man's property*. Among the ancient Babylonians and Hebrews, women and their assailants were equally likely to be punished. These are not only ancient notions. Even contemporary judges and police frequently assume that rapes have been victim-precipitated (Feldman-Summers & Palm, 1980). A Minnesota judge was recently removed from the bench for declaring that a teenaged boy could not be blamed for raping his 15-year-old victim. After all, noted the judge, she had dressed provocatively. Who could blame an impressionable boy for being inspired to sexual assault?

In court, victims are likely to find that their entire sexual histories may be trotted out before strangers (which is one reason why so many women do

This statue, "The Rape of the Sabine Women," portrays a theme that has been darkly disturbing to women, and those who care for them, since the dawn of history.

not report rapes). The more sexually experienced they are, the more likely it is that they will be considered responsible for the rape (Cann and others, 1979).

Women are apparently expected to remain demure, passive, and virginal. When there is any deviation from these unwritten standards—as in being socially outspoken, sexually assertive, or even going out alone in the evening or unescorted to a bar—society seems ready to blame women for whatever men do to them.

Conditions That Lead to Rape Many social critics argue that our culture socializes men into becoming rapists (Albin, 1977; Burt, 1980). Males, who are often reinforced for aggressive and competitive behavior, could be said to be asserting culturally expected dominance over women.

QUESTIONNAIRE

Cultural Myths That Create a Climate That Supports Rape

Martha Burt (1980) has compiled a number of statements concerning rape. Read each of them and indicate whether you believe it to be true or false by writing a T or F on the line provided. Then turn to Appendix B to learn of the implications of your answers.

T   F

_____ 1. A woman who goes to the home or apartment of a man on their first date implies that she is willing to have sex.

_____ 2. Any female can get raped.

_____ 3. One reason that women falsely report a rape is that they frequently have a need to call attention to themselves.

_____ 4. Any healthy woman can successfully resist a rapist if she really wants to.

_____ 5. When women go around braless or wearing short skirts and tight tops, they are just asking for trouble.

_____ 6. In the majority of rapes, the victim is promiscuous or has a bad reputation.

_____ 7. If a girl engages in necking or petting and she lets things get out of hand, it is her own fault if her partner forces sex on her.

_____ 8. Women who get raped while hitchhiking get what they deserve.

_____ 9. A woman who is stuck-up and thinks she is too good to talk to guys on the street deserves to be taught a lesson.

_____ 10. Many women have an unconscious wish to be raped, and may then unconsciously set up a situation in which they are likely to be attacked.

_____ 11. If a woman gets drunk at a party and has intercourse with a man she's just met there, she should be considered "fair game" to other males at the party who want to have sex with her too, whether she wants to or not.

_____ 12. Many women who report a rape are lying because they are angry and want to get back at the man they accuse.

_____ 13. Many, if not most, rapes are merely invented by women who discovered they were pregnant and wanted to protect their reputation.

Women, on the other hand, may be socialized into the victim role. The stereotypical feminine role (discussed previously in this chapter) encourages passivity, nurturance, warmth, and cooperation. Women are often taught to sacrifice for their families, and not to raise their voices. Thus a woman may be totally unprepared to cope with an assailant. She may lack aggressive skills and believe that violence is inappropriate for women. She may not know how to raise her voice to shout for help.

Social Attitudes and Myths That Encourage Rape   Many people, including professionals who work with rapists and victims, believe a number of myths about rape. These include "Only bad girls get raped," "Any healthy woman can resist a rapist if she wants to," and "Women only cry rape when they've been jilted or have something to cover up" (Burt, 1980, p. 217). These myths tend to deny the impact of the assault, and also to place blame on the victim rather than her assailant. They contribute to a social "climate" that is too often lenient toward rapists and unsympathetic toward victims.

Do you believe cultural myths that have the effect of supporting rape? Why not take the questionnaire on p. 522 and find out?

Preventing Rape   In *Our Bodies, Ourselves*, The Boston Women's Health Book Collective (1979) lists a number of suggestions that women can use to lower the likelihood of rape: Establish signals and arrangements with other women in an apartment building or neighborhood. List only first initials in the telephone directory or on the mailbox. Use dead-bolt locks. Keep windows locked and obtain iron grids for first-floor windows. Keep entrances and doorways brightly lit. Have keys ready for the front door or the car. Do not walk alone in the dark. Avoid deserted areas.

Also: Never allow a strange man into your apartment or home without checking his credentials. Drive with the car windows up and the door locked. Check the rear seat of the car before entering. Avoid living in an unsafe building. Do not pick up hitchhikers. Do not talk to strange men in the street. Shout "Fire!" not "Rape!" People crowd around fires but avoid scenes of violence.

The Sexual Response Cycle

During the 1960s William Masters and Virginia Johnson became renowned for their research in human sexual response and sexual problems, or dysfunctions. They disdained the standard questionnaire and interview approaches to sex research. Instead, they arranged for volunteers to engage in sexual activity in the laboratory while their physiological responses were monitored by elaborate recording equipment.

Masters and Johnson (1966) found that sexual stimulation leads to many types of responses. Two of them are largely reflexive: **myotonia,** or muscle tension, and **vasocongestion,** or the flow of arterial blood into the genitals and other parts of the body, such as the breasts. These responses, and others, can be described in terms of a sexual response cycle that applies to both men and women. The four phases of this cycle are the excitement, plateau, orgasm, and resolution phases (Figure 13.1). Much of our discussion of sexual response is based on the findings of Masters and Johnson.

Myotonia
(my–oh–TONE–knee–uh). Muscle tension. (From the Greek *myos*, meaning "muscle.")

Vasocongestion
(vaz–oh–con–JEST–shun). Accumulation of blood, particularly in the genital region. (From the Latin *vas*, meaning "vessel," as in "blood vessel.")

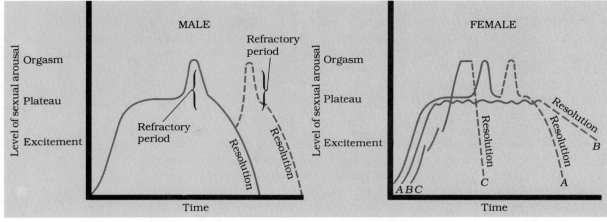

Figure 13.1   The Male and Female Sexual Response Cycles. The pattern of male sexual response shows that men undergo a refractory period following orgasm during which they are not responsive to further sexual stimulation. But they may be restimulated to orgasm after sufficient time passes. Pattern A, for women, shows that women may be restimulated to orgasms in quick succession (multiple orgasms). In Pattern B, a woman has been highly excited for a protracted period, but has not reached orgasm. Eventually her excitement subsides. In Pattern C, a woman quickly reaches orgasm and her excitement also rapidly subsides. Men may also experience patterns B and C. Source: Masters and Johnson (1966).

Excitement phase The first phase of the sexual response cycle, in which erection occurs in the male, and vaginal lubrication and clitoral swelling occur in the female.

Penis The male organ of coitus. (A Latin word meaning "tail.")

Clitoris A female sexual organ that is highly sensitive to sexual stimulation.

Vagina (vuh–JY–nuh). The female organ of coitus. (A Latin word meaning "sheath.")

Sex flush A reddish hue on body surfaces that is caused by vasocongestion.

Plateau phase (plat–toe). An advanced state of sexual arousal that precedes orgasm.

Penile glans The tip of the penis, which is highly sensitive to sexual stimulation. (From the Latin *glans*, meaning "acorn"—referring to the appearance of the end of the penis.)

Testes Organs that produce sperm cells and male sex hormones. Also called *testicles*.

The Excitement Phase

The **excitement phase** is the first phase of physiological response to sexual stimulation. The heart rate, blood pressure, and respiration rate increase. In the male, blood vessels in chambers of loose tissue within the **penis** dilate reflexively to allow blood to flow in. This filling or engorgement with blood results in erection. Despite the slang terms for an erection, "boner" and "muscle," the process of erection relies neither on bone nor muscle.

In the female, the breasts swell and the nipples become erect. Blood engorges the genital region and the **clitoris**—a protrusion on the genitals that is highly sensitive to sexual stimulation—expands. The inner part of the **vagina**—the tubelike organ that contains the penis during coitus—lengthens and dilates. Within ten seconds to half a minute vaginal lubrication reflexively appears. A **sex flush,** or mottling of the skin, may appear late in this phase.

The Plateau Phase

The **plateau phase** describes a heightening of sexual arousal that prepares the body for orgasm. The heart rate, blood pressure, and respiration rate continue to rise. In the man, further engorgement causes the ridge around the head of the penis, or **penile glans,** to turn a deep purple. The **testes** increase in size and elevate in order to allow a full ejaculation.

In the woman, the outer vagina becomes so engorged that its diameter is reduced about one-third. Engorgement of the area around the clitoris causes the clitoris to "withdraw" beneath a fold of skin called the clitoral hood. Further swelling of the breasts causes the nipples to appear to have become smaller, although they have not. The sex flush becomes pronounced.

The Orgasm Phase

Semen (SEE–men). The fluid that is ejaculated during coitus, containing sperm.

Refractory period A period following orgasm when a male is insensitive to further sexual stimulation.

Multiple orgasms The experiencing of one or more additional orgasms as a result of sexual stimulation during the resolution phase. Two or more orgasms in rapid succession.

Resolution phase The final phase of the sexual response cycle, during which the body returns gradually to its prearoused state.

During orgasm, breathing, blood pressure, and heart rate reach a peak, and there are involuntary muscle contractions throughout the body. In the man, muscles at the base of the penis contract and expel **semen** through the penis. In the woman, muscles surrounding the outer third of the vagina contract rhythmically. Most authorities agree that there is no female ejaculation, just vaginal lubrication—but see Ladas and her colleagues (1982) for a divergent view. For both sexes the initial contractions are most intense and spaced at about 0.8-second intervals (five contractions every four seconds). Subsequent contractions are weaker and spaced farther apart.

Following orgasm, men enter a **refractory period** during which they are unresponsive to further sexual stimulation, although some men are capable of reaching orgasm twice before sexual arousal subsides. Women can experience numerous or **multiple orgasms,** as many as 50 in rapid succession! This capacity has given some women the feeling that they ought not be satisfied with only one—the flip side of the old myth that sexual pleasure is meant for men only. In sex, as in other areas of life, our oughts and shoulds often place arbitrary demands on us that evoke anxiety and feelings of inadequacy (Rathus & Nevid, 1983).

Orgasm is a reflex. We can set the stage for it by receiving adequate sexual stimulation of a physical and, perhaps, cognitive nature (by focusing on the attractiveness of our partner, erotic fantasies, and so forth). Sexual cognitions can indirectly heighten arousal by relaying "messages" to the genitals through the spinal cord (see Chapter 8 in Rathus [1983] for a fuller explanation of neural mechanisms in sexual response). But we cannot force or will an orgasm to happen. Efforts to force orgasm can be counterproductive, as we shall see in our discussion of the sexual dysfunctions.

The Resolution Phase

After an orgasm that is not followed by additional sexual stimulation, a **resolution phase** occurs in which the body gradually returns to its resting state. The heart rate, blood pressure, and respiration rate all return to normal levels. Blood that has engorged the genitals is dispelled from this region throughout the body.

If a lengthy plateau phase is not followed by orgasm (as in pattern B in Figure 13.1), genital engorgement may take longer to dissipate, leading to pelvic tension or discomfort. In men this discomfort has been labeled "blue balls."

Sexual Response and the Aging

"Just because there's snow on the roof doesn't mean there's no fire in the furnace"—so goes the saying. Yet, for various reasons, we may think of sex as for young people only. It may be difficult for us to imagine our parents engaged in sexual activity; we may not understand why the elderly would be attracted to one another; and we may link sex with reproduction (Rathus, 1983). Still, Kinsey and his colleagues (1948) found that three-fourths of the 70-year-old men in his sample and half the men aged 75 achieved erections regularly. Masters and Johnson (1966) found women at these ages capable of multiple orgasms.

Some changes do occur with advancing age. By age 50 or so, men may require increased sexual stimulation to achieve erection and may not be able to reattain erection for from eight to 24 hours after ejaculation (Kaplan & Sager, 1971). But from the woman's perspective, her mate may become the perfect lover. It may take older men longer to ejaculate, and so the couple may be able to prolong intercourse. Many men continue to have intercourse into their 80s, but some lose the ability to perform sexually. This falloff may stem from decreased production of testosterone and physical problems, but can also reflect psychological factors, such as commitment to one's sex partner.

Along with **menopause,** women may experience vaginal dryness and loss of elasticity that reflects decreased estrogen production. This condition may be corrected through use of artificial lubrication or estrogen-replacement therapy (ERT). However, ERT is controversial because prolonged use has been linked to cancer. Menopause signals the end of a woman's reproductive capacity, but certainly not of her sexual capacity. Women in their 80s can reach orgasm. Men and women with positive sexual attitudes can enjoy sexual activity for a lifetime.

Sexual Dysfunctions and Sex Therapy

Perhaps most of us will be troubled by some form of **sexual dysfunction,** or difficulty in becoming sexually aroused or reaching orgasm, at one time or another. Masters and Johnson (1970) estimate that at least half the marriages in this nation are sexually dysfunctional. Fourteen to 15 percent of the middle-class married men and women surveyed by Frank and his colleagues (1978) reported their sexual relations as "not very satisfying" or "not satisfying at all." The incidence of sexual dysfunction may be higher among single people since they are less likely to feel secure in their sexual relationships and to be familiar with their partner's sexual preferences.

In this section we define the various sexual dysfunctions, then discuss their origins and their treatment.

Types of Sexual Dysfunctions

Male sexual dysfunctions include **erectile dysfunction** (inability to attain or sustain erection long enough for coitus), **premature ejaculation** (ejaculation prior to plan or the wishes of the couple), and **ejaculatory incompetence** (difficulty reaching orgasm). Erectile dysfunction was once called "impotence," a term that has been changed because of its implication that a man is weak or sterile. Ejaculatory "incompetence" has such a negative ring to it that we shall refer to it as "ejaculatory dysfunction."

In women, sexual dysfunctions include **orgasmic dysfunction** (difficulty reaching orgasm) and **vaginismus** (involuntary muscle contractions in the vagina that prevent entry of the penis). There are two types of orgasmic dysfunction. In "primary" orgasmic dysfunction the woman has never reached orgasm. In "situational" orgasmic dysfunction, the problem reflects specific circumstances, such as a particular sex partner or fatigue. Orgasmic dysfunction was once unfortunately called "frigidity," implying that women with this sexual dysfunction were disinterested in sex or "cold" as people. However, women with this problem may be quite frustrated and concerned.

Menopause The cessation of menstruation.

Sexual dysfunction A problem in becoming sexually aroused or in reaching orgasm.

Erectile dysfunction Inability to achieve or sustain an erection long enough to have coitus. Also called *impotence.*

Premature ejaculation Ejaculation that occurs before the couple are satisfied with the duration of coitus.

Ejaculatory incompetence Inability to ejaculate within the vagina.

Orgasmic dysfunction Difficulty reaching orgasm.

Vaginismus (vadge–in–IS–muss). Involuntary contraction of the muscles surrounding the outer part of the vaginal barrel.

Both sexes may encounter **dyspareunia** (painful coitus) and **sexual apathy** (lack of interest).

Origins of Sexual Dysfunctions

It was once assumed that sexual dysfunctions stemmed from organic or physical causes. But there has been recent recognition that most dysfunctions reflect psychosocial factors like troubled relationships, lack of sexual skills, irrational beliefs, and anxiety. Physical factors may also interact with psychological factors. For instance, anxiety has physiological correlates like rapid heart and respiration rates. In small doses, as typical of a first date, anxiety may enhance sexual excitement, but severe anxiety can block sexual response. Let us now examine various physical and psychological causes of sexual dysfunction.

Physical Factors　Since perhaps 10 to 20 percent of sexual dysfunctions stem from disease, people seeking sex therapy usually receive a thorough physical examination. Erectile dysfunction, for example, can reflect diabetes and diseases of the heart and lungs.

The single most common cause of dyspareunia in women is lack of sufficient vaginal lubrication which, in turn, usually reflects inadequate foreplay, marital dissatisfaction, anxiety, or other factors (Marmor, 1976; Wabrek & Wabrek, 1975). But dyspareunia may also result from a vaginal infection, an **episiotomy** scar, collection of secretions underneath the clitoral hood, and other physical causes. Dyspareunia in men can reflect infection of the **prostate gland, gonorrhea,** or even high sensitivity to the natural acidity of the vagina.

Fatigue may lead to erectile and ejaculatory dysfunctions in men, and orgasmic dysfunction and dyspareunia (because of inadequate lubrication) in women. But these will be isolated incidents unless we attach too much meaning to them and become overly concerned about future sexual performance.

Depressants like alcohol, narcotics, and tranquilizers may impede sexual response. Antiadrenergic drugs (used to treat high blood pressure), adrenal steroids like cortisone and ACTH (used to treat allergic reactions and inflammation), and anticholinergic drugs (used to treat ulcers and glaucoma) may contribute to sexual dysfunctions (see Rathus [1983] for a fuller discussion).

Traditional Attitudes　Certain traditional attitudes suggest that although men may find sex pleasurable, sex is a duty for women. Women who share these sex-negative attitudes may be so anxious about sex that they become a self-fulfilling prophecy. Men, too, may be handicapped by misinformation and sexual taboos.

Psychosexual Trauma　**Psychosexual trauma** refers to physically or psychologically painful sexual experiences that cause future sexual response to be blocked by anxiety. Rape victims may encounter sexual adjustment problems such as vaginismus or orgasmic dysfunction. Masters and Johnson (1970) report several cases of men with erectile dysfunction who had had extremely anxiety-evoking encounters with prostitutes.

Troubled Relationships　A sexual relationship is usually no better than other aspects of the relationship or marriage (Perlman & Abramson, 1982). Com-

Dyspareunia (dis–par–OO–knee–uh). Painful coitus.

Sexual apathy (AP–uh–thee). Lack of interest in sexual activity. (From Greek roots meaning "without feeling.")

Episiotomy (ep–peas–ee–OTT–to–me). A surgical incision that eases childbirth.

Prostate gland A gland that secretes the bulk of seminal fluid (semen).

Gonorrhea (gone–no–REE–uh). A sexually transmitted disease that can inflame the pelvic region.

Psychosexual trauma A distressing sexual experience that may have lingering psychological effects.

munication problems are an excellent predictor of marital dissatisfaction (Markman, 1981; Snyder, 1979; Schultz, 1980). Couples who have problems expressing their sexual desires are at a disadvantage in teaching their partners how to provide pleasure. We shall see that sex-therapy techniques enhance communication skills. Couples who communicate are also less likely to build resentments over nonsexual issues that spill over into the bedroom.

People who cannot express resentments verbally may "withhold" orgasm to make their partners feel guilty or inadequate. In one case (Rathus, 1978), a man who was angered by his wife's failure to appreciate his material provisions developed ejaculatory dysfunction.

Psychoanalytic Factors Within psychoanalytic theory, sexual dysfunctions are assumed to reflect unconscious conflicts primarily of the phallic stage—that is, the Oedipus and Electra complexes (Fenichel, 1945; Meissner, 1980). A man may unconsciously equate interest in a certain woman with the urge to possess his mother. This wish may stir unconscious fear of retaliation by the father. Resultant castration anxiety may cause erectile dysfunction (without erection the man cannot possess the mother substitute), premature ejaculation (early withdrawal may avert castration), or ejaculatory dysfunction (averting the possibility of impregnating the mother substitute).

A woman with unresolved penis-envy may avoid orgasm to express her unconscious jealousy of her partner's penis. Vaginismus may reflect unconscious denial of the fact that her partner has a penis.

In Chapter 9 we noted that psychoanalytic theory has been criticized for its reliance on undetectable processes, like presumed unconscious conflicts. Many psychoanalysts have specifically criticized Freud's views on penis-envy (Blum, 1976; Horney, 1967; Schafer, 1974). If Freud's views were correct, only long-term psychoanalysis which dealt with the roots of sexual dysfunction would be effective. But short-term sex-therapy techniques have been quite successful, as we shall see. And psychoanalytic methods have been unsuccessful unless supplemented by sex therapy (Kaplan, 1974).

Lack of Sexual Skills Sexual skills, as other behavioral competencies, are learned largely from operant conditioning and observational learning (see Chapters 5 and 9). We learn what makes us and others feel good through exploration (trial and error), reading about sex, and, perhaps, by watching sex films. But many people do not acquire sexual skills because they lack the opportunity to experiment. Or perhaps anxiety that stems from traditional sex-negative beliefs inhibits their exploration.

Sex therapy addresses the teaching of sexual skills, and also deals with anxiety that may interfere with their acquisition.

Irrational Beliefs Albert Ellis and other cognitive psychologists (Ellis & Harper, 1975; Ellis, 1977) point out that irrational beliefs and attitudes may contribute to sexual dysfunctions as well as other problems. For instance, if we believe that we need others' approval at all times, we may catastrophize the importance of one disappointing sexual episode. Similarly, if we believe that events are essentially beyond our control, we may assume that we are powerless to change our sexual "fates." Each of the 10 basic irrational beliefs discussed in Chapter 10 may be applied to sexual behavior. Sex therapists attempt to be sensitive to client's anxiety-evoking, self-defeating irrational beliefs.

Performance Anxiety Two thousand years ago it was said, "All roads lead to Rome"—the heart of the empire. In most cases of sexual dysfunction, the physical and psychological factors we have discussed lead to yet another psychological factor—**performance anxiety,** or fear as to whether we shall be able to perform sexually. People with performance anxiety may focus on recollections of past failures and expectations of another disaster rather than lose themselves in their erotic sensations and fantasies.

Performance anxiety, as other forms of anxiety, can make it difficult for a man to attain erection, yet spur him to ejaculate prematurely (see Chapter 2). Erectile dysfunction and premature ejaculation are often found in the same man. Performance anxiety, as other forms of anxiety, can prevent a woman from becoming adequately lubricated or contribute to vaginismus.

At the heart of performance anxiety is the cognition that something is being sexually *demanded* of someone. Therefore, sex-therapy programs suggest that an individual or a couple begin retraining themselves under nondemanding circumstances.

Treatment of Sexual Dysfunctions

When Kinsey was making his surveys of sexual behavior in the 1940s, there was no effective treatment for the sexual dysfunctions. But a number of treatments based on the behavioral model, collectively called **sex therapy,** have been developed during the past two decades.

Sex therapists assume that sexual dysfunctions can be treated by directly modifying the problem behavior that occurs in the bedroom. Treatment of most dysfunctions is enhanced by the cooperation of a patient sex partner, so it may be necessary to work on the couple's relationship before sex therapy is undertaken. But it is not considered necessary to gain insight into possible deep-seated roots of dysfunctions through lengthy, insight-oriented therapy such as psychoanalysis.

Sex therapy focuses on (1) reducing performance anxiety; (2) changing self-defeating expectations; and (3) learning sexual skills or behavioral competencies. When possible, both sex partners are involved in therapy, although, as we shall see, individual treatment may be preferable for primary orgasmic dysfunction. The sex therapists, often a male and female therapy team, educate the couple and guide them through a series of homework assignments. Masters and Johnson have a standard two-week treatment format that they use with couples who live in residence at their clinic during this period. However, in many instances "bibliotherapy"—or treatment of problems through reading self-help manuals—has also been helpful in sexual dysfunctions (e.g., Dodge and others, 1982).

Let us have a look at a sample of the techniques that have been effective in treating erectile dysfunction, premature ejaculation, and orgasmic dysfunction.

Erectile Dysfunction A man with erectile problems learns that he need not "do" anything to attain erection. He need only receive sexual stimulation under relaxed circumstances, so that anxiety does not inhibit the erectile reflex.

In order to reduce performance anxiety, the partners engage in contacts that do not demand that the man attain erection. At first they use **sensate focus exercises** in which they massage one another without touching the genitals. Each partner learns to "pleasure" the other and to "be pleasured"

Performance anxiety Excessive concern about whether one will be able to become sexually aroused or reach orgasm. Extreme anxiety can inhibit sexual response.

Sex therapy A collection of predominantly behavioral methods that treat sexual dysfunctions by (1) reducing performance anxiety; (2) changing self-defeating expectations; and (3) teaching sexual skills.

Sensate focus exercises Planned sessions in which couples take turns giving and receiving physical pleasure.

The Sexual Anxiety Inventory

While a little anxiety of the sort we experience on a first date can enhance sexual response, severe anxiety can block it. Factors like traditional sex-negative beliefs, psychosexual trauma, troubled relationships, irrational beliefs, and concerns about performance can all contribute to our sexual anxiety.

The following questionnaire, constructed by psychologists Louis Janda and Kevin O'Grady, will allow you to compare your level of sexual anxiety to that of other college students. Read each item and choose the answer, a or b, that best describes your feelings. Work rapidly and leave no item blank—even if the choice is difficult.

Then turn to the scoring key in Appendix B to interpret your answers.

Sexual Anxiety Inventory

1. Extramarital sex . . .
   a. is O.K. if everyone agrees
   b. can break up families
2. Sex . . .
   a. can cause as much anxiety as pleasure
   b. on the whole is good and enjoyable
3. Masturbation . . .
   a. causes me to worry
   b. can be a useful substitute
4. After having sexual thoughts . . .
   a. I feel aroused
   b. I feel jittery
5. When I engage in petting . . .
   a. I feel scared at first
   b. I thoroughly enjoy it
6. Initiating sexual relationships . . .
   a. is a very stressful experience
   b. causes me no problem at all
7. Oral sex . . .
   a. would arouse me
   b. would terrify me
8. I feel nervous . . .
   a. about initiating sexual relations
   b. about nothing, when it comes to members of the opposite sex
9. When I meet someone I'm attracted to . . .
   a. I get to know him or her
   b. I feel nervous
10. When I was younger . . .
    a. I was looking forward to having sex
    b. the thought of sex scared me
11. When others flirt with me . . .
    a. I don't know what to do
    b. I flirt back
12. Group sex . . .
    a. would scare me to death
    b. might be interesting
13. If in the future I committed adultery . . .
    a. I would probably get caught
    b. I wouldn't feel bad about it
14. I would . . .
    a. feel too nervous to tell a dirty joke in mixed company
    b. tell a dirty joke if it were funny
15. Dirty jokes . . .
    a. make me feel uncomfortable
    b. often make me laugh
16. When I awake from sex dreams . . .
    a. I feel pleasant and relaxed
    b. I feel tense
17. When I have sexual desires . . .
    a. I worry about what I should do
    b. I do something to satisfy them
18. If in the future I committed adultery . . .
    a. it would be nobody's business but my own
    b. I would worry about my spouse's finding out
19. Buying a pornographic book . . .
    a. wouldn't bother me
    b. would make me nervous
20. Casual sex . . .
    a. is better than no sex at all
    b. can hurt many people
21. Extramarital sex . . .
    a. is sometimes necessary
    b. can damage one's career
22. Sexual advances . . .
    a. leave me feeling tense
    b. are welcomed
23. When I have sexual relations . . .
    a. I feel satisfied
    b. I worry about being discovered
24. When talking about sex in mixed company . . .
    a. I feel nervous
    b. I sometimes get excited
25. If I were to flirt with someone . . .
    a. I would worry about his or her reaction
    b. I would enjoy it

Source: Janda & O'Grady, 1980.

In order to overcome sexual dysfunctions, couples must learn to communicate.

by receiving and giving verbal instructions and guiding the other's hands. Thus communication skills as well as sexual skills are acquired. After a couple of sessions, sensate focus extends to the genitals. When the man attains erection the couple does not immediately attempt coitus, since this might recreate performance anxiety. Once erection is attained reliably, the couple engages in a graduated series of sexual activities, culminating in intercourse.

Masters and Johnson (1970) report that this technique resulted in a "reversal" of erectile dysfunction in about 72 percent of the couples they treated for the problem. But it should be noted that Masters and Johnson have been criticized for their evaluation of the effectiveness of their treatments. Their shortcomings include (1) failure to operationally define degrees of improvement in clients; and (2) inadequate follow-up of treated clients to determine whether treatment "reversals" remain reversed (Adams, 1980; Zilbergeld & Evans, 1980).

Premature Ejaculation Sensate focus exercises are also often used in treatment of premature ejaculation so that couples will learn to give and receive pleasure under relaxed, rather than sexually demanding, circumstances. Then, when the couple is ready to begin sexual interaction, Masters and Johnson (1970) teach them the "squeeze technique," in which the tip of the penis is squeezed when the man feels he is about to ejaculate. This method, which can be learned only through personal instruction by sex therapists, prevents ejaculation. Gradually the man learns to prolong coitus without ejaculating. Masters and Johnson report this technique successful with 182 of 196 men treated.

In 1956, urologist James Semans suggested a simpler method called the "stop-and-go" technique, in which a man simply suspends sexual stimulation whenever he feels he is about to ejaculate. With this method, too, the man learns gradually to prolong sexual stimulation without ejaculating.

Primary Orgasmic Dysfunction Women who have never experienced orgasm often harbor beliefs that sex is dirty and may have been taught never to touch themselves. They are anxious about their sexuality, and have not had the chance to learn, through trial and error, what types of sexual stimulation will excite them and bring them to climax.

Masters and Johnson have treated primary orgasmic dysfunction by working with the couples involved, but other sex therapists suggest that it is preferable to use masturbation (Andersen, 1981; Barbach, 1975; Heiman and others, 1976; LoPiccolo & Lobitz, 1972; McMullen & Rosen, 1979). Masturbation provides women with a chance to learn about their own bodies and to give themselves pleasure without depending on a sex partner. Once women can masturbate to orgasm, they may need additional treatment to transfer their training to sex with a partner (Leiblum & Ersner-Hershfield, 1977; Schneidman & McGuire, 1976; Zeiss and others, 1977).

The actual masturbation programs have several elements in common. Women first learn about their own anatomy through reading, discussion groups, and use of a mirror. They experiment with self-caresses at their own pace, learning gradually to bring themselves to orgasm while pleasure helps countercondition sexual anxiety.

Situational Orgasmic Dysfunction When situational orgasmic dysfunction reflects a woman's relationship with or feelings about her sex partner, treatment requires dealing with the couple—if the woman chooses to maintain the relationship. Masters and Johnson again begin with sensate focus exercises to decrease performance anxiety, open communication channels, and enhance the couple's sexual skills. During genital massage and then coitus, the woman guides her partner in the caresses and movements that she finds sexually exciting. Masters and Johnson (1970) report that the dysfunctions of 81 percent of 183 women treated for this problem were reversed.

Sex therapists tend to agree that success rates for treating these problems would be much greater if every person and couple they worked with were fully committed to productive change. In a sense, this observation applies to every area of life. Aren't we generally more successful at those undertakings to which we are fully committed?

Summary

Sex is a natural function that has found varied expression with different cultures and individuals. Since the late 1940s, America has experienced a sexual revolution. Americans, especially younger Americans, have become more likely to seek sexual satisfaction through masturbation, petting, and premarital coitus—although they appear to maintain a sex-with-affection standard. Various activities once considered deviant are practiced more frequently, such as oral sex and a variety of coital positions. But it may be that the percentage of Americans who engage in extramarital sex has not increased markedly, and most Americans still disapprove of affairs.

A sex role is a cluster of stereotypical traits ascribed to men or women. The masculine sex-role stereotype includes aggressiveness, skill in business, interest in math and science, logic, and decisiveness. The feminine sex role includes dependence, warmth, vanity, nurturance, and expression of feelings. Research subjects including college students and mental-health professionals have shown sexism. Students assume that men create superior works, and mental-health workers (at least in 1970) did not equate the traits of the healthy woman with those of the healthy adult.

Despite stereotypes, sex differences in intellect and personality seem rather small. Still, men seem somewhat better versed in math and spatial relations, while women excel in verbal skills. Men are more aggressive, although experiments suggest that aggression in women seems inhibited by cultural expectations.

Pornography appears to sexually arouse women as well as men, but there is no reliable evidence that pornography contributes to antisocial behavior. However, recent experiments suggest that aggressive-erotic (rape) films may lead to increased aggression by men toward women.

Homosexuality is sexual preference for members of one's own sex. Homosexual episodes do not necessarily reflect a homosexual orientation. Few homosexuals fit the stereotypes of the swishy gay male and the butch lesbian. Homosexuals are generally as well-adjusted as heterosexuals, although homosexuals who lead different life styles show different levels of adjustment. The causes of homosexuality are complex and mysterious, but it may be that prenatal hormonal influences combined with subsequent learning experiences are implicated in homosexuality.

Forcible rape is a violent crime. Throughout history society has frequently blamed the victim for rape. Various cultural myths help maintain a climate that has the effect of supporting rape.

The human sexual response cycle consists of four phases: excitement, plateau, orgasm, and resolution. The responses of these phases occur reflexively when adequate sexual stimulation is received in the absence of inhibitory anxiety. Women are capable of multiple orgasms. The elderly usually retain the physical capacity to respond sexually, although many discontinue sex for psychological reasons.

Sexual dysfunctions are problems in becoming sexually aroused or reaching orgasm. Men's dysfunctions include erectile dysfunction, premature ejaculation, and ejaculatory dysfunction. Women's dysfunctions include orgasmic dysfunction and vaginismus. Both sexes may experience dyspareunia and sexual apathy. Sexual dysfunctions now and then reflect physical factors, like disease, but most reflect psychosocial factors like traditional sex-negative beliefs, psychosexual trauma, troubled relationships, lack of sexual skills, and irrational beliefs. Any of these may lead to performance anxiety, which compounds sexual problems.

Sex therapy is based largely on the behavioral model. It deals with the sexual dysfunctions through brief treatment programs that reduce performance anxiety, challenge irrational expectations and beliefs, and impart sexual skills. Many programs involve a dysfunctional couple in sensate focus exercises, but these programs are quite varied.

Truth or Fiction Revisited

- *Excessive masturbation can lead to mental illness.* False. There is no evidence that masturbation is physically or mentally harmful.
- *Most Americans learn about the birds and the bees through school sex education programs.* False. Most of us learn about sex from friends.
- *Most women have entertained fantasies about imaginary lovers while engaging in sexual relations with their husbands.* True, according to surveys such as that by E. Barbara Hariton.
- *Men behave more aggressively than women do.* True. The question is whether their greater aggressiveness is innate or reflects cultural expectations.
- *Men show greater math and spatial relations abilities than women do.* True, but the differences are small. Differences within the sexes also exceed differences between the sexes.
- *Sex offenders have histories of repeated exposure to pornography.* False. Surveys of offenders report that they have less exposure to pornography than nonoffenders. Of course, these surveys are prone to problems in self-reporting.
- *Homosexuals suffer from hormonal imbalances.* False. Their current levels of sex hormones do not differ from those of heterosexuals. However, prenatal imbalances in sex hormones may be implicated in homosexuality.
- *Sexual dysfunctions are rather rare occurrences.* False. It may be that most of us will encounter some sexual dysfunction at one time or another.

FOURTEEN

OUTLINE

Social Psychology

TRUTH OR FICTION?

- Beauty is in the eye of the beholder.
- Liberal women are more attracted to men with long hair, while conservative women prefer short-haired men.
- Juries are less likely to find attractive individuals guilty of burglary or of cheating on an exam.
- We often see ourselves as victims of circumstances, while we assume that other people act as they do out of choice.
- Most people would refuse to deliver painful electric shock to an innocent party, even under powerful social pressure.
- Business executives acting as a group are more likely to gamble a sizable sum of money on a risky venture than would the average group member, when acting as an individual.
- Nearly 40 people stood by and did nothing while a woman was being stabbed to death.
- Auto fumes may lower your children's IQ.

Candy and Stretch. A new technique for controlling weight gains? No, these are the names Bach and Deutsch (1970) give two people who have just met at a camera club that doubles as a meeting place for singles.

Candy and Stretch stand above the crowd—literally. Candy, an attractive woman in her early 30s, is almost six feet tall. Stretch is more plain-looking, but wholesome, in his late 30s, and six feet five inches.

Stretch has been in the group for some time. Candy is a new member. Let's listen in on them as they make conversation during a coffee break. As you will see, there are some differences between what they say and what they are thinking:

THEY SAY

STRETCH: Well you're certainly a welcome addition to our group.

CANDY: Thank you. It certainly is friendly and interesting.

STRETCH: My friends call me Stretch. It's left over from my basketball days. Silly, but I'm used to it.

CANDY: My name is Candy.

STRETCH: What kind of camera is that?

CANDY: Just this old German one of my uncle's. I borrowed if from the office.

STRETCH: May I? (He takes her camera, brushing her hand and then tingling with the touch.) Fine lens. You work for your uncle?

CANDY: Ever since college. It's more than being just a secretary. I get into sales, too.

STRETCH: Sales? That's funny. I'm in sales, too, but mainly as an executive. I run our department. I started using cameras on trips. Last time it was in the Bahamas. I took—

CANDY: Oh! Do you go to the Bahamas, too? I love those islands.

STRETCH:

I did a little underwater work there last summer. Fantastic colors. So rich in life.

CANDY:

I wish I'd had time when I was there. I love the water.

THEY THINK

(Can't I ever say something clever?)

(He's cute.)

(It's safer than saying my name is David Stein.)

(At least my nickname is. He doesn't have to hear Hortense O'Brien.)

(Why couldn't a girl named Candy be Jewish? It's only a nickname, isn't it?)

(He could be Irish. And that camera looks expensive.)

(Now I've done it. Brought up work.)

(So okay, what if I only went for a year. If he asks what I sell, I'll tell him anything except underwear.)

(Is there a nice way to say used cars? I'd better change the subject.)

(Great legs! And the way her hips move—)

(So I went just once, and it was for the brassiere manufacturers convention. At least we're off the subject of jobs.)

(She's probably been around. Well, at least we're off the subject of jobs.)

(And lonelier than hell.)

(Look at that build. He must swim like a fish. I should learn.)

(Well, I do. At the beach, anyway, where I can wade in and not go too deep.)

And so begins a relationship. Candy and Stretch have a drink and talk, sharing their likes and dislikes. Amazingly, they seem to agree on everything—from cars to clothing to politics. The attraction is very strong, and neither is willing to risk turning the other off by disagreeing.

They spend the weekend in Stretch's apartment and feel that they have fallen in love. They still agree on everything they discuss, but they scrupulously avoid one topic: religion. Their religious differences became apparent when they exchanged last names. But that doesn't mean they have to talk about it.

They also put off introducing each other to their parents. The O'Briens and the Steins are narrow-minded about religion. If the truth be known, so are Candy and Stretch. They narrow their relationships to avoid tension with one another, and as the romance develops, they feel progressively isolated from family and friends.

What happens in this tangled web of deception? Candy becomes pregnant. After some deliberation, and not without misgivings, the couple decides to marry. Do they live happily ever after? We cannot say—"ever after" hasn't arrived yet.

We may not have all the answers, but we do have some questions. Candy and Stretch's relationship began with a powerful attraction. What is *attraction?* How do we determine who is attractive? Candy and Stretch pretended to share each other's attitudes? What are *attitudes?* Why were Candy and Stretch so reluctant to disagree?

Candy and Stretch were prejudiced about religion. What is *prejudice?* Why didn't Candy and Stretch introduce each other to their parents? Did they fear that their parents would want them to *conform* to their own standards? Would their parents try to *persuade* them to date within their religions? Would they *obey?*

And—as long as we're asking questions—what do you think might have happened if their parents had tried to break up the relationship? Would they have succeeded, or would Candy and Stretch, like the star-crossed lovers in *Romeo and Juliet*, have been pressed closer by family opposition?

Social Psychology and Environmental Psychology

Attraction, attitudes, prejudice, conformity, persuasion, obedience. These and related topics are the province of the branch of psychology called **social psychology.** Social psychologists study the ways in which people's thoughts, feelings, and behaviors are influenced by other people.

In this chapter we first discuss attitudes, social perception, obedience to authority, and the nature of group behavior. We shall examine theory and research that concerns many of the questions posed about Candy and Stretch. Then we explore some of the issues that have been raised in a new area of inquiry, **environmental psychology.** Environmental psychologists study relationships between people and their physical environment, such as the effects of noise, air pollution, and city life.

There is some controversy about environmental psychology. Some psychologists regard it as a subfield of social psychology, while others consider it a field of its own. I am firmly determined to avoid taking a stand on this matter.

Social psychology The field of psychology that studies the ways in which people and groups influence the behavior of other people.

Environmental psychology The field of psychology that studies the ways in which behavior influences, and is influenced by, the environment.

Attitude An enduring system of beliefs, feelings, and behavioral tendencies concerning people, objects, or ideas.

Attitude-discrepant behavior Behavior that is inconsistent with an attitude.

Classical conditioning A simple form of learning in which one stimulus acquires the capacity to elicit the response usually brought forth by a second stimulus by being paired repeatedly with the second stimulus. See Chapter 5.

Operant conditioning A simple form of learning in which reinforcement increases the frequency of a response. See Chapter 5.

Attitudes: What They Are, How They Develop, How They Change

Psychologists are a rather independent bunch, so it is not surprising to find different definitions of **attitudes.** Some view attitudes primarily as cognitive evaluations. Others consider attitudes feelings with an evaluative, cognitive component. We define attitudes in terms of (1) cognitive, (2) emotional, and (3) behavioral components—as enduring systems of beliefs, feelings, and behavioral tendencies concerning people, groups, religion, politics, and so on.

Attitudes can change, but they tend to remain stable unless shoved a little. Most people do not change their religion or political affiliation without serious deliberation.

This definition implies that our behavior is consistent with our beliefs and feelings. When we are free to do as we wish, it often is, even though social psychologists have found that the relationships between attitudes and behavior are quite complex (Bagozzi, 1981; Bentler & Speckart, 1981; Borgida & Campbell, 1982). But just as Candy and Stretch were reluctant to express attitudes that might turn each other off, we may be influenced to behave in ways that are inconsistent with our beliefs. Such behavior is termed **attitude-discrepant behavior.** As we shall see in the case of Patty Hearst, attitude-discrepant behavior may actually change our beliefs (Bem, 1972). Finally, in this section we explore the nature of a particularly troublesome type of attitude—prejudice.

Origins of Attitudes

You were not born a Republican or Democrat. You were not born a Catholic or a Jew—although your parents may have practiced one of these religions when you came along. Political, religious, and other attitudes are learned.

Classical and Operant Conditioning Conditioning may play a role in the acquisition of attitudes. For instance, children who enjoy slim hamburgers and slimmer French fries could acquire a positive attitude toward one emblem of the new American architecture—the McDonald's golden arches. Through **classical conditioning,** the golden arches may lead children to respond positively because they have been repeatedly associated with eating. Laboratory experiments have shown that attitudes toward national groups can be influenced simply by associating them with positive words (like "gift" or "happy") or negative words (like "ugly" and "failure") (Lohr & Staats, 1973).

In examples of **operant conditioning,** parents often reward children for saying and doing things consistent with their own attitudes. Children may be shown approval for wearing Daddy's "No nukes" button or carrying Mommy's "My body is my own" placard. Experiments have shown that people who are rewarded consistently for favorable descriptions of even nonexistent groups will later express more positive attitudes toward these groups (Kerpelman & Himmelfarb, 1971). How much more positive would they be if the groups did exist?

Observational Learning We also acquire attitudes from friends and the mass media. The approval or disapproval of peers molds adolescents to prefer short or long hair, or blue jeans or preppy sweaters. Television shows us that body odor, bad breath, and the frizzies are dreaded diseases—and, perhaps, that people who use harsh toilet paper are vaguely un-American.

Logic and "Cognitive Anchors"   Yet all is not so mechanical. Now and then we also evaluate information and attitudes on the basis of evidence. Occasionally we may modify an attitude that we find to be illogical. Still, early attitudes tend to serve as cognitive "anchors." In this way, attitudes we learn about later are often judged in terms of how much they "deviate" from the first set. Accepting larger deviations appears to require greater adjustments in information-processing (Quattrone, 1982; Tversky & Kahneman, 1974). For this reason, perhaps, they are more likely to be resisted. Yet attitudes can be changed by persuasion, as we see in the following section.

Changing Attitudes through Persuasion

There are at least two routes to persuading others to change attitudes (Petty & Cacioppo, 1981). The first, or central route, views attitude change as resulting from careful consideration of arguments and evidence. The second, or peripheral route, involves association of the objects of attitudes with positive or negative "cues." These cues include rewards (like McDonald's French fries) and punishments (like parental disapproval), and factors such as the trustworthiness and attractiveness of the communicator. In this section we examine several central and peripheral factors in persuasion: (1) the message; (2) the person delivering the message; (3) the context in which the message is delivered; and (4) the audience.

The Persuasive Message: Say What? Say How? Say How Often?   How do we respond when television commercials are repeated until we have memorized every dimple on the actors' faces? Research suggests that familiarity breeds content, not contempt.

You might not be crazy about *zabulons* and *afworbus* at first, but Zajonc (1968) found that people began to react favorably toward these bogus Turkish words on the basis of repeated exposure. Political candidates who become highly familiar to the public through frequent television commercials attain more votes (Grush, 1980). People respond more favorably to abstract art (Heingartner & Hall, 1974), classical music (Smith & Dorfman, 1975), even photographs of black people (Hamm and others, 1975) simply on the basis of repetition. Love for classical art and music may begin through exposure in the nursery—not the college appreciation course. The more complex the stimuli, the more likely it is that frequent exposure will have favorable effects (Saegert & Jellison, 1970; Smith & Dorfman, 1975). The 100th repetition of a Bach concerto may be less tiresome than the 100th repetition of a pop tune.

Two-sided arguments, in which the communicator recounts the arguments of the opposition in order to refute them, can be especially effective when the audience is at first uncertain about its position (Hass & Linder, 1972). Theologians and politicians sometimes expose their followers to the arguments of the opposition. By refuting them one by one, they give their followers a sort of psychological immunity to them. Swinyard found that two-sided product claims, in which advertisers admitted their product's weak points as well as highlighting its strengths, were most believable (in Bridgwater, 1982).

Emotional appeal A type of persuasive communication that influences behavior on the basis of feelings that are aroused, instead of rational analysis of the issues.

It would be nice to think that people are too sophisticated to be persuaded by an **emotional appeal.** However, grisly films of operations on cancerous lungs are more effective than matter-of-fact presentations at changing smoking attitudes (Leventhal and others, 1972). Films of bloodied gums and decayed teeth are also more effective than logical discussions at increasing toothbrushing (Evans and others, 1970). Guilt as well as fear facilitates persuasion (Regan and others, 1972; Wallington, 1973).

Audiences also tend to believe arguments that appear to run counter to the personal interests of the communicator. People may pay more attention to a whaling fleet owner's claim, than to a conservationist's, that whales are becoming extinct. If the president of General Motors complained that auto fumes were becoming increasingly poisonous, you can bet we would prick up our ears.

The Persuasive Communicator: Whom Do You Trust? Would you buy a used car from a person convicted for larceny? Would you attend weight-control classes run by a 350-pound leader? Would you leaf through fashion magazines with ungainly models? Probably not. Research shows that persuasive communicators show expertise (Mills & Harvey, 1972), trustworthiness (Walster and others, 1966a), attractiveness, or similarity to their audiences (Eagly and others, 1978; Zimbardo and others, 1977).

Health professionals enjoy high status in our society and are considered experts. It is not surprising that toothpaste ads boast that their products have the approval of the American Dental Association.

Trustworthiness, or credibility, also sells. Sam Ervin, former senator from North Carolina, became a prominent public figure during the investigation of the Watergate affair. Televised senate sessions created his image of a "simple country lawyer" with impeccable integrity and a mind like a steel trap. In recent years, American Express Company has paid Ervin to endorse their credit cards on television.

Even though we are raised not to judge books by their covers, we are more likely to find attractive people persuasive. Corporations do not gamble millions on the physically unappealing to sell their products. Some advertisers seek out the perfect combination of attractiveness and plain, simple folksiness with which the audience can identify. Ivory Soap commercials sport "real" people with attractive features who are so freshly scrubbed that you may think you can smell Ivory Soap in their hair through the TV set.

The Context of the Message: "Get 'Em in a Good Mood" You are too clever and insightful to allow someone to persuade you by buttering you up, but perhaps someone you know would be influenced by a sip of wine, a bite of cheese, and a sincere compliment. Seduction attempts usually come at the tail end of a date—after the Szechuan tidbits, the nouveau Fresno film, the disco party, and the wine that was sold at its time. An assault at the outset of a date would be viewed as . . . well, an assault. Experiments suggest that food and pleasant music increase acceptance of persuasive messages (Janis and others, 1965; Galizio and Hendrick, 1972).

It is also counterproductive to call your dates fools when they disagree with you—even though their views are bound to be foolish if they do not agree with yours. Agreement and praise are more effective at encouraging others to accept your views (Baron, 1971; Byrne, 1971). Appear sincere, or else you will look manipulative. It seems a bit immoral to give out this information.

Baseball great Joe DiMaggio sells a coffee-maker in a TV commercial. Why does a manufacturer gamble millions that an athlete can sell coffee-makers? Probably because athletes tend to be perceived as wholesome, competent, and attractive. They are also familiar public figures.

Former CBS News anchorperson Walter Cronkite was recently rated as having more credibility than any other public figure in the United States. How much would corporations pay him to endorse deodorant, toothpaste, or paper towels in TV commercials?

The Persuaded Audience: Are You a Person Who Can't Say No?   Why do some people have "sales resistance," while others enrich the lives of every door-to-door salesperson? People with high self-esteem and low social anxiety are more likely to resist social pressure (Santee & Maslach, 1982). A study by Schwartz and Gottman (1976) suggests that the social anxiety that makes it difficult for some of us to say no is linked to what we are thinking when requests are made.

Schwartz and Gottman found that people who comply with unreasonable requests are more likely to report thinking: "I was worried about what the other person would think of me if I refused," "... it is better to help others

You Wouldn't Mind if We Ransacked Your Home, Would You?

How would you respond if a man from a consumer group phoned and asked if a six-man crew could drop by your home to inventory every product? It could take several hours to complete the chore.

In an experiment by Freedman and Fraser (1966), only 22 percent of women phoned acceded to this rather troublesome request. But 53 percent of another group of women agreed to a visit from this wrecking crew. Why? The more compliant group had been phoned a few days earlier and agreed to answer a few questions about the soap products they used. They had been primed for the second request. The caller had gotten his "foot in the door." The

foot-in-the-door technique is also effective in persuading people to make charitable contributions (Pliner and others, 1974) and to sign petitions (Baron, 1973).

The results of one study (Snyder & Cunningham, 1975) suggest that people who have acceded to a small request become more likely to accede to a larger one because they come to view themselves as the "type of person" who helps others by acceding to requests. Regardless of how the foot-in-the-door technique works, it seems that giving an inch now makes it more likely that later you will give a yard.

than to be self-centered," or "... the other person might be hurt or insulted if I refused." People who did not comply reported thoughts like "... it doesn't matter what the other person thinks of me," "... I am perfectly free to say no," or "This request is an unreasonable one" (p. 916).

In Chapter 10 we noted cognitive strategies that may be used by people who are concerned that irrational attitudes—such as fearing the disapproval of the person who makes the request—lower their sales resistance. Assertiveness training, discussed in Chapter 12, focuses both on client attitudes as well as fostering social skills.

Let us now turn our attention to the issue of what happens when we perceive our own attitudes to be inconsistent or imbalanced.

Balance Theory and Cognitive Dissonance

According to **balance theory** (Heider 1958), we are motivated to maintain harmony among our perceptions, beliefs, and attitudes. When people we like share our attitudes, there is balance and all is well. If we dislike others, we do not care about their attitudes. They may disagree with us, but this state of **nonbalance** leaves us indifferent (Newcomb, 1971).

But when someone you care about expresses a discrepant attitude, you are likely to be concerned. The relationship will survive if you like chocolate and your friend prefers vanilla, but what if the discrepancies concern important attitudes about religion, politics, or raising children? Now a state of **imbalance** exists. Candy was Catholic and Stretch Jewish. Each was painfully aware of the imbalance in religious preferences. How did they handle the imbalance? At first they misperceived the other's preference. Later they tried not to think about it.

What else can people do to end a state of imbalance? We can try to convince others to change their attitudes. (Candy and Stretch could have asked each other to change religions.) Or we can change our feelings about the other person. (Candy or Stretch might have "realized" that the other was a jerk, after all.) Cognitive dissonance theory, however, might suggest that Candy and Stretch's feelings for one another could grow even stronger as a result of discovering their religious differences, as we shall see.

Cognitive Dissonance According to cognitive dissonance theory, which was originated by Leon Festinger (Festinger, 1957; Festinger & Carlsmith, 1959), awareness that two cognitions—thoughts, attitudes, or beliefs—are dissonant motivates us somehow to reduce the discrepancy.

Consider a typical study on cognitive dissonance. One group of college students is paid a great deal to engage in a boring task. This group rates the task as dull. Other students are paid less to engage in the same boring task, but the underpaid group rates the task as enjoyable. From a learning theory point of view, this result would be confusing; after all, shouldn't we learn to like that which is highly rewarding? But cognitive dissonance theory would suggest that the cognitions "I was paid very little" and "This task is dull" are dissonant. Students would be able to justify their participation to themselves only by deciding that the task was interesting in its own right.

Concerning Candy and Stretch, cognitive dissonance theory might predict that their discovery that they held different religious views might have *strengthened* rather than destroyed their relationship. Why? After finding out about the other's religion, each might have thought, "Stretch (Candy) must be

Balance theory The view that people have a need to organize their perceptions, opinions, and beliefs in a harmonious manner.

Nonbalance In balance theory, a condition in which persons whom we dislike do not agree with us.

Imbalance In balance theory, a condition in which persons whom we like disagree with us. We are motivated to bring such a discrepancy into "balance."

When the World (Almost) Ended, or, Close Encounters of *No* Kind

The Seekers were quite a group. Their leader, Marian Keech, dutifully recorded the messages she received from "the Guardians" in outer space. One particular message was somewhat disturbing—namely that a great flood would bring the world to an end on December 21.

Then came the good news. Mrs. Keech had received word from the Guardians that the Seekers would be spared the flood because of their faith. Flying saucers would arrive for them at the stroke of midnight on the morning of the 21st.

In *When Prophecy Fails*, Festinger and his colleagues (1956) relate how they managed to be present at this fateful hour by pretending to belong to the faithful. But their sole purpose was to observe the Seekers during and after the prophecy's failure. At that time there would be two dissonant cognitions: (1) Mrs. Keech is a prophet, and (2) Mrs. Keech is wrong. The researchers predicted that the group would resolve this cognitive dissonance by taking action to spread the word and finding additional converts, rather than by losing faith in Mrs. Keech.

Otherwise, the group would be embarrassed.

Many Seekers had quit their jobs and gone on spending sprees before the end. Now they had all gathered. They fidgeted as midnight approached, waiting for the flying saucers. Midnight came. There were anxious glances back and forth. Silence. Coughs. A few minutes after there were more glances. Watches were checked. Faces looked concerned. Time passed painfully. At 4:00 A.M. an anxious and bitter Mrs. Keech complained that group members were doubting her. At 4:45, however, she was relieved. She had received another message! The world would be allowed to continue in its sinful ways for a while longer, for with the Seekers there was hope.

You guessed it. Their faith was renewed. They called the wire services and newspapers to spread the word. All but three psychologists from the University of Minnesota. They went home, weary but enlightened, and wrote a book.

Mr. Keech? He was a tolerant sort. He slept through it all.

---

very important to me if I can feel this way about him (her), knowing that he (she) is Jewish (Catholic)."

Can One's Self-Identity Be Converted through Attitude-Discrepant Behavior? The Strange Case of Patty Hearst   In February 1974 newspaper heiress Patty Hearst, an undergraduate student at Berkeley, was abducted by a revolutionary group known as the Symbionese Liberation Army (SLA). Early messages from the SLA directed the Hearst family to distribute millions of dollars' worth of food to the poor if they wished their daughter to live. There was no suggestion that Patty was a willing prisoner.

But after a couple of months, SLA communiqués contained statements by Patty that she had joined the SLA. She declared her revolutionary name to be Tania and sent a photograph in which she wore a guerrilla outfit and held a machine gun. She expressed contempt for her parents' capitalist values and called them pigs. But her family did not believe that Patty's attitudes had changed. They had raised her for 20 years. She had been with the SLA for only two months. Surely her statements were designed to earn good treatment from her captors.

In April, Patty and other SLA members robbed a San Francisco bank. Patty was videotaped brandishing a rifle. She was reported to have threatened a guard. But, the Hearsts maintained, the rifle could have been unloaded. Patty might still have been acting out of fear of losing her life. Then Patty became involved in another incident. She acted as a cover for SLA members William and Emily Harris, firing an automatic rifle as they fled from a store they had robbed. Patty seemed unsupervised at the time.

Patty and the Harrises were captured in San Francisco late in 1975. At first Patty was defiant. She gave a revolutionary salute and identified herself

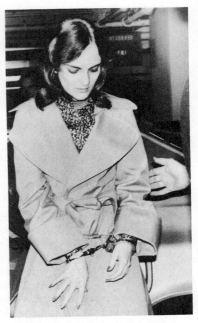

Effects of Attitude-Discrepant Behavior. Patty Hearst as the "urban guerrilla" Tania (left), and in manacles (right) on her way to testify in court. After her abduction by the Symbionese Liberation Army, Patty was forced into attitude-discrepant revolutionary behavior. Engaging in antisocial acts like armed robbery appears to have converted her self-identity from that of a typical college student to that of a revolutionary. After her capture, her identity appeared to revert to that of Patty. Patty's experience raises a challenging question: How can any of us know where the influences of others end and our "real selves," or true identities, begin?

as Tania. But once she was in prison, her identity appeared to undergo another transformation. She asked to be called Patty. At her trial she seemed quite remorseful. The defense argued that had it not been for the social influence of the SLA, Patty would never have engaged in criminal behavior or adopted revolutionary values. When President Jimmy Carter signed an order for Patty's early release from prison in 1979, he was operating under an admission from Patty's original prosecutors that they, too, believed that Patty would not have behaved criminally without being abducted by the SLA and experiencing dread in the days that followed.

How is it that a college undergraduate with typical American values came to express attitudes that were opposed to her lifelong ideals?

It may be that such conversions in identity can be explained through cognitive dissonance theory. After Patty's kidnapping, she was exposed to fear and fatigue and forced into attitude-discrepant behavior. She had to express agreement with SLA values, make love to SLA members, and train for revolutionary activity. So long as she clung firmly to her self-identity as Patty, these repugnant acts created great cognitive dissonance. But by adopting the suggested revolutionary identity of Tania, Patty could look upon herself as "liberated" rather than as a frightened captive or criminal. In this way her cognitive dissonance would be reduced and behavior would no longer be distressful. Supportive research shows that we do draw conclusions about our attitudes from our decisions to engage in particular behavior (Fazio and others, 1982; Nisbett & Ross, 1980).

Cognitive dissonance theory is not without its critics (e.g., Bem, 1967; Chapanis & Chapanis, 1964). But it leads to the hypothesis that we can change people's attitudes by getting them somehow to behave in a manner consistent with the attitudes we wish to promote. Research does show that people may indeed change attitudes when attitude-discrepant behavior is rewarded (Calder and others, 1973; Cooper and others, 1974). It is at once a frightening and promising concept. For instance, it sounds like a prescription for totalitarianism. Yet it also suggests that prejudiced individuals who are prevented from discriminating—who are compelled, for example, by open-housing laws to allow people from different ethnic backgrounds to buy homes in their neighborhoods—may actually become less prejudiced. In the following section, we turn our attention to the problems of prejudice and discrimination.

Prejudice

A few years ago Iowa schoolteacher Jane Elliot taught her all-white class of third-graders some of the effects of prejudice. She divided the class into blue-eyed and brown-eyed children. The brown-eyed children were labeled inferior, made to wear collars that identified their group, and denied classroom privileges. After a few days of discrimination, the brown-eyed children lost self-esteem and earned poorer grades. They cried often and expressed the wish to stay at home.

Then the pattern was reversed. Blue-eyed children were assigned the inferior status. After a few days they, too, learned how painful it is to be victims of discrimination. Weiner and Wright (1973) later found that making children victims of discrimination in this fashion led them to show less discrimination toward blacks.

Prejudice is an attitude toward a group that leads people to negatively evaluate members of that group. On a cognitive level, prejudice is linked to expectations that the target group will behave badly, as on a job or as in engaging in criminal activity. On an affective level, prejudice is associated with negative feelings like dislike or hatred. Behaviorally, prejudice is associated with avoidance behavior, aggression, and, as we shall see, discrimination. There is an interaction between our cognitions, affects, and behaviors. In one recent study, nonangered white people apparently adopted new **egalitarian** norms by acting less aggressively toward blacks than toward other whites. But angered whites acted more aggressively toward blacks than whites, suggesting persistence of underlying prejudices (Rogers & Prentice-Dunn, 1981).

Sexism and Racism In Chapter 13 it was noted that women are often expected to produce inferior work. This form of prejudice is called sexism. In **racism,** one race or ethnic group holds negative attitudes toward members of another. For instance, research suggests that whites are more likely to assume that blacks are guilty of crimes such as rape, while blacks may also be more likely to attribute guilt for such crimes to whites (Ugwuegbu, 1979).

Ageism In recent years we have become more aware of the effects of a form of prejudice called **ageism.** "Ageists" assume that the elderly will be less capable of performing adequately on the job, that they will hold "old-fashioned" moral and political views, and that they will be easily irritated, or "crotchety." Ageists may even believe that senior citizens cannot (or should

Prejudice The belief that a person or group, on the basis of assumed racial, ethnic, sexual, or other features, will possess negative characteristics or perform inadequately. An attitude toward members of a group that is not supported by facts.

Egalitarian Descriptive of the belief that all people should have equal rights.

Racism The prejudgment on the basis of race or ethnic background that a person will possess negative traits or perform inadequately.

Ageism (AGE–izm). The prejudgment on the basis of age that a person will possess negative traits or perform inadequately.

Discrimination The denial of privileges to a person or group on the basis of prejudice. A behavioral aspect of prejudice.

Reverse discrimination The denial of privileges to members of a group that was privileged in the past—notably white males.

Stereotype A fixed, conventional idea about a group.

not) engage in sexual activity (Rathus, 1983). None of these expectations necessarily conforms to the facts. Unfortunately, senior citizens may also acquire these expectations, and may disqualify themselves from productive work or enjoyable sexual activity.

Discrimination　One form of negative behavior that results from prejudice is called **discrimination.** Many groups have been discriminated against from time to time in the United States. They include, but are not limited to, Jews, Catholics, blacks, Native Americans, Hispanic Americans, homosexuals, and women. Discrimination takes many forms, including denial of access to certain jobs, housing, even the voting booth. Many people have forgotten that American blacks gained the right to vote several decades before it was obtained by American women.

Reverse Discrimination　In recent years **reverse discrimination** has also emerged—in part as a result of laws intended to overturn the effects of years of discrimination. In reverse discrimination, groups that had previously been privileged, notably white males, now find that racial minorities and women are often given preference in hiring practices, purely because they are minorities or women.

Stereotypes　Are Jews shrewd and ambitious? Are blacks superstitious and musical? If you believe any of these, you are falling for a **stereotype**—a prejudice about a group that can lead us to interpret observations in a biased fashion. In one experiment, subjects who watched videotapes of a child taking an academic test rated her performance as superior when told that she came from a high socioeconomic background. Other subjects were told that she came from a low socioeconomic background. They watched the same videotape but rated her performance as below grade level (Darley & Gross, 1983).

Stereotypes have changed over the years. Between 1933 and 1967 Princeton students came to stereotype Jews as less shrewd but as more ambitious (Karlins and others, 1969). Blacks became less likely to be labeled superstitious, but more likely to be considered musical. Americans have become seen as more materialistic, but as less intelligent. Princeton students have increased their favorability ratings of blacks and Jews over the years, while decreasing favorability ratings of Americans as a whole.

Some stereotypes persist. In one recent study (Smedley & Bayton, 1978), whites viewed middle-class blacks as ambitious, intelligent, conscientious, and responsible, but saw *lower-class* blacks as ignorant, rude, rebellious, and self-pitying. Blacks shared whites' negative impressions of lower-class individuals of the other race. But blacks also negatively evaluated *middle-class* whites as biased, sly, and deceitful, even though they also considered middle-class whites conscientious and ambitious.

Sources of Prejudice　The sources of prejudice are many and varied. Let us briefly consider several possible contributors.

As we shall see later in the chapter, we are prone to feeling attracted to and liking people who share our attitudes. In forming impressions of others, we are influenced by attitudinal similarity and dissimilarity as well as by race (Goldstein & Davis, 1972; Rokeach and others, 1960). People of different religions and races often have different backgrounds and values, giving rise to dissimilar attitudes. But even when people of different races share important values, they are likely to assume that they will not.

There is also a lengthy history of social and economic conflict between people of different races and religions. Conflict and competition lead to negative attitudes (Sherif, 1966). In their description of a lynching, Miller and Dollard (1941) argue that much white hatred of blacks in the South during the days of the Great Depression stemmed from fear that blacks would take low-level jobs and deprive many white people of an income. Similar fears in recent years may have led Sunbelt inhabitants, including blacks, to develop negative attitudes toward Hispanic and Asian immigrants.

Based on psychoanalytic theory and their interpretation of the **holocaust,** some social scientists (e.g., Adorno and others, 1950) have argued that racial and religious minorities serve as **scapegoats** for majority groups. The Germans, for instance, submitted to Nazi **authoritarianism** because they had been raised to submit to authority figures. They then displaced unconscious hostility toward their fathers onto Jews. These Freudian concepts have been criticized by many psychologists, but authoritarian people do appear to harbor more prejudices than nonauthoritarians (e.g., Stephan & Rosenfield, 1978).

As noted in Chapter 8, children tend to acquire certain attitudes from others, especially parents, through identification and socialization. Children often broadly imitate their parents, and parents often reinforce their children for doing so. In this way, prejudices are likely to be transmitted from generation to generation.

A recent information-processing view of prejudice suggests that stereotypes do not always reflect negative feelings. They often simply make it easier for us to process information about new individuals (Taylor, 1978). That is, we cut down on our "work" if we limit our search for an architect to men and our search for a babysitter to women. Unfortunately, processing information according to stereotypes often leads to incorrect conclusions and denies many people equal opportunity.

Let us now turn our attention to some of the factors involved in our formation of impressions of other people.

Holocaust The name given the Nazi murder of millions of Jews during World War II. A great or total destruction of life, especially by fire. (From the Greek *holos*, meaning "whole," and *kaustos*, meaning "burnt.")

Scapegoat A person or group upon whom the blame for the mistakes or crimes of others is cast. (From the ancient Jewish practice of confessing sins over a goat that was subsequently allowed to escape.)

Authoritarianism Belief in the importance of unquestioning obedience to authority. A characteristic of a society that demands unquestioning obedience.

Social perception A subfield of social psychology that studies the ways in which we form and modify impressions of others.

Social Perception

Getting to know you,
Getting to know all about you . . .

So goes the song from *The King and I.* How do we get to know other people, get to know all about them? In this section we explore some factors that contribute to **social perception:** primacy and recency effects, attribution theory, and body language. In the following section we explore determinants of attraction to others.

Primacy and Recency Effects: The Importance of First Impressions

Why do you wear your best outfit to an interview for an attractive job? Why do defense attorneys dress their clients immaculately before they are seen by the jury? Because first impressions are important.

When I was a teenager, a young man was accepted or rejected by his date's parents the first time they were introduced. If he was considerate and made small talk, her parents would allow them to stay out past curfew, even to attend submarine races at the beach. If he was boorish or uncommunicative, he was a cad forever. Her parents would object to him no matter how hard he worked to gain their favor later on.

First impressions often make or break us. This is the **primacy effect.** As noted in Chapter 9, we infer traits from behavior. If we act considerately at first, we are labeled considerate. The trait of considerateness is used to explain and predict our future behavior. If, after being labeled considerate, one keeps a date out past curfew, this behavior is likely to be seen as an exception to a rule—as justified by circumstances or external causes. But if at first one is seen as inconsiderate, several months of considerate behavior may be perceived as a cynical effort to "make up for it."

In an experiment on the primacy effect, Luchins (1957) had subjects read different stories about "Jim." The stories consisted of one or two paragraphs. One-paragraph stories portrayed Jim as friendly or unfriendly. These paragraphs were also used in the two-paragraph stories, but presented to different subjects in opposite order. Of subjects reading only the "friendly" paragraph, 95 percent rated Jim as friendly. Of those who read just the "unfriendly" paragraph, three percent rated him as friendly. Seventy-eight percent of those who read two-paragraph stories in the "friendly-unfriendly" order labeled Jim as friendly. But when they read the paragraphs in the reverse order, only 18 percent rated Jim as friendly.

How can we encourage people to pay more attention to more recent impressions? Luchins accomplished this by allowing time to elapse between presenting the paragraphs. In this way, fading memories allowed more recent information to take precedence. This is the **recency effect.** Luchins found a second way to counter first impressions: He simply counseled subjects to avoid snap judgments and to weigh all the evidence.

Attribution Theory

Dispositional and Situational Attributions   When parents and children argue about the children's choice of friends or dates, the parents tend to see their children as being stubborn, difficult, and independent. The children may perceive their parents as bossy and controlling. Parents and children alike attribute the others' behavior to internal causes. That is, they make **dispositional attributions** about the behavior of others.

But how do the parents and children perceive themselves? The parents probably see themselves as forced into conflict by their children's foolishness. If they become insistent, it is in response to their children's stubbornness. The children probably see themselves as responding to peer pressures, and, perhaps, to sexual urges which may be within but do not seem "of their own making." The parents and children tend to see their own behavior as motivated by external factors. That is, they make **situational attributions** about their own behavior.

Biases in the Attribution Process   Our inference of the motives and traits of others through the observation of their behavior is called the **attribution process.** The attribution process is often biased by the tendency to attribute the behavior of others to internal, dispositional factors, and our own behavior to external, situational influences (Jellison & Green, 1981; Jones, 1979; Reeder, 1982; Safer, 1980). We often see others as willful, but perceive ourselves as victims of circumstances.

Other biases also seem to be at work in the attribution process. As noted in Chapter 10, we are more likely to attribute our successes to internal, dispositional factors, but our failures to external, situational influences. When we have done well on a test or impressed a date, we are more likely to attribute these outcomes to our intelligence and charm. But when we fail, we are more likely to attribute these outcomes to bad luck, an unfairly difficult test, or our date's "bad mood."

There are some exceptions. We are more likely to own up to our responsibility for our failures when we think that other people will not accept situational attributions (Reiss and others, 1981). And, as noted in Chapter 11, depressed people are more likely than nondepressed people to attribute their failures to internal factors, even when dispositional attributions are not justified. Of course, people who accurately attribute their failures to internal or external factors will be more capable of taking corrective action. If you have been boorish and turned off your date, blaming the date will not encourage you to examine your social behavior. The inability to accept appropriate blame for shortcomings prevents many people from analyzing themselves and fostering more effective behavior. Depressed people, by contrast, overly blame themselves and feel helpless to improve their lots.

Another interesting bias in attribution is a sex difference in attributions for friendly behavior. Men are more likely than women to interpret a woman's friendliness toward men as a sign of promiscuity or seductiveness (Abbey, 1982). Traditional sex-role expectations apparently still lead men to believe that "decent" women are socially passive.

Consensus, Consistency, and Distinctiveness   According to Kelley (1973), our attribution of behavior to internal or external causes is influenced by three factors: *consensus*, *consistency*, and *distinctiveness*. We are surprised to find that our dull classmate, Morris, is on a date with a woman for whom many sovereign nations would go to war. The question: Does Morris have a secret way with women? (Is his success due to internal causes?) Or did Morris luck out on a blind date (an external cause)? As you see in Table 14.1, behavior that is low in **consensus**, high in consistency, and low in distinctiveness is more likely to be attributed to internal, dispositional factors.

Morris's dating experience ranks low in consensus, low in consistency, and high in distinctiveness. Few men have such attractive dates; Morris has not dated this woman before; and, in fact, Morris rarely dates at all. That's two out of three (consistency and distinctiveness) in favor of an external attribution. The chances are that we shall infer that Morris's date was a fluke, and that his date may have had to go out with him because she lost a bet. If they go out again (and consistency thereby increases), and we observe her accepting an engagement ring from Morris, we may begrudgingly reconsider.

Body Language

Body language is an important factor in our perception of others. At an early age we learn that the ways that people carry themselves provide cues as to how they feel and are likely to behave. For instance, when people are "uptight," their bodies may also be rigid and straight-backed. People who are relaxed are more likely to literally "hang loose."

When people face us and lean toward us, we may assume that they like us or are interested in what we are saying. If we are privy to a conversation

Consensus (con–SEN–suss). General agreement. (From the Latin *com-*, meaning "with," and *sentire*, meaning "to feel.")

TABLE 14.1   Factors Leading to Internal or External Attributions of Behavior

	Internal Attribution	External Attribution
Consensus	Low: Few people behave this way.	High: Most people behave this way.
Consistency	High: The person behaves this way frequently.	Low: The person rarely behaves this way.
Distinctiveness	Low: The person behaves this way in many situations.	High: The person behaves this way in few situations.

We are more likely to attribute behavior to internal, dispositional factors when it is low in consensus, high in consistency, and low in distinctiveness. In the example given in the text, we will be most likely to attribute Morris's dating of a beautiful woman to internal factors if few men date beautiful women, but Morris does so frequently and generally acts as if such behavior is typical of him.

between a couple and observe that the woman is leaning toward the man but that he is sitting back and toying with his hair, we are likely to infer that he is not having any of what she is selling (Clore and others, 1975; DePaulo and others, 1978).

Touching also communicates. In one touching experiment, Kleinke (1977) showed that appeals for help can be more effective when the distressed person engages in physical contact with people being asked for aid. A woman received more dimes for phone calls when she touched the person whom she was asking for money on the arm. In another experiment, women about to undergo operations reported lower anxiety and showed lower blood pressure when nurses explaining the procedures touched them on the arm (Whitcher & Fisher, 1979). But men who were touched while the procedures were explained reported higher anxiety and showed elevated blood pressure. How do we account for this sex difference? Female patients may have interpreted touching as a sign of warmth while male patients may have seen it as a threatening sign of the nurse's superior status in the hospital.

Body language can also be used to establish and maintain territorial control (Brown & Altman, 1981), as anyone who has had to step aside because a football player was walking down the hall can testify. Werner and her colleagues (1981) found that players in a game arcade used touching as a way of signaling others to keep their distance. Solo players engaged in more touching than did groups, perhaps because they were surrounded by strangers.

Gazing and Staring: The Eyes Have It   We usually feel we can learn much from eye contact. When others "look us squarely in the eye," we may assume that they are assertive or open with us. Avoidance of eye contact may suggest deception or depression (Knapp, 1978; Siegman & Feldstein, 1977). In a study designed to validate a scale to measure romantic love, Rubin (1970) found that couples who attained higher "love scores" also spent more time gazing into each other's eyes.

Gazes are different, of course, from persistent "hard" stares. Hard stares are interpreted as provocations or signs of anger (Ellsworth & Langer, 1976). Adolescent males sometimes engage in "staring contests" as an assertion of dominance. The male who looks away first "loses."

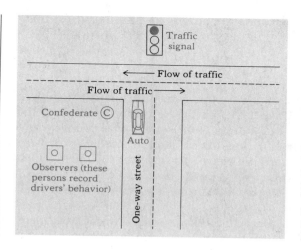

Diagram of an Experiment in Hard Staring and Avoidance. In the Greenbaum and Rosenfeld (1978) study, the confederate of the experimenter stared at some drivers and not at others. Those stared at drove across the intersection more rapidly once the light turned green. Does this surprise you?

Hard staring is found among many primates and may elicit instinctive responses. Rhesus monkeys use hard stares to establish and maintain dominance hierarchies (Exline, 1972). High status in these hierarchies affords privileges in feeding and mating. Exline has found that when people venture hard stares at a rhesus monkey, the monkey first returns the stare. Then it opens its mouth and begins to bob its head. If these "threats" fail to induce withdrawal, the rhesus literally springs to the attack. A submissive rhesus monkey shows more "discretion" than an occasional experimental psychology student; it suspends hard staring before eliciting an attack.

In a series of field experiments, Ellsworth and his colleagues (1972) subjected drivers stopped at red lights to hard stares from riders of motor scooters. Recipients of the stares crossed the intersection more rapidly than nonrecipients when the light changed. Greenbaum and Rosenfeld (1978) found that recipients of hard stares from a man seated near an intersection also drove off more rapidly after the light turned green. Other research shows that recipients of hard stares show higher levels of physiological arousal than people who do not receive the stares (Strom & Buck, 1979). It may be that many of us rapidly leave situations in which we are stared at in order to achieve pleasant declines in arousal and avoid the threat of danger.

Interpersonal Attraction

Whether we are talking about a pair of magnetic toy animals or a couple in a singles bar, **attraction** is a force that draws bodies, or people, together. In social psychology, attraction has been defined as an attitude of liking or disliking (Berscheid, 1976). Factors such as *physical appearance, attitudinal similarity, complementarity, family opposition, reciprocity, propinquity,* and whether the other person seems "hard to get" all contribute to interpersonal attraction.

Physical Attractiveness: How Important Is Looking Good?

You might like to think that we are all so intelligent and sophisticated that we rank physical appearance low on the roster of qualities we seek in a date—below sensitivity and warmth, for example. But in experimental "Coke dates" and computer dates, physical appearance has been found the central

Attraction A force that draws bodies or people together. In social psychology, an attitude of liking or disliking (negative attraction). (From the Latin *ad-*, meaning "to," and *trahere*, meaning "to draw" or "to pull.")

factor in attraction and consideration of partners for future dates, sexual activity, and marriage (Byrne and others, 1970; Walster and others, 1966b).

What determines physical attractiveness? Are our standards fully subjective, or is there broad agreement on what is attractive?

Is Beauty in the Eye of the Beholder?   It may be that there are no universal standards for beauty (Ford & Beach, 1951), but there are some common standards for physical attractiveness in our culture. Both sexes prefer people who are slender (Lerner & Gellert, 1969). Tallness is an asset for men (Berkowitz and others, 1971), but tall women are not viewed so positively. Women generally prefer men with a V-taper, whose backs and shoulders are medium-wide, but whose waists, buttocks, and legs taper from medium-thin to thin (Lavrakas, 1975; Horvath, 1981).

Men, weaned on *Playboy* magazine perhaps, desire women with larger-than-average breasts, medium-length legs, and small to medium buttocks (Wiggins and others, 1968). Yet women with medium bust sizes are better liked than women with large or small busts. Women with large breasts are also often viewed as less intelligent, competent, moral, and modest than women with smaller breasts (Kleinke & Staneski, 1980).

Gentlemen and gentlewomen seem to prefer brunettes, not blonds, at least according to a study from upstate New York (Lawson, 1971). Women's preference for long or short hair in men seems to be linked to general liberalism or conservatism. Women who prefer long-haired men are more likely to have experimented with drugs. They have dated more men and are more sexually experienced. They attend church less frequently and are more self-assertive (Peterson & Curran, 1976).

Today Victoria Principal contributes to setting the standard for female beauty in our culture. Are attractive people more successful? Do they make better spouses and parents?

Do Good Things Come in Pretty Packages? According to psychologist Karen Dion and her colleagues (1972), we rate what is beautiful as good. We expect attractive people to hold prestigious jobs, be good parents, feel fulfilled, and have stable marriages. The good looking are assumed to be more popular and persuasive (Berscheid & Walster, 1974).

But attractive people are also seen as more self-centered and likely to have extramarital affairs (Dermer & Thiel, 1975). Yet even these "negative" assumptions have a positive side. After all, don't they mean that we think attractive people have more to be self-centered about, and that their affairs reflect their greater sexual opportunities?

Attractive people are more likely to be found innocent of burglary and cheating in mock jury experiments. When found guilty, they are handed down less severe sentences (Efran, 1974). Perhaps we assume that more attractive people are less likely to need to resort to deviant behavior to achieve their goals. Even when they have erred, perhaps they will have more opportunity for personal growth and be more likely to change their evil ways.

The beautiful are also perceived as more talented. In one experiment, students rated essays as higher in quality when their authorship was attributed to a more attractive woman (Landy & Sigall, 1974).

Attractive children learn early of the high expectations of others. Parents, teachers, and other children expect them to do well in school and be popular, well behaved, and talented. Since our self-esteem reflects the admiration of others, it is not surprising that the physically attractive have higher self-esteem (Maruyama & Miller, 1975).

More attractive people seem to develop greater social skills. Goldman and Lewis (1977) found that attractive people were more likely to be rated by telephone partners as socially skillful and likable, even though their conversants were blind to their appearance. It may be that our expectations of attractive people somehow induce socially skillful behavior. In one experiment, male telephone callers were told that their telephone partner was attractive or unattractive, although all women were equal in appearance (Snyder and others, 1977). Judges listening to the women's side of the conversation only rated women who had been labeled attractive as more likable, sociable, and friendly. But remember: All women were equal in appearance, and judges were unaware of the bogus ratings. Yet somehow the expectations of their male conversants had elicited more competent social behavior from women who were labeled attractive.

Attractive college men engage in more social interaction with women and less interaction with men than do their less attractive peers (Reis and others, 1980, 1982). Their increased contacts with women appear to be at the expense of relationships with men. There is no such link between attractiveness and social interactions among college women. More attractive college women spend more time on dates and at parties than do their less attractive peers, but increased heterosexual interactions do not spill over into other areas of social contact. The satisfaction derived from opposite-sex interactions is positively related to attractiveness for both sexes.

The Matching Hypothesis: Who Is "Right" for You? Have you ever refrained from asking out an extremely attractive person for fear of rejection? Do you feel more comfortable with someone who's a bit less attractive?

If so, you're not alone. Although we may rate highly attractive people as most desirable, we are more likely to try to construct relationships with and

Two Types of Similarity. According to the matching hypothesis, we tend to form relationships with people who are similar to ourselves in attractiveness (photo left). We also tend to be more attracted to people who possess similar attitudes, whether the relationship is a love relationship or a friendship (photo right).

marry people who are similar to ourselves in attractiveness (Murstein & Christy, 1976). This tendency is predicted by the **matching hypothesis** (Berscheid and others, 1971). A major motivating factor is fear of rejection by more attractive people. In a recent study, Shanteau and Nagy (1979) found that college women chose prospective dates who were moderately attractive but highly likely to accept the date, as opposed to more attractive men who were considered likely to reject them.

But the process of "settling" for someone other than the local Robert Redford or Cheryl Tiegs look-alike need not be an unhappy one. We tend to rate our mates as slightly more attractive than ourselves—as if we had somehow "gotten the better of the deal" (Murstein, 1972). We tend to idealize loved ones (see Chapter 7), but other explanations are also possible. By focusing on their positive features we may feel happier with our marriages. Too, we may be aware of our own struggles to present ourselves to the world each day, but take our mates' appearance more or less for granted.

There are exceptions. Now and then we find a beautiful woman married to a plain man, or vice versa. How do we explain it? According to Bar-Tal and Saxe (1976), we may assume that such men are wealthy—as in the Jackie Kennedy-Aristotle Onassis match—highly intelligent, or otherwise successful. We seek an unseen factor that will maintain the balance in the match. Similarly, a recent study of lonely hearts advertisements, published under the provocative title "Let's Make a Deal" (Harrison & Saeed, 1977), found that there were exceptions to the matching rule of only attractive people seeking attractive partners. For instance, physically unappealing but wealthy men and women often advertised for physically attractive partners. Wealth and physical appeal are both positively valued in our society. In this way it could be argued that such couples were "matches," after all.

Matching hypothesis The view that people tend to choose persons similar to themselves in attractiveness in the formation of interpersonal relationships.

Attitudinal Similarity: Birds of a Feather Flock Together

Birds of a feather flock together—especially when they are good-looking. Byrne and his colleagues (1970) found that college students were most attracted to computer match-ups who were physically appealing and expressed similar attitudes. Ratings of physically attractive dates with dissimilar attitudes approximated those of unattractive dates with similar attitudes. This finding suggests that physical appeal and attitudes may be comparable in importance.

But there is also evidence that we may tend to *assume* that physically attractive people share our attitudes (Marks and others, 1981). Can this be a sort of wish-fulfillment? When physical attraction is very strong, as it was with Candy and Stretch, perhaps we like to think that all the kinks in a relationship will be small, or capable of being ironed out. Similarly, we tend to assume that preferred presidential candidates share our political and social attitudes (Brent & Granberg, 1982). Once they are in office, we may become disillusioned when they swerve from our expectations.

Not all attitudes are necessarily equal. Men on computer dates at the University of Nevada were more influenced by sexual than religious attitudes (Touhey, 1972). But women were more attracted to men whose religious views coincided with their own. These findings suggest that women may have been less interested than men in a physical relationship, but more concerned about creating a family with cohesive values. Considering changing values and the ongoing "sexual revolution," it would be interesting to learn whether these findings would hold in the 1980s.

Grush and Yehl (1979) found that nontraditional college women (who, for example, endorsed the views of the National Organization for Women) and traditional college men were more attracted to opposite-sex strangers who they believed shared their sex-role attitudes. They showed stronger preferences for dating, marriage, and work partners who shared their beliefs. Traditional women and nontraditional men were not so strongly influenced by attitudinal similarity. These findings may seem confusing at first, but recall from Chapter 13 that the traditional (stereotypical) masculine role includes traits of competitiveness and outspokenness. These traits are more likely shared by *non*traditional than traditional women. Thus, traditional men and nontraditional women may be less tolerant of people who disagree with them, or at least more willing to confront others who disagree.

Complementarity: Every Comic Needs a Straight Man, or Woman

There are some occasions on which opposites do attract. In terms of sex roles, the historical attraction between man and woman has been viewed as a natural intermingling of the active and the passive, the dominant and the submissive. Now that stereotypical sex roles are fading, it is no longer easy to predict whether someone will be active or dominant on the basis of gender. But a dominant person will still often be attracted to someone who is submissive. A needy person will be attracted to someone who is giving.

With **complementarity,** opposing traits reinforce each other, so that each person benefits from the interaction. A relationship based on complementarity can run aground if one party wishes to change a complementary role. The formerly submissive wife of a domineering husband may decide that times are changing and begin to assert herself. The "student" in a student-teacher type of romance may eventually mature.

Complementarity A feature of a relationship, or source of attraction, characterized by the reinforcement value of opposing traits.

When Parents Say No: The "Romeo and Juliet Effect"

Would parental opposition drive a wedge between you and your date, or would you fight to maintain the relationship? In the Shakespearean play, the young lovers, Romeo and Juliet, drew closer against the bloody backdrop of a family feud. But that was literature. What about real life?

Psychologists sought an answer through a survey of dating and married couples at the University of Colorado (Driscoll and others, 1972). Student questionnaires suggested that parental opposition intensified feelings of love between couples during the first six to 10 months of the relationship. But parental opposition did not affect feelings between married couples.

During the early stages of a relationship, parental opposition may intensify needs for security within a couple so that they cling together more strongly. But for couples who have already made a strong commitment, as in a lengthy courtship or a marriage, parental opposition may become irrelevant.

Reciprocity: If You Like Me, You Must Have Excellent Judgment

Has anyone told you how good-looking, brilliant, and mature you are? That your taste is refined? If so, have you been impressed by his or her fine judgment?

When people praise us, we are more susceptible to the messages they are delivering. When we are admired and complimented, we tend to return these feelings and behaviors. This is **reciprocity.** When people tell you that you are terrific, you may wonder why you didn't pay more attention to them before.

Propinquity: If You're Near Me, I Must Be Attracted to You

Why did Sarah Abrams walk down the aisle with Allen Ackroyd and not Danny Schmidt? Sarah and Danny actually had more in common. But Sarah and Al exchanged smoldering glances throughout eleventh-grade English because their teacher had used an alphabetical seating chart. Danny sat diagonally across the room. Sarah, to him, was only a name called when attendance was taken.

Propinquity. People who are placed in frequent contact with one another are more likely to develop relationships than those who are not.

Attraction is more likely to develop between people who are placed in frequent contact with one another. This is the effect of nearness, or **propinquity.** Students are more likely to develop friendships when they sit next to one another (Segal, 1974). Homeowners are most likely to become friendly with next-door neighbors, especially those with adjacent driveways (Whyte, 1956). Apartment dwellers tend to find friends among those who live nearby on the same floor (Nahemow & Lawton, 1975).

Propinquity (pro–PINK–quit–tea). Nearness. (From the Latin *prope*, meaning "near.")

Playing Hard To Get: "I Only Have Eyes for You"

Are you likely to be more or less attracted to people who play "hard to get"?

Elaine Walster and her colleagues (1973) recruited male subjects for an experiment in which they were given the opportunity to rate and select dates. They were given phony initial reactions of their potential dates to them and to the other men in the study. One woman was generally hard to get. She reacted indifferently to all the men. Another woman was uniformly easy to get. She responded positively to all male participants. A third showed the fine judgment of being attracted to the rater only. Men were overwhelmingly more attracted to this woman—the one who had eyes for them only. She was selected for dates 80 percent of the time.

Obedience to Authority

Richard Nixon resigned the presidency of the United States in August 1974. For two years the business of the nation had almost ground to a halt while Congress investigated the burglary of a Democratic party campaign office in the Watergate office and apartment complex. It turned out that people close to Nixon had authorized the break-in during the 1972 election campaign. Nixon himself might have been involved in the cover-up of this connection later on. For two years Nixon and his aides had been investigated by the press and by Congress. Now it was over. Some of the bad guys were thrown in jail. Nixon was exiled to the beaches of Southern California. The nation returned to work. The new president, Gerald Ford, declared "Our national nightmare is over."

But was it over? Have we come to grips with the implications of the Watergate affair?

According to Yale University psychologist Stanley Milgram (*APA Monitor,* January 1978), the Watergate cover-up, like the Nazi slaughter of the Jews, was made possible through the compliance of people who were more concerned about the approval of their supervisors than about their own morality. Otherwise they would have refused to abet these crimes.

People try to rationalize their misconduct. H. R. Haldeman, Nixon's chief of staff, told CBS's Mike Wallace that he had prevented certain facts from coming to light to protect "the presidency" of the US. Presidential aide John Dean communicated requests for "hush money" to his supervisors. But he rationalized that he was not personally doing the dirty work of the cover-up. He was only an agent, a middleman, an administrator (*APA Monitor,* 1978, p. 23). Nazi war criminals also rationalized their actions. They were only "following orders," or there was nothing they could do to halt the slaughter anyhow.

Shocking Stuff at Yale: The Milgram Studies

Were the crimes of Nazi Germany historical flukes? How pressing is the need to obey authority figures?

Stanley Milgram also wondered how many of us would resist authority figures who made immoral requests. To find out, he ran a series of experiments at Yale. In an early phase of his work, Milgram (1963) placed ads in New Haven newspapers for subjects for studies on learning and memory. He enlisted 40 men ranging in age from 20 to 50—teachers, engineers, laborers, salespeople, men who had not completed elementary school, men with graduate degrees. The sample was truly a cross section of the population of this small Connecticut city some 75 miles to the northeast of New York City.

Let us suppose you had answered an ad. You would have shown up at the university for a fee of $4.50, for the sake of science and your own curiosity. You might have been impressed. After all, Yale was a venerable institution with an almost magical name. It dominated the city. You would not have been less impressed by the elegant labs where you would have met a distinguished behavioral scientist dressed in a white laboratory coat and another newspaper recruit—like you. The scientist would have explained that the purpose of the experiment was to study the *effects of punishment on learning.* The experiment would require a "teacher" and a "learner." By chance you would be appointed the teacher, and the other recruit the learner.

You, the scientist, and the learner would enter a laboratory room with a rather threatening chair with dangling straps. The scientist would secure the learner's cooperation and strap him in. The learner would express some concern, but this was, after all, for the sake of science. And this was Yale University, was it not? What could happen to a person at Yale?

You would follow the scientist to an adjacent room from which you would do your "teaching." This teaching promised to be effective. You would punish the "learner's" errors by pressing levers marked from 15 to 450 volts on a fearsome looking console (Figure 14.1). Labels described 28 of the 30 levers as running the gamut from "Slight Shock" to "Danger: Severe Shock." The last two levers resembled a film unfit for anyone under age 17: They were rated simply "XXX." Just in case you had no idea what electric shock felt like, the scientist gave you a sample 45-volt shock. It stung. You pitied the fellow who might receive more.

Your learner was expected to learn word pairs. Pairs of words would be read from a list. After hearing the list once, the learner would have to produce

FIGURE 14.1   The "Aggression Machine." In the Milgram studies on obedience to authority, pressing levers on the "aggression machine" was the operational definition of aggression.

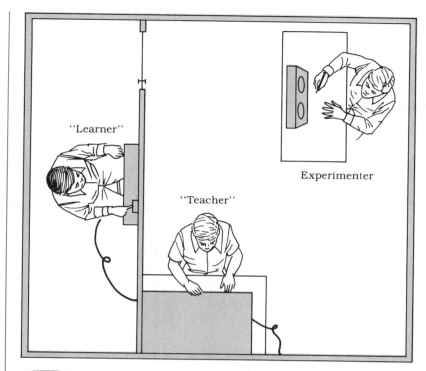

The Experimental Set-Up in the Milgram Studies. When the "learner" makes an error, the experimenter prods the "teacher" to deliver a painful electric shock.

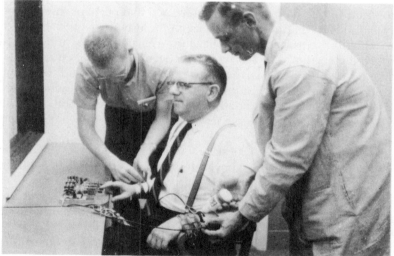

A "Learner" in the Milgram Studies on Obedience to Authority. This man could be in for quite a shock.

the word that was paired with the stimulus word. He would do so by pressing a switch that would signify his choice from a list of four alternatives. The switch would light one of four panels in your room. If it was the correct panel, you would proceed to the next stimulus word. If not, you would deliver an electric shock. With each error, you would increase the voltage of the shock.

You would probably have some misgivings. Electrodes had been strapped to the learner's wrists, and the scientist had applied electrode paste to "avoid blisters and burns." You were also told that the shocks would cause "no permanent tissue damage" although they might be extremely painful. Still, the learner was going along, and, after all, this was Yale.

The learner answered some items correctly and then made some errors. With mild concern you pressed the levers up through 45 volts. You had tolerated that much yourself. Then a few more mistakes were made. You pressed the 60-volt lever, then 75. The learner made another mistake. You paused and looked at the scientist. He was reassuring: "Although the shocks may be painful, there is no permanent tissue damage, so please go on." Further errors were made, and quickly you were up to a shock of 300 volts. But now the learner was pounding on the other side of the wall! Your chest tightened and you began to perspire. Damn science and the $4.50, you thought. You hesitated and the scientist said, "The experiment requires that you continue." After the delivery of the next stimulus word, there was no answer at all. What were you to do? "Wait for five to 10 seconds," the scientist instructed, "and then treat no answer as a wrong answer." But after the next shock, there was again that pounding on the wall! Now your heart was racing and you were convinced that you were causing extreme pain and discomfort. Was it possible that no lasting damage was being done? Was the experiment that important, after all? What to do? You hesitated again. The scientist said, "It is absolutely essential that you continue." His voice was very convincing. "You have no other choice," he said, "you *must* go on." You could barely think straight and for some unaccountable reason you felt laughter rising in your throat. Your finger shook above the lever. What were you to do?

On Truth at Yale   Milgram (1963, 1974) found out what most people would do. Prior to the study, seniors at Yale had predicted that perhaps three percent of the population would administer shocks all the way through 450 volts, the maximum. Milgram's professional colleagues—psychologists and psychiatrists—had predicted that very few would go beyond 200 volts. But of the 40 men in this phase of his research, only five refused to go beyond the 300-volt level, at which the learner first pounded the wall. Nine more teachers defied the scientist within the 300-volt range. But 26 of the 40 participants complied with the scientist throughout the series, believing that they were delivering 450-volt, XXX-rated shocks.

Were these newspaper recruits simply unfeeling? Not at all. Milgram was impressed by their signs of stress. They trembled, they stuttered, they bit their lips. They groaned, they sweated, they dug their fingernails into their flesh. There were fits of laughter, though laughter was inappropriate. One 46-year-old salesperson's laughter was so convulsive that he could not continue with the experiment.

Milgram wondered if college students, heralded for independent thinking, would show more defiance. But a replication of the study with Yale undergraduates yielded similar results. What about women, who were supposedly less aggressive than men? Women, too, shocked the "learners." But surely this could only happen within the walls of Yale, where subjects would be overpowered by the prestige of the setting! Not so. Milgram attained the same results in a dingy storefront in a nearby town. All this in a nation that values independence and the free will of the individual. Our "national nightmare" may not be over at all.

On Deception at Yale   You are probably skeptical enough to wonder whether the "teachers" in the Milgram study actually shocked the "learners" when they pressed the levers on the console. They didn't. The only real shock in this experiment was the 45-volt sample given the teachers. Its purpose was to lend credibility to the procedure.

The learners in the experiment were actually confederates of the experimenter. They had not answered the newspaper ads, but were in on the truth from the start. "Teachers" were the only real subjects. Teachers were led to believe that they were chosen at random for the teacher role, but the choosing was rigged so that newspaper recruits would always become teachers.

Milgram had no interest in the effects of punishment on learning. Rather, he wished to learn how many people would obey an authority figure in an immoral undertaking. This frightening tendency to obey authority figures is not limited to Germanic and American cultures. The Milgram study was recently replicated in Jordan with children aged six to 16 (Shanab & Yahya, 1977) and university students (Shanab & Yahya, 1978). The results were all too familiar.

Milgram's research has alerted us to a real and present danger—the tendency of most people to obey authority figures, even when their demands contradict their moral attitudes and values. It has happened before. Unhappily, unless we remain alert, it may happen again. Who are the authority figures in your life? How do you think you would have behaved if you had been a "teacher" in the Milgram studies? Are you sure?

Group Behavior

To be human is to belong to groups. Families, classes, religious groups, political parties, circles of friends, bowling teams, sailing clubs, conversation groups, therapy groups—to how many groups do you belong? How do groups influence the behavior of individuals?

Social Facilitation

One effect of groups on individual behavior is **social facilitation,** or increased performance that results from being a group member. We tend to eat more rapidly when we eat with others. Runners tend to run more rapidly in groups, when others "pace" them.

The presence of others engaged in similar activity often appears to increase the individual's level of motivation (Zajonc, 1965). But there are exceptions. Bibb Latané and his colleagues (e.g., Latané, Williams, and Harkins, 1979; Williams, Harkins, and Latané, 1981) have found that working in a group may sometimes lead to lowered performance, or "social loafing," as noted on p. 562. That is, workers sometimes seem to "goof off" when they feel that they will not be held accountable for their performance.

Polarization and the Risky Shift

You might think that a group decision would be more conservative than an individual decision. After all, a few "mature" individuals should be able to balance the opinions of daredevils. But in general you would be wrong.

As an individual, you might recommend that your company risk $10,000 on a new product. Other company executives, polled individually, might risk similar amounts. But if you were gathered for a group decision, it is likely that you would either recommend well above this figure or nothing at all (Myers & Lamm, 1976). This group effect is called **polarization,** or the taking of an

Social facilitation The process by which a person's performance is increased when other members of a group engage in similar behavior.

Polarization In social psychology, the taking of an extreme position or attitude on an issue.

Peril of Work within Group: Social Loafing

Science works its wonders in homely ways. Alexander Fleming saw a mold growing in a dish—and came upon penicillin. Benjamin Franklin flew a kite in a thunderstorm, and demonstrated that lightning is electricity.

Professor Bibb Latané listened to a bunch of college kids hollering and clapping—and decided that he had uncovered a root cause of America's slowing productivity: social loafing.

Dr. Latané is a professor of psychology at Ohio State University and co-author of a study that won the 1980 socio-psychological prize of the American Association for the Advancement of Science. The study's conclusion is that people tend to slack off, or loaf, when they work in a group more than they do when working alone.

The Presence of Others   Dr. Latané concludes that there is a "diffusion of responsibility" in groups. Each person feels less responsibility to help because others are present.

Much of the latest experimentation has been done by Latané and his colleagues.... The researchers organized Buckeye student volunteers into groups of varying sizes and asked them to clap or shout as loud as they could. In some tests, students wore blindfolds and headphones, and the headphones sometimes transmitted taped sounds of yelling and clapping so students couldn't judge the sound output of other subjects.

The researchers measured the volume generated by students alone and in groups. In one experiment, students were told over the headphones that they would shout in pairs, but in fact they shouted alone. In other trials they were told they would shout alone, and did. In this and other experiments, the researchers found that when subjects either were in a group or believed they were, they consistently made less noise per person than when they shouted or clapped alone.

The Work Place   Dr. Latané says his group plans to extend its basic research into the work place by examining a secretarial pool, an executive committee meeting and an air traffic control center.

Commenting on the research, Harry Levinson, a psychologist and consultant on organizational behavior, says clapping and shouting "is a kind of inane task, if you ask me." A psychologist at a New York bank points out that students didn't have real-life motivations. "Those people weren't out earning money to pay their mortgages or feed their families," he comments.

People Are Consistent   Dr. Latané acknowledges that his work has a way to go. But, he says, "Until you try something in the field, you don't know how it will work." He adds, "I think it's also true that the nature of human beings is relatively consistent along certain lines."

Despite what his research suggests, Dr. Latané doesn't think the solution to social loafing is breaking up groups and turning the US work force into a collection of loners. Rather, the researchers suggest that managers channel group motivation to intensify rather than diffuse individual effort.

A Japanese Idea   Many corporate managers already endorse that conclusion. Dr. Levinson notes the "almost fad-like move to quality circles," the teamwork concept many companies have imported from Japan. General Motors is one of them. Its Fitzgerald, Georgia, battery-making plant has run on a team system since it opened in 1975. There, semiautonomous teams set their own production goals and work schedules, administer their own discipline and evaluate their own performance—with great success.

Social Facilitation or Social Loafing?   Does working in a group facilitate performance or promote social loafing?

---

extreme position. Yet if you had to gamble on which way the decision would go, you would do better to place your money on movement toward the higher sum—that is, to bet on a **risky shift.** Why?

One possibility is that a group member may reveal information which the others had not been aware of (Ebbesen & Bowers, 1974), and that this information clearly points in one direction or the other. With doubts removed, the group becomes polarized—moving decidedly in the appropriate direction. It may also be that social facilitation occurs in the group setting, and that increased motivation prompts more extreme decisions.

But why do groups tend to take greater rather than smaller risks than those that would be ventured by their members? One answer is **diffusion of responsibility.** If the venture flops, it will not be you alone to blame. You can always say (and tell yourself) that it was, after all, a group decision. And if the venture pays off handsomely, I have no doubt that you will trumpet abroad your influential role in the group decision-making process.

Diffusion of responsibility The spreading or sharing of responsibility for a decision or behavior among a group.

Deindividuation (dee–in–div–vid–you–AY–shun). The process by which group members may discontinue self-evaluation and adopt group norms and attitudes.

Mob Behavior and Deindividuation: Do Crowds Bring Out the Beast in Us?

Gustave Le Bon (1960), the French social thinker, did not endear himself to feminists and liberals when he wrote that men in mobs show the gullibility and ferocity of "primitive beings" like women, children, members of the lower classes, and savages. He branded mobs and crowds irrational, like a "beast with many heads." Mob actions like race riots and lynchings sometimes seem to operate on a psychology of their own. Do mobs elicit the beast in us? How is it that mild-mannered people will commit mayhem as members of a mob? In seeking an answer, let us examine a lynching and the baiting type of crowd that often seems to attend threatened suicides.

The Lynching of Arthur Stevens In *Social Learning and Imitation*, Neal Miller and John Dollard (1941) vividly described a southern lynching. Arthur Stevens, a black man, was accused of murdering his lover, a white woman, when she wanted to break up with him. Stevens was arrested and confessed to the crime. The sheriff feared violence and moved Stevens to a town 200 miles distant during the night. But his location was uncovered. The next day a mob of 100 stormed the jail and returned Stevens to the scene of the crime.

Outrage spread from person to person like a plague bacillus. Laborers, professionals, women, adolescents, and law-enforcement officers alike were infected. Stevens was tortured and emasculated. His corpse was dragged through the streets. Then the mob went on a rampage in town, chasing and assaulting other blacks. The riot ended only when troops were sent in to restore law and order.

Deindividuation When we act as individuals, fear of consequences and self-evaluation tend to prevent antisocial behavior. But as members of a mob, we may experience **deindividuation,** a state of reduced self-awareness and lowered concern for social evaluation (Mann and others, 1982). Many factors lead to deindividuation, including anonymity, diffusion of responsibility, arousal due to noise and crowding (Zimbardo, 1969), and focusing of individual attention on the group process (Diener, 1980). Individuals also tend to adopt the emerging norms and attitudes of the group (Turner & Killian, 1972). Under these circumstances, crowd members behave more aggressively than they would as individuals.

Police know that mob actions are best averted early, by dispersing the small groups that may gather into a crowd. On an individual level, perhaps we can resist deindividuation by instructing ourselves to stop and think whenever we begin to feel highly aroused as group members. If we dissociate ourselves from such groups when they are in the formative process, we shall be more likely to retain critical self-evaluation and avoid behavior that we shall later regret.

The Baiting Crowd in Cases of Threatened Suicide   As individuals, we often feel compassion when we observe people who are so distressed that they are considering suicide. Why is it, then, that when people who are considering suicide threaten to jump from a ledge the crowd often baits them, urging them on?

Such baiting occurred in 10 of 21 cases of threatened suicide studied by Leon Mann (1981). Analysis of newspaper reports suggested a number of factors that might have prompted deindividuation among crowd members, all contributing to anonymity: The crowds were large. It was dark out (past 6 P.M.). The victim and the crowd were distant from one another (with the victim, for example, on a high floor). Baiting by the crowd was also linked to high temperatures (the summer season) and a long duration of the episode, suggestive of stress and fatigue among crowd members.

Perhaps feelings of stress and fatigue should also warn us to separate ourselves from ugly crowds as early as possible.

Helping Behavior and the Bystander Effect: Some Watch While Others Die

In 1964 America was shocked by the murder of Kitty Genovese in New York City. Murder was not unheard of in the big apple. But Kitty had screamed for help as her killer had repeatedly stabbed her. Nearly 40 neighbors had heard the commotion. Many watched. Nobody helped. Why? As a nation are we a callous, unempathetic bunch who would rather watch then help when others are in trouble? What factors determine whether we will come to the aid of others who are in trouble?

The Helper: Who Helps?   Some psychologists (e.g., Hoffman, 1981) suggest that **altruism** is a part of human nature. In keeping with sociobiological theory (see Chapter 1), they argue that self-sacrifice will sometimes help guarantee that a close relative will succeed. In this way, self-sacrifice is actually "selfish" from a genetic point of view: It helps us perpetuate a genetic code similar to our own in future generations.

But this is a minority view. Most psychologists focus on the roles of helper mood and personality traits. By and large, we are more likely to help others when we are in a good mood (Cunningham and others, 1980; Rosenhan and others, 1981). Yet we may help others when we are miserable ourselves if our own problems work to increase our empathy or sensitivity to the plights of others (Batson and others, 1981; Thompson and others, 1980). People with a high need for approval may act "altruistically" in order to earn approval from others (Satow, 1975). Conversely, fear of making a social blunder (and looking foolish) inhibits helping behavior.

People who believe that others "get" what they deserve may rationalize not helping by thinking that a person would not be in trouble unless this outcome was just (Lerner and others, 1975). A sense of personal responsibility increases the likelihood of helping. Such responsibility may stem from having made a verbal commitment to help (e.g., Moriarty, 1975) or from having been designated by others as responsible for carrying out a helping chore (Maruyama and others, 1982).

Altruism (AL–true–izm). Unselfish concern for the welfare of others. (From the Latin *alter,* meaning "another.")

The Victim: Who Is Helped?   It is traditional for men to help women in our society although, as noted in Chapter 13, sex roles have been changing in recent years. Latané and Dabbs (1975) found that women were more likely than men to receive help, especially from men, when they dropped coins in Atlanta (a southern city) than in Seattle or Columbus (northern cities). The researchers explain this difference by noting that traditional sex roles are persevering more strongly in the South.

Women are also more likely than men to be helped when their cars have broken down on the highway or they are hitchhiking (Pomazal & Clore, 1973). There may be sexual overtones to some of this "altruism." Women are most likely to be helped by males when they are attractive and they are alone (Snyder and others, 1974; Benson and others, 1976).

Situational Determinants of Helping: "Am I the Only One Here?"   It may seem logical that a group of people would be more likely to have come to the aid of Kitty Genovese than would a lone person. After all, a group could more effectively have overpowered her attacker. Yet research by Darley and Latané (1968) suggests that a lone person may have been more likely to try to help.

In their experiment, male subjects were performing meaningless tasks in cubicles when they heard a (convincing) recording of a person apparently having an epileptic seizure. When the subjects thought that four other persons were immediately available to help, only 31 percent made an effort to help the victim. But when they thought that no one else was available, 85 percent of them tried to offer aid. As in other areas of group behavior, it seems that diffusion of responsibility inhibits helping behavior in groups or crowds. When we are in a group, we are often willing to let George (or Georgette) do it. When George isn't around, we are more willing to help others ourselves.

Other situational factors also influence the likehood of helping behavior. We are more likely to help others when we can clearly see what is happening (for instance, if we can see clearly that the woman whose car has broken down is alone), and when the setting is familiar to us (for instance, when we are in our home town rather than a strange city).

Conformity

Most of us would be reluctant to wear blue jeans to a funeral, to walk naked on city streets in summer, or, for that matter, to wear clothes at a nudist colony. Groups can exert enormous pressure on us to **conform,** or to behave in accord with group norms. This is often a good thing. Some group norms have evolved because they favor comfort and survival. But group pressure can also promote maladaptive behavior, such as wearing coats and ties in summer in buildings cooled only to 78° F. At that high temperature the main motive for conforming to a dress code may be to show that we have been adequately socialized and are not threats to social rules.

Let us have a look at a classic experiment on conformity run by Solomon Asch in the early 1950s. Then we shall examine factors that promote conformity.

Seven Line Judges Can't Be Wrong: The Asch Study

Do you believe what you see with your own eyes? Seeing is believing, is it not? Not if you were a participant in the Asch (1952) study.

Conform To behave in accordance with group norms and expectations.

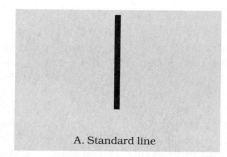
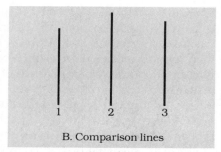

A. Standard line   B. Comparison lines

FIGURE 14.2   Cards Used in the Asch Study on Conformity. Which line on card B—1, 2, or 3—is the same length as the line on card A? Line 2, right? But would you say "2" if you were a member of a group and six people answering ahead of you all said "3"? Are you sure?

You would enter a laboratory room with seven other subjects for an experiment on visual discrimination. If you were familiar with psychology experiments, you might be surprised: There were no rats and no electric shock apparatus in sight, only a man at the front of a room with some cards with lines drawn on them.

The eight of you would be seated in a series. You would be given the seventh seat, a minor fact at the time. The man would explain the task. There was a single line on the card on the left. Three lines were drawn on the card at the right (Figure 14.2). One line was the same length as the line on the other card. You and the other subjects need only call out, one at a time, which of the three lines—1, 2, or 3—was the same length. Simple.

You would try it out. Those to your right spoke out in order: "3," "3," "3," "3," "3," "3." Now it was your turn. Line 3 was clearly the same length as the line on the first card, so you said "3." Then the fellow after you chimed in "3." That's all there was to it. Then two other cards were set up in the front of the room. This time line 2 was clearly the same length as the line on the first card. "2," "2," "2," "2," "2," "2." Your turn again. "2," you said, and perhaps your mind began to wander. Your stomach was gurgling a bit. That night you would not even mind dorm food particularly. "2," said the fellow after you.

Another pair of cards was held up. Line 3 was clearly the correct answer. The 6 people on your right spoke in turn: "1," "1 . . ." Wait a second! ". . . 1,"

The Set-Up of the Asch Experiment in Conformity.   The experimenter is at the right, and the unsuspecting subject is seated sixth from the left. All other "subjects" are actually in league with the experimenter.

"1—" You forgot about dinner and studied the lines briefly. No, 1 was too short, by a good half an inch. ". . . 1," "1," and suddenly it was your turn. Your hands had quickly become sweaty and there was a lump in your throat. You wanted to say 3, but was it right? There was really no time and you had already paused noticeably. "1," you said. "1," the last fellow confirmed matter-of-factly.

Now your attention was riveted on the task. Much of the time you agreed with the other seven line judges, but sometimes you did not. And for some reason beyond your understanding, they were in perfect agreement, even when they were wrong—assuming that you could trust your eyes. It was a nightmare, and you began to doubt your judgment.

The nightmare in the Asch study was the pressure to conform. Actually, the other seven recruits were confederates of the experimenter. They prearranged a number of incorrect responses. The sole purpose of the study was to see whether you would conform to the erroneous group judgments.

How many of Asch's subjects caved in? How many went along with the crowd rather than assert what they thought to be the right answer? Seventy-five percent. *Three of four agreed with the majority wrong answer at least once.*

What about you? Would you wear blue jeans if everyone else wore slacks and skirts? A number of more recent experiments (Wheeler and others, 1978) show that the tendency to conform did not go out with the Fabulous Fifties.

Factors Influencing Conformity: Numbers, Support, and Sex

Several personal and situational factors promote conformity. Personal factors include low self-esteem, high self-consciousness, social shyness (Krech and others, 1962; Santee & Maslach, 1982), gender (Cooper, 1979), and familiarity with the task. As noted in Chapter 13, women who accept the feminine sex role stereotype are more likely than men to conform (Bem, 1975). One interesting recent experiment (Eagly and others, 1981) found that men conform to group opinions as frequently as women do when their conformity or independence will be private. But when their conformity would be made known to the group, they conform less often than women do, apparently because nonconformity is more consistent with the masculine sex role stereotype of independence. That is, men may often show independence just to conform with the male sex role stereotype of rugged individualism. It's a little bit like "doublethink" in the Orwell novel *1984:* "Nonconformity is conformity." (As with experiments showing that we are more "altruistic" when we are rewarded for being altruistic, sometimes you just can't win.)

Familiarity with the task at hand promotes self-reliance (Eagly, 1978). In one experiment, for example, Sistrunk and McDavid (1971) found that women were more likely to conform to group pressure on tasks involving identification of tools (such as wrenches) that were more familiar to men. But men were more likely to conform on tasks involving identification of cooking utensils, with which women, in our society, are usually more familiar.

Situational factors include the number of people who hold the majority opinion and the presence of at least one other who shares the discrepant opinion. Probability of conformity, even to incorrect group judgments, increases rapidly as a group grows to five members. Then it increases at a slower rate up to eight members (Gerard and others, 1968; Wilder, 1977), at which point maximum probability of conformity is reached. But finding just one other person who supports your minority opinion is apparently enough to encourage you to stick to your guns (Morris and others, 1977). In a variation of the Asch experiment, recruits were provided with just one confederate who agreed with their minority judgments (Allen & Levine, 1971). Even though this confederate seemed to have a visual impairment, as evidenced by thick glasses, his support was sufficient to lead actual subjects not to conform to incorrect majority opinions.

Environmental Psychology

Pollution, overpopulation, the quality of life in the cities—these and other vital issues are the province of environmental psychologists. Only recently have psychologists begun to study systematically how people and the environment influence each other. This is an important field of inquiry, for it is within the environment that we survive from day to day and hope to enhance the quality of life.

Let us explore some findings of environmental psychology concerning the effects of noise, heat, air pollution, and crowding.

Noise: Of Rock 'n' Roll, Traffic, and Low-Flying Aircraft

Noise, especially loud noise, can be aversive. How do you react when chalk is scraped on the blackboard or when an airplane shrieks low overhead?

The unit for expressing the loudness of noise is the **decibel** (dB). The hearing threshold is defined as zero dB. Your school library is probably about 30–40 dB. A freeway is about 70 dB. One hundred forty dB is painfully loud and 150 dB can rupture your eardrums. After eight hours of exposure to 110–120 dB your hearing may be damaged (rock groups play at 110–120 dB). High noise levels lead to increases in blood pressure and other signs of stress.

Children who are exposed to greater traffic noise on the lower floors of apartment complexes (Cohen and others, 1973), or to loud noise from low-flying airplanes in their schools (Cohen and others, 1980), show signs of stress, hearing loss, and impairments in learning and memory. Time to adjust and subsequent noise abatement do not seem to reverse their cognitive and perceptual deficits (Cohen and others, 1981).

Couples may enjoy high noise levels at the disco, but less desirable noises of 80 dB seem to decrease feelings of attraction, causing couples to space themselves farther apart. Loud noise also puts a damper on helping behavior. People are less likely to help pick up a dropped package when the background noise of a construction crew is at 92 dB than when it's at 72 dB (Page, 1977). They're even less willing to make change for a quarter.

If you and your date have had a fight and are then exposed to a sudden blowout, look out. Angered people are more likely to behave aggressively when exposed to an sudden noise of 95 dB than one of 55 dB (Donnerstein & Wilson, 1976).

Heat: A Hot Day in July

Is keeping your cool more difficult when the midsummer sun bakes the sidewalks? Campus and city riots broke out with regularity during the broiling summers of the 1960s (Figure 14.3). Each spring, news commentators won-

Decibel A unit expressing the loudness of a sound. Abbreviated *dB*. See Chapter 3.

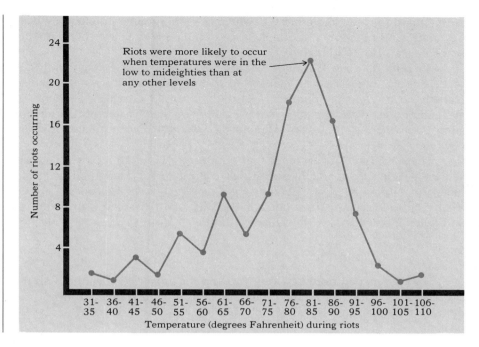

FIGURE 14.3 The "Long, Hot Summer Effect." Most riots of the 1960s occurred when temperatures were in the uncomfortable mid-80s. There was a rapid decrease in the incidence of rioting as temperatures increased further. When the heat is really on, perhaps people "cool it" by themselves.

Riots were more likely to occur when temperatures were in the low to mideighties than at any other levels

dered whether we would be in for another "long, hot summer." Yet it can also be too hot for a riot. The United States Riot Commission (1968) found that riots occurred only rarely in temperatures exceeding 100° F.

Air Pollution: Fussing and Fuming

Auto fumes, industrial smog, cigarette smoke, fireplaces, burning leaves—these are a handful of the sources of air pollution that affect us each day. The lead in auto fumes may impair children's intellectual functioning in the same way chewing lead paint does (Fogel, 1980). Carbon monoxide, a colorless, odorless gas found in cigarette smoke and auto fumes, decreases the capacity

"Here Comes the Sun": A Time for Favors and Big Tips?

Do our dispositions vary with the sunshine? Do we become bright and open, or grim and cloudy, as do the skies? Recent research suggests that we may indeed become more cooperative and generous when the sun shines down upon us (Cunningham, 1979).

Student passers-by at the University of Minnesota were more likely to agree to fill out a lengthy public opinion poll when the sun was shining than on cloudy days of equal temperature. Temperature, wind velocity, and humidity also played roles. Helping behavior peaked when the temperature was an ideal 65° F and dropped off when the thermometer moved up or down. Wind velocity was positively linked to helping in the summer, when cooling breezes are favored, but negatively linked in winter,

when the wind-chill factor also chilled the hearts of passers-by. Students were also more helpful when the humidity was low.

Sunshine streaming in through restaurant windows also apparently warms customers' hearts as measured by the size of tips. Waitresses at a Chicago restaurant with large windows tracked their tips for several weeks. The temperature and humidity in the restaurant were kept constant throughout the period. But when the sun shone, it shone into the restaurant as well, and tips were significantly larger.

If misfortune should befall us so that we are in need of help, let us hope that the sun is shining, the temperature is 65° F, and the humidity is low.

of the blood to carry oxygen (see Chapter 4). Carbon monoxide impairs learning ability and perception of the passage of time (Beard & Wertheim, 1967). It may also contribute to highway accidents.

Air pollution can kill more directly. In December 1952 stagnation of industrial smog over London was linked to 3,500 deaths, with sulfur dioxide considered the specific culprit (Goldsmith, 1968). Los Angeles residents are accustomed to warnings to remain indoors or inactive to reduce air consumption when atmospheric inversions allow smog to accumulate for several days near ground level.

There is mounting evidence that odorous air pollutants, like other forms of aversive stimulation, decrease feelings of attraction and heighten aggression (Bell and others, 1978). In people who are sensitive, even the atmospheric electricity that accompanies changing weather patterns can lead to tension and irritability (Charry & Hawkinshire, 1981).

Crowding and Personal Space

Sometimes you do everything you can for mice. You give them all they can eat, sex partners, a comfortable temperature, and protection from predators like owls and pussycats. And how do they reward you? By acting like, well, animals.

Calhoun's "Mouse Universe"   Calhoun (1962) allowed mice to reproduce with no constraints but for the limited space of their laboratory environment (Figure 14.4). At first all was bliss in mouse city. The males scurried about, gathered females into harems, and defended territories. They did not covet their neighbors' wives. They rarely fought. The females, unliberated, built nests and nursed their young. They resisted the occasional advance of the passing male.

But unrestricted population growth proved to be the snake in mouse paradise. Beyond a critical population, the **mortality** rate rose. Family structure broke down, packs of delinquent males assaulted inadequately defended females. Some males shunned all social contact. Some females avoided sexual advances and huddled with fearsome males. Upon dissection, many mice showed bodily signs of stress—unhealthy changes in organs and gland malfunctions.

Meanwhile, Back at the Dorm . . .   People are also influenced by crowding. You may have been shoehorned with several roommates into a dorm room intended for two. Under such crowded conditions, students are less satisfied with their roommates and rate them as less cooperative (Baron and others, 1976). But women seem to find such crowding less aversive than men do. This may be because women, in contrast to men, who are socialized into keeping feelings to themselves, feel freer to express their discomfort (Karlin and others, 1976).

Dorm architecture can do much to eliminate the feelings of stress that often attend crowding. Students in suite arrangements, who share a common gathering place and bathroom, find their roommates more cooperative and encounter less stress than do students who live along a lengthy central hall (Baum & Davis, 1980). The suite arrangement allows them to exercise more control over their social contacts.

Mortality Death, especially on a large scale, as from disease or war. (From the Latin *mortis,* meaning "death.")

FIGURE 14.4   The "Mouse Universe." In John Calhoun's "mouse universe," an unlimited food supply and easy access between compartments (with the exception of compartments 1 and 4, between which there was no direct access) caused compartments 2 and 3 to become a "behavioral sink." The "sink" was characterized by overpopulation, breakdown of the social order, and a higher mortality rate. Do some human cities function as behavioral sinks?

Some Effects of City Life   As compared with suburbanites and rural folk, people who live in the big city encounter greater stimulus overload and fear of crime. Overwhelming crowd stimulation, bright lights, shop windows, and so on cause them to narrow their perceptions to a particular face, destination, or job.

City dwellers are less willing to shake hands with (Milgram, 1977), make eye contact with (Newman & McCauley, 1977), or help strangers (Glass & Singer, 1972; Milgram, 1970). People who move to the city from more rural areas adjust by becoming more deliberate in their daily activities (Franck and others, 1974). They plan ahead to take safety precautions, and they increase their alertness to potential dangers.

Farming, anyone?

Personal Space: "Don't Burst My Bubble, Please"   One aversive effect of crowding is the invasion of **personal space**. Personal space is an invisible boundary, something like a bubble, that surrounds you. You are likely to become anxious and, perhaps, angry when others invade your space, as in sitting

Personal space A psychological boundary that surrounds a person and permits that person to maintain a protective distance from others.

down across from or next to you in an otherwise empty cafeteria, or standing too close in an elevator.

Personal space appears to serve protective and communicative functions. Violent people are likely to expect violent reactions from others, and violent prisoners require three times the personal space sought by nonviolent prisoners (Kinzel, 1970). Anxious people position themselves farther from others than do nonanxious people (Karabenick & Meisels, 1972). We need more personal space when we are in small rooms with others (White, 1975) or indoors rather than outdoors (Pempus and others, 1975). We apparently seek a safe distance from others when escape or exit could be a problem. Persons with an internal locus of control (see Chapter 10) require less personal space than externals (Duke & Nowicki, 1972). Perhaps they feel more competent to handle potential threats.

As a form of communication, the distance between people limits the possible interactions (Hall, 1968). Up to one and one half feet permits an intimate relationship in which touch is important, as in lovemaking, comforting, and contact sports like wrestling. Close friends and everyday acquaintances tend to remain from one and one half to four feet apart. Impersonal business contacts remain four to 12 feet distant and formal contacts, as between performer and audience or lawyer and judge, remain at least 12 feet apart.

People sit and stand closer to people of the same race, similar age, or similar socioeconomic status. Dating couples come closer together as the attraction between them increases. As noted in Chapter 13, men are made more uncomfortable by strangers who sit across from them, while women feel more "invaded" by strangers who sit next to them. In libraries men tend to pile books protectively in front of them, while women strategically place books and coats to discourage others from taking adjacent seats (Bell and others, 1978). Consider the possibilities for miscommunicating your intentions to the opposite sex. A man might seat himself next to a woman rather than across from her in order to avoid threatening her. Yet she might find his behavior forward and offensive.

Perhaps such communications problems have a bright side. They help keep a number of psychologists in business.

"Space Invaders" and Arousal, *or* **Psychology Goes to the John** *Up periscope!* was the thrilling cry of submarine warfare during World War II. These cigar-shaped vessels poked their periscopes above the water to search for prey without alerting their victims.

Recently a periscope was used in a less dramatic but more unusual theater of action: a men's room (Figure 14.5). Psychologists (Middlemist and others, 1976) were pioneering an ingenious method for seeing whether personal space invasions lead to stress, as reflected by higher levels of arousal. High arousal, you see, interferes with urinating. When people are aroused, it takes them longer to begin to urinate (there is "delay of onset"), and the duration of urinating is shorter.

The men's room had three urinals and a toilet stall. When a male subject was about to urinate in the urinal next to the stall, his personal space was invaded by another male who was a confederate of the experimenter. The "space invader" would use either the urinal adjacent to his or the one at the far end of the row. While this drama was taking place, an unseen experimenter in the innocent-looking stall used a periscope to observe time of onset and

FIGURE 14.5   Research on "Space Invaders" in a Campus Restroom. A periscope is quite obvious in the photo at the left. But in the experiment by Middlemist and his colleagues, the periscope was hidden from view by the wall of a stall, enabling the researchers to observe subjects' bathroom behavior surreptitiously.

duration of urination. Sure enough, close encounters led to increased delay of onset and shorter duration of urination—the target signs of heightened arousal (Figure 14.6).

This experiment received some acid commentary from other psychologists. Gerald Koocher (1977), for one, complained that it invaded the privacy as well as the space of the subjects. The subjects might also have suffered psychological damage if they had known they were being observed. Middlemist and his colleagues (1977) replied that men in a pilot study reported no concern when they were told that they had been secretly observed while urinating.

It is hard to determine whether some experiments are ethically justified. Some experiments can only be run by secretly observing or deceiving subjects.

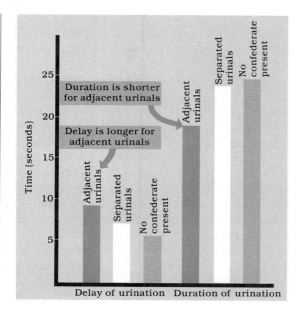

FIGURE 14.6   Effects of the Restroom "Space Invaders." The graph shows that men whose personal space was invaded by a person using the adjacent urinal showed (1) delay of onset and (2) shorter duration of urination. Both effects are interpreted as signs of stress.

In each case we must weigh the value of the potential knowledge to be gained against the possible negative consequences to the people involved.

In any case, I'm sure that the restroom down the hall from you is free from experimenters.

Summary

Social psychologists study ways in which we are influenced by other people and by the environment. Areas of inquiry include attitudes, social perception, attraction, obedience to authority, group behavior, conformity, and environmental psychology.

Attitudes are cognitive evaluations with affective and behavioral components. Attitudes may be acquired through principles of learning and logical processes. Attitudinal change may be induced by persuasive communicators (who may show expertise, trustworthiness, attractiveness, or similarity to the audience), repetition, emotional appeals, and attitude-discrepant behavior. People apparently wish to organize their beliefs in a balanced, harmonious manner. Attitude-discrepant behavior apparently induces cognitive dissonance which people then can reduce by changing their attitudes. People who see themselves as helpful or who are highly concerned about the approval of others show low sales resistance.

Prejudice is an attitude toward a group that includes negative evaluations, negative affect, and avoidance behavior or discrimination. Three forms of prejudice are racism, ageism, and sexism. Sources of prejudice include attitudinal dissimilarity, social conflict, social learning, authoritarianism, and information processing strategies.

Social perception concerns our perception of others. We often perceive others in terms of first impressions (primacy effect), although recent impressions (recency effect) can become important when time passes between observations. We tend to attribute our own behavior to external (situational) factors, but to attribute the behavior of others to internal (dispositional) factors. At an early age we learn to "read" body language. People who feel positively toward one another position themselves close together and touch. Gazing into another's eyes can be a sign of love, but a "hard stare" is an aversive challenge.

We are more attracted to good-looking people and assume that they are more likely to be talented and less likely to engage in criminal behavior. We tend to seek dates and mates at our own level of attractiveness, according to the matching hypothesis, largely because of fear of rejection. Attitudinal similarity, propinquity, reciprocity, parental opposition, and playing hard to get can all enhance feelings of attraction.

Most people comply with the demands of authority figures, even when these demands seem immoral, as shown in the Milgram studies on obedience.

Group behavior may facilitate our performance or induce social loafing, depending on circumstances. Group decisions tend to be more polarized and risky than individual decisions, largely because groups diffuse responsibility. We are more likely to help people in need when we think we are the only one available, have a clear view of the situation, and are not afraid that we shall be committing a social blunder. Presence of others again diffuses responsibility. Highly emotional crowds may induce attitude-discrepant aggressive behavior through deindividuation.

People experience increasing pressure to conform to group norms and opinions as groups grow to eight persons. The presence of a person who shares one's minority view and familiarity with the task at hand decreases conforming behavior.

Studies in environmental psychology show that high noise levels can lead to stress and to cognitive and perceptual deficits. Uncomfortable levels of heat increase the risk of aggressive behavior, unless heat is too extreme (above 90° F). Air pollution can be physically harmful, foster aggression and decrease feelings of attraction. Crowding is stressful and leads people to rate others as less cooperative. We seek a certain amount of personal space, which seems to serve both protective and communicative functions. Invasions of our personal space can lead to anxiety and irritation.

Truth or Fiction Revisited

- *Beauty is in the eye of the beholder.* False. There are some rather consistent cultural standards for beauty.
- *Liberal women are more attracted to men with long hair, while conservative women prefer short-haired men.* True. Hair length and style can be an emblem of one's political attitudes. So it is not surprising that others may respond to one's hair style on this basis.
- *Juries are less likely to find attractive individuals guilty of burglary or of cheating on an exam.* True. Attractive people are also seen as talented, and thus as not needing to resort to deviant behavior to achieve their goals.
- *We often see ourselves as victims of circumstances, while we assume that other people act as they do out of choice.* True. This tendency is a major bias in attribution.
- *Most people would refuse to deliver painful electric shock to an innocent party, even under powerful social pressure.* False. The great majority complied with an authority figure in the Milgram studies.
- *Business executives acting as a group are more likely to gamble a sizable sum of money on a risky venture than would the average group member, when acting as an individual.* True. The group decision apparently diffuses responsibility.
- *Nearly 40 people stood by and did nothing while a woman was being stabbed to death.* True. We are more likely to help others when we believe we are the only ones available to do so.
- *Auto fumes may lower your children's IQ.* True. Auto fumes contain lead, carbon monoxide, and other pollutants.

Appendix A: Statistics

Imagine that some visitors from outer space arrive outside Madison Square Garden in New York City. Their goal, this dark and numbing cold winter evening, is to learn all they can about the inhabitants of planet Earth. They are drawn inside the Garden by lights, shouts, and warmth. The spotlighting inside rivets their attention to a wood-floored arena where the New York Knicks are hosting the Los Angeles Lakers in a briskly contested basketball game.

Our visitors use their sophisticated instruments to take some measurements of the players. Some surprising **statistics** are sent back to the planet of their origin: (1) It appears that 100 percent of Earthlings are male, and (2) the height of Earthlings ranges from six feet one inch to seven feet two inches.

Statistics is the name given the science that is concerned with obtaining and organizing numerical measurements or information. Our imagined visitors have sent home some statistics about the sex and size of human beings that are at once accurate and misleading. They accurately measured the basketball players, but their small **sample** of Earth's **population** was quite distorted. Fortunately for us Earthlings, about half of us are female. And the **range** of heights observed by the aliens, of six feet one to seven feet two, is both restricted and too high. People vary in height by more than one foot and one inch. And our **average** height is not between six one and seven two but is several inches below.

Psychologists, like our imagined visitors, are vitally concerned with measuring human as well as animal characteristics and traits—not just physical characteristics like sex and height, but also psychological traits like intelligence, aggressiveness, anxiety, or self-assertiveness. By observing the central tendencies (averages) and variations in measurements from person to person, psychologists can state that some person is average or above average in in-

Statistics (stuh–TISS–ticks). Numerical facts assembled in such a manner that they provide significant information about measures or scores. (From the Latin word *status*, meaning "standing" or "position.")

Sample. Part of a population.

Population. A complete group from which a sample is selected.

Range. A measure of variability; the distance between extreme measures or scores.

Average. Central tendency of a group of measures, expressed as mean, median, and mode.

telligence, or that another person is less assertive than, say, 60 percent of the population.

But psychologists, as compared to our aliens, are more careful in their attempts to select a sample—on which they will make their measurements and base their calculations—which accurately represents the entire population. Professional basketball players do not represent the human species. They are taller, stronger, and more agile than the rest of us, and they make more shaving cream commercials.

In this appendix we shall survey some of the statistical methods used by psychologists to draw conclusions about the measurements they take in research activities. First we shall discuss *descriptive statistics* and learn what types of statements we can make about the height of basketball players and some other human traits. Then we shall discuss the *normal curve* and learn why basketball players are abnormal—at least in terms of height. We shall explore *correlation coefficients* and provide you with some less-than-shocking news: More intelligent people attain higher grades than less intelligent people. Finally, we shall have a brief look at *inferential statistics* and see why we can be bold enough to say that the difference in height between basketball players and other people is not just a chance accident, or fluke. Basketball players are in fact *statistically significantly* taller than the general population.

"He's a 17.63 on a scale of minus 42 to plus 29."

Descriptive Statistics

Being told that someone is a "Ten" is not very descriptive unless you know something about how possible scores are distributed and how frequently one finds a Ten. Fortunately—for Tens, if not for the rest of us—one is usually informed that someone is a Ten on a scale of one to ten, and that ten is the positive end of the scale. If this is not sufficient, one will also be told that Tens are few and far between—rather unusual statistical events.

This business of a scale from one to ten is not very scientific, to be sure, but it does suggest something about **descriptive statistics.** We can use descriptive statistics to clarify our understanding of a distribution of scores, such as heights, test grades, IQs, or increases or decreases in measures of sexual arousal following drinking of alcohol. For example, descriptive statistics can help us to determine measures of central tendency, or averages, and to determine how much variability there is in the scores. Being a Ten loses some of its charm if the average score is an eleven. Being a Ten is more remarkable in a distribution whose scores range from one to ten than in one that ranges from nine to ten.

Let us now examine some of the concerns of descriptive statistics: the *frequency distribution, measures of central tendency* (types of averages), and *measures of variability.*

The Frequency Distribution

A **frequency distribution** takes scores, or items of raw data, puts them into order, as from lowest to highest, and groups them according to class intervals. Table A.1 shows the rosters for a Boston Celtics–Los Angeles Lakers basketball game. The members of each team are listed according to the numbers of their uniforms. Table A.2 shows a frequency distribution of the heights of the players of both teams combined, with a class interval of one inch.

Descriptive statistics. The branch of statistics that is concerned with providing information about a distribution of scores.

Frequency distribution. An ordered set of data that indicates how frequently scores appear.

TABLE A.1 Lakers vs. Celtics at Boston, a Recent Season

Los Angeles		Boston	
7 Byrnes	6-7	7 Archibald	6-1
9 Chones	6-11	12 Chaney	6-5
10 Nixon	6-2	18 Cowens	6-9
14 Holland	6-3	30 Carr	6-6
21 Cooper	6-5	31 Maxwell	6-8
25 Mack	6-3	32 Judkins	6-6
31 Haywood	6-9	33 Bird	6-9
32 Johnson	6-8	42 Ford, C.	6-5
33 Abdul-Jabbar	7-2	43 Henderson	6-2
35 Ford. D.	6-9	45 Fernsten	6-10
52 Wilkes	6-6	53 Robey	6-10

A glance at the rosters for a Boston Celtics–Los Angeles Lakers basketball game shows you that the average heights of the teams, combined, ranged from six feet, one inch to seven feet, two inches. Are the average heights of the teams representative of the average heights of the general population?

It would also be possible to use three-inch class intervals, as in Table A.3. In determining how large a class interval should be, a researcher attempts to collapse that data into a small enough number of classes to ensure that they will appear meaningful at a glance, but attempts also to maintain a large enough number of categories to ensure that important differences are not obscured.

Table A.3 obscures the fact that no players are six feet four inches tall. If the researcher feels that this information is extremely important, a class interval of one inch may be maintained.

Figure A.1 shows two methods for representing the information in Table A.3 with graphs. Both in frequency **histograms** and frequency **polygons** the class intervals are typically drawn along the horizontal line, or X-axis, and the number of scores (persons, cases, or events) in each class is drawn along the

Histogram (HISS–toe–gram). A graphic representation of a frequency distribution that uses rectangular solids. (From the Greek *historia*, meaning "narrative," and *gramma*, meaning "writing" or "drawing.")

Polygon (POLL–ee–gone). A closed figure. (From the Greek *polys*, meaning "many," and *gōnia*, meaning "angle.")

TABLE A.2 Frequency Distribution of Heights of Basketball Players, with a One-inch Class Interval

Class Interval	Number of Players in Class
6-1 to 6-1.9	1
6-2 to 6-2.9	2
6-3 to 6-3.9	2
6-4 to 6-4.9	0
6-5 to 6-5.9	3
6-6 to 6-6.9	3
6-7 to 6-7.9	1
6-8 to 6-8.9	2
6-9 to 6-9.9	4
6-10 to 6-10.9	2
6-11 to 6-11.9	1
7-0 to 7-0.9	0
7-1 to 7-1.9	0
7-2 to 7-2.9	1

TABLE A.3 Frequency Distribution of Heights of Basketball Players, with a Three-inch Class Interval

Class Interval	Number of Players in Class
6-1 to 6-3.9	5
6-4 to 6-6.9	6
6-7 to 6-9.9	7
6-10 to 7-0.9	3
7-1 to 7-3.9	1

vertical or Y-axis. In a histogram the number of scores in each class interval is represented by a rectangular solid, so that the graph resembles a series of steps. In a polygon the number of scores in each class interval is plotted as a point, and the points are then connected to form a many-sided geometric figure. Note that class intervals were added at both ends of the horizontal axis of the frequency polygon so that the lines could be brought down to the axis to close the geometric figure.

Measures of Central Tendency

There are three types of measures of central tendency, or averages: *mean, median,* and *mode.* Each tells us something about the way in which the scores in a distribution may be summarized by a typical or representative number.

The **mean** is what most people think of as "the average." The mean is obtained by adding up all the scores in a distribution and then dividing this sum by the number of scores. In the case of our basketball players it would be advisable first to convert all heights into one unit, such as inches (6'1" becomes 73", and so on). If we add all the heights in inches, then divide by the number of players, or 22, we obtain a mean height of 78.73", or 6'6.73".

The **median** is the score of the middle case in a frequency distribution. It is the score beneath which 50 percent of the cases fall. In a distribution with an even number of cases, such as the distribution of the heights of the twenty-two basketball players in Table A.2, the median is determined by find-

Mean. A type of average calculated by dividing the sum of scores by the number of scores. (From the Latin *medius,* meaning "middle.")

Median. The score beneath which 50 percent of the cases fall. (From the Latin *medius,* meaning "middle.")

FIGURE A.1. Two Graphical Representations of the Data in Table A.3.

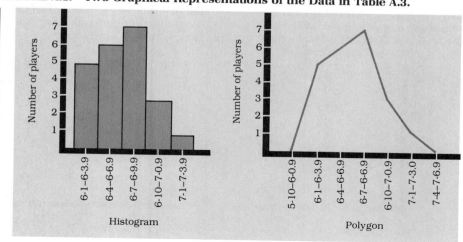

Histogram

Polygon

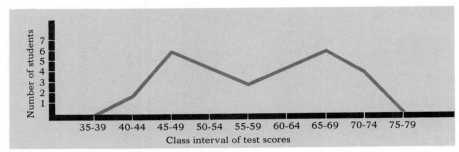

FIGURE A.2   A Bimodal Distribution. This hypothetical distribution represents the scores of students on a test. The mode at the left represents the central tendency of students who did not study, and the mode at the right represents the mode of students who studied.

ing the mean of the two middle cases. Listing these twenty-two cases in ascending order, we find that the eleventh case is 6′6″ and the twelfth case is 6′7″. Thus the median is (6′6″ + 6′7″)/2, or 6′6½″.

In the case of the heights of the basketball players the mean and the median are similar, and either serves as a useful indicator of the central tendency of the data. But suppose we are attempting to determine the average savings of thirty families living on a suburban block. Let us assume that twenty-nine of the thirty families have savings between $8,000 and $12,000, adding up to $294,000. But the thirtieth family has savings of $1,400,000! The mean savings for a family on this block would thus be $56,467. A mean can be greatly distorted by one or two extreme scores, and for such distributions the median is a better indicator of the central tendency. The median savings on our hypothetical block would lie between $8,000 and $12,000, and so would be more representative of the central tendency of savings. Studies of the incomes of American families usually report median rather than mean incomes just to avoid the distortions that would result from treating incomes of the small numbers of multimillionaires in the same way as other incomes.

The **mode** is simply the most frequently occurring score in a distribution. The mode of the data in Table A.1 is 6′9″ because this height occurs most often. The median class interval for the data in Table A.3 is 6′6½″ to 6′9½″. In these cases the mode is somewhat higher than the mean or median height.

Mode. The most frequently occurring number or score in a distribution. (From the Latin *modus*, meaning "measure.")

FIGURE A.3   Hypothetical Distributions of Student Test Scores. Each distribution has the same number of scores, the same mean, and even the same range, but the standard deviation is greater for the distribution on the left because the scores tend to be farther from the mean.

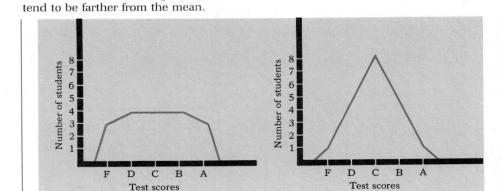

In some cases the mode is a more appropriate description of a distribution than the mean or median. Figure A.2 shows a **bimodal** distribution, or a distribution with two modes. In this hypothetical distribution of the test scores the mode at the left indicates the most common class interval for students who did not study, and the mode at the right indicates the most frequent class interval for students who did. The mean and median test scores would probably lie within the 55–59 class interval, yet use of that interval as a measure of central tendency would not provide very meaningful information about the distribution of scores. It might suggest that the test was too hard— not that a number of students chose not to study. One would be better able to visualize the distribution of scores if it is reported as bimodal. Even in similar cases in which the modes are not exactly equal, it might be more appropriate to describe a distribution as being bimodal or even multimodal.

Measures of Variability

Measures of variability of a distribution inform us about the spread of scores, or about the typical distances of scores from the average score. Measures of variability include the *range* of scores and the *standard deviation*.

The **range** of scores in a distribution is defined as the difference between the highest score and the lowest score, and it is obtained by subtracting the lowest score from the highest score. The range of heights in Table A.2 is 7′2″ minus 6′1″, or 1′1″. It is important to know the range of temperatures if we move to a new climate so that we may anticipate the weather and dress appropriately. A teacher must have some understanding of the range of abilities or skills in a class in order to teach effectively. Classes of gifted students or slow learners are formed so that teachers may attempt to devise a level of instruction that will better meet the needs of all members of a particular class.

The range is an imperfect measure of variability because of the manner in which it is influenced by extreme scores. In our earlier discussion of the savings of thirty families on a suburban block, the range of savings is $1,400,000 to $8,000, or $1,392,000. This tells us little about the typical variability of savings accounts, which lie within a restricted range of $8,000 to $12,000. The standard deviation is a statistic that indicates how scores are distributed about a mean of a distribution.

The standard deviation considers every score in a distribution, not just the extreme scores. Thus the standard deviation for the distribution on the right in Figure A.3 would be smaller than that of the distribution on the left. Note that each distribution has the same number of scores, the same mean, and the same range of scores. But the standard deviation for the distribution on the right will be smaller than that of the distribution on the left because the scores tend to cluster more closely about the mean.

The **standard deviation** (S.D.) is calculated by the following formula:

$$\text{S.D.} = \sqrt{\frac{\text{Sum of } d^2}{N}}$$

where d equals the deviation of each score from the mean of the distribution, and N equals the number of scores in the distribution.

Let us find the mean and standard deviation of the IQ scores listed in column 1 of Table A.4. To obtain the mean, we add all the scores, attain 1500, and then divide by the number of scores (15) to obtain a mean of 100. We

TABLE A.4   Hypothetical Scores Attained from an IQ Testing

IQ Score	d (Deviation Score)	d² (Deviation Score Squared)
85	15	225
87	13	169
89	11	121
90	10	100
93	7	49
97	3	9
97	3	9
100	0	0
101	−1	1
104	−4	16
105	−5	25
110	−10	100
112	−12	144
113	−13	169
117	−17	289

Sum of IQ scores = 1500   Sum of d^2 scores = 1426

$$\text{Mean} = \frac{\text{Sum of scores}}{\text{Number of scores}} = \frac{1500}{15} = 100$$

$$\text{Standard Deviation (S.D.)} = \sqrt{\frac{\text{Sum of } d^2}{\text{Number of scores}}} = \sqrt{\frac{1426}{15}} = \sqrt{95.07} = 9.75$$

obtain the deviation score (d) for each IQ score by subtracting the score from 100. The d for an IQ of 85 equals 100 minus 85, or 15, and so on. Then we square each d and add these squares. The S.D. equals the square root of the sum of squares (1426) divided by the number of scores (15), or 9.75.

As an additional exercise, we can show that the S.D. of the test scores on the left (in Figure A.4) is greater than that for the scores on the right by assigning the grades points according to a 4.0 system. Let A = 4, B = 3, C = 2, D = 1, and F = 0. The S.D. for each distribution of test scores is computed in Table A.5. The greater S.D. for the distribution on the left indicates that the scores in that distribution are more variable, or tend to be farther from the mean.

The Normal Curve

Normal distribution. A symmetrical distribution in which approximately 68 percent of cases lie within a standard deviation of the mean.

Normal curve. Graphic presentation of a normal distribution, showing a bell shape.

Many human traits and characteristics, such as height and intelligence, seem to be distributed in a pattern known as a normal distribution. In a **normal distribution** the mean, median, and mode all fall at the same data point or score, and scores cluster most heavily about the mean, fall off rapidly in either direction at first—as shown in Figure A.4—and then taper off more gradually.

The curve in Figure A.4 is bell-shaped. This type of distribution is also called a **normal curve.** It is hypothesized to reflect the distribution of variables in which different scores are determined by chance variation. Height is

TABLE A.5 Computation of Standard Deviations for Test Score Distributions in Figure A.3

Distribution at Left:				Distribution at Right:		
Grade	d	d^2		Grade	d	d^2
A (4)	2	4		A (4)	2	4
A (4)	2	4		B (3)	1	1
A (4)	2	4		B (3)	1	1
B (3)	1	1		B (3)	1	1
B (3)	1	1		B (3)	1	1
B (3)	1	1		C (2)	0	0
B (3)	1	1		C (2)	0	0
C (2)	0	0		C (2)	0	0
C (2)	0	0		C (2)	0	0
C (2)	0	0		C (2)	0	0
C (2)	0	0		C (2)	0	0
D (1)	−1	1		C (2)	0	0
D (1)	−1	1		C (2)	0	0
D (1)	−1	1		D (1)	−1	1
D (1)	−1	1		D (1)	−1	1
F (0)	−2	4		D (1)	−1	1
F (0)	−2	4		D (1)	−1	1
F (0)	−2	4		F (0)	−2	4

Sum of grades = 36

Mean grade = 36/18 = 2

Sum of d^2 = 32

S.D. = $\sqrt{\dfrac{32}{18}}$ = 1.33

Sum of grades = 36

Mean grade = 36/18 = 2

Sum of d^2 = 16

S.D. = $\sqrt{\dfrac{16}{18}}$ = 0.94

thought to be largely determined by chance combinations of genetic material. A distribution of the heights of a random sample of the population approximates normal distributions for men and women, with the mean of the distribution for men a few inches higher than the mean for women.

Test developers traditionally assumed that intelligence was also randomly or normally distributed among the population. For that reason they constructed intelligence tests so that scores would be distributed as close to "normal" as possible. In actuality, IQ scores are also influenced by environmental factors and chromosomal abnormalities, so the resultant curves are not perfectly normal. Most IQ tests have means defined as scores of 100 points, and the Wechsler scales are constructed to have standard deviations of 15 points, as shown in Figure A.4. This means that 50 percent of the Wechsler scores fall between 90 and 110 (the "broad average" range), about 68 percent (or two of three) fall between 85 and 115, and more than 95 percent fall between 70 and 130—that is, within two S.D.'s of the mean. The Stanford-Binet Intelligence Scale has an S.D. of 16 points.

The Scholastic Aptitude Tests (SATs) were constructed so that the mean scores would be 500 points, and an S.D. would be 100 points. Thus a score of 600 would equal or excel that of some 84 to 85 percent of the test takers. Because of the complex interaction of variables determining SAT scores, the distribution of SAT scores is not exactly normal either. The normal curve is an idealized curve.

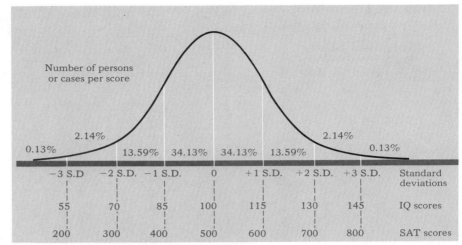

FIGURE A.4 A Bell-Shaped or Normal Curve. In a normal curve approximately 68 percent of the cases lie within a standard deviation (S.D.) from the mean, and the mean, median, and mode all lie at the same score. IQ tests and Scholastic Aptitude Tests have been constructed so that distributions of scores would approximate the normal curve.

Skewed Distributions

Skewed distributions are variations of normal distributions. A skewed distribution may be skewed, or slanted, to the left or to the right, as in Figure A.5. In skewed distributions the mean, median, and mode lie at different scores or data points and are arranged in alphabetical order (MEAn, MEDian, MOde). The mean always lies farthest out in the direction of the skewness. In a skewed distribution there is usually some systematic influence at work that interferes with the normality of the distribution.

The curve at left in Figure A.5 could reflect IQ scores among a population of test takers that included persons who had difficulty understanding the language in which the test was administered, or a population that included individuals with genetic abnormalities (see Chapter 2) that resulted in mental retardation. The curve at right in Figure A.5 could reflect SAT scores among a population of test takers that included individuals who had attended classes that directly taught the skills assessed by the SATs, or who had taken a number of practice tests. In all these examples a factor systematically influences the distribution of scores in such a way that the resultant curve is skewed.

Skewed distribution. A slanted distribution, drawn out to the left or right.

FIGURE A.5 Skewed Distributions. In a skewed distribution the scores are slanted to the left or the right, and the mean, median, and mode fall at different scores.

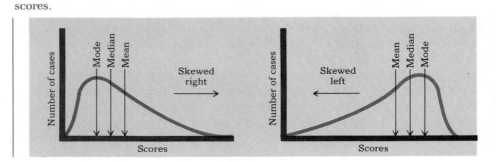

In the example given earlier, savings of twenty-nine families ranged from $8,000 to $12,000, but a thirtieth family on the same block had saved more than a million dollars. While the mean and median savings remain between $8,000 and $12,000, the thirtieth family's savings skew the distribution upward so that the mean savings is dramatically increased.

The Correlation Coefficient

What is the relationship between intelligence and educational achievement? Between cigarette smoking and lung cancer in human beings? Between introversion and frequency of dating among college students? We cannot run experiments to determine whether the relationships between these variables are causal because we cannot manipulate the independent variable. For example, we cannot randomly assign a group of people to cigarette smoking and another group to nonsmoking. People must be permitted to make their own choices, and so it is possible that the same factors that lead people to choose to smoke may also lead to lung cancer. However, the **correlation coefficient** may be used to show that there is a relationship between smoking and cancer. If a strong correlation is shown between the two variables, and we add supportive experimental evidence with laboratory animals who are assigned to conditions in which they inhale tobacco smoke, we wind up with a rather convincing indictment of smoking as a determinant of lung cancer.

The correlation coefficient is a statistic that describes the relationship between two variables. It varies from +1.00 to −1.00; therefore a correlation coefficient of +1.00 is called a perfect positive correlation, a coefficient of −1.00 is a perfect negative correlation, and a coefficient of 0.00 shows no correlation between variables. In order to examine the meanings of different correlation coefficients, let us first discuss the *scatter diagram*.

The Scatter Diagram

A **scatter diagram**, or scatter plot, is a graphic representation of the relationship between two variables. As shown in Figure A.6, a scatter diagram is typically drawn with an *X* axis (horizontal) and *Y* axis (vertical).

Let us assume that we have two thermometers. One measures temperature according to the Fahrenheit scale and one measures temperature according to the centigrade scale. Over a period of several months we record the temperatures Fahrenheit and centigrade at various times of the day. Then we randomly select a sample of eight Fahrenheit readings and jot down the corresponding centigrade readings, as shown in Figure A.6.

Figure A.6 shows a perfect positive correlation. One variable increases as the other increases, and the points on the scatter diagram may be joined to form a straight line. We usually do not find variables forming a perfect positive (or perfect negative) correlation, unless they are related according to a specific mathematical formula. The temperatures Fahrenheit and centigrade are so related (degrees Fahrenheit = 9/5 degrees centigrade + 32).

A positive correlation of about +0.80 to +0.90, or higher, between scores attained on separate testings is usually required to determine the **reliability** of psychological tests. Intelligence tests such a the Stanford-Binet Intelligence Scale and the Wechsler scales have been found to yield **test-retest reliabilities** that meet these requirements. Somewhat lower correlation coefficients are

Correlation coefficient. A number between −1.00 and +1.00 that indicates the degree of relationship between two variables.

Scatter diagram. A graphic presentation showing the plotting of points defined by the intersections of two variables.

Reliability. Consistency; see Chapter 6.

Test-retest reliability. Consistency of a test as determined by a comparison of scores on repeated testings.

The Correlation Coefficient   **585**

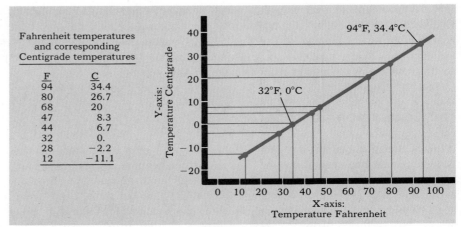

FIGURE A.6 A Scatter Diagram Showing the Perfect Positive Correlation between Fahrenheit Temperatures and the Corresponding Centigrade Temperatures. Scatter diagrams have *X* and *Y* axes, and each point is plotted by finding the spot where an *X* value and the corresponding *Y* value meet.

Validity. The degree to which a test measures what it is supposed to measure; see Chapter 6.

usually accepted as indicators that a psychological test is **valid,** when test scores are correlated with scores on an external criterion. Figure A.7 shows a hypothetical scatter diagram that demonstrates the relationship between IQ scores and academic averages for children in grade school. The correlation coefficient that would be derived by mathematical formula would be between +0.60 and +0.70. Remember that correlation does not show cause and effect. Figure A.7 suggests a relationship between the variables but cannot be taken as evidence that intelligence causes achievement.

Figure A.8 shows a scatter diagram in which there is a correlation coefficient of about 0.00 between the *X* and *Y* variables, suggesting that they are

FIGURE A.7 A Hypothetical Scatter Diagram Showing the Relationship between IQ Scores and Academic Averages. Such correlations usually fall between +0.60 and +0.70, which is considered an adequate indication of validity for intelligence tests, since such tests are intended to predict academic performance.

FIGURE A.8 A scatter diagram showing a correlation coefficient of 0.00 between the *X* and *Y* variables.

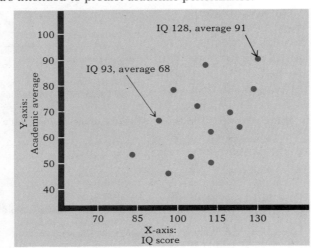

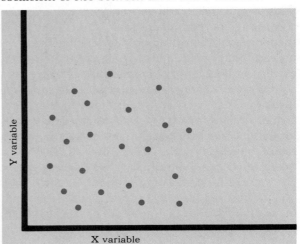

fully independent of each other. A person's scores on spelling quizzes taken in California ought to be independent of the daily temperatures in Bolivia. Thus we would expect a correlation coefficient of close to 0.00 between the variables.

Figure A.9 shows a scatter diagram in which there is a perfect negative correlation between two variables: As one variable increases, the other decreases systematically.

Correlations between 0.80 and 1.00 are considered very high (whether they are positive or negative). Correlations between 0.60 and 0.80 are high, between 0.40 and 0.60 moderate, from 0.20 to 0.40 weak, and between 0.00 and 0.20 very weak.

It cannot be overemphasized that correlation coefficients do not show cause and effect. For instance, a relationship between intelligence and academic performance could be explained by suggesting that the same cultural factors that lead some children to do well on intelligence tests also lead them to do well on academic tasks. According to this view, intelligence does not cause high academic performance. Instead, a third variable determines both intelligence and academic performance.

However, many psychologists undertake correlational research as a first step in attempting to determine causal relationships between variables. Correlation does not show cause and effect; but a lack of correlation between two variables suggests that it may be fruitless to undertake experimental research in order to determine whether they are causally related.

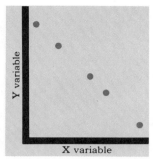

FIGURE A.9 A scatter diagram showing a correlation coefficient of −1.00 between the *X* and *Y* variables, or a perfect negative relationship.

FIGURE A.10 A scatter diagram showing the relationship between income of a student's family and the student's score on the Scholastic Aptitude Test (SAT) taken during 1980–1981. Scores are a combination of scores on the Verbal and Mathematics subtests, and may vary from 400–1600. Scores shown are for white students only. SAT scores predict performance in college. Note the strong positive correlation between SAT scores and parental income. Does the relationship show that a high-income family is better able to expose children to concepts and skills measured on the SAT? Or that families who transmit genetic influences that may contribute to high test performance also tend to earn high incomes? Correlation is *not* cause and effect. For this reason, the data cannot answer these questions.

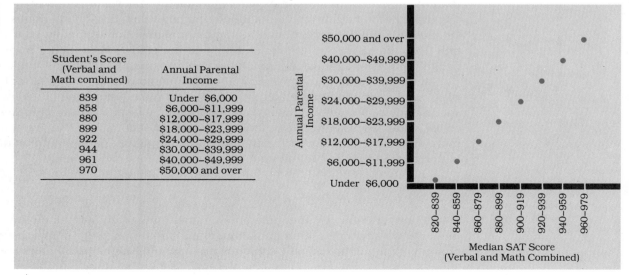

Student's Score (Verbal and Math combined)	Annual Parental Income
839	Under $6,000
858	$6,000–$11,999
880	$12,000–$17,999
899	$18,000–$23,999
922	$24,000–$29,999
944	$30,000–$39,999
961	$40,000–$49,999
970	$50,000 and over

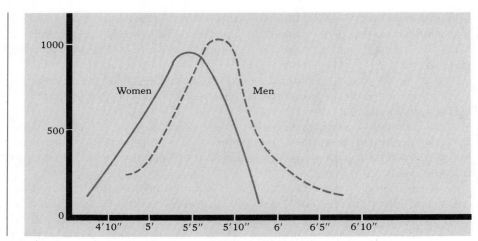

FIGURE A.11 Distribution of Heights for Random Samples of Men and Women. Inferential statistics permit us to apply our findings to the populations sampled.

Inferential Statistics

In a study reported in Chapter 6 children enrolled in a Head Start program earned a mean IQ score of 99, whereas children similar in background who were not enrolled in Head Start earned a mean IQ score of 93. Is this difference of six points in IQ significant, or does it represent chance fluctuation of scores? In a study reported in Chapter 1, subjects who believed they had drunk alcohol chose higher levels of electric shock to be applied to persons who had provoked them than did subjects who believed they had not drunk alcohol. Did the difference in level of shock chosen reflect an actual difference between the two groups of subjects, or could it have been a chance fluctuation? Inferential statistics help us make decisions as to whether differences found between such groups reflect real differences or just fluctuations.

Figure A.11 shows the distribution of heights of a thousand men and a thousand women selected at random. The mean height for men is greater than the mean height for women. Can we draw the conclusion, or **infer,** that this difference in heights represents the general population of men and women? Or must we avoid such an inference and summarize our results by stating only that the sample of a thousand men in the study had a higher mean height than that of the sample of a thousand women in the study?

If we could not draw inferences about populations from studies of samples, our research findings would be very limited indeed—limited only to the specific subjects studied. However, the branch of statistics known as **inferential statistics** uses mathematical techniques in such a way that we can make statements about populations from which samples have been drawn, with a certain level of confidence.

Statistically Significant Differences

In determining whether differences in measures taken of research samples may be applied to the populations from which they were drawn, psychologists use mathematical techniques that indicate whether differences are

Infer. To draw a conclusion, to conclude. (From the Latin *in,* meaning "in," and *ferre,* meaning "to bear.")

Inferential statistics. The branch of statistics concerned with the confidence with which conclusions drawn about samples may be extended to the populations from which they were drawn.

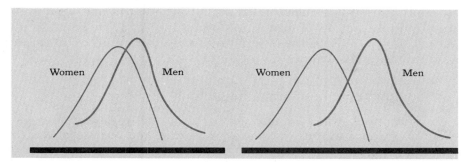

FIGURE A.12 Psychologists use group means and standard deviations in order to determine whether the difference between group means is statistically significant. The difference between the means of the groups on the right is greater and thus more likely to be statistically significant.

statistically significant. Was the difference in IQ scores for children attending and those not attending Head Start significant? Did it represent only the children participating in the study, or can it be applied to all children represented by the sample? Is the difference between the height of men and the height of women in Figure A.11 statistically significant? Can we apply our findings to all men and women?

Psychologists use formulas involving the means and standard deviations of sample groups in order to determine whether group differences are statistically significant. As you can see in Figure A.12, the farther apart the group means are, the more likely it is that the difference between them is statistically significant. This makes a good deal of common sense. After all, if you were told that your neighbor's car had gotten one-tenth of a mile more per gallon of gasoline than your car had last year, you might assume that this was a chance difference. But if the differences were farther apart, say fourteen miles per gallon, you might readily believe that this difference reflected an actual difference in driving habits or efficiency of the automobiles.

As you can see in Figure A.13, the smaller the standard deviations (a measure of variability) of the two groups, the more likely it is that the difference of the means is statistically significant. As an extreme example, if all women sampled were exactly 5′5″ tall, and all men sampled were exactly 5′10″, we would be highly likely to assume that the difference of five inches in group

FIGURE A.13 The variability of the groups on the left is smaller than the variability of the groups on the right. Thus it is more likely that the difference between the means of the groups on the left is statistically significant.

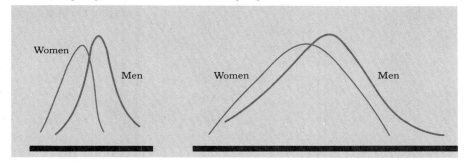

means is statistically significant. But if the heights of women varied from 2′ to 14′, and the heights of men varied from 2′1″ to 14′3″, we might be more likely to assume that the five-inch difference in group means could be attributed to chance fluctuation.

Samples and Populations

Inferential statistics are mathematical tools that psychologists apply to samples of scores in order to determine whether they can generalize their findings to populations of scores. Thus they must be quite certain that the samples involved actually represent the populations from which they were drawn.

As you saw in Chapter 1, psychologists often use the techniques of random sampling and stratified sampling of populations in order to draw representative samples. If the samples studied do not accurately represent their intended populations, it matters very little how sophisticated the statistical techniques of the psychologist may be. We could use a variety of statistical techniques on the heights of the Boston Celtics and Los Angeles Lakers, but none would tell us much about the height of the general population.

Appendix B: Answer Keys for Questionnaires

This appendix contains scoring keys, answer keys, and normative data for the various Questionnaires presented in the text.

Scoring Key for the "Social Desirability Scale" (Chapter 1, pp. 30–31)

Place a check mark on the appropriate line of the scoring key each time your answer *agrees* with the one listed on the scoring key. Add the check marks and place the total number of check marks in the box marked "Total Score."

SCORING KEY

1. T ____	12. F ____	23. F ____
2. T ____	13. T ____	24. T ____
3. F ____	14. F ____	25. T ____
4. T ____	15. F ____	26. T ____
5. F ____	16. T ____	27. T ____
6. F ____	17. T ____	28. F ____
7. T ____	18. T ____	29. T ____
8. T ____	19. F ____	30. F ____
9. F ____	20. T ____	31. T ____
10. F ____	21. T ____	32. F ____
11. F ____	22. F ____	33. T ____

TOTAL SCORE

Interpreting your score. LOW SCORERS (0–8). About one respondent in six earns a score between 0 and 8. Such respondents answered in a socially *undesirable* direction much of the time. It may be that they are more willing than most people to respond to tests truthfully, even when their answers might meet with social disapproval.

AVERAGE SCORERS (9–19). About two respondents in three earn scores between 9 and 19. They tend to show an average degree of concern for the social desirability of their responses, and it may well be that their actual behavior represents an average degree of conformity to social rules and conventions.

HIGH SCORERS (20–33). About one respondent in six earns a score between 20 and 33. These respondents may be highly concerned about social approval and respond to test items in such a way as to avoid the disapproval of people who may read their responses. Their actual behavior may show high conformity to social rules and conventions.

Scoring Key for the "Why Do You Drink?" Questionnaire (Chapter 4, pp. 144–145)

Why do you drink? Score your questionnaire by seeing how many items you answered for each of the following reasons for drinking. Consider the key as *suggestive* only. For example, if you answered several items in such a way that you scored on the *addiction* factor, it may be wise to seriously examine what your drinking means to you. However, a few test item scores cannot be interpreted as binding evidence of addiction.

Addiction	Anxiety/Tension Reduction	Pleasure/Taste	Transforming Agent
1. T	7. T	2. T	2. T
6. F	9. T	5. T	4. T
32. T	12. T	16. T	19. T
38. T	15. T	27. T	22. T
40. T	18. T	28. T	28. T
	26. T	35. T	30. T
	31. T	37. T	34. T
	33. T		36. T

Social Reward	Celebration	Religion	Social Power
3. T	10. T	11. T	2. T
8. T	24. T		13. T
23. T	25. T		19. T
			30. T

Scapegoating (Using alcohol as an excuse for failure or social misconduct)	Habit
14. T	17. T
15. T	29. T
20. T	
21. T	
39. T	

Scoring Key for "Are You a Sensation Seeker?" (Chapter 7, pp. 272–273)

Since this is a shortened version of a questionnaire, no norms are available. However, the following answers are suggestive of sensation seeking:

1. A	5. A	8. A	11. A
2. A	6. B	9. B	12. A
3. A	7. A	10. B	13. B
4. B			

Norms for the Love Scale (Chapter 7, p. 289)

Table B.1 gives the scores of 220 undergraduate students at Northeastern University, aged between 19 and 24, with the largest single age group 21. Students were asked to indicate whether they were absolutely in love, probably in love, not sure, probably not in love, or definitely not in love. Scores of men and women in the five conditions did not differ, so they are lumped together. A number of students broke into arguments after taking the Love Scale: their love for one another "differed" by a couple of points! Please do not take scales like this too seriously. They are fun, but will not hold up in court as grounds for divorce. Rely on your feeling, not your scores.

A number of students were also asked how they knew when they were in love. This is what some of them said:

> When I feel that nobody else matters.
> When I go out and I stop checking out other people that are there.
> When I lust after my love in my heart.
> When my feet turn blue.
> I know that I am in love when I start to make plans for us as a unit, hoping we can spend a lifetime together.
> When I stop wanting to pick up other people.
> When I hear the Platters singing "Heart of Mine."
> I'm willing to bet that more than three-quarters of the group didn't even take a crack at this question. Why? Either they're lazy, they didn't have enough time, or they don't know what love is, or unconsciously they were bombarded with an unacceptable impulse from the Id and they tamped it down with a solid dose of repression to protect them from their own ignorance.
> When I can't thiink about anything or anybody else all day long.

TABLE B.1   Love-Scale Scores of Northeastern University Students

Condition	N*	Mean Scores
Absolutely in love	56	89
Probably in love	45	80
Not sure	36	77
Probably not in love	40	68
Definitely not in love	43	59

*N = Number of students.

Answer Key for "Are You Type A or B" Questionnaire
(Chapter 10, pp. 398–399)

Yesses suggest the Type A behavior pattern, which is marked by a sense of time urgency and constant struggle. In appraising your "type," you need not be overly concerned with the precise number of "yes" answers; we have no normative data for you. But as Freidman and Rosenman note, you will have little difficulty spotting yourself as "hard core" or "moderately afflicted" (1974, p. 85)—that is, if you are honest with yourself.

Scoring Key for the "Locus of Control Scale"
(Chapter 10, pp. 408–409)

Credit yourself with one point each time your answer agrees with the answer on the scoring key below. Write the total number of answers in agreement in the box marked "Total Score."

SCORING KEY

1.	Yes ____	11.	Yes ____	21.	Yes ____	31.	Yes ____
2.	No ____	12.	Yes ____	22.	No ____	32.	No ____
3.	Yes ____	13.	No ____	23.	Yes ____	33.	Yes ____
4.	No ____	14.	Yes ____	24.	Yes ____	34.	No ____
5.	Yes ____	15.	No ____	25.	No ____	35.	Yes ____
6.	No ____	16.	Yes ____	26.	No ____	36.	Yes ____
7.	Yes ____	17.	Yes ____	27.	Yes ____	37.	Yes ____
8.	Yes ____	18.	Yes ____	28.	No ____	38.	No ____
9.	No ____	19.	Yes ____	29.	Yes ____	39.	Yes ____
10.	Yes ____	20.	No ____	30.	No ____	40.	No ____

TOTAL SCORE

Interpreting your score. LOW SCORERS (0–8). About one respondent in three earns a score of from 0 to 8. Such respondents tend to have an internal locus of control. They see themselves as responsible for the reinforcements they attain (and fail to attain) in life.

AVERAGE SCORERS (9–16). Most respondents earn from 9 to 16 points. Average scorers may see themselves as partially in control of their lives. Perhaps they see themselves as in control at work, but not in their social lives—or vice versa.

HIGH SCORERS (17–40). About 15 percent of respondents attain scores of 17 or above. High scorers largely tend to see life as a game of chance, and success as a matter of luck.

Scoring the "Rathus Assertiveness Schedule"
(Chapter 12, pp. 484–485)

Tabulate your score as follows: Change the signs of all items followed by an asterisk (*). Then add the 30 item scores. For example, if the response to an asterisked item was 2, place a minus (−) sign before the 2. If the response to an asterisked item was −3, change the minus sign to a plus sign (+) by adding a vertical stroke.

Scores on this test can vary from +90 to −90. Table B.2 below will show you how your score compared with those of 764 college women and 637

TABLE B.2 Percentiles of Scores on the Rathus Assertiveness Schedule for College Women and Men

Women's Scores	Percentile	Men's Scores	Women's Scores	Percentile	Men's Scores
55	99	65	6	45	8
48	97	54	2	40	6
45	95	48	−1	35	3
37	90	40	−4	30	1
31	85	33	−8	25	−3
26	80	30	−13	20	−7
23	75	26	−17	15	−11
19	70	24	−24	10	−15
17	65	19	−34	5	−24
14	60	17	−39	3	−30
11	55	14	−48	1	−41
8	50	11			

Source: Nevid & Rathus (1978).

college men from 35 campuses all across the United States. For example, if you are a woman and your score was 26, it exceeded that of 80 percent of the women in the sample. A score of 15 for a male exceeds that of 55–60 percent of the men in the sample.

Answer Key for "Cultural Myths that Support Rape" Questionnaire (Chapter 13, p. 522)

Actually, each item on the questionnaire, with the exception of number 2, represents a cultural myth that tends to support rape. Agreement with any of these items shows endorsement of such a myth.

Scoring Key for the "Sexual Anxiety Inventory" (Chapter 13, p. 530)

For each of the following answers, credit yourself with a point of sexual anxiety:

1. b	6. a	11. a	16. b	21. b
2. a	7. b	12. a	17. a	22. a
3. a	8. a	13. a	18. b	23. b
4. b	9. b	14. a	19. b	24. a
5. a	10. b	15. a	20. b	25. a

TOTAL SCORE

In their studies with 95 males and 135 females, Janda and O'Grady (1980) found the average score for males to be 8.09 and the average score for females to be 11.76. Approximately 2 of every 3 scores for men fell within the range from 3 to 13. Approximately 2 of every 3 women's scores fell between 7 and 17.

Don't take your own score too seriously. You are comparing it to only a small and rather unrepresentative sample of individuals. But if you are concerned about your score, you may wish to discuss it with your professor.

References

Abbey, A. Sex differences in attributions for friendly behavior. *Journal of Personality and Social Psychology*, 1982, 42, 830–838.

Abramowitz, C. V., Abramowitz, S. I., Roback, H. B., & Jackson, C. Differential effectiveness of directive and nondirective group therapies as a function of client internal-external control. *Journal of Consulting and Clinical Psychology*, 1974, 42, 849–853.

Abramson, P. R., & Mosher, D. L. Development of a measure of negative attitudes toward masturbation. *Journal of Consulting and Clinical Psychology*, 1975, 43, 485–490.

Abse, D. W. *Hysteria and related mental disorders.* Baltimore: Williams & Wilkins, 1966.

Adams, V. Sex therapies in perspective. *Psychology Today*, August 1980, 35–36.

Adams, V. Mommy and I are one. *Psychology Today*, May 1982, 24–36.

Adelman, M. R. A comparison of professionally employed lesbians and heterosexual women on the MMPI. *Archives of Sexual Behavior*, 1977, 6, 193–202.

Adelson, J. Still vital after all these years. *Psychology Today*, April 1982, 52–59.

Adolph, E. F. The internal environment and behavior: Water content. *American Journal of Psychiatry*, 1941, 97, 1365–1373.

Adorno, T. W., Frenkel-Brunswick, E., & Levinson, D. J. *The authoritarian personality.* New York: Harper, 1950.

Akil, H., Mayer, D. J., & Liebeskind, J. L. Antagonism of stimulation-produced analgesia. *Science*, 1976, 191, 961–962.

Albert, M. S. Geriatric neuropsychology. *Journal of Consulting and Clinical Psychology*, 1981, 49, 835–850.

Albin, R. S. Psychological studies of rape. *Signs*, 1977, 3, 423–435.

Allen, V. L., & Levine, J. M. Social support and conformity: The role of independent assessment of reality. *Journal of Experimental Social Psychology*, 1971, 7, 48–58.

Allgeier, A. R., & Byrne, D. Attraction toward the opposite sex as a determinant of physical proximity. *Journal of Social Psychology*, 1973, 90, 213–219.

Allport, G. W. *Personality: A psychological interpretation.* New York: Holt, Rinehart and Winston, 1937.

Allport, G. W. *Pattern and growth in personality.* New York: Holt, Rinehart and Winston, 1961.

Allport, G. W., & Odbert, H. S. Trait names: A psycholexical study. *Psychological Monographs*, 1936, 47, 2–11.

American Psychiatric Association. *Diagnostic and statistical manual–III.* Washington, D. C.: Author, 1980.

American Psychological Association. Ethical principles of psychologists. *American Psychologist*, 1981, 36, 633–638.

Amir, M. *Patterns in forcible rape.* Chicago: University of Chicago Press, 1971.

Andersen, B. L. A comparison of systematic desensitization and directed masturbation in the treatment of primary orgasmic dysfunction in females. *Journal of Consulting and Clinical Psychology*, 1981, 49, 568–570.

Andersson, B. Thirst—and brain control of water balance. *American Scientist*, 1971, 59, 408.

Angrist, B., Lee, H. K., & Gershon, S. The antagonism of amphetamine-induced symptomology by a neuroleptic. *American Journal of Psychiatry*, 1974, 131, 817–819.

APA *Monitor*, February 1978, 4.

APA *Monitor*, January 1978, 5, 23.

Ariam, S., & Siller, J. Effects of subliminal oneness stimuli in Hebrew on academic performance of Israeli high school students. *Journal of Abnormal Psychology*, 1982, 91, 343–349.

Arkin, R. M., Detchon, C. S., & Maruyama, G. M. Roles of attribution, affect, and cognitive interference in test anxiety. *Journal of Personality and Social Psychology*, 1982, 43, 1111–1124.

Asch, S. E. *Social psychology.* Englewood Cliffs, N. J.: Prentice-Hall, 1952.

Ascher, L. M., & Efran, J. S. Use of paradoxical intention in a behavioral program for sleep onset insomnia. *Journal of Consulting and Clinical Psychology*, 1978, 46, 547–550.

Athanasiou, R., Shaver, P., & Tavris, C. Sex. *Psychology Today*, 1970, 4, 39–52.

Atkinson, K., MacWhinney, B., & Stoel, C. An experiment on recognition of babbling. In *Papers and Reports on Child Language Development.* Stanford, Calif.: Stanford University Press, 1970.

Atkinson, R. C. Mnemotechnics in second-language learning. *American Psychologist*, 1975, 30, 821–828.

Averill, J. R. A constructivist view of emotion. In R. Plutchik & H. Kellerman (eds.), *Theories of Emotion.* New York: Academic Press, 1978.

Ayllon, T., & Haughton, E. Control of the behavior of schizophrenic patients by food. *Journal of the Experimental Analysis of Behavior*, 1962, 5, 343–352.

Bach, G. R., & Deutsch, R. M. *Pairing.* New York: Peter H. Wyden, 1970.

Bach-y-Rita, P., et al. Display techniques in a tactile vision-substitution system. *Medical and Biological Illustration*, 1972, 20, 7, 11.

Bagozzi, R.P. Attitudes, intentions, and behaviors: A test of some key hypotheses. *Journal of Personality and Social Psychology*, 1981, 41, 607–627.

Bahrick, H. P., Bahrick, P. O., & Wittlinger, R. P. Those unforgettable high-school days. *Psychology Today*, December 1974.

Bandura, A. *Aggression: A social learning analysis.* Englewood Cliffs, N. J.: Prentice-Hall, 1973.

Bandura, A. *Social learning theory.* Englewood Cliffs, N. J.: Prentice-Hall, 1973.

Bandura, A. Self-referrant thought: A developmental analysis of self-efficacy. In J. H. Flavell & L. Ross (eds.), *Social Cognitive Development: Frontiers and Possible Futures.* Cambridge, England: Cambridge University Press, 1981.

Bandura, A. The psychology of chance encounters and life paths. *American Psychologist*, 1982, *37*, 747–755.

Bandura, A. Self-efficacy mechanism in human agency. *American Psychologist*, 1982, *37*, 122–147.

Bandura, A., Blanchard, E. B., & Ritter, B. The relative efficacy of desensitization and modeling approaches for inducing behavioral, affective, and cognitive changes. *Journal of Personality and Social Psychology*, 1969, *13*, 173–199.

Bandura, A., Reese, L., & Adams, N. E. Microanalysis of action and fear arousal as a function of differential levels of perceived self-efficacy. *Journal of Personality and Social Psychology*, 1982, *43*, 5–21.

Bandura, A., & Rosenthal, T. L. Vicarious classical conditioning as a function of arousal level. *Journal of Personality and Social Psychology*, 1966, *3*, 54–62.

Bandura, A., Ross, D., & Ross, S. A. A comparative test of the status envy, and the secondary reinforcement theories of identificatory learning. *Journal of Abnormal and Social Psychology*, 1963a, *67*, 527–534.

Bandura, A., Ross, S. A., & Ross, D. Imitation of film-mediated aggressive models. *Journal of Abnormal and Social Psychology*, 1963b, *66*, 3–11.

Banyai, E. I., & Hilgard, E. R. A comparison of active-alert hypnotic induction with traditional relaxation induction. *Journal of Abnormal Psychology*, 1976, *85*, 218–224.

Barbach, L. G. For yourself: The fulfillment of female sexuality. Garden City, N. Y.: Doubleday, 1975.

Barber, T. X. *LSD, marihuana, yoga, and hypnosis.* Chicago: Aldine, 1970.

Barber, T. X., Spanos, N. P., & Chaves, J. F. *Hypnosis, imagination, and human potentialities.* New York: Pergamon Press, 1974.

Bard, P. The neurohumoral basis of emotional reactions. In C. A. Murchison (ed.), *Handbook of General Experimental Psychology.* Worcester, Mass.: Clark University Press, 1934.

Bardwick, J. M. *Psychology of women: A study of biocultural conflicts.* New York: Harper & Row, 1971.

Baron, R. A. Behavioral effects of interpersonal attraction: Compliance with requests from liked and disliked others. *Psychonomic Science*, 1971, *25*, 325–326.

Baron, R. A. The "foot-in-the-door" phenomenon: Mediating effects of size of first request and sex of requester. *Bulletin of the Psychonomic Society*, 1973, *2*, 113–114.

Baron, R. A., & Byrne, D. *Social psychology: Understanding human interaction.* Boston: Allyn & Bacon, 1981.

Baron, R. A., Mandel, D. R., Adams, C. A., & Griffen, L. M. Effects of social density in university residential requirements. *Journal of Personality and Social Psychology*, 1976, *34*, 434–446.

Barraclough, B. M., Nelson, B., Bunch, J., & Sainsbury, P. The diagnositc classification and psychiatric treatment of 100 suicides. Proceedings of the Fifth International Conference for Suicide Prevention. London, 1969.

Bart, P. B. Mother Portnoy's complaints. *Trans-action*, 1970, *8*, 69–74.

Bar-Tal, D., & Saxe, L. Perceptions of similarly and dissimilarly physically attractive couples and individuals. *Journal of Personality and Social Psychology*, 1976, *33*, 772–781.

Bartell, G. D. Group sex among the mid-Americans. *Journal of Sex Research*, 1970, *6*, 113–130.

Batson, C. D., Duncan, B. D., Ackerman, P., Buckley, T., & Birch, K. Is empathic emotion a source of altruistic motivation? *Journal of Personality and Social Psychology*, 1981, *40*, 290–302.

Baucom, D. H., & Aiken, P. A. Effect of depressed mood on eating among obese and nonobese dieting and nondieting persons. *Journal of Personality and Social Psychology*, 1981, *41*, 577–585.

Bauer, R. H., & Fuster, J. M. Delayed-matching and delayed-response deficit from cooling dorsolateral prefrontal cortex in monkeys. *Journal of Comparative and Physiological Psychology*, 1976, *90*, 293–302.

Baum, A., & Davis, G. E. Reducing the stress of high density living: An architectural intervention. *Journal of Personality and Social Psychology*, 1980, *38*, 471–481.

Bauman, K. E., & Wilson, R. R. Premarital sexual attitudes of unmarried university students. *Archives of Sexual Behavior*, 1976, *5*, 29–37.

Bazar, J. Catching up with the ape language debate. *APA Monitor*, January 1980, 4–5, 47.

Beard, R. R., & Wertheim, G. A. Behavioral impairment associated with small doses of carbon monoxide. *American Journal of Public Health*, 1967, *57*, 2012–2022.

Beauchamp, G. Paper presented to the Conference on the Determination of Behavior by Chemical Stimuli. Hebrew University, Jerusalem, 1981.

Beck, A. T. *Cognitive therapy and the emotional disorders.* New York: International Universities Press, 1976.

Beck, A. T., Ward, C. H., Mendelson, M., Mock, J. E., & Erbaugh, J. K. Reliability of psychiatric diagnoses II: A study of consistency of clinical judgments and ratings. *American Journal of Psychiatry*, 1962, *119*, 351–357.

Beck, J., Elsner, A., & Silverstein, C. Position uncertainty and the perception of apparent movement. *Perception and Psychophysics*, 1977, *21*, 33–38.

Becker, R. D. Brain pollution. *Psychology Today*, February 1979, 124.

Beers, T. M., & Karoly, P. Cognitive strategies, expectancy, and coping style in the control of pain. *Journal of Consulting and Clinical Psychology*, 1979, *47*, 179–180.

Bell, A. P., & Weinberg, M. S. *Homosexualities: A study of diversity among men and women.* New York: Simon & Schuster, 1978.

Bell, A. P., Weinberg, M. S., & Hammersmith, S. K. *Sexual preference: Its development in men and women.* Bloomington, Ind.: University of Indiana Press, 1981.

Bell, P. A., Fisher, J. D., & Loomis, R. J. *Environmental psychology.* Philadelphia: Saunders, 1978.

Bem, D. J. Self-perception: An alternative interpretation of cognitive dissonance phenomena. *Psychological Review*, 1967, 74, 183–200.

Bem, D. J. Self-perception theory. In L. Berkowitz (ed.), *Advances in Experimental Social Psychology*, Vol. 6. New York: Academic Press, 1972.

Bem, D. J., & Allen, A. On predicting some of the people some of the time: The search for cross-situational consistencies in behavior. *Psychological Review*, 1974, 81, 506–520.

Bem, S. L. The measurement of psychological androgyny. *Journal of Consulting and Clinical Psychology*, 1974, 42, 151–162.

Bem, S. L. Sex role adaptability: One consequence of psychological androgyny. *Journal of Personality and Social Psychology*, 1975, 31, 634–643.

Bem, S. L., & Bem, D. J. Training the woman to know her place: The power of a nonconscious ideology. In L. S. Wrightsman & J. C. Brigham (eds.), *Contemporary Issues in Social Psychology*, 2d ed. Monterey, Calif.: Brooks/Cole, 1973.

Bem, S. L., & Lenney, E. Sex typing and the avoidance of cross-sexed behaviors. *Journal of Personality and Social Psychology*, 1976, 33, 48–54.

Bem, S. L., Martyna, W., & Watson, C. Sex typing and androgyny: Further explorations of the expressive domain. *Journal of Personality and Social Psychology*, 1976, 34, 1016–1023.

Benedict, R. *Patterns of culture.* Boston: Houghton Mifflin, 1934.

Benson, H. *The relaxation response.* New York: Morrow, 1975.

Benson, H., Manzetta, B. R., & Rosner, B. Decreased systolic blood pressure in hypertensive subjects who practiced meditation. *Journal of Clinical Investigation*, 1973, 52, 8.

Benson, P. L., Karabenick, S. A., & Lerner, R. M. Pretty pleases: The effects of physical attractiveness, race, and sex on receiving help. *Journal of Experimental Social Psychology*, 1976, 12, 409–415.

Bentham, J. Introduction to the principles of morals and legislation. In M. Warnock (ed.), *John Stuart Mill: Utilitarianism, on Liberty, Essay on Bentham.* Cleveland: Meridian, 1962. (Essay first published in 1822.)

Bentler, P. M. A typology of transsexualism: Gender identity theory and data. *Archives of Sexual Behavior*, 1976, 5, 567–584.

Bentler, P. M., & Speckart, G. Attitudes "cause" behaviors: A structural equation analysis. *Journal of Personality and Social Psychology*, 1981, 40, 226–238.

Berko, J. The child's learning of English morphology. *Word*, 1958, 14, 150–177.

Berkowitz, L., & Donnerstein, E. External validity is more than skin deep: Some answers to criticisms of laboratory experiments. *American Psychologist*, 1982, 37, 245–257.

Berkowitz, W. R., Nebel, J. C., & Reitman, J. W. Height and interpersonal attraction: The 1960 mayoral election in New York City. Paper presented at the annual convention of the American Psychological Association. Washington, D. C., 1971.

Berne, E. *Beyond games and scripts.* New York: Grove, 1976a.

Berne, E. *Games people play.* New York: Ballantine, 1976b.

Bernheim, M. *Hypnosis and suggestion.* New Hyde Park, N. Y.: University Books, 1964.

Bernstein, B. E. Effect of menstruation on academic performance among college women. *Archives of Sexual Behavior*, 1977, 6, 289–296.

Berscheid, E. Theories of interpersonal attraction. In B. B. Wolman & L. R. Pomeroy (eds.), *International Encyclopaedia of Neurology, Psychiatry, Psychoanalysis, and Psychology.* New York: Springer, 1976.

Berscheid, E., Dion, K., Walster, E., & Walster, G. W. Physical attractiveness and dating choice: A test of the matching hypothesis. *Journal of Experimental Social Psychology*, 1971, 7, 173–189.

Berscheid, E., & Walster, E. A little bit about love. In T. L. Huston (ed.), *Foundations of Interpersonal Attraction.* New York: Academic Press, 1974a.

Berscheid, E., & Walster, E. Physical attractiveness. In L. Berkowitz (ed.), *Advances in Experimental Social Psychology*, Vol. 7. New York: Academic Press, 1974b.

Berscheid, E., & Walster, E. *Interpersonal attraction.* Reading, Mass.: Addison-Wesley, 1978.

Bersoff, D. N. Testing and the law. *American Psychologist*, 1981, 36, 1159–1166.

Betz, N. E., & Hackett, G. The relationships of career-related self-ef-ficacy expectations to perceived career options in college women and men. *Journal of Counseling Psychology*, 1981, 28, 399–410.

Bexton, W. H., Heron, W., & Scott, T. H. Effects of decreased variation in the sensory environment. *Canadian Journal of Psychology*, 1954, 8, 70–76.

Bieber, I. A. Discussion of "Homosexuality: The ethical challenge." *Journal of Consulting and Clinical Psychology*, 1976, 44, 163–166.

Bieber, I. A., Dain, H., Dince, P., Drellich, M., Grand, H., Gundlach, R., Kremer, M., Rifkin, A., Wilbur, C., & Bieber, T. *Homosexuality.* New York: Vintage Books, 1962.

Biglan, A., & Craker, D. Effects of pleasant-activities manipulation on depression. *Journal of Consulting and Clinical Psychology*, 1982, 50, 436–438.

Biran, M., & Wilson, G. T. Treatment of phobic disorders using cognitive and exposure methods: A self-efficacy analysis. *Journal of Consulting and Clinical Psychology*, 1981, 49, 886–899.

Birch, H. G., & Rabinowitz, H. S. The negative effect of previous experience on productive thinking. *Journal of Experimental Psychology*, 1951, 42, 121–125.

Blanchard, E. B., Andrasik, F., Ahles, T. A., Teders, S. J., & O'Keefe, D. M. Migraine and tension headache: A meta-analytic review. *Behavior Therapy*, 1980, 11, 613–631.

Blanchard, E. B., Andrasik, F., Neff, D. F., Arena, J. G., Ahles, T. A., Jurish, S. E., Pallmeyer, T. P., Saunders, N. L., Teders, S. J., Barron, K. D., & Rodichok, L. D. Biofeedback and relaxation training with three kinds of headache: Treatment effects and their prediction. *Journal of Consulting and Clinical Psychology*, 1982, 50, 562–575.

Bland, J. The junk-food syndrome. *Psychology Today*, January 1982, 92.

Blank, M. Cognitive functions of language in the preschool years. *Developmental Psychology*, 1974, 10, 229–245.

Blittner, M., Goldberg, J., & Merbaum, M. Cognitive self-control factors in the reduction of smoking behavior. *Behavior Therapy*, 1978, 9, 553–561.

Bloch, V., Hennevin, E., & Leconte, P. Relationship between paradoxical sleep and memory processes. In

M. A. B. Braszier (ed.), *Brain Mechanisms in Memory and Learning: From the Single Neuron to Man.* New York: Raven Press, 1979.

Block, J., & Block, J. An investigation of the relationship between intolerance of ambiguity and ethnocentrism. *Journal of Personality,* 1951, *19,* 303–311.

Blum, H. P. Masochism, the ego ideal, and the psychology of women. *Journal of the American Psychoanalytic Association,* 1976, *24,* 157–191.

Borgida, E., & Campbell, B. Belief relevance and attitude-behavior consistency: The moderating role of personal experience. *Journal of Personality and Social Psychology,* 1982, *42,* 239–247.

Bornstein, M. H., Kessen, W., & Weiskopf, S. The categories of hue in infancy. *Science,* 1976, *191,* 201–202.

Bornstein, M. H., & Marks, L. E. Color revisionism. *Psychology Today,* January 1982, 64–73.

Boston Women's Health Book Collective. *Our bodies, ourselves.* New York: Simon & Schuster, 1979.

Bourne, L. E., Ekstrand, B. R., & Dominowski, R. L. *The psychology of thinking.* Englewood Cliffs, N. J.: Prentice-Hall, 1971.

Bower, D. W., & Christopherson, V. A. University student cohabitation: A regional comparison of selected attitudes and behavior. *Journal of Marriage and the Family,* 1977, *39,* 447–452.

Bower, G. H. Mood and memory. *American Psychologist,* 1981, *36,* 129–148.

Boyatzis, R. E. The effect of alcohol consumption on the aggressive behavior of men. *Quarterly Journal for the Study of Alcohol,* 1974, *35,* 959–972.

Brant, E., & Granberg, D. Subjective agreement with the presidential candidates of 1976 and 1980. *Journal of Personality and Social Psychology,* 1982, *42,* 393–403.

Bray, D. W. The assessment center and the study of lives. *American Psychologist,* 1982, *37,* 180–189.

Brazleton, T. B. Effects of prenatal drugs on the behavior of the neonate. *American Journal of Psychiatry,* 1970, *126,* 95–100.

Brecher, E. M., & Editors of *Consumer Reports.* Marijuana: The legal question. *Consumer Reports,* 1975, *40,* 265–266.

Brehm, J. W. *Responses to loss of freedom: A theory of psychological reactance.* Morristown, N. J.: General Learning Press, 1972.

Briddell, D. W., & Wilson, G. T. Effects of alcohol and expectancy set on male sexual arousal. *Journal of Abnormal Psychology,* 1976, *85,* 225–234.

Bridges, K. M. B. Emotional development in early infancy. *Child Development,* 1932, *3,* 324–334.

Bridgwater, C. A. What candor can do. *Psychology Today,* May 1982, 16.

Bronfenbrenner, U. Freudian theories of identification and their derivatives. *Child Development,* 1960, *31,* 15–40.

Bronfenbrenner, U. The dream of the kibbutz. In *Readings in Human Development.* Guilford, Conn.: Dushkin Publishers, 1973.

Brooks, J., Ruble, D. N., & Clarke, A. E. College women's attitudes and expectations concering menstrual-related changes. *Psychosomatic Medicine,* 1977, *39,* 288.

Brown, B. B. *Stress and the art of biofeedback.* New York: Harper & Row, 1977.

Brown, B. B., & Altman, I. Territoriality and residential crime. In P. A. Brantingham & P. L. Brantingham (eds.), *Urban Crime and Environmental Criminology.* Beverly Hills: Sage, 1981.

Brown, M., Amoroso, D., & Ware, E. Behavioral aspects of viewing pornography. *Journal of Social Psychology,* 1976, *98,* 235–245.

Brown, R. The first sentences of child and chimpanzee. In R. Brown (ed.), *Psycholinguistics.* New York: Free Press, 1970.

Brown, R., & Hanlon, C. Derivational complexity and order of acquisition in child speech. In J. R. Hayes (ed.), *Cognition and the Development of Language.* New York: Wiley, 1970.

Brown, R. W., & McNeill, D. The tip-of-the-tongue phenomenon. *Journal of Verbal Learning and Verbal Behavior,* 1966, *5,* 325–337.

Brown, S. A., Goldman, M. S., Inn, A., & Anderson, L. R. Expectations of reinforcement from alcohol. *Journal of Consulting and Clinical Psychology,* 1980, *48,* 419–426.

Brown, W. A., Monti, P. M., & Corriveau, D. P. Serum testosterone and sexual activity and interest in men. *Archives of Sexual Behavior,* 1978, *7,* 97–103.

Brownell, K. D. Obesity: Understanding and treating a serious, prevalent, and refractory disorder. *Journal of Consulting and Clinical Psychology,* 1982, *50,* 820–840.

Brownmiller, S. *Against our will.* New York: Simon & Schuster, 1975.

Bruner, J. S., Goodnow, J. J., & Austin, G. A. *A study of thinking.* New York: Wiley, 1956.

Brunson, B. I., & Matthews, K. A. The Type-A coronary-prone behavior pattern and reactions to uncontrollable stress. *Journal of Personality and Social Psychology,* 1981, *40,* 906–918.

Burt, M. R. Cultural myths and supports for rape. *Journal of Personality and Social Psychology,* 1980, *38,* 217–230.

Buss, A. H., & Plomin, R. *A temperament theory of personality development.* New York: Wiley, 1975.

Byrne, D. *The attraction paradigm.* New York: Academic Press, 1971.

Byrne, D., Baskett, G. D., & Hodges, L. Behavioral indicators of interpersonal attraction. *Journal of Applied Social Psychology,* 1971, *1,* 137–149.

Cadoret, R. J. Psychopathology in adopted-away offspring of biologic parents with antisocial behavior. *Archives of General Psychiatry,* 1978, *35,* 176–184.

Cahalan, D. *Problem drinkers: A national survey.* San Francisco: Jossey-Bass, 1970.

Calder, B. J., Ross, M., & Inkso, C. A. Attitude change and attitude attribution: Effects of incentive, choice, and consequences. *Journal of Personality and Social Psychology,* 1973, *25,* 84–99.

Calhoun, J. B. Population density and social pathology. *Science,* 1962, *206,* 139–148.

Calne, D. B., Developments in the pharmacology and therapeutics of Parkinsonism. *Annals of Neurology,* 1977, *1,* 111–119.

Campbell, A. The American way of mating: Marriage si, children only maybe. *Psychology Today,* 1975, *8,* 37–43.

Campos, J. J., Langer, A., & Krowitz, A. Cardiac responses on the visual cliff in prelocomotor infants. *Science,* 1970, *170,* 196–197.

Cann, A., Calhoun, L. G., & Selby, J. W. Attributing responsibility to the victim of rape. *Human Relations,* 1979, *32,* 57–67.

Cannon, D. S., & Baker, T. B. Emetic

and electric shock alcohol aversion therapy. *Journal of Consulting and Clinical Psychology*, 1981, *49*, 20–33.

Cannon, W. B. The James-Lange theory of emotions: A critical examination and an alternative theory. *American Journal of Psychology*, 1927, *39*, 106–124.

Cannon, W. B. *Bodily changes in pain, hunger, fear, and rage.* New York: Appleton, 1929.

Cannon, W. B. Voodoo death. *Psychosomatic Medicine*, 1957, *19*, 182–190.

Cantor, P. C. Personality characteristics found among youthful female suicide attempters. *Journal of Abnormal Psychology*, 1976, *85*, 324–329.

Carlson, N. R. *Physiology of behavior.* Boston: Allyn & Bacon, 1981.

Carrington, P. Dreams and schizophrenia. *Archives of General Psychiatry*, 1972, *26*, 343–350.

Carrington, P. *Freedom in meditation.* New York: Anchor Press/Doubleday, 1977.

Cartwright, R. D. *A primer on sleep and dreaming.* Reading, Mass.: Addison-Wesley, 1978.

Cattell, R. B. *The culture-free intelligence test.* Champaign, Ill.: Institute for Personality and Ability Testing, 1949.

Cattell, R. B. *The scientific analysis of personality.* Baltimore: Penguin, 1965.

Cattell, R. B. Personality pinned down. *Psychology Today*, 1973, 7, 40–46.

Cattell, R. B., Kawash, G. F., & DeYoung, G. E. Validation of objective measures of ergic tension: Response of the sex erg to visual stimulation. *Journal of Experimental Research in Personality*, 1972, *6*, 76–83.

Cautela, J. R. Covert reinforcement. *Behavior Therapy*, 1970, *1*, 33–50.

Cautela, J. R. Covert sensitization. *Psychological Reports*, 1967, *74*, 459–468.

Centor, A. Criminals and amnesia: Comment on Bower. *American Psychologist*, 1982, 37, 240.

Cermak, L. *Improving your memory.* New York: McGraw-Hill, 1978.

Chapanis, N. P., & Chapanis, A. C. Cognitive dissonance: Five years later. *Psychological Bulletin*, 1964, *61*, 1–22.

Charry, J. M., & Hawkinshire, F. B. W., Jr. Effects of atmospheric electricity on some substrates of disordered social behavior. *Journal of Personality and Social Psychology*, 1981, *41*, 185–197.

Chase, M. H. The secret life of neurons. *Psychology Today*, August 1978, 104.

Chase, M. H. The dreamer's paralysis. *Psychology Today*, November 1981, 108.

Chesler, P. *Women and madness.* Garden City, N. Y.: Doubleday, 1972.

Chesno, F. A., & Kilmann, P. R. Effects of stimulation intensity on sociopathic avoidance learning. *Journal of Abnormal Psychology*, 1975, *84*, 144–151.

Chomsky, N. *Aspects of the theory of syntax.* Cambridge: M.I.T. Press, 1965.

Chomsky, N. *Language and mind.* New York: Harcourt Brace Jovanovich, 1968.

Chomsky, N. Rules and representations. *Behavior and Brain Science*, 1980, *3*, 1–15.

Christiansen, B. A., Goldman, M. S., & Inn, A. Development of alcohol-related expectancies in adolescents. *Journal of Consulting and Clinical Psychology*, 1982, *50*, 336–344.

Cialdini, R. B., Borden, R. J., Thorne, A., Walker, M. R., Freeman, S. & Sloan, L. R. Basking in reflected glory: Three (football) field studies. *Journal of Personality and Social Psychology*, 1976, *34*, 366–375.

Cipolli, C., & Salzarulo, P. Sleep and memory: Reproduction of syntactic structures previously evoked within REM-related reports. *Perceptual and Motor Skills*, 1978, *46*, 111–114.

Clark, H. H., & Clark, E. V. *Psychology and language: An introduction to psycholinguistics.* New York: Harcourt Brace Jovanovich, 1977.

Clark, M., Gosnell, M., Shapiro, D., & Hager, M. The mystery of sleep. *Newsweek*, July 13, 1981, 48–55.

Cleckley, H. *The mask of sanity, 4th ed.* St. Louis: Mosby, 1964.

Cline, V. B., Croft, R. C., & Courrier, S. The desensitization of children to television violence. *Journal of Personality and Social Psychology*, 1973, 27, 360–365.

Clore, G. L., Wiggins, N. H., & Itkin, S. Gain and loss in attraction: Attributions from nonverbal behavior. *Journal of Personality and Social Psychology*, 1975, *31*, 706–712.

Cochran, W. G., Mosteller, F., & Tukey, J. *Statistical problems of the Kinsey report on sexual behavior in the human male.* Washington, D. C.: American Statistical Association, 1954.

Coggins, W. J. The general health status of chronic cannabis smokers in Costa Rica. In S. Szara & M. Braude (eds.), *Psychopharmacology of Marihuana.* New York: Raven Press, 1976.

Cohen, D. B. Sex-role orientation and dream recall. *Journal of Abnormal Psychology*, 1973, *82*, 246–252.

Cohen, D. B. Dark hair and light eyes in female college students: A potential biologic marker for liability to psychopathology. *Journal of Abnormal Psychology*, 1978, *87*, 455–458.

Cohen, E. J., Motto, A., & Seiden, R. H. An instrument for evaluating suicide potential: A preliminary study. *American Journal of Psychiatry*, 1966, *122*, 886–891.

Cohen, R. Answers to hard questions. *New York*, May 15, 1978.

Cohen, S., Evans, G. W., Krantz, D. S., & Stokols, D. Physiological, motivational, and cognitive effects of aircraft noise on children. *American Psychologist*, 1980, *35*, 231–243.

Cohen, S., Evans, G. W., Krantz, D. S., Stokols, D., & Kelly, S. Aircraft noise and children: Longitudinal and cross-sectional evidence on adaptation to noise and the effectiveness of noise abatement. *Journal of Personality and Social Psychology*, 1981, *40*, 331–345.

Cohen, S., Glass, D. C., & Singer, J. E. Apartment noise, auditory discrimination, and reading ability in children. *Journal of Experimental Social Psychology*, 1973, 9, 407–422.

Colby, C. Z., Lanzetta, J. T., & Kleck, R. E. Effects of the expression of pain on autonomic and pain tolerance response to subject-controlled pain. *Psychophysiology*, 1977, *14*, 537–540.

Comarr, A. E. Sexual function among patients with spinal cord injury. *Urologia Internationalis*, 1970, *25*, 134–168.

Condiotte, M. M., & Lichtenstein, E. Self-efficacy and relapse in smoking cessation programs. *Journal of Consulting and Clinical Psychology*, 1981, *49*, 648–658.

Conger, J. J. *Adolescence and youth: Psychological development in a changing world.* New York: Harper & Row, 1977.

Connor, J. Olfactory control of aggressive and sexual behavior in the mouse. *Psychonomic Science*, 1972, *27*, 1–3.

Conway, E., & Brackbill, Y. Delivery medication and infant outcome: An empirical study. *Monographs of the Society for Research in Child Development*, 1970, *35*(4), 24–34.

Cooper, A. J. Neonatal olfactory bulb lesions: Influences on subsequent behavior of male mice. *Bulletin of the Psychonomic Society*, 1978, *11*, 53–56.

Cooper, H. M. Statistically combining independent studies: A meta-analysis of sex differences in conformity research. *Journal of Personality and Social Psychology*, 1979, *37*, 131–146.

Cooper, J., Zanna, M. P., & Goethals, G. R. Mistreatment of an esteemed other as a consequence affecting dissonance reduction. *Journal of Experimental Social Psychology*, 1974, *10*, 224–233.

Cooper, R., & Zubek, J. Effects of enriched and restricted early environments on the learning ability of bright and dull rats. *Canadian Journal of Psychology*, 1958, *12*, 159–164.

Cotton, W. L. Masturbation frequencies of men and women. *Medical Aspects of Human Sexuality*, 1975, *9*, 31.

Cowan, P. A. *Piaget with feeling*. New York: Holt, Rinehart and Winston, 1978.

Cozby, P. C. Self-disclosure: A literature review. *Psychological Bulletin*, 1973, *79*, 73–91.

Craik, F. I. M., & Watkins, M. J. The role of rehearsal in short-term memory. *Journal of Verbal Learning and Verbal Behavior*. 1973, *12*, 599–607.

Crawford, C. George Washington, Abraham Lincoln, and Arthur Jensen: Are they compatible? *American Psychologist*, 1979, *34*, 664–672.

Crawford, H. J. Hypnotizability, daydreaming styles, imagery vividness, and absorption: A multidimensional study. *Journal of Personality and Social Psychology*, 1982, *42*, 915–926.

Crockenburg, S. B. Creativity tests: A boon or boondoggle for children? *Review of Educational Research*, 1972, *42*, 27–45.

Cronbach, L. J. Five decades of public controversy over mental testing. *American Psychologist*, 1975, *30*, 1–14.

Cronholm, B., & Otosson, J. O. "Counter-shock" in electroconvulsive therapy. *Archives of General Psychiatry*, 1961, *4*, 254–258.

Crowe, R. R. An adoption study of antisocial personality. *Archives of General Psychiatry*, 1974, *31*, 785–791.

Cummings, N. A. Turning bread into stones: Our modern antimiracle. *American Psychologist*, 1979, *34*, 1119–1129.

Cunningham, M. R. Weather, mood, and helping behavior. *Journal of Personality and Social Psychology*, 1979, *37*, 1947–1956.

Dale, P. S. Language development: Structure and function. Hinsdale, Ill.: Dryden Press, 1976.

Dalton, K. Menstruation and examinations. *Lancet*, 1968, 2, 1386–1388.

Dalton, K. *The menstrual cycle*. New York: Warner Books, 1972.

Dalton, K. Cyclical criminal acts in premenstrual syndrome. *Lancet*, 1980, 2, 1070–1071.

Darley, J. M., & Gross, P. H. A hypothesis-confirming bias in labeling effects. *Journal of Personality and Social Psychology*, 1983, *44*, 20–33.

Darley, J. M., & Latané, B. Bystander intervention in emergencies: Diffusion of responsibility. *Journal of Personality and Social Psychology*, 1968, *8*, 377–383.

Darwin, C. A. *The expression of the emotions in man and animals*. London: J. Murray, 1872.

Davison, G. C. Homosexuality: The ethical challenge. *Journal of Consulting and Clinical Psychology*, 1976, *44*, 157–162.

Davison, G. C., & Neale, J. M. *Abnormal psychology*, 3d ed. New York: Wiley, 1982.

Davitz, J. R. *The language of emotion*. New York: Academic Press, 1969.

Deaux, K. *The behavior of men and women*. Monterey, Calif.: Brooks/Cole, 1976.

Delahunt, J., & Curran, J. P. Effectiveness of negative practice and self-control techniques in the reduction of smoking behavior. *Journal of Consulting and Clinical Psychology*, 1976, *44*, 1002–1007.

Delgado, J. M. R. *Physical control of the mind*. New York: Harper & Row, 1969.

Dement, W. Sleep and dreams. In A. M. Freedman & H. I. Kaplan (eds.), *Human Behavior: Biological, Psychological, and Sociological*. New York: Atheneum, 1972.

DePaulo, B. M., Rosenthal, R., Eisenstat, R. A., Rogers, P. L., & Finkelstein, S. Decoding discrepant nonverbal cues. *Journal of Personality and Social Psychology*, 1978, *38*, 313–323.

Depue, R. A., Slater, J. F., Wolfstetter-Kausch, H., Klein, D., Goplerud, E., & Farr, D. A behavioral paradigm for identifying persons at risk for bipolar depressive disorder. *Journal of Abnormal Psychology*, 1981, *90*, 381–438.

Dermer, M., & Thiel, D. L. When beauty may fail. *Journal of Personality and Social Psychology*, 1975, *31*, 1168–1176.

Derner, G. Biofeedback Workshop. Adelphi University, Garden City, N. Y., May 7, 1977.

Dethier, V. G. Other tastes, other worlds. *Science*, 1978, *201*, 224–228.

Diamond, M. C. Aging and cell loss: Calling for an honest count. *Psychology Today*, September 1978, 126.

Diener, E. Deindividuation: The absence of self-awareness and self-regulation in group members. In P. Paulus (ed.), *The Psychology of Group Influence*. Hillsdale, N. J.: Erlbaum, 1980.

Dion, K. K., Berscheid, E., & Walster, E. What is beautiful is good. *Journal of Personality and Social Psychology*, 1972, *24*, 285–290.

Dobelle, W. H., Mladejovsky, M. G., Evans, J. R., Roberts, T. S., & Girvin, J. P. "Braille" reading by a blind volunteer by visual cortex stimulation. *Nature*, 1976, *259*, 111–112.

Dodge, L. J. T., Glasgow, R. E., & O'Neill, H. K. Bibliotherapy in the treatment of female orgasmic dysfunction. *Journal of Consulting and Clinical Psychology*, 1982, *50*, 442–443.

Doerr, H. O., & Hokanson, J. E. A relation between heart rate and performance in children. *Journal of Personality and Social Psychology*, 1965, *2*, 70–76.

Dollard, J., Doob, L. W., Miller, N. E., Mowrer, O. H., & Sears, R. R. *Frustration and aggression*. New Haven, Conn.: Yale University Press, 1939.

Donnerstein, E. Aggressive erotica and violence against women. *Journal of Personality and Social Psychology*, 1980, *39*, 269–277.

Donnerstein, E., & Wilson, D. W. Effects of noise and perceived control on ongoing and subsequent aggressive behavior. *Journal of Personality and Social Psychology,* 1976, *34,* 774–781.

Doob, A. N., & Wood, L. Catharsis and aggression: The effects of annoyance and retaliation on aggressive behavior. *Journal of Personality and Social Psychology,* 1972, *22,* 236–245.

Doyle, N. C. The facts about second-hand cigarette smoke. *American Lung Association Bulletin,* 1974, *60,* 13–15.

Driscoll, R., Davis, K. E., & Lipetz, M. E. Parental interference and romantic love. *Journal of Personality and Social Psychology,* 1972, *24,* 1–10.

Duke, M. P., & Nowicki, S. A new measure and social learning model for interpersonal distance. *Journal of Experimental Research in Personality,* 1972, *6,* 119–132.

Durden-Smith, J. How to win the mating game by a nose. *Next,* November/December 1980, 85–89.

Eagly, A. H. Comprehensibility of persuasive arguments as a determinant of opinion change. *Journal of Personality and Social Psychology,* 1974, *29,* 758–773.

Eagly, A. H. Sex differences in influenceability. *Psychological Bulletin,* 1978, *85,* 86–116.

Eagly, A. H., Wood, W., & Chaiken, S. Causal inferences about communicators and their effect on opinion change. *Journal of Personality and Social Psychology,* 1978, *36,* 424–435.

Eagly, A. H., Wood, W., & Fishbaugh, L. Sex differences in conformity: Surveillance by the group as a determinant of male conformity. *Journal of Personality and Social Psychology,* 1981, *40,* 384–394.

Ebbeson, E. B., & Bowers, J. B. Proportion of risky to conservative arguments in a group discussion and choice shift. *Journal of Personality and Social Psychology,* 1974, *29,* 316–327.

Edwards, A. L. *Edwards personal preference schedule.* New York: Psychological Corporation, 1954.

Edwards, D. J. A. Approaching the unfamiliar: A study of human interaction differences. *Journal of Behavioral Sciences,* 1972, *1,* 249–250.

Efran, M. G. The effect of physical ap-

pearance on the judgment of guilt, interpersonal attraction, and severity of recommended punishment in a simulated jury task. *Journal of Research in Personality,* 1974, *8,* 45–54.

Eibl-Eibesfeldt, I. *Love and hate: The natural history of behavior patterns.* New York: Schocken Books, 1974.

Eidelson, R. J., & Epstein, N. Cognition and relationship maladjustment: Development of a measure of dysfunctional relationship beliefs. *Journal of Consulting and Clinical Psychology,* 1982, *50,* 715–720.

Ekman, P., & Oster, H. Facial expressions of emotion. *Annual Review of Psychology, Vol. 30.* Palo Alto, Calif.: Annual Reviews, 1979.

Elkins, R. L. Covert sensitization treatment of alcoholism. *Addictive Behaviors,* 1980, *5,* 67–89.

Ellis, A. The basic clinical theory of rational-emotive therapy. In A. Ellis & R. Grieger (eds.), *Handbook of Rational-Emotive Therapy.* New York: Springer, 1977.

Ellis, A., & Harper, R. A. *A new guide to rational living.* Hollywood, Calif.: Wilshire Books, 1975.

Ellison, G. D. Animal models of psychopathology: The low-norepinephrine and low-serotonin rat. *American Psychologist,* 1977, *32,* 1036–1045.

Ellsworth, P. C., Carlsmith, J. M., & Henson, A. The stare as a stimulus to flight in human subjects. *Journal of Personality and Social Psychology,* 1972, *21,* 302–311.

Ellsworth, P. C., & Langer, E. J. Staring and approach: An interpretation of the stare as a nonspecific activator. *Journal of Personality and Social Psychology,* 1976, *33,* 117–122.

English, H. B. Three cases of the "conditioned fear response." *Journal of Abnormal and Social Psychology,* 1929, *34,* 221–225.

Erikson, E. H. *Childhood and society.* New York: Norton, 1963.

Erikson, E. H. *Life history and the historical moment.* New York: Norton, 1975.

Eriksson, K. Behavior and physiological differences among rat strains specially selected for their alcohol consumption. *Annals of the New York Academy of Science,* 1972, *197,* 32–41.

Eron, L. D. Parent-child interaction,

television violence, and aggression of children. *American Psychologist,* 1982, *37,* 197–211.

Ervin-Tripp. S. Imitation and structural change in children's language. In E. H. Lenneberg (ed.), *New Directions in the Study of Language.* Cambridge: M.I.T. Press, 1964.

Erwin, J., Maple, T., Mitchell, G., & Willott, J. Follow-up study of isolation-reared rhesus monkeys paired with preadolescent cospecifics in late infancy: Cross-sex pairings. *Developmental Psychology,* 1974, *6,* 808–814.

Essen-Möller, 1941. Reported in G. C. Davison & J. M. Neale, *Abnormal Psychology,* 3d ed. New York: Wiley, 1982.

Estes, W. K. An associative basis for coding and organization in memory. In A. W. Melton & E. Martin (eds.), *Coding Processes in Human Memory.* Washington, D. C.: Winston, 1972.

Evans, R. B. Sixteen personality factor questionnaire scores of homosexual men. *Journal of Consulting and Clinical Psychology,* 1970, *34,* 212–215.

Evans, R. I., Rozelle, R. M., Lasater, T. M., Demborski, T. M., & Allen, B. P. Fear arousal, persuasion, and actual versus implied behavioral change: New perspective utilizing a real-life dental hygiene program. *Journal of Personality and Social Psychology,* 1970, *16,* 220–227.

Exline, R. V. Visual interaction: The glances of power and preference. In J. K. Cole (ed.), *The Nebraska Symposium on Motivation, Vol. 19.* Lincoln, Neb.: University of Nebraska Press, 1972.

Eysenck, H. J. Classification and the problem of diagnosis. In H. J. Eysenck (ed.), *Handbook of Abnormal Psychology.* London: Pitman, 1960.

Eysenck, H. J. Obscenity—officially speaking. *Penthouse,* November 1972, 95–102.

Eysenck, H. J., & Rachman, S. *The causes and cures of neurosis.* San Diego: Knapp, 1965.

Fairbanks, L. A., McGuire, M. T., & Harris, C. J. Nonverbal interaction of patients and therapists during psychiatric interviews. *Journal of Abnormal Psychology,* 1982, *91,* 109–119.

Fantz, R. L. The origin of form perception. *Scientific American*, 1961, *204*(5), 66–72.

Fazio, R. H., Sherman, S. J., & Herr, P. M. The feature-positive effect in the self-perception process: Does not doing matter as much as doing? *Journal of Personality and Social Psychology*, 1982, *42*, 404–411.

Feldman-Summers, S., & Palmer, G. C. Rape as viewed by judges, prosecutors, and police officers. *Criminal Justice and Behavior*, 1980, *7*, 19–40.

Felsenthal, N. *Orientations to mass communications*. Chicago: Science Research, 1976.

Feltz, D. L. Path analysis of the causal elements in Bandura's theory of self-efficacy and an anxiety-based model of avoidance behavior. *Journal of Personality and Social Psychology*, 1982, *42*, 764–781.

Fenichel, O. *The psychoanalytic theory of the neuroses*. New York: Norton, 1945.

Fenigstein, A. Does aggression cause a preference for viewing media violence? *Journal of Personality and Social Psychology*, 1979, *37*, 2307–2317.

Fenigstein, A., Scheier, M. F., & Buss, A. H. Public and private self-consciousness: Assessment and theory. *Journal of Consulting and Clinical Psychology*, 1975, *43*, 522–527.

Festinger, L. *A theory of cognitive dissonance*. Evanston, Ill.: Row, Peterson, 1957.

Festinger, L., & Carlsmith, J. M. Cognitive consequences of forced compliance. *Journal of Abnormal and Social Psychology*, 1959, *58*, 203–210.

Fink, M., Kety, S., McGaugh, J., & Williams, T. A. (eds.). *Psychobiology of convulsive therapy*. New York: Halsted Press, 1974.

Fisher, D. F., & Karsh, R. Modality effects and storage in sequential short-term memory. *Journal of Experimental Psychology*, 1971, *87*, 410–414.

Fisher, J. D., & Byrne, D. Too close for comfort: Sex differences in response to invasions of personal space. *Journal of Personality and Social Psychology*, 1975, *32*, 15–21.

Fisher, K. Debate rages on 1973 Sobell study. *APA Monitor*, November 1982, 8–9.

Fisher, L. E. Relationships and sexuality in contexts and culture: The anthropology of eros. In B. B. Wolman & J. Money (eds.), *Handbook of Human Sexuality*. Englewood Cliffs, N. J.: Prentice-Hall, 1980.

Fisher, S. *Female orgasm: Psychology, physiology, fantasy*. New York: Basic Books, 1973.

Fisher, W. A., & Byrne, D. Individual differences in affective, evaluative, and behavioral responses to an erotic film. *Journal of Applied Social Psychology*, 1978a, *8*, 355–365.

Fisher, W. A., & Byrne, D. Sex differences in response to erotica? Love versus lust. *Journal of Personality and Social Psychology*, 1978b, *36*, 117–125.

Fitch, G. Effects of self-esteem, perceived performance, and choice on causal attribution. *Journal of Personality and Social Psychology*, 1970, *16*, 311–315.

Flaherty, J. F., & Dusek, J. B. An investigation of the relationship between psychological androgyny and components of self-concept. *Journal of Personality and Social Psychology*, 1980, *38*, 984–992.

Fleming, J. D. Field report: The state of the apes. *Psychology Today*, 1974, *7*, 31–46.

Fleming, M. Z., MacGowan, B. R., Robinson, L., Spitz, J., & Salt, P. The body image of the postoperative female-to-male transsexual. *Journal of Consulting and Clinical Psychology*, 1982, *50*, 461–462.

Fodor, E. M., & Smith, T. The power motive as an influence on group decision making. *Journal of Personality and Social Psychology*, 1982, *42*, 178–185.

Fodor, J. A., Bever, T. G., & Garrett, M. F. *The psychology of language*. New York: McGraw-Hill, 1974.

Fogel, M. L. Warning: Auto fumes may lower your kid's IQ. *Psychology Today*, January 1980, 108.

Ford, C. S., & Beach, F. A. *Patterns of sexual behavior*. New York: Harper & Row, 1951.

Foulkes, D. Longitudinal studies of dreams in children. In J. Masserman (ed.), *Science and Psychoanalysis*. New York: Grune & Stratton, 1971.

Franck, K. D., Unseld, C. T., & Wentworth, W. E. Adaptation of the newcomer: A process of construction. Unpublished manuscript, City University of New York, 1974.

Frank, E., Anderson, C., & Rubinstein, D. Frequency of sexual dysfunction in "normal" couples. *New England Journal of Medicine*, 1978, *299*, 111–115.

Frankl, V. E. Paradoxical intention and dereflection. *Psychotherapy: Theory, Research, and Practice*, 1975, *12*, 226–236.

Freedman, J. L., & Fraser, S. C. Compliance without pressure: The foot-in-the-door technique. *Journal of Personality and Social Psychology*, 1966, *4*, 195–202.

Freedman, J. L., Wallington, S. A., & Bless, E. Compliance without pressure: The effect of guilt. *Journal of Personality and Social Psychology*, 1967, *7*, 117–124.

Freedman, R. R., & Sattler, H. L. Physiological and psychological factors in sleep-onset insomnia. *Journal of Abnormal Psychology*, 1982, *91*, 380–389.

French, G. M., & Harlow, H. F. Variability of delayed-reaction performance in normal and brain-damaged rhesus monkeys. *Journal of Neurophysiology*, 1962, *25*, 585–599.

Freud, S. (1909). Analysis of a phobia in a five-year-old boy. In *Collected Papers*, Vol. 3, translated by A. and J. Strachey. New York: Basic Books, 1959.

Freud, S. (1927). A religious experience. In *Standard Edition of the Complete Psychological Works of Sigmund Freud, Vol. 21*. London: Hogarth Press, 1964.

Freud, S. (1930). *Civilization and its discontents*, translated by J. Strachey. New York: Norton, 1961.

Freud, S. (1933). New introductory lectures. In *Standard Edition of the Complete Psychological Works of Sigmund Freud, Vol. 22*. London: Hogarth Press, 1964.

Friedman, M., & Rosenman, R. H. *Type A behavior and your heart*. New York: Knopf, 1974.

Friedman, M. I., & Stricker, E. M. The physiological psychology of hunger: A physiological perspective. *Psychological Review*, 1976, *83*, 409–431.

Fromm, E. *The art of loving*. New York: Harper & Row, 1956.

Funkenstein, D. The physiology of fear and anger. *Scientific American*, May 1955.

Galanter, E. Contemporary psychophysics. In R. Brown et al. (eds.), *New Directions in Psychology*. New York: Holt, Rinehart and Winston, 1962.

Galassi, J. P., Frierson, H. T., & Sharer,

R. Behavior of high, moderate, and low test anxious students during an actual test situation. *Journal of Consulting and Clinical Psychology*, 1981, *49*, 51–62.

Galizio, M., & Hendrick, C. Effect of musical accompaniment on attitude: The guitar as a prop for persuasion. *Journal of Applied Social Psychology*, 1972, *2*, 350–359.

Garcia, J. The logic and limits of mental aptitude testing. *American Psychologist*, 1981, *36*, 1172–1180.

Gardner, B. T., & Gardner, R. A. Two-way communication with an infant chimpanzee. In A. M. Schrier & F. Stollnitz (eds.), *Behavior of Nonhuman Primates, Vol. 4.* New York: Academic Press, 1972.

Gardner, R. A., & Gardner, B. T. Comparative physiology and language acquisition. In K. Salzinger & F. Denmark (eds.), *Psychology: The State of the Art.* New York: Annals of the New York Academy of the Sciences, 1977.

Garfield, S. L. Psychotherapy: A 40-year appraisal. *American Psychologist*, 1981, *36*, 174–183.

Garfield, S. L. Eclecticism and integration in psychotherapy. *Behavior Therapy*, 1982, *13*, 610–623.

Gash, D. M. Brain transplants are next. *Psychology Today*, December 1981, 116.

Gatchel, R. J., & Proctor, J. D. Effectiveness of voluntary heart rate control in reducing speech anxiety. *Journal of Consulting and Clinical Psychology*, 1976, *44*, 381–389.

Gazzaniga, M. S. The split brain in man. *Scientific American*, 1967, *217*, 24–29.

Gazzaniga, M. S. One brain—two minds? *American Science*, 1972, *60*, 311–317.

Gebhard, P. H. The institute. In M. S. Weinberg (ed.), *Sex Research: Studies from the Kinsey Institute.* New York: Oxford University Press, 1976.

Geen, R. G. Behavioral and physiological reactions to observed violence: Effects of prior exposure to aggressive stimuli. *Journal of Personality and Social Psychology*, 1981, *40*, 868–875.

Geen, R. G., Stonner, D., & Shope, G. L. The facilitation of aggression by aggression: Evidence against the catharsis hypothesis. *Journal of Personality and Social Psychology*, 1975, *31*, 721–726.

Gerard, H. B., Wilhelmy, R. A., & Conolley, E. S. Conformity and group size. *Journal of Personality and Social Psychology*, 1968, *8*, 79–82.

Gerbner, G., & Gross, L. The scary world of TV's heavy viewer. *Psychology Today*, 1976, *9*, 41–45.

Getzels, J. W., & Jackson, P. W. *Creativity and intelligence: Explorations with gifted students.* New York: Wiley, 1962.

Gilmartin, B. G. That swinging couple down the block. *Psychology Today*, 1975, *8*, 54.

Gittelman-Klein, R., Klein, D. F., Katz, S., Saraf, K., & Pollack, E. Comparative effects of methylphenidate and thioradizine in hyperkinetic children. *Archives of General Psychiatry*, 1976, *33*, 1217–1231.

Glass, D. C. *Stress and coronary-prone behavior.* Hillsdale, N. J.: Erlbaum, 1977.

Glass, D. C., & Singer, J. E. *Urban stress.* New York: Academic Press, 1972.

Gleason, H. A., Jr. *An introduction to descriptive linguistics*, rev. ed. New York: Holt, Rinehart and Winston, 1961.

Glick, P., & Spanier, G. B. Married and unmarried cohabitation in the United States. *Journal of Marriage and the Family*, 1980, *42*, 19–30.

Gmelch, G. Baseball magic. *Trans-action*, June 1971.

Gold, P. E., & King, R. A. Retrograde amnesia: Storage failure versus retrieval failure. *Psychological Review*, 1974, *81*, 465–469.

Goldberg, L. W. Differential attribution of trait-descriptive terms to oneself as compared to well-liked, neutral, and disliked others. *Journal of Personality and Social Psychology*, 1978, *36*, 1012–1028.

Goldfoot, D. A., Essock-Vitale, S. M., Asa, C. S., Thornton, J. E., & Leshner, A. I. Anosmia in male rhesus monkeys does not alter copulatory activity with cycling females. *Science*, 1978, *199*, 1095–1096.

Goldfried, M. R., Linehan, M. M., & Smith, J. L. Reduction of test anxiety through cognitive restructuring. *Journal of Consulting and Clinical Psychology*, 1978, *46*, 32–39.

Goldman, W., & Lewis, P. Beautiful is good: Evidence that the physically attractive are more socially skillful. *Journal of Experimental Social Psychology*, 1977, *13*, 125–130.

Goldsmith, J. R. Effects of air pollution on human health. In A. C. Stearn (ed.), *Air Pollution*, 2d ed. New York: Academic Press, 1968.

Goldstein, M., & Davis, E. E. Race and belief: A further analysis of the social determinants of behavioral intentions. *Journal of Personality and Social Psychology*, 1972, *22*, 345–355.

Goldstein, M. J. Exposure to erotic stimuli and sexual deviance. *Journal of Social Issues*, 1973, *29*, 197–219.

Goldstein, M. J., Kant, H., Judd, L., Rice, C., & Green, R. Experience with pornography: Rapists, pedophiles, homosexuals, transsexuals, and controls. *Archives of Sexual Behavior*, 1971, *1*, 1–15.

Goleman, D. J. Special abilities of the sexes: Do they begin in the brain? *Psychology Today*, November 1978, 48–120.

Goleman, D. J. Staying up. *Psychology Today*, March 1982, 24–35.

Goleman, D. J., & Schwartz, G. E. Meditation as an intervention in stress reactivity. *Journal of Consulting and Clinical Psychology*, 1976, *44*, 456–466.

Golub, S. The effect of premenstrual anxiety and depression on cognitive function. *Journal of Personality and Social Psychology*, 1976, *34*, 99–104.

Goodwin, D. W. Alcoholism and heredity. *Archives of General Psychiatry*, 1979, *36*, 57–61.

Goodwin, D. W., Schulsinger, F., Hermansen, L., Guze, S. B., & Winokur, G. A. Alcohol problems in adoptees raised apart from alcoholic biological parents. *Archives of General Psychiatry*, 1973, *128*, 239–243.

Gordon, E. W., & Terrell, M. D. The changed social context of testing. *American Psychologist*, 1981, *36*, 1167–1171.

Gormally, J., Sipps, G., Raphael, R., Edwin, D., & Varvil-Weld, D. The relationship between maladaptive cognitions and social anxiety. *Journal of Consulting and Clinical Psychology*, 1981, *49*, 300–301.

Gotlib, I. H. Self-reinforcement and depression in interpersonal interaction: The role of performance level. *Journal of Abnormal Psychology*, 1982, *91*, 3–13.

Gough, H. G. *A preliminary guide for the use and interpretation of the California Psychological Inventory.* Berkeley, Calif.: University of California Institute for Personality Assessment and Research, 1954.

Gould, R. Adult life stages: Growth toward self-tolerance. *Psychology Today*, 1975, *8*, 74–81.

Goy, R. W., & Goldfoot, D. A. Neuroendocrinology: Animal models and problems of human sexuality. In E. A. Rubenstein et al. (eds.), *New Directions in Sex Research*. New York: Plenum, 1976.

Graham, J. *The MMPI: A practical guide.* New York: Oxford University Press, 1977.

Green, B. F. A primer of testing. *American Psychologist*, 1981, *36*, 1001–1011.

Green, R. Homosexuality as mental illness. *International Journal of Psychiatry*, 1972, *10*, 77–98.

Greenbaum, P., & Rosenfeld, H. M. Patterns of avoidance in response to interpersonal staring and proximity: Effects of bystanders on drivers at a traffic intersection. *Journal of Personality and Social Psychology*, 1978, *36*, 575–587.

Greenberg, D. J., & Blue, S. Z. The visual-preference technique in infancy: Effect of number of stimuli presented upon experimental outcome. *Child Development*, 1977, *48*(1), 131–137.

Greene, J. The gambling trap. *Psychology Today*, September 1982, 50–55.

Gregory, R. L. *Eye and brain*, 2d ed. New York: World Universities Library, 1973.

Grush, J. E. The impact of candidate expenditures, regionality, and prior outcomes on the 1976 Democratic presidential primaries. *Journal of Personality and Social Psychology*, 1980, *38*, 337–347.

Grush, J. E., & Yehl, J. G. Marital roles, sex differences, and interpersonal attraction. *Journal of Personality and Social Psychology*, 1979, *37*, 116–123.

Guilford, J. P. Traits of creativity. In H. H. Anderson (ed.), *Creativity and Its Cultivation*. New York: Harper & Row, 1959.

Guilford, J. P. *The nature of human intelligence*. New York: McGraw-Hill, 1967.

Guilford, J. P., & Hoepfner, R. *The analysis of intelligence*. New York: McGraw-Hill, 1971.

Haber, R. N. Eidetic images. *Scientific American*, 1969, *220*, 36–55.

Haber, R. N. Eidetic images are not just imaginary. *Psychology Today*, November 1980, 72–82.

Haber, R. N., & Hershenson, M. *The psychology of visual perception*. New York: Holt, Rinehart and Winston, 1980.

Hackett, T. P., & Cassem, N. H. Psychological reactions to life-threatening illness: Acute myocardial infarction. In H. S. Abram (ed.), *Psychological Aspects of Stress*. Springfield, Ill.: Charles C Thomas, 1970.

Hall, C. *The meaning of dreams*. New York: McGraw-Hill, 1966.

Hall, E. T. Proxemics. *Current Anthropology*, 1968, *9*, 83–107.

Halperin, K. M., & Snyder, C. R. Effects of enhanced psychological test feedback on treatment outcome: Therapeutic implications of the Barnum effect. *Journal of Consulting and Clinical Psychology*, 1979, *47*, 140–146.

Hamm, N. H., Baum, M. R., & Nikels, K. W. Effects of race and exposure on judgments of interpersonal favorability. *Journal of Experimental Social Psychology*, 1975, *11*, 14–24.

Hammen, C., & Mayol, A. Depression and cognitive characteristics of stressful life-event types. *Journal of Abnormal Psychology*, 1982, *91*, 165–174.

Hansel, C. E. M. *ESP and parapsychology*. Buffalo, N.Y.: Prometheus Books, 1979.

Hansen, G. O. Meeting house challenges: Involvement—the elderly. In *Housing Issues*. Lincoln, Neb.: University of Nebraska Press, 1975.

Harbeson, G. E. *Choice and challenge for the American woman*, rev. ed. Cambridge: Schenckman, 1971.

Harburg, E., Erfurt, J. C., Hauenstein, L. S., Chape, C., Schull, W. J., & Schork, M. A. Socioecological stress, suppressed hostility, skin color, and black-white male blood pressure: Detroit. *Psychosomatic Medicine*, 1973, *35*, 276–296.

Harder, D. W., Gift, T. E., Strauss, J. S., Ritzler, B. A., & Kokes, R. F. Life events and two-year outcome in schizophrenia. *Journal of Consulting and Clinical Psychology*, 1981, *49*, 619–626.

Hariton, E. B., & Singer, J. L. Women's fantasies during sexual intercourse: Normative and theoretical implications. *Journal of Consulting and Clinical Psychology*, 1974, *42*, 313–322.

Harlow, H. F. Love in infant monkeys. *Scientific American*, 1959, *200*, 68–86.

Harlow, H. F. Sexual behavior in the rhesus monkey. In F. Beach (ed.), *Sex and Behavior*. New York: Wiley, 1965.

Harlow, H. F., & Harlow, M. K. Learning to love. *American Scientist*, 1966, *54*, 244–272.

Harlow, H. F., Harlow, M. K., & Meyer, D. R. Learning motivated by a manipulation drive. *Journal of Experimental Psychology*, 1950, *40*, 228–234.

Harlow, H. F., & Zimmermann, R. R. Affectional responses in the infant monkey. *Science*, 1959, *130*, 421–432.

Harlow, M. K., & Harlow, H. F. Affection in primates. *Discovery*, 1966, *27*, 11–17.

Harrell, T. W., & Harrell, M. S. Army General Classification Test scores for civilian occupations. *Educational and Psychological Measurement*, 1945, *5*, 229–239.

Harris, G. W., & Levine, S. Sexual differentiation of the brain and its experimental control. *Journal of Physiology*, 1965, *181*, 379–400.

Harris, T. A. *I'm OK—You're OK*. New York: Harper & Row, 1967.

Harrison, A. A., & Saeed, L. Let's make a deal: An analysis of revelations and stipulations in lonely hearts advertisements. *Journal of Personality and Social Psychology*, 1977, *35*, 257–264.

Hart, B. Sexual reflexes and mating behavior in the male dog. *Journal of Comparative and Physiological Psychology*, 1967, *66*, 388–399.

Hartmann, E. L. *The functions of sleep*. New Haven, Conn.: Yale University Press, 1973.

Hartmann, E. L. The strangest sleep disorder. *Psychology Today*, April 1981, 14–18.

Hartmann, E. L., & Stern, W. C. Desynchronized sleep deprivation: Learning deficit and its reversal by increased catecholamines. *Physiology and Behavior*, 1972, *8*, 585–587.

Harvey, J. H., Ickes, W. J., & Kidd, R. F. (eds.). *New directions in attributional research, Vol. 1*. Hillsdale, N.J.: Erlbaum, 1976.

Harvey, J. H., Ickes, W. J., & Kidd, R. F. (eds.). *New directions in attributional research, Vol. 2*. Hillsdale, N.J.: Erlbaum, 1978.

Harvey, J. R. Diaphragmatic breathing: A practical technique for breath control. *The Behavior Therapist*, 1978, *1*(2), 13–14.

Haspel, K. C., & Harris, R. S. Effect of tachistoscope stimulation of subconscious Oedipal wishes on competitive performance: A failure to replicate. *Journal of Abnormal Psychology*, 1982, *91*, 437–443.

Hass, R. G., & Linder, D. E. Counterargument availability and the effects of message structure on persuasion. *Journal of Personality and Social Psychology*, 1972, *23*, 219–233.

Hassett, J. Sex and smell. *Psychology Today*, 1978, *11*(10), 40–42, 45.

Hatfield, E., Sprecher, S., & Traupman, J. Men's and women's reaction to sexually explicit films: A serendipitous finding. *Archives of Sexual Behavior*, 1978, *6*, 583–592.

Havighurst, R. J. *Developmental tasks and education*, 3d ed. New York: McKay, 1972.

Hayes, S. L. Single case design and empirical clinical practice. *Journal of Consulting and Clinical Psychology*, 1981, *49*, 193–211.

Haynes, S. N., Adams, A., & Franzen, M. The effects of presleep stress on sleep-onset insomnia. *Journal of Abnormal Psychology*, 1981, *90*, 601–606.

Haynes, S. N., Follingstad, D. R., & McGowan, W. T. Insomnia: Sleep patterns and anxiety level. *Journal of Psychosomatic Research*, 1974, *18*, 69–74.

Haynes, S. N., Sides, H., & Lockwood, G. Relaxation instructions and frontalis electromyographic feedback intervention with sleep-onset insomnia. *Behavior Therapy*, 1977, *8*, 644–652.

Haynes, S. N., Woodward, S., Moran, R., & Alexander, D. Relaxation treatment of insomnia. *Behavior Therapy*, 1974, *5*, 555–558.

Heaton, R. K., & Victor, R. G. Personality characteristics associated with psychedelic flashbacks in natural and experimental settings. *Journal of Abnormal Psychology*, 1976, *85*, 83–90.

Heber, R., Garber, H., Harrington, S., & Hoffman, C. Rehabilitation of families at risk for mental retardation. Progress report, University of Wisconsin at Madison, December 1972.

Heiby, E., & Becker, J. D. Effect of filmed modeling on the self-reported frequency of masturbation. *Archives of Sexual Behavior*, 1980, *9*, 115–122.

Heider, F. *The psychology of interpersonal relations*. New York: Wiley, 1958.

Heiman, J. R. The physiology of erotica: Women's sexual arousal. *Psychology Today*, 1975, *8*, 90–94.

Heiman, J. R., LoPiccolo, L., & LoPiccolo, J. *Becoming orgasmic: A sexual growth program for women*. Englewood Cliffs, N. J.: Prentice-Hall, 1976.

Heingartner, A., & Hall, J. V. Affective consequences in adults and children of repeated exposure to auditory stimuli. *Journal of Personality and Social Psychology*, 1974, *29*, 719–723.

Helmreich, R. L., Spence, J. T., & Holahan, C. K. Psychological androgyny and sex-role flexibility: A test of two hypotheses. *Journal of Personality and Social Psychology*, 1979, *37*, 1631–1644.

Hendrick, C., Wells, K. S., & Faletti, M. V. Social and emotional effects of geographical relocation on elderly retirees. *Journal of Personality and Social Psychology*, 1982, *42*, 951–962.

Hendrick, J., & Hendrick, C. D. *Aging in mass society: Myths and realities*. Cambridge: Winthrop Publishers, 1977.

Hennigan, K. M., DelRosario, M. L., Heath, L., Cook, T. D., Wharton, J. D., & Calder, B. J. Impact of the introduction of television on crime in the United States. *Journal of Personality and Social Psychology*, 1982, *42*, 461–477.

Herrell, J. M. Sex differences in emotional responsiveness to "erotic literature." *Journal of Consulting and Clinical Psychology*, 1975, *43*, 921.

Herrnstein, R. IQ. *Atlantic Monthly*, September 1971, 43–64.

Hess, E. H. Attitude and pupil size. *Scientific American*, 1965, *212*, 46–54.

Hess, E. H. *The tell-tale eye*. New York: Van Nostrand, 1975.

Heston, L. L. Psychiatric disorders in foster-home-reared children of schizophrenic mothers. *British Journal of Psychiatry*, 1966, *112*, 819–825.

Hilgard, E. R. *Divided consciousness: Multiple controls in human thought and action*. New York: Wiley-Interscience, 1977.

Hirsch, J. Jensenism: The bankruptcy of "science" without scholarship. *Educational Theory*, 1975, *25*, 3–28.

Hirsch, J., & Keniston, K. Psychological issues in talented college dropouts. *Psychiatry*, 1970, *33*, 1–20.

Hite, S. *The Hite report: A nationwide study on female sexuality*. New York: Macmillan, 1976.

Hite, S. *The Hite report on male sexuality*. New York: Knopf, 1981.

Hobson, J. A., & McCarley, R. W. The brain as a dream state generator: An activation-synthesis hypothesis of the dream process. *American Journal of Psychiatry*, 1977, *134*, 1335–1348.

Hoffman, M. L. Is altruism part of human nature? *Journal of Personality and Social Psychology*, 1981, *40*, 121–137.

Hokanson, J. E., & Burgess, M. The effects of three types of aggression on vascular processes. *Journal of Abnormal and Social Psychology*, 1962, *64*, 446–449.

Hokanson, J. E., Burgess, M., & Cohen, M. F. Effects of displaced aggression on systolic blood pressure. *Journal of Abnormal and Social Psychology*, 1963, *67*, 214–218.

Hokanson, J. E., Willers, K. R., & Koropsak, E. Modification of autonomic responses during aggressive interchange. *Journal of Personality*, 1968, *36*, 386–404.

Hollingshead, A. B., & Redlich, F. C. *Social class and mental illness: A community study*. New York: Wiley, 1958.

Holmes, T. H., & Rahe, R. H. The social readjustment rating scale. *Journal of Psychosomatic Research*, 1967, *11*, 213–218.

Holroyd, K. A., Westbrook, T., Wolf, M., & Badhorn, E. Performance, cognition, and physiological responding in test anxiety. *Journal of Abnormal Psychology*, 1978, *87*, 442–451.

Hooker, E. The adjustment of the male overt homosexual. *Journal of Projective Techniques and Personality Adjustment*, 1957, *21*, 18–23.

Horner, M. Toward an understanding of achievement-related conflicts in women. *Journal of Social Issues*, 1972, *28*, 157–175.

Horney, K. *Feminine psychology*. New York: Norton, 1967.

Horton, D. L., & Turnage, T. W. *Human learning*. Englewood Cliffs, N. J.: Prentice-Hall, 1976.

Horvath, T. Physical attractiveness: The influence of selected torso parameters. *Archives of Sexual Behavior*, 1981, *10*, 21–24.

Howard, J. L., Liptzin, M. B., & Reifler, C. B. Is pornography a problem? *Journal of Social Issues*, 1973, *29*, 133–145.

Hull, J. G. A self-awareness model of the causes and effects of alcohol consumption. *Journal of Abnormal Psychology*, 1981, *90*, 586–600.

Hunt, M. *Sexual behavior in the 1970s*. Chicago: Playboy Press, 1974.

Hursch, C. J. *The trouble with rape*. Chicago: Nelson-Hall, 1977.

Hurvich, L. M. Two decades of opponent processes. In F. W. Billmeyer & G. Wyszecki (eds.), *Color 77*. Bristol, England: Adam Hilger, 1978.

Hurvich, L. M., & Jameson, D. Opponent processes as a model of neural organization. *American Psychologist*, 1974, *29*, 88–102.

Hutchings, B., & Mednick, S. A. Registered criminality in the adoptive and biological parents of registered male adoptees. In S. A. Mednick, F. Schulsinger, J. Higgins, & B. Bell (eds.), *Genetics, Environment, and Psychopathology*. New York: Elsevier, 1974.

Huxley, A. *Brave new world*. New York: Harper & Row, 1939.

Hyde, J. S. How large are cognitive gender differences? *American Psychologist*, 1981, *36*, 892–901.

Ibrahim, A. The home situation and the homosexual. *Journal of Sex Research*, 1976, *12*, 263–282.

Istvan, J., & Griffitt, W. Emotional arousal and sexual attraction. Unpublished manuscript, Kansas State University, 1978.

Ivey, M. E., & Bardwick, J. M. Patterns of affective fluctuation in the menstrual cycle. *Psychosomatic Medicine*, 1968, *30*, 336–345.

Izard, C. E. On the development of emotions and emotion-cognition relationships in infancy. In M. Lewis & L. Rosenblum (eds.), *The Development of Affect*. New York: Plenum, 1978.

Jacobson, E. *Progressive relaxation*. Chicago: University of Chicago Press, 1938.

James, W. *The principles of psychology*. New York: Henry Holt and Company, 1890.

James, W. Does "consciousness" exist? *Journal of Philosophy, Psychology, and Scientific Methods*, 1904, *1*, 477–491.

Janda, L. H., & O'Grady, E. E. Development of a sex anxiety inventory. *Journal of Consulting and Clinical Psychology*, 1980, *48*, 169–175.

Janda, L. H., O'Grady, E. E., & Capps, C. F. Fear of success in males and females in sex-linked occupations. *Sex Roles*, 1978, *4*, 43–50.

Janis, I., & Mann, L. *Decision-making*. New York: Free Press, 1977.

Janis, I., & Wheeler, D. Thinking clearly about career choices. *Psychology Today*, December 1978, 66–76, 121–122.

Janis, I., Kaye, D., & Kirschner, P. Facilitating effects of "eating while reading" on responsiveness to persuasive communications. *Journal of Personality and Social Psychology*, 1965, *1*, 181–186.

Jannoun, L., Oppenheimer, C., & Gelder, M. A self-help treatment program for anxiety state patients. *Behavior Therapy*, 1982, *13*, 103–111.

Janowitz, H. D., & Grossman, M. I. Effect of variations in nutritive density on intake of food in dogs and cats. *American Journal of Physiology*, 1949, *158*, 184–193.

Jellison, J. M., & Green, J. A self-presentation approach to the fundamental attribution error: The norm of internality. *Journal of Personality and Social Psychology*, 1981, *40*, 643–649.

Joffee, C. Sex-role socialization and the nursery school: As the twig is bent. *Journal of Marriage and the Family*, 1971, *33*, 467–475.

Johns, M. W., Masterson, J. P., & Bruce, D. W. Relationship between sleep habits, adrenocortical activity and personality. *Psychosomatic Medicine*, 1971, *33*, 499–507.

Johnson, D. M. A modern account of problem solving. *Psychological Bulletin*, 1944, *41*, 201–229.

Johnson, P. B. Achievement motivation and success: Does the end justify the means? *Journal of Personality and Social Psychology*, 1981, *40*, 374–375.

Johnson, S. M., & White, G. Self-observation as an agent of behavioral change. *Behavior Therapy*, 1971, *2*, 488–497.

Jones, E. *The life and work of Sigmund Freud*. New York: Basic Books, 1961.

Jones, E. The rocky road from acts to dispositions. *American Psychologist*, 1979, *34*, 107–117.

Jones, H. E., & Jones, M. C. Fear. *Childhood Education*, 1928, *5*, 136–143.

Jones, M. Community care for chronic mental patients: The need for a reassessment. *Hospital and Community Psychiatry*, 1975, *26*, 94–98.

Jones, M. C. Elimination of children's fears. *Journal of Experimental Psychology*, 1924, *7*, 381–390.

Jones, R. T., Benowitz, N., & Bachman, J. Clinical studies of cannabis tolerance and dependence. *Annals of the New York Academy of Sciences*, 1976, *282*, 221–239.

Jong, E. *How to save your own life*. New York: Holt, Rinehart and Winston, 1977.

Julien, R. M. *A primer of drug action*. San Francisco: Freeman, 1978.

Jung, C. G. *Man and his symbols*. Garden City, N. Y.: Doubleday, 1964.

Jus, A., Pineau, R., Lachance, R., Pelchat, G., Jus, K., Pires, P., & Villeneuve, R. Epidemiology of tardive dyskinesia. *Diseases of the Nervous System*, 1976, *37*, 210–214.

Kagan, J. The plasticity of early intellectual development. Paper presented at the meeting of the Association for the Advancement of Science, Washington, D. C., 1972.

Kagan, J. Acquisition and significance of sex-typing and sex-role identity. In M. L. Hoffman & L. W. Hoffman (eds.), *Review of Child Development Research, Vol. 1*. New York: Russell Sage, 1964.

Kagan, J., 1982. Quoted in Turkington, C. Nature wins round in studies on infants. APA *Monitor*, March 1982, 14, 41.

Kagan, J., Kearsley, R. B., & Zelazo, P. R. The effects of infant day-care on psychological development. Paper presented at the meeting of the Association for the Advancement of Science, Boston, 1976.

Kagan, J., Kearsley, R. B., & Zelazo, P. R. *Infancy: Its place in human development*. Cambridge: Harvard University Press, 1980.

Kahn, M. The physiology of catharsis. *Journal of Personality and Social Psychology*, 1966, *3*, 278–286.

Kallmann, F. J., 1946. Reported in G. C. Davison & J. M. Neale, *Abnormal Psychology*. New York: Wiley, 1982.

Kallmann, F. J. Comparative twin study on the genetic aspects of male homosexuality. *Journal of Nervous and Mental Disease*, 1952, *115*, 283–298.

Kamens, L. Cognitive and attribution factors in sleep-onset insomnia. Unpublished doctoral dissertation, Southern Illinois University at Carbondale, 1980.

Kanfer, F., & Goldfoot, D. Self-control and tolerance of noxious stimulation. *Psychological Reports*, 1966, *18*, 79–85.

Kanin, E. J., & Parcell, S. R. Sexual aggression: A second look at the offended female. *Archives of Sexual Behavior*, 1977, *6*, 67–76.

Kanin, G. *It takes a long time to become young*. Garden City, N. Y.: Doubleday, 1978.

Kaplan, H. S., & Sager, C. J. Sexual patterns at different ages. *Medical Aspects of Human Sexuality*, 1971, *5*(6), 10–23.

Kaplan, R. M., & Singer, R. D. Television violence and viewer aggression: A reexamination of the evidence. *Journal of Social Issues*, 1976, *32*, 35–70.

Karabenick, S. A., & Meisels, M. Effects of performance evaluation on interpersonal distance. *Journal of Personality*, 1972, *40*, 275–286.

Karacan, I. Advances in the psychophysiological evaluation of male erectile impotence. In J. LoPiccolo & L. LoPiccolo (eds.), *Handbook of Sex Therapy*. New York: Plenum, 1978.

Karam, J. H. Obesity: Fat cells—not fat people. *Western Journal of Medicine*, 1979, *130*, 128–132.

Karlin, R. A., McFarland, D., Aiello, J. R., & Epstein, Y. M. Normative mediation of reactions to crowding. *Environmental Psychology and Nonverbal Behavior*, 1976, *1*, 30–40.

Karlins, M., Coffman, T. L., & Walter, G. On the fading of social stereotypes: Studies in three generations of college students. *Journal of Personality and Social Psychology*, 1969, *13*, 1–16.

Kazdin, A. E. Drawing valid inferences from case studies. *Journal of Consulting and Clinical Psychology*, 1981, *49*, 183–192.

Kazdin, A..E., & Wilcoxin, L. A. Systematic desensitization and nonspecific treatment effects: A methodological evaluation. *Psychological Bulletin*, 1976, *83*, 729–758.

Keating, C. F., Mazur, A., Segall, M. H., Cysneiros, P. G., Divale, W. T., Kilbride, J. E., Komin, S., Leahy, P., Thurman, B., & Wirsing, R. Culture and the perception of social dominance from facial expression. *Journal of Personality and Social Psychology*, 1981, *40*, 615–626.

Keele, S. W. *Attention and human performance*. Santa Monica, Calif.: Goodyear, 1973.

Keesey, R. E. A set-point analysis of the regulation of body weight. In A. J. Stunkard (ed.), *Obesity*. Philadelphia: Saunders, 1980.

Keesey, R. E., & Powley, T. L. Hypothalamic regulation of body weight. *American Scientist*, 1975, *63*, 558–565.

Kelley, C. K., & King, G. D. Behavioral correlates of the 2–7–8 MMPI profile type in students at a university mental health center. *Journal of Consulting and Clinical Psychology*, 1979, *47*, 679–685.

Kelly, H. H. The processes of causal attribution. *American Psychologist*, 1973, *28*, 107–128.

Kelly, C. New NIDA studies document dramatic rise in drug abuse. *ADAMHA News*, July 11, 1980.

Kennell, J., Jerauld, R., Wolfe, H., Chesler, D., Kreger, N., McAlpine, W., Steffa, M., & Klaus, M. Maternal behavior one year after early and extended post-partum contact. *Developmental Medicine and Child Neurology*, 1974, *16*, 172–179.

Kerpelman, J. P., & Himmelfarb, S. Partial reinforcement effects in attitude acquisition and counterconditioning. *Journal of Personality and Social Psychology*, 1971, *19*, 301–305.

Kesey, K. *One flew over the cuckoo's nest*. New York: Viking, 1962.

Keuthen, N. Subjective probability estimation and somatic structures in phobic individuals. Unpublished manuscript, State University of New York at Stony Brook, 1980.

Keverne, E. B. Pheromones and sexual behavior. In J. Money & H. Musaph (eds.), *Handbook of Sexology*. Amsterdam: Excerpta Medica, 1977.

Kiesler, C. A. Mental hospitalization and alternative care. *American Psychologist*, 1982, *37*, 349–360.

Kihlstrom, J. F. Posthypnotic amnesia for recently learned material: Interactions with "episodic" and "semantic" memory. *Cognitive Psychology*, 1980, *12*, 227–251.

Kimmel, D. C. *Adulthood and aging: An interdisciplinary developmental view*. New York: Wiley, 1974.

Kinsey, A. C., Pomeroy, W. B., & Martin, C. E. *Sexual behavior in the human male*. Philadelphia: Saunders, 1948.

Kinsey, A. C., Pomeroy, W. B., Martin,

C. E., & Gebhard, P. H. *Sexual behavior in the human female*. Philadelphia: Saunders, 1953.

Kinzel, A. S. Body buffer zone in violent prisoners. *American Journal of Psychiatry*, 1970, *127*, 59–64.

Kleinke, C. L. Compliance to requests made by gazing and touching experimenters in field settings. *Journal of Experimental Social Psychology*, 1977, *13*, 218–223.

Kleinke, C. L., & Staneski, R. A. First impressions of female bust size. *Journal of Social Psychology*, 1980, *110*, 123–134.

Kleinke, C. L., & Walton, J. H. Influence of reinforced smiling on affective responses in an interview. *Journal of Personality and Social Psychology*, 1982, *42*, 557–565.

Klineberg, O. Emotional expression in Chinese literature. *Journal of Abnormal and Social Psychology*, 1938, *33*, 517–520.

Knapp, M. L. *Nonverbal communication in human interaction*. New York: Holt, Rinehart and Winston, 1978.

Knox, V. Cognitive strategies for coping with pain: Ignoring versus acknowledging. Doctoral dissertation, University of Waterloo, 1972.

Koffka, K. *The growth of the mind*. New York: Harcourt Brace Jovanovich, 1925.

Kohen, W., & Paul, G. L. Current trends and recommended changes in extended care placements of mental patients: The Illinois system as a case in point. *Schizophrenia Bulletin*, 1976, *2*, 575–594.

Kohlberg, L. *Stages in the development of moral thought and action*. New York: Holt, Rinehart and Winston, 1969.

Köhler, W. *The mentality of apes*. New York: Harcourt Brace Jovanovich, 1925.

Kohn, P. M., Barnes, G. E., & Hoffman, F. M. Drug-use history and experience seeking among adult male correctional inmates. *Journal of Consulting and Clinical Psychology*, 1979, *47*, 708–715.

Kolb, L. C. *Modern clinical psychiatry*, 9th ed. Philadelphia: Saunders, 1977.

Komacki, J., & Dore-Boyce, K. Self-recording: Its effects on individuals high and low in motivation. *Behavior Therapy*, 1978, *9*, 65–72.

Konecni, V. J. Annoyance, type and duration of postannoyance activity, and aggression: The "cathartic" effect. *Journal of Experimental Psychology: General*, 1975, *104*, 76–102.

Koocher, G. P. Bathroom behavior and human dignity. *Journal of Personality and Social Psychology*, 1977, *35*, 120–121.

Kramer, C. Women's speech: Separate but unequal? *Quarterly Journal of Speech*, February 1974, 14–24.

Krapfl, J. E. Differential ordering of stimulus presentation and semi-automated versus live treatment in the systematic desensitization of snake phobia. Doctoral dissertation, University of Missouri, 1967.

Krech, D., Crutchfield, R. S., & Ballachey, E. L. *Individual in society.* New York: McGraw-Hill, 1962.

Krulewitz, J. E., & Nash, J. E. Effects of sex-role attitudes and similarity on men's rejection of male homosexuals. *Journal of Personality and Social Psychology*, 1980, *38*, 67–74.

Kübler-Ross, E. *On death and dying.* New York: Macmillan, 1969.

Kutchinsky, B. Deviance and criminality: The case of a voyeur in a peeper's paradise. *Diseases of the Nervous System*, 1976, *37*, 145–151.

LaChance, C. C., Chestnut, R. W., & Lubitz, A. The "decorative" female model: Sexual stimuli and the recognition of advertisements. *Journal of Advertising*, 1978.

Ladas, A. K., Whipple, B., & Perry, J. D. *The G spot and other recent discoveries about human sexuality.* New York: Holt, Rinehart and Winston, 1982.

Laing, R. D. Is schizophrenia a disease? *International Journal of Social Psychiatry*, 1964, *10*, 184–193.

Laird, J. D. Self-attribution of emotion: The effects of expressive behavior on the quality of emotional experience. *Journal of Personality and Social Psychology*, 1974, *29*, 475–486.

Landreth, C. *Early childhood.* New York: Knopf, 1967.

Landy, D., & Sigall, H. Beauty is talent: Task evaluation as a function of the performer's physical attractiveness. *Journal of Personality and Social Psychology*, 1974, *30*, 299–304.

Lang, A. R., Goeckner, D. J., Adesso, V. J., & Marlatt, G. A. Effects of alcohol on aggression in male social drinkers. *Journal of Abnormal Psychology*, 1975, *84*, 508–518.

Lang, A. R., Searles, J., Lauerman, R., & Adesso, V. J. Expectancy, alcohol, and sex guilt as determinants

of interest in and reaction to sexual stimuli. *Journal of Abnormal Psychology*, 1980, *89*, 644–653.

Langer, E. J., Rodin, J., Beck, P., Weinman, C., & Spitzer, L. Environmental determinants of memory improvement in late adulthood. *Journal of Personality and Social Psychology*, 1979, 37, 2003–2013.

Lansky, D., & Wilson, G. T. Alcohol, expectations, and sexual arousal. *Journal of Abnormal Psychology*, 1981, *90*, 35–45.

Lanzetta, J. T., Cartwright-Smith, J., & Kleck, R. E. Effects of nonverbal dissimulation on emotional experience and autonomic arousal. *Journal of Personality and Social Psychology*, 1976, *33*, 354–370.

Larson, C. C. Taub conviction revives centuries-old debate. APA *Monitor*, January 1982, 1, 12–13.

Lashley, K. S. In search of the engram. In *Symposium of the Society for Experimental Biology, Vol. 4.* New York: Cambridge University Press, 1950.

Latané, B., & Dabbs, J. M. Sex, group size, and helping in three cities. *Sociometry*, 1975, *38*, 180–194.

Latané, B., Williams, K., & Harkins, S. Many hands make light the work: The causes and consequences of social loafing. *Journal of Personality and Social Psychology*, 1979, *37*, 822–832.

Lau, R. R., & Russell, D. Attributions in the sports pages. *Journal of Personality and Social Psychology*, 1980, *39*, 29–38.

Lavin, D. E. *The prediction of academic performance: A theoretical analysis and review of research.* New York: Russell Sage, 1965.

Lavrakas, P. J. Female preferences for male physiques. Paper presented at the Midwestern Psychological Association, Chicago, May 1975.

Lawson, E. D. Hair color, personality, and the observer. *Psychological Reports*, 1971, *28*, 311–322.

Layne, C. The Barnum effect: Rationality versus gullibility? *Journal of Consulting and Clinical Psychology*, 1979, *47*, 219–221.

Leak, G. K., & Christopher, S. B. Freudian psychoanalysis and sociobiology: A synthesis. *American Psychologist*, 1982, *37*, 313–322.

LeBon, G. (1895). *The crowd.* New York: Viking, 1960.

LeBow, M. D., Goldberg, P. S., & Collins, A. Eating behavior of over-

weight and nonoverweight persons in the natural environment. *Journal of Consulting and Clinical Psychology*, 1977, *45*, 1204–1205.

Lefcourt, H. M., Miller, R. S., Ware, E. E., & Sherk, D. Locus of control as a modifier of the relationship between stressors and moods. *Journal of Personality and Social Psychology*, 1981, *41*, 357–369.

Leiblum, S., & Ersner-Hershfield, R. Sexual enhancement groups for dysfunctional women: An evaluation. *Journal of Sex and Marital Therapy*, 1977, *3*, 139–152.

Lenneberg, E. H. *Biological foundations of language.* New York: Wiley, 1967.

Lenneberg, E. H. On explaining language. *Science*, 1969, *164*, 635–643.

Leonard, C. V. Depression and suicidality. *Journal of Consulting and Clinical Psychology*, 1974, *42*, 98–104.

Leonard, C. V. The MMPI as a suicide predictor. *Journal of Consulting and Clinical Psychology*, 1977, *45*, 367–377.

Lerner, M. J., Miller, D. T., & Holmes, J. G. Deserving versus justice: A contemporary dilemma. In L. Berkowitz & E. Walster (eds.), *Advances in Experimental Social Psychology, Vol. 12.* New York: Academic Press, 1975.

Lerner, R. M., & Gellert, E. Body build identification, preference, and aversion in children. *Developmental Psychology*, 1969, *1*, 456–462.

Leslie, G. R., & Leslie, E. M. *Marriage in a changing world.* New York: Wiley, 1977.

Leventhal, H. Findings and theory in the study of fear communication. In L. Berkowitz (ed.), *Advances in Experimental Social Psychology, Vol. 5.* New York: Academic Press, 1970.

Leventhal, H., & Avis, N. Pleasure, addiction, and habit: Factors in verbal report or factors in smoking behavior? *Journal of Abnormal Psychology*, 1976, *85*, 478–488.

Leventhal, H., Watts, J. C., & Paogano, F. Effects of fear and instructions on how to cope with danger. *Journal of Personality and Social Psychology*, 1967, *6*, 313–321.

Levinson, D. J., Darrow, C. N., Klein, E. B., Levinson, M. H., & McKee, B. *The seasons of a man's life.* New York: Knopf, 1978.

Levitt, R. A. *Physiological psychology.* New York: Holt, Rinehart and Winston, 1981.

Lewinsohn, P. M. The behavioral study and treatment of depression. In M. Hersen, R. M. Eisler, & P. M. Miller (eds.), *Progress in Behavior Modification, Vol. 1.* New York: Academic Press, 1975.

Lewinsohn, P. M., & Amenson, C. S. Some relations between pleasant and unpleasant mood-related events and depression. *Journal of Abnormal Psychology*, 1978, *87*, 644–654.

Lewinsohn, P. M., & Graf, M. Pleasant activities and depression. *Journal of Consulting and Clinical Psychology*, 1973, *41*, 261–268.

Lewinsohn, P. M., & Libet, J. Pleasant events, activity schedules, and depression. *Journal of Abnormal Psychology*, 1972, 79, 291–295.

Lichtenstein, E. The smoking problem: A behavioral perspective. *Journal of Consulting and Clinical Psychology*, 1982, *50*, 804–819.

Lichtenstein, E., & Glasgow, R. E. Rapid smoking: Side effects and safeguards. *Journal of Consulting and Clinical Psychology*, 1977, *45*, 815–821.

Lichtenstein, E., Harris, D., Birchler, G., Wahl, J., & Schmahl, D. Comparison of rapid smoking, warm, smoky air, and attention placebo in the modification of smoking behavior. *Journal of Consulting and Clinical Psychology*, 1973, *40*, 92–98.

Lick, J. R., & Heffler, D. Relaxation training and attention placebo in the treatment of severe insomnia. *Journal of Consulting and Clinical Psychology*, 1977, *45*, 153–161.

Lieberman, M. A., Yalom, I. D., & Miles, M. *Encounter groups: First facts.* New York: Basic Books, 1973.

Lieberman Research, Inc. The teenager looks at cigarette smoking. Study conducted for the American Cancer Society, November 1967.

Lipinski, D. P., Black, J. L., Nelson, R. O., & Ciminero, A. R. Influence of motivational variables on the reactivity and reliability of self-recording. *Journal of Consulting and Clinical Psychology*, 1975, *43*, 637–646.

Loehlin, J. C., Willerman, L., & Horn, J. M. Personality resemblances between unwed mothers and their adopted-away offspring. *Journal of Personality and Social Psychology*, 1982, *42*, 1089–1099.

Logan, D. D. Variations on "the curse": Menstrual euphemisms in other countries. Paper presented at the meeting of the American Psychological Association, Toronto, August 1978.

Lohr, J. M., & Staats, A. Attitude conditioning in Sino-Tibetan languages. *Journal of Personality and Social Psychology*, 1973, *26*, 196–200.

LoPiccolo, J., & Lobitz, C. The role of masturbation in the treatment of sexual dysfunction. *Archives of Sexual Behavior*, 1972, 2, 163–171.

Lorenz, K. *King Solomon's ring.* London: Methuen, 1962.

Lorenz, K. *On aggression.* New York: Harcourt Brace Jovanovich, 1966.

Luborsky, L., & Spence, D. P. Quantitative research on psychoanalytic therapy. In A. E. Bergin & S. L. Garfield (eds.), *Handbook of Psychotherapy and Behavior Change: An Empirical Analysis.* New York: Wiley, 1971.

Luchins, A. S. Primacy-recency in impression formation. In C. I. Hovland (ed.), *The Order of Presentation in Persuasion.* New Haven, Conn.: Yale University Press, 1957.

Lykken, D. T. A study of anxiety in the sociopathic personality. *Journal of Abnormal and Social Psychology*, 1957, *55*, 6–10.

Lykken, D. T. *A tremor in the blood: Uses and abuses of the lie detector.* New York: McGraw-Hill, 1981.

Lykken, D. T. Fearlessness: Its carefree charm and deadly risks. *Psychology Today*, September 1982, 20–28.

Maccoby, E. E., & Feldman, S. S. Mother-attachment and stranger reactions in the third year of life. *Monographs of the Society for Research in Child Development*, 1972, *37*(1).

Maccoby, E. E., & Jacklin, C. N. *The psychology of sex differences.* Stanford, Calif.: Stanford University Press, 1974.

Macklin, E. D. Cohabitation in college: Going very steady. *Psychology Today*, November 1974, 53–59.

Macklin, E. D. Nonmarital heterosexual cohabitation: A review of the recent literature. *Marriage and Family Review*, 1978, *1*, 1–12.

Maddi, S. R. The existential neurosis. *Journal of Abnormal Psychology*, 1967, *72*, 311–325.

Maddi, S. R. *Personality theories: A comparative analysis.* Homewood, Ill.: Dorsey, 1980.

Mahoney, M. J. *Cognition and behavior modification.* Cambridge: Ballinger, 1974.

Mahoney, M. J. *Abnormal psychology.* New York: Harper & Row, 1980.

Maier, N. R. F., & Schneirla, T. C. *Principles of animal psychology.* New York: McGraw-Hill, 1935.

Maital, S. The tax-evasion virus. *Psychology Today*, March 1982, 74–78.

Malamuth, N. M. Rape fantasies as a function of exposure to violent sexual stimuli. *Archives of Sexual Behavior*, 1981, *10*, 33–48.

Malamuth, N. M., Heim, N., & Feshbach, S. Sexual responsiveness of college students to rape depictions: Inhibitory or disinhibitory effects. *Journal of Personality and Social Psychology*, 1980, *38*, 399–408.

Malatesta, V. J., Sutker, P. B., & Treiber, F. A. Sensation seeking and chronic public drunkenness. *Journal of Consulting and Clinical Psychology*, 1981, *49*, 292–284.

Mankiewicz, F., & Swerdlow, J. *Remote control.* New York: Quadrangle, 1977.

Mann, J., Sidman, J., & Starr, S. Evaluating social consequences of erotic films: An experimental approach. *Journal of Social Issues*, 1973, *29*, 113–131.

Mann, L. The baiting crowd in episodes of threatened suicide. *Journal of Personality and Social Psychology*, 1981, *41*, 703–709.

Mann, L., Newton, J. W., & Innes, J. M. A test between deindividuation and emergent norm theories of crowd aggression. *Journal of Personality and Social Psychology*, 1982, *42*, 260–272.

Markman, H. J. Prediction of marital distress: A five-year follow-up. *Journal of Consulting and Clinical Psychology*, 1981, *49*, 760–762.

Marks, G., Miller, N., & Maruyama, G. Effect of targets' physical attractiveness on assumption of similarity. *Journal of Personality and Social Psychology*, 1981, *41*, 198–206.

Marks, I. M. Toward an empirical clinical science: Behavioral psychotherapy in the 1980s. *Behavior Therapy*, 1982, *13*, 63–81.

Marks, P. A., & Monroe, L. J. Correlates of adolescent poor sleepers. *Journal of Abnormal Psychology*, 1976, *85*, 243–246.

Marlatt, G. A., & Gordon, J. R. Determinants of relapse: Implications for the maintenance of behavior change. In P. O. Davidson & S. M.

Davidson (eds.), *Behavioral Medicine: Changing Health Lifestyles.* New York: Brunner/Mazel, 1980.

Marlatt, G. A., & Rohsenow, D. J. The think-drink effect. *Psychology Today,* December 1981, 60–69.

Marmor, J. Frigidity, dyspareunia, and vaginismus. In B. J. Sadock et al. (eds.), *The Sexual Experience.* Baltimore: Williams & Wilkins, 1976.

Marshall, D. S. Sexual behavior on Mangaia. In D. S. Marshall & R. C. Suggs (eds.), *Human Sexual Behavior: Variations in the Ethnographic Spectrum.* New York: Basic Books, 1971.

Marston, A. R., London, P., Cohen, N., & Cooper, L. M. In vivo observation of the eating behavior of obese and nonobese subjects. *Journal of Consulting and Clinical Psychology,* 1977, *45,* 335–336.

Martin, B. *Abnormal psychology: Clinical and scientific perspective.* New York: Holt, Rinehart and Winston, 1983.

Maruyama, G., Fraser, S. C., & Miller, N. Personal responsibility and altruism in children. *Journal of Personality and Social Psychology,* 1982, *42,* 658–664.

Maruyama, G., & Miller, N. *Physical attractiveness and classroom acceptance.* Social Science Research Institute Report no. 75–2, University of Southern California, 1975.

Maslach, C. Emotional consequences of arousal without reason. In C. E. Izard (ed.), *Emotions and psychopathology.* New York: Plenum, 1978.

Maslow, A. H. The need to know and the fear of knowing. *Journal of General Psychology,* 1963, *68,* 111–124.

Maslow, A. H. *Motivation and personality,* 2d ed. New York: Harper & Row, 1970.

Maslow, A. H. *The farther reaches of human nature.* New York: Viking, 1971.

Masters, W. H., & Johnson, V. E. *Human sexual response.* Boston: Little, Brown, 1966.

Masters, W. H., & Johnson, V. E. *Human sexual inadequacy.* Boston: Little, Brown, 1970.

Masters, W. H., & Johnson, V. E. *Homosexuality in perspective.* Boston: Little, Brown, 1979.

Matefy, R. Role-playing theory of psychedelic flashbacks. *Journal of Consulting and Clinical Psychology,* 1980, *48,* 551–553.

Matthews, K. A., Krantz, D. S., Dembroski, T. M., & MacDougall, J. M. Unique and common variance in structured interview and Jenkins Activity Survey measures of the Type A behavior pattern. *Journal of Personality and Social Psychology,* 1982, *42,* 303–313.

Maurer, D. M., & Maurer, C. E. Newborn babies see better than you think. *Psychology Today,* October 1976, 85–88.

Mausner, B. Report on a smoking clinic. *American Psychologist,* 1966, *121,* 251–255.

May, P. R. A follow-up study of treatment of schizophrenia. In R. L. Spitzer & D. F. Klein (eds.), *Evaluation of psychological therapies.* Baltimore: The Johns Hopkins University Press, 1975.

McArthur, L. Z., & Resko, B. G. The portrayal of men and women in American film commercials. *Journal of Social Psychology,* 1975, *97,* 209–220.

McBurney, D. H., & Collings, V. *Introduction to sensation/perception.* Englewood Cliffs, N. J.: Prentice-Hall, 1977.

McBurney, D. H., Levine, J. M., & Cavanaugh, P. H. Psychophysical and social ratings of human body odor. *Personality and Social Psychology Bulletin,* 1977, *3,* 135–138.

McCall, R. B. *Intelligence and heredity.* Homewood, Ill.: Learning Systems Company, 1975.

McCaul, K. D., & Haugvedt, C. Attention, distraction, and cold-pressor pain. *Journal of Personality and Social Psychology,* 1982, *43,* 154–162.

McCaul, K. D., Holmes, D. S., & Solomon, S. Voluntary expressive changes and emotion. *Journal of Personality and Social Psychology,* 1982, *42,* 145–152.

McClearn, G. E., & DeFries, J. C. *Introduction to behavioral genetics.* San Francisco: Freeman, 1973.

McClelland, D. C. Methods of measuring human motivation. In J. W. Atkinson (ed.), *Motives in Fantasy, Action, and Society.* Princeton, N. J.: Van Nostrand, 1958.

McClelland, D. C. Achievement and entrepreneurship: A longitudinal study. *Journal of Personality and Social Psychology,* 1965, *1,* 389–392.

McClelland, D. C. Inhibited power motivation and high blood pressure in man. *Journal of Abnormal Psychology,* 1979, *88,* 182–190.

McClelland, D. C. Understanding psychological man. *Psychology Today,* May 1982, 55–56.

McClelland, D. C., Alexander, C., & Marks, E. The need for power, stress, immune functions, and illness among male prisoners. *Journal of Abnormal Psychology,* 1982, *91,* 61–70.

McClelland, D. C., Atkinson, J. W., Clark, R. A., & Lowell, E. L. *The achievement motive.* New York: Appleton, 1953.

McClelland, D. C., Davidson, R. J., Floor, E., & Saron, C. Stressed power motivation, sympathetic activation, immune function, and illness. *Journal of Human Stress,* 1980, *6*(2), 11–19.

McClelland, D. C., & Jemmott, J. B., III. Power, motivation, stress, and physical illness. *Journal of Human Stress,* 1980, *6*(4), 6–15.

McClintock, M. K. Menstrual synchrony and suppression. *Nature,* 1971, *229,* 244–245.

McClintock, M. K. Estrous synchrony and its mediation by airborne chemical communication. *Hormones and Behavior,* 1979, *10,* 264.

McConaghy, N., & Blaszczynski, A. A pair of monozygotic twins discordant for homosexuality: Sex-dimorphic behavior and penile volume responses. *Archives of Sexual Behavior,* 1980, *9,* 123–132.

McConnell, J. V., Jacobson, A. L., & Kimble, D. P. The effects of regeneration upon retention of a conditioned response in the planarian. *Journal of Comparative and Physiological Psychology,* 1959, *52,* 1–5.

McConnell, J. V., Shigehisa, T., & Salive, H. Attempts to transfer approach and avoidance responses by RNA injections in rats. In K. H. Pribram & D. E. Broadbent (eds.), *Biology of Memory.* New York: Academic Press, 1970.

McGaugh, J. L., Martinez, J. L., Jr., Jensen, R. A., Messing, R. B., & Vasquez, B. J. Central and peripheral catecholamine function in learning and memory processes. In *Neural Mechanisms of Goal-Directed Behavior and Learning.* New York: Academic Press, 1980.

McGinnies, E. Emotionality and perceptual defense. *Psychological Review,* 1949, *56,* 244–251.

McGrath, J. J., & Cohen, D. B. REM sleep facilitation of adaptive waking behavior: A review of the literature. *Psychological Bulletin*, 1978, *85*, 24–57.

McGurk, H., Turnura, C., & Creighton, S. J. Auditory-visual coordination in neonates. *Child Development*, 1977, *48*, 138–143.

McMullen, S., & Rosen, R. C. Self-administered masturbation training in the treatment of primary orgasmic dysfunction. *Journal of Consulting and Clinical Psychology*, 1979, *47*, 912–918.

McNeill, D. The development of language. In P. H. Mussen (ed.), *Carmichael's Manual of Child Psychology, Vol. 1*, 3d ed. New York: Wiley, 1970.

Mead, M. *Sex and temperament in three primitive societies.* New York: Morrow, 1935.

Mednick, M. T. S., & Puryear, G. R. Race and fear of success in college women: 1968 and 1971. *Journal of Consulting and Clinical Psychology*, 1976, *44*, 787–789.

Mednick, S. A. The associative basis of the creative process. *Psychological Review*, 1962, *69*, 220–232.

Mehr, J. J. *Abnormal psychology.* New York: Holt, Rinehart and Winston, 1983.

Meichenbaum, D. Toward a cognitive theory of self-control. In G. Schwartz & D. Shapiro (eds.), *Consciousness and Self-Regulation: Advances in Research.* New York: Plenum, 1976.

Meichenbaum, D. *Cognitive behavior modification: An integrative approach.* New York: Plenum, 1977.

Meichenbaum, D., & Butler, L. Toward a conceptual model for the treatment of test anxiety: Implications for research and treatment. In I. G. Sarason (ed.), *Test Anxiety: Theory, Research, and Application.* Hillsdale, N. J.: Erlbaum, 1980.

Meissner, W. W. Psychoanalysis and sexual disorders. In B. B. Wolman & J. Money (eds.), *Handbook of Human Sexuality.* Englewood Cliffs, N. J.: Prentice-Hall, 1980.

Mellstrom, M., Jr., Cicala, G. A., & Zuckerman, M. General versus specific trait anxiety measures in the prediction of fear of snakes, heights, and darkness. *Journal of Consulting and Clinical Psychology*, 1976, *44*, 83–91.

Melzack, R. *The puzzle of pain.* New York: Basic Books, 1973.

Melzack, R., & Scott, T. H. The effects of early experience on the response to pain. *Journal of Comparative and Physiological Psychology*, 1957, *50*, 155–161.

Mendelson, J. H., Rossi, A. M., & Meyer, R. E. (eds.). *The use of marihuana: A psychological and physiological inquiry.* New York: Plenum, 1974.

Messenger, J. C. Sex and repression in an Irish folk community. In D. S. Marshall & R. C. Suggs (eds.), *Human Sexual Behavior: Variations in the Ethnographic Spectrum.* New York: Basic Books, 1971.

Meyer-Bahlburg, H. F. L. Sex hormones and male homosexuality in comparative perspective. *Archives of Sexual Behavior*, 1977, *6*, 297–326.

Meyer-Bahlburg, H. F. L. Sex hormones and female homosexuality: A critical examination. *Archives of Sexual Behavior*, 1979, *8*, 101–120.

Michael R. P., Keverne, E. B., & Bonsall, R. W. Pheromones: Isolation of male sex attractants from a female primate. *Science*, 1971, *172*, 964–966.

Middlemist, R. D., Knowles, E. S., & Matter, C. F. Personal space invasions in the lavatory: Suggestive evidence for arousal. *Journal of Personality and Social Psychology*, 1976, *33*, 541–546.

Middlemist, R. D., Knowles, E. S., & Matter, C. F. What to do and what to report: A reply to Koocher. *Journal of Personality and Social Psychology*, 1977, *35*, 122–124.

Milgram, S. Behavioral study of obedience. *Journal of Abnormal and Social Psychology*, 1963, *67*, 371–378.

Milgram, S. The experience of living in cities. *Science*, 1970, *167*, 1461–1468.

Milgram, S. *Obedience to authority.* New York: Harper & Row, 1974.

Milgram, S. *The individual in a social world.* Reading, Mass.: Addison-Wesley, 1977.

Milgram, S. Understanding psychological man. *Psychology Today*, May 1982, 49–51.

Miller, G. A. The magical number seven, plus or minus two: Some limits on our capacity for processing information. *Psychological Review*, 1956, *63*, 81–97.

Miller, I. W., Klee, S. H., & Norman, W. H. Depressed and nondepressed inpatients' cognitions of hypothetical events, experimental tasks, and stressful life events. *Journal of Abnormal Psychology*, 1982, *91*, 78–81.

Miller, N. E. Learning of visceral and glandular responses. *Science*, 1969, *163*, 434–445.

Miller, N. E. Understanding psychological man. *Psychology Today*, May 1982, 51–52.

Miller, N. E., & Dollard, J. *Social learning and imitation.* New Haven, Conn.: Yale University Press, 1941.

Miller, P. H., Heldmeyer, K. H., & Miller, S. A. Facilitation of conservation of number in young children. *Developmental Psychology*, 1975, *11*, 253.

Miller, P. M., & Mastria, M. A. *Alternatives to alcohol abuse: A social learning model.* Champaign, Ill.: Research Press, 1977.

Miller, R. L., & Carson, G. L. Playboy stuff and other variables: Scholarship, athletics, and girl friends. *Journal of Social Psychology*, 1975, *95*, 143–144.

Miller, S. M. Why having control reduces stress: If I can stop the roller coaster I don't want to get off. In J. Garber & M. E. P. Seligman (eds.), *Human Helplessness: Theory and Research.* New York: Academic Press, 1980.

Miller, W. R. Treating problem drinkers: What works? *The Behavior Therapist*, 1982, *5*(1), 15–18.

Miller, W. R., & Hester, R. K. Treating the problem drinker. In W. R. Miller (ed.), *The Addictive Behaviors.* New York: Pergamon Press, 1980.

Miller, W. R., & Lief, H. I. Masturbatory attitudes, knowledge, and experience. Data from the Sex Knowledge and Attitude Test (SKAT). *Archives of Sexual Behavior*, 1976, *5*, 447–468.

Miller, W. R., & Muñoz, R. F. *How to control your drinking*, 2d ed. Albuquerque: University of New Mexico Press, 1983.

Mills, J., & Harvey, J. Opinion change as a function of when information about the communicator is received and whether he is attractive or expert. *Journal of Personality and Social Psychology*, 1972, *21*, 52–55.

Mirsky, I. A. Physiologic, psychologic, and social determinants in the etiology of duodenal ulcer. *American Journal of Digestive Diseases*, 1958, *3*, 285–315.

Mischel, W. On the future of personality measurement. *American Psychologist*, 1977, *32*, 246–254.

Mischel, W. *Introduction to personality.* New York: Holt, Rinehart and Winston, 1981.

Money, J. Phantom orgasm in the dreams of paraplegic men and women. *Archives of General Psychiatry*, 1960, *3*, 373–382.

Money, J. Prenatal hormones and posthormonal socialization in gender identity differentiation. In J. K. Cole & R. Dienstbier (eds.), *Nebraska Symposium on Motivation*. Lincoln, Neb.: University of Nebraska Press, 1974.

Money, J. Human hermaphroditism. In F. A. Beach (ed.), *Human Sexuality in Four Perspectives*. Baltimore: The Johns Hopkins University Press, 1977.

Money, J., & Ehrhardt, A. *Man and woman, boy and girl*. Baltimore: The Johns Hopkins University Press, 1973.

Monroe, L. J. Psychological and physiological differences between good and poor sleepers. *Journal of Abnormal Psychology*, 1967, *72*, 255–264.

Monroe, L. J., & Marks, P. A. MMPI differences between adolescent poor and good sleepers. *Journal of Consulting and Clinical Psychology*, 1977, *45*, 151–152.

Monroe, S. M. Life events and disorder: Event-symptom associations and the course of disorder. *Journal of Abnormal Psychology*, 1982, *91*, 14–24.

Monte, C. F. *Beneath the mask: An introduction to theories of personality*. New York: Holt, Rinehart and Winston, 1980.

Moos, R. The development of the Menstrual Distress Questionnaire. *Psychosomatic Medicine*, 1968, *30*, 853.

Moriarty, T. Crimes, commitment, and the responsive bystander: Two field experiments. *Journal of Personality and Social Psychology*, 1975, *31*, 370–376.

Morin, S. F., & Garfinkle, E. M. Male homophobia. *Journal of Social Issues*, 1978, *34*, 29–47.

Morris, N. M., & Udry, J. R. Pheromonal influences on human sexual behavior: An experimental search. *Journal of Biosocial Science*, 1978, *10*, 147–157.

Morris, W. N., Miller, R. S., & Spangenberg, S. The effects of dissenter position and task difficulty on conformity and response conflict. *Journal of Personality*, 1977, *45*, 251–256.

Morse, W., & Skinner, B. F. A second type of "superstition" in the pigeon. *American Journal of Psychology*, 1957, *70*, 308–311.

Mosher, D. L., & O'Grady, K. E. Homosexual threat, negative attitudes toward masturbation, sex guilt, and males' sexual and affective responses to explicit sexual films. *Journal of Consulting and Clinical Psychology*, 1979, *47*, 860–873.

Motowidlo, S. T. Sex role orientation and behavior in a work setting. *Journal of Personality and Social Psychology*, 1982, *42*, 935–945.

Mowrer, O. H. *Learning theory and the symbolic processes*. New York: Wiley, 1960.

Murray, H. A. *Explorations in Personality*. New York: Oxford University Press, 1938.

Murstein, B. I. Physical attractiveness and marital choice. *Journal of Personality and Social Psychology*, 1972, *22*, 8–12.

Murstein, B. I., & Christy, P. Physical attractiveness and marital adjustment in middle-aged couples. *Journal of Personality and Social Psychology*, 1976, *34*, 537–542.

Myers, A. M., & Gonda, G. Utility of the masculinity-femininity construct: Comparison of traditional and androgyny approaches. *Journal of Personality and Social Psychology*, 1982, *43*, 514–523.

Myers, D. G., & Lamm, H. The group polarization phenomenon. *Psychological Bulletin*, 1976, *85*, 602–627.

Naffziger, C. C., & Naffziger, K. Development of sex role stereotypes. *Family Coordinator*, 1974, *23*, 251–258.

Nahemow, L., & Lawton, M. P. Similarity and propinquity in a friendship formation. *Journal of Personality and Social Psychology*, 1975, *32*, 205–213.

National Institute of Mental Health. Television and behavior: Ten years of scientific progress and implications for the eighties. Washington, D.C.: Author, 1982.

Neugarten, B. Grow old with me, the best is yet to be. *Psychology Today*, May 1971, 45–49.

Neugarten, B. Understanding psychological man. *Psychology Today*, May 1982, 54–55.

Neuringer, C. Affect configurations and changes in women who threaten suicide following a crisis. *Journal of Consulting and Clinical Psychology*, 1982, *50*, 182–186.

Nevid, J. S., & Rathus, S. A. Multivariate and normative data pertaining to the RAS with the college population. *Behavior Therapy*, 1978, *9*, 675.

Newcomb, T. M. Dyadic balance as a source of clues about interpersonal attraction. In B. I. Murstein (ed.), *Theories of Attraction and Love*. New York: Springer, 1971.

Newman, J., & McCauley, C. Eye contact with strangers in city, suburb, and small town. *Environment and Behavior*, 1977, *9*, 547–558.

Newmark, C. S., Frerking, R. A., Cook, L., & Newmark, L. Endorsement of Ellis's irrational beliefs as a function of psychopathology. *Journal of Clinical Psychology*, 1973, *29*, 300–302.

Newport, E. Motherese: The speech of mothers to young children. In N. J. Castellan, D. B. Pisoni, & G. R. Potts (eds.), *Cognitive Theory, Vol. 2*. Hillsdale, N. J.: Erlbaum, 1976.

Nicassio, P., & Bootzin, R. A comparison of progressive relaxation and autogenic training as treatments for insomnia. *Journal of Abnormal Psychology*, 1974, *83*, 253–260.

Niesser, U. Understanding psychological man. *Psychology Today*, May 1982, 44–48.

Nisbett, R. E., & Ross, L. *Human inference: Strategies and shortcomings of social judgment*. Englewood Cliffs, N. J.: Prentice-Hall, 1980.

Nolan, J. D. Self-control procedures in the modification of smoking behavior. *Journal of Consulting and Clinical Psychology*, 1968, *32*, 92–93.

Novaco, R. A treatment program for the management of anger through cognitive and relaxation controls. Doctoral dissertation, Indiana University, 1974.

Novaco, R. A stress inoculation approach to anger management in the training of law enforcement officers. *American Journal of Community Psychology*, 1977, *5*, 327–346.

Novin, D., Wyrwick, W., & Bray, G. A. (eds.). *Hunger: Basic mechanisms and clinical implications*. New York: Raven Press, 1976.

Nowlis, G. H., & Kessen, W. Human newborns differentiate differing concentrations of sucrose and glucose. *Science*, 1976, *191*, 865–866.

Olds, J. The central nervous system and the reinforcement of behavior.

American Psychologist, 1969, *24*, 114–132.

Olds, J., & Milner, P. Positive reinforcement produced by electrical stimulation of the septal area and other regions of the rat brain. *Journal of Comparative and Physiological Psychology*, 1954, *47*, 419–427.

Olson, R. P., Ganley, R., Devine, D. T., & Dorsey, G. Long-term effects of behavior versus insight-oriented therapy with inpatient alcoholics. *Journal of Consulting and Clinical Psychology*, 1981, *49*, 866–877.

Opstad, P. K., Ekanger, R., Nummestad, M., & Raabe, N. Performance, mood, and clinical symptoms in men exposed to prolonged, severe physical work and sleep deprivation. *Aviation Space and Environmental Medicine*, 1978, *49*, 1065–1073.

Orne-Johnson, D. Autonomic stability and transcendental meditation. *Psychosomatic Medicine*, 1973, *35*, 341–349.

Ornstein, R. E. *The psychology of consciousness*, 2d ed. New York: Harcourt Brace Jovanovich, 1977.

Osborn, D. K., & Endsley, R. C. Emotional reactions of young children to TV violence. *Child Development*, 1971, *42*, 321–331.

Page, R. A. Noise and helping behavior. *Environment and Behavior*, 1977, *9*, 311–334.

Paige, K. E. Effects of oral contraceptives on affective fluctuations associated with the menstrual cycle. *Psychosomatic Medicine*, 1971, *33*, 515–537.

Paige, K. E. Women learn to sing the menstrual blues. *Psychology Today*, 1973, *7*(4), 41.

Paige, K. E. Sexual pollution: Reproductive sex taboos in American society. *Journal of Social Issues*, 1977, *33*, 144.

Paige, K. E. The declining taboo against menstrual sex. *Psychology Today*, July 1978, 50–51.

Palmer, F. H. *The effects of minimal early intervention on subsequent IQ scores and reading achievement.* Report to the Education Commission of the States, contract 13–76–06846, State University of New York at Stony Brook, 1976.

Papalia, D. E., & Olds, S. W. *Human development.* New York: McGraw-Hill, 1981.

Parke, R. D., Berkowitz, L., Leyens, J.

P., West, S. G., & Sebastian, R. J. Some effects of violent and non-violent movies on the behavior of juvenile delinquents. In L. Berkowitz (ed.), *Advances in Experimental Social Psychology*, Vol. 10. New York: Academic Press, 1977.

Parker, N. Homosexuality in twins: A report on three discordant pairs. *British Journal of Psychiatry*, 1964, *110*, 489–495.

Parloff, M. B., Waskow, I. E., & Wolfe, B. E. Research on therapist variables in relation to process and outcome. In S. L. Garfield & A. E. Bergin (eds.), *Handbook of Psychotherapy and Behavior Change*, 2d ed. New York: Wiley, 1978.

Patterson, F. Conversations with a gorilla. *National Geographic*, 1978, *154*, 438–465.

Pattison, E. M. Confusing concepts about the concept of homosexuality. *Psychiatry*, 1974, *47*, 340–349.

Paul, G. L. Outcome of systematic desensitization II: Controlled investigations of individual treatment, technique variations, and current status. In C. M. Franks (ed.), *Behavior Therapy: Appraisal and Status.* New York: McGraw-Hill, 1969a.

Paul, G. L. Physiological effects of relaxation training and hypnotic suggestion. *Journal of Abnormal Psychology*, 1969b, *74*, 425–437.

Pavlov, I. *Conditioned reflexes.* London: Oxford University Press, 1927.

Pearlman, C. A., & Greenberg, R. Post-trial REM sleep: A critical period for consolidation of shuttlebox avoidance. *Animal Learning and Behavior*, 1973, *1*, 49–51.

Pempus, E., Sawaya, C., & Cooper, R. E. "Don't fence me in": Personal space depends on architectural enclosure. Paper presented to the American Psychological Association, Chicago, 1975.

Penfield, W. Consciousness, memory, and man's conditioned reflexes. In K. H. Pribram (ed.), *On the Biology of Learning.* New York: Harcourt Brace Jovanovich, 1969.

Pennebaker, J. W., & Skelton, J. A. Selective monitoring of physical sensations. *Journal of Personality and Social Psychology*, 1981, *41*, 213–223.

Perlman, S. D., & Abramson, P. R. Sexual satisfaction among married and cohabiting individuals. *Journal of Consulting and Clinical Psychology*, 1982, *50*, 458–460.

Perls, F. S. *Gestalt therapy verbatim.* New York: Bantam, 1971.

Perri, M. G., Richards, C. S., & Schultheis, K. R. Behavioral self-control and smoking reduction: A study of self-initiated attempts to reduce smoking. *Behavior Therapy*, 1977, *8*, 360–365.

Perry, D. G., & Bussey, K. The social learning theory of sex differences: Imitation is alive and well. *Journal of Personality and Social Psychology*, 1979, *37*, 1699–1712.

Person, E., & Ovesey, L. The psychodynamics of male transsexualism. In R. Friedman et al. (eds.), *Sex Differences in Behavior.* New York: Wiley, 1974.

Pervin, L. A., & Yatko, R. J. Cigarette smoking and alternate methods of reducing dissonance. *Journal of Personality and Social Psychology*, 1965, *2*, 20–36.

Peterson, C., Schwartz, S. M., & Seligman, M. E. P. Self-blame and depressive symptoms. *Journal of Personality and Social Psychology*, 1981, *41*, 253–259.

Peterson, K., & Curran, J. P. Trait attribution as a function of hair length and correlates of subjects' preferences for hair style. *Journal of Psychology*, 1976, *93*, 331–339.

Peterson, L. R., & Peterson, M. J. Short-term retention of individual verbal items. *Journal of Experimental Psychology*, 1959, *58*, 193–198.

Petty, R. E., & Cacioppo, J. T. *Attitudes and persuasion: Classic and contemporary approaches.* Dubuque, Iowa: Wm. C Brown, 1981.

Piaget, J. *The moral judgment of the child.* New York: Collier, 1962.

Piaget, J. *The origins of intelligence in children.* New York: Norton, 1963.

Piaget, J. *The construction of reality in the child.* New York: Ballantine, 1971.

Piaget, J. *The grasp of consciousness.* Cambridge: Harvard University Press, 1976.

Pierrel, R., & Sherman, J. G. Train your pet the Barnabus way. *Brown Alumni Monthly*, February 1963, 8–14.

Pines, M. Head start. *New York Times Magazine*, October 26, 1975.

Pitts, F. N., & McClure, J. N. Lactate metabolism in anxiety neurosis. *New England Journal of Medicine*, 1967, *277*, 1329–1336.

Pliner, P., Hart, H., Kohl, J., & Saari, D. Compliance without pressure: Some further data on the foot-in-the-door technique. *Journal of Experimental Social Psychology*, 1974, *10*, 17–22.

Plomin, R. (1982). Quoted in Pines, M. Behavior and heredity: Links for specific traits are growing stronger. *New York Times*, June 29, 1982, C1–C2.

Plomin, R., & DeFries, J. C. Genetics and intelligence: Recent data. *Intelligence*, 1980, *4*, 15–24.

Plutchik, R. *The emotions: Facts, theories, and a new model*. New York: Random House, 1962.

Podlesny, J. A., & Raskin, D. C. Physiological measures and the detection of deception. *Psychological Bulletin*, 1977, *84*, 782–799.

Pomazal, R. J., & Clore, G. L. Helping on the highway: The effects of dependency and sex. *Journal of Applied Social Psychology*, 1973, *3*, 150–164.

Pomeroy, W. B. Parents and homosexuality: I. *Sexology*, 1966, *32*, 508–511.

Pool, J. L. *Your brain and nerves*. New York: Scribner, 1973.

Postman, L. Verbal learning and memory. *Annual Review of Psychology*, 1975, *26*, 291–335.

Powley, T. L. The ventromedial hypothalamic syndrome, satiety, and a cephalic phase hypothesis. *Psychological Review*, 1977, *84*, 89–126.

Premack, A. J., & Premack, D. Teaching language to an ape. *Scientific American*, 1972, *227*, 92–99.

Premack, A. J., & Premack, D. Teaching language to an ape. In R. C. Atkinson (ed.), *Psychology in Progress*. San Francisco: Freeman, 1975.

Premack, D. Mechanisms of self-control. In W. A. Hunt (ed.), *Learning Mechanisms in Smoking*. Chicago: Aldine, 1970.

Press, A., Clausen, P., & Contreras, J. The trials of hypnosis. *Newsweek*, October 19, 1981, 96.

Prewett, M. J., van Allen, P. K., & Milner, J. S. Multiple electroconvulsive shocks and feeding and drinking behavior in the rat. *Bulletin of the Psychonomic Society*, 1978, *12*, 137–139.

Provence, S., & Lipton, R. C. *Infants in institutions*. New York: International Universities Press, 1962.

Qualls, P. J., & Sheehan, P. W. Imagery encouragement, absorption capacity, and relaxation during electromyographic feedback. *Journal of Personality and Social Psychology*, 1981, *41*, 370–379.

Quattrone, G. A. Overattribution and unit formation: When behavior engulfs the person. *Journal of Personality and Social Psychology*, 1982, *42*, 593–607.

Rabkin, J. G. Stressful life events and schizophrenia: A review of the literature. *Psychological Bulletin*, 1980, *87*, 408–425.

Rabkin, L. Y., & Rabkin, K. Children of the kibbutz. In *Readings in Psychology Today*, 3d ed. Del Mar, Calif.: CRM Books, 1974.

Rada, R. T., & Kellner, R. Drug treatment in alcoholism. In J. Davis & D. J. Greenblatt (eds.), *Recent Developments in Psychopharmacology*. New York: Grune & Stratton, 1979.

Randell, J. Preoperative and postoperative status of male and female transsexuals. In R. Green & J. Money (eds.), *Transsexualism and Sex Reassignment*. Baltimore: The Johns Hopkins University Press, 1969.

Randrup, A., & Munkvard, I. Evidence indicating an association between schizophrenia and dopaminergic hyperactivity in the brain. *Orthomolecular Psychiatry*, 1972, *1*, 2–7.

Raps, C. S., Peterson, C., Reinhard, K. E., Abramson, L. Y., & Seligman, M. E. P. Attributional style among depressed patients. *Journal of Abnormal Psychology*, 1982, *91*, 102–108.

Rathus, S. A. A 30-item schedule for assessing assertive behavior. *Behavior Therapy*, 1973, *4*, 398–406.

Rathus, S. A. Treatment of recalcitrant ejaculatory incompetence. *Behavior Therapy*, 1978, *9*, 962.

Rathus, S. A. *Human sexuality*. New York: Holt, Rinehart and Winston, 1983.

Rathus, S. A., & Nevid, J. S. *Behavior therapy*. Garden City, N. Y.: Doubleday, 1977.

Rathus, S. A., & Nevid, J. S. *Adjustment and growth: The challenges of life*, 2d ed. New York: Holt, Rinehart and Winston, 1983.

Reckless, J., & Geiger, N. Impotence as a practical problem. In J. LoPiccolo & L. LoPiccolo (eds.), *Handbook of Sex Therapy*. New York: Plenum, 1978.

Reeder, G. D. Let's give the fundamental attribution error another chance. *Journal of Personality and Social Psychology*, 1982, *43*, 341–344.

Rees, L. The significance of parental attitudes in childhood asthma. *Journal of Psychosomatic Research*, 1964, *7*, 253–262.

Regan, D. T., Williams, M., & Sparling, S. Voluntary expiation of guilt: A field experiment. *Journal of Personality and Social Psychology*, 1972, *24*, 42–45.

Rehm, L. P. Mood, pleasant events, and unpleasant events. *Journal of Consulting and Clinical Psychology*, 1978, *46*, 854–859.

Reich, J. W., & Zautra, A. Life events and personal causation: Some relationships with satisfaction and distress. *Journal of Personality and Social Psychology*, 1981, *41*, 1002–1012.

Reich, W. The world of Soviet psychiatry. *The New York Times Magazine*, January 30, 1983, 20–26, 50.

Reichelt, P. A. Coital and contraceptive behavior of female adolescents. *Archives of Sexual Behavior*, 1979, *8*, 159–172.

Reis, H. T., Nezlek, J., & Wheeler, L. Physical attractiveness in social interaction. *Journal of Personality and Social Psychology*, 1980, *38*, 604–617.

Reis, H. T., Wheeler, L., Spiegel, N., Kernis, M. H., Nezlek, J., & Perri, M. Physical attractiveness in social interaction: II. Why does appearance affect social experience? *Journal of Personality and Social Psychology*, 1982, *43*, 979–996.

Reiss, B. F., Safer, J., & Yotive, W. Psychological test data on female homosexuality: A review of the literature. *Journal of Homosexuality*, 1974, *1*, 71–85.

Reiss, I. L. *The social context of premarital sexual permissiveness*. New York: Holt, Rinehart and Winston, 1967.

Reiss, M., Rosenfeld, P., Melburg, V., & Tedeschi, J. T. Self-serving attributions: Biased private perceptions and distorted public descriptions. *Journal of Personality and Social Psychology*, 1981, *41*, 224–231.

Renwick, P. A., & Lawler, E. L. What you really want from your job. *Psychology Today*, May 1978, 53–65, 118.

Reschly, D. J. Psychological testing in educational classification and placement. *American Psychologist*, 1981, *36*, 1094–1102.

Restak, R. José Delgado: Exploring inner space. *Saturday Review*, August 9, 1975.

Rheingold, H. F., Gewirtz, J. L., & Ross, H. W. Social conditioning of vocalizations in the infant. *Journal of Comparative and Physiological Psychology*, 1959, *51*, 68–73.

Rhine, J. B. (ed.). *Progress in parapsychology*. Durham, N.C.: Parapsychology Press, 1971.

Rice, B. Brave new world of intelligence testing. *Psychology Today*, September 1979, 27.

Richardson, D. C., Bernstein, S., & Taylor, S. P. The effect of situational contingencies on female retaliative behavior. *Journal of Personality and Social Psychology*, 1979, *37*, 2044–2048.

Richter, C. P. On the phenomenon of sudden death in animals and man. *Psychosomatic Medicine*, 1957, *19*, 191–198.

Ridon, J., & Langer, E. J. Long-term effects of control-relevant intervention with the institutionalized aged. *Journal of Personality and Social Psychology*, 1977, *35*, 897–902.

Rieser, J., Yonas, A., & Wilkner, K. Radial localization of odors by human newborns. *Child Development*, 1976, *47*, 856–859.

Ringler, N., Kennell, J., Jarvella, R., Navojosky, B., & Klaus, M. Mother-to-child speech at two years—Effects of early postnatal contact. *Journal of Pediatrics*, 1975, *86*(1), 141–144.

Rizley, R. Depression and distortion in the attribution of causality. *Journal of Abnormal Psychology*, 1978, *87*, 32–48.

Roberts, A. H. Self-control procedures in the modification of smoking behavior: A replication. *Psychological Reports*, 1969, *24*, 675–676.

Robins, E. J., Gassner, J., Kayes, J., Wilkinson, R., & Murphy, G. E. The communication of suicidal intent: A study of 134 successful (completed) suicides. *American Journal of Psychiatry*, 1959, *115*, 724–733.

Robinson, M. H., & Robinson, B. By dawn's early light: Matutinal mating and sex attractants in a neotropical mantid. *Science*, 1979, *205*, 825–826.

Rock, I., & Victor, J. Vision and touch: An experimentally created conflict between the two senses. *Science*, 1964, *143*, 594–596.

Rodin, J. Menstruation, reattribution, and competence. *Journal of Personality and Social Psychology*, 1976, *33*, 345.

Rodin, J., & Slochower, J. Externality in the obese: The effects of environmental responsiveness on weight. *Journal of Personality and Social Psychology*, 1976, *33*, 338–344.

Rogers, C. R. *Client-centered therapy*. Boston: Houghton Mifflin, 1951.

Rogers, C. R. A theory of therapy, personality, and interpersonal relationships, as developed in the client-centered framework. In S. Koch (ed.), *Psychology: A Study of Science, Vol. 3*. New York: McGraw-Hill, 1959.

Rogers, C. R. The actualizing tendency in relationship to "motives" and to consciousness. In M. R. Jones (ed.), *Nebraska Symposium on Motivation*. Lincoln, Neb.: University of Nebraska Press, 1963.

Rogers, C. R. In retrospect: 46 years. *American Psychologist*, 1974, *29*, 115–123.

Rogers, C. R., & Dymond, R. F. (eds.). *Psychotherapy and personality change*. Chicago: University of Chicago Press, 1954.

Rogers, R. W., & Deckner, C. W. Effects of fear appeals and physiological arousal upon emotions, attitudes, and cigarette smoking. *Journal of Personality and Social Psychology*, 1975, *32*, 222–230.

Rogers, R. W., & Prentice-Dunn, S. Deindividuation and anger-mediated interracial aggression: Unmasking regressive racism. *Journal of Personality and Social Psychology*, 1981, *41*, 63–73.

Rokeach, M., Smith, D. W., & Evans, R. I. Two kinds of prejudice or one? In M. Rokeach (ed.), *The open and closed mind*. New York: Basic Books, 1960.

Rorschach, H. *Psychodiagnostics*. Berne: Hans Huber, 1921.

Rosch, E. Linguistic relativity: In A. Silverstein (ed.), *Human Communication: Theoretical Perspectives*. New York: Halsted Press, 1974.

Rose, R. M. Testosterone, aggression, and homosexuality: A review of the literature and implications for future research. In E. J. Sachar (ed.), *Topics in psychoendocrinology*. New York: Grune & Stratton, 1975.

Rosen, G. M., Glasgow, R. E., & Barrera, M., Jr. A controlled study to assess the efficacy of totally self-administered systematic desensitization. *Journal of Consulting and Clinical Psychology*, 1976, *44*, 208–217.

Rosenhan, D. On being sane in insane places. *Science*, 1973, *179*, 250–258.

Rosenhan, D. L., Salovey, P., & Hargis, K. The joys of helping. *Journal of Personality and Social Psychology*, 1981, *40*, 899–905.

Rosenthal, D. *Genetic theory and abnormal behavior*. New York: McGraw-Hill, 1970.

Rosenthal, D. M. The modularity and maturation of cognitive capacities. *Behavior and Brain Science*, 1980, *3*, 32–34.

Rosenzweig, M. R. Effects of heredity and environment on brain chemistry, brain anatomy, and learning ability in the rat. In M. Manosovitz et al. (eds.), *Behavioral genetics*. New York: Appleton, 1969.

Rotter, J. B. Generalized expectancies for internal versus external control of reinforcememt. *Psychological Monographs*, 1966, *80*(609).

Rotter, J. B. External control and internal control. *Psychology Today*, 1971, *5*, 37–42, 58–59.

Rotter, J. B. Beliefs, social attitudes, and behavior: A social learning analysis. In J. B. Rotter, J. E. Chance, & E. J. Phares (eds.), *Applications of a Social Learning Theory of Personality*. New York: Holt, Rinehart and Winston, 1972.

Rotter, J. B. Some problems and misconceptions related to the construct of internal versus external control of reinforcement. *Journal of Consulting and Clinical Psychology*, 1975, *43*, 56–67.

Rubin, V., & Comitas, L. *Ganja in Jamaica*. The Hague: Mouton, 1975.

Rubin, Z. Measurement of romantic love. *Journal of Personality and Social Psychology*, 1970, *16*, 265–273.

Rumbaugh, D. M. (ed.). *Language learning by a chimpanzee: The Lana project*. New York: Academic Press, 1977.

Rumbaugh, D. M., Gill, T. V., & Von Glaserfeld, E. C. Reading and sentence completion by a chimpanzee (PAN). *Science*, 1973, *182*, 731–733.

Rumbaugh, D. M., & Savage-Rumbaugh, S. Chimpanzee language research: Status and potential. *Behavior Research Methods and Instrumentation*, 1978, *10*, 119–131.

Rundus, D. Analysis of rehearsal processes in free recall. *Journal of*

Experimental Psychology, 1971, *89*, 63–77.

Ruppenthal, G. C., Arling, G. L., Harlow, H. F., Sackett, G. P., & Suomi, S. J. A ten-year perspective of motherless-mother monkey behavior. *Journal of Abnormal Psychology*, 1976, *85*, 341–349.

Russell, J. A., & Mehrabian, A. Evidence for a three-factor theory of emotions. *Journal of Research in Personality*, 1977, *11*, 273–294.

Russell, M. J., Switz, G. M., & Thompson, K. Olfactory influences on the human menstrual cycle. Paper presented at the meeting of the American Association for the Advancement of Science, June 1977.

Rutter, M. Separation experiences: A new look at an old topic. *Pediatrics*, 1979, *95*(1), 147–154.

Sachs, D. P. L., Hall, R. G., Pechacek, T. F., & Fitzgerald, J. Clarification of risk-benefit issues in rapid smoking. *Journal of Consulting and Clinical Psychology*, 1979, *47*, 1053–1060.

Saegert, S. C., & Jellison, J. M. Effects of initial level of response competition and frequency of exposure to liking and exploratory behavior. *Journal of Personality and Social Psychology*, 1970, *16*, 553–558.

Safer, M. A. Attributing evil to the subject, not the situation: Student reactions to Milgram's film on obedience. *Personality and Social Psychology Bulletin*, 1980, *6*, 205–209.

Saghir, M. T., & Robins, E. *Male and female homosexuality: A comprehensive investigation.* Baltimore: Williams & Wilkins, 1973.

Salapatek, P. Pattern perception in early infancy. In L. B. Cohen & P. Salapatek (eds.), *Infant Perception: From Sensation to Cognition, Vol. 1.* New York: Academic Press, 1975.

Santee, R. T., & Maslach, C. To agree or not to agree: Personal dissent amid social pressure to conform. *Journal of Personality and Social Psychology*, 1982, *42*, 690–700.

Sapir, E. *Language.* New York: Harcourt, 1921.

Sarason, I. G. The test anxiety scale. In C. D. Spielberger & I. G. Sarason (eds.), *Stress and Anxiety, Vol. 5.* New York: Halsted-Wiley, 1978.

Sarbin, T. R., & Coe, W. C. *Hypnosis: A social psychological analysis of influence communication.* New York: Holt, Rinehart and Winston, 1972.

Sarbin, T. R., & Nucci, L. P. Self-reconstitution processes: A proposal for reorganizing the conduct of confirmed smokers. *Journal of Abnormal Psychology*, 1973, *81*, 182–195.

Satir, V. *Conjoint family therapy.* Palo Alto, Calif.: Science and Behavior Books, 1967.

Satow, K. L. Social approval and helping. *Journal of Experimental Social Psychology*, 1975, *11*, 501–509.

Sawrey, W. L., Conger, J. J., & Turrell, E. S. An experimental investigation of the role of psychological factors in the production of gastric ulcers in rats. *Journal of Comparative and Physiological Psychology*, 1956, *49*, 457–461.

Sawrey, W. L., & Weisz, J. D. An experimental method of producing gastric ulcers. *Journal of Comparative and Physiological Psychology*, 1956, *49*, 269–270.

Scarr, S. Testing *for* children: Assessment and the many determinants of intellectual competence. *American Psychologist*, 1981, *36*, 1159–1166.

Scarr, S., Webber, P. L., Weinberg, R. A., & Wittig, M. A. Personality resemblance among adolescents and their parents in biologically related and adoptive families. *Journal of Personality and Social Psychology*, 1981, *41*, 885–898.

Scarr, S., & Weinberg, R. A. IQ test performance of black children adopted by white families. *American Psychologist*, 1976, *31*, 726–739.

Scarr, S., & Weinberg, R. A. Intellectual similarities within families of both adopted and biological children. *Intelligence*, 1977, *1*, 170–191.

Schaar, K. On advertising by psychologists. APA *Monitor*, November 1978, 9, 17.

Schachter, S. *The psychology of affiliation.* Stanford, Calif.: Stanford University Press, 1959.

Schachter, S. *Emotion, obesity, and crime.* New York: Academic Press, 1971a.

Schachter, S. Some extraordinary facts about obese humans and rats. *American Psychologist*, 1971b, *26*, 129–144.

Schachter, S. Recidivism and self-cure of smoking and obesity. *American Psychologist*, 1982, 37, 436–444.

Schachter, S., & Gross, L. P. Manipulated time and eating behavior. *Journal of Personality and Social Psychology*, 1968, *10*, 98–106.

Schachter, S., Kozlowski, L. T., & Silverstein, B. Effects of urinary pH on cigarette smoking. *Journal of Experimental Psychology: General*, 1977, *106*, 13–19.

Schachter, S., & Latané, B. Crime, cognition, and the autonomic nervous system. In D. Levine (ed.), *Nebraska Symposium on Motivation.* Lincoln, Neb.: University of Nebraska Press, 1964.

Schachter, S., & Rodin, J. *Obese humans and rats.* Washington, D.C.: Erlbaum/Halsted, 1974.

Schachter, S., & Singer, J. E. Cognitive, social, and physiological determinants of emotional state. *Psychological Review*, 1962, *69*, 379–399.

Schafer, R. Problems in Freud's psychology of women. *Journal of the American Psychoanalytic Association*, 1974, *22*, 459–485.

Scheier, M. F., Buss, A. H., & Buss, D. M. Self-consciousness, self-report of aggressiveness, and aggression. *Journal of Research in Personality*, 1978, *12*, 133–140.

Schiavi, R. C., Davis, D. M., Fogel, M., White, D., Edwards, A., Igel, G., Szechter, R., & Fisher, C. Luteinizing hormone and testosterone during nocturnal sleep: Relation to penile tumescent cycles. *Archives of Sexual Behavior*, 1977, *6*, 97–104.

Schleidt, M., & Hold, B. Paper presented to the conference on the determination of behavior by chemical stimuli. Hebrew University, Jerusalem, 1981.

Schmahl, D. P., Lichtenstein, E., & Harris, D. E. Successful treatment of habitual smokers with warm, smoky air and rapid smoking. *Journal of Consulting and Clinical Psychology*, 1972, *38*, 105–111.

Schmauk, F. J. Punishment, arousal, and avoidance learning in sociopaths. *Journal of Abnormal Psychology*, 1970, *76*, 443–453.

Schmidt, G. Male-female differences in sexual arousal and behavior during and after exposure to sexually explicit stimuli. *Archives of Sexual Behavior*, 1975, *4*, 353–364.

Schmidt, G., & Sigüsch, V. Sex differences in response to psychosexual stimulation by films and slides. *Journal of Sex Research*, 1970, *6*, 268–283.

Schmidt, G., Sigüsch, V., & Schafer, S. Responses to reading erotic stories: Male-female differences. *Archives of Sexual Behavior*, 1973, *2*, 181–199.

Schneidman, B., & McGuire, L. Group therapy for nonorgasmic women: Two age levels. *Archives of Sexual Behavior*, 1976, *5*, 239–247.

Schotte, D. E., & Clum, G. A. Suicide ideation in a college population: A test of a model. *Journal of Consulting and Clinical Psychology*, 1982, *50*, 690–696.

Schulsinger, F. Psychopathy: Heredity and environment. *International Journal of Mental Health*, 1972, *1*, 190–206.

Schultz, D. P. *Psychology and industry today*. New York: Macmillan, 1978.

Schultz, T. Does marriage give today's women what they really want? *Ladies' Home Journal*, June 1980, 89–91, 146–155.

Schwab, J. J., Fennell, E. B., & Warheit, G. J. The epidemiology of psychosomatic disorders. *Psychosomatics*, 1974, *15*, 88–93.

Schwartz, J. L., & Dubitsky, M. One year follow-up results of a smoking cessation program. *Canadian Journal of Mental Health*, 1968, *59*, 161–165.

Schwartz, M. *Physiological psychology*. Englewood Cliffs, N. J.: Prentice-Hall, 1978.

Schwartz, R. M., & Gottman, J. M. Toward a task analysis of assertive behavior. *Journal of Consulting and Clinical Psychology*, 1976, *44*, 910–920.

Scott, J. P., & Fuller, J. L. *Genetics and the social behavior of the dog*. Chicago: University of Chicago Press, 1965.

Sebeok, T., & Umiker-Sebeok, J. *Speaking of apes*. New York: Plenum, 1980.

Seer, P. Psychological control of essential hypertension: Review of the literature and methodological critique. *Psychological Bulletin*, 1979, *86*, 1015–1043.

Segal, M. W. Alphabet and attraction: An unobtrusive measure of the effect of propinquity in the field setting. *Journal of Personality and Social Psychology*, 1974, *30*, 654–657.

Segovia-Riquelma, N., Varela, A., & Mardones, J. Appetite for alcohol. In Y. Israel & J. Mardones (eds.), *Biological Basis of Alcoholism*. New York: Wiley, 1971.

Seligman, M. E. P. Fall into helpless-ness. *Psychology Today*, 1973, *7*, 43–48.

Seligman, M. E. P., Abramson, L. Y., Semmel, A., & von Baeyer, C. Depressive attributional style. *Journal of Abnormal Psychology*, 1979, *88*, 242–247.

Selye, H. *The stress of life*. New York: McGraw-Hill, 1976.

Semans, J. Premature ejaculation: A new approach. *Southern Medical Journal*, 1956, *49*, 353–358.

Shadish, W. R., Hickman, D., & Arrick, M. C. Psychological problems of spinal injury patients: Emotional distress as a function of time and locus of control. *Journal of Consulting and Clinical Psychology*, 1981, *49*, 297.

Shanab, M. E., & Yahya, K. A. A behavioral study of obedience in children. *Journal of Personality and Social Psychology*, 1977, *35*, 530–536.

Shanab, M. E., & Yahya, K. A. A cross-cultural study of obedience. *Bulletin of the Psychonomic Society*, 1978, *11*, 267–269.

Shanteau, J., & Nagy, G. Probability of acceptance in dating choice. *Journal of Personality and Social Psychology*, 1979, *37*, 522–533.

Shapira, A., & Madsen, M. C. Between and within group cooperation and competitive behavior among kibbutz and nonkibbutz children. *Developmental Psychology*, 1974, *10*, 140–145.

Shapiro, D., & Goldstein, I. B. Behavioral perspectives on hypertension. *Journal of Consulting and Clinical Psychology*, 1982, *50*, 841–859.

Sheehy, G. *Passages: Predictable crises of adult life*. New York: Dutton, 1976.

Sheehy, G. *Pathfinders*. New York: Morrow, 1981.

Sheldon, W. H., in collaboration with S. S. Stevens. *The varieties of temperament: A psychology of constitutional differences*. New York: Harper & Row, 1942.

Shenker, R. Adult communication patterns with children. *New York Times*, October 10, 1971.

Sherif, M. *In common predicament: Social psychology of intergroup conflict and cooperation*. Boston: Houghton Mifflin, 1966.

Shaw, J. S. Psychological androgyny and stressful life events. *Journal of Personality and Social Psychology*, 1982, *43*, 145–153.

Shiffman, S. Relapse following smok-ing cessation: A situational analysis. *Journal of Consulting and Clinical Psychology*, 1982, *50*, 71–86.

Shipley, R. H. Maintenance of smoking cessation: Effect of follow-up letters, smoking motivation, muscle tension, and health locus of control. *Journal of Consulting and Clinical Psychology*, 1981, *49*, 982–984.

Shipley, R. H., Butt, J. H., Horwitz, B., & Farbry, J. E. Preparation for a stressful medical procedure: Effect of amount of stimulus preexposure and coping style. *Journal of Consulting and Clinical Psychology*, 1978, *46*, 499–507.

Shneidman, E. S., Farberow, N. L., & Litman, R. E. (eds.). *The psychology of suicide*. New York: Science House, 1970.

Siegelman, M. Adjustments of male homosexuals and heterosexuals. *Archives of Sexual Behavior*, 1972, *1*, 9–25.

Siegelman, M. Parental background of male homosexuals and heterosexuals. *Archives of Sexual Behavior*, 1974, *3*, 3–18.

Siegelman, M. Psychological adjustments of homosexual and heterosexual men: A cross-national replication. *Archives of Sexual Behavior*, 1978, *7*, 1–11.

Siegelman, M. Adjustment of homosexual and heterosexual women: A cross-national replication. *Archives of Sexual Behavior*, 1979, *8*, 121–126.

Siegler, R. S., & Liebert, R. M. Effects of presenting relevant rules and complete feedback on the conservation of liquid quantity task. *Developmental Psychology*, 1972, *7*, 133–138.

Siegman, A. W., & Feldstein, S. (eds.). *Nonverbal behavior and communication*. Hillsdale, N. J.: Erlbaum, 1977.

Silverman, L. H., Lachmann, F. M., & Milich, R. H. *The search for oneness*. New York: International Universities Press, 1982.

Silverstein, B. Cigarette smoking, nicotine addiction, and relaxation. *Journal of Personality and Social Psychology*, 1982, *42*, 946–950.

Silverstein, B., Kozlowski, L. T., & Schachter, S. Social life, cigarette smoking, and urinary pH. *Journal of Experimental Psychology: General*, 1977, *106*, 20–23.

Singer, J. *The inner world of day-*

dreaming. New York: Harper & Row, 1975.

Singular, S. A memory for all seasonings. *Psychology Today*, October 1982, 54–63.

Sirota, A. D., Schwartz, G. E., & Shapiro, D. Voluntary control of human heart rate: Effect on reaction to aversive stimulation: A replication and extension. *Journal of Abnormal Psychology*, 1976, *85*, 473–477.

Sistrunk, F., & McDavid, J. W. Sex variable in conforming behavior. *Journal of Personality and Social Psychology*, 1971, *17*, 200–207.

Sjøstrøm, L. Fat cells and body weight. In A. J. Stunkard (ed.), *Obesity*. Philadelphia: W. B. Saunders Co., 1980.

Skeels, H. M. Adult status of children with contrasting early life experiences: A follow-up study. *Monographs of the Society for Research in Child Development*, 1966, *31*(3), 1–65.

Skeels, H. M., & Dye, H. B. A study of the effects of differential stimulation on mentally retarded children. *Proceedings of the American Association for Mental Deficiency*, 1939, *44*, 114–136.

Skinner, B. F. *The behavior of organisms: An experimental analysis*. New York: Appleton, 1938.

Skinner, B. F. *Walden two*. New York: Macmillan, 1948.

Skinner, B. F. *Verbal behavior*. New York: Appleton, 1957.

Skinner, B. F. Pigeons in a pelican. *American Psychologist*, 1960, *15*, 28–37.

Skinner, B. F. *Beyond freedom and dignity*. New York: Knopf, 1972.

Skinner, B. F. *The shaping of a behaviorist*. New York: Knopf, 1979.

Slade, M., & Biddle, W. Ideas and trends: Scientists find key to growth. *New York Times*, October 31, 1982, E7.

Slater, E., & Shields, J. Genetic aspects of anxiety. In M. H. Luder (ed.), *Studies of Anxiety*. Ashford, England: Headley Brothers, 1969.

Slobin, D. I. *Psycholinguistics*. Glenville, Ill.: Scott, Foresman, 1971.

Slobin, D. I. Cognitive prerequisites for the development of grammar. In C. A. Ferguson & D. I. Slobin (eds.), *Studies of Child Development*. New York: Holt, Rinehart and Winston, 1973.

Slobin, J. F., & Depue, R. A. The contribution of environmental events and social support to serious suicide attempts in primary depressive disorder. *Journal of Abnormal Psychology*, 1981, *90*, 275–285.

Sluckin, W. *Early learning in man and animal*. London: G. Allen, 1970.

Smedley, J. W., & Bayton, J. A. Evaluative race-class stereotypes by race and perceived class of subjects. *Journal of Personality and Social Psychology*, 1978, *36*, 530–535.

Smith, B. M. The polygraph. *Scientific American*, January 1967.

Smith, B. M. *The polygraph in contemporary psychology*. San Francisco: Freeman, 1971.

Smith, C. P., & Graham, J. R. Behavioral correlates for the MMPI *F* scale and for a modified *F* scale for black and white psychiatric patients. *Journal of Consulting and Clinical Psychology*, 1981, *49*, 455–459.

Smith, D. Trends in counseling and psychotherapy. *American Psychologist*, 1982, *37*, 802–809.

Smith, D., King, M., & Hoebel, B. G. Lateral hypothalamic control of killing: Evidence for a cholinoceptive mechanism. *Science*, 1970, *167*, 900–901.

Smith, G. F., & Dorfman, D. The effect of stimulus uncertainty on the relationship between frequency of exposure and liking. *Journal of Personality and Social Psychology*, 1975, *31*, 150–155.

Smith, T. W., Snyder, C. R., & Handelsman, M. M. On the self-serving function of an academic wooden leg: Test anxiety as a self-handicapping strategy. *Journal of Personality and Social Psychology*, 1982, *42*, 314–321.

Snow, C. Mothers' speech to children learning language. *Child Development*, 1972, *43*, 549–565.

Snyder, D. Multidimensional assessment of marital satisfaction. *Journal of Marriage and the Family*, 1979, *41*, 813–823.

Snyder, M., & Cunningham, M. R. To comply or not to comply: Testing the self-perception explanation of the "foot-in-the-door" phenomenon. *Journal of Personality and Social Psychology*, 1975, *31*, 64–67.

Snyder, M., Grether, J., & Keller, K. Staring and compliance: A field experiment on hitchhiking. *Journal of Applied Social Psychology*, 1974, *4*, 165–170.

Snyder, M., Tanke, E. D., & Berscheid, E. Social perception and interpersonal behavior: On the self-fulfilling nature of social stereotypes. *Journal of Personality and Social Psychology*, 1977, *35*, 656–666.

Snyder, S. H., Banerjee, S. P., Yamamura, H. I., & Greenberg, D. Drugs, neurotransmitters, and schizophrenia. *Science*, 1974, *184*, 1243–1253.

Sobell, L. C., Sobell, M. B., & Christelman, W. C. The myth of "one drink." *Behaviour Research and Therapy*, 1972, *10*, 119–123.

Sobell, M. B., & Sobell, L. C. Individualized behavior therapy for alcoholics. *Behavior Therapy*, 1973, *4*, 49–72.

Sommer, B. Menstrual cycle changes and intellectual performance. *Psychosomatic Medicine*, 1972, *34*, 263–269.

Sommer, B. The effects of menstruation on cognitive and perceptual motor behavior: A review. *Psychosomatic Medicine*, 1973, *35*, 515–534.

Sommer, R. *Personal space*. Englewood Cliffs, N. J.: Prentice-Hall, 1969.

Sommers, S. Emotionality reconsidered: The role of cognition in emotional responsiveness. *Journal of Personality and Social Psychology*, 1981, *41*, 553–561.

Spanier, G. B., & Cole, C. L. Mate swapping: Perceptions, value orientations, and participation in a midwestern community. *Archives of Sexual Behavior*, 1975, *4*, 143–159.

Spanos, N. P., Jones, B., & Malfara, A. Hypnotic deafness: Now you hear it—now you still hear it. *Journal of Abnormal Psychology*, 1982, *91*, 75–77.

Spanos, N. P., Radtke, H. L., & Dubreuil, D. L. Episodic and semantic memory in posthypnotic amnesia: A reevaluation. *Journal of Personality and Social Psychology*, 1982, *43*, 565–573.

Spanos, N. P., & Radtke-Bodorik, H. L. Integrating hypnotic phenomena with cognitive psychology: An illustration using suggested amnesia. *Bulletin of the British Society for Experimental and Clinical Hypnosis*, April 1980, 4–7.

Spence, J. T., Helmreich, R., & Stapp, J. Ratings of self and peers on sex-role attributes and their relation to self-esteem and concepts of masculinity and femininity. *Journal of Personality and Social Psychology*, 1975, *32*, 29–39.

Sperling, G. The information available in brief visual presentations. *Psychological Monographs*, 1960, *74*, 498.

Sperry, R. W. Lateral specialization in the surgically separated hemispheres. In F. O. Schmitt & F. G. Worden (eds.), *The Neurosciences: Third Study Program*. Cambridge: M.I.T. Press, 1974.

Spielberger, C. D. The effects of anxiety on complex learning and academic achievement. In C. D. Spielberger (ed.), *Anxiety and Behavior*. New York: Academic Press, 1966.

Spielberger, C. D. Anxiety as an emotional state. In C. D. Spielberger (ed.), *Anxiety: Current Trends in Theory and Research, Vol. 1*. New York: Academic Press, 1972.

Spitz, R. A., & Wolff, K. M. Anaclitic depression: An inquiry into the genesis of psychiatric conditions in early childhood: II. In A. Freud et al. (eds.), *The Psychoanalytic Study of the Child, Vol. 2*. New York: International Universities Press, 1946.

Spitzer, R. L., Forman, J. B. W., & Nee, J. DSM–III field trials: Initial interrater diagnostic reliability. *American Journal of Psychiatry*, 1979, *136*, 815–817.

Squire, L. R., Slater, P. C., & Chace, P. M. Retrograde amnesia: Temporal gradient in very long term memory following electroconvulsive therapy. *Science*, 1975, *187*, 77–79.

Stapp, J., & Fulcher, R. The employment of APA members. *American Psychologist*, 1981, *36*, 1263–1314.

Staub, E., Tursky, B., & Schwartz, G. Self-control and predictability: Their effects on reactions to aversive stimulation. *Journal of Personality and Social Psychology*, 1971, *18*, 157–162.

Steck, L., Levitan, D., McLane, D., & Kelley, H. H. Care, need, and conceptions of love. *Journal of Personality and Social Psychology*, 1982, *43*, 481–491.

Steele, C. M., Southwick, L. L., & Critchlow, B. Dissonance and alcohol: Drinking your troubles away. *Journal of Personality and Social Psychology*, 1981, *41*, 831–846.

Steffensmeier, D., & Steffensmeier, R. Sex differences in reactions to homosexuals: Research continuities and further developments. *Journal of Sex Research*, 1974, *10*, 52–67.

Stengel, E. *Suicide and attempted suicide*. Baltimore: Penguin, 1964.

Stephan, W. G., & Rosenfield, D. Effects of desegregation on racial attitudes. *Journal of Personality and Social Psychology*, 1978, *36*, 795–804.

Stericker, A., & LeVesconte, S. Effect of brief training on sex-related differences in visual-spatial skill. *Journal of Personality and Social Psychology*, 1982, *43*, 1018–1029.

Sternberg, R. J. Who's intelligent? *Psychology Today*, April 1982, 30–39.

Sternberg, R. J., Conway, B. E., Ketron, J. L., & Bernstein, M. People's conceptions of intelligence. *Journal of Personality and Social Psychology*, 1981, *41*, 37–55.

Stock, M. B., & Smythe, P. M. Does undernutrition during infancy inhibit brain growth and subsequent intellectual development? *Archives of Disorders in Childhood*, 1963, *38*, 546–552.

Storms, M. D. Sexual orientation and self-perception. In P. Plier et al. (eds.), *Advances in the Study of Communication and Affect, Vol. 5*. New York: Plenum, 1978.

Storms, M. D. Theories of sexual orientation. *Journal of Personality and Social Psychology*, 1980, *38*, 783–792.

Strahan, R. F. Time urgency, Type A behavior, and effect strength. *Journal of Consulting and Clinical Psychology*, 1981, *49*, 134.

Strauss, M. A., Gelles, R., & Steinmetz, S. *Behind closed doors: A survey of family violence in America*. Garden City, N. Y.: Doubleday, 1979.

Strom, J. C., & Buck, R. W. Staring and participants' sex: Physiological and subjective reactions. *Personality and Social Psychology Bulletin*, 1979, *5*, 114–117.

Stunkard, A. J. Obesity and the denial of hunger. *Psychosomatic Medicine*, 1959, *1*, 281–289.

Suinn, R. M. How to break the vicious cycle of stress. *Psychology Today*, 1976, *10*, 59–60.

Suomi, S. J., & Harlow, H. F. Social rehabiliation of isolate-reared monkeys. *Developmental Psychology*, 1972, *6*, 487–496.

Suomi, S. J., Harlow, H. F., & McKinney, W. T. Monkey psychiatrists. *American Journal of Psychiatry*, 1972, *128*, 927–932.

Sussman, N. M., & Rosenfeld, H. M. Influence of culture, language, and sex on conversational distance.

Journal of Personality and Social Psychology, 1982, *42*, 66–74.

Szasz, T. J. The myth of mental illness. *American Psychologist*, 1960, *15*, 113–118.

Szasz, T. J. The myth of mental illness: Three addenda. *Journal of Humanistic Psychology*, 1974, *14*, 11–19.

Szucko, J. J., & Kleinmuntz, B. Statistical versus clinical lie detection. *American Psychologist*, 1981, *36*, 488–496.

Tart, C. *On being stoned*. Palo Alto, Calif.: Science and Behavior Books, 1971.

Tasto, D. L., & Hinkle, J. E. Muscle relaxation treatment for tension headaches. *Behaviour Research and Therapy*, 1973, *11*, 347–350.

Tavris, C., & Sadd, S. *The Redbook report on female sexuality*. New York: Delacorte, 1977.

Taylor, C. B., Farquhar, J. W., Nelson, E., & Agras, D. Relaxation therapy and high blood pressure. *Archives of General Psychiatry*, 1977, *34*, 339–343.

Taylor, S. E. A developing role for social psychology in medicine and medical practice. *Personality and Social Psychology Bulletin*, 1978, *4*, 515–523.

Taylor, S. P., & Epstein, S. Aggression as a function of the interaction of the sex of the aggressor and the sex of the victim. *Journal of Personality*, 1967, *35*, 474–486.

Télégdy, G. Prenatal androgenization of primates and humans. In J. Money & H. Musaph (eds.), *Handbook of Sexology*. Amsterdam: Excerpta Medica, 1977.

Terkel, J., & Rosenblatt, J. S. Humoral factors underlying maternal behavior at parturition: Cross transfusion between freely moving rats. *Journal of Comparative and Physiological Psychology*, 1972, *80*, 365–371.

Terrace, H. *Nim*. New York: Knopf, 1980.

Thomas, M. H., Horton, R. W., Lippincott, E. C., & Drabman, R. S. Desensitization to portrayals of real-life aggression as a function of exposure to television violence. *Journal of Personality and Social Psychology*, 1977, *35*, 450–458.

Thompson, W. C., Cowan, C. L., & Rosenhan, D. L. Focus of attention mediates the impact of negative affect on altruism. *Journal of Per-*

sonality and Social Psychology, 1980, 38, 291–300.

Thurstone, L. L. Primary mental abilities. *Psychometric Monographs*, 1938, *1*.

Thurstone, L. L., & Thurstone, T. G. *SRA primary abilities.* Chicago: Science Research, 1963.

Tobias, S. Sexist equations. *Psychology Today*, January 1982, 14–17.

Tolman, E. C., & Honzik, C. H. Introduction and removal of reward, and maze performance in rats. *University of California Publications in Psychology*, 1930, *4*, 257–275.

Toufexis, A. Coping with Eve's curse. *Time Magazine*, July 27, 1981, 59.

Toufexis, A. Report from the surgeon general. *Time Magazine*, March 8, 1982, 72–73.

Touhey, J. C. Comparison of two dimensions of attitude similarity on heterosexual attraction. *Journal of Personality and Social Psychology*, 1972, *23*, 8–10.

Touhey, J. C. Effects of additional women professionals on ratings of occupational prestige and desirability. *Journal of Personality and Social Psychology*, 1974, *29*, 86–89.

Triandis, H. C. *Interpersonal behavior.* Monterey, Calif.: Brooks/Cole, 1976.

Tryon, R. C. Genetic differences in maze learning in rats. *Yearbook of the National Society for Studies in Education*, 1940, *39*, 111–119.

Tucker, J. A., Vuchinich, R. E., & Sobell, M. B. Alcohol consumption as a self-handicapping strategy. *Journal of Abnormal Psychology*, 1981, *90*, 220–230.

Turnbull, C. M. Notes and discussions: Some observations regarding the experiences and behavior of the Bambute pygmies. *American Journal of Psychology*, 1961, *7*, 304–308.

Turner, J. S., & Helms, D. B. *Life span development.* Philadelphia: Saunders, 1979.

Turner, R. H., & Killian, L. M. *Collective behavior.* Englewood Cliffs, N. J.: Prentice-Hall, 1972.

Turner, R. J., & Wagonfield, M. O. Occupational mobility and schizophrenia. *American Sociological Review*, 1967, *32*, 104–113.

Turner, R. M., & Ascher, L. M. Controlled comparison of progressive relaxation, stimulus control, and paradoxical intention therapies for insomnia. *Journal of Consulting and Clinical Psychology*, 1979, *47*, 500–508.

Tversky, A., & Kahneman, D. Judgment under uncertainty: Heuristics and biases. *Science*, 1974, *185*, 1124–1131.

Twain, M. *The mysterious stranger and other stories.* New York: Harper & Brothers, 1916.

Udry, J. R. *The social context of marriage.* Philadelphia: Lippincott, 1971.

Ugwuegbu, D. C. E. Racial and evidential factors in juror attribution of legal responsibility. *Journal of Experimental Social Psychology*, 1979, *15*, 133–146.

Underwood, B., & Moore, B. S. Sources of behavioral consistency. *Journal of Personality and Social Psychology*, 1981, *40*, 780–785.

Ullman, C. Cognitive and emotional antecedents of religious conversion. *Journal of Personality and Social Psychology*, 1982, *43*, 183–192.

Ullmann, L. P., & Krasner, L. *A psychological approach to abnormal behavior.* Englewood Cliffs, N. J.: Prentice-Hall, 1975.

United States Riot Commission. *Report of the National Advisory Commission on civil disorders.* New York: Bantam, 1968.

Vaillant, G. E. *The natural history of alcoholism.* Cambridge: Harvard University Press, 1982.

Vaillant, G. E., & Milofsky, E. S. The etiology of alcoholism. *American Psychologist*, 1982, *37*, 494–503.

Valenstein, E. S. Science-fiction fantasy and the brain. *Psychology Today*, July 1978, 28–39.

Valins, S. Cognitive effects of false heart-rate feedback. *Journal of Personality and Social Psychology*, 1966, *4*, 400–408.

Verplanck, W. S. The control of the content of conversation: Reinforcement of statements of opinion. *Journal of Abnormal and Social Psychology*, 1955, *51*, 668–676.

Von Békésy, G. The ear. *Scientific American*, August 1957, 66–78.

Wabrek, A. J., & Wabrek, C. J. Dyspareunia. *Journal of Sex and Marital Therapy*, 1975, *1*, 234–241.

Wachtel, P. L. What can dynamic therapies contribute to behavior therapy? *Behavior Therapy*, 1982, *13*, 594–609.

Wales, E., & Brewer, B. Graffiti in the 1970s. *Journal of Social Psychology*, 1976, *99*, 115–123.

Walker, A. M., Rablen, R. A., & Rogers, C. R. Development of a scale to measure process changes in psychotherapy. *Journal of Clinical Psychology*, 1960, *16*, 79–85.

Walker, J. M., Floyd, J. C., Fein, G., Cavness, C., Lualhati, R., & Feinberg, I. Effect of exercise on sleep. *Journal of Applied Physiology*, 1978, *44*, 945–951.

Wallington, S. A. Consequences of transgression: Self-punishment and depression. *Journal of Personality and Social Psychology*, 1973, *29*, 1–7.

Walstedt, J. J., Geis, F. L., & Brown, V. Influence of television commercials on women's self-confidence and independent judgment. *Journal of Personality and Social Psychology*, 1980, *38*, 203–210.

Walster, E., Aronson, E., & Abrahams, D. On increasing the persuasiveness of a low prestige communicator. *Journal of Experimental Social Psychology*, 1966a, *2*, 325–342.

Walster, E., Aronson, E., Abrahams, D., & Rottman, L. Importance of physical attractiveness in dating behavior. *Journal of Personality and Social Psychology*, 1966b, *4*, 508–516.

Walster, E., & Walster, G. W. *A new look at love.* Reading, Mass.: Addison-Wesley, 1978.

Walster, E., Walster, G. W., Piliavin, J., & Schmidt, L. "Playing hard to get": Understanding an illusive phenomenon. *Journal of Personality and Social Psychology*, 1973, *26*, 113–121.

Waterman, A. S., Geary, P. S., & Waterman, C. K. A longitudinal study of changes in ego identity status from the freshman to the senior year at college. *Developmental Psychology*, 1974, *10*, 387–392.

Waterman, A. S., & Waterman, C. K. A longitudinal study of changes in ego identity status during the freshman year in college. *Developmental Psychology*, 1971, *5*, 167–173.

Waterman, C. K., & Nevid, J. S. Sex differences in the resolution of the identity crisis. *Journal of Youth and Adolescence*, 1977, *6*, 337–342.

Watkins, M. J., Ho, E., & Tulving, E. Context effects on recognition memory for faces. *Journal of Verbal Learning and Verbal Behavior*, 1976, *15*, 505–518.

Watson, J. B. Psychology as the behaviorist views it. *Psychological Review*, 1913, *20*, 158–177.

Watson, J. B. *Behaviorism.* New York: Norton, 1924.

Watson, J. B., & Rayner, R. Conditioned emotional reactions. *Journal of Experimental Psychology*, 1920, *3*, 1–14.

Watson, S. J., Berger, P. A., Akil, H., Mills, M. J., & Barchas, J. D. Effects of naloxone on schizophrenia: Reduction in hallucinations in a subpopulation of subjects. *Science*, 1978, *201*, 73–76.

Watt, N. F., Grubb, T. W., & Erlenmeyer-Kimling, L. Social, emotional, and intellectual behavior among children at high risk for schizophrenia. *Journal of Consulting and Clinical Psychology*, 1982, *50*, 171–181.

Webb, W. *Sleep: The gentle tyrant*, 1975.

Wechsler, D. *The measurement of adult intelligence.* Baltimore: Williams & Wilkins, 1939.

Wechsler, D. Intelligence defined and undefined: A relativistic appraisal. *American Psychologist*, 1975, *30*, 135–139.

Wegner, D. M. Hidden Brain Damage Scale. *American Psychologist*, 1979, *34*, 192–193.

Weil, G., & Goldfried, M. R. Treatment of insomnia in an eleven-year-old child through self-relaxation. *Behavior Therapy*, 1973, *4*, 282–294.

Weinberg, R. S., Yukelson, S., & Jackson, A. Effect of public and private efficacy expectations on competitive performance. *Journal of Sport Psychology*, 1980, *2*, 340–349.

Weinberg, S. L., & Richardson, M. S. Dimensions of stress in early parenting. *Journal of Consulting and Clinical Psychology*, 1981, *49*, 688–693.

Weiner, H., Thaler, M., Rieser, M. F., & Mirsky, I. A. Relation of specific psychological characteristics to rate of gastric secretion. *Psychosomatic Medicine*, 1957, *17*, 1–10.

Weiner, M. J., & Wright, F. E. Effects of undergoing arbitrary discrimination upon subsequent attitudes toward a minority group. *Journal of Applied Social Psychology*, 1973, *3*, 94–102.

Weir, J. M. Male student perceptions of smokers. In S. V. Zagona (ed.), *Studies and Issues in Smoking Behavior.* Tucson: University of Arizona Press, 1967.

Weiss, J. M. Psychological factors in stress and disease. In R. C. Atkin-son (ed.), *Psychology in Progress.* San Francisco: Freeman, 1975.

Wender, P. H., Rosenthal, R., Kety, S., Schulsinger, S., & Weiner, J. Cross-fostering: A research strategy for clarifying the role of genetic and experiential factors in the etiology of schizophrenia. *Archives of General Psychiatry*, 1974, *30*, 121–128.

Werner, C. M., Brown, B. B., & Damron, G. Territorial marking in a game arcade. *Journal of Personality and Social Psychology*, 1981, *41*, 1094–1104.

Wexler, D. A., & Butler, J. M. Therapist modification of client expressiveness in client-centered therapy. *Journal of Consulting and Clinical Psychology*, 1976, *44*, 261–265.

Wheeler, L., Deci, L., Reis, H., & Zuckerman, M. *Interpersonal influence.* Boston: Allyn & Bacon, 1978.

Whitcher, S. J., & Fisher, J. D. Multidimensional reaction to therapeutic touch in a hospital setting. *Journal of Personality and Social Psychology*, 1979, *37*, 87–96.

White, G. L., Fishbein, S., & Rutstein, J. Passionate love and the misattribution of arousal. *Journal of Personality and Social Psychology*, 1981, *41*, 56–62.

White, M. Interpersonal distance as affected by room size, status, and sex. *Journal of Social Psychology*, 1975, *95*, 241–249.

Whorf, B. *Language, thought, and reality.* New York: Wiley, 1956.

Whyte, W. W. *The organization man.* New York: Simon & Schuster, 1956.

Wiggins, J. S., Wiggins, N., & Conger, J. C. Correlates of heterosexual somatic preference. *Journal of Personality and Social Psychology*, 1968, *10*, 82–90.

Wilcoxon, L. A., Shrader, S. L., & Sherif, C. W. Daily self-reports on activities, life events, moods, and somatic changes during the menstrual cycle. *Psychosomatic Medicine*, 1976, *38*, 399.

Wilder, D. A. Perception of groups, size of opposition, and social influence. *Journal of Experimental Social Psychology*, 1977, *13*, 253–268.

Willerman, L. *The psychology of individual and group differences.* San Francisco: Freeman, 1977.

Williams, K., Harkins, S., & Latané, B. Identifiability as a deterrant to social loafing. *Journal of Personality and Social Psychology*, 1981, *40*, 303–311.

Williams, R. L. Scientific racism and IQ: The silent mugging of the black community. *Psychology Today*, May 1974.

Williams, R. M., Goldman, M. S., & Williams, D. L. Expectancy and pharmacological effects of alcohol on human cognitive and motor performance: The compensation for alcohol effect. *Journal of Abnormal Psychology*, 1981, *90*, 267–270.

Wilson, G. T. Psychotherapy process and procedure: The behavioral mandate. *Behavior Therapy*, 1982, *13*, 291–312.

Wilson, G. T., & Lawson, D. M. Expectancies, alcohol, and sexual arousal in women. *Journal of Abnormal Psychology*, 1978, *87*, 358–367.

Wilson, G. T., Lawson, D. M., & Abrams, D. B. Effects of alcohol on sexual arousal in male alcoholics. *Journal of Abnormal Psychology*, 1978, *87*, 609–616.

Wilson, G. T., Leaf, R. C., & Nathan, P. E. The aversive control of excessive alcohol consumption by chronic alcoholics in the laboratory setting. *Journal of Applied Behavior Analysis*, 1975, *8*, 13–26.

Wilson, M. L., & Greene, R. L. Personality characteristics of female homosexuals. *Psychological Reports*, 1971, *28*, 407–412.

Wilson, T. D., & Linville, P. W. Improving the performance of college freshmen: Attribution therapy revisited. *Journal of Personality and Social Psychology*, 1982, *42*, 367–376.

Wing, R. R., Epstein, L. H., & Shapira, B. The effect of increasing initial weight loss with the Scarsdale diet on subsequent weight loss in a behavioral treatment program. *Journal of Consulting and Clinical Psychology*, 1982, *50*, 446–447.

Witkin, H. A., Mednick, S. A., Schulsinger, F., Bakkestrom, E., Christiansen, K. O., Goodenough, D. R., Hirschhorn, K., Lundsteen, C., Owen, D. R., Philip, J., Rubin, D. B., & Stocking, M. Criminality in XYY and XXY men. *Science*, 1976, *193*, 547–555.

Wolfe, L. *The Cosmo report.* New York: Arbor House, 1981.

Wolinsky, J. Responsibility can delay aging. APA *Monitor*, March 1982, *14*, 41.

Wolpe, J. *Psychotherapy by reciprocal inhibition.* Stanford, Calif.: Stanford University Press, 1958.

Wolpe, J. *The practice of behavior therapy.* New York: Pergamon Press, 1973.

Wolpe, J., & Lazarus, A. A. *Behavior therapy techniques.* New York: Pergamon Press, 1966.

Wolpe, J., & Rachman, S. Psychoanalytic "evidence": A critique based on Freud's case of Little Hans. *Journal of Nervous and Mental Disease,* 1960, *131,* 135–147.

Wurtman, R. Brain muffins. *Psychology Today,* October 1978, 140.

Yankelovich, D. New rules in American life: Searching for self-fulfillment in a world turned upside down. *Psychology Today,* April 1981, 35–91.

Yarnold, P. R., & Grimm, L. G. Time urgency among coronary-prone individuals. *Journal of Abnormal Psychology,* 1982, *91,* 175–177.

Yessler, P. G., Gibbs, J. J., & Becker, H. A. On the communication of suicidal ideas. *Archives of General Psychiatry,* 1961, *5,* 12–29.

Youkilis, H. D., & Bootzin, R. R. A psychophysiological perspective on the etiology and treatment of insomnia. In S. N. Haynes & L. R. Gannon (eds.), *Psychosomatic Disorders.* New York: Praeger, 1981.

Zajonc, R. B. Social facilitation. *Science,* 1965, *149,* 269–274.

Zajonc, R. B. Attitudinal effects of mere exposure. *Journal of Personality and Social Psychology,* Monograph Supplement 2, 1968, *9,* 1–27.

Zeiss, A., Rosen, G., & Zeiss, R. Orgasm during intercourse: A treatment strategy for women. *Journal of Consulting and Clinical Psychology,* 1977, *45,* 891–895.

Zigler, E., & Butterfield, E. C. Motivational aspects of change in IQ test performance of culturally deprived nursery school children. *Child Development,* 1968, *39,* 1–14.

Zilbergeld, B., & Evans, M. The inadequacy of Masters and Johnson. *Psychology Today,* August 1980, 29–34, 47–53.

Zimbardo, P. G. The human choice: Individuation, reason, and order versus deindividuation, impulse, and chaos. In W. J. Arnold & D. Levine (eds.), *Nebraska Symposium on Motivation, Vol. 17.* Lincoln, Neb.: University of Nebraska Press, 1969.

Zimbardo, P. G., Ebbesen, E. B., & Maslach, C. *Influencing attitudes and changing behavior.* Reading, Mass.: Addison-Wesley, 1977.

Zubek, J. P. Review of effects of prolonged deprivation. In J. E. Rasmussen (ed.), *Man in isolation and confinement.* Chicago: Aldine, 1973.

Zuckerman, M. The sensation-seeking motive. In B. Maher (ed.), *Progress in Experimental Personality Research, Vol. 7.* New York: Academic Press, 1974.

Zuckerman, M. Sensation seeking. In H. London & J. Exner (eds.), *Dimensions of Personality.* New York: Wiley, 1980.

Zuckerman, M., Eysenck, S., & Eysenck, H. J. Sensation seeking in England and America: Cross-cultural, age, and sex comparisons. *Journal of Consulting and Clinical Psychology,* 1978, *46,* 139–149.

Zuckerman, M., Klorman, R., Larrance, D. T., & Spiegel, N. H. Facial, autonomic, and subjective components of emotion. *Journal of Personality and Social Psychology,* 1981, *41,* 929–944.

Zuger, B. Monozygotic twins discordant for homosexuality: Report of a pair and significance of the phenomenon. *Comprehensive Psychiatry,* 1976, *17,* 661–669.

right 1967 by Pergamon Press, Inc. Maxwell House. Reprinted by permission of Publisher.

QUESTIONNAIRE (pp. 408–409) Reprinted by permission. Copyright 1973 by Stephen Nowicki and Bonnie Strickland.

TABLE 10.4 (p. 412) Data from Galassi, J. P., Frierson, H. T. and Sharer, R. "Behavior of Big, Moderate, and Low Test Anxious Students During An Actual Test Situation." JOURNAL OF CONSULTING AND CLINICAL PSYCHOLOGY, 49, pp. 51–62. Copyright 1981 by American Psychological Association. Reprinted by permission of Publisher.

NEWS ITEM (p. 416) Copyright 1980 by The New York Times Company. Reprinted by permission.

QUESTIONNAIRE (pp. 484–485) From Rathus, Spencer "A 30 Item Schedule for Assessing Assertive Behavior," BEHAVIOR THERAPY, pp. 398–406. Copyright 1973 by Academic Press, Inc. Association for Advancement of Behavior Therapy. Reprinted by permission.

TABLE 13.1 (p. 502) Data from Hunt, M. SEXUAL BEHAVIOR IN THE 1970s, pp. 91–93. Copyright 1974 by Playboy Press, a Division of BEI Books, Inc. Reprinted by permission.

TABLE 13.2 (p. 503) Data from Hunt, M. SEXUAL BEHAVIOR IN THE 1970s, p. 122. Copyright 1974 by Playboy Press, a Division of BEI Books, Inc. Reprinted by permission.

TABLE 13.3 (p. 504) From Hunt, M. SEXUAL BEHAVIOR IN THE 1970s, p. 150. Copyright 1974 by Playboy Press, a Division of BEI Books, Inc. Reprinted by permission.

TABLE 13.5 (p. 508) Adaptation reprinted by permission of publisher. Copyright by Society for the Psychological Study of Social Issues.

NEWS ITEM (p. 510) Copyright 1981 by Newsweek, Inc. All Rights Reserved. Reprinted by Permission.

TABLE 13.6 (p. 514) Data reprinted by permission. Copyright 1974 Stanford University Press.

QUESTIONNAIRE (p. 522) From Burt, M. R. "Cultural Myths and Supports for Rape." JOURNAL OF PERSONALITY AND SOCIAL PSYCHOLOGY, 38, pp. 217–230. Copyright 1980 by American Psychological Association. Reprinted by permission of Publisher.

QUESTIONNAIRE (p. 530) From Janda, L. H. and O'Grady, E. E. "Development of a Sex Anxiety Inventory." JOURNAL OF CONSULTING AND CLINICAL PSYCHOLOGY, 48, pp. 169–175. Copyright 1980 by American Psychological Association. Reprinted by permission of Publisher.

NEWS ITEM (p. 562) Reprinted by permission of THE WALL STREET JOURNAL © Dow Jones & Company, Inc. 1981. All Rights Reserved.

FIGURE 14.6 (p. 573) Data from Middlemist, R. D., Knowles, E. S. and Matter, C. F. "Personal Space Invasions in the Lavatory: Suggestive Evidence for Arousal." JOURNAL OF PERSONALITY AND SOCIAL PSYCHOLOGY, 33, pp. 541–546. Copyright 1976 by American Psychological Association. Reprinted by permission of Publisher.

TABLE B-2 (p. 595) From Nevid, J. S. and Rathus, S. A. "Multivariate and Normative Data Pertaining to the RAS with the College Population." BEHAVIOR THERAPY, 9, p. 675. Copyright 1978 by Academic Press, Inc. Association for Advancement of Behavior Therapy. Reprinted by permission.

Photo Credits

Chapter 1: *Chapter Opening*, EPA/Alinari-Scala; *page 4*, EPA/Alinari-Scala; *page 9*, Museum of Modern Art/Film Stills Archive; *page 11*, Wide World Photos; *page 12*, courtesy of B. F. Skinner; *page 13*, Peter Schaaff/*Time Magazine*; *page 14*, Jim Amos/Photo Researchers; *page 15*, The Bettmann Archive; *page 16*, The Bettmann Archive; *page 17*, Three Lions; *page 20*, The Bettmann Archive; *page 21*, (left), Yale Joel/Life Picture Service (right), Animal Behavior Enterprises, Inc.; *page 24*, National Geographic Society; *page 28*, John Sotomayor/NYT Pictures; *page 32*, The New Yorker Magazine, Inc.; *page 35*, Jeff Albertson/Stock, Boston, Inc.

Chapter 2: *Chapter Opening*, United Press International; *page 43*, United Press International; *page 59*, courtesy of Roger Sperry; *page 60*, courtesy of Dr. Jose M. R. Delgado; *page 68*, courtesy of Wisconsin Primate Center; *page 71*, Omikron/Photo Researchers, Inc.

Chapter 3: *Chapter Opening*, courtesy of Victor Vasarley; *page 87*, Scanning electron microphotograph of Necturus rods and cones by Frank Werblin and Edwin Lewis, University of California, Berkeley; *page 89*, Erika Stone; *page 91*, copyright © 1971 by *Playboy* Magazine. Reprinted by special permission of *Playboy* Magazine; *page 92*, (top), drawing by Tobey; © 1978 by The New Yorker Magazine, Inc.; *page 93*, courtesy of Victor Vasareley; *page 94*, from King, 1976; *page 95*, Michael Stratford; *page 100*, Collection, The Museum of Modern Art, New York. Philip Johnson Fund.

Chapter 4: *Chapter Opening*, Nick Passmore/Stock, Boston; *page 128*, photos by Theodore Spagna, from Dreamstage Exhibit Catalog, copyright © 1977 by Allan Hobson and Hoffman-LaRoche, Inc.; *page 132*, Culver Pictures; *page 136*, Chris Springman; *page 137*, Charles Gatewood; *page 142*, Michael Weisbrot; *page 147*, (left),

Inc.; *page 504*, (left), Fung Lam (right), Tim Carlson/Stock, Boston; *page 510*, ''B.C.'' by permission of Johnny Hart and Field Enterprises, Inc.; *page 511*, Eric Kroll/Taurus Photos; *page 517* (all photos), courtesy of Spencer Rathus; *page 519*, (left) Peter Southwick/Stock, Boston (right), Ellis Herwig/Stock, Boston; *page 521*, courtesy of Spencer A. Rathus; *page 531*, John R. Maher/EKM-Nepenthe.

Chapter 14: *Chapter Opening*, © 1980 John Blaustein/ Woodfin Camp & Associates; page 541 (left), © Donald Dietz 1976/Stock, Boston (right), CBS News Photo; *page 544* (right and left), Wide World Photos; *page 552*, Wide World Photos; *page 554* (left), Frederick Bodin/Stock, Boston; (right), Mark Jones/The Stockmarket and The Burton Holmes Collection; *page 556*, Robert Eckert/EKM-Nepenthe; *page 558 and 559*, © 1965 by Stanley Milgram from the film *Obedience* distributed by the NYU Film Library; *page 562*, © 1980 John Blaustein/Woodfin Camp & Associates; *page 566*, William Vandivert; *page 573*, photos by Eric Knowles.

Color insert: *Plate 2.1* (left, top and bottom), from Leeson and Leeson, *Descriptions and Explanations: Practical Histology, A Self-Instructional Laboratory Manual in Filmstrip*, Philadelphia, W.B. Saunders Company, 1973 (right), from Curtis, Jacobson, and Marcus, *An Introduction to the Neurosciences* (filmstrip), Philadelphia, W.B. Saunders Company, 1972; *Plate 2.2*, from Curtis, Jacobson, and Marcus, *An Introduction to the Neurosciences* (filmstrip), Philadelphia, W.B. Saunders Company, 1972; *Plate 3.2*, Inmont Corporation; *Plate 3.4*, American Optical Corporation from their AO Pseudo-Isochromatic Color Tests; *Figures 1 and 2*, courtesy of Jennifer Loch; *Figure 3*, courtesy Kenneth M. Lansing.

Name Index

Subject Index

Displacement, in memory theory, **199**
Displacement as a defense mechanism,
    350, **406**
    coping and, 406
Dispositional attributions, **548**
Dissension, Soviet method of dealing
    with, 431
Dissociative disorders, 439–441
    theories of, 440–441
Dissociative neurosis, **432**
Dissonant, **107**
Distribution
    normal, **582**
    skewed, **584**–585
Disulfuram, 143
Divergent thinking, **236**
Dizygotic twins, **71**
DNA, 70, 208, 335–336, 430
Dominant trait, **71**
Dopamine, **46,** 450, 451
    schizophrenia and, 450, 451
Double approach-avoidance conflict,
    395–396
Double-blind study, **26**
Down's syndrome, **71**–72, 300
Dream, the, 332
Dream analysis, 468
Dream symbols in psychoanalytic theory,
    131
Dreamer's paralysis, 133
Dreams, **130**–133
    content of, 131–132
Drinking, reasons given for, 144–145
    See also Alcohol; Alcoholism
Drives, **257**
    hunger, 259–265
    maternal, 268–269
    physiological, 258–267
    primary, 258
    sex, 267–268
    thirst, 266–267
Drugs, 137–156
    abstinence syndrome, **138**
    abuse of, 138
    addiction to, **138**
    antidepressant, 445, **493**
    coping and, 401–402
    dependence on, **138,** 139
    hallucinogenic, **144,** 156
    psychedelic, **144**
    physiological effects and expecta-
        tions, 138
    use of, 138
Ductless glands, 62–69
Duos, **215,** 223–224
Dying, 336–337
Dyslexia, **8**
Dyspareunia, **527**
Dysthymic disorder, **442**–443

Ear, 105
    semicircular canals, **115**
Eardrum, **107**
Eclecticism, **432**
Ectomorphic, **361**
Educational psychologists, 8
Edwards Personal Preference Schedule,
    376
EEG, *see* Electroencephalograph

Effect, law of (Thorndike), **179**
Efferent neurons, **42**
Ego, **347,** 353, 467, 468
Ego analysts, **406**
Ego-dystonic homosexuality, **427**
Ego identity, **288,** 326–327
Ego integrity, **337**
Egocentric, **319**
Eidetic imagery, **199**–200
Ejaculation, premature, 53–54, **526,** 528,
    529, 531
Ejaculatory incompetence, **526,** 528
Elaborative rehearsal, **201**
Elavil, 493
Elderly, living arrangements of the, 336
Electra complex, **350,** 353
Electrical stimulation of the brain, 60–62
Electroconvulsive therapy, **494**–495
Electroencephalograph, **126**
Electromyograph, **161**
Embryonic period, **298**
Emetic, **479**
Emotion(s), **279**–290
    Cannon-Bard theory of, 284
    classification of, 280
    expression of, 280–282
    facial feedback and, 282
    James-Lange theory of, 282–283
    Schachter-Singer theory of, 284–285
Emotional appeal, **540**
Empathetic understanding, **471**
Empathy, **145**
Empty nest syndrome, **333**
Encephalitis, **435**
Encoding, **196,** 197
Encounter groups, 18, 462, **488**–489, 491
Endocrine system, 40–41, **62**–63, 69
Endomorphic, **361**
Endorphins, **115**
Engram, **207**
Environment, intelligence and, 250–251
Environmental engineering, using, to
        lower stress, 416–417
Environmental psychologists, 10
Environmental psychology, **537,** 568–574
Epidural anesthetic, **300**
Epilepsy, **52,** 58–59
Epinephrine, *See also* Adrenalin, 46, **149**
Epiphyseal closure, **326**
Episiotomy, **527**
Erectile dysfunction, **526,** 527, 528, 529
        treatment, 529, 531
Erogenous zones, **348**
Eros, **287,** 348, 350, 351
Erotica, **515**
ESP, *see* Extrasensory perception
Esteem needs, 257
Estrogen, **66,** 326
Estrus, **267,** 311
Ethics, 6, **34**–36
        psychology and, 6, 33–36
Ethologists, **308**
Exaltolide, 111
Excitatory synapse, **46**
Excitement phase (sexual response
        cycle), **524**
Exhaustion stage, 398
Exhibitionism, 438, **454**–455
Existential neurosis, **403**

Exorcism, 429, **463**
Expectancies, **365**
Experiment, **25**
Experimental method, 25–29
Experimental psychologists, 11
Experimental subjects, **25**
Experimenter bias, **362**
Exploration, **271**
External eaters, 262
Extinction, **22,** 175–176, 183, 439, 477
Extramarital sex, **507**–508
Extrasensory perception, **116**–117
Extraversion, **70,** 358, 361
Eye, 83–103
        structure, 85
Eye contact, 550–551

Facial feedback hypothesis, **282**
Fallopian tube, **294**
Family therapy, **489**–490
Fantasy
        coping and, 403
        sleep and, 135
Farsightedness, **88**
Fear
        coping with, 437
        of success, **512**
        See also Phobias
"Feel-O-Vision," 114
Fellatio, **503,** 507
Fetishism, **454**–455
Fetus, **295,** 298, 300
        sex of the, 300
Fight-or-flight reaction, **397,** 399
Figure-ground perception, 97–98
First impressions, importance of, 547–548
Fissures, **53**
Fixation time, **303**
Fixations, **349**
Fixed interval schedule, **187**
Fixed ratio schedule, **187**
Flashbacks, **155**
Flextime, **11**
Fogging, **482**
Food, 47
        taste and, 111–113
Forced-choice format, **376**
Forensic psychologist, **439**
Foreplay, 503, 506
Forgetting, 203–206
Formal operations stage (cognitive devel-
        opment), **321**–322
Fovea, **85**
Frame of reference, **373,** 471
Fraternal twins, 71
Free association, 466, **468**
Free-floating anxiety, **391**
Free will, 366
Freedom, 366–367
Frequency distribution, **577**–579
Frequency theory (sound), **109**
"Frigidity," 526
Frontal lobe, **55**
Frustration, 367, 368, **393**
        stress and, 393–394
        tolerance for, **394**
Functional analysis, **483**–484, 485
Functional fixedness, **234**–235